D0142186

MEXICO
An Encyclopedia of
Contemporary Culture and History

About the Authors

Don M. Coerver (Ph.D., Tulane University, 1973) is professor of history at Texas Christian University. Author of a number of books and articles dealing with modern Mexico and U.S.–Latin American relations (especially the U.S.–Mexico border), his most recent book (with Linda B. Hall) is *Tangled Destinies: Latin America and the United States* (Albuquerque: University of New Mexico Press, 1999). He is a longtime contributing editor to the *Handbook of Latin American Studies* and a consultant to the Hispanic Division of the Library of Congress. His current research involves book-length studies of the role of the Texas Rangers in the Mexican Revolution and of Mexican political figure Lázaro Cárdenas.

Suzanne B. Pasztor (Ph.D., University of New Mexico, 1994) is associate professor of history and international studies at the University of the Pacific in northern California. Her first book, *The Spirit of Hidalgo: The Mexican Revolution in Coahuila,* was published by the University of Calgary Press in 2002. Since 1994 she has been a contributing editor for the *Handbook of Latin American Studies* and a consultant for the Hispanic Division of the Library of Congress. In addition to publishing in the field of Latin American history, Pasztor has served as a consultant/ historian for the United States Department of Energy and the government of Sweden. Her current research deals with the history of homeopathic medicine in Mexico and Latin America.

Robert M. Buffington (Ph.D., University of Arizona, 1994) is an associate professor of history at Bowling Green State University. His publications include *Criminal and Citizen in Modern Mexico* (Lincoln: University of Nebraska Press, 2000); a coedited volume (with Carlos Aguirre), *Reconstructing Criminality in Latin America* (Wilmington, DE: Scholarly Resources, 2000); and several articles. Current research includes two book-length projects: "The Sentimental Education of the Mexican Working Class" explores changing gender relations in the turn-of-the-century Mexico City penny press. "'A Touch of Evil': Tales from the U.S.–Mexico Borderlands" analyzes the way public narratives about the borderlands have reflected and constructed public attitudes and public policies in the United States and Mexico since the 1920s.

MEXICO

An Encyclopedia of
Contemporary Culture and History

Don M. Coerver, Suzanne B. Pasztor,
and Robert M. Buffington

A B C **CLIO**

Santa Barbara, California
Denver, Colorado
Oxford, England

Library of Congress Cataloging-in-Publication Data
Coerver, Don M., 1943–
Mexico: an encyclopedia of contemporary culture and history / Don M. Coerver,
Suzanne B. Pasztor, and Robert M. Buffington.
    p.   cm.
  Includes bibliographical references and index.
    ISBN 1-57607-132-4 (hardcover : alk. paper)   ISBN 1-85109-517-9 (e-book)
    1. Mexico—Civilization—20th century—Encyclopedias.   I. Pasztor, Suzanne B.,
1964–   II. Buffington, Robert, 1952–   III. Title.

F1234.C67   2004
972.08'2'03—dc22   2004014738

08   07   06   05   04   10 9 8 7 6 5 4 3 2

This book is also available on the World Wide Web as an eBook. Visit abc-clio.com for details.

ABC-CLIO, Inc.
130 Cremona Drive, P.O. Box 1911
Santa Barbara, California 93116-1911
This book is printed on acid-free paper.

For Linda Hall
—DMC

For Mom and Dad, and for Tim and Olaf
—SBP

For Megan, Sam, Owen, Celina, and Frances
—RMB

CONTENTS

PREFACE

Mexico entered the twentieth century as a model example of the modernization process. Mexico's long-serving President Porfirio Díaz (1877–1880, 1884–1911) was hailed as one of the great statesmen of the period. The centennial celebration of Mexico's independence in 1910 provided a showcase for the major advances that had taken place during the "Porfiriato"—the Age of Porfirio. The centennial celebrations had hardly subsided, however, before Mexico experienced the beginnings of the first great social revolution of the twentieth century, the Revolution of 1910, always spelled with a capital "R" in Mexican history. The upheaval that was "the Revolution" sent Díaz into exile in 1911 and influenced virtually all aspects of Mexico's domestic and international affairs. Long after the major fighting stopped in 1916, Mexicans continued to struggle over what the Revolution should be. Revolutionary change peaked in the 1930s during the administration of President Lázaro Cárdenas, but by the 1940s there was already public discussion that "the Revolution was dead." During World War II, Mexico embarked on a new approach to economic development, which it would pursue into the 1980s. This new approach emphasized government-guided industrialization and led critics to claim that Mexico was experiencing the "New Porfiriato," a conservative era in which the prosperity of modernization was enjoyed by only a few. The dominant official party, the Partido Revolucionario Institucional (the In-stitutional Revolutionary Party, or PRI), maintained control despite growing popular demands for major economic and political reforms. Growing popular frustration vented itself in the bloody confrontation between students and government forces in the Tlatelolco Massacre of October 1968 in Mexico City. It appeared that both the postwar development scheme and PRI control were unraveling when major new oil discoveries in the mid-1970s postponed the day of economic and political judgment. The government, however, badly mismanaged the new oil wealth as corruption reached unprecedented levels. The oil boom of the 1970s gave way to the "debt crisis" of the 1980s, which saw a substantial decline in the standards of living for almost all Mexicans. Major economic reforms were unavoidable as the PRI leadership dismantled the development scheme that had guided the economy since the 1940s. Political reforms were slower to appear, but there were enough changes in the political system in the 1980s and the 1990s to undermine the dominant role played by the PRI. The most important symbolic sign of political change was the presidential election of 2000, which saw an opposition candidate win the presidency for the first time since the establishment of the official party in the late 1920s. Mexico exited the twentieth century looking for new ways to promote economic development and struggling with the problems of an emerging democracy.

Mexico: An Encyclopedia of Contemporary Culture and History deals primarily with these twentieth-century events, developments, and personalities, although the background for some entries may require a pre–twentieth-century treatment. When appropriate, the narrative takes the entry into the twenty-first century. Any words in Spanish are translated immediately following in the text. Entries deal with a complete range of topics: politics, economics, cultural activities, international relations, military affairs, religious issues, and social developments. There are individual entries for each Mexican president; there are also comprehensive entries on each of the thirty-one Mexican states and the Federal District. All entries are accompanied by cross-references and suggestions for further reading on the topic.

TWENTIETH-CENTURY MEXICO: AN OVERVIEW

Mexico entered the twentieth century as a country apparently moving rapidly toward modernization. Under the lengthy rule of General Porfirio Díaz, who held the presidency almost continuously from 1877 on, Mexico experienced an unusual degree of political stability and economic development. Díaz's accomplishments were in stark contrast to the first fifty years of Mexican independence, which had witnessed economic dislocation, foreign invasions, loss of half of the national territory, and civil wars. As Mexico approached the centennial celebration of its independence in 1910, symbols of progress seemed to abound. Mexico enjoyed an extensive rail system and modernized ports; long an important mining center, Mexico was also in the forefront of the rapidly expanding oil industry. Mexico's urban areas—especially Mexico City—in particular reflected Porfirian progress and prosperity. Motor cars, electric street cars, and European-style clothing and manners were all seen as signs of modernization. Much of Mexico's transformation owed itself to foreign investment and technology. Even sports reflected the growing foreign influence as cycling, roller-skating, baseball, and even polo were adopted by the Porfirian elite. The traditional cockfights and bullfighting were increasingly left to the lower classes.

Behind the façade of Porfirian progress, another Mexico coexisted uneasily with the modernization process. Porfirian prosperity bypassed most Mexicans, even those who saw their lives affected by the economic and technological changes taking place. There was growing criticism of foreign penetration of the economy and its political results. An expanding middle class demanded a greater political voice the Porfirian elite were not prepared to permit. In general terms, Mexico's political modernization had not kept pace with its economic modernization. Mexico's growing integration with the international economy had its positive aspects, but Mexicans saw its downside when an economic downturn in the United States in 1907 quickly transferred to Mexico. Crop failures between 1907 and 1909 heightened the misery in the countryside. Even some members of the Porfirian elite saw the need for change and were uneasy at the prospect of the aging Díaz (80) running for yet another term as president in 1910. The interest in imitating European culture was giving way to a rising tide of cultural nationalism. Years of Porfirian stability were about to collide with a perennial Mexican political problem: a crisis over presidential succession.

Díaz viewed the presidential elections of July 1910 as a public relations opportunity to confirm the wisdom of his rule and as an appropriate lead-in to the major celebrations of Mexico's centennial in September 1910. Certainly the president never expected to encounter any significant opposition. Francisco Madero, a member of the elite, became the focus of growing opposition to yet another reelection to the presidency of Díaz. Madero originally supported the reelection of Díaz in 1910 but asked the aging dictator to permit a free election for the vice-president who, presumably, would succeed Díaz. When Díaz refused, Madero decided to run for the presidency himself and soon became a rallying point for a number of different political persuasions. Díaz eventually jailed Madero until the elections were concluded, with Díaz enjoying an appropriately large margin of victory. Upon his release from jail, Madero went into exile in San Antonio, Texas. He later issued a call for revolution to start on 20 November 1910.

Madero entered northern Mexico to lead the Revolution but was disappointed by the response he received and returned to San Antonio. Revolts did break out in Mexico, especially in the north under Pascual Orozco and Pancho Villa. Madero later returned to Mexico to resume nominal leadership of the Revolution, but in the key rebel victory at Ciudad Juárez in May 1911, it was Orozco and Villa who made the decision to attack in defiance of Madero's orders to withdraw. It was an early preview of the problems Madero would encounter in trying to establish his leadership. The fall of Juárez led to the resignation of Díaz, who went into a comfortable exile in France.

After a brief interim government presided over by the Porfirian technocrat, Francisco León de la Barra, Madero assumed the presidency as the result of new elections. From the time he took office in November 1911 until his assassination in February 1913, Madero was under attack from a variety of political factions. Madero was basically a political reformer rather than a revolutionary and was not prepared to deliver the major changes being sought in labor and agrarian affairs. His administration was the target of a number of revolts from both the political left and right. His assassination in February 1913 assured him a position in Mexican history as the "apostle of democracy," but his brief and tumultuous tenure in the presidency did not provide the Revolution with any long-term direction.

The overthrow of Madero put the old-line Porfirian general, Victoriano Huerta, in the presidency. Huerta's administration did not represent a full-scale counterrevolution; in fact, Huerta took a more progressive position on agrarian reform, education, and labor than had Madero. Huerta, however, was considered a "usurper" and aroused major military opposition from the different Revolutionary factions. He also encountered increasing hostility from the United States, which embargoed arms, refused recognition, and even intervened militarily to hasten Huerta's ouster. Huerta did not endure long against such a collection of opponents and resigned in August 1914. Huerta's removal from office, however, ushered in the bloodiest phase of the Revolution of 1910 as the different Revolutionary factions fought each other for control of Mexico.

The principal opposition to Huerta had come from the "Men of the North" (Venustiano Carranza, Alvaro Obregón, and Francisco "Pancho" Villa) and the man of the south, Emiliano Zapata. A Revolutionary convention in October 1914 could not resolve the competing claims to power; the result was a bloody civil war with Carranza and Obregón fighting Villa and Zapata. Obregón's superior military skills prevailed; in 1915 he inflicted a series of defeats on Villa who was reduced to the status of a regional leader in the north. At the same time, Obregón's forces were able to confine Zapata to his original base in the south. Obregón's military victories put Carranza in the presidency; Obregón was willing to await what he thought would be his turn.

To confirm the triumph of the Revolution, a new constitution went into effect in February 1917. Part blueprint for government and part statement of Revolutionary goals, the Constitution of 1917 set down four major themes that would be the criteria for judging presidential administrations for years to come. Those four themes were land and agrarian reform, workers' rights and social welfare, anticlericalism, and antiforeignism. The willingness of a president to implement or ignore these themes became the basis for determining how "revolutionary" his regime was. The Constitution of 1917 also—hopefully—indicated that the military phase of the Revolution had passed, and a new era of political order had begun. Carranza was the first president to be elected under the new constitution, with his term ending in 1920.

Carranza had not wanted such a radical constitution and showed little enthusiasm for implementing its themes. In the area of agrarian reform, Carranza was unenthusiastic about the emphasis on communal ownership of property as called for under the new constitution and moved forward slowly on the distribution of land. There was no progress on the welfare provisions of the Constitution of 1917. Carranza did promote the creation of a government-sponsored national labor confederation (the Confederación Regional Obrera Mexicana [the Regional Confederation of Mexican Workers or CROM]) but only to prevent the organization of an independent workers union. Carranza was not particularly anticlerical and was not interested in provoking a confrontation with the Roman Catholic Church. The highly nationalistic Carranza feuded regularly with the United States and U.S. investors, but there was no effort at a comprehensive implementation of the antiforeign provisions of the Constitution. His nationalistic stance reflected a rising sense of cultural nationalism that intensified after the Revolution of 1910. The drive to define a national culture—to identify what it meant to "be Mexican"—would eventually influence every aspect of cultural production: art, novels, essays, theater, poetry, music, and newspapers.

Once again the issue of presidential succession led to a major crisis. The Constitution prevented Carranza from running for a second term in 1920. Obregón assumed that Carranza would support his candidacy in 1920 in return for Obregón's role in putting Carranza in the presidency in the first place. Instead, Carranza attempted to impose another candidate, sparking a revolt by Obregón's supporters in 1920. The revolt led to Carranza's assassination and to the election of Obregón to the presidency for the 1920–1924 term.

When Obregón took office, the principal contenders for power during the military phase of the Revolution of 1910 had mostly been eliminated. Carranza contrived the assassination of Emiliano Zapata in 1919. Carranza, in turn, was assassinated in 1920. Also in 1920 Pancho Villa reached an agreement with the government in which he promised to cease his military and political activities in return for a large estate and other benefits. It was under Obregón that the four Revolutionary themes of the Constitution of 1917 first received serious implementation. He had played a key role in getting the more radical provisions of the Constitution enacted, but he was still restricted in his actions by the need to consolidate political power and by the financial problems of the government. Obregón sped up the pace of land distribution but still favored a gradual approach that would minimize disruption in agricultural production. Church and state competed to organize groups such as women, workers, and the youth, but there was no major confrontation between the two. Obregón worked to receive diplomatic recognition by the United States, to satisfy Mexico's foreign creditors, and to reach an agreement on the status of oil properties. The Bucareli Agreements of 1923 between the United States and Mexico dealt with these issues temporarily. In the interest of political stability, Obregón was willing to give most state governors considerable freedom in determining how far they wanted reform measures to be implemented in their state, as long as there was no direct challenge to his authority.

Mexico appeared to be heading toward political stability and economic recovery when yet another crisis over presidential succession developed in 1923. Obregón selected Plutarco Elías Calles to succeed him, prompting a major revolt on behalf of the other principal contender, Adolfo de la Huerta. Although Obregón crushed the revolt, it shook domestic and foreign confidence in the progress that appeared to be taking place. The revolt gave Obregón the opportunity to eliminate a number of rival generals, but it forced him to create an even greater number of new generals to ensure the loyalty of the military. The professionalization of the military (getting the military out of politics) became a major concern of Calles, who easily won election to the presidency in 1924. Calles was a ruthless politician, using violence against his political opponents and removing some twenty-five state governors between 1925 and 1927. While increasing the distribution of land, Calles also tried to modernize agriculture by establishing agrarian credit banks and reorganizing the administration of communal lands. In labor affairs, the government continued to favor the CROM, although the corruption and abuse of power by CROM leader Luis Morones was a growing embarrassment for the administration. When Calles cracked down on the Roman Catholic Church, he provoked a full-scale civil war known as the Cristero Rebellion between 1927 and 1929. Calles also reignited the feud between the Mexican government and the foreign-owned oil companies.

Calles was still trying to cope with the Cristero Rebellion when an additional political crisis presented itself over the question of presidential succession in 1928. The restriction on reelection had been removed, thus permitting Obregón to run for reelection in 1928; later the presidential term was extended to six years. Calles was politically astute enough to jump on the Obregón bandwagon, but other military leaders challenged Obregón's return, which led to a rebellion against the government in late 1927. After the execution of the two principal rebel leaders, Obregón easily won the election. The crisis surrounding the presidential succession

in 1928, however, was not over. In August 1928, President-elect Obregón was assassinated. While some urged Calles to continue in the presidency, Calles realized that such a move would almost certainly spark new revolts. The president decided to step down while continuing to control politics from behind the scenes. Calles continued to dominate the political process through a series of three "puppet" presidents between 1928 and 1934; this period is now known as the "Maximato," a term derived from Calles's honorific title of "Maximum Leader." Calles also moved to establish an official party, one of whose principal functions would be to eliminate the perennial crisis over presidential succession. The new party—the Partido Nacional Revolucionario (the National Revolutionary Party, or PNR)—was established in 1929.

Calles maintained his control throughout the 1928–1934 period. The Cristero Rebellion concluded with the government as the victor. The feud with the foreign-owned oil companies subsided. Calles had to cope with the financial and economic effects of the Great Depression, including the repatriation of Mexican workers from the United States. The government slowed down the program of land distribution, convinced that the land was being divided into uneconomically small holdings. The Maximum Leader collected increasing criticism that he was abandoning the principles of the Revolution.

Calles intended to continue in his dominant role beyond 1934, although he was legally prevented from running again for the presidency. He selected the man he intended to be his fourth puppet president, Lázaro Cárdenas. Calles even set down a "Six-Year Plan" to guide the Cárdenas administration between 1934 and 1940. Cárdenas, however, quickly moved to assert his independence, provoking a power struggle with the Maximum Leader. Cárdenas purged the official party of the followers of Calles, created new organizations to support the administration, and even forced Calles himself into exile in 1936.

The Revolution moved dramatically to the left under Cárdenas, a change already called for in the Six-Year Plan. This was most evident in the areas of agrarian reform and labor relations. In particular, Cárdenas greatly accelerated the distribution of land, a move dictated by political needs (attracting peasant support) rather than economic considerations. Cárdenas strictly enforced prolabor legislation, encouraged strikes, and even turned some business enterprises over to workers to operate under collective ownership. Cárdenas also created two important new groups to organize peasants and workers and to incorporate them more effectively into the official party. In 1938 he established the Confederación Nacional Campesina (the National Peasant Confederation, or CNC) to unite various local, state, and regional peasant groups. The new Confederación de Trabajadores de México (the Mexican Workers' Confederation, or CTM) replaced the discredited CROM as the government-supported labor confederation. Cárdenas incorporated the CNC and the CTM into a reorganized official party, renamed the Partido de la Revolución Mexicana (the Party of the Mexican Revolution, or PRM) in 1938. Cárdenas encountered problems with the Roman Catholic Church over his educational programs but avoided the level of conflict that had been reached under Calles. The peak of the antiforeign theme of the Constitution of 1917 came in 1938 with the nationalization of the foreign-owned oil companies.

Even as social reform was peaking in 1938, Cárdenas made a decision to push the Revolution and the country in a much different direction. Government finances were in drastic need of a major overhaul. The agrarian reform program had been a political success but an economic failure. It was painfully evident that government programs aimed at redistributing Mexico's wealth would not substantially improve the standard of living for Mexico's masses. New developmental approaches that would increase Mexico's wealth, not simply reallocate it, were required. The onset of World War II also pushed Mexico in the direction of new economic choices. Closer relations with the United States were unavoidable. More emphasis on industrialization was needed both to cope with the wartime situation and to promote postwar growth. The interests of labor would have to be subordinated to the needs of business. Even the long-running conflict between Church and State was seen as increasingly outdated, as the two parties developed a new working relationship.

The new approach to economic development became embodied in the term "import substitution industrialization" (ISI). The government consciously fostered a policy of rapid industrialization by imposing tariffs, employing import quotas, allocating credit, improving transportation and communication, and encouraging but guiding foreign investment. ISI produced spectacular results in the immediate post–World War II years, as the international community marveled at Mexico's "economic miracle." Mexico's development policies were seen as a model for other developing countries. But the new vision of a modern, urban, industrial society came at a price. The growth spurt was partially fueled by keeping wages low, so little of the benefits of the new prosperity filtered down to the masses. Rapid industrialization was accompanied by rapid urbanization, with cities unable to provide basic services to the rapidly expanding urban slums. Foreign penetration of the economy again became a major concern. The old problem of corruption achieved new dimensions. There was growing criticism that ISI was leading to a "new Porfiriato" in which a small elite reaped a disproportionate amount of the benefits of prosperity. By the late 1960s and early 1970s, the "miracle" was losing its luster. Growth slowed dramatically as the limits of ISI became more apparent.

Also in the 1960s and the 1970s, Mexican cultural production became increasingly diverse and even transnational as it shook off its preoccupation with cultural nationalism and began to engage more directly with "foreign" influences—many of them from its traditional competitor, the United States. The spread of international mass culture—from cinema to television to rock and roll—played a major role in this shift. So, also, did dissatisfaction with the authoritarian politics of the ruling party, the PRI. The 1968 Tlatelolco massacre of protesters by the army came to symbolize the growing disillusionment of Mexicans in general and of Mexican writers, artists, and other intellectuals in particular. This growing disillusionment had a profound effect on their responses to the officially sanctioned and sponsored cultural nationalism of earlier decades. Writers, artists, and intellectuals increasingly rejected cultural nationalism and embraced international trends in their respective fields. Artisans moved freely from traditional villages to modern markets to "postmodern" exhibition spaces and back again. Even the traditional icons, such as the Virgin of Guadalupe and *charros* (singing cowboys), developed new meanings as they took on new forms such as rub-on tattoos and music videos.

By the mid-1970s, it appeared that the day of economic reckoning was at hand for Mexico, but Mexico enjoyed a brief reprieve as the result of major new oil discoveries in the south and offshore. These new oil discoveries coincided with a long-term upswing in oil prices in the 1970s. The perils of oil prosperity, however, soon became evident: unprecedented corruption, government mismanagement, extensive foreign borrowing, and lavish subsidies for consumer items. The free-spending of the 1970s ended in the debt crisis of the 1980s. Austerity and economic reforms were now the order of the day. Under Presidents Miguel de la Madrid (1982–1988) and Carlos Salinas de Gortari (1988–1994), government adjustments to the debt crisis evolved into full-scale economic reforms that not only involved the abandonment of ISI but also the cherished ideals of the Revolution, most notably land reform. The 1980s became known as "the

lost decade" as most Mexicans experienced a decline in their standard of living. Mexico appeared to be on the road to economic recovery late in the Salinas administration, only to see those hopes evaporate with the collapse of the peso in late 1994. The North American Free Trade Agreement (NAFTA) went into effect in 1994, but continuing economic problems reduced its anticipated benefits. Salinas's claim that Mexico was on the verge of becoming a "First-World" country rang hollow for most Mexicans.

Mexico's economic problems and attempted reforms accelerated demands for political reforms. The reforms being sought were encapsulated in the phrase, "the democratization process." The demand for political reforms had been growing since the 1960s. In the Mexican context, democratization did not mean getting the military out of politics as it did in other Latin American countries; that had largely been accomplished already. Democratization required the internal and external reform of the official party, which had received a new name in 1946: the Partido Revolucionario Institucional (the Institutional Revolutionary Party, or PRI). There was growing criticism of the PRI for being unresponsive, undemocratic, and corrupt. The sorry state of the economy also encouraged political opposition. The PRI attempted to satisfy its critics by allowing opposition parties greater representation in the national Congress beginning in the 1960s. This was done through the use of "proportional representation," in which a certain number of seats in the lower house of the Congress (the Chamber of Deputies) were awarded based on the percentage of the national vote won by individual parties. Subsequent reforms in 1977 and 1986 led to greater opposition representation, but the perception existed that the government was "allocating" seats rather than the opposition "winning" them. Opponents concluded that the PRI was willing to allow the opposition a greater role in the political system as long as the opposition did not actually pose a threat to PRI control.

The continuing economic crisis, however, forced even greater concessions on the democratization process. During the Salinas administration, there were restrictions placed on campaign expenditures, which hurt the well-financed PRI, and the opposition was given greater access to the media, which was usually pro-PRI. The political reforms led to a greater opposition presence in local and state offices as well as in the national Congress. The PRI, however, still dominated the political process as a whole. In particular, there was widespread skepticism that the PRI would ever permit an opposition candidate to win the presidency. This conviction was particularly an outgrowth of the hotly disputed election of 1988, which many believed had been won by the opposition candidate, Cuauhtémoc Cárdenas, rather than by the PRI candidate, Carlos Salinas.

The election of the PRI candidate to the presidency in 1994, Ernesto Zedillo, was generally viewed as a true reflection of the voting results. Zedillo promised he would emphasize political reforms and preside over an honest election for the presidency in 2000. In 1996 the Federal Election Institute, which was responsible for conducting the election process, was made an autonomous agency; previously it had been under the control of the government and had come under heavy criticism for its supposed rigging of the presidential elections in 1988. Zedillo also indicated that he would not "tap" his choice for the PRI nomination for the presidency in 2000 as had been the practice since the 1920s but would permit real political competition for the nomination. Zedillo delivered on his political promises. The clearest evidence was the presidential victory in 2000 by opposition candidate Vicente Fox.

While the election of Fox was the end of a long struggle, it was also the beginning of a lengthy political process. One presidential election did not mean that "democracy" was established in Mexico. Political parties and leaders were not used to functioning in a democracy and often had trouble figuring out the "lessons" to be learned from the elections of 2000. The PRI no longer held the presidency, but it was still the dominant political party in terms of positions held at all levels of government. Fox did not have a working majority in either house of the national Congress—a situation made worse by the 2003 elections—and found it difficult to get his major reforms approved. Efforts to implement the "new federalism"—a shift in power from the central government to state and local governments—were encountering problems. Many Mexicans were still waiting for the economy to "recover." While trying to adjust to a global economy, Mexicans also had to adjust to growing transnational cultural influences viewed by many as a new type of "cultural imperialism." Old problems still remained: immigration, drug-trafficking, and corruption. The energy, enthusiasm, and optimism of the early months of the Fox administration seemed to wane. At least the air of crisis—which characterized so much of the 1970s, 1980s, and 1990s—was no longer in evidence. Mexico entered the twenty-first century much as it had entered the twentieth century: still pursuing the elusive goal of modernization.

CHRONOLOGY OF KEY EVENTS

1901   February. Founding of Partido Liberal Mexicano (PLM), early group opposing President Porfirio Díaz

1907   "Panic" of 1907 leads to recession in Mexico, hurting rich and poor alike

1910   September. Centennial of Mexican Independence

       20 November. Beginning of "The Revolution" against Porfirio Díaz as called for by Francisco Madero

1911   25 May. Resignation of President Porfirio Díaz; Francisco León de la Barra becomes interim president

       1 October. First post-Revolution presidential elections

       6 November. Francisco Madero assumes presidency

       28 November. Revolt by agrarian leader Emiliano Zapata against Madero administration

1912   3 March. Revolt by prominent Revolutionary general, Pascual Orozco, against Madero administration

1913   21 February. Assassination of President Francisco Madero as a result of military coup by General Victoriano Huerta

       Assumption of power by General Victoriano Huerta

       26 March. Plan of Guadalupe in opposition to Huerta administration issued by Governor Venustiano Carranza of Coahuila

1914   April–November. U.S. occupation of key Mexican port of Vera Cruz

       15 July. Resignation of Victoriano Huerta as president

       August. World War I begins in Europe

       October–November. Failure of Convention of Revolutionary leaders at Aguascalientes leads to civil war among Revolutionary factions

1916   9 March. Attack on Columbus, New Mexico, by forces of Revolutionary leader Francisco "Pancho" Villa leads to Pershing Expedition

1917   5 February. New, Revolutionary Constitution in effect

Last troops of Pershing Expedition leave Mexico

1 March. Publication of Zimmermann Telegram, which calls for Mexican–German alliance

April. The United States enters World War I on side of England and France

May. Election of Venustiano Carranza as first president under new Constitution

1918 May. Founding of Confederación Regional Obrera Mexicana, first national labor confederation affiliated with central government

1919 10 April. Assassination of Revolutionary leader Emiliano Zapata by supporters of President Venustiano Carranza

1920 April. Plan of Agua Prieta calls for overthrow of Carranza administration

21 May. Assassination of President Venustiano Carranza

1920–1924. Presidency of Revolutionary General Alvaro Obregón

1923 Bucareli Agreements between Mexico and the United States bring at least temporary settlement of major issues

20 July. Assassination of Revolutionary leader Francisco "Pancho" Villa

December. Adolfo de la Huerta, longtime ally of Obregón, revolts

against Obregón administration over issue of presidential succession in 1924

1924 1924–1928. Presidency of Revolutionary leader Plutarco Elías Calles

1925 January. Banco de México, Mexico's central bank, established

1928 17 July. Assassination of President-elect Alvaro Obregón

1928–1930. Mexican Congress selects Emilio Portes Gil to serve as interim president until new elections can be held and successor takes office

1928–1934. Period known as "The Maximato" after Calles (the "Maximum Leader") steps down from presidency but continues to control political scene

1929 Establishment of the Partido Nacional Revolucionario (official party, forerunner of current Partido Revolucionario Institucional)

June. Church-State agreement ends Cristero Rebellion

1930 1930–1932. Presidency of Revolutionary General Pascual Ortiz Rubio, first official party nominee elected to presidency

1932 3 September. President Ortiz Rubio resigns, citing health problems and "grave political reasons"

1932–1934. Mexican Congress selects Revolutionary General Abelardo Rodríguez to finish out presidential term through 1934

1934   1934–1940. Presidency of Revolutionary General Lázaro Cárdenas

1936   February. Confederación de Trabajadores de México established to serve as new national labor confederation supported by central government

April. Former President Plutarco Elías Calles exiled by President Cárdenas

1938   Confederación Nacional Campesina established to organize peasant organizations at local, state, and regional levels; later becomes peasant component of reorganized official party

PNR reorganized and renamed the Partido de la Revolución Mexicana (PRM)

18 March. Expropriation of foreign-owned oil companies

July. Petróleos Mexicanos (PEMEX)—government-owned oil company—begins operations

1939   September. Founding of the Partido de Acción Nacional (PAN)

World War II in Europe begins

1940   1940–1946. Presidency of General Manuel Avila Camacho, the last of the military presidents

1942   Beginning of *bracero* program (ends 31 December 1964)

22 May. Mexico enters World War II

1946   Partido de la Revolucion Mexicana (official party) renamed the Partido Revolucionario Institucional (PRI)

1946–1952. Presidency of Miguel Alemán

1952   1952–1958. Presidency of Adolfo Ruiz Cortines

1954   Devaluation of the peso (12.5 pesos to the dollar)

1958   1958–1964. Presidency of Adolfo López Mateos

1963   Chamizal Treaty

1964   1964–1970. Presidency of Gustavo Díaz Ordaz

1968   October. Summer Olympics in Mexico City

2 October. Tlatelolco "Massacre"

1970   1970–1976. Presidency of Luis Echeverría Alvarez

1971   10 June. Corpus Christi Day "massacre" of demonstrating students in Mexico City by police and paramilitary units

1976   September. Peso devalued for first time since 1954 (20.5 pesos to the dollar)

1976–1982. Presidency of José López Portillo

Exploitation of new oil resources leads to runaway boom and unprecedented corruption

1982   August. Announcement by Mexican government on debt problem

September. Nationalization of the banks

1982–1988. Presidency of Miguel de la Madrid

1985   19 September. Mexico City earthquake

1986   Immigration Reform and Control Act providing major changes in immigration laws goes into effect

1988   1988–1994. Presidency of Carlos Salinas de Gortari

1990   January. Debt settlement

1992   January. Provisions of Constitution relating to Church-State relations amended

September. Mexico and the Vatican establish diplomatic relations

1993   June. Cardinal Juan Jesús Posadas Ocampo murdered

1994   1 January. North American Free Trade Agreement goes into effect

Zapatista rebellion begins in southern Mexico

23 March. Assassination of PRI presidential candidate Luis Donaldo

Colosio; replaced by Ernesto Zedillo Ponce de León

May. First televised debate in presidential elections

September. Assassination of PRI official José Francisco Ruiz Massieu

December. Peso "crisis" and devaluation

1994–2000. Presidency of Ernesto Zedillo Ponce de León

1995   28 February. Arrest of Raúl Salinas, brother of former president, on murder conspiracy charges

2000   July. Presidential elections result in victory by PAN candidate Vicente Fox; first loss of presidential election by official party (PRI) since its establishment in 1929

2000–2006. Presidency of Vicente Fox

2003   July. Congressional elections strengthen PRI, weaken PAN

2004   February. Arrest of Miguel Nazar Haro, former security official who led "dirty war" against leftists in the 1960s and 1970s.

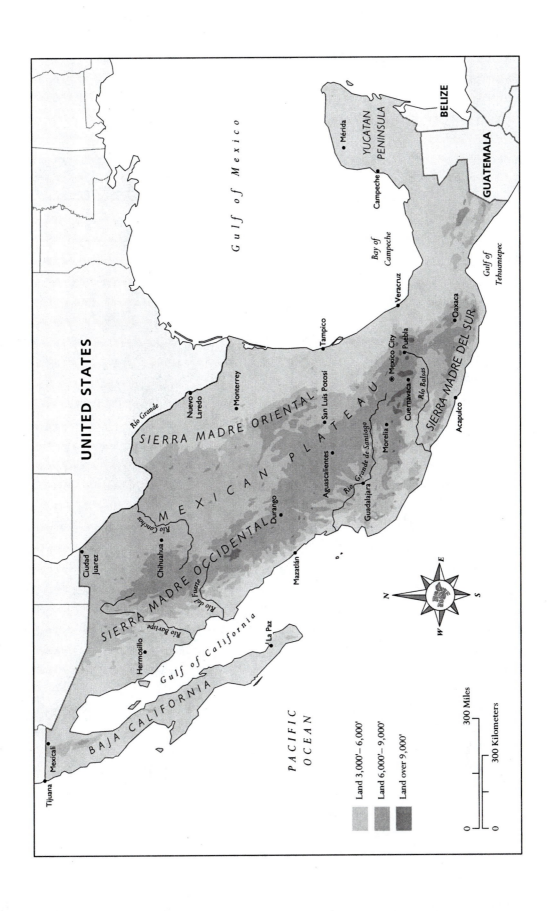

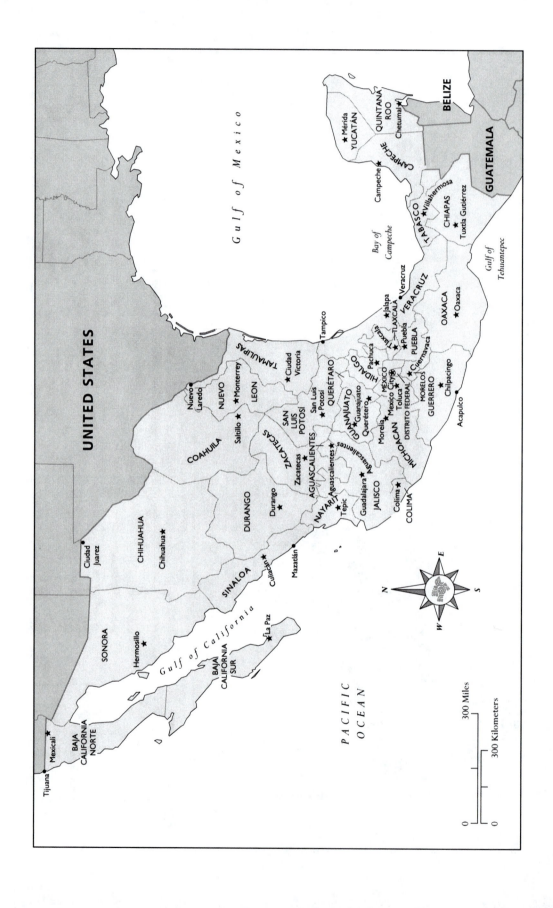

Agrarian Reform/Land and Land Policy

The history of land tenure and land policy in Mexico is a complex one. Agrarian reform, a prominent theme of the Mexican Revolution, is a key to contemporary Mexico and has made the term *ejido* (land granted to a specific group for communal cultivation) common-place. The ongoing importance of the agrarian question is evident in the numerous peasant revolts and conflicts that are a part of Mexico's history, including the Zapatista rebellion that emerged during the last decade of the twentieth century. At the heart of Mexican agrarian reform and land policy has been the debate over the existence of and right to communal property, as well as Mexico's ongoing attempt to grapple with the legacy of *latifundio*, or large-scale landholding.

The concept of communal land was embraced by both pre-Hispanic cultures and by the Spanish conquerors of Mexico. The *calpulli*, the basic unit of social organization among the Aztecs, included not only lands for cultivation assigned to each head of a family, but also lands held and worked in common by *calpulli* members. In the same way, the Spanish Crown granted lands for individual use as well as the collective use of a town. Only grants to Spaniards were recognized as pri-

vate property, while those to Indian villages were simply grants to use the land. As the colonial era progressed, land grants to Spaniards as well as Spanish policies that enabled Spaniards to acquire Indian lands, contributed to the growth of large landholdings or *latifundio*, and the large estate, or hacienda, became a permanent fixture of the Mexican economy.

The Catholic Church also contributed to the concentration of land during the colonial era. In fact, because many *hacendados* (owners of large estates) left parts of their lands to the Church in their wills, by the time of Mexican Independence, the Church had become Mexico's principal landowner. Church lands were usually left fallow and were said to be in *manos muertos* or "dead hands." By the beginning of the nineteenth century, land distribution was skewed in favor of large and often inefficient estates owned by *hacendados* and the Church. At the same time, several Indian and peasant communities clung precariously to the communal lands that helped secure their livelihood, while Mexican leaders in the liberal tradition began a long debate over the future of communal and corporate landholding.

Mexico's struggle for independence that began in 1810 provided evidence that the agrarian question had become a significant one in Mexican society. Followers of the early popular revolts led by Miguel Hidalgo and José María Morelos were often peasants affected by the gradual disappearance of community lands during the colonial era, and the agrarian question compelled both Hidalgo and Morelos to call for the protection of community lands. Immediately after independence, however, liberal leaders determined that the key to Mexico's progress lay in the creation of an economy based on private property and the yeoman farmer. Hence they staged a multipronged attack on communal landholding that targeted both the Church and Indian communities. The first step in the liberal attack was the Ley Lerdo of 1856, included in the 1857 Constitution as Article 27. This law opened for sale and private ownership Church and community lands, including Indian *ejidos.* Although the Catholic Church was often able to protect its lands by, for example, selling to trusted friends, many Mexican peasants saw their lands, both family and communal, threatened.

Bitter conflict over the liberal agenda provoked a civil war from 1858 to 1861, which was soon followed by the French occupation of Mexico. Such unrest, particularly because it underscored the rebellious potential of Mexico's peasants, forced liberals to stall their agrarian plans. As Mexico emerged from the nineteenth century, a full-scale and largely successful assault on Church lands was completed, but political exigencies had halted the liberal assault on community lands and on the Indian *ejido.* Furthermore, nothing was done about *latifundio,* and Mexico remained a country characterized by the existence of large estates owned by a wealthy few.

The period from 1876 to 1910, presided over by Porfirio Díaz, was one of impressive economic growth and national integration. The agrarian question was central to Díaz's plans for transforming Mexico, as he envisioned the growth of Mexico's agrarian export sector and sought the enhancement of Mexico's rural economy through the incorporation of vacant or untitled lands. To this end, Díaz passed laws in 1875, 1883, and 1884

that provided for the transfer of such *terrenos baldíos* to private ownership. Two mechanisms aided Díaz in this transfer. The first involved concessions to private survey companies in which untitled lands were surveyed and companies received one-third of the land marked. In this way, survey companies were especially important in bringing the previously isolated lands of the northern states into the national economy. The second mechanism that aided the transfer of land involved legal proceedings by which untitled lands were claimed and passed into private hands. In both cases, communities and private owners were given the opportunity to present the title or deed that would protect their lands from such transfers. Since most lacked such papers, however, dispossession was a common result of the Porfirian land program.

The effect of Porfirian policies on land tenure in Mexico was twofold. In the first place, Díaz's laws intensified the concentration of landed wealth, so that by 1910, 87 percent of Mexico's rural lands were owned by less than 1 percent of its landowners. Thus the problem of *latifundio* persisted. Secondly, Díaz's approach to the agrarian question increased the number of Mexicans without land. Indeed, by 1910, approximately 90 percent of the population was landless. While Porfirian policies enhanced Mexico's economy and were central to the transformation and integration of the Mexican nation, they also ensured that peasant grievances would continue to grow. Not surprisingly, such grievances were an important part of the Mexican Revolution and were central to the crafting of the postrevolutionary Mexican state.

When Francisco I. Madero called for revolt against the dictatorship of Porfirio Díaz in 1910, he included in his revolutionary Plan of San Luis Potosí a pledge to restore to their original owners untitled lands unjustly taken by survey companies and courts of law during the Porfiriato. But as a wealthy landowner from the northern state of Coahuila, Madero's commitment to true agrarian reform was always in doubt. His hesitancy to act on an issue that drew scores of peasants into the Mexican Revolution was a key element in his downfall. Peasants in Mexico's central/eastern section especially rallied around the land question and found in Emiliano Zapata a potent agrarian leader.

Zapata was a small-scale landowner from the central Mexican state of Morelos, a state affected by the growth of the sugar-export industry during the Porfiriato—growth that entailed the expansion of large sugar estates at the expense of the peasantry. In the 1911 Plan of Ayala, Zapata pledged to help those Mexicans needing land through the restoration of lands previously taken from villages, and through the expropriation of one-third of all hacienda properties. As it developed, Zapatista agrarian policy came also to include limits on the amount of land an individual could hold (an attempt to address the problem of *latifundio*) and pledged to protect village lands. Zapatista reform moved beyond words and included the occupation of several large haciendas by Zapatista soldiers. The popular success of the Zapatista rebellion in Mexico ensured that Mexico's persistent agrarian problem would have to be addressed by each of the main revolutionary factions. Each crafted its own approach to land reform.

By 1915, Pancho Villa and Venustiano Carranza, both important revolutionaries from the north, had added their voices to the agrarian debate. Although Villa called for an end to *latifundio*, he placed his faith in small-scale private plots, rather than communal or *ejido* lands. And although he joined Zapata in his pledge to help peasants dispossessed of their lands, Villista land expropriations were largely political measures designed to punish enemies and generate revenue. Pressured by the success of Zapatismo, in 1915 Carranza reluctantly announced his own Agrarian Law, guaranteeing the restoration of stolen *ejido* lands and the granting of *ejidos* to peasant villages in need. Carranza also established national and local mechanisms for processing petitions for land.

While the Zapatista faction would eventually be defeated on the battlefield, it was Zapata's vision of rural Mexico that ultimately triumphed. In Article 27 of the Constitution of 1917, the idea of the *ejido* was officially sanctioned. The Mexican state assumed responsibility for restoring lands taken from peasants, and granting *ejidos* to peasant communities that needed them. Only plots of good land not exceeding fifty hectares were exempt from expropriation, and the idea that subsoil resources (including oil) ultimately belonged to the nation was endorsed.

Despite the strength of Article 27, its implementation varied widely and was dependent upon the personal outlook of each Mexican president and the political exigencies faced. Indeed, the first three presidents under the new constitution—Carranza, Alvaro Obregón, and Plutarco Elías Calles—were lukewarm in their efforts to distribute lands, favoring private property over *ejidos*. Furthermore, landowners could, through the courts or through the use of force, effectively halt land distribution. (The landowner's right to legally suspend expropriation of his properties was revoked only in 1931.) When it occurred, land reform had a clearly political motive and the process was often tainted with corruption. The favored region for *ejido* grants was East-Central Mexico, the stronghold of Zapatismo, which included the states of Morelos, Puebla, Tlaxcala, Mexico, Hidalgo, and the Federal District.

While the period from 1917 to 1934 amounted to only a minor assault on Mexican *latifundio*, the presidency of Lázaro Cárdenas (1934 to 1940) represented the heyday of agrarian reform. Economic difficulties and the increasing militancy of peasant groups confronted Cárdenas as he assumed power. Unlike his predecessors, Cárdenas embraced the idea of the *ejido* and increased state support for *ejidatarios* through such things as the Ejido Credit Bank. Cárdenas also sealed his reputation as champion of the Mexican *campesino* (peasant) by distributing twice as much land as his predecessors. By the end of his term, 49 million acres had been distributed to the benefit of more than 700,000 peasants. One of the most impressive expropriations occurred in the Laguna region along the border of the northern states of Coahuila and Durango. There, in 1936, Cárdenas took nearly 150,000 hectares and distributed it to more than 30,000 *campesinos*. The Laguna became a kind of showcase of Cardenista reform, and the federal government supplied schools and other social services to the region's *ejidatarios*.

Agrarian reform under Cárdenas, however, retained a high degree of political motivation. In 1939, Cárdenas established the National Campesino Confederation (CNC), bringing together local peasant groups into a national organization beholden to him. At the same time, Cárdenas's agrarianism encouraged the continued growth of landowner resistance and militancy. Indeed, many large landowners divided their lands among relatives and friends to avoid expropriation. In this way, Mexico's wealthy elite somewhat ironically contributed to the ongoing dissolution of *latifundio* in Mexico. Finally, despite and perhaps because of its scope, Cardenista agrarian reform, like that of the 1917 to 1934 era, was accompanied by a certain degree of corruption. But it was the decline in Mexico's agricultural productivity, a by-product of the initial disruption caused by agrarian reform, that helped inspire a post-1940 shift away from the *ejido* and back to the idea of small-scale, privately owned plots.

For the next twenty-five years, legal reforms increased the amount of agricultural land an individual small landowner could hold, while continuing the protection for cattle ranchers and the cattle industry that was actually begun under Cárdenas. Most importantly, as the Mexican government embraced industrial development and agricultural modernization, financial support of the ejidal sector declined. By the mid-1960s, this, along with Mexico's steady population growth, contributed to a situation in which the country could no longer feed itself.

From 1964 to 1976, Mexico experienced another wave of agrarian reform as Presidents Gustavo Díaz Ordaz and Luís Echeverría sought to revive the agrarian sector, bolster the country's agricultural productivity, and respond to a new wave of peasant mobilization. The amount of land distributed under these two leaders was twice that distributed under Cárdenas, and it included a significant portion of northern Mexico, where *latifundio* was especially persistent. Little was solved, however, and it was increasingly obvious that in Mexico the problem of *latifundio* had been replaced by that of *minifundio:* plots too small to produce well, especially in an increasingly global market.

By the 1980s, as Mexico wrestled with a general economic crisis and attempted to respond to international pressures to open up its economy, the limits of the *ejido* became especially apparent. It was left to Carlos Salinas de Gortari, president from 1988 to 1994, to make the changes necessary to end Mexico's long history of agrarian reform. In 1992, Salinas announced reforms to Article 27 of the Constitution, granting *ejidatarios* legal titles to the lands previously held in trust for them by the nation, and thus providing the opportunity to sell or rent such lands. Land reform was effectively ended, and the hope was that the Mexican agricultural sector would embark upon a new era of growth and productivity.

Predictably, Salinas's determination to end the redistribution of land sparked criticism and protest. The most visible resistance to change came in the form of the Zapatista uprising in the southern state of Chiapas. This rebel movement began in 1994 and included as part of its agenda the defense of Article 27. Despite changes to the Consitution, however, Mexico experienced no significant change in landholding patterns during the last years of the twentieth century, and the *ejido* is still a significant part of the rural landscape. Whether agrarian reform is truly dead is a question left to the twenty-first century.

—*SBP*

See also: Confederación Nacional Campesina (CNC); Constitution of 1917; North American Free Trade Agreement (NAFTA); Revolution of 1910; Zapata, Emiliano; Zapatista National Liberation Army (EZLN).
References:
Craig, Ann L. *The First Agraristas: An Oral History of a Mexican Agrarian Reform Movement.* Berkeley: University of California Press, 1983.
DeWalt, Billie R., Martha W. Rees, and Arthur D. Murphy. *The End of Agrarian Reform in Mexico: Past Lessons, Future Prospects.* San Diego: Center for U.S.–Mexican Studies, University of California, San Diego, 1994.
Gledhill, John. *Casi Nada: A Study of Agrarian Reform in the Heartland of Cardenismo.* Albany, NY: Institute for Mesoamerican Studies, 1991.
Harvey, Neil. *The New Agrarian Movement in Mexico, 1979–1990.* London: Institute of Latin American Studies, 1990.
Markiewicz, Dana. *The Mexican Revolution and the Limits of Agrarian Reform.* Boulder, CO: Lynne Rienner, 1993.
Randall, Laura, ed. *Reforming Mexico's Agrarian Reform.* Armonk, NY: M. E. Sharpe, 1996.
Sanderson, Steven E. *Agrarian Populism and the Mexican State: The Struggle for Land in Sonora.* Berkeley: University of California Press, 1981.
Sanderson, Susan Walsh. *Land Reform in Mexico, 1910–1980.* Orlando, FL: Academic Press, 1984.
Simpson, Eyler N. *The Ejido: Mexico's Way Out.* Chapel Hill: University of North Carolina Press, 1937.
Tannenbaum, Frank. *The Mexican Agrarian Revolution.* New York: Macmillan, 1929.

Aguascalientes, Convention of

In August 1914 the combined military pressure of various Revolutionary groups forced General Victoriano Huerta to resign as president and go into exile. There was a widespread fear that the overthrow of the common enemy would soon give way to fighting among the different Revolutionary factions. A noticeable split had already taken place in the ranks of the Constitutionalists, the northern and most important group which had opposed Huerta. The "First Chief of the Constitutionalist Army," Venustiano Carranza, was feuding with his most famous general, Francisco "Pancho" Villa. The Constitutionalists

also lacked any kind of agreement with the followers of Emiliano Zapata, the leader of the major rebel force in the south. Many of the Revolutionary factions operated with little direct control from Carranza, Villa, or Zapata. Carranza further confused the situation by ignoring his own Revolutionary program, the Plan of Guadalupe, which called for Carranza either to become provisional president or to designate a provisional president once Huerta was defeated. Instead Carranza continued to function as "First Chief," which gave him a free hand in making decisions. With the ouster of Huerta, the Revolutionary groups needed to gather to work out the appointment of a provisional president and develop a transition to a regular government. Failure to do so almost certainly meant renewed and even bloodier civil war.

Carranza tried to deal with the situation by calling for certain Revolutionary leaders to meet in Mexico City on 1 October 1914. The meeting did not really serve the cause of Revolutionary unity. First, Carranza made a concerted effort to exclude any military chiefs loyal to either Villa or Zapata. While this did not ensure that only pro-Carranza leaders would attend, it did create the perception that Carranza was "packing" the meeting with his own supporters. Second, Carranza also made it clear that he considered the meeting to be strictly an advisory body that could make recommendations to him (a "junta") rather than a group that could make independent decisions on Mexico's political, economic, and social problems (a "convention"). Carranza's views on the gathering disappointed even his supporters, most of whom wanted the calling of a "convention." Before the junta met, Villa broke publicly with Carranza. On 30 September Villa issued a manifesto denouncing the proposed gathering and calling for the removal of Carranza. That same day, Carranza's top general, Alvaro Obregón, informed Carranza that he and other leading military figures had reached an agreement that a "convention" of Revolutionary chieftains would take place in the city of

Aguascalientes beginning on 10 October. Unlike the meeting scheduled for Mexico City, the convention at Aguascalientes would be open to all Revolutionary factions.

Despite these developments, the junta convened as scheduled on 1 October in Mexico City. The some 80 delegates supposedly did not include any who were obviously anti-Carranza, but most at the meeting indicated a willingness to dump Carranza if it would prevent civil war. Some civilians were present at the meeting, but the military dominated, with Obregón playing a leading role. Carranza made a speech to the junta, during which he offered his resignation. The junta did not accept the resignation but did so in a way that left open the possibility of Carranza resigning. Instead of rejecting the resignation and supporting Carranza's actions, the junta voted overwhelmingly to delay consideration of the resignation until the Convention at Aguascalientes. The junta also reached two other important decisions. The large majority of delegates voted to attend the Convention at Aguascalientes and also agreed that only military leaders would be permitted to attend the Convention at Aguascalientes. Although the meeting of the junta had been both planned and denounced as a pro-Carranza gathering, the discussions were often bitter, and most delegates indicated a willingness to sacrifice Carranza in the interest of domestic peace. The meeting at Mexico City proved to be a good preview of what was to come at Aguascalientes.

In October 1914 Aguascalientes was a thriving city of approximately 40,000 people that had escaped the worst effects of the Revolutionary disorders. The city was supposed to be a neutral site, and there was an agreement among the Revolutionary factions that there would be no troop movements during the convention. The reality was that there were not only troop movements but also fighting in a number of locations. In addition, Villa had a force of approximately 40,000 men within a day's travel of Aguascalientes and some 15,000 troops who could reach the city within two hours. This military presence created the impression—if not the reality—of a convention dominated by Villa.

Furthermore, there were problems concerning the composition of the convention. Attendance was supposedly restricted to military commanders with representation based on the number of troops in the field. Some of the military leaders were notable for their absence. Neither Carranza nor Zapata attended sessions of the convention. Villa made only a brief, ceremonial appearance. Many other military leaders sent their representatives rather than attending in person; in fact, most of the participants fell into this category. The decision to restrict the meeting to military leaders was also evaded; several of the representatives were civilians or persons who were given a military rank for the occasion but who had never led troops in combat. Also missing at the start were delegates from Zapata. Drawing the Zapatistas into the process was considered crucial; although the convention convened as scheduled on 10 October, there was little substantive action until the delegation from Zapata arrived on 26 October. Most of the Zapatista delegates were in fact civilians, although they all had an official military rank. The Zapatistas further confused the situation by refusing to present their credentials but still demanding the right to speak and even vote in convention sessions. Of a total convention membership of some 150, Villa controlled 37 delegates and Zapata 26. The remainder—a large majority—were not necessarily pro-Carranza. Carranza had alienated many military leaders by his firm stand for *civilismo*, civilian control of politics. Most of the military leaders were convinced that politics was too important to be left exclusively to the politicians and envisioned a major role for themselves in ruling a post-Revolutionary Mexico.

Carranza's attitude toward the convention was crucial to its outcome, even though he was not in attendance. Carranza declined to attend the convention because to do so would have reduced his role to that of one more delegate in terms of influence. Carranza also consistently refused to recognize that the convention had any independent power to make decisions. His attitude was that the Convention of Aguascalientes was just like the recently held junta in Mexico City: an advisory body and nothing more. Carranza declined an invitation by the convention to attend but did send a message to the convention which was read by Obregón. In the message Carranza denounced his critics at the convention as "reactionaries." He said that he was "disposed to retire" as First Chief but would do so only if Villa and Zapata retired at the same time. Carranza also offered a threat; he was ready to mobilize Constitutionalist forces against the "enemies of the Mexican people." In a secret session, the convention accepted what it called the "resignations" of Villa and Carranza. The vote on Carranza was revealing on two counts. First, Carranza had never tendered his resignation; he had indicated only that he was considering retirement under certain conditions, which still had to be met. Second, only 20 delegates voted for Carranza to continue in his present capacity, a clear indication of how few delegates were truly pro-Carranza.

Without even considering the possibility of Carranza continuing as First Chief, the convention moved to the selection of a provisional president. With the major figures canceling each other out, Obregón on 1 November took the lead in having the provisional presidency bestowed on General Eulalio Gutiérrez, who had played a minor role in the struggle against Huerta and was currently the military governor of San Luis Potosí. To appease the Zapatista representatives who claimed that their full delegation had not yet arrived, Gutiérrez's term was to run only to 20 November when his continuation in office would have to be confirmed by the convention.

Any unity produced by the appointment of Gutiérrez soon vanished on 2 November when Villa arrived in Aguascalientes with some 6,000 troops, including artillery.

Gutiérrez tried to limit the damage by claiming that Villa had his permission to come to town to purchase supplies. The presence of Villa's troops, however, violated the most important promise made about the security of the convention and cast considerable doubt on the independence of Gutiérrez. Villa's forces continued to move in, bringing the total to some 30,000 troops in the immediate area by 7 November. With the independence of the convention hopelessly compromised and with Carranza supporters withdrawing from the convention, delegates voted on 5 November to send an ultimatum to Carranza demanding that he step down no later than 10 November. When the deadline passed without a response from Carranza, the delegates declared that Carranza was "in rebellion" against the convention.

On 1 November, Carranza had already started to respond to the actions of Villa and the convention by beginning a slow-motion evacuation of Mexico City. Carranza began a withdrawal to the east of the civilian government, which was followed by a military withdrawal of Constitutionalist forces from the capital under the leadership of Obregón, who had sided with Carranza in the coming struggle. Sides had been chosen for what was to become the bloodiest phase of the Revolution between 1910 and 1920.

All three of the major Revolutionary leaders were unwilling to submit their respective movements to outside authority, and all three played a key role in the convention's failure. Carranza did not want the convention in the first place, considered it only an advisory body, and had no intention of cooperating with it if it moved in a direction against his wishes. Villa's use of his troops went from compromising the convention to bringing about its collapse. By the time the convention officially adjourned, the image of a convention dominated by Villa had largely become reality. Zapata's uncompromising stance and the demanding attitude of his representatives also undercut any possibility of success. The Zapatistas arrived late, demanded much, and were more interested in forging links with Villa than in making the convention a success. The Mexican people ultimately paid the price for the convention's failure. In the year following the convention, approximately 200,000 Mexicans died in the fighting among the Revolutionary factions.

—DMC

See also: Carranza, Venustiano; Constitutionalists; Huerta, Victoriano; Militarism; Obregón, Alvaro; Revolution of 1910; Vera Cruz, Occupation of (1914); Villa, Francisco "Pancho"; Zapata, Emiliano.

References:
Cumberland, Charles C. *Mexican Revolution: The Constitutionalist Years.* Austin: University of Texas Press, 1972.
Knight, Alan. *The Mexican Revolution.* 2 vols. Cambridge: Cambridge University Press, 1986.
Quirk, Robert E. *The Mexican Revolution, 1914–1915.* Bloomington: Indiana University Press, 1960.

Aguascalientes (State)

One of Mexico's smallest states, Aguascalientes is located in central Mexico. The state's name means "hot waters" and is a reference to the numerous hot springs that attract swimmers and bathers to the area. The city of Aguascalientes serves as the capital, and other main urban areas are Jesús María, Calvillo, and Rincón de Ramos. Aguascalientes developed in the shadow of Zacatecas, colonial Mexico's lucrative silver mining region. Its struggle for autonomy (and eventual statehood) continued well into the nineteenth century, and its central location placed Aguascalientes at the center of Mexico's revolutionary upheaval during the early part of the twentieth century. Indeed, the state hosted (and gave its name to) the revolutionary convention that sought to create a new government and chart a new course for Mexico. A predominantly agricultural state for most of its history, Aguascalientes developed a more urban, industrial base during the latter part of the twentieth century.

During the Spanish colonial era, Aguascalientes was part of the province of Zacatecas and was incorporated into the broader juris-

diction of Nueva Galicia. The search for, and discovery of, lucrative silver mines in Zacatecas ensured a constant flow of Spaniards through the territory of Aguascalientes. As elsewhere in Nueva Galicia, Indian peoples resisted the Spanish advance, and from 1541 to 1542 the province experienced a bloody conflict known as the Mixtón War. Indian resistance continued beyond the Mixtón War, and it prevented the city of Aguascalientes (established in 1575) from experiencing any real growth until the end of the sixteenth century. Meanwhile, war, disease, and slavery caused a dramatic decline in the region's Indian population. Many who survived became workers on Spanish haciendas, while a few groups managed to establish their own settlements.

For most of the colonial period, Aguascalientes served primarily as a way station for those on their way to Zacatecas from Guadalajara (Jalisco) and Mexico City. The region developed some cattle ranching and agriculture, though it struggled to feed its people. Periodic famine compelled the opening to cultivation of more land during the eighteenth century. The early 1700s also saw the emergence of silver mining in Aguascalientes, which was centered in the mining community of Asientos. Though Asientos did not enjoy a boom similar to that in Zacatecas, its development did help to transform the city of Aguascalientes into a more dynamic commercial area.

After Mexico achieved its independence in 1821, Aguascalientes remained a part of Zacatecas. It was the most populous section of that state, and it also emerged as a productive agricultural zone. While some in Aguascalientes argued that, because of the area's small size and limited resources, it was better to remain a part of Zacatecas, the broader trend was toward autonomy, though it was not easily achieved. In 1835, Aguascalientes was separated from its northern master as a reward for aid given to the central government during a Zacatecas rebellion. For the next two decades, however, Zacatecas resisted Aguascalientes's independence and the latter region alternated between being a federal territory and remaining a part of its stronger neighbor. Not until the promulgation of Mexico's 1857 constitution was Aguascalientes finally recognized as an independent state. Its central location within Mexico, however, ensured that an independent Aguascalientes would continue to feel the effects of broader political events. In the 1860s, French troops occupied the state and a decade later, soldiers supporting the revolt of Porfirio Díaz gained control of its capital city.

Economic developments during the late nineteenth and early twentieth centuries helped to transform and diversify the still predominantly rural structure of Aguascalientes. The arrival of the railroad encouraged modernization of the agricultural sector, which produced increasing amounts of corn, wheat, beans, and meat. These foodstuffs helped to supply the workers who labored in factories that were built in the state's capital. Aguascalientes City became a center of Mexico's tanning industry, and it emerged as one of Mexico's most important railroad centers, with connections to Mexico City, the border town of El Paso, and the Gulf Coast port city of Tampico. On the eve of the Mexican Revolution, Aguascalientes had also become one of Mexico's most important producers of copper and lead. The Guggenheim family was instrumental in this development, investing money, hiring thousands of workers, and opening the Great Central Mexican Smelter just north of the state capital.

The inhabitants of Aguascalientes experienced economic growth unevenly. While wealthier elements took advantage of land laws to further concentrate their holdings, others lost land and many chose to leave the state. And while foreign investors such as the Guggenheims created thousands of jobs, workers laboring in the Great Central Mexican Smelter and other factories were often poorly paid and poorly treated. As in many areas of Mexico during the Díaz dictatorship, political and economic power was concentrated in a few hands, and the corruption inherent in that monopoly was often glaringly evident. On the eve of the Mexican Revolu-

tion, Aguascalientes's governor, Alejandro Vázquez del Mercado, became embroiled in a very public scandal when he embarked upon a costly project to bring drinking water and a drainage system to the state capital. The project promised to funnel large sums of money to Vázquez's friends at a time when most residents of the state were experiencing lower wages, political repression, and even famine.

Despite the concentration of land and power, Aguascalientes did not host any significant uprisings during the Mexican Revolution. It did, however, experience the effects of that upheaval. In the early phase of the Revolution, Alberto Fuentes Dávila (a native of Coahuila) became the state's governor. Fuentes worked to undercut the privileges of Aguascalientes's large landowners, and although his reforms were later nullified, Fuentes gained a reputation as a particularly radical leader. In October 1914, the spotlight fell on the city of Aguascalientes, which hosted the leaders of the revolution as they chose a new government. With the split between this "convention" government and Venustiano Carranza's Constitutionalist movement, Aguascalientes remained strategically important. The forces of Pancho Villa (representing the convention) occupied the capital until July of 1915, when Constitutionalist general Alvaro Obregón captured the city.

The dislocations of the Mexican Revolution encouraged many in Aguascalientes to emigrate, a factor that discouraged any further revolutionary activity and that enabled the state's traditional elite to regain much of its power during the 1920s. Aguascalientes, like the neighboring state of Jalisco, resisted radical reforms for a time. It was also a center of conservative Catholic activism, and of the church-state struggle known as the Cristero Rebellion (1926–1929). Though local demands for change were temporarily muted, President Lázaro Cárdenas and governors Enrique Osornio and Juan G. Alvarado finally answered them during the 1930s. Petitions for land received a favorable response, and railroad workers, as well as workers in the state's mining and smelting industry, found that their views were increasingly represented in the political arena.

In the decades after the Mexican Revolution and the reforms of the 1930s, Aguascalientes entered a period of economic development and urbanization. From 1940 to the 1990s, the state's rural population experienced a gradual decline as mechanized agriculture took hold, displacing some farmers and rural workers. At the same time, industry grew, particularly in the capital city. During the 1980s, Aguascalientes began to attract more foreign capital, particularly in the electronics industry, which was geared toward external markets. The capital housed a large Texas Instruments factory, and it also developed a clothing industry that employed primarily female labor. By the end of the twentieth century, Aguascalientes continued to depend on commercial agriculture and cattle ranching. Erosion and drought, however, were presenting new problems for farmers and ranchers. Meanwhile, the constant migration of the state's inhabitants toward more urban areas was beginning to have negative effects, with the capital city struggling to provide housing and services to increasing numbers of new residents.

—SBP

See also: Catholic Church; Cristero Rebellion; Jalisco (State); Revolution of 1910; Zacatecas (State)

References:

Esparza, Victor M. González. *Cambio y continuidad: la revolución mexicana en Aguascalientes.* Mexico City: CIEMA, 1998.

———. *Jalones modernizadores: Aguascalientes en el Siglo XX.* Aguascalientes: Instituto Cultural de Aguascalientes, 1992.

Rojas, Beatríz, et al. *Cambio y continuidad: la revolución mexicana en Aguascalientes.* Mexico City: El Colegio de Mexico, 1994.

Official state web site: www.ags.gob.mx

Alemán, Miguel (1900–1983)

President from 1946 to 1952, Miguel Alemán was born in the Gulf Coast state of Veracruz. He was unable to attend schools in his hometown of Sayula because of the "radical" political views of his father, a storekeeper who later become a Revolutionary general. Alemán attended the prestigious National Preparatory School in Mexico City and later received his law degree from the National School of Law in 1928. He became the legal advisor to the secretary of agriculture, but suffered a personal and political blow in 1929 when his father—now a Revolutionary general—revolted unsuccessfully against the regime of Plutarco Elías Calles and was killed. From 1930 to 1935, Alemán served as a judge on the Higher Tribunal of Justice of the Federal District. The rise of Lázaro Cárdenas and the simultaneous decline of Calles helped Alemán's career. In 1934 he won election to the national senate from the state of Veracruz and served as governor of the state from 1936 to 1939. In 1939 he became national director for the presidential campaign of General Manuel Avila Camacho, the nominee of the official party. After Avila Camacho was elected president, he rewarded Alemán by appointing him to the key cabinet position of secretary of the interior (internal security). Avila Camacho then tapped Alemán in 1945 to succeed him as president. With the nomination of the official party, Alemán easily won election to the presidency in 1946, the first civilian to be elected president since 1917.

Labor support for Alemán in 1945–1946 led some to believe that Alemán might deviate from the policies followed during the administration of Avila Camacho. Alemán, however, built on those policies and became identified with them both politically and historically. Agrarian reform, labor rights, anticlericalism, and economic nationalism gave way to import substitution industrialization, close ties with business, accommodation with the Roman Catholic Church, and encouragement of foreign investment. This shift in policy—although started in 1938—became known as "Alemanismo."

The attitude of the new administration became evident early on with changes in the agrarian reform program. Alemán had the Congress pass new legislation giving landowners greater legal protection against expropriation and increasing the maximum legal size of landholdings. Alemán was more

Miguel Alemán, candidate for the Mexican presidency, is surrounded by supporters on his way to make a speech. Mexico City, 1946. (Library of Congress)

concerned with the modernization of agriculture than with land redistribution. Credit was reduced for the communal landholdings created in the 1920s and 1930s and increased for large-scale agricultural producers geared to the export market.

Alemán also showed that he was much more concerned with business than with labor. The strong commitment to industrialization encouraged the president's probusiness attitude. Wealthy businessmen had made large contributions to Alemán's presidential campaign, and Alemán himself was a big businessman in the making while serving as president. Alemán encouraged divisions within the ranks of organized labor and made it clear he would not tolerate strikes or other work stoppages interfering with the industrialization program. The new president was in of-

fice less than a month when he took on the powerful union of oil workers, using the army to end a work stoppage in that industry. Alemán made it clear he would not tolerate independent unions and used his power to impose progovernment union leaders. He ended experiments with worker administration of businesses begun under Cárdenas. The president did try to pacify the workers by expanding Social Security.

A growing accommodation between the government and the Roman Catholic Church also characterized the Alemán administration. Although Alemán had been anticlerical earlier in his career, he had followed a restrained course as secretary of the interior. As President Alemán reached out to the Church in a number of ways. The government helped in the construction of new churches and did not strictly enforce regulations prohibiting public religious functions. Alemán even supported the construction of a boulevard from Mexico City to the shrine of the Virgin of Guadalupe. Conservative elements also approved of the educational policy pursued by Alemán. The old socialist education gave way to a policy aimed at putting the educational system in harmony with the new economic development scheme. Although education in general had a lower priority, Alemán considered his greatest achievement to be the construction of a new campus for the National Autonomous University of Mexico (Universidad Nacional Autónoma de México, or UNAM).

Alemán made it clear that the economic nationalism of the Revolution that had peaked under Cárdenas in 1938 with the expropriation of the foreign-owned oil companies was no longer fashionable. Alemán considered the attraction of foreign capital to be crucial to Mexico's industrialization, and he cultivated close ties with international business leaders, especially from the United States. Alemán suspended enforcement of the regulation prohibiting foreigners from holding a majority interest in Mexican firms. At the same time, the degree of government control over business activity—such as price controls on certain products—dictated that businesses maintain good relations with the government as well. Anti-U.S. sentiment was always just below the surface, but Alemán continued the close relations developed during World War II. Alemán exchanged presidential visits with President Truman, and the Mexican government's anticommunist (actually antileftist) campaign set well with U.S. authorities who were involved in an anticommunist crusade of their own. Although Alemán resisted persistent U.S. efforts to get Mexico to furnish troops for the Korean War, his administration strongly supported the United States in the Cold War.

Mexico's commitment to industrialization required improved transportation, communication, and power sources, and Alemán put considerable emphasis on public works programs. Alemán modernized the railroads, finished Mexico's segment of the Pan American Highway, completed construction of a highway across the Isthmus of Tehuantepec, and expanded road construction in general. A series of hydroelectric projects permitted Mexico to triple its electrical output capacity. Cheap electricity and oil literally fueled Mexico's industrial expansion.

By the end of his administration, Alemán could point to impressive economic gains resulting from his policies. There was talk of "the Mexican economic miracle," and Mexico was considered a model for development by the less-developed countries of the world. Critics, however, charged that Alemán was presiding over the creation of a "new Porfiriato," a reference to the policies followed by the lengthy dictatorship of Porfirio Díaz overthrown by the great Revolution of 1910. Indeed, criticism of Alemán echoed the criticism of Díaz. Although Mexico was experiencing prosperity, only a small elite benefited. Foreign penetration of the economy endangered Mexico's independence as the country became too dependent on foreign capital and technology. One of the most serious charges against the Alemán administration was the rampant corruption that existed. Corruption was nothing new to the Mexican political scene, but its scale under Alemán aroused public opinion. As the government's role in the economy expanded, the opportunities for corruption likewise increased. Corruption took a variety of forms: direct looting of public funds, kickbacks on government contracts, payment for special government "services," and the use of government information for personal profit. Charges of corruption reached the presidency itself, with Alemán accused of being one of the most corrupt officials of an unusually corrupt administration. One of Alemán's most high-profile construction projects was a superhighway from Mexico City to the growing resort of Acapulco, where Alemán himself had extensive investments.

The corruption scandal had a major influence on the choice of a successor for Alemán in 1952. It was difficult to find potential successors who were not tainted by the corruption of the Alemán administration. The choice fell to Adolfo Ruiz Cortines, Alemán's secretary of the interior. With the nomination of the official party, Ruiz Cortines went on to an easy and predictable victory.

After retiring from the presidency, Alemán had his many business interests to occupy at least part of his time. His investments literally stretched from coast to coast, from real estate in Acapulco to a luxury hotel in Mexico City to a pineapple plantation in Veracruz. He continued to be an influential figure in the right wing of the official party. Several of Alemán's interests came together when he became director general of the National Board of Tourism in 1958, a position he held until his death in 1983.

The corruption of the Alemán years has strongly tainted his historical reputation. His notoriety should not obscure the important role he played in the economic and political development of Mexico. Alemán accelerated the policies started late in the Cárdenas administration and continued by the wartime administration of Avila Camacho. For better or worse, these policies conditioned government action until the 1980s. Alemán—a civilian who had not played a major role in the early Revolutionary years—represented a major departure from the Revolutionary generals who had ruled Mexico in the preceding decades. In the future, the National University, rather than the barracks, became the recruiting ground for Mexico's leaders. Alemán continued the long-term trends of political centralization and concentration of power in the presidency. Although the majority of Mexican citizens could at least observe the transformation that was taking place, only a minority actually benefited from the pursuit of Alemán's vision of an urban, industrial, modernized Mexico.

—DMC

See also: Agrarian Reform / Land and Land Policy; Avila Camacho, Manuel; Cárdenas, Lázaro; Corruption; Import Substitution Industrialization (ISI); Korean War; Lombardo Toledano, Vicente; Presidents of the Twentieth Century; United States, Relations with.

References:

Niblo, Stephen R. *Mexico in the 1940s: Modernity, Politics, and Corruption.* Wilmington, DE: Scholarly Resources, 1999.

————. *War, Diplomacy, and Development: The United States and Mexico, 1938–1954.* Wilmington, DE: Scholarly Resources, 1995.

Torres, Blanca. *Historia de la Revolución Mexicana, Periodo 1940–1952.* Vol. 21. *Hacia la utopía industrial.* Mexico City: El Colegio de México, 1984.

Anarchism

In the late nineteenth and early twentieth centuries, anarchism exercised an important influence on both the urban labor movement and agrarian movements. It also shaped political thought leading to and following the Revolution of 1910. Mexican anarchism had its roots in European thinking but also reflected the changes caused by the Mexican environment. At the heart of anarchism was the belief that people were inherently good but were corrupted and oppressed by the machinery of state. Government, therefore, should be abolished. French philosopher Pierre Joseph Proudhon (1809–1865) greatly influenced anarchist thinking with his concept of "mutualism," which posited that both farmers and workers be organized into small communes or cooperatives that would interact politically and economically within contracts of exchange. An opponent of both private property and violent change, Proudhon advocated equal distribution of any surplus production. Russian revolutionary Mikhail Bakunin (1814–1876) was another major figure in the anarchist movement. Unlike Proudhon, Bakunin advocated violent change and favored revolutionary overthrow of existing governments. Bakunin envisioned a society organized into larger groups of workers based on voluntary "collectivism." In western Europe, anarchism was often linked with syndicalism, which called for ownership of the means of production by groups of workers or syndicates. Syndicalists typically viewed the state as a tool of oppression to be abolished and favored the transformation of society through the relatively peaceful methods of the general strike, the boycott, and industrial sabotage.

As anarchism moved from western Europe to Mexico in the second half of the nineteenth century, it found a receptive environment but also one that would partially transform it. Mexico was experiencing its own industrial revolution on a smaller scale, which was changing working relationships and placing new pressures on different socioeconomic groups. Two groups in particular were influenced by these changes: the agricultural workers and the urban workers. The traditional communal landholdings of the indigenous people of Mexico came under fierce attack because of the legal requirement to break up "corporate" landholdings. Indigenous groups that had successfully defended their lands through the Spanish Conquest, the colonial period, and the upheaval of the early decades of independence lost their lands in the name of modernization in the second half of the nineteenth century. The indigenous traditions of local autonomy and communal ownership were highly compatible with anarchist thinking, which increasingly shaped the agrarian movement. At the same time, the industrial revolution increased the number of urban workers who were encountering worsening labor conditions. The mutualist self-help approach characteristic of earlier artisan production gave way to a growing collectivism and eventually to anarcho-syndicalism. Aiding this transition was a major increase in immigration to Mexico from Spain, where anarchist and syndicalist views were among the strongest of any area in Europe. By the late 1870s, a "Congress of Workers" had evolved representing approximately 50,000 workers. Anarchism influenced both the leadership and the emerging ideology of the Congress, which split in 1880 into anarchist and nonanarchist groups. In 1882 the government of President Manuel González cracked down on the labor movement in general. Although competing with and often confused with marxism and socialism, Mexican anarchism remained the dominant ideology among workers through 1917.

After 1900 anarchism was increasingly associated with Ricardo Flores Magón and the Mexican Liberal Party (the Partido Liberal Mexicano, or PLM). Using his newspaper, *Regeneración,* Flores Magón originally advocated

reform rather than revolution. Constantly harassed and frequently arrested, Flores Magón went into exile in the United States where his views became increasingly radical. In 1906, Flores Magón's *Regeneración* published the "Program and Manifesto of the Mexican Liberal Party," a Revolutionary but not anarchist document that called for reforming rather than abolishing government. Flores Magón's legal problems continued in the United States, pushing him toward a public statement of his now-anarchist views. When revolution began in 1910 under the leadership of Francisco Madero, the PLM engaged in military operations against the government of Porfirio Díaz but refused to align itself with the Madero revolt. Flores Magón's movement toward anarchism led to major splits in the PLM and contributed to his constant legal problems in the United States, which limited his role as an anarchist leader.

While Flores Magón attempted to promote his anarchist views from the United States, other anarchists in Mexico were organizing urban workers. One of the most notable anarchist leaders was Amadeo Ferrés, a Spanish immigrant, who in 1912 helped to organize the "House of the Worker" (Casa del Obrero), a workers' group based on anarcho-syndicalist ideas. Unlike the supporters of Flores Magón, the Casa took sides in the factional struggle among the revolutionary groups that began in 1914. The Casa not only politically supported the Constitutionalist faction under Venustiano Carranza; it also provided fighters—the "Red Battalions"—which served under Constitutionalist General Alvaro Obregón. In return for the Casa's military and political support, the Casa was promised a free hand in organizing the workers.

After the triumph of the Constitutionalists, the Casa soon came into conflict with Carranza and Obregón. In the face of food shortages and rampant inflation, the Casa called a general strike for Mexico City in May 1916. The strike quickly brought government promises to address the problems, but the promises were not fulfilled. This led the Casa to call a second general strike in August 1916.

This time the government responded in a much different fashion. Carranza called in the army to raid the Casa's headquarters, arrest its anarchist leaders, and disarm its members. To ensure the demise of the Casa, in 1918 the government set up a rival union organization, the Regional Mexican Workers' Confederation (the Confederación Regional Obrero Mexicano, or CROM). The CROM supported radical goals but was not anarchist; indeed, it was designed to work closely with the government rather than for the abolition of the government. In 1921 anarchist leaders established a new labor organization, the General Confederation of Workers (the Confederación General de Trabajadores, or CGT). Although the leadership of the CGT was anarcho-syndicalist, its membership held a variety of radical views, including marxism and socialism. In attempting to organize workers during the 1920s, the CGT found itself in an uneven competition with the government-backed CROM. The passage of a new federal labor law in 1931 brought all labor organizations under tighter government control, effectively co-opting or cutting out the anarchist leadership of the CGT.

Although the anarchists briefly sided with the winning faction in the post-1910 revolutionary struggles, they were defeated in terms of their basic goal of forming a classless society based on voluntary associations of factory workers or peasants in which government would be unnecessary. Urban workers were typically disunited and—although increasing in numbers—still made up a relatively small percentage of the total workforce. The tradition of government control of labor movements developed early, making it difficult for more radical views such as anarchism to take hold. Urban workers even wound up fighting peasants when the Casa's "Red Battalions" supported Carranza and Obregón against the forces of Emiliano Zapata and Pancho Villa. The leading national peasant and workers organizations that emerged in the 1930s were under government control. The student movement of 1968 and the Zapatista rebellion in Chiapas in 1994 hint at the continuing ap-

peal of some anarchist ideas. Anarchism, however, lost to the emerging revolutionary elite dedicated to strengthening government control over the very groups that the anarchists sought to liberate.

—DMC

See also: Constitutionalists; Díaz, Porfirio; Flores Magón, Ricardo; Labor Movements; Partido Liberal Mexicano (PLM); Tlatelolco Massacre; Zapatista National Liberation Army (EZLN).

References:

Hart, John M. *Anarchism and the Mexican Working Class, 1860–1931.* Austin: University of Texas Press, 1978.

Hodges, Donald C. *Mexican Anarchism after the Revolution.* Austin: University of Texas Press, 1995.

Langham, Thomas C. *Border Trials: Ricardo Flores Magón and the Mexican Liberals.* El Paso: Texas Western Press, 1981.

MacLachlan, Colin M. *Anarchism and the Mexican Revolution: The Political Trials of Ricardo Flores Magón in the United States.* Berkeley: University of California Press, 1991.

Anthropology and Archeology

It is hardly surprising that a country as culturally diverse and historically rich as Mexico should have a strong anthropological and archeological tradition. Indeed, since the early twentieth century, Mexican anthropologists and archeologists have been regarded as among the best in the world. More surprising is their considerable impact on government policies, especially regarding Mexico's sizeable Indian population. This dual role as preservers of the national patrimony and as advisors on social policy has contributed to their prestige as nation-builders; it has also left them open to criticism as agents of the state and internal colonizers. In recent years, dissident anthropologists and grassroots Indian rights movements have begun to challenge this dual role. As a result, Mexican anthropologists in general (and to a lesser extent archeologists) have become more independent of and outspoken about government policies. Nevertheless, policymaking in Mexico is still a highly centralized affair with both financial largesse and social reform tending to flow from the top down. With this in mind, anthropologists and archeologists have been reluctant to completely sever their ties to government, and they continue to exert an importance influence on public policy.

Mexico has always had its ethnographers and antiquarians. Since 1521 when Hernán Cortés defeated the Aztec empire at Tenochtitlán and proceeded to dismantle the Aztec city to build his own capital, scholarly "amateurs" have played a crucial role in preserving the nation's cultural heritage. During the colonial period (1521–1821), priests such as Bernardino de Sahagún produced extensive studies of Indian cultures and languages in hopes of facilitating the "spiritual conquest" of New Spain (as Mexico was called before independence), and intellectuals such as seventeenth-century scientist Carlos de Sigüenza y Góngora took great care to study and preserve pre-Hispanic antiquities. For *criollo* elites (*criollos* were whites born in the New World), as resentful of Spanish discrimination as they were proud of their homeland, these studies became a vital part of an emerging sense of American identity. Some went so far as to blame Spanish colonial policy for the degraded state of the colony's Indians. In his monumental *Ancient History of Mexico* (1780–1781), for example, Mexican-born Jesuit historian Francisco Javier Clavigero insisted that "if their upbringing were carefully supervised, if they were educated in schools by competent teachers, and if they were encouraged by rewards, one would see among the Indians philosophers, mathematicians, and theologians who would vie with the most famous of Europe." Father Servando Teresa de Mier, a prominent agitator for independence, laid the blame directly on the Roman Catholic Church, whose attacks on indigenous religious practices, he argued, had undermined Indian culture and contributed to their degradation during the colonial period.

The struggle for independence ensured that these pro-Indian sentiments would play an important role in official ideology. Concerned to separate Mexico's historical experience from Spain, *criollo* intellectuals like Father Mier attempted to rewrite history by suggesting that the nation's glorious past, symbolized by the Aztec and Mayan empires, had been cut short by a brutal Spanish Conquest and three hundred years of colonial exploitation. Independence, then, marked a restoration of preconquest glory albeit with *criollo* rather than Indian leadership. If some intellectuals argued for Indian redemption through education, most were content to associate themselves with past splendors and ignore present conditions. An important step in that process of identification was the founding of the National Museum in 1825, which functioned as a central site for the construction of a "national" past in which all Mexicans could take pride and around which they could unite in common purpose. Still, the political struggles that dominated most of the nineteenth century precluded much progress in either ethnographic study or archeological preservation even as anthropology had begun to emerge in Europe and the United States as a recognized "discipline" with professional standards for scholarly rigor and training.

By the turn of the century, the relative stability that resulted from Porfirio Díaz's long tenure as president (1876–1880, 1884–1910) had produced both the political will and the economic means to develop Mexican archeology and anthropology. Aware of Mexico's exotic appeal to Europeans and Americans, the regime devoted most of its energies to archeology: in 1886, the professional journal *Anales del Museo Nacional* (Annals of the National Museum) appeared; in 1896 and 1897, laws protecting monuments and declaring all archeological sites to be property of the nation were passed; and in 1906 archeologist Leopoldo Bartres began a massive excavation and reconstruction project at Teotihuacán, a spectacular pre-Aztec site conveniently located just outside Mexico City, which included the massive Pyramid of Sun that would become (with no intentional irony) a symbol of the solidity and power of the Porfirian regime. If reconstructed pyramids were insufficient, exhibitions at international expositions and world's fairs played up the nation's Indian past with exhibition halls in the shape of temples, lavish displays of artifacts, and beautifully illustrated archeological treatises. Mexico even sent live Indians to demonstrate their everyday "customs" and perform indigenous rituals in simulated villages. (This was common practice at the turn of the century—the most notorious example being the New York City Natural History Museum's live Eskimo exhibit.)

Despite the emphasis on the publicity potential of archeology and anthropology, efforts were made to professionalize the two disciplines. American anthropologists like Frederick Starr and Aleš Hrdlička had been conducting ethnographic studies on Mexican Indians for some time, but Mexican studies were relatively scarce, in part because the country lacked well-trained anthropologists. Finally, in 1900, the National Museum appointed Nicolás León (a student of Hrdlička's) to head its physical anthropology section; he became its first professor of anthropology and ethnology three years later. In 1906, Minister of Education Justo Sierra encouraged the National Museum to reorganize its departments, classification systems, and training programs to conform to the latest international standards. Then, in 1911, on the eve of the Revolution, Mexico signed an international agreement to invite scholars from Harvard, Columbia, and the University of Pennsylvania to found an International School of American Archeology and Ethnography under the auspices of the National Museum. At the International School and in subsequent study at American and European universities, Mexican anthropologists and archeologists learned the latest advances in their fields from internationally recognized anthropologists such as Eduard Seler and Franz Boas. Although revolutionary turmoil made work at the International School difficult, some pioneering studies resulted nonetheless, many of them by Mexican anthropologists. Perhaps the most important of these studies—Manuel Gamio's "discovery" of a sequence of civilizations in Mexico (postulated but not proven by his mentor at Columbia University, Franz Boas)—produced the notion of "Mesoamerica" as a coherent cultural area, a concept that has structured archeological work in the region ever since.

The end of the Revolution marked the beginning of a new era in Mexican anthropology. Spearheaded by the peripatetic Gamio, anthropologists came to play a preeminent role in postrevolutionary nation-building as new political leaders, determined to avoid the mistakes of their predecessors, sought ways to bring Mexico's many different ethnic groups into the national project. (Ethnicity is defined in different ways, but in Mexico definitions are generally cultural rather than biological; using linguistic differences as a marker, it has nearly sixty distinct Indian ethnic groups.) Incorporation, however, was no simple matter. In his influential 1916 treatise, *Forjando patria* (Forging the Fatherland), Gamio insisted that "we not only need to know how many men, women, and children there are in the Republic, the languages they speak, and how they control their ethnic groups. We need to know many other things: geography, geology, meteorology, flora and fauna . . . also language, religion, industry, art, commerce, folklore, clothing, food, strength, physical-anthropological type, etc., etc."

A project of this magnitude in an ethnically heterogeneous country the size of Mexico was a daunting prospect requiring legions of trained anthropologists. To that end, Gamio founded the Directorate of Archeological and Ethnographic Studies (later renamed the Directorate of Anthropology) in 1917. Operating under the auspices of the powerful Secretariat of Agriculture and Development, Gamio envisioned a series of comprehensive regional studies that would include archeological digs, ethnographic studies, local museums to foster popular historical awareness, and even political consciousness-raising. These studies would then provide the essential knowledge base for government efforts at economic and social development. His own remarkable 1922 study of Teotihuacán—Gamio conceived of the project and wrote the overview, other scholars contributed studies on different topics—would serve as a model for subsequent work throughout Mexico.

In 1920, to publicize his politically and socially "engaged" anthropology among nonacademics, Gamio founded *Ethnos,* "a magazine dedicated to the study and betterment of the indigenous population of Mexico." This eugenic-sounding slogan was no accident. Although a cultural relativist like his mentor Boas and much less racist than most of his American and European contemporaries, Gamio nevertheless favored a progressive eugenics (as opposed to the more drastic "eliminationist" approach associated with the Nazis) that would "better" Mexico's Indian races both biologically—mostly through better hygiene and nutrition—and culturally—mostly through education. His successor at *Ethnos,* Lucio Mendieta y Núñez shared this sentiment, insisting that the purpose of anthropological study was "to obtain a complete and exact as possible knowledge of the principal indigenous populations of the Republic, past and present, in order to uncover the causes of their present vices and the scientific means of correcting them." Progressive eugenics or not, the notion that Mexican Indians had vices in need of correction had ominous implications that were sometimes realized in government policies.

The most intrusive of these policies was public education. Since policymakers generally constructed ethnic difference in cultural terms, the bulk of their Indian "reform" projects focused on what they saw as the negative aspects of indigenous culture (rather than on race or genetics per se). Under the direction of Mexico's influential Secretary of Education José Vasconcelos (1920–1924), efforts to educate Indians were blatantly assimilationist. A great admirer of the early Spanish missionaries who had converted the Indians to Christianity, Vasconcelos went about his task with a similar zeal as well as a similar confidence in the superiority of European civilization and the Spanish language. These "cultural missions" represented a commitment to rural education and an embracing of previously marginalized ethnic groups that was without precedent in Mexican history. They also showed little regard for cultural difference even among non-Indian subcultures. Needless to say, rural education encountered considerable resistance throughout Mexico.

Modifications to Vasconcelos's extreme approach by his successors, including anthropologist Moisés Sáenz, proved more workable, although resistance from indigenous communities and local *caciques* (bosses) continued to plague rural education programs. A Boas student like Gamio, Sáenz became the dean of official *indigenismo* (Indian integrationist policy) after political difficulties forced both Vasconcelos and Gamio into American exile. Under Sáenz's guidance, the Directorate of Anthropology (which had been transferred from the National Museum to the Secretariat of Public Education) was renamed the Department of Rural Schools and Indigenous Cultural Incorporation and transformed into the principal vehicle for the government's *indigenista* policies. Rural education became more practical and less blatantly Eurocentric than it had been under Vasconcelos: teachers and agricultural extension agents attempted to instruct Indians in basic literacy, proper hygiene, and modern farming techniques while anthropologists sought to continue Gamio's regional studies model (although with only limited success). Nevertheless, the anticlerical attitudes of most educators (excepting Vasconcelos), who blamed the Roman Catholic Church for the degradation of Indian culture, continued to provoke resistance among Mexico's mostly Catholic Indians.

Resistance to public education aside, *indigenismo's* ideological importance as a symbol of revolutionary commitments to a more inclusive social policy meant considerable government support for anthropology, especially during the relatively radical presidency of Lázaro Cárdenas (1934–1940). In 1935, the Cárdenas administration supported the creation of the Summer Linguistic Institute to study and teach indigenous languages under the direction of William Cameron Townsend, an American linguist and Protestant minister. (Sáenz, his principal sponsor was also a Protestant.) The next year, a separate Department of Indigenous Affairs (DIA) was created to study contemporary indigenous cultures and coordinate government social welfare programs. In 1939, the National Institute of Anthropology and History (INAH) was founded to oversee archeological sites and museums. A year after that, Mexico hosted an Inter-American Indigenist Conference during which specialists from all over the continent discussed Indian affairs. Some argued for a multiethnic approach, but most agreed with Cárdenas, whose opening speech stressed his administration's commitment "not to Indianize Mexico but to Mexicanize the Indian." Manuel Gamio even returned from exile to head a new Inter-American Indigenist Institute.

Archeology continued to flourish after the Revolution, but in the intensely ideological climate of the 1920s and 1930s, it had taken a back seat to the nation-building projects of social anthropologists like Gamio and Sáenz. Nevertheless, major archeological projects on Mayan sites supported by American institutions such as the Smithsonian, the Carnegie Foundation, and Tulane University and staffed with Mexican anthropologists like Carlos Basauri, and ambitious INAH projects on various sites, including Monte Albán, Oaxaca (by the institute's prominent director Alfonso Caso), contributed not only to scholarship on pre-Hispanic Indian civilizations but to national pride in the Indian past and to a rapidly growing tourist industry as well. Although less spectacular and of little ideological value, INAH's administration and development of colonial era buildings and monuments was also of considerable importance to scholarly endeavors and tourism.

With Cárdenas's departure in 1940, the influence of official *indigenismo* declined markedly. To be sure, policymakers continued to promote the government's commitment to indigenous Mexicans. For example, the presidential administration of notorious modernizer Miguel Alemán (1946–1952), which generally favored urban over rural development and industry over agriculture, also oversaw the creation of a National Indigenist Institute

under the direction of Alfonso Caso. Although it was still state-sponsored and closely linked to nation-building, Mexican anthropology had matured and diversified as a discipline: the era of simplistic slogans and a naïve belief in forced assimilation—at least on the part of most anthropologists—was over. The Institute's principal goal might have been to transform unproductive Indians into trained workers, but Institute anthropologists such as Gonzalo Aguirre Beltrán had begun to question the top-down integrationist model favored by most bureaucrats.

In place of "assimilation" that had attempted to integrate Indians into mainstream *mestizo* Mexican society, Aguirre Beltrán proposed "acculturation," which would bring Indians into the national project through empowerment rather than coercion—on terms of their own choosing (with guidance from anthropologists) rather than on those of the state. Inspired in part by the marxist notion that economic relations determine culture, acculturationists argued that indigenous communities had been oppressed for years by local *mestizo* and *ladino* (hispanicized Indian) elites and that oppression had produced a corrupt indigenous culture based on Roman Catholic superstition and deference to power patrons, which facilitated their exploitation. Their comprehensive solution to this vicious cycle of oppression involved more anthropological study (as always) and state intervention in the form of regional Coordinating Centers for Indigenist Action that would promote agrarian reform, hygiene, education, and even political organizing. Even though acculturation still sought to integrate Indians into the national economy and eventually into a national culture through state intervention, its focus on empowerment was extraordinarily progressive for the 1950s and 1960s, especially when compared to segregationist policies in the United States.

As official *indigenismo* waned, innovative work like Aguirre Beltrán's further increased the stature of Mexican anthropology. This international reputation for progressive anthropology took an academic turn in the 1960s as

Mexican and American anthropologists collaborated to produce the definitive study of Mesoamerica, the multivolume *Handbook of Middle American Indians*. Additionally, the opening of the National Museum of Anthropology and History, a world-class museum in Mexico City dedicated to the nation's past and present indigenous cultures, publicly attested to the international stature and disciplinary maturity of Mexican anthropology.

Political events would put both to the test. A national legitimacy crisis prompted by the 1968 massacre of student (and other) demonstrators in Mexico City hit Mexican anthropologists especially hard. For one thing, the traditional *nahuatl* (Aztec) name of the neighborhood, Tlatelolco, and name of the actual site of the massacre, the Plaza of Three Cultures, had tremendous resonance for anthropologists, and their desecration by government forces dispelled whatever illusions progressive anthropologists may have harbored for their redemptive projects. For another, dissidents from within the discipline had already begun to critique its close ties to Mexico's one-party state and to American institutions. In 1970, they issued a manifesto with the provocative title, *On So-Called Mexican Anthropology*, which condemned mainstream anthropologists and archeologists for their support of the state's integrationist policies and massive reconstruction projects aimed more at increasing revenues from tourism than expanding knowledge of the indigenous past.

Concerned by these signs of independence, the newly elected President Luis Echeverría Alvarez (1970–1976) made a concerted effort to win them back into the government fold. The progressive Aguirre Beltrán replaced Alfonso Caso as head of the National Indigenist Institute and under his guidance the number of regional coordinating centers swelled to nearly a hundred. In another conciliatory gesture, at Aguirre Beltrán's behest, Guillermo Bonfil Batalla, one of the most prominent dissidents, was named head of INAH. In this more open environment, anthropological scholarship also blossomed with the development of more sophisticated marxist theories about the relationship between economic relations and cultural production that inspired new studies in everything from Aztec ideology to the transformation of rural peasants into rural proletarians.

This political opening also encouraged Mexican anthropologists to turn their attention to urban areas and non-Indian populations. North American anthropologist Oscar Lewis's popular studies of Mexico City's barrios, *Five Families: Mexican Case Studies in the Culture of Poverty* (1959) and *The Children of Sanchez: Autobiography of a Mexican Family* (1961), had provoked considerable controversy with their riveting narratives of recent migrants struggling to survive in a dysfunctional urban jungle. In response, Mexican anthropologists like Larissa Adler Lomnitz, Lourdes Arizpe, and Jorge Alonso produced carefully researched and theoretically informed studies of different urban communities that went beyond Lewis's rather simplistic "culture of poverty" argument to explore the role of social networks, migrant culture, and political activism in the lives of the urban poor.

Secure in international reputation and disciplinary diversity, Mexican anthropology and archeology have continued to flourish and innovate into the twenty-first century. Monumental reconstruction and renovation projects have kept archeology in the public eye. The most visible of these projects was the Templo Mayor (principal temple of the Aztec capital, Tenochtitlán), discovered by workmen during subway construction in 1978 and excavated under the direction of the appropriately named Eduardo Matos Moctezuma. Located just off the Zócalo (main square) in Mexico City, the Templo Mayor and its opulent museum opened with great fanfare in 1987. The considerable expenditure involved, especially in an era of economic crisis and natural disasters, signaled the government's continued commitment to monumental archeology as a source of national pride, public education, and tourist revenue.

Less showy but just as impressive (at least to international scholars) was the appearance of thoughtful analyses of Mexican and Latin American society by some of the leading lights of Mexican anthropology. Roger Bartra's *Cage of Melancholy,* for example, revisited the much-debated issue of Mexican national identity not to affirm a "national inferiority complex" as Octavio Paz had done in the 1950s but to explore the constructed nature of nationalist discourses about culture. Claudio Lomnitz-Adler's *Exits from the Labyrinth* used comparative regional studies to critique Mexican nationalist ideology as an anthropological practice crucial to the maintenance of political legitimacy. Guillermo Bonfil's *México Profundo* (deep Mexico) extended his critique of assimilation and acculturation by insisting that deeply rooted indigenous spiritual and communitarian values still lingered in Mexico (and Mesoamerica) despite centuries of "ethnocide" and that those values held a redemptive promise for a nation fractured by the wrenching changes of a never-quite-realized modernity. The "hybrid" quality of Latin American modernity received its definitive treatment in Néstor García Canclini's provocative *Hybrid Cultures: Strategies for Entering and Leaving Modernity,* which argued that the region had never become fully modern; that traditional, modern, and postmodern sectors existed simultaneously; and that social actors entered and exited these sectors on a regular basis. Taken together, these influential works—all of them available in English or English translation—have forced anthropologists (as well scholars working in related disciplines, such as history and cultural studies) throughout the world to reconsider the meanings and uses of "culture" as well as their own complicity in the production of national ideologies.

—*RMB*

See also: Cárdenas, Lázaro; Echeverría Alvarez, Luis; *Mestizaje* and *Indigenismo*; Vasconcelos, José.

References:

Bartra, Roger. *The Cage of Melancholy: Identity and Metamorphosis in the Mexican Character.* Trans. Christopher Hill. New Brunswick, NJ: Rutgers University Press, 1992.

Bonfil Batalla, Guillermo. *México Profundo: Reclaiming a Civilization.* Trans. Philip Dennis. Austin: University of Texas, 1996.

Buffington, Robert M. "*Forjando Patria:* Anthropology, Criminology, and the Post-Revolutionary Discourse on Citizenship," in *Criminal and Citizen in Modern Mexico,* pp. 141–164. Lincoln: University of Nebraska Press, 2000.

García Canclini, Néstor. *Hybrid Cultures: Strategies for Entering and Leaving Modernity.* Trans. Christopher Chiappari and Silvia López. Minneapolis: University of Minnesota Press, 1995.

Knight, Alan. "Racism, Revolution, and *Indigenismo:* Mexico, 1910–1940," in Richard Graham, ed., *The Idea of Race in Latin America, 1870–1940,* pp. 71–113. Austin: University of Texas Press, 1990.

Lomnitz, Larissa Adler. *Networks and Marginality: Life in a Mexican Shantytown.* Trans. Cinna Lomnitz. New York: Academic Press, 1977.

Lomnitz-Adler, Claudio. *Exits from the Labyrinth: Culture and Ideology in the Mexican National Space.* Berkeley: University of California Press, 1992.

Tenorio-Trillo, Mauricio. *Mexico at the World's Fair: Crafting a Modern Nation.* Berkeley: University of California Press, 1996.

Architecture

Of all the arts, architecture is probably the most inherently ideological and nationalistic. The considerable expense, planning, and coordination needed to carry out a major building project usually requires some form of government involvement, particularly in "developing" countries like Mexico that rely on extensive state planning and investment to catch up to the "developed" world. It is hardly surprising that governments would favor projects that reflect official concerns about national identity and the direction of national development. In Mexico, government involvement in architecture has a long and distinguished tradition that reached a peak in the 1950s with the massive "city" constructed for the National Autonomous University of Mexico (UNAM) and has only recently begun to cede ground to the architectural interests of private investors.

Coming after a century of turmoil and two foreign invasions, the thirty-five years of relative stability and economic growth during

Porfirio Díaz's regime (1876–1880, 1884–1911) saw a dramatic increase in new construction. During this period, modernizing elites favored the European Beaux-Arts style in public buildings as a symbol of the nation's modern, cosmopolitan identity. Certainly, the best of the Porfirian Beaux-Arts buildings were worthy of any European or North American city. The design and initial construction of Mexico City's sumptuous Palacio de Bellas Artes (Palace of Fine Arts) was even overseen by internationally renowned Italian architect Adamo Baori (1863–1928). Begun with great fanfare in 1904 but delayed by foundation problems and the Revolution, it was finally completed in 1934 under the direction of Mexican architect and architectural theorist Federico Mariscal (1881–1971). Another Beaux-Arts treasure, the smaller but no less elegant Juárez Theater in Guanajuato (begun 1873, finished 1903), was opened by no less a personage than the president himself. Other public buildings, such as the national penitentiary (1900) and a new mental hospital (1910), were less overtly stylish but also represented the most recent advances in institutional architecture.

Nor did Porfirian modernizers ignore city planning in the manner of French urban architect Baron Haussmann, whose spacious boulevards had cleared out Paris's crowded and politically volatile center for open vistas and easier policing during the mid-nineteenth century. In Mexico City, swanky new neighborhoods sprang up along the capital's principal boulevard, the Paseo de la Reforma, which runs from the downtown district to the presidential residence in Chapultepec Park. City planners even included a history-civics lesson with strategically placed monuments along the Paseo de la Reforma to national heroes like Aztec emperor Cuauhtémoc and Díaz's great liberal predecessor Benito Juárez. State and local officials followed suit as best they could with modern theaters, penitentiaries, boulevards, and monuments of their own.

Outside Mexico, however, national architecture presented a more exotic image as Porfirian publicists attempted to woo tourists and foreign investors. For the 1889 Paris Exposition, for example, Mexico built an Aztec palace at the foot of the Eiffel Tower. The indigenous architecture was merely a façade: the structure itself was quite modern and visitors attracted by its "primitive" allure were bombarded with books, statistics, and maps that stressed the successes of Mexico's modernization efforts. Although styles within Mexico would undergo considerable changes over the course of the twentieth century, the nation's international architectural style would continue to exploit the indigenous or, less often, neocolonial themes that foreigners had come to appreciate and expect.

After the Revolution of 1910, as government officials and policymakers struggled to distance themselves from their Porfirian predecessors, neocolonial architecture enjoyed a resurgence of sorts. The prime instigator was dynamic Secretary of Education José Vasconcelos, whose somewhat idiosyncratic views of Mexican civilization included a deep appreciation of the Hispanic contribution to national development. Other influential public intellectuals, such as sociologist Andrés Molina Enríquez and anthropologist Manuel Gamio, were less enthusiastic about Spanish colonialism but shared Vasconcelos's view that *mestizo* culture with its mixture of Hispanic and indigenous elements had given the nation its unique character. Architecture, they agreed, should reflect that *mestizo* character, as they felt had been the case during the colonial era when Spanish architects and Indian artisans collaborated to produce uniquely Mexican architectural styles. To this end, Vasconcelos contracted an engineer, Federico Méndez Rivas, to design and build the new Secretariat of Education building, a three-story colonial-style palace modeled on Mexico City's eighteenth-century Law School with two spacious interior courtyards. To further mark the building as a national space, Vasconcelos brought in painter Diego Rivera to decorate the interior walls of the courtyards with Mexican themes. Rivera's brilliant murals not only exalted Mexican culture, their popularity ensured the building's landmark status and established a linkage between decorative arts and public buildings—*integración plástica* (plastic intergration) architectural theorists called it—that would come to distinguish mid-twentieth-century Mexican architecture. In most cases, the didactic nature of most murals further enhanced the ideological and nationalistic impact of the architecture.

More important on its own merits was the work of architect Carlos Obregón Santacilia (1896–1961), whose Benito Juárez Elementary School (1923–1925), with its arched façade in colonial hacienda style, and Secretariat of Health building (1926–1927), with its subtle mixture of neocolonialism and Art Deco (complete with Mexican eagle above the entrance), helped define the new postrevolutionary style. Another of Vasconcelos's favorite architects, José Villagrán García (1902–1992), designed a National Stadium (1924) that could seat 60,000 people. A massive stone structure with colonial-style arches and a grand stairway entrance, it elicited from Vasconcelos the admission that "I detest those iron buildings, in the style of American skyscrapers, that will have to be demolished in fifty years. I admire peoples who build for eternity . . . like the Romans . . . like the Babylonians . . . like the Inca of Peru."

The inauguration of the National Stadium, however, marked the end of Vasconcelos's controversial tenure as secretary of education. Although neocolonial buildings continued to be designed and built, new architectural trends began to surface. Art Deco was easily subsumed within the neocolonial aesthetic by architects like Obregón Santacilia, "functionalism"—the quintessential modern style—was a different matter altogether. Unlike the decorative façades of neocolonial architecture, functionalist buildings were characterized by efficient simplicity; the use of unfinished materials, exposed structural elements, and low-cost materials gave buildings a pared-down ultramodern look that appealed to a new generation of architects dedicated to producing a new people's architecture in the populist style of postrevolutionary presidents like

Plutarcho Elías Calles (presidential term, 1924–1928) and Lázaro Cárdenas (presidential term, 1934–1940). The inspiration behind functionalism may well have come from Europe via French theorist Le Corbusier and German Bauhaus director Hannes Meyer (who emigrated to Mexico in 1939), but Mexican architects soon gave it their own distinctive stamp. They were aided in this endeavor by *Cemento,* the widely distributed promotional magazine of the Tolteca Cement Company, which featured articles and advertisements on the latest advances in modern construction techniques and equipment.

One of the earliest, most influential, and least doctrinaire converts to functionalism was Villagrán García, architect of the National Stadium and professor of architectural theory at the National School of Architecture from 1926 to 1976. Although the National Stadium reflected Vasconcelos's neocolonial inclinations, García's subsequent work for the Secretariat of Public Health (1924–1935) demonstrated more modern concerns about architecture's social function. The Institute of Hygiene at Popotla (1925), for example, was a simple reinforced concrete structure with flat roofs, unadorned façades, and vertical and horizontal angles. The functionalist emphasis on convenience, efficient use of space, and moderate costs would become a hallmark of García's many hospitals and sanatoria. From the Public Health secretariat's perspective, these architectural qualities represented the government's commitment to affordable, hygienic, modern health care for all Mexicans.

The most passionate early advocate of functionalism, Juan O'Gorman (1905–1982), was a student at the National School of Architecture who had worked with both Obregón Santacilia and Villagrán García. Inspired by his reading of Le Corbusier's pathbreaking *Towards a New Architecture* (1923), O'Gorman built a prototype functionalist house for himself in Mexico City's swanky San Angel district. With its modern construction techniques, attention to the human use of space, and careful orientation to local conditions, O'Gorman's house attracted the attention of both horrified traditionalists (to his great delight) and influential artists like muralist Diego Rivera, who commissioned a pair of adjoining house-studios for himself and his wife, Frida Kahlo. Completed in 1932, the Rivera-Kahlo complex was a triumph of functionalist principles—low cost, modern materials, "honest" design—of a distinctively Mexican type—raised construction (on *pilotis* or pillars), huge windows, open interior spaces, vivid colors, local materials. This combination of functionalist efficiency and Mexican style attracted the attention of Narciso Bassols (1897–1959), the dynamic new secretary of education, who appointed O'Gorman head of the secretariat's architectural office. In that capacity and in just three years, O'Gorman designed and built twenty-four new public schools for the Federal District. His innovative design (based on three-meter modules) produced schools for underserved urban working-class neighborhoods and outlying rural areas that were inexpensive, easy to maintain, hygienic, and colorful—often with murals painted by local artists. To critics, who complained about their uniformity and lack of "style," he responded by contrasting technical and academic architecture: "The technician is useful to the majority and the academic useful to the minority . . . an architecture which serves humanity, or an architecture that serves money."

A colleague, Juan Legarreta (1908–1934), who worked for the Department of Communications and Public Works designing low-cost housing for workers, went even further. In a 1933 speech to the Society of Mexican Architects, he insisted that "a people that lives in huts and round shacks cannot talk of architecture." Architecture or not, Legarreta's design for a "minimalist worker's house" (1930) was hardly devoid of nationalist ideology: the front door opened into the kitchen-dining room, the space of "the mother-worker . . . center and symbol of the family"; just to the right was an airy, light "family" living room. The emphasis on nuclear families leading hygienic, productive, if modest lives—there were no servants quarters, a feature of even

middle-class Mexican housing—was right in step with the progressive, prolabor elements of the postrevolutionary program. At the same time, a small walled patio and lots of bare walls meant that occupants could provide the Mexican touches—birds, flowers, bright colors—that would nationalize the otherwise nondescript space.

By 1940, the Cardenista experiment had pretty much run its course. Moreover, rapid urbanization had produced an acute housing shortage unlikely to be resolved by single-family dwellings however economical. To address the problem, the Mexican government offered architect Mario Pani (1911–1993)—indoctrinated with modernist notions of urban planning during his architecture studies in Paris—several commissions for large-scale public housing. His Centro Urbano Presidente Alemán (President Alemán Urban Center, 1947–1949) mixed three-story and thirteen-story buildings raised on *pilotis,* gardens, schools, day care, swimming pool, laundry, and an assortment of commercial outlets in a one of Latin America's first planned communities. Needless to say, there were walls for the ubiquitous murals, including José Clemente Orozco's uncompleted last work. Pani's no less ambitious Centro Urbano Presidente Juárez (President Juárez Urban Center, 1950–1952) included colored mosaics by the renowned Guatemalan painter Carlos Mérida. As in buildings by colleagues such as O'Gorman and Legarreta, the combination of local materials, Mexican art, and architectural flair helped mitigate the impersonal utilitarian feel of the functionalist style.

Even Catholic churches, so rich in colonial architectural traditions, began to adapt to more modern styles. (Innovative religious architecture had, of course, been quite common in the colonial period as Mexico's remarkable variety of church styles attests.) Enrique de la Mora's Church of Mary in Monterrey (1948) with its intersecting parabolic concrete shells in the shape of a cross, is an important early example. The modern churches of Félix Candela (1917–1997) set the standard, especially the Church of the Miraculous Virgin in Mexico City (1954) with its dramatic interior arches subtly inscribed by wood patterns from the concrete forms. The more modest Chapel of the Missionaries of the Holy Ghost in Coyoacán (1956), designed by de la Mora and built by Candela, is an especially fine example of modern church architecture in which functionalist minimalism combined with excellent acoustics provides a sense of lightness and grace—a contemplative, "modern" spirituality uninhibited by traditional life-size representations of the tortured Christ and side altars crammed with icons of the saints.

The greatest achievement of the Mexican modernist style to grow out of functionalism is the massive University City (1950–1956) constructed on the volcanic lava beds or *pedregal* south of Mexico City as the new home for the National Autonomous University of Mexico (UNAM). Directed by Mario Pani and Enrique del Moral (1906–1987), the project sought to meld the different architectural and decorative styles of the previous two decades into a coherent, albeit eclectic, national style. For President Miguel Alemán, its principal sponsor, University City represented his regime's commitment to fostering higher education, modernizing Mexico through massive state investment, and imposing technocrat rationality on traditional institutions. The removal of potentially troublesome students from the central city was a less publicized benefit. Of these ambitious goals, the consolidation of a national architectural style was probably the least controversial, in part because Pani and del Moral encouraged architects to put a personal stamp on their different buildings and let the grand plan provide a sense of aesthetic and ideological cohesion. The Central Library, covered with stone mosaics by O'Gorman (who was also one of the architects) that incorporated an array of historical and mystical symbols of Mexicanness, represented the intellectual core (despite the shortcomings of its holdings). The Administration Building with its dramatic sculpture-painting-mosaic by muralist David Álfaro Siqueiros, "From the People to the University—From the University to the People: For a New Hu-

manist National Culture of Universal Profundity," captures somewhat pedantically the project's ideological pretensions. The massive Olympic Stadium (designed to seat over 100,000 spectators) and the pre–Columbian-looking handball courts were no less ideological, although both were linked architecturally and decoratively to Mexico's indigenous past. Diego Rivera's spectacular stone mural on an Aztec theme for the stadium entrance, for example, resignified the ancient Greek roots of the Olympic games. Even the whimsical Pavilion for Cosmic Ray Research resembled the modern Mexican churches of its builder, Félix Candela. Taken as a whole, these very different buildings (along with their more nondescript companions) represented the vigorous hybrid Mexican spirit that University City sponsors and planners hoped would propel their "developing" nation into the modern age. The forced expropriation of communal lands held by local residents who stood in the way of progress hinted at the sometimes ruthless nature of that vision.

The eclectic national style developed for the University City project has continued to exercise a powerful influence on Mexican architecture, especially in public and private educational institutions. The National Anthropology Museum (1963), for example, combines the clean horizontal lines of modernist architecture with indigenous decorative elements like the magnificent carved central pillar with its fountain and huge aluminium canopy and a vivid jaguar mural by Rufino Tamayo. The San Gerónimo Hospital (1975), modeled after the pyramids of the pre-Columbian religious center of Monte Albán, seamlessly integrates modernist and indigenous aesthetics. Private educational institutions like El Colegio de Mexico (1975) and Universidad Iberoamericana (1981–1987) preferred to explore the intersection of modernist and colonial uses of interior spaces like courtyards, walkways, and natural light. More recently, the National Center for the Arts complex, a pet project of President Carlos Salinas de Gortari (presidential term, 1988–1994), revived some of the grandeur of the University City project, grouping together distinct buildings by some of Mexico's most distinguished architects in an effort to consolidate a new hybrid postmodern national style. More cynical commentators also noted the coincidence of architectural ambition and rampant corruption that characterized both the Alemán and Salinas regimes.

Not all architecture, however, reflected the nationalist obsession of projects like University City or the National Center for the Arts. Major buildings from the early 1950s such as the Torre de Seguros Latinoamericanos (Latin American Insurance Tower, 1950) and the Mexico City Airport (1953), for example, were done in a classic international style that emphasized sleek design and lots of glass, aluminium, and steel. Likewise, Mexico City's tallest "skyscraper," the Insurance Tower, referenced comparable buildings in foreign cities, such as New York's Empire State Building, more so than its Mexican neighbors. A playful version of the internationalist style appears in the famous multicolored towers designed by sculptor Mathías Goeritz (1915–1991) for the entrance to a huge suburban housing development outside Mexico City with the up-to-date name of Satellite City (1958).

At the opposite end of the architectural spectrum from the international style, some Mexican architects rejected modernism for a more personal style. After his initial enthusiasm for functionalism, Juan O'Gorman abruptly changed gears in 1940s and began to espouse a nativist style in design and construction (reflected in his contribution to the University City project). In the Anacahualli Museum (1943–1957), designed by Rivera for his pre-Columbian art collection, and especially in O'Gorman's own house (1956), O'Gorman used local materials, designs, and spaces to construct unique, even idiosyncratic buildings "purified" of architectural theory. The O'Gorman house, built directly into the lava beds of the *pedregal* was a marvel of construction and covered throughout with colorful stone mosaics on Mexican themes. At the same time, it followed no known style and held out few possibilities for an architectural

program other than whimsy and creative engagement with local conditions.

The work of residential architects like Luis Barragán (1902–1988) and Max Cetto (1903–1980) (and the versatile Mario Pani), on the other hand, produced an influential if eclectic style that drew on a variety of modern and traditional currents. From functionalism and modernism, these architects took an appreciation of open spaces and natural materials; from American master architect Frank Lloyd Wright (and others), the desire to create a vernacular architecture inspired by local conditions; from Mexican colonial buildings, the use of courtyards and decorative touches like *vigas* (exposed ceiling beams) and plastered walls; from Japanese Zen gardens, the subtle manipulation of natural elements, especially water, stone, and plants. The rocky, volcanic terrain of the *pedregal,* one of the few "open" spaces left near Mexico City, was their principal site and they filled it with a remarkable collection of residences designed to provide private retreats for the more sophisticated members of Mexico's growing bourgeois managerial class. A far cry from the "minimalist worker's house" of the 1930s but no less ideological, the *pedregal* style acknowledged the growing separation of work and leisure in everyday life as Mexican elites used the ever-expanding highway system to link their urban workplaces to their rural residences—the urban colonial elite had always maintained rural haciendas; new modes of transportation allowed their modern counterparts to enjoy the rural life on a regular basis. As Barragán explained in his 1980 acceptance speech for the prestigious international Pritzker Architecture Award: "In my work, I have always tried to adapt the magic of those remote nostalgic years [on my father's ranch] to the needs of modern living." As the middle classes continued to expand during the 1960 boom years of the Mexican economic "miracle," the *pedregal* style spread quickly throughout Mexico. Also, as mainstream Mexican architecture began to attract international attention thanks to projects like University City, this new residential style began to have an influence abroad as well.

The *pedregal* style has become even more influential in recent years as private capital supersedes public funding in major building projects like resort hotels and office complexes. At the forefront of the institutionalization of the *pedregal* style is Ricardo Legorreta (1931–), the architect behind the most daring building of the National Center for the Arts, the National School of Plastic Arts (1994). In a series of luxury hotels—Hotel Camino Real, Mexico City (1968), Hacienda Cabo San Lucas, Baja California (1972), Hotel Camino Real, Ixtapa (1981)—Legorreta adapted the intimate residential style of Barragán and Cetto with its emphasis on the interplay of light, texture, and color to larger institutional settings and the international modernist-postmodernist idiom preferred by most developers. The new style was a raging success and, by the 1980s, he was designing hotels and office complexes throughout the world. Legorreta's potent mix of *pedregal*-modernism combined with a certain postmodern playfulness continues to inspire architects and to represent a contemporary Mexican architectural style based not on the exotic appeal of pre-Columbian and colonial traditions or the practical needs of workers or the ambitions of a developing nation, but on the leisured sophistication of an elite national and international clientele.

—*RMB*

See also: Art since 1950; Muralist Movement; Orozco, José Clemente; Rivera, Diego; Siquieros, David Álfaro; Tamayo, Rufino; Vasconcelos, José.

References:
Beacham, Hans. *The Architecture of Mexico, Yesterday and Today.* New York: Architectural Book Publishing, 1969.

Cetto, Max L. *Modern Architecture in Mexico.* New York: Praeger, 1961.

Damaz, Paul F. *Art in Latin American Architecture.* New York: Reinhold Publishing, 1963.

Eggener, Keith. *Luis Barragán's Gardens of El Pedregal.* New York: Princeton Architectural Press, 2001.

Fraser, Valerie. *Building the New World: Studies in the Modern Architecture of Latin America, 1930–1960.* New York: Verso, 2000.

Tenorio-Trillo, Mauricio. *Mexico at the World's Fairs: Crafting a Modern Nation.* Berkeley: University of California Press, 1996.

Art since 1950

The muralist movement that emerged from the Revolution of 1910 thrust Mexican art onto the international stage. For postrevolutionary policymakers, eager to demonstrate their commitment to social progress, public murals on national and revolutionary themes seemed an effective means to get their message to ordinary people (or at least to represent themselves as popular, nationalistic, and progressive). As a result of this official support (combined with their own extraordinary talent), the "big three" muralists—Diego Rivera (1886–1957), José Clemente Orozco (1883–1949), and David Álfaro Siquieros (1898–1974)—dominated Mexican visual arts for the first half of the twentieth century. That domination, however, was far from absolute. By the middle of the twentieth-century, it was openly contested by artists seeking a more personal, less ideological approach to art. From this "rupture" would develop a vibrant art scene, impossible to categorize perhaps, but no less artistically dynamic or distinctly Mexican than that of the muralists.

Muralism, especially in its later incarnations, was often overtly nationalistic and sometimes crudely ideological. At the same time, Mexican artists, including the muralists, actively participated in the major international artistic currents of the time, most of which were neither. During the 1920s and 1930s, a cosmopolitan artistic avant-garde provided an important counterpoint to the dominant national style. *Estridentismo,* although mostly a poetic movement, produced visual art that exalted modern urban industrial society, regardless of nationality, rather than pre-Colombian cultures or *campesino* (peasant) revolutionaries after the fashion of official art. Contributors included muralists Rivera and Orozco along with printmaker Leopoldo Méndez (1902–1969), evidence that even at the height of muralism, artistic categories were hard to define and artists difficult to pigeonhole. The *Contemporaneos,* another avant-garde poetry group, were less interested in the aesthetics of modernity than in a visual art that would allow more scope for personal rather than social expression. Artists connected to the *Contemporaneos,* such as Rufino Tamayo (1899–1991) and Antonio Ruiz Cortines (1897–1964), may have been less politically radical than the *Estridentistas* (with the possible exception of Orozco), but their artistic agenda was more subversive of official art. In Ruiz's famous *The Dream of Malinche* (1939), for example, an Indian woman (Malinche was Cortés's interpreter during the conquest of Mexico) lies sleeping on a bed with a bucolic scene of the Mexican countryside nestled into her blanket—a national allegory to be sure but more problematic than celebratory, especially considering Malinche's reputation as a traitor to her people. Moreover, Tamayo's growing international reputation and Ruiz's popular La Esmerelda art school would provide touchstones and training for young artists looking for alternative modes of representation.

Another alternative, surrealism, was not so much a rebuttal of official muralism as a complementary style that respected its expressive power but focused on the ambiguities of representation and social "reality," issues that muralism only rarely acknowledged. As an artistic movement (as opposed to artistic practice), Mexican surrealism dates from the visits of French surrealist guru André Breton (1938) to Mexico City. One of surrealism's most respected voices, Breton was instantly taken with a country and culture that he considered naturally surreal. More important, his collaborations with Mexican artists like Diego Rivera, Frida Kahlo (1907–1952), and photographer Manuel Álvarez Bravo (1902–2002) along with his insistence that artists like Kahlo, Ruiz, and María Izquierdo (1902–1955) were already practicing a native surrealism, provided an important external endorsement of a Mexican artistic practice that was not directly linked to the already well-known muralist movement. Among other things, that external endorsement encouraged a surrealist migration to Mexico. One of the first to arrive was Austrian painter Wolfgang Paalen (1902–1959), with whom Breton organized the 1940 International Surrealist Exposition in Mexico

City, an event that included several contemporary Mexican artists as well as displays of folk art and objects from Diego Rivera's famous pre-Columbian collection. Later arrivals, such as Remedios Varo (1908–1963) and Leonora Carrington (1917–)—although neither developed a particularly Mexican style—helped keep the surrealist tradition alive in Mexico well into the second half of the twentieth century even as it declined elsewhere in the world.

The first major challenge to official muralism was mounted in the 1950s by artists associated with an unofficial, loosely defined movement they called *Ruptura* (Rupture). *Ruptura* artists shared a common disdain for the overt nationalism and radical politics of muralists like Rivera and Siquieros, arguing instead for a more personal art capable of reflecting the ambiguities of the human experience. In 1956, the group's combative self-appointed spokesman, José Luis Cuevas (1934–), published a polemic, "The Cactus Curtain," in which he attacked the national government's art bureaucracy for inhibiting free artistic expression through its support for a suffocating cultural nationalism. Angered by Siquieros's insistence that "there is no other route but ours" and his aggressive policing of less doctrinaire muralists like Orozco (hardly surprising in a hard-core Stalinist), Cuevas condemned midcentury muralism as an artistically bankrupt movement that generated nothing but nationalist or, in the case of Siquieros, communist propaganda.

In the early 1960s, a new group, *Nueva Presencia* (New Presence), that included Cuevas and several other prominent antiestablishment artists, extended Cuevas's critique to all academic art. Prominent poet and essayist Octavio Paz, in his influential meditations on national identity, *Labyrinth of Solitude* (1950), had argued that most Mexicans, unable to confront the traumas of conquest and domination from which the national culture emerged, hid behind "masks" of reserved courtesy, disdain for death, and macho domination of women. For *Nueva Presencia* artists,

Paz's vivid formulation held immense artistic promise and much of their work reflected similar preoccupations with the existential dilemmas that shaped the human condition. Cuevas, for example, achieved early international acclaim for his exquisitely rendered watercolor-drawings of criminals, prostitutes, dead bodies, and monsters inspired by earlier artists like Francisco Goya and novelists like Franz Kafka and Fyodor Dostoyevsky—hardly the optimistic images of human progress favored by most muralists (with the notable exception of Orozco). *Nueva Presencia* painters like Rafael Coronel (1932–) favored a similar "neofigurative" approach and a respect for artistic tradition as in his well-known portrait of the Italian Renaissance master, *Titian* (1969), depicted in profile with a huge smudge of a hat that contrasts strikingly with the carefully rendered face and hands. This neofigurative strand has continued to play a prominent role in Mexican art, although usually in conjunction with other styles as in the cubist rendition of Jacques Louis David's *Death of Marat* by *Nueva Presencia* founder Arnold Belkin (1930–1992); the pop surrealist homage to Diego Velázquez by *Ruptura* artist Alberto Gironella (1929–1999); or, more recently, in the multicultural "magical realism" of Robert Márquez (1959–).

An important factor in the successful promotion of *Ruptura-Nueva Presencia* artists and their successors was a midcentury expansion of Mexico City's art gallery scene. In these unofficial spaces, geared to upscale private buyers eager to demonstrate their artistic sensibilities, new art styles could develop and thrive. More adventuresome gallery owners even sponsored the work of artistic rabble-rousers like the neo-Dadaist group, *Los Hartos* (The Fed-Up), which mounted still more attacks on the failings of contemporary art while relentlessly promoting their own. The 1964 opening of the Museum of Modern Art in Mexico City and a series of important artistic expositions demonstrated that even the art bureaucracies had accepted the exciting new developments in the visual arts.

The rousing success of these assaults on the muralist movement opened Mexican art as never before to a broad spectrum of artistic styles that continues to defy any attempt at strict classification. Nevertheless, several strands do stand out and most artists demonstrate enough stylistic consistency to allow for some generalization. Two of the most difficult artists to categorize are Carlos Mérida (1891–1984) and Rufino Tamayo (1899–1991). Although both belong to the same generation as the big three muralists, both painted public murals, and both drew artistic inspiration from Mexico's indigenous cultures (Mérida was Mayan, Tamayo was Zapotec), neither expressed much interest in the politically charged art of the muralist movement. Instead they focused on the subtle manipulation of color, shapes, and symbols in a variety of styles that ranged from impressionism (Tamayo) to cubism (Mérida) to near abstraction (both). Tamayo, in particular, had a profound influence on fellow Oaxacan artist Francisco Toledo (1940–), whose rich colors, grainy textures, and ambiguous symbols reflect both a stylistic debt to his predecessor and their common indigenous roots. In works like *Turtle* (1963) and *Lazy Dog* (1972), Toledo exploits the symbolic power of traditional images while using subtle shifts in color and unusual composition to hint at deeper, timeless layers of meaning inaccessible to modern, rationalist understanding. An internationally acclaimed artist in his own right, Toledo has disciples of his own, especially the prolific and popular Sergio Hernández (1959–). Some critics regard Toledo and especially Hernández as artisans who craft beautiful but facile images rather than as "serious" artists, but the distinction is difficult to sustain and suggests a suspicion of uncontroversial, popular art that borders on snobbism. Alejandro Colunga (1948–), whose colorful images derive more from traditional Mexican childhood stories— La Llorona, the weeping woman perpetually searching for her children, and Chamuco, a devil who murders children—than from the indigenous past, suggests the breadth of

Mérida's and Tamayo's ongoing influence on Mexican art.

If Mérida, Tamayo, and their successors have flirted at times with abstraction, other artists have taken things much further. One of the first, Gunther Gerzso (1915–), began as a surrealist; by the 1950s, however, his distinctive paintings of overlapping geometric planes had become increasingly abstract. Gerzso himself rejected the label, insisting on figurative connections to Mexican landscapes and pre-Columbian design. Regardless, his work opened the way for abstractionists such as Fernando García Ponce (1933–1987) and Lilia Carillo (1930–1974), whose work explored color, shape, and texture without figuration. García Ponce, for example, mixed carefully composed collage with "accidental" drips and daubs, while Carillo experimented with swirls and smudges of paint that seemed deliberate but impossible to decipher. The current generation of abstractionists, including Irma Palacios (1943–) and Francisco Castro Leñero (1956–), have introduced "expressive" elements into their work with suggestive titles like *Mirror of the Earth* (1992) and *Black and White* (1992) that suggest emotional content and hidden meanings (rather than the "pure" aesthetics of strict abstractionists) while continuing to resist figurative elements.

The decline of official muralism since the 1950s has not discouraged artists from making political statements or socially aware art. Disgusted with political corruption and repression, especially in the wake of the 1968 Tlatelolco massacre of unarmed protesters by Mexican soldiers, student groups like *Suma* (1976) and the *Pentagon Process Group* (1976) attacked the commodification of mainstream and commercial art by using popular forms of representation and reproduction—graffiti, photocopying, mail art—to bring their art to the less privileged sectors of Mexican society. More recently, conceptual artists like Sylvia Gruner have expanded those methods through multimedia installations and performance art in order to critique the role of representation

itself—whether official, commercial, or high art—in producing social inequality.

Contemporary Mexican art also includes some postmodern elements, namely, the rejection of master narratives of social progress (including in art) and playful juxtaposition of stylistic elements. Alfredo Castañeda (1938–), for example, has developed a hyperrealist style that goes beyond surrealism and neorealism into visual paradox. In *The Great Birth* (1983)—a painting that resembles a turn-of-the-century circus poster of the bearded artist giving birth to himself—Castañeda borrows the birth motif from pre-Columbian pottery not as an antiquarian or as evidence of a personal existential crisis but rather to reflect on the relentless and cyclical craziness of modern life. On the other hand, Nahum B. Zenil (1947–) ironically deploys images from popular culture (Virgin of Guadalupe) and folk art (*retablos*) to explore questions of personal-national identity. His *Ex voto* (1987) and *Bloodiest Heart* (1990), for example, depict the artist with an exposed sacred bleeding heart, a Catholic image that references both popular religion and Frida Kahlo's frequent use of the same symbol in her own self-portraits. Julio Galán's (1958–) less personalized use of popular icons in works such as *Where There Is No Sex* (1985) and *What's Missing?* (1990) achieves an even more complex referential effect that suggests a shifting multiplicity of possible meanings. Germán Venegas (1959–) and Javier Marín (1962–) incorporate postmodern aesthetics into the construction of their compositions by combining plastic arts such as painting, collage, and sculpture. Venegas's *Natural Color* (1991), for example, incorporates folk techniques, especially "primitive" wood carving of popular images from the colonial era, while Marín's pottery sculpture, *This Heart Is Not Mine* (1995), uses the traditional clays of indigenous folk art for a stitched-together classical head and torso with the cryptic title scrawled over its heart. Marín's message seems more ironic than sincere, however, a symptom perhaps of a contemporary Mexican art that revels in postmodern play and its own Mexicanness even as it rejects the hope of ever defining what that might mean.

—RMB

See also: Architecture; Kahlo, Frida; Muralist Movement; Orozco, José Clemente; Paz, Octavio; Photography; Poetry; Rivera, Diego; Siquieros, David Álfaro; Tamayo, Rufino; Tlatelolco Massacre.

References:

Ades, Dawn. *Art in Latin America: The Modern Era, 1820–1980.* New Haven, CT: Yale University Press, 1989.

Del Conde, Teresa. "Mexico," in Edward J. Sullivan, ed., *Latin American Art in the Twentieth Century*, pp. 17–50. London: Phaidon, 1996.

Goldman, Shifra M. *Contemporary Mexican Painting in a Time of Change.* Austin: University of Texas Press, 1981.

Lucie-Smith, Edward. *Latin American Art of the Twentieth Century.* New York: Thames and Hudson, 1993.

Assassinations

Assassinations have played a major role in the course of Mexican history during the twentieth century. Being president was a dangerous occupation, especially during the early decades of the century.

Even the lengthy dictatorship of General Porfirio Díaz (1877–1880, 1884–1911)—known for bringing law and order to Mexico—witnessed an assassination attempt on Díaz. Díaz was participating in ceremonies in connection with Mexico's Independence Day celebration on 16 September 1897 when a man from the crowd attacked him. Improbably, the assailant used a rock as a weapon, striking the president on the back of his neck. Díaz was unharmed, but the incident caused a major scandal when the would-be assassin was himself killed while in police custody. Public opinion linked the assassination attempt to a conspiracy involving two members of Díaz's cabinet, and the Mexico City police chief confessed to ordering the murder of the assailant and later committed suicide.

The Revolution of 1910 brought forth a number of political leaders who would later be assassinated. The first president to emerge from the Revolution, Francisco Madero (1911–1913), also became the Revolution's first presidential casualty. Elected to the presidency in late 1911, Madero was overthrown in a military coup led by General Victoriano Huerta on 18 February 1913. Three days later, Madero and his vice-president, José María Pino Suárez, were murdered. Francisco Madero's brother, Gustavo, was also assassinated as part of the coup. These assassinations would set the tone for dealing with presidential rivals for the next fifteen years.

In July 1914 a collection of Revolutionary factions overthrew Huerta, who went into exile. The four leading figures of this next phase of the Revolution—Emiliano Zapata, Venustiano Carranza, Francisco "Pancho" Villa, and Alvaro Obregón—would all become assassination victims.

The first of the group to be assassinated was Emiliano Zapata. Zapata had revolted against every government in Mexico City from 1910 to 1919 in the name of agrarian reform. In 1919 he found himself at odds with the administration of President Venustiano Carranza (1917–1920). In April 1919 Zapata was lured into an elaborate trap set by one of Carranza's officers, who claimed he wanted to defect to Zapata's cause. When Zapata arrived for a conference to finalize the defection, the supposed honor guard gunned him down.

Carranza himself soon fell victim to Revolutionary violence. Carranza provoked a revolt when he attempted to impose his successor in the presidential elections of 1920. Carranza bypassed the most obvious choice and the man who had done the most to put him in the presidency: General Alvaro Obregón. Obregón and his supporters revolted; when Carranza fled from Mexico City in May 1920, Obregón's supporters caught up with Carranza en route to Veracruz and assassinated him.

Francisco "Pancho" Villa had been an antagonist of both Carranza and Obregón since 1914. Reduced to a regional figure, Villa reached an agreement with the government in 1920 in which he would withdraw from political life. The agreement reflected Villa's concern for his own physical welfare; under the arrangement Villa was permitted to maintain a personal bodyguard of fifty men. Even in retirement, fear of assassination haunted Villa, who took extensive security precautions. Tensions rose in 1923 over the issue of who would succeed Obregón as president in 1924. Correctly or not, Villa was connected with one of the contenders, Adolfo de la Huerta, who as interim president had been the major force behind Villa's retirement agreement. On 20 July 1923, Villa—accompanied by only his driver, an aide, and three bodyguards—was attacked by a group of eight armed men. Hit nine times, Villa died instantly.

Many attributed Villa's assassination either to Obregón or his designated successor as president, Plutarco Elías Calles (1924–1928). Assassination would also play a major role in Calles's return of the presidency to Obregón in 1928. When the Constitution of 1917 was amended in 1926 to permit reelection to nonconsecutive terms, it struck at one of the fundamental principles of the Revolution and provoked substantial opposition to Obregón, the obvious beneficiary of the amendment. Obregón's principal competition for the presidency came from two other Revolutionary generals, Arnulfo Gómez and Francisco Serrano. Calles—fearing another revolt—ordered the arrest of Serrano, who was executed along with thirteen of his supporters on 3 October 1927. The following month, Gómez was captured and quickly executed.

The violence surrounding the election of 1928 would claim as its most significant victim President-elect Obregón. Although Obregón's main competitors were removed through execution, arrest, or exile, violence still punctuated the campaign. Obregón himself was the target of an unsuccessful assassination attempt while campaigning, and bombs exploded in the lower house of the Mexican Congress in May 1928. Obregón

easily won the elections in July and was scheduled to take office in December. One of his most-pressing concerns was to bring to an end the small-scale civil war that had arisen from a confrontation between Calles and the Roman Catholic Church. At a banquet in his honor in Mexico City on 17 July, Obregón was shot five times by a religious fanatic, José de León Toral. Obregón died almost immediately. Onlookers quickly seized León Toral, who was executed by firing squad in February 1929.

Although Obregón's death was to be the last assassination of a major leader of the Revolution, the fallout from the presidential election of 1928 continued to provoke violence. An interim president was appointed until new presidential elections could be held in November 1929. The campaign featured the first nominee of the newly formed official party, Pascual Ortiz Rubio. Voting was a hazardous activity, with nineteen people killed in Mexico City alone on election day. Although Ortiz Rubio easily won the election, he had little opportunity to celebrate his victory; within hours of his inauguration on 5 February 1930, Ortiz Rubio was shot in the jaw by a lone assailant outside the National Palace. The would-be assassin, Daniel Flores, was quickly captured, tried, and sentenced in March 1931 to almost twenty years in jail; he died, however, in prison in April 1932. Authorities tried unsuccessfully to link Flores to other conspirators; nevertheless, military officers still executed en masse some sixty opponents of the regime.

Repression continued to be a basic part of political life in the 1930s, but no major political figures were assassinated. The presidential elections of 1940 proved particularly violent, with several assassination attempts directed against the principal opposition candidate, General Juan Andreu Almazán, who survived but lost the election. The winner of the 1940 presidential election, General Manuel Avila Camacho (1940–1946), was himself the target of an assassin. In April 1944 a longtime friend of the president and fellow army officer, Antonio de la Lama, fired at Avila Camacho as he was arriving at the National Palace. The bullet hit the president's coat but not the president himself, who helped subdue the assailant. According to official accounts, on the night of the assassination attempt, guards shot de la Lama as he tried to escape; he died two days later from his wounds.

During the post–World War II period, violence continued to be a fact of political life at local and state levels but bypassed top-ranking political leaders. This undercurrent of political violence came dramatically to the surface in October 1968 in what became known as the Tlatelolco Massacre. Student demonstrations against the government had been escalating during the summer of 1968. With Mexico scheduled to host the Summer Olympics in October 1968, the government was more security-conscious than usual. On 2 October 1968 another student protest took place in the Tlatelolco district of Mexico City. The administration of President Gustavo Díaz Ordaz responded by calling out the riot police and the army. The demonstration turned into a violent confrontation, with an estimated 300 to 400 people killed and perhaps 2,000 injured.

While the government and its critics argued over the responsibility for and the casualties connected with the incident, the Tlatelolco Massacre indicated the growing economic and political disenchantment with the official Revolutionary party, the PRI, which under various names had effectively dominated Mexican politics since 1929. The postwar economic boom had turned sour, and there were growing demands for both political and economic reforms. The political elite were more likely to be the instigators, than the targets, of political violence. One possible exception was Carlos Madrazo, who, after being appointed head of the PRI by Díaz Ordaz, attempted to promote the internal democratization of the party. Madrazo's reform efforts provoked the opposition of PRI bosses, and he was forced to resign in 1965.

Madrazo, however, refused to retire from politics and became a public advocate of democratization; Madrazo died in a suspicious plane crash in 1969.

Mexico's economic problems reached crisis proportions in the 1980s, leading to promises by the PRI of economic and political reforms. While the administrations of Miguel de la Madrid (1982–1988) and Carlos Salinas de Gortari (1988–1994) pressed forward with economic reforms, there was persistent criticism of the slow pace of political reforms. The presidential election of 1988 proved controversial but featured minimum violence; even though the election was a closely contested three-way race, there was no violence directed against the major candidates. The presidential election of 1994, however, took place in a much more violent context.

On 1 January 1994, a serious antigovernment uprising took place in the southern state of Chiapas with the rebels (calling themselves "Zapatistas") attacking army outposts and seizing several towns. The government of Carlos Salinas de Gortari quickly isolated but could not end the rebellion. Other armed groups staged highly publicized attacks in other parts of the country. Mexico's role in the growing international drug trade led to public fears that the country was on the verge of becoming another "narco-state" like Colombia. Responding to growing political opposition, the PRI had nominated as its presidential candidate in 1994 the highly popular and energetic Luis Donaldo Colosio. In March 1994, Colosio was assassinated during a campaign stop in the border city of Tijuana. The alleged gunman, Mario Aburto Martínez, was immediately detained by authorities. Conspiracy theories abounded, including one that said Colosio had been killed because of his opposition to the drug traffickers and another that maintained he had been murdered because he was connected to the drug traffickers. A more sinister explanation offered was that Colosio's assassination had been ordered by opponents within the PRI itself. Aburto Martínez proved to be the only person charged and convicted of the crime. Additional controversy arose in September 1994 when another prominent PRI politician, José Francisco Ruiz Massieu, was also assassinated. Ruiz Massieu held the second highest position in the PRI and was majority leader-elect in the Senate. The accused assassin—Daniel Aguilar Treviño—was captured almost immediately. The case quickly took some unusual turns. President Salinas appointed the assassination victim's brother, Mario Ruiz Massieu, to head the investigation of the assassination. Raul Salinas, the president's brother, was arrested in February 1995 on charges that he had masterminded the assassination. The case took an even more bizarre turn when Mario Ruiz Massieu fled the country amid charges that he had engaged in a cover-up of his own brother's assassination and was laundering money for drug dealers. In January 1999 a Mexican court found Raul Salinas guilty of planning and ordering the assassination of José Francisco Ruiz Massieu and gave him the maximum sentence of fifty years in prison.

The violent events of the 1990s proved to be a shock to the Mexican political system. Optimistic talk of Mexico joining the ranks of the advanced countries crumbled in the face of political assassinations and unprecedented corruption.

—DMC

See also: Corruption; Elections; Presidents of the Twentieth Century; Revolution of 1910; Villa, Francisco "Pancho"; Zapata, Emiliano.

References:

Dulles, John W. F. *Yesterday in Mexico: A Chronicle of the Revolution, 1919–1936*. Austin: University of Texas Press, 1961.

Guadalupe Garcia, Clara. *Rojo: del asesinato político en México*. Barcelona, Spain: Plaza & Janés, 1997.

Meyer, Michael C. *Huerta: A Political Portrait*. Lincoln: University of Nebraska Press, 1972.

Avila Camacho, Manuel (1897–1955)

President from 1940 to 1946, Manuel Avila Camacho was born in the state of Puebla to a middle-class ranching family. He attended local schools and then the National Preparatory School in Mexico City. He joined the Revolutionary ranks in 1914 as a second lieutenant in the Constitutionalist forces of Venustiano Carranza. Avila Camacho rose rapidly through the ranks, becoming a colonel in 1920. That same year he served as chief of staff for the state of Michoacán under future president Lázaro Cárdenas, the beginning of an association that would serve Avila Camacho well throughout his career. Avila Camacho held a series of military positions in the 1920s and early 1930s, fighting against the de la Huerta rebels in 1923–1924, the Cristeros in 1927, and later against the Escobar rebellion in 1929. When Cárdenas became secretary of war in 1933, Avila Camacho served as his chief of staff. After Cárdenas became president, he appointed Avila Camacho secretary of war in 1937.

As the 1940 presidential elections approached, Cárdenas was faced with the choice of tapping a successor. Cárdenas had vigorously pursued a program of reforms between 1934 and 1937, but a combination of domestic and international factors had forced him to deemphasize reform and redirect the government's economic policy away from agrarian reform to a greater emphasis on industrialization. In picking his successor, Cárdenas had to decide whether to choose someone who would renew the reform program or to select a more moderate candidate who could reduce the political divisions within the country that Cárdenas's controversial program had worsened. Cárdenas opted for the moderate choice, selecting Avila Camacho to be the candidate of the official party, the Party of the Mexican Revolution (Partido de la Revolución Mexicana, or PRM). Although critics dismissed Avila Camacho as the "Unknown Soldier," his nomination by the PRM guaranteed his election. In an election marked by violence and fraud, Avila Camacho defeated Juan Andreu Almazán, a former Revolutionary general but the conservative candidate.

Avila Camacho continued the transition to new government policies Cárdenas had started late in his administration. The Revolutionary themes of agrarian reform, labor, economic nationalism, and anticlericalism were to be deemphasized in favor of new approaches.

The redistribution of land had reached its peak under Cárdenas, who had distributed some 49 million acres with the stress on land going to communal holdings, the *ejidos*. Large-scale land redistribution had been a political success, winning the support of the peasantry for Cárdenas and the official party. There was, however, a growing concern about the economic impact of the program as more and more marginal land was distributed. The program also proved costly to implement, leading even Cárdenas to slow down the process late in his administration. Avila Camacho continued the de-emphasis of agrarian reform, distributing only some 12 million acres. He also shifted the focus of distribution from communal holdings to heads of families. Even with this substantial de-emphasis, the Avila Camacho administration still ranked second in land distribution compared with all administrations since 1911.

There were also important changes in the area of labor relations. Cárdenas had helped to establish a major new labor organization, the Confederation of Mexican Workers (the Confederación de Trabajadores Mexicanos, or CTM) under the leadership of the marxist Vicente Lombardo Toledano. Avila Camacho ousted Lombardo Toledano in favor of the more conservative and cooperative Fidel Velázquez. Velázquez helped to curb labor demands even though real wages deteriorated badly during World War II due to inflation. Velázquez continued to head the CTM and to play a moderating role until his death in 1997. Unlike the prounion days under Cárdenas, government officials were quicker to side with management in labor-management disputes. There was one major gain for labor under Avila Camacho. In 1943 the president supported the establishment of the Mexican Institute of Social Security (Instituto Mexicano de Seguro Social or IMSS). Social Security coverage was to be phased in so that, by the end of the Avila Camacho administration in 1946, some 250,000 workers were covered. The Social Security system would later be expanded to include rural areas as well as the operation of clinics and hospitals.

During the presidential campaign, Avila Camacho had been asked about his attitude toward the Roman Catholic Church. He shocked many by replying, "I am a believer." This was a clear indication of the de-emphasis of anticlericalism that was to follow. The anticlerical provisions of the Constitution of 1917 were increasingly ignored, and socialist education—offensive to conservative elements—was officially abandoned.

Economic nationalism also had to take a backseat to wartime demands. The wartime situation dictated closer economic ties with the United States as Mexico found it increasingly difficult to maintain normal economic and financial relations with Europe. Mexico became even more economically dependent on the United States as both a market for its products and a supplier of its needs. The Avila Camacho administration also agreed to let Mexican laborers (*braceros*) work in the United States under regulated conditions to help ease the labor shortage caused by the war.

The government's new development approach, which stressed import substitution industrialization, also represented a major change in economic thinking. Agrarian reform had placed the emphasis on redistributing existing wealth. The new approach emphasized the creation of new wealth, rather than redistribution of existing wealth, as the only way to raise the standard of living for most Mexicans. For Mexican leaders, the appeal of an affluent, urban, industrial lifestyle proved irresistible. Although the Avila Camacho administration represented a move to the right politically, the new development policy actually meant a more active role for the national government in the economy. The government provided credit, allowed tax exemptions, and established protective tariffs to encourage domestic industry. Legislation passed in 1944 encouraged foreign investment in Mexico's industrialization but with the restriction that Mexicans must own a majority of the stock in any joint venture. As a further incentive to industrialization, the government also worked with labor leaders to keep wages low. Just as political power was becoming increasingly centralized, government planning called for industrialization to be centralized in the Federal District, despite early warnings about air pollution and shortages of public services.

Mexico's actions during World War II were another indication of the new directions in government policy under Avila Camacho. Anti-U.S. sentiment had been a strong component of Revolutionary thinking since 1910. During World War I, President Venustiano Carranza had kept Mexico neutral and had defied U.S. pressure to take a more active role in the conflict. During World War II, President Avila Camacho adopted a decidedly pro-U.S. stance. After the United States entered the war, Mexico broke relations with Japan and Germany. In May 1942, after German submarine attacks on Mexican oil tankers, Mexico issued a formal declaration of war. In addition to the *bracero* program that furnished Mexican workers for the U.S. economy, Mexico reached an agreement with the United States, permitting the United States to draft Mexican citizens residing in the United States. The Avila Camacho administration even let the United States establish recruiting stations in Mexico. As a result, approximately 250,000 Mexican citizens served in the U.S. armed forces during the war. Mexico received military supplies under the U.S. Lend-Lease Act and even furnished a small military force—a fighter squadron equipped and trained by the United States—for service in the Philippines.

The new direction of the government and the official party was demonstrated by the renaming of the official party and by its selection for the presidency in 1946. The Party of the Mexican Revolution was renamed the Institutional Revolutionary Party (Partido Revolucionario Institucional, or PRI) both to signify that the Revolution had generated the institutions needed to sustain it and to indicate the new official policies that were being pursued. Avila Camacho tapped as his successor Miguel Alemán, a civilian who had not played an active role in the early years of the Revolution. Alemán—Avila Camacho's secretary of the interior (internal security)—was committed to the continuation and the expansion of the policies that Avila Camacho had been pursuing.

In 1940 Manuel Avila Camacho was one of Mexico's less well-known Revolutionary generals (the "Unknown Soldier"). He then went on to become one of Mexico's less well-known presidents. This lack of historical notoriety, however, does not indicate that his term in the presidency was unimportant. On the contrary, Avila Camacho helped to develop some of the basic policies that guided the government and the official party for the next forty years. The Avila Camacho administration proved to be a key period as Mexico made the transition to its post-Revolutionary era.

—DMC

See also: Agrarian Reform/Land and Land Policy; Alemán, Miguel; Assassinations; *Bracero* Program; Cárdenas, Lázaro; de la Huerta, Adolfo; Import Substitution Industrialization (ISI); Partido Revolucionario Institucional (PRI); Presidents of the Twentieth Century; Velázquez Sánchez, Fidel; World War II.

References:
Niblo, Stephen R. *Mexico in the 1940s: Modernity, Politics, and Corruption.* Wilmington, DE: Scholarly Resources, 1999.
———. *War, Diplomacy, and Development: The United States and Mexico, 1938–1954.* Wilmington, DE: Scholarly Resources, 1995.
Torres, Blanca. *Historia de la Revolución Mexicana, Periodo 1940–1952.* Vol. 21. *Hacia la utopia industrial.* Mexico City: El Colegio de México, 1984.

B

Baja California Norte and Baja California Sur (States)

Baja California Norte and Baja California Sur are two states in northeastern Mexico that occupy the peninsula of Baja California and include within their jurisdictions several islands off the Pacific coast and in the Gulf of California. Mexicali serves as the current capital of Baja California Norte, and La Paz is the capital of Baja California Sur. Both areas achieved statehood only after World War II, and Baja California Sur has the distinction of being Mexico's newest state. Characterized by aridity and rugged terrain, the entire peninsula of Baja California remained sparsely populated until the twentieth century. Its physical location, in turn, proved an obstacle to Baja's integration with the rest of the Mexican nation. During the latter part of the twentieth century, Baja California developed a thriving tourist industry. It also became a center of the drug trade.

Three tribal groups, the Pericúes, Guaycuras, and Chochimíes, inhabited the peninsula of Baja California upon the arrival of the Spaniards. Spanish exploration of the area was spurred on by the news that pearls could be found in the area and the peninsula (initially believed to be an island) was dubbed "Island of Pearls" for a time. Despite the rugged terrain and inhospitable environment, the Spanish Crown made continuous attempts to colonize Baja California, largely in response to threats from English and Dutch pirates who plied the coastal region, spying on the Manila Galleons as they made their way (loaded with silver and other valuables) to and from Asia. Effective settlement came largely at the hands of missionaries, who attended to a steadily declining Indian population. Beginning in the seventeenth century, the Jesuits established a string of missions in the peninsula. Dominican and Franciscan missionaries assumed control of this work after the Jesuits were expelled from Spanish domains in the eighteenth century. The colonial period, in short, was one of gradual development and frequent setbacks for Baja California. Poor land and isolation from the Mexican colony discouraged settlement and encouraged plotting by Spain's rivals.

Baja California remained isolated after Mexican Independence, when it became part of the Territory of the Californias. Its isolation left it open to foreign threats and in the 1820s Englishman Thomas Cochrane sailed two ships to the peninsula in an attempt to make the Californias independent. La Paz, which was designated the peninsular capital in 1828, bore the brunt of several such foreign invasions. U.S. forces occupied the port during the Mexican War, as did William Walker, an American filibusterer who attempted to proclaim an independent "Republic of Baja California" during the 1850s. Amid such threats, the Mexican government attempted to colonize the area by issuing land grants. The most significant of these was the Leese Concession, given to an American in the 1860s. Like several concessions granted by Mexico during the nineteenth century, the Leese grant did not bring the desired colonists, and the land thus reverted to Mexican control.

The focus on rapid economic growth that characterized the regime of Porfirio Díaz generated additional attempts to populate Baja California during the late nineteenth and early twentieth centuries. Díaz provided foreigners, including Americans and the British, with generous land concessions. Although speculation and fraudulent activity by Mexican and foreign investors was common, the peninsula did experience a modest growth in economic activity (including agriculture and cattle ranching) and in population. It was also during the Díaz era that Baja California was divided into two zones, thus beginning the distinct political histories of Baja California Norte and Baja California Sur.

Economic and demographic growth in the southern district occurred primarily around La Paz and included development in pearl fishing and mining. Baja California Norte, however, experienced more dramatic changes around the turn of the century. The northwestern portion of the district, particularly the area around the port city of Ensenada, grew with U.S. and Mexican investment, and in 1889 a short-lived gold strike at El Alamo (southeast of Ensenada) attracted workers from the U.S. state of California and from other parts of Mexico. Meanwhile, in the northeastern section of the peninsula, development was spurred on by activities on the other side of the international border. As Americans harnessed the waters of the Col-

orado River to create the rich agricultural region of the Imperial Valley, small towns emerged on the Mexican side of the line, including the future state capital of Mexicali. The American-owned Colorado River Land Company, which spearheaded growth in the Imperial Valley, acquired lands in the neighboring Mexicali Valley and thus encouraged its growth. Many Mexicans migrated to this border region to work as rural laborers, especially in the cotton fields that flourished on both sides of the border. Economic development in the Mexicali-Imperial Valley zone, as well as the creation of railroad lines and boat connections that linked Baja California Norte with the United States, underscored the peninsula's historical orientation away from the Mexican mainland.

Baja California's isolation from the rest of Mexico, as well as its closer links to the United States, became especially apparent during the early phase of the Mexican Revolution. In 1911, the Mexican Liberal Party (PLM) of Ricardo and Enrique Flores Magón used their base in Los Angeles, California, to stage an invasion of the northern section of the peninsula. Their efforts, which were part of a broader rebellion against the Mexican government, failed. The PLM movement generated additional concerns, however, because of rumors that an independent Baja California might emerge and perhaps even be annexed by the United States. To a much greater extent than Baja California Norte, Baja California Sur was largely isolated from the Mexican Revolution. In 1913, however, General Félix Ortega began a rebellion against Victoriano Huerta, who claimed the presidency of Mexico after the assassination of Francisco I. Madero. Baja California Sur became one of many arenas in which the Revolution played itself out.

Economic recovery and additional growth characterized the history of Baja California in the aftermath of the Mexican Revolution. Baja California Sur, historically the lesser populated and developed of the two peninsular zones, became the target of a government colonization program during the 1930s, which used irrigation to open up more land to cultivation. At the same time, the south's once-lucrative pearl fishing industry declined because of a disease that affected mother-of-pearl shells. Development in Baja California Norte in the aftermath of the Mexican Revolution was more impressive. During the 1920s, the region experienced a boom when Prohibition in the United States brought business to Tijuana and other border towns. Gambling, prostitution, and drug trafficking also became part of the borderlands economy. The economic future of most residents of Baja California Norte, however, depended on a successful resolution of the agrarian problem.

The Colorado River Land Company continued to control most of the land in the Mexicali Valley, renting it to Mexican farmers. In 1915 those farmers began a struggle to reclaim that land, and in 1937 they occupied company properties in what became known as the "Assault on the Land." President Lázaro Cárdenas responded to the movement in the peninsula by redistributing some of the land, and in 1946 the Mexican government acquired all of the Mexican lands of the Colorado River Land Company and began to redistribute them.

World War II was a pivotal event for Baja California Sur and Norte since it highlighted the peninsula's strategic importance. Baja California became central to Mexican attempts to protect its Pacific coast zone and the government invested more money in the region. Migration to the peninsula increased and particularly affected Baja California Norte as Mexican agricultural workers came to the Imperial and Mexicali valleys in greater numbers. The *Bracero* Program, initiated in 1942 to encourage Mexican laborers to work in American fields, attracted additional migrants. Population growth continued after the war and economic growth throughout the peninsula received a boost from the emerging tourist industry, which brought new prosperity to La Paz, Ensenada,

Tijuana, and other urban areas. At the dawn of the twenty-first century, Baja California continued to welcome over one million tourists each year, many of them drawn to the peninsula's offshore attractions, including coral reefs and lagoons that serve as the winter home for gray whales.

World War II and the development that followed encouraged Mexico's leaders to consider a change in the territorial status of the peninsula. Baja California Norte became a state in 1952 and Baja California Sur, which lagged behind in its growth and experienced little in the way of industrial development, achieved statehood in 1974. During the last decades of the twentieth century, growth in both states depended primarily on tourism, agriculture, and fishing. The illegal traffic in drugs, however, remains an important part of the peninsula's economy and has given Baja's northern border zone a reputation for violence and corruption. During the 1990s, Tijuana was a center of drug gangs, including the infamous Arellano Félix cartel. Police and judicial officials were murdered on a regular basis, and in 1994 Luis Donaldo Colosio (a candidate for the presidency) was assassinated in Tijuana, an incident that some linked to the drug trade.

While the drug economy has compromised the safety of the border zone and provided the newest obstacle to Mexico's control of Baja California, other economic developments during the second half of the twentieth century have had a negative effect on the region. In the Mexicali-Imperial Valley area, overcultivation of the land, as well as overuse of the waters of the Colorado River, have generated international disputes and environmental decline. In response to Mexican complaints that Americans monopolized the waters of the Colorado River, the United States and Mexico signed a treaty regulating the use of that river in 1944. Steady immigration to the region, and its unrestricted development, however, strained the water supply so that, by the 1960s, salinity, pollution, and water shortages were common problems.

The *maquiladora* industry, which brought industry to Mexico's border region beginning in the 1960s, exacerbated the situation by producing more waste and toxins and placing additional demands on the water supply.

In the twenty-first century, the fate of Baja California may well depend on how it addresses the problems of overdevelopment and environmental decline. At the same time, Mexico's success in controlling this distant frontier will depend on its ability to confront the drug trade.

—*SBP*

See also: *Bracero* Program; Drug Trafficking; Partido Liberal Mexicano (PLM).

References:

Blaisdell, Lowell L. *The Desert Revolution: Baja California, 1911.* Madison: University of Wisconsin Press, 1962.

Martínez, Pablo L. *A History of Lower California.* Mexico City: Editorial Baja California, 1960.

Ward, Evan. "Two Rivers, Two Nations, One History: The Transformation of the Colorado River Delta since 1940," *Frontera Norte* 11, no. 22 (July/December 1999): 113–140.

Worster, Donald. *Rivers of Empire: Water, Aridity, and the Growth of the American West.* New York: Pantheon, 1985.

Official web site: http://www.bajacalifornia.gob.mx

Banking and Finance

For much of the nineteenth century, the absence of financial institutions severely restricted Mexico's efforts to achieve financial stability and economic development. An inadequate tax structure forced the central government to depend on foreign and domestic borrowing. The Mexican government found it difficult to borrow from foreign creditors after an early default (1827) on a loan from British financiers, forcing it to rely on domestic lending sources. These domestic lenders were known as *agiotistas*—speculators or loan sharks—who specialized in short-term, high-interest loans to the government. The *agiotistas* constituted an informal financial network, and some made the transition to entrepreneurial status. They did not, however, charter formal financial institutions. The government tried its own hand at organizing a bank in 1830 when it created the Banco de Avío, which used a portion of the government's tariff revenues to make long-term loans to promote manufacturing activity. Mexico's ongoing political, financial, and military problems led to the dissolution of the Banco de Avío in 1842. The first major private bank in Mexico was the Banco de Londres y México (the Bank of London and Mexico) established in 1864. As the title indicated, it was financed by British capital. The state of Chihuahua granted charters to two private banks in the 1870s. The only other significant financial institution in the 1870s was the Monte de Piedad, the National Pawnshop. The Monte had functioned as a pawnshop since 1775; in 1879 it expanded its activities to include the receipt of deposits, the negotiation of discounts, and the issuance of notes, which the government accepted for the payment of fees or taxes.

The emphasis on economic development during the administrations of Presidents Porfirio Díaz (1877–1880, 1884–1911) and Manuel González (1880–1884) required and supported an expansion in Mexico's financial institutions. The González administration took a major step toward the establishment of a true banking system in 1882 when it issued a charter for the Banco Nacional Mexicano (the Mexican National Bank). Despite its name, the bank was actually a branch of the Franco-Egyptian Bank of Paris. The bank was to have a minimum capital of 6 million pesos and was authorized to issue notes acceptable in payment at all federal offices. It served as the fiscal agent for the Mexican government and also provided a line of credit from which the central government could borrow up to 4 million pesos per fiscal year at an interest rate of 4 to 6 percent.

At its establishment, the Banco Nacional Mexicano was the most important financial institution in Mexico. It soon, however, achieved even greater importance when it merged in 1884 with the Banco Mercantil

Mexicano (the Mexican Mercantile Bank) to form the Banco Nacional de México (the National Bank of Mexico). The Mexican government—in need of additional domestic loans—encouraged the merger of the two banks. The Banco Nacional de México had a capital of 20 million pesos and could issue notes acceptable in payment at all government offices. The central government was to have a line of credit at the bank allowing it to borrow up to 8 million pesos per year at an interest rate of 6 percent. Two government supervisors were to oversee general operations at the bank; in addition, the bank had to file monthly financial reports with the government.

In 1884 the federal government also issued a new commercial code that provided for federal regulation of banking. The federal government assumed responsibility for chartering and regulating banks. No bank could be established without prior approval by the minister of the treasury. All banks had to have a minimum capital of 500,000 pesos. Banks could not own land except for property used for bank buildings. If a bank acquired property through foreclosure, the bank was required to sell the property within two years. A federal inspector was to be appointed for each bank, and all banks had to submit monthly financial reports to the federal government. Banks could issue notes, but they had to be backed by gold or silver on deposit in the national treasury. All notes had to be approved by the minister of the treasury before circulating; notes were not considered legal tender. Financial institutions that did not meet the requirements of the commercial code could be liquidated by the federal government. The Bank of London and Mexico had to appeal to the Mexican Supreme Court to avoid liquidation.

The financial structure also was affected by a crisis involving the Monte de Piedad and government plans to issue new nickel coinage. The Monte had moved far beyond its pawning functions into mortgage lending, the discounting of business paper, savings ac-

counts for the public, and the issuance of its own notes, which were accepted in payment of federal taxes. The Monte soon ran into trouble by issuing too many notes and becoming too dependent on mortgage lending. The Monte had also made major loans to the federal government. Rumors that the government was seeking an additional loan from the Monte caused fears that the Monte would not have sufficient metallic reserves to redeem its notes. The result was a run on the Monte, which forced it to close temporarily in April 1884. The closing of the Monte frightened those who held notes from other banks, and a run on other financial institutions ensued. The Monte soon reopened but restricted its future financial services to its original pawning function.

The introduction of a new system of nickel coinage also provoked public concern and financial disorder. Mexico's expanding commercial activity required additional coinage. The issuance of the new nickel money (actually a nickel-copper alloy) also addressed the frequent problem of the metallic value of Mexican coinage being greater than its legal value; this difference led to coinage being taken out of circulation and used for industrial purposes. The González administration, however, made two major mistakes when 4 million pesos of the new nickel coins were introduced beginning in December 1882. First, there was no limit on the amount of the new money that had to be accepted in any one transaction. González asked for a one-peso limit, but Congress omitted the restriction in the final legislation. Second, in order to get the coinage into circulation as quickly as possible, the government sold large quantities of the new coins at a discount to certain commercial establishments. As a result of these two mistakes, the new coinage depreciated rapidly. The government tried to salvage the new coinage by belatedly introducing a limit on the amount that had to be accepted in any transaction. Public disenchantment with the new coinage was so great that the government ordered the complete withdrawal of the new nickel money in February 1884.

The federal government under Porfirio Díaz continued to promote the establishment of new banks and the creation of a banking system. A new commercial code in 1889 called for a suspension on any new banking regulations pending a comprehensive study of Mexican financial institutions. New banks could be established under the provisions of the commercial code of 1884; several new provincial banks were established in the 1890s. No new bank legislation was forthcoming until 1897.

The new legislation of 1897 reflected the thinking and influence of Minister of the Treasury José Yves Limantour. The previous year Limantour had guided the Mexican government to the first balanced budget in its history, an accomplishment that brought Limantour national and international acclaim. The general law of credit institutions passed in 1897 confirmed the control of the federal executive over bank concessions. It established three basic categories of banks: emissions, auxiliary development, and mortgage. Emissions banks were authorized to issue their own notes and to make loans not to exceed nine months; they provided short-term credit to finance business activities. Auxiliary development banks (*refaccionarios*) provided intermediate-term credit of up to two years to support mining, manufacturing, and agriculture. Mortgage (*hipotecario*) banks made loans secured by real estate for periods of up to forty years. The law required auxiliary development banks to have a minimum capital of 200,000 pesos, while emission and mortgage banks were required to have a minimum capital of 500,000 pesos. Operating as a bank of emission, the National Bank of Mexico retained its special position under the new legislation. It served as the fiscal agent of the federal government, could conduct operations throughout Mexico, and its notes circulated throughout the country.

The legislation of 1897 did lead to an expansion of the Porfirian banking system. Most of the new banks were banks of emission, with many located in the provinces. A relatively small number of Mexico City banks led by the National Bank of Mexico, however, dominated banking in terms of capital controlled and notes issued. Representatives of the major banks strongly influenced the drafting of the new legislation, so it was not surprising that it protected their privileged positions. Weak enforcement of the law also meant that the specialized division of financial institutions based on length and object of lending was often not observed; banks frequently violated their restrictions on duration and types of loans.

Although the banking system had expanded, the international financial crisis of 1907 exposed the weaknesses of many Mexican financial institutions. Even Limantour himself—still minister of the treasury—believed that most Mexican banks were not financially sound. After conferring with the banking community, Limantour issued a new set of reforms in 1908. The reforms prohibited emissions banks from establishing new branches and encouraged emissions banks to transform themselves into auxiliary development or mortgage banks to provide additional intermediate- and long-term lending. Many of the emissions banks were already illegally engaged in such lending anyway. Another indication of abuses in the banking system was the reform prohibiting emissions banks from making loans to administrators or stockholders during their first year of operations.

The various efforts to reform and to promote the Porfirian financial structure produced mixed results. The number of chartered banks went from just nine in 1897 to thirty-two in 1910; the combined capital of the chartered banks increased from 35 million pesos to more than one billion pesos over the same time period. The Porfirian elite, however, had a disproportionate access to these increased financial resources. In addition, a handful of Mexico City banks dominated the financial landscape, and foreigners played a major role in the financial sector as they did in many areas of the economy. Limantour's switching of Mexico from the silver standard to the gold standard in 1905 helped exporters and foreign investors but hurt importers and domestic commerce, as the currency was devalued. Mexican financial institutions were already badly shaken by the financial decline that set in in 1907. An even greater trauma lay ahead—the impact of the Revolution of 1910 on the financial system. Limantour labored over the public finances to the bitter end. Even as the Porfirian regime crumbled in 1910–1911, Limantour was renegotiating Mexico's external debt and predicting a surplus for the fiscal year.

As the Revolution of 1910 escalated into a full-scale civil war that ravaged Mexico in 1914 and 1915, normal banking operations were impossible. Revolutionary generals issued their own paper money, which was backed up only by the threat of violence against those who refused to accept it. Porfirian legislation continued to regulate the banking system until 1915 and the triumph of the Constitutionalist Revolutionary faction under Venustiano Carranza. Carranza had been angered by the refusal of the private banks to honor his Constitutionalist currency and had responded in kind by refusing to recognize the notes issued by the private banks. In October 1916, Carranza appointed a special commission to examine the solvency of the banks and to make recommendations for liquidating insolvent banks; the commission reported back that fifteen of the twenty-four emissions banks examined were insolvent. Carranza also ordered the seizure of banks with insufficient reserves. One of the biggest threats to the surviving banks was Carranza's effort to wring massive forced loans out of them. Carranza favored the creation of a government-controlled central bank with the exclusive right to issue notes. The Constitution of 1917 provided for such a bank, but economic and financial problems delayed its establishment until 1925. Although Carranza's actions further weakened the banking

system inherited from Porfirio Díaz, much of the Porfirian elite survived the Revolution and were prepared to bargain with post-Carranza Revolutionary governments.

The administrations of Alvaro Obregón (1920–1924) and Plutarco Elías Calles (1924–1928) needed to normalize relations with the bankers as part of their broader effort to reconstruct the economy and centralize political power after years of revolution and dislocation caused by World War I and its aftermath. The refusal of the United States to extend recognition to Obregón also undermined Mexico's financial position. In 1921 Obregón ordered that the banks seized by Carranza be restored to their owners. In 1922 Obregón reached an agreement on Mexico's foreign debt with the International Committee of Bankers on Mexico, which represented the leading French, British, and U.S. banks. The agreement left Mexico heavily indebted—almost one billion pesos after consolidation. It did, however, offer some breathing space for the Mexican government, which did not have to resume full servicing of the debt until 1 January 1928. Obregón's inability to get new loans forced him to suspend the agreement in June 1924. Likewise, lack of finances continued to delay the establishment of a central bank.

In February 1924 the first National Banking Convention was held, bringing together leading private bankers as well as government officials. Both groups were ready for an accommodation that would evolve into a long-term alliance. The convention endorsed such key concepts as government regulation of private banking, a government commitment to pay its bank debts, and the establishment of a central bank. The legislative outgrowth of the convention was the General Law of Credit Institutions passed in January 1925. The law prohibited banks from owning stocks in other banks and eliminated the tax-exemption enjoyed by banks under the old Porfirian system. The National Banking Commission within the Ministry of the Treasury would exercise overall supervision of the banking system. The law also called for the creation of a central bank with exclusive authority to issue notes.

The organic law and statutes establishing the new central bank, the Banco de México (or Bank of Mexico), were issued in August 1925. The bank was to be a mixed-capital venture with the government owning 51 percent of the shares and the remaining 49 percent of the shares being offered for sale to private banks or individuals. The government would appoint five of the nine members of the bank's board of directors. The minister of the treasury had the power to veto board decisions if they were deemed to affect the national interest or broader government policy. The bank had exclusive control over the issue of notes and also regulated interest rates, exchange rates, and money in circulation. The bank was the fiscal agent for the federal government and supplied a line of credit against which the federal government could borrow up to 10 percent of the bank's paid-in capital.

In operation, the bank had to overcome an initial shortage of capital and of public confidence in it. The general public was slow to accept the notes issued by the bank; only two private banks initially associated themselves with the bank in 1925, compared with the forty-one financial institutions participating in the National Banking Convention in 1924. The presence of private bankers on the Bank of Mexico's board, however, assured a linkage between the public and private banking sectors. The International Committee of Bankers strongly opposed the establishment of the bank on the grounds that it would delay renewal of payments on the foreign debt. On a more somber note, by the end of 1927, the bank had already exceeded the legal limit on the amount of money it could lend the federal government. The bank and the new banking legislation substantially reduced the role played by foreign bankers in the banking system. The bank was an important tool that the government could use to ensure that the banking system supported government development policies. Although the bank helped

to regulate the private banking system, it was also a mechanism for cooperation between an evolving private banking system and an emerging centralized state. A striking symbol of the relation between the state and the private banking system was the temporary location of the central offices of the Bank of Mexico in the headquarters of the Bank of London and Mexico.

Legislation passed in 1932 further strengthened the position of the Bank of Mexico in the overall banking structure. Under the law, all banks were required to associate themselves with the Bank of Mexico and to invest their capital in Mexico. This legislation led three of the six foreign banks to cease operations in Mexico. The new legislation also provided for the establishment of investment banks (*financieras*) to provide long-term financing for agriculture and industry. The result of the legislation was to hasten the "Mexicanization" of the banking system, which had been a government goal since the Carranza administration.

One of the most important financial changes of the 1920s and 1930s was the growing role of government development banks. These banks were designed to promote government development plans and to provide credit to groups that normally would find it difficult or impossible to obtain credit. They were also intended to gain the political loyalty of the groups receiving the credit. One of the earliest and most important of these institutions was the Banco Nacional de Crédito Agrícola (the National Agricultural Credit Bank) established in 1926. This bank was set up to help finance the needs of the small farmers and *ejido* members who received land under the government's expanding agrarian reform program. The Banco Nacional Hipotecario Urbano y de Obras Públicas (the Public Works Bank) helped to finance road construction and irrigation systems. Crédito Hotelero, established in 1937, provided financing for hotel construction by private firms. The most important of these institutions was the Nacional Financiera (the

National Development Bank, or NAFINSA). NAFINSA was particularly important in promoting industrial development through the extension of loans, the purchase of stock in private companies, and the placement of government securities.

The growing alliance between the state and the private banks was made clear in 1937 when bank employees tried to unionize. The administration of Lázaro Cárdenas (1934–1940) had a well-established record for encouraging workers to organize and strike to get their demands. Bankers and some administration officials maintained that a strike by bank employees might undermine public confidence in the banking system as a whole. A new regulation that went into effect in November 1937 specifically prohibited strikes by bank employees and required that bank employees have individual contracts rather than the collective work contracts, which the Cárdenas administration usually supported. Labor-management disputes would be referred to the Ministry of the Treasury or to the federal arbitration board. One of the principal authors of the new regulation was Luis Montes de Oca, director of the central bank.

In the post-1940 period, the Mexican government embarked on a new development scheme—import substitution industrialization (ISI)—that would influence banking and finance. ISI called for the government to become even more actively involved in the economy to promote domestic manufacturing through a number of measures, including protective tariffs and import quotas. Rapid industrialization required increased foreign investment, bank lending, and direct government financial support. The regulatory powers of the central bank were strengthened, and NAFINSA became a key allocator of credit to the private sector by making loans, purchasing corporate stock, facilitating industrial access to foreign sources of credit, and working with international lending agencies such as the World Bank and the International Monetary Fund. Government policies

were a factor in growing inflationary pressures, which led to devaluations of the peso in 1948 and 1954. Mexico would not experience another devaluation until 1976.

As the Mexican economic "miracle" unfolded in the 1940s and 1950s, the banking system expanded along with the economy. The number of bank branches increased rapidly in the 1950s, almost tripling during the decade. The banking system also became more concentrated; that is, controlled by fewer banks. In 1950 fourteen banks controlled 60 percent of bank resources; by 1960 just seven banks controlled 60 percent of resources. Within the overall expansion of the system, the fastest growing segment was the *financieras,* originally established to provide long-term credit for industry. During the 1960s, the economic miracle began to fade, but concentration in the private banking industry continued at a high rate. By 1968 just seven bank groups controlled 78 percent of bank resources and accounted for 72 percent of bank profits.

The growing importance of bank groups—often connected with industrial groups—was a major feature of Mexican banking in the post-1940 period. Mexican banking law did not allow the "full-service" banking we are accustomed to today. Instead, separate institutions were required for commercial banking, investment banking, and mortgage lending. The formation of bank groups helped to circumvent these legal restrictions. Two groups provide examples of the type of financial combinations that were assembled: the Banamex Group and the Serfin Group. The two principal components of the Banamex Group were the Banco Nacional de Mexico, a commercial bank started in 1884, and Financiera Banamex, an investment bank originally established as the Crédito Bursatil in 1936. The Serfin Group was made up of: the Bank of London and Mexico, the oldest commercial bank in the country; Financiera Aceptaciones, one of the country's largest investment banks, and Monterrey, Compania de Seguros, one of Mexico's leading insurance companies. Serfin, in turn, was connected to the Garza Sada industrial group in Monterrey, which was involved in a broad range of business activities from beer to steel. These groups wielded tremendous financial, economic, and political power that made them obvious targets for attack when the economic miracle and the oil boom turned sour in the 1970s and 1980s.

By the early 1970s, import substitution industrialization had reached its limits as a development policy. Income distribution was badly skewed, and a growing population threatened to increase the already high levels of unemployment and underemployment. Inflation was a growing problem, and the government found it increasingly difficult to maintain a stable peso. Both the government and private companies were becoming more dependent on foreign financing, and Mexican banks became more actively involved in international financial markets. Government credit institutions and government-owned business operations (*paraestatales*) also became more dependent on foreign debt. Much of this foreign debt was contracted through Mexican private banks. Government policies in the 1970s continued the process of concentration in the banking sector. The worsening financial picture was made clear in 1976 when Mexico devalued the peso for the first time since 1954.

The oil boom of the late 1970s temporarily relieved the growing economic, financial, and political pressures. When the oil boom turned bust in 1981, financial crisis soon followed. Even before the break in oil prices, Mexican officials were already worried by the growing signs of capital flight (capital—both foreign and Mexican—leaving Mexico for investment elsewhere). Capital flight was estimated at $36 billion between 1978 and 1982. Private banks experienced a decline in capital and a major upswing in overdue loans between 1980 and 1982. The heavy borrowing of the 1970s culminated in the debt crisis of August 1982 when the Mexican government announced it could no longer meet its debt obligations.

Facing political disgrace, outgoing President José López Portillo (1976–1982) increasingly focused on the banks as the villains of the piece. López Portillo had entered office as the financial technocrat who would straighten out Mexico's financial and economic problems. It now appeared he would leave office in 1982 with Mexico in a greater economic crisis than when he entered. The banks were directly involved in—and often profiting from—two of the most controversial aspects of the crisis: capital flight and speculation in the peso. As early as March 1982 government officials were considering the possibility of the nationalization (government ownership and operation) of the private banks. There was a growing conviction that the banks had acted in a socially irresponsible manner and were no longer promoting national development. The banks in turn argued that it was the government's own policies that encouraged capital flight and speculation and that the banks were only doing what they were legally permitted to do. A massive devaluation of the peso (70 percent) in early 1982 heightened the crisis atmosphere. The August 1982 announcement by the government that it could not meet its debt obligations was accompanied by another major devaluation. The value of the peso had gone from 12.5 to the dollar in 1976 to 37.7 in February 1982 to 69 in August 1982.

As the Mexican government worked to avoid a formal default, the López Portillo administration was moving toward a decision to nationalize the banks. In his last report to the nation as president on 1 September 1982, López Portillo announced the nationalization of the banks and the imposition of exchange controls by executive decree. The president justified his actions on the grounds that the banks had been involved in a massive "looting" of the nation and that this action was necessary to bring an end to capital flight and to speculation in the peso. Many interpreted López Portillo's actions as motivated more by political concerns—a failed presidency and a crisis of legitimacy for the official party—than by financial and economic considerations.

Reaction to the nationalization was immediate. The director of the Mexican central bank, the head of the government-owned foreign trade bank, and the minister of the treasury all tendered their resignations. López Portillo refused to accept the resignation of his treasury minister, Jesús Silva Herzog, who was involved in crucial negotiations with Mexico's international creditors. Silva Herzog worked to limit the impact of the nationalization, influencing the appointment of government officials who took over administration of the nationalized banks. President-elect Miguel de la Madrid was not enthusiastic about the nationalization of the banks and was opposed to the imposition of exchange controls.

The bankers who had their institutions nationalized had two main concerns. First, the nationalized banks held stock in a number of private companies; the ex-bankers were interested in having the government sell off these stocks, especially those in nonbank financial institutions. Second, the government was supposed to compensate the banks for their assets; the ex-bankers were concerned about how the government would value these assets and what the terms of compensation would be. The government indicated that the shares in private companies held by the nationalized banks would be sold off, with the ex-bankers getting the first opportunity to purchase them. Indemnization would be in the form of government bonds with valuation based on the adjusted capital of the bank.

The bank nationalization had as its stated goals the curbing of speculation, the reduction of capital flight, and the channeling of credit into productive activities, especially small- and medium-sized operations. The nationalization met with limited success in achieving these goals. There was continued speculation in and a rapid decline of the peso during the de la Madrid administration (1982–1988). Capital flight declined slightly but continued at levels that aggravated Mex-ico's financial problems; capital flight for the 1983–1985 period was approximately $16 billion. Small- and medium-sized businesses still found credit expensive and hard to obtain. In addition, the government found itself stuck with the shares of stock in private companies that were heavily indebted and not performing well; this necessitated a major program in which the government assumed responsibility for a large portion of private-sector debts. The nationalization also left the government responsible for some $10 billion worth of foreign debt, which it "inherited" from the nationalized banks.

A partial "reprivatization" of the banking system began almost immediately. De la Madrid extended the sale of stock held by nationalized banks to include the sale of stock in nonbank financial institutions. This permitted ex-bankers to regain control of institutions such as insurance companies and stock brokerages. This permitted the development of a parallel, private financial market, with stock brokerages in particular booming. In 1982, stock brokerages managed less than 10 percent of total public savings; by 1986, they managed almost 30 percent of total public savings.

Miguel de la Madrid's successor, Carlos Salinas de Gortari (1988–1994), envisioned a comprehensive reprivatization of the banking system. Salinas was a fan of privatization in general and believed that many of Mexico's economic and financial problems were a result of excessive government involvement in the economy. Salinas started the process in late 1989 with a major deregulation of the financial sector. In May 1990 Salinas called for the reprivatization of the nationalized banking system, which was quickly implemented. Proceeds from the sale of the banks went to reducing the debt, improving the infrastructure, and expanding social programs. The reprivatization of the banking system produced minimal opposition given the limited benefits of the initial nationalization and the dedication of the proceeds of the sales to specific and socially beneficial purposes.

The reprivatization of the banking system did not guarantee debt relief, financial stability, or economic development. Salinas's successor, Ernesto Zedillo (1994–2000) was in office for less than three weeks when he had to deal with a major devaluation of the peso. The peso lost almost half of its value in December 1994 and January 1995 and then continued its slide after that. The devaluation, in turn, led to a crash of the Mexican stock market and massive capital flight. A large number of short-term government bonds also came due in early 1995. Zedillo had to resort to a $20 billion international bailout arranged by the United States and to implement the toughest austerity program since the original debt crisis of 1982. With interest rates and inflation climbing, Mexico plunged into a deep and lengthy recession. The 1994–1995 financial crisis led to a major solvency and liquidity crisis for the Mexican banking system. Problems with the banking system added to the debt burden of the government, which insured bank deposits through the Instituto de Protección al Ahorro Banacario (the Institute for the Protection of Bank Savings, or IPAB); liabilities accrued by IPAB were estimated at $76 billion by the end of 1999. The economy began to rebound by late 1996 and early 1997; even the peso recovered much of its lost value. The Mexican government, however, continued to labor under a heavy debt load, and the role of the banks in creating or relieving the debt load continued to be a major point of public controversy. The costly bailout of the banks by the government proved especially controversial.

—DMC

See also: Calles, Plutarco Elías; Carranza, Venustiano; Debt, Mexico's Foreign; Díaz, Porfirio; Economy; Import Substitution Industrialization (ISI); Madrid (Hurtado), Miguel de la; Obregón, Alvaro; Salinas de Gortari, Carlos; Zedillo Ponce de León, Ernesto.

References:
Giugale, Marcelo M., Olivier Lafourcade, and Vinh H. Nguyen, eds. *Mexico: A Comprehensive Development Agenda for the New Era.* Washington, DC: The World Bank, 2001.
Maxfield, Sylvia. *Governing Capital: International Fiance and Mexican Politics.* Ithaca, NY: Cornell University Press, 1990.
White, Russell N. *State, Class, and the Nationalization of the Mexican Banks.* New York: Taylor & Francis, 1992.

Boundary Conflicts

Mexico has had major boundary conflicts with both its northern neighbor, the United States, and its southern neighbor, Guatemala. The disagreement over the boundary between Mexico and Texas was a major factor in bringing war between the United States and Mexico in 1846. The Treaty of Guadalupe Hidalgo ended that conflict in 1848 and established the boundary from the Gulf of Mexico to the Pacific Ocean. Once the boundary was defined, marking it and maintaining it became points of contention between the two countries. An adequate marking of the boundary dragged on into the 1880s. Changes in the channel of the Rio Grande also caused problems, an issue addressed with partial success by a treaty signed in 1884. Mexico and Guatemala haggled over the boundary of the Mexican state of Chiapas for most of the nineteenth century, finally ratifying a treaty in 1883; surveying the southern boundary carried over into the 1890s.

The shifting nature of the Rio Grande was the source of most boundary disputes between the United States and Mexico in the twentieth century. These shifts could occur slowly through a process of erosion and accretion or suddenly and violently in a process known as avulsion. The treaty of 1884 had prescribed that a gradual change in the river's course would lead to a change in the boundary but that the old boundary would be retained in the event of a sudden change in the river. The Rio Grande's tendency to wander detached a number of small parcels of land from each country, known as *bancos*. In 1905 Mexico and the United States agreed to assign these parcels based on the concept that they had all been created slowly through erosion rather than individually determine how each was detached. This meant that the boundary itself would change; as a result, Mexico received title to all *bancos* on the right bank, with all those on the left going to the United States. By 1970 some 247 changes in the boundary had taken place using the concept established in 1905.

One piece of real estate in the Rio Grande that was not covered under this arrangement was the Chamizal, a disputed area created by sudden shifts in the river in the El Paso-Ciudad Juárez area caused by floods in the 1850s and 1860s. The United States claimed jurisdiction over the Chamizal, a position challenged by Mexico since 1867. The Chamizal proved impervious to the series of agreements assigning the *bancos*. In 1910, Mexico and the United States agreed to arbitrate the issue, bringing in a Canadian jurist as a third party. In a 1911 decision, the Canadian representative sided with the Mexican view that the change in the river's course had been sudden and that the old boundary should be observed, meaning that the Chamizal would revert to Mexico. The United States rejected the arbitration decision on technical grounds. A new treaty signed in 1933 called for "rectifying" the course of the Rio Grande through the construction of levees and even provided for land swaps between the two countries; the Chamizal area, however, was not covered in the treaty. The dispute continued until the conclusion of a treaty in 1963 in which the United States essentially recognized the 1911 arbitration decision that awarded most of the disputed area to Mexico. The 1963 treaty even provided for the construction of a new concrete-lined channel for the Rio Grande. In 1970, Mexico and the United States entered into another treaty that superseded all previous agreements dealing with changes in the Rio Grande, settled existing disputes, and provided detailed guidelines for dealing with similar problems in the future. Although the United States and Mexico continue to have a number of problems relating to the border area, boundary disputes are not among them.

Even though Mexico has had periodic diplomatic disagreements with Guatemala, these disagreements generally have not related to the international boundary. The Guatemalan dictator, General Manuel Estrada Cabrera, briefly (1911 to 1917) and unsuccessfully provided assistance to separatist forces in Chiapas. Mexico and Guatemala also had an indirect boundary dispute of sorts over Belize, the former colony of British Honduras. Mexico, which itself had previously claimed part of Belize, opposed Guatemala, which claimed all of Belize. The dispute was effectively neutralized by Britain's announcement that it was prepared to use force to preserve the territorial integrity of an independent Belize. As is the case with the United States, Mexico continues to experience border problems with Guatemala, but they do not relate to boundary disputes.

—*DMC*

See also: Chiapas (State); Foreign Policy; United States, Relations with.

References:

Liss, Sheldon B. *A Century of Disagreement: The Chamizal Conflict, 1864–1964*. Washington, DC: University Press, 1965.

Martínez, Oscar J. *Troublesome Border*. Tucson: University of Arizona, 1988.

Mueller, Jerry E. *Restless River: International Law and the Behavior of the Rio Grande*. El Paso: Texas Western Press, 1975.

Zorrilla, Luis G. *Relaciones de México con la República de Centro América y con Guatemala*. Mexico City: Porrúa, 1984.

Bracero **Program**

Mexican migrant workers have long played a major role in U.S. agriculture. When the United States imposed immigration restrictions in 1917, the legislation was later modified specifically to exempt Mexican workers. Mexican temporary workers played an important role in meeting the labor needs of the U.S. southwest in World War I. Likewise the labor demands of World War II led U.S. agricultural interests to seek Mexican workers as a solution to labor shortages; this time, however, workers would be recruited through an official system of contract labor that became know as the "*bracero* program."

The *bracero* program was actually a series of programs, starting as a response to an emergency situation in 1942 and continuing until the end of 1964. The program received its name from the Spanish word for "arm" (*brazo*)—which hinted at the manual labor aspect of the program—and evolved in response to changes in U.S. legislation and a series of labor agreements between the U.S. and Mexican governments.

The program began in 1942 to deal with labor shortages caused by the entry of the United States into World War II. The agreement provided for the recruitment of Mexican workers by the Mexican government with the workers' transportation, living expenses, and repatriation costs guaranteed. The U.S. government served as primary contractor and guarantor; the U.S. government, in turn, would subcontract workers to individual employers. *Braceros* were to be paid the prevailing wage rate in the area, with thirty cents per hour the minimum acceptable rate. Employers were to provide housing and medical care as well as reimburse the U.S. government for travel expenses. Texas—traditionally the greatest center for Mexican workers—was specifically excluded from the program at the request of the Mexican government, which cited a history of abuse of Mexican workers in the state. The 1942 agreement set down the general guidelines for the program until 1947. Between 1942 and 1947, more than 200,000 *braceros* worked in the United States, earning approximately $200 million.

The *bracero* program continued after 1947 but under different terms. Between 1948 and 1951 the U.S. government ceased to be the official contractor and was no longer legally responsible for contract fulfillment; this role now fell to individual employers. Also there was no guaranteed minimum wage as had been the case under the wartime program. Although the new arrangement favored the

employers, the number of *braceros* actually increased under the new system, with 200,000 employed between 1948 and 1950. Both the U.S. and Mexican governments favored a return to the government-to-government system, but the U.S. Congress would not support such an approach.

It would take another wartime emergency—the Korean War—to bring about major changes in the program. Even before the war, the program had come under growing pressure. There was particular criticism of employers "legalizing" illegal aliens by giving them *bracero* contracts. The setting and payment of wages also stirred controversy. The U.S. Congress laid the foundation for a new *bracero* program by passing Public Law 78 in July 1951, which provided the general framework within which the program would operate until its official end in 1964. P.L. 78 did away with the direct recruitment followed between 1948 and 1951 and reinstated the U.S. government as the official guarantor of *bracero* contracts. Workers were to be paid the prevailing wage in the area, and no state would be prohibited from importing *braceros*. P.L. 78 led to immediate negotiations between the U.S. and Mexican governments, with a new labor agreement being signed in August 1951. The new agreement reflected the provisions of P.L. 78 with detailed worker guarantees, including insurance and housing.

Importation of Mexican workers continued to generate controversy during the 1950s, especially in regard to recruitment and the role of illegal workers, known as *mojados* or "wetbacks." Despite these issues, approximately 2.5 million *braceros* were employed between 1954 and 1959, reaching a peak of almost 450,000 in 1956. The *bracero* program had a concentrated impact on U.S. agriculture in several ways. First, although *braceros* worked in more than twenty states, just two states—Texas and California—accounted for a large majority of the workers. (The same was true at the supply end, where a small number of Mexican states such as Guanajuato and Michoacán provided a disproportionate number of *braceros.*) Second, *bracero* labor tended to be seasonal, with late summer and fall being the most active periods. Third, *bracero* employment was also concentrated on a small percentage of farms; by the late 1950s, less than 2 percent of U.S. farms had *bracero* workers. Finally, *braceros* also were concentrated in certain crops, such as lettuce and cotton.

Throughout the 1950s and 1960s, extensions of Public Law 78 continued to provide the legal basis for labor agreements between the United States and Mexico. At the same time, the program came under growing criticism from a variety of different sources. Agricultural employers were increasingly uneasy with efforts by the U.S. government to enforce more strictly contract provisions involving housing, transportation, and wages. Opponents of the program maintained that it depressed wages paid to U.S. workers and cited widespread failure of employers to fulfill their contractual obligations. Organized labor in the United States had consistently opposed the *bracero* program. At the same time, the growing mechanization of farming reduced the need for manual labor. There had been a steady decline in the use of *bracero* labor as well. As late as 1959, approximately 440,000 *braceros* found employment in the United States; by 1963, employment had dropped to about 190,000. In Texas alone, the use of *braceros* declined from 123,000 in 1960 to 30,000 in 1962 primarily because of mechanization of cotton farming. Paralleling the decline in use of *braceros* was a decline in political support for the *bracero* program in the U.S. Congress. In 1963 the U.S. Congress gave the last extension to P.L. 78, and the U.S. and Mexican governments provided for a final extension of the labor agreement. Both P.L. 78 and the labor agreement expired on 31 December 1964, bringing an official end to the *bracero* program.

The *bracero* program—which had started as a response to a wartime emergency—evolved into a system that outlasted World War II by almost two decades. It was always a program that reflected the varying needs and demands of the U.S. government, the Mexican government, and powerful domestic interest groups in both countries. Under the various *bracero* programs, almost five million Mexican workers found legal employment in the United States. Supporters of the program in both Mexico and the United States early on drew a connection between *braceros* and illegal workers, hoping or claiming that legal importation of workers would reduce the influx of illegal workers. In fact, the influx of illegal workers typically kept pace with or exceeded the flow of *braceros;* in addition, many *braceros* were originally illegal workers who had their status regularized by receiving a contract. Over the life of the program, there were about as many illegal aliens apprehended (approximately five million) as there were *braceros* legally imported. As the problem of illegal immigration worsened in the 1970s and 1980s, there was periodic discussion of—but no action on—implementing an updated *bracero* program. President Vicente Fox (2000–2006) made an immigration treaty with the United States a top priority of his administration, and there was some support in the United States for an updated and revised version of the *Bracero* Program. As of mid-2004, however, security concerns on the part of the United States blocked any comprehensive agreement on the movement of workers across the U.S.–Mexican border.

—DMC

See also: Immigration/Emigration; Korean War; United States, Relations with; World War II.

References:
Calavita, Kitty. *Inside the State: The Bracero Program, Immigration, and the I.N.S.* New York: Routledge, 1992.
Craig, Richard B. *The Bracero Program: Interest Groups and Foreign Policy.* Austin: University of Texas Press, 1971.
García, Juan Ramón. *Operation Wetback: The Mass Deportation of Mexican Undocumented Workers in 1954.* Westport, CT: Greenwood Press, 1980.
Kiser, George C., and Martha Woody Kiser, eds. *Mexican Workers in the United States: Historical and Political Perspectives.* Albuquerque: University of New Mexico Press, 1979.

C

Calles, Plutarco Elías (1877–1945)

President from 1924 to 1928, Plutarco Elías Calles was born in Guayamas, Sonora, in 1877. Orphaned at the age of four, he was adopted by relatives and grew up in the state capital of Hermosillo. Calles showed an early interest in education, becoming first a teacher and later a school inspector. After inheriting some land, Calles focused on farming from 1898 to 1909. He became involved in the Anti-reelection Movement of Francisco Madero in 1910 but did not participate in the fighting in the first phase of the Revolution in 1910–1911. Calles became mayor of the border town of Agua Prieta in 1911. His military career began in 1912 in the struggle against the rebels led by Pascual Orozco. With the overthrow of Madero by General Victoriano Huerta in February 1913, Calles joined the anti-Huerta Constitutionalist forces headed by "First Chief" Venustiano Carranza. Calles rose rapidly in rank from captain in 1913 to brigadier general in October 1914; at the same time, he was cementing his relationship with fellow Sonoran and Constitutionalist general, Alvaro Obregón.

Following the unsuccessful effort to unite the Revolutionary factions at the Convention of Aguascalientes in October 1914, Calles continued to support the Constitutionalists led by Carranza and Obregón against the loose military coalition led by Emiliano Zapata and Pancho Villa. In 1915 Calles became provisional governor and military commander of the state of Sonora. As military commander Calles defeated Sonoran forces allied with Pancho Villa. As governor he introduced a number of radical and often controversial reforms. Calles established a minimum wage and implemented a number of changes in education, including the founding of a teachers' college and a technical school for children orphaned as a result of the Revolution. He cracked down on producers, sellers, and consumers of alcoholic beverages. Calles also expelled all Roman Catholic priests from the state, a preview of the bitter church-state struggle that would take place when he was president. Calles also launched a ruthless campaign to suppress the rebellious Yaqui Indians of Sonora. Despite controversy over his reforms, Calles was elected governor in his own right in 1917.

Calles left the governorship in 1919 to accept the position of minister of industry, commerce, and labor in the administration of President Carranza. Carranza had already decided not to support Alvaro Obregón for the presidency in 1920 and hoped to split Obregón and Calles. Carranza's strategy

Plutarco Elías Calles, ca. 1931. Calles was a prominent figure in the Mexican Revolution and president of Mexico from 1924 to 1928. After his term, he continued to control the presidency until 1934. (Library of Congress)

quickly failed when Calles resigned in February 1920 to become manager of Obregón's presidential campaign. When Carranza moved against Obregón and Governor Adolfo de la Huerta of Sonora, Calles and de la Huerta issued a call for revolution, the Plan of Agua Prieta, in April 1920. The revolt led to the overthrow and assassination of Carranza in May. Calles became minister of war in the government of interim president Adolfo de la Huerta in 1920. When Obregón officially assumed the presidency in December 1920, Calles was given the key position of minister of the interior (internal security) while Adolfo de la Huerta became minister of the treasury.

During his three years as minister of the interior, Calles built alliances with political, military, and labor leaders. In September 1923 Calles resigned in order to campaign for the presidency in 1924 with the blessing of President Obregón. The "Sonoran Trian-gle" of Obregón, Calles, and de la Huerta came apart when de la Huerta also decided to contest for the presidency. De la Huerta's campaign turned into a revolt in December 1923. Both Obregón and Calles took the field against the rebels who were defeated in early 1924. With de la Huerta in exile in the United States, Calles easily won the election and became president on 1 December 1924.

President Calles pushed forward and expanded on Obregón's reforms. As a long-time and not particularly successful farmer, Calles was interested in agrarian reform. His experience as a northerner, however, gave him a different view of the problems of the countryside; in particular, Calles saw Mexico's agricultural future in the small farmer rather than in the communal (*ejido*) approach that had been emphasized in the Constitution of 1917. Calles sped up the distribution of land, allocating approximately six million acres between 1924 and 1928. Lands would still go to the *ejidos* but would then be subdivided for individual cultivation. Calles also established a system of agricultural credit, set up agricultural education programs, and expanded irrigation projects. Calles also cultivated good relations with labor, continuing the established policy of promoting the national labor organization, the CROM, and even appointing the head of the CROM—Luis Morones—as his minister of labor. Calles reignited the dispute with the foreign-owned oil companies over control of subsoil resources in 1925 but had to back down in 1927 in the face of external pressure and growing domestic problems.

Many of his domestic problems were a product of his crackdown on the Roman Catholic Church. Calles was the first president to enforce strictly the anticlerical provisions of the Constitution of 1917, sparking a major confrontation with the Church and a civil war. Calles had a reputation for anticlericalism dating back to his years as governor of Sonora. His goal was to subordinate the Roman Catholic Church to the State, creating a kind of Mexican Catholic Church with the president as its head. The Church's response was to announce that all services requiring a priest would be suspended as of 31 July 1926. The "strike" soon escalated into armed resistance, the Cristero Rebellion, which lasted until 1929.

One of Calles's most important reforms was to have the Constitution amended in 1926, thereby permitting reelection of the president to nonconsecutive terms. There was no doubt about the immediate beneficiary of the change; Alvaro Obregón announced he would be a candidate for the presidency in 1928. His principal opposition came from two other prominent generals: Arnulfo Gómez and Francisco Serrano. After a halting attempt at revolution by supporters of Gómez and Serrano, both were arrested and executed in the fall of 1927. Obregón easily won the elections held on 1 July 1928 but was assassinated just sixteen days later in Mexico City. The death of Obregón produced a new political crisis, with some attributing the assassination to Calles or Morones. The situation led Calles to take one of his most important actions: the founding of an official Revolutionary party.

Shortly before his death, Obregón had talked about the need to create a permanent political organization that could continue the pursuit of Revolutionary goals, train future leaders, and help reduce the personalism that characterized politics. With Obregón's assassination, the establishment of such a party became even more pressing for Calles. On the day Obregón would have taken office—1 December 1928—there was an announcement of the formation of the National Revolutionary Party (the Partido Nacional Revolucionario, or PNR), which would bring together the various Revolutionary elements. The party was formally organized in 1929; this new official party would become a primary force in Mexican politics.

Calles left office as scheduled on 1 December 1928, leaving the government in the hands of an interim president selected by the Congress, Emilio Portes Gil, lawyer and staunch supporter of Calles. Although Calles was out of office, he continued to dominate Mexican politics from 1928 to 1934 by operating through a series of three puppet presidents. Calles acquired the title of *Jefe Máximo* ("Maximum Leader") of the Revolution, leading the period from 1928 to 1934 to be described as "the Maximato," the era of the Maximum Leader. Calles, however, ran afoul of the person who was supposed to be the fourth puppet president, Lázaro Cárdenas, whose assertion of an independent position led to Calles being unceremoniously shuffled into exile in the United States in 1936. Calles maintained contact with anti-Cárdenas elements, but Cárdenas had effectively broken the Maximum Leader's grip on Mexican politics. In an effort to promote national unity during World War II, President Manuel Avila Camacho reintegrated Calles into the army in 1942 and invited him to return to Mexico. Calles accepted the offer; he died in Mexico City on 19 October 1945.

—DMC

See also: Agrarian Reform/Land and Land Policy; Assassinations; Avila Camacho, Manuel; Cárdenas, Lázaro; Carranza, Venustiano; Cristero Rebellion; Morrow, Dwight; Orozco, Pascual; Partido Revolucionario Institucional (PRI); Presidents of the Twentieth Century; Religion; Sonora; World War II.

References:
Camp, Roderic Ai. *Mexican Political Biographies, 1884–1935.* Austin: University of Texas Press, 1991.
Córdova, Arnaldo. *La Revolución en crisis: La aventura del maximato.* Mexico City: Cal y Arena, 1995.
Meyer, Jean, Enrique Krauze, and Cayetano Reyes. *Historia de la Revolución Mexicana, Periodo 1924–1928.* Vol. 11. *Estado y Sociedad con Calles.* Mexico City: El Colegio de México, 1977.

Campeche (State)

Located in the western section of the Yucatán Peninsula, Campeche shares borders with Quintana Roo, Yucatán, Tabasco, and the neighboring countries of Guatemala and Belize. The city of Campeche serves as the capital, and Ciudad del Carmen, an active oil port, is the state's other main urban center. Campeche was established as a state in 1857, but because of the creation, dissolution, and reestablishment of neighboring Quintana Roo, its borders were not definitively set until 1940. Never densely populated, Campeche always struggled to create a viable economy. In the last decades of the twentieth century, the discovery of oil brought significant change to the state. Campeche remains a major producer of Mexico's oil.

The Yucatán Peninsula, of which Campeche is a part, was a center of the Mayan culture. In 1517, Francisco Hernández de Córdoba made contact with the peninsula and its native peoples. The encounter between Spaniard and Indian was not always peaceful, and the Spanish presence in the Yucatán was not definitive until 1540 with the establishment of San Francisco de Campeche (today's Campeche City). This settlement became a key port of entrance for Spanish explorers and settlers, and it developed as a commercial hub that exported tobacco, sugar, indigo, cochineal, and other products.

The forests of Campeche and the Yucatán Peninsula held special economic promise, particularly because of the dyes that could be extracted from certain trees for use in Europe's textile industry. This lucrative resource encouraged competition, and for nearly a century, the Spaniards of Campeche were challenged by English pirates for control of Campeche's forests. Pirates occupied Carmen Island (off the southwest coast of Campeche) in 1558, seizing control of part of the dyewood trade. The Spaniards responded to the English threat with the construction of defensive barriers around San Francisco de Campeche. By the eighteenth century, the town was heavily fortified, and it effectively supported the trade in dyewood and other products. At the same time, the port emerged as a center for the repair and building of ships. The English were expelled from Carmen Island in the early eighteenth century, and the Spaniards solidified their control there with the establishment of the city of Carmen.

Although local intellectuals engaged in the debates that arose during Mexico's struggle for independence, the Yucatán Peninsula experienced no real insurgency. Independence did little to change Campeche's political status. As in the colonial period, it remained part of the broader province of Yucatán, of which Mérida was the capital. Campeche's push for autonomy, however, finally bore fruit in 1857 when a new state (with its capital at Campeche City) was carved out of the peninsula. The Mexican government formally recognized the new state in 1862. Carmen Island remained a disputed land for several more years. It was both a federal territory and a part of the state of Yucatán before being officially absorbed into Campeche.

Campeche, unlike neighboring Yucatán and Quintana Roo, escaped the worst violence of the Caste War, an uprising of Maya Indians that began in 1847 and claimed thousands of lives. The state's location, however, ensured that it would not escape France's assault on Mexico during the 1860s. As they began to assert their control over Mexico, paving the way for an empire, French troops occupied Campeche's capital and Carmen Island. Campeche and Yucatán were also reunited into one political unit. Campeche regained its autonomy shortly after the French withdrew from Mexico and their empire dissolved.

Political instability characterized the last decades of the nineteenth century in Campeche. During the reign of Mexico's dictator Porfirio Díaz (1876–1911), the state had twenty-five governors. Campeche's economy, however, did experience some growth, aided and encouraged by Díaz's emphasis on economic expansion and foreign investment. Railroad lines began to break the isolation of the Yucatán Peninsula, and foreign investors became increasingly involved in the region's wood and wood products industry. Foreign money also supported the development of another of the Yucatán's lucrative resources: henequen or sisal. At the same time, Campeche struggled to augment its sparse population by recruiting Chinese and Japanese laborers, as well as workers from other parts of Mexico.

As the twentieth century opened, Campeche faced economic problems despite several years of growth. International prices of sisal and dyewood (now being replaced by synthetic dyes) decreased, underscoring the state's dependence on the export of a few raw materials. At the same time, social unrest increased, particularly among the rural workers whose labor supported the extractive industries of the Yucatán Peninsula. Debt peonage was a particular problem, and its elimination became a goal for those who joined in the Mexican Revolution.

Although Campeche was not a center of Francisco I. Madero's 1910–1911 revolt against Porfirio Díaz, it did experience unrest. After Díaz's fall, the state made a peaceful political transition under Governor Manuel Castillo Brito, a rebel leader, who promised a new era. Change for Campeche's workers, however, came only after another round of violence, in which Venustiano Carranza emerged as Mexico's new leader. Carranza's forces entered Campeche City in 1915, and Joaquín Mucel Acereto became governor. Mucel decreed an end to debt peonage, and he also eliminated the company store (which kept many workers in debt through its monopoly on the local sale of food, clothing, and other items). Mucel also pursued a limited agrarian reform.

Several socialist governors controlled both Campeche and Yucatán during the 1920s and 1930s. Reforms that further benefited workers, as well as efforts to undermine the power of the Roman Catholic Church, characterized this era. Campeche's economy remained underdeveloped, however, and many left the state, seeking work and a better life in Mexico City or in Mérida, the capital of Yucatán. Governors since the 1940s have focused much of their efforts on developing the state's economic base, particularly through the expansion of infrastructure and through the promotion of agriculture and industry.

In the 1960s, Governor José Ortiz Avila attempted to address the problem of Campeche's population, which was still an impediment to economic growth. He presided over a significant redistribution of land and offered that land to thousands of *campesinos* (rural workers) who migrated from other areas of Mexico. Ortiz's efforts were continued by his successors but with mixed results. The state's population remains low and its rural economy underdeveloped.

During the last two decades of the twentieth century, two enterprises provided at least temporary hope for the state's economy. The fishing industry, which reached a peak during the early 1980s, established Campeche as a main exporter of fish, particularly to markets in the United States. More important were the large oil reserves discovered off the coast of Campeche in the 1970s. With Mexico's oil boom, Campeche enjoyed an unprecedented prosperity, as significant revenues poured in. The city of Carmen, which became a main oil port, especially benefited from these developments.

Despite the new wealth that accompanied the oil boom, Campeche (like other oil-producing states) felt the negative effects of the oil industry. An international decline in oil prices beginning in 1982 caused a significant downturn in the local economy and underscored the problems inherent in Campeche's (and Mexico's) heavy dependence on the export of this resource. Environmental problems also accompanied the exploitation of oil. Oil spills have destroyed marine life and threatened Campeche's other key economic sector: the fishing industry.

—*SBP*

See also: Oil Industry; Quintana Roo (State); Revolution of 1910; Yucatán (State).

References:

Sierra, Carlos Justo. *Breve historia de Campeche.* Mexico City: El Colegio de Mexico, 1998.
Official state web site: http://www.campeche.gob.mx

Cantinflas (1911–1993)

On 12 August 1911, Mario Moreno Reyes was born in a working-class Mexico City neighborhood and into a country on the

Actor and comedian Cantinflas relaxes in a director's chair. (C. John Springer Collection / Corbis)

carpas specialized in Mexico's version of vaudeville variety shows and included everything from song-and-dance numbers (usually crude and lewd) to acrobatics, short melodramatic skits, and comic routines. The irreverent, improvisational style of *carpa* comedy encouraged audience participation and provided the ideal place for Moreno to develop his comedic alter ego, Cantinflas. A composite of stock characters from Mexico's burlesque theater tradition, Cantinflas's name combined the Spanish words, *cantina* (bar) and *inflas* (you get drunk); his getup included a skimpy mustache (in the land of seriously mustachioed Revolutionary icons such as Emiliano Zapata and Pancho Villa), sagging pants, an undersized hat (in the land of big sombreros), and a tattered vest he inevitably referred to as a *gabardina* (overcoat); his shtick was a nonsensical verbosity Moreno later claimed occurred accidentally as a result of stage fright.

If singing *charros* (cowboys) like midcentury film stars Pedro Infante and Jorge Negrete portrayed idealized macho men—brave, strong, straight-shooting, well-bred, handsome, sentimental—Moreno's great comic creation, Cantinflas, represented their opposite, the urban *pelado* (tramp). For "respectable" Mexicans, especially in the decades preceding the Revolution, *pelados* were the subhuman dregs of a rapidly urbanizing society:

> Unhappy men and women that lack a normal, secure means of subsistence: they live in the streets and sleep in public dormitories; huddled in vestibules, in doorways, in the trash of houses under construction, in some tavern if they can afford three or four centavos to sleep on the floor, or put up in the house of some relative or friend. . . . They dress in tatters, they scratch incessantly, and their matted hair is covered with the dust and mud of all the city's barrios. . . . They have lost all control of their lives; their language is of the tavern; they live in sexual promiscuity; they inebriate themselves daily . . . they quarrel and are the principal instigators of scandal . . . from their

verge of revolution. On 20 April 1993, the funeral of Cantinflas—a wealthy international celebrity and Mexico's most beloved comedian—attracted one-quarter million people, including President Carlos Salinas de Gortari. In a bittersweet eulogy, novelist Carlos Fuentes noted that although "laughter has left this country . . . up there he's making those who went before us laugh." Moreno's own epitaph read simply: "It seems like he's gone, but it's not true" (quoted in Herschfield and Maciel, *Mexico's Cinema*, pp. 49–50). True or not, the remarkable career of the man Charlie Chaplin called the greatest comic of his time helped Mexicans (not to mention Latin Americans and Latinos) from all walks of life to laugh at themselves through his antics and to see themselves in his eyes.

Born and raised near Mexico City's famous Garibaldi Square—the center of mariachi culture, another important symbol of Mexican national identity—it is hardly surprising that young Mariano Moreno chose to become a performer in one of the capital's many provisional tent theaters (*carpas*). The bosom petty thieves are recruited and they are hidden perpetrators of serious crimes. Insensible to moral suffering, indifferent to physical deprivation and pain, and little responsive to pleasure, . . . they are indifferent to other's feelings and egotistical after the fashion of animals. (Julio Guerrero, *La génesis del crimen en México,* 1901)

These accusations were repeated by prominent public intellectuals after the Revolution but with a significant new twist. Social psychologist Samuel Ramos's influential *Profile of Man and Culture in Mexico* (1934), for example, insisted that while "the *pelado* belongs to the most vile category of social fauna . . . [and is] a form of human rubbish," he nevertheless "constitutes the most elemental and clearly defined expression of national character." Octavio Paz's classic analysis of Mexican society, *The Labyrinth of Solitude* (1950), further developed the notion of a national inferiority complex that derived from the *pelado's* "servant mentality." "The Mexican is always a problem," Paz argued, "both for other Mexicans and for himself." (Women's exclusion from discussions of national identity is typical of the era, and not just in Mexico.)

For prominent social critics, then, *pelados* represented a dire threat to the nation's political, economic, and social development. But while Cantinflas—scruffy, often drunk, sometimes belligerent, outrageous, uneducated, lazy—could only reinforce these concerns, he also humanized and empowered (at least temporarily) the much-reviled *pelado*. In the face of this barrage of elite disapproval and despair, Moreno's bumbling, ingenious, openhearted *peladito* (little tramp) provided redemption and good spirits. If Mexico was indeed a *pelado* country, then the optimistic Cantinflas rather than gloomy public intellectuals like Ramos and Paz would be its popular spokesperson. And in forty-two feature films from 1936 to 1981, he was indeed the country's most recognizable, although not always comprehensible, voice.

Whatever his origins, Cantinflas proved a huge hit with audiences. In 1934, after a stint in small-town *carpas,* Moreno married the boss's daughter and left the family tent for Mexico City's burlesque theaters. Two years later he headlined at the new Follies Bergère with an all-star cast that included Mexico's best-known singer-songwriter Agustín Lara. He also made his film debut as a cabaret comedian in the family melodrama, *No te engañes, corazón* (Don't Kid Yourself, Sweetheart, 1936). It was just the beginning. Over the course of a film career of fifty-five years, Mexico's quintessential *pelado,* Cantinflas, would reach millions all over the world and win over prominent fans like Charlie Chaplin, Gabriel García Márquez (Colombia's Nobel Prize–winning novelist), and Fidel Castro.

Most critics and biographers (fans are less picky) prefer the early films, beginning with Cantinflas's first feature, *Así es mi tierra* (My Country's Like That, 1937), and ending with the tedious *El analfabeto* (The Illiterate, 1960). Given his decidedly un-macho persona, it seems appropriate and hardly coincidental that the first target of his humor was that most manly of Mexican film genres, *comedia ranchera*. In *Así es mi tierra,* set in the time of the Mexican Revolution, renowned Russian émigré director, Arcady Boytler, inserts Cantinflas as a local bumpkin into two love triangles that include a pair of Revolutionary officers and a haughty lawyer whose pompous style prompts the awed bumpkin to respond: "I hear you speak and it makes me jealous because suddenly I say what I don't want to, and I don't want to say what I say, and everything gets mixed up." Subsequent films continued to poke fun at national myths and conventional morality. Especially outrageous was *El signo del muerte* (The Sign of Death, 1939). Written by the acerbic and flamboyantly effeminate social critic Salvador Novo (with music by prominent composer Silvestre Revueltas), the film mocked macho, postrevolutionary *indigenistas* (Indianists) like artist Diego Rivera by having Cantinflas serve as a verbally challenged museum guide and staging an Aztec human sacrifice of a bare-breasted maiden. More shocking still is a dream sequence in which Cantinflas in drag plays a coy Carlotta to a fellow comedian's amorous Emperor Maximillian.

The film that made Cantinflas a major star was *Ahí está el detalle* (There's the Point, 1940), a biting satire of Mexico's pretentious upper classes and bureaucratic legal culture. In the final scene of this signature film, the comedian, on trial for a murder he did not commit, so confounds the authorities with his verbal assault on legal discourse that they too are reduced to incoherence. Thus, the marginalized *pelado* exposes the most important privilege of the powerful—their "right" to speak and be heard in public—as an often nonsensical cover for their exercise of political and economic power. The message appealed to everyone from the truly marginal to political cynics, women annoyed by macho posturing, and businessmen frustrated by bureaucratic red tape. In fact, Moreno's verbal virtuosity proved popular enough to merit its own officially recognized Spanish verb, *cantinflear*: to talk a lot without saying anything. Asked about his unique style, Moreno replied:

> Ah!, but let me make one thing clear, I have moments of lucidity, and I speak very clearly. And now I will speak with clarity . . .
> Friends! There are moments in life that are really momentary. . . . And it's not because one says it, but because we must see it! What do we see? That's what we must see . . . because, what a coincidence, friends, that supposing that in the case—let's not say that it could be—but we must think about it and understand the psychology of life to make an analogy of the synthesis of humanity. Right? Well, that's the point! (quoted in Herschfield and Maciel, *Mexico's Cinema*, p. 54)

Nor was Moreno the only source of *cantinfladas;* Mexican President Luis Echeverría Alvarez was said to have explained the ruling party's political philosophy as: "We are neither of the left, nor of the right, but entirely the opposite" (quoted in Stavans, *The Riddle of Cantinflas,* p. 41). True or not, the anecdote suggests the subversive potential of Cantinflas's humor.

In subsequent films, Cantinflas pokes fun at a wide range of cultural icons and authority figures: bullfighters, boxers, policemen, firemen, photographers, professors, playboys, scientists, oil executives, priests, Satan, Romeo, Don Quixote, and the Three Musketeers. Invariably, the *peladito* triumphs over adversity, usually through the manipulation – and abuse of language and despite his own inept scheming. That the message was more irreverent than radical, the resolution more accidental than intentional, likely increased the films' popularity. Even Cuban revolutionary leader Fidel Castro—notorious for interminable political speeches and impenetrable marxist jargon—confessed that "the way of speaking, the nonsense that he says, make me laugh" (quoted in Herschfield and Maciel, *Mexico's Cinema*, p. 59). His star turn as David Niven's sidekick, Passepartout, in the Hollywood blockbuster, *Around the World in Eighty Days* (1955), introduced Cantinflas to English-speaking audiences and won him a Golden Globe nomination as best comedian. His Hollywood career quickly floundered—hardly surprising since so much of his humor depended on mangled Spanish—but by 1960 his fame was secure and his image enshrined in a huge Diego Rivera mosaic façade for Mexico City's luxurious Insurgentes Theater.

For some critics, however, Cantinflas's cockeyed optimism and satiric ambiguity coupled with Moreno's political aspirations, considerable wealth, and growing conservatism made the comedian a puppet of an oppressive, undemocratic political system. Moreno had played a central role (along with *charro* star Jorge Negrete) in the National Actors Association and Union of Cinema Production Workers' battles with rival unions affiliated with the powerful union boss Fidel Velázquez. While the successful resolution of these struggles provided some autonomy within the ruling party's complex union structure, political compromises undermined any real independence or democratic decision-making processes. Corrupt union politicians favored producers with connections and blacklisted controversial directors, which contributed to a serious decline in the artistic quality of Mexican cinema by the late 1950s. The taint of political corruption along with his growing wealth and declining artistry has discredited Moreno, especially in the eyes of leftist critics. Even his legendary generosity seems to them more like charity than true concern for Mexico's poor. "Although at times there would appear to be in the movies of Cantinflas a certain mockery of authority and the police," one critic notes, "the result is customarily a symbiosis between the people and their repressors, who are united in meaninglessness" (Roger Bartra, *The Cage of Meloncholy*, New Brunswick, NJ: Rutgers University Press, 1992, p. 129). Not all critics share this assessment. Some embrace his politically ambiguous, lowbrow antics as an authentic reflection of Mexican national character and point to legions of loyal fans from all social classes as evidence of his continued cultural relevance. The final word on his controversial career rightly belongs to Cantinflas himself: "It seems like he's gone, but it's not true."

—RMB

See also: Cinema from 1930 to 1960: The Golden Age; Echeverría Alvarez, Luis; Fuentes, Carlos; Paz, Octavio; Rivera, Diego; Salinas de Gortari, Carlos.

References:
Herschfield, Joanne, and David R. Maciel, eds. *Mexico's Cinema: A Century of Film and Filmmakers.* Wilmington, DE: Scholarly Resources, 1999.
Pilcher, Jeffrey M. *Cantinflas and the Chaos of Mexican Modernity.* Wilmington, DE: Scholarly Resources, 2001.
Stavans, Ilan. *The Riddle of Cantinflas: Essays on Hispanic Popular Culture.* Albuquerque: University of New Mexico Press, 1990.

Cárdenas, Cuauhtémoc (1934–)

The only son of one of Mexico's most famous presidents—Lázaro Cárdenas—and three times an unsuccessful candidate for the presidency in his own right, Cuauhtémoc Cárdenas was born in Mexico City on 1 May 1934, seven months before his father assumed the presidency (1934–1940). The younger Cárdenas became active in politics early in life and met a broad range of Mexico's leading politicians and power brokers. The elder Cárdenas continued to be a major force in Mexican political life until his death in 1970. As a result, Cuauhtémoc Cárdenas had advantages unique to Mexican political life but also had to labor in the shadow of his more famous father.

Cuauhtémoc Cárdenas often assisted or represented his father in various political activities. At the age of seventeen, Cuauhtémoc became involved in his first effort to promote the internal democratization of the official party, the Institutional Revolutionary Party (Partido Revolucionario Institucional, or PRI). He assisted his father who was attempting to limit the traditional practice of outgoing presidents designating their successors and who also wanted a less conservative party candidate for the presidency in 1952. This initial effort to promote internal democratization of the PRI and push its policies farther to the left did not succeed, but the Cárdenases continued to try to build support for these changes.

In the early 1960s both of the Cárdenases actively resumed their efforts to democratize the PRI and to have it adopt more leftist policies. They participated in the formation of the National Liberation Movement (Movimiento de Liberación Nacional, or MLN), with Cuauhtémoc serving on its national committee. The MLN favored a more leftist approach in both foreign and domestic affairs. The MLN supported Cuba in its escalating conflict with the United States; it also called for the internal democratization of the PRI and a greater stress on agrarian reform, a major theme of the presidency of the elder Cárdenas. The MLN—like many leftist parties before and since—experienced major problems with maintaining a unified position.

A split took place over actively participating in the presidential elections of 1964, a move which both of the Cárdenases opposed. Although the MLN did not achieve its goal of democratizing the PRI, it did help Cuauhtémoc Cárdenas expand his contacts with more leftist elements on the Mexican political scene, connections which would help him later in his political career.

Cuauhtémoc Cárdenas continued his political path within the PRI, while periodically opposing its general direction. With an engineering degree from the National Autonomous University of Mexico, Cárdenas served on the technical council of the National Peasant Confederation (Confederación Nacional Campesina, or CNC). The CNC had been established in 1938 by Lázaro Cárdenas to promote his agrarian reform program and to organize peasant support behind his administration. Cuauhtémoc Cárdenas also participated in a lengthy study of development projects for the Las Balsas River basin region between 1963 and 1974. In 1974 Cárdenas publicly sought the PRI nomination for the governorship of the state of Michoacán, a position which his father held from 1928 to 1932. When the PRI leadership failed to support him, Cárdenas was forced to withdraw his candidacy.

Cárdenas still enjoyed considerable prestige and influence in the PRI despite his father's death in 1970 and his disagreement over the governorship in 1974. Cárdenas served briefly as a federal senator in 1976 but resigned to become a subsecretary in the Ministry of Agriculture. In 1979 the PRI selected him as its candidate for governor of Michoacán, which was equivalent to his appointment to the position. While serving as governor from 1980 to 1986, Cárdenas became more vocal in his criticism of the PRI, especially the economic and financial policies being adopted following the debt crisis that began in 1982. The austerity program adopted by President Miguel de la Madrid (1982–1988) led to major cuts in federal spending, the sale of government enterprises, and a greater opening in the economy for foreign trade and investment. These measures meant a declining standard of living for most Mexicans during the 1980s. The series of "technocrats" in the presidency from 1976 on also reduced the power of the more left-wing members of the PRI such as Cárdenas.

Opponents of the direction of government policy began to organize within the PRI to influence the PRI nomination for the presidency in 1988. Given his earlier experience with efforts at democratization and his family's political heritage, Cuauhtémoc Cárdenas soon became one of the leaders of this new reform group within the PRI, dubbed the "Democratic Current." Members of the Democratic Current worked publicly and privately to influence the PRI nomination for the presidency in 1988. Cárdenas increasingly took on the role of unofficial candidate of the Current for the nomination. Cárdenas was actively moving toward a break with the PRI, especially after publicly denouncing the party leadership in early 1987 as undemocratic and unresponsive to social needs. The Democratic Current and Cárdenas experienced a crushing and bitter defeat when President Miguel de la Madrid tapped as his successor, Carlos Salinas de Gortari, a fellow financial technocrat and one of the principal architects of the government's unpopular austerity program.

Cárdenas responded by leaving the PRI and accepting the presidential nomination of a collection of leftist parties and movements eventually organized into the National Democratic Front (Frente Democrático Nacional, or FDN). Cárdenas proved a diligent, if not especially charismatic, candidate. With a high degree of name recognition, Cárdenas soon emerged as the leading opposition candidate to the PRI's Carlos Salinas, who had never run for elective office before. The election held in July 1988 produced widespread claims of electoral fraud ranging from computer manipulation to the burning of ballots. According to the final results, Salinas won with just under 51 percent of the vote, the poorest showing ever by a PRI nominee. Cárdenas came in second with 31 percent of the vote, the highest "official" vote ever garnered by an opposition candidate.

Cárdenas claimed victory in the election, and the FDN joined with the conservative National Action Party (Partido de Acción Nacional, or PAN) in an unsuccessful effort to block confirmation of Salinas's victory. Many supporters of Cárdenas favored direct action, such as civil disobedience, to force recognition of Cárdenas's claim to victory. Cárdenas himself, however, opposed such an escalation in political opposition; he recognized the organizational limitations of the FDN and feared a violent confrontation with a government that had demonstrated its ability and willingness to use repressive force.

The presidential elections of 1988 were scarcely concluded before Cárdenas began to organize for the presidential elections of 1994. Soon after the elections, the FDN was replaced by the Democratic Revolutionary Party (Partido Revolucionario Democrático, or PRD), with the hope that this would be a more unified and better organized mechanism for opposing the PRI. Cárdenas was elected the first president of the new party. While Cárdenas's political prestige helped to form and hold the party together, the personalistic nature of the party also restricted its development. It was hard for the PRD to escape the public perception that it was simply a vehicle for Cárdenas's personal political ambitions. Elections held in 1991 indicated considerable slippage in popular support for the PRD. Many who had left the PRI in 1988 to support Cárdenas returned to the PRI in 1991; in addition, the PAN regained its status as the leading opposition party. The PRD received only 8 percent of the votes cast in 1991 and did not achieve a majority vote in any single state.

Although the 1991 elections did not auger well for Cárdenas's chances for the presidency in 1994, the presidential elections of 1994 still seemed up for grabs. On 1 January 1994 armed insurrection broke out in south-ern Mexico, clouding the day that was supposed to be known for the implementation of the North American Free Trade Agreement (NAFTA). An even bigger shock occurred in March when Luis Donaldo Colosio, the popular PRI nominee for the presidency, was assassinated while campaigning. His hasty replacement by another financial technocrat who had never held elective office, Ernesto Zedillo, created further uncertainty about the elections as well as Mexico's political stability. Recent electoral reforms—including campaign spending limits and greater opposition access to the media—were supposed to improve opposition chances for a victory. The new media access included Mexico's first televised presidential debate, featuring Zedillo for the PRI, Cárdenas for the PRD, and Diego Fernández de Cevallos of the PAN. Cárdenas fared badly in the debate, quickly slipping to number three in the polls. In the presidential elections in July, Mexicans opted for stability. Zedillo finished first with approximately 50 percent of the vote; Fernández de Cevallos came in second with 26 percent of the vote; and Cárdenas came in a distant third with 17 percent of the vote. The results were particularly disappointing for the populist Cárdenas since the elections featured the highest voter turnout in a presidential election in Mexican history (78 percent) and were generally considered to have been fairly conducted.

Cárdenas's second defeat in a presidential election did not signal the end of his political prominence. New political reforms were implemented in 1996, including a provision for the election in 1997 of the mayor of the Federal District, a position that previously had been appointed by the president. Presiding over most of the populous Mexico City area, the mayor would be a national and not just a local leader. In the 1997 elections, Cárdenas ran for mayor, winning a big victory. In addition, the PRD had a large majority on the Federal District Assembly (city council), and the PRD substantially increased its representation in the national Congress, especially in the Chamber of Deputies where the PRD was the second-largest party. Many thought that Cárdenas would be able to use the mayor's position as a stepping-stone to the presidency.

Cárdenas, however, found governing Mexico City a difficult proposition. Mexico City's chronic problems with economic development, population growth, crime, and pollution forced Cárdenas to deal with the details of administering one of the world's largest cities rather than articulating his left-of-center plans for a national program. With the 2000 presidential elections approaching, Cárdenas easily won the nomination of the PRD, but the lack of competition within the PRD for the nomination was in stark contrast to the opening up of competition for the presidential nominations of the PRI (won by Francisco Labastida Ochoa) and the PAN (won by Vicente Fox). There was public support for a coalition of opposition parties to unite behind one candidate to try to end the PRI's long-running control of the presidency. If the opposition did unite behind one candidate, it most likely would have been the PAN's Fox, who had a substantial lead over Cárdenas in presidential polls. Cárdenas was determined to run again for the presidency so a broad coalition of opposition forces never developed. Both the PAN and the PRD entered into minor alliances, but the presidential contest became a three-way race among Fox, Cárdenas, and Labastida Ochoa. Fox finished first with approximately 43 percent of the vote, Labastida Ochoa second with 36 percent, and Cárdenas third with 17 percent of the vote. The PRD also suffered a major loss of seats in the Chamber of Deputies and in the Federal District Assembly.

Following his third defeat for the presidency, Cárdenas found himself without an elected position. His close political ally and president of the PRD, Andrés Manuel López Obrador, won election as the mayor of the Federal District in the 2000 elections. Cárdenas also found himself publicly feuding with the newly inaugurated President Fox over the financial condition in which Cárdenas left Mexico City when he stepped down from the mayorship. Cárdenas's future political role is uncertain. There is no tradition of a "loyal opposition" in Mexican politics. The age factor may also become an issue if he attempts another campaign for the presidency. Ernesto Zedillo was 48 years old when he completed his term as president in 2000; Cárdenas will be 72 when presidential elections are held in 2006. Even if Cárdenas does not play a major political role in the twenty-first century, he played an important role in shaping the Mexican left in the twentieth century.

—*DMC*

See also: Cárdenas, Lázaro; Confederación Nacional Campesina (CNC); Democratization Process; Elections; Fox, Vicente; Madrid (Hurtado), Miguel de la; North American Free Trade Agreement (NAFTA); Partido de Acción Nacional (PAN); Partido Revolucionario Institucional (PRI); Salinas de Gortari, Carlos; Zedillo Ponce de León, Ernesto.

References:

Bruhn, Kathleen. *Taking on Goliath: The Emergence of a New Left Party and the Struggle for Democracy in Mexico.* University Park: Pennsylvania State University Press, 1997.

Camp, Roderic Ai. *Politics in Mexico.* 2d ed. New York: Oxford University Press, 1996.

Schultz, Donald E., and Edward J. Williams, eds. *Mexico Faces the 21st Century.* New York: Praeger, 1995.

Cárdenas, Lázaro (1895–1970)

President from 1934 to 1940, Lázaro Cárdenas was born in Jiquilpan, Michoacán, in 1895. Because of the death of his father, Cárdenas had to conclude his formal education after primary school. He did not participate in the first phase of the Revolution (1910–1911) but joined in the revolt against the dictatorship of Victoriano Huerta in 1913. He rose rapidly through the ranks, becoming a lieutenant colonel in 1915. He fought against legendary figures Francisco "Pancho" Villa and Emiliano Zapata. More important, he fought under the command of two future presidents: Alvaro Obregón and Plutarco

Lázaro Cárdenas (ca. 1962) led Mexico as a bold and talented president between 1934 and 1940. His political coalition and reforms reshaped the nation and continue to influence its development. (Library of Congress)

Elías Calles. In 1920 he supported Obregón and Calles in their successful revolt against President Venustiano Carranza. In 1923 he fought against forces supporting the failed revolt of presidential aspirant Adolfo de la Huerta, who opposed Obregón's selection of Calles as his successor.

Cárdenas continued to rise in the army, reaching the highest rank of general of division in 1928. That same year, he was elected governor of Michoacán. As governor he provided a preview of what he would do later as president; he promoted workers' organizations and vigorously championed agrarian reform, going so far as to arm the peasants in their struggle against the landowners. Cárdenas held a series of important posts in the early 1930s. In 1930 he became president of the recently founded official party, the National Revolutionary Party (the Partido Nacional Revolucionario, or PNR). He served in the key position of sec-

retary of the interior (internal security) in the administration of President Pascual Ortiz Rubio (1931) and held the sensitive post of secretary of war in the cabinet of President Abelardo Rodríguez (1933).

As the presidential elections of 1934 approached, there was growing support for Cárdenas to run for president. Cárdenas received the approval, but not the official endorsement, of the power behind the presidency, former president and "Maximum Leader" Plutarco Elías Calles. Calles indicated that Cárdenas was one of three candidates he considered acceptable. Cárdenas gained the nomination of the PNR, campaigned vigorously, and easily won election in 1934.

Calles assumed that Cárdenas would be the latest in a series of presidents (Emilio Portes Gil, Pascual Ortiz Rubio, Abelardo Rodríguez) he had dominated since 1928. Cárdenas, however, had distinctly different ideas and early on tried to stake out an independent position. Cárdenas actively encouraged workers to organize and to strike if necessary to improve their conditions. The president also fostered industrial unionism, the organization of all workers in a particular industry into one union. These labor policies led to an unprecedented level of strikes involving so many workers that there were fears for the economy and public order. It also provoked public criticism by Calles, who was already becoming nervous about the independent path Cárdenas was following. Cárdenas also moved against the powerful national labor confederation connected to Calles, the Regional Mexican Workers' Confederation (Confederación Regional Obrera Mexicana, or CROM). Cárdenas attacked the CROM and its corrupt leader, Luis Morones, by establishing a rival labor organization, the Mexican Workers' Confederation (Confederación de Trabajadores Mexicanos, or CTM), under the leadership of Vicente Lombardo Toledano.

Cárdenas also pursued an aggressive agrarian reform program that provoked considerable controversy. He dramatically accelerated the redistribution of land, distributing more acreage than all of the administrations since 1910 combined. Cárdenas also changed the type of land being expropriated and distributed. Previous administrations had been reluctant to divide the large commercial operations out of fear of hurting production. Cárdenas, however, did not exempt these commercial estates from expropriation. Most of the land distributed went to the *ejidos,* the communal landholding system of indigenous Mexico. The scale and nature of Cárdenas's agrarian reform program aroused considerable opposition, including that of Calles. Cárdenas also strengthened the rural sector by integrating the existing regional and state peasant groups into one national organization, the National Peasant Confederation (the Confederación Nacional Campesina, or CNC). He also provided loans to peasant groups and even armed the peasants as he had done earlier as governor.

Cárdenas worked to expand Mexico's educational system, especially in rural areas, and to implement the recently adopted policies of socialist education and sex education. These activities were aimed not only at promoting education but also at undermining the traditional social and cultural influence of the Roman Catholic Church. The Church and other conservative social groups (including many peasants) strongly opposed these educational initiatives, eventually forcing Cárdenas to abandon sex education and to de-emphasize socialist education.

Cárdenas's labor and agrarian policies supported his major reorganization of the official party in 1938. The restructuring of the party began in 1935 with the removal of Calles's supporters, culminating in April 1936 with the forced exile of Calles and the labor leader Luis Morones. The reorganized and renamed official party, the Party of the Mexican Revolution (Partido de la Revolución Mexicana, or PRM) was divided into four sectors: agrarian, labor, "popular," and military. The new National Peasant Confederation comprised the agrarian sector, while the new

Mexican Workers' Confederation was the foundation for the labor sector. The "popular" sector was a miscellaneous collection of groups including youth and women's organizations as well as government workers. One of the most controversial aspects of the realignment was giving the military a sector of its own, although Cárdenas maintained it actually reduced the role of the military in political decision making. While the realigned party supposedly gave the groups involved greater input into party policy, it actually promoted the centralization of power in the hands of the president.

The defining act of the Cárdenas administration was his expropriation of the foreign-owned oil companies in March 1938. U.S. and British companies dominated the Mexican oil industry from its beginnings in the early twentieth century. The oil companies had been involved in periodic confrontations with the Mexican government since the passage of the Constitution of 1917. The latest confrontation grew out of Cárdenas's labor policies. As part of his policy of promoting industrial unionism, Cárdenas had encouraged the twenty-one unions representing different types of workers in the oil industry to merge into one giant union capable of confronting the multinational companies dominating the industry. The new union immediately demanded a substantial pay raise, additional benefits, and greater control over working conditions. When the companies rejected the demands, the matter was referred to the federal Arbitration Board, which reached a decision that basically favored the workers. The owners then appealed the matter to the Mexican Supreme Court, which also ruled in favor of the union. When the oil companies publicly announced that they would not abide by the Supreme Court's decision, Cárdenas expropriated all of the foreign-owned oil companies on 18 March 1938. The expropriation enjoyed broad public support, even among conservative groups. Cárdenas had correctly guessed that the international situation prevented a strong response by either the U.S. or British governments (although Great Britain did break diplomatic relations) and that Mexico could sell its oil to other customers if the oil companies boycotted Mexican oil (which they did). While the date of the expropriation became known as "Mexico's economic independence day," the international situation that had encouraged the expropriation in the first place would soon force Mexico into even greater economic dependency on the United States.

Even as Mexicans celebrated the oil expropriation, the Cárdenas administration was in the process of redirecting its policies away from the reforms that had brought the social revolution to its peak. Reforms in education and the agrarian sector proved expensive, and by 1937 the Cárdenas administration was in the midst of a major financial crisis. His policies also alarmed investors, leading to a critical problem with capital flight. Cárdenas dramatically reduced his reform activities and began to think in terms of a new development approach with an emphasis on industrialization. Although the transition to this new approach was not complete until after Cárdenas left office, its foundation was laid in the last years of his presidency. The international situation also played a major role in the de-emphasis of reform. The Spanish Civil War (1936–1939) in particular influenced Cárdenas, who saw in it a preview of World War II as well as a possible scenario for domestic upheaval in Mexico as conservative-reform tensions grew. The new direction being taken by Cárdenas evidenced itself in his choice of a successor. Those who favored a continuation or even expansion of reforms supported the candidacy of General Francisco Múgica, Cárdenas's secretary of public works and long-time supporter of extensive agrarian reform. Cárdenas, however, designated the more conservative and less controversial General Manual Avila Camacho as his choice. The PRM dutifully nominated Avila Camacho, who went on to an easy—but violence-plagued—victory in the 1940 elections.

Although he soon became a political icon, Cárdenas continued to be an important political figure after he left the presidency in December 1940. Cárdenas became the leading symbol for what many considered the "authentic revolution" of agrarian reform, labor rights, nationalism, and anticlericalism. Mexico's involvement in World War II soon brought Cárdenas back into public life. He served as commander of the specially created "Pacific Defense Zone" in 1941–1942 and as secretary of national defense from 1942 to 1945. Although Cárdenas had played a crucial role in setting the Revolution on a new and more conservative course, he remained until his death in 1970 a mythic symbol for the left wing in the official party and in Mexican politics in general.

Contemporary and historical evaluations of Cárdenas have provoked conflict and controversy. Categorizing Cárdenas has proven difficult. He has been called a socialist, a social democrat, a marxist, a populist, an authoritarian, a corporatist, and a reformer. Although Cárdenas granted political asylum to the famous communist exile Leon Trotsky in 1936, Trotsky dismissed Cárdenas as a "bourgeois reformer." Cárdenas's agrarian reform program distributed land on an unprecedented scale and helped to gain the loyalty of the peasants for both his government and for the official party. Whether the agrarian reform program actually did much to raise the standard of living of most peasants is still a hotly debated topic. Cárdenas promoted labor organization while simultaneously trying to extend greater government control over the labor movement. His expropriation of the foreign-owned oil companies in 1938 is the supreme expression of Mexican economic nationalism in the twentieth century, but developments soon proved that it was not Mexico's "economic independence day." His pursuit of socialistic and sex education may very well have hurt his overall efforts to expand education. Cárdenas's reorganization of the official party was a major step in the establishment of the political system that dominated

Mexican politics throughout the rest of the century. Ironically, it was that very system that was bitterly denounced by Cárdenas's son, Cuauhtémoc Cárdenas, as he campaigned for the presidency in the elections of 1988, 1994, and 2000.

—DMC

See also: Agrarian Reform/Land and Land Policy; Avila Camacho, Manuel; Calles, Plutarco Elías; Cárdenas, Cuauhtémoc; Confederación de Trabajadores de México (CTM); Confederación Nacional Campesina (CNC); Confederación Regional Obrera Mexicana (CROM); Education; Labor Movements; Lombardo Toledano, Vicente; Morones, Luis; Oil Industry; Partido Revolucionario Institucional (PRI); Presidents of the Twentieth Century.

References:
Bantjes, Adrian A. *As if Jesus Walked on Earth: Cardenismo, Sonora, and the Mexican Revolution.* Wilmington, DE: Scholarly Resources, 1997.
Becker, Marjorie. *Setting the Virgin on Fire: Lázaro Cárdenas, Michoacán Peasants, and the Redemption of the Mexican Revolution.* Berkeley: University of California Press, 1995.
Gledhill, John. *Casi Nada: A Study of Agrarian Reform in the Homeland of Cardenismo.* Albany: State University of New York Press, 1991.

Carranza, Venustiano (1859–1920)

President from 1917 to 1920, Carranza was born in 1859 in Cuatro Ciénegas, Coahuila. His family was part of the northern landholding class, and Carranza received a good education, including attendance at the prestigious National Preparatory School and National School of Medicine in Mexico City. His first political position was as municipal president of his hometown. Although part of the Porfirian power structure, Carranza violently opposed the reelection of Díaz's choice for governor in 1893. Carranza later went on to serve in the national senate from 1904 to 1912. Carranza was an early champion of the principle of anti-reelection and originally supported General Bernardo Reyes as the logical successor to Porfirio Díaz. Later, Carranza supported Francisco Madero for the presidency in 1910 and served in Madero's Revolutionary cabinet as minister of war. In 1912, with Madero in the presidency, Carranza became governor of Coahuila.

As governor of Coahuila, Carranza implemented a progressive, but not radical, program. He introduced a new tax structure, permitted unionization, reformed education, and improved public health. Carranza was in the governorship in February 1913 when Madero was overthrown and assassinated by General Victoriano Huerta. Carranza refused to recognize Huerta's government and issued his Revolutionary Plan de Guadalupe in March 1913. The Plan did not address the social or economic goals to be pursued; it simply prescribed a process of political transition to a new government. In the Plan, Carranza called on his fellow governors to renounce recognition of the Huerta regime; it also appointed Carranza the "first chief of the Constitutionalist army" and provided that Carranza would be provisional president once the Revolution triumphed. The Plan put Carranza in the leadership of the most serious military opposition to Huerta; key Revolutionary generals in the north, such as Alvaro Obregón and Francisco "Pancho" Villa, promised to follow Carranza's lead.

Despite his title, Carranza found it difficult to control his generals, especially Villa, who was suspicious of Carranza's Revolutionary commitment, and Carranza never reached any arrangement with the principal rebel leader in the south, Emiliano Zapata. Carranza restricted the flow of supplies to Villa to ensure that troops under Obregón's command would beat Villa's forces to Mexico City. Obregón won the race to Mexico City in August 1914, but the growing friction between Carranza and Villa was an indicator of the bloody struggle for power among the different Revolutionary factions that emerged after the resignation and exile of Huerta in July 1914.

In an effort to promote unity among the Revolutionary groups, Carranza called a meeting of military chieftains in October 1914 at Aguascalientes. Instead of uniting the military factions, the convention at Aguascalientes polarized the major Revolutionary groups into followers of Villa and Zapata on the one hand and supporters of Carranza and Obregón on the other. The Revolution of 1910 was about to enter its bloodiest phase.

The struggle initially went against Carranza, who had to abandon Mexico City and set up an alternate capital in Veracruz. Under the able leadership of Obregón, Carranza's forces soon recaptured Mexico City and inflicted a series of defeats on Villa, who retreated to the north. Carranza's forces were unable to inflict a decisive defeat on Zapata but did generally succeed in containing Zapata in his home state of Morelos. The United States acknowledged the dominant position of Carranza and his Constitutionalist forces by extending diplomatic recognition to the Carranza regime in October 1915.

Although Villa had been reduced to a regional leader, his strength in the north enabled him to further trouble the Carranza administration. He provoked a major crisis between Carranza and the U.S. government by invading Columbus, New Mexico, on 9 March 1916. The United States responded by sending a "punitive expedition" under General John J. Pershing deep into Mexico in pursuit of Villa and his forces. Initially, Carranza's forces did not oppose the movement of U.S. forces into northern Mexico. As the punitive expedition grew in size and moved deeper into Mexico, Carranza ordered military force to be used to block any further movement south by the expedition. Two of the biggest battles engaged in by the expedition were with Carranza's forces. War was avoided, and Pershing's forces returned to U.S. soil in February 1917.

At the same time that Pershing was withdrawing the last of his forces, Carranza promulgated a new constitution that had been under discussion since late 1916. Carranza tried to control the actions of the constitutional convention but eventually had to accept a more radical document than he had wished for. Carranza easily won the first

presidential election held under the new Constitution and took office as Constitutional president on 1 May 1917.

Although Carranza accepted the Constitution of 1917, he did not have to enforce it. Like Madero, Carranza believed that Mexico's greatest need was for political reform, not for sweeping social and economic reforms as Mexico struggled to recover from years of civil war. Carranza moved slowly—if at all—to implement the Constitution's more radical provisions. Agrarian reform was one of the more hotly contested issues. A large landowner himself, Carranza was a defender of private property and was reluctant to cause further economic dislocation by large-scale redistribution of land. He distributed only about 450,000 acres, an amount less than the individual landholdings of many large landowners in the north. Most of the acreage distributed was taken from Carranza's personal political enemies and given to his political supporters rather than to landless peasants. He also approved a plan that resulted in the assassination of the principal exponent of agrarian reform, Emiliano Zapata, in 1919. The Constitution called for regulation of working conditions and protection for unionization, provisions largely ignored by Carranza. Carranza used the army and the police to put down strikes. He permitted the formation of a national labor confederation (the Confederación Regional Obrera Mexicana, or CROM) but tried to bring it under government control from its inception. Carranza did act out the growing nationalism connected with the Revolution, including maintaining Mexico's neutrality during World War I despite pressure from the United States, which had entered the conflict in April 1917. Carranza also started the process of recentralizing political power in Mexico after the extensive decentralization caused by years of fighting and civil war.

Carranza's presidency and his life came to an end as part of a familiar political crisis: presidential succession. The Constitution prohibited Carranza from being reelected, so he worked to impose his own candidate, the diplomat Ignacio Bonillas. This went directly against the aspirations and expectations of Alvaro Obregón, who had assumed that Carranza would reward Obregón's crucial role in putting Carranza in the presidency by supporting Obregón's bid for the presidency in 1920. When it became obvious that Carranza was not going to back Obregón for the presidency, Obregón's followers rose in revolt in April 1920. Carranza decided to leave Mexico City and establish his government at Veracruz as he had done in 1914, but some of Obregón's forces overtook Carranza's party en route to Veracuz and killed Carranza on 21 May 1920. Under Carranza, the Revolution had passed through the important phase of establishing Revolutionary goals in the Constitution of 1917. It would take other—and more radical—presidents to pursue those goals.

—DMC

See also: Agrarian Reform/Land and Land Policy; Assassinations; Confederación Regional Obrera Mexicana (CROM); Díaz, Porfirio; Labor Movements; Madero, Francisco; Obregón, Alvaro; Presidents of the Twentieth Century; Revolution of 1910; United States, Relations with; Villa, Francisco "Pancho"; Zapata, Emiliano.

References:

Hall, Linda B. *Oil, Banks, and Politics: The United States and Postrevolutionary Mexico, 1917–1924.* Austin: University of Texas Press, 1995.

Katz, Friedrich. *The Secret War in Mexico: Europe, the United States, and the Mexican Revolution.* Chicago: University of Chicago Press, 1981.

Richmond, Douglas W. *Venustiano Carranza's Nationalist Struggle, 1893–1920.* Lincoln: University of Nebraska Press, 1983.

Castellanos, Rosario (1925–1974)

Since she first arrived on the Mexican literary scene as a member of the "Generation of 1950," critics have held Rosario Castellanos in high regard. In 1957 her first novel, *Balún Canán,* won the prestigious Mexican Critics' Award, in 1967 she was proclaimed the nation's Woman of the Year and awarded a professorship at the National Autonomous University, and from 1971 until her death in 1974 she served as Mexico's ambassador to Israel. Castellanos's reputation has continued to grow since midcentury and she is now considered one of twentieth-century Mexico's literary giants. One obvious reason is that she serves as a role model for new generations of Mexican women writers and readers. Another is her tragic early death at age 49. More important than these incidentals, however, is her pioneering engagement with the issues of race, class, and gender, and her decidedly feminine/feminist vision of those issues. As another of Mexico's great twentieth-century chroniclers (and personal friend), Elena Poniatowska remarked: "Rosario used literature the way the majority of us women still use it, as a form of therapy. We turn to writing to free ourselves, to empty ourselves, to confess, to explain the world to ourselves, to understand what is happening to us" (quoted in Schaefer, *Textured Lives,* p. 39). Whatever the reasons, the contemporary feel of both her political concerns and her personal style continues to attract new fans.

By her own admission, Castellanos's ambiguous social position deeply influenced her literary work. Born on 25 May 1925 in Mexico City but raised on the family *hacienda* (ranch) in Chiapas near Mexico's border with Guatemala, Castellanos experienced all the privileges of a white, upper-class child in Mexico's poorest and most Indian state. These included her own Indian "nana" (nanny) and trips in a sedan chair carried by Indian porters. An elite education that produced a master's degree in philosophy from the National Autonomous University and entrée into Mexico City literary society compounded her sense of privilege. Nevertheless, coming of age in a politicized era of Revolutionary rhetoric and economic modernization, Castellanos rejected the comforts of an upper-class feminine lifestyle. A six-year stint (1951–1957) with the National Indigenous Institute in her native Chiapas, provided a firsthand glimpse at pervasive racism and rural poverty. If that was not enough, her position as a woman in a macho (male-dominated) society further encouraged her commitment to social justice. In a 1970 essay on President Lázaro Cárdenas (1934–1940), whose land redistribution policies so alienated her parents' generation during her childhood, Castellanos wrote gratefully that "possibilities were available to me, doors were opened to me, all because of one government official's concept of justice and the consistency of his desire to see the law equally applied" (Castellanos, *Another Way to Be,* p. 119).

Rejecting the exploitation of Indian labor, Castellanos drew instead on the region's indigenous rich Mayan cultures to produce a "Chiapas cycle" of novels and short stories that first brought her national attention: *Balún Canán* (Nine Guardians, 1957), *Ciudad real* (City of Kings, 1960), *Oficio de tinieblas* (Office of Tenebrae, 1962), and *Los convidados de agosto* (The Guests of August, 1964). Told mostly from the perspective of a seven-year-old white girl—unnamed but perhaps Castellanos herself—initiated into Mayan culture by her Indian nana, *Balún Canán,* combines a contemporary awareness of social inequalities and cultural conflict with an ethnographer's eye for indigenous customs and a poet's appreciation for their strange beauty. "As she has done since I was born," the little girl tells us, "Nana draws me onto her lap. It is warm and caring. But it has a wound, a wound that we have caused" (Castellanos, *Another Way to Be,* p. 61). Similar concerns with the double oppression of Indian women (as Indians and as women) characterize the rest of the Chiapas cycle as well. Her second novel, *Oficio de tinieblas,* for example, uses indigenous notions of circular time to transport a 1867 Chamula Indian uprising into the Cárdenas era in order to explore the long-standing inequalities of power that structured the region's complex racial and social divisions. Furthermore, in the stories of *Ciudad real,* Castellanos even critiques the anthro-pologists, doctors, and linguists of the National Indigenous Institute (and other government agencies) whose well-meaning efforts to modernize the Maya inevitably end in cultural misunderstanding and failure. Noteworthy in all her prose is the presence of strong women, like the shaman Catalina Díaz Puijla in *Oficio de tinieblas,* who help organize their communities to fight oppression. Despite an evident pro-Indian bias, Castellanos rejected the simple good-Indian/bad-Spaniard dichotomies of official *indigenismo* (Indianism). "This simplicity makes me laugh," she insisted:

> Indians are human beings absolutely equal to whites except [they've been] placed in circumstances that are unique and unfavorable. Because they are weaker they can be worse—more violent, more treacherous, or more hypocritical—than white people. Indians do not seem mysterious or poetic to me. What happens is that they live in atrocious poverty. It's necessary to describe how that poverty has atrophied their best qualities. (Castellanos, *A Rosario Castellanos Reader,* p. 32)

Nor did she restrict this admirable frankness to the analysis of Mayan society. The short stories in *Los convidados de agosto,* for example, deal mostly with provincial *ladino* (culturally hispanic) culture and expose women's complicity in their own oppression both as active enforcers and passive victims of a patriarchal society. Like Indians, women's oppression "has atrophied their best qualities."

Although her novels and short stories first attracted the general public's attention, Castellanos's great love was poetry. *Oficio de tinieblas* (1962) was her last novel, but she wrote and published poetry throughout her life from the youthful *Apuntes para declaración de fe* (Notes for a Declaration of Faith) in 1948 to the collection *Poesía no eres tú* (You Are not Poetry) in 1972. In her poetry, Castellanos explores with great ambivalence, candor, and wit the personal side of race, class, and especially gender inequalities. Her most consistent theme—developed years before it became a central theme in European academic discourse—was the self's encounter with the other. In a poem from the collection *Poesía no eres tú,* for example, Castellanos implies that only through that encounter can the self take on a sense of identity and purpose:

> The other: mediator, judge, balance
> between opposites, witness,
> knot that binds up all that had broken
> The other, muteness begging a voice
> from the speaker,
> claiming an ear
> from the listener.
> The other. With the other
> humanity, dialogue, poetry begin. (Castellanos, *A Rosario Castellanos Reader,* p. 109)

This intimate connection between self and other has political implications. Borrowing from French activist and feminist thinker Simone Weil, Castellanos insists that "The sword of injustice is a two-edged sword that wounds the one who yields it just as brutally as it does its intended victim" (Castellanos, *Another Way to Be,* p. xxvii). Seen in this light, all human relationships are fraught with ambivalence. In a poem about her son Gabriel, she confessed:

> Ugly, sick, bored,
> I felt him grow at my expense,
> rob my blood of its color, add
> a secret weight and volume
> to my condition on this earth. (Castellanos, *A Rosario Castellanos Reader,* p. 102)

Castellanos's response to this ambivalence about human relationships, especially in her later poetry, was humor. In a poem constructed as a series of mock interviews after the style of prominent U.S. sexologist Alfred Kinsey, a "married women" describes sex with her husband:

> At a rate I can regularly predict
> my husband makes use of his rights,

> or, as he likes to say, he pays the conjugal
> debt. Then he turns his back on me and
>   snores.
> I always resist. Out of decency.
> But then I always give in. Out of obedience.
> No, I don't like anything special.
> Anyhow, I'm not supposed to like it.
> Because I'm a decent woman; and he's so
>   gross! (Castellanos, *A Rosario Castellanos Reader,* p.112)

This "claw of ferocious humor," as she called it, is particularly evident in her many essays—after 1960 she wrote regularly for Mexico City newspapers—and a in dramatic farce, *El eterno feminino* (The Eternal Feminine, 1975), published just after her death. Set in a Mexico City beauty parlor with appearances by mythical-historical figures like the Virgin of Guadalupe (symbolic mother and protector of Mexico), Malinche (Cortes's translator and concubine), Sor Juana (great Mexican seventeenth-century poetess), Carlota (wife of doomed emperor Maximillian), and Adelita (legendary prostitute from a famous Revolutionary ballad), *El eterno feminino* mocks the contradictory stereotypes of women as virgins or whores, self-sacrificing wives and mothers or brainless consumers, eternal victims or betrayers of men.

The problem, Castellanos ultimately decided, was language itself, which had become, in the hands of male conquerors and domineering patriarchs, "an instrument of domination." "We have to create another language," she argued, "we have to find another starting point, search for the pearl within each shell, the pit beneath the peel, because the shell holds still another treasure, the peel another substance" (Castellanos, *A Rosario Castellanos Reader,* p. 252). To that end, her efforts were truly heroic. And yet, she would have appreciated the symbolic implications of her accidental death in a Tel Aviv apartment, electrocuted while turning on a light.

—*RMB*

See also: Gender and Sexuality; *Mestizaje* and *Indigenismo*; Novel since 1960; Poetry; Poniatowska, Elena.

References:

Castellanos, Rosario. *A Rosario Castellanos Reader: An Anthology of Her Poetry, Short Fiction, Essays, and Drama*. Edited and translated by Maureen Ahern. Austin: University of Texas Press, 1988.

———. *Another Way to Be: Selected Works of Rosario Castellanos*. Edited and translated by Myralyn Allgood. Athens: University of Georgia Press, 1990.

Schaefer, Claudia. *Textured Lives: Women, Art and Representation in Modern Mexico*. Tucson: The University of Arizona Press, 1992.

Chávez, César (1927–1993)

Among the most visible elements of the Chicano movement in the United States, César Chávez and the farmworkers' union he helped establish played an important role in encouraging activism among Mexican Americans. Like the League of United Latin American Citizens (LULAC), which was established in Texas in 1929, the United Farm Workers (UFW) fought against the discrimination that had been part of the lives of Mexican Americans since the end of the Mexican War. Yet while LULAC focused on the assimilation of Mexican Americans into U.S. society and represented the reformist voice of middle-class Hispanics, the UFW waged a more radical struggle for workers' rights and was led by a man whose background was as humble as the people his union came to represent.

A grandson of Mexican immigrants, César Chávez was born in Arizona in 1927. Financial difficulties caused Chávez's parents to lose their plot of land near Yuma, pushing the family to California in search of work. Arriving in California during the Great Depression, the Chávez family joined thousands of other migrants (including Mexicans and Americans) who became farm laborers. They followed a seasonal round of work that took them to many areas of the state, including the vast Central/San Joaquín Valley and the Imperial Valley. César spent his teenage years doing the hard labor of a field-worker and encountering firsthand the blatant discrimination that was the lot of Mexican Americans

(and other ethnic groups, including Filipinos and blacks) in California and elsewhere. This discrimination, as well as poor pay and working conditions, encouraged Chávez's parents to support efforts at unionization and to participate in strikes. Chávez thus received an early exposure to the workers' struggle.

After a brief stint in the U.S. Navy during World War II, Chávez returned to farmwork in California and married Helen Fabela. Beginning in the 1950s, he embarked on a life of activism that was especially inspired by Gandhi's idea of nonviolence and by the doctrine of social justice that was embraced by some reformists within the Roman Catholic Church. Initially, Chávez worked with the Community Service Organization (CSO), a group organized by Fred Ross, who had earlier helped mobilize the poor in the city of Chicago. Chávez helped the CSO register Mexican American voters in California, particularly in the San Joaquín Valley. He also became involved in the ongoing struggle to prevent the state's growers from hiring *braceros* (Mexican laborers initially welcomed to the United States to help with a World War II labor shortage). This tactic was often used to break strikes and to discourage farmworkers from organizing.

Convinced of the need for a separate union to challenge California's growers, Chávez quit the CSO and organized a group that became the United Farm Workers. The union was officially established at a meeting in 1962, with Chávez as its president and Dolores Huerta and Gilbert Padilla as vice-presidents. Dolores Huerta, raised in Stockton, California, became Chávez's most important partner in the UFW, helping to organize and develop the union and lobbying on its behalf in Washington, D.C., and Sacramento. At its founding meeting, the UFW also adopted a union flag, featuring a black eagle on a red background, and it declared its official slogan to be "Viva la Causa" ("Long Live the Cause"). The union headquarters was located in Delano, a Central Valley town near Bakersfield.

The birth of the UFW coincided with the end of the *bracero* program, which eliminated one of the main obstacles to workers' strikes. Beginning in 1965, Chávez and the UFW supported Filipino workers who struck for better pay against grape growers in the San Joaquín Valley. This strike spread rapidly and eventually involved thousands of farmworkers. It became a general struggle against grape growers for guaranteed wages, better working conditions, and formal contracts between growers and workers. The strike culminated in a national boycott of California table grapes that halted the shipment of grapes to major cities in the United States (as well as Canada) and encouraged picket lines outside supermarkets that carried "nonunion grapes."

The grape strike and boycott generated support from churches (both Catholic and Protestant), from national unions (including the United Auto Workers), and from students, many of whom were also involved in the Civil Rights Movement of the 1960s. The UFW and Chávez became a central feature of the broader Chicano movement, and the black and red union flag was seen regularly at Chicano rallies. National political figures, including Martin Luther King Jr. and Robert F. Kennedy, also lent their support to Chávez, acknowledging a place for the UFW in the Civil Rights Movement and underscoring the growing political importance of the Mexican American population.

Chávez himself was a central figure in the strike, and he gained local attention with his speeches, many at California colleges. A march from Delano to Sacramento in the middle of the strike brought national media attention, which intensified when Chávez introduced another tactic that became a hallmark of his UFW leadership: the hunger strike. Chávez saw this first hunger strike as a part of his emphasis on nonviolent protest. He continued to use the tactic, often fasting for weeks at a time.

By 1970 the grape strike and boycott had succeeded in getting most California grape growers to negotiate contracts with the UFW. Despite this victory, however, Chávez and the farmworkers continued to battle growers and their supporters (often including the local police). In this ongoing struggle, the Teamsters' Union became especially problematic. Though it initially indicated support for the UFW, the Teamsters' Union was ultimately a rival that sought to block the UFW strikes that would hurt packers and truckers who were Teamster members. During the 1970s the Teamsters also colluded with growers to block the UFW, using violence and intimidation to discourage farmworker activism. In this, the Teamsters had the backing of President Richard Nixon, who supported Teamster efforts to undermine the UFW.

Even amid such repression, Chávez continued his tireless efforts. In 1975 he won a significant victory with the passage of the California Agricultural Labor Relations Act, which protected workers' right to boycott and secured the right of seasonal workers (abundantly represented in the UFW) to vote in labor elections. The UFW also continued to spread its influence, establishing some thirty union centers in California. These centers provided members with access to clinics, a credit union, legal services, and other benefits. In 1973, the UFW drafted a constitution that included a bill of rights and that did not distinguish between those born in Mexico and those born in the United States. This was a significant step: despite the union always having had many immigrants (legal and undocumented) in its ranks, it had often been pushed to oppose Mexican immigration in order to strengthen its own position.

The 1980s and 1990s were decades of mixed success for the UFW, particularly since unionism in the United States declined during that period. The UFW also faced financial problems and union membership dropped. Growers in California signed fewer contracts with the UFW and boycotts and strikes failed to generate the public support they once did. During the late 1980s, the

UFW briefly revived public interest in the plight of farmworkers by producing the film *The Wrath of Grapes,* which called attention to the birth defects and cancers caused by pesticide use in the fields. Chávez himself traveled to cities in the Midwest and eastern U.S. to further publicize the danger of pesticides to workers and consumers. Chávez continued his tireless efforts on behalf of farmworkers until his unexpected death on 23 April 1993.

—SBP

See also: *Bracero* Program; Chicano/a; League of United Latin American Citizens (LULAC).

References:
Acuña, Rodolfo. *Occupied America: A History of Chicanos.* 2d ed. New York: Harper and Row, 1981.
Griswold del Castillo, Richard, and Richard A. García. *César Chávez: A Triumph of Spirit.* Norman: University of Oklahoma Press, 1995.
Matthiesen, Peter. *Sal Si Puedes. César Chávez and the New American Revolution.* Berkeley: University of California Press, 2000.

Chiapas (State)

Mexico's southernmost state, Chiapas has its capital at Tuxtla Gutiérrez and shares a border with Guatemala. It has a varied terrain, including a high central plateau (the Meseta Central), the Central Valley, the Highlands, and the Pacific coastal plain of Soconusco. Chiapas is often acknowledged to be the poorest state in Mexico, despite its wealth in natural resources. Although it remains, as in the colonial era and nineteenth century, an agricultural and ranching state, Chiapas is also Mexico's largest generator of hydroelectric energy and a major producer of oil and gas. At the same time, the state is burdened with high illiteracy and infant mortality rates. The majority of its people, one-third of whom are Indians of Mayan descent, live in poverty. During the last decade of the twentieth century, Chiapas was one of Mexico's most visible states. Since 1994, it has hosted a major rebellion, led by the Zapatista National Liberation Army (EZLN), which has highlighted the issues of poverty, land reform, and indigenous rights.

Spanish attempts to lay claim to "La provincia de Chiapa" began in the 1520s when Pedro de Alvarado conquered the Pacific coast section of Soconusco. To Diego de Mazariegos was left the task of conquering the Chiapas highlands and establishing the first Spanish town, Villa Real, now known as San Cristóbal de las Casas. In Chiapas, a center of the ancient Mayan civilization, Spanish settlers encountered a large indigenous population and attempted to subdue it by forcing Indians into several concentrated settlements. This contributed to a dramatic decline in Chiapas's Indian population, as epidemic diseases spread rapidly among the congregated Indians. Only by the eve of Mexican independence had the Indian population made a significant recovery.

Since Chiapas lacked mineral wealth, the provincial economy came to be based on agriculture, with Indian labor and tribute supporting the new Spanish population. The Roman Catholic Church and its missionaries were also active in the province, their interests often clashing with the more material ones of Spanish colonists. Despite the pervasive presence of the Spaniards, many Indians remained outside Spanish control, often fleeing into the jungle. Early on, the province of Chiapas gained a reputation for the intransigence of its Indian peoples.

Mexico's independence movement saw Chiapas elites divided over the issue of joining Mexico or neighboring Guatemala. The conflict brought Chiapas to the brink of civil war but ended peacefully in 1824 with incorporation as a Mexican state. As the nineteenth century progressed, the modern boundaries of Chiapas took shape, with the annexation of a border between Chiapas and neighboring Guatemala.

Elite competition was a hallmark of nineteenth-century Chiapas. Struggle for control of the state's rich agricultural land and for control of Indian labor encouraged the growth of regional factions and in particular fostered a split between wealthy landowners of the Central Highlands and those of the Central Valley. Politics mirrored this situation, with power held by several regional bosses who tended to be the owners of large estates. Left out of this economic and political equation were the Indians, many of whom lost their lands to the Spanish-speaking elites and were forced into debt peonage. The Indian resistance that had been a part of the colonial era, however, persisted into the nineteenth century. In the 1860s a "Caste War" occurred, as Chamula Indians laid siege to San Cristóbal de las Casas, demanding the release of their leader Pedro Díaz Cuscat, who had been imprisoned by the Spanish-speaking "*ladino*" leaders of San Cristóbal. A ceremony in which a young Indian boy was crucified in a symbolic "creation" of an Indian Jesus, precipitated this conflict, which ended after several months with the Indians' defeat.

The late nineteenth and early twentieth centuries represented a time of economic modernization for Chiapas. Under the governorship of Emilio Rabasa, handpicked by Mexico's dictator Porfirio Díaz, the state embarked on a program of "regeneration and progress." The arrival of the railroad and Rabasa's ambitious efforts to build an infrastructure in this previously isolated state helped set the stage for an influx of foreign investment. Chiapas developed an export economy based on hardwoods, rubber, sugarcane, cacao, and most important, coffee. In 1892 Rabasa moved the government seat from the highland city of San Cristóbal to the fast-growing commercial center of Tuxtla Gutiérrez in the Central Valley.

Although impressive in its scope, Rabasa's program of modernization, continued by his successors, benefited relatively few. It included a project of agrarian reform that actually increased large landholdings at the expense of small-scale farmers and communal Indian villages. Those displaced as a result of Rabasa's agrarian program were often forced into debt peonage or became migrant workers.

The Mexican Revolution in Chiapas was characterized primarily by a continuation of conflict and competition between regional elites. Wealthy residents of highland San Cristóbal attempted unsuccessfully to undermine the power of their Central Valley counterparts. The state's popular classes, however, were not particularly active, and despite the poor conditions of the peasantry, Chiapas experienced no popular revolution from below. In the end, owners of the largest estates successfully weathered the Revolution, preserving both their economic and political power.

In the aftermath of the Mexican Revolution, the pattern of land concentration and consequent displacement of small-scale farmers continued as modern commercial agriculture flourished. Coffee cultivation remained the state's dominant economic activity, with cattle ranching assuming a new importance as well. Local political bosses, allied with the Institutional Revolutionary Party, or PRI, encouraged this pattern of economic growth and personally benefited from it. Workers and peasants who attempted to organize were successfully co-opted by state and local political machines, while limited agrarian reform and federal programs of assistance helped prevent widespread popular resistance to the postrevolutionary regime.

Not until the 1970s did a significant agrarian struggle begin in Chiapas. The continued loss of land to commercial agriculture and cattle ranching pushed Maya Indians and other peasants to seize property and stage demonstrations. In the Lacandón jungle, located in the eastern part of the state, settlers displaced from other areas of the state began to organize, aided in some cases by the activism of Bishop Samuel Ruíz, a supporter of Liberation Theology. It was in this section of Chiapas that the Zapatista movement and the EZLN began to emerge during the early 1980s.

The local and national government response to the Chiapas situation was to increase the military presence in that state.

During the 1980s, the PRI helped place Absalón Castellanos Domínguez, an influential cattle rancher and career military man, into the governor's seat. Castellanos quickly gained a reputation for repression and was considered responsible for human rights abuses.

Mexico's official end to agrarian reform and the signing of the North American Free Trade Agreement (NAFTA) during the 1990s pushed many peasants to a higher level of opposition. In 1994 the Zapatista movement began a military offensive, capturing four towns and encouraging peasants to invade privately owned lands. Several rounds of negotiations between the Zapatista rebels and the Mexican government failed to bring a resolution to the conflict, and a particular sticking point was the rebel insistence on official recognition of indigenous rights, including the right of Indians to form their own local governments. Meanwhile, the Mexican army and right-wing paramilitary groups, sponsored by local landowners, worked to undermine the Zapatista base of support.

As the twentieth century drew to a close, Chiapas had gained the attention of Mexico's national government and of the international community. An uneasy truce between Zapatista rebels and the government was a reminder that, despite its tremendous natural wealth and economic potential, this southern state continued to struggle with issues that date back to the colonial era.

—SBP

See also: Agrarian Reform/Land and Land Policy; North American Free Trade Agreement (NAFTA); Ruíz, Bishop Samuel; Zapatista National Liberation Army (EZLN).

References:
 Benjamin, Thomas. *A Rich Land, a Poor People: Politics and Society in Modern Chiapas.* Albuquerque: University of New Mexico Press, 1989.
 Collier, George A., and Elizabeth Lowery Quaratiello. *Basta! Land and the Zapatista Rebellion in Chiapas.* Oakland, CA: Food First Books, 1994.
 Gerhard, Peter. *The Southeast Frontier of New Spain.* Norman: University of Oklahoma Press, 1993.

Official state web site: http://www.chiapas. gob.mx

Chicano/a

A truncated form of the word "Mexicano," this term was popularized during the 1960s and 1970s and was embraced by many Mexican Americans. The origin of the word "chicano" is a matter of dispute. It was used in the early part of the twentieth century as a disparaging reference to working-class Mexicans. In the 1960s and 1970s it became a term used proudly by Mexican Americans, particularly by political activists pushing for rights and recognition of the sizeable and growing U.S. population of Mexican Americans. Many of these activists wished to emphasize their Indian or *mestizo* (mixed Spanish and Indian) roots, and the term "Chicano," derived from the Nahuatl Indian word for "Mexican," provided a means of doing so. For many activists, "Chicano" was a more acceptable and powerful self-referent than the term "Hispanic," which the United States government began using in the 1970s to refer to the sizeable and growing Mexican American population.

The Chicano movement, which reached its height in the 1960s and 1970s, underscored the significant presence of Mexican Americans and sought redress for several things. Since the sixteenth century, people of Spanish and later Mexican descent had occupied areas that were later incorporated into the United States. The Treaty of Guadalupe Hidalgo (1848), which ended the Mexican War, delineated the boundary between Mexico and the United States while transforming some 50,000 Mexicans into American citizens. Although the Treaty guaranteed these former Mexicans civil rights, clashes with the Anglo world, particularly over property and political rights, became the rule rather than the exception. In New Mexico, Texas, Arizona, and California (the areas where Mexican Americans were concentrated) Mexican Americans fought an uphill battle for economic and political rights while enduring various forms of discrimination. As one historian has remarked, Mexican Americans became "foreigners in their native land."

As the twentieth century began, the Mexican population of the United States grew dramatically. Largely as a result of the unrest caused by the Mexican Revolution, the Mexican population of the U.S. had reached 1.5 million by 1930. Mexican immigrants flocked to the western states, particularly New Mexico, Texas, Arizona, and California (areas that already had sizeable Mexican American populations). Many became the cheap labor that fueled the expanding agribusiness sector of the southwest. Discrimination continued, however, and the U.S. Congress tried to limit the number of Mexican immigrants entering the country. The Great Depression simply heightened discrimination, and many Mexican Americans, viewed as taking jobs away from Americans, were forcibly repatriated to Mexico.

During World War II, Mexican laborers were once again welcomed into the United States through the *bracero* program, an attempt to address the labor shortage created by the war. Some remained in the United States, becoming part of the still-growing Mexican American population. Mexican Americans also served in the U.S. military in record numbers. Their experience as soldiers contributed to a greater self-awareness and a determination to do something about the discrimination that continued to affect Mexican Americans. In Los Angeles, where the Mexican American population had experienced significant growth since the turn of the century, racial tensions found expression in the "Zoot Suit" riots of 1943, which responded to discrimination against Mexican Americans and in particular to police harassment and brutality leveled against the local Mexican American population.

Activism among Mexican Americans began in the late nineteenth and early twentieth centuries as peoples of Mexican descent organized in various ways to protect their rights and to protest against political, economic, and social discrimination and disfranchisement. One of the most visible of the early groups was the League of United Latin American Citizens (LULAC). Established in 1929 in Texas (a state with a particularly poor record of discrimination), LULAC sought to end discrimination and to help people of Mexican descent to assert themselves as full citizens of the United States.

Organization and activism among Mexican Americans increased after World War II and culminated in the Chicano movement of the 1960s and 1970s. The Chicano movement drew on Aztec mythology to unify Mexican Americans and to encourage their participation in a fight against political, economic, and social discrimination. In particular, the movement equated the U.S. southwest with Aztlán, the ancestral homeland of the Mexicans. This powerful symbol gave many peoples of Mexican descent a sense of belonging to a place that many felt had been taken from them after the Mexican War. It also contributed to a collective identity based on a shared history of invasion and conquest.

The Chicano movement took various forms and counted among its ranks several leaders. Colorado activist Corky González spearheaded the Crusade for Justice, which took up the cause of poverty and briefly joined with Martin Luther King Jr. in a multiracial campaign for economic justice. González was also the author of the poem "I Am Joaquín," a literary centerpiece of the Chicano movement. In New Mexico, Reyes López Tijerina led a fight for lands that had been taken away from the descendants of Spanish settlers of the area. In 1967 López Tijerina and his followers in the Alianza Federal de Mercedes (Federal Alliance of Land Grants) invaded a portion of the Kit Carson National Forest in northern New Mexico, demanding a return of lands taken away by American courts. The Alianza movement was unsuccessful and faded away by the 1970s. In Texas, José Angel Gutiérrez helped found La Raza Unida as a separate political party for Chicanos (in 1970).

California was perhaps the most visible center of Chicano activism during the 1960s. High school and college students led a fight for equal rights and opportunities in the schools and demanded the inclusion of Mexican American history, literature, and art, as well as the Spanish language in the curriculum. Demonstrations for such reforms began in East Los Angeles when high school students staged "blowouts" by walking out of their classes. This tactic inspired a National Chicano walkout in 1969 and encouraged students at the University of California-Berkeley to stage a sit-in of the president's office. Demand for educational reform by Chicano high school and college students met with limited success, but it did help encourage the passage in 1968 of the Bilingual Education Act, which reversed state laws that prohibited teaching classes in languages other than English. The Chicano movement for educational reform also inspired the creation of Chicano/Mexican American studies courses, and it helped foster a greater awareness of Mexican American culture. At a 1969 conference at the University of California-Santa Barbara, Chicano students from various campuses joined together to create the Movimiento Estudiantil Chicano de Aztlán (MECHA), a Chicano student group that remains active on many college and high school campuses throughout the United States.

The Chicano movement in California also included a fight for the rights of farmworkers and their families, who endured harsh working and living conditions and lived in poverty. In 1962, César Chávez began organizing farmworkers into what eventually became the United Farm Workers (UFW). UFW activism focused on nonviolence, and Chávez led several hunger strikes to draw attention to the demands of farmworkers. The most visible and successful of UFW's activities was a national boycott of California table grapes, which was used to demand guaranteed wages, better working conditions (including protection against pesticides), and formal contracts between growers and farmwork-

ers. The boycott began in 1967 and ended in 1970 with California growers conceding most of the farmworkers' demands (negotiating contracts with the UFW/AFL-CIO).

The California Chicano movement also spawned the most militant group of the Chicano movement—the Brown Berets. Established in East Lost Angeles in 1967, the Brown Berets were modeled on the Black Panthers (a militant branch of the African American civil rights movement). The Brown Berets were initially seen as a humanitarian group that pushed for better housing, employment opportunities, and social services for Mexican Americans. However, they soon gained a reputation for violence, and Brown Berets were linked to incidents of arson, rioting, and confrontations with police.

Mexican American women, or Chicanas, were visible participants in the Chicano movement. Even before the 1960s, Chicanas participated in local organizations, sometimes in leadership roles. Many working Chicanas experienced a double discrimination based on their ethnicity and gender and several became active in unions. During the 1960s and 1970s, Chicanas continued and expanded their activism. Mexican American women were among the founders of La Raza Unida and Dolores Huerta, perhaps the most visible Chicana during the Chicano movement, served as vice-president of the UFW. As the movement entered the 1970s, Chicanas began to organize among themselves, calling attention to their subordinate status and championing women's issues, such as child welfare and reproductive freedom. Women also assumed leadership positions in MECHA and other student organizations.

. The last two decades of the twentieth century have witnessed the continued growth of the Mexican American population of the United States, which is now approaching 20 million. Although the momentum of the earlier Chicano movement has faded somewhat, Chicanas/Chicanos remain active, and many of the earlier Chicano groups continue their work of empowering Mexican Americans. By the end of the twentieth century, Chicanos were emerging as a particularly important political group, with more members registering to vote, running for public office, and being appointed to political posts. At the same time, lessening official support for bilingual education, affirmative action, and other measures threatened to undermine some of the gains of the 1960s and 1970s. At the start of the new millennium, Chicanos/ Chicanas continued to face the familiar problem of discrimination at the same time that their numbers and their political and economic clout were growing.

—SBP

See also: *Bracero* Program; Chávez, César; League of United Latin American Citizens (LULAC).
References:
Acuña, Rodolfo. *Occupied America: A History of Chicanos.* 3d ed. New York: Harper and Row, 1988.
Chávez, John R. *The Lost Land: The Chicano Image of the Southwest.* Albuquerque: University of New Mexico Press, 1984.
Maciel, David R., and Isidro D. Ortiz, eds. *Chicanas/Chicanos at the Crossroads: Social, Economic, and Political Change.* Tucson: University of Arizona Press, 1996.
Weber, David J., ed. *Foreigners in Their Native Land: Historical Roots of the Mexican Americans.* Albuquerque: University of New Mexico Press, 1973.

Chihuahua (State)

Located in northern Mexico and sharing an extensive border with the United States, Chihuahua is Mexico's largest state. It contains several major urban centers, including Ciudad Juárez (across the border from El Paso, Texas), Parral, Delicias, and Chihuahua City (the capital). During much of the colonial period and well into the nineteenth century, Chihuahua was a volatile Indian frontier, and the region struggled to maintain its population and its economy amid Indian rebellions and raids. During the Mexican Revolution, the state was a major theater of conflict, and it produced several important Revolutionary figures, including Pancho Villa. Chihuahua experienced impressive economic growth during the latter part of the twentieth century, but it also experienced the growth of the drug trade and increasing environmental problems, especially along the northern border.

The rich silver mines of Zacatecas, which drew Spaniards north from central Mexico, encouraged settlement of this remote frontier. Chihuahua became part of the larger province of Nueva Vizcaya, and the development of mining was accompanied by the growth of several Spanish towns. Silver discoveries helped make Parral Chihuahua's most important Spanish settlement during the seventeenth century, and for a time it was the political seat of Nueva Vizcaya. Chihuahua City, also established as a result of mining strikes, was founded in 1709. This urban center occupied a privileged position on the Camino Real, which linked central Mexico with remote New Mexico. Chihuahua City became a commercial center, through which a variety of goods passed between Santa Fe, New Mexico, and central Mexico.

While the Spaniards' northward advance was encouraged by mining and facilitated by the Camino Real, it was hampered by Indian resistance. Chihuahua's native groups, including the Tarahumaras, Conchos, and Tepehuanes, often responded to the Spanish presence and Spanish demands for labor with raids and rebellions. By the eighteenth century, nomadic Apache Indians to the north were adding to the region's unrest. The Spaniards answered the challenges of native groups with the establishment of *presidios,* or military outposts (including El Paso), and during the late colonial period they further increased their military presence on the northern frontier. It was a policy of negotiation and gifts (including alcohol and firearms), however, that brought the Spaniards a brief era of peace. After Mexican independence, the gifts stopped, and Apache raids resumed.

Chihuahua remained loyal to the Spanish Crown during Mexico's independence era.

Francisco "Pancho" Villa and followers pass his home in Chihuahua, Mexico, 1914. (Library of Congress)

Indeed, Miguel Hidalgo and other leaders of the early anti-Spanish insurgency were tried and executed here. In 1824, three years after Mexico achieved independence from Spain, Chihuahua became a state. Initially, it enjoyed a prosperity that was created largely by the region's silver, copper, and gold mines. Chihuahua also maintained its commercial links with Santa Fe and with the rapidly expanding United States. The decades after independence were far from peaceful, however. Indian raids resumed in the 1830s and attempts to subdue the Apaches dominated much of the nineteenth century. The Mexican War added to the volatile situation: American troops established themselves in El Paso, and they occupied Chihuahua City twice.

After the war, Chihuahua became a border state, and with the subsequent Gadsden Purchase of 1853, it lost a sizeable slice of territory to the United States. The drawing of the international border simply exacerbated the problem of Indian raids since Indians could now retreat to the United States after striking on the Mexican side of the line. The unrest of the Mexican War and especially the persistence of nomadic raiders, devastated Chihuahua's economy and hampered the growth of its population.

It was in this context that Luis Terrazas, the dominant figure of nineteenth-century Chihuahua, emerged. A successful entrepreneur who gradually amassed a fortune in agriculture, cattle ranching, banking, industry, and commerce, Terrazas linked his business interests and his family (through strategic marriages) to the state's other wealthy groups. His economic success paralleled his accomplishments in the political arena. Terrazas served as the state's governor from 1861 to 1873 and from 1880 to 1884. In 1903 his son-in-law Enrique Creel became governor, assuring the continuation of Terrazas's political influence.

Terrazas participated in Chihuahua's final offensive against the Apaches (which was aided by an 1882 treaty with the United States that allowed transborder pursuit of raiders), even as he presided over the growth of the state's economy and his own personal fortune. Although Terrazas resisted both of Porfirio Díaz's rebellions against the central government, he remained a political force and commanded Díaz's respect. The development, which Terrazas and his fellow oligarchs encouraged, however, brought uneven prosperity to Chihuahua. As wealth became increasingly concentrated in the hands of a small group of Mexicans and foreign investors, civil unrest among peasants, miners, and smallholders grew. Protests and rebellions were brutally suppressed, encouraging popular resentment of Terrazas and of President Porfirio Díaz. That resentment would make Chihuahua a center of the Mexican Revolution and would help produce one of the Revolution's most visible figures: Francisco "Pancho" Villa.

Workers, members of the middle class, and enemies of the Terrazas clan all joined in Francisco Madero's revolt against Díaz in 1910–1911. Chihuahua was a pivotal state in this phase of the Revolution and the 1911 rebel capture of Ciudad Júarez (across the border from El Paso) sealed Díaz's fate and compelled his resignation. Abraham González, Pascual Orozco, and Pancho Villa all joined Madero's revolt, and in the aftermath of Madero's victory, González became the state's governor. González faced continuing unrest, however. In 1912 Pascual Orozco rebelled against Madero, embracing a plan of significant reforms with a focus on workers' rights. Villa, who remained loyal to Madero, aided in the suppression of the Orozco rebellion.

In 1913, with Madero's overthrow and death, Abraham González was captured and killed. Villa joined Venustiano Carranza's Constitutionalist movement and he assembled an army, which became known as the Division of the North. In December 1913 Villa captured Chihuahua City and declared himself gover-

nor. He ordered the confiscation of the properties of Chihuahua's elites. Among those affected was Luis Terrazas who, at the age of 85, fled to El Paso. In 1914, Villa broke with Carranza and joined Morelos rebel Emiliano Zapata in challenging Carranza's leadership of the Revolution. Villa controlled much of Chihuahua until the end of 1915, when Constitutionalist troops assumed control. Among the beneficiaries of Carranza's victory in Chihuahua was Luis Terrazas, who recovered his properties after Carranza nullified Villa's previous confiscations.

Villa remained a problem for Carranza, who became Mexico's leader and who received the recognition of the United States. In 1916, Villa and his followers retaliated with raids on Santa Isabel, Chihuahua, and Columbus, New Mexico. These raids, which resulted in several American deaths, precipitated the Pershing Expedition, an unsuccessful attempt by American soldiers to capture Villa. Villa remained belligerent until Carranza's own overthrow and death in 1920, when he withdrew to his hacienda. In 1923 Villa was assassinated, the same year that his enemy, Luis Terrazas, died.

The 1920s and 1930s were marked by a struggle between Chihuahua's elites and popular classes and by the attempts of the central government to control the state's leaders. Chihuahua's wealthier residents, many of whom had (like Terrazas) gone into exile during the Revolution, returned. They were joined by a new group of elites emerging from the Revolution and equally determined to protect their wealth and privilege. While Chihuahua's oligarchs, both old and new, succeeded for a time in resisting Revolutionary reforms and monopolizing local power, they could no long ignore the popular voices that had emerged during the Revolution. During the 1930s, President Lázaro Cárdenas pursued land and labor reforms, and he organized workers and *campesinos* (peasants) as a counterweight to Chihuahua's conservative elites. By 1940, Chihuahua's oligarchs could no longer operate autonomously. State leaders were now compelled to look to the national government and to Mexico's official party (eventually known as the PRI) for support and legitimacy.

By the middle of the twentieth century, Chihuahua's economy was enjoying a new era of growth. Both agriculture and the cattle industry expanded, and forestry became an important part of the local economy. After World War II, the state also became part of the international drug trade, smuggling marijuana, heroin, and cocaine to the U.S. market. Despite earlier reforms that had favored Chihuahua's *campesinos,* agrarian tensions remained. Beginning in the 1960s, *campesinos* participated in land invasions, challenging the special protections given to the state's large cattle ranchers and owners of forest lands. President Luis Echeverría (1970–1976) sought to quiet this unrest by carving out Mexico's largest *ejido* (community land grant) in Chihuahua.

The last decades of the twentieth century brought increased urbanization and industrial growth to Chihuahua. The population became concentrated in several cities, including the capital, Parral, and Ciudad Juárez. The growth of the border city of Ciudad Juárez was particularly remarkable. Much of that expansion accompanied the growth of the *maquiladora* industry, which began in the 1960s. Under special arrangement with the Mexican government, foreign (mostly U.S.) companies built assembly plants along Mexico's northern border. These plants took advantage of low-cost labor to assemble goods for reexport.

In addition to population growth, the state's *maquiladora* industry brought some significant changes. Increasing numbers of women (who could be hired for less than men) joined the *maquila* workforce. Border industry also brought environmental problems, as emissions from *maquila* plants and the use of toxic industrial chemicals in those plants polluted air and water on both sides of the international line. The incidence of cancer and birth defects linked to environmental toxins grew at an alarming rate in the Ciudad Juárez-El Paso area. Thus, while the *maquiladora* industry brought new jobs and growth to Chihuahua, it also bequeathed serious problems to Chihuahuans as the twenty-first century began.

—*SBP*

See also: Drug Trafficking; *Maquiladora* Industry; Pershing Expedition; Revolution of 1910; Villa, Francisco "Pancho."

References:

Aboites, Luis. *Breve historia de Chihuahua.* Mexico City: El Colegio de Mexico, 1994.

Altamirano, Graziella, and Guadalupe Villa. *Chihuaha: Una historia compartida, 1824–1921.* Mexico City: Instituto de Investigaciones Dr. José María Luis Mora, 1988.

Beezley, William H. *Insurgent Governor: Abraham González and the Mexican Revolution in Chihuahua.* Lincoln: University of Nebraska Press, 1973.

Katz, Friedrich. *The Life and Times of Pancho Villa.* Palo Alto, CA: Stanford University Press, 1998.

Wasserman, Mark. *Capitalists, Caciques, and Revolution: The Native Elite and Foreign Enterprise in Chihuahua, Mexico, 1854–1911.* Chapel Hill: University of North Carolina Press, 1984.

———. *Persistent Oligarchs: Elites and Politics in Chihuahua, Mexico, 1910–1940.* Durham, NC: Duke University Press, 1993.

Official state web site: http://www.chihuahua.gob.mx

Científicos

The term *científicos* (the "scientific ones") was applied to a group of advisors and technocrats who were prominent in the administration of Mexico's long-serving President Porfirio Díaz (1877–1880, 1884–1911). The *científicos* were most influential in the closing years of Díaz's rule.

The *científicos* received their name because of their belief in the positivist doctrines of the French intellectual Auguste Comte. Supporters of positivism wanted to move Mexico into the "scientific stage" of development through the application of scientific methods to society's institutions and problems. The popularization of positivist thinking began in the late 1860s with Gabino Barreda, founder of the National Preparatory School in Mexico City, which would produce many of Mexico's future leaders. Positivist thinking also converged with social Darwinism, which was increasingly popular in the late nineteenth century both in Latin America and in the United States.

The *cientfícos* believed that the scientific approach must be applied to politics and that technocrats should be more important than politicians in determining Mexico's future. They took on the difficult task of trying to reconcile traditional liberal views on political freedom with traditional conservative demands for political order and stability. The *cientfícos* did not envision any early involvement in political decision making by Mexico's mostly illiterate masses. Mexico would still be ruled by an elite group; but, for the *cientfícos,* it would be a technocratic elite in tune with the scientific thinking of the day.

The growth of *cientfíco* influence was connected with two important figures: Justo Sierra and Manuel Romero Rubio. Sierra was rapidly becoming one of Mexico's leading intellectuals and was a professor at the National Preparatory School. Sierra spread positivist thinking to educated urban groups through his publications in a number of Mexico City newspapers, especially *La Libertad.* Manuel Romero Rubio was the father-in-law of President Díaz as well as one of the president's most-trusted advisors. Sierra and Romero Rubio helped to transform *cientfíco* thinking into a philosophical rationale for Díaz's emerging policies of centralization, political conciliation, and economic development.

The *cientfícos* saw in Díaz's continuation in office the best hope of achieving their vision of a "scientific" Mexico. In 1892 they formed a political group, the Liberal Union, to promote Díaz's reelection that year. In addition to Díaz's reelection, the group also called for the creation of the position of vice-president and an independent judiciary. These latter proposals represented the ongoing efforts by the *cientfícos* to harmonize political stability

with political freedom. Díaz and some of his non-*cientfíco* supporters rejected these suggestions. It was in the debate over these reforms that the government-subsidized newspaper, *El Siglo XIX,* employed the term *cientfícos* to describe Sierra and his group in an unfavorable way.

The *cientfícos* hoped that the political group they created in 1892 would evolve into a national political party that could reshape Mexico's political system. Instead, it became one more interest group contending for influence with the president and hoping to provide the successor to the aging Díaz. The principal rival group to the *cientfícos* was one identified with General Bernardo Reyes, a prominent military figure and an important promoter of the economic development of Monterrey. As Díaz became increasingly nervous about the influence of Reyes, he moved to offset it by giving a greater role to those identified with the *cientfícos.* While Sierra continued to be one of the most prominent of the *cientfícos,* José Yves Limantour, Díaz's minister of the treasury, was also a major figure. Limantour gained both national and international celebrity for balancing the Mexican budget and renegotiating the Mexican debt. Limantour played a leading role in many of the technocratic reforms of the era that embodied *cientfíco* thinking, ranging from improved drinking water for Mexico City to monetary stabilization.

The economic and financial policies favored by the *cientfícos* accounted for much of the political controversy at the time and much of the historical controversy later. These policies were aimed at benefiting the existing elites and had little if anything to offer the large majority of Mexicans, especially in rural areas. There was particularly strong criticism that *cientfíco* policies encouraged foreign—especially U.S.—penetration of the economy. The *cientfícos* defended their approach, claiming that Mexico lacked the financial, technological, and human resources needed for rapid development. They also worked to counterbalance the dominant role of U.S. investors in the economy by encouraging European investment. Limantour himself opposed the signing of a special commercial treaty with the United States. *Científico* financial and economic policies were also seen as self-serving. They promoted a skewed economic growth, benefiting primarily the elite groups, most notably the *científicos* themselves. Some of the *científicos* were also involved in the corruption associated with the development scheme being followed, manipulating the political and legal systems in exchange for payments from foreign investors.

In 1904 the *científicos* achieved a political reform they had been pursuing for some time: the creation of the office of vice-president. They even succeeded in having one of their own put into the position: Ramón Corral, Díaz's minister of the interior. The aging Díaz (74) finally agreed to the creation of the position as a means of maintaining political stability; his appointment of Corral, however, indicated that Díaz still was not prepared to designate his successor. Instead, the appointment demonstrated that Díaz was nevertheless following his longtime practice of playing one group or individual against another. Díaz retained his close ties to the *científicos* but took on as vice-president a member of the group whose prestige was considerably less than that of Limantour or Sierra.

The decline and collapse of *científico* influence paralleled that of the Díaz regime. In 1907 Mexico experienced a major financial crisis, which called into question the wisdom of *científico* development policies. The economic downturn likewise personally hurt the financial positions of individual *científicos*. The *científicos* also had championed centralization, which put them at odds with many local and regional leaders. The *científicos* were so closely identified with and connected to the Díaz regime that its decline and ultimate collapse in 1911 could not have left them unaffected. Some *científico* thinking even showed up in the first post-Revolution administration of Francisco Madero. This was not surprising since the Madero family originally had strong

ties to the *científico* group. General Victoriano Huerta's successful coup against the Madero government in February 1913 briefly revived *científico* hopes, but Huerta's forced resignation in 1914 brought a definitive end to the *científicos* as a major interest group in Mexican politics. Just as the role of the *científicos* provoked contemporary controversy, their role is still debated today by historians. Certainly, it is an oversimplification to equate *científico* policies with Díaz's policies. Díaz did not always follow the advice of the *científicos,* who constituted only one group vying for the attention and the confidence of the president. Likewise, the "Porfirian elite" was made up of more than just the *científicos,* who were the political and economic rivals of other elite groups within the Porfirian circle of supporters. Even the origin of the term *científico* demonstrated the complexity of the Porfirian political structure; it originated in the 1890s as a derisive term used by one group of Díaz's supporters against another group of his supporters. In the post–World War II era, the development policies pursued by supposedly Revolutionary governments led many critics to claim that a "neo-Porfiriato" was being presided over by "neo-científicos." This sentiment was reinforced by the rise to prominence of the technocratic presidents from 1976 to 2000: José López Portillo, Miguel de la Madrid, Carlos Salinas, and Ernesto Zedillo. The *científicos* ultimately foundered for the same reason that many reformers after the Revolution would. They tried to get close to the center of power to make changes, but in getting close they were ultimately co-opted by the very system they hoped to change.

Obsessed with the "cult of modernity," the *científicos* never succeeded in transcending or transforming the Porfirian system. They could impose a more modern style on traditional structures but could not deal with the internal contradictions this represented. Lacking mass or even military support, the *científicos* became the most visible apologists for a regime they knew needed changing.

—DMC

See also: Corruption; Díaz, Porfirio; Huerta,
Victoriano; López Portillo, José; Madero,
Francisco; Madrid (Hurtado), Miguel de la;
Monterrey Group; Salinas de Gortari, Carlos;
Zedillo Ponce de León, Ernesto.

References:
Hale, Charles A. *The Transformation of Liberalism in
Late Nineteenth-Century Mexico.* Princeton, NJ:
Princeton University Press, 1989.
Sierra, Justo. *The Political Evolution of the Mexican
People.* Austin: University of Texas Press, 1969.
Zea, Leopoldo. *Positivism in Mexico.* Austin:
University of Texas Press, 1974.

Cinema to 1930: The Silent Era

Mexico's ongoing love affair with movies
began early. On 6 August 1896, within
months of the Paris debut of the Lumière
brothers' new cinematograph, French promoters gave President Porfirio Diáz and his
entourage an extended private exhibition of
their new invention and received his hearty
endorsement. At a public screening a few days
later in downtown Mexico City, a mostly
elite audience—tickets for these first showings were quite expensive—responded with
similar enthusiasm. That initial excitement
was compounded in subsequent weeks by the
addition of new footage depicting the president strolling in Chapultepec Park and other
Mexico City scenes.

Nor did support decline when the Lumière empresarios left town a few months
later. In the capital, the opening of 22 theaters by the turn of the century (although
most were tent shows and relatively short-
lived) reflected continued public interest.
Moreover, intense competition resulted in
much lower ticket prices, which made
moviegoing accessible to nearly everyone.
The September 1910 centennial celebrations saw the opening of twenty-seven new
theaters in Mexico City, several with the capacity to seat over 500 viewers. The phenomenon was not confined to the capital.
Movie mania spread quickly throughout the
country as enterprising, mostly Mexican,
entrepreneurs opened theaters and tent

shows in provincial capitals such as Puebla,
Mérida, Guanajuato, and Guadalajara with
an occasional excursion into more remote
rural communities.

Novelty certainly explains much of cinema's appeal for turn-of-the-century Mexicans. But it was more than just new, it was
also modern. Of all the modern technologies in an era committed (at least by official
slogans) to "order and progress," cinema was
one of the few accessible to and appreciated
by Mexicans from all walks of life: rich and
poor, urban and rural, young and old. Cars
and bicycles were strictly for elite consumption; electric trolleys were mocked in the
popular press as pedestrian-killing machines; and the rapid expansion of trains and
telegraphs had thrown peasants off their
lands and encouraged the national government to meddle in local affairs. But, with
the exception of an occasional priest offended by French films of women in tights
and government officials worried about possible threats to public order, movies provided a much-needed diversion in an unsettled and unsettling world. In Mexico, as
elsewhere, cinema was modern entertainment for modern times.

If novelty and modernity were not enough,
cinema entrepreneurs found local applica-
tions for the new technology that further increased its considerable appeal. The Lumière
empresarios had stroked the presidential ego,
local vanity, and national pride by screening
clips of the president, his family, and Mexico
City attractions. There were other, increasingly compelling, reasons to shoot new films
in Mexico. Early movies were quite short,
often under three minutes long, and public
screenings typically included at least eight
films. Under these circumstances, an avid
moviegoer could tire rather quickly of the
limited stock of imported movies. So,
spurred by local interest and a shortage of
imported films, Mexican promoters became
avid directors and producers despite the considerable expense of cameras and projectors
and the need to have their film processed in

France. Aside from the ubiquitous presidential clips and a rare disaster like the 1905 Guanajuato flood, early films tended to favor scenes from everyday life—weddings, bullfights, rodeos, dances, weekend promenades, religious processions, and public festivals—with a special fondness for the rural settings and "colonial" customs of Mexico before the onslaught of modernity. Thanks to these early movies, Mexican audiences could begin to envision a national culture grounded in nostalgia for an idyllic past most of their great grandparents never experienced. After 1906, the development of extensive distribution networks, and even a pair of fledgling Mexico City studios, guaranteed that Mexicans, even in the nation's remotest corners, could share in the lives of their compatriots and revel in their collective past. For a country as diverse as Mexico, the development and spread of a national cinematic identity had truly revolutionary potential.

Not that early Mexican cinematographers recognized the radical possibilities inherent in a popular medium that allowed audiences so much interpretive freedom. Most of the important early documentaries depicted the glories of late-Porfirian public spectacles: Enrique Rosas and Salvador Toscano's 1906 chronicles of a presidential visit to Yucatán, the Alva brothers' 1909 interview between Porfirio Díaz and American President William Howard Taft, extensive coverage of the September 1910 centennial. Still, filmmakers could hardly control how audiences received these images of opulence in a country on the brink of revolution. The 1910 centennial, in particular, was widely regarded as excessive and insensitive in light of Mexico's growing social inequalities. Once the Revolution started, however, filmmakers played an instrumental role in bringing it home to eager audiences throughout Mexico. Films with titles like *The Assault and Taking of Ciudad Juárez, Triumphal Journey of Revolutionary Chief Francisco Madero from Ciudad Juárez to Mexico City, The Oroquista Rebellion or Glorious Deeds of the National Army,* and *Revolution in Veracruz*

provided national audiences with news and moving images (literally and figuratively) of Revolutionary chiefs, battles, devastation, and death.

Alert to the possibilities of the new medium, most Revolutionary chiefs recruited in-house cinematographers to record their trials, tribulations, and triumphs. Pancho Villa's entourage alone included ten North American filmmakers. These propaganda efforts, however, did not always turn out as planned. In a partisan era, audiences took interpretations into their own hands even more than before. In his classic novel of the Mexican Revolution, *The Eagle and the Serpent,* Martín Luis Guzmán recounted an incident in which Villista soldiers shot their pistols at the film image of rival Revolutionary chief Venustiano Carranza and cheered the photogenic Villa as if the two men were stock characters in a classic melodrama. Some Mexicans eschewed Revolutionary rivalries altogether: one of the most popular films of the period, *General Don Porfirio Díaz in Paris,* reminded nostalgic viewers of "the exceptional vigor of this great expatriate" (quoted in Paranaguá, *Mexican Cinema,* p. 71). Regardless of audience reception, extensive cinematic coverage of the Revolution gave some coherence to the extremely fragmented experiences of most participants. If the Revolution brought Mexicans together as a nation for the first time, as novelist Carlos Fuentes insists, then cinema played an indispensable role in that process.

As Revolutionary violence subsided, Mexican producers and directors like Mimí Derba sought to develop a national cinema that would "illustrate the real customs of the Mexican people . . . stimulate the public and orient it toward the social practices required by our civilization" (quoted in Paranaguá, *Mexican Cinema,* p. 72). Noble intentions aside, most of these early efforts merely transposed Italian-style melodramas to Mexico settings. Even the film adaptation of Mexican novelist Federico Gamboa's *Santa* (1918), the story of a young woman's rape, fall into prostitution, and a tragic death, reflected the turn-of-the-century cosmopolitan nationalism—French novelist Émile Zola's *Nana* was Gamboa's obvious inspiration—of its Porfirian author rather than any identifiably Mexican style. The notable exception was Enrique Rosas's film, *El automóvil gris* (The Grey Car, 1919), which recounted the true story of a notorious Mexico City gang that had used a gray car, stolen military uniforms, and official complicity to rob wealthy residents under the cover of Revolutionary turmoil. In the style of earlier documentaries, the movie was shot on location and included actual footage of gang members' executions. Rosas's willingness to modify events into episodes and other innovations, such as tracking shots, fades, and zooms, adapted from North American filmmakers demonstrated a growing awareness of cinema's dramatic requirements. Still, *El automóvil gris* had little success outside Mexico and marked the beginning of a serious decline in Mexican efforts to establish a national cinema. As early as 1919, North American film distributors like Universal and Fox had opened offices in Mexico City. Their films would dominate the Mexican market until the end of the silent era. Between 1920 and 1930, Hollywood contributed nearly 80 percent of the films shown in Mexico City; Mexican producers managed only 6.5 percent (Berg, *Cinema of Solitude,* p. 13).

—*RMB*

See also: Díaz, Porfirio; Novel of the Revolution; Revolution of 1910.

References:

Berg, Charles Ramírez. *Cinema of Solitude: A Critical Study of Mexican Film, 1967–1983.* Austin: University of Texas Press, 1992.

Herschfield, Joanne, and David R. Maciel, eds. *Mexico's Cinema: A Century of Film and Filmmakers.* Wilmington, DE: Scholarly Resources, 1999.

King, John. *Magic Reels: A History of Cinema in Latin America.* New York: Verso, 2000.

Mora, Carl J. *Mexican Cinema: Reflections of a Society, 1896–1980.* Berkeley: University of California Press, 1982.

Noriega, Chon A., and Steven Ricci, eds. *The Mexican Cinema Project.* Los Angeles: UCLA Film and Television Archive, 1994.

Paranaguá, Paulo Antonio, ed. *Mexican Cinema,* Trans. Ana M. López. London: British Film Institute / IMCINE, 1995.

Cinema from 1930 to 1960: The Golden Age

Throughout the 1920s, Hollywood productions dominated Mexican markets. The introduction of talkies (movies with sound) in the late 1920s made North American control of Mexican cinema more difficult. Concerned about losing lucrative markets south of the border, Hollywood responded by producing movies in Spanish for Latin American audiences, especially in Mexico. Most of these films, however, were box-office flops. Mexican producers, directors, actors, and actresses—many of them trained in Hollywood—stepped in to fill the void. A successful 1931 sound remake of Gamboa's *Santa,* starring American-trained Lupita Tovar and Donald Reed (Ernesto Guillén), with songs by Augustín Lara, Mexico's most popular songwriter, inaugurated a resurgence in Mexican cinema.

The timing was good. Internationally renowned Soviet director Sergei Eisenstein, hard at work on his never-to-be-completed visionary masterpiece *¡Que viva México!,* provided inspiration and stylistic innovations that encouraged a generation of Mexican directors to move beyond hackneyed Hollywood formulas. The opening of major studios in Mexico City supplied much needed infrastructure; the Mexican government under populist president Lázaro Cárdenas provided moral support, protectionist polices, and an occasional subsidy.

This conjunction of creative, practical, and political forces produced a series of important movies that laid the groundwork for an internationally recognized Mexican cinema and foreshadowed the important themes of the "golden age" that followed. Director Fernando de Fuentes's revolutionary trilogy, *El prisionero trece* (Prisoner 13, 1933), *El compadre Mendoza* (Compadre Mendoza, 1933), and ¡*Vámonos con Pancho Villa!* (Let's Go with Pancho Villa!, 1935) explored the dramatic possibilities of the Revolution, especially the heroism of ordinary soldiers in the face of tragic betrayals. (It also included footage of Villa's assassination so bloody that the moralistic Cárdenas asked him to take it out.) Carlos Novarro's *Janitzio* (1934) condemned the abuse of Mexico's indigenous peoples, in this case a fisherman played by future director Emilio "El Indio" Fernández, whose own films would further develop the *indigenista* (Indianist) genre. Eager to redeem Mexico's oppressed Indians, the Cárdenas government got into the act with subsidies for *Redes* (Nets, 1934), another film about abused Indian fishermen but with an activist twist: this time they struggle to form a union to counter exploitation. On a less overtly political note, several directors, including Eisenstein protégé Arcady Boytler (*La mujer del puerto,* The Woman of the Port, 1935) and Mexico's first female director of sound movies, Adela Sequeyro (*La mujer de nadie,* Nobody's Woman, 1937), produced *caberateras* (cabaret-brothel melodramas) that chronicled the tragic fates of loose women denied the protection of male-dominated family and social structures.

None of these budding genres could begin to rival the soaring popularity of the *comedia ranchera* (Mexico's version of the singing cowboy films of Roy Rogers) that followed the 1936 release of Fernando de Fuentes's *Allá en el Rancho Grande* (Over on the Big Ranch). De Fuentes's film about traditional male honor and female virtue on a "typical" hacienda struck a responsive chord throughout Mexico and Latin America. Delighted investors promptly funded a host of imitators and Mexican cinema was on its way (with some help from Hollywood distributors like United Artists) to becoming the world's most important producer of Spanish-language films.

The advent of World War II (1940–1945) played a crucial role in the ascendancy of Mexican cinema. Mexico's special relationship with the United States—based on politi-cal alliance, price controls for strategic metals, access to Mexican labor, and even an Air Force squadron in the Philippines—translated into access to film stock, and Hollywood's logistical and technical support, including the joint venture that produced a state-of-the-art film studio, Estudios Churubusco. Combined with an endless procession of Hollywood war movies of little interest to most Latin Americans and the success of *comedia ranchera,* support from the United States provided Mexican cinema a huge comparative advantage over hemispheric rivals like neutral Argentina. Mexican producers responded with pro-Allied films like *Espionaje en el golfo* (Espionage in the Gulf, 1942).

At the same time, the sea change in Mexican politics from the populist nationalism of the Cárdenas administration to the probusiness, pro-U.S. policies of subsequent administrations meant increased government support for commercial (rather than Revolutionary) cinema. The creation of a film bank (1942) supplied Mexican producers with an important source of credit, the National Film Industry Council (1943) provided promotion and lobbying efforts, and the Mexican Academy of Cinematographic Arts and Sciences (1945) began presenting Ariel awards (Mexico's version of the Oscar) to highlight the industry's achievements. The result was a "Golden Age" of Mexican cinema that lasted from the late 1930s until the reassertion of Hollywood dominance in the late 1950s. During this period, Mexican film production soared from 29 films in 1940 to a peak of 125 in 1950!

This dramatic increase in film production gave Mexican cinematographers ample opportunity to further develop earlier genres and, in the process, to play an even greater role in forging a national cinematic identity. Instant classics like Joselito Rodríguez's ¡*Ay Jalisco, no te rajes!* (Oh Jalisco, Don't Back Down!, 1941) and Emilio Fernández's *Flor Silvestre* (Wild Flower, 1943) guaranteed the continued success of the *comedia ranchera.* So did its social conservatism. An antimodern message in a modern medium, the *comedia ranchera*'s nostalgic portrayal of honorable *charros* (cowboys) and virtuous women, even its decidedly un-Revolutionary representation of Mexico as a land of unquestioned social divisions, patriarchy, and machismo (aggressive male posturing) made it the Golden Age's dominant genre and a potent source of gender stereotypes that would profoundly impact subsequent generations of Mexican men and women. Innovations like the use of technicolor in de Fuentes's *Así se quiere en Jalisco* (That's How They Love in Jalisco, 1942) further enhanced *comedia ranchera*'s prestige and helped wrap its reactionary values in a modern cloak.

Traditional morality also permeated other popular genres. In the conservative political climate of the 1940s and 1950s, family dramas proved a huge hit, especially following the success of *Cuando los hijos se van* (When the Children Leave, 1941). This unabashedly sentimental story of a father's doubts about and a mother's unwavering love for a wayward son would inspire two remakes (1957, 1969) and a 1980s television soap opera. The most popular Mexican film of the Golden Age, *Nosotros somos pobres* (We the Poor, 1947) took the family drama into a marginal urban neighborhood where the quiet Christian dignity of a poor carpenter transcended the many degradations of poverty and oppression. Even films like Emilio Fernández's *indigenista* classics, *María Candelaria* (1943) and *Río Escondido* (Hidden River, 1948), revolved around the virtue and religiosity of their female protagonists. On the other side of same coin, the typical *caberetera* related the betrayal of a beautiful young woman into the seedy urban world of nightclub singers, rumba dancers, and prostitutes. However, titles like *Las abandonadas* (The Abandoned Women, 1944), *Humo en los ojos* (Smoke in the Eyes, 1946), *Aventurera* (Adventurer, 1949), *Sensualidad* (Sensuality, 1950), and *No niego mi pasado* (I Don't Deny My Past, 1951) were more suggestive than didactic. Sumptu-

ously choreographed dances, heartrending *boleros* (love ballads) by singer-songwriters like Agustín Lara, and an endless parade of glamorous stars made the genre an unlikely vehicle for traditional moralism.

As in Hollywood, Mexican movie "stars" became international celebrities and ensured an audience even for mediocre pictures. Some like *comedia ranchera* star Jorge Negrete, Cuban-born *rumbera* (rumba dancer) Ninón Sevilla, and "Mexico's [self-sacrificing] mother" Sara García were closely associated with a single genre; others lent their considerable talents to several. Pedro Infante's huge success as a *charro* star carried over to family dramas like *Nostros los pobres* and the antiracist melodrama *Angelitos negros* (Little Black Angels, 1948). Director Emilio Fernández's favorite couple, Pedro Armendáriz and Dolores del Río, brought their on-screen chemistry to everything from the *indigenista* film (*María Candelaria*) to *comedia ranchera* (*Flor silvestre*) to *caberetera* (*Las abandonadas*). Armendáriz and del Río were just as versitile in their solo careers, which included extensive stints in Hollywood. No less impressive was María Félix, whose many different roles often tested genre boundaries as in de Fuentes's *Doña Bárbara* (1943), where she played a domineering Venezuelan hacienda owner and Fernándéz's *caberetera*, *Salon México* (1948), in which her character embodied the contradiction between a poor woman's virtue and the need to provide for her family.

The star system also carried over into comedies, one of the Golden Age's most important contributions to Mexican cinema. The films of great comedians like Cantinflas (Mario Moreno) and Tin-Tan (Germán Valdés) were box-office smashes throughout the Spanish-speaking world despite their very different styles and very Mexican brands of humor. Cantinflas's first hit *Ahí está el detalle* (There's the Hitch, 1940) laid the groundwork for a string of extraordinarily popular films that would stretch into the early 1980s! In this typical Cantinflas vehicle, his *pelado* (urban tramp) character, falsely accused of

El Médico de las Locas *poster, created in 1950 (Swim Ink/Corbis)*

murdering a gangster, talks his way out of trouble with a jumble of meaningless phrases that leaves policemen, lawyers, and judges hopelessly confused. This ability to manipulate language (one of the principal mechanisms of elite power over the lower classes), along with his comic appearance (scruffy mustache, sagging pants, undersized hat) and gentle mocking of middle-class respectability appealed to a broad spectrum of Mexican society perhaps because the underlying message of most Cantinflas films was humorous acceptance of social differences—a message rich and poor alike could embrace. Language "abuse," eccentric fashion, and social satire played a key role in the success of the Golden Age's other great comedian, Tin Tan. This time, however, it was the language of the northern border and its *pochismos* (idioms that mixed Spanish and English), flashy zoot suits, and criminal tendencies that gave Tin Tan's characters their *pachuco* (Latino youth gang) flair. In his most successful film, *El rey del barrio* (King of the Neighborhood, 1949), Tin Tan, as the head of a Mexico City pickpocket ring, sings, dances, and talks his way into respectability with a comedic style that one critic called "contemporary in attitude and as anachronistic as the neighborhoods that will soon be demolished, like the crooks in the pool halls and the corner stores" (quoted in Herschfield and Maciel, *Mexico's Cinema,* p. 76). Unfortunately, neither comedian could resist the temptations of success and as the Golden Age drew to a close their films would become increasingly formulaic and considerably less subversive.

It is hardly surprising given the conservative political climate in Mexico after 1940 that Golden Age cinema emphasized entertainment value and commercial success over social awareness and artistic integrity. That the best Golden Age films managed to entertain and instruct, make money and art, is testimony to the tremendous talent of directors like Fernando de Fuentes and Emilio Fernández and stars like Cantinflas, Tin Tan, Pedro Armendáriz, Dolores del Río, and María Félix.

In addition to their efforts, the Golden Age of Mexican cinema also produced its share of provocative, noncommercial films. Movies like Julio Bracho's *Distinto amanecer* (Different Dawn, 1943) about an honest young labor leader (Armendáriz) pursued by a corrupt governor's henchmen and his later adaptation of Martín Luis Guzmán's novel *La sombra del caudillo* (The Shadow of the Caudillo, 1960), which dramatized the vicious political in-fighting that surrounded the birth of the PRI (Mexico's ruling party from 1929 to 2000), continued the cinematic critique of the Mexican Revolution inaugurated during the 1930s by de Fuentes's *¡Vámanos con Pancho Villa!* Like its distinguished predecessor, *La sombra del caudillo* attracted the attention of government censors, who refused to permit the screening of an uncut version until 1990! Censors also blocked the release of Alejandro Galindo's *Las mojadas* (The Wetbacks, 1953) because its vivid portrayal of oppressed undocumented workers offended U.S. government sensibilities.

The Golden Age's most internationally renowned director was Luis Buñuel, an exile from fascist Spain who arrived in Mexico in 1946. During his Mexican sojourn (1946–1965), Buñuel would make twenty films, several on Mexican themes. Although he had attracted early critical attention with his surrealist classic, *Un chien andalou* (Andalucian Dog, 1928), it was the release of his third Mexican film, *Los olvidados* (The Forgotten Ones, 1950), for which he received the 1951 best director award at the prestigious Cannes Film Festival, that made Buñuel's international reputation. This grim portrayal of Mexico's street children as hopelessly mired in poverty, degradation, and violence put the lie to official promoters of the "Mexican miracle" of economic development. In *Los olvidados,* modernization brings not progress and prosperity but urban decay and social disintegration. Even the efforts of benevolent government officials—a Lázaro Cárdenas look-alike as a paternalistic reform school director—seem doomed to failure in the face of negligent mothers, drunken fathers, and abandoned children. Broad social commentary, however, took second place to psychodrama in subsequent films like *Ensayo de un crimen* (Rehearsal for a Crime, 1955), *Nazarín* (1958), *Viridiana* (1961), *El ángel exterminador* (The Exterminating Angel, 1962), and *Simón del desierto* (Simon of the Desert, 1965). Although Buñuel's reputation added luster to Mexican cinema in the declining years of the Golden Age, he had many admirers but few imitators.

By 1960 the Golden Age of Mexican cinema was over. From the mid-1940s onward, North American entrepreneur William O. Jenkins and his Mexican partners dominated film distribution networks and, by the late 1950s, Mexico City had only two major studios. Moreover, production costs had skyrocketed as union demands escalated and blockbusters like the international hit *Around the World in Eighty Days* (starring the ever-popular Cantinflas in his Hollywood debut) raised audience expectations for quality cinema. In response to these pressures, Mexican studios fell back on tried-and-true formulas or developed inexpensive serials. *Comedia ranchera* knock-offs, Cantinflas and Tin Tan comedies, and the *Santo* series with its professional wrestler superhero raked in considerable profits and entertained countless Mexicans. For highbrow critics, however, the paucity of "serious" Mexican films suggested that something was amiss. Regardless, by 1960, the vital energies of Golden Age cinema with its heady mixture of popular appeal and artistic pretension had given way to a commercial cinema more concerned with giving audiences what they wanted to see than with developing a national style or winning international awards.

—*RMB*

See also: Cantinflas; Cárdenas, Lázaro; Gender and Sexuality; *Mestizaje* and *Indigenismo*; Novel of the Revolution; Popular Music.

References:

Berg, Charles Ramírez. *Cinema of Solitude: A Critical Study of Mexican Film, 1967–1983.* Austin: University of Texas Press, 1992.

Fein, Seth. "Myths of Cultural Imperialism and Nationalism in Golden Age Mexican Cinema," in Gilbert Joseph, Anne Rubenstein, and Eric Zolov, eds., *Fragments of a Golden Age: The Politics of Culture in Mexico since 1940,* pp. 159–198. Durham, NC: Duke University Press, 2001.

Herschfield, Joanne. *Mexican Cinema / Mexican Woman, 1940–1950.* Tucson: University of Arizona Press, 1996.

Herschfield, Joanne, and David R. Maciel, eds., *Mexico's Cinema: A Century of Film and Filmmakers.* Wilmington, DE: Scholarly Resources, 1999.

King, John. *Magic Reels: A History of Cinema in Latin America.* New York: Verso, 2000.

Mora, Carl J. *Mexican Cinema: Reflections of a Society, 1896–1980.* Berkeley: University of California Press, 1982.

Noriega, Chon A., and Steven Ricci, eds. *The Mexican Cinema Project.* Los Angeles, CA: UCLA Film and Television Archive, 1994.

Paranaguá, Paulo Antonio, ed. *Mexican Cinema,* Trans. Ana M. López. London: British Film Institute / IMCINE, 1995.

Pilcher, Jeffrey M. *Cantinflas and the Chaos of Mexican Modernity.* Wilmington, DE: Scholarly Resources, 2001.

Rubenstein, Anne. "Bodies, Cities, Cinema: Pedro Infante's Death as Political Spectacle," in Gilbert Joseph, Anne Rubenstein, and Eric Zolov, eds. *Fragments of a Golden Age: The Politics of Culture in Mexico since 1940,* pp. 199–233. Durham, NC: Duke University Press, 2001.

———. "Mass Media and Popular Culture in the Postrevolutionary Era," in Michael C. Meyer and William H. Beezley, eds. *The Oxford History of Mexico,* pp. 637–670. New York: Oxford University Press, 2000.

Cinema after 1960: Contemporary Mexican Film

By 1960, the Golden Age of Mexican cinema, which had begun in the late 1930s, was over. During that era, the creative tension between experimental and commercial filmmaking (often by the same people) had produced some remarkable work and considerable international recognition. But after midcentury, rising production costs and increasingly exclusive industry policies discouraged innovation and rewarded complacency. As a result, Mexican films reverted to proven formulas like *comedia ranchera* (singing cowboy movies), comedic farces (a la Cantinflas), and melodramas; difficult directors like Emilio "El Indio" Fernández faced blacklisting by cautious producers. The artistic contributions of the period, serial movies, especially the still popular *Santo* series with its professional wrestler superhero and titles like *Santo versus el cerebro diabólico* (Santo versus the Diabolic Brain, 1961), and comedy-fantasies like Carlos Vela's *Cinco de chocolate y uno de fresa* (Five Chocolates and One Strawberry, 1967) with its super-spy heroine, Brenda, were designed to entertain rather than challenge or enlighten audiences. For highbrow critics, if not the general public, the 1960s represented (and still represent) one of the "dark ages" of Mexican cinema.

One problem was the officially sanctioned union, the Sindicato de Trabajadores de la Producción Cinematográfica, or STPC (Union of Cinematic Production Workers), which represented the directors, performers, and technicians involved in feature films. With strong ties to the official party (PRI) apparatus, the STPC kept production costs high, restricted membership, and controlled access to funding. Producers responded by shifting their operations to television production studios (controlled by a rival union) and even to other Latin American countries, but neither solution proved satisfactory. Another problem was the Banco Cinematográfico, a government-funded bank that lent money to Mexican film producers. While the bank did help prevent Hollywood control of Mexican cinema by providing capital and bringing distribution networks back under national control, it also solidified the power of well-connected Mexican producers with few incentives other than the bottom line. On top of these local difficulties, film production costs had skyrocketed: by 1967 the average Hollywood film cost $3 million to produce compared with a paltry $80,000 for a Mexican production (Berg, *Cinema of Solitude*, p. 38). The unavoidable difference in quality that resulted from this disparity placed Mexican producers at a considerable disadvantage, especially in the fierce competition for international markets. As Hollywood films increased their already substantial domination of international markets, the demand for Mexican films declined precipitously. From a 1958 high of 138 films, Mexican film production had fallen to 72 by 1970.

Although genre films and serials provided a steady source of income under increasingly adverse circumstances, even the STPC acknowledged that "we cannot aspire to improve the returns on Mexican films either in the domestic or foreign markets as long as their quality is not improved" (quoted in Martin, *New Latin American Cinema*, p. 38). To that end, the union sponsored an experimental film festival in 1965. Meanwhile, a new generation of aspiring filmmakers and critics, shut out of the national film industry and inspired by Brazil's *Cinema novo* and a resurgent Cuban cinema (in the aftermath of Fidel Castro's 1959 socialist revolution), had begun to agitate for a serious national cinema that would confront head-on the dramatic transformations of twentieth-century Mexican society rather than lulling the masses with mindless fantasies. Although these efforts met with some modest successes—a short-lived journal (*Nuevo cine*), an underfunded film archive, a cinema department at the National Autonomous University of Mexico— the outlook was still far from rosy.

The shocking massacre of student protestors at Tlatelolco in October 1968, however, prompted a major change in Mexican cinema. Desperate to undo the severe damage done to the government's image by the brutal massacre, the Luis Echeverría administration (1970–1976) attempted to co-opt young Mexican intellectuals by initiating new social programs and promoting the arts. To demonstrate his sincerity to a new generation of filmmakers, the president put his brother Rodolfo in charge of the Banco Cinematográfico. Under Rodolfo's guidance, the bank financed a new film school, created a national film archive, nationalized studios, and increased government control of film distribution. Even more important were the three state-run production companies that provided funding for serious films like Paul Leduc's Revolutionary saga *Reed: México insurgente* (Reed: Insurgent Mexico, 1971); Luis Alcoriza's attack on Mexico City's crass lower middle class, *Mecánica nacional* (National Mechanic, 1971); Arturo Ripstein's disturbing real-life tale of a family sequestered by an obsessive father, *El castillo de pureza* (Castle of Purity, 1972); Alejandro Galindo's complex retelling of the treason trial of Cortés's *mestizo* (mixed race) son, *El juicio de Martín Cortés* (The Trial of Martín Cortés, 1973); and Felipe Cazals's damning critique of the anticommunist paranoia that led to Tlatelolco, *Canoa* (1975). As promised, new filmmakers confronted contemporary issues head-on; class conflict, racism, machismo, and Cold War politics were all subjected to their critical gaze. To be sure, state producers insisted on occasional propaganda films—*Historia del PRI, Compañero presidente*—and commercial producers continued to churn out serials—*Santo versus la hija de Frankenstein* (Santo versus the Daughter of Frankenstein), *Bikini y Rock*—but the overall quality of Mexican cinema improved dramatically. Quantity, however, was in serious decline. As government subsidies for commercial films dried up, so did commercial production. In 1971, joint ventures which combined government and private capital had produced 63 (of 75) films; by 1976, there were none (of 42). Exclusive state production meanwhile had risen from 5 to 37 (Martin, ed., *New Latin American Cinema*, p. 50).

For incoming president José López Portillo (1976–1982), this decline coupled with a growing national debt provided sufficient grounds for a reevaluation of the government's role in film production. His sister Margarita, head of the newly formed Directorate of Radio, Television, and Cinema, reversed course, reviving the practice of joint sponsorship and favoring the production of films with commercial potential. As in the 1960s, directors who balked at serials and melodramas were blacklisted. As expected, quality declined while production and profits rebounded. The entrance of television giant *Televisa* into film production during this period helped expand the market for Mexican films in Latin America and the United States but did little to encourage innovative filmmaking. Sometimes, Mexican films transcended their limited aspirations as in India María comedies like *Sor Tequila* (Sister Tequila, 1974), which revolved around the adventures of a quick-witted Indian heroine whose antics subvert the cinematic stereotype of passive, self-sacrificing women. But, for the most part, the López Portillo years marked another low point for ambitious Mexican filmmakers.

In the long run, however, declining government support did not spell the end of serious Mexican cinema. Filmmakers continued to turn out internationally acclaimed films often with little or no government help. Some films, like Paul Leduc's imaginative, feminist biography of Frida Kahlo, *Frida: Naturaleza viva* (1983), and Nicolás Echeverría's magical realist interpretation of explorer Álvar Núñez Cabeza de Vaca's eight-year trek, *Cabeza de Vaca* (1990), achieved national and international critical acclaim for their innovative treatment of historical subjects. Others have transformed traditional genres: comedic farces, *comedia ranchera*, *cabareteras* (cabaret dramas), horror, and melodrama. In *Doña Herlinda y su hijo* (Doña Herlinda and Her Son, 1984), for example, director Jaime Humberto Hermosillo constructs a "typical" comedy of errors around a respectable upper-middle-class woman's efforts to marry off her gay son while concealing his affair with a young musician. Alfonso Arau takes similar liberties with the *comedia ranchera* in *Como agua para chocolate* (Like Water for Chocolate, 1991), which views ranch life from the kitchen through women's eyes and severely burns its singing *charro*. Likewise, *El mariachi* (1992), the debut work of Chicano filmmaker Robert Rodríguez, follows its hand-

A close-up from Like Water for Chocolate, *directed by Alfonso Arau (Howard Jacqueline / Corbis Sygma)*

some mariachi hero through the violent underworld of border drug trafficking. The female perspective dominates María Novaro's version of the *cabaretera, Danzón* (1991), the story of a telephone operator's search for her missing dance partner that becomes a journey of self-renewal. Guillermo del Toro's *Cronos* uses a vampire tale to critique the corporate greed. Also, Jorge Fons's sprawling multigenerational soap opera, *Callejón de los milagros* (Midaq Alley, 1995) subtly explores complex issues of male and female sexuality in modern Mexico City. The international recognition (and distribution) accorded these films suggests that Mexican cinema just might be poised for a second Golden Age.

Most recently, Mexican films have begun to attract attention for their innovative cinematography and startling subject matter. Alejandro González Iñárritu's *Amores perros* (Love's a Bitch, 2000), for example, is structured around a bloody car crash that brings together three distinct plot lines, all related somehow to dogs and their human owners. In *Amores perros*, the distinction between human and animal violence shrinks, while the visceral impact of that violence is heightened by the use of dogs. Alfonso Cuarón's *Y tu mamá también* (And Your Mother Too, 2001) uses the classic road trip format to explore the intersection of eroticism and death as the protagonists—two teenage boys and a sexy older woman—move through a Mexican countryside filled with narco-traffickers and grinding poverty on their way to a mythical beach community. The international success of both films despite the "handicap" of subtitles—usually fatal in the huge American market—suggests that the once almost moribund Mexican film industry has once more come into its own.

—*RMB*

See also: Cinema from 1930 to 1960: The Golden Age; Echeverría Alvarez, Luis; Kahlo, Frida; López Portillo, José; Popular Music; Tlatelolco Massacre.

References:

Berg, Charles Ramírez. *Cinema of Solitude: A Critical Study of Mexican Film, 1967–1983.* Austin: University of Texas Press, 1992.

Herschfield, Joanne, and David R. Maciel, eds. *Mexico's Cinema: A Century of Film and Filmmakers*. Wilmington, DE: Scholarly Resources, 1999.

King, John. *Magic Reels: A History of Cinema in Latin America*. New York: Verso, 2000.

Martin, Michael T., ed. *New Latin American Cinema*. Detroit, MI: Wayne State University Press, 1997.

Mora, Carl J. *Mexican Cinema: Reflections of a Society, 1896–1980*. Berkeley: University of California Press, 1982.

Noriega, Chon A., and Steven Ricci, eds. *The Mexican Cinema Project*. Los Angeles: UCLA Film and Television Archive, 1994.

Classical Music

Classical music has difficulty flourishing under adverse economic circumstances. The cost of training and paying musicians or building symphony halls and opera houses is often beyond the means of developing nations. Given its rather turbulent political history and uneven economic development, Mexico has done surprisingly well. Several Mexican composers and musicians have achieved international recognition and most major cities boast both orchestra and opera. Moreover, a promising crop of new composers, directors, and musicians—most notable in a spate of recent opera productions—suggests that classical music's future in Mexico is secure.

Mexico has a rich classical music tradition. During the colonial period, the Roman Catholic Church dominated musical practice and most classical music served a religious function. With some interesting exceptions, musical practices reflected European techniques and aesthetics. After independence in 1821, church music took a backseat to Italian and French opera and Spanish light musical theater, especially *zarzuela*. Touring companies such as Domenico Ronzani's Italian-Mexican Opera Company brought music to Mexico City and the major provincial cities on a regular basis and included international stars like Italian tenor Enrico Tamberlink and soprano Angela Peralta (1845–1883), "The Mexican Nightingale." Most Mexican opera composers favored a European style. Melesio Morales (1838–1908), perhaps the most successful Mexican opera composer, wrote works based on stories about Cleopatra and Romeo and Juliet with Italian librettos (scripts). One exception stands out: the 1871 premiere of Aniceto Ortega de Villar's (1823–1875) *Guatimotzín*, based on the tragic story of the last Aztec emperor Cuauhatémoc (the accepted modern spelling), captured, tortured, and executed by Hernán Cortés. Ortega's opera had a Spanish libretto, included some recognizable snippets of Mexican folk songs, and featured Angela Peralta (although Tamberlink played the title role).

As in Europe and the United States, the piano was crucial to the development of classical music in Mexico. Like their opera counterparts, Mexican piano composers generally wrote in the accepted European mode, as in the popular Austrian-style waltzes of Juventino Rosas (1868–1894). Some did hint at the beginnings of a national style. Tomás León (1826–1893) and Felipe Villanueva (1862–1893), for example, wrote several *danzas mexicanas* (Mexican dances). But even these "exceptional" composers were still wedded to a typical turn-of-the-century cosmopolitan nationalism that embellished a solidly European style with an occasional dash of Mexican spice. The presence of an occasional "eccentric" like Julián Carrillo (1875–1965), who was experimenting with microtones or *sonido trece* (sound thirteen) as early as 1895, only highlights the conservative approach of most of his colleagues.

Classical music's popularity, at least among Mexican elites, provided the impetus for the development of a musical infrastructure. In 1866, a private Mexico City Conservatory dedicated to the training of classical musicians opened its doors. Eleven years later, in one of Porfirio Díaz's first acts as president, it became the National Conservatory of Music. (Later directors would include some of the most important figures in Mexican classical music, such as Manuel Ponce,

Carlos Chávez, and Silvestre Revueltas.) To ensure the high quality of musical life in the short term, the Díaz administration also subsidized European educations for promising Mexican musicians. In 1900, to mark the turn of the new century, work was begun on an extravagant Palacio de Bellas Artes (Palace of Fine Arts) in downtown Mexico City, which was intended to serve as the centerpiece of Mexican musical culture. (Construction difficulties and the outbreak of the Revolution of 1910 delayed its opening until 1930.)

After the Revolution of 1910 (1910–1920), the development of a national style took on new importance as composers responded to the cultural nationalism of the era as embodied by the world-renowned Mexican muralist movement. Most still worked well within the Western classical music tradition but took much more seriously than their turn-of-the-century counterparts the need to Mexicanize that tradition in a meaningful way. The pivotal figure of this transition period was Manuel Ponce (1882–1948). The details of Ponce's career—piano studies in Europe, conducting the National Symphony (1917–1919), studying composition in Paris, directing the National Conservatory—were not so different from his contemporaries. Ponce, however, was a gifted and prolific music critic as well. Beginning with a 1913 public lecture on "Music and the Mexican Song," he became an enthusiastic advocate for Mexican folk and popular music, even establishing a chair in folk music at the National School of Music to help recover and preserve the nation's rich musical legacy. As Ponce's interests shifted from performance to composition, folk themes and popular songs began to appear with some regularity in works like the impressionistic *Chapultepec* (1934) and *Suite en estilo antiguo* (Suite in the Old Style, 1935). Several of his pieces, especially those written for Spanish guitar virtuoso Andrés Segovia, such as the *Concierto del Sur* (Concerto of the South, 1941), brought him an international reputation and enhanced

his stature at home. As a result, Ponce's intriguing blend of Mexican, Latin American, and international styles would exercise a profound influence on subsequent generations of Mexican composers.

One of the best-known composers of this new generation, Silvestre Revueltas (1899–1940), was, like Ponce, a great mixer of genres and styles. In scores for some of the most important films of Mexican cinema's "golden age"—*Redes* (Nets, 1935), *Vámanos con Pancho Villa* (Let's Go with Pancho Villa, 1936), *Los de abajo* (The Underdogs, 1940)—Revueltas freely combined Mexican popular music with a complex "international" orchestral style. Like Ponce, he often wrote on Latin American (rather than just Mexican) themes. His often-played *Sensemaya* (1938), a piece for voice and orchestra set to Afro-Cuban writer Nicolas Guillen's poem about killing a snake, is often compared to Igor Stravinsky's *Rite of Spring* for its rhythmic complexity and drive. A complex talent, Revueltas's range extended from humorous songs for orchestra like *Duo para pato y canario* (Duo for Duck and Canary, 1931) and *Ranas y el tecolote* (Frogs and the Owl, 1931) to radical politics as in his *Homenaje a García Lorca* (Homage to García Lorca, 1935), which was composed in honor of the martyred Spanish poet and playwright Federico García Lorca, whose republican sympathies (in the Spanish Civil War) he shared.

The most important figure of the postrevolutionary generation was Carlos Chávez (1899–1978). A student of Ponce, Chávez made his Mexico City debut at age thirteen, playing the piano music of French impressionist composer Claude Debussy. After the Revolution of 1910, encouraged by influential secretary of education José Vasconcelos, he embraced *indigenismo*—a movement that sought to revive and revalorize indigenous cultures—with Aztec ballets like *El fuego nuevo* (1921), *Los cuatro soles* (1925), and his masterwork *Sinfonia India* (1936), which included Aztec melodies and Indian percussion instruments. Chávez also integrated musical themes from Mexican folk culture as in his ambitious *Caballos de vapor* (Horses of Vapor, 1932), premiered in Philadelphia by conductor Leopold Stowkowski and featuring sets by muralist Diego Rivera. Like Revueltas, Chávez wrote political music that reflected the radical populism of the Lázaro Cárdenas administration in works such as *Llamadas: Sinfonía proletaria* (Calls: Proletarian Symphony, 1934) and *Chapultepec: Obertura Republicana* (Chapultepec: Republican Overture, 1935). These programmatic works attracted considerable attention, but it was the mature, more "international" style of later works like the Violin, Piano, Cello, and Trombone concertos and *Solis I-IV* that cemented his credentials as major twentieth-century composer. In addition to the music itself, his gift for music criticism (and advocacy) along with close friendships with prominent American and European composers, contributed to Chávez's growing international fame and produced an invitation to give the prestigious Harvard Norton lectures in 1958–1959. (These were later published as *Musical Thoughts* in 1960.) Also, Chávez was a tireless institution builder: he directed the National Conservatory (1928–1934), founded and directed the Mexican Symphony Orchestra (1928–1949), and developed the Musical Research Section of the National Institute of Fine Arts (1946–1952). Chávez's students, especially the celebrated "Group of Four," continued his efforts to create a national style with works like Daniel Ayala Pérez's (1906–1975) *U kayil chaac* (Mayan Rain Song, 1934); Salvador Contreras's (1910–1982) *Cantata a Juárez* (Cantata to Juárez, 1967); Blas Galindo Dimas's (1910–1993) *Sones de Mariachi* (1953); and José Pablo Moncayo's (1912–1958) *Huapango* (1941). At the same time, like their mentor, they often wrote in an international idiom that had little obvious connection to cultural nationalism.

This tension between cosmopolitanism and nationalism—less compelling than in the visual arts but apparent nonetheless in classical music—persisted and intensified in the next generation of Mexican musicians. Better training in modern musical idioms was one reason. In 1939, Spanish émigré Rodolfo Halftter (1900–1987) moved to Mexico after the defeat of the republican cause. An influential journalist and music theory teacher at the National Conservatory (1941–1981), Halftter gravitated toward the serialism and atonality of composer-theorist Arnold Schoenberg and many of his students followed suit. Some gained prominence primarily as musicians, such as Eduardo Mata (1943–1995), longtime conductor of the Dallas Symphony Orchestra and champion of twentieth-century music, and Alicia Urreta (1933–1987), whose piano performances of the avant-garde European, American, and Mexican repertoire introduced national audiences to the latest advances in modern classical music.

In the second half of the twentieth century, composers responded as well, often melding the musical nationalism of previous generations with the latest international styles. Manuel Enríquez (1926–1994) mixed pieces in the international style that sometimes included aleatory procedures (which allow the performer freedom to improvise certain sections within a piece) with more conventional "Mexican" pieces like *Obertura sobre temas de Juventino Rosas* (Overture on Themes of Juventino Rosas, 1989). Mario Kuri-Aldana (1931–) adapted the compositional techniques of French composer Olivier Messiaen to Native American musical forms and brought new compositional techniques to bear on Mexican popular music forms, such as *mariachi, bolero,* and *danzón.* Hector Quintanar (1936–) produced mixed media performances (although with few overtly Mexican traits) and promoted new music as the director of the National Conservatory's electronic music studio. Arturo Márquez (1950–) has written music for tape, video, and computer in the best avant-garde tradition along with extremely popular orchestral *danzones* that provide nostalgic glimpses of Mexico City's vibrant 1930s dance hall culture. Recent works by Gabriela Ortíz (1964–), such as *Altar de neon* (Neon Altar, 1995) and *Altar de muertos* (Altar of the Dead, 1996) written for the world-famous Kronos Quartet, reference Mexican spiritual practices in order to address complex issues of cultural hybridity with international implications.

Of special note is the resurgence of opera in the waning years of the twentieth century. Earlier attempts—Miguel Bernál Jiménez's (1910–1956) *Tata Vasco* (1941) on Bishop Vasco de Quiroga's 1541 arrival in Michoacán and José Pablo Moncayo's *La mulata de Córdoba* (1943) on a legendary colonial beauty—provided important precedents, but the difficulties and expense of staging operas along with a general preference for more "serious" symphonic music discouraged imitators. By the 1980s, the economic situation and musical tastes had changed. One result was an impressive string of major operas by Mexican composers. One reason for opera's growing popularity and prestige was its affinity for national subjects—less easily incorporated into instrumental music. And indeed most Mexican operas from the 1980s and 1990s were based on national or regional themes. For example: Carlos Jiménez Mabarek's (1916–1994) *La güerra Rodríguez* (1982) was a famous figure of Mexican independence; Mario Lavista's (1943–) *Aura* (1988) and Julio Estrada's (1943–) *Pedro Páramo* (1992) were based on important Mexican novels by Carlos Fuentes and Juan Rulfo; and Daniel Catán's (1949–) *Florencia en el Amazonas* (1996) echoed the magic realist style associated with Colombian novelist Gabriel García Márquez. The economic crash of 1995 discouraged further major productions—*Florencia en el Amazonas* premiered in Houston—but the wealth of creative talent revealed by the late twentieth-century opera boom suggests that classical music in Mexico is in good hands.

—RMB

See also: Art since 1950; Fuentes, Carlos; *Mestizaje* and *Indigenismo*; Muralist Movement; Popular Music; Rulfo, Juan.

References:

Béhague, Gerard. *Music in Latin America: An Introduction.* Englewood Cliffs, NJ: Prentice-Hall, 1979.

Chávez, Carlos. *Musical Thought.* Cambridge, MA: Harvard University Press, 1961.

Parker, Robert L. *Carlos Chávez: Mexico's Modern-day Orpheus.* Boston: Twayne, 1983.

Coahuila (State)

Mexico's third largest state, Coahuila is located in the northeastern section of the country and shares an extensive border with Texas. Officially known as "Coahuila de Zaragoza," it has its capital at Saltillo. Coahuila's history is that of a region that began as a sparsely populated frontier, experienced rapid economic growth during the nineteenth century, made a significant contribution to the Mexican Revolution, and by the end of the twentieth century was a dynamic, industrializing region.

Several nomadic Indian groups inhabited Coahuila prior to Spanish Conquest. The Spanish Crown laid formal claim to the area in 1577 with the founding of Saltillo. Tlaxcalan Indians from central Mexico aided in the early settlement of Coahuila, and missions and military colonies were created in an attempt to solidify the Spanish presence. Despite such efforts, however, Coahuila remained an isolated frontier. The problem of Indian raids, lack of a sedentary population that might serve as a labor force, and the region's aridity and limited economic potential ultimately discouraged effective settlement. Coahuila remained far from the center of colonial power and it emerged from the independence era with a strong tradition of political and economic autonomy.

Coahuila's status as a frontier region persisted for much of the nineteenth century. Until the Mexican War, it was part of the state of "Coahuila and Texas" with Saltillo serving as the administrative capital of this large territory. Based on agriculture and ranching, the local economy was supplemented by a healthy trade, both legal and illegal, with the United States. Several figures involved in this trade became part of a dynamic entrepreneurial class emerging in northeastern Mexico. Investing their newly earned fortunes in mining, agriculture, and other economic activities, these entrepreneurs helped begin Coahuila's economic transformation. The arrival of the railroad and the growth of foreign investment also helped define this transformation. On the eve of the Mexican Revolution, Coahuila was Mexico's most important source of coal, and the city of Torreón, in the southwestern corner of the state, was one of the country's premier industrial centers. The border zone had also assumed a new importance.

Increasing competition for Coahuila's resources, as well as elite political competition and resistance to political centralization by the regime of Porfirio Díaz (1876–1911) encouraged the growth of reform movements after 1900. Francisco I. Madero, a member of one of Coahuila's wealthiest families, became leader of one such movement and the figurehead of the Mexican Revolution of 1910. Coahuila also counts Venustiano Carranza, a member of another prominent local family, as a native son. Carranza served as the state's governor during the early phase of the Revolution and he called for the rebellion against President Victoriano Huerta in 1913. Using Coahuila as his base, Carranza established the so-called Constitutionalist movement. The victory of this Revolutionary faction propelled Carranza into Mexico's presidential seat.

Coahuila experienced the early phase of the Revolution as a largely spontaneous popular revolt, encouraged by a major economic crisis and by the dislocations that resulted from the state's economic transformation. After 1913, Carranza succeeded in recruiting many of these early rebels to his Constitutionalist army. Coahuilan elites, however, remained split throughout the Revolution, often supporting counterrevolutionary factions. In addition, many of the state's residents cast their lot with Francisco "Pancho" Villa, another prominent Revolutionary from northern Mexico. When Villa broke with Carranza in 1914, the state was split into two zones. Supporters of both leaders wrestled for control of the state until September of 1915, when Villa finally abandoned Coahuila.

Although unrest and periodic local rebellions continued to plague the state after the Constitutionalist victory, Coahuila began an era of reconstruction and reform. President Carranza worked closely with Governor Gustavo Espinosa Mireles to stabilize the economy and bring peace to the state. Espinosa Mireles responded to popular pressures with a series of moderate reforms, including an equalization of taxes and the expansion and improvement of the state's educational system. The governor also acknowledged the importance of Coahuila's workers by establishing a ministry of labor. In 1918, the state hosted a national meeting of labor unions at which the Confederation of Mexican Workers (CROM) was established.

While Coahuila did experience significant changes in the aftermath of the Revolution, the land reform that some hoped for was not immediately forthcoming. Indeed, in the immediate aftermath of the Revolution and through the 1920s, Coahuila remained one of the states in which land concentration was most persistent. In the southwestern, or Laguna, region, wealthy landowners worked with political authorities to halt land reform, and in the north, cattle ranchers were equally successful in defending their large landholdings, thus protecting the state's cattle industry. Coahuila did not experience true land reform until the 1930s, when President Lázaro Cárdenas ordered the expropriation and redistribution of agricultural lands in the fertile Laguna.

Coahula's postrevolutionary history has been characterized by relative political stability and, particularly since the 1940s, impressive economic growth. Industrial development has been of particular importance. Coahuila remained an important mining center, and it developed a thriving iron and steel industry. Foreign investment has been a crucial component in Coahuila's contemporary growth. Beginning in the 1970s, General Motors and the Chrysler Corporation established plants in the environs of Saltillo, transforming the area and attracting many workers, including those from other states. By the middle of the 1980s, the automobile industry had become Coahuila's most important economic sector. Also beginning in the 1970s, *maquiladora* plants (foreign-owned plants that use Mexican labor to assemble goods for re-export) emerged in Coahuila's border zone. *Maquiladoras* had also been established in other areas of the state by the 1980s. By the end of the twentieth century, the North American Free Trade Agreement (signed in 1994) was facilitating the continuing influx of foreign investment.

Just as the latter part of the twentieth century was characterized by economic growth, so was it marked by the continuing mobilization of Coahuila's workers and *campesinos*. Demands for land persisted beyond the era of Lázaro Cárdenas, compelling additional distributions of land and an extension of land reform to the cattle ranching areas of northern Coahuila. The state also remained a center of the Mexican workers' movement. At midcentury, mine workers staged a well-publicized strike against the American Smelting and Refining Company (ASARCO). Government and company repression, which included a blockade on foodstuffs, generated a protest march from Coahuila to Mexico City in 1951. Although the strike was ultimately suppressed, the so-called Caravan of Hunger became an important event in the history of Coahuila's workers.

Popular mobilization and protest continued to be a part of Coahuila's history as the twenty-first century dawned. The workers' movement remained fairly strong, and increasingly, the state's citizens protested against industrial pollution, a by-product of the state's impressive growth. Opposition political parties also assumed a role, taking advantage of popular discontent to challenge

Mexico's official party, the PRI (Institutional Revolutionary Party). By the 1980s, the National Action Party (PAN) had emerged as a major political force, and was successfully challenging the PRI in local elections.

—SBP

See also: Agrarian Reform/Land and Land Policy; Cárdenas, Lázaro; Confederación Regional Obrera Mexicana (CROM); Constitutionalists; Diaz, Porfirio; Labor Movements; Madero, Francisco; Partido de Acción Nacional (PAN); Partido Revolucionario Institucional (PRI); Revolution of 1910; Villa, Francisco "Pancho."

References:
 Cuéllar Valdés, Pablo M. *Historia del estado de Coahuila.* Saltillo, Coahuila: Biblioteca de la Universidad Autónoma de Coahuila, 1979.
Enríquez Terrazas, Eduardo, and José Luis García Valero. *Coahuila: Una historia compartida.* Mexico City: Instituto de Investigaciones Dr. José María Luis Mora, 1989.
Meyers, William K. *Forge of Progress, Crucible of Revolt: The Origins of the Mexican Revolution in La Comarca Lagunera, 1880–1911.* Albuquerque: University of New Mexico Press, 1994.
Pasztor, Suzanne B. *The Spirit of Hidalgo: The Mexican Revolution in Coahuila.* Calgary: University of Calgary Press, 2002.
Santoscoy, María Elena, et al. *Breve historia de Coahuila.* Mexico City: El Colegio de Mexico, 2000.
Official state web site: http://www.coahuila. gob.mx

Colima (State)

Pacific coast state with a capital of the same name. Colima is home to the bustling port of Manzanillo, which has taken part in the commercial trade of the Pacific since the colonial era. During the last decades of the twentieth century, Manzanillo's beaches became a tourist attraction. For much of its history, Colima has been an isolated area, remote from Mexico's main political and economic centers. Although the state is rich in natural resources, its prosperity has been hard won and unevenly shared.

Colima felt the influence of several Indian groups (including the Otomí, Toltecs, and Chichimecs) in the centuries before the arrival of the Spaniards. Native peoples beat back Spanish expeditions to this corner of Mexico three times before Gonzálo de Sandoval and his men overwhelmed them. In 1523, Sandoval established San Sebastián de Colima (today's capital), using the name of a local Indian leader, Coliman. Francisco Cortés, a relative of the Spanish explorer Hernán Cortés, consolidated Spanish control over Colima, and he used it as a starting point for land and sea expeditions to other areas. It was from this base that Spanish control was extended into Jalisco and Nayarit. Several ports, including Manzanillo, developed along Colima's coastline, and they became key points for the provisioning and repair of ships. Colima's ports also provided refuge from the hurricanes that frequently appeared in this part of the Pacific.

Briefly during the sixteenth century Colima enjoyed a gold rush, attracting settlers from Peru, Spain's other major American colony. The region's colonial economy, however, was based primarily on cattle ranching and on the cultivation of cocoa, cotton, sugar, and coconut. Colima also provided salt for Mexico's mining communities. Economically and politically, Colima was linked to Guadalajara (in neighboring Jalisco), the commercial hub of western Mexico. Despite its natural resources, this small area lacked real wealth and autonomy, and Manzanillo was dwarfed by the main Pacific port of San Blas, in today's Nayarit.

Mexico's independence era brought sporadic rebel activity to Colima. In 1811 insurgents made prisoners of several Spanish residents of the city of Colima, which remained in rebel hands for a time. Spanish properties also were attacked. In the aftermath of independence, Colima was both a federal territory and a part of Michoacán before achieving statehood in 1857. The status of Manzanillo was contested again during the nineteenth century, and the port was closed twice because of contraband trading. Manzanillo was finally recognized as both an official port and urban center in 1873.

Colima remained something of a backwater during the nineteenth century owing to its isolation and the lack of a well-developed link between the capital city and Manzanillo. It was not, however, aloof from Mexico's major political developments. President Benito Juárez took advantage of the state's remoteness in 1858 as he sought refuge during the War of Reform (a civil conflict between Mexico's liberal and conservative factions). When France established an empire in Mexico, Colima was subdued, and its capital occupied by French troops from 1864 to 1867.

During the second half of the nineteenth century, Colima's economy began to expand and the state, along with the port of Manzanillo, became a center from which goods were distributed to the interior of Mexico. Towns grew and Mexican and foreign immigrants arrived, drawn by the promise of the state's natural resources. Many of those resources were shipped to the United States. Indeed, Colima supplied the United States with cotton during the American Civil War. The railroad, which first linked Colima City to Manzanillo, was crucial to the continued growth of the state, and it helped solidify Manzanillo's status as a permanent port.

Colima's economic development was accompanied by greater political stability. This stability was encouraged by President Porfirio Díaz, who worked closely with the state's governors in the years before the Mexican Revolution. Francisco Santa Cruz and Enrique O. de la Madrid were the most important governors of this era. Santa Cruz served for thirteen nonconsecutive years. De la Madrid held power for nine years before the 1910–1911 revolt of Francisco I. Madero against President Díaz compelled de la Madrid's resignation.

With Madero's ascension to the presidency, Trinidad Alamillo became Colima's governor. After Madero's death in 1913, Alamillo joined Venustiano Carranza's Constitutionalist rebellion and aided in the capture of the state capital. Under Juan José Rios, who governed the state from 1914 to 1917,

Colima witnessed its first round of Revolutionary reform. Rios distributed land to the state's *campesinos* (rural workers) and he took an anticlerical stance, limiting the influence of the Roman Catholic Church in local schools. Rios's anticlericalism was echoed by his successors, angering many in a state where Catholic activism had become an important force in the years before the Revolution. Colima thus experienced directly the violence of the Cristero Rebellion (1926–1929). Pro-Church rebels grew steadily in number during the conflict, and they frequently raided the capital city. Cristero insurgents also attacked and briefly controlled Manzanillo.

In addition to the changes resulting from the Revolution (including another round of land reform in the 1930s), Colima's twentieth-century history has been characterized by an ongoing attempt to expand and modernize the state's economy. In the 1980s, President Miguel de la Madrid (a Colima native) announced the Plan Colima. This attempt to improve the state's productivity focused on expanding infrastructure, promoting agro-industry, and developing a tourist sector. Plan Colima also provided large sums of money to modernize the port and urban center of Manzanillo. Although national attention to Colima's development did bring impressive gains (Manzanillo, for example, became Mexico's most important commercial port on the Pacific) the benefits of growth were unevenly shared. Foreign investors, for example, were the primary beneficiaries of Colima's new tourist industry.

By the end of the twentieth century, poverty, crime, and an underground drug economy underscored the lopsided nature of Colima's development. Indeed, the state gave birth to its own drug cartel, which helped move cocaine and marijuana to the United States as part of a larger Pacific coast trade. Politically, Colima's contemporary history has been marked by the growth of political opposition. By the 1990s, more of the state's voters were challenging the dominance of the Institutional Revolutionary Party (PRI), which controlled Mexican politics for much of the twentieth century.

—*SBP*

See also: Cristero Rebellion; Drug Trafficking; Jalisco; Michoacán; Nayarit; Revolution of 1910.

References:

Romero de Solís, José Miguel. *Breve historia de Colima*. Mexico City: El Colegio de Mexico, 1994.

Official state web site: http://www.colima.gob.mx

Comic Books

Mexicans are among the world's most enthusiastic producers and consumers of *historietas* or comic books. Each month around 40 million *historietas* are sold at newsstands all over the country. Studies suggest that each issue is read by an average of five other people, which means that as many as 200 million *historietas* are read each month in a country of just over 90 million! (This is possible only because most readers read more than one a month.) Moreover, comic books account for about 80 percent of all printed material in Mexico, considerably more than books and newspapers combined. Critics argue that the simplistic, sensationalistic, melodramatic style of most *historietas*—combined in recent years with generous servings of violence and quasi-pornography—panders to baser instincts, undermines family values, and encourages the introduction of foreign cultural symbols like *El Pato Donald* (Donald Duck) and Superman. Supporters point out that they introduce readers to "modern" ideas, promote literacy (especially for those with inadequate educations), and represent a decidedly Mexican aesthetic that sometimes incorporates but is hardly subservient to American influences. Both groups agree that Mexican *historietas* have played and continue to play a key role in the development and dissemination of mass culture in Mexico and throughout Latin America (including the Spanish-speaking regions of the United States).

The historical origins of *historietas* are complicated. During the colonial period (1521–1821), the combination of images and text to tell stories was a favorite strategy of priests and friars eager to spread the Roman Catholic faith and to control the meaning of complex Indian images (frequently used in divination) by providing explanatory captions in both Spanish and Indian languages. Another colonial legacy—*ex-votos* or religious pictures painted on tin with captions thanking some intercessor (the Virgin of Guadalupe, for example) for a miraculous cure—employs similar means to more personal ends. After independence from Spain (1821), satirical political cartoons became quite popular as competing political groups sought to undermine each other's pretensions to legitimacy. This tradition culminated at the turn of the century with the brilliantly satirical and often sensationalistic images of printmakers such as José Guadalupe Posada. Posada even produced one the first serial cartoon characters, the hapless Don Chepito Marihuano, whose misadventures—mostly of his own making—mirrored the cultural confusion of early twentieth-century Mexico City life. Around the same time, innovative advertisers, responding to a rapidly expanding consumer culture, turned to cartoons to sell their products. The tobacco company, El Buen Tono, for example, provided "Historia de una mujer" (History of a Woman) and "Ranilla" (Little Frog) inserts in cigarette packages. The *historietas'* immediate and most important predecessors, however, were the *dominicales* or Sunday comics initiated in 1918 by Mexico City's biggest daily newspaper, *El Universal*. The *dominicales* were newspaper supplements rather than comic books and favored American imports like *Tarzan*, but their considerable popularity prompted adventuresome publishers to try their hand at self-contained publications.

The first widely popular Mexican comic book, *Paquín*, appeared in 1934. Its success encouraged others, most notably *Paquito* (1935), *Chamaco* (1936), and *Pepín* (1936).

Emboldened by rapidly rising sales, *Chamaco* went to daily issues in 1939 and *Pepín* followed suit the next year. The latter proved so popular—daily sales reached over one million copies during its heyday—that it added a second Sunday edition and lent its name, *pepines,* to the comic book genre.

These comic books were typically around 60 pages long and generally included several different serials. Sometimes the serials were American imports like *Phantom* or *Superman* but the most popular strips like "Adelita y las Guerrillas" and "Supersabios (Wisemen)" were homegrown and they went on from one cliff-hanging adventure to the next for years. The range of subjects was broad, including strips about Revolutionary heroes, noble bandits, superheroes, detectives, and movie stars in genres like science fiction, melodrama, and historical romance.

To encourage reader loyalty, *historieta* editors ran contests, printed readers' pictures, and even solicited readers' life stories as possible story plots. They also carefully tailored vocabulary and grammar (but not the often confusing and always complicated plot lines) to the capabilities of less-educated readers. Although *historietas* tended to be more escapist than socially aware, they nonetheless often addressed—either through melodrama as in *Lágrimas, Risas y Amor* (Tears, Laughs, and Love) or comedy as in *La Familia Burrón*—contemporary issues like urban migration and changing gender roles that readers confronted in their daily lives. Moralists of all political persuasions, however, saw little of value in the increasingly popular *historietas,* and after persistent lobbying, especially by Roman Catholic conservatives, the government established a censorship commission to monitor the industry. The commission had little impact on the major Mexican comics but did serve a protectionist role by denying American competitors easy entrance into the Mexican market.

By the early 1950s, *historietas* had become a major industry employing thousands of editors, writers, artists, and printers. Sometimes writers themselves became publishers. For example, Yolanda Vargas Dulché, writer for the popular *Lágrimas, Risas y Amor,* helped found Editorial Vid, one of the major *historieta* publishing houses. José Cruz, writer of *Pepín's* "Adelita y las Guerrillas," produced his own hugely successful *El Santo,* the adventures of a crime-fighting professional wrestler presented in the form of a *fotonovela* (illustrated with photographs rather than the traditional pictures). New approaches like *El Santo,* however, were the exception. Industry expansion generally meant more competition and less innovation as business managers and production teams came to replace individual artists as the driving forces behind *historieta* production. Under pressure from new publications, the great daily comics of the 1930s and 1940s gradually died off. Nevertheless, best-selling weeklies like *El Santo, Kalimán, Memín Pengüin,* and *Lágrimas, Risas y Amor* continued to thrive for decades, often aided by expansion into other media. *El Santo* became one of Mexico's biggest B-movie stars and *Kalimán* used a popular radio show (and a couple films) to expand its readership to two million copies a week by the early 1980s.

The general stagnation of the industry, abetted by the growing concentration of *historieta* production in the hands of just a few major production companies, did not completely inhibit innovation. During the social turmoil of the 1960s and 1970s, the biting political critiques of Eduardo del Río (Rius) in *Los Supermachos* and *Los Agachados* as well as Carlos Vigil in *Torbellino* made their way into popular culture via comic books. Ruis even attacked the comic book industry, insisting that "merchandise-peddling publishers . . . make only comics that are alienating and in bad taste, pornographic and disgustingly sentimental." And indeed Mexican *historietas* in general have become increasingly pornographic and violent since the 1960s.

After peaking in the 1980s, *historieta* production in Mexico has declined somewhat in recent years. Lack of innovation is probably one reason, but competition from television is probably the biggest factor. Moreover, these factors are closely linked. Media giant Televisa's increased presence in the *historieta* market, for example, has further industrialized the production process and encouraged the subordination of comic books to television. Nevertheless, the decline of Mexican comic books must be seen in relative terms. *Historietas* such as *El Libro Vaquero* (Book of Cowboys) and *El Libro Policiaco* (mostly about American police departments in places like Miami, New Orleans, San Francisco, and New York) sell 1.5 million copies a week. Melodrama continues to attract readers with titles like *El Libro Rosa, El Libro Sentimental,* and *El Libro Pasional.* Any rumor of the *historietas'* imminent demise is decidedly premature.

—*RMB*

See also: Newspapers and Magazines; Posada, José Guadalupe; Radio; Television.

References:

Hinds, Harold E., Jr., and Charles M. Tatum. *Not Just for Children: The Mexican Comic Book in the Late 1960s and 1970s.* Westport, CT: Greenwood Press, 1992.

Rubenstein, Anne. *Bad Language, Naked Ladies, and Other Threats to the Nation: A Political History of Comic Books in Mexico.* Durham, NC: Duke University Press, 1998.

Communism in Mexico

Communism has exerted a lengthy if uneven influence on Mexican politics throughout the twentieth century. Revolutionary leaders at different times have supported and suppressed communism. Communism has been popular among intellectuals and students but has not been able to develop a mass base among either the peasants or the urban workers. Communism often competed with and was confused with anarchism, socialism, and revolutionary nationalism. Various political parties have claimed the communist banner over the years. Like many parties on the political left in Mexico, the communists have found it difficult to remain unified. The communist movement has often been racked by internal disagreements, leading to a series of expulsions or defections. Most important, communism has had to compete with the ideology and propaganda of the Mexican Revolution as well as the corporatist state and official party produced by the Revolution. Mexican communism has also been influenced by a series of international forces, including the Communist International, the Communist Party of the United States, and more recently the Cuban revolution under Fidel Castro.

The first and most durable communist party in Mexico was the Partido Comunista de México, later known as the Partido Comunista Mexicano (the Communist Party of Mexico, or PCM). The PCM grew out of a congress of Mexican socialists held in Mexico City in August and September 1919. The more radical elements of the congress soon formed the PCM around the small Mexican Socialist Party, which had originally called the congress. The PCM officially aligned itself with and was recognized by the international communist movement, the Communist International or Comintern, which was a product of the Bolshevik revolution in Russia in 1917. Anarchism and syndicalism were strong influences in the new party. This was especially apparent in the forceful stance the PCM took against participation in elections ("electoralism"), a position the Moscow-controlled Comintern strongly advocated at the time. The PCM attempted to develop a base among the urban workers but could not compete with the government-backed Confederación Regional Obrera Mexicana (the Regional Mexican Workers' Confederation, or CROM), which espoused a radical doctrine but was strongly anticommunist.

The PCM followed a shifting path in working with what it called "reformist" organizations. In the early 1920s the PCM opposed cooperating with reformists groups like the CROM but reversed itself in 1926, calling on communists to work within reformist groups to gain control of them. In 1928, however, the Communist International abandoned its support for this "united front" approach of cooperating with and within reformist organizations. The PCM faithfully implemented this reversal in strategy, severing its ties with reformist groups. The PCM even formed its own national labor-peasant organization, the Confederación Sindical Unitaria de México (the Mexican Unitary Trade Union Confederation, or CSUM).

The PCM's movement to the left also put it increasingly at odds with the government. The PCM was incorrectly implicated in a major revolt against the government in 1929, which led to a major repression of communists and the PCM by the new administration of President Emilio Portes Gil. A number of communist leaders were killed or imprisoned, PCM offices were closed, the party newspaper was closed down, and later the party's printing plant was destroyed. The government exiled foreign communists, broke relations with the Soviet Union, and used army troops to put down communist-led strikes. The remnants of the PCM had to operate underground until the advent of the friendlier administration of President Lázaro Cárdenas in late 1934.

A change in tactics by the Comintern and a change in government policy by Cárdenas produced a rapid revival in the political fortunes of communism and the PCM. The rapidly changing international situation in Europe caused the Comintern to call for a "popular front" strategy in which communists would unite with other leftist and liberal parties to form an antifascist coalition. At the same time, Cárdenas was determined to push the Revolution farther to the left and found the communists useful in this effort. In June 1935 the communist-backed CSUM signed an agreement with other noncommunist labor unions to form a new national trade confederation that would be supported by the government. Cárdenas was grooming Vicente Lombardo Toledano to head this new confederation. Lombardo was not a member of the PCM but was a self-proclaimed marxist who had visited the Soviet Union and supported Stalin's policies in the 1930s. The new labor organization came into existence in 1936 with the establishment of the Confederación de Trabajadores de México (the Confederation of Mexican Workers, or CTM). The new organization disappointed the communists as it soon became evident the CTM would be controlled by Lombardo and his supporters, with a limited role for the communists.

The PCM enthusiastically endorsed the reforms of Cárdenas and gained greater access to labor unions, peasant organizations, and government agencies. In some respects, Cárdenas frustrated the communists. He refused to renew diplomatic relations with the Soviet Union and granted asylum to Leon Trotsky, who sought exile after losing in a power struggle to Stalin. Trotsky continued his criticism of Stalin's regime until his assassination in Mexico City in 1940. Cárdenas also excluded the communists from official participation in the reorganized official party.

As World War II approached, many Mexican communists found it increasingly difficult to go along with the changes in policies advocated by the Comintern. The signing of a nonaggression pact between Germany and the Soviet Union in August 1939 led to a dramatic change in the official view of Hitler, who had been considered the epitome of the fascist enemy. PCM members who refused to accept the new party line were expelled from the party. The political casualties included the PCM's chief official, Secretary General Hernán Laborde, who was expelled first from the party executive committee and then from the party itself in 1940. His replacement was the influential peasant leader Dionisio Encina, who would head the PCM for the next twenty years.

During Encina's tenure, the PCM underwent a prolonged decline caused by external and internal forces. One of the principal problems was that the Mexican government was moving closer to the United States in international affairs and also adopted a new development policy—import substitution industrialization—requiring worker discipline imposed by the CTM. The radical demands of

the communists did not sit well with the growing conservatism of the government. The government embarked on a sustained and a successful effort to remove communist leaders from labor unions, including the CTM. Even the powerful and popular former leader of the CTM, Vicente Lombardo Toledano, was expelled from the CTM along with his supporters. This was done despite Lombardo's support of the government's new development scheme and his consistent claims that he was a marxist but not a communist. The government also cracked down on communist propaganda and unionization activities. The PCM also faced new political competition on the left in 1947–1948 when Lombardo formed a new party, the Partido Popular (the People's Party, or PP). Like Lombardo himself, the PP was presented as marxist but not communist. An additional communist party also appeared on the political scene in 1950, the Partido Obrero-Campesino Mexicano (the Mexican Worker-Peasant Party, or POCM). The PCM also suffered from internal dissension brought on by the personalistic rule of Encina and his dogmatic adherence to the international communist line. Expulsions and defections produced a dramatic reduction in PCM membership, which dropped from approximately 30,000 in 1940 to around 2,000 in 1960.

The PCM and other Mexican communists were operating in a much changed political environment in the 1960s. After a bitter internal fight, the PCM ousted Encina as secretary general in 1960. The PCM began to place more emphasis on agricultural workers, students, youth groups, and state workers. The success of Fidel Castro's revolution in Cuba in 1959 and its rapid movement toward Marxism-Leninism encouraged Mexican communists. Many Mexican communists were also adopting a more critical view of the Soviet Union. When the Soviets intervened in Hungary in 1956, the PCM strongly supported the intervention; the PCM, however, condemned the Soviet intervention in Czechoslovakia in 1968. Government repression of the communists continued in the 1960s, especially under the administration of conservative President Gustavo Díaz Ordaz (1964–1970). In 1965 the government arrested a number of PCM leaders and raided the offices of the PCM.

The PCM played a minimal role in the student-popular movement of 1968. The government attributed the unrest to "foreign" and "subversive" elements and raided PCM headquarters and shut down its newspaper. Communists had little influence on student leaders, and the PCM supported negotiations with the government, a position that later led to charges that the PCM sold out the movement. The severity of the government's repression of the movement caught all of the government's opponents by surprise and led to the jailing of some communists. In the early 1970s, the PCM returned to its policy of boycotting elections. Abstentions from elections had increased in general, and there was growing criticism of the political legitimacy of the government and the official party, the Partido Revolucionario Institucional (the Institutional Revolutionary Party, or PRI). The government and the PRI responded by giving the opposition a larger number of representatives in the lower house of the Mexican Congress, the Chamber of Deputies. The PCM decided to return to the electoral struggle, and in 1978 the government recognized it as a legally registered party. The PCM also entered into a coalition with other leftist parties for the congressional elections of 1979, the coalition emerging from the elections with eighteen seats in the Chamber of Deputies. The coalition of 1979 was the background to a merger of the PCM in 1981 with four other left-wing groups to form a new organization, the Partido Socialista Unificado de México (the Unified Mexican Socialist Party, or PSUM). At the time of the merger and its dissolution, the PCM was the oldest political party in Mexico.

The PSUM soon encountered a problem common to left-wing parties in Mexico: internal dissension. The PCM had been the largest of the five groups involved in the mergers, and there were suspicions from the start by non-PCM members that the PSUM was simply a convenient way to expand PCM influence. The PSUM experienced major defections in its early years and did not make strong showings in the congressional races of either 1982 or 1985. PSUM was unable to turn the worsening economic situation to its political advantage and made few converts among workers, peasants, or the new social action groups. The PSUM merged with four other leftist organizations in 1987 to form the Partido Mexicano Socialista (the Mexican Socialist Party, or PMS). The PMS, in turn, became part of the Partido de la Revolución Democrática (the Party of the Democratic Revolution, or PRD) in 1989. The PRD was the vehicle for the unsuccessful presidential campaigns in 1994 and 2000 of Cuauhtémoc Cárdenas, the former PRI leader.

Communism in Mexico has often exercised an influence greater than the number of its official supporters might indicate. Communism has been particularly influential among artists and intellectuals. Ideologically, communism found it difficult to compete with the nationalistic ideology that came out of the Mexican Revolution. Organizationally, the communists found it difficult to compete for the loyalties of the workers and the peasants who were under the corporatist control of the official party and the state. This inability to connect with the masses has continued to the present and is most visible in the communists' inability to exploit the economic problems Mexico has experienced since 1970. Indeed the biggest political beneficiary of Mexico's economic difficulties has not been an organization of the left but rather an organization of the right, the Partido de Acción Nacional (the National Action Party, or PAN). The dissolution of the Soviet bloc followed by the dissolution of the Soviet Union has undercut most of the foreign support for a domestic communist movement.

—DMC

See also: Anarchism; Cárdenas, Cuauhtémoc; Cárdenas, Lázaro; Confederación de Trabajadores de México (CTM); Confederación Regional Obrera Mexicana (CROM); Democratization Process; Elections; Labor Movements; Lombardo Toledano, Vicente; Partido Revolucionario Institucional (PRI); Tlatelolco Massacre.

References:

Carr, Barry. *Marxism and Communism in Twentieth-Century Mexico.* Lincoln: University of Nebraska Press, 1992.

Millon, Robert P. *Mexican Marxist: Vicente Lombardo Toledano.* Chapel Hill: University of North Carolina Press, 1966.

Schmitt, Karl M. *Communism in Mexico: A Study in Political Frustration.* Austin: University of Texas Press, 1965.

Confederación de Trabajadores de México (CTM)

The most important labor organization in Mexico from the 1930s to the present, the Confederación de Trabajadores de México (the Mexican Workers' Confederation, or CTM), has played a major role in the economic and political life of the country. The Revolutionary leaders who dominated Mexico following the implementation of the Constitution of 1917—Carranza, Obregón, Calles, Cárdenas—recognized the need to permit labor organization; they were unwilling, however, to permit the rise of powerful independent labor organizations that might threaten their control. Instead, they permitted labor to organize in return for the labor organization's unfailing support of government policies. The first to employ this approach was President Venustiano Carranza, who sponsored the formation in 1918 of the Confederación Regional Obrera Mexicana (the Regional Confederation of Mexican Workers, or CROM). With government support, the CROM grew rapidly, assuming a dominant role in the labor movement. The CROM was also an important source of political support for the government; the CROM leader, Luis Morones, became a powerful political figure, eventually becoming

minister of labor in the administration of President Plutarco Elías Calles (1924–1928).

The decline of the CROM was a result of the events surrounding the presidential elections of 1928. Morones intended to run for the presidency but had to revise his plans when the Constitution was amended to permit former president Alvaro Obregón to run for reelection. Morones and the CROM made a series of political blunders that soon ended their favored position. The CROM originally opposed efforts to amend the Constitution to permit Obregón's reelection. Morones and the CROM compounded their problems by initially supporting Obregón and then withdrawing their support. When President-elect Obregón was assassinated in July 1928, there were widespread rumors that Morones and the CROM were behind the assassination. The final blow came when Morones and the CROM unsuccessfully opposed the formation of an official Revolutionary party by outgoing president Calles.

The late 1920s and early 1930s were a time of political and economic crisis for Mexico and the labor movement. Former President Calles continued to dominate the political scene between 1928 and 1934 through a series of three presidential puppets. He hoped to avoid further political instability by creating the new official party, the Partido Nacional Revolucionario (the National Revolutionary Party, or PNR). Amid this political uncertainty, Mexico began to feel the effects of the depression of the 1930s, which brought massive layoffs of workers and wage cuts. From this confused situation emerged two important labor leaders, Vicente Lombardo Toledano and Fidel Velázquez, who would shape the labor movement for decades to come and play a key role in the creation of the CTM.

Lombardo Toledano was one of Mexico's emerging left-wing intellectuals as well as a prominent figure in the CROM. He led a reform faction within the CROM, which opposed the arbitrary rule and the corruption of the Morones leadership. Lombardo Toledano broke with Morones in 1932 and then formed what he called the "purified" CROM in 1933. Rather than trying to promote an independent labor movement, Lombardo Toledano worked to establish a relationship with the government. Fidel Velázquez was also an important figure within the CROM who broke with the CROM leadership in January 1929. He played a leading role in the establishment of the Federación Sindical de Trabajadores del Distrito Federal (the Federated Union of Workers of the Federal District, or FSTDF). The FSTDF brought together most of the important labor unions in Mexico City that had broken with the CROM. Velázquez also sought a partnership with the government. In 1933 Lombardo Toledano and Velázquez combined their efforts to form a new national labor organization, the Confederación General de Obreros y Campesinos de México (the General Confederation of Workers and Peasants of Mexico, or CGOCM).

A new political crisis soon had a major impact on labor organization. Calles selected what he thought was a fourth puppet president to take office in 1934—Lázaro Cárdenas. A political conflict soon developed when Cárdenas asserted his independence from Calles. Calles was particularly disenchanted with Cárdenas's encouragement of strikes, and he publicly criticized the new president. Cárdenas needed allies in the coming showdown with Calles, and organized labor was eager to oblige. In June 1935 Lombardo Toledano and Velázquez helped to establish a new and even larger labor organization, the Comité Nacional de Defensa Proletaria (the National Committee for Proletarian Defense, or CNDP). The CNDP mobilized the workers behind the Cárdenas administration, including a massive march of some 80,000 workers in Mexico City in December 1935.

When the CNDP had first been formed, its leaders had agreed there would be a national convention of workers and peasants to create a new, national labor confederation. The convention took place in Mexico City in February 1936. Although the convention highlighted the divisions existing within the Mexican labor movement, the convention did produce a new national labor organization, the Confederación de Trabajadores de México (the Mexican Workers' Confederation, or CTM). Setting an anticapitalist and nationalist tone, the convention—with little disagreement—selected Vicente Lombardo Toledano to serve as secretary general of the CTM. The competition for the position of organizational secretary of the CTM showed the internal divisions of the new organization, particularly the split between the communists and the supporters of Fidel Velázquez. Velázquez became organizational secretary after some of his supporters threatened to leave the CTM if he was not chosen. The CTM brought together some 3,000 organizations with approximately 600,000 members. Lombardo Toledano and Fidel Velázquez would play key roles in the development of the CTM. Both came from a union background that stressed cooperation with the government, and both effectively allied themselves with the emerging winner in the presidential power struggle—Lázaro Cárdenas. Buoyed by CTM support, Cárdenas exiled both Calles and Morones in April 1936.

The alliance between the CTM and the state—as well as the ability of the CTM to contain the labor movement—was soon tested by a series of major strikes involving the railroad, electrical, and petroleum workers. In May 1936, 45,000 members of the railroad workers union—a CTM affiliate—struck the government-owned Mexican National Railroad over the issue of paid holidays. Cárdenas had earlier rejected the union's demands, and the federal committee on conciliation and arbitration declared the strike illegal. The railroad workers insisted that the CTM call a national solidarity strike in support of its demands, but the CTM refused to confront the Cárdenas administration. Instead, the CTM called for a thirty-minute sympathy strike and urged workers to end the confrontation. In June 1936, some

3,000 members of the electrical workers' union struck the foreign-owned Mexican Light Company, which supplied electricity to central Mexico. The issue was a simple one—wage increases. CTM workers marched in support of the strikers, but CTM general secretary Vicente Lombardo Toledano rejected the strikers' request that the CTM call a general strike. Cárdenas finally intervened personally in the dispute, ordering the company to meet the workers' demands.

The difficulty of harmonizing the interests of the workers, the CTM leadership, and the government became apparent in the petroleum workers' strike of 1937 and its aftermath. When Cárdenas came to power, the petroleum workers were divided into a number of different unions based on geography and on skill. Cárdenas wanted to create one large industrial union that would represent all workers in the oil industry and that would be affiliated with the CTM. This would give Cárdenas additional leverage with the powerful, foreign-owned oil companies as well as greater control over the workers. In 1935 the diverse unions came together to form the Sindicato de Trabajadores Petroleros de la Republica Mexicana (the Union of Petroleum Workers of the Mexican Republic, or STPRM). The STPRM joined the CTM in 1936 and in 1937 called for an industrywide strike, which was supported by the CTM. The oil companies refused to accommodate workers' demands, even when directed by the Mexican Supreme Court to do so. At that point, Cárdenas expropriated the foreign-owned oil companies. The union wanted the workers to administer the expropriated properties, but Cárdenas rejected the request, a rejection backed by the CTM.

The alliance between the government and the CTM was put into institutionalized form with Cárdenas's reorganization and renaming of the official party, the PNR, in 1938. The new party—the Partido de la Revolución Mexicana (the Party of the Mexican Revolution, or PRM)—was divided into four sectors: agrarian, labor, military, and "popular."

The CTM was the dominant force in the labor sector, but the reorganization ultimately led to the creation of new organizations that restricted the power of the CTM. The CTM originally had been involved in the organization of peasants and government employees. Cárdenas, however, blocked further CTM involvement with these important groups by establishing separate federations to organize the peasants and the bureaucrats and then incorporating these organizations into the official party.

The CTM continued to work closely with the government in response to wartime demands and a changing national development policy. In 1942 the CTM offered to sign a "workers' solidarity pact" with business in which they pledged to settle peacefully all labor-management disputes in the interest of the war effort. When the pact was rejected by business, the CTM offered a "no-strike" pledge anyway. A number of strikes still occurred as the workers' real wages declined dramatically. This decline was a product of the CTM's efforts to hold down wages while Mexico was experiencing a high inflation rate. When the government decided to make a basic change in development policy to one emphasizing industrialization, the CTM once again offered its support. In April 1945 the CTM signed a "Labor-Industry Pact," in which it promised to continue the wartime collaboration with business in order to promote national development. While the CTM said that it was returning to the use of the strike as a weapon, the CTM leadership felt its main contribution to industrial growth would be to keep wages low and to maintain labor peace.

The CTM's alliance with business and government, as well as its chronic internal dissension, led to major problems in the 1940s. The willingness of the CTM leadership to sacrifice workers' wages for government development policy led to important defections from the federation. Major industrial unions—the oil workers, the electrical workers, the railway workers, and the miners—

left the CTM. The ongoing internal problems of the CTM finally led to a definitive split between Vicente Lombardo Toledano and Fidel Velázquez. Lombardo Toledano and Velázquez had been rivals for power since the birth of the CTM. Lombardo Toledano turned over the position of secretary general to Velázquez in 1941, setting in motion a steady decline in his influence over the federation. Velázquez gradually forced out Lombardo's supporters. This gradual process turned into a full-scale purge in 1947–1948 when the marxist Lombardo Toledano and his "communist" supporters were expelled from the CTM.

The CTM's dependency on the government grew during the presidency of Miguel Alemán (1946–1952). Alemán's commitment to the new industrialization policy led him to demand greater government control over the labor force, with the CTM as his principal tool for containing worker discontent. Alemán was even more prepared than his predecessors to intervene in the internal affairs of individual unions and to use repression if necessary. This new approach became known as *"charrismo"* after Alemán's intervention in the railway workers union to impose as its secretary general Jesús Díaz de León, who was fond of wearing the fancy attire of the Mexican cowboy, the *charro*. The railway workers' union had left the CTM in 1947 and had publicly opposed the government's new development policy. Alemán used a combination of legal action and police repression to keep Díaz de León in office. Similar tactics—rigged elections, police action, even use of the army—were used to impose progovernment leaders on the independent-minded petroleum workers' union, which had left the CTM in 1946, and on the miners union, which had also defected from the CTM. The government and the CTM also worked together to block the rise of any significant national labor organization that might be a rival to the CTM. The linkage between the government and the CTM became stronger, but the position of the CTM in the alliance also became weaker.

The rise in real wages in the 1950s helped to reduce worker discontent, as it appeared that the government's development scheme was working. Under the continuing leadership of Fidel Velázquez, the CTM retained its dominant position in the national labor movement as well as its close relationship with the government and the official party, now known as the Partido Revolucionario Institucional (the Institutional Revolutionary Party, or PRI). Despite the signs of economic progress, independent-minded workers still challenged *charrismo* and the role of the CTM. There was a major confrontation between the government and railroad workers in 1958–1959 over wages and *charro* leadership. In 1958 the workers struck for a large wage increase and overthrew the *charro* leadership of the union. The government refused, initially, to recognize the new independent leadership and called out the police and the army to emphasize its position. The government later relented and permitted the independent leadership to retain control. The CTM launched a propaganda campaign against the independent leaders, who were described as being communistic and unpatriotic. Railway workers struck again in February 1959, prompting the CTM's Velázquez to claim that the union leaders were communist inspired. When worker militancy continued, the government arrested the union leaders, sponsored the election of new *charro* leadership, and began a process that would eventually result in the firing of some 20,000 workers. The CTM leadership fully supported the government crackdown, even taking out full-page ads in major newspapers denouncing the strikers as communists. The government later used police repression, the army, and even a sizeable loan to the union to keep the *charro* leadership in power.

As the so-called Mexican economic miracle began to tail off in the 1960s and the 1970s, new pressures were felt by the CTM from both the government and an increasingly unhappy workforce. President Luis Echeverría (1970–1976) was eager to establish his credentials as a "populist" president in the mode of Lázaro Cárdenas, whose name he frequently invoked. To promote this image, Echeverría decided to distance himself from the labor confederation Cárdenas had helped to create, the CTM. The president tolerated the rise of a limited number of independent unions, especially among the automobile workers of central Mexico. This willingness to permit independent unionism had its limits, most notably with the rise of what was called the "Democratic Tendency" in the early 1970s. The Democratic Tendency was a grassroots workers' movement beyond the control of the CTM, which was highly critical of government economic policy and the *charro* leadership supported by the CTM. When the Democratic Tendency began to attract too much popular support, the government and the CTM combined to crush it as a major labor movement.

The Echeverría administration ended amid financial and economic crises, which, in various forms, would afflict Mexico through the 1990s. These crises forced the Mexican government to abandon its postwar economic development scheme and adopt economic reforms that contradicted the Revolutionary heritage of the previous sixty years. Through these major changes, the CTM, under the leadership of Velázquez, continued to be a key source of support for the government and the official party, the PRI. The introduction of government austerity programs and a decline in real wages led to tremendous rank-and-file pressure for the CTM leadership to take a more aggressive stance in defending workers' interests. The economic reforms of a series of presidents in the 1980s and 1990s—Miguel de la Madrid, Carlos Salinas de Gortari, and Ernesto Zedillo—made the traditional relationship between the government and the CTM increasingly irrelevant and even insupportable. The aging Fidel Velázquez retained his conservative control of the CTM amid mounting criticism of his leadership. Although increasingly critical of government policies, Velázquez faithfully supported the financial and economic reforms being implemented even when it meant sacrificing labor demands for higher wages. The rapidly changing economic structure produced a major decline in union membership, especially in key industries such as oil, railways, and mining.

The death of Velázquez in 1997—after more than a half-century as the dominant figure in the CTM—ushered in a new and uncertain era for the labor organization. Although the influence and the power of the CTM declined substantially, it was still the most important labor organization in Mexico. The future of the CTM was further clouded by its lengthy association with the PRI, which also was in decline but still Mexico's most important political party. Whether the CTM and the PRI—working together or separately—can revive their economic and political fortunes—is unclear. As yet, no leader has emerged for the CTM who can fulfill the role played for so many decades by Fidel Velázquez.

—DMC

See also: Alemán, Miguel; Avila Camacho, Manuel; Calles, Plutarco Elías; Cárdenas, Lázaro; Confederación Regional Obrera Mexicana (CROM); Echeverría Alvarez, Luis; Import Substitution Industrialization (ISI); Lombardo Toledano, Vicente; Madrid (Hurtado), Miguel de la; Morones, Luis; Partido Revolucionario Institucional (PRI); Salinas de Gortari, Carlos; Velázquez Sánchez, Fidel; Zedillo Ponce de León, Ernesto.

References:

Caulfield, Norman. *Mexican Workers and the State: From the Porfiriato to NAFTA.* Fort Worth: Texas Christian University Press, 1998.

La Botz, Dan. *The Crisis of Mexican Labor.* New York: Praeger, 1988.

Roxborough, Ian. *Unions and Politics in Mexico: The Case of the Automobile Industry.* Cambridge: Cambridge University Press, 1984.

Confederación Nacional Campesina (CNC)

The early presidents who emerged from the Revolution of 1910—Francisco Madero,

Venustiano Carranza, Alvaro Obregón, and Plutarco Elías Calles—found it difficult to control a mobilized peasantry demanding immediate land distribution. There was an early effort by the Revolutionary government to harness the industrial worker; in 1918 the Carranza administration sponsored the formation of the Confederacion Regional Obrera Mexicana (the Regional Mexican Workers' Confederation, or CROM) with a view to ensuring formation of a national labor organization under government control.

Efforts to bring the peasants into a national organization under government direction was a longer and more complex process. The two main early Revolutionary leaders who were perceived as champions of agrarian reform—Pancho Villa and Emiliano Zapata—suffered military defeat and assassination. A number of local peasant organizations sprang up, but the development of a national organization proved more difficult. In 1920 followers of Zapata established a short-lived national agrarian party. A more serious organizational move took place in 1926 with the establishment of the Liga Nacional Campesina (the National Peasant League, or LNC). The LNC brought together peasant organizations from fifteen states as well as the Federal District. The LNC soon suffered defections, a problem that would affect many later peasant organizations. When Calles formed the new official party in 1929, the Partido Nacional Revolucionario (the National Revolutionary Party, or PNR), LNC leaders were divided over how to respond to it. Many LNC members were disenchanted with what they saw as the increasingly conservative direction of the Calles administration, particularly its waning enthusiasm for land redistribution. Most LNC leaders, however, elected to join the PNR.

In 1933 there was further movement toward the establishment of a national peasant organization. That year a group of peasant leaders established the Confederación Campesina Mexicana (the Mexican Peasant Confederation, or CCM). The CCM affiliated itself with the official party, the PNR, and helped to ensure a greater emphasis on agrarian reform in the presidential campaign of 1934. In the 1934 campaign, the PNR candidate was General Lázaro Cárdenas, who was dedicated to reviving the lagging agrarian reform program and creating a new national peasant organization. While governor of the state of Michoacán between 1928 and 1932, Cárdenas had engaged in extensive land redistribution and had promoted the formation of peasant leagues.

As president from 1934 to 1940, Cárdenas wanted to speed up the distribution of land, primarily through the use of the *ejido,* or communal landholding system. All *ejido* members in turn would be organized into a new national peasant organization under the control of the official party and the government. Thus, two of Cárdenas's main concerns converged: agrarian reform and centralization of political power. Cárdenas ordered the establishment of a "League of Agrarian Communities" in each state; these leagues would form the foundation for the new national organization. To control peasant organization, Cárdenas specifically prohibited national labor organizations such as the CROM and the Confederación de Trabajadores de México (the Mexican Workers' Confederation, or CTM) from attempting to organize the peasantry. In 1938 Cárdenas officially established the Confederación Nacional Campesina (the National Peasant Confederation, or CNC) as the national organization to bring together the various state, regional, and local peasant groups. Cárdenas also reorganized and renamed the official party. He divided the official party into four sectors, with the CNC as the foundation for the agrarian sector of the party, now called the Partido de la Revolución Mexicana (the Party of the Mexican Revolution, or PRM). The CNC succeeded—when previous attempts had failed—in organizing the peasantry because it could count on the support of the official party, the government, and an active program of agrarian reform. The CNC became the principal intermediary between the government and the individual peasant. Government programs such as land distribution, rural credit, and irrigation were conducted through the CNC. For the individual peasant, it became increasingly difficult to distinguish among the policies of the government, the CNC, and the PRM.

Ironically, Cárdenas began to scale back his commitment to agrarian reform at about the same time that the CNC was founded. Financial problems, world war, and shifting government development policies all served to deemphasize agrarian reform; the emphasis increasingly was on industrialization and modernization of the agricultural sector. The supporters of agricultural modernization often took a dim view of agrarian reform, especially the *ejido,* which was seen as backward and inefficient. The government reduced the amount and quality of land distributed and cut back support services for the *ejidos* such as the provision of credit. Like its industrial counterpart, the CTM, the CNC as part of the official party was committed to backing the new development approach, even if it meant sacrificing the interests of the peasants. One of the key supports of the CNC had been an active land distribution program; with land distribution on the decline, the CNC suffered a loss of legitimacy in the eyes of the peasants. The CNC faced growing internal dissent and efforts to develop rival, independent peasant organizations during the 1940s and 1950s. There were also growing problems with corruption in the CNC as its officials used their positions to promote their personal financial and economic interests.

One of the strongest challenges to the CNC came from the Unión General de Obreros y Campesinos de México (the General Union of Workers and Peasants of Mexico, or UGOCM), which was founded in 1949. One of the leaders of the UGOCM was Vicente Lombardo Toledano, former head of the CTM who had been blocked by Cárdenas in his earlier efforts to organize the

peasants. As happened with other peasant organizations, the UGOCM suffered from internal dissension and eventually split into three different organizations. In 1963 another major independent peasant organization, the Central Campesino Independiente (the Independent Peasant Central, or CCI), challenged the CNC. The CCI enjoyed the support of Cárdenas himself but soon fell victim to factionalism. It suffered various splits, with some of its members going over to the CNC and affiliating with the official party. The government also harassed CCI leaders, briefly jailing some of them.

By 1970 there was sufficient concern about the rural sector and the status of the CNC that the government turned its attention in earnest to these two areas. One of the clearest indicators of rural distress was the growing number of land invasions, or the unauthorized occupation of private property by peasants. The CNC originally supported some of these land invasions; as the takeovers became more numerous, however, the CNC came out in opposition to all land invasions. The growing discontent of the peasants also led to greater demands from independent peasant organizations. President Luis Echeverría (1970–1976) implemented a policy of devoting more resources to the rural sector as well as reorganizing the institutions that dealt with the peasantry. In 1973 the government supported the formation of the Congreso Permanente Agrario (the Permanent Agrarian Congress, or CONPA). CONPA included the CNC as well as other major peasant organizations. The groups constituting CONPA agreed the following year to create one large peasant union centered on the CNC. Echeverría, however, was not really interested in a fundamental restructuring of peasant organization, and the CNC's credibility and legitimacy continued to erode despite Echeverría's greater attention to rural matters.

The CNC tried with minimal success to adapt to Mexico's changing financial and economic conditions in the late 1970s and 1980s. With private producers and private investors playing a growing role in agriculture, the CNC tried to broaden its membership beyond its core group of *ejido* members; despite these efforts, the CNC was still basically an organization of *ejiditarios*. The reforms introduced by President Miguel de la Madrid (1982–1988) and expanded on by President Carlos Salinas de Gortari (1988–1994) reduced the role of the government in the agricultural sector, at the same time reducing the importance of the CNC as a mediator between the government and the peasantry. The changes introduced in 1992 under Salinas in particular struck at the traditional role of the CNC. The Agrarian Law of 1992 ended land redistribution as a basic policy of the government and gave *ejido* members the right to sell, rent, mortgage, or sharecrop their land. *Ejido* members could enter into joint ventures with private investors, including foreign investors. The *ejidos,* in effect, could choose to dissolve, with *ejido* members receiving individual title to former communal lands. These changes affected some of the basic functions previously performed by the CNC, especially land redistribution and mediation between the government and *ejido* members. The CNC could no longer supply many of the benefits that had enabled its control of the peasantry in the past. Any decline in the number of *ejido* members struck at the heart of CNC membership. Salinas also supported the creation of independent producer organizations, which undercut CNC efforts to attract new members or retain existing members.

Throughout its history until 2000, the CNC had been able to count on the support of the government and of the official party, known since 1946 as the Partido Revolucionario Institucional (the Institutional Revolutionary Party, or PRI). The CNC had been able to rely on the government to use a combination of co-optation and harassment to divide and weaken its rivals, but it can no longer depend on the government to perform those functions. The declining position of the CNC both reflected and contributed to

the decline of the PRI. The PRI retains its connection to the CNC and still has its strongest support from rural areas. The economic reforms that drastically changed the countryside and the PRI loss of the presidency in 2000, however, call into question the political and economic relevance of the CNC. The CNC can no longer play the role it was designed to play when it was established in 1938. Whether the CNC can adapt to the rapidly changing political and economic situation in Mexico remains to be seen.

—DMC

See also: Agrarian Reform/Land and Land Policy; Cárdenas, Lázaro; Confederación de Trabajadores de México (CTM); Confederación Regional Obrera Mexicana (CROM); Echeverría Alvarez, Luis; Lombardo Toledano, Vicente; Madrid (Hurtado), Miguel de la; Partido Revolucionario Institucional (PRI); Rural Labor; Salinas de Gortari, Carlos.

References:

Barry, Tom. *Zapata's Revenge: Free Trade and the Farm Crisis in Mexico.* Boston: South End Press, 1995.

Hellman, Judith Adler. *Mexico in Crisis.* 2d ed. New York: Holmes & Meier Publishers, Inc., 1988.

Levy, Daniel C., Kathleen Bruhn, and Emilio Zebadúa. *Mexico: The Struggle for Democratic Development.* Berkeley: University of California Press, 2001.

Confederación Regional Obrera Mexicana (CROM)

The first major national labor confederation to emerge after the implementation of the Constitution of 1917, the Confederación Regional Obrera Mexicana (the Regional Confederation of Mexican Workers, or CROM), set a pattern for relations between the government and organized labor that would be followed for most of the twentieth century. As Mexico industrialized under the administration of President Porfirio Díaz (1877–1880, 1884–1911), urban workers first joined together to form mutual-aid societies. In the insecure world of the industrial worker, these societies could provide assistance for workers who were injured on the job or who became unemployed. Some of these societies evolved into or inspired the formation of unions, organizations to bargain collectively on the behalf of workers. Díaz was content to let the mutualist societies operate since many of their leaders had connections to his administration. He saw in the mutualist associations an alternative to unions rather than the early stages of union development. Díaz made it clear he would not permit the development of independent unions. When copper miners went on strike at Cananea, Sonora, in 1906, the government used force to crush the strike. Similarly, federal troops put down a strike by textile workers in 1907. Díaz viewed strikes as a threat to public order and as disruptions of his economic development plans.

Shortly after the overthrow of Díaz in 1911, the Casa del Obrero Mundial (The House of the World Worker, or COM) was established in Mexico City. Influenced by anarchist thinking, the Casa originally rejected political action in favor of direct action such as strikes and sabotage. The Casa developed branches throughout Mexico and claimed to have 50,000 members at its peak. Although the Casa was the most important labor association until the formation of the CROM in 1918, the Casa lacked centralized organization and was not a true national labor confederation. The radicalism of the Casa disturbed the first Revolutionary president, Francisco Madero (1911–1913). Fearing the growing influence of the Casa, Madero closed it down, suppressed its newspaper, and expelled its foreign leaders, including the founder of the Casa, the Spanish anarchist Juan Francisco Moncaleano. After Madero's overthrow by General Victoriano Huerta in 1913, the Casa remained suppressed. Huerta, in turn, was forced from office in July 1914. The ensuing civil war among the Revolutionary factions gave the Casa a new lease on life. After considerable internal dissension, the Casa aligned itself with the Constitutionalist faction under the leadership of Venustiano Carranza and Alvaro Obregón. Both the Casa and Carranza were reluctant

allies, but in early 1915 the Casa reached a formal agreement to furnish troops—later dubbed the "Red Battalions"—for the Constitutionalists in return for Carranza's support for a prolabor policy. As soon as the Constitutionalists triumphed, Carranza moved quickly to disband the Red Battalions in early 1916.

The Casa had little time to enjoy the benefits of its alliance with Carranza. The deteriorating financial and economic situation led to strikes or strike threats in early 1916. When workers in the Federal District went on strike, Carranza responded by sending troops to disperse the strikers and to occupy the headquarters of the Casa in Mexico City. Carranza used the occasion to launch a full-scale assault on the Casa, closing down its offices outside of Mexico City and arresting its leaders.

Although the Casa had been vanquished, there was still enough labor pressure on Carranza to force him to accept strongly prolabor provisions in Article 123 of the new Constitution of 1917. Article 123 helped to stimulate labor activism and organization, forcing Carranza to take action. As the first president elected under the new Constitution, Carranza decided that labor organization was inevitable; therefore, the best approach from his viewpoint was to ensure that any developing labor organizations were under his control. Even prolabor members of the Carranza administration opposed the creation of radical independent unions. Carranza tried to head off the rise of an independent union movement by sponsoring the creation of a national labor confederation under his control.

In March 1918 a Carranza supporter, Governor Gustavo Espinosa Mireles of Coahuila, invited labor leaders to attend a convention in the state capital of Saltillo in May. The federal government was to pay all expenses for those attending the meeting. Representatives from 113 organizations attended the meeting and expressed a variety of views on establishing a national labor confederation. After considerable debate, the CROM was established. The CROM committed itself to a program that was Revolutionary, at least in apparent intent: direct action instead of political action, class warfare, worker control of industry, and land for the peasants. The person selected to head the CROM as its secretary general was Luis Morones, who had organized electrical workers in the Federal District. Although the CROM officially called for direct action rather than political action, Morones was convinced that the CROM need to be involved politically. He soon had the opportunity to act on this conviction.

With another crisis over presidential succession on the horizon, Morones and other CROM leaders had to decide which candidate to support. Obregón believed that President Carranza would back him for the presidency in 1920, but Carranza threw his support behind Ignacio Bonillas, a civilian and ambassador to the United States. The pragmatic Morones saw an opportunity to promote the CROM and his personal interests by aligning with Obregón. In exchange for CROM support in the coming struggle with Carranza, Obregón promised to create a separate ministry of labor, implement labor legislation, and promote and protect the particular interests of the CROM. In 1919 Morones established the Labor Party as the political arm of the CROM, and the Labor Party threw its support behind Obregón, whose supporters revolted against and overthrew Carranza in 1920. Having helped to put Obregón in the presidency, the CROM now waited to see if Obregón would deliver on his promises.

Obregón's ability and willingness to follow through on his promises to Morones and the CROM met with an unfavorable economic situation, the involvement of state governments in labor matters, and Obregón's interest in developing support among agrarian elements. Continued economic difficulties required Obregón to follow a pragmatic and gradualist approach in introducing major changes. His plans for economic recovery de-

pended heavily on private enterprise that would be discouraged by a strongly prolabor stance. The new government provided federal funds for the CROM; the CROM and the Labor Party were also permitted to require "contributions" from government employees. In addition, several CROM leaders received positions in the government. The most notable appointments went to Morones, who became director of the federal munitions industry, and to Celestino Gasca, who held the prominent position of governor of the Federal District. When Obregón intervened in labor disputes, it was usually in favor of the CROM; Obregón, however, often delegated decisions regarding labor disputes to officials at lower levels, such as state governors, whose views on labor might vary considerably. Indeed, when Obregón urged Congress to create a separate cabinet post of minister of labor as he had promised, Congress rejected the request on the grounds that the Constitution of 1917 gave responsibility for labor matters to state governments. While Obregón had enjoyed labor support between 1915 and 1920, he was increasingly looking to agrarian groups for future support.

As Obregón's affinities gravitated toward agrarian groups, the CROM increasingly identified with his designated successor, Plutarco Elías Calles. When disappointed presidential hopeful Adolfo de la Huerta revolted in 1923, the CROM once again had a chance to position itself on the winning side in the struggle over presidential succession. The Calles presidency (1924–1928) gave the CROM its apex of power and influence. CROM leaders held a number of positions, with Morones being appointed to the cabinet-level position of minister of industry, trade, and labor. The CROM also controlled two state governorships as well as a number of seats in the national Congress. The CROM was able to use its new power against rival unions, especially the more radical and independent Confederación General de Trabajadores (the General Confederation of Workers, or CGT). The CROM attack on the CGT included large-scale police repression of the CGT in 1925. CROM members even served as strikebreakers against rival unions. The blatant power exercised by the CROM made it easier to attract new members to CROM-affiliated unions. The CROM even unionized lottery-ticket sellers, bullfighters, and Mexico City prostitutes.

The growing power and wealth of the CROM and its leaders, especially Luis Morones, drew increasing public criticism. The strong-arm tactics of the CROM against rival unions operated side by side with extortion of employers, who were threatened with strikes if they did not pay. The upper-class lifestyles of Morones and the CROM elite—the Grupo Acción (Action Group)—were in stark contrast to the lower-class existence of most urban workers, even those who benefited from CROM membership. The dominant role played by Morones in the CROM had been a problem from the start, with defections from the CROM by groups who disagreed with Morones's tactics, personal power, and accumulating wealth. The CROM had become notoriously corrupt and abusive and was increasingly seen as a political liability by other supporters of Calles, and even by Calles himself.

The CROM's rise to power had revolved around crises over presidential succession in 1920 and 1924. Its descent from power was the product of the crisis resulting from the presidential succession of 1928. Morones fancied himself as a presidential possibility in 1928, but everyone had to reshape their thinking when the Constitution was amended to permit reelection to the presidency, paving the way for Obregón's return to power. The CROM had opposed amending the Constitution to permit reelection when the proposal was first presented in the national Congress and had little expectation of receiving favors from Obregón even if it campaigned actively for him. After initially supporting Obregón, the CROM and its affiliate, the Labor Party, withdrew their support of Obregón, leading to large-scale defections

from both organizations by Obregón supporters. Obregón's easy reelection signaled major problems for the CROM, but CROM prospects dimmed all the more when President-elect Obregón was assassinated in July 1928.

Within a few days after the assassination, all CROM leaders holding positions in the Calles administration resigned, including Morones as minister of industry, commerce, and labor. Many supporters of Obregón believed that Morones was linked to the assassination even though the assassin—a religious fanatic—had been apprehended immediately and had no discernible link to Morones or the CROM. There were further problems for the CROM when the national Congress elected Emilio Portes Gil to serve as interim president. Portes Gil was a long-time antagonist of Morones and the CROM. As governor of Tamaulipas, Portes Gil had worked successfully to replace the CROM with a labor organization under his own control. The power of the government used in behalf of the CROM for a decade now turned against it. Labor unions continued to desert the CROM at a rapid rate. A congressional investigation into CROM finances further discredited the CROM and Morones. Relations between the CROM and Calles deteriorated further when the CROM opposed the creation of an official Revolutionary party by Calles, the National Revolutionary Party. Ironically, both Calles and Morones would be sent into exile together by President Lázaro Cárdenas in 1936.

Although the CROM never recovered from the decline that began in 1928, it set a pattern in the 1920s for relations between the government and organized labor that would ensue into the 1990s. The government and organized labor worked together as partners to their mutual benefit, but organized labor was always the junior partner in the relationship. A new labor organization, the Confederación de Trabajadores de México (the Confederation of Mexican Workers, or CTM) arose in the 1930s to occupy the position formerly held by the CROM, but the CTM was never truly independent and remained the junior partner in its relationship with the government.

—DMC

See also: Anarchism; Calles, Plutarco Elías; Cárdenas, Lázaro; Carranza, Venustiano; Confederación de Trabajadores de México (CTM); Constitution of 1917; Constitutionalists; Díaz, Porfirio; Labor Movements; Madero, Francisco; Morones, Luis; Obregón, Alvaro; Portes Gil, Emilio.

References:
Ashby, Joe C. *Organized Labor and the Mexican Revolution under Lázaro Cárdenas.* Chapel Hill: University of North Carolina Press, 1967.
Clark, Marjorie Ruth. *Organized Labor in Mexico.* Chapel Hill: University of North Carolina Press, 1934.
Dulles, John W. F. *Yesterday in Mexico: A Chronicle of the Revolution, 1919–1936.* Austin: University of Texas Press, 1961.
Middlebrook, Kevin J., ed. *Unions, Workers, and the State in Mexico.* San Diego: University of California, San Diego, 1991.

Constitution of 1917

The Constitution of 1917 is considered by many Mexicans to be the central document of their modern history and the highest expression of the ideals of the Mexican Revolution. In fact, the Constitution was both a product of the Revolution and a result of debates that had been occurring for nearly a century on key social, political, and economic issues. Throughout the twentieth century, Mexico's Constitution has been revised, reinterpreted, and often selectively implemented. The last two decades of the twentieth century saw major changes in this important document; changes that some welcomed as a sign of progress and others vilified as a "sell-out" of the Mexican Revolution and its principles.

The Constitution of 1917 is the fourth constitution Mexico has had. Constitutional conventions during the nineteenth century concerned themselves primarily with the question of government structure and with the role of the Roman Catholic Church in Mexican society. The Church was a particular concern since it had emerged from the colonial era as Mexico's major landowner, and its social clout had become a form of significant political power. The 1824 Constitution embraced a federalist structure; created a balance of power among an executive, judicial, and legislative branch (while allowing for the extraordinary exercise of power by the president); and maintained the privileged position of the Roman Catholic Church in Mexican society. The 1836 Constitution embraced the idea of centralism and a strong executive. The Constitution of 1857 returned to the federalist model. More important, it included a bill of rights, endorsed the idea of no reelection, abolished the privileged position of the Roman Catholic Church, and restricted Church ownership of property. Further attempts to erode Church power would continue until the era of Porfirio Díaz (1876–1911).

When delegates to the next constitutional convention convened at Querétaro in 1916, the Mexican Revolution was well under way. President Venustiano Carranza submitted a draft constitution that simply reworded the 1857 document, with few significant changes. Yet while some delegates endorsed such a moderate remaking of the Mexican state, others were determined to create a new constitution that would reflect the popular voice of the Revolution and bring about more significant change. In its final form, the Constitution of 1917 reflected the wishes of the latter group, just as it echoed many ideas included in the 1857 document.

Mexico's new Constitution endorsed the ideals of a federal system, separation of powers, and no reelection. It created a bicameral legislature, included a bill of rights, and retained the restrictions on the Roman Catholic Church that had been put in place during the nineteenth century. The Constitution should also be viewed as a blueprint for reform that grew out of specific grievances expressed in the Mexican Revolution. The struggle of Emiliano Zapata and other revolutionaries to address the economic inequities of Mexican society found expression in the new document, as did the struggle of Mexican workers for a better life. The Constitution was also reflective of Mexico's attempt to reclaim its economic sovereignty. The nineteenth century, and particularly the years of Porfirio Díaz, were years of tremendous foreign (especially U.S.) investment in Mexico. Foreign investors came to control many parts of the economy and enjoyed generous concessions and special treatment.

Mexico's ongoing quest for Church-State separation, along with the Revolutionary struggles for land reform, workers rights, and economic sovereignty, found expression in three specific articles of the 1917 Constitution: Article 3, Article 27, and Article 123. Articles 3 and 27 completed the work of nineteenth-century Mexican liberals by restricting the activities of the Roman Catholic Church (and other religious organizations) and by attempting to undermine the political and social power of such institutions. Under these articles, Church involvement in primary education was prohibited, and private elementary and secondary schools were to be secularized. The Roman Catholic Church was also blocked from owning or administering property. Clergy were forbidden to vote, hold political office, or assemble for political purposes, and the wearing of clerical garb in pubic was forbidden. Finally, Mexican states were given the power to license (and therefore limit the number of) clergy.

The promise of land was at the heart of Article 27, which proclaimed that Mexico's land and resources ultimately belonged to the government, and which recognized the concept of the *ejido* (communal plot of land). Article 27 became the justification for the expropriation and redistribution of Mexican land on a significant scale, and it helped create a system of communal properties that have only recently begun to be dismantled. Article 27 also endorsed the 1938 expropriation of Mexico's oil fields, which had come under foreign control during the Díaz era.

Indeed, it was Article 27 that gave voice to the nationalism of the Mexican Revolution and provided the means by which Mexico could assert its sovereignty. This section of the Constitution restricts where foreigners may own property and places specific limits on ownership in border zones and coastal areas (the two places where non-Mexican investment was concentrated on the eve of the Revolution). Special treatment for foreign entrepreneurs was explicitly rejected by the Constitution, which now required foreigners to agree to abide by Mexican laws if they wished to do business in the country.

The historically poor treatment of Mexican workers was addressed in Article 123 of the new Constitution. Mexican workers gained the right to unionize, bargain collectively, and strike against employers. The government guaranteed a minimum wage, a maximum workday of eight hours, and other benefits and protections for workers, including a social security system. Workers also benefited from Article 5, which ended the practice of debt peonage (the virtual enslavement of workers through the practice of extending credit).

The gradual implementation of the Constitution characterized the period from 1917 to 1940. It was Lázaro Cárdenas, president from 1934 to 1940, who paid perhaps the most attention to the Constitution and who used it in an attempt to bring about major social and economic change. Under Cárdenas, agrarian reform reached new heights, the labor movement was reorganized and strengthened, and the properties of foreign oil companies were expropriated. Cárdenas also continued in the path of his predecessors by using Article 3 to remake Mexican schools in such a way that religion was excluded from education.

As Mexico's leaders attempted an aggressive program of economic development after 1940, implementation of key provisions of the Constitution slowed. Agrarian reform (and Article 27) was de-emphasized, foreign investment was gradually welcomed back into the country, and a more probusiness stance lessened the government's interest in the Mexican worker. That anticlericalism would no longer be a central political theme was indicated by President Manuel Avila Camacho's announcement *"soy creyente"* ("I am a believer"). Since 1940, the relationship between the Church and the Mexican State has been characterized by cooperation. In the 1988 presidential election, Carlos Salinas de Gortari was endorsed by the Mexican Church hierarchy, which was represented at Salinas's inauguration. In 1991, the Mexican Congress did away with Constitutional prohibitions on religious education, Church ownership of property, and clerical voting. In 1992, Salinas reestablished diplomatic relations with the Vatican, which had been broken as a result of earlier implementation of the anticlerical provisions of the Constitution of 1917.

Other significant changes to the Constitution occurred in the last decade of the twentieth century, and particularly under the administration of Salinas (1988–1992). Salinas's efforts (which would culminate in the signing of the North American Free Trade Agreement) were part of an attempt to push Mexico into a global economy and to enhance foreign investment by removing legal barriers to outside ownership and control of Mexican land and resources. In 1992, Salinas announced the revision of Article 27, effectively ending agrarian reform and allowing the owners of *ejidos* to sell their properties. Although this constitutional revision eliminated the admittedly inefficient system of land tenure, it drew significant protest and was criticized as a "sell-out" of the Mexican Revolution. Salinas's overtures to foreign businesses were likewise denounced as a return to the pre-Revolutionary days of Porfirio Díaz. Perhaps the most striking complaint against the revision of Article 27 came from the southern state of Chiapas, where a rebellion that claimed land reform as one of its central issues began in 1994.

Although changes to Article 3 and Article 27 were of particular importance, other important revisions have occurred. Suffrage, which was restricted in the original document to literate males (eighteen years old if married and twenty-one if single), was extended in 1954 to women and in 1975 to all Mexicans eighteen years or older. Since the 1960s, constitutional reforms have also created more space for opposition parties in the Mexican Congress, although at the end of the twentieth century the political system continued to be dominated by the official PRI party and the governmental system remained "presidentialist" (dominated by the figure of the president). Another notable reform occurred in 1998, when the Constitution was amended to grant dual citizenship to Mexicans residing abroad, 95 percent of whom live in the United States. The effect of this new law is yet to be seen (some Mexican Americans hope it will allow them to vote in Mexican elections). Of more immediate consequence was a revision during the Salinas presidency that allows the sons and daughters of foreigners to run for president in Mexico. The first beneficiary of this amendment was Vicente Fox, son of a Spanish mother, who won the presidency in 2000 as a candidate for the National Action Party (PAN).

Since it was first drafted in 1917, the Mexican Constitution has been amended and reinterpreted countless times. It has served as a blueprint for significant social and economic reform and has inspired some of the major political initiatives of the twentieth century. As Mexico enters the next millennium, the Constitution will surely continue to evolve.

—*SBP*

See also: Agrarian Reform/Land and Land Policy; Education; Labor Movements; North American Free Trade Agreement (NAFTA); Revolution of 1910; Salinas de Gortari, Carlos; Zapatista National Liberation Army (EZLN).

References:
Cumberland, Charles C. *The Mexican Revolution: The Constitutionalist Years.* Austin: University of Texas Press, 1972.
Niemeyer, E. V. *Revolution at Querétaro: The Mexican Constitutional Convention of 1916–1917.* Austin: University of Texas Press, 1974.

Constitutionalists

The Constitutionalists made up the principal Revolutionary faction opposing the military regime of General Victoriano Huerta, who ruled from February 1913 until forced from office in August 1914. Once Huerta was ousted, the Constitutionalists eventually emerged as the winning group in the bitter civil war from 1914 to 1916 among the different Revolutionary factions.

In February 1913, General Victoriano Huerta staged a coup in Mexico City that led to the overthrow and, soon thereafter, the assassination of President Francsico Madero, the first democratically elected president of the Revolutionary period. Venustiano Carranza, governor of the northern border state of Coahuila, refused to recognize the Huerta regime and instead called for the return to constitutional order as represented by the Constitution of 1857. This emphasis on constitutionality gave those who rallied to Carranza their name, the "Constitutionalists." The limited goals of the Constitutionalists were set down in the Plan of Guadalupe, issued on 26 March 1913. The Plan refused to recognize Huerta as president and also called for withdrawal of recognition from any state governor who did not reject the Huerta regime within thirty days. Carranza would immediately assume the position of "First Chief of the Constitutionalist Army." Once the Constitutionalist Revolution had triumphed, Carranza or someone designated by him would become provisional president and preside over new elections. The Plan was criticized for its failure to address social and economic problems. Carranza, however, believed that the narrow Revolutionary goals of the Plan would make it easier to unite the various Revolutionary factions behind him; he also thought that the restoration of constitutional order had to have priority over advancing social and political reforms. The Plan helped to create the image of Carranza as the leader of an organized, national revolution in contrast to the numerous local and regional leaders who were also in revolt against Huerta.

The Constitutionalists succeeded in attracting diverse Revolutionary groups to their cause. This diversity, however, made it difficult for Carranza to assert his authority over the movement and meant that the Constitutionalists were divided from the beginning. Several of the leading Constitutionalist generals—Alvaro Obregón, Francisco "Pancho" Villa, and Pablo González—held strong individual views about military strategy and Revolutionary goals that did not always agree with those of Carranza. Villa, in particular, was frequently at odds with Carranza. The cautious Carranza found it difficult to deal with the impetuous Villa, who jealously guarded his dominant political and military position in the state of Chihuahua. Villa and Carranza also clashed publicly over the U.S. intervention at Vera Cruz in April 1914; Villa was the only Constitutionalist general to support the intervention, viewing it as one more way to pressure Huerta. As the Constitutionalist armies in the north drove south toward Mexico City, Carranza deliberately withheld crucial supplies needed by Villa's forces in order to ensure that Obregón would beat Villa to Mexico City. Prominent supporters of the assassinated Madero found a new home in the Constitutionalists ranks but were often looked on as failed Revolutionaries by those who identified more closely with Carranza than with the martyred president. This introduced yet another division in Constitutionalist ranks, particularly when some of the Madero veterans began to gravitate toward Villa.

While northerners such as Villa and Obregón were at least nominally in the Constitutionalist ranks, the most important leader of Revolutionary forces in the South—Emiliano Zapata—refused to recognize Carranza as the leader of the anti-Huerta forces. Zapata did not consider Carranza to be sufficiently Revolutionary and was also aware of the growing difficulties between Villa and Carranza. Zapata essentially wanted the Constitutionalists to join his ranks rather than the reverse. Carranza, for his part, considered Zapata to be too radical and too provincial. Repeated efforts to negotiate an agreement failed. In June 1914 Zapata ordered the execution of any person supporting Carranza's Plan of Guadalupe. When forces of Obregón took control of Mexico City in August 1914, Obregón used troops of the defeated Huerta to block any advance by Zapata's forces on the capital.

When the Constitutionalists took power in Mexico City in August 1914, they did not immediately attempt to restore constitutional order. Carranza did not become provisional president nor did he designate someone else to take the post as the Plan of Guadalupe had prescribed. Carranza instead continued in his role of "First Chief of the Constitutionalist Army in Charge of the Executive Power." This permitted Carranza to rule without the restrictions of a congress or courts. Also, under Mexican law, if Carranza had declared himself provisional president, he would not have been eligible to run for election to the presidency for a regular term in his own right, which was his main goal. Although leader of the Constitutionalists, once in power, Carranza suspended the legal guarantees provided by the Constitution of 1857.

With Zapata in open opposition and Villa threatening to break ranks, Carranza tried to keep the Constitutionalist coalition together by calling a meeting of military chieftains in Mexico City for 1 October 1914. Obregón risked his own life conducting personal negotiations aimed at achieving an agreement between Carranza and Villa. Villa, however, withdrew his recognition of Carranza as "First Chief" and on 30 September called for Carranza's replacement by a civilian who would hold presidential elections as soon as possible. The meeting in Mexico City took place as scheduled but with no representatives from either Villa or Zapata. Even before the meeting took place, a decision had already been made that a larger convention of Revolutionary leaders would take place in the neutral city of Aguascalientes beginning on 10 October. The Mexico City meeting did

take one important action. It restricted participants at the Convention of Aguascalientes to military leaders only; no civilians would be permitted to take part.

The Convention at Aguascalientes differed from the Mexico City meeting in another significant way. While the Mexico City meeting was limited to supporters of Carranza, military leaders affiliated with Villa and Zapata were allowed to participate at Aguascalientes. Neither Carranza nor Zapata attended the convention. Villa made a brief appearance to make the oath of allegiance to the convention and give a short speech. Most of the Constitutionalist representatives at the Convention—including Obregón—demonstrated a willingness to dump Carranza to avoid a civil war among the Revolutionary factions. Even though the Constitutionalists represented a majority of the delegates, the Convention voted to bypass all the major Revolutionary leaders and selected as provisional president the inoffensive but not highly respected Eulalio Gutiérrez, military governor of the state of San Luis Potosí.

Even before the Convention formally elevated Gutiérrez to the provisional presidency on 6 November, Carranza started a low-profile withdrawal from Mexico City. Carranza was uncertain about the loyalties of some of his generals, including Obregón, who had played a prominent role in the selection of Gutiérrez. Carranza refused to recognize the actions taken by the Convention and ordered his representatives to withdraw from the Convention. In a crucial move for the long-term development of the Revolution, Obregón decided to stick with Carranza even though on several earlier occasions he had indicated a willingness to sacrifice him to avoid military conflict among the Revolutionary factions. Obregón resumed command of Carranza's forces and on 19 November made a public declaration of war on Villa. The long-feared civil war among the Revolutionaries was now at hand.

The civil war pitted what remained of the Constitutionalists against the forces of Villa and Zapata. Although Villa and Zapata were nominally allies, there was little in the way of mutual assistance or coordination of military operations. The two groups were simply fighting the common enemy, Carranza and the Constitutionalists. The early fighting went against the Constitutionalists, who had to abandon Mexico City and establish their capital in the port city of Vera Cruz, which had only recently witnessed the end of the U.S. occupation there. Zapata's army was reluctant to operate very far from its home base in the state of Morelos. Zapata failed to follow through on his victory at the key city of Puebla on the Mexico City–Vera Cruz road while Villa also failed to deliver on his earlier promise to Zapata to attack Vera Cruz. Villa and Zapata unwittingly gave Obregón both the time and the space he needed to launch a successful counterattack.

Constitutionalist forces led by Obregón soon recaptured Mexico City, isolated Zapata's forces in the south, and forced Villa's forces to retreat to the north. By late 1915 the two main threats to the Constitutionalists had both been reduced to regional military concerns. In the year following the resignation of Huerta (July 1914 to July 1915), perhaps as many as 200,000 Mexicans died as a result of the falling out of the Revolutionaries. The Constitutionalists emerged as the winning Revolutionary faction in the bitter civil war, but Revolutionary factionalism did not come to an end. The political leader of the Constitutionalists, Carranza, and the military leader of the Constitutionalists, Obregón, split over the issue of who should succeed to the presidency in 1920. A revolt led by Obregón resulted in the overthrow and assassination of Carranza in May 1920. Carranza was killed while trying to flee to Vera Cruz, where he had hoped to establish a government as the Constitutionalists had done in 1914.

—DMC

See also: Aguascalientes, Convention of; Assassinations; Carranza, Venustiano; Constitution of 1917; Huerta, Victoriano; Madero, Francisco; Obregón, Alvaro; Orozco, Pascual; Revolution of 1910; Vera Cruz, Occupation of (1914); Villa, Francisco "Pancho"; Zapata, Emiliano.

References:
Cumberland, Charles C. *The Mexican Revolution: The Constitutionalist Years*. Austin: University of Texas Press, 1972.

Knight, Alan. *The Mexican Revolution*. 2 vols. Cambridge: Cambridge University Press, 1986.

Quirk, Robert E. *The Mexican Revolution, 1914–1915*. Bloomington: Indiana University Press, 1960.

Richmond, Douglas W. *Venustiano Carranza's Nationalist Struggle, 1893–1920*. Lincoln: University of Nebraska Press, 1983.

Corruption

Corruption has been a pervasive part of the Mexican political system for centuries. The Revolutionary upheavals and economic development schemes of the twentieth century provided new dimensions for this old practice. Historically, this corruption has taken on a variety of forms and has affected all levels of the political system. Corruption can range from the neighborhood police official seeking a payoff to overlook a parking violation to the president of the nation asking for kickbacks on multimillion-dollar government contracts. The concept of a "public office as a public trust" has never taken root in Mexico. The more typical view is that a public office is a private concession. There is a built-in expectation that public officials will exploit their positions for personal gain. Corruption is viewed as an important element keeping the system together and permitting it to function, even thought the waste and inefficiency connected with such a system are also generally recognized. Although corruption is credited with promoting political stability, it has also led to a deep-seated cynicism on the part of the public toward politics and politicians. In dealing with officials, the average citizen is more likely to think in terms of "seeking favors" than "demanding rights."

The Revolutionary generals who survived the upheavals of the 1910–1920 period felt they had conquered the positions that they had achieved and were determined to exploit them as they saw fit. Many Revolutionary leaders used their political and military positions to engage in business activities, seize land, eliminate their competitors, and obtain government contracts. The first president elected under the Revolutionary Constitution of 1917, Venustiano Carranza, set a pattern that would be followed by later presidents. Carranza personally exploited his position and permitted other political and military officials to do likewise. When forced to flee Mexico City in 1920, he had to commandeer a train to carry off the loot.

Another tradition also was soon established: a presidential call to end corruption. These anticorruption campaigns began in the 1920s and have become a staple of presidential politics. They help to disassociate the new administration from the old one, to distract the public from other pressing problems, to establish the control of the new president, and to discourage the old president from meddling in politics. They also stress that corruption is a result of particular individuals gone wrong rather than a characteristic of the system itself. These campaigns generally produce little in the way of significant results. The campaign cannot be carried out too thoroughly for fear of destabilizing the political system. Also, former presidents have always been exempted as targets from these campaigns no matter how extravagant the corruption of their administrations.

In those periods when the government becomes more active in the economy, corruption is likely to be more pronounced. One of the most corrupt administrations was that of Miguel Alemán, president from 1946 to 1952. In the name of rapid industrialization, the government was playing a more prominent role in the economy. Federally sponsored construction projects provided ample opportunity for kickbacks on contracts and profitable land deals using inside information. Alemán also used his position to promote Acapulco as an important tourist resort, a development in which he was reported to have a major personal interest. Alemán also encouraged the military to engage in illegal enrichment activities in order to keep them out of politics. Alemán's departure from the presidency resulted in an unusually large number of resignations and transfers in both the political and military ranks amid charges that some $200 million was unaccounted for during his term.

Corruption continued as a chronic problem during the 1950s and 1960s and emerged as a major political issue in the 1970s and 1980s. The crisis over corruption was again connected with a significant increase in government involvement in the economy during the administration of José López Portillo (1976–1982). López Portillo had started his administration with the usual anticorruption campaign, targeting several senior officials in the previous administration of Luis Echeverría (1970–1976). López Portillo, however, soon became involved in a major corruption scandal of his own brought on by the oil boom of the late 1970s. Oil revenue led to a major increase in government spending, with much of the funds making their way into the pockets of government officials. The state-owned oil company, PEMEX, and the president himself were at the center of the growing controversy over corruption. PEMEX was spending as well as earning large amounts of money. PEMEX administrators routinely demanded kickbacks on the numerous contracts they were giving out, and many contracts went to companies owned by prominent politicians, including the director of PEMEX, Jorge Díaz Serrano. López Portillo himself was also caught up in an expanding web of corruption, favoritism, and nepotism. The president found lucrative government positions for his wife, son, two sisters, and even his mistress. One sister built a mansion on federal property using government equipment. The president bought two mansions in Acapulco: one for his wife, the other for his

Jorge Díaz Serrano, a former PEMEX Oil Company Director and Mexican senator, is released from prison following a 1984 conviction for corruption. Mexico City, 1989. (Sergio Dorantes / Corbis)

mistress. This personal housing binge concluded with the president building a five-mansion complex on the edge of Mexico City while the country was in the midst of a major financial crisis. Critics charged López Portillo with making off with between $1 and $3 billion.

When Miguel de la Madrid became president in 1982, he put out a call for "moral renovation." New legislation, government regulations, and presidential instructions were issued to deal with corruption. A special agency—the Office of the Controller General—was established to lead the anticorruption campaign. The president appointed an army general to head the notoriously corrupt Mexico City police force. The de la Madrid administration prosecuted two of the most blatant symbols of corruption in the López Portillo administration: PEMEX Director Jorge Díaz Serrano and Mexico City Police Chief Arturo Durazo Moreno. Díaz Serrano was accused of pocketing $34 million on the purchase of two tankers while Durazo had accumulated millions of dollars in assets on a salary of about $1,600 per month as police chief. Miguel de la Madrid, however, refused to go after López Portillo himself and later had to deal with charges that he was earning illegal millions as president.

One of the factors affecting the public perception of corruption was the ongoing financial and economic problems confronting Mexico in the 1980s. The oil bust, the debt crisis, an austerity program, and major economic reforms had led to a major decline in the standard of living for most Mexicans. When economic hard times coincided with unprecedented levels of corruption, it elevated corruption from a "problem" to a "crisis." The public began to link their sinking economic situation directly to increasing corruption, with its accompanying waste and mismanagement. The few who were benefiting directly from corruption found themselves competing harder for a diminishing pool of resources. Even the elite had to consider the possibility that corruption—previously seen as a stabilizing political influence—had turned into excessive corruption and was perhaps a threat to the system itself.

Corruption once again reached the level of national scandal during the administration of President Carlos Salinas de Gortari (1988–1994). Early in his administration Salinas launched an anticorruption campaign that included the arrest of the corrupt and powerful leaders of the oil union as well as prominent business figures involved in a stock market scandal. Salinas declined to pursue corruption charges made against Miguel de la Madrid and feared that the issue of corruption was undermining his efforts to reach a trade agreement with the United States. The connection between corruption and the drug trade also embarrassed Salinas. The growing controversy over corruption hit close to home when the president's brother, Raúl Salinas, was linked to massive corruption as well as the drug trade. Raúl used his presidential connections to profit from government contracts and the sell-off of government-owned businesses, earning him the nickname, "Mr. Ten Percent." He was also linked to multimillion-dollar payoffs to protect the narcotics trafficking of Colombia's notorious Medellín drug cartel. Later disclosures indicated that Raúl had deposited $84 million in Swiss bank accounts under a false name. The top Swiss official investigating the affair estimated that Raúl had pocketed about $500 million during his brother's presidential administration. Although President Salinas was not directly linked to any of Raúl's activities, a number of officials had warned the president about his brother's business dealings, warnings which the president ignored. In July 2001 the Mexican Attorney General's Office charged that Raúl received 239 payments totaling $13.6 million from the Office of the Presidency between 2 August 1989 and 2 August 1994, years that his brother Carlos was president. Raúl finally wound up being sentenced to fifty years in prison in a murder

plot—a sentence later reduced—while Carlos Salinas went into self-imposed exile in Ireland shortly after stepping down from the presidency.

The legal actions concerning the Salinas soap opera played themselves out during the administration of President Ernesto Zedillo. Although Zedillo had numerous financial and economic problems with which to deal, his administration largely escaped the spectacular scandals of more recent years. Corruption continued to be a major issue, especially drug-related corruption, with some observers claiming that Mexico was on the verge of becoming a "narco-state" like Colombia.

Although corruption will continue as a major problem, there are economic and political changes taking place that will affect its future nature and extent. The economic reforms of the 1980s and 1990s have substantially reduced the role of the government in the economy and, thus, the possibilities for corruption. The erosion of the dominant position of the old official party, the PRI, will also influence corruption. In the past, PRI control of the national Congress has restricted that body's role in exposing and correcting corrupt practices; for example, PRI members of Congress have consistently blocked any efforts to investigate corruption charges against former presidents. The loss of the PRI majority in the lower house of Congress offered the possibility of new congressional investigations into corrupt activities. In late 1999 a special committee of the lower house investigated the state agency, CONASUPO, which provides heavily subsidized food products and other basic commodities to the poor. After studying CONASUPO's activities over the previous thirteen years, the committee concluded that the agency had lost billions of dollars through corruption, nepotism, influence peddling, and dealing in contaminated food products. As opposition politicians win positions at all levels of government, they will be eager to turn the spotlight on the corrupt practices of the official party. As the reformers have discovered already, the fight against corruption will be a long one. It will also involve more than simply reducing the control of the long-dominant PRI. It will be necessary to deal with the "culture of corruption," which goes beyond any one party and beyond the political system.

—*DMC*

See also: Alemán, Miguel; Drug Trafficking; Government; López Portillo, José; Madrid (Hurtado), Miguel de la; Salinas de Gortari, Carlos.

References:

Morris, Stephen D. *Corruption and Politics in Contemporary Mexico.* Tuscaloosa: University of Alabama Press, 1991.

Niblo, Stephen R. *Mexico in the 1940s: Modernity, Politics, and Corruption.* Wilmington, DE: Scholarly Resources, 1999.

Riding, Alan. *Distant Neighbors: A Portrait of the Mexicans.* New York: Alfred A. Knopf, 1985.

Cristero Rebellion

A popular movement that affected parts of Mexico from 1926 to 1929, the Cristero Rebellion (so called because of the rebel battle cry, *"Viva Cristo Rey!"*—long live Christ the King!) reflected discontent with the administration of Plutarco Elías Calles. The rebellion was touched off by Calles's attempt to undermine the position of the Roman Catholic Church in Mexico, and it underscored the long-standing tension between Church and State that is an integral part of Mexico's history.

Mexico's Church-State struggle has its roots in the colonial era, when the Spanish Crown acted as supervisor of the Roman Catholic Church through the *patronato real* or royal patronage. The colonial Church assumed a privileged position in Mexican society, monopolizing the educational system, serving as the chief financial institution, and exerting a general social influence through its regular contact with the people. Clergy also enjoyed the *fuero,* which provided a kind of legal immunity. The Roman Catholic Church emerged from the colonial period with con-

siderable wealth and prestige. Its strength was the concern of politicians throughout the nineteenth century, and this issue ultimately helped precipitate a civil war. Through the Constitution of 1857 and the Laws of Reform (issued in 1859), Mexican liberals attempted to curtail clerical privileges and to severely undermine the economic and social clout of the Roman Catholic Church. Their attempts were only partly successful, and by the end of the nineteenth century, President Porfirio Díaz opted for a truce between the Mexican State and the Roman Catholic Church. The uneasy truce held until the Mexican Revolution.

The anticlerical sentiment that was a part of Mexico's nineteenth-century history resurfaced during the Revolution, with many Revolutionaries viewing the Church as an enemy and targeting clergy and Church property in their campaigns. This sentiment was expressed in Articles 3, 5, 127, and 130 of the Constitution of 1917. The architects of the Constitution sought a weak Church that would be subordinate to a strong Mexican State. To this end, the Constitution prohibited Church involvement in primary education, forbade the Church from owning or controlling real property, and prevented clergy from voting, holding political office, or assembling for political purposes. The Constitution also provided for the state regulation of clergy, which would allow local officials to restrict the Church's presence within their jurisdictions.

Encouraged by Pope Leo XII's call for Roman Catholic social activism in the encyclical *Rerum Novarum* (1891), Mexican Roman Catholics had already begun to organize on the eve of the Revolution. The anticlerical provisions of the Constutition of 1917 encouraged such organization, as women, workers, and Roman Catholic youth banded together to resist implementation of the Constitution. In 1925, Roman Catholic organizations combined to establish the National League for the Defense of Religious Liberty (LNDLR). Confrontation finally came when Calles, who had proven his anticlerical bent as governor of Sonora, became Mexico's president in 1924. Calles invited state officials to regulate their clergy, and he even encouraged an effort, ultimately unsuccessful, to establish a schismatic "Mexican Catholic Church." Finally, in 1926 he decreed that he would enforce the anticlerical provisions of the Constitution. The Church responded with a general strike that suspended Mass and other religious ceremonies. The LNDLR responded with militancy. Calles faced a guerrilla war that would last for three years and result in the death and exile of thousands of Mexicans.

The Cristero Rebellion was a localized uprising, concentrated primarily in western Mexico and especially affecting the states of Jalisco, Guanajuato, Guerrero, Michoacán, Zacatecas, and Colima. At its height it included perhaps as many as 50,000 rebels. Although precipitated by the Church-State issue and ostensibly led by the LNDLR, the rebellion attracted those with motives independent of the religious question. Former Revolutionaries who had followed Pancho Villa, Emiliano Zapata, and Venustiano Carranza joined the rebel ranks, as did peasants fighting for land and Mexicans expressing their frustration over Calles's ambitious plan to expand and secularize rural education. Indeed, the rebellion may be seen as part of a more general resistance to the intrusion of an increasingly powerful and ambitious Mexican central government.

The guerrilla warfare and more coordinated efforts of Cristero rebels provided a significant challenge to the Federal Army and forced Calles to look abroad for help in financing the government's counterrevolutionary campaign. After an impressive rebel victory at the Battle of Tepatitlán in April 1929, Cristeros and the Federal Army reached a stalemate. The stalemate was broken with the help of United States Ambassador Dwight Morrow. Morrow's careful cultivation of Calles, and his good reputation among Mexicans, enabled him to arrange and supervise successful negotiations between the Church hierarchy and the Mexican government. Under Calles's successor, Emilio Portes Gil, an agreement was reached in which the constitutional articles relating to the Church remained intact, but the government agreed to respect the integrity and spiritual role of the Church.

While the Roman Catholic Church remains a popular and revered institution in the eyes of many Mexicans, the agreement that ended the Cristero Rebellion was ultimately a victory for the idea of a Church excluded from the political arena and subordinated to a secular state. In this sense, the Cristero Rebellion represents the culmination of a historical process that began in the nineteenth century with the first attempts to curtail a Roman Catholic Church that had become politically powerful, economically wealthy, and socially influential.

—SBP

See also: Constitution of 1917; Education; Religion.

References:
Bailey, David. *Viva Cristo Rey!: The Cristero Rebellion and the Church-State Conflict in Mexico.* Austin: University of Texas Press, 1974.
Quirk, Robert. *The Mexican Revolution and the Catholic Church, 1910–1929.* Bloomington: Indiana University Press, 1973.
Tuck, Jim. *The Holy War in Los Altos: A Regional Analysis of Mexico's Cristero Rebellion.* Tucson: University of Arizona Press, 1982.

D

de la Huerta, Adolfo (1881–1955)

Interim president in the crucial year of 1920, Adolfo de la Huerta was born in Guaymas, Sonora, on 26 May 1881. De la Huerta's father was an important local businessman, and his son received a good education emphasizing accounting and music. He studied accounting at the National Preparatory School in Mexico City and later worked as an accountant for the National Bank of Mexico. De la Huerta was caught up in the Anti-reelection Movement of the late Porfirian period, supporting for the presidency General Bernardo Reyes in 1909 and Francisco Madero in 1910. He was elected to the state legislature of Sonora in 1911 and supported in local campaigns two persons who would figure prominently in his future and that of Mexico: future Presidents Alvaro Obregón and Plutarco Elías Calles.

De la Huerta was in Mexico City in February 1913 when the coup that overthrew Madero began. He returned to the north to participate in the growing opposition to the new regime of General Victoriano Huerta, recognizing Venustiano Carranza as leader of Revolutionary forces. After General Huerta resigned in July 1914, Carranza appointed de la Huerta to the position of chief of staff in the Ministry of the Interior (Internal Secu-

rity). In August 1915, de la Huerta became minister of the interior, one of the most important and sensitive posts in Carranza's government.

De la Huerta continued his rise through the Revolutionary ranks with his appointment as interim governor of Sonora in May 1916. As governor, de la Huerta introduced a number of reforms relating to land, labor, and the legal system. After the election of Carranza as the first president under the new Constitution of 1917, Adolfo de la Huerta returned to his old position of chief of staff at the Ministry of the Interior. He was elected to the national Senate from Sonora in 1918, later was appointed Consul General of Mexico in New York, and in 1919 was elected governor of Sonora.

When de la Huerta became governor on 1 September 1919, a major national crisis was brewing over the question of the presidential succession in 1920. Carranza was attempting to impose a civilian, Ignacio Bonillas, as president; this conflicted with the presidential ambitions of de la Huerta's fellow Sonoran, General Alvaro Obregón, whose military successes had put Carranza in the presidency in the first place. Carranza tried to undercut Obregón's candidacy by attacking his base of support in Sonora. This brought the Carranza

Adolfo de la Huerta, former provisional president of Mexico, photographed while living in exile at his Los Angeles home, May 1929 (Bettmann/Corbis)

administration into direct conflict with de la Huerta's state administration. Although de la Huerta had held a series of important positions under Carranza, de la Huerta supported Obregón in the showdown for the presidency. In April 1920, de la Huerta and yet another Sonoran, General Plutarco Elías Calles, issued the Plan of Agua Prieta, which withdrew recognition from Carranza's government and appointed de la Huerta commander of Revolutionary forces. When most of the army came out in favor of the revolt, Carranza was finished. While trying to move his government from Mexico City to Vera Cruz, Carranza was overtaken and killed on 21 May 1920 by forces loyal to Obregón. The Mexican Congress then named de la Huerta interim president until new elections could be held and the new president could take office on 1 December 1920.

Although the presidency of de la Huerta lasted only six months, there were a number of important developments under his brief administration. De la Huerta provided a major impetus to pacification by reaching political agreements with both the Zapatistas and the Villistas. The most controversial conciliatory deal involved Pancho Villa, who had continued to cause trouble in the north, including an unsuccessful attempt to take Ciudad Juárez in 1919. Villa went into retirement in return for a large estate, a government-paid bodyguard, and other financial considerations. Obregón's antagonism toward Villa was so great that he recognized the deal but refused to endorse it officially. De la Huerta did not have time to deal with two other pressing issues: the national finances and the lack of diplomatic recognition by the United States. De la Huerta completed his most important function by presiding over new presidential elections and handing over power to Obregón on schedule.

Obregón appointed de la Huerta minister of the treasury, an important position given Mexico's chaotic national finances and international debt problems. De la Huerta made some progress in both areas. He restored order to the federal budget and reached a long-term agreement with Mexico's foreign creditors in 1922.

De la Huerta found himself increasingly at odds with President Obregón. The president approved but disliked the 1922 agreement with the international bankers. Obregón supported a package of agreements—the Bucareli Agreements—being put together with the United States government dealing with financial claims, oil concessions, property expropriations, and recognition of the Obregón administration. De la Huerta was not involved in the negotiations and objected to the final agreements based on the belief that they sacrificed Revolutionary goals. More threatening was the question of presidential succession in 1924. Obregón could not run for reelection and had to chose between his two fellow Sonorans: de la Huerta and Plutarco Elías Calles. Obregón opted for Calles, a move that angered de la Huerta's supporters as well as a number of army generals who outranked Calles. In December 1923 there was a revolt on behalf of de la Huerta, with major elements of the army coming over to his side. The rebels were unable to coordinate their activities, and Obregón skillfully mobilized political and military support from labor, peasants, and the remaining elements of the army. The revolt carried over into 1924 but failed. De la Huerta went into exile in the United States while many of the generals who supported his revolt were executed.

De la Huerta spent most of his U.S. exile in Los Angeles, supporting himself by giving violin and voice lessons. In 1927 de la Huerta's younger brother, General Alfonso de la Huerta, died during a failed revolt against the Calles regime. Developments took an ironic twist during the presidential administration of Lázaro Cárdenas (1934–1940). In 1935 Cárdenas granted amnesty to de la Huerta and in 1936 appointed him inspector general of Mexican consulates in the United States; in 1936 Cárdenas sent Calles into exile, with Calles settling in California. De la Huerta served as inspector general from 1936 to 1946; in 1946 he returned to Mexico to serve as director general of civil pensions and retirement. He died in Mexico City in 1955.

—*DMC*

See also: Assassinations; Calles, Plutarco Elías; Cárdenas, Lázaro; Debt, Mexico's Foreign; Díaz, Porfirio; Huerta, Victoriano; Madero, Francisco; Obregón, Alvaro; Presidents of the Twentieth Century; Revolution of 1910; Villa, Francisco "Pancho"; Zapata, Emiliano.

References:
Camp, Roderic A. *Mexican Political Biographies, 1884–1935.* Austin: University of Texas Press, 1991.

Dulles, John W. F. *Yesterday in Mexico: A Chronicle of the Revolution, 1919–1936.* Austin: University of Texas Press, 1972.

Debt, Mexico's Foreign

The foreign debt has played an important part in the national life of Mexico since independence in 1821. Mexico contracted for its first foreign loan from a British firm in 1823; the Mexican government defaulted on the debt owed to British bondholders in 1827. These credit problems became diplomatic problems as European governments were prepared to intervene on behalf of their nationals to force Mexico to pay its debts. After three years of civil war from 1858 through 1860, the government of Benito Juárez reluctantly suspended payment on both the foreign and domestic debts in July 1861. This led to intervention in early 1862 by the forces of Britain, Spain, and France to force collection of debts owed to their nationals. This triple alliance soon broke up; Britain and Spain removed their troops from Mexico, while France attempted to impose the empire of Archduke Maximilian. The French Intervention led to a break in relations between Mexico and the nations representing its principal foreign creditors. Although the intervention ended in 1867, Mexico's problems with the foreign debt continued into the 1870s and 1880s.

During the 1870s, the Mexican government punctually paid money owed under a claims agreement with the United States, but Mexico's major European creditors found debt collection difficult given the extended break in diplomatic relations between Mexico and Great Britain and France consequent to the intervention of the 1860s. Although Mexico renewed relations with France in October 1880, a renewal of relations with Britain was delayed; Britain wanted a settlement of the debt to precede a renewal of relations while the Mexican government saw a renewal of relations as the key step to reaching an agreement on the debt. Britain and Mexico finally agreed to renew relations in October 1884 without any prior agreement on the debt question.

Seeking new foreign loans and investment, President Porfirio Díaz (1877–1880, 1884–1911) emphasized the need to reach a settlement of the foreign debt. This led in 1888 to the so-called Dublán Convention, named for the Mexican secretary of the treasury, Manuel

Dublán. The convention provided for a consolidation of past debts held by British and German bondholders through the issuance of new bonds paying 6 percent interest for a 35-year period. The convention had the desired effect of attracting foreign investment and promoting modernization but left Mexico with the largest debt of any Latin American country when Díaz was overthrown in 1911.

The upheaval of the Revolution of 1910 interrupted payments on the foreign debt while simultaneously forcing the various political factions to contract additional debt. As Mexico began to experience more peaceful conditions in 1917, the administration of newly elected president Venustiano Carranza turned its attention to Mexico's financial problems. Mexico's Ministry of the Treasury hired the well-known U.S. accountant, Thomas R. Lill, to make a comprehensive audit of the government's financial situation. Lill calculated Mexico's total debt at almost $865 million; his audit would serve as the basis for negotiations over Mexico's debt for years to come. After World War I ended in November 1918, the international financial community was again able to turn its attention to Mexico. In February 1919 the International Committee of Bankers on Mexico was formed, made up of representatives from leading French, British, and U.S. banks. The U.S. banks dominated the committee, and its most important figure was Thomas Lamont of the New York banking firm, J. P. Morgan and Company.

Efforts to settle Mexico's foreign debt in the early 1920s became entangled in disagreements over property rights, Mexico's desire for new loans, and U.S. refusal to extend recognition to the government of President Alvaro Obregón (1920–1924). Despite these obstacles, Thomas Lamont and Mexico's Secretary of the Treasury Adolfo de la Huerta reached a complex agreement in the summer of 1922. The Lamont–de la Huerta agreement left Mexico heavily indebted (almost one billion pesos after consolidation), but it also gave the Obregón administration until 1

January 1928 to resume full servicing of the debt. The agreement later contributed to a split between Obregón and de la Huerta that culminated in a revolt by de la Huerta in December 1923. The expense of putting down the rebellion and the failure of the banks to provide new loans led Obregón to suspend the Lamont–de la Huerta agreement in June 1924. A modified version of the 1922 agreement was approved in October 1925. The continuing financial problems of the Mexican government led to new efforts at negotiation, with Mexico stressing that any new agreement take into account its "capacity to pay." Even without new loans, by 1929 Mexico's total foreign debt—including bonds and claims—had reached 1.4 billion pesos.

The onset of the Great Depression of the 1930s found Mexico in the unwanted position of being Latin America's largest debtor. Early in the Depression, the Mexican government unsuccessfully tried to gain U.S. acceptance of a moratorium on debt payments. President Lázaro Cárdenas (1934–1940) recognized Mexico's foreign debt and did not formally default on financial obligations but indicated that he would not divert government revenues from developmental programs to debt payments. World War II created a great demand for many strategic products, which Mexico furnished, enabling the government to reduce its foreign debt. Wartime economic cooperation between the United States and Mexico led to new negotiations on the foreign debt. Thomas Lamont and the International Committee of Bankers on Mexico still represented Mexico's major creditors, and a new agreement was concluded in 1942. The agreement took into account the irregularity of Mexico's earlier interest payments on the debt, the low market value of Mexico's bonds, and the need to emphasize Mexico's ability to pay. The new accord reduced Mexico's acknowledged foreign debt from more than $1 billion to $117 million, a reduction of approximately 90 percent.

In the years immediately after World War II, the Mexican economy experienced a period of spectacular growth that came to be called the "Miracle." By the mid-1960s the "miracle" had run its course, and by the mid-1970s the foreign debt had once again become a major problem. The discovery of large, new oil reserves in the mid-1970s, however, changed both international and domestic attitudes about Mexico's debt. The administration of José López Portillo (1976–1982) spent lavishly and borrowed heavily, assuming that current and future oil revenues could cover the bills. In the early 1980s this approach began to unravel because of an international recession, higher interest rates, and a drastic decline in oil prices. A domestic debt problem became an international debt crisis in August 1982 when the Mexican government publicly announced that it could not service its debt. The U.S. government moved quickly to prevent an official default by Mexico, fearing that a default might lead to a series of defaults by other Third-World countries that could threaten the entire international financial structure. The United States provided an aid package totaling almost $3 billion while the International Monetary Fund agreed to provide new loans if Mexico adopted an "austerity program." This program included a major reduction in government spending, increased taxes, a devaluation of the peso, the easing of restrictions on foreign investment, and the sale of unprofitable government-owned businesses. Mexico reluctantly agreed to the austerity program, which produced the worst economic downturn since the Great Depression of the 1930s. Faced with mounting social pressures and political opposition, the government of President Miguel de la Madrid (1982–1988) fell off the austerity bandwagon in 1985 only to climb back on in 1986 as Mexico's foreign debt approached $100 billion.

Mexico finally reached a comprehensive settlement with its creditors in January 1990. Under the complex agreement, creditors were given three options. First, they could swap their loans for an equal amount of new Mexican bonds paying a fixed rate of 6.25 per-

cent, far below the rates at which most creditors were supposed to be repaid. Second, they could exchange their old loans for new Mexican bonds at a 35 percent discount but with an interest rate closer to the current market rate. Third, creditors could retain their existing loans but had to provide new loans equal to 25 percent of the existing loans. The Mexican government—eager for new loans—hoped that creditors would take option three. Instead banks holding almost 90 percent of the debt elected either option one or two, meaning there was little in the way of new lending. The agreement did provide the government with enough relief that the debt crisis became once again the debt problem, a problem which continues into the twenty-first century.

The debt crisis and subsequent recession forced the Mexican government to abandon most of the economic development scheme it had been following since World War II. The crisis adversely affected almost all Mexicans, especially the lower and middle classes. For Mexican workers, real wages in 1986 were at virtually the same level they had been at in 1967; for many, a generation of economic progress had been wiped out by the "lost decade" of the 1980s. The debt problem had been resolved but not solved. After almost two centuries of independence, Mexico was still struggling with its foreign debt.

—*DMC*

See also: Economy; Presidents of the Twentieth Century; United States, Relations with; World War II.

References:

Bazant, Jan. *Historia de la deuda exterior de México (1823–1946).* Mexico: El Colegio De México, 1968.

Hall, Linda B. *Oil, Banks, and Politics: The United States and Postrevolutionary Mexico, 1917–1924.* Austin: University of Texas Press, 1995.

Turlington, Edgar. *Mexico and Her Foreign Creditors.* New York: Columbia University Press, 1930.

Democratization Process

For many Latin American countries in the late twentieth century, the "democratization process" meant the replacement of military governments with civilian governments. In Mexico, with the last general in the presidency having stepped down in 1946, democratization has taken on a much different meaning. It means ending one-party rule by the Institutional Revolutionary Party (Partido Revolucionario Institucional, or PRI) and opening up the PRI itself to greater political competition. While elections have regularly been held at all levels of government, they typically have not been contests for power but rather opportunities to gauge public support for the policies of the PRI and the government. The rigging of elections became a fundamental part of the political system. Opponents of the PRI were often denied access to the media.

The movement toward greater political competition began in the 1960s, brought on by growing criticism that the PRI was unrepresentative of and unresponsive to a large part of the population. Problems with the government's economic development scheme also encouraged demands for greater democracy in the system. The first of the reforms came in 1964 with the assignment of thirty to forty seats in the lower house of the Mexican Congress, the Chamber of Deputies, to opposition parties based on their percentage of votes in national elections (proportional representation). This approach was expanded in 1977 when the number of seats in the Chamber of Deputies was increased to 400 with a minimum of 100 going to opposition parties. Electoral reform in 1986 again increased the size of the Chamber, from 400 to 500, with 200 of the seats to be assigned by proportional representation; in addition, no one party could hold more than 70 percent of the seats in the Chamber. All of these reforms were aimed at reducing criticism of one-party rule without actually threatening the control of the PRI. Also, the government was awarding seats in the Chamber without actually guaranteeing more effective suffrage in elections. In fact, the PRI continued to "win" almost all of the 300 seats involving di-

rect competition by district. The administration of President Miguel de la Madrid (1982–1988) showed a greater willingness to permit legitimate competition for power at the municipal level, with the PRI conceding defeat in reasonably clean elections in a number of major cities.

The presidential elections of 1988 proved to be a watershed in the democratization process, even though there were widespread charges of electoral fraud. The PRI candidate, Carlos Salinas, found himself in a three-way race involving Manuel Clouthier, the candidate of the National Action Party (Partido Acción Nacional, or PAN), and Cuauhtémoc Cárdenas, the nominee of a coalition of leftist parties. Cárdenas had led an unsuccessful effort to reform the PRI from within, known as the Democratic Current. When the party leadership made it clear there would be no internal reforms and after Cárdenas lost out on the PRI presidential nomination, Cárdenas and several other prominent members of the PRI left the party. Salinas barely received a majority of the votes, the worst showing ever by an official party candidate. Congressional elections in 1988 left the PRI with a slight majority in the Chamber of Deputies, 260 out of 500 seats.

The democratic opening widened with PAN victories in governorship races in Baja California in 1989 and San Luis Potosí and Guanajuato in 1991. The victory in Baja California represented the first governor's race officially won by an opposition candidate since the 1930s. Congressional elections in 1991, however, led to a slight increase in the PRI majority in the Chamber of Deputies from 260 to 321 of 500 seats. The PRI continued its overwhelming domination of elections by district in 1991, winning 290 of the 300 directly contested seats. President Salinas also sponsored electoral reforms imposing restrictions on party financing, limits on campaign spending, and providing greater opposition access to the media.

There was considerable uncertainty as the 1994 presidential elections approached. The leftist coalition of the 1988 election had evolved into a new party, the Democratic Revolutionary Party (Partido Revolucionario Democrático, or PRD), but was experiencing problems with party unity and organization. The North American Free Trade Agreement had gone into effect on 1 January 1994. That same day, the Zapatista uprising took place in Chiapas. Adding to the electoral anxiety was the March assassination of the PRI's presidential nominee, Luis Donaldo Colosio. The PRI hastily put forward as its new nominee Colosio's campaign manager, Ernesto Zedillo, who was being prepared for a possible run for the presidency in 2000. Zedillo won with a narrow majority of the votes but with the added benefit of having participated in what was generally viewed as an honest election.

The democratization process continued after 1994 but with unpredictable results. Reforms passed in 1996 increased the autonomy of the Federal Election Institute, the organization responsible for conducting elections, and provided for the election of the mayor of Mexico City. The position of mayor of Mexico City was seen as a possible stepping-stone to the presidency in 2000; the mayoral election took place in 1997, resulting in a victory for Cuauhtémoc Cárdenas, who had finished a distant third in the presidential elections of 1994. Cárdenas's party, the PRD, also controlled a majority of the seats on the Mexico City council. Congressional elections in 1997 resulted in the PRI winning only 239 seats in the Chamber of Deputies, leaving it without an absolute majority in the lower house for the first time. The PRI maintained a majority in the Senate, but the percentage of opposition senators increased to 40 percent representing five different parties. Although the once-dominant position of the PRI was eroding, it still was able to win seven of the ten races for governor in 1998.

Many saw the ultimate test of democratization in the contest for the presidency in 2000. While the PRI has been willing to recognize election losses at all levels of government, the official party always retained control of the presidency. Ironically, it was the PRI that displayed the most democratic energy in selecting a presidential nominee in 2000. For the first time since the founding of the official party, the outgoing president did not "tap" his successor. Instead the PRI permitted an open campaign for the presidential nomination, leading to a lively contest for the designation. Meanwhile, the two leading opposition parties—the PRD and the PAN—found it difficult to generate much internal political competition. The leading candidate for the PRD nomination was Cuauhtémoc Cárdenas, who was finding his position as mayor of Mexico City to be as much a political swamp as a stepping-stone to the presidency. There was further embarrassment for the PRD when a vote for party leader had to be thrown out due to widespread voting irregularities. Governor Vicente Fox of Guanajuato was virtually unopposed for the PAN nomination. Fox's victory in the election marked the first victory for an opposition candidate in a presidential election since the founding of the official party in 1929. The PRI also experienced a substantial decline in its dominant position in the national Congress.

Congressional elections in 2003 sent mixed signals about the progress of democratization. Perhaps, the most telling fact was that only 41 percent of the eligible voters cast their ballots. Election results continued the division in the lower house of the Congress, the Chamber of Deputies, in which no party had a majority. The PRI continued to be the dominant party in the Chamber but lacked a simple majority. PAN strength in the Chamber declined as a result of the elections. The divided Congress that had blocked Fox's efforts at reform between 2000 and 2003 would be even more divided between 2003 and 2006. With the major parties already maneuvering for the 2006 presidential elections, the prospect for cooperation between the president and the Congress was slim.

There is no guarantee that Mexico will evolve steadily in the direction of greater democracy. Democratization is hindered by a number of longstanding characteristics of the political system: lack of respect for the rule of the law, corruption, opportunism, political violence, and presidentialism. While democratization is most evident at local and state levels, there are signs of it at the national level. The loss of its absolute majority in the Chamber of Deputies forced the PRI to seek out allies, leading to significant opposition involvement in financial and economic matters. There is still doubt as to whether political leaders of all parties are committed to playing the political game according to democratic rules. While the PRI established a national primary for the presidential nomination in 2000, the reform required that the nomination go to the candidate who won a majority of the country's 300 electoral districts rather than to the candidate receiving the highest popular vote. The most prominent political reform movement within the PRI—the "Renovating Current"—was highly critical of many of the key liberalizing economic reforms of the 1980s and 1990s. After regularly criticizing the PRI for voter fraud, the PRD found itself with a major voting fraud scandal in its own internal elections. The PAN worked with the PRI in the Congress on economic and financial matters while trying unsuccessfully to negotiate a coalition with the PRD aimed at defeating the PRI for the presidency in 2000. In recent years the Mexican government has been more responsive to foreign criticism of undemocratic practices, especially from the United States. There is little doubt that Mexico—pushed by both internal and external forces—is moving in the direction of greater political participation. Whether this will lead to democratic practices and structures similar to those in the United States is considerably less certain.

—DMC

See also: Assassinations; Militarism; Presidents the Twentieth Century; Zapatista National Liberation Army (EZLN).

References:

Butler, Edgar W., and Jorge A. Bustamante, eds. *Sucesión Presidencial: The 1988 Mexican Presidential Election.* Boulder, CO: Westview Press, 1990.

Camp, Roderic Ai. *Politics in Mexico.* 2d ed. New York: Oxford University Press, 1996.

Morris, Stephen D. *Political Reformism in Mexico.* Boulder, CO: Lynne Rienner Publishers, 1995.

Rodríguez, Victoria E., and Peter M. Ward, eds. *Opposition Government in Mexico.* Albuquerque: University of New Mexico Press, 1994.

Díaz, Porfirio (1830–1915)

Dictator of Mexico from 1876 to 1911, Porfirio Díaz is generally considered a villain in Mexican history. His manipulation of the political system, use of strong-arm tactics to control the Mexican people, and economic policies that promoted foreign dominance and worked to the detriment of Mexico's popular classes, encouraged dissent. In 1910, this dissent burst forth in the Mexican Revolution.

Díaz, of Mixtec Indian and Spanish blood, was born into a poor Oaxaca family in 1830. After several years of study in the local seminary, Díaz rejected the priesthood and enrolled in the Institute of Arts and Sciences of Oaxaca. There he experienced a curriculum influenced by the liberal philosophy that attracted the likes of Benito Juárez and that emphasized the rule of law and constitutional freedoms. Mexico's volatile political situation, however, ultimately settled Díaz on a military career. As a soldier, Díaz quickly distinguished himself as both a good commander and a staunch supporter of liberalism. He gained fame as a member of the liberal forces that fought in the 1850s War of Reform, and he participated in resisting the French invasion of Mexico in the 1860s.

Díaz's liberal stripes soon turned him into a rebel. In 1871, after Benito Juárez manipulated elections to allow himself another term as president, Díaz staged the Revolt of La Noria. Failing to gain military or popular support, Díaz briefly retired to Veracruz. When Juárez's successor, Miguel Lerdo de Tejada, likewise attempted to continue in office, Díaz revolted again. The 1876 Rebellion

Mexican dictator Porfirio Díaz was a towering figure in Mexican history who ruled from 1876 until being deposed in the Mexican Revolution of 1910. (Library of Congress)

of Tuxtepec, which took as its slogan "Effective Suffrage, No Reelection," succeeded, and it ushered in a thirty-five-year period known as the "Porfiriato."

Although Díaz revolted under the banner of constitutionalism and democratic rule, he was soon convinced that economic development supervised by a strong central government was the key to Mexico's future. Ultimately, he relegated political democracy to a backseat as he sought to create a stable country conducive to economic modernization. In a similar way, Díaz (who coined the phrase "Poor Mexico, so far from God and so close to the United States") rejected the antiforeign sentiments of many Mexicans and embraced foreign investment as a key to economic growth. The Díaz system stressed peace, order, and stability while pursuing policies designed to usher Mexico into a modern industrial age.

Individual Mexican states provided the key to the Porfirian political system as Díaz sought to rule through local elites while playing them against each other. He also encouraged regional military leaders to serve as a counterbalance to local political machines. From Mexico City, Díaz directly intervened in state affairs, helping to fashion electoral slates and rigging elections. He also amended the Constitution to allow the central government to intervene in states in the event of a "breakdown" of order. *"Pan o palo"*—bread or the stick—is often used to describe the Díaz political system. While Díaz preferred a conciliatory approach toward potential rivals, he was willing to use force against enemies and troublemakers.

As a career military man, Díaz used the army as a tool of coercion, offering promotions and economic incentives to soldiers who helped put down rebellions and otherwise maintained order. The *Rurales,* a federal police agency established under the Juárez regime, continued to be used to control banditry and other forms of criminal activity in the Mexican countryside. Through the widespread use of the *"Ley de Fuga"* or law of flight, by which troublemakers and suspected enemies were summarily executed, the *Rurales* sought to intimidate Mexicans into submission. A final tool in the Díaz arsenal was the *Bravi,* a presidential bodyguard and intelligence service.

The philosophy of Positivism reinforced the Porfirian quest for order and progress in Mexico. Developed in France during the mid-nineteenth century, Positivism embraced a scientific view of things and looked forward to a golden age in which the laws of science would be used to govern and regulate society. In Mexico, President Díaz was surrounded by a group of Positivists, known as *científicos*—the "scientific ones." Many Mexican *científicos* also adopted social Darwinism, arguing that certain sectors of society (most notably the poor and the Indian population) were destined to die out. The racism and classism inherent in Mexican Positivism prevented a serious consideration of some of Mexico's most pressing social problems during the Porfiriato and ensured that they would become issues in the Mexican Revolution.

Foreign capital held the key to the Porfirian dream of economic development in Mexico. In addition to providing a stable environment in which to invest, Díaz courted foreigners in a variety of ways. In 1884, a new mining code reversed the old colonial practice that prevented private ownership of subsoil resources. The new law encouraged foreign investment in mining and in the young Mexican oil industry. Porfirian land policies also increased the foreign presence in Mexico's economy. Díaz began a policy of surveying, dividing, and selling public lands to private owners. In some areas of Mexico, the real estate speculation that ensued adversely affected smallholders who found themselves cut off from the resources needed for survival. Díaz also presided over the great era of railroad building in Mexico. Here, too, foreign investment was crucial, and the major Mexican railroad lines linked Mexico to outside markets. Finally, Díaz smoothed relations with the United States by addressing the issue of the volatile border region, agreeing to a pact that allowed American forces to cross the international line in hot pursuit of outlaws.

Porfirian economic policies helped Mexico develop its infrastructure and achieve a degree of financial stability. Porfirian growth, however, did not benefit all Mexicans. In fact, Díaz's policies favorably affected only a fraction of the Mexican people, and some even experienced a decline in living standards as a result of the displacement that accompanied many Porfirian programs. The export orientation of the new economy made Mexico vulnerable, and, coupled with the lack of foreign investment in agriculture, actually caused a decline in Mexico's ability to feed its people. It is not surprising that modern Mexico condemns Díaz as a man who "sold out" Mexico to foreigners.

On the eve of the Mexican Revolution of 1910, the Porfirian system was increasingly out of touch with a country that had experienced significant changes during Díaz's six terms as president. The aging Díaz slipped into the role of elder statesman, while the *científicos* controlled the country. Political dissent grew among all sectors of society. Local elites, including Francisco I. Madero of Coahuila, who had experienced persecution under the Díaz regime, chaffed under the restrictive political system. Mexico's nascent middle class protested its lack of political clout, and members of the lower class grew restless as the benefits of Porfirian policies continued to elude them. An international recession complicated the picture and exposed the vulnerability of Mexico's export-oriented economy. On the eve of the 1910 elections, Díaz himself added more confusion with the Creelman Interview, in which he hinted to American journalist James Creelman that he might relinquish power and that he would welcome competition for the position of president.

Díaz's words were taken seriously by Francisco Madero, who advanced himself as a presidential candidate. Madero's arrest, followed by the predictable rigged elections that awarded Díaz yet another term, served as a catalyst for revolt. By 1911, many areas of Mexico were in a state of rebellion. With the capture of the border town of Ciudad Juárez in June of that year, Díaz finally relinquished power. Although he went quietly into exile in Paris, where he died in 1915, Díaz's presence continued to be felt in the persistence of a Porfirian bureaucracy and army and in the survival of an economic system with a life of its own. Indeed, the Mexican Revolution, particularly in its early phase, was largely a struggle to undo the legacy of Porfirio Díaz.

—SBP

See also: Madero, Francisco; Revolution of 1910.
References:
Ballard Perry, Laurens. *Juárez and Díaz: Machine Politics in Mexico.* DeKalb: Northern Illinois University Press, 1978.

Beals, Carleton. *Porfirio Díaz: Dictator of Mexico.* Philadelphia: J. B. Lippincott, 1932.

Díaz Ordaz, Gustavo (1911–1979)

President from 1964 to 1970, Gustavo Díaz Ordaz was born in the state of Puebla. After primary and secondary studies in Oaxaca City and Guadalajara, he studied law at the University of Guadalajara and then the University of Puebla, where he received his degree in 1937. He held a series of government positions at different levels that would lead him to the presidency. He served as a prosecuting attorney, a judge, and a labor arbitrator at the local and state levels. From 1943 to 1946 he served as a member of the lower house of the national Congress from Puebla; between 1946 and 1952 he was a member of the national Senate from Puebla. Díaz Ordaz then advanced through a series of positions in the key government department of the Secretariat of the Interior (internal security). He served first as director general of legal affairs

President Gustavo Díaz Ordaz acknowledges the cheers of a joint session of Congress after delivering his second State of the Union address. Mexico City, Mexico. (Corbis)

for the secretariat and then as chief of staff for the department from 1956 to 1958. President Adolfo López Mateos (1958–1964) then appointed him secretary of the interior, the position that had been the stepping-stone to the presidency for two of the last three presidents (Miguel Alemán and Adolfo Ruiz Cortines). When it came time for López Mateos to designate his successor, the nod went to his Secretary of the Interior Díaz Ordaz. As the nominee of the official party, the Institutional Revolutionary Party (Partido Revolucionario Institucional, or PRI), Díaz Ordaz went on to an easy victory in the elections of 1964.

Although Díaz Ordaz had said he would continue the policies of his predecessor, who had pushed the government program to the left, he turned out to be one of the most conservative presidents put forward by the official party up to that time. López Mateos had substantially sped up the redistribution of land during his presidency, and Díaz Ordaz distributed some 22 million acres, a respectable figure for post-1940 presidents. Mexico even became briefly self-sufficient in agricultural products. The main emphasis of the administration remained on industrialization, which continued to post impressive growth but with little of the benefits filtering down to the masses. As López Mateos had done, Díaz Ordaz enforced the Constitutional provision requiring employers to share profits with industrial workers. Federal spending on education continued to rise, and the government launched major urban renewal projects.

The contemporary and historical evaluation of the Díaz Ordaz administration was permanently tarnished by the failure of political reform. Early in his administration, Díaz Ordaz appointed the reform-minded Carlos Madrazo as head of the PRI. Madrazo recommended a number of reforms aimed at promoting the internal democratization of the party, including greater efforts to recruit young people and women. In particular he wanted to reduce the extensive power exercised by local and state political bosses by conducting party primaries to nominate candidates. When Madrazo started introducing the reforms in 1965, the bosses created such opposition that Díaz Ordaz rolled back the reforms and fired Madrazo. Madrazo then became one of the most outspoken critics of the PRI until his death in a suspicious plane crash in 1969.

Even if Madrazo's reforms had been enacted, they would have only promoted the internal democratization of the PRI; they would not have opened the political system as a whole to greater democracy. There were growing voices outside the PRI calling for more general reform. University students—especially those in Mexico City—were in the forefront of the growing opposition to the PRI. At the same time, the government was becoming increasingly security conscious as the Olympic Games scheduled for the fall of 1968 approached. Mexico would be the first Latin American country and the first developing country to host the Olympics. The Díaz Ordaz administration was determined to use the Olympics to showcase Mexico's development and saw political opposition as a threat to the Olympics.

There had been a number of confrontations between students and authorities in Mexico City beginning in the summer of 1968. Students formed a National Student Strike Committee, which issued a number of demands to the government. The Díaz Ordaz administration was prepared to negotiate in secret, but the students demanded a public airing of their grievances, which the government rejected. The different players were to converge in a violent confrontation on 2 October 1968 in the Plaza of the Three Cultures in the Tlatelolco district of Mexico City. When about 5,000 protestors gathered in the plaza, police and army units moved in to break up the demonstration. In the clash that followed, the army troops fired on the crowd at close range. Government authorities officially admitted that 43 demonstrators were killed; a more realistic figure probably would be 300 to 400. Some 2,000 demonstrators were jailed.

The "massacre at Tlatelolco" became the great divide in both the administration of Díaz Ordaz and in recent Mexican history. Those working inside and outside the PRI for reform became disillusioned with the regime and pessimistic about the prospects for change. In particular, the students and intellectuals gave up on the PRI as a force for social and economic change. The massacre called into question both the political system and the development policies that had evolved since 1940. The president and the party both suffered a major loss of stature. The military also took much of the criticism, and military leaders were determined to avoid being put in the position of having to repress their fellow citizens in the future. To further add to the general feeling of gloom, Díaz Ordaz tapped as his successor Luis Echeverría Alvarez, secretary of the interior and a central figure in the massacre. After leaving the presidency, Díaz Ordaz briefly returned to public life with his appointment as ambassador to Spain in 1977. There was such a public outcry against the appointment that Díaz Ordaz resigned the post without ever having served in it. He then retired permanently to private life, dying in July 1979.

—DMC

See also: Democratization Process; Echeverría Alvarez, Luis; Import Substitution Industrialization (ISI); Intellectuals; López Mateos, Adolfo; Partido Revolucionario Institucional (PRI); Presidents of the Twentieth Century; Tlatelolco Massacre.

References:
Camp, Roderic Ai. *Generals in the Palacio: The Military in Modern Mexico.* New York: Oxford University Press, 1992.
Hansen, Roger D. *The Politics of Mexican Development.* Baltimore: Johns Hopkins University Press, 1971.
Hellman, Judith Adler. *Mexico in Crisis.* 2d ed. New York: Holmes and Meier, 1983.

Drug Trafficking

Drug trafficking has figured prominently in Mexico's domestic and foreign affairs for much of the twentieth century and into the twenty-first. In the 1920s, Mexican workers in the U.S. southwest were linked to the use of marijuana, a linkage which served as part of the rationale for their forced repatriation during the Depression years of the 1930s. In addition to marijuana, Mexico was also a producer of heroin and a transshipment point for other drugs. As early as the 1940s, U.S. drug agents were operating in Mexico with the informal approval of Mexican officials. It was not until the 1960s with the growing demand for drugs in the United States that drug trafficking became a major domestic and international problem for Mexico. The growing drug traffic also complicated other important issues, such as immigration and trade. During the 1970s the United States government increased its efforts to intercept drugs crossing the U.S.–Mexican border and pressured Mexican officials to take sterner measures against the drug trade. On two different occasions U.S. officials implemented "Operation Intercept," a detailed inspection of all vehicles crossing the international boundary. Legitimate border traffic was thrown into chaos, leading the Mexican government to announce a "permanent campaign" against drugs.

Although both Mexico and the United States intensified their efforts to interrupt drug trafficking, the drug trade continued to grow in the 1980s. The status of the drug trade brought growing complications for Mexico both internationally and domestically. Mexico and the United States bickered endlessly over the their relative commitments to drug enforcement and on the amount of emphasis that should be placed on interrupting the supply of drugs coming across the border versus reducing demand for drugs in the United States. It became increasingly difficult to separate the drug controversy from the issues of immigration and trade. The Mexican government even feared that the drug dispute might derail efforts to get approval for the North American Free Trade Agreement.

Cadets hoping to become members of the Mexican Federal Investigation Agency take part in training exercises in Mexico City, November 2003. (Daniel Aguilar/Reuters/Corbis)

The domestic implications for Mexico of the expanding drug trade were also worrisome. The consumption of drugs within Mexico was on the rise. At the same time, drug-related corruption of political and law enforcement institutions raised the possibility of Mexico becoming a "narco-state" along the lines of Colombia. Two incidents drove home the dangers involved. In June 1993 one of the highest ranking officials of the Roman Catholic Church in Mexico, Cardinal Juan Jesús Posadas Ocampo, was shot and killed at the airport in Guadalajara. Investigators were never able to determine conclusively whether the cardinal was the target of the attack or whether he died in a shootout between drug gangs. The cardinal, however, had spoken out earlier against the drug traffickers. In March 1994 the candidate of the official party for the presidency, Luis Donaldo Colosio, was assassinated in the border town of Tijuana during a campaign appearance. Authorities struggled over an official explanation for the assassination, but the killing was linked almost immediately with drug traffickers. The assassination shortly afterward of the Tijuana police chief, who had angered the local drug cartel, heightened speculation about a drug connection to Colosio's assassination.

The assassinations of Cardinal Posadas and Colosio led Mexico's president, Carlos Salinas de Gortari, to press for tougher action against drug traffickers. Soon after Salinas left the presidency in December 1994, a major political and legal controversy developed over the possible involvement of Salinas's older brother, Raul, with drug traffickers. Raul Salinas became the target of an international investigation involving the Mexican, U.S., and Swiss governments. Salinas was accused of having accumulated a personal fortune conservatively estimated at $500 million, much of it gained by using his high-level political connections to provide protection for drug traffickers. In October

1998 the Swiss government officially ended a lengthy investigation into the finances of Raul Salinas by ordering the confiscation of $114 million of Salinas's assets on the grounds that they represented drug payoffs. Salinas in the meantime was in a Mexican jail, charged with corruption and murder.

Both Mexico and the United States have moved toward a greater militarization of the drug war. Stung by continuing criticism of corruption among civilian law enforcement officials, the Mexican government turned more of the antidrug effort over to the military on the grounds that it was not tainted by corruption. An army officer, General Jesús Gutiérrez Rebollo, was made Mexico's antidrug chief. Two months after assuming his new position, the general found himself under arrest on charges of taking a bribe from the leader of one of Mexico's biggest drug cartels, Amado Carrillo Fuentes. General Gutiérrez proclaimed his innocence but at the same time accused several other high-ranking army officers of taking bribes to protect drug dealers. U.S. efforts to get its armed forces more actively involved in the drug war also proved controversial. Critics claimed that the armed forces had the hardware but not the training to engage in what was essentially police work. When a military patrol along the border accidentally killed a shepherd, the United States cut back on its use of the military in intercept operations.

Even the more optimistic officials on both sides of the U.S.–Mexico border admitted that the war on drugs was far from being won. Drug traffickers were adept at shifting production locations and supply routes in response to pressure from authorities. It was clear that the drug problem would continue to be a major factor in the domestic and diplomatic affairs of Mexico well into the twenty-first century.

—DMC

See also: Corruption; Immigration/Emigration; Militarism; North American Free Trade Agreement (NAFTA); United States, Relations with.

References:
González, Guadalupe, and Marta Tienda. *The Drug Connection in U.S.–Mexican Relations.* San Diego: Center for U.S.–Mexican Studies, University of California, San Diego, 1989.
Shannon, Elaine. *Desperados: Latin Drug Lords, U.S. Lawmen, and the War America Can't Win.* New York: Viking, 1988.
Smith, Peter H., ed. *Drug Policy in the Americas.* Boulder, CO: Westview Press, 1992.

Durango (State)

One of Mexico's biggest states, Durango is located in northern Mexico. It has a rugged, mountainous terrain and an arid climate. Historically, the state's largest cities have been Durango (the capital), Gómez Palacio, Ciudad Lerdo, and Mapimí. The latter three are located in the Laguna region, a rich agricultural area in northeastern Durango and southwestern Coahuila (a neighboring state). Francisco "Pancho" Villa is perhaps the state's most famous son, and he had a significant following in Durango during the Mexican Revolution. Durango early distinguished itself as a center of mining, and to the north of the capital city lies one of the world's largest deposits of iron ore.

Spanish colonization of Durango was driven by the discovery of rich mines in the neighboring state of Zacatecas. Agriculture and cattle ranching developed to supply the mining communities, and Franciscan and Jesuit missionaries worked among Durango's native peoples, including the Tarahumara and Guachichiles. Land concentration and the development of *haciendas* inevitably displaced Durango's native peoples, many of whom became laborers in the mines. Durango became part of the province of Nueva Vizcaya, and the city of Durango (established in 1563) served as provincial capital and as a center of the Catholic Church. Durango also housed one of Nueva Vizcaya's assay houses and became a center for the distribution of mercury used in the processing of silver extracted from the mines of northern Mexico.

Toward the end of the colonial period, Durango enjoyed a brief mining boom of its own, centered on Guarisamey. This mining boom encouraged additional growth in Durango's cattle ranching and agricultural economies, but it also helped to transform the city of Durango into a flourishing economic center, complete with small-scale industry. European and Asian imports made their way to Durango's elites, as the city was drawn into a global economy driven by the export of silver.

Durango's economic boom did not survive Mexico's independence movements. The unrest of the early nineteenth century caused many mines to be abandoned, and Durango had difficulty attracting investors who would replace the capital resources that disappeared as Mexico broke from Spain. An exception was the Cerro de Mercado, where mining and smelting of iron ore began in earnest during the 1820s and expanded up until the Mexican Revolution disrupted this enterprise. Agriculture also struggled with the dislocations of the post-independence era. Nomadic Indian raids, which affected most of northern Mexico during the nineteenth century, encouraged a pattern of land concentration that had begun during the colonial period. Small-scale holdings were often sold to the large landowners or *hacendados* who had the means to defend their properties against attack. Yet while land concentration aided in the defense of this part of Mexico's northern frontier, it did not necessarily lend itself to agricultural productivity. At the same time, large amounts of land had fallen into the hands of the Catholic Church since the colonial period. Much of this land remained uncultivated. New laws restricting the Church's wealth took effect at mid-century, but lands thus released were acquired primarily by *hacendados*. Only in the fertile Laguna region did Durango's agricultural economy exhibit any real dynamism. There, cotton farming developed and grew to meet the demand from Mexico's expanding textile industry. Durango eventually became a major cotton producer, second only to the state of Veracruz.

The dynamism of the Laguna region continued during the dictatorship of Porfirio Díaz (1876–1911). The arrival of the railroad encouraged development, and Gómez Palacio and its Laguna sister city of Torreón (in neighboring Coahuila) became centers of banking, industry, and commerce. Mining enjoyed a revival during the Porfiriato, aided by the railroad, by the end of Indian raiding, and by national policies that encouraged foreign investment. Mapimí and Velardeña emerged as Durango's chief mining and smelting centers, and while the state's mines continued to produce silver and some gold, they also shifted increasingly to the production of industrial metals including iron, copper, lead, mercury, and zinc.

As in many areas of Mexico, the economic wealth generated in Durango during the Porfirian era was monopolized by foreigners and by a few local elites. The Gurza and Flores families were particularly important, and their investments extended to industry, mining, and cotton cultivation. The Flores clan was most successful in translating its economic clout into political power. General Juan M. Flores (who had aided Porfirio Díaz's rise to power) served as Durango's governor, and his relatives and friends acquired other political posts.

The concentration of economic wealth and political power in a few hands, as well as the overwhelming foreign presence in Durango's economy, generated some significant tensions on the eve of the Mexican Revolution. Ocuila Indians in the municipality of Cuencamé resisted the encroachment of *hacendados* who sought more land on which they could cultivate guayule, a rubber plant that became a lucrative export during the Porfirian era. Out of such resistance emerged a small band of outlaws that, under the leadership of Calixto Contreras, wandered armed and mounted in the Laguna region as the Mexican Revolution began. The mining community of Velardeña was the scene of another popular protest, this time by mine workers resentful of their treatment at the hands of the American-owned mining company. After officials suppressed a religious procession, Velardeña miners lashed out at local authorities, precipitating the intervention of the army and the assassination of sixteen miners. A final important conflict revolved around the waters of the Nazas River, which were used by farmers in Durango and Coahuila, and by the powerful foreign-owned Tlahualilo Company. Competition for this resource, crucial to cotton cultivation and other economic activities, generated several clashes among elite landowners and frequently drew in peasants, or *campesinos,* as well.

The Cuencamé, Velardeña, and Nazas conflicts underscored the social tensions that had emerged as a result of Durango's rapid economic development. With an economy that was heavily dependent on the international price of metals, and with an agricultural sector that suffered periodic problems due to drought and other climatic changes, Durango was vulnerable. In 1907, when an international economic crisis began, this vulnerability was underscored. A drop in the price of metals hurt mining companies, and workers experienced lowered wages and unemployment. At the same time, farmers were affected by a drought and by frosts that plagued the Laguna region.

Because social tensions and the repercussions of the 1907 crisis were particularly severe in the Laguna, it was this region that experienced the most significant activity as the Mexican Revolution began. The Mexican Liberal Party (PLM) found recruits in Durango's Laguna region, and Ocuila Indians took part in a PLM raid on Viesca, Coahuila, in 1908. Laguna rebels were among the first to rise up against Porfirio Díaz in 1910, responding to the call of Francisco I. Madero (son of a prominent family in neighboring Coahuila who had blood ties to Durango's wealthy Gurza family). Calixto Contreras was one of the insurgents who joined Madero. In neighboring Chihuahua, Pancho Villa, another Durango native who had been born to sharecropper parents on one of the state's largest haciendas, participated in the movement that finally toppled Díaz in 1911.

Although Francisco Madero's rebellion began a process that would transform Mexico, significant change did not come to Durango until after Madero's own overthrow and death in 1913. Porfirian politicians continued to hold prominent positions, and promises of economic and social reform languished. Many who had joined in the fight against Díaz expressed their frustration by joining the movement of Pascual Orozco, a mule skinner from Chihuahua who rebelled against Madero's government. Madero's demise and death simply complicated the situation, as Durango insurgents declared themselves opposed to Madero's assassin, Victoriano Huerta, and immediately captured the state's capital in the name of the nascent Constitutionalist movement led by Venustiano Carranza. As the Constitutionalists gained control of Durango, Pastor Rouaix, an engineer, became governor. Rouaix dismissed old Porfirian officials, and he began the process of agrarian reform, responding to a major grievance that had caused Durango campesinos to revolt. Rouaix's reforms also included a law ending the old practice of debt peonage.

In 1914, as the gulf between revolutionary leaders Venustiano Carranza and Pancho Villa widened, Durango became a battleground between followers of these two leaders. And although Carranza's forces had gained control of the state by the end of 1916, the Laguna region experienced ongoing unrest as Pancho Villa continued his rebellion. With Carranza serving as Mexico's president, Domingo Arrieta assumed the governorship and continued the slow process of agrarian reform in Durango. He abandoned his post in 1920, when Carranza was deposed and then killed in the Plan of Agua Prieta.

Land reform remained a central issue in Durango in the decades after the revolution, and Mexican presidents were compelled to respond to agrarian grievances with expropriations and redistribution of land. The Laguna in particular was the focus of official attention, and in 1936 President Lázaro Cárdenas divided its land into a series of *ejidos,* or communal plots. By the end of the twentieth century, the Laguna's cotton farms were incorporated into a large cooperative controlled by Durango and Coahuila. Durango remains one of Mexico's major producers of cotton.

Although cattle ranching, agriculture, and mining all recovered in the decades after the Mexican Revolution, Durango's fortunes have wavered since the mid-twentieth century. Because of the state's aridity, the agricultural sector remains vulnerable to drought and especially to variations in the price of cotton. And although Durango continues to mine (and explore for) gold, copper, silver, lead, and other metals, production in some mines (including the Cerro de Mercado) has declined. Beginning in the 1970s, Durango emerged as a major producer of wood products and it is the home of Grupo Industrial Durango, Latin America's largest paper producer. Yet while the wood products industry has added a new component to the local economy, a general lack of economic opportunity has encouraged Durango's inhabitants to leave. As the twenty-first century began, Durango, like neighboring Zacatecas, had one of Mexico's highest levels of emigration.

—*SBP*

See also: Carranza, Venustiano; Coahuila (State); Revolution of 1910; Villa, Francisco "Pancho."

References:
Altamirano, Graziella, et al. *Durango: Una historia compartida.* 2 vols. Mexico City: Instituto de Investigaciones Dr. José María Luis Mora, 1997.
Guzmán, Gabino Martínez, and Juan Angel Chávez Ramírez. *Durango: Un volcán en erupción.* Mexico City: Fondo de Cultura Económica, 1998.
Official state web site: www.durango.gob.mx

E

Echeverría Alvarez, Luis (1922–)

President from 1970 to 1976, Luis Echeverría was born in Mexico City and attended the National Preparatory School there. After studying in Argentina, Chile, France, and the United States on scholarship in 1941, he studied law at the National University and received his law degree in 1945. The following year he became the private secretary of General Rodolfo Sánchez Taboada, the president of the official party, the Institutional Revolutionary Party (Partido Revolucionario Institucional, or PRI). Echeverría served in a variety of positions for the PRI during the administration of President Miguel Alemán (1946–1952), although he did not campaign for any public office. From 1952 to 1954 he was director of accounts for the Secretariat of the Navy and later became chief of staff for the Secretariat of Public Education. In 1958 he was appointed subsecretary in the Secretariat of the Interior (internal security); in 1964 President Gustavo Díaz Ordaz appointed him secretary of the interior. As secretary of the interior, Echeverría was at the center of the controversy over the "Tlatelolco Massacre" in October 1968 when police and army troops fired on a group of demonstrators, killing an estimated 300 to 400 people. As the PRI nominee for the presidency in

1970, Echeverría followed the example set by Lázaro Cárdenas in the 1934 presidential contest and seriously campaigned for the presidency. Unlike Cárdenas in 1934, however, there was little indication that this campaigning earned the allegiance of the increasingly skeptical Mexican public. The election results were a foregone conclusion at any rate; Echeverría was an easy winner.

Despite his hard-line background and reputation, Echeverría as president began to use a populist rhetoric reminiscent of Cárdenas and tried to move his administration to the left. Early on he indicated there would be greater emphasis on the rural sector. The new emphasis was highlighted by a major increase in spending on agriculture and the creation of a new cabinet-level post, the secretary of agrarian reform. Much of the money would go toward expanding the rural road system and rural electrification. The administration also permitted an increase in the prices paid to agricultural producers in hopes that they would respond with increased production, permitting Mexico to reduce its food imports. Critics noted that the most immediate result of this new agricultural policy was an increase in the federal bureaucracy. Agricultural producers were not able to expand their production in response to the

Former Mexican president Luis Echeverría during a meeting with reporters and legislators on 3 February 1998 (Reuters/ Corbis)

higher prices offered by the government. The Echeverría administration also used fiscal policy to pursue its populist approach. The personal income tax was increased and a luxury tax introduced. The president implemented strict price controls on basic commodities in an effort to ease the impact of inflation on the poor. Echeverría also directed that all urban workers receive a one-third pay increase to help them cope with inflationary pressures. The government also initiated a new housing program financed by a tax on employers. In an effort to respond to worker agitation, Echeverría tried unsuccessfully to reduce the power of the conservative Confederation of Mexican Workers (Confederación de Trabajadores Mexicanos, or CTM) under its longtime leader Fidel Velázquez, even though the CTM and Velázquez were traditionally firm supporters of the PRI and the government. The president even harkened back to the economic nationalism of the 1930s by tightening restrictions on foreign investment.

In an effort to make people forget his role in the Tlatelolco Massacre of October 1968, Echeverría released most of the students still in prison early in his administration. The students had scarcely been released, however, when a new confrontation took place between the authorities and striking students. On 10 June 1971—the feast of Corpus Christi, which would give the incident its name—student demonstrators in Mexico City clashed with the police and paramilitary forces financed by wealthy business interests. Some fifty students were killed in this latest "massacre." The clash was only one aspect of the growing violence afflicting the Mexican political scene. Urban and rural guerrillas began operations, engaging in politically motivated bank robberies, bombings, and kidnappings. In one incident, a group kidnapped Echeverría's father-in-law, a former governor of the state of Jalisco. These guerrilla groups were small and did not threaten the dominant position of either the president or the PRI. They did serve as an embarrassing reminder of the growing discontent with Echeverría and the official party. Partially as an effort to distract from his domestic problems, Echeverría pursued an active and controversial foreign policy. He couched his foreign policy statements in leftist terms and tried to project Mexico as a leader of the developing nations. Echeverría presented himself as a defender of Third-World interests and was reported to be "campaigning" for the position of secretary general of the United Nations. His postpresidential ambitions were undone by his anti-U.S. rhetoric and his support for the U.N. resolution equating Zionism with racism, a move which led to a boycott of Mexico by Jewish tourists.

Although Echeverría might periodically take refuge in foreign policy, there was no escaping the mounting financial and economic problems at home. His administration was unsuccessful in curbing inflation, with basic food products such as beans and tortillas experiencing dramatic increases in prices in 1974 and 1975. Mexico's trade deficit grew worse, and the government had to borrow heavily in order to avoid devaluing the currency, which had held its value for more than twenty years. The government's development plan—in place since the late 1930s—had run its course; by the 1970s the limits of import substitution industrialization had been reached. Echeverría's political swing to the left had alienated conservative elements without winning over leftist elements who considered it primarily rhetoric rather than reality.

As Echeverría approached the end of his term and the time to pick a presidential successor, Mexico was in a state of political and economic crisis. Echeverría recognized the extent of Mexico's financial and economic problems by picking as his successor José López Portillo, one of the rising group of financial technocrats in the government. There was even talk of a military coup, although differing rumors had the coup being directed by and against Echeverría. One rumor that did come true was the devaluation of the peso, which had not been devalued since 1954. Postwar governments not only took pride in the soundness of the peso but also considered it an indicator of the correctness of their development policies. In September 1976 Echeverría devalued the peso, which fell from 12.5 pesos to the dollar to 20.5 to the dollar. There was another major devaluation before Echeverría left office on 1 December 1976. Land seizures by peasants added to the chaotic final days of the Echeverría administration. Even though the Mexican court system was adjudicating the seizures, Echeverría abruptly confirmed the seizures, transferring some 250,000 acres from large landowners to peasant communities. Echeverría established the dubious tradition of closing out presidential terms amid financial and economic crisis, a tradition which continued through 1994.

While Echeverría did move politics to the left, his populist policies did not make him "the new Cárdenas" as he had hoped. Instead, Echeverría launched the era of financial technocrats in the presidency, which continued through the presidential elections of 1994. The Revolutionary generals of the pre-1946 period and the *"políticos"* (politicians) of the postwar era were giving way to the *"técnicos"* (technicians) of the post-1970 period. The road to power, which once ran through the military and later through the official party, now ran through the federal bureaucracy.

—*DMC*

See also: Agrarian Reform/Land and Land Policy; Alemán, Miguel; Cárdenas, Lázaro; Debt, Mexico's Foreign; Díaz Ordaz, Gustavo; Foreign Policy; López Portillo, José; Partido Revolucionario Institucional (PRI); Presidents of the Twentieth Century; Tlatelolco Massacre.

References:

Bailey, John J. *Governing Mexico: The Statecraft of Crisis Management.* New York: St. Martin's, 1988.

Schmidt, Samuel. *The Deterioration of the Mexican Presidency: The Years of Luis Echeverría.* Tucson: University of Arizona Press, 1991.

Economy

The political and financial instability that plagued Mexico from the 1820s to the 1870s made it difficult to achieve economic growth or to pursue coherent economic and financial policies. Although the conservative-liberal political feud had its economic dimension, there was some agreement on basic economic views. Both called for improvements in transportation and communication. Liberals and conservatives both recognized the need for foreign capital in promoting economic development. Both sought improvements in agriculture and more efficient government administration. Conservatives and liberals firmly believed in the right of private property and the responsibility of the government to protect it.

The economy with which the liberals and conservatives had to contend was one that had been badly dislocated by the lengthy struggle for independence from 1810 to 1821. The economy revolved around agricultural production, mining, and trade. The wars for independence were particularly disruptive for agriculture and mining. Crops were lost, stolen, or destroyed; livestock was killed or driven off. Many of the mines had to be abandoned owing to the fighting. Neglected mines quickly flooded, making it difficult to resume operations once the fighting ended. The decline in silver production led to a contracting money supply that damaged the entire economy. Most Mexicans had little or no cash income and therefore provided a domestic market for only the most basic necessities. Mexico's population growth was slow, and the country attracted few immigrants, further retarding the domestic market. An additional catastrophic blow to the economy was the loss of almost half of the national territory as a result of the war with the United States from 1846 to 1848. That

territory helped fuel the growth of the United States—rather than Mexico—in the second half of the nineteenth century.

The general environment in which the economy operated also retarded development. The legal framework within which business had to be conducted was constantly changing. Mexico had four constitutions between 1824 and 1857, going from liberal to conservative to more conservative back to liberal. The rules of the game for business people were constantly changing; further confusion was caused by uncertainty over enforcement of the changing legislation. The precarious financial position of the federal government also poisoned the economic environment. The central government found it difficult to collect revenues, and the revenues collected often had to be devoted to nonproductive purposes, most notably the military. Early on, the Mexican government started borrowing from foreign creditors and was equally quick to encounter debt problems, defaulting for the first time in 1827. The principal source of revenue for the government—customs duties, or taxes on imports and exports—soon became pledged to pay past debts and could not be used to meet current expenses. This downward spiral in government finances seemed unstoppable; the Mexican government operated at a deficit until the 1890s.

The 1850s saw the triumph of the liberals politically and militarily, a victory with important implications for the economy. The liberals supported free trade and private property, but their views on landholding ultimately had the greatest effect on the economy. The liberals did not oppose the existence of large landholdings, but they did want to bring to an end "corporate" ownership of property by the Roman Catholic Church and the Indian communities. The liberals wanted to make this property available to create a class of family farmers, which would produce both economic growth and political stability. This view found its way into the Constitution of 1857, but it took years for the full impact of the legislation to be felt. Instead of creating a group of family farmers, the action intensified the problem of large landholdings. The federal government did not provide any financial assistance to the landless peasants seeking property, so only those with capital or access to credit (the wealthy or large landowners) were able to purchase the land released under the program. The liberals were also moving in the direction of greater government involvement in the economy and the attraction of foreign investment, especially for infrastructure projects such as the railroads. The liberal program actually had little time to take effect before civil war and foreign intervention in the 1860s accentuated the existing economic and financial instability.

While the liberals were able to outlast the French intervention, their ultimate triumph in 1867 did little to get the country moving again economically. Liberal factionalism reasserted itself, and a more authoritarian brand of liberalism—exemplified by Benito Juárez—took hold following 1867. Efforts to reshape the land system caused confusion and encountered opposition in rural areas. The liberal program to "modernize" Mexico would be left to a new generation of liberals to implement, most notably Porfirio Díaz.

Díaz's lengthy rule (1877–1880, 1884–1911) gave him an opportunity to consolidate power, establish order, and pursue a coherent program of economic development. Like a later generation of Mexican leaders, Díaz and his supporters believed that Mexico's economic future lay in industrialization, much of it to be financed by foreign investment. Mexico needed to create a favorable political and legal environment that would be attractive to foreign investors. There were major changes in the land laws and mining code aimed at increasing investment. The Porfirians believed that the transfer of public lands into private hands was crucial to Mexico's economic growth. New legislation permitted private companies to survey unoccupied public lands, with companies receiving one-third of the land surveyed as their compensation. The law led to extensive speculation and the concentration of much of the land in large-scale holdings; on the positive side it stimulated investment in commercial agriculture geared to the export market. The Porfirians also wanted to rejuvenate the mining sector of the economy, especially the exportation of silver. Once again the problem was attacked primarily through legislation. The Constitution of 1857 had placed regulation of mining under the control of state governments, so each state formulated its own mining ordinances. In 1883 the Constitution was amended, giving the national Congress the exclusive power to regulate the mining industry. Congress responded the following year by passing a new mining code, which for the first time in Mexican history gave private individuals the right to acquire legal title to subsoil resources rather than functioning as concessionaires as they had in the past. The new legislation attracted major inputs of foreign capital and technology, converting the Mexican mining industry into a capital-intensive, large-scale operation using modern technology to exploit low-grade deposits. The Mining Code of 1884 also played a key role in the development of Mexico as a major oil producer in the early 1900s.

The Díaz years also brought Mexico's great boom in railroad construction. As in land and mining, government policy and foreign investment played key roles. The federal government provided subsidies and tax exemptions for railroad construction, with foreign companies dominating the scene. Most of the railroad construction was geared to the export market, especially in the United States. The expansion of the rail network was a crucial factor in the growth of the mining industry and of commercial agriculture.

Gains in manufacturing, however, were harder to achieve. Manufacturers could not compete in the international market, needed government-provided tariffs to fend off imports, and had only a small domestic market to tap. Despite the expansion of the railroad system, domestic transportation problems often prevented the development of a true national market for producers. Foreign technology was expensive and often difficult to apply to the Mexican scene. Mexican workers often resisted the industrial discipline needed for factory production. Lack of financial institutions also hampered manufacturers. There were few lending institutions, and most of those made short-term loans to finance real estate transactions. Despite tariff protection, tax exemptions, and government subsidies, there were still important limits on the expansion of manufacturing.

Díaz's export-led development scheme registered important gains in a number of areas, especially railroads, mining, and oil. It also had the effect of integrating Mexico more tightly into the international economy; economic downturns in other parts of the world, especially in the United States, could be quickly transferred to the Mexican economy. The "Panic" (recession) of 1907 that started in the United States had a particularly unsettling effect, even for the Porfirian elite. Another basic problem with the government's development scheme was that few of its benefits filtered down to the masses. Rural workers in particular found their standard of living declining as a result of the land and agricultural policies being followed. There was growing resentment of the prominent role played by foreigners in the economy, especially U.S. investors. Even Díaz and his top advisors were uneasy about the growing power of U.S. companies in Mexico. Díaz responded, however, by trying to diversify foreign investment rather than by reducing the importance of foreign investment in his development plans.

The outbreak of the Revolution in 1910 did not immediately lead to major disruptions in the economy. The years from 1910 to 1913 did not witness extensive fighting or destruction. With the overthrow of President Francisco Madero in February 1913, the Revolution entered a bloodier phase with the national opposition to the regime of General Victoriano Huerta, who was forced into exile in July 1914. The ouster of Huerta led to full-scale civil war from 1914 to 1916 as various Revolutionary factions fought for control. Revolutionary activity had an uneven effect on economic activity. The mining industry was severely damaged by the Revolution; most of the major mining activity was in the north, which was the scene of some of the most bitter and prolonged fighting. Revolutionaries turned to the mines for cash, supplies, explosives, and even recruits. The closing of mines for even a brief period of time often led to flooding, which made renewal of operations difficult and expensive. Despite similar problems, the oil industry actually expanded substantially between 1910 and 1920; annual production increased from 3.6 million barrels in 1910 to 157 million barrels in 1920, making Mexico one of the world's leading producers. Oil represented immense profits for the foreign companies involved in its production as well as a crucial source of revenue for Revolutionary factions. Between 1910 and 1920 legal trade between Mexico and the United States increased substantially; in addition there was a brisk illegal trade in the border area.

The Revolutionary struggle produced a new constitution, the Constitution of 1917, which had major implications for the economy and business activities. The new document assumed that the federal government had an interventionist and nationalistic role to play in the economy. The Constitution of 1917 restored the principle that all subsoil resources ultimately belonged to the nation. The Constitution also established the concept that all property must serve a "social function," meaning that it was subject to government regulation in the public interest. The Constitution of 1857 had provided for the abolition of the *ejido*, the traditional, communal landholding of the indigenous population; the Constitution of 1917 specifically restored the *ejido*. The Constitution also committed the government to a program of expropriation and redistribution of land on a large scale. There were Constitutional restrictions on foreigners owning property, including an outright ban on ownership in border and coastal areas. During the Porfirian period, foreign investors received preferential treatment in Mexican courts. Under the new Constitution of 1917, foreigners could expect to be treated on the same basis as Mexican companies; foreigners had to agree to abide by Mexican laws and be subject to Mexican courts in order to conduct business. The Constitution also had a long list of prolabor provisions with major economic implications. Debt peonage came to an end through the simple expediency of abolishing all workers' debts contracted prior to 1917. Workers had the right to organize and to bargain collectively. The Constitution also prescribed minimum wages and maximum hours for workers and even established a social security system. Like earlier constitutions, the Constitution of 1917 would be subject to revision, interpretation, and uneven enforcement.

The provisions of the Constitution immediately collided with the economic reality of Mexico in 1917. Mexico was far from having recovered from the massive destruction and dislocation caused by Revolutionary activity since 1910. In addition the outbreak of World War I in 1914 caused further dislocation in traditional trade and investing patterns. Inflation became a major problem as numerous Revolutionary leaders issued their own currency, making all currencies devalue rapidly. Radical political philosophies abounded—marxism, socialism, anarchism, and syndicalism; but most of the Revolutionary leaders—regardless of their official views—showed an enthusiasm for capitalism and entrepreneurship, at least when it came to their own personal fortunes. The first president to implement the new Constitution of 1917 was Venustiano Carranza (1917–1920). Carranza had little enthusiasm for the more radical provisions of the Constitution, but his nationalistic sentiments did lead to disagreements with the foreign-owned oil companies. Carranza wanted to use the foreign-owned oil companies as a major source of revenue, a move that led the companies to claim that the government was engaging in discriminatory taxation. The Carranza administration also failed to reach an agreement with the oil companies over the issue of whether the subsoil provisions of the Constitution would be applied retroactively.

The administrations of President Alvaro Obregón (1920–1924) and Plutarco Elías Calles (1924–1928) saw some effort to implement the more advanced economic provisions of the Constitution, but both administrations were limited in their efforts by continuing financial and political problems. Obregón reached a complex settlement with Mexico's international creditors in 1922 only to have to suspend the agreement in 1924. In 1923 Obregón reached an agreement with the U.S. government that dealt with the issues of expropriation of land and compensation. There was even a temporary settlement of the issue of subsoil resources. A postwar international recession and a major revolt against his administration in 1923 brought an end to the limited economic progress and brief political peace. The economic program of Calles was able to produce some limited results. Calles had as a top priority the reordering of government finances and the monetary system. He was able to balance the budget and in 1925 established Mexico's first true central bank, the Banco de México, which could influence the private banking system to support government policy. Calles also established a National Banking Commission to further extend government influence over the banking system and created the Bank of Agricultural Credit to provide credit to the rural sector of the economy. Calles also promoted an active program of highway construction and of irrigation projects.

Once again the budding economic revival was interrupted by major political and economic upheavals. In 1928 Obregón was elected to another term in the presidency, only to be assassinated before he could take office. This led to a series of three presidents, each mostly dominated by Calles, who continued to be the prevailing political force. Preventing further political disintegration became a top priority, as Mexico was already caught up in a smaller-scale civil war known as the Cristero Rebellion. In 1929 the stock market crash in the United States soon gave way to the Great Depression of the 1930s. Mexico's dependence on export-led growth collided with declining foreign demand for its exports. Bad harvests in 1929 and 1930 further aggravated Mexico's economic situation. Although the Mexican economy declined sharply in the early 1930s, Mexico did not suffer as much or as long from the Depression as did the United States or even many other Latin American countries. The impact of the Depression was lessened by the fact that a majority of Mexico's workers were involved in the agricultural sector of the economy, which was not as hard hit as exports and manufacturing.

The Depression led Calles in 1933 to call for the formulation of a "Six-Year Plan" to guide government economic activity. Calles wanted the federal government to play a more active and nationalistic role in the economy, especially in the regulation of the large export industries. The Six-Year Plan—soon referred to as the Plan Calles—called for a socialistic form of education in the schools. It also provided for greater federal control over the program of land redistribution with a view toward accelerating the distribution process. Under the Plan, the government was to encourage Mexican investors to become more actively involved in the key fields of mining, oil, and power production. Calles believed that the state should be an "active agent" in the economy and not merely a "custodian." The actual implementation of the Plan Calles would be up to the new president, Lázaro Cárdenas, who was supposed to be another political puppet of Calles.

As president (1934–1940), Cárdenas proved an enthusiastic supporter of the Plan but not of Calles, who was sent into exile in 1936. Cárdenas accelerated the distribution of land, giving away more acres than all of his predecessors combined. He also embraced the mechanism of the *ejido*, something for which earlier Revolutionary presidents had little or no enthusiasm. Cárdenas championed socialistic education and encouraged workers to strike. The peak of the economic nationalism of his administration came with the expropriation of the foreign-owned oil companies in March 1938, ending an off-and-on feud between the government and the companies that had lasted for more than two decades. Cárdenas's economic program literally came at a price. His educational and agrarian reforms were not only controversial; they were also expensive. His extensive agrarian reform program led to a decline in agricultural production. His economic nationalism led to capital flight and an international boycott by foreign oil companies. Mexico avoided a formal default on its international debt but made little progress on a settlement with its foreign creditors. Ironically, late in his administration, Cárdenas started the transition to a much different economic policy, one which stressed industrialization and the attraction of foreign investment.

This new policy evolved into "import substitution industrialization" (ISI), which would be at the heart of government development policy from the 1940s to the 1980s. The administration of President Manuel Avila Camacho (1940–1946) implemented the basics of ISI while the administration of President Miguel Alemán (1946–1952) was most closely associated with the policy. ISI called for increasing the pace of industrialization by encouraging the domestic production of previously imported products; the federal government played an activist role in the economy through a variety of measures: protective tariffs, import licenses, customs regulations, allocation of credit, and restrictions on foreign investment. This more active role even came to include greater government ownership and operation of certain businesses such as the film industry, airlines, and power production.

Until the mid-1960s, ISI produced impressive growth statistics as well as stable development, including a sound peso and low inflation. By 1970 top government officials were increasingly convinced that ISI had reached its limits as a development strategy and that new approaches should be examined. There were some modifications in ISI during the administration of President Luis Echeverría, but a final decision on the policy was postponed by the oil boom of the late 1970s. When the oil boom turned bust in the early 1980s, the administrations of Presidents Miguel de la Madrid (1982–1988) and Carlos Salinas de Gortari (1988–1994) began a process of dismantling ISI. The abandonment of ISI was partially a response to the need to implement an austerity program in order to get financial aid from the International Monetary Fund; it also represented a conviction that ISI had run its course. The protectionist policies of the last four decades came tumbling down as Mexico joined the General Agreement on Tariffs and Trade and the North American Free Trade Agreement.

The policy the government embraced—and has continued to the present—is one of "neoliberalism" or market-guided economic growth. This approach calls for a much reduced role for the government in the economy, leading to a sell-off ("privatization") of hundreds of government-owned companies, ranging from the national telephone company to the national banking system, which had been nationalized as recently as 1982. This new approach has survived the transition to the presidency of an opposition candidate—President Vicente Fox (2000–2006), who had supported the earlier reforms of the 1980s and 1990s. Given Mexico's lengthy tradition of government involvement in the economy, there is no guarantee that this new approach will not subsequently undergo modification or replacement.

—DMC

See also: Agrarian Reform / Land and Land Policy; Alemán, Miguel; Avila Camacho, Manuel; Calles, Plutarco Elías; Cárdenas, Lázaro; Constitution of 1917; Debt, Mexico's Foreign; Díaz, Porfirio; Echeverría Alvarez, Luis; Import Substitution Industrialization (ISI); Madrid (Hurtado), Miguel de la; Monterrey Group; North American Free Trade Agreement (NAFTA); Obregón, Alvaro; Salinas de Gortari, Carlos.

References:

Grayson, George W. *Mexico: From Corporatism to Pluralism?* Fort Worth, TX: Harcourt Brace & Company, 1998.

Haber, Stephen H. *Industry and Underdevelopment: The Industrialization of Mexico, 1890–1940.* Palo Alto, CA: Stanford University Press, 1989.

Hamilton, Nora. *The Limits of State Autonomy: Post-Revolutionary Mexico.* Princeton, NJ: Princeton University Press, 1982.

Snyder, Richard. *Politics after Neoliberalism: Reregulation in Mexico.* Cambridge: Cambridge University Press, 2001.

Education

The contemporary history of education in Mexico reflects challenges that the country has been facing for centuries. The problems of illiteracy, absenteeism, lack of schools, and shortage of well-trained teachers have persisted as obstacles to Mexican development. Historically, education has also been used as a political tool, reflective of ideological struggles and of broader policy agendas. Presidents throughout the twentieth century, like their predecessors, have sought to shape Mexican society through a variety of educational programs and ideas. The effect of the Mexican Revolution on educational thought and policymaking was a particularly notable trend during the twentieth century.

The education of Mexico's indigenous peoples was central to the early colonial era, as Roman Catholic missionaries (most notably the Franciscans and Jesuits) sought to bring Christianity and Spanish ways to native groups. Other schools (or *colegios* as they were known) provided an education in religion and other subjects for the colony's mestizo (Spanish-Indian) and creole (American-born Spaniard) populations. Mexico's first university was established in 1551. In general, colonial education placed a strong emphasis on religion, and many secondary-level schools focused on the training of young men for the priesthood. Education reflected the biases inherent in colonial society: better and higher level schools were reserved for wealthier and more Spanish elements of society, and women's education was limited by social expectations that consigned them to marriage or the convent. In fact, by the end of the colonial period, Mexico's network of schools was quite limited and most Mexicans did not even have access to primary education.

After Mexican independence, and continuing throughout the nineteenth century, many policymakers attempted to increase the availability of primary schooling while lessening the influence of the Roman Catholic Church on education. Particularly under the leadership of Mexican liberals, ideas of government regulation and oversight of schools emerged, as did the idea of using education as a tool for building national unity and fostering national progress. Mexican conservatives, who continued to cling to the idea of a traditional and Roman Catholic Mexico, joined the educational debate as well. The 1857 Constitution endorsed the idea of secular and free primary education, and at the height of the liberal-conservative struggle that characterized much of the nineteenth century, liberal President Benito Juárez decreed the secularization of higher education as well. The University of Mexico (successor to the colonial institution) became a particular point of contention between liberals and conservatives. Several times during the nineteenth century it was suppressed and reestablished, serving as a political football for Mexico's two dominant political factions.

The focus on official oversight of schools and the attempt to deemphasize religious education in Mexico continued into the twentieth century and found additional support in the philosophy of Positivism, which influenced policymaking during the long reign of Porfirio Díaz. Positivist thinkers sought to create an educational system based heavily on the sciences, and they rejected the idea of religious education. The impressive economic growth that characterized the Porfirian era was reflected in the expansion of primary and vocational schools (including schools for women) and in the general increase in school enrollment. Such progress, however, was skewed in favor of the wealthier northern states and in favor of urban areas. In fact, little of the federal budget was earmarked for education, and Mexico's illiteracy rate (around 85 percent) remained high. On the eve of the Mexican Revolution, the results of over a century's worth of attempts to expand educational opportunities for Mexicans and to centralize control over schools were decidedly mixed. The country continued to have a motley collection of public and private schools, and federal control did not extend very far from Mexico City.

Several leaders of the Mexican Revolution saw the education issue as crucial to the formation of a "new" Mexico. The issues of secularization and federal control continued to be central to the educational debate, and the Revolution also brought a specific call for rural (including Indian) education. The rural school was viewed as part of a broader attempt to unify and democratize Mexican society, and (at least until 1940) was intended to complement the agrarian reform agenda. Article 3 of the Constitution of 1917 reiterated the nineteenth-century idea of free, secular, and compulsory primary education, blocked the ability of religious organizations to establish or direct primary schools, and promised national supervision of private schools. It became the main vehicle through which several generations of Revolutionary and post-Revolutionary leaders would seek to shape Mexico's educational system.

The country's first viable system of public education emerged in the 1920s with the establishment of the Secretary of Public Education (SEP) and the initiation of a system of federally controlled primary schools. Under José Vasconcelos, the first Minister of SEP, the rural school idea came to fruition with the establishment of Casas del Pueblo: rural schools designed to promote literacy and provide vocational training for both children and adults. Mexico's rural schools, which continued to be a cornerstone of educational policy during the 1920s and 1930s, became the focus of pedagogical experiments. Until the mid-1930s, for example, Mexican educational leaders embraced the ideas of American educator John Dewey, transforming the rural school into the "School of Action," which stressed hygiene, athletics, education in social problems (such as alcoholism), and other nonacademic activities. But pedagogy was only one part of the equation during the Revolutionary 1920s and 1930s. Mexico's rural school, and Article 3 of the new Constitution, also served as ideological battlegrounds.

During the presidency of Plutarco Elías Calles (1924–1928) and continuing into the 1930s, left-leaning political leaders, including members of Mexico's growing and influential labor movement, gained the upper hand in the educational debate. At the insistence of Narciso Bassols (1897–1959), secretary of education from 1931 to 1934, the national government took an increasingly activist approach to education and moved toward more strict enforcement of the educational provisions of the Constitution of 1917. In 1934, through a revision of Article 3, Mexico officially embraced the idea of the "socialist" school. This rather ill-defined concept coincided with a peak in Mexico's agrarian reform and was intended to reinforce that program. Perhaps more important, the socialist education agenda sought to definitively exclude religion from Mexican schools, public and private. All religious doctrine was to be excluded from the classroom, and religious groups and personnel were prohibited from intervening in primary, secondary, and normal schools. Bassols and his supporters insisted on schools that would create a "rational" citizenry, and they emphatically rejected religious thought as an obstacle to that goal.

It was also during the Revolutionary period that Mexico's National University emerged in its modern form. Officially established in 1910 at the end of the Díaz era, the National University in Mexico City was intended to provide all Mexicans with the opportunity for a higher education. By the 1920s, the University had become politicized, and it participated in the controversy surrounding the attempt to secularize schools and to create a socialist educational system. Governmental pressure on the university to participate in the national education agenda brought a fight for university autonomy. Limited autonomy was granted in 1929, giving the institution its current name: Universidad Nacional Autónoma de México (National Autonomous University). At the same time, however, the federal government reserved the right to participate in the governance of the country's largest school of higher education and would help select the rector and oversee the university budget.

Attempts by Bassols and other policymakers to push the socialist and anticlerical line in Mexican education, predictably, met with resistance. The Roman Catholic Church, many parents, and even some teachers objected to this sweeping (and somewhat impractical) attempt to transform Mexican society. Indeed, protest over the issue of secularizing schools played a significant role in the Cristero Rebellion of the 1920s. Such protest continued into the 1930s and reached a new height when Bassols attempted to introduce sex education in the schools. Bassols' resignation soon followed, and President Lázaro Cárdenas (1934–1940) de-emphasized the anticlerical aspects of the educational issue. The federal government remained active, however, and the SEP continued to view schools and teachers as important allies in the campaigns for agrarian reform and national unity.

The decades from the beginning of the Mexican Revolution to 1940 brought significant changes to the Mexican educational system. More schools (primary, secondary, and technical/vocational) were established, more teachers were trained, and a greater portion of the federal budget was earmarked for educational purposes. As the Revolutionary era ended, however, Mexico's report card was mixed. Enrollment and literacy rates had risen overall, but certain states (most notably in the south) and many rural areas continued to struggle with the basic issue of bringing primary education to their people. The financing of schools continued to be problematic, and despite the expansion of normal schools and teacher training programs, Mexico remained short of well-qualified teachers. Particularly in rural areas, absenteeism persisted—a function of economic conditions that required children to contribute to the family income from an early age. Constant changes in the educational agenda, and regular introduction of new pedagogical styles by federal authorities, likewise confused the teacher's situation and inhibited the effectiveness of reform. Finally, Mexican leaders had given only limited attention to the problem of educating and integrating the country's indigenous peoples, many of whom continued to speak only native languages. Both Vasconcelos and Bassols had established special schools for Indian students, with decidedly limited results.

The next revision in Mexico's educational agenda began around 1940 and was in many ways a reflection of the country's push to industrialize and the consequent de-emphasis of agrarian reform. The idea of using schools to help establish national unity remained, but now that unity was to be used to help modernize the country. In the minds of Mexico's new and more conservative leaders, such modernization depended on an urban model of education and on professional and technical schools. Under the presidency of Manuel Avila Camacho and the SEP leadership of Jaime Torres Bodet, Article 3 of the Constitution was again modified, this time to erase the idea of socialist education. The ideal of secular education remained in place, but the federal government no longer followed an aggressive policy of anticlericalism. Indeed, parochial schools continued to operate in Mexico City.

Educational initiatives during the next several decades included literacy campaigns, programs to promote adult education, attempts to improve teacher training and salaries, and efforts to build more primary schools. Beginning in the early 1960s, the Mexican government introduced the Free Textbook program. Official texts in history, language, math, and science were produced and distributed under the auspices of the SEP and were obligatory in all schools, public and private. The intent was to ensure a "democratic" educational system and to contribute to the ongoing creation and indoctrination of a unified and educated citizenry. The establishment of government agencies such as the National Institute of Anthropology and History (INAH) and the National Institute of Fine Arts (INBA) also indicated the ongoing attempt of the federal government to extend its control over educational endeavors. Indian education continued to receive some official attention as well. An Office of Indian Affairs and the National Indianist Institute, both established in the 1940s, helped extend educational opportunities, including training in the Spanish language, to Mexico's native peoples.

Higher education expanded in Mexico after the 1950s. Regional public universities and additional private universities provided Mexicans with alternatives to UNAM and the National Polytechnic Institute, which was established in 1937. University enrollments increased as Mexico experienced an economic boom, although demand for university graduates did not keep pace. By 1990, about one million Mexicans were enrolled in universities.

Even at a time when Mexico's economy was experiencing an impressive level of growth, its educational system continued to lag behind. By the 1970s a population boom had outstripped the steadily increasing government expenditures on education. Over half of all Mexican adults still lacked a complete primary education. High dropout rates, particularly in rural areas, continued to be the norm, primary and secondary schools were overcrowded and underfunded, and despite the teacher-training initiatives of the past decades, instructors were scarce and often ill-prepared. One obstacle to teacher training and innovation was the politically powerful National Teachers Union (SNTE), which resisted reform. Many Mexican universities also lacked an adequate budget and frequently relied on inadequately trained faculty.

During the 1980s and 1990s, education remained a central political issue in Mexico. The anticlericalism inherent in earlier educational policies was largely abandoned and in 1991 the Mexican Congress ended the Constitutional prohibition on religious education. At the same time, the country's renewed efforts to modernize its economy, this time through privatization and participation in the global marketplace (including the North American Free Trade Agreement/ NAFTA) lent renewed urgency to the education question and called attention to the continuing problems plaguing the educational system. In fact, NAFTA includes guidelines for academic certification among the United States, Canada, and Mexico.

The last two presidents of the twentieth century, Carlos Salinas de Gortari (1988–1994) and Ernesto Zedillo (1994–2000) focused more attention on schools and, in particular, sought to make schools, universities, and teachers more accountable while providing incentives for improvement. Salinas's Solidarity program provided funds for the improvement of schools, particularly in poor rural areas, while Zedillo's Progresa program provided financial incentives to poor families so that their children would remain in school. Both presidents also sought to decentralize the educational system, and a 1992 law (the National Agreement for the Modernization of Basic Education) expressed the government's intention to give administrative freedom to the states. Salinas also pressured public universities and their faculty to improve through more official oversight and financial incentives for teachers. Broader attempts to privatize the economy and end government subsidies had also begun to affect the public university system by the end of the twentieth century. In 1999, an attempt to raise tuition at UNAM resulted in a strike. Many students and their parents insisted on a continuation of free and government-supported university education for all Mexicans while policymakers argued that such a model was obsolete and inefficient.

Also indicative of the challenges faced by Mexican policymakers as they sought to push Mexico into a global economy and do away with the structures (including agrarian reform and government-subsidized higher education) deemed incompatible with the "neoliberal" model was the controversy over a new set of history texts introduced in 1992 as part of the Free Textbook program. The texts were commissioned and written during the Salinas presidency and while his successor Ernesto Zedillo served as secretary of education. The obligatory texts for the fourth, fifth, and sixth grades were immediately criticized as a biased rewriting of Mexican history that placed Salinas's controversial free-market reforms in a more favorable light. In particular, the new books treated Porfirio Díaz more kindly than earlier texts, underscoring his efforts to modernize the country and to welcome foreign investment during his 35-year rule. The Mexican Revolution, particularly the struggle for land reform embodied by Emiliano Zapata, was de-emphasized in comparison to earlier texts. Although this new version of history received support from several elements of Mexican society, it also drew biting criticism and protest from important groups, including the Federal Army (which was definitively linked in the new texts to the massacre of Mexican students in 1968) and a sizeable group within the National Teachers Union (SNTE). Within a year, the Salinas administration had abandoned the new history books.

As Mexico enters the new millennium, education is sure to remain a central political issue and a pressing social problem. Throughout the country, the dropout rate remains high and the average Mexican completes only eight years of schooling. Despite increasing levels of federal spending on education, resources for teachers and schools remain inadequate. Candidates in the presidential race of 2000 featured education as a major part of their campaigns and helped underscore the fact that, despite impressive gains made during the past century, Mexico continues to struggle with the basic issue of educating its citizens.

—SBP

See also: Constitution of 1917; Cristero Rebellion; Vasconcelos, José.

References:
Gilbert, Dennis. "Rewriting History: Salinas, Zedillo and the 1992 Textbook Controversy." *Mexican Studies/Estudios Mexicanos.* 13, no. 2 (Summer 1997): 271–298.

Ruíz, Ramón. *Mexico: The Challenge of Poverty and Illiteracy.* San Marino, CA: Huntington Library, 1963.

Vaughan, Mary Kay. *Cultural Politics in Revolution.* Tucson: University of Arizona Press, 1997.

———. *The State, Education and Social Class in Mexico, 1880–1928.* DeKalb: Northern Illinois University Press, 1982.

Elections

Elections—local, state, federal—were an accepted feature of political life in Mexico throughout the twentieth century. In most cases these elections did not play a meaningful role in who exercised political power or in what governmental policies were pursued. Voters assumed—often with good reason—that the elections were rigged. Charges of electoral fraud followed virtually every election, but typically no action was ever taken. Many voters responded by not voting in elections; low voter turnout was often a better indicator of political opposition than the

number of votes garnered by the losing candidate. After 1929 the dominant role played by the official party, the Institutional Revolutionary Party (Partido Revolucionario Institucional, or PRI), discouraged political competition. The PRI could draw on its own resources as well as those of the government, making meaningful opposition virtually impossible. Political competition took place within the PRI rather than between the PRI and other political parties. PRI nominees were selected by party bosses, not through a primary-election system. Elections were more important as an occasion for the rotation of offices among PRI politicians than as an opportunity to contest for political power.

The role played by elections began to change in the 1960s in the face of growing public pressure for greater democracy within the PRI and in the political system in general. PRI leaders squelched efforts at internal reform but wanted, at least, to create the impression of a willingness to compete for political power. They accomplished this purpose by reforming the electoral code in 1964 to introduce the concept of proportional representation. Under this system opposition parties could win representation in the Chamber of Deputies, the lower house of the Mexican Congress, based on the total percentage of votes won in national elections, even if they did not win any of the direct elections for congressional seats based on geographical districts. This approach provided some semblance of political competition without threatening the PRI's dominant control of politics. Electoral reform in 1977 guaranteed 25 percent of the seats in the Chamber of Deputies (100 out of 400) to opposition parties. Further reforms in 1986 provided that no single party would control more than 70 percent of the seats in the Chamber of Deputies and that 200 of the now 500 seats in the Chamber would come from proportional representation; the remaining 300 seats would be based on geographical districts where elections almost always went to the PRI. These reforms provided for greater opposition representation in the Chamber but did not address fundamental problems in the electoral system that gave rise to charges of vote fraud.

The presidential elections of 1988 focused unprecedented attention on the question of elections and election fraud. PRI candidates not only consistently won presidential elections; they also typically won with big majorities, often being credited with more than 90 percent of the vote. In the 1988 election, the PRI candidate, Carlos Salinas de Gortari, barely won a majority of the vote amid widespread charges of electoral fraud. Also in 1988, congressional elections left the PRI with its smallest majority ever in the Chamber of Deputies, 260 out of 500 seats. The improving electoral results of the opposition partially reflected a willingness on the part of the government and the PRI to refrain from electoral manipulation in contests where fraud might provoke an unacceptable level of popular criticism and perhaps even political action. Even this limited amount of electoral honesty was unacceptable to a conservative element in the PRI, soon dubbed the "dinosaurs." The dinosaurs wanted to continue the traditional fraudulent election practices even if it meant public criticism and even violent opposition. The dinosaurs pointed to growing opposition gains at municipal and state levels as proof that permitting even limited electoral competition was a threat to PRI control. Particularly notable were election victories in races for the governorship by the opposition party, the National Action Party (Partido Acción Nacional, or PAN). The PAN won a series of elections for governor in Baja California-Norte (1989), San Luis Potosí (1991), Guanajuato (1991), and Chihuahua (1992).

Additional electoral reforms continued to make elections more competitive. Electoral modifications in 1993 and 1996 included limits on campaign expenditures, greater opposition access to the media, the election of the mayor of Mexico City, and a nonpartisan and autonomous Federal Electoral Institute to monitor federal elections. These reforms all undercut the power of the PRI in elections, which was quickly demonstrated in the 1997 elections. In 1997 an opposition party won the mayorship of Mexico City as well as control of the Mexico City assembly; the PRI for the first time in its history did not have a majority in the Chamber of Deputies; and the PAN won governorships in the states of Nuevo León and Querétaro.

While there was widespread recognition of the growing significance of elections at all levels, there was still the ultimate test of a presidential election being won by a non-PRI candidate. The 1994 presidential race had resulted in a victory for the PRI nominee, Ernesto Zedillo, who was generally considered to have been the actual winner as well as the official winner of a campaign that had seen the assassination of the original PRI candidate, Luis Donaldo Colosio. Zedillo promised there would be honest presidential elections in 2000, despite opposition from within his own party. Zedillo also declined to name the PRI presidential nominee, permitting a modified primary system to select the party nominee, Francisco Labastida Ochoa. The 2000 election resulted in the first non-PRI president, Vicente Fox Quesada, since the founding of the official party in 1929. While opposition politicians heaped praise on Zedillo for presiding over honest elections, Zedillo's fellow PRI members bitterly denounced his role in the proceedings. Zedillo and the PRI found themselves in a no-win situation; the only way they could demonstrate that the election was honest was to lose it.

Congressional elections in 2003 led to modest PRI gains in the Congress, with the PAN suffering a major decline in representation. There were few charges of election irregularities. Perhaps, the most telling thing about the 2003 elections was the low voter turnout; only 41 percent of eligible voters cast their ballots.

There is little doubt that Mexican elections are the most open and competitive that they have ever been. Political observers—especially in the United States—are quick to point out that an honest presidential election does not mean that democracy is firmly established in Mexico. There are still considerable local and regional variations in the democratic aspects of elections; running for mayor of Mexico City offers different obstacles to honest elections than running for governor of the state of Chiapas. The absence of a two-party system affects the role of elections in Mexican politics. Both politicians and voters have little experience with a truly democratic political culture or the role of a "loyal opposition." Honest elections make political outcomes unpredictable, as former President Ernesto Zedillo can attest.

—*DMC*

See also: Calles, Plutarco Elías; Cárdenas, Cuauhtémoc; Democratization Process; Fox, Vicente; Government; Partido de Acción Nacional (PAN); Partido Revolucionario Institucional (PRI).

References:

Camp, Roderic Ai. *Politics in Mexico: Democratizing Authoritarianism.* 3d ed. New York: Oxford University Press, 1999.

Rodríguez, Victoria E., and Peter M. Ward, eds. *Opposition Government in Mexico.* Albuquerque: University of New Mexico Press, 1995.

Story, Dale. *The Mexican Ruling Party: Stability and Authority.* New York: Praeger, 1986.

Environmental Issues

As the twenty-first century began, President Vicente Fox announced a "national crusade for forests and water" and declared environmental issues to be a matter of national security. Fox's words acknowledged problems that had been building in Mexico throughout the twentieth century, including deforestation, pollution, exhaustion of groundwater resources, erosion, and soil depletion. Industrial and urban growth, as well as a "Green Revolution," have resulted in the overexploitation of resources, a loss of biodiversity, and an increase in air, water, soil, and even noise pollution. The price of economic growth was readily apparent by the time of Fox's election in 2000. Indeed, some now estimate that Mexico loses 11 percent of its Gross Domestic Product (GDP) yearly because of environmental degradation. Even as Mexico's leaders have continued to embrace economic modernization and the country's integration into a global economy, many Mexicans have experienced deterioration in their quality of life. This is particularly true in Mexico City and the United States–Mexico border region, where phenomenal population growth has strained already inadequate local services while largely unregulated industrial expansion has contributed to an increasingly toxic environment.

The alteration of Mexico's environment and exploitation of its resources are not new phenomena. Spanish colonists in particular altered woodlands, waters, and soil as they introduced cattle ranching, new food crops, as well as mining and other industrial activities. While the first century after independence saw the enactment of Mexico's first forestry law (under President Benito Juárez), the broader trend was toward land concentration and the intensified exploitation of natural resources. Under the regime of Porfirio Díaz (1876–1911), alteration of the environment accelerated as the government welcomed foreign investment and sought to push the country into a "modern" economic age. Mexico's forests were particularly affected by growth as they increasingly provided fuel and raw materials for industrial development, including the construction of a railroad system.

As the historic hub of population and development, central Mexico experienced a significant transformation of its landscape during the late nineteenth and early twentieth centuries. The cutting of forests and construction of irrigation works in this area reflected the expansion of agriculture and manufacturing. The growth of textile factories in the Valley of Mexico brought especially significant changes. Textile production demanded water and wood for steam engines, and factories claimed nearby lands for worker housing. A notable environmental change also occurred in and around Mexico City, which had emerged during the Spanish colonial period at the expense of the lakes that had once dotted the Valley of Mexico. Convinced that the lakes gave the city an unhealthy climate, Spaniards began draining them in the seventeenth century. The diversion of water from Mexico's capital was an ongoing task, and it culminated in the *desagüe* (drainage) project of the late nineteenth century. Completed in 1900, the *desagüe* project involved the construction of a large tunnel and a canal, which by 1920 had drained significant amounts of water from the city and its environs. The removal of standing water allowed Mexico City to expand, but it also altered the valley's ecosystem. Drainage removed many plant and animal species native to the area. It also left the city sitting atop dry lake beds in a valley that was surrounded by mountains, thus creating problems that have persisted, including (ironically) lack of water and inadequate sewage disposal for an ever-expanding population.

The 1940s marked the beginning of Mexico's next wave of economic growth as the country sought to lessen its dependence on other countries for manufactured goods. A series of national leaders embraced a policy of import substitution industrialization (ISI), which brought with it additional environmental challenges. While the government promoted rapid industrialization, the country's urban centers grew and a significant migration of people from countryside to city occurred. Mexico City, Guadalajara, and Monterrey were the main areas of industrial growth, and they absorbed a disproportionate number of migrants. After the 1950s, however, other areas were also transformed, including Acapulco, Coatzacoalcos, Tijuana, and Ciudad Juárez. Acapulco's growth reflected the development of Mexico's tourist industry, while that of Coatzacoalcos (in Veracruz) was tied largely to the exploitation of Mexico's oil resources. The expansion of the border towns of Tijuana and Ciudad Juárez was encouraged by the *maquiladora* industry,

which began in 1965 and welcomed foreign companies and their assembly plants to the border region.

Tourism, the petroleum industry, and *maquiladoras,* as well as the growth affecting Mexico City, Guadalajara, and Monterrey transformed the landscape. In all areas, population increases and the growth of factories strained municipal services (including wastewater treatment) and contributed to an increase in pollution. Tourism presented the danger of overusing coastal ecosystems, and the oil industry raised the specter of oil spills and other forms of contamination related to the drilling and processing of petroleum. Indeed, in 1978 a major oil spill occurred off the coast of Campeche, contaminating the ocean floor and coating nearby beaches. By the late twentieth century, Mexico's state-run petroleum industry was a major polluter, threatening marine life and contributing to water and soil contamination in coastal areas.

In Mexico's rural areas, a Green Revolution took hold after midcentury, promoting intensive agricultural production through the application of new technologies, including pesticides, intensive irrigation, and plant hybrids. Cattle ranching also expanded, particularly into the fragile tropical ecosystems of southeastern Mexico. Both agribusiness and cattle ranching contributed to the exhaustion of soil, depletion and contamination of groundwater, and deforestation. Meanwhile, Mexico's fishing industry also intensified, encouraging the overexploitation of marine resources.

One area that was especially transformed by economic growth and the intensified use of natural resources was the southernmost state of Chiapas, an area of great biodiversity and natural wealth. Chiapas had begun to feel the effects of commercial logging in the nineteenth century, but it experienced more significant change beginning in the 1940s as landless peasants from other areas of Mexico flooded into the state. After the 1960s, the forest industry expanded, as did cattle ranching. By the late twentieth century, Chiapas's forests, including the Lacandón, were devastated by development. At the same time, overhunting threatened the extinction of some of the area's unique species.

During the last two decades of the twentieth century, Mexico experienced yet another wave of urban and industrial expansion. National leaders embraced neoliberal policies, privatizing important sectors of the economy and (as in the era of Porfirio Díaz) encouraging foreign investment. These efforts culminated in the North American Free Trade Agreement (NAFTA) signed in 1994 by Mexico, Canada, and the United States. In many ways, neoliberal policies have exacerbated environmental problems. Rural to urban migration has continued, now encouraged in part by the concentration of land in the hands of large mechanized enterprises that can best meet international demand for certain crops. Agribusiness, with its use of intensive irrigation and chemical fertilizers and pesticides, increasingly alters rural ecosystems, depleting soil and groundwater and releasing toxins into the environment.

While economic growth in urban and rural areas has affected most regions of Mexico, by the late twentieth century Mexico City and the U.S.–Mexico border zone were the areas that had experienced the most significant environmental deterioration. During the 1990s, Mexico City and the surrounding metropolitan region were home to some 20 million people, many lacking adequate services, including potable water and sewage disposal. With over 3 million vehicles and countless factories, Mexico City was also arguably the world's most polluted city. In the 1980s and early 1990s, ozone was frequently measured at dangerous levels, seriously threatening the health of residents and prompting intervention by the national government. Beginning in 1989 car use was regulated and factories ordered to cut back on production and to take measures against pollution. Driving rules were further restricted

A veil of smog hangs over Mexico City in the early 1990s. (Liba Taylor/Corbis)

over the next few years, and several high-polluting factories were closed. Although Mexico City could report some improvement in air quality as the twenty-first century began, it continued to face significant environmental problems.

In the U.S.–Mexico border region, the expansion of the *maquiladora* industry beginning in the 1980s resulted in a similar crisis. Thousands of *maquilas* were built, as foreign companies sought to take advantage of cheap labor and the relatively lax enforcement of Mexican environmental laws. The population of the border also grew as Mexicans migrated north in search of better economic opportunities. The most serious environmental issue emerging in the border zone was related to so-called *aguas negras,* or black waters: wastewater from residential areas and factories. Because of the lack of adequate sewage and wastewater treatment facilities, "black waters" flowed freely into the environment, contaminating soil, rivers (including the Rio Grande), and even drinking water. A lack of industrial waste treatment facilities, particularly for *maquiladora* plants, also contributed chemical waste to the "black waters," adding to the toxic environment. Air pollution began to plague the borderlands, with car emissions, industrial pollutants (including sulfur dioxide from smelters), and dust all contaminating the air. "Black waters" and air pollution have helped to create a public health crisis on both sides of the U.S.–Mexico border. Hepatitis, tuberculosis, and various cancers have proliferated, and the incidence of birth defects, including *anacephaly* and *spina bifida,* has increased. Such health problems have been directly linked to exposure to toxic chemicals, such as those used in the *maquiladora* industry. Understandably, the difficulties facing the *maquiladora* zone prompted significant concern during the negotiation of the North American Free Trade Agreement, eventually resulting in an environmental side agreement to that accord. While some have successfully used NAFTA regulatory provisions to challenge development projects in Mexico, efforts to clean up the border have had a limited effect thus far.

Since most of Mexico's national leaders have prioritized economic growth and modernization, official environmental policy in the country has a rather short and uneven history. Although clearly supporting economic development over environmental protection, Porfirio Díaz agreed to the preservation of forestland in the Valley of Mexico. He did so on the urging of Miguel Angel de Quevedo, Mexico's first great conservationist. Quevedo gained a post in the Ministry of Public Works, a position he also used to create parks in Mexico City. Quevedo's efforts at preservation continued during and after the Mexican Revolution. Under President Lázaro Cárdenas (1934–1940) Quevedo was appointed to the new Department of Forestry, Fish, and Game. He oversaw efforts to protect and restore Mexico's forests, while the Cárdenas administration also took steps to protect wildlife and to expand the national park system. While Quevedo's efforts at forest preservation were of limited success, they, along with Cárdenas's own proconservation stance, represented a brief departure from past attitudes, in which economic modernization clearly took precedence over conservation.

It was not until the 1970s that the Mexican government began a more comprehensive effort to protect the environment. Federal laws passed in the 1970s and 1980s sought to address specific environmental problems that had intensified with industrial development and urbanization. In 1982 the first cabinet-level ministry (SEDUE, the Ministry of Urban Development and Ecology) was created. In 1992 it was replaced with SEDESOL (the Ministry of Social Development). Mexican leaders also worked with the United States on the difficulties facing border communities, and with the 1983 La Paz agreement, both countries pledged themselves to cooperate in alleviating the border environmental crisis. During the 1990s, joint commissions tried to address

A woman washes clothes in a polluted stream near the United States–Mexico border. The polluted water is suspected of causing serious illnesses, including cancer. (Annie Griffiths Belt / Corbis)

specific border issues, and the environmental side agreement of NAFTA resulted in the establishment of the Border Environmental Cooperation Commission (BECC).

Federal attention to environmental issues during the latter part of the twentieth century was accompanied (and encouraged) by the growth of an environmental movement in Mexico. Several proconservation groups were established in the 1970s and 1980s, including the Mexican Ecologist Movement (MEM). In 1987, many environmental groups joined together to establish the Partido Verde Mexicana (Mexican Green Party). By the end of the 1990s, Mexico's Green Party had a visible presence in national and local politics. The attempt to close down the Laguna Verde Nuclear Power Plant, located along the Gulf of Mexico in Veracruz State, was perhaps the most important campaign of Mexico's environmental movement. Construction of Laguna Verde began in 1972 and continued throughout the 1980s. Built on a

geologic fault, Laguna Verde emitted radioactive materials even before it was fully operational. In 1987, thousands of protestors symbolically closed the plant. Laguna Verde remained open, however, and questions about its safety persist.

As a new century begins, Mexico faces daunting environmental problems. Deforestation claims nearly 600,000 hectares of wooded land each year. Land, water, and soil contamination, as well as erosion, have reached critical levels in several areas of the country while the overuse of natural resources threatens biodiversity. Population growth and urban and industrial expansion also continue to produce grim results: over half of all urban and industrial wastewater returns untreated to the environment, and millions of Mexicans lack access to potable water or adequate sewage treatment facilities. While national leaders have paid more serious attention to the environment in recent years, Mexico's history of development, as well as the desire of many

Mexicans to remain competitive in a global economy, may well limit future efforts at conservation and environmental regulation.

—SBP

See also: Import Substitution Industrialization (ISI); Lacandón; Mexico City; North American Free Trade Agreement (NAFTA); Oil Industry; Petróleos Mexicanos (PEMEX); Tourism; Urbanization.

References:

Barry, Tom. *The Challenge of Cross-Border Environmentalism: The U.S.–Mexico Case.* Albuquerque, NM, and Bisbee, AZ: Resource Center Press/Border Ecology Project, 1994.

Hernández, Lucina, et al. *Historia ambiental de la ganadería en Mexico.* Xalapa, Veracruz: Instituto de Ecología, 2001.

López Portillo y Ramos, Manueled. *El medio ambiente en Mexico: Temas, Problemas, y Alternativas.* Mexico City: Fondo de Cultura Económica, 1982.

Melville, Elinore G. K. *A Plague of Sheep: Environmental Consequences of the Conquest of Mexico.* New York: Cambridge University Press, 1994.

Ortiz Monasterio, Fernando, et al. *Tierra profanada: Historia ambiental de México.* Mexico City: Instituto Nacional de Antropología e Historia, 1987.

Simonian, Lane. *Defending the Land of the Jaguar: A History of Conservation in Mexico.* Austin: University of Texas Press, 1995.

Tortolera Villaseñor, Alejandro, ed. *Tierra, agua y bosques: Historia y medio ambiente en el México Central.* Mexico: CEMCA/University of Guadalajara, 1996.

Vázquez Botello, Alfonso, and Federico Páez. *El problema crucial: La contaminación.* Mexico City: Centro de Ecodesarrollo, 1987.

Flores Magón, Ricardo (1873–1922)

Reformer turned revolutionary turned anarchist, Ricardo Flores Magón was born in the poor southern state of Oaxaca of humble parents with liberal ideas. Ricardo had two brothers—the elder Jesús and the younger Enrique—who at various times joined him in his political activism. Despite his background, Ricardo received a good education in Mexico City, including at the prestigious National Preparatory School. He began his studies for a law degree but never completed them.

Flores Magón's political involvement began in 1892 when he joined brother Jesús in opposing the reelection of long-running president, Porfirio Díaz (1877–1880, 1880–1911). Both brothers were arrested but quickly released. Unfortunately for Ricardo it was only the first in a long series of arrests, imprisonments, and trials. In 1893 Ricardo started his journalistic career by joining the Mexico City newspaper, *El Demócrata*, a liberal opposition newspaper highly critical of the Díaz regime, which soon had the paper suppressed. In 1900 Ricardo and Jesús established their own newspaper, *Regeneración,* which would be identified with Ricardo for the rest of his career. Ricardo also joined in

the movement headed by Camilo Arriaga, a wealthy reformer who promoted the establishment of Liberal Clubs throughout Mexico. Flores Magón attended the first Liberal Congress held in February 1901 and also turned *Regeneración* into a semiofficial organ of the budding Mexican Liberal Party (Partido Liberal Mexicano, or PLM).

Díaz soon moved to silence his growing group of critics. In May 1901 authorities closed down *Regeneración* and arrested both Ricardo and Jesús Flores Magón for defaming public officials. Both remained in jail until April 1902 when they were released without ever having stood trial. While Jesús ended his connection with the liberal movement, Ricardo—now with younger brother, Enrique—joined another liberal opposition newspaper, *El Hijo del Ahuizote.* Officials soon closed this newspaper as well, with both Ricardo and Enrique being jailed from 12 September 1902 to 23 January 1903. The Flores Magón brothers did not stay out of jail very long. They were arrested again in April 1903 for defaming public officials; authorities released them in October 1903, again without having brought them to trial. This constant legal harassment radicalized Ricardo Flores Magón, convincing him to pursue Revolution rather than reform; it also convinced him to follow other liberals into exile where he could continue his opposition beyond the reach of Mexican government officials.

Ricardo and Enrique Flores Magón arrived in Texas in January 1904. They established themselves in San Antonio and began publishing *Regeneración* again in November 1904. Mexican agents in Texas kept Flores Magón under observation, and in December there was an unsuccessful effort to assassinate Ricardo. This convinced Ricardo to move farther away from the border to St. Louis, Missouri. Part of the financing for the move came from Francisco Madero, a wealthy landowner in the northern Mexican state of Coahuila, who was in the early stage of developing opposition to the Díaz regime.

In February 1905, Flores Magón completed the move to St. Louis, and *Regeneración* renewed publication. Splits began to appear in the liberal exile group, provoked by the growing radicalism of Flores Magón. Camilio Arriaga, one of the most important liberal leaders, broke with Flores Magón and returned to San Antonio, Texas. Francisco Madero also ceased his funding of Flores Magón's activities. In September 1905 Ricardo Flores Magón announced the establishment of the "Organizing Junta of the Mexican Liberal Party," with himself as president and brother Enrique as treasurer. This completed the break with Arriaga, who had established the foundation for the Liberal Party years earlier.

Flores Magón's radicalism also attracted the attention of U.S. authorities. In October 1905 St. Louis police raided the offices of *Regeneración* and arrested the Flores Magón brothers for defamation. They remained in jail until supporters raised enough money for their bail in December. Harassed by police and private security agents hired by Mexican officials, the liberals decided to move even farther north, fleeing first to Toronto and then Montreal, Canada.

On 1 July 1906, *Regeneración* published the "Program and Manifesto of the Mexican Liberal Party," a list of some 52 political, social, and economic reforms representing the collective views of the Flores Magón brothers and other liberal exiles. Among other things, these reforms called for restrictions on the Roman Catholic Church, prohibition on foreign ownership of land, and redistribution by the state of unused lands. In September 1906 Ricardo returned to the United States, establishing his revolutionary headquarters in El Paso, Texas. The liberals were linked to strikes and small guerrilla raids in Mexico, prompting a crackdown on them by both U.S. and Mexican officials.

Ricardo Flores Magón moved to California to avoid arrest, arriving in November 1906. With *Regeneración*—which had continued to publish in St. Louis—again shut down by authorities, Flores Magón helped to start a new publication in California called *Revolución* in June 1907. This newspaper continued to stress the need for revolutionary action to overthrow the Díaz government but was becoming increasingly radical in its pronouncements. On 23 August 1907, private investigator Thomas Furlong arrested Flores Magón in Los Angeles without a warrant, but local officials held him as a fugitive from justice. Federal officials decided to try Flores Magón for violating U.S. neutrality laws in connection with a liberal revolutionary movement launched from Douglas, Arizona, in September 1906. Flores Magón endured a lengthy stay in jail while unsuccessfully fighting extradition on the federal charges. In March 1909 he was transferred to Arizona. In May his trial began in Tombstone, Arizona. He was found guilty of violating the neutrality laws and sentenced to eighteen months in the federal penitentiary.

When Flores Magón was released in August 1910, he returned to Los Angeles to renew his revolutionary activities. At the time there was still a warrant for his arrest in Texas on another charge of violating the U.S. neutrality laws in connection with liberal activity in 1908. Flores Magón revived *Regeneración* in September with an even more radical tone. This renewed activity took place just as a new call for Revolution was issued by Francisco Madero, Flores Magón's former financial supporter and unsuccessful candidate for the presidency in 1910. Flores Magón dismissed Madero's Revolutionary program as insufficiently radical because it emphasized political rather than social and economic reforms. This attitude reflected Flores Magón's growing anarchism, which saw the government as an obstacle to improving the condition of the masses. It may also have reflected Flores Magón's resentment at Madero's challenge to his Revolutionary leadership. Whether for personal or political reasons, Flores Magón never supported Madero's cause.

Madero's revolution also posed other problems for Flores Magón. Some of the liberals advocated an alliance with Madero, a move which Flores Magón strongly opposed. The public split between Madero and Flores Magón also cost Flores Magón support among his U.S. followers, such as the socialists and the labor unions. There was also pressure on Flores Magón to return to Mexico and become more directly involved in the military effort to overthrow Díaz. The major military effort of the liberals during the Madero revolution of 1910–1911 was an effort to seize Baja California. The Baja campaign not only proved unsuccessful; it was also criticized as a filibustering expedition because of the uncertainty surrounding its goals. Madero's revolution even led to a family split. Jesús Flores Magón became a successful attorney in Mexico City after leaving the liberal movement. In June 1911, after the overthrow of Díaz, Madero sent Jesús to Los Angeles to try to win over Ricardo. Ricardo rejected the overtures, and Jesús returned to Mexico.

On 14 June 1911—the day after the failed meeting between Jesús and Ricardo—police raided liberal headquarters and arrested both Ricardo and Enrique Flores Magón on federal warrants charging them with violating the neutrality laws in connection with the failed campaign in Baja California. Released

on bail, Ricardo claimed that his arrest was instigated by brother Jesús and Madero in retaliation for his refusal to join them. The Liberal Party issued a new manifesto in September 1911, which was openly anarchistic in its views, advocating an end to private property and the establishment of communal work groups in both industry and agriculture.

The Flores Magón trial finally got under way in June 1912. Ricardo and Enrique were accused of violating the neutrality laws, specifically of recruiting men for the failed military expedition to Baja California in 1911. The trial ended in a guilty verdict, and on 25 June 1912 both were sentenced to twenty-three months in the federal penitentiary. A pardon appeal was made based on the contention that the convictions were gained through perjured testimony, but President Woodrow Wilson refused to grant the appeal in July 1913.

After their release from prison in January 1914, Ricardo and Enrique returned to Los Angeles to resume their work with *Regeneración*. Madero was gone from the Mexican scene, overthrown by a coup and later assassinated while the Flores Magóns were in prison. A new and more bloody round of revolution was under way in Mexico as the Flores Magóns resumed their work. The publication of *Regeneración* met with little official opposition until February 1916, when Ricardo and Enrique were arrested under a federal law prohibiting the sending of "indecent matter" (reading materials calling for murder, assassination, or arson) in the U.S. mails. The brothers could not afford bail, so they remained in jail until their trial began in May 1916. The "indecent matter" sent through the mails consisted of articles from *Regeneración*. They were found guilty in June. Because of health problems, Ricardo was sentenced to serve one year and one day in the federal penitentiary; Enrique received a three-year term. Both were released under bail while their case was appealed.

While Ricardo's 1916 conviction was still working its way through the appeal process, he was arrested in March 1918 for violating the Espionage Act and the Trading-with-the-Enemy Act that had been passed after the United States entered World War I in April 1917. When Ricardo came to trial in July 1918, he was quickly convicted and sentenced to twenty years and one day in addition to the sentence of one year and one day he received for the 1916 conviction. On 21 November 1922 Ricardo Flores Magón died in the federal prison at Leavenworth, Kansas.

Contemporaries of Flores Magón as well as later historians disagreed over his importance to the coming of revolution to Mexico beginning in 1910. The Mexican Liberal Party failed in its military goals. The party also suffered from major organizational problems and internal divisions, many of them attributed to Flores Magón. His lengthy stay in exile, even after the Revolution began to unfold in 1910, provoked contemporary and historical criticism. Although committed to a brand of agrarian reform, Flores Magón's reliance on newspaper propaganda made it difficult for the liberal message to reach the illiterate masses in the Mexican countryside. Despite these problems, the Mexican Liberal Party under Ricardo Flores Magón was able to provide a sustained, revolutionary opposition to the government of Porfirio Díaz in the years leading up to the Revolution of 1910. Many of the reforms suggested by Flores Magón influenced changes after the Revolution of 1910. Flores Magón's importance as a precursor has long been recognized, even by the political heirs of the revolutionaries he earlier opposed. In 1945 the Mexican government had Flores Magón's remains reinterred in the nation's Rotunda of Illustrious Men, a belated recognition of his struggle to improve the lives of the Mexican people.

—DMC

See also: Anarchism; Díaz, Porfirio; Juárez, Benito; Madero, Francisco; Partido Liberal Mexicano (PLM).

References:
Albro, Ward. *Always a Rebel: Ricardo Flores Magón and the Mexican Revolution.* Fort Worth, TX: Texas Christian University Press, 1992.
Langham, Thomas C. *Border Trials: Ricardo Flores Magón and the Mexican Liberals.* El Paso: Texas Western Press, 1981.
MacLachlan, Colin M. *Anarchism and the Mexican Revolution: The Political Trials of Ricardo Flores Magón in the United States.* Berkeley: University of California Press, 1991.

Folk Art

Mexico has long been internationally renowned for its varied and inventive folk art. The exquisite textiles, feather work, pottery, and jewelry that Cortés brought back from the recently conquered territories sparked the European imagination and produced a taste for Mexico's exotic wares that persists to this day. Nearly five hundred years later, some of these folk arts still bear striking resemblance to their pre-Hispanic predecessors. Most, however, have taken on new forms, incorporated new technologies, and adapted themselves to new markets. Plus, some Mexican folk art is of relatively recent invention. Government sponsorship, especially since the Revolution of 1910, has played an important role in maintaining and promoting folk art. In the process, it has further commercialized traditional arts and crafts by connecting them to national and international markets where local meanings, uses, and practices no longer pertain, despite advertisements that promise "genuine Mexican popular art." The result is a hybrid folk art that is simultaneously traditional, modern, and postmodern—in which, for example, an indigenous artisan who lives and works in a *traditional* space might sell his wares in a *modern* market for upscale consumers who might display it alongside contemporary art in order to represent themselves as *postmodern* sophisticates. To further complicate matters, the increased acceptance of Mexican kitsch, like lotto cards, calendar Aztecs, professional wrestling action figures, and Barney piñatas as a legitimate form of popular art has stretched the concepts of "folk" art and cultural hybridity to their limits and beyond.

Since Cortés, foreign travelers have marveled at the variety and quality of Mexican arts and crafts. Still, it was not until near the end of the nineteenth century, with the expansion of modern transportation networks and the spread of international expositions and world's fairs, that folk art made the transition from handicrafts for a local market to cottage "industry." Government support played a key role in this transition as turn-of-the-century promoters sought to turn European and American fascination with exotic cultures to Mexico's comparative advantage. The administration of president Porfirio Díaz (1876–1880, 1884–1911) even allowed Mexican Indians to be exhibited abroad—as long as they were not "mistreated"—carrying out their daily tasks in mock villages for the edification of curious fairgoers. These tasks typically included the production of traditional arts and crafts. Even long-standing export-oriented cottage industries such as *Talavera* pottery from Puebla expanded to meet the increased demand of national and international markets. Extensive promotion and market expansion altered traditional modes of production by encouraging the introduction of new technologies and a new kind of market savvy oriented toward nonlocal consumers. These changes, in turn, affected folk art's traditional uses and meanings.

After the Revolution of 1910, determined to redeem Mexico's much-abused indigenous population, policymakers like influential Secretary of Education José Vasconcelos turned to traditional arts and crafts. For one thing, folk art could provide an immediate and much-needed source of income for poor communities; for another, it could begin the process of cultural assimilation by drawing those communities into the national economy and providing a useful complement to the ambitious educational reforms government officials hoped would transform the nation's Indians (and other marginalized groups) into productive citizens. To begin this redemptive project, the government sponsored an extensive folk art exposition in Mexico City for the

1921 centennial of Mexican independence. Organized and later written up by well-known Revolutionary artist, Dr. Atl (Gerardo Murillo), the centennial exposition introduced urban Mexicans to an impressive popular artistic tradition and encouraged them to rethink long-standing prejudices against lazy, apathetic, and unproductive Indians. For more sensitive souls, folk art held out the promise of reverse redemption, this time of the dominant groups in Mexican society. To these enthusiasts, the "authentic" arts and crafts of marginalized groups captured the essence of the national soul—*México profundo* (deep Mexico) some called it—before it was tainted by the alienation and commodification that accompanied modernity. A series of subsequent expositions in Mexico and abroad (including the Museum of Modern Art in New York City) further developed the general public's appreciation of folk art. So did the endorsement of important artists—Diego Rivera, Roberto Montenegro, Miguel Covarrubias—and renowned collectors like Nelson Rockefeller, whose extraordinary collection of Mexican folk art (now at the San Antonio Museum of Art and San Francisco's Mexican Museum) provided external validation for an artistic tradition some Mexicans still considered primitive.

Folk art's redemptive possibilities and growing international prestige lent some urgency and prestige to official promotion efforts. Beginning in the economic boom years of the 1950s, government support expanded from folk art expositions and an occasional new museum to the creation of official agencies—Foundation for Popular Arts and Industries (1951), Foundation for the Development of Artisanry (1961, FONART after 1974), General Directorship of Popular Cultures (1971)—and an extensive national museum system that included a Museum of Popular Arts and Industries (1951). These official institutions did much to promote and legitimize folk arts even among the generally conservative Mexican middle class. Thanks in part to these efforts, folk art saturates Mexican daily life from the ubiquitous street vendors with their cut-glass idols and calendar stones to the sugar skulls and pop-up coffins of Day of the Dead to the paper cutouts that decorate festive occasions of all kinds.

Folk art might be everywhere in Mexico, but it is often used in very different ways. Although most traditional arts and crafts derive from the utilitarian objects of everyday life, in the hands of talented and imaginative artisans, these objects far transcend their practical uses. Folk ceramics gives some indication of the different artistic possibilities inherent in the everyday. All over Mexico, clay jars, pitchers, and water coolers are gracefully shaped, imaginatively colored, cleverly painted, and carefully designed both for function and aesthetic appeal. Results, however, are quite varied. For example, artisans like the Nahua Indian potters of Tulimán, Guerrerro, still use pre-Hispanic techniques and materials, while *Talavera* pottery from Puebla, popular since the colonial era, derives from a Spanish style introduced into Mexico during the colonial period, a style already heavily indebted to European, Chinese, and Moorish ceramics. At the same time, Nahua potters often decorate their jars with *charro* (cowboy) figures, while their *Talavera* counterparts stick almost exclusively to colonial era motifs. Variety also characterizes the fabric arts. They run the gamut from the traditional *huipiles* and beaded blouses of indigenous women from southern Mexico to the elegant *serapes* (blanket-cloaks) of northern Saltillo weavers. As with potters, Mexican weavers and embroiderers often adapt modern cloth, thread, tools, and motifs to their "traditional" arts.

Ceremonial objects, especially those connected to folk religious practices, show even more variation. According to poet-essayist Octavio Paz's well-known characterization in *Labyrinth of Solitude,* Mexico is a land of masks behind which people disguise their resentments and insecurities. True or not, nearly every Mexican subculture incorporates masks into ceremonial life. For indigenous groups, masks often represent spiritual forces such as the *nahual,* a shaman's animal counterpart, usually a jaguar. European and especially Christian icons are even more common, ranging from devils and saints to Roman centurions, black men, and nineteenth-century dandies. In nearly all cases, ceremonial masks were originally intended for religious rituals—whether Indian, Christian, or a mixture of both—but their popularity with collectors and tourists has detached them from local contexts even in the rare cases where the masks are accompanied by anthropological explanations of their significance.

Another favorite of collectors (including Frida Kahlo) are private religious images, *retablos* and *ex-votos,* usually painted on tin and intended to honor a religious figure—the Virgin of Guadalupe and Santo Niño (Holy Child) are frequent subjects—or to give thanks for an answered prayer. *Ex-votos* with their personalized message inscribed on the painting itself by the artist are too specialized for effective mass marketing but the increased availability and low cost of "commercial" images of the religious figures in placards, medallions, and figurines has mostly supplanted the *retablo* tradition as well as the carving of wooden *santos* or saints (although both are sold as specialty items to connoisseurs). Nevertheless, the tradition of household and neighborhood altars assembled from carefully chosen items selected by the shrine builder allows considerable leeway for artistic interpretation—even if a tendency to include commercially produced images, soft drink bottles, and Christmas lights offends traditionalists.

Although grounded in everyday life, folk art does not always serve a primarily practical or religious purpose. For example, candlesticks shaped like dinosaurs, mermaids, or flower trees might hold candles; molded sugar figurines, pop-up coffins, or costumed skeletons might commemorate the Day of the Dead, but in these cases the artist's imagination has far exceeded the demands of practical application. The same can be said of lacquered boxes from Guerrero or elaborate pineapple-shaped water jars from Michoacán or the fanciful clay market women and animal bands (seeded with chia, they grow "fur" when watered) of Oaxaca potters like the renowned Teodora Blanco.

Some folk art, especially in recent years, has a taken on a purely decorative function, such as the *papel picado* (paper cutouts) that appears on most festive occasions or bright bark paintings of "traditional" life done in modern acrylics or tin Christmas tree ornaments colored with magic markers. Moreover, despite folk art's supposedly timeless quality, new "traditions" are emerging all the time. Especially popular these days are the painted, carved wood Mexican animals first produced in the late 1960s by Oaxaca woodcarver, Manuel Jiménez, which are now a regular feature in art galleries and import shops throughout Mexico and the United States. Commercial images also figure prominently in contemporary Mexican folk art, although traditionalists still reject things like lotto cards, Aztec calendar scenes, prepackaged-prewired Virgin of Guadalupe shrines, and plastic wrestling figures (of famous Mexican wrestlers like El Santo and Blue Demon) as modern mass-produced "popular" art unworthy to be grouped with tradition artisancrafted "folk" art. Artistic fancy, however, has a way of blurring these boundaries, even when it means undermining the "authenticity" of artistic practice. The fame of folk artists like Blanco and Jiménez suggests that the traditional folk art of anonymous village artisans is already a thing of the past.

—*RMB*

See also: Anthropology and Archeology; Holy Days and Holidays; Kahlo, Frida; *Mestizaje* and *Indigenismo*; Murillo, Gerardo "Dr. Atl"; Vasconcelos, José; Virgin of Guadalupe.

References:
Espejel, Carlos, ed. *The Nelson A. Rockefeller Collection of Mexican Folk Art.* San Francisco: Chronicle Books—The Mexican Museum of San Francisco, 1986.
García Canclini, Néstor. *Transforming Modernity : Popular Culture in Mexico.* Trans. Lidia Lozano. Austin: University of Texas Press, 1993.
Gutiérrez, Ramón A., ed. *Home Altars of Mexico.* Albuquerque: University of New Mexico Press, 1998.
Harvey, Marian. *Mexican Crafts and Craftspeople.* Philadelphia: The Art Alliance Press, 1987.
Oettinger, Marion, Jr. *Folk Treasures of Mexico.* New York: Harry Abrams, 1990.
Sayer, Chloë. *Arts and Crafts of Mexico.* San Francisco: Chronicle Books, 1990.
Tenorio-Trillo, Mauricio. *Mexico at the World's Fairs: Crafting a Modern Nation.* Berkeley: University of California Press, 1996.

Food

Mexico is well known throughout the world for its unique cuisine. Salsa now outsells catsup in the United States and $5 billion worth of tortillas are sold internationally each year. This popularity, however, has come at a price: the increased standardization of an impressive variety of regional and local cuisines within Mexico. Knowledgeable consumers in the United States, for example, might be able to distinguish among Tex-Mex (from Texas), Sonoran (from the northern Mexican state), and New Mexican (from New Mexico) food but would have difficulty identifying basic differences between the cuisines of Sonora, Veracruz, and Oaxaca. At one level, standardization is the inevitable by-product of international marketing strategies developed by American chains like Taco Bell. At another, it reflects the symbolic power of food to construct identity. Indeed, "classic" Mexican cookbooks that assemble distinct regional cuisines into a definitive text have played an important role in forging a national community bound together by the ties of shared recipes, even as they help preserve those regional differences in the process. To complicate matters further, changes in food production, distribution networks, and food-processing technologies, along with the introduction of mass-produced food products, including "junk" food, has significantly altered Mexican eating habits and Mexican cuisine. Still, Mexican food has managed to preserve its distinct (if hard to categorize) identity and to thrive in the face of internal and external challenges. People from Toronto to Patagonia to Sydney would agree that, standardized or not, Mexican food has vastly improved the international culinary landscape.

Long before the age of industrial and cultural standardization, the development of Mexican cuisine was already a hybrid affair. The cultural clash between Native American cultures and their Spanish overlords was reflected symbolically in the dramatic differences between traditional Native American diets based on corn, beans, squash, and chili peppers and a Spanish diet based on wheat, olives (especially olive oil), grapes (for wine), and meat (cows, pigs, sheep, and chickens were all imports from Europe). As colonizers, the Spanish sought to impose their food preferences, whether by forcing Indians communities to grow wheat for bread rather than corn for tortillas or by letting livestock run loose on Indian fields. Nevertheless, indigenous resistance and the need to reach an accommodation with Mexico's colonized peoples, encouraged the development of hybrid cuisines. This hybridization generally took place within households as Spanish men entered into relationships (mostly informal) with Indian women who were expected to do the cooking—an arrangement guaranteed to preserve basic Indian culinary traditions even as it inevitably opened the door to the incorporation of Spanish foods. Given choices, Indian cooks preferred to retain their own cuisine while adopting the most useful elements of the Spanish diet. (Hardy pigs and chickens could live anywhere and provided a ready source of protein; wheat, however, was a much riskier crop than corn and made little nutritional difference.) On the other hand, differences in food consumption continued to mark and thus reinforce class and racial distinctions, in particular among the status-conscious, European-oriented upper classes. This elite prejudice discouraged the mixing of foods (at least in any obvious way) probably because it symbolized the greatly feared but ever growing *mestizaje* (race mixing) that had come to characterize colonial society.

In the years following independence from Spain (1821), Mexican policymakers were often highly critical of indigenous cuisine as "barbaric" and "unworthy" of a modern nation. At the same time, the need to distinguish Mexican from Spanish culture in order to legitimize the severing of colonial ties led them to accept and even exalt certain hybrid culinary creations like *mole poblano* and *chiles en nogada*. Each had an origin myth, however, that stressed *creole* (European-American) control over the hybridization process: *mole poblano*, its signature sauce a subtle mixture of chili and chocolate, was attributed to seventeenth-century nuns in Puebla; *chiles en nogada*, a stuffed chili pepper with walnut sauce and pomegranate seeds—green, white, and red like the Mexican flag—was said to have been inspired by Agustín de Iturbide, the architect of national independence. This qualified acceptance of a *mestizo* cuisine by *creole* elites had its limits even in cookbooks dedicated to national cuisine. These *creole* experts still considered distinctly Indian dishes like *tamales*—to say nothing of corn tortillas and beans—as culturally and nutritionally inferior to European food. Also, in their social commentary, they repeatedly conjured up images of Indian women slaving over the *metate* (household grinding stone) and sullen, apathetic, unproductive *campesinos* (rural workers) to prove their foregone conclusions.

The *científico* (technocratic or scientific) elites who held important government positions under authoritarian President Porfirio Díaz (1876–1880, 1884–1910) used the authority of their "scientific" educations to further legitimize this dismissive attitude toward indigenous culinary traditions. (Modern nutritional studies have demonstrated that the traditional Native American diet is in fact quite healthy.) A few enlightened policymakers, like Minister of Education Justo Sierra, saw the main problem as lack of adequate caloric intake rather than an inferior diet per se. Others, like his *científico* colleague Francisco Bulnes, insisted that all the world's truly great civilizations were based on a wheat and meat diet; excessive corn tortilla consumption, he argued, was "incompatible with human life." Still, more derogatory were *científico* attitudes toward *pulque,* the mildly alcoholic but highly nutritious fermented maguey cactus juice consumed in huge quantities by the lower classes, a drink that even the tolerant Sierra considered the "evil of the century."

These attitudes persisted well after the Revolution of 1910 despite the efforts of public intellectuals like sociologist Andrés Molina Enriquez to redeem the indigenous foods that "represented in an absolutely indubitable manner the national cuisine." Sierra's influential postrevolutionary successor, Secretary of Education José Vasconcelos, repeated Bulnes assertions about the nutritional superiority of wheat and national census officials inquired into Mexican eating habits in order to gauge poverty—a preference for corn tortillas over wheat bread was considered a sure sign (as was a preference for sandals over shoes). By the 1940s, however, scientific studies by groups like the Rockefeller Foundation and the National Institute of Nutrition had proven the fundamental soundness of the indigenous diet (provided, of course, that people had enough to eat). Meanwhile, Revolutionary ideologies like *indigenismo,* which highlighted indigenous contributions to Mexican society, worked to undermine long-standing prejudices against Indian foods and even to make them fashionable among Mexico City's artistic avantgarde. Without scientific or cultural support, criticism of indigenous culinary traditions tapered off and paved the way for their inclusion in the national cuisine.

The decisive step in construction of truly *mestizo* (as opposed to *creole*) cuisine was the 1946 publication of the "classic" Mexican cookbook, *Platillos regionales de la República mexicana* (Regional Dishes of the Mexican Republic) by Josefina Velazáquez de León. Previous cookbook authors—especially the women who produced more informal collections of family recipes—had often ignored elite prejudices against corn-based dishes like *tamales, enchiladas,* and *posole* (hominy stew). Velazáquez's book, however, brought a broad and diverse spectrum of regional cuisines together as *the* national cuisine and insisted that these corn-based dishes represented its culinary center. Nor did she ignore the practical needs of Mexican women. A tireless campaigner for Mexican cuisine, Velazáquez included, among her more than 150 cookbooks, several publications geared toward middle- and lower-class housewives and working women with titles like *Popular Cooking: 30 Economical Menus* and *How to Cook in Hard Times.* Her influential work inspired a host of imitators and set the tone for family magazines aimed at middle-class Mexican women. By the 1950s, *mestizo* cuisine—as defined by authors like Velazáquez and folklorist Virginia Rodríguez Rivera, author of another "classic" cookbook, *La cocina en el México antiguo y moderno* (Cooking in Old and Modern Mexico, 1968)—had become Mexican food. The reception of *Like Water for Chocolate* (1989), Laura Esquivel's best-selling novel (along with the well-regarded movie version directed by her husband Alfonso Arau), which she structures around a series of traditional recipes, testifies to the ongoing popularity of that culinary identity both in Mexico and the United States.

But even as Mexican food was emerging as an essential component of modern national identity, technological changes and market integration were dramatically altering the culinary landscape. One drawback of a corn-based diet was that it required women to invest as much as five hours a day in grinding corn by hand on a stone *metate* in order to feed their families. Corn tortillas were then cooked in small batches on a *comal* (griddle). This laborious process was central to women's identities and the skillful tortilla maker was widely admired (and easily married). It was also tedious and time-consuming. Urban consumers could usually find alternatives—a common solution was to switch to wheat breads like the ubiquitous *bolillos* (rolls) that still grace Mexican tables. These alternatives, however, were not always available to rural women. Thus the spread of relatively inexpensive and efficient mills during the 1930s revolutionized women's lives as many chose to accept what most considered an inferior product in order to make "free" time for other things, including work outside the home. Better-off rural women who could afford household servants to do their grinding for them often clung stubbornly to "the old ways." But, as mills became more common, as tortilla machines (beginning in the 1950s and 1960s) allowed for local mass production of fresh tortillas, and as *masa harina* or corn flour appeared in grocery stores throughout Mexico, most women's lives changed dramatically. If some lamented the loss of handcrafted tortillas, the majority adapted quickly to the new culinary realities. Less dramatic but just as important was the spread of blenders and pressure cookers. These appliances greatly reduced the time needed to grind up chili sauces, mix fruits, and cook beans, again "freeing" women to take on other sorts of tasks.

Beginning with railroads in the last decades of the nineteenth century, improvements in the nation's transportation infrastructure facilitated these technological changes by opening local markets to outside goods and services. The expansion of the road system after the Revolution of 1910 meant that even the most remote regions could participate in these advances. It also gave national and international food-processing giants like Maseca (the nation's largest corn flour supplier) and Pepsico access to rural consumers so that they too could enjoy the benefits of processed foods like *masa harina* and soft drinks. The considerable cost of setting up and maintaining distribution networks favored larger companies, which encouraged standardization and undermined local culinary traditions. Sometimes, consumers responded in "peculiar" ways. The Mayan Indian community of San Juan Chamula, for example, has adopted

Pepsi as the drink of choice for community rituals, in part because the local *cacique* (boss) controls Pepsi distribution in the region. For the most part, however, the concentration of processed food distribution meant that everyone's tortillas tasted pretty much the same, just like the soda and beer that washed them down.

The expanding transportation infrastructure also increased the mobility of Mexican workers, exposing them to different kinds of foods and eating habits. Perhaps the most pernicious of these habits was the rapid rise in the consumption of junk food, everything from Sabritas chips to Fanta orange soda. Successful companies were careful to cater to national tastes by developing products like apple-flavored soda, tropical fruit juices, and colorfully decorated cookies, but for poorer Mexicans, the switch from corn and beans to junk food was a nutritional disaster. For huge urban areas like Mexico City, Guadalajara, Monterrey, Juárez, and Tijuana, the extra trash generated by packaged foods has clogged dumps, created environmental problems, and strained municipal services.

Another, often overlooked, factor in the development of Mexican cuisine has been the government's food production policies. Before the Revolution of 1910 (1910–1920), policymakers took a laissez faire approach that was mostly restricted to propaganda efforts against "backward" diets in the lower classes. Laws were passed to prevent the adulteration of food and efforts were made to clean up markets and slaughterhouses, but enforcement was rather spotty where it existed at all and then it was aimed mostly at protecting middle- and upper-class urban consumers. Post-Revolutionary regimes, however, had staked their legitimacy on social justice, promising (among other things) agrarian reform, better education, and adequate food for all. The process of land redistribution from large landholders to *campesinos* took off during the administration of president Lázaro Cárdenas (1934–1940). In addition to land, the government also provided access to capital and agricultural extension programs to teach modern farming and livestock raising techniques. Coupled with the onset of the Green Revolution in farming, government policies resulted in a dramatic rise in food production—especially of staples like beans, corn, wheat, and rice—and, more important for poorer Mexicans, in food consumption. By the 1960s, Mexico was more or less self-sufficient in staple food production.

Self-sufficiency declined steadily after the 1960s as the population exploded and national economic development began to take precedence over Cardenista-style social engineering. For most policymakers, national economic development required Mexico's integration into global markets and that, in turn, required competitive industrial and agricultural sectors. During the 1940s, a series of prodevelopment administrations shifted resources from small-scale *campesino* agriculture to "agribusiness." Huge dams were constructed to irrigate the arid but fertile northern plains, road building was concentrated in "productive" areas, and investment capital made available to large-scale agricultural operations. To make matters worse for small-scale rural farmers, the demands of urban consumers for cheap food underwritten by government subsidies kept prices low for staples like corn and beans— the only crops poorer farmers with little access to water and fertilizer could afford to grow. Moreover, as the demand for staples quickly outstripped the supply, imported grains from the United States flooded the Mexican market. Those who could afford it made the switch from staples to export crops like lettuce, broccoli, and tomatoes.

A string of government institutions with acronyms like CONASUPO and SAM, designed to regulate the national food supply, generally preferred to deal with national and international suppliers, especially in times of economic crisis—an increasing influential "fact of life" in Mexico in the last decades of the twentieth century. Even when government policies were adjusted to favor staple production, it was generally agribusinesses— because they could afford the risks associated with shifting crops—rather than small farmers who reaped most of the benefits. In 1991, when President Carlos Salinas de Gortari made the controversial decision to remove Constitutional restrictions on selling *ejido* (communally held) land, many hard-pressed *campesinos* sold off plots to large-scale cultivators concerned more with appealing to national and international markets than catering to local tastes. In addition, Salinas's compensatory food-subsidy program, Solidarity, relied heavily on imported foods to keep prices low.

Although, policymakers directed these diverse governmental programs primarily at farmers and consumers rather than cooks, they have had a noticeable impact on Mexican cuisine. Even ordinary consumers insist that corn from the American Midwest tastes different than Mexican corn and the widespread distribution of foods by companies like Maseca and Pan Bimbo (Bimbo Bread) has favored standardization of flavors and textures over diversity. So has the introduction of American-style Mexican food into Mexico, whether by returning workers with an acquired taste for American-style Mexican food or by fast-food chains like Taco Bell that seem clean and modern compared to a typical street vendor's cart. Nevertheless, the discriminating consumer can still find "authentic" regional cuisines most places in Mexico and even in the southwestern United States. Moreover, the modern obsession with novelty in all things, even when exploited for commercial purposes, just might push traditional Mexican ingredients and regional cuisines into the international mainstream.

—*RMB*

See also: *Mestizaje* and *Indigensimo*.
References:
Esquivel, Laura. *Like Water for Chocolate*. Trans. Carol Christensen and Thomas Christensen. New York: Doubleday, 1992.

Fox, Jonathan. *The Political Dynamics of Reform: State Power and Food Policy in Mexcio*. Ithaca, NY: Cornell University Press, 1991.

Pilcher, Jeffery M. "Mexico's Pepsi Challenge: Traditional Cooking, Mass Consumption, and National Identity," in Gilbert Joseph, Anne Rubenstein, and Eric Zolov, eds. *Fragments of a Golden Age: The Politics of Culture in Mexico Since 1940*. Durham, NC: Duke University Press, 2001.

————. *¡Que vivan los tamales! Food and the Making of Mexican National Identity*. Albuquerque: University of New Mexico Press, 1998.

Foreign Policy

While Mexico's foreign relations increasingly revolve around its bilateral relationship with the United States, Mexico has also pursued a broad-based foreign policy guided by an interrelated set of principles. These principles include national sovereignty, nonintervention, the juridical equality of all nations, peaceful resolution of conflicts, participation in international organizations, and the search for counterbalances to U.S. dominance. Mexico also has special regional concerns relating to the Caribbean and especially Central America. Indeed, Central American nations on a number of occasions have criticized Mexico for acting toward them the way the United States has acted toward Mexico. Mexico's foreign policy also has been shaped by domestic concerns such as governmental development policy and the need to pacify critics of the regime.

The outbreak of Revolution in 1910 forced both Mexico and the major foreign powers to rethink and reshape their policies. While the Revolution was still in progress, World War I began in August 1914, further complicating foreign relations. The major foreign powers sought to exploit the Revolution for their own purposes; in particular, there was great concern over access to Mexico's oil resources. With Venustiano Carranza in the presidency, Mexico maintained its neutrality during the conflict. Although Carranza rejected the offer of a military alliance with Germany, he was still considered "pro-German" by the U.S. government. The highly nationalistic Carranza attempted to stake out an independent foreign policy position for post Revolutionary Mexico in what became known as the "Carranza doctrine." Carranza called for the rejection of the U.S. Monroe Doctrine, foreign respect for Mexico's laws, an absolute ban on intervention, and closer Mexican ties to Latin America and Europe.

Although Carranza was overthrown and assassinated in 1920, his so-called doctrine would influence later administrations. His immediate successor, Alvaro Obregón (1920–1924), however, had to focus his attention on relations with the United States, including lengthy negotiations for recognition. The regime of Plutarco Elías Calles (1924–1934) also had significant problems with the United States but was able to return to some of the themes set down by Carranza and even contested with the United States for influence in Central America.

Both Carranza and Obregón supported unsuccessful efforts to establish a union of the Central American nations. This Central American policy was not an attempt to export the Mexican Revolution; it was aimed instead at blocking growing U.S. political and military influence in the region. Mexico feared being caught between U.S. pressure from both the north and the south. Calles continued an active Mexican role in the area, primarily in Nicaragua. The United States ended its intervention in Nicaragua in August 1925, leading to renewed civil war between conservatives and liberals. Calles provided military assistance to the liberals but was forced to curtail his involvement when the United States intervened again in 1926. Mexico later offered political asylum to the most famous of the liberal generals, Augusto Sandino.

During the Calles years, Mexico also expanded its concept of nonintervention with the "Estrada Doctrine" in 1930. Mexican Minister of Foreign Relations Genaro Estrada called for the diplomatic recognition of governments regardless of how they had come to power. This policy reflected Mexico's frequent difficulties in obtaining recognition from the United States as well as the contemporary problem of revolutionary governments coming to power as a result of the world depression.

The administration of President Lázaro Cárdenas (1934–1940) confronted growing foreign policy problems brought about by the Depression and the coming of war in both Europe and Asia. The Cárdenas years also witnessed a greater professionalization of foreign policy as technocrats in the Ministries of Foreign Relations and the Treasury increasingly shaped foreign policy, especially economic relations. Mexico also became more actively involved in international organizations. Mexico had not joined the League of Nations until 1931 because of its disenchantment with the League's acceptance of the Monroe Doctrine. Mexico's first action as a League member was to challenge the provision of the League covenant recognizing the Monroe Doctrine. Under Cárdenas, Mexico would use the League as a forum for its leftist nationalism and its opposition to the spread of fascist influence. Mexico tried to rally League support for the republican government in Spain after the outbreak of civil war there in 1936. The League established a "Committee of Non-Intervention" to try to confine the struggle; Mexico unsuccessfully challenged this action, claiming that it prevented the legitimate government of Spain from gaining access to international assistance it had a right to under international law. Mexico also welcomed a large number of refugees from the Spanish Civil War.

Cárdenas's decision to nationalize the foreign-owned oil companies in 1938 also had major international repercussions. Efforts to export oil to democratic governments failed in the face of an international boycott. Mexico then turned to barter deals with Nazi Germany and fascist Italy, causing further international alarm. The German conquest of France in June 1940 essentially cut Mexico off from its European markets but also helped to produce a settlement of the oil controversy.

By 1940 international developments made Mexico largely reliant on its bilateral economic relationship with the United States. Mexico maintained limited contact with the Axis powers until the United States entered the war in December 1941. Mexico subsequently broke diplomatic relations with the Axis but did not declare war until May 1942 after German submarine attacks on Mexican oil tankers. The war led to an unprecedented level of cooperation between Mexico and the United States but also led Mexico to renew relations with Britain and the Soviet Union.

Mexico's postwar foreign policy increasingly reflected its commitment to a new national strategy for economic development based on industrialization through import substitution. The government introduced protectionist tariff policies and encouraged but guided foreign investment. This new approach led to impressive economic gains that were described as the "Mexican miracle." With the United States emphasizing the need to "meet the communist threat," postwar Mexican governments maintained an anticommunist stance, supporting the United States in the United Nations and maintaining generally cool relations with the Soviet Union. Mexico, however, was still prepared to stand up for its traditional foreign policy principles, especially nonintervention. Mexico refused to support the growing pressure exerted by the United States on the left-wing government of Guatemala, which culminated in U.S. support for its military overthrow in 1954. The triumph of Fidel Castro's revolution in Cuba in 1959 posed particular problems. As Castro aligned Cuba with the Soviet bloc and proclaimed himself a Marxist-Leninist, the U.S. moved to mobilize the hemisphere against Castro. The Mexican government was initially enthusiastic about Castro's revolution. After Castro embraced communism, the Mexican government restrained its enthusiasm for the Cuban revolution but still defended the right of Cuba to national self-determination and freedom from outside intervention. President Adolfo López Mateos in 1962 criticized Castro for letting the Soviets introduce nuclear missiles into Cuba but opposed any military action by the United States. When the Organization of American States (OAS) recommended in 1964 that all member nations break relations with Cuba, Mexico refused to go along.

President Luis Echeverría (1970–1976) set Mexico on a more assertive approach in foreign policy as well as a more leftward swing in domestic politics. Echeverría wanted Mexico to assume a leadership role among the developing nations. In pursuit of this goal, he visited 36 countries, initiated relations with 67 additional nations, and signed 160 international pacts and agreements. He also pursued greater trade relations with the European Economic Community, Japan, and the Soviet bloc. Echeverría was one of the leading forces behind the establishment of the Latin American Economic System (SELA) aimed at promoting and protecting Latin regional economic interests. The United States was excluded from the grouping. In a similar vein, Echeverría championed the "Charter of the Economic Rights and Duties of States" aimed at protecting the economic rights of underdeveloped countries. Although the United Nations General Assembly overwhelmingly approved the Charter, it was a nonbinding resolution which lacked the support of the advanced western industrial nations. Mexico also played a leading role in softening the stance of the OAS on Cuba; in 1975 the OAS voted to let each member determine what level of relations it wanted with the Castro regime. Echeverría even injected himself into the Arab-Israeli conflict, offering to mediate and supporting a controversial U.N. resolution equating "Zionism with Racism." He also deviated from the "Estrada Doctrine" by refusing to recognize the military government of Chile, which had overthrown the marxist Salvador Allende in 1973. Echeverría hoped to become the next secretary general of the United Nations and perhaps even receive a Nobel Peace Prize. His hopes went unfulfilled as his administration ended in the midst of a major financial crisis in 1976.

Echeverría's successor, José López Portillo (1976–1982), continued an activist international approach, aided by a substantial increase in Mexico's oil wealth. New oil policy limited the amount of oil Mexico would export as well as the amount that would be sold to any one country (that is, the United States). Mexico also declined to join the Organization of Petroleum Exporting Countries (OPEC), preferring an independent position in international oil politics. López Portillo was particularly interested in Central America, which was becoming increasingly unstable. Mexico broke relations with the dictatorial government of Anastasio Somoza in Nicaragua in May 1979. When the Sandinista rebels overthrew Somoza in July 1979, Mexico became one of the most visible supporters of the new marxist-leaning government. López Portillo also injected himself into the civil war in El Salvador where the right-wing government was confronting marxist guerrillas. He caused considerable controversy by recognizing the rebels as a "representative political force." This led nine Latin American governments to criticize Mexico for interfering in the internal affairs of El Salvador. López Portillo's actions were in keeping with the long-standing policy of supporting Central American factions friendly to Mexico while simultaneously trying to reduce U.S. influence in the region. Mexico had to scale back its involvement in the face of declining oil revenues and growing evidence that the United States was willing to use military force to influence events in the region.

Mexico's accumulating financial and economic problems largely shaped the environment in which Mexico's foreign policy unfolded in the 1980s and 1990s. The heady days when Echeverría pitched Mexico as a leader of the third world and López Portillo made Mexico a regional power quickly receded into the background. Mexico's chronic economic and financial problems dictated a closer relationship with the United

States and reaching agreements with the International Monetary Fund and the international banking community. President Miguel de la Madrid (1982–1988) had to cut back, then cut out, economic aid to the Sandinista government of Nicaragua. Mexico retained a modest role in Central American affairs by joining the Contadora group (Panama, Colombia, and Venezuela) in an effort to promote a comprehensive regional peace. The hope was that peace in Central America would reduce the flow of refugees that was provoking problems with Guatemala on Mexico's southern boundary.

Madrid and his successor Carlos Salinas (1988–1994) set in motion economic reforms that broke down Mexico's tariff barriers and provided a greater opening to foreign investment. Instead of seeking counterbalances to North American influences, Salinas effectively tied Mexico's economic future to the United States and Canada in the North American Free Trade Agreement (NAFTA), which went into effect in 1994. More traditional principles of Mexican foreign policy made sporadic appearances. Searching for some counterbalance to growing U.S. economic influence, Mexico signed a free trade agreement with Chile in 1991 and also pursued free trade with Central America. Mexico was critical of the U.S. military intervention in Panama in 1989 and unenthusiastic about U.S. intervention in Haiti in 1994. Mexico continued to separate itself from the United States on Cuban policy; Salinas criticized Castro for human rights abuses but—upholding the traditional principle of nonintervention—refused to pressure Castro to democratize. President Ernesto Zedillo (1994–2000) entered office amid yet another financial crisis, leaving him little choice but to pursue ever-closer relations with the United States. While most of Mexico's traditional principles of foreign policy remained intact, they clearly had to be subordinated to the new development approach of the 1980s and 1990s.

—DMC

See also: Debt, Mexico's Foreign; Economy; Korean War; North American Free Trade Agreement (NAFTA); Revolution of 1910; World War II.

References:

Ojeda, Mario. *Alcances y límites de la política exterior de México*. México: El Colegio de México: 1976.

Roett, Riordan, ed. *Mexico's External Relations in the 1990s*. Boulder, CO: Lynne Rienner Publishers, 1991.

Schuler, Friedrich E. *Mexico between Hitler and Roosevelt: Mexican Foreign Relations in the Age of Lázaro Cárdenas*. Albuquerque: University of New Mexico Press, 1998.

Fox, Vicente (1942–)

Elected president for the 2000–2006 period, Vicente Fox Quesada was born in Mexico City but grew up in the state of Guanajuato, where his family had been involved in ranching activities since 1913. Fox's ancestral roots were in Ireland and Spain, and his grandfather grew up in Ohio. Unlike many of his predecessors in the presidency who attended the National Preparatory School and the National Autonomous University of Mexico (UNAM), Fox was educated in local schools and graduated from the Jesuit-affiliated Iberoamerican University in Mexico City, where he studied business administration. In 1964 he joined Coca-Cola de México as a route supervisor and worked his way up the corporate ladder to president of Coca-Cola's Latin American operations. Fox left Coca-Cola to pursue his own business and political interests. He directed Grupo Fox, a group of companies involved in agribusiness and the manufacture of footwear and cowboy boots. Grupo Fox was interested in the export market, and Fox himself served as a board member for the United States–Mexico Chamber of Commerce. Fox did not become actively involved in politics until the 1980s, when he joined the long-standing opposition party in the Mexican political system, the Partido Acción Nacional (the National Action Party, or PAN).

The PAN was making the transition from nominal opposition to legitimate competitor for power with the official party, the Partido Revolucionario Institucional (the Institutional Revolutionary Party, or PRI). In 1988 Fox was elected to the lower house of the Mexican Congress from Guanajuato. In 1991 he lost a controversial election for governor of Guanajuato. In 1995 Fox ran again for the governorship, winning handily. Fox was one of the few non-PRI state governors in Mexico; this fact—along with the controversy leading up to his election—made Fox a national figure and a leading candidate for the PAN nomination for the presidency in 2000.

Fox won the PAN nomination for the presidency in 2000 with very little opposition within his own party. There was brief talk of Fox joining in a coalition with the other leading opposition party candidate, Cuauhtémoc Cárdenas, the nominee for the Partido de la Revolución Democrática (the Party of the Democratic Revolution, or PRD). Uniting the two leading opposition parties behind one candidate offered the best opportunity to defeat the PRI nominee, Francisco Labastida Ochoa. This alliance fell through when it became clear that it would have to be Cárdenas who dropped out, a concession he refused to make. PAN did enter into a coalition with Mexico's small "green" party, the Partido Verde Ecologista de México (the Ecologist Green Party of Mexico, or PVEM). This coalition of the PAN and the PVEM—with the PAN the clearly dominant partner—was known as the Alianza por Cambio, the Alliance for Change. During the campaign, Fox emphasized the themes of economic development, educational change, security and justice, and good government. In the elections held in July 2000, Fox won the presidency with 42 percent of the vote to 36 percent for Labastida, and approximately 17 percent for Cárdenas. There was no requirement that the victor receive a majority of the votes, and the popular vote determined the winner.

The Fox victory was a landmark in Mexican political history. For the first time since the establishment of the official party in 1929, an opposition candidate had won the presidency. The Fox victory was tempered by the results of the congressional elections held at the same time. The PAN made impressive gains in the lower house of Congress, the Chamber of Deputies, but was unable to gain a majority; the PAN-PVEM coalition controlled 223 of the 500 seats in the Chamber. The former official party, the PRI, held 210 and the PRD 67. The remaining seats were divided among a series of smaller parties. In the upper house of the Congress—the Senate with 128 seats—the PAN-PVEM coalition held 51 seats, but the PRI was still the largest party with 60. This congressional lineup meant that it would be difficult for Fox to get many of his reform measures passed by the Congress. Congressional opposition to presidential wishes was not something about which most presidents in the twentieth century needed to worry. The largest party in the Congress—the PRI—was badly disunited after its unprecedented defeat, and there was a great deal of uncertainty about what "lessons" the PRI should learn from the 2000 elections and how they should be applied. Certainly the PRI was poorly prepared to assume the role of "loyal opposition."

Fox's relations with the PRI members of Congress ran into problems almost immediately. PRI members challenged the legality of Fox's taking of the oath as president on the grounds that he had deviated from the wording specifically set down in the Constitution. Fox added a reference about protecting the interests of "the poor and the marginalized of the country." Fox ignored the complaints and pressed on with his legislative program. It was not, however, an encouraging start for a president who needed to win over significant opposition support for his program.

With a cabinet composed primarily of business people and numerous political outsiders, Fox set out on his reform program. One of the first important indicators as to how Fox might fare with Congress was his proposed tax reform. Fox had called for a balanced budget by 2003, and the government needed additional revenue to shore up its credit rating in international financial markets. Fox's proposed reforms included a reduction in the maximum personal income tax rate from 40 percent to 32 percent. The corporate tax rate would rise slightly from 30 percent to 32 percent, but the 10 percent tax on dividend income would also be abolished. The most controversial aspect of the reform was the call for an end to the exemption from the 15 percent value-added tax for items such as food and medicine. To counter charges that this last change would hurt the poorest of Mexico's population, Fox offered increased subsidies for Mexico's poorest 25 million people and also provided for a personal income tax exemption on the first $5,250 of income. Fox said that these changes would stimulate the economy and improve tax collection. In an effort to win PRI support, he also indicated that about one-third of the new revenues would go to state governments, most of which were still under PRI control. One high-ranking PRI member of Congress denounced the plan as "fiscal terrorism," a preview of the rough road ahead for fiscal reform. Congress did provide additional funding for antipoverty programs, but the tax reform package itself became stalled in the Congress, primarily because of opposition to the extension of the 15 percent value-added tax to items that were previously exempt.

Fox enjoyed one advantage no Mexican president had experienced since 1970; he took office without the accompanying financial and economic crises that had overtaken presidential transitions beginning in 1976. Fox, however, encountered mixed results in achieving other financial and economic goals. To a great extent, Fox was restricted during his first year in office by budget decisions made before he assumed the presidency. On 1 January 2001 new minimum wages, which varied depending on the region of the country involved, went into effect. Fox—with labor support—called for a single, national minimum wage. The growth in the Mexican economy was already slowing before Fox took office, although the growth for the year 2000 as a whole was an impressive 7 percent, which exceeded the government's target rate of 4.5 percent. By early 2001 oil prices were in decline, threatening major budgetary problems since oil revenues accounted for almost one-third of all government revenues. There were also worries about export sales to Mexico's best foreign customer, the United States, as the economy declined there as well. While the inflation rate for 2000 was almost 9 percent, the Fox administration set a target inflation rate for 2001 of 6.5 percent; by late 2001, it appeared that the rate might be less than 6 percent. Unlike the peso crisis that marked the transition of his predecessor, Ernesto Zedillo, the peso was strong throughout Fox's first year in office; it was one of the few currencies in the world to gain against the dollar in 2001. A strong currency had advantages and disadvantages. It helped attract foreign investment for the Mexican economy, but it also made it more difficult for Mexico to export.

Fox the international businessman sometimes found himself in conflict with Fox the domestic politician. While supporting continued privatization, he made it clear that there would be no effort made to privatize PEMEX, electricity, or water. In an effort to stimulate the economy by providing cheaper energy, Fox implemented through PEMEX a "Mexican price" for natural gas sold domestically, which was less than half the market price. The special price would be in effect for a three-year period beginning 1 January 2001. At the same time, Fox vetoed a rural development law because it called for a greater government role in agriculture. The veto was particularly noteworthy because Mexican presidents have rarely had to resort to the veto and because members of Fox's own party in the Chamber of Deputies had earlier voted unanimously for the measure.

Closely connected to the poor conditions in rural areas was the issue of indigenous rights, especially the ongoing (since 1 January 1994) Zapatista "rebellion" in the southern state of Chiapas. Fox assigned a high priority to dealing with the Zapatista uprising and indicated that he supported the San Andrés accords, an agreement between the Zapatistas and the previous administration of PRI President Ernesto Zedillo signed in 1996. Although Zedillo agreed to the accords, which recognized most of the indigenous demands, he never got Congress to pass the legislation necessary to put them into effect. Fox said that he would submit the necessary legislation to Congress, including needed revisions in the Constitution. Fox also created the Office for the Development of Indigenous Peoples to deal more effectively with problems of the indigenous population. Fox closed the last of the military bases set up to deal with the Zapatista rebellion, converting some of them into rural development communities. He also freed a number of political prisoners who had been jailed in the wake of the uprising. Even more controversial was Fox's support for a "march" by Zapatistas from Chiapas to Mexico City to present their demands in person to Congress. Fox publicly urged Congress to give the Zapatistas a hearing, a move opposed by many members of Congress, including a number from the PAN. Congressional leaders agreed to let the Zapatistas address a gathering of three joint congressional committees but not a formal session of both houses of Congress. The Zapatista leaders made their presentation in late March 2001. Fox offered to meet with Zapatista leaders while they were in Mexico City, but the Zapatistas rejected the offer.

Although Fox urged Congress to pass legislation to implement Zapatista demands, there were legitimate concerns about the effect of such an action on Mexico's national unity. These demands included government recognition of indigenous "autonomy" and "free determination" of their political, cultural, and economic activities. Critics of the plan said that it would lead to the creation of "states within the state" and the "Balkanization" of Mexico. Congress later passed legislation aimed at improving indigenous rights;

this new legislation, however, did not meet the demands made by the Zapatistas who rejected the congressional offering. The most famous of the Zapatista leaders, Subcomandante Marcos, said that a renewal of the armed struggle would be a failure but that the Zapatistas were not prepared to accept peace as matters stood. Fox had rashly predicted during the presidential campaign that he could solve the Chiapas conflict in "15 minutes." Although he was unable to do that, his political position was not damaged since he could demonstrate that he had done all he could do as president and that he had urged the Congress to meet the demands of the indigenous population.

During the campaign Fox emphasized the need to deal with the issues of corruption and human rights. Anticorruption campaigns were nothing new; Mexican presidents early in their administrations often talked of reducing corruption. Fox was in a somewhat different position; since he was not connected with the PRI, he could attack corruption without attacking his own party. The downside of his position was that he needed PRI support to pass new legislation dealing with corruption. Fox made public his own finances and assets, which included a Dodge pickup truck and a Honda motorcycle. One of the key government agencies in the fight against corruption was the Secretaría de la Contraloría y Desarrollo Administrativo (the Ministry of the Controller General and Administrative Development, or SECODAM). SECODAM asked the different government agencies to provide a list of areas under their jurisdiction with the greatest incidence of corruption; many unit heads initially refused to comply. With the anticorruption campaign under way, several high-ranking members of government agencies resigned, including SECODAM's own chief auditor. The controller general, Francisco Barrio, indicated that it was difficult to tie corruption directly to top-level administrators because these administrators typically let lower-level officials sign off on government contracts

Mexican president Vicente Fox meets with indigenous people. Fox came to present Indian women with microcredits for their businesses. He wears a smock presented by Mayan Indians from Zinacantan. San Cristobal de las Casas, Chiapas, Mexico, January 2001. (Keith Dannemiller / Corbis)

and orders for use of official resources. Fox did remove all of the directors of Mexico's 47 regional customs offices, many of which were notorious for corruption and abuse of the public. The president admitted that it would take years to root out the corruption that has plagued Mexico for generations. In the area of human rights, Fox announced that he would open government archives on the "Tlatelolco Massacre" of 1968 and the "dirty war" of the 1970s and 1980s waged by the government against political dissidents. During the campaign Fox called for the establishment of a "truth commission" to investigate and punish human rights violations. He had also indicated, however, that in other Latin American countries such truth commissions often caused more problems than they have solved. Fox still has not established a truth commission, but he has appointed a special prosecutor to investigate the "disappearances" of government oppo-

nents going all the way back to the 1960s and promised to establish a five-member independent citizens' panel to keep an eye on the special prosecutor.

Fox placed a premium on developing good relations with the United States. The new president of the United States, George W. Bush, was a former governor of Texas who was interested in giving a higher priority to relations with Mexico. In February 2001 Fox and Bush held a "summit" at Fox's ranch, where they discussed such controversial issues as drug trafficking, immigration, and energy policy. Although no major agreements came out of the meeting, it was clear that Fox and Bush got along well personally and would work closely together in the future. In April 2001, the U.S. Senate Foreign Relations Committee came to Mexico City to meet with their Mexican Senate counterparts on issues between the United States and Mexico. The meeting was unusual by any measure, but particularly so since the head of the Foreign Relations Committee was Senator Jesse Helms, one of the most vocal critics of Mexico in Washington. Helms was well known for his annual efforts to block "certification" by the U.S. government that Mexico was cooperating in the war on drugs. Helms was generous in his praise for the new administration of President Fox and indicated that he believed the annual certification process should be modified to put less pressure on Mexico.

Two of the most difficult issues in U.S.–Mexican relations were immigration and drug trafficking. Fox's home state of Guanajuato was a major source of immigrants to the United States, and the new president made highly publicized Christmas visits to the border in December 2000 and December 2001 to show his support for improved treatment of Mexican citizens working in the United States who were returning to Mexico for the holidays. Fox was pushing for a completely open border between the United States and Mexico within twenty years and for a new amnesty program for Mexicans illegally in the United States similar to the one implemented in 1986. There was little support for either idea on the U.S. side, but there was agreement on the possibility of a new guest worker program. The events of 11 September 2001 also cast the issue of border control in a different light. The emphasis on the U.S. side shifted more toward monitoring and controlling the flow of people across the border rather than making it easier. The drug trade along the U.S.–Mexican border continued to flourish, bringing with it violence and corruption. Fox called for a "National Campaign against Drug Trafficking and Organized Crime" while he also lobbied to get the United States to end its practice of annual certification of Mexico's cooperation in the war on drugs. In his efforts to improve law enforcement along the border, Fox ousted some 80 federal agents in the key northern state of Chihuahua in February 2001. The difficulty of controlling the border

became evident when Mexican officials announced that a 3-ton elephant named Benny had been successfully smuggled from Texas into Mexico.

Fox also proposed a national debate on drafting a new constitution for Mexico. Fox believed that Mexico needed to address the problem of trying to evolve toward a democratic society while following a constitution that provided for many authoritarian institutions. From a more practical standpoint, there had been almost 400 changes in the Constitution, approximately half of which had been introduced in the 1980s and 1990s. Given the divided nature of Mexican politics, President Fox faced a difficult struggle in getting a national consensus on a new constitution or for major renovation of the Constitution of 1917.

After three years in office, Fox has been able to implement few of the numerous reforms he called for in the presidential campaign and in his early days in office. The excitement generated by the defeat of the long-ruling PRI in the 2000 presidential elections resulted in unrealistic expectations about and by Fox. Fox's energy, charisma, and frenetic pace could not make up for a lack of congressional support for his proposed reforms. Fox was doing a good job of selling Mexico domestically and internationally as an emerging democracy. Fox took office just as the Mexican economy was slowing after five years of growth. He delivered on his promise of a freer media, only to have much of the media use this new-found freedom to criticize his activities. Fox has still not pushed through Congress his fiscal-reform plan, which he considered central to his other reform efforts. Economic recovery did not live up to Fox's promises or the public's expectations. On the plus side for Fox, he still enjoyed an approval rating of more than 60 percent. The initial optimism surrounding the ouster of the PRI from the presidency has given way to a more sober and realistic view that it will take years to implement fundamental reforms in Mexican society and that it may take many additional years for those reforms to produce noticeable effects. The midterm congressional elections of 2003 made Fox's political position even more difficult. The elections slightly strengthened the position of the PRI—the largest party—in the Chamber of Deputies while Fox's PAN suffered a major decline. No party could command a majority in the Chamber, and the parties were already maneuvering for the 2006 presidential elections. A badly divided Congress made it unlikely that Fox would be able to gain approval for major reforms. No matter how long—or short—the final list of Fox's accomplishments, he will always hold a special place in Mexico's political history as the man who beat the PRI.

—DMC

> **See also:** Cárdenas, Cuauhtémoc; Constitution of 1917; Corruption; Democratization Process; Drug Trafficking; Immigration/Emigration; Partido de Acción Nacional (PAN); Partido Revolucionario Institucional (PRI); Petróleos Mexicanos (PEMEX); Tlatelolco Massacre; Zapatista National Liberation Army (EZLN).
> **References:**
> Instituciones Mexicanas/Mexican Institutions web site: http://www.un.int/mexico/INSTIT.HTM.
> Internet System of the Mexican presidency: http://www.presidencia.gob.mx/.
> *Reforma* newspaper: http://www.reforma.com/.

Fuentes, Carlos (1928–)

Many twentieth-century Mexican intellectuals have written about the tension between national and international concerns, between provincial and cosmopolitan identities. But none have explored those tensions as forthrightly as Carlos Fuentes. In numerous novels, short stories, dramas, essays, and public lectures, the prolific Fuentes has pondered questions of Mexican identity with great tenacity and virtuosity. At the same time, his preoccupation with universal concerns such as the nature of historical time and the intersection of history and myth has attracted a huge international audience that includes some of the century's most important writers: Milan Kundera, Gabriel García Márquez, Norman Mailer, and Salman Rushdie. More than that, he has made frequent appearances on American (North and South) and European television as an expert on everything from the North American Free Trade Agreement and the Chiapas uprising to the Balkan crisis and Latin American democracy, all of which has made him something of an international celebrity.

The explanation for this astonishing versatility comes in large part from Fuentes's formative years. The son of a prominent Mexican diplomat, he was born in Panama City on 11 November 1928 and raised in a series of foreign capitals: Washington, D.C., Santiago (Chile), Buenos Aires (Argentina), Rio de Janeiro (Brazil), Montevideo (Uruguay), Quito (Ecuador). By the time he returned to Mexico City at age sixteen, he had attended some of the best preparatory schools in the Americas, achieved equal fluency in English and Spanish, and taken the first steps toward a literary career. By 1950, still in his early twenties, Fuentes had graduated with a law degree from the National Autonomous University and entered postgraduate studies in international law in Geneva, Switzerland. Later in life, he would serve in Mexico's diplomatic corps—as United Nations press secretary, head of cultural relations for the Secretariat of Foreign Affairs, ambassador to France (1974–1977)—and as visiting professor of literature at some of the world's most prestigious universities, including Harvard, Princeton, and Cambridge. Certainly, his resume would be impressive enough without the literary achievements.

Those literary achievements, however, are astonishing in their own right. At last count, his fiction works alone included fifteen novels, six short story collections, five plays, and a book of poetry. Nonfiction works, mostly collections of his many essays, number over twenty. Three of his novels—*La region más transparente del aire* (Where the Air Is Clear), *La muerte de Artemio Cruz* (The Death of Artemio Cruz), *Terra Nostra* (Our Land)—

Carlos Fuentes at his home in the San Geronimo neighborhood of Mexico City, 10 April 2003 (Reuters/Corbis)

would have a place in any short list of important twentieth-century world fiction. Here too, early life experience played a key role in a seemingly charmed life. Gregarious, generous, and talented, the young Fuentes moved in Mexico City's highest intellectual circles: his mentors included the great poet-essayists Alfonso Reyes and Octavio Paz, and he counted among his immediate peers soon-to-be literary and political stars such as writer Elena Poniatowska and future president Miguel de la Madrid. His university group felt confident enough to found their own journal for law students, *Medio Siglo* (Mid-Century), in which they published essays on literature, culture, and politics—subjects Fuentes has continued to write about throughout his career—and insisted that Mexican writers could address universal themes without the loss of their national identities. In 1954, Fuentes helped bring these ideas to an international audience with a new journal, the *Revista Mexicana de Liter-*

atura (Journal of Mexican Literature), which quickly became one of Latin America's most important literary magazines. Reflecting back on these years, Fuentes credited Octavio Paz with teaching him "that there were no privileged centers of culture, race, or politics; that nothing should be left out of literature, because our time is a time of deadly reduction" (quoted in Williams, *The Writings of Carlos Fuentes,* p. 20).

Fuentes's fascination with the creative tension produced by Mexicanizing universal concerns (or universalizing Mexican concerns) was evident from the beginning. One of his earliest stories, "Chac Mool," explores the hazy boundaries between reality, history, and myth through the person of a clerk in a government office who buys a statue of the Mayan rain god, Chac Mool, that gradually takes over his life. On one level, Chac Mool's takeover represents the return of a repressed Indian culture and its victory over the conqueror (in the guise of a minor bureaucrat), but, in an ironic twist, the god adapts a middle-class lifestyle (and a fondness for cheap cologne) that robs him of the awesome dignity of his indigenous past. As with much of Fuentes's later fiction, the subject matter in this story is emphatically Mexican while the themes speak to universal (or at least Western) concerns about the psychology of repression and mythical intrusions into everyday life, concerns derived from the work of psychoanalysts Sigmund Freud and Carl Jung.

Fuentes considerably expanded the scope of his investigations with his first novel, *La region más transparente del aire* (1958). The novel is set in mid–twentieth-century Mexico City during the heyday of the "Mexican Miracle" when optimistic government officials were trumpeting the inevitability of economic modernization. Although a great lover of the capital's vibrant night life—from chic restaurants to night clubs to El Buen Tono (The Good Taste) whorehouse—Fuentes harbored no illusions about economic progress. In *La region más transparente,* ex-revolutionaries lose their youthful idealism, becoming corrupt politicians, scheming bankers, and crooked labor lawyers whose self-centered lives reflect their moral and spiritual bankruptcy. Even the heroes, the moralistic poet-journalist Zamacona and the cruel Indian executioner Ixca Cienfuegos, are tainted by arrogance and self-righteousness. According to Fuentes himself, the novel "reflected . . . the excessive, and somewhat mythical preoccupation over nationality, ancestry, and patrimony rampant at the time in Mexico" (quoted in Harss and Dohmann, *Into the Mainstream,* p. 292). Indeed, in the spirit of Octavio Paz's influential essays on national identity in *Laberinto de la soledad* (Labyrinth of Solitude, 1950), *La region más transparente* implied that progress was little more than a mask that covered the deep social rifts produced by the primordial act of violence—the Spanish Conquest—that had produced the Mexican nation.

His next two major novels, *Aura* (1962) and *La muerte de Artemio Cruz* (The Death of Artemio Cruz, 1962), further developed the themes of moral degeneration and history as myth. *Aura* is a short gothic novel about a young historian who takes a room in an old house in Mexico City, falls in love with a young woman who may or may not be a projection of his elderly landlady (probably a witch), and gradually takes on the persona of the landlady's dead husband, one of the emperor Maximilian's generals during the French occupation of Mexico. In this novel, Mexico's turbulent history controls the historian (rather than vice versa) and thus defeats any attempt to make sense of the past in order to progress beyond it. In *La muerte de Artemio Cruz,* on the other hand, Fuentes deals not with the mythical power of history over individuals but with its tangible effects on individuals, in this case the once idealistic revolutionary, now cynical powerbroker Artemio Cruz. Probably the best known of his books, the novel's bitter critique of the Mexican Revolution's failure to live up to its promises of social justice attracted immediate attention in Mexico. But *La muerte de Artemio Cruz* is more than just a political critique. Fuentes uses a broad range of novelistic techniques—flashbacks, interior monologues, shifting tenses, and even a personified "conscience"—to give Cruz an emotional depth and self-awareness that transcend his obvious corruption and cynicism. This combination of political engagement, psychological subtlety, and innovative narrative style secured Fuentes's reputation as a star of the international "boom" in Latin American literature, a position he shared with Cuba's Alejo Carpentier, Colombia's Gabriel García Márquez, Peru's Mario Vargas Llosa, and Argentina's Julio Cortázar.

The 1967 publication of *Cambio de piel* (Change of Skin) and *Zona sagrada* (Sacred Zone) signaled a more experimental turn in Fuentes's literary style. This turn would produce another masterwork, *Terra nostra* (Our Land, 1975), a thriller, *La cabeza de la hidra* (The Hydra's Head, 1978), a romance, *El gringo viejo* (The Old Gringo, 1985), and end fittingly enough with a new Columbus, *Cristóbal nonato* (Christopher Unborn, 1987). Central to most of these works is a disjointed, self-referential narrative style that keeps the reader off balance by refusing to reconcile the ambiguities—of perspective, of morality, of truth—that Fuentes sees as fundamental to the human condition. Appalled by the ravages of global capitalism and inspired by the 1959 Cuban revolution, Fuentes declared (somewhat prematurely) that "the end of the cycle of bourgeois fiction coincides with the death throes of the bourgeoisie itself." Drawing on modernist writers like James Joyce, John Dos Passos, and William Faulker, the earlier novels had played with form but without challenging the conventional boundary that separates external reality and literary text. By 1967, however, Fuentes aspired to a new "language of alarm, renovation, disorder and humor. The language, in sum, of ambiguity: the plurality of signifieds: of the constellation of allusions: of openness." In *Cambio de piel,* for example, violence is transformed into spectacle—exploited workers as singing mariachis—and horrendous historical events become sources of perverse humor—a black man who defends the Nazis as liberators from "centuries of Judeo-Christian barbarism that has mutilated mankind" (quoted in Van Delden, *Carlos Fuentes, Mexico, and Modernity*, pp. 77, 83, 107). *Zona sagrada,* uses a twisted mix of Greek mythology and Freudian psychology to explain a fictionalized relationship between a Mexican movie diva, María Felix, and her son. *La cabeza de la hidra* plays with the spy thriller genre in a tale about Mexican oil, Arabs, and Israelis that undermines the simplistic dichotomies that characterize most analyses of Middle Eastern politics. *El gringo viejo*—later made into a Hollywood film— toys with conventional stereotypes of uptight gringos and macho Mexicans as it explores the erotics of cultural difference. In *Cristóbal nonato,* the narrator, an unborn fetus (scheduled to be born on the Columbus quincentenary in 1992 and win a contest to become Mexico's president on his twenty-second birthday), mercilessly exposes the environmental and economic devastation that threatens to undermine Mexico's cultural and political sovereignty.

The major work of this period is the ambitious, sprawling *Terra nostra.* The central themes that hold the novel together are power—symbolized by the Spanish monarchy, especially Philip II (1556–1598) and his palace, El Escorial—and violence—symbolized by the Spanish Conquest of the Americas. For Fuentes, the conquistadors were "heroes only because they would not disdain their own passions but rather, would follow them through to their disastrous conclusion, master of the entire realm of passion but mutilated by the cruelty and the narrowness of the religious and political reasoning that turned their marvelous madness, their total excess, into a crime: their pride, their love, their madness, their dreams—all punishable offenses." These punishable offenses included reproducing Spain's problems in Mexico: "the same social order . . . , the same rigid, vertical hierarchies, the same sort of government: for the powerful every right and no duty; for the weak, no right and every duty" (Fuentes, *Terra nostra,* pp. 10–11). Thus, in *Terra nostra,* the violent imposition of Spanish power is the primordial sin that pollutes time and space as it cycles madly through Latin American history. The result is a fragmented society, permeated with inequalities—an effect mirrored in the novel's loose, enigmatic structure with its shifting narrators and countless references to the classics of Spain's sixteenth-century Golden Age (Miguel de Cervantes and Diego Velázquez are favorites). Fuentes is characteristically unapologetic: "Every storyteller reserves the right not to clear up mysteries," one of his character asserts, "in order that they may remain mysteries; and anyone whom this displeases may ask for his money back" (Fuentes, *Terra nostra,* p. 24).

In his most recent works, Fuentes has adopted a more conventional style and a more overtly political agenda. His historical novel, *La campaña* (The Campaign, 1990), historical essays, *The Buried Mirror: Reflections on Spain and the New World* (1992), political essays, *Nuevo tiempo Mexicano* (A New Time for Mexico, 1994), and ruminations on the U.S.–Mexico border, *La frontera de cristal: Una novela en nueve cuentos* (The Crystal Frontier, 1995), all reflect a straightforward commitment to the democratization of contemporary Mexican society. In the conclusion to *The Buried Mirror,* Fuentes argues for the construction of a civil society no longer dominated by the authoritarian institutions of government: "professionals, intellectuals, technocrats, students, trade unions, agricultural co-ops, business associations, women's organizations, religious groups, neighborhood communities—the whole spectrum of our society—are quickly becoming the protagonists of our history, outflanking the state, the army, the church, even the traditional political parties" (Fuentes, *The Buried Mirror,* p. 355). An essay from *Nuevo tiempo Mexicano* highlights the creative aspects of that dramatic social change: "The history of Mexico and Latin America is that of a deep cleavage between a vigorous continuous culture and a fragmented, failed, weak political and economic life. To breathe the culture's vigor into political and economic institutions would be the primary answer to our present-day dilemma" (Fuentes, *New Time for Mexico,* p. 207). His latest fiction tries to do just that. *La campaña,* the first in a proposed trilogy of historical novels about the Independence era in Latin America (1810–1821), recaptures the cultural and intellectual vitality of that turbulent period before the region's plunge back into authoritarianism. *La frontera de cristal,* proposes to do the same for the culture clash at the U.S.–Mexico border. Because of its unique position between Latin America and the United States, Fuentes argues, Mexico is the ideal site for a new "inclusive" modernity that respects cultural differences. His final words in *Nuevo tiempo Mexicano* serve as both an artistic manifesto and a prescription for a better future: "We must not tie ourselves to any dogma, any essence, any exclusive goal. We should rather embrace the emancipation of signs; the human scale of things; inclusion; the dreams of others. This, I think, is the only way to found, every day, a new Mexican time" (Fuentes, *New Time for Mexico,* p. 207). In his work as in his life, Fuentes has done his best to make this "Mexican time" a reality for Mexico and for the world.

—RMB

See also: Intellectuals; Novel of the Revolution; Novel since 1960; Paz, Octavio; Poniatowska, Elena.

References:
Brody, Robert, and Charles Rossman. *Carlos Fuentes: A Critical View.* Austin: University of Texas Press, 1982.
Harss, Luis, and Barbara Dohmann. *Into the Mainstream: Conversations with Latin American Writers.* New York: Harper and Row, 1967.
Stavans, Ilan. "Carlos Fuentes in His Labyrinth," in *The Riddle of Cantinflas: Essays on Hispanic Popular Culture.* Albuquerque: University of New Mexico Press, 1990.
Van Delden, Maarten. *Carlos Fuentes, Mexico, and Modernity.* Nashville, TN: Vanderbilt University Press, 1998.
Williams, Raymond Leslie. *The Writings of Carlos Fuentes.* Austin: University of Texas Press, 1996.

Gender and Sexuality

Mexico has an international reputation as a country of domineering men and submissive women. Indeed, the word used in many languages to describe a particularly virulent brand of aggressive masculinity, *machismo* (or *macho* behavior) comes from Mexico. Some scholars have also argued for a female counterpart, *marianismo,* named after the Virgin Mary (María in Spanish) that stresses women's passivity and suffering in the face of *macho* aggression. To suggest, as some observers do, that these gender stereotypes are somehow typical of Mexican men and women is absurd: Mexicans, like people everywhere, exhibit a broad spectrum of male and female behaviors in their daily lives. Nevertheless, these stereotypes play an undeniably important role in the way Mexicans construct their gendered identities so that even those who deliberately reject *machismo* and *marianismo* in their own lives feel compelled to address these stereotypes in some way. At the same time, the ongoing impact of social forces ranging from industrialization, urbanization, and immigration to the growth of women's and gay rights movements has begun to challenge their hold over the Mexican imagination.

As one of Mexico's most powerful myths, it is hardly surprising that *machismo* received its most compelling definition from the nation's most famous poet, Octavio Paz. According to Paz, "one word sums up the aggressiveness, insensitivity, invulnerability and other attributes of the *macho:* power. It is force without the discipline of any notion of order: arbitrary power . . . that almost always reveals itself as a capacity for wounding, humiliating, annihilating" (Paz, *Labyrinth of Solitude,* pp. 81–82). Paz traces the roots of that undisciplined power to the Spanish Conquest of Mexico and especially to the violation of Indian women (whether physical or psychic) by the victorious conquistadors. Mexico's *mestizo* (mixed race) national identity, he argues, derived from the "union" of the male Spanish aggressor symbolized by Hernán Cortés and his female Indian "victim" symbolized by La Malinche, Cortés's Indian concubine and the mother of his son, Martín, the "first Mexican *mestizo.*" Because La Malinche (or Doña Marina as the Spaniards called her) served as Cortés's interpreter and thus played an important role in the conquest, she has also become a symbol of betrayal to foreigners of her fellow Indians and, by extension, of Mexico itself. Even today, Mexicans who betray their culture by becoming too European, too Americanized, or just too modern are condemned as *malinchistas.* For Paz, La Malinche's "passivity is abject: she does not resist violence, but is an inert heap of bones, blood, and dust" (Paz, *Labyrinth of Solitude,* p. 85). Moreover, this negative image of women as passive victims, he argues, carries over into the *macho's* relationships with men, women, children, and society in general.

Not all Mexicans, however, accept Paz's definition of either *machismo* or La Malinche. Recent anthropological studies, for example, suggest that Mexican men and women hold contradictory notions of *machismo.* On one hand, they recognize the bad macho: a violent, boastful, arrogant, irresponsible, unfaithful man who fights with other men, abuses women, neglects his many children (often by different women), and breaks the law with impunity. On the other, they argue for the good macho: a brave, soft-spoken, modest, responsible, faithful man who fights only under duress, respects women, provides for his family, and conscientiously fulfills the obligations of citizenship (including resistance to the abuses of power by other men). The good macho is unquestionably a patriarchal figure but he nevertheless recognizes and even embraces the responsibilities that come with his masculine power.

In addition to a more nuanced view of *machismo,* anthropologists and historians have noted that far from being deeply rooted in the Mexican psyche, *machismo* (at least as a term) is relatively new—more a product of Mexican *charro* (singing cowboy) films from the 1940s and 1950s than a legacy of Spanish Conquest. They agree that Mexican culture has long been obsessed with manliness and that women have often paid the price of that obsession. In the colonial period, for example, a man's honor revolved around both the protection of the women in his own extended family—mothers, sisters, wives, daughters, aunts, nieces, female in-laws, etc.—and the conquest of women "belonging" to other men. Protected or conquered, women were caught in the middle of these male power struggles. It is important to note

that social class made a considerable difference: since only well-off men could afford to keep their wives at home, poorer men were often seen by elites as without honor even in legal proceedings. Gender made a difference too: women, especially from the "decent" classes, had not honor but shame or *vergüenza* to protect. Concern about male honor and female shame persisted in different guises into the national period and continues to influence attitudes today. Still, it was not until the middle of the twentieth century that the cluster of behaviors associated with manhood coalesced into a full-blown stereotype and the Mexican *macho* was born.

The image of La Malinche has been contested as well. Disgusted with Paz's decidedly male view of the Mexican national psyche, feminist scholars have sought to restore La Malinche's tarnished reputation. They point out that there was no pan-Indian identity at the time of the conquest, only rival Indian groups who regularly fought with each other, that La Malinche had no reason to be loyal to the Aztecs especially after they sold her into slavery, and that she managed to survive and even thrive at a very difficult time in Mexican history by using the only tools at her disposal: her facility with Indian languages and her sexuality. For these scholars, La Malinche was not a passive victim of Spanish aggression but a strong, intelligent woman confronted with hard choices (none of them "decent") who triumphed over adversity in the face of overwhelming odds—a role model for oppressed women rather than the passive, abject, violated mother of *mestizo* Mexico described by Paz.

To further complicate matters, some Latin Americanists have argued for a different kind of female counterpart to *machismo, marianismo,* that is based not on female betrayal like La Malinche (Mexico's version of the biblical Eve), but on female acceptance of suffering in imitation of the Virgin Mary. Although the idea is somewhat controversial because it lacks *machismo's* popular acceptance (as a term), *marianismo* works well for Mexico because the Virgin Mary's Mexican manifestation, the much revered Virgin of Guadalupe, is regarded both in popular culture and by the Roman Catholic Church as the nation's patroness and the paragon of female virtue. Guadalupe, according to Paz, "is pure receptivity, and the benefits she bestows are of the same order: she consoles, quiets, dries tears, calms passions" (Paz, *Labyrinth of Solitude,* p. 85). *Marianismo* thus stresses the spiritual virtues of patient suffering and unqualified love whether in the face of life's sorrows or at the hands of violent or unfaithful men. As might be expected, opinion is divided on this view of women. Those who see the self-sacrificing woman as a positive female image argue that the Virgin's example provides genuine consolation for real woes and empowers women by validating their spirituality and even their presumed moral superiority to men. Detractors insist that it encourages female passivity, denies female sexuality, and supports the patriarchal attitudes of both men and women. Some even argue for a patriarchal pact lasting well into the twentieth century between wealthy landowners and Roman Catholic priests that encouraged abused male workers to accept their miserable situation by allowing them to dominate women whose suffering would then be compensated (at least morally and spiritually) by comparisons to the Virgin. Patriarchal pact or not, male domination of women has indeed been the rule in Mexico and if not always openly endorsed or even accepted (as in the case of physical abuse of women, for example), it is still widely expected.

Expectations of male domination are also reflected in men's interactions with each other. Male honor and macho power are everyday practices that might require the domination of women but whose real audience is almost always other men. Thus male domination of women provides a model for male competition with and domination of each other. This is especially noticeable in male attitudes toward effeminacy and homosexuality, according to which men who appear passive or weak are linked symbolically to women and often persecuted. In everyday life this persecution runs the gamut from endless teasing among men about each other's sexual orientation to outright homophobia, sometimes accompanied by violence. In politics, it becomes a way to demean and humiliate a political opponent as in the 2000 election when Vicente Fox, the eventual winner, publicly accused his principal opponent of being a sissy and a mama's boy. In this instance, Fox's cowboy boots, massive belt buckle, and imposing stature emphasized his manliness. Nevertheless, as a middle-aged bachelor, he also felt compelled to marry during the election campaign, presumably to fend off charges of being either a playboy or a homosexual. The first charge might well have enhanced his popularity since Mexicans tend to be less puritanical than Americans about male politicians' philandering; the second would have stopped his presidential bid in its tracks.

In a society that places a high premium on the public performance of fairly rigid gender roles, it should come as no surprise that ideas about male domination would affect homosexual relations as well. During the colonial period, sex between men was identified as sodomy and condemned by the Roman Catholic Church as a sin. The focus, however, was on the sinful act and not on the sexual orientation of its perpetrators (since "sodomites" engaged in a wide range of practices including oral sex and bestiality). But, while the Church condemned both parties, society at large focused its disapproval on the passive partner in anal intercourse because that man took on a female role and thus voluntarily accepted an inferior social position. The active partner might be a sinner but his masculinity remained intact because he never relinquished his male position of power. This attitude has proven remarkably resilient and even today anthropologists report that men who routinely perform male gender roles and assume (or at least claim) the active role in sexual relations with other men usually deny being homosexuals.

By the end of the nineteenth century in Mexico, as elsewhere, sociologists and psychologists had begun to label men who behaved "like women" and women who behaved "like men" (generally of much less concern) as sexual inverts and biological deviants. As the Church's influence waned, this scientific identification helped justify the continued persecution of homosexual behaviors by linking them to a personality type, the sexual invert, whose sexual orientation defined their social identity. Despite these scientific interventions, however, in Mexico at least, homosexual acts remained legal between consenting adults as long as they did not become public and thereby offend "good customs." Historians, including well-known cultural commentator Carlos Monsiváis, argue that male homosexuality in the modern sense was "invented" in Mexico in 1901 when police raided a private ball and arrested 41 men, half of them dressed as women. The resulting scandal received massive press coverage and prompted a series of widely circulated prints by José Guadalupe Posada that depicted the dance, the public humiliation of the cross-dressers (they were forced to sweep the streets under police guard), and the exile of some of the men to work in the army barracks in Yucatán. Rumors that the president's nephew had attended the dance but was permitted to escape further added to the scandal's notoriety. Since that time, the number 41 has come to symbolize male homosexuality in Mexican popular culture, figuring frequently in jokes and in casual teasing. Because of its symbolic importance, the 41 scandal also became the foundational myth of male homosexual subculture in Mexico as gay men began to construct sexual identities around the powerful images it generated.

The birth of modern female homosexuality is much harder to locate. Latin America has a long tradition of women who dress as men and claim male privileges. The most famous is the seventeenth-century "lieutenant nun," Catalina de Erauso, whose adventures, related in her widely read memoirs, so riveted the Spanish-speaking world that he/she received papal permission to live as man after the ruse was discovered. According to some accounts, he/she ended up in Mexico as a mule-skinner on the treacherous Mexico City–Vera Cruz route. Similar instances have been recorded as late as the Mexican Revolution in which women not only supported male soldiers as *soldaderas* (camp followers) but fought and led troops into battle sometimes as men. Often, they maintained male identities throughout their lives. In none of these cases, however, is there any sense of a consciously acknowledged lesbian identity—a sexual orientation or identity available to women only in recent years—and male-identified women behaved like men in their public relationships with other women.

The impact of social changes, especially since the late nineteenth century, has finally begun to challenge gender stereotypes like *machismo* and *marianismo* and prevailing attitudes toward homosexuality. Chief among these social changes are industrialization, urbanization, and immigration. During the Porfirian era (1876–1910) and beginning again in the 1940s, Mexico's economy became increasingly industrialized. The prospect of gainful employment in industry attracted huge numbers of *campesinos* (rural workers), many of them dispossessed by land fraud and the expansion of commercial agriculture, to the nation's major cities. Included in this massive migration were growing numbers of women. Given the opportunity, they entered the workforce in greater and greater numbers. In 1940, women comprised 7.3 percent of the economically active population; by 1960 they were 17.9 percent; by 1990 they were 32 percent. Even in the more conservative rural sector, women's participation in the workforce grew from 9.2 percent in 1970 to 14.2 percent in 1990. Since 1982, repeated economic crises and declining real wages (wages adjusted for inflation) have kept women in the workforce, including the married middle-class women traditionally expected to raise children at home. Women, especially from the lower classes, had always contributed to family incomes, sometimes with factory work but most often by selling in the local market or by taking in laundry. Yet for many of these women, and especially for their middle-class counterparts, salaried work in designated workplaces was a new and sometimes liberating experience, even if liberation too often led to misery at the hands of abusive bosses, poor working conditions, and wages significantly lower than those paid to men. Regardless, these experiences have given growing numbers of women more economic and social independence than ever before.

Women's grassroots political activism—most often tied to women's issues like demanding services and education for their children, lobbying the government on public health issues, or protecting squatters' settlements—has further reinforced women's sense of independence and entitlement. Coupled with fewer children (due mostly to better and more accessible birth control) and higher literacy rates (although still lower than men's in rural areas), this growing sense of empowerment on the part of women has had a significant impact on traditional gender roles in Mexico because it directly challenges the male monopoly on power that characterizes gender stereotypes like *machismo.*

Immigration to the United States, an experience shared by millions of Mexicans, has also had a profound influence on gender relations. In the middle decades of the twentieth century when the majority of immigrants were men, the absence of the male head-of-household forced many women to manage on their own. More recently, women have immigrated in even greater numbers than men, a symbol perhaps of their growing independence at home. In addition, the American experience—reinforced by the influx of American popular culture into Mexico through movies, television, tourism, etc.—has altered male and female expectations, through exposure to more open attitudes toward pre-

marital sex (especially for women) to more open negotiation of domestic duties. This is not to say that female sexuality is less repressed in the United States than in Mexico or that American men do more housework than Mexican men—although there is some anecdotal evidence to support both claims—but that these things are more openly debated in the United States.

Another factor in changing gender relations are the women's and gay rights movements that have provided a political and ideological voice for the concerns of Mexican women and homosexuals. Although different women's groups had been active since the Porfirian era, the first big push for women's rights came in the 1930s with the United Front for Women's Rights (*Frente Único Pro Derechos de la Mujer*), a broad-based women's organization that claimed as many as 50,000 members at its height. Male politicians, such as President Lázaro Cárdenas, voiced public support but, concerned that female suffrage would increase the influence of the Roman Catholic Church, failed to follow through on their promises until 1953 when President Adolfo Ruiz Cortines finally granted women the right to vote in national elections. Although women's groups continued to agitate for women's rights, it was not until the 1970s that Mexican feminists began to attract serious attention on the national scene. As women's participation in public life has increased dramatically, feminist ideas have begun to affect the everyday lives of Mexican men and women. The gay rights movements that followed in the wake of 1970s feminism have had an effect as well. By providing alternative sexual identities that called into question not just the heterosexual imperative but also the rigid gendering that has characterized Mexican homosexuality until now, gay rights movements have challenged the validity of all gender stereotypes. Whether feminism and gay rights movements pose a serious threat to *machismo* and *marianismo,* however, remains to be seen.

—*RMB*

See also: Cinema from 1930 to 1960; Fox,
Vicente; *Mestizaje* and *Indigenismo*; Monsiváis,
Carlos; Paz, Octavio; Virgin of Guadalupe;
Women's Movement.

References:

Anzaldúa, Gloria. *Borderlands / La Frontera: The New
Mestiza.* San Francisco: Aunt Lute Press, 1987.

Carrier, Joseph M. *De los Otros: Intimacy and
Homosexuality among Mexican Men.* New York:
Columbia University Press, 1995.

Fowler-Salamani, Heather, and Mary K. Vaughan,
eds. *Women of the Mexican Countryside,
1850–1990.* Tucson: University of Arizona
Press, 1994.

Gutmann, Matthew C. *The Meanings of Macho:
Being a Man in Mexico City.* Berkeley: University
of California Press, 1996.

Irwin, Robert McKee. "The Famous 41: The
Scandalous Birth of Modern Mexican
Homosexuality," *GLQ* (Gay and Lesbian
Quarterly) 6 (2000): pp. 353–376.

Melhuus, Marit, and Kristi Anne Stølen, eds.
*Machos, Mistresses, Madonnas: Contesting the Power
of Latin American Gender Imagery.* New York:
Verso, 1996.

Mirandé, Alfredo. *Hombres y Machos: Masculinity and
Latino Culture.* Boulder, CO: Westview Press,
1997.

Paz, Octavio. *The Labyrinth of Solitude and Other
Writings.* Trans. Lysander Kemp, Yara Milos,
and Rachel Phillips Belash. New York: Grove
Press, 1985.

Prieur, Annick. *Mema's House, Mexico City: On
Transvestites, Queens, and Machos.* Chicago:
University of Chicago Press, 1998.

Tuñón Pablos, Julia. *Women in Mexico: A Past
Unveiled.* Trans. Alan Hynds. Austin: University
of Texas Press, 1999.

Government

For most of its history as an independent nation, Mexico has had, at least in theory, a political system based on federalism as in the United States; under a federalist system, powers and responsibilities are divided among local, state (or provincial), and national governments. This system was embodied in various forms in the Constitutions of 1824, 1857, and 1917. Despite this commitment to federalism, there has in fact been an almost constant effort to centralize power in the national government and, in particular, in the presidency.

This struggle between the centralists and the federalists was most obvious during the nineteenth century as part of the larger struggle between the conservatives and the liberals. The conservatives were typically associated with centralism and the liberals with federalism. The political breakdown, however, was not really that simple. The centralist-federalist conflict was also influenced by factors such as political opportunism, personalism, militarism, and regionalism. Many of those involved in politics were more concerned with promoting their own interests than in pursuing some political philosophy or program. Political loyalties were directed toward persons rather than toward political parties with their platforms and ideologies. Military involvement in politics often made the federalist-centralist struggle irrelevant. Regional concerns also influenced the centralist-federalist struggle. Identification with a particular region rather than with the nation was an important characteristic of indigenous Mexico, colonial Mexico, and modern Mexico. Despite improved transportation / communication and government efforts to promote nationalism, regionalism continues as an important political factor into the twenty-first century.

Even those with federalist sentiments often became centralists when they were actually in power. Benito Juárez was a good example of such a political figure. Although originally famous as a federalist in the 1850s, Juárez became increasingly centralist in the 1860s and 1870s. Another liberal and federalist figure of the 1860s and 1870s who turned increasingly centralist was Porfirio Díaz, president from 1877 to 1880 and from 1884 to 1911. Although Díaz came into office on a program of "no reelection," he later went on to be reelected on seven different occasions. Díaz skillfully used a blend of coercion and conciliation to promote centralization.

The careers of Juárez and Díaz illustrate another important feature of the Mexican political system: presidentialism or the concentration of political power in the presidency. Presidentialism relates to the issue of centralization as well as to the issue of separation of powers: the division of powers among the executive, legislative, and judicial branches of the national government. The roots of presidentialism can be traced back as far as the colonial period. The more recent foundations for it lie in the Constitution of 1917. Under the Constitution of 1917, the president has broad powers of appointment, ranging from cabinet ministers to high-ranking members of the armed forces. Historically, the Mexican Congress made up of a Chamber of Deputies and a Senate has done little to counterbalance presidential power. Until the 1990s, most members of Congress directly or indirectly owed their positions to the president and rarely went against his wishes. The prohibition on members of Congress being elected to consecutive terms also reduced the power of the Congress in relation to the presidency. The president also determined the party leadership in the Congress for the now-former official party, the Partido Revolucionario Institucional (the Institutional Revolutionary Party, or PRI). The legislative initiative also resided with the president; more than 90 percent of legislation originated in the executive branch. The political reforms of the 1980s and 1990s have not only given greater congressional representation in Congress to non-PRI parties; they have also strengthened the position of the Congress in relation to the presidency. The president can no longer assume that Congress will automatically approve any legislation presented to it. The judiciary also has played a limited role in restricting the power of the presidency. Judges were not appointed for life, and the concept of judges setting legal precedents is not as important in Mexico as it is in the U.S. system. A general disrespect for the law and the well-known corruption of the judicial system also limit the ability of the judiciary to restrain presidential action.

The president also exercised broad economic powers as the role of the state in the economy expanded in the late nineteenth and twentieth centuries. This expansive power was particularly evident in the growing number of state-owned businesses (*paraestatales*) from the 1940s to the 1980s; the president appointed the heads of these government agencies and also determined the policies that they followed. The most important example of this type of agency was the government-owned oil company, Petróleos Mexicanos (Mexican Petroleum, or PEMEX). The economic powers of the president were clearly demonstrated when President José López Portillo nationalized the entire banking system in 1982 by decree.

The role of the president in the political system is also affected by the fact that he cannot be reelected. The problems that arose in connection with the efforts of Alvaro Obregón (1920–1924) to serve a second term in the presidency led to an outright prohibition on presidential reelection. This ban eliminated the possibility of a president continuing in office (*continuismo*) as Porfirio Díaz did from 1884 to 1911. The ban on reelection was partially offset by the practice of the outgoing president "tapping" (selecting) his successor and then imposing his selection on the official party—the PRI—and using the resources of the government to ensure his chosen successor's election.

The dominant role played by the official party, the PRI, for most of the twentieth century has also greatly influenced the operation of the political system. The PRI evolved along corporatist lines; that is, the group to which a person belonged—peasant, labor, business, military—defined that person's relationship to the government. Specific organizations were established and incorporated into the PRI to represent these corporatist interests. For example, peasants were organized into the Confederación Nacional Campesina (the National Peasant Confederation, or CNC) while industrial workers were organized into the Confederación de Trabajadores de México (the Mexican Workers' Confederation, or CTM). Both the CNC and the CTM became part of the PRI. Independent peasant or workers' organizations were either refused support or repressed by the government. The military even briefly (1938–1940) had corporate representation through the PRI. The government encouraged the formation of progovernment business groups, although these were not officially incorporated into the PRI.

This corporatist approach to organization was connected with an active policy of co-optation, the recruiting of individuals or groups who might potentially oppose the PRI or the government. The offering of political positions or economic opportunities to potential opponents often not only blocked the rise of significant opposition but also incorporated opposition leaders into the ranks of the PRI or the government. This co-optation policy was so successful for so long that it greatly reduced the need for the outright repression of political opponents. Aspiring political leaders soon learned the value of working with the PRI and the government.

Also affecting the operation of the political system was the role played by the camarilla in Mexican politics. A camarilla is a group of individuals with common political interests who unite to promote their political careers. Each camarilla has a leader who serves as a mentor to the other members of the group; in this sense, the camarilla is a variation on the patron-client relationship that traditionally has played such an important role in Mexican political history. As the camarilla leader makes his way up the political ladder, he brings his fellow camarilla members along with him by appointing them to political positions. The most successful camarilla is the one whose leader reaches the presidency. Individuals can be members of more than one camarilla, and it is not unusual for members to leave a camarilla if the political career of the leader becomes stalled. The two most important camarillas in recent Mexican history were those fostered by two very different presidents, Lázaro Cárdenas (1934–1940) and Miguel Alemán (1946–1952). The

factors involved in the formation of camarillas have changed over the years. Military experience was an important factor in the formation of many early camarillas. Later a background in law became important; in the 1980s and 1990s the emphasis shifted to economics and finance.

A federalist system implies that significant powers and responsibilities are reserved for state and local governments. In practice it has been difficult for either state or local governments to play an important political role for most of the twentieth century. Since the formation of the official party, almost all state governors have been members of the PRI and are usually politically beholding—at least indirectly—to the president for their position. Presidents have often used local military officials to undercut the power of state governors. Under the Constitution of 1917, the president has the power to declare the "disappearance of constitutional powers" in a state, to remove the governor, and to appoint a provisional governor until new elections can be held. State governments are typically short on financing and have to depend on the central government for most of their funding. Local or municipal governments operate under many of the same constraints. Municipal officials often owe their position to the governor who in turn is dependent on the president. In some states, governors had the legal power under the state constitution to remove municipal officials. The PRI has used its dominant position at the local level to restrict action by local officials. Municipal governments are chronically short of funds and must depend on the state and especially the central governments for much of their financing.

The Mexican political system is currently undergoing a major transition with an uncertain conclusion that may fundamentally alter the way Mexico is governed. The democratization process, especially the PRI loss of the presidency in 2000 to Vicente Fox, has produced a situation where there is no longer an official party. One party controls the presidency, the Partido de Acción Nacional (the National Action Party, or PAN); the PRI is still the dominant party in the Congress, although it does not have a majority. Both the PRI and the principal leftist party, the Partido de la Revolución Democrática (the Party of the Democratic Revolution, or PRD), are suffering major internal problems of leadership and direction. The role of Congress in the political equation is also changing. Democratization broke the PRI stranglehold on the presidency, but it also created a Congress that will not automatically follow the lead of the president. Even the judiciary is beginning to show greater signs of independence. As a former governor, Fox has stressed the need to revitalize federalism, especially relations between the president and the state governors. There is still, however, no comprehensive plan for this decentralization process, especially one that could bring the powers of taxation into line with the responsibilities for spending. Fox has called for a major restructuring of the political system, citing the contradiction in trying to establish a "democratic society with authoritarian institutions." Ironically, an increasingly independent Congress has largely ignored his calls for fundamental constitutional reforms. The role of the PRI in the political system has been permanently altered by the political developments of the last two decades. How Mexico will be governed in the future and by whom are two issues still very much in doubt.

—DMC

See also: Alemán, Miguel; Banking and Finance; Confederación de Trabajadores de México (CTM); Confederación Nacional Campesina (CNC); Constitution of 1917; Democratization Process; Díaz, Porfirio; Fox, Vicente; Juárez, Benito; López Portillo, José; Militarism; Obregón, Alvaro.

References:

Aguilar Camín, Hector, and Lorenzo Meyer. *In the Shadow of the Mexican Revolution: Contemporary Mexican History, 1910–1989.* Austin: University of Texas Press, 1993.

Camp, Roderic Ai. *Politics in Mexico.* 2d ed. New York: Oxford University Press, 1996.

Giugale, Marcelo M., Olivier Lafourcade, and Vinh H. Nguyen, eds. *Mexico: A Comprehensive Development Agenda for the New Era.* Washington, DC: The World Bank, 2001.

Guanajuato (State)

Located in central Mexico, Guanajuato is part of Mexico's fertile Bajío region. In addition to Guanajuato City, the capital, principal cities include León, Irapuato, Celaya, and Salamanca. The state also contains Dolores Hidalgo, a town whose name commemorates the rebellion of Father Miguel Hidalgo, which began on 16 September 1810. This is officially acknowledged as the beginning of Mexico's movement for independence. Because of its location and proximity to Mexico City, Guanajuato has played a central role in Mexico's political struggles. During the latter part of the twentieth century, the state distinguished itself as an area of active opposition to the PRI, the official party that emerged from the Mexican Revolution and that dominated the country's political scene for over 70 years.

Tarascan Indians, as well as various groups of nomadic and seminomadic Chichimec peoples inhabited the Guanajuato region on the eve of Spanish contact. Many of these natives were killed in the early military campaigns of the Spaniards. The sixteenth century was one of consistent conflict between Europeans and natives, particularly because of the growth of mining. Guanajuato lay along the path from Mexico City to the rich mining region of Zacatecas, and Guanajuato itself was home to lucrative silver mines. Spaniards used a variety of tactics to subdue the local Indian population, including war and enslavement, the establishment of military outposts or presidios, and attempts to buy off native groups with land and other gifts. Franciscan, Augustinian, and Jesuit missionaries also played a role in pacifying and settling Guanajuato.

By the beginning of the seventeenth century, conflict between Spaniards and Indian groups had subsided and a handful of Spanish towns, including San Miguel el Grande (later San Miguel Allende), Silao, Celaya, León, and Guanajuato City, had emerged. For the next two centuries, Guanajuato experienced rapid growth in its population and corresponding economic growth. Mining, concentrated in and around the city of Guanajuato and utilizing both Indian and black labor, was central to the region's prosperity. Of special importance was the Valenciana mine, discovered in 1767. Agriculture, which flourished in the fertile Bajío, and a textile industry (also based in the Bajío and producing for markets as distant as Texas) added to the area's wealth.

Despite, and in part because of, its economic success, Guanajuato and the Bajío region became a center of insurgency at the beginning of the nineteenth century. Particularly as landowners began to consolidate and use their holdings to produce goods for wealthier urban dwellers, Bajío residents faced higher prices for subsistence crops such as corn, which became increasingly scarce. Drought and famine ultimately encouraged many to join Father Miguel Hidalgo's call for rebellion against the Spanish colonial government. For several months, Hidalgo's followers roamed the Bajío, capturing towns, destroying property, and killing many Peninsulars (native-born Spaniards). Ignacio Allende, another prominent figure in Mexico's independence movement and whose name was later attached to that of his native town of San Miguel el Grande, joined Hidalgo's insurgency. The Hidalgo rebellion was ultimately suppressed, and the severed heads of its leaders were displayed in Guanajuato City. The destruction wrought by this movement was extreme, and it delayed until 1821 Mexico's separation from Spain.

Guanajuato achieved statehood in 1824, though its economy continued to struggle, and it never regained its status as a wealthy mining center. Moreover, because of its central location and proximity to Mexico City, Guanajuato experienced directly the effect of the numerous political struggles that charac-terized the nineteenth century. During the midcentury war between conservatives and liberals, the capital served briefly as the seat of Mexico's government, and several important battles took place within the state. From 1863 to 1867 forces loyal to the French invaders who established a short-lived empire in Mexico occupied most of Guanajuato. The state also experienced popular unrest in the decades after Mexican independence. The sierra region of Guanajuato's northeast was the center of several uprisings, which were most often precipitated by thefts of land.

The last three decades of the nineteenth century were characterized by the renewal of political stability and by economic modernization and growth. Railroad lines linked Guanajuato City with the state's other important towns, including Celaya, León, Salamanca, Irapuato, and Silao. Additional links eased communication with Mexico City and beyond. Foreign investment played an important role in economic expansion. In the mining sector, for example, American companies dominated, and they actually replaced some Mexican families that had established their mining fortunes during the colonial era. Agriculture also expanded, and as in many areas of Mexico, land became concentrated in fewer and fewer hands. The city of León especially benefited from the economic growth that characterized turn-of-the-century Guanajuato. By 1910 it was the state's most populous town, and a center of agricultural and industrial production.

Guanajuato's growth was aided by the long and often-repressive reign of Mexican President Porfirio Díaz, who during his 1876 revolt against the federal government established his military headquarters at Salamanca. Joaquín Obregón González was Díaz's chief representative in Guanajuato, and he served as the state's governor for nineteen years. In response to the heavy hand of Díaz and his local representatives, opposition groups had begun to emerge by the early twentieth century. These groups supported Francisco Madero's call for Díaz's overthrow in 1910. Cándido Navarro, a schoolteacher from Guanajuato, was perhaps the state's most outstanding figure in this early phase of the Mexican Revolution, commanding troops that captured Silao and León. Navarro was a prominent rebel figure until his death in 1913.

Though Francisco Madero's national victory against Díaz helped install a new regime in Guanajuato, the state remained divided, with workers and *campesinos* pushing for reform while the state's large landowners and businessmen resisted significant change. Guanajuato also became a center of the conservative National Catholic Party, which similarly resisted change, while seeking to protect the Roman Catholic Church from the anticlericalism that was part of the Revolution. Madero's death and the beginning of Venustiano Carranza's Constitutionalist movement did little to clarify Guanajuato's political situation. Constitutionalist forces gained control of several areas of Guanajuato in 1914 and Carranza installed as governor Pablo A. de la Garza. Although Garza's reforms won favor with workers, he alienated more conservative elements with his anticlerical measures, including the prohibition of confession.

Guanajuato remained a strategic prize throughout the Mexican Revolution, particularly when Carranza's Constitutionalists parted company with Pancho Villa, another prominent Revolutionary leader. Villa's forces briefly held Guanajuato in 1914 and early 1915 before being dislodged in the pivotal battles of Celaya. José Siurob briefly represented the victorious Constitutionalists as the state's governor, issuing decrees to benefit workers and beginning the process of land reform. Siurob and his successors continued to confront a state that was bitterly divided over the direction of revolutionary reform, particularly over the issues of land redistribution and the relationship between the Roman Catholic Church and the Mexican state. Resistance to agrarian reform and to the anticlerical provisions of the new Mexican Constitution of 1917 made the state a center of both the Cristero Rebellion (1926–1929) and the reactionary *sinarquista* movement, both of which opposed the more radical tendencies of the post-Revolutionary period.

The conservative tendencies represented by the Cristero Rebellion and the *sinarquista* movement have colored Guanajuato's political history for most of the twentieth century and have made the state a center of opposition to the Institutional Revolutionary Party (PRI). They have also provided a particularly strong political base for the National Action Party (PAN). In 1945, *sinarquists* joined with the PAN to protest the outcome of municipal elections in León, which favored a PRI candidate. The protest brought a showdown between the national and local governments and resulted in the deaths of several protestors. Another notable clash occurred in 1991 when businessman and PAN candidate Vicente Fox ran for the governorship and was defeated by Ramón Aguirre Velázquez of the PRI. Protests against the questionable election results forced Aguirre's resignation and a special election was set for 1995. Appealing to business interests and playing to the state's strong Roman Catholic heritage by referring to his training at a Jesuit-run school, Fox won the 1995 election. He resigned his post in 1999 to run for the presidency of Mexico.

While Guanajuato's political history in the latter part of the twentieth century has been characterized by volatility, the state's economy has felt the effects of industrialization and commercialization. The agricultural sector has been steadily converted to commercial production, and Guanajuato has become a leading producer of winter vegetables such as broccoli and cauliflower, which are primarily grown for export to the United States. Foreign companies, including Campbell's, have come to dominate this economic sector. Growth in industry and manufacturing has been concentrated in the state's central region, and an industrial corridor has emerged among the cities of León, Celaya, Salamanca, and Irapuato. Metalworking, and the manufacture of clothing, shoes, and chemicals are among the activities within this zone.

While Guanajuato's economic development has contributed to a steady growth in population (which is concentrated in urban areas and particularly in the industrial corridor), it has not occurred without costs. By the beginning of the twenty-first century, the state faced significant problems of erosion, deforestation, and water contamination. While its economy has become increasingly modern and mechanized, Guanajuato has failed to produce the jobs needed for its expanding population. As a result, Guanajuato has a high level of immigration to United States.

—SBP

See also: Cristero Rebellion; Fox, Vicente; Partido de Acción Nacional (PAN); Revolution of 1910.

References:

Blanco, Mónica, Alma Parra, and Ethelia Ruíz Medrano. *Breve historia de Guanajuato*. Mexico City: El Colegio de Mexico, 2000.
Official state web site: http://www.guanajuato.gob.mx

Guerrero (State)

Guerrero is a southwestern Mexican state situated along the Pacific coast, with Chilpancingo as its capital. Guerrero is home to Acapulco and Ixtapa-Zihuatanejo, resort areas that attract thousands of tourists each year. The state also contains Taxco, which has been famous for its silver since the colonial era. Guerrero is one of Mexico's poorest states and its history is one of uneven development and marginalization. It has played a key role in the major events of Mexico's history, however. Twentieth-century Guerrero has been characterized by endemic violence as popular movements and rebellions have sought fundamental changes while wealthier elements have resisted such change.

Many inhabitants of modern Guerrero speak an indigenous language, and the state contained several Indian groups in the centuries before the Spaniards arrived. On the eve of conquest, Guerrero was controlled by the Aztec Empire, to which its peoples paid tribute. Spanish exploration of the region began in 1523 and in 1531 the port of Acapulco was established. Silver was discovered in Taxco in 1534, attracting more settlers. Taxco and Acapulco were central to Guerrero's colonial economy, tying it to global markets. Silver left Acapulco for Spain and Asia on the Manila Galleons, which brought goods destined for the interior of New Spain. Although agriculture developed to serve the needs of Taxco, and cotton was grown to support a local textile industry, the rest of Guerrero remained underdeveloped and peripheral to colonial Mexico.

Despite the marginalization of much of the region, Guerrero played a central role in the political struggles of the nineteenth century. José María Morelos, who joined Miguel Hidalgo's revolt against Spanish control in 1810, assembled an army in Guerrero. In 1813, Chilpancingo hosted a congress that formally declared Mexico's independence. After Morelos's capture and execution in 1815, the independence struggle continued and Vicente Guerrero (for whom the state is named) emerged as a main insurgent leader in southern Mexico. Along with Nicolás Bravo, Guerrero played a key role in postindependence politics, briefly serving as Mexico's president.

Guerrero achieved statehood in 1847, though Chilpancingo was not chosen as the capital until 1871. The new state remained a player in national events, and in 1854 the Plan of Ayutla (by which President Antonio López de Santa Anna was overthrown) was declared here. Guerrero was also central to the struggle between Mexico's liberal and conservative factions during the War of Reform (1858–1861). Finally, Acapulco and other parts of the state were captured and held during the French occupation of Mexico (1862–1867).

During the era of Porfirio Díaz (1876–1911), Guerrero had a series of leaders, most imposed with the help of Mexico's central government. Diaz's attempts to bring economic growth and foreign investment to Mexico, however, affected Guerrero only marginally. Meanwhile the state's *campesinos* (rural workers) grew increasingly restive in response to poor working and living conditions. Agrarian tensions, also a part of the earlier independence struggle, intensified, and soon spilled over into the violence of the Mexican Revolution.

Led by the prominent Figueroa family, the state's *rancheros* (small independent farmers) were the first to challenge the Díaz regime. This group joined Francisco I. Madero's 1910–1911 revolt against Díaz, and they assembled the forces that captured Chilpancingo, compelling the resignation of Guerrero's last Porfirian governor. *Campesinos* also joined Madero's revolt, although they were drawn primarily to the movement of Emiliano Zapata, who demanded land reform. Jesús Salgado and Julián Blanco led the local Zapatista movement, and they challenged the leadership of the more conservative Figueroa clan. In 1914, Zapata's forces captured Chilpancingo and Salgado became the state's governor. The expropriation of haciendas, elimination of company stores, and declaration of a minimum wage were among Salgado's reforms. Zapatista dominance of Guerrero was short-lived, however, and with the triumph of Venustiano Carranza's Constitutionalist movement, Zapata's followers were marginalized.

Despite Zapata's failure to maintain control in Guerrero, the state continued to produce popular movements that sought the more radical change Zapata represented. In 1919 Juan Ranulfo Escudero established the Workers' Party of Acapulco, which pushed for better wages, protection for workers, and land reform. Escudero's election and reelection as Acapulco's municipal president alarmed local elites and Mexico's central government. In 1921, Escudero was seriously wounded in an assassination attempt. Acapulco was also the scene of a rebellion against the Spanish-owned companies that controlled the port and the coastal economy. This revolt ended when President Emilio Portes Gil distributed lands to the insurgents.

The popular unrest that characterized Guerrero's Revolutionary years encouraged President Lázaro Cárdenas (1934–1940) to distribute more land, particularly in the state's coastal region. Land reform angered *rancheros* (including the Figueroa family) and they responded with violence. Advocates of land reform also organized. A cycle of popular unrest and official repression was reinforced by the state's political instability. From 1925 to 1996 only six governors completed their terms. Perhaps most important, Guerrero failed to develop a well-balanced and equitable economic system in the decades after the Mexican Revolution.

Beginning in the 1940s, Mexican and foreign investment began to develop Guerrero's tourist industry. By the 1950s, Acapulco was an internationally famous resort. By the 1990s, Ixtapa and Zihuatanejo had also emerged as major tourist attractions. Yet while tourism brought revenue and jobs for some, its benefits were limited to the coastal region. Taxco's silver mining industry was the only other economic alternative to agriculture, and neither tourism nor silver could create the jobs needed for an expanding (and increasingly landless) population. Many inhabitants of Guerrero responded to the situation by leaving, others by organizing to protest poverty and the repression and unresponsiveness of the state government.

One of the most visible protest groups to emerge in Guerrero was the Partido de los Pobres (Party of the Poor, or PP). The PP developed in the state's highlands during the late 1960s. Its leader was Lucio Cabañas Barrientos, a teacher and member of Mexico's Communist Party. Cabañas took up arms after his brother and six other rural teachers were killed in a clash with local officials. He molded the PP into a guerrilla organization, which enjoyed support particularly in the coastal region south of Acapulco, a poverty-stricken area in which violent competition over resources was common. The PP financed its activities through bank robberies and kidnapping. One kidnapping victim was Rubén Figueroa Figueroa, a senator who attempted to negotiate with Cabañas. Figueroa was freed in a shootout, and he went on to become Guerrero's governor. Cabañas was killed in a confrontation with army troops in 1974.

Popular protest and official repression showed no signs of ending in the last decade of the twentieth century. In 1995, seventeen members of the Southern Sierra Peasant Organization, a group mobilized to challenge logging operations that threatened the livelihood of *campesinos,* were massacred on their way to a protest meeting. Videotaped footage of the massacre at Aguas Blancas revealed that soldiers had opened fire on the unarmed activists. This evidence compelled the resignation of Governor Rubén Figueroa Alcócer (Figueroa Figueroa's son). An official investigation sentenced several people to jail, but the sentences were brief. The Aguas Blancas massacre encouraged the formation of another guerrilla organization, the Ejército Popular Revolucionario (EPR or the People's Revolutionary Army), which emerged in 1996. The EPR staged raids on army installations and provided, for a brief period, a threat to the local and national government that was compared to the Zapatista movement in Chiapas, another poor southern state.

—SBP

See also: Agrarian Reform/Land and Land Policy; Revolution of 1910; Tourism; Zapata, Emiliano; Zapatista National Liberation Army (EZLN).

References:

Illades, Carlos. *Breve historia de Guerrero.* Mexico City: El Colegio de Mexico, 2000.

Jacobs, Ian. *Ranchero Revolt: The Mexican Revolution in Guerrero.* Austin: University of Texas Press, 1982.

Official state web site: http://www.guerrero.gob.mx

Hidalgo (State)

Located in central Mexico, Hidalgo is one of the country's most mountainous areas. Historically, the state has been one of Mexico's most important mining regions, and it continues to produce silver, lead, copper, zinc, and other minerals. Hidalgo's past has been marked by popular unrest, and the state has a long history of worker activism. Hidalgo's *campesinos* (peasants), including members of its sizeable Indian population, have also waged a long struggle to preserve their lands and autonomy. This battle was still being fought in the last decades of the twentieth century.

Hidalgo was a center of Mexico's Toltec culture and the state contains the ruins of Tula, the Toltec capital distinguished by its large Atlas columns, which depict famous warriors. Huastec and Otomí Indians were among the many groups that inhabited the area prior to Spanish contact, and on the eve of the Spaniards' arrival, parts of Hidalgo had been drawn into the Aztec Empire. Hernán Cortés passed through Hidalgo on his way to the Aztec capital and Spanish settlement, complete with missionaries, soon followed.

Pachuca (the current capital of the state) was one of New Spain's first settlements. Located in a rich mining zone, it quickly be-

came a mining capital. The patio process of amalgamation was perfected in Pachuca by Bartolomé de Medina, and the Real del Monte mine, in the Pachuca district, became one of the colony's most important. Mining was central to Hidalgo's colonial economy, and it utilized the labor of Indians and Africans. Agriculture and commerce emerged as a complement to the mines. In Hidalgo's southeast, haciendas devoted to the cultivation of maguey used in the production of *pulque* (a popular fermented drink derived from cactus juice) supplied the mining communities and gradually expanded to serve the central Mexican market as well.

On the eve of Mexico's independence, Hidalgo enjoyed a thriving economy based on mining and the hacienda system. Poor treatment of miners and hacienda workers, however, ensured conflict. In 1766, for example, a nine-year labor dispute in Real del Monte began, as miners protested the manner in which they were paid and called attention to other conditions of their work. As Mexico's independence era began, miners and *campesinos* in Hidalgo provided recruits for the popular insurrection that began in Guanajuato in 1810. José Francisco Osorno and Julián Villagrán were among those who organized the local insurgency and who seconded Father

Miguel Hidalgo's challenge to the Spanish colonial regime. The independence period brought significant destruction to Hidalgo, forcing some mines to close and hampering production on the haciendas.

With Mexico's independence, Hidalgo became a part of the state of Mexico, along with Morelos, Guerrero, the Federal District, and Tlaxcala. It gained statehood only in 1869. Economic recovery and expansion characterized the years after independence. Mining in particular benefited from foreign investment as U.S., British, and German investors established mining companies and employed thousands of workers. After mid-century, railroad lines linked the state to other points in central Mexico and to the port of Vera Cruz. This development aided not only the mining sector but also the state's *pulque* industry, which thus gained an efficient and less expensive means of marketing its product to other areas of Mexico.

Although the nineteenth century was one of relatively uninterrupted economic growth, Hidalgo's political situation was volatile. Its central location, proximity to Mexico City, and industrial wealth made the state a battleground during the civil conflict between Mexico's liberal and conservative factions. Pachuca and Tulancingo (the main areas of commerce and industry) were especially prized. Hidalgo also experienced unrest during the Mexican War (when U.S. troops invaded Mexico and marched toward the capital) and during the 1860s, when invading French troops (that would pave the way for a French empire in Mexico) occupied Pachuca. The struggles of Hidalgo's *campesinos* also marked the nineteenth century, particularly as economic expansion robbed many Indians of their lands. Miners were restive as well, and their livelihood was increasingly undercut by the depletion of mineral deposits and by a decline in the price of silver. During the 1870s, the Real del Monte mine was once again the site of a worker's movement focused on better pay and working conditions.

Popular unrest was met with increasing repression in Hidalgo during the reign of President Porfirio Díaz (1876–1911). Determined to create the stability needed to attract foreign investment and encourage economic modernization, Díaz encouraged local leaders to quell dissent. In Hidalgo, the Cravioto brothers provided the firm hand. Rafael, Simón, and Francisco controlled the state from 1877 to 1897 and they paid particular attention to crushing those who fought for the return of lands. Under Rafael's leadership, for example, dozens of *campesinos* in the community of El Zaquital were massacred when they pushed for the return of their lands.

Such repression continued into the twentieth century under the governorship of Pedro Rodríguez, who also faced a growing political opposition to the Díaz's regime. In Hidalgo, this opposition took the form of support for the Mexican Liberal Party (Partido Liberal Mexicano, or PLM) and Francisco I. Madero's Anti-reelection Movement. Among those who joined the call for an end to the Díaz regime was Alfonso Cravioto, son of former governor Rafael. Alfonso was a student leader who worked with the PLM and was later jailed for his activism.

Miners and *campesinos* were among the initial supporters of Francisco Madero's 1910–1911 rebellion against Díaz. The Madero revolt also attracted the predominantly Indian population of Hidalgo's Huasteca region. Maderista rebels eventually captured both Pachuca and Tulancingo, and Jesús Silva and Ramón Rosales (leaders of Pachuca's Anti-reelection Movement) served brief terms as governor after Madero's national victory. With the fall of Madero's government, Hidalgo experienced another wave of violence as Venustiano Carranza, Pancho Villa, and other insurgents sought control over the course of Mexico's Revolution. Pachuca was a prize for all factions and it changed hands three times before 1920. Carranza eventually asserted his authority over Hidalgo, and Nicolás Flores assumed the governorship.

Flores attempted a limited agrarian reform, courted the state's workers, and challenged the historically strong position of the Roman Catholic Church.

After Carranza's own deposition and death in 1920, Hidalgo experienced additional unrest. Although *campesinos* in particular sought to have their demands for change included in the Revolution, landowners resisted any real transformation. In the Sierra Alta region, for example, *rancheros* (midsized landowners) successfully manipulated the process of land reform to their own advantage. The grievances of *campesinos* thus persisted well beyond the Revolutionary era. During the 1970s, the demand for land reform again erupted in violence, particularly in the Huasteca region. There, landowners responded to *campesino* demands with the formation of "white guards," which used brute force to silence the cries for reform. In the 1980s the state government finally responded to the situation by distributing lands to *campesinos* in the Huasteca. Hidalgo's workers also remained active in the decades after the Mexican Revolution.

Although the Mexican Revolution disrupted the state's economy, it did not halt development. Industrial growth increased after 1940 and irrigation helped expand agricultural production. During the last decades of the twentieth century, the Pachuca-Mineral del Monte region was still one of Mexico's most important mining zones. Hidalgo's future as a mining region was somewhat uncertain, however, owing to overexploitation and a decline in some of the state's mineral resources. The cement industry (which had emerged at the turn of the twentieth century) also remained an important economic activity and two of Mexico's major cement makers (Cruz Azul and Cementos Tolteca) operated in Hidalgo.

—SBP

See also: Carranza, Venustiano; Díaz, Porfirio; Revolution of 1910; Villa, Francisco "Pancho."

References:
Lau Jaiven, Ana, and Ximena Sepúlveda Otaiza. *Hidalgo: Una historia compartida.* Mexico City: Instituto de Investigaciones José María Luis Mora, 1994.

Rubluo, Luis. *Historia de la revolución mexicana en el Estado de Hidalgo.* 2 vols. Mexico City: Instituto Nacional de Estudios Históricos de la Revolución Mexicana, 1983.

Schryer, Frans J. *The Rancheros of Pisaflores: The History of a Peasant Bourgeoisie in Twentieth-Century Mexico.* Toronto: University of Toronto Press, 1980.

Official state web site: http://www.hidalgo.gob.mx

Holy Days and Holidays

As in most modern nations, special days in Mexico fall into two general categories: religious holy days and civic holidays. Religious holy days typically predate the modern nation-state and represent the primordial bonds of shared cultural experiences while civic holidays generally begin with its formation and represent the more specific bonds of national citizenship. Together they serve to bind people together as families, communities, and nations. In Mexico (and elsewhere), holy days and holidays are more complicated than this simple schematic suggests. Vestiges of Native American religious practices provide subtle undercurrents to the accepted Roman Catholic interpretation of religious celebrations. Folk Catholicism with its insistence on local control of religious symbols and practices has often been even more subversive of official church doctrine. To make matters worse (for the historian at least), three hundred years of colonial rule, during which State and Church often intermingled provide historical precedents for the introduction of political concerns into religious celebrations and vice versa. More recently, intense commercialization and frequent cultural transfers have significantly altered the traditional meaning of some of Mexico's most important celebrations, including Christmas, Day of the Dead, and Cinco de Mayo. The ambiguity and flexibility inherent in popular culture are, however, also a source of considerable strength,

Participants in a Day of the Dead pageant march in a mock funeral procession towards the main square. (Andrew Winning/ Reuters/Corbis)

and it is unlikely that Mexico's vibrant ritual life will succumb to the temptations of either religious orthodoxy or crass modernity.

Religious holy days in Mexico, as in most predominantly Roman Catholic countries, revolve around the annual celebrations of the birth and death of Jesus Christ, Christmas and Easter. Christmas Day is a fixed "feast" celebrated every December 25, while Easter is a moveable "feast" celebrated in midspring. Both religious holy days are extended celebrations composed of distinct stages in which the event itself represents the climax of days (weeks if one counts Advent and Lent) of elaborate preparation. Both events and their preparatory stages—especially in villages, smaller towns, and some urban barrios—involve much of the population (sometimes at considerable expense) and serve to strengthen community ties by providing a model of social reciprocity that enhances the status of those major contributors who choose to recognize their obligations by financing the cele-

brations. That these elaborate ceremonies occur simultaneously throughout Mexico also strengthens national ties as participants perform shared primordial rituals—rituals the origins of which are considered mythical rather than historical—that predate and thus confer inevitability on the modern nation-state.

The Christmas cycle begins with Advent in late November and concludes with the Baptism of Christ in January. The first major event in the Mexican Christmas cycle, the December 12 feast day of the Virgin of Guadalupe, the nation's patron saint, is especially important in Mexico (although celebrated throughout Latin America) and serves to link Roman Catholic and national celebrations at the beginning of the first major cycle of the religious calendar—a practice that echoes the elaborate joint Church-State rituals of the colonial period (1521–1821). This concession to a religious image on the part of an often anticlerical state reflects a pragmatic willingness to embrace the Virgin of Guadalupe's symbolic power as the "mother" of Mexico despite strong reservations about the Church's role in Mexican society. Indeed the Church, for all its efforts to fix the meaning of religious symbols, has been unable to control devotional practices associated with the Virgin of Guadalupe, including her deployment as a patriotic symbol or beliefs like the widely accepted link between the Virgin and Aztec goddess Tonantzín.

The popular "folk" celebration, *Las posadas* (the inns), begins on December 16 and runs through Christmas Eve. Inspired by early missionary efforts to make Christianity accessible and acceptable to their Indian converts through community-staged performances of bible stories, *Las posadas* reenacts the familiar story of Mary and Joseph's search for lodging in Bethlehem so that Mary could give birth to Jesus. A locally controlled musical-theatrical celebration staged all over Mexico and the southwestern United States, *Las posadas* has many different variants. In most, young girls carry images of Mary, Joseph, and Jesus through the streets accompanied by a chorus, usually of older women. The procession involves at least two stops, during which the Holy Family are rejected by uncharitable innkeepers before they reach their final destination where the image of the baby Jesus is gently laid in the manger. In many places, the procession is repeated every evening through Christmas Eve. It typically concludes with the distribution of the *agüinaldo* (small bags of candy, nuts, and fruit) and the breaking of *piñatas* (papier-mâché decorated pots filled with treats) by the community's younger boys. Christmas Day, by contrast, is typically devoted to more orthodox Roman Catholic rituals, such as Christmas Mass directed by priests and taking place mostly in churches. The Christmas cycle concludes with the Adoration of the Magi on the Sunday after Christmas followed by the Baptism of Christ a week later.

The moveable Easter cycle that celebrates Jesus's death and resurrection is a more solemn affair. It officially begins in midwinter with Ash Wednesday and runs through Easter Sunday in midspring. The day before Ash Wednesday is, of course, Mardi Gras, the traditional day of Carnival. During Mardi Gras, participants get a chance to release their inhibitions and invert social hierarchies before the start of Lent, the long period of purification and self-denial that precedes Easter. Some scholars have argued that the freedoms of Mardi Gras represent a challenge to the established social order and thus hold out the possibility of a more equitable society. Others point out that social hierarchies are invariably restored and ultimately reinforced by this annual ritual of social dissolution and reconstruction. Certainly Lent and the special days of Holy Week—Palm Sunday, Maundy Thursday, Good Friday, etc.—are intended to remind participants of the sacrifice made for their salvation and the need to attend to their souls or risk eternal damnation. Although less common in the twentieth century, Lenten retreats in Mexico sometimes led to ritual self-flagellation as believers sought to subdue their sinful flesh in imitation of the sufferings of Christ—an image graphically represented in the bloody, tortured, life-sized crucifixion figures that grace most Mexican churches. At the conclusion of Holy Saturday, Mexicans sometimes break the Lenten silences with rowdy public Judas burnings, in which effigies of Christ's betrayer are filled with treats (sausages and coins are special favorites), wrapped in firecrackers, and then exploded. At times, Judas figures have taken on the visages of political figures considered as traitors to the community in some way. During the administration of president Porfirio Díaz (1876–1880, 1884–1910), attempts were made to push Judas burnings and their potentially volatile politic messages out of urban public spaces and to replace them with more orderly parades that encouraged passive spectatorship rather than active participation. On Easter Day, the traditional purple mantels on the holy images for Lent are taken off and the holy icons are carried in elaborate processions through the streets for public veneration. The restoration of the icons to the church marks the end of the Easter season.

The religious calendar between Easter and Advent is filled with individual Saints' days, several moveable feasts, and the Day of the Dead celebrations (All Saints' and All Souls') on the first two days of November. The principal national saints' days are for Saint Joseph on March 19 (which falls appropriately during the Easter cycle) and Saints Peter and Paul on June 29. However, each city, town, village, and barrio has its own patron saint. The preparation for and celebration of these different saints' days provide an important marker of community identity and often spawn fierce rivalries between villages and neighborhoods. At the same time, the layers of spiritual patronage—barrios might construct rivalries around their respective saints but both tend to venerate the town or city saint—serve to bind these different entities together. Aside from individual saints' days, moveable feast days such as Pentecost and Corpus Christi ensure a rich ritual life. During Corpus Christi celebrations in Mexico City, for example, children decked out in Indian costumes gather outside the Cathedral of Mexico on the Zócalo to have their baskets of fruit and other foods blessed by the priest while hundreds of street vendors ply them with fruit tamales called *mulitas* (little mules).

The most distinctly Mexican holy day is unquestionably Day of the Dead. Encompassing two consecutive holy days, All Saints' on November 1 and All Souls' on November 2, Day of the Dead celebrations far exceed the official liturgical requirements of these feast days—the most important of which are the Office of the Dead and Requium Masses said on All Souls' to aid in the purification of souls seeking to enter into heaven. For Mexicans, these two days take on complex and apparently contradictory meanings. On one hand, attention to the dead is taken very seriously. Many families, especially in more traditional Indian communities, mark the occasion by cleaning the gravesites of their deceased relatives, making *ofrendas* or offerings (of food and flowers, especially the yellow marigold-like *cempasúchil*), holding all-night vigils, and constructing home altars to honor dead family members. Although November 1 is officially All Saints', for many participants, it's also a special day devoted to mourning the death of children, especially *angelitos,* whose pure souls are said to watch over their families like guardian angels. Both days end with lugubrious bell tolling and ritualized begging to remind participants of their tenuous hold on life and the inevitability of death. On the other hand, Day of Dead celebrations also include a considerable dose of "black" humor. *Pan de muerto* (death bread), sugar candy in the shape of skulls, miniature wooden coffins with pop-up skeletons, and satirical *calaveras* (literally "skulls")—poems, caricatures, and figurines ridiculing political figures and celebrities—appear everywhere. For some observers, this obsession with death has indigenous roots in Aztec culture with its human sacrifices and skeletal iconography (minus, of course, the sense of humor). Others stress the influence of early modern Roman Catholicism, especially the apocalyptic sort espoused by the sixteenth-century Franciscan and Dominican friars and priests who proselytized so much of Indian Mexico. Regardless of its origins, in the past few decades, Day of Dead has become the symbol of a uniquely Mexican approach to life and thus an important marker of national identity. As a result, the elaborate Day of the Dead rituals practiced by specific, mostly Indian, communities in places like Oaxaca and villages around Lake Pátzcuaro have spread throughout Mexico and even spilled over into Mexican communities in the United States. At the same time, foreign customs have begun to intrude on traditional Day of the Dead practices. Children used to beg for treats with a request for *mi muertito* (little dead one), now they ask instead for *mi Halloween.*

Civic holidays are both more recent and more overtly nationalistic than religious holy days. As in most modern nation-states, the most important civic celebration is Independence Day, celebrated on September 16. In strictly historical terms, Mexico became officially independent of Spain on 27 September 1821 when General Agustín de Iturbide rode into Mexico City at the head of his army. The day just happened to coincide with Iturbide's birthday and when the increasingly unpopular general-turned-emperor was deposed in 1823, Independence Day was changed to September 16, the day on which Father Miguel Hidalgo gave the famous 1810 speech, the Grito de Dolores, which began the wars for independence in Mexico. Father Hidalgo's revolt was crushed and its leader executed, but the nobility of his martyr's cause seemed more inspiring than Iturbide's crass self-promotion, so the date stuck and Hidalgo became the Father of Mexico, the first secular saint in the liberal pantheon (despite his excommunication by the Roman Catholic Church). One hundred years later, efforts by the administration of President Porfirio Díaz (1876–1880, 1884–1911) to link the celebration to the President Díaz's birthday (September 15) failed as his opponents used the massive expenditures for elaborate building projects and gaudy history parades to condemn the regime's callous disregard for the more pressing needs of the Mexico's undereducated, underfed, and underemployed people. (Díaz was ousted just a few months after the centenary celebrations.) Post Revolutionary celebrations are less pretentious but probably more effective at inspiring national unity. Each year just before midnight on the night before Independence Day, Mexico's president repeats a reconstructed version of Hidalgo's speech (based on eyewitness accounts) and ends with the cheer *"Viva México,"* to which the crowd responds defiantly, *"Viva México, hijos de la chingada"* (Long live Mexico, you sons of bitches).

The second most important civic holiday, Cinco de Mayo (May 5), reflects a similar defiance in the face of foreign threats. A celebration of the 1862 victory of Mexican forces over an invading French army near the city of Puebla, Cinco de Mayo commemorates an ultimately unsuccessful effort to prevent the French occupation of Mexico a year later. For liberal forces fighting the French-imposed emperor Maximilian, however, it represented (and for most Mexicans still represents) the willingness to fight for freedom in the face of seemingly impossible odds. The cult of the *niños héroes* (heroic children), military cadets who, according to stories, threw themselves off the cliffs of Chapultepec Castle wrapped in Mexican flags rather than surrender to U.S. invaders during the Mexican War (1846–1848), is another such symbol. With the enthusiastic support of president Porfirio Díaz, whose courage and skill during the battle of Puebla made him a national hero, Cinco de Mayo quickly became a major civic holiday. The sponsorship of beer companies, eager to promote sales, further increased its popularity, especially in the United States where Budweiser successfully used the holiday to market to Mexican American consumers. Other secular holidays—Benito Juárez's birthday (March 21), Constitution Day (February 2), Anniversary of the Mexican Revolution Day (November 20)—are less popular but nonetheless function like saints' days to remind participants and observers of their national history and imbue a general feeling of civic responsibility in the ritual spaces between the two major celebrations.

Not all holidays, however, directly celebrate the nation-state. Labor Day (May 1), for example, is an international holiday that honors the contributions and sacrifices of workers throughout the world (although as a national holiday, it focuses on Mexican workers). Other holidays are more commercial than ideological. This is especially true of popular foreign imports like Valentine's Day and Mother's Day that link bourgeois sentimentality and family values to consumption—a more "modern" configuration than either religious holy days or civic holidays. At some level, these imported traditions represent an erosion of Mexican ritual life, but, as Mexico's homegrown Day of the Child attests, the tradition and richness of that ritual life works against the forces of cultural imperialism and Mexicans are more likely to bend imported traditions to their own purposes than to succumb without a fight.

—*RMB*

See also: Folk Art; Virgin of Guadalupe.

References:

Beezley, William H. *Judas at the Jockey Club and Other Episodes of Porfirian Mexico.* Lincoln: University of Nebraska Press, 1987.

Beezley, William H., Cheryl English Martin, and William E. French, eds. *Rituals of Rule, Rituals of Resistance: Public Celebrations and Popular Culture in Mexico.* Wilmington, DE: Scholarly Resources, 1994.

Carmichael, Elizabeth, and Chloë Sayer. *The Skeleton at the Feast: The Day of the Dead in Mexico.* Austin: University of Texas Press, 1992.

Ingham, John M. *Mary, Michael, and Lucifer: Folk Catholicism in Central Mexico.* Austin: University of Texas Press, 1986.

Huerta, Adolfo de la

See de la Huerta, Adolfo

Huerta, Victoriano (1845–1916)

President of Mexico in the tumultuous years of 1913 and 1914, Victoriano Huerta was born in Colotlán, Jalisco, in 1845. Huerta had a limited education and limited prospects until he became the personal secretary of General Donato Guerra, who used his influence to get Huerta an appointment to the National Military College. Huerta distinguished himself in mathematics and astronomy and received his commission in 1877, the beginning of a lengthy military career that would eventually lead to the presidency. After participating in pacification campaigns in western Mexico in 1878 and 1879, Huerta began a lengthy assignment as part of team preparing a new military map of Mexico, a job which took him to nearly every state in Mexico. Huerta proved an able defender of the Porfirian regime, putting down revolts from Sonora to Yucatán. Huerta was promoted to brigadier general in 1901.

When the Revolution of 1910 broke out, Huerta was sent to quell the rebels under Emiliano Zapata; however, he was recalled to Mexico City before leading the federal forces against the rebels. After Díaz resigned, Huerta commanded the troops escorting the former president from Mexico City to Vera Cruz, the port from which Díaz would embark on his European exile. Interim President Francisco León de la Barra sent Huerta to Morelos to speed up the demobilization of Zapata's forces. Huerta was unsuccessful in trying to disarm and, later, in trying to defeat Zapata's forces.

When Francisco Madero became president, Huerta's fortunes briefly faded. Madero disliked Huerta's connections with General

Group portrait, standing left to right: Jose C. Delgado, Victoriano Huerta, Abraham F. Ratner. (Library of Congress)

Bernardo Reyes, who had provided the only real competition for Madero in the 1911 presidential campaign; Madero was also disenchanted with Huerta's performance in regard to Zapata and his forces. The situation changed rapidly in 1912 when Pascual Orozco, the key military figure in Madero's overthrow of Porfirio Díaz, rebelled against Madero. When early efforts to crush the revolt failed, Madero reluctantly called on Huerta to lead a force to suppress Orozco. Huerta defeated the rebels and also tried to have Pancho Villa, who was serving under Huerta, shot by a firing squad for theft. Madero's intervention saved Villa at the last minute.

Assigned a military command in Mexico City, Huerta was aware of the plotting taking place among various generals in late 1912 and early 1913 to overthrow the Madero government. Huerta initially refused to join the conspiracy headed by Generals Bernardo Reyes and Félix Díaz, nephew of the former dictator. When the revolt began on 9 February 1913, it immediately took a wrong turn; Reyes was among the first killed in a failed attempt to take the National Palace. Heavy fighting followed, with major casualties among both civilians and military forces. Huerta was in command of the troops defending Madero but saw in the revolt an opportunity to advance his own agenda. He secretly negotiated an agreement with Félix Díaz in which Huerta would go over to the rebellion in return for becoming provisional president. Huerta arrested Madero and his vice-president, José María Pino Suárez, and forced their resignations on 19 February 1913. Three days later both Madero and Pino Suárez were murdered while being transferred from the National Palace to a military prison. There was no direct evidence—but plenty of circumstantial evidence—linking Huerta to the assassinations.

Huerta then faced the problem of consolidating his position as president against considerable domestic and foreign opposition. Huerta moved against his supposed political ally, Félix Díaz, by forcing out cabinet officials connected with Díaz. He then removed Díaz

from the scene by first appointing him ambassador to Japan and later forcing him into exile in the United States. Huerta's seizure of power put the Revolution of 1910 into a new and bloodier phase. Major revolts broke out in the north under Venustiano Carranza, Pancho Villa, and Alvaro Obregón and in the south under Emiliano Zapata. In the face of congressional criticism, Huerta dissolved the Congress and arrested more than one hundred of its members. Huerta also had to contend with growing opposition from the United States government under President Woodrow Wilson, which escalated its policy from pressuring Huerta to resign to taking active measures to throw him out, including U.S. military intervention at Vera Cruz in April 1914.

Although under tremendous military and diplomatic pressure, Huerta did attempt to implement new domestic programs. Despite his reputation as a "counterrevolutionary," Huerta provided additional funding for education, reached out for labor support, and started a modest agrarian reform program. Although authoritarian in his approach, Huerta realized that he could not turn the clock back to the days of Porfirio Díaz.

Huerta resorted to desperate military efforts to defeat his various enemies, including implementation of the dreaded *leva,* a system in which the urban and rural poor were forcibly recruited, given little or no training, and then sent to fight the rebels. Lacking in morale and discipline, these unfortunate draftees often deserted or defected to the rebels. The United States also played a role in Huerta's downfall by blocking Huerta's efforts to purchase arms in the United States but permitting Huerta's opponents to do so. With the economy in shambles and his military fortunes in decline, Huerta resigned from the presidency on 15 July 1914 and fled the country for European exile.

Like many Mexican exiles, Huerta plotted to return to Mexico. With German support, Huerta planned to use El Paso, Texas, as a revolutionary base for regaining the presidency. Huerta was to meet with his former enemy, but now political ally, Pascual Orozco, in the small town of Newman, New Mexico, presumably away from the prying eyes of state and federal authorities. Federal officials, however, had been monitoring Huerta's movements closely and on 28 June 1915 arrested both Huerta and Orozco at Newman. After transfer to El Paso, both Huerta and Orozco were released on bond. When Orozco jumped bail, Huerta was once again taken into custody. Huerta died on 13 January 1916 while still under detention by U.S. federal authorities.

—DMC

See also: Assassinations; Díaz, Porfirio; Madero, Francisco; Obregón, Alvaro; Orozco, Pascual; Presidents of the Twentieth Century; Revolution of 1910; United States, Relations with; Villa, Francisco "Pancho"; Zapata, Emiliano.

References:

Grieb, Kenneth J. *The United States and Huerta.* Lincoln: University of Nebraska Press, 1969.

Katz, Friedrich. *The Secret War in Mexico: Europe, the United States, and the Mexican Revolution.* Chicago: University of Chicago Press, 1981.

Meyer, Michael C. *Huerta: A Political Portrait.* Lincoln: University of Nebraska Press, 1972.

I

Immigration/Emigration

Although Mexican history has been influenced by the movement of people into and out of the country, most of the historical and political focus has been on Mexicans leaving the country. In particular the emphasis has been on the impact of Mexican citizens moving from Mexico to the United States.

The first major "movement" of Mexican citizens to the United States was involuntary. The war between Mexico and the United States, which started in 1846 and ended in 1848, resulted in a massive transfer of real estate from Mexico to the United States. Mexican citizens living in an area stretching from Texas to California now found themselves residents of the United States.

For almost a half-century after the war, there was little population movement from Mexico into the United States. By the late 1890s, major socioeconomic changes in Mexico began to encourage a substantial migration from Mexico to the United States. This movement was a product of the development policies being pursued by the administration of President Porfirio Díaz (1877–1880, 1884–1911) as well as changes in the southwestern part of the United States. Díaz's pursuit of agricultural modernization led to large-scale displacement of

much of the rural population, depressed agricultural wages, and promoted the continuation of debt peonage. The expansion of the railroads also disrupted rural labor and landholding patterns while simultaneously offering some rural workers a way out of their rural poverty.

At the same time that economic changes encouraged workers to leave Mexico, there were economic developments in the southwestern United States that attracted workers. The expanding railroad, mining, and agricultural sectors in that region offered attractive work alternatives to Mexico's unskilled workers. The early development of large-scale commercial agriculture created a demand for a seasonal labor force. With restrictions on Asian immigration, U.S. growers turned to Mexico for migrant labor. Although the U.S. Immigration Act of 1885 prohibited immigration based on labor contracts, U.S. growers regularly recruited Mexican workers, especially in the border area. The growing national opposition in the United States to "non Anglo-Saxon" immigration did not strongly affect the flow of immigrants from Mexico. Although Americans did not try to hide their feelings of superiority toward Mexicans, they had greater experience with Mexicans than they had with the

Chinese or Japanese. In addition, Americans saw Mexicans as less of a threat because Mexican migrants could—and did—easily return to their native country. When immigration legislation passed in 1903 and 1907 levied a head tax on immigrants, southwestern business interests lobbied successfully for an exemption for Mexican immigrants. There was growing criticism in Mexico about the outflow of its citizens, but the Díaz administration saw the population movement as economically beneficial to both Mexico and the United States. By the time of the Revolution of 1910, U.S. economic interests in the southwest were heavily dependent on Mexican migrant labor; this was especially the case with agriculture.

The Revolution of 1910 had a major impact on population flows. The period from 1910 to 1920 witnessed widespread physical destruction, civil wars, political instability, and the uprooting of a large part of Mexico's population. Many of the uprooted looked to the United States as at least a temporary refuge and possibly a permanent new home. Perhaps as many as 1.5 million Mexicans—more than 10 percent of Mexico's total population—crossed into the United States in the Revolutionary decade of 1910 to 1920. Although Revolutionary upheaval caused increased immigration by professionals and skilled workers, the large majority of immigrants were still unskilled workers. Most of those who legally entered the country—approximately two-thirds of the total—indicated that they were staying only temporarily.

The passage of new immigration legislation in 1917 had the potential for disrupting the flow of Mexican immigrants. The Immigration Act of 1917 imposed a literacy test and an $8 head tax on immigrants legally entering the country; in addition, it repeated the prohibition against contract labor as a basis for immigration. Most Mexican immigrants could not pass the literacy test and could not afford the head tax. Southwestern business interests immediately began to pressure the government to exempt Mexican workers from the provisions of the law. When the United States entered World War I in April 1917, the possibility of a labor shortage became even more pressing. In May 1917 the U.S. government exempted Mexican agricultural workers from the provisions of the 1917 act; the exemption was later extended to include Mexicans working in the railroad, construction, and mining industries. The exemptions continued until March 1921, more than two years after the war ended. These exemptions demonstrated the continuing ability of business groups in the southwest to influence immigration policy as it applied to Mexicans; it also reflected the continuing perception of Mexicans as a special case in formulating immigration policy.

The entry of the United States into World War I created another problem relating to Mexican immigration. Under the Selective Service Act of 1918, foreigners were required to register with their local draft board but were not subject to military service. There were no prior government efforts to educate Mexican workers about the provisions of selective service, and rumors soon circulated among Mexican immigrants in the southwest that they were to be drafted and sent to fight in France. A large—but brief—exodus of Mexican workers took place in the early summer of 1917. The U.S. government then launched a large-scale program to educate the Mexican workers about the law; in July 1918 the U.S. government even exempted Mexican workers from the requirement to register for the draft. Many of those who had fled to Mexico soon returned, along with new waves of Mexican immigrants.

The number of Mexican immigrants entering the United States continued to increase during the 1920s, driven by negative factors in Mexico and positive ones in the United States. Although the most violent phase of the Mexican Revolution had passed by 1920, there was still considerable political instability and economic dislocation plaguing the country. Revolutionary governments labored to consolidate power, and Mexico was

Mexicans immigrating to U.S., Nuevo Laredo, Mexico, 1912 (Library of Congress)

slow to recover from a decade of economic destruction and disruption. Rural workers in particular suffered from food shortages and low wages. The economic boom in the United States held out the possibility of higher wages and a more secure environment. Mexican workers continued to play a key role in agriculture, mining, and railroads in the southwest. During the 1920s Mexican workers showed greater mobility in employment. While most workers were still located in the U.S. southwest, significant numbers were beginning to appear in states such as Illinois and Ohio. This geographic change in-

dicated another important trend. Mexican workers were increasingly moving out of agriculture into industrial employment; by 1930, approximately 50 percent of Mexican workers lived in urban areas.

During the 1920s the United States tightened its immigration laws but again tended to deal with Mexico as a special case. In 1921 and in 1924, the U.S. Congress passed legislation establishing national quotas for legal immigration but specifically exempted the Western Hemisphere from any quotas. Mexico was the most obvious beneficiary of this exemption. The 1924 act specifically prohibited the entry of any persons with more than 50 percent Indian blood, a restriction that could have had a major impact on emigration from Mexico. U.S. officials got around this restriction by classifying all Mexicans as "white." In an effort to crack down on illegal immigration, the U.S. Congress in 1924 authorized the funds to create the Border Patrol. Although the Border Patrol expanded during the 1920s, it remained difficult to control immigration along the border with Mexico, which is almost 2,000 miles long, with approximately 400 men. Even this limited effort at control drew criticism from business interests in the southwest.

U.S. attitudes toward the role of the Mexican immigrant changed dramatically with the onset of the Great Depression of the 1930s. With unemployment rapidly rising (eventually to reach 25 percent in 1933), there was growing pressure for Americans to hold the jobs that remained. Mexican workers were among the first to be laid off, and there was growing criticism that Mexican workers were a welfare burden. The idea of repatriating Mexican workers was a popular solution to the unemployment problem as well as the welfare burden. Local and state governments sponsored the repatriation of Mexican immigrants, some going voluntarily but others under pressure. Community groups, charitable agencies, and Mexican consular officials also helped to finance repatriation. The federal government had little involvement in repatriation activities but increased its efforts at formal deportation— the removal of an alien who has violated some law. The time and expense of a formal deportation proceeding often led federal officials to encourage deportable aliens to depart voluntarily. Repatriated immigrants received assistance from the Mexican federal government once they reached the border. Repatriates were permitted to bring their possessions into Mexico without paying any duties. The Mexican government also provided free rail transportation from the border to the interior. There were also offers of government

land for repatriates, but these "colonization" schemes involved only about 5 percent of the repatriates and were generally unsuccessful. Repatriation peaked in 1931; by 1935 an estimated 500,000 had been repatriated. Among the repatriates were a number of children born in the United States of Mexican parents who were thus U.S. citizens.

The U.S. economy did not show substantial improvement until the late 1930s when the buildup to and the outbreak of World War II substantially increased the demand for American products. From 1938 to 1941, the United States went from having an unemployment problem to anticipating major labor shortages after U.S. entry into the conflict in December 1941. To deal with the labor shortages in agriculture, the U.S. and Mexican governments in 1942 created the "*bracero*" program. Under the arrangement, the Mexican government permitted the recruitment of Mexican laborers to work in the United States, with the U.S. government guaranteeing the workers' transportation, living expenses, and repatriation costs. The U.S. government, in turn, was to subcontract the Mexican workers to individual employers. The employers had to furnish housing and medical care, as well as reimburse the U.S. government for transportation costs. The 1942 agreement regulated the flow of *bracero* workers until 1947; from 1942 to 1947, more than 200,000 *braceros* entered the United States. The program continued after 1947, but the U.S. government was no longer a guarantor of work contracts. Problems with U.S. employers adhering to contracts led to the reinstatement of the U.S. government as the contract guarantor in 1951. The U.S. government continued in that role throughout the remaining years of the *bracero* agreement. The demand for *bracero* labor remained strong throughout the 1950s but entered a pronounced decline in the early 1960s as mechanization of agriculture accelerated. The *bracero* program officially came to an end on 31 December 1964. During the life of the program, almost 5 mil-

Mexicans entering the United States. United States immigration station, El Paso, Texas. ca. 1938 (Library of Congress)

lion Mexican workers found employment in U.S. agriculture.

Supporters of the *bracero* program claimed—or hoped—that providing a legal mechanism for immigration would reduce the growing problem with illegal immigration from Mexico into the United States. There was little indication that the *bracero* program had that desired effect. One of the earliest criticisms of the program was that many *braceros* were originally illegal immigrants whose status had been legalized by receiving a work contract. During the life of the *bracero* program (1942–1964), the number of illegal aliens apprehended (approximately 5 million) was almost exactly the same as the number of legal workers imported under the system. Critics further claimed that the number of illegal aliens apprehended was considerably less than the number of Mexican workers illegally entering the United States.

Despite the end of the *bracero* program, Mexico continued to be a major source of legal immigrants to the United States. Changes in immigration laws, however, re-

duced Mexico's special status under earlier legislation. Until 1965 Mexico as a Western Hemisphere nation was exempt from any quota restrictions on legal immigration. In 1965 new legislation established a quota of 120,000 immigrants per year for the Western Hemisphere. In 1976 Mexico came under general restrictions limiting any single nation to a maximum of 20,000 immigrants a year. One of the most important changes involving immigration law took place in 1986 with the passage of the Immigration Reform and Control Act (IRCA). IRCA combined two important features: an amnesty provision for illegal immigrants and sanctions for employers who knowingly hired illegal aliens. Under the amnesty provisions, more than 1 million Mexicans illegally in the United States became legal residents with a process for becoming full citizens if they wished. Further changes in immigration laws in 1990 raised Mexico's annual quota to 25,620. Immigration legislation has also typically contained provisions providing for preferential admission of close relatives of U.S. citizens or those who have permanent resident status;

such preferences favor the legal admission of additional Mexicans not covered by the quota systems. The Legal Immigration and Family Equity Act, which went into effect in December 2000, continued and expanded on policies that favored legal Mexican immigration. The net effect of all of this legislation has been to make Mexico an important source of legal immigration to the United States.

Although Mexico figures prominently in terms of legal immigration, the focus in recent decades has been on illegal immigration from Mexico into the United States. Mexico experienced a series of economic and financial crises beginning in the 1970s at the same time that its population was expanding rapidly. The Mexican economy could not generate enough new jobs to absorb new entries into the workforce much less reduce the high rate of existing unemployment. These economic conditions pushed ever larger numbers of Mexicans north to find employment. The Mexican government publicly indicated that it considered this migration to be an important social "safety valve" for Mexico and had no intention of trying to stop it. Mexican workers entering the United States were violating U.S. law but were not doing anything illegal by Mexican standards. Those apprehended by U.S. authorities were typically returned to the border where they could easily recross into the United States. Since the passage of IRCA in 1986, employer sanctions have been in place, but these have been poorly enforced and do not impose any major legal penalties on the illegal immigrants themselves. Although IRCA caused a brief decline in illegal immigration from Mexico, the flow of illegal immigrants soon returned to pre-1986 levels, with U.S. officials making more than 1 million apprehensions a year.

In the late 1980s and early 1990s, discussions relating to the North American Free Trade Agreement (NAFTA) raised the issue of the flow of Mexican workers into the United States. Mexican officials hoped that NAFTA's provisions for a freer flow of goods and capital would also include a freer flow of labor. NAFTA, however, did not call for any major changes in immigration restrictions. With Vicente Fox's assumption of the presidency in 2000, there was renewed emphasis on reaching a new agreement on immigration. Fox came from the Mexican state of Guanajuato, which had a long history of sending large numbers of illegal workers to the United States. Fox called for a legalized, orderly, and circular flow of workers from Mexico to the United States and back. Fox met with President George W. Bush at Fox's ranch in Guanajuato in February 2001. The two agreed to the creation of a high-level commission on migration headed by the U.S. secretary of state and the Mexican minister of foreign relations. The events of 11 September 2001, however, shifted the emphasis to tighter control of immigration into the United States rather than easing controls. U.S. officials specifically cited the porous U.S.–Mexican border as a major security problem. A downturn in the U.S. economy after a lengthy period of prosperity also undercut support for more liberal immigration policies. As of early 2004, the special commission had not produced any major framework for a new immigration agreement.

New trends are evident in the nature of the flow of illegal immigrants to the United States. Traditionally, workers came from rural backgrounds seeking seasonal employment in American agriculture. Most immigrants now come from urban backgrounds and find employment in nonagricultural sectors of the U.S. economy. Workers are also more likely to come intending to stay for a longer period of time or even to settle permanently. Historically, Mexicans were the least likely of the major immigrant groups to seek U.S. citizenship; but there is now a greater trend toward seeking citizenship, primarily because of legal changes. Certain Mexican states still provide a disproportionate number of illegal migrants, but the migratory movement to the United States has become a nationwide phenomenon for Mexico. Illegal immigrants increasingly depend on the services of "coyotes," professional smugglers of people who are often also involved in the drug trade. While officials in Mexico and the United States increasingly see migration as a permanent part of the bilateral relationship, there are a number of experts who believe that this migration must be viewed in a global context and not simply as a bilateral problem involving Mexico and the United States.

While Mexican migration has typically been thought of in terms of outflows of population, migration into Mexico has also played an important role. For most of the nineteenth century, Mexico offered little to attract substantial foreign immigration. Chronic political instability scared off many potential immigrants. Mexico was also experiencing major financial and economic problems; in particular, the landholding system of Mexico, which concentrated land in the hands of a relatively small number of people, discouraged immigration. In attracting foreigners, Mexico found it difficult to compete with other hemispheric nations such as the United States, Canada, Brazil, and Argentina. Early government efforts to promote immigration proved unsuccessful or even disastrous as in the case of Texas in the 1820s and 1830s. The government of Porfirio Díaz (1877–1880, 1884–1911) viewed immigration as a key component in its larger program of modernization. The government provided land and financial support for a number of rural colonization schemes that were almost uniformly unsuccessful. There were also changes in land, mining, and immigration laws aimed at attracting more foreigners to Mexico. While these changes led to a growing foreign role in the economy, they did not bring in significant numbers of immigrants; certainly they did not attract enough immigrants to produce the "civilizing" effect on Mexican society envisioned by Díaz's policymakers. The Mexican census of 1895 indicted that the largest group of foreigners in Mexico were the Guatemalans, not the Euro-

peans the Porfirian elite hoped to attract. The few immigrants who came tended to resist assimilation and tried to isolate themselves from the Mexican population; such foreign "enclaves or colonies" contributed little to the "uplifting" of Mexican society envisioned by the government. Díaz himself became disenchanted with the results of his efforts to promote immigration; in the closing years of his regime, he moved to a more restrictive immigration policy.

The outbreak of Revolution in 1910 led to a lengthy period of political, economic, and social upheaval that not only discouraged immigration but also led to an exodus of foreigners from Mexico. The pronounced nationalist theme of the Revolution often took on an antiforeign character, especially directed against U.S. and Spanish citizens. World War I (1914–1918) further interrupted international migration. The 1920s brought some political stability and national reconstruction, including a modest increase in immigration. The onset of the Great Depression of the 1930s caused further interruption in immigration to Mexico. Faced with a declining economy and the need to absorb some 500,000 Mexican workers repatriated from the United States, the Mexican government moved to a more restrictive immigration policy. The Mexican government wanted to block the influx of indigent immigrants who would only add to the country's financial and economic problems. This more restrictive policy had its exceptions. The administration of President Lázaro Cárdenas (1934–1940) did admit some Jewish refugees fleeing Nazi persecution in Europe and especially refugees from the civil war in Spain (1936–1939). The Spanish refugees in particular had an important influence on Mexico's cultural and intellectual life, as many remained permanently in Mexico. The advent of World War II led to further changes in immigration and to the partial breakdown of the foreign enclaves that had developed in earlier years. In particular the Mexican government—urged on by the United States—

cracked down on activities by the Germans, Italians, and Japanese, even seizing their business operations after Mexico officially entered the war against the Axis powers. During the postwar period, there were further changes in Mexico's attitude toward immigration. Postwar administrations abandoned the idea that immigration could and should play a major role in economic development and modernization. The Ley General de Población (the General Law of Population) passed in 1947 downplayed immigration and emphasized natural population growth as the key to Mexico's economic development. Instead of trying to attract foreign immigrants, the emphasis was on promoting the return of Mexican nationals working outside the country, especially in the United States. The law wanted to admit immigrants who could make an immediate, positive impact on the economy, not those who might compete with Mexicans for jobs. With both its population and its economic problems growing rapidly, Mexico further restricted immigration in 1973. The new legislation made it difficult for immigrants to get permanent work authorization; some groups such as foreign retirees and tourists were specifically prohibited from working while in Mexico. The Mexican government did admit political refugees, even permitting them to work; but this policy encountered problems in the 1980s when political and military upheavals in Central America sent large numbers of refugees into southern Mexico.

For most of its recent history, Mexico has been a net exporter of people on a major scale. The 1990 Mexican census indicated that slightly more than 340,000 foreign citizens resided in Mexico, with U.S. citizens accounting for more than half of the total (200,000). Those figures are dwarfed by the number of persons born in Mexico and living in the United States, a figure that one Mexican government agency currently places at 8.5 million, including some 3 million undocumented workers. Mexico is also an important transit point for non-Mexican workers;

the Mexican government estimates that as many as 200,000 foreign workers a year pass through Mexico en route to a third country, usually the United States. In January 2002 officials in the Mexican state of Hidalgo detained 42 undocumented persons traveling through Mexico to the United States. Of the group, 25 were from Honduras, 14 from Guatemala, and 3 from El Salvador. The migration of workers—in a variety of forms—will continue to play an important role in Mexico's future.

—*DMC*

See also: *Bracero* Program; Fox, Vicente; North American Free Trade Agreement (NAFTA); Revolution of 1910.

References:

Cardoso, Lawrence A. *Mexican Emigration to the United States, 1897–1931: Socio-Economic Patterns.* Tucson: University of Arizona Press, 1980.

Hoffman, Abraham. *Unwanted Mexican Americans in the Great Depression: Repatriation Pressures, 1929–1939.* Tucson: University of Arizona Press, 1974.

Reisler, Mark. *By the Sweat of Their Brow: Mexican Immigrant Labor in the United States, 1900–1940.* Westport, CT: Greenwood Press, 1976.

Mexico, Consejo Nacional de Población (National Council on Population): http://www.conapo.gob.mx/

Import Substitution Industrialization (ISI)

Import substitution industrialization (ISI) was a set of economic policies implemented with varying degrees of emphasis by a succession of presidential administrations from the 1940s to the 1980s. Although Mexico had been fitfully pursuing industrialization since the nineteenth century, ISI had its immediate origins in the financial and economic problems of the closing years of the Cárdenas administration (1934–1940). The expense and economic limitations of his extensive agrarian reform program encouraged Cárdenas to think in terms of a new development approach that placed greater emphasis on speeding up the rate of industrialization. The interruptions in trade patterns caused by World War II accentuated the need for Mexico to produce manufactured products it had been importing previously. The outlines of ISI were clearly present in the policies pursued by the administration of President Manuel Avila Camacho (1940–1946). The Avila Camacho administration used allocation of credit, tax exemptions, and protective tariffs to encourage domestic industrial growth. Foreign investment in Mexico's industrialization was permitted—even encouraged—but with the restriction that Mexican investors must control a majority of the stock in any joint venture.

Although ISI was basically in place by the end of World War II, it is most closely associated with the presidency of Miguel Alemán (1946–1952). Under Alemán, ISI became a fundamental part of the government's vision of a future Mexico as a modern, urban, industrial country. ISI required an active role for the federal government in the economy. In addition to providing credit, licensing imports, and setting the conditions for foreign investment, the central government's ownership of the oil industry provided a source of cheap fuel for Mexico's industrialization. Alemán also emphasized infrastructure development to support the industrialization process, including expansion of the highway system and modernization of railroads. He also used government control of labor unions to keep wages low.

The Mexican government's embrace of ISI took place at a time when other Latin American nations were being encouraged to do the same by the United Nations' Economic Commission for Latin America (ECLA) under the leadership of Argentine economist Raúl Presbisch. The ECLA and Prebisch maintained that the international "terms of trade" (the prices a country receives for its exports vs. the prices it pays for its imports) operated against the Latin American nations, which depended heavily on the exportation of commodities; they identified a long-term trend in the twentieth century in which the terms of

trade worked in favor of nations exporting industrial products and against nations exporting commodities. Therefore, the best development path for the Latin American nations to pursue was industrialization, with the central government playing a key role. (Prebisch would later criticize the excessively protectionist type of industrialization taking place in Mexico and other Latin American countries because it fostered and protected highly inefficient industries.)

The correctness of Mexico's development scheme seemed to be confirmed by the impressive economic statistics registered in the early years of ISI. Mexico experienced striking growth rates, a stable currency, and low inflation. Economists raved about the "Mexican Miracle" and presented Mexico as an example for other underdeveloped countries looking for a development plan. Most Mexicans experienced an improvement in their standard of living, although there were early concerns about a disproportionate amount of the profits of the new industrialization going to a small minority in society. Foreign investment—especially from the United States—poured into Mexico. Rapid industrialization was accompanied by rapid urbanization, with Mexico City at the center of both processes by government design.

By the mid-1960s, there were growing signs that ISI was losing momentum as a development strategy. One of the most important criticisms of ISI was that its benefits were not filtering down to the masses but were being co-opted by a small minority at the top of the social pyramid. There was also concern that ISI was not generating as many new jobs as expected, a major issue given Mexico's rapid population growth. The explosive urbanization accompanying ISI—especially in Mexico City—was creating a host of new social, political, and economic problems. There was continuing uneasiness over the expanding role of foreign capital in the economy. Critics charged that ISI was encouraging the development of inefficient and excessively diversified industries that could contribute little to real economic growth. Opponents of ISI maintained that the policy was producing neglect of the agricultural sector, especially the small communal farmers. Even ECLA's enthusiasm for ISI was on the decline. ECLA feared that long-term implementation of ISI had made it difficult for countries like Mexico to import the capital goods and other industrial inputs needed to continue industrial progress.

President Luis Echeverría (1970–1976) continued ISI but with major modifications. Echeverría moved to silence critics of growing foreign control of the economy by tightening the rules for foreign investors. A law passed in 1973 provided that all business firms must have majority Mexican ownership and established a special commission to enforce the restriction. The law eliminated an earlier provision that permitted foreigners to have 100 percent ownership in certain business fields. Echeverría also called for an end to the indiscriminate granting of tariff protection and subsidies to developing industries. Government protection and assistance would now be extended only to Mexican companies producing lower priced goods for the domestic market. Echeverría's ability to reform ISI, however, was greatly undercut by rising political unrest, recession, and financial crises.

A final decision on the status of ISI was postponed by the temporary economic boom of the late 1970s brought on by new oil discoveries and a rapid increase in oil prices. Instead of using the breathing space to evaluate its basic development scheme, the administration of José López Portillo (1976–1982) went on a massive spending spree, which included the financing of a number of questionable industrial activities, such as a major steel mill at a time when the world market for steel was already glutted. The equally rapid decline in oil prices in the early 1980s sealed the fate of López Portillo and ISI. López Portillo left office amid a long list of financial and economic woes: skyrocketing inflation, unprecedented corruption, capital flight, deval-uation of the peso, high unemployment, and a looming debt crisis.

The administrations of Miguel de la Madrid (1982–1988) and Carlos Salinas de Gortari (1988–1994) saw the final dismantling of ISI. This dismantling reflected both the growing belief that ISI had run its course as well as the need to implement an austerity program required by the International Monetary Fund in order for Mexico to get new loans. Mexico abandoned its protectionist trade policies and even joined the General Agreement on Tariffs and Trade (GATT), a comprehensive agreement calling for a reduction in obstacles to trade. Restrictions on foreign investment were also substantially reduced. The government implemented a program for dispersal of industry. Mexico City under ISI had been a target for industrial growth; under the new reforms, it became a special target for industrial dispersal. Large numbers of government businesses, which had been acquired by the government as a secondary effect of ISI, were sold (a move toward "privatization"). These reforms were continued under Salinas, most notably in the North American Free Trade Agreement, which provided a schedule for eliminating almost all obstacles to trade and investment. ISI had no place in an era where market-guided economies were increasingly in vogue.

—*DMC*

See also: Alemán, Miguel; Avila Camacho, Manuel; Cárdenas, Lázaro; Debt, Mexico's Foreign; Echeverría Alvarez, Luis; Economy; Madrid (Hurtado), Miguel de la; Monterrey Group; North American Free Trade Agreement (NAFTA); Salinas de Gortari, Carlos; Urbanization.

References:

Aguilar Camín, Hector, and Lorenzo Meyer. *In the Shadow of the Mexican Revolution: Contemporary Mexican History, 1910–1989.* Austin: University of Texas Press, 1993.

Bethell, Leslie, ed. *The Cambridge History of Latin America.* Volume 6. *Part I. Economy and Society.* Cambridge: Cambridge University Press, 1994.

Hellman, Judith Adler. *Mexico in Crisis.* 2d ed. New York: Holmes and Meier, 1988.

Niblo, Stephen R. *War, Diplomacy, and Development: The United States and Mexico, 1938–1954.* Wilmington, DE: Scholarly Resources, 1995.

Intellectuals

In Mexico, the role of intellectuals in public life is taken very seriously. Moreover, from conservative statesman Lucas Alamán during the first years of nationhood to turn-of-the-century "scientific" politicians to contemporary rebel leader Subcomandante Marcos, intellectuals have often crossed over into politics where their ability to shape and manipulate political discourse sometimes translates into "real" political power. This has been especially important in a country where, until very recently, electoral politics have provided few opportunities for meaningful political change. While intellectuals have not always advocated progressive causes or democratic reform, their commitment to open inquiry and civil dialogue (at least within elite circles) has more often than not served as a corrective to the power mongering and corruption of public officials. Equally important has been their ongoing engagement with issues of national identity, especially in the years that followed the Revolution of 1910 as policymakers attempted to transform a country fractured by region, ethnicity, class, culture, and even language into a modern nation-state.

Although Mexican intellectuals of all political persuasions made important contributions to nineteenth-century nation-building, political instability undermined efforts to develop coherent and effective public policies. As a result, most of their contributions served not practical but ideological purposes for different factions—liberals and conservatives, federalists and centralists, monarchists and republicans—struggling to legitimize their different agendas. By the late 1860s, with liberal centralists firmly in power (at least at the national level), the opportunity to transform ideological programs into public policy had finally arrived. The intellectual call to arms was delivered, appropriately enough, on Independence Day (September 16) in 1867 by Gabino Barreda (1818–1881), a disciple of French positivist philosopher Auguste Comte. Infused with a positivist faith in the power of science to transform the world, Barreda's "Civic Oration" heralded the advent of "Liberty, Order, and Progress" for Mexico. That same year, he founded the National Preparatory School in Mexico City to train future generations of Mexican leaders, not in traditional subjects such as law, rhetoric, and theology that encouraged discursive haggling and metaphysical musings but in modern scientific methods that could be brought to bear on everything from social engineering to railroad construction. True to its purpose, the National Preparatory School indoctrinated a new generation of Mexican intellectuals whose "scientific" educations inspired the moniker by which they have been known ever since: *científicos* (men of science or technocrats). With Porfirio Díaz firmly in power after 1876, the *científicos* became in-house intellectuals who provided crucial technological and ideological expertise to a regime committed at least in its slogans to "Order and Progress" (if not Liberty) and "Administration over Politics."

The most respected of the *científicos* was Justo Sierra (1848–1912). A student and later teacher at the National Preparatory School, founder of the National University, Supreme Court Justice, and minister of education, the peripatetic Sierra was also a prominent historian. His 1905 biography of former President Benito Juárez helped consolidate the liberal version of Mexican history, which still appears in most history textbooks (and helped downplay President Díaz's disagreements with his popular predecessor), while his monumental *México: Su evolución social* (Mexico: Its Social Evolution, 1910), written in conjunction with *científico* colleagues, sought to ground the national project in historical and sociological context. Sierra's contribution on political evolution was especially noteworthy for its warning that Mexico was falling behind in the international "struggle for life" and risked absorption by "fitter" nations like the United States. This Darwinian argument (likely inspired by English social theorist, Herbert Spencer) blamed the nation's "backwardness" on political immaturity, economic shortsightedness, and social inequality. These attributes in turn provided a convincing and convenient argument for Díaz's authoritarian regime since, according to Sierra, only prolonged stability could ensure the economic development needed to foster the growth of democratic institutions. Chief among those institutions was public education, the sine qua non of responsible citizenship and a prerequisite of "Liberty" (which regime propagandists had dropped from Barreda's original slogan). This liberal faith in the transforming power of education—so evident in Sierra's public service—caused him to reject the racist doctrines of influential European thinkers like the Comte de Gobineau and Mexico's own Francisco Bulnes and to insist that, with proper schooling and better living conditions, Mexico's much-maligned Indians could become "social assets" and its hotheaded *mestizos* (people of mixed race) could become a positive "dynamic force."

Because of their ideological contributions to the Porfirian regime and because several of them reaped huge profits from government positions, the *científicos* attracted bitter criticism from independent intellectuals and a disaffected citizenry who despised their intellectual pretensions and self-serving development schemes. (Sierra was generally exempted from these attacks because of his personal integrity, liberal commitment to education, and advocacy of gradual democratization.) For example, Yucatecan sociologist Andrés Molina Enríquez (1868–1940), although a positivist himself, blamed Mexican underdevelopment not on racial inferiority or lack of education, but on a neofeudal hacienda system that favored large landholders over small proprietors, an arrangement that blocked the development of a rural middle class by reducing *campesinos* (rural agricultural workers) to peonage and poverty. His provocative analysis of *Los grandes problemas nacionales* (The Great National Problems, 1909), published on the eve of the Revolution, argued for extensive land reform even as prominent *científicos* such as Finance Minister José Limantour and Yucatecan Governor Olegario Molina were amassing huge estates. Meanwhile, in Mexico City, positivism itself was under attack as young intellectuals belonging to the *Ateneo de la juventud* (Young Athenians) began publishing essays that criticized not just the material excesses of the Porfirian regime but its materialist philosophy as well. Nor did they restrict their criticism to philosophical disputes in newspapers and literary journals: they sought substantive revisions of the positivist curriculums of the National Preparatory School and the National University and opened an experimental University of the People in Mexico City to take their humanistic message to lower middle-class and working-class Mexicans with no access to these elite institutions.

The outbreak of the Revolution in 1910 hampered efforts at institutional change but did little to dampen these new intellectual trends. Molina Enríquez's book, for example, inspired drafters of the Constitution of 1917 to write agrarian reform into the new national charter. And, in 1916, a young anthropologist, Manuel Gamio (1883–1960), published *Forjando patria* (Forging the Fatherland), which preached a doctrine of social inclusion that would form the backbone of official policies toward Indians and other ethnic minorities for years to come. Former members of the Ateneo also weighed in on the crucial question of national identity. In *Visión de Anáhuac* (Vision of Anáhuac, 1917), Alfonso Reyes (1889–1959) argued that the country's unique environment, in particular its high desert plateaus and "transparent" air, had produced a collective identity that united Mexicans despite obvious differences of class, ethnicity, and language. Antonio Caso (1883–1940) provided a humanistic philosophy in *La existencia como economía, como desinterés y como caridad* (Existence as Economy, as Disinterest, and as Charity, 1919) through which the crude self-interest and materialism of Porfirian positivism might give way to more communitarian forms of social organization—a welcome, optimistic message in the wake of a devastating civil war.

In addition to his intellectual contributions to the national project, the most prominent of the ex-Ateneo triumvirate, José Vasconcelos (1881–1959), revived the public intellectual as public servant role that Sierra had played so well. First, as rector of the National University and then as Mexico's first Secretary of Education, Vasconcelos's programs had a huge impact in the years immediately following the Revolution, especially his "cultural missions" to the nation's previously ignored rural areas and his promotion of the muralist movement, which brought powerful visual images to the Mexican masses and international prestige to its government sponsors. The temperamental Vasconcelos quit government service in 1924 to run unsuccessfully for governor of Oaxaca and went into American exile shortly thereafter. Disgusted with politics, he returned to philosophy. In two influential books, *La raza cósmica* (The Cosmic Race, 1925) and *Indología* (1926), Vasconcelos argued (among other things) that the mixing of different races in Latin America was producing a "cosmic race"—"the definitive race, the synthetical race, the integral race, made up of the genius and the blood of all peoples and, for that reason, more capable of true brotherhood and of a truly universal vision." These books quickly became foundational texts for a modern Mexican (and Latin American) identity that celebrated its racial hybridity in the face of European racist doctrines that denigrated people of color as biologically inferior and people of mixed race as embodying the worst traits of both races. Along with Gamio's *Forjando Patria* and Reyes *Visión de Anáhuac*, Vasconcelos's works also supplied a philosophical underpinning for post-Revolutionary

indigenista policies that sought to redeem Mexico's much abused Indian population through assimilation into a multiracial society defined by *mestizaje* (race mixture).

The Ateneo's influence was strongest on the self-proclaimed "Generation of 1915" despite (or perhaps because of) their training at the National Preparatory School and the National University. Initially, the Generation of 1915 expended most of their energies advocating for university autonomy—one of Vasconcelos's pet causes—in order to guarantee an open intellectual environment free from governmental meddling and several served under him at the Secretariat of Education in the early 1920s. Despite these youthful demonstrations of group solidarity and a common commitment to active public service, the most prominent members of the Generation of 1915 took very different paths. Vicente Lombardo Toledano (1894–1968), for example, went from Vasconcelos protégé to labor organizer. In 1936, encouraged by prolabor president Lázaro Cárdenas, he founded the Confederation of Mexican Workers (CTM), the most powerful labor umbrella organization of the time with over a million members by the 1940s. In 1947, as the official party became increasing conservative under president Miguel Alemán, he moved into opposition politics as founder of the Popular Party. The Popular Party vice-presidential candidate, another Generation of 1915 alumnus, Narciso Bassols (1897–1959), also had a distinguished career in public service—dean of the National University Law School, secretary of education (1930–1934), high-ranking diplomat—before breaking with the official party. Yet another Generation of 1915 luminary, Manuel Gómez Marín (1897–1972), followed a similar path from eager Revolutionary to political opponent, although to the opposite side of the political spectrum. During the 1920s, he had served as the Bank of Mexico advisor charged with revising Mexico's outdated credit and tax laws but, disillusioned by Vasconcelos's defeat in the 1929 presidential election, he left the official ranks to found the conservative National Action Party (PAN), the party that would ultimately defeat the Institutional Revolutionary Party (PRI) in the 2000 presidential elections.

The most traditionally academic member of the Generation of 1915 was Daniel Cosío Villegas (1898–1976). Educated at some of the world's most prestigious universities—Harvard, London School of Economics, Ecole Libre des Sciences Politiques—and a Vasconcelos protégé, Cosío Villegas focused his energies on higher education rather than politics and government service. In 1929, he helped created the economics department at the National University, and then in collaboration with an illustrious group of Spanish émigrés (in exile from the fascist regime of dictator Francisco Franco), he helped found the Colegio de México, which would become (and remains) one of Latin America's premier graduate schools. To help disseminate scholarly work, he started an important publishing house, Fondo de Cultura Económica, and a series of academic journals, including *Historia Mexicana*. Like many of his generation, Cosío Villegas grew increasing skeptical of the Revolutionary legacy and in 1947, he published a damning critique, *La crisis en México* (Crisis in Mexico) that accused the official party of betraying the spirit of the Revolution by putting its own interests ahead of the country's need for social justice and political democratization. To get at the historical roots of the nation's current democratic crisis, he embarked on his crowning achievement as a scholar, a five-volume *Historia Moderna de México* (History of Modern Mexico) that took nearly twenty years and a team of prominent historians to complete—a work that continues to set the standard for historical research on Mexico.

Cosío Villegas was not the only one concerned about the Mexican condition at midcentury, nor were the Generation of 1915 the only ones concerned about national identity. In 1934, philosopher Samuel Ramos (1897–1957) published a provocative study of Mexican society, *Perfil del hombre y la cultura en México* (Profile of Man and Culture in Mexico), in which he posited a national "inferiority complex" produced by a variety of factors, some environmental (the overwhelming landscape that dwarfed human achievements), some historical (especially the "birth trauma" of conquest), and some sociological (a society characterized by the touchy *pelado* or underclass urban male with his lingering resentments and exaggerated masculinity). The psychoanalytic approach to national identity found its greatest expression in a stunning collection of essays by poet Octavio Paz (1914–1998) with the suggestive title, *El laberinto de la soledad* (Labyrinth of Solitude, 1950). In these essays, Paz grappled with the social pathologies he thought plagued Mexican identity: failure to come to grips with the past, impenetrable masks that covered up repressed feelings and desires, latent masculine insecurity and violence manifested in everyday profanity, the Revolution as a carnival characterized by violent excess, social inversion, and an orgiastic coming together that only partially compensated for everyday lives of alienation and solitude. The elegance and explanatory power of *El laberinto de la soledad,* to say nothing of the poetry that won him the 1990 Nobel Prize, thrust Paz into the national limelight, a position he used to agitate for the democratization of Mexican society and against "extremism" from either side of the political spectrum until his death in 1998.

By the middle of the twentieth century, a new generation of intellectuals had begun to appear on the scene. Like Paz, this generation would keep its distance from the ruling party, accepting official honors and an occasional ambassadorship but without unduly compromising its critical distance. The brightest new star was a young writer, Carlos Fuentes (1928–), whose brilliant novels, such as *La region más transparente del aire* (Where the Air Is Clear, 1958) and *La muerte de Artemio Cruz* (The Death of Artemio Cruz, 1962), helped launch a "boom" in Latin

American literature that would garner worldwide accolades. In Mexico City literary circles, his new journals, such as *Medio Siglo* (Mid Century) and *Revista Mexicana de Literatura* (Journal of Mexican Literature), provided support and notoriety for up-and-coming writers.

Thanks in part to the support of high-powered intellectuals like Paz and Fuentes, by the 1960s, the intellectual scene had expanded to include yet another generation of public intellectuals like cultural critic *par excellence,* Carlos Monsiváis (1938–). According to Monsiváis, the 1960s represented "the new spirit, the rejection of conventions and prejudices, the creation of a new morality . . . the advance of social militants . . . their longing for another Renaissance." Certainly, their more critical and more playful take on perennial issues such as national identity suggested that the intellectuals' role in Mexican society was changing despite official efforts at co-optation. Moreover, mostly friendly competition among literary "mafias" headed by "capos" like Paz, Fuentes, and Monsiváis made the 1960s something of a golden age for Mexican intellectual life (at least in the capital).

The 1968 government massacre of student and other demonstrators at Tlatelolco's Plaza of the Three Cultures in an effort to pacify Mexico City before the Summer Olympics put a dramatic end to the celebratory mood. Paz immediately resigned his ambassadorship to India in protest and, in 1970, published a book, *Posdata,* in which he denounced the nation's return to violence and advocated for democratization of political and social life. In a collection of essays, *Días de guardar* (Days of Remembrance, 1970), published that same year, Monsiváis wrote that "after a misfortune as unjust, irreparable, and unpunished, as the massacre of Tlatelolco, things were never again the same. . . . Certitude disappeared, security was eliminated . . . fear obliged us to dispense with intelligence, skepticism was confused with cynicism that was mixed in turn with a sense of abandonment that contaminated an indifference that

was blended with lethargy." His colleague and fellow "new chronicler" Elena Poniatowska (1933–) followed suit with a devastating literary montage of eyewitness accounts of the massacre, *La noche de Tlatelolco* (The Night of Tlatelolco, 1971), that further undermined the credibility of the regime and widened the gap between the government and most intellectuals. These acts of witness and outrage made Tlatelolco a defining moment for a generation. Certainly, Paz, Monsiváis, and Poniatowska have maintained their political independence and their the pressure on the ruling party ever since. (Paz died in 1998.)

In an effort to win back intellectuals and relegitimize the regime's commitment to Revolutionary ideals, later presidents actively courted their goodwill with leftist pronouncements (and regular visits to Fidel Castro), diplomatic appointments, and government subsidies for academic research. In 1970, President Luis Echeverría appointed Carlos Fuentes ambassador to Paris and, in 1984, President José López Portillo opened the National Research Center that still continues to fund 2,000 "favored" intellectuals each year. These efforts, however, have never been completely successful as occasional "clients" like Fuentes have lent their support only to policies they actually endorsed and continue to openly criticize authoritarian politics, corruption, and the ravages of global capitalism.

During the 1970s, serious political rifts developed between leftist intellectuals focused on social justice, such as Fuentes and Monsiváis, and liberals focused on political democratization, such as Octavio Paz and his protégé Enrique Krauze (1947–). But, although infighting persisted (and persists), by the 1980s, intellectuals from across the political spectrum began to unite in support of an expansion of a civil society, independent of government control. The catalyzing event was probably the 1982 Mexico City earthquake, in which ordinary citizens banded together to cope with the catastrophe in the face of official apathy and ineptitude. A seemingly endless series of economic crises and a growing sense among intellectuals that the ruling party was beyond redemption further reinforced these attempts at solidarity. Monsiváis, who published an influential book on Mexico's emerging civil society, *Entrada libre: cronicas de la sociedad que se organiza* (Free Admission: Chronicles of a Society that Is Getting Organized, 1987), noted that "it was the first time that intellectuals of all the various ideological tendencies came together to take a common position in defense of democracy." Even Krauze, whose attacks on Fuentes and other leftists could be quite bitter, admitted that "we are on ambiguous terrain now, in a period of transition. Many intellectuals have not been able to rid themselves of old ideas and relationships to power, but others are realizing that independence is better."

At the turn of the twenty-first century, Mexican intellectuals are more independent, more vocal, and more diverse than ever before—although Mexico City continues to dominate the country's intellectual life. Political liberals like Krauze, who assumed Paz's directorship of the influential journal *Vuelta* (and changed its name to *Letras Libres*), have continued to agitate for Western-style democracy and against what they perceive to be extremism on the part of leftist intellectuals. Like Sierra and Cosío Villegas before him, Krauze has turned to history and especially "biographies of power" in order to understand Mexico's current situation and to warn against traditional authoritarian solutions to social problems. Frequent *Vuelta* and *Letras Libres* contributor, poet-economist Gabriel Zaid (1934–) has taken a similar political tack but with a bit more humor. In books like *El progreso improductivo* (Unproductive Progress, 1978) and *La economía presidencial* (The Presidential Economy, 1987), Zaid has attacked political and economic centralization with charts, graphs, and wicked sarcasm—suggesting, for example, that the government levy a tax on the traditional *mordida* (bribe). Nor does he spare the hypocrisies of the political left. "Mexico is a country where radical-

ism increases with income," he points out, "To be a leftist and live in the Pedregal, have a house in Cuernavaca, travel abroad . . . is something forgivable." At the same time, the reclusive Zaid tempers his critique of gentleman marxists with an even greater disgust for Mexico's new bourgeoisie, whose conspicuous consumption and slavish adherence to American models of social organization and economic, he finds particularly reprehensible.

The traditional left is well represented by public intellectuals like political scientist Jorge Castañeda (1953–), a frequent contributor (along with Monsiváis) to the muckraking journal *Proceso* and longtime critic of authoritarian politics. A desire for political change, however, has forced Castañeda to reconsider some of the left's agenda: he has participated regularly on government advisory panels, supported probusiness PAN candidate, Vicente Fox, in the 2000 presidential race, and even served as Fox's foreign minister until 2003. Another prominent leftist activist is Homero Aridjis (1940–), perhaps the most versatile of Mexico's current crop of public intellectuals, whose many careers include poet, novelist, political scientist, and environmental activist. As leader of the Group of 100, founded in 1985 to protest Mexico City's many environmental problems (especially air pollution), Aridjis has taken on environmental issues as diverse as nuclear power and the disruption of whale breeding grounds. While he, too, has accepted government positions as ambassador to the Netherlands and Switzerland, it has done little to temper his criticism of authoritarian politics. In a 1987 interview, for example, he insisted that "by raising questions about abuse of power, corruption, and favoritism, we have established a direct linkage between politics and ecology in Mexico." Nor is he unaware of the dilemma facing public intellectuals in Mexico: "for people like us, the main problem is how to defend ourselves against the temptations and invitations of the government. It is traditional for the intellectual to represent public opinion, but the system is always seeking ways to disarm any serious movement."

Still, as with Castaneda, frequent negotiations with the government have softened his critique. When, after a public protest by the Group of 100, President Miguel de la Madrid invited them to lunch, he acknowledged that "in some other place, maybe they would have thrown us in jail."

One leftist intellectual and political activist who has resolutely maintained his distance from the regime is Zapatista leader, Subcomandante Marcos, who serves as the public voice (his face is always covered by a ski mask) of a rebel army that still occupies territory in the southern state of Chiapas. Marcos's clever parables about Mexican politics and society combined with his brilliant use of modern technology, especially the Internet, has proven quite effective at limiting government repression of the Zapatista movement and at undermining the regime's cynical claims to represent the Revolutionary legacy of Emiliano Zapata. Moreover, his example has helped energize less radical (or at least more pacifistic) and widely respected leftist intellectuals like Monsiváis and Poniatowska to open a public dialogue about long-standing social inequalities and the nature of Mexican society.

—RMB

See also: Anthropology and Archeology; *Científicos;* Fuentes, Carlos; Marcos, Subcomandante; *Mestizaje* and *Indigenismo*; Monsiváis, Carlos; Novel of the Revolution; Novel since 1960; Paz, Octavio; Poetry; Poniatowska, Elena; Vasconcelos, José.

References:
Stabb, Martin S. "The Essay," in David William Foster, ed., *Mexican Literature: A History,* pp. 305–340. Austin: University of Texas Press, 1994.

J

Jalisco (State)

Located in west-central Mexico, Jalisco contains the cosmopolitan city of Guadalajara (Jalisco's capital and Mexico's second largest city) and the well-known resort of Puerto Vallarta. Lake Chapala, Mexico's largest natural lake, is also located in Jalisco, and its northern shore is populated with thousands of American and Canadian residents, most of whom have chosen to retire in Mexico because of the climate and the low cost of living. Jalisco is acknowledged as the home of two of Mexico's most distinctive cultural inventions: mariachi music and tequila. Much of the state's historical importance is due to Guadalajara, which since the colonial era has served as the economic center of western Mexico while rivaling Mexico City as a cultural hub. During the last decade of the twentieth century, the Guadalajara region became Mexico's "Silicon Valley" as a boom in the electronics industry and information technology took hold. Meanwhile, the tequila industry struggled to keep pace with the rising global demand for this quintessentially Mexican product.

Jalisco's pre-Columbian heritage is evident today in the several Indian languages (including Nahuatl, Huichol, and Mixtec) that are still spoken in the state. The Spanish Conquest of this part of Mexico's western frontier, however, was hardly accommodating for indigenous peoples. The Spanish search for gold, silver, and good seaports brought them to Jalisco, which became a part of the province of Nueva Galicia. Nuño Beltrán de Guzmán led a brutal campaign against the Indians of Nueva Galicia, spurring Indian resistance and, eventually, the Mixtón War of 1541–1542. Many of Jalisco's Indians were parceled out as a labor force for the area's expanding hacienda system while Franciscan (and later Dominican and Jesuit) missionaries sought converts among them.

In 1560, Guadalajara (which was first established by the Spaniards in 1531 and relocated several times because of pressure from Indian groups) became the capital of Nueva Galicia. It emerged not only as a political and commercial center, but also as a center for the Roman Catholic Church. With the Spanish advance into northwestern Mexico, and the development of the Pacific coast region, Guadalajara became a commercial hub and a way station for people and goods. The city also earned its reputation as a center of intellectual and cultural activity, and it became the home of Mexico's second oldest university, the University of Guadalajara.

Although Guadalajara's commercial activity dominated the economy of Jalisco, agriculture and cattle ranching also emerged as important activities during the colonial period. Sugarcane, tobacco, cotton, and wheat were among the crops produced. By the end of the eighteenth century, the region of Tequila (just northwest of Guadalajara) was becoming wealthy through the exploitation of its agave plants. Mescal wine and, more important, tequila (derived from Jalisco's signature blue agave) were produced from the fermented juices of these plants. During the nineteenth century, Jalisco families, including the Cuervo and Sauza clans, participated in the production of tequila and responded to a growing demand for their product; a demand that reached into California during the gold rush of the mid-1800s. Thus Jalisco became the birthplace of Mexico's most famous drink, which gave rise to an industry that has steadily increased in importance.

Jalisco became a state in 1823, just two years after Mexican independence. For a time, it included Nayarit, Colima, and a portion of Zacatecas within its borders. For much of the nineteenth century, the new state was plagued by unrest and thousands left because of insecurity and economic destruction. Jalisco was a center of the struggle between Mexico's dominant political factions, and the state was particularly resistant to the liberal laws that sought to curtail the historically strong position of the Mexican Roman Catholic Church. In 1861, the bishop of Guadalajara was expelled from Mexico because of his resistance to such liberal reforms. During the French intervention in Mexico, the capital city of Guadalajara was occupied from 1864 to 1866. Jalisco also struggled to contain banditry during the nineteenth century. Manuel Lozada, an Indian leader from Nayarit, was a particular problem. He attempted to capture Guadalajara in 1873.

By the end of the nineteenth century, Jalisco remained an agricultural state in which land concentration and debt peonage were typical. Industry, including distilleries for mescal along with soap and textile factories, was concentrated in the Guadalajara region, and commerce struggled to recover from several decades of unrest. Mining, never as significant in Jalisco as in neighboring Zacatecas, experienced a decline as prices and capital investment fell. When the region of Tepic (today's Nayarit state) was designated a federal military district, Jalisco also lost a large piece of its territory, along with the lucrative textile factories located there.

Jalisco weathered such challenges, however, and its economic development continued during the era of Porfirio Díaz (1876–1911). Railroad lines aided in that development, linking Guadalajara with western Mexico, Mexico City, and the Tequila region. Political stability, not always peacefully achieved, also facilitated growth. Under the governorship of Francisco Tolentino, repression was used to heel Jalisco's banditry. At the same time, the Roman Catholic Church (long a vocal participant in Jalisco politics) regained some of the privileges lost during the nineteenth century and became an increasingly visible presence through the formation of local Catholic organizations and, on the national level, the National Catholic Party (PCN).

Some have suggested that the strong (and conservative) presence of the Roman Catholic Church in Jalisco prevented that state from experiencing the Revolution that began in 1910. Indeed, there was little organized protest against the Díaz dictatorship and a lukewarm response to Francisco Madero's call for rebellion in 1910. In the aftermath of Madero's victory, the National Catholic Party made a strong showing in state elections, and many in the party supported Victoriano Huerta, a Huichol Indian and a native of Jalisco, who overthrew Madero in 1913. With Huerta's own fall and the emergence of the Constitutionalist movement, Revolutionary leaders captured Guadalajara and, under Governor Manuel M. Diéguez, the Church's power was directly challenged. Guadalajara's archbishop, Francisco Orozco y Jiménez, who defied Diéguez's anticlerical decrees and openly opposed Mexico's new Constitution (which included significant restrictions on the Church's role in education, the economy, and politics) was expelled from Mexico on Diéguez's orders.

The tension between Church and State ensured that Jalisco would be a center of the Cristero Rebellion, a conflict that affected parts of Mexico from 1926 to 1929 and that was precipitated by official attempts to enforce the anticlerical provisions of Mexico's Constitution. Within Jalisco, Governor José Guadalupe Zuna's efforts to rein in the Church encouraged Archbishop Orozco y Jiménez to support this armed movement. Indeed, the archbishop joined armed rebels in the mountains of Jalisco. Even after the conflict had been settled, Orozco y Jiménez remained defiant. He was again expelled from Mexico in the early 1930s for attempting to foment another rebellion against the Mexican government, which was increasingly criticized by the Church and the National Catholic Party for its pursuit of "socialist" goals, especially in the realm of education.

Jalisco's political situation had begun to stabilize by the 1940s, and during World War II, its economy received a boost as local industry responded to wartime demand for clothing. Guadalajara, the center of most industry, grew markedly. Jalisco's rural areas, however, grew only marginally after the mid-twentieth century. Only the tequila industry and the wood products industry have injected Jalisco's rural economy with any real dynamism, and the broader trend has been migration to Guadalajara, which in population and economic productivity has come to dwarf the rest of the state. (The only other area to experience significant growth during the latter half of the twentieth century has been Puerto Vallarta, which developed as a tourist resort beginning in the 1960s and now welcomes millions of visitors each year.) During the 1990s, the Guadalajara region experienced yet another boom as a flourishing electronics industry attracted thousands of workers and gave the area a reputation as Mexico's Silicon Valley. The success of the 1990s was marred, however, by the arrival of the drug trade (which claimed the life of Cardinal Jesús Posadas Ocampo in 1993) and by a huge gas explosion in 1992, which claimed the lives of over 200 residents of Jalisco's capital city.

As the twenty-first century began, Guadalajara and its industrial base were showing signs of strain. Overpopulation had given rise to slums surrounding the city, and an economic slowdown was causing significant layoffs in Jalisco's electronics, textile, and footwear industries. In the countryside, the tequila industry was struggling with its own success, as the demand for this product, now truly global in scope, strained the supply of blue agave plants (which take up to twelve years to mature).

—SBP

See also: Cristero Rebellion; Religion; Revolution of 1910.
References:
María Muría, José. Breve historia de Jalisco. Mexico City: Fondo de Cultura Económica, 1994.
Martínez Limón, Enrique. Tequila: The Spirit of Mexico. New York: Abbeville Press, 1998.
Official state web site: http://www.jalisco.gob.mx

Juárez, Benito (1806–1872)

President from 1858 to 1872, Benito Juárez was a Zapotec Indian born in the village of Guelatao, Oaxaca. An orphan at age three, Juárez lived with his uncle until he was twelve, when he moved to the state capital of Oaxaca City. Juárez spoke little Spanish but found a home with a Franciscan lay brother who promoted his education. Juárez briefly attended the seminary in Oaxaca City but abandoned his ecclesiastical career for the legal profession. He worked his way through law school, receiving his law degree in 1834.

As he was completing his studies, Juárez was also becoming more active in politics. In the 1828 presidential campaign, he supported the candidacy of Vicente Guerrero, a liberal hero of the wars for independence. As

A statue of Benito Juárez, reformist President of Mexico between 1858 and 1872, Mexico City (Nancy Carter/North Wind Picture Archives)

liberals and conservatives contested for power at the national level, Juárez embarked on his own political career when he became a member of the city council of Oaxaca City in 1832. The following year he was elected to the state legislature. Juárez continued to practice law, often defending impoverished Indians without charging fees. During the war with the United States (1846–1848), Juárez served in the national Congress and as interim governor of the state of Oaxaca.

In 1848 Juárez won a four-year term as governor of Oaxaca. As governor, he promoted rural education, engaged in public-works projects, reduced the state bureaucracy, and brought some order to state finances. Shortly after Juárez completed his term, General Antonio López de Santa Anna returned to power in Mexico City. Santa Anna returned to power as a conservative and centralist, which placed him at odds with Juárez, a prominent provincial liberal. Santa Anna also had a personal grudge against Juárez; in 1848, following the military loss to the United States, Santa Anna sought refuge in Oaxaca but was turned away by Governor Juárez. "Emperor" Santa Anna had Juárez arrested and later sent into exile.

Settling in New Orleans, Juárez joined other leading liberal exiles, such as Melchor Ocampo, who were plotting the overthrow of Santa Anna's government. In 1854 liberals in Mexico under the leadership of veteran guerrilla leader Juan Alvarez revolted against Santa Anna. The liberals in New Orleans provided military supplies to the rebels, and in 1855 Juárez returned to Mexico to join Alvarez as a political advisor. The liberal movement triumphed in August 1855, making Juárez a national political figure.

Juárez received the position of minister of justice in the government of provisional President Juan Alvarez. One of the main goals of the liberals was equality before the law for all Mexicans. This meant the elimination of legal privileges (*fueros*) held by the clergy and the military under which all legal matters involving those two groups would be heard in their

court systems rather than in the regular civil or criminal courts. As minister of justice, Juárez's name was attached to the first major piece of legislation to come out of the liberal revolt. The Ley Juárez (the Juárez Law)—issued in November 1855—restricted the jurisdiction of military and church courts to cases involving violations of military or church law. Civil or criminal cases involving members of the military or the Church would be tried in the regular courts. The law adversely affected two of the most important interest groups in Mexican society at the time. The law aroused such strong opposition that Juárez was forced to resign his position. Despite the uproar, the Ley Juárez was incorporated into the new liberal Constitution that went into effect in early 1857. Juárez in the meantime spent most of 1856 and 1857 serving once again as governor of Oaxaca.

In elections held under the new Constitution, Juárez was elected president of the Supreme Court. With no position of vice-president, Juárez constitutionally was also first in line to succeed to the presidency of Mexico in the event of the incapacity of the newly elected President Ignacio Comonfort. Comonfort was a moderate caught between the more radical liberals and the conservatives. In December 1857 Comonfort joined in a conservative rebellion under General Félix Zuloaga, which called for an end to the Constitution of 1857 but the continuation in office of Comonfort with emergency powers. The alliance between Comonfort and Zuloaga was brief. In January 1858 Zuloaga dumped Comonfort and proclaimed himself president. From the standpoint of Mexican liberals, the presidency was now vacant, meaning that Juárez automatically succeeded to the position.

With two presidents and two governments, Mexico embarked on a three-year civil war, known as the War of the Reform. The conservatives attempted to rule from Mexico City, while the liberals established their government in the key port of Vera Cruz. The war led to more radical actions by the liberals (The Laws of the Reform), including the nationalization of all property held by the Roman Catholic Church. Early fighting favored the conservatives, but by 1860 the liberal forces increasingly controlled the situation. The conservatives were particularly hurt by two failed efforts to take the liberal capital of Vera Cruz. In December 1860 liberal forces under General Jesús González Ortega retook Mexico City, and in January 1861 Juárez returned as president to the national capital he had fled three years earlier.

One of the first things confronting Juárez was new presidential elections. Juárez had served as president for more than three years, but he had succeeded to the position rather than being elected to it. Although Juárez might have seemed the logical choice for the presidency, the liberals were badly divided, and he faced major opposition from General Jesús González Ortega and from the leading radical liberal, Miguel Lerdo de Tejada. The death of Lerdo during the campaign helped to swing the election to Juárez. Even then, a resolution calling for Juárez's resignation was defeated by only one vote in the lower house of the Mexican Congress in September 1861.

The new Juárez administration also faced major financial problems. Even before the War of the Reform, government finances were a mess; during the war, two governments were running up expenses. Finally, Juárez was forced to take an action he had considered during the war but rejected: the suspension of debt payments. In July 1861 Juárez announced a two-year suspension in payments on the government's debt. One of the main fears of the Juárez administration in canceling the debt was the threat of foreign intervention. In more normal times Juárez might have been able to turn to the United States for financial and possibly military assistance to head off European intervention. But these were not normal times. Mexico had just ended a civil war, and the United States had just started one. In October 1861 England, France, and Spain signed an agreement

calling for a joint military intervention in Mexico for the sole purpose of collecting debts.

The intervention actually began in late 1861, with the landing of Spanish troops at Vera Cruz. It soon became obvious that the French had political designs that went well beyond debt collection. The French emperor, Napoleon III, had conceived of a plan to place an "emperor" in Mexico under his control. British and Spanish forces soon abandoned the intervention, leaving the French to go on alone. As the overconfident French forces marched from Vera Cruz toward Mexico City, they suffered a surprising defeat at the major city of Puebla on 5 May 1862, the famous Cinco de Mayo. A reinforced French Army won the Second Battle of Puebla in May 1863, forcing Juárez and his government to abandon Mexico City. Just before evacuating Mexico City, Juárez was granted extraordinary powers by the Congress to conduct the resistance against the French intervention.

Mexican conservatives and high officials of the Roman Catholic Church welcomed the intervention and the new ruler it produced, the Austrian Archduke Maximilian. After his arrival in May 1864, Maximilian soon proved a disappointment to both groups. Maximilian proclaimed a general amnesty and endorsed the liberal measures of the Juárez government. Maximilian even directed a conciliatory policy toward Juárez, who rejected his peace overtures. Juárez, in the meantime, presided over a government on the run, waging a decentralized guerrilla war against French and conservative forces. Imperial forces controlled most of the major urban areas but could not inflict a decisive defeat on liberal guerrilla forces. The Juárez government also enjoyed continuing diplomatic recognition by the United States. Once the U.S. Civil War ended in the spring of 1865, U.S. diplomatic pressure on the French—including the threat of military action—quickly escalated. The French also felt threatened at home by the rising power of Germany, and their Mexican intervention had proved a financial failure as well. As French troops began to withdraw in late 1866, Maximilian's empire quickly collapsed.

The liberal military victory led to one of the most controversial acts of Juárez's lengthy political career. In a final stand at Querétaro in May 1867, Maximilian himself had been captured by liberal forces. Juárez decided that Maximilian would be tried by a military court for treason; after a brief trial, Maximilian was sentenced to death. His execution on 19 June 1867 provoked widespread international criticism of Juárez, especially when Juárez later delayed the release of Maximilian's body to Austrian officials.

When Juárez returned to Mexico City on 15 July 1867, he had to contend with the aftermath of almost a decade of civil war, foreign intervention, economic destruction, and financial dislocation. As had been the case in 1861, Juárez had to address almost immediately the question of his presidential position. Elected to a four-year term in 1861, his presidential term was extended in late 1865 until such time as the French could be expelled. With the French gone, Juárez stood for election in 1867, defeating two military opponents: General Jesús González Ortega, who had opposed Juárez in 1861, and General Porfirio Díaz, a political newcomer who had distinguished himself in the resistance against the French. Although Juárez won the election, his simultaneous effort to strengthen the presidency failed, and he found a powerful new enemy in Díaz.

Although Juárez was beginning what was, in effect, his third term, his first two periods in office had involved a lengthy civil war and a foreign intervention that prevented him from effectively ruling large parts of the country. The period from 1857 to 1867 saw a decentralization of power. Local, state, and military officials by default took over many of the central government's functions, including tax collection and distribution of nationalized Church property. Juárez wanted to reassert the authority of the central government, strengthen the presidency, and place greater emphasis on economic development. One of his most important measures was to reduce the size of the army from 60,000 to 20,000 troops. This move not only lessened the possibility of military intervention in political affairs; it also cut down on government expenses. To promote law and order in the countryside, Juárez expanded and reorganized the Rurales, a rural police force he had established earlier. The Rurales could also be used to influence elections.

After 1867, Juárez placed greater emphasis on economic development and educational reform. The desire for improved transportation was an issue that found support across the political spectrum. One of the major accomplishments of Juárez's administration was the completion in 1872 of the Vera Cruz to Mexico City railroad, which had been started in 1837. To bring the railroad to completion, Juárez provided cash subsidies and overlooked the fact that the railroad company had supported Maximilian's empire. Juárez also called for a restructuring of public education along more practical and scientific lines. The key figure in this educational reform was Gabino Barreda; Barreda's studies in France had exposed him to the "positivist" philosophy of Auguste Comte, who stressed the application of scientific methodology to society's problems. Educational policy called for primary education to be free and mandatory, but financial limitations restricted the impact of educational reforms.

Juárez also moved to lessen tensions between Church and state, which had been at the center of so much of the controversy in the 1850s and 1860s. This new accommodation saw Juárez reduce the strict enforcement of the reform laws in return for the Roman Catholic Church reducing its public criticism of Juárez's policies. The emergence of this new relationship was clearly demonstrated when the archbishop of Mexico participated in the public ceremonies commemorating the completion of the Mexico City–Vera Cruz railway line.

Juárez's efforts to centralize power in the presidency and to perpetuate himself in office continued to cause divisions in liberal ranks. With presidential elections scheduled for 1871, Juárez decided to seek yet another term in office. He faced two strong liberal opponents: General Porfirio Díaz and Sebastián Lerdo de Tejada, brother of Miguel Lerdo de Tejada, who had contested for the presidency against Juárez in 1861. When none of the candidates obtained a majority of the votes in the regular presidential election, it was the responsibility of the Congress under the Constitution of 1857 to select the president. Although Congress chose Juárez for another term, his failure to win the election outright demonstrated the president's eroding political support. Díaz soon launched an unsuccessful revolt, criticizing Juárez's indefinite reelection to the post. Lerdo was elected president of the Supreme Court, making him first in line to succeed to the presidency. The political uproar caused by Juárez's continuation in office soon proved unnecessary; on 18 July 1872 Juárez died suddenly from heart problems. Lerdo succeeded to the presidency, with an increasingly impatient General Díaz awaiting his turn for the presidency.

Historical evaluations of Juárez are made difficult by the mythology that has grown up around him, a mythology often promoted by the Mexican government. In a time of civil war and foreign intervention, Juárez was a powerful symbol of national unity. As an Indian, Juárez epitomized the importance of the indigenous heritage in Mexican history. As a reformer, he embodied the search for legal equality and modernization. The mythical Juárez is essentially the pre-1867 Juárez. The mythology largely ignores or plays down the post-1867 Juárez who promoted centralization, presidentialism, and perpetuation in office. Juárez was a practical, and often ruthless, politician who—like many political leaders—came to think of himself as indispensable to the cause. In this case, the cause was liberalism, an evolving and often disputed concept, which both shaped and was shaped by Juárez.

—*DMC*

See also: *Científicos;* Díaz, Porfirio; Education; Elections; Religion; *Rurales.*

References:

Hamnett, Brian. *Juárez.* New York: Longman, 1994.

Perry, Laurens Ballard. *Juárez and Díaz: Machine Politics in Mexico.* DeKalb: Northern Illinois University Press, 1978.

Roeder, Ralph. *Juárez and His Mexico: A Biographical History.* 2 vols. New York: Viking Press, 1947.

Scholes, Walter V. *Mexican Politics during the Juárez Regime, 1855–1872.* Columbia: University of Missouri Press, 1957.

Kahlo, Frida (1907–1954)

"Frida," her husband and mentor Diego Rivera once wrote, "is the only example in the history of art of someone who tore out her own breast and heart to tell the biological truth of what she feels in them." Rivera often played loosely with facts, but the visual evidence for this insight is indisputable. Indeed, the biological vividness of Frida Kahlo's images is riveting, especially her self-portraits with their thick eyebrows, slight moustache, umbilical cords, surgical apparatus, and bleeding hearts. In recent years, after a life and artistic career spent in Rivera's formidable shadow, the power of her unique and decidedly female vision has captured the imagination of artists throughout the world and propelled her to the forefront of modern Mexican art. Now, at the turn of the twentieth century, as Rivera's influence wanes a bit, Kahlo's reputation and influence continue to grow.

Magdalena Carmen Frida Kahlo Calderón was born on 6 July 1907 in Coyoacán (now part of Mexico City). In a 1936 painting, *My Grandparents, My Parents, and I (Family Tree)*, Kahlo depicts herself as a giant, naked young girl, standing in the courtyard of the house her father built, the beloved *Casa Azul* (blue house), and holding a red ribbon that connects her to parents and grandparents. Over the girl's left shoulder is her German-Jewish-Hungarian father, a recent immigrant to Mexico and professional studio photographer, and his European parents; over her right, her Mexican mother, a devout Roman Catholic obsessed with respectability, and the obviously *mestizo* (part-Indian) grandparents. Kahlo's obsession with origins and belonging would stay with her throughout her life. This lifelong struggle to define herself would make Kahlo one of the most self-consciously Mexican artists of the twentieth century.

The first defining moment in Kahlo's life—the bus accident that nearly killed her, resulted in 32 separate surgical operations, turned her life into a constant struggle with pain, and contributed to her early death at age 48—came on 17 September 1925, when she was just nineteen years old. Until that moment she had been a gifted student at the prestigious National Preparatory School with a vague interest in art and a penchant for doodling in her notebooks. The prolonged inactivity that followed her accident turned vague interest into a vocation. "I was bored as hell," she wrote later to an American gallery director, "in bed with a plaster caster cast . . . so I . . . stoled [sic] from my father some oil paints, and my mother ordered up for me a

Studio of artist Frida Kahlo (The Art Archive / Dagli Orti)

special easel because I couldn't sit [up], and I started to paint" (quoted in Herrera, *Frida,* pp. 63–64).

The second defining moment was a 1928 meeting with the by-then world-famous painter and muralist Diego Rivera. Although they probably met at a party given by a mutual friend, both reconstructed the event as an artistic encounter that began with a fearless Frida accosting the great man hard at work on his Department of Education murals. "Without more ado," she later recalled, "I said: Diego, come down [he was working on a scaffold]. . . . Look, I have not come to flirt or anything even if you are a woman chaser. I have come to show you my painting. If you are interested in it, tell me so, if not, likewise, so that I will go to work at something else to help my parents." To this audacious demand, Rivera replied: "In my opinion, no matter

how difficult it is for you, you must continue to paint" (quoted in Herrera, *Frida,* pp. 87–88). The next year, they married; Rivera was forty-three, Kahlo twenty-two. Although Rivera continued to chase women, including Frida's sister (she retaliated with several affairs of her own); and although they separated, divorced, and remarried between 1935 and 1940; their admiration and support for each other's artistic vision never diminished.

As artists, however, Rivera and Kahlo could not have been more different. Rivera's huge murals favored the grand statements on the evolution of the human spirit or the mobilization of the masses. Kahlo's art was intimate, often personal: her favorite genre was the portrait, her favorite model was herself. Some critics have labeled her unique style "primitivistic" in part because it deliberately drew on traditional Mexican folk art, especially religious ex-votos that depicted scenes of divine intercession and usually included an explanatory text. For example, a 1940 *Self-Portrait with Cropped Hair* painted during her divorce from Rivera included a song lyric with music painted across the top of the picture that read "Look, if I loved you, it was for the hair / Now that you're bald, I love you no longer." Several other self-portraits show the artist in traditional Mexican dress—the Tehuana costume was a favorite because of the region's reputation for strong women—sometimes with images painted on her forehead (Rivera, death) to represent her thoughts. Other pictures, her gruesome 1935 picture of a murderer standing over his murdered lover, *A Few Small Nips,* and the 1938–1939 *Suicide of Dorothy Hale,* a New York socialite, drew on the sensational broadside tradition of José Guadalupe Posada. Also, the 1940s *The Dream* includes a traditional Judas figure wired with firecrackers for the popular Easter celebration.

But if Kahlo's style drew on Mexican popular culture, it was far from primitive. When the French surrealist poet André Breton, a renowned art theorist, encountered her work on a 1938 trip to Mexico, he declared that she had achieved "pure surreality" and arranged to show her work in Paris. Moreover, her paintings demonstrated a sophisticated sensibility and sureness of technique that, regardless of its borrowings from popular culture, was clearly crafted for the cosmopolitan connoisseur. The 1939 *The Two Fridas,* for example, showed the artists (she's holding hands with herself) dressed in traditional Mexican fashions with exposed hearts, a popular religious motif. Nevertheless, the hearts' anatomical correctness, the surgical clamp, and the ambivalent symbolism produced a decidedly modern effect. Kahlo's art was authentically Mexican to be sure, but it was a Mexicanness grounded in the present rather than mired in the past. Appropriately enough, her last public act before her death on 13 July1954 was to protest the United States' intervention in Guatemala. In the second half of the twentieth century, an era increasingly obsessed with the constructed nature of personal identities, Kahlo's unique approach to both life and art has become more influential than ever, especially in the wake of a well-received Hollywood film version of her colorful life, featuring Mexican film star Salma Hayek.

—*RMB*

See also: Art since 1950; Posada, José Guadalupe; Rivera, Diego.
References:
Billeter, Erika. *The Blue House: The World of Frida Kahlo.* Houston TX: Museum of Fine Arts, 1993.
Frida. Directed by Julie Taymor. USA, 2002.
Herrera, Hayden. *Frida: A Biography of Frida Kahlo.* New York: Harper & Row Publishers, 1983.
Zamora, Martha. *Frida Kahlo: The Brush of Anguish.* Trans. Marlyn Sode Smith. San Francisco: Chronicle Books, 1990.

Korean War

During World War II, Mexico had worked closely with the United States economically and was one of only two Latin American nations to furnish combat troops. Once the war ended, Mexico wanted to maintain the close wartime economic ties but was reluctant to maintain the close military ties of World War II and was unenthusiastic about U.S. efforts to create closer military links in the name of hemispheric defense. Mexico was disenchanted with the U.S. emphasis on strategic concerns and doubted the seriousness of the communist threat to the hemisphere in general or to Mexico in particular.

After the North Korean invasion of South Korea in June 1950, Mexico supported the U.S. position on the major resolutions relating to the war in the U.N. General Assembly and offered to provide foodstuffs and medical supplies for the conflict. The United States, however, wanted a Mexican troop commitment, hoping that a Mexican contribution of troops might encourage contributions from other Latin American countries. In April 1951, U.S. officials made a formal request to Mexican Foreign Minister Manuel Tello that Mexico contribute a division to the fighting in Korea. Tello replied that public opinion in

Mexico would not support the sending of Mexican troops outside of Mexican territory and emphasized the problem of sending Mexican troops to Korea with presidential elections scheduled in Mexico for July 1952. The Mexican Senate would have to approve any commitment of Mexican forces outside the country, a process that would almost certainly spark a major debate over the constitutionality of such a move as well as raise the volatile question of national sovereignty. Tello also indicated that Mexico would not be able to bear the cost of supporting a division in the field since the United States had a policy of requiring reimbursement for any expenses incurred by the U.S. government in equipping, training, transporting, or maintaining troops of other nations in connection with Korean service.

The United States continued to work for a promise of Mexican troops, hoping that the growing economic ties between the two countries might produce a change in Mexico's position. The United States had granted Mexico "most-favored-nation" status in trade, even though no trade agreement was in force. The United States also backed loans to Mexico from the U.S. Export-Import Bank and the World Bank, as well as a growing program of technical assistance under the U.S. Point IV Program. The United States made a final effort to enlist Mexican military support at a meeting in Mexico City in early 1952. The United States wanted to reach an agreement with Mexico under the U.S. Mutual Security Act of 1951, which provided U.S. military assistance in exchange for a promise from the recipient country to participate in "missions important to the defense of the Western Hemisphere." Mexican officials were so nervous about the appearance of making a military commitment that the joint press release announcing the meeting put the emphasis on improving Mexico's defensive capabilities rather than on hemispheric defense. When negotiations got under way in February 1952, the Mexican delegation again cited domestic political and constitutional problems that prevented the signing of a standard military assistance agreement. After negotiations reached an impasse, the United States delegation announced that it was returning to Washington for further consultation. Mexico never signed a military assistance pact and never provided troops for U.N. operations in Korea.

While the United States unsuccessfully attempted to gain Mexico's military support, Mexico continued to provide diplomatic support for U.S. efforts. One of the most important developments in this area was Mexico's proposal at the United Nations aimed at breaking the deadlock over repatriation of prisoners of war, which had become the single biggest obstacle to an armistice. The proposal was never voted on by the General Assembly, but its submission did help to promote an eventual resolution of the POW controversy. Although Mexico never provided the kind of military support that the United States thought appropriate, it did provide important economic and diplomatic support for the goals being pursued by the United States and the United Nations in Korea. It was perhaps unrealistic for U.S. officials to expect that Mexico would make a major military contribution to the Korean War, which Mexico considered distant and nonthreatening. Mexico had also undergone a lengthy process of reducing military influence in politics; Mexican politicians feared that military involvement in Korea ran the risk of returning the military to politics with a larger portion of the national budget.

—DMC

See also: Foreign Policy; Militarism; United States, Relations with; World War II.

References:

Dozer, Donald Marquand. *Are We Good Neighbors?: Three Decades of Inter-American Relations, 1930–1960.* Gainesville: University of Florida Press, 1959.

Parkinson, F. *Latin America, the Cold War, and the World Powers, 1945–1973.* Beverly Hills, CA: Sage Publications, 1974.

L

Labor Movements

The regime of President Porfirio Díaz (1877–1880, 1884–1911) actively pursued the industrialization of Mexico. Despite these efforts to accelerate the industrialization process, by 1910 only about 15 percent of Mexico's workforce was made up of nonagricultural workers. These industrial workers had to deal with long hours, low pay, and dangerous working conditions; they enjoyed none of the benefits that workers today typically expect: medical coverage, unemployment benefits, workers' compensation, life insurance, retirement plans, and social security. There was no network of charitable organizations and governmental agencies to provide workers with assistance. To cope with this hostile environment, workers in Mexico did what workers in many industrializing societies did; they formed mutual aid societies. These mutualist groups offered some protection for the workers in the absence of a more formal social and economic "safety net." Workers regularly contributed a small amount of their pay to these societies, which in turn would assist them if the workers encountered employment or health problems. In many countries, these societies evolved into or provided the foundation for true labor unions, organizations that represent and bargain collectively on behalf of the workers. The

Díaz administration permitted the development of mutualist societies, especially if they had ties to the government. He strongly opposed, however, the development of true independent unions.

The Partido Liberal Mexicano (the Mexican Liberal Party, or PLM) led some of the earliest efforts to organize Mexican workers. The PLM advocated government regulation of working conditions, an eight-hour workday, a guaranteed minimum wage, and the abolition of child labor. The PLM tried to organize workers in Mexico and in the southwestern region of the United States. The Díaz administration refused to tolerate such an independent-minded and radical group and forced the PLM leadership into exile in the United States. Even with its leaders in exile, the PLM inspired major strikes by copper workers in Cananea, Sonora, in 1906 and by textile workers in Rio Blanco, Veracruz. In both cases the Díaz regime used force to break the strikes. The PLM saw itself as leading a revolutionary movement, not simply a labor movement. It never created a national labor organization, and its leaders were constantly harassed by officials in both Mexico and the United States.

The outbreak of Revolution in 1910 gave workers new opportunities to organize for political and economic purposes. The first major labor organization to develop in the wake of the Revolution of 1910 was the Casa del Obrero Mundial (the House of the World Worker, or COM). The COM had strong anarchist tendencies, which led to internal dissension over whether it should use political action or employ direct action, such as strikes and sabotage. The COM established branch offices throughout Mexico, but it was not a national labor organization because it did not have centralized control. The COM was regarded as too radical for the first president to emerge from the Revolution, Francisco Madero (1911–1913). Madero suppressed the COM and its newspaper and expelled its foreign leaders from the country. After the overthrow of Madero in 1913, his successor—General Victoriano Huerta—continued the suppression of the COM. The ouster of Huerta in July 1914 ushered in a chaotic period of civil war among Revolutionary factions. The COM returned to action and eventually decided to align itself with the Revolutionary faction known as the Constitutionalists under the leadership of Venustiano Carranza and Alvaro Obregón. The COM even provided troops for the Constitutionalists—known as the "Red Battalions"—which played an important role in the eventual victory of the Constitutionalists over the forces led by Emiliano Zapata and Francisco "Pancho" Villa.

If the COM was expecting to benefit from its support of the Constitutionalists, it was soon disappointed. After the Constitutionalists prevailed in the civil war, Carranza quickly disbanded the "Red Battalions," seeing them as a potential threat to his consolidation of power. The end for the COM came when it helped to provoke a strike by workers in the Federal District. Carranza responded by sending troops to occupy COM headquarters in Mexico City, closing down COM branches throughout the country, and arresting COM leaders. The COM never recovered.

The passage of the Constitution of 1917 provided a new direction to the labor move-

ment in Mexico. Article 123 of the Constitution guaranteed a number of benefits for workers, including the right to organize and bargain collectively. Convinced that labor organization was unavoidable, Carranza, as the first president elected under the new Constitution, decided to promote labor organization but to ensure that the organization was under government control. Carranza was no more disposed to accept an independent labor movement than Porfirio Díaz had been. In 1918 the federal government sponsored a national convention of labor leaders who founded the Confederación Regional Obrera Mexicana (the Regional Confederation of Mexican Workers, or CROM). The person elected to head the new organization as its secretary general was Luis Morones, a former member of the COM who had risen to prominence as a labor leader in Mexico City. Although CROM policy placed the emphasis on direct action rather than political action, Morones was convinced that the CROM needed to be involved politically. In 1919 Morones set up the Partido Laborista (the Labor Party, or PL) as the political arm of the CROM. In the growing struggle for power between Carranza and Obregón in 1919–1920, the CROM and the PL sided with the eventual winner, Obregón.

Obregón, who was president from 1920 to 1924, was prepared to reward Morones and the CROM for their support but only within his broader views of the reconstruction of the nation after almost a decade of destruction and dislocation. In return for CROM support for his policies, Obregón provided a number of benefits for the CROM. The CROM received funds directly from the government and also was permitted to extract "contributions" from federal employees. The government gave the CROM control of the federal committees for arbitration and conciliation; these committees rendered decisions on recognition of unions, the legality of strikes, and helped to resolve labor-management disputes. The government also intervened to block the rise of rivals to the CROM. In 1921 more radical labor leaders formed the Confederación General de Trabajadores (the General Confederation of Workers, or CGT) in open opposition to the CROM and its pro-government position. The anarcho-communist views of the new CGT were hardly in tune with the policies of Obregón, who needed the support of the private sector and even foreign capital to promote economic recovery. When the CGT sponsored a strike by transit workers in Mexico City in 1923, the Obregón administration sent in troops, created a CROM-affiliated union to organize the workers, recruited strikebreakers from Mexico City jails, and arrested more than 100 CGT leaders and members.

The CROM expanded and the CROM leadership prospered under the protection of the government. The peak of the CROM's power and influence came during the administration of President Plutarco Elías Calles (1924–1928). Calles appointed Morones to the cabinet-level position of minister of industry, trade, and labor, the government ministry charged with supervising labor affairs. CROM leaders were elected to governorships in two states and to several seats in the national Congress. The rise of the CROM began with a presidential election in 1920; the decline of the CROM began with another presidential election in 1928. The power of the CROM was so great that Morones himself considered campaigning for the presidency in 1928. Morones had to abandon his presidential aspirations when a constitutional amendment permitted former president Obregón to run for reelection. The CROM compromised itself politically by originally opposing the constitutional amendment permitting reelection and then waffling in its public support for Obregón; after initially supporting Obregón, the CROM and its political affiliate, the Labor Party, withdrew their support for his candidacy. When President-elect Obregón was assassinated in August 1928, suspicion fell on Morones and the CROM for involvement in the killing. All CROM leaders holding positions in the Calles administration resigned, including Morones as minister of industry, trade, and labor. The final blow to the position of the CROM came when it unsuccessfully opposed the efforts by Calles to form an official party to try to prevent civil war in the wake of Obregón's assassination.

The decline of the CROM did not lead immediately to the rise of another national labor organization to assume its position in the alliance with the government. Defections from the CROM were the central features of the labor movement in the years immediately after 1928. The authoritarian and corrupt rule of Morones and the post-1928 decline of the CROM led to a series of defections from the organization. Two former CROM leaders were particularly important: Fidel Velázquez Sánchez and Vicente Lombardo Toledano. Velázquez broke with the CROM in January 1929, establishing the Federación Sindical de Trabajadores del Distrito Federal (the Federated Union of Workers of the Federal District, or FSTDF). The FSTDF united most of the major unions in the Federal District that had broken with the CROM. Lombardo broke with the CROM in 1932, creating what he called the "Purified" CROM in 1933, a collection of unions that had splintered from the CROM. Also competing to unionize workers in the early 1930s were a much subdued CGT and a labor group organized by the Communist Party, the Confederación Sindical Unitaria de México (the United Union Confederation of Mexico, or CSUM).

In 1933 Velázquez and Lombardo combined efforts to establish a new national labor organization, the Confederación General de Obreros y Campesinos de México (the General Confederation of Workers and Peasants of Mexico, or CGOCM). The CGOCM was the basis for an even larger labor organization, the Comité Nacional de Defensa Proletaria (the National Committee for Proletarian Defense, or CNDP) founded in 1935. The CNDP played a prominent role in the growing power struggle between former President Calles and President Lázaro

Cárdenas (1934–1940). Calles had mostly controlled the political affairs of Mexico from 1928 to 1934 through a series of puppet presidents. When Cárdenas balked at being the latest puppet and tried to assert his independence, a major political crisis developed. Cárdenas turned to the CNDP to mobilize labor support for his government against Calles, whose only source of labor support was the much-weakened CROM.

As the conflict between Calles and Cárdenas neared a conclusion, a labor convention called earlier by the CNDP met to form yet another and bigger labor organization. In February 1936, labor leaders formed a new national labor organization, the Confederación de Trabajadores de México (the Mexican Workers' Confederation, or CTM). The new organization had familiar leadership. The convention selected Vicente Lombardo Toledano as secretary general and Fidel Velázquez as organizational secretary. The CTM represented some 3,000 organizations with approximately 600,000 members. With CTM support, President Cárdenas brought a definitive end to the conflict with Calles; Cárdenas exiled both Calles and Morones in April 1936.

A series of strikes by railroad, electrical, and petroleum workers in 1936–1937 tested the budding alliance between the CTM and the Cárdenas administration as well as the ability of the CTM to contain the labor movement within government-approved bounds. When the interests of the workers clashed with the interests of the government, the CTM leadership made it clear that it would side with the government. This show of loyalty was rewarded in 1938 when the alliance was institutionalized with the reorganization and renaming of the official party. The new official party was called the Partido de la Revolución Mexicana (the Party of the Mexican Revolution, or PRM). The PRM was divided into four sectors along corporate lines: agrarian, labor, military, and "popular." Cárdenas assigned the dominant role in the labor sector to the CTM. This preferential position

came with a price. The CTM had already started the process of organizing the peasants and government employees. Cárdenas, however, blocked further organizational efforts among these two groups by the CTM, fearing that the CTM might become too powerful and threaten the government's dominant role in the alliance between the state and labor. Cárdenas organized the peasants into a separate group, the Confederación Nacional Campesina (the National Peasant Confederation, or CNC); the CNC was larger than the CTM. Government employees also ended up in a labor organization beyond the CTM's control, the Federación de Sindicatos de Trabajadores al Servicio del Estado (the Federation of Unions of Workers in Service to the State, or FSTSE). Both the CNC and the FSTSE were established in 1938, when the CTM was incorporated into the official party.

Like the CROM before it, the CTM faced internal dissension and defections as it tried to harmonize the interests of the workers, the confederation leadership, and the government. The demands of World War II and later the government's postwar development policy both required that workers' wages be kept low and that labor peace be maintained. During the war the CTM attempted to follow a no-strike policy and in 1945 signed a labor industrial pact pledging to work with business in pursuit of government development policies. The apparent willingness of the CTM leadership to sacrifice workers' wages to help business and the government led to massive defections from the CTM by the industrial unions: the oil workers, the railway workers, the electrical workers, and the miners. The long-simmering rivalry between Lombardo and Velázquez for control of the CTM came to a head in 1947–1948 with the expulsion of Lombardo and his followers for their "communistic" views.

The government continued its policy of undercutting labor unions that represented potential rivals for the CTM. In 1947 defectors from the CTM organized an alternative national labor organization, the Confederación Unica de Trabajadores (the Sole Confederation of Workers, or CUT). The CUT drew support from the industrial unions, such as the railway workers and oil workers, which had defected from the CTM. The CUT denounced the CTM as corrupt, rejected cooperation with the government, and demanded wage increases, which the government considered a threat to its development plans. The government responded by using force to impose a progovernment leader on the union of railway workers, which had led in the establishment of the CUT. The CUT never recovered from this attack and later merged with another labor organization, which unsuccessfully challenged the domination of the CTM. The intervention by the government in the internal affairs of the railway workers union was only one of several instances in which the administration of President Miguel Alemán (1946–1952) used repression and rigged elections to put progovernment, pro-CTM leaders into office in independent-minded unions. The alliance between the government and the CTM grew stronger but with the CTM assuming an even more subordinate position.

In 1950 Fidel Velázquez returned to his position as secretary general of the CTM, a position he would hold until his death in 1997. Velázquez assured the dominant position of the CTM by maintaining close ties to both the government and the official party, now known as the Partido Institucional Revolucionario (the Institutional Revolutionary Party, or PRI). Velázquez became an indispensable part of the PRI elite and even served two terms in the national Congress as the PRI senator from the Federal District (1946–1952, 1958–1964). The relationship between the Velázquez-led CTM on the one hand and the government and the official party on the other was not static. The economic boom of the 1950s and 1960s gave way to a series of economic crises beginning in the 1970s that have continued to the present. The economic crises forced the govern-

ment to abandon its postwar development policies in the 1980s and shift to a much different market-guided approach to development. Fidel Velázquez sometimes criticized this new approach, but nevertheless he steadfastly kept the CTM behind the government's shifting policies even at the sacrifice of the workers' standard of living. The government generally supported the CTM against rival union organizations but also had to show some flexibility in the face of the changing economic situation. For example, in the 1970s the government permitted the development of a non-CTM labor organization, the Unidad Obrera Independiente (the Independent Worker Unity, or UOI) to organize workers in the automobile, textile, chemical, and transportation industries. The UOI was used to block organizational efforts by a more radical and more independent labor organization, the Frente Auténtico del Trabajo (the Authentic Labor Front, or FAT). Although the government generally favored the CTM, it was prepared to let non-CTM labor organizations develop as long as they operated within the existing state-labor coalition.

As Mexico's financial and economic problems continued into the 1990s, there were new efforts in the labor movement to establish national organizations to rival the CTM. In 1995 dissident labor leaders established the Foro Sindicalismo ante la Nación (the Labor Forum before the Nation, or Foro). The Foro was mildly critical of the government's economic policies and called for the creation of a rival organization to the CTM. The Foro played a key role in the creation of the Unión Nacional de Trabajadores (the National Workers' Union, or UNT). The UNT called for the reversal of the market-guided economic policies being pursued, the protection of government social programs, and the independence of unions from both government and PRI control. As the UNT was organizing, the CTM's Fidel Velázquez died in 1997 after a half century at the head of the labor organization. The death of Velázquez called into question the role of the CTM in the government-labor alliance and the close connection between the CTM and the PRI, which was also seeing its dominant position slide in the 1990s. The death of Velázquez and the decline of the PRI almost certainly signal a change in relations between the government and the labor movement. Whether that change will involve the rise of a truly independent labor movement is still not clear.

—DMC

See also: Alemán, Miguel; Avila Camacho, Manuel; Calles, Plutarco Elías; Cárdenas, Lázaro; Confederación de Trabajadores de México (CTM); Confederación Regional Obrera Mexicana (CROM); Constitutionalists; Import Substitution Industrialization (ISI); Lombardo Toledano, Vicente; Morones, Luis; Obregón, Alvaro; Partido Liberal Mexicano (PLM); Partido Revolucionario Institucional (PRI); Velázquez Sánchez, Fidel.

References:

Caulfield, Norman. *Mexican Workers and the State: From the Porfiriato to NAFTA.* Fort Worth: Texas Christian University Press, 1998.

Collier, Ruth Berins. *The Contradictory Alliance: State-Labor Relations and Regime Change in Mexico.* Berkeley: University of California Press, 1992.

Middlebrook, Kevin J. *The Paradox of Revolution: Labor, the State, and Authoritarianism in Mexico.* Baltimore: Johns Hopkins University Press, 1995.

Lacandón

A tropical rain forest in southeastern Chiapas, the Lacandón Forest emerged during the second half of the twentieth century as a major center of agrarian unrest. During the 1980s the area became the home of the Zapatista movement, and in 1994, the Lacandón gained attention as the heartland of the Zapatista rebellion against the Mexican government. From the colonial period, when it was a remote Indian frontier, to the twentieth century, when it became the scene of significant conflict, the Lacandón has witnessed an ongoing struggle over labor, land, and resources.

As a frontier area for Spanish colonists, and then as a part of Mexico's sparsely populated and underdeveloped southern border region, the Lacandón received relatively little attention until the nineteenth century. On the eve of the Spanish Conquest, the area was home to members of the Maya-Quiché Indian group, which resisted colonization. Throughout the colonial period, and into the nineteenth century, Indians from other areas of Chiapas, the Yucatán, and neighboring Guatemala joined this native group, seeking refuge from the labor and tribute demands that accompanied the Spanish Conquest. Today's Lacandón Maya, who are estimated to be some 500 in number, are descendents of these refugees (particularly those from Guatemala) and refer to themselves as "Hach Winik" (True People).

After Mexican independence, national leaders took a greater interest in the country's southern region, which looked like it might become a part of Guatemala for a brief period of time. The Lacandón's mahogany trees promised wealth for those who would exploit them, and by the late nineteenth century, timber barons (both Mexican and foreign) were engaged in the process of extracting the trees and shipping them to markets in Europe and the United States. Nineteenth-century laws, including those implemented during the dictatorship of Porfirio Díaz, encouraged the timber industry by opening up unoccupied lands for settlement and cultivation. On the eve of the Mexican Revolution, concessions to Mexicans and foreign businessmen (including Americans) had helped the industry lay claim to much of the Lacandón, which was still a sparsely populated area. Labor for the timber companies was largely servile, with Indians from Chiapas and beyond secured as workers through the system of debt peonage. At the same time that the timber industry developed, additional lands were cleared to produce sugarcane, coffee, and cacao. Thus began the deforestation that would intensify over time and contribute to the Lacandón's explosive history.

As with the rest of Chiapas, the Lacandón experienced the Mexican Revolution primarily as a continuation of elite competition for land and resources. Isolated popular struggles did occur, however, and in 1912 workers in the Lacandón revolted against conditions in the lumber camps. Chiapas's elites predictably resisted the land reform that was promised by the new Mexican Constitution, and continuing land concentration eventually converted over half of the state's Indians into landless workers. Meanwhile, the Lacandón continued to play its historic role as a safety valve. In the several decades after the Revolution, indigenous peoples from other parts of Chiapas streamed into the forest, seeking land. Most had been robbed of their lands elsewhere as Chiapas's economic elites monopolized the state's resources. Many of the new immigrants attempted to regularize their claims to Lacandón lands, and several utilized that land to cultivate coffee and raise cattle. With additional development, the deforestation problem in the Lacandón continued apace.

By the 1970s, the population of the Lacandón had more than tripled, even as the prospects for new migrants were increasingly uncertain. President Luis Echeverría (1970–1976) added to the volatile situation by announcing another round of agrarian reform for Mexico and promising government subsidies to those who would settle lands communally. The government also set aside land (in the form of a national park) for the Hach Winik. At the same time, a state-owned timber company secured a ten-year concession to exploit mahogany and cedar trees in the Lacandón. This concession affected the Hach Winik, who agreed to sell lumbering rights on their lands (an arrangement that still exists as of this writing). Finally, in 1978, Echeverría's successor, José López Portillo, declared 200,000 hectares of the Lacandón a biosphere reserve. The efforts of Echeverría and López Portillo, coupled with the continuing interests of the commercial timber industry and the continuing immigration of dispossessed Indians, heightened tensions in an area that could no longer sustain the subsistence and commercial demands of its inhabitants. Violent evictions of people from their lands, sometimes aided by the Mexican military, became a part of the Lacandón's history, encouraging Indians to organize for protection.

The virtual lack of state control in the Lacandón (as compared with the more highly populated areas of Chiapas) facilitated the growth of grassroots organizations that began in earnest in the 1970s. Some of this activity was encouraged by Samuel Ruíz, a proponent of Liberation Theology who became Bishop of Chiapas in 1960. Ruíz and his followers in the Roman Catholic Church encouraged Indians to organize and protect their lands and their culture. The Lacandón also hosted several leftist groups whose leaders came primarily from outside Chiapas. All of these groups experienced repression, and many had been eliminated by the end of the 1970s.

During the 1980s, the Lacandón experienced yet another wave of settlement as the government renewed its efforts to secure and populate its southern border. Civil war in neighboring Guatemala, which caused thousands of refugees to stream into Mexico, helped motivate such government efforts. At the same time, people from other areas of Chiapas who had been evicted from their own lands, continued to migrate to the Lacandón. Now plagued by regular and often-violent clashes over land and resources, Chiapas came increasingly into the public eye, and the Mexican government was compelled to address the agrarian issue. Yet even as the country's leaders designated several areas, including the Lacandón, for the redistribution of lands, they were moving toward a free trade agreement with the United States and Canada. Thus Mexico embraced neoliberal ideas and announced an end to agrarian reform and to government subsidies for agricultural activities. The official end to agrarian reform (announced in 1992) was especially problematic for inhabitants of the Lacandón since many lacked titles to their lands and thus did not have the legal means to control their holdings.

It was in this context that the Zapatista National Liberation Army (EZLN) emerged in Chiapas. With the help of Subcomandante Marcos, a *ladino* (non-Indian) from central Mexico, the EZLN found ready recruits in the Lacandón, particularly among those who had experienced, or were threatened with, eviction from their lands. Indian membership and leadership grew naturally from earlier grassroots activism, and it was from this Lacandón base that Marcos and the Zapatistas declared a rebellion against the Mexican government, deliberately timed to coincide with the day on which the North American Free Trade Agreement (NAFTA) took effect: 1 January 1994.

Throughout the Zapatista rebellion, which has sought to improve the conditions and enhance the rights of the indigenous peoples of Chiapas, the Lacandón has been a center of rebel activity and organization. It has also been the scene of counterrevolutionary repression by the Mexican military and by the numerous paramilitary organizations that are supported by economic elites. At the same time, the Lacandón has hosted international meetings sponsored by the EZLN and designed to draw attention to the Zapatista movement, to indigenous rights, and to the costs of neoliberalism. The first such meeting, the National Democratic Convention, was held in 1994 and drew thousands of people. Interestingly, while the Zapatistas have succeeded in recruiting to their cause most of the indigenous people in the Lacandón, the Hach Winik have resisted the EZLN, which they have treated with their characteristic wariness toward outsiders.

As Mexico enters the new millennium, the Lacandón remains a volatile area. With its long history as a refuge for the dispossessed, this once-remote section of southern Mexico has experienced the twentieth century as one of increasing conflict and violence. As its resources have been overexploited, and its natural base destroyed, the Lacandón has become a center of agrarian unrest in Mexico. It has also become a center of popular activism and rebellion.

—*SBP*

See also: Chiapas; Ruíz, Bishop Samuel; Zapatista National Liberation Army (EZLN).

References:

Benjamin, Thomas. *A Rich Land, a Poor People: Politics and Society in Modern Chiapas.* Albuquerque: University of New Mexico Press, 1989.

Boremanse, Didier. *Hach Winik: The Lacandón Maya of Chiapas, Southern Mexico.* Albany, NY: Institute for Mesoamerican Studies, 1998.

Collier, George A., and Elizabeth Lowery Quaratiella. *Basta!: Land and the Zapatista Rebellion in Chiapas.* Oakland CA: Food First Books, 1994.

Gerhard, Peter. *The Southeast Frontier of New Spain.* Norman: University of Oklahoma Press, 1993.

Harvey, Neil. *The Chiapas Rebellion: The Struggle for Land and Democracy.* Durham, NC: Duke University Press, 1998.

Wasserstrom, Robert. *Class and Society in Central Chiapas.* Berkeley: University of California Press, 1983.

League of United Latin American Citizens (LULAC)

Arguably the most important and historically most visible Mexican American organization in the United States, LULAC was founded in 1929 in Corpus Christi, Texas. From its inception, LULAC echoed the voices of middle-class Mexican Americans and embraced a reformist, rather than radical, approach to change. LULAC leaders have always stressed patriotism and the effective assimilation of Mexican Americans into mainstream American society. The organization's work to end discrimination against people of Mexican descent resulted in several significant victories during the twentieth century and inspired change at the local and national levels. Although LULAC's fortunes have waxed and waned over the years, it remains a viable organization, headquartered in Washington, D.C., with chapters throughout the United States as well as in Puerto Rico, Guam, Mexico, and even on a U.S. military base in West Germany.

The violence of the Mexican Revolution, as well as the labor demands created in the United States as a result of World War I, encouraged many Mexicans to immigrate during the early decades of the twentieth century. By the 1920s, and particularly with the onset of the Depression, peoples of Mexican descent became the target of discrimination. As the Depression took hold, Mexican immigrants, as well as some Mexican Americans living in the southwest became the targets of campaigns that forcibly repatriated them to Mexico. It was in this context that a group of middle-class Mexican Americans in south Texas (some of whom could trace their Texas roots back for generations) decided to form LULAC. Their immediate aim was to distinguish themselves from the new Mexican arrivals and to lessen the discrimination that threatened to undermine the gains that Mexican Americans had made.

LULAC's initial "Statement of Aims and Purposes" declared that the organization would "develop within the members of our race the best, purest, and most perfect type of a true and loyal citizen of the United States of America." The new organization stressed its patriotism (and sought to draw a distinction between Mexican Americans and newly arrived Mexican immigrants) in a variety of ways. Members pledged loyalty to the U.S. Constitution and U.S. laws, promising to push for change peacefully and legally. English was embraced as the official language of LULAC, and only U.S. citizens were accepted as members. The organization used legal and political pressure to combat discrimination while it sought to attain the goal of full citizenship for Mexican Americans primarily through voter registration drives and campaigns to make public schools (viewed as a key to assimilation) more accessible to Mexican Americans.

During the first two decades of its existence, LULAC won important legal victories, particularly in the area of school desegregation. It also successfully pressured the U.S. Census Bureau to reclassify as "white" Americans of Mexican descent. By World War II, LULAC's membership had grown to around 2,000 and the organization had expanded from its base in south Texas to include groups in New Mexico, Colorado, and California.

The post–World War II period witnessed another wave of LULAC activism, encouraged by the determination of returning veterans to continue the struggle against discrimination. LULAC sponsored legal efforts to end segregation in public schools and other public facilities throughout the southwest. LULAC attorneys also sought to end discrimination within the U.S. legal system, and they won a crucial victory in 1953 when the U.S. Supreme Court declared unconstitutional the exclusion of Mexican Americans from jury selection in a Texas murder trial. The patriotic line of LULAC persisted as well. Members continued to distinguish themselves from Mexican immigrants, and they supported citizenship and English classes in an ongoing effort to promote assimilation. In 1957 LULAC launched its "Little School of the 400" program, which taught Mexican children 400 basic English words before they entered the first grade. During the 1960s, this program was transformed into Project Headstart and received the endorsement of the federal government.

During the 1960s and with the emergence of the Chicano movement, LULAC's dominant position within the Mexican American community was challenged. From the beginning, elements within the Mexican American population had criticized LULAC for its insistence on assimilation and accused it of a kind of elitism. Chicano activists of the 1960s and 1970s likewise insisted on a more radical response to discrimination within American society and embraced a separate "Mexicano" identity. At the same time, LULAC's membership base was declining, and the organization was compelled to look for outside sources of support. Its name recognition and high profile helped LULAC secure funding from government and corporate sources, enabling the organization to continue with its own brand of activism. In 1965 a Houston LULAC chapter piloted a job placement program that eventually became the federally funded SER-Jobs for Progress program. Government support also helped establish the Mexican American Legal Defense and Educational Fund (MALDEF) in 1968.

The new reliance on corporate support was not without problems. In 1977 the LULAC Foundation (established as a tax-exempt body that could solicit corporate grants) began what would become a long-standing link with the Adolph Coors Brewing Company. The company was known for its anti-union policies and employed few minorities. It drew the ire of other Mexican American groups and heightened criticism of LULAC. Throughout the 1980s, LULAC leaders would work (with some success) to encourage the Coors Company to initiate more minority hiring.

Despite continuing difficulties with establishing a sizeable and active membership base, and despite financial and legal scandals involving the LULAC Foundation and LULAC leadership, LULAC remained a high-profile group during the last two decades of the twentieth century. It continued its efforts on the legal and educational fronts, and its leaders issued public criticisms of the English Only Movement and the anti-affirmative action sentiments that took hold among some politicians and voters during the 1980s and 1990s. As the twenty-first century began, LULAC remained an influential voice for Mexican Americans.

—SBP

See also: *Bracero* Program; Chicano/a.
References:

Márquez, Benjamin. *LULAC: The Evolution of a Mexican American Political Organization.* Austin: University of Texas Press, 1993.

San Miguel, Guadalupe. *"Let all of them take heed": Mexican Americans and the Campaign for Educational Equality in Texas, 1910–1981.* Austin: University of Texas Press, 1987.

Sandoval, Moisés. *Our Legacy: The First Fifty Years.* Washington, DC: LULAC, 1979.

León de la Barra, Francisco (1863–1939)

Interim president in 1911 during the crucial transition from the old regime of Porfirio Díaz to the Revolutionary regime of Francisco Madero, Francisco León de la Barra was born in the city of Querétaro on 16 June 1863. From a wealthy family, he excelled in his studies and received an appointment as instructor in mathematics and logic at the prestigious National Preparatory School in Mexico City at the age of twenty-one. After obtaining his law degree, León de la Barra served three terms in the national Congress before embarking on a career as a diplomat. Rising through the diplomatic ranks, he received Mexico's most important diplomatic post, ambassador to the United States, in 1908. Impressed by León de la Barra's performance, President Díaz appointed him minister of foreign relations in April 1911 as the old regime was crumbling. When Díaz and his vice-president, Ramón Corral, resigned in May 1911, León de la Barra became president under the provisions of the Constitution, an action that had also been agreed to by Díaz and the Revolutionary leader, Francisco Madero.

In his brief inaugural address, León de la Barra emphasized his desire to provide a peaceful transition to democracy and indicated that he would not be a candidate for either president or vice-president in the coming elections. Although a loyal Porfirian technocrat, León de la Barra shared many of the reformist views of Madero and his less-radical followers. As interim president, León de la Barra began to address such pressing issues as labor, education, and agrarian reform. His greatest problems involved the effort to disarm and demobilize the Revolutionary forces in accordance with the agreement reached by Madero and Díaz leading to Díaz's resignation. The mustering out of the Revolutionary forces was mostly successful, although the continued resistance of troops under Emiliano Zapata produced new fighting and worsened relations between León de la Barra and Madero.

One of León de la Barra's most important responsibilities was to preside over new elections scheduled for 1 October 1911. He

Francisco León de la Barra (Library of Congress)

strongly endorsed freedom of speech and assembly as essential to a democratic campaign. He resisted efforts to postpone the elections and rejected requests that he be a presidential candidate. The National Catholic Party (PCN) did nominate León de la Barra for vice-president, although without his approval; he still finished second in the balloting in October. The elections themselves produced a number of irregularities but were reasonably honest given Mexico's authoritarian tradition.

León de la Barra's diplomatic and political careers did not end when he turned over the presidency to Madero on 6 November 1911. Madero gave him a diplomatic assignment to Italy, and there were discussions about his becoming ambassador to France. He returned to Mexico in 1912 and soon won a seat in the national Senate from the state of Mexico as a member of the National Catholic Party.

León de la Barra might have retired with his diplomatic and democratic credentials in-

tact except for his association with the regime of General Victoriano Huerta. In February 1913 Generals Bernardo Reyes and Félix Díaz led a coup in Mexico City aimed at overthrowing the Madero government. León de la Barra sought refuge in the British Embassy, fearful that Madero would crack down on all opponents of his administration. León de la Barra offered to mediate between the government and the rebels, an offer accepted by Madero. Negotiations fell apart over rebel demands that Madero resign; León de la Barra later led a delegation of his fellow senators to the National Palace to seek Madero's resignation. The military stalemate ended when General Victoriano Huerta—commander of the troops defending Madero—went over to the rebels and had Madero and his vice-president, José María Pino Suárez, arrested, and took the position of president for himself. León de la Barra agreed to serve as Huerta's minister of foreign relations. When Madero and Pino Suárez were murdered on 22 February 1913, some of the blame attached to León de la Barra as a prominent member of Huerta's cabinet. León de la Barra strenuously denied any involvement in the decision to kill Madero and Pino Suárez, a denial supported by the available evidence.

Huerta and León de la Barra had a parting of the ways after Huerta became impatient over the failure to achieve diplomatic recognition by the United States and became uneasy about León de la Barra's possible links to Huerta's rival, Félix Díaz. In July 1913 León de la Barra resigned as minister of foreign relations and accepted a position as ambassador to France. León de la Barra was in France in July 1914 when Huerta—under military pressure—resigned as president. The Revolutionary government in Mexico relieved León de la Barra the following month and confiscated his property in Mexico.

Although León de la Barra spent the rest of his life in exile, he avoided exile politics and carved out a new legal and diplomatic career for himself. A successful international lawyer and professor of international law at the University of Paris, León de la Barra served as a legal consultant to the French government at the Versailles conference in 1919 and later served on several of the tribunals created under the Treaty of Versailles. A champion of the principal of international arbitration, he tried unsuccessfully to promote a negotiated settlement of the conflict between Italy and Ethiopia in 1935 and regarding the Spanish Civil War in 1938. León de la Barra died in Biarritz, France, on 22 September 1939.

—DMC

See also: Díaz, Porfirio; Huerta, Victoriano; Madero, Francisco; Presidents of the Twentieth Century; Revolution of 1910; Zapata, Emiliano.

References:

Henderson, Peter V. N. *In the Absence of Don Porfirio: Francisco León de la Barra and the Mexican Revolution.* Wilmington, DE: Scholarly Resources, 2000.

Knight, Alan. *The Mexican Revolution.* 2 vols. Cambridge: Cambridge University Press, 1986.

Meyer, Michael C. *Huerta: A Political Portrait.* Lincoln: University of Nebraska Press, 1972.

Lombardo Toledano, Vicente (1894–1968)

Prominent intellectual and labor leader, Vicente Lombardo Toledano was born in Teziutlán, Puebla. He attended a local primary school with future general and president Manuel Avila Camacho. From a solid middle-class background, his parents were able to send Lombardo to Mexico City for his later education. Lombardo graduated from the prestigious National Preparatory School in 1915 and then enrolled in both the Law School and the School of Graduate Studies at the National University. While a university student, he was greatly influenced by his professors, especially Antonio Caso, who was known for his humanistic, antipositivist philosophy. Lombardo received both his master's degree and his law degree in 1919. Although Lombardo would become Mexico's most famous marxist, he adopted an antimarxist attitude in his law-degree thesis entitled "Public Law and the New Philosophical Currents." Lombardo soon established a career path in education, becoming a professor at the Law School of the National University and, in 1922, director of the National Preparatory School. In 1923 he established the National Preparatory School's night program.

While Lombardo was involved in educational activities throughout the 1920s and 1930s, he was also active in labor affairs and political life. In 1917 Lombardo had become secretary of the Universidad Popular, an educational institution designed to acquaint the general public, especially workers, with humanistic ideas. It was as a representative of the Universidad Popular that Lombardo in 1918 attended the organizational meeting of the Confederación Regional Obrera Mexicana (the Regional Confederation of Mexican Workers, or CROM). With government support, the CROM under its leader Luis Morones soon emerged as the most powerful labor organization in Mexico. In 1920, Lombardo organized Mexico's first teachers' union. In the early 1920s he became the CROM's secretary of education, responsible for educating the workers in areas ranging from labor law to world history. Lombardo's presence provided an aura of intellectual legitimacy to an increasingly corrupt and abusive organization. In his position Lombardo championed popular, nationalistic, and socialistic education. During the 1920s Lombardo also held a series of political positions. In 1921 he became secretary of the government of the Federal District. In 1923 Lombardo supported the government of President Alvaro Obregón against the rebellion led by Adlofo de la Huerta and briefly served as interim governor of his native state of Puebla. He served on the city council of the Federal District in 1924–1925 and also served two terms (1924–1928) in the lower house (Chamber of Deputies) of the Mexican Congress.

Lombardo emerged as one of the principal leaders of a reform group within the CROM, which was becoming notorious for the corrupt leadership of Morones and his close associates. In 1928 Lombardo proposed that the political arm of the CROM, the Partido Laborista (Labor Party, or PL) be disbanded, a move rejected by Morones. As a result of its wavering policies in the 1928 presidential elections, the CROM and Morones went into a prolonged decline. Lombardo continued to work for reform within the CROM but finally resigned from the organization in September 1932 after a bitter public dispute with Morones. In March 1933 Lombardo helped to organize what was called the "Purified CROM," a collection of unions that had defected from the CROM. Lombardo was elected secretary general of the new organization and immediately went to work organizing an even larger labor group. In October 1933 Lombardo was a key figure in the establishment of the Confederación General de Obreros y Campesinos de México (the General Confederation of Workers and Peasants of Mexico, or CGOCM). The CGOCM united the Purified CROM with several other important unions; Lombardo was elected secretary general of this new labor confederation.

Lombardo and the CGOCM were soon part of a growing crisis over the presidency. As had been the case in 1923, Lombardo once again chose the winning side. Following the assassination of President-elect Alvaro Obregón in 1928, former President Plutarco Elías Calles maintained political control through a series of three puppet presidents between 1928 and 1934. For the 1934–1940 presidential term, Calles had selected what he thought was a fourth puppet, Lázaro Cárdenas. When Cárdenas tried to establish an independent position, a struggle for political control soon developed, with the CGOCM and Lombardo supporting Cárdenas. One of the biggest points of contention between Calles and Cárdenas was the new president's encouragement of strikes. Calles publicly criticized Cárdenas and Lombardo for the wave of strikes Calles believed threatened Mexico's political stability. Cárdenas prevailed in the struggle, sending both Calles and Morones into exile in April 1936.

Shortly before the exile of Calles and Morones, a major labor convention took place in Mexico City; this led to the formation of the Confederación de Trabajadores de México (the Mexican Workers' Confederation, or CTM). Lombardo Toledano was elected secretary general of the new confederation, which brought together some 3,000 worker and peasant organizations with a total membership of approximately 600,000. The CTM was not only the largest labor organization in Mexico; it also enjoyed the official support of the Cárdenas administration. When Cárdenas reorganized and renamed the official party in 1938, the CTM was a major force in the new political organization. Now known as the Partido de la Revolución Mexicana, the official party was divided into four sectors, with the CTM as the dominant force in the labor sector. Lombardo became the leading intellectual figure in enunciating the nationalistic and socialist goals of the Cárdenas regime and was part of Cárdenas's inner circle. The price of this privileged relationship was the subordination of the CTM to the government. Cárdenas also blocked Lombardo from organizing two key groups Lombardo had targeted: the peasants and government employees. Both of these groups were organized into separate federations beyond the control of Lombardo.

In 1938 Lombardo made important moves in both the national and international arenas. Lombardo and the CTM were prominent supporters of Cárdenas in his showdown with the oil companies, which led to the expropriation of March 1938. The year 1938 also saw the culmination of Lombardo's dream of establishing an international labor organization that would unite the workers of the hemisphere and establish an antifascist front. With leadership from Lombardo and financial help from the Mexican government, a convention was held in Mexico City in September 1938 that drew workers' representatives from thirteen Latin American nations. This group established the Confederación de Trabajadores de América Latina (the Confederation of Latin American Workers, or CTAL). The convention selected Lombardo to be president of the new organization. The CTAL became the main focus of Lombardo's labor activities in the early 1940s.

Lombardo's growing involvement in the CTAL accompanied his declining influence in the CTM. In 1941 he stepped down as secretary general of the CTM and was replaced by the more conservative Fidel Velázquez, who would go on to dominate the organization for more than fifty years. Lombardo supported the government's wartime policy of industrialization, no strikes, and no wage increases. Lombardo also backed the transformation of this wartime policy into a long-range development scheme, including the industrial labor pact of April 1945, which called for cooperation between labor and management in the interest of economic development.

Although Lombardo strongly supported the successful presidential candidacy of the official party's Miguel Alemán in 1946, his marxist views were increasingly out of sync with a government that was becoming more conservative and experiencing Cold War chills of its own. For many years Lombardo had long drawn a distinction between being a marxist and being a communist. In fact, he had frequent disagreements with Mexican communists. Lombardo, however, found it increasingly difficult to defend his connection to the Soviet Union, which he had visited in 1935. Lombardo was also fond of the "popular front" approach to political action advocated by the Soviets in the 1930s and 1940s. In a rare break with the Mexican government, Lombardo had denounced the offering of exile to Soviet dissident, Leon Trotsky. Lombardo had also supported the shifting Soviet policy toward Germany between 1939 and 1941.

Lombardo's enthusiasm for the popular front approach, which dated to the late 1930s, found an outlet almost a decade later in his formation of a new political party. In 1947 Lombardo founded the Partido Popular (Popular Party, or PP). The new party positioned itself to the left of the official party, the name of which had been changed recently to the Partido Revolucionario Institucional (the Institutional Revolutionary Party, or PRI). Lombardo originally hoped that the CTM would support this project, but the CTM leadership prohibited its members from supporting the new party, pulled the CTM out of Lombardo's CTAL, expelled Lombardo from the CTM, and then purged his supporters from the labor organization. Although the Partido Popular generally supported the PRI, the official party refused to return the favor, considering the PP a threat on the left to its mass support. Although the new party was considered a potential rallying point for more left-wing groups, it did not prove to be a major factor in Mexican politics. Lombardo's tight control over the party led to a series of intraparty squabbles and defections. Lombardo was the PP's nominee for the presidency in 1952, but his candidacy had little impact on the campaign. In 1960 the PP transformed itself into the Partido Popular Socialista (the Popular Socialist Party, or PPS) but continued its support for PRI policies and candidates.

Lombardo continued to favor close ties between the labor movement and the government, even when the partnership operated against him. Lombardo defended government intervention to impose union leaders and criticized the student movements of 1968 with their strong anti-PRI stance. As one of the leading ideologues of the Mexican Revolution, Vicente Lombardo Toledano exercised great influence over a generation of intellectuals, politicians, and government bureaucrats. From the 1940s on, however, he found it increasingly difficult to translate that influence into political power as he had earlier, although he did once again occupy a seat in the lower house of the Mexican Congress between 1964 and 1967. He also lost out in the struggle to lead Mexico's most powerful labor organization—the CTM—to the durable Fidel Velázquez, who controlled the CTM from 1947 to 1997.

—DMC

See also: Alemán, Miguel; Avila Camacho, Manuel; Calles, Plutarco Elías; Cárdenas, Lázaro; Confederación de Trabajadores de México (CTM); Confederación Regional Obrera Mexicana (CROM); Import Substitution Industrialization (ISI); Morones, Luis; Partido Revolucionario Institucional (PRI); Velázquez Sanchez, Fidel.

References:

Caulfield, Norman. *Mexican Workers and the State: From the Porfiriato to NAFTA.* Fort Worth: Texas Christian University Press, 1998.

La Botz, Dan. *The Crisis of Mexican Labor.* New York: Praeger, 1988.

Millon, Robert Paul. *Mexican Marxist: Vicente Lombardo Toledano.* Chapel Hill: University of North Carolina Press, 1966.

López Mateos, Adolfo (1910–1969)

President from 1958 to 1964, Adolfo López Mateos was born in the state of Mexico and received his early education in Mexico City and Toluca, the capital of the state of Mexico. His involvement in politics began at eighteen when he became the private secretary of Colonel Filiberto Gómez, governor of the State of Mexico. He went on to study law at the National University. In the 1929 presidential campaign to select a successor for the assassinated Alvaro Obregón, he supported José Vasconcelos against the candidate of the official party, Pascual Ortiz Rubio. After the defeat of Vasconcelos, López Mateos briefly went into self-imposed exile in Guatemala. In 1934 he received his law degree from the National School of Law and became private secretary to Carlos Riva Palacio, president of the official party. López Mateos worked his way through the party ranks. In 1946 he worked in the presidential campaign of Miguel Alemán; that same year, he was elected to the national Senate from his home state of Mexico. López Mateos was the campaign manger for Adolfo Ruiz Cortines's suc-

cessful run for the presidency in 1952. The new president appointed López Mateos to the position of secretary of labor. As labor secretary, he established a reputation for being able to mediate labor-management disputes. Ruiz Cortines tapped López Mateos to succeed him in the presidency, and López Mateos went on to the typical lopsided victory enjoyed by the official candidate in the presidential election of 1958.

López Mateos began his presidency on a conservative note, using force to end a dispute with railroad workers and jailing their leaders. He also continued to operate within the general development approach followed since the late 1930s. This approach dictated an emphasis on industrialization and a major role for the central government in the economy. Although seeking foreign investment, he strictly enforced the legal provision requiring Mexicans to own a majority of the stock in business firms. The government also extended its ownership of business activities; López Mateos nationalized the telephone system, the electric power industry, the motion picture industry, mining, and petrochemicals. His administration continued the expansion of the national transportation system, especially the construction of highways. Industrial production continued to show growth, and exports also increased. By 1964 Mexico was essentially self-sufficient in such basic industries as oil, iron, and steel.

Although Mexico's conservative development approach continued, López Mateos was determined to move the general direction of Mexican politics to the left. He was concerned about the growing disunity in the country and the inability of the development program—despite its successes—to improve substantially the standard of living of most Mexicans. This concern was most evident in the greater attention paid to the rural sector. López Mateos vigorously revived the land-redistribution program, distributing approximately 30 million acres; this figure made his administration second only to that of Lázaro Cárdenas (1934–1940) in total acreage distributed. Additional acreage was opened to cultivation through extensive irrigation projects. Rural income was increased by raising the guaranteed prices for agricultural products. There was a major expansion in social security benefits and services, with rural areas especially targeted.

Despite his early confrontation with the railroad workers, López Mateos also moved to improve the standard of living of urban workers. During his administration Mexico made the official transition to being an urban country, with the urban population exceeding the rural population for the first time in the early 1960s. Rapid population growth and urbanization led to the growth of slums and shantytowns in urban areas, especially in the Mexico City vicinity. Demands for government services increased dramatically, and the urban poor posed a much greater threat to political stability than the rural poor. López Mateos responded by launching a major program of low-cost public housing in the leading industrial cities. He also implemented the long-ignored provision of the Constitution of 1917 that called for employers to share profits with industrial workers. The government increased its subsidies for low-cost food and other basic necessities for the poor. There was greater emphasis on education, with spending for education becoming the single biggest item in the budget. The education program emphasized rural education and a cooperative effort between the central government and local communities. In the construction of new schools, the central government provided building materials and technical assistance while local communities provided land and labor. López Mateos also established a system of free—but required—textbooks for primary schools. While the free textbooks were welcomed by the financially strapped schools, they also provoked opposition from conservative elements, who objected to the political slant of the textbooks.

López Mateos pursued a more leftist foreign policy while simultaneously maintaining good relations with the United States. His ad-ministration settled the long-running Chamizal controversy with the United States over some 600 acres of land that had originally been claimed by Mexico but had ended up north of the Rio Grande as the result of a shift in the riverbed in the 1860s. In 1964 the United States agreed to return most of the disputed real estate to Mexico. Relations between the United States and Mexico were considerably less cordial over the status of Cuba. Revolutionary leader Fidel Castro—who had been in exile in Mexico in the 1950s—seized power in Cuba in 1959 and steadily aligned Cuba with the Soviet bloc. The United States wanted the other nations of Latin America to isolate Cuba diplomatically and economically. Mexico, however, followed an independent path and refused to participate in economic sanctions against Cuba or to cut diplomatic relations. López Mateos also emphasized Mexico's independent foreign policy by making numerous trips abroad to countries representing a variety of political views and by welcoming visits to Mexico by heads of state ranging from U.S. President Dwight Eisenhower to the King of Nepal.

López Mateos also attempted to deal with growing demands for reforms to break the official party's monopoly of political power. His response was to support a constitutional amendment introducing proportional representation for the lower house of the national Congress, the Chamber of Deputies. Under proportional representation, political parties could receive representation in the Chamber based on achieving a certain percentage of the national vote even if they did not win any of the races for geographical districts. When the reform was first introduced in 1964, opposition parties won thirty seats. Even then, critics of the reform accused the official party of "assigning" seats in the Chamber and of trying to create the impression of democracy without actually risking its dominant position. Despite the critics, proportional representation would be expanded in later years.

Adolfo López Mateos (right), president from 1958 to 1964, is greeted by Prince Bernhard of the Netherlands during ceremonies in Mexico City inaugurating the 19th Congress of the International Chamber of Commerce, 22 April 1963. (Bettmann/Corbis)

While the energetic López Mateos recognized the need for major changes in government policy, he was not able to deal successfully with the fundamental problems that had evolved in postwar Mexico: the population explosion, urbanization, the growing gap between rich and poor, chronic difficulties in the rural sector, and growing demands for political reform. The person López Mateos chose to succeed him—Gustavo Díaz Ordaz—would prove even less responsive to demands for political and economic change. After finishing his presidential term, López Mateos served briefly as head of the Olympic Committee organizing the Summer Games to be held in Mexico City in 1968 but soon resigned because of poor health. He died in September 1969 in Mexico City.

—*DMC*

See also: Agrarian Reform/Land and Land Policy; Alemán, Miguel; Avila Camacho, Manuel; Cárdenas, Lázaro; Democratization

Process; Díaz Ordaz, Gustavo; Foreign Policy; Labor Movements; Partido Revolucionario Institucional (PRI); Presidents of the Twentieth Century; Ruiz Cortines, Adolfo; Urbanization.

References:

Aguilar Camín, Héctor, and Lorenzo Meyer. *In the Shadow of the Mexican Revolution: Contemporary Mexican History, 1910–1989.* Austin: University of Texas Press, 1993.

Story, Dale. *The Mexican Ruling Party: Stability and Authority.* New York: Praeger, 1986.

López Portillo, José (1920–)

President from 1976 to 1982, José López Portillo was born in Mexico City and attended the National Preparatory School there. He received his law degree from the National School of Law in 1946 where he attended classes with his longtime friend and future president, Luis Echeverría Alvarez. López Portillo rose to power through the government bureaucracy rather than through the military or through the official party, the Institutional Revolutionary Party (the Partido Revolucionario Institucional, or PRI). After more than a decade as a professor at the National School of Law, he began his government career in 1959 as a technical advisor in the Secretariat of National Patrimony. Under President Gustavo Díaz Ordaz (1964–1970), López Portillo served as legal counsel to the Secretariat of the Presidency and subsecretary of the presidency. In the early 1970s he held the positions of subsecretary of government properties and director general of the Federal Electric Commission, the state-owned electric utility. As Mexico's financial and economic situation worsened, López Portillo became secretary of the treasury in 1973. Amid continuing financial decline, President Echeverría designated as his successor his longtime friend and financial technocrat, José López Portillo. As the official party candidate, López Portillo easily won election to the presidency in 1976.

Although Mexico was in the midst of a major crisis when Echeverría stepped down, Mexico's financial situation was about to take a

José López Portillo, president from 1976 to 1982, greets the crowds with outstretched arms during his campaign for the presidency. Mexico City, Mexico, 14 October 1975. (Corbis)

dramatic turn. Major new oil discoveries had been made as early as 1974, but their impact was delayed until the López Portillo administration. At the same time that Mexico's known oil reserves were expanding, the price of oil in the international market was rising rapidly as a result of the Arab oil embargo of 1973 and later manipulation of production and pricing by the Organization of Petroleum Exporting Countries (OPEC). Since the Mexican government owned the oil industry, it would be the one who would reap the profits from the increase in oil production and prices.

There was tremendous pressure on Mexico from oil-consuming countries, especially the United States, to increase its production rapidly and bring down oil prices. The López Portillo administration resisted such pressures and announced that it would follow a policy of "digestible exploitation" of its newfound oil wealth. Mexico declared that it would limit its total oil production, the amount of oil exported, and the amount sold to any one country (that is, the United

States). By gradually introducing oil profits into the economy, Mexico would avoid the waste, inflation, and corruption that rapid exploitation had brought to oil-producing countries such as Venezuela and Iran.

This restrained approach to oil development in theory soon gave way in fact to an unprecedented level of government spending, using not just oil profits but also money borrowed implicitly against future oil profits. Spending by the federal government shot up dramatically, increasing at a rate five times the rate of increase in the gross national product. Government involvement in the economy grew, with the emphasis on capital-intensive industries such as steel and petrochemicals rather than on labor-intensive industries needed to provide jobs for Mexico's rapidly expanding workforce. There was a boom in the construction of public works, as well as a major expansion in government subsidies for consumer goods. Government spending helped to maintain industrial growth, but agricultural production continued to lag behind the population increase, forcing Mexico to spend part of its oil profits on food imports.

Mexico's oil wealth permitted it to play a more independent and prominent role in international affairs. In particular, Mexico played a more assertive role in its relations with the United States. When President Jimmy Carter called for a boycott of the 1980 Moscow Olympics after the Soviet invasion of Afghanistan, López Portillo quickly announced that Mexico would not support the boycott. The Carter and López Portillo administrations had a public dispute over the price of Mexican natural gas, leading López Portillo to announce that Mexico would burn off the natural gas before selling it at the price sought by the United States. Mexico's policy toward leftist guerrilla movements in Central America also put it at odds with U.S. policy in that region.

Under López Portillo, "digestible exploitation" of oil wealth had given way to massive deficit spending, which might have proved sustainable had oil prices continued to rise as the Mexican government believed they would. Instead, oil prices began a major decline in 1981, leading to yet another financial and economic crisis for Mexico. Corruption—always present—had reached new dimensions under López Portillo and touched the president himself. Mexican capital was being taken out of the country at an alarming rate. Mexico was laboring under an unpayable international debt and high domestic unemployment. Inflation rose from 18 percent in 1979 to 60 percent in 1982, López Portillo's last year in office. Also in 1982, there was another massive devaluation of the peso. In a desperate bid to resurrect his political and historical reputation, López Portillo nationalized the banks in September 1982. Rather than rallying the country behind him, the nationalization intensified Mexico's financial problems. José López Portillo had entered the presidency in 1976 as the financial technocrat who could deliver Mexico from crisis. After riding the wave of oil prosperity, he left the presidency in 1982 amid another financial crisis for which he had to share much of the blame. The "financial savior" of 1976 had become the "financial scapegoat" of 1982. To save Mexico from its latest financial predicament, López Portillo turned for his successor to another financial technocrat—Miguel de la Madrid—who had risen to prominence in the Secretariat of Planning and Budget, a new federal agency created by López Portillo.

—DMC

See also: Corruption; Debt, Mexico's Foreign; Díaz Ordaz, Gustavo; Foreign Policy; Madrid (Hurtado), Miguel de la; Oil Industry; Partido Revolucionario Institucional (PRI); Presidents of the Twentieth Century.

References:

Aguayo, Sergio. *Myths and [Mis]perceptions: Changing U.S. Elite Visions of Mexico.* La Jolla, CA: University of California, San Diego, 1998.

Bailey, John J. *Governing Mexico: The Statecraft of Crisis Management.* New York: St. Martin's, 1988.

Newell, G., Roberto, and Luis Rubio F. *Mexico's Dilemma: The Political Origins of Economic Crisis.* Boulder, CO: Westview Press, 1984.

M

Madero, Francisco (1873–1913)

The first Revolutionary president of Mexico from 1911 to 1913, Madero was born on 30 October 1873 in Parras, Coahuila. The Madero family was part of the Porfirian elite with interests in agriculture, ranching, mining, and banking. He received an excellent education, including studies in Paris from 1888 to 1892 and at the University of California at Berkeley in 1893. Madero returned to Mexico in 1893 with an enthusiasm for American-style democracy, an interest in spiritism, and new ideas for improving his family's agricultural operations. Managing one of the family's cotton farms, he implemented new techniques of cultivation and introduced irrigation. He also showed a concern for the poor unusual among the landed class, establishing housing, schools, and centers of homeopathic medicine to serve the rural workers and their families.

Madero's involvement in politics began in 1904 with the formation of a local political club to back an opposition candidate for municipal office. In 1905 Madero tried unsuccessfully to block the reelection of the official candidate for governor of Coahuila. Madero's frustration with trying to buck the Díaz political machine at the state and local levels convinced him of the need for effective suf-frage and no reelection. It also helped to persuade him that the solution to Mexico's problems lay in political reform at the national level. In 1909, Madero's book, *The Presidential Succession in 1910,* appeared, making him a leading figure in the growing group of those who were calling for changes in the Porfirian system. The book was scarcely a Revolutionary tract. While Madero criticized the Porfirian system, he did not attack Porfirio Díaz personally and even said that it would be "convenient" for Díaz to be reelected yet again in 1910. Madero did call for complete freedom in selecting the vice-president, members of Congress, and state governors and for recognition of the principle of no reelection. The ever-idealistic Madero even sent a copy of the work to Díaz, asking him to reflect on its contents.

It became apparent that Díaz—at age 80—was going to run again in 1910 and had no intention of introducing major reforms. As a result, Madero transformed himself from a critic of the regime to an official opponent of Díaz for the presidency, becoming the presidential candidate of the Anti-Reelectionist Party. Díaz at first welcomed Madero's candidacy, believing that Madero posed no threat and would help create the illusion of a democratic contest for power. As

Madero rapidly gained support, Díaz decided to remove Madero from the scene until the elections were concluded. Madero was arrested on trumped-up charges, spending election day—21 June 1910—in jail. With the elections over and Díaz overwhelmingly reelected, Madero was permitted to post bail and go free.

It was at this point that Madero made the transition from reformer to revolutionary. He went into exile in San Antonio, Texas, and issued a call to revolution, the Plan of San Luis Potosí, named for the Mexican city where he had been jailed. The Plan dealt primarily with political concerns, nullifying the recent presidential elections and making Madero provisional president. It also set a specific date for the Revolution to begin: 20 November 1910. Madero expected to find a Revolutionary army awaiting him when he returned to Mexico on the night of 19 November. When he found only a small band of poorly armed supporters, Madero returned to San Antonio without firing a shot.

Although Madero's portion of the Revolution got off to a bad start, other Revolutionary leaders answered the call and actually started military operations. The most important of these leaders were in the north, Pancho Villa and Pascual Orozco, who were operating in the border state of Chihuahua. Madero returned to Mexico in February 1911, briefly and unsuccessfully assuming military leadership; after suffering a major defeat, Madero returned responsibility for military operations to Orozco and Villa. The two Revolutionary generals targeted the key border city of Ciudad Juárez, across the Rio Grande from El Paso, Texas. Madero, however, was afraid that an attack on Juárez might spill over into El Paso, provoking U.S. military intervention. When Madero ordered Orozco and Villa to move south, they attacked anyway, rapidly conquering Juárez. This insubordination on the part of his two top generals was a good indication of problems to come. Revolutionary factionalism and conflict between civilian and military

leaders would influence the course of the Revolution for years to come.

In May 1911, Madero reached an agreement with the Díaz government, usually referred to as the Treaty of Ciudad Juárez. Under the agreement, Díaz and his vice-president, Ramón Corral, would resign before the end of May. Francisco León de la Barra, Díaz's minister of foreign relations, would serve as interim president until new elections could be held. The most surprising and controversial feature of the agreement was that the, Revolutionary forces would be demobilized while the old Porfirian army would continue as the federal army. This move outraged many of Madero's military commanders, who were expecting to be incorporated into a new army with their Revolutionary ranks recognized.

Between the Treaty of Juárez in May 1911 and the presidential elections of October 1911, Madero focused his attention on the presidential campaign, although at times he intervened in the affairs of the León de la Barra interim administration. The demobilization of Revolutionary forces produced major problems, including a cabinet crisis and outright rebellion by Emiliano Zapata's forces. For Madero the Revolution had succeeded with the overthrow of Díaz; for many of his followers, the end of the Porfirian regime was the beginning of the Revolution, not its end. Madero easily won election to the presidency in October and took office on 6 November 1911.

As president, Madero thought primarily in terms of political reforms; most notable was his abolition of the Porfirian system of local political bosses who had dominated municipal government. When it came to socioeconomic matters such as the demands of urban workers and the call for agrarian reform, Madero proceeded with caution if at all. Madero was not well prepared to deal with the demands of urban labor. He believed in limited agrarian reform but within an established legal framework, a view which guaranteed a slow process of land distribution. Like

Francisco Madero (third from right) with his rebel leaders, 1911 (Library of Congress)

many a political moderate, Madero found himself under attack from more radical elements who thought he was doing too little and more conservative elements who thought he was doing too much. The first to revolt was Emiliano Zapata, in November 1911, who believed that Madero was moving too slowly on agrarian reform. Old-line Porfirian Generals Bernardo Reyes and Félix Díaz, nephew of the former dictator, also revolted against Madero. The most serious threat to the Madero regime was the revolt in 1912 by Pascual Orozco, who was disenchanted with Madero's lack of reforms and also with Madero's perceived lack of gratitude for Orozco's role in putting him in power. All the revolts failed, but they distracted the Madero administration from more productive activities and caused a major drain on the treasury.

The failure of these provincial revolts encouraged anti-Madero forces to think in terms of a more traditional coup in Mexico City as the method for overthrowing Madero. Both Reyes and Félix Díaz were in jail in Mexico City, which facilitated their conspiring with other army generals who were also interested in overthrowing Madero. On 9 February 1913 the coup began with the release of Reyes and Díaz from jail but quickly unraveled when Reyes was killed in an attack on the National Palace. This led to ten days of fighting, including the exchange of artillery fire, in the heart of Mexico City. The bloody struggle came to an end when the commander of the troops defending the Madero government, General Victoriano Huerta, reached an agreement with Díaz to end the Madero government. Madero and Vice-President Pino Suárez were arrested. On 22 February 1913 Madero and Pino Suárez were assassinated while being transferred from the National Palace to a military prison. It is unclear whether Huerta or Félix Díaz directly ordered the killings. The unlikely official explanation put out by the new provisional government of General Huerta was that Madero and Pino Suárez were killed in the crossfire that erupted when supporters of Madero attempted to free him.

Despite the limited accomplishments of the Madero administration, Madero remained a heroic figure of the Revolution, the "apostle of democracy." Although he enjoyed substantial popular support, he was never able to consolidate his administration or corral the diverse personal ambitions and Revolutionary movements unleashed by the Revolution of 1910. With his limited view of the Revolution, Madero would likely have been the target of further revolts even if his administration had survived the events of February 1913. Madero's assassination proved an appropriate prelude to the bloody civil wars to follow when the Revolutionary factions turned first on Huerta and then later on each other.

—DMC

See also: Assassinations; Carranza, Venustiano; Díaz, Porfirio; Flores Magón, Ricardo; Huerta, Victoriano; Orozco, Pascual; Revolution of 1910; Zapata, Emiliano.

References:

Cumberland, Charles C. *Mexican Revolution: Genesis under Madero.* Austin: University of Texas Press, 1952.

LaFrance, David G. *The Mexican Revolution in Puebla, 1908–1913: The Maderista Movement and the Failure of Liberal Reform.* Wilmington, DE: Scholarly Resources Books, 1989.

Ross, Stanley R. *Francisco I. Madero, Apostle of Mexican Democracy.* New York: Columbia University Press, 1955.

Madrid (Hurtado), Miguel de la (1934–)

Born in the western state of Colima where his family had been prominent for generations, Miguel de la Madrid (Hurtado) studied in private schools in Mexico City and then received his law degree from the National School of Law in 1957. After serving as advisor to the administration of the Bank of Mexico where his uncle had served as director general, he went on to study in the United States; he received his master's degree in public administration from Harvard University in 1965.

Like Luis Echeverría and José López Portillo before him, Miguel de la Madrid worked his way up to the presidency through a series of government positions rather than through the military or the official party, the Institutional Revolutionary Party (Partido Revolucionario Institucional, or PRI). He carved out a career as a financial technocrat in a series of posts in the Secretariat of the Treasury; while serving as subsecretary of the treasury in 1979, he was appointed to the recently created cabinet position of secretary of planning and budget. With Mexico in the midst of one of the gravest financial and economic crises of the twentieth century, President José López Portillo tapped Madrid to be his successor in 1982. Although the economic situation was so critical that it threatened the social order, Madrid easily won election as the nominee of the PRI.

Miguel de la Madrid's domestic agenda was basically dictated by the austerity program he followed to deal with Mexico's crushing international debt. The new president had to reduce federal spending drastically. Curbing the expanding government bureaucracy was a major priority. Madrid first imposed a freeze on further hiring and later eliminated more than 50,000 jobs. Many of the federal employees remaining had their salaries reduced. Madrid increased federal taxes and let the peso "float," or seek its market level in international trading. The floating peso soon became the sinking peso. When Madrid took office in December 1982, the exchange rate was 150 pesos to the dollar; by December 1987 the rate was an astounding 2,300 pesos to the dollar. The president also began an active program of "privatization," the sell-off of government-owned businesses to private individuals or corporations. His administration also initiated a program of dispersal of industry, especially from the overindustrialized and heavily polluted Federal District. Madrid made Mexico more attractive to foreign investors, as the *maquiladora* industries along the border boomed. Mexico also abandoned its long-established policy of protective tariffs and joined the General Agreement on Tariffs and Trade. These measures were confirmed in an agreement with

Miguel de la Madrid, ca. 1983. Madrid was president from 1982 to 1988. (Bettmann/Corbis)

the International Monetary Fund in exchange for short-term loans to keep Mexico from defaulting on its international debt.

Even nature seemed to conspire against Mexico's economic recovery when a major earthquake struck Mexico City on 19 September 1985. The quake left an estimated 8,000 to 12,000 dead and property damage of more than $4 billion. Madrid came under heavy criticism for the slowness of the federal government's response as small groups of residents took the lead in rescue and recovery operations. The earthquake also jolted the peso as well as the national capital, with the value of the currency quickly dropping some 30 percent.

Confronted with the unprecedented corruption of the López Portillo administration, Miguel de la Madrid had called for a "moral renovation." Although Madrid's anti-corruption campaign bypassed López Portillo, two high-profile figures from the previous administration were indicted and convicted. Jorge Díaz Serrano—the former director of the government oil monopoly,

PEMEX—was convicted and sentenced to ten years in jail for embezzling $43 million in the purchase of oil tankers. More colorful and more notorious was the case of Mexico City's Chief of Police Arturo Durazo Moreno. Durazo was a boyhood friend of Presidents Luis Echeverría and José López Portillo, both of whom promoted his career in law enforcement. While serving as police chief, Durazo carved out his own criminal empire, ranging from cocaine trafficking to charging a personal "tax" for each license plate issued in the capital. On an official salary of about $1,600 per month, Durazo by 1982 was worth an estimated $200 million to $600 million. Durazo fled from Mexico but was later extradited from the United States. Although accused of monumental graft and implicated in some fifty murders, Durazo was finally sentenced on a series of lesser charges in 1989. These well-publicized prosecutions provided good examples of the extremes of corruption, but there was little indication that "moral renovation" was having a substantial impact on overall corruption. One virtue of the government's austerity program was that it meant fewer opportunities for officials to engage in graft.

Despite major cuts in federal spending, inflation became an even greater problem. Inflation rose from 64 percent in 1985 to 106 percent in 1986 to 159 percent in 1987. To curb inflation, Madrid brought together leaders of the four interest groups involved—labor, business, agriculture, and government—and obtained agreement on an anti-inflationary pact. The federal government promised to reduce spending further and to continue the process of selling-off government businesses. Union leaders promised to reduce their wage demands while business and agriculture promised to restrict prices and profits. All the parties involved were pleasantly surprised by how well the pact worked in operation. Inflation dropped to 52 percent in 1988, prompting an extension of the pact into 1990.

The decline in the rate of inflation was one of the few bits of good financial news. As Mexico's foreign debt grew, topping $100 billion in 1988, the government continued to struggle to reach an agreement with its creditors. Under strong political and social pressures to increase spending, the Madrid administration found it hard to stay on the austerity bandwagon and was uneasy with the U.S. government's depiction of Mexico as a "model debtor." The United States was becoming more restrained in its offers of financial aid and more demanding in linking additional financing with economic reforms. The Madrid administration sought to end the lengthy negotiations by making a new debt-exchange proposal in 1988 that would have involved the exchange of loans at a discount for new Mexican bonds, which in turn would be backed by U.S. government bonds purchased by the Mexican government. The proposal was not finalized, but it did help to lead to a settlement of the debt issue early in the administration of Madrid's successor.

Mexico's ongoing economic problems led to a major increase in illegal immigration from Mexico to the United States, further straining relations between the two countries. Madrid made it clear to U.S. officials that Mexico was not going to take action to stop the illegal immigration, which was considered an important social and economic "safety valve" for his country. The United States responded by passing new immigration legislation in 1986 that provided amnesty for illegal aliens who had resided in the United States for an extended period of time and established penalties for U.S. employers who knowingly hired illegal aliens. The measure also provided for an increase in the U.S. border patrol to stem the flow of new illegal aliens. The new legislation produced a dramatic—but brief—drop in illegal immigration, but continuing economic problems in Mexico soon produced a new rise in illegal immigration.

The drug problem also took on greater prominence during the Madrid administration. Mexico was under growing criticism as both a producer and transshipper of drugs. The murder of a U.S. drug enforcement agent near Guadalajara brought unusual levels of public criticism from U.S. officials and politicians. A particularly sensitive issue was the question of corruption of Mexican law enforcement officials and the lack of cooperation extended by Mexican officers in suppressing the drug trade. The anti-Mexico sentiment reached a peak in 1988 when the U.S. Senate refused to "certify" Mexico as cooperating in the war against drugs, making Mexico ineligible for U.S. economic aid. The increasing power of a small number of Mexican drug cartels led to public speculation about whether Mexico was becoming a "narco-state" along the lines of Colombia or Bolivia. It was clear that the drug problem was one that would extend well beyond any one presidential administration.

In 1986, faced with increasing demands to open the political system, Madrid supported electoral reforms that would show immediate effects in the elections of 1988. The reforms related to the composition of the lower house of the Mexican Congress, the Chamber of Deputies. The total number of seats in the Chamber was increased from 400 to 500 with 200 of the seats being awarded on the basis of proportional representation, the assigning of seats based on the percentage of votes that a party received in the election. No one party (meaning the PRI) could hold more than 70 percent of the seats in the Chamber. While the reforms affected the Congress, the real interest was in the presidential elections scheduled for 1988. With Mexico's financial and economic problems still unresolved, Miguel de la Madrid selected as his successor Secretary of Planning and Budget Carlos Salinas de Gortari, the driving force behind many of the economic reforms of the Madrid administration. In 1988, however, getting the nomination of the PRI would not mean an easy ride to the presidency. The 1988 presidential election would become one of the most hotly contested and controversial presidential elections since 1940.

When Miguel de la Madrid took office in December 1982, Mexico was beset with financial and economic crises; when he left office in December 1988, the country was still suffering from major financial and economic problems. The economic reforms of Madrid, however, represented the official end of the development policy that had guided Mexico for fifty years. These reforms would be accelerated and expanded by his successor. Sandwiched between the scandal-ridden regimes of José López Portillo (1976–1982) and Carlos Salinas de Gortari (1988–1994), the administration of Miguel de la Madrid looked good, at least by comparison. Madrid's reforms would shape the economy into the next century, but for most Mexicans there was little if any relief from economic decline. A deteriorating standard of living for the masses and an endless stream of financial "crises" already had ordinary citizens referring to the 1980s as the "lost decade." Miguel de la Madrid will never be able to escape the historical fact that he was president during most of that period.

—DMC

See also: Cárdenas, Cuauhtémoc; Corruption; Debt, Mexico's Foreign; Democratization Process; Drug Trafficking; Immigration/Emigration; Import Substitution Industrialization (ISI); López Portillo, José; Partido Revolucionario Institucional (PRI); Presidents of the Twentieth Century; Salinas de Gortari, Carlos; United States, Relations with.

References:
Bailey, John J. *Governing Mexico: The Statecraft of Crisis Management*. New York: St. Martin's, 1988.
Purcell, Susan K. *Mexico in Transition: Implications for U.S. Policy*. New York: Council on Foreign Relations, 1988.

Marcos, Subcomandante

The acknowledged leader of the Zapatista movement in the southern state of Chiapas, Subcomandante Marcos is one of the most visible figures in Mexico's recent history. His charismatic guerrilla image, complete with mask and pipe, attracted immediate international attention with the beginning of the Zapatista rebellion of 1994. Since that time, although the Zapatistas have faded from public view, Marcos has remained a highly visible figure, and his writings against neoliberalism and in favor of human rights issues (including indigenous rights) have continued to find an audience.

Marcos's identity has been a source of contention since his emergence on the national and international scene. Because Marcos, like the other members of the EZLN (Zapatista National Liberation Army) conceals his identity with a mask, which he says he will remove only when Mexico removes its own (thus acknowledging the seriousness of the country's problems and inequalities), his biography is largely a matter of conjecture. He was first described as a "green-eyed foreigner" with a Mexico City accent, an allusion to his presence as a non-Indian leader of the predominantly indigenous Zapatista movement. During the administration of President Ernesto Zedillo (1994–2000), the Mexican government revealed Marcos to be Rafael Sebastián Guillén Vicente, a thirty-seven year old former university professor from Tampico, Tamaulipas, who received a doctorate in philosophy from the National Autonomous University of Mexico (UNAM). According to Zedillo, Guillén was a member of a marxist guerrilla group prior to his arrival in Chiapas.

Marcos himself no longer denies that he is Rafael Sebastián Guillén. He claims to be a *ladino* (non-Indian) from central Mexico, the son of Spanish parents (both schoolteachers) who immigrated to Mexico, and who early on instilled in him a love of literature. He also speaks of time spent in the southwestern United States, including stints as a taxi driver and a waiter. To queries about his identity, however, Marcos has offered a more philosophical answer: "I am gay in San Francisco . . . a Black in South Africa . . . an Asian in Europe . . . a Palestinian in Israel."

Marcos, in other words, sees himself, and the Zapatista movement, as representing the dispossessed. Although the Mexican government has insisted on branding him a marxist, Marcos claims that the Zapatista movement represents a coming together of many doctrines and ideologies. He is also quick to stress the indigenous nature of the Zapatista movement, noting his own struggle within the movement to learn and appreciate the Indian way of seeing and explaining the world.

Despite the still-incomplete picture of Marcos's identity and biography, the story of his participation in what eventually became the Zapatista movement is fairly clear. In the early 1980s, he came to Chiapas with a small group of Mexicans who had been active in the Forces of National Liberation (FLN). Indeed, Marcos adopted the name of one of his FLN friends, who was gunned down at a police blockade in Chiapas. The FLN, established in 1969, was one of numerous leftist groups that arose in Mexico during the 1960s and 1970s in response to an economic downturn and government corruption and repression.

When Marcos and his FLN colleagues arrived in Chiapas, they became part of a situation that was already highly politicized. Throughout Chiapas, but particularly in the Lacandón Forest, where Marcos would help create the base of the Zapatista movement, Indian peasants had been struggling for decades to acquire and retain lands. Peasant organizations had emerged to combat land concentration and to protect against the threat of eviction. Some of these organizations received help and encouragement from Samuel Ruíz, Bishop of Chiapas; and while many were repressed, their members provided ready recruits for the Zapatistas.

The EZLN was formally established in the Lacandón at the end of 1983 and in the wake of a new round of violence in which several peasants were evicted from their lands. In its original form, it consisted of self-defense units intended to protect Chiapas Indians from further abuse and encroachment on their lands. The movement emerged as Mexico increasingly adopted the tenets of neoliberalism, ending land reform, opening the agrarian sector to private investment, and thus encouraging the land concentration that had already become a central problem in Chiapas. As the EZLN grew, Marcos emerged as a leader, working alongside Chiapas's Indian peoples, learning to speak their languages, and coming to understand their culture. As it became increasingly clear that peasants would need to defend their lives and their lands with force, Marcos (because of his knowledge of both the Indian and non-Indian worlds) was designated a leader and spokesman of the EZLN. Marcos assumed the title of "Subcomandante" (subcommander), suggesting that his leadership was largely titular, and was acknowledged within the context of a fairly egalitarian movement.

On 1 January 1994, the Zapatistas began a rebellion that deliberately coincided with the first day of the North American Free Trade Agreement (NAFTA). Marcos, who called NAFTA "a death certificate for the ethnic peoples of Mexico," immediately emerged as the mouthpiece of the revolt, arguing for land reform and indigenous rights, and criticizing free trade and neoliberalism. His ability to speak both Spanish and English encouraged international media coverage of the rebellion. The press (including the American television show *60 Minutes*) flocked to Chiapas in hopes of interviewing Marcos who, complete with fatigues, mask, gun, and pipe, was an intriguing figure. Indeed, Marcos soon became a sex symbol, and he received a flood of love letters. As the mystique of Marcos captured the imagination of Mexicans and non-Mexicans, the Zapatista rebellion garnered more attention. The EZLN helped foster that attention through its use of the internet and an official web page that often featured the letters, communiqués, and poetry of Subcomandante Marcos. At the same time, Marcos and the Zapatista movement inspired a variety of commercial items, including Zapatista dolls,

Subcomandante Marcos, acknowledged leader of the Zapatista movement, holds up an indigenous leadership staff given to him by a troupe of dancers after he arrived in Mexico City, concluding a fifteen-day caravan through thirteen Mexican states, March 2001. (Reuters / Corbis)

T-shirts, and "Marcondones" (Marcos condoms, complete with a ski-mask imprint).

Through writings and interviews, Subcomandante Marcos broadcast the grievances and demands of the Zapatista movement. He condemned the Mexican government for its role in disenfranchising Mexico's Indian peoples and making a mockery of the democratic process. In a letter to U.S. President Bill Clinton, he hinted that American aid intended for antidrug activities was being used to help the Mexican army repress the Zapatista rebels. Marcos also sent several letters to individuals in which he expressed Zapatista solidarity for the universal struggle for human rights. In 1999, he wrote a letter of support to Mumia Abu-Jamal, a black man imprisoned in Pennsylvania and condemned to death in a controversial case that many believe involved racism and police corruption.

The Zapatista movement, and Marcos's crusade on behalf of human rights and economic justice, attracted many international figures who flocked to the Lacandón to meet with the rebel leader. Marcos played host to Oliver Stone, American filmmaker, and to former French First Lady Danielle Mitterand in the early phase of the Zapatista rebellion. In the summer of 1994, Marcos presided over the National Democratic Convention, an international meeting that attracted Mexicans and non-Mexicans to Chiapas to engage in a dialogue about democracy, neoliberalism, and human rights. Marcos personally invited several Mexican notables, including authors Carlos Fuentes and Elena Poniatowska; and he penned invitations to international figures, including South African leader Nelson Mandela.

Since the 1994 uprising, Marcos has been the main representative for the EZLN in negotiations with the Mexican government. As the conflict in Chiapas has reached a stalemate, however, the public attention paid to Marcos and the Zapatistas has diminished. Nonetheless, Marcos's message and the EZLN struggle have not lost their allure. Indeed, Marcos's writings, including stories that attempt to convey the indigenous realities that lie at the heart of the Zapatista movement, have been preserved in a handful of books. Many Mexicans are now familiar with one of Marcos's key literary characters, Don Durito: a talking beetle with glasses and a pipe who converses with Marcos on a variety of topics, including the evils of neoliberalism. Marcos's literary compositions also have continued to draw international attention. In 1999, *The Story of Colors,* an English translation of a children's tale inspired by the indigenous culture in which Marcos has lived for almost twenty years, was published in the United States. The book's publisher, Cinco Puntos Press, received a production grant from the National Endowment for the Arts. The grant was withdrawn, however, when conservative U.S. congressmen were informed of the author's identity. Publication of *The Story of Colors,* which had now captured media attention, proceeded with alternative funding, and sales of the book soared.

As Mexico enters the next millennium, the fate of the Zapatistas and of Marcos is uncertain. Since the rebellion has lost momentum and dialogue between the rebels and the Mexican government has largely halted, the EZLN has lost its central position on the Mexican stage. Marcos's appeal, however, continues to be tangible. His ability to capture the imagination of many Mexicans, and to call international attention to a relatively small movement in the poorest state of Mexico, ensures Marcos an enduring place in Mexican history.

—*SBP*

See also: Agrarian Reform / Land and Land Policy; Chiapas; Lacandón; North American Free Trade Agreement (NAFTA); Ruíz, Bishop Samuel; Zapatista National Liberation Army (EZLN).

References:

Collier, George A., and Elizabeth Lowery Quaratiello. *Basta! Land and the Zapatista Rebellion in Chiapas.* Oakland, CA: Food First Books, 1994.

Harvey, Neil. *The Chiapas Rebellion: The Struggle for Land and Democracy.* Durham, NC: Duke University Press, 1998.

Katzenberger, Elaine, ed. *First World, Ha Ha Ha!: The Zapatista Challenge.* San Francisco, CA: City Lights, 1995.

Marcos, Subcomandante (Rafael Sebastián Guillén Vicente). *Our Word Is Our Weapon.* New York: Seven Stories Press, 2001.

————. *Shadows of Tender Fury: The Letters and Communiques of Subcomandante Marcos and the Zapatista Army of National Liberation.* Trans. Frank Bardacke and Leslie López. New York: Monthly Review Press, 1995.

————. *The Story of Colors.* Trans. Anne Bar Din. El Paso, TX: Cinco Puntos Press, 1999.

Ross, John. *Rebellion from the Roots: Indian Uprising in Chiapas.* Monroe, ME: Common Courage Press, 1995.

————. *The War against Oblivion: The Zapatista Chronicles.* Monroe, ME: Common Courage Press, 2000.

Mestizaje and *Indigenismo*

In Mexico as in the United States, questions of race and ethnicity are hotly debated whether in terms of public policy or popular culture. Unlike the United States, however, where most of these debates involve the black-white divide, in Mexico race and ethnicity are more likely to focus on *mestizaje* (race mixture) and the ongoing Indian "problem," topics most Americans prefer to ignore. Moreover, since the Revolution of 1910, policymakers—politicians, bureaucrats, academics, public intellectuals—have successfully encouraged Mexicans to acknowledge and even embrace their *mestizaje.* As part of this successful identification of Mexico as a nation of *mestizos* (people of mixed race), many of these same policymakers have attempted to incorporate the nation's sizeable but historically marginalized Indian population through *indigenismo,* a mixed bag of policies, programs, and rhetoric intended to facilitate that incorporation. While *indigenismo* has represented a more inclusive approach to the Indian "problem," its appreciation for Indian culture is usually more concerned with preconquest glories and current tourist potential than any desire to include Indians in a truly multicultural society. The ongoing Mayan Indian-based Zapatista movement that broke out in 1994 when Mexico signed the North American Free Trade Agreement (NAFTA) served notice that questions of race and ethnicity would continue to dominate public discourse into the twenty-first century.

Although the Spanish, like their English counterparts, imposed their colonies on lands that had previously "belonged" to various indigenous groups, the colonial experience with these conquered peoples was very different. This was especially true in Mexico, where Hernán Cortés's 1521 victory over the Aztecs gave Spain control of their empire and its well-developed tribute system. Most historical accounts stress the mineral wealth—gold and silver—that followed out of Mexico to Spain but an equally important source of wealth was Indian labor. The presence of an easily exploitable tribute system and the need for Indian labor to keep it producing gave the Spanish ample incentive to incorporate Indians into their empire rather than push them aside as the English and, later, the Americans did in their colonies. In the process, the administrative category of Indian, which lumped together hundreds of distinct cultures, would come to signify a racial identity that European colonists used to explain cultural differences (and thus to define themselves against) but that Indians tended to ignore until the development of pan-Indian movements in the late twentieth century.

Another concern of Spanish colonial administrators was the scarcity of European women, especially in the first decades after the conquest. As a reward for service and to facilitate conquest, prominent conquistadors were wedded to Indian princesses and already married men, like Cortés himself, often took Indian women as concubines. His soldiers followed suit, sometimes treating Indian women as the spoils of war, at other times developing informal "voluntary" relationships of different kinds. Cortés's union with his famous translator, La Malinche (or Doña Marina, as the Spanish called her), produced a son, Martín, who became a symbol of the mixing of the European and the Indian in terms of both blood and culture. Martín might have been Mexico's "first" *mestizo* but he was hardly alone and as the population of New Spain (Mexico's colonial name) grew, so did the proportion of *mestizos*. Legitimate *mestizos* from high-status families or the acknowledged but illegitimate children of prominent fathers, like Martín, were legally defined as "white" and retained the status of their parents (although it was Cortés's legitimate son by his Spanish wife who inherited his lands and titles). But, for the most part, in the colonial period, *mestizaje* was considered a marker of illegitimacy and *mestizos* were generally treated as social inferiors by Spaniards and *criollos* (whites born in the new world). Moreover, since Spanish law also recognized social distinctions, *mestizos* and Indians were usually prohibited from holding high positions in government and in the Church, from owning or carrying weapons, or from exhibiting any other signs of high status. They could also be whipped in public as punishment for a crime, a humiliation usually spared those of "pure" European descent. Under these circumstances, although some *mestizos* and Indians managed to rise to positions of prominence and wealth during 300 years of colonial rule, most continued to occupy the lower ranks in Mexican society. In some ways, *mestizos* had the worst of it since they were denied the legal protections accorded to Indians under Spanish law—Indians were classed as minors (along with women and children) and had their own court system—as well as the social privileges associated with whiteness.

The situation changed dramatically with Independence in 1821 and the liberal 1824 Constitution's codification of legal equality. Now, all Mexicans, including *mestizos* and Indians, were to be citizens—equal under the law and thus entitled, at least on paper, to all the privileges and duties of full citizenship. Moreover, both groups had played a central role in the independence struggles, producing their share of genuine heroes, such as *mestizo*

priest José María Morelos. However, these gains affected only a few, and it would be tempting to dismiss these legal advances as mere window-dressing were it not for that fact that two of the nation's most important nineteenth-century leaders, Benito Juárez and Porfirio Díaz, could not have held high public office in the colonial period because the former was Indian and the latter *mestizo*. Nevertheless, for the most part, both groups were still considered socially (if not constitutionally) inferior to whites and widely discriminated against. Since *mestizos* and Indians tended to belong to the lower classes, they were seen to embody all the negative traits traditionally ascribed to the poor by the *gente decente* (decent folk). Although stereotypes could vary, most commentators agreed that *mestizos* were highly emotional and prone to violence while Indians tended to be lazy and sneaky. Thus, for every success story, there were hundreds of less flattering accounts of *mestizo* and Indian perfidy and degradation. To make matters worse, educated elites influenced by European ideas about inferior races and the dangers of race mixture sometimes argued that these traits were essential or biological in origin—a position that implied the futility of any attempts at redemption through education or an improved standard of living.

The need to distinguish independent Mexico from Spain, however, favored more tolerant attitudes. For one thing, the Spanish colonial administration had discriminated against *criollos*, too, partly because they doubted their loyalty to Spain and partly because eighteenth-century racial theory held that climate and geography determined character, a theory that tainted *criollos* with inborn "tropical" inclinations to sensuality and sloth. For another, historical and cultural differences between Spain and Mexico were closely linked to race since it was Indian-ness past and present that most distinguished the colony from its colonizer. In this context, independence-minded *criollos* sought to glorify preconquest Indian "civilizations" and to represent themselves as its cultural heirs.

The demands of nineteenth-century nation-building, in particular the need to develop feelings of citizenship in all Mexicans, also encouraged more optimistic and inclusive attitudes toward nonwhite citizens. Humiliating defeats at the hands of the United States and France, the first resulting in the loss of half the national territory, the second in a three-year occupation, made even racist elites painfully aware of the dangers of an apathetic or disloyal underclass. If that were not enough, the stirring examples of Benito Juárez and Porfirio Díaz, both heroes of the French intervention, served as reminders of the potential greatness of the nation's *mestizo* and Indian populations. Still, the racial attitudes of policymakers on the eve of the Revolution of 1910 can only be described as mixed. On one hand, commentators like Francisco Bulnes insisted that over the centuries the Indians' corn-based diet had produced a biologically inferior or degenerate civilization incapable of meeting the demands of modern life. On the other hand, Minister of Education Justo Sierra argued that education and better living conditions could transform the Indians into "social assets." Whatever their opinion on Indians, most agreed that its was *mestizos* like president Díaz who represented Mexico's future. According to Sierra: "The *mestizo* family . . . in spite of the errors and vices that youth [as a "race"] and lack of education more than explain, has constituted the dynamic factor in our history." Sociologist Andrés Molina Enríquez even argued for a *mestizo* hybrid vigor, the product of years of struggle against man-made and environmental adversity and supplemented by frequent infusions of "Indian blood." Even the most sympathetic analysts, like Sierra, nonetheless favored increased European immigration to "whiten" the nation's racial stock.

The Revolution pushed racial policies to the forefront of the national agenda. Although accurate numbers for race are nearly impossible to extract from census data, a reasonable guess for early twentieth-century Mexico would be a national population that was 50 percent *mestizo*, 35 percent Indian, and 15 percent white. The percentage of *mestizos* would continue to expand as the other categories contracted. Thus, any hope at developing a unified national culture, at least in the eyes of most post-Revolutionary policymakers, resided with the *mestizo* population. In his influential and aptly titled 1916 tract on nation-building, *Forjando patria* (Forging the Fatherland), anthropologist Manuel Gamio insisted that "fusion of races, convergence and fusion of cultural manifestations, linguistic unification and economic balance of social elements . . . ought to characterize the Mexican population, so that it constitute and incarnate a powerful Fatherland and a coherent and defined nationality." José Vasconcelos, Mexico's first secretary of education, agreed, noting that "whether we like it or not the *mestizo* is the dominant element of the Latin American continent." In his widely read 1925 book, *La raza cósmica* (The Cosmic Race), Vasconcelos went further, arguing that race mixture in Latin America was producing a universal "cosmic race" that would eventually supersede the overly materialistic and arrogant white races. Late nineteenth-century criminological treatises had characterized *mestizos* as overly sensual and prone to violence; now they had become the Mexican national "type." If some commentators like philosopher Samuel Ramos and poet-essayist Octavio Paz would later suggest that *mestizos* as a group suffered from inferiority complexes and hid those insecurities behind masks, they clearly acknowledged these traits as inherent in the national character, as typically Mexican, rather than as the social pathologies of a marginalized subculture. Whiteness had by no means lost its privileged position in Mexican society, but the official "cult of the *mestizo*" represented a huge advance over previous official attitudes toward race and ethnicity, which had ranged from liberal condescension to outright racism. Coupled with a national Revolutionary experience that touched nearly every Mexican's life and the expansion of state power into the most isolated regions of the country, this official recognition of a *mestizo* Mexico helped develop the strong sense of national identity and purpose that had eluded pre-Revolutionary policymakers.

The very success of the cult of the *mestizo* raised questions about the place of Indians in post-Revolutionary Mexico. As one of principal cultural and biological components of *mestizaje,* Indians were recognized and even embraced by Mexican policymakers, who acknowledged that they had been unfairly left out of national development in the past. Post-Revolutionary policymakers promised to do better and devised comprehensive anthropological studies to provide the necessary data. Gamio noted that "we not only need to know how many men, women, and children there are in the Republic, the languages they speak, and how they control their ethnic groups. We need to know many other things: geography, geology, meteorology, flora and fauna . . . also language, religion, industry, art, commerce, folklore, clothing, food, strength, physical-anthropological type, etc., etc." With this kind of knowledge, he argued, the Mexican state could better "understand our needs, aspirations, deficiencies, and qualities . . . to procure the betterment of diverse ethnic groups." Although the intention seemed benevolent enough, Gamio's project was decidedly top-down: the Mexican government guided by expert anthropologists and sociologists would use the knowledge collected in these studies to "better" the nation's diverse ethnic groups but with little apparent interest in the concerns of those groups that did not fit the national agenda.

As memories of Revolutionary battles between Emiliano Zapata's "Indians" and the victorious Constitutionalists faded, *indigenismo* became an important component of official ideology, a symbol of Revolutionary promises to forge a Mexico that benefited all Mexicans regardless of race or ethnicity. Opinion within the *indigenista* movement was split from the beginning. Some argued that

Mexico's many Indian groups (official figures based on linguistic differences include nearly sixty distinct ethnicities) represented an invaluable national patrimony and should be accorded cultural autonomy. The more radical even argued for a degree of legal autonomy. Most favored varying degrees of assimilation. Official policy, at least until very recently, has generally insisted on their eventual integration into the *mestizo* majority. For Vasconcelos, assimilation began with education in the Spanish language and an introduction to European culture. To achieve this end, as secretary of education between 1920 and 1924, he opened over a thousand rural schools, staffed by "cultural missionaries." Sensing a threat to their way of life (which included the need for children's labor), Indian resistance to these cultural missions was widespread and strong. Subsequent programs taught in Indian languages and stressing practical skills such as basic literacy, hygiene, and modern farming techniques proved a bit more successful. Still, schoolteachers as government "agents" often got embroiled in local controversies and alienated many of their intended clients, especially during the more radical years of the Lázaro Cárdenas administration when "socialist education" attempted to undermine the authority of the Roman Catholic Church and local bosses. Official efforts to teach Indians about Indian culture were often inept, as educators typically failed to distinguish among groups, teaching a pan-Indian culture that sometimes bore little or no resemblance to local practices (even if it occasionally produced useful skills for the growing tourist industry). Efforts to incorporate Indian languages into the school curriculum were equally compromised as Cárdenas's Secretary of Education Moisés Sáenz turned the project over to an American Protestant minister, William Cameron Townsend, and his Summer Linguistic Institute. Assimilation programs failed to achieve their goals even when they worked: an Institute for Indigenous Students opened by the Secretariat of Education in Mexico City in

1926 did indeed train Indian students in a variety of useful skills, but most students refused to return home once they completed their studies because they felt more comfortable in the city.

But if live Indians resisted official *indigenismo,* dead Indians proved quite amenable. Mexican anthropologists like Manuel Gamio and Alfonso Caso reclaimed the glories of preconquest Mexico with massive reconstruction projects at Teotihuacán (outside Mexico City) and Monte Albán (outside Oaxaca). Mexican museums like the National Museum of Anthropology and History, which opened in 1964, became world-renowned repositories of Indian art and culture. The equally well-known Ballet Folclórico included "traditional" Indian dances in its repertoire. These practices spilled over into popular culture as entrepreneurs throughout Mexico began to produce and sell Indian relics—real (often stolen), faked, reproduced—and Mexico City *mestizos* began to don gaudy feathered costumes and dance to drums outside the national cathedral. As tourists flocked to Mexico in search of exotic customs and trinkets, the Indian "problem" was transformed into a thriving business. The fortuitous discovery and reconstruction of the Templo Mayor—the main temple in the Aztec capital—just off the Zócalo (main square) in Mexico City further cemented the connection between official *indigenismo,* monuments, and the tourist industry.

Since the 1970s, official *indigenismo* has come under public attack from dissident anthropologists and increasingly from Indian groups themselves. Beginning in the 1950s, anthropologists had begun to back away from their support for assimilation in favor of an "acculturation" model that stressed cultural and political reciprocity. To facilitate this reciprocal process, Gonzalo Aguirre Beltrán, appointed director of the National Indigenist Institute in 1970, established dozens of regional coordinating centers intended to provide the necessary training and support to break the cycles of Indian oppression fostered by local powerbrokers. By 1980, anthropologists like Guillermo Bonfil (a protégé of Aguirre Beltrán's) were prepared to go even further, condemning official *indigenismo* as a "ethnocide" and arguing for Indian cultural autonomy. Growing agitation from within Indian communities contributed as well. Official *indigenismo* had always been a top-down project conceived of and implemented by non-Indians (sympathetic or not). By the end of the twentieth century, the situation had shifted enough to warrant a constitutional change. Since 1992, Article 4 of the Mexican Constitution has guaranteed that "the law will protect and promote the development of [indigenous] languages, cultures, uses, customs, resources, and specific forms of social organization and will guarantee [indigenous peoples] effective access to the jurisdiction of the state." This constitutional emphasis on state jurisdiction, however, has been contested by Indian groups. Recent Indian demands for political autonomy, represented most forcefully by the Zapatistas in Chiapas, may well force the Mexican government to confront the Indian "problem" once again.

—RMB

See also: Anthropology and Archeology; Constitution of 1917; Vasconcelos, José; Zapatista National Liberation Army (EZLN).

References:

Buffington, Robert M. *"Forjando Patria:* Anthropology, Criminology, and the Post-Revolutionary Discourse on Citizenship," in *Criminal and Citizen in Modern Mexico.* Lincoln: University of Nebraska Press, 2000.

Knight, Alan. "Racism, Revolution, and *Indigenismo:* Mexico, 1910–1940," in Richard Graham, ed. *The Idea of Race in Latin America, 1870–1940,* pp. 71–113. Austin: University of Texas Press, 1990.

Mexico (State)

Located in central Mexico and surrounding the Federal District, Mexico State includes the valleys of Mexico and Toluca. The modern boundaries of the state were set in 1869 and Toluca became the capital city. The history and development of Mexico State are tied intimately to those of Mexico City. During the twentieth century, population growth overwhelmed this area, and by the 1990s, the state struggled with poverty and uneven development.

Mexico State was part of a broader area that gave rise to several urban cultures before the colonial period. Important population centers included Teotihuacán, Tula, Chalco, and Texcoco, and many areas had come under Aztec domination on the eve of Spanish Conquest. Spaniards arrived in central Mexico in 1519 and soon captured the Aztec capital (which became Mexico City). With help from Indian allies, the area surrounding the city was subdued. Hernán Cortés parceled out lands and Indian laborers to the conquerors, including himself. Texcoco was the largest grant, and it included over 16,000 Indians. Such grants were only grudgingly accepted by the Spanish Crown, which took steps to bring Indians under royal control. These efforts were aided by Franciscan and Dominican missionaries, who established Indian settlements that were intended to keep native and Spanish worlds separate. Although such efforts sought to protect Indians, their ultimate effect was to give Spanish mine owners and landowners easier access to a concentrated pool of labor.

The colonial economy of Mexico State was based on agriculture and cattle ranching. The large and growing market of Mexico City provided consistent demand for crops produced with the help of native labor. Silver mining also developed in the area, with mines at Zacualpán, Sultepec, and Temascaltepec utilizing Indian labor. The revolt of Miguel Hidalgo and José María Morelos, which began Mexico's struggle for independence in 1810, attracted some of the region's natives, whose lives were increasingly affected by labor and tribute demands. There were several insurgent victories here, including the brief capture of Toluca.

In 1824, statehood was granted to a large entity that included today's Mexico State, Hidalgo, Morelos, the Federal District, and much of Guerrero. Mexico City was initially the capital, and the new state contained the most significant population center in the new country. As the nineteenth century progressed, Mexico State assumed its modern shape. Mexico City was separated and Toluca chosen as the permanent capital. Guerrero was carved out in 1849, and in 1869 Hidalgo and Morelos were established.

Surrounding Mexico's capital and located in the center of the country, Mexico State directly experienced the political struggles of the nineteenth century. During the War of Reform (1858–1861), representatives of Mexico's conservative political faction controlled the region. From 1863 to 1867, the area was controlled by French forces, which supported a short-lived empire in Mexico. The Tuxtepec rebellion that brought Porfirio Díaz to power in 1876 also affected the state, which saw its governors imposed by the Porfirian regime (1876–1911).

Despite the autocratic nature of its political system, the Porfiriato brought remarkable progress to Mexico State. Mining and industry expanded with the help of foreign investment and the railroad enhanced the region's links with the Federal District and other areas of the country. Governor José Vicente Villada (who served four terms as governor from 1889 to 1904) helped foster these developments while also maintaining a degree of popular support through construction of new schools and declaration of laws that benefited the working class. But Villada and other state leaders also witnessed increasing opposition to the Díaz regime and its model of development, which did not benefit all sectors of society.

In 1909, Andrés Molina Enríquez, a teacher from Mexico State, wrote a pointed critique of Mexico's social problems, including peonage and land concentration. Molina was among those who supported Francisco I. Madero's rebellion against Díaz in 1910–1911. Molina, however, was then blocked in his bid for the governor's post, and he was captured and imprisoned. Several of his followers, upset with Madero's lack of attention to land reform, joined the movement of Morelos rebel Emiliano Zapata. The state's Zapatista movement, led by Genovevo de la O and Francisco Pacheco, grew in importance, and after Madero's death, it challenged Venustiano Carranza's Constitutionalist movement for control of the state. Briefly in 1915, Mexico's Convention government (with which Zapata sided) dominated, and Governor Gustavo Baz embraced Zapata's Plan of Ayala, which called for sweeping agrarian reform. Carranza's Constitutionalists soon occupied Toluca, however, and hopes for radical reform diminished.

During the 1920s and 1930s, state leaders focused on pacifying the region, which experienced more unrest during the Cristero Rebellion (1926–1929). The economy worsened and *campesinos* (rural workers) became more aggressive in their demands for land. During the presidency of Lázaro Cárdenas (1934–1940) and under Governor Wenceslao Labra, Mexico State finally experienced a round of agrarian reform. Through such reform, many *ejidos* (state grants of land cultivated by a community) were established in this part of central Mexico.

After 1940, as Mexico's leaders shifted attention from Revolutionary reform to development and economic modernization, Mexico State (along with the Federal District) experienced an industrial transformation. Private investment in electricity, steel, textiles, construction, and tourism all aided in this transformation. During the late 1950s and early 1960s, Governor Gustavo Baz welcomed the establishment of several automotive plants (including General Motors and Ford). Baz also promoted the creation of industrial zones in the Toluca Valley, Texcoco, and Chalco. Mexico State's impressive economic growth did not affect agriculture, which attracted little investment and remained technologically backward. Additionally, the economic boom did not benefit all areas of the state. The south

in particular remained rural, agricultural, and underdeveloped.

Urbanization accompanied the industrial boom, and during the last three decades of the twentieth century, Mexico State witnessed a steady and overwhelming growth in its population. People poured into the state to fill the jobs created by industry, and many more spilled in from the congested Federal District. Just as Mexico's capital city found it increasingly difficult to provide housing and services to its inhabitants, so did Mexico State struggle to accommodate its people. The dynamic growth of both areas also brought environmental problems (particularly air pollution and the depletion of water resources) and a steady decline in living conditions for many. When Mexico began experiencing an economic crisis during the 1980s, rising crime rates were added to the picture. The future of Mexico State, like that of the Federal District, will largely depend on how its leaders manage the urban growth that has overwhelmed this section of central Mexico.

—*SBP*

See also: Cristero Rebellion; Mexico City; Revolution of 1910; Urbanization.

References:

Jarquín O., María Teresa, and Carlos Herrejón Peredo. *Breve historia del Estado de Mexico.* Mexico City: El Colegio de Mexico, 1995.

Official state web site: http://www.edomex.gob. mx

Mexico City

A sprawling metropolis situated in the Valley of Mexico, Mexico City serves as the nation's capital. Strictly speaking, the city consists of only the historic center (including the Zócalo or main plaza) and four "delegations," or sections. But the Federal District (D.F.) extends beyond this to include several other delegations while the metropolitan area extends farther still to include contiguous areas of the State of Mexico. Mexico City has historically served as the country's political and economic center. It has also served as a cultural hub, with impressive museums and an active musical and artistic scene. Particularly as the twentieth century began, Mexico City became a magnet for Mexicans from other parts of the country. It continued to attract migrants during Mexico's midcentury economic boom. By the 1990s, Mexico City was the largest city in the world with a metropolitan population of some 20 million. It was also one of the world's poorest urban areas, and it faced significant environmental problems.

Mexico City was the center of the Aztec culture before the arrival of the Spaniards in 1519. Indeed, the Zócalo sits atop the ancient Aztec capital of Tenochtitlán. According to legend, the nomadic Aztecs (or Mexica) settled here when they saw an eagle perched on a cactus grasping a snake (a scene depicted on today's Mexican flag). After the Spaniards defeated the Aztecs, they began to build their own city, destroying and burying temples, and other signs of native culture. Mexico City became the headquarters of the colony of New Spain, and it developed a grid pattern, with the Zócalo (site of the main government buildings and a cathedral) at the center.

Mexico City retained its position as the seat of power after 1821, when Mexico achieved independence from Spain. The volatile and often violent nature of Mexican politics during the nineteenth century directly affected the capital city as a series of rulers occupied (and were often forcibly deposed from) the presidential seat. During the Mexican War (1846–1848), U.S. troops briefly controlled the city, and from 1864 to 1867 Austrian Archduke Maximilian and his wife, Carlotta, ruled from the capital, supported by French troops that first invaded Mexico in 1862.

Because of such political unrest, Mexico City remained insecure and underdeveloped. By midcentury, however, the capital began to experience limited growth. This first wave of

Mexico City's Zócalo and cathedral (Nik Wheeler / Corbis)

development was encouraged by the so-called Reform Laws, which forced the Roman Catholic Church (owner of nearly half of the city's buildings) to sell its properties. This had the effect of expanding settlement to the west of the Zócalo (where most Church holdings were located). Members of the working class first occupied this area, but the wealthy soon claimed the city's west side as its own.

A second wave of growth began in the 1880s and coincided with an export-oriented economic boom presided over by President Porfirio Díaz (1876–1911). Under Díaz, Mexico City became the financial and business center of the country and home to major import houses and foreign investors. Many of Mexico's wealthiest landowners also kept a residence in the capital. Meanwhile, the city took on a more modern appearance as federal money (and foreign expertise) helped pave streets, build sewers, expand railroad lines, and wire the city for electricity. As the country's celebration of the centennial of independence approached, Díaz also invested in monuments designed to depict Mexico's "official" heroes. Thus, statues of Columbus, Cuahtémoc (the last Aztec emperor), and Benito Juárez (nineteenth-century president and architect of the Reform Laws) were erected, as was the Angel of Independence, one of the city's most famous landmarks.

Despite its impressive growth around the turn of the century, however, Mexico City continued to struggle with problems related to its geographical location in a wet valley with poor drainage and flooding problems. While a British-built drainage system was completed in 1900, disease was a constant problem and many residents continued to live without potable water or access to an adequate sewage system. Conditions were especially challenging for the growing numbers of workers and the city's poorer residents.

Many peasants migrated to Mexico City in the last two decades of the nineteenth century, having lost their lands because of the expansion of the railroad and of large estates.

By 1900, nearly half of the capital's population of over 500,000 were peasants from rural areas. These recent migrants, as well as the city's working class were increasingly pushed to the city's eastern edges as wealthier residents established themselves west of the Zócalo. The pattern of a rich west and poor east would persist, with the east characterized by slums and poor living conditions. As Díaz sought to make the capital a showcase of Mexican modernization, the poor were further marginalized and even punished for their poverty. Mass arrests of petty thieves and beggars occurred, and many peasants were rounded up and sent back to rural areas to serve as laborers.

On the eve of the Mexican Revolution of 1910, workers in Mexico City were beginning to mobilize against the continuation of the Díaz regime. The city's sizeable middle class was also increasingly vocal, often basing their demands for change on the concept of municipal autonomy, which had been eliminated by Díaz as the national government centralized its control over the capital. While the heavy hand of Díaz prevented supporters of Francisco Madero from taking up arms in 1910 and 1911, the popular classes eventually took to the streets to push for Díaz's resignation.

As president, Madero did restore a degree of political autonomy to Mexico's capital. Significant reforms for workers and the urban poor did not occur, however. Workers in particular became radicalized, and in 1912 they established the Casa del Obrero Mundial, which brought together several workers' groups as well as members of the middle class. Increasingly the capital's workers became a political force that could not be ignored by Revolutionary leaders. Through strikes and interruptions in electrical and transport services, workers demanded better pay, improved living conditions, and a permanent voice in the administration of the city. Women also added to the fray, playing a major role in the food riots that became common as Revolutionary unrest took its toll.

The violence of the Mexican Revolution touched the capital first during the Decena Trágica (Tragic Ten Days) of 1913. During this brief period, soldiers loyal to President Madero exchanged fire in the heart of the city with forces trying to overthrow the president. The security of many residents was also affected by the struggle between Venustiano Carranza's Constitutionalist forces and those of Emiliano Zapata and Pancho Villa. Between 1914 and 1915, these two factions competed for control of the capital and the government.

Unlike Zapata and Villa, whose interests lay in rural areas, Carranza and his most important general, Alvaro Obregón, recognized the importance of gaining the support of Mexico City's residents, particularly its workers. They thus attempted to provide some material relief to the city, which was often cut off from supplies of food as fighting elsewhere disrupted the railroad system. Carranza and Obregón also fashioned an alliance with the Casa del Obrero Mundial, promising workers housing and other benefits in return for their support. Despite this pact, however, once Carranza was firmly established in power, he catered more to the capital's business interests. Workers' restiveness was expressed in the general strike of 1916, which threatened to paralyze the city. Carranza's response to worker militancy was repression, and he extended martial law throughout the city, jailing many workers and union leaders.

Carranza's actions were the beginning of a long trend: that of a recentralization of federal control over Mexico City. By the end of the 1920s, Mexico City was once again controlled by the national government and by Mexico's official party, eventually known as the PRI. The capital's mayor was chosen directly by the president. Organized labor (as well as the city's middle class) remained an important political force, but it increasingly competed with business and industrial interests as Mexico's leaders debated the future of the city's development.

Beginning in the 1940s, the federal government embraced industrial development. By the 1960s, Mexico was in the middle of an economic boom, with Mexico City at the center of that boom. Federal money helped expand the capital's infrastructure, and a service economy grew to meet the demand of an expanding middle class. The city's population grew, nearly tripling in size from 1940 to 1960. This demographic boom was primarily due to migration, as poorer groups from the countryside came to the city seeking better opportunities. Many of these migrants entered a city that was already straining to provide housing and essential services. Some of the recent arrivals incurred the wrath of Ernesto P. Uruchurtu, who served as the city's mayor for fourteen years beginning in 1952. Uruchurtu's administration had a highly moralistic tone, and he sought to cleanse the capital of street vendors and squatters, members of the lower classes whose options were few.

As Mexico City's population grew and the city expanded outward, transportation became a key issue. Traffic congestion in the central city and the growth of peripheral areas finally encouraged the national government to embrace the idea of a subway system, as did the prospect of hosting the world at the 1968 Olympics. The METRO, as it was called, was built in the late 1960s and later expanded. While it quickly gained a reputation as an efficient and reliable means of transportation, the METRO also assured the additional and rapid growth of the city and its suburbs, exacerbating urban problems. These problems became especially obvious as Mexico's economy began to deteriorate.

Under President Luis Echeverría (1970–1976) an attempt was made to slow the capital's growth by halting expansion of the METRO and encouraging industrial development in other parts of the country. Such efforts largely failed to halt Mexico City's phenomenal expansion, and subsequent presidents fought a losing battle to provide services, even as the country's economy worsened and resources for its capital city diminished. The national government's inability to control urban growth mirrored the PRI's inability to gain the approval of the city's middle classes, workers, and urban poor. Beginning in the 1970s, the PRI steadily lost electoral support in Mexico City.

Significant popular challenges to the PRI surfaced in 1968, with protests that called attention to the government's lavish spending on the Olympics and its neglect of urban poverty. Protestors also lamented the very real limitations to political participation under the one-party system. Students were especially active as demonstrators and on 2 October 1968 many were massacred by police on the order of President Gustavo Díaz Ordaz and the Minister of the Interior Luis Echeverría. Citizen activism continued in the 1980s and 1990s, spurred on by Mexico's poor economy. A steady decrease in public money for the capital city, as well as the PRI's mismanagement of the 1985 earthquake, which leveled parts of the city and caused

thousands of deaths, further emboldened residents. Voters demanded a greater voice in local politics, and in 1988 they voted overwhelmingly for Cuahtémoc Cárdenas, who unsuccessfully challenged PRI candidate Carlos Salinas for the presidency. Finally in 1997, Mexico City's voters were given the right to elect directly their mayor. They chose Cárdenas in the first popular vote for mayor since 1928.

The popular activism that was successfully challenging the PRI by the end of the twentieth century helped call attention not only to the limits of one-party rule but also to two of the capital's most significant problems: crime and environmental deterioration. Particularly as the economy worsened, Mexico City experienced a crime wave. Violent crime and theft made the city a particularly dangerous place, and the police seemed unable (and even unwilling) to act. Many residents identified the police as part of the problem, and some officers were implicated in criminal

Rescue workers stand before a building completely demolished in the 1985 earthquake in Mexico City. (Owen Franken / Corbis)

acts and corruption. Cleaning up the capital's police force and lowering the city's crime rate remained concerns as the twenty-first century began. In 2002, a group of Mexico City entrepreneurs took the novel step of hiring former New York City mayor Rudolph Guliani to advise the city on crime prevention.

Environmental deterioration is an equally alarming problem in today's Mexico City. By the end of the twentieth century, the capital faced a significant water shortage, so that millions of gallons of water had to be pumped into the city each day. As the area's underground aquifers have been depleted, the land underneath the city has sunk, causing significant structural damage to buildings, including the national cathedral. Air pollution, however, has been Mexico City's most visible environmental problem. By the late 1980s the capital (with over 3 million vehicles and countless factories) was considered one of the most polluted cities in the world, with ozone levels frequently reaching dangerous levels. Officials began to address this problem in earnest in 1989 by requiring every car to sit idle for one weekday and by ordering the dirtiest factories to curtail their production. In the early 1990s, several high-polluting factories were shut down, and the government introduced unleaded gasoline and catalytic converters. While some of these actions had a decidedly limited effect (many people, for example, bought a second car to get around the once-weekly driving restriction), by the year 2000 there had been some improvement in air quality.

—SBP

See also: Cárdenas, Cuahtémoc; Carranza, Venustiano; Díaz, Porfirio; Environmental Issues; Labor Movements; Madero, Francisco; Mexico (State); Partido Revolucionario Institucional (PRI); Revolution of 1910; Tlatelolco Massacre; Urbanization.

References:

Davis, Diane E. *Urban Leviathan: Mexico City in the Twentieth Century.* Philadelphia: Temple University Press, 1994.

Johns, Michael. *The City of Mexico in the Age of Díaz.* Austin: University of Texas Press, 1997.

Kandell, Jonathan. *La Capital: The Biography of Mexico City.* New York: Random House, 1988.

Lear, John. *Workers, Neighbors, and Citizens: The Revolution in Mexico City.* Lincoln: University of Nebraska Press, 2001.

Michoacán (State)

A central-western state with Morelia as its capital, Michoacán has a varied terrain, including valleys, highlands, and coastal lowlands. The state is home to several large lakes, including Lake Pátzcuaro. It also houses Latin America's largest steel factory and contains one of Mexico's most important Pacific ports, which is named after Lázaro Cárdenas, a native son. Michoacán has always played a central role in Mexico's history. It produced the main leaders of the independence movement, and during the Revolutionary period of the early twentieth century, Lázaro Cárdenas carried out sweeping reforms here, which anticipated his efforts at the national level. In the latter part of the twentieth century, Michoacán struggled to create a viable economy, and it became a center of opposition to the Institutional Revolutionary Party (PRI).

An area of great cultural diversity, Michoacán hosted several native groups in the centuries before Spanish contact. Among the most important were the Purepecha or Tarascan peoples, who arrived in the twelfth century. The Tarascans extended their influence throughout much of the state, establishing an empire with urban centers at Pátzcuaro and Tzintzuntzán. This empire was a rival of the Mexica-Aztec kingdom, which unsuccessfully sought the help of the Tarascans in resisting Spanish conquest.

Initial contact between the Spaniards and Tarascans was peaceful, though many Indians fled from Spanish control. Missionaries arrived in the 1530s to begin the work of converting Michoacán's native peoples. Vasco de Quiroga led these efforts, and he was named Bishop of Michoacán in 1536. Quiroga gained a reputation as a defender and champion of the Indians. He established a college in Pátzcuaro that was devoted to the study and preservation of native languages, and he encouraged Indians to develop the artisanal skills that earned Pátzcuaro its reputation as a center of native crafts (a reputation that has persisted).

An economy based on mining and the production of sugar, indigo, cotton, and other crops emerged, and the city of Valladolid (today's Morelia) became Michoacán's political and economic hub. By the seventeenth century, Valladolid was a prosperous area, and many wealthy miners and landowners chose to live here. Their wealth helped produce the art and architecture that continues to draw visitors to today's capital city. Valladolid was also a center of the Roman Catholic Church, with which the economic elite had strong ties. Many of Michoacán's native peoples were drawn into the colonial economy as a labor force for the haciendas and mines. Indian lands, meanwhile, came under attack as Spaniards sought to build larger estates. By the late colonial period, Indian discontent over labor demands and land disputes was encouraging rebellion.

Indian unrest helped produce recruits for the anti-Spanish revolt of Miguel Hidalgo and José María Morelos, both of whom were natives of Michoacán. In this early phase of Mexico's independence movement, many mestizos (people of Spanish and Indian ancestry) also joined the Hidalgo-Morelos insurgency. Valladolid remained a center of support for the Spanish Crown, however. In 1821, Agustín de Iturbide, another native son, occupied the city and imposed independence on its reluctant elites. Iturbide became the country's first leader, though his Mexican Empire lasted only briefly. Michoacán gained statehood in 1824. Valladolid was designated the capital, and its name was soon changed to Morelia, in honor of José María Morelos.

Michoacán did not easily recover from the considerable destruction of the independence era, and the political unrest of Mexico's early years as a nation delayed any re-

covery. The state was a center of the War of Reform (1858–1861), in which liberal and conservative factions clashed. The liberal Laws of Reform, which included attacks on communal (e.g., Indian and Church) lands added to the volatile situation, generating Church protest and agrarian unrest. Finally, in the 1860s, Michoacán was partially occupied by invading French forces, which briefly established an empire on Mexican soil. Rebel groups resisted the French, bringing another round of violence to the state.

Under the national regime of President Porfirio Díaz (1876–1911), Michoacán enjoyed greater stability and prosperity. Foreign investment helped build the state's railway lines and expand industrial production, particularly in mining and wood products. Foreigners also invested in land, bringing mechanized agriculture to some areas of the state. This latter development, aided by national laws that encouraged land concentration, occurred at the expense of the state's campesinos (rural workers), who became increasingly restive on the eve of the Revolution of 1910.

Several outstanding figures provided leadership in Michoacán during the Revolution. Salvador Escalante was among the first to support Francisco Madero's 1910–1911 revolt against Díaz, and his forces captured Morelia in 1911. After Madero's death, Gertrudis Sánchez led the local rebellion against Victoriano Huerta, who was responsible for Madero's demise. Sánchez joined Venustiano Carranza's Constitutionalist movement. He captured Morelia in 1914 and briefly served as the state's governor. In 1920, after the death of Carranza, Francisco Múgica became governor. An opposition journalist during the Díaz years, Múgica had supported the revolts of both Madero and Carranza, and he served as a representative to the congress that drafted Mexico's Constitution of 1917. Múgica was a dedicated reformer, and during his term as governor, he began the process of land distribution. Múgica also established a friendship with Lázaro Cárdenas, who assumed the governorship in

1928. Cárdenas continued Múgica's work, organizing urban workers and *campesinos,* carrying out land reform, and reigning in the power of the Roman Catholic Church. With his reputation as a social reformer well established, Cárdenas moved into national politics, serving as Mexico's president from 1934 to 1940. As a national leader, Cárdenas included the like-minded Múgica in his cabinet.

The land reform that was championed by Múgica and Cárdenas was also encouraged by the figure of Primo Tapia de la Cruz. A member of the Tarascan community of Naranja, Tapia spent time working in the United States, where he was exposed to the radicalism of the International Workers of the World (IWW). Tapia also allied himself with the Mexican Liberal Party (PLM), which sought significant social reform and which was a leading critic of the Díaz regime on the eve of the Revolution of 1910. When he returned to Michoacán in 1921, Tapia became the state's main agrarian leader, helping to organize *campesinos* and resisting the attempts of the Mexican government to co-opt them. Tapia became increasingly dissatisfied with the pace and nature of agrarian reform and he led others in seizing lands in the Naranja region. On the order of President Plutarco Elías Calles, Tapia was captured, tortured, and shot in 1926.

After the era of reform that characterized the 1920s and 1930s, Michoacán, like many areas of Mexico, turned its attention to economic modernization. Under a series of governors, social reform was deemphasized in favor of development. Irrigation and the application of science and technology to agriculture helped Michoacán become an important producer of fruits and vegetables for U.S. markets. Cattle ranching expanded, as did the state's fishing industry. Forestry also remained important, and in 1973 the Mexican government established Productos Forestales de Michoacán to promote the wood products industry. Although such developments did expand the state's economy, Mi-

choacán never fully industrialized, and it remained dependent on outside markets for its agriculture and forestry products. The growth of the agro-export sector was also accompanied by a resurgence of land concentration. Finally, Michoacán failed to produce the jobs needed for a growing population. By the late twentieth century, Michoacán's people were migrating to the United States in increasing numbers in search of work and better opportunities.

Politically, contemporary Michoacán is known for its defiance of the PRI, the official party that dominated Mexico for most of the twentieth century. Particularly in the last two decades of the century, the state became a center of opposition. In 1987, Cuauhtémoc Cárdenas (son of the former president) withdrew from the PRI to protest its selection of Carlos Salinas de Gortari as Mexico's next president. In 1988, Cárdenas unsuccessfully challenged Salinas in an election riddled with fraud, though he gained the support of voters in Michoacán. One year later, Cárdenas helped establish the Party of the Democratic Revolution (PRD), which became Mexico's main left-of-center party. The PRD proved especially strong in Cárdenas's home state, and the PRI's efforts to suppress it led to political violence. Rigged municipal elections in 1989, for example, encouraged PRD sympathizers to occupy government buildings. Soldiers and tanks were sent to dislodge the protestors, several of whom were arrested and killed. The 1992 governor's election was also volatile, with the PRD defying the questionable election results that favored the PRI and installing their own candidate, Cristóbal Arías, as the leader of a rival government.

—*SBP*

See also: Agrarian Reform/Land and Land Policy; Cárdenas, Cuauhtémoc; Cárdenas, Lázaro; Revolution of 1910.

References:
Florescano, Enrique, ed. *Historia general de Michoacán,* 4 vols. Morelia, Michoacán: Instituto Michoacana de Cultura, 1989.
Friedrich, Paul. *Agrarian Revolt in a Mexican Village.* Englewood Cliffs, NJ: Prentice Hall, 1970.

Official state web site: http://www.michoacán.gob.mx

Militarism

Militarism—the involvement of the armed forces in political affairs—has played a major role in shaping Mexico's development in the nineteenth and twentieth centuries. Although political ideologies and politicians contested for power, the real political players were the generals who dominated the presidency or the presidents from 1821 to 1946. The upheaval of the Revolution of 1910 ended the old militarism, only to give birth to a new Revolutionary militarism. It would take the rise of well-organized civilian groups and the determination of a series of Revolutionary presidents who were also generals to curb the power of the military by the 1940s.

Porfirio Díaz—who dominated Mexican politics from 1876 to 1911—was a good example of the career soldier who came to the presidency through military action. Díaz, however, realized the importance of curbing the power of the regional military leaders and used a variety of techniques ranging from salary increases to military force to bring the generals into line. While these actions curbed provincial militarism, they also created a corrupt, politicized, and aging military commanded by an officer corps out of touch with the troops they commanded and the masses in general.

When the Revolution of 1910 produced scattered regional revolts, the Federal Army quickly demonstrated its inability to suppress the uprisings. Díaz had substantially reduced the size of the army, from 35,000 in 1900 to 20,000 in 1910. In a matter of months (November 1910 to May 1911), the combined Revolutionary forces nominally led by Francisco Madero forced Díaz to resign and go into exile.

Madero's peace pact with Díaz, however, kept the Federal Army intact while disbanding most of the Revolutionary forces. After his election to the presidency in late 1911,

Madero had to depend primarily on the old Federal Army to defend his new administration. In addition, Madero violated an earlier promise that all those who fought for the Revolution would be incorporated into the regular army at their permanent ranks. Thus, Madero alienated the very forces that had helped put him in power. Revolts against his government soon developed, including some led by former rebel commanders who had supported him in 1910–1911. Madero believed that his election to the presidency represented the triumph of civilian rule over militarism. His failure of judgment became clear in February 1913 when prominent generals in the old Federal Army overthrew his government and assassinated Madero and his vice-president.

The new president of Mexico was General Victoriano Huerta, a military holdover from the Díaz era. Huerta's actions quickly sparked new and more extensive Revolutionary activity. Although Huerta desperately tried to increase the size of the army, the Revolutionaries outnumbered federal forces in every major battle. The most powerful of the Revolutionary forces was the Constitutionalist army, which contained such prominent leaders as Venustiano Carranza, Pancho Villa, and Alvaro Obregón. In July 1914 Huerta went into exile; the following month the Revolutionary victors formally dissolved the old Federal Army. The defeat of Huerta signaled the end of the old-style militarism; it created, however, a new Revolutionary militarism that would take decades to curb.

While the Revolutionary generals would soon fall out and start fighting each other, there was one thing on which they could agree: the Revolutionary generals—not the civilian politicians—should run the country. When Revolutionary military leaders met in October 1914, they were unable to reach a political agreement, which led to civil war and the bloodiest phase of the Revolutionary struggle in 1914 and 1915. The main military contest was between the forces of Pancho Villa and those loyal to Carranza but led by

Obregón. After Carranza's forces eliminated Villa as a national political contender, Carranza faced the problem of dealing with Revolutionary militarism.

Although calling himself the "First Chief of the Constitutionalist Army," Carranza left the fighting to his other generals and basically represented civilian leadership for the Revolution. After his election to the presidency in 1917, Carranza faced the same task that Porfirio Díaz had many years earlier: subduing the regional military leaders. Military officers held the governorships of eighteen of the thirty states, often ignored orders from the central government, and commanded the personal loyalty of their troops. Carranza had to deal with a military establishment far larger than the one confronting Madero just four years earlier. The "Constitutionalist" army consisted of more than 200,000 troops commanded by approximately 50,000 officers, of whom more than 5,000 claimed the rank of general. The process of substantially reducing the size of the army started in 1916. On 1 May 1917 a shrunken Constitutionalist army (approximately 150,000) became the new federal army. Despite the reduction in force of more than 100,000, the military still took up two-thirds of the total national budget.

While the army had been reduced, the political ambitions of the Revolutionary generals had not. Carranza could not constitutionally succeed himself so he attempted to impose a civilian, Ignacio Bonillas, as his successor in the 1920 presidential elections. This move was challenged by Obregón and his supporters, who revolted in April 1920, leading to the assassination of Carranza. The elections went forward, and Obregón assumed the presidency in December 1920.

Although Obregón was a Revolutionary general who enjoyed strong support among the military, the new president soon moved to curb the political role of the military. Military officers who supported Carranza lost their military and political posts. Obregón also had to deal with the military leaders who had supported him in the 1920 revolt. He ordered that all his supporters who claimed the rank of general be incorporated in the regular army at that rank. Obregón also provided generous financial incentives to officers willing to curb their political ambitions. At the same time, Obregón moved in a much different direction. He reduced the size of the army by some 40,000 troops and the army's share of the national budget from 61 percent in 1921 to only 36 percent in 1924. Obregón also attempted to promote greater professionalism in the military through improvements in military education.

Obregón's efforts to reduce militarism were rudely interrupted by a major revolt in 1923 caused by disenchantment with the military reforms and disagreement over who would succeed Obregón in 1924. The suppression of the revolt provided mixed results as far as the long-term goal of reducing militarism was concerned, producing about as many new political generals as it eliminated. The defeat of the rebellion of 1923 indicated that the end of regional military power was nearing as the central government increased its control.

Obregón's successor in the presidency, Plutarco Elías Calles, was another Revolutionary general who continued the process of reducing the role of the military in political life. A key figure in this process was General Joaquín Amaro, minister of war from 1924 to 1930. Amaro reduced the size of the army, setting a maximum of 55,000 troops, and temporarily suspended all promotions. The military percentage of the national budget declined from 36 percent in 1924 to 25 percent in 1927. Amaro also instituted reforms affecting the mission of the armed forces, promotion policies, and retirement and pensions. There was an effort to instill greater professionalism in the military by improving education at all levels of the army. Amaro even went to the extreme of completely closing the Military College—Mexico's only source of trained officers—for a year to overhaul completely its physical plant, staff, and curriculum.

Obregón's decision to return to the presidency in 1928 provoked a crisis among the military elite. Obregón's move frustrated the political ambitions of several other generals who aspired to the presidency. Two of the army's most prominent generals—Arnulfo Gómez and Francisco Serrano—announced their candidacies. Facing certain electoral defeat, Gómez and Serrano revolted in October 1927. The revolt was quickly crushed, with both leaders being executed.

A dispute between Calles and the Roman Catholic Church was also producing military problems for Calles. Calles's feud with the Church had provoked a small-scale civil war that was attracting support from some of the Revolutionary generals who saw it as an opportunity to pursue their own political ambitions. The crisis over presidential succession and the conflict with the Church came together in July 1928 when a religious fanatic assassinated President-elect Alvaro Obregón. So many generals wanted to assume the presidency that a civilian candidate—Emilio Portes Gil—had to be selected as provisional president by Congress. It was the top generals, however, who told the Congress who the civilian president would be. The real winner was the outgoing president, Calles, who continued to dominate politics after leaving office.

In a new move to bring the generals into line, Calles founded the official party, originally called the Partido Nacional Revolucionario, or PNR. The PNR brought together the main interest groups of the Revolution—agrarian, labor, and military—into an organized structure Calles hoped would curb regional militarism. Instead, the generals soon came to control the new party; its first head was yet another general, Pascual Ortiz Rubio. This effort at political reorganization also prompted the last major uprising by Revolutionary generals against the central government in March 1929. Calles personally directed the government's successful campaign against the rebels, whose defeat led to yet another purge of the officer corps.

After the provisional presidency of the civilian Portes Gil from 1928 to 1930, two generals—Pascual Ortiz Rubio and Abelardo Rodríguez—served the remaining years of the presidential term (1930–1934). Calles and a small group of top-ranking officers, however, continued to control political affairs as the military dominated both the government and the new official party. Despite the political role played by the generals, the portion of the budget allotted to the military actually declined from 32 percent in 1930 to 25 percent in 1933.

With another presidential succession scheduled for 1934, the ruling generals were divided over who should be the next president. Calles tapped as the new president General Lázaro Cárdenas, who easily defeated his two opponents, who were also military officers. Calles and Cárdenas soon split; Cárdenas prevailed in the ensuing power struggle, removing Calles's supporters at all levels of the officer corps and effectively sending Calles himself into exile.

Cárdenas's reworking of the military went far beyond the simple expediency of removing officers who supported Calles. Cárdenas implemented a "Six-Year Plan" for reforming and reorganizing the military establishment. To promote greater professionalism, Cárdenas established a promotion plan based on competitive examination and tightened provisions for mandatory retirement. He also improved general living conditions for the military through higher pay, better housing, and expanded educational facilities. Cárdenas still succeeded in reducing the military's share of the national budget from 25 percent in 1934 to 19 percent in 1938. He also replaced the volunteer system of recruitment, which had encouraged regional militarism, with one calling for a lottery system that would draw from a broader social and geographic base. His reform and reorganization of the military establishment redirected the loyalty of junior officers and military personnel from their immediate superiors to the president. Cárdenas also encouraged the creation of agrarian and labor militias to counterbalance the power of the army. By 1938 the labor militia alone numbered 100,000, making it considerably larger than the entire regular army. Cárdenas also reorganized the official party into four sectors; although one sector was reserved for the military, it was counterbalanced by the creation of agrarian, labor, and popular sectors. The reorganization also restricted the representation of the military to the national level, eliminating it from regional party councils where Revolutionary officers often played leading roles.

The 1940 presidential election was a contest between two generals, the official party candidate, General Manuel Avila Camacho, and a distinguished Revolutionary general, Juan Andreu Almazán. Avila Camacho won easily, among the usual charges of electoral fraud. Avila Camacho, however, was not a typical Revolutionary general turned president. He had not reached the rank of general until the 1920s and had made his military reputation as an effective administrator rather than a combat commander. Avila Camacho was not popular among the Revolutionary generals and continued the long-term process of curbing their political power. One of his first actions as president was to eliminate the military sector of the official party.

Despite Mexico's entry into World War II in 1942, the military share of the national budget actually decreased under Avila Camacho from 21 percent in 1940 to 15 percent in 1945. Once the wartime emergency was over, Avila Camacho implemented the mandatory retirement policies established under Cárdenas, forcing more than 500 aging Revolutionary generals into retirement. The declining political power of the military was evident in the 1946 presidential campaign when the official party nominated as its candidate, Miguel Alemán, a civilian.

Although a civilian, Alemán had special ties to the military; his father had been a Revolutionary general and had been executed after a failed revolt in 1929. Alemán hastened the political decline of the Revolutionary generals by rapidly promoting a new generation of officers who were products of the more professional military academies of the 1920s and 1930s. Mexico maintained a modest military establishment into the 1950s and 1960s. The size of the armed forces was held at about 50,000, while military expenditures accounted for about 7 percent of the total budget. The growing role of the military in maintaining internal security, however, eventually produced a major crisis in civil-military relations in 1968.

A series of student demonstrations took place in Mexico City during the summer of 1968 aimed at forcing the official party to democratize. With Mexico City scheduled to host the Summer Olympics in October, the administration of President Gustavo Díaz Ordaz was especially conscious of security matters and of the government's international image. When government officials became alarmed by a major demonstration at Tlatelolco Plaza on 2 October 1968, the army moved in to clear the square, killing an estimated 300 to 400 people. The key figure in the decision to clear the square was the minister of defense, General Marcelino García Barragán. Barragán believed that the army was being forced to clean up what was essentially a political mess made by the civilian leadership. The military's reputation had been badly tarnished by its role in the "Tlatelolco Massacre," and civilian leaders hastened to compensate the military for this loss of prestige. The president authorized the creation of a new zone command, three new army battalions, and the expansion of the presidential guard. Most of the troops received new weapons, and the air force acquired thirty-seven new planes. The president also gave out an unusually high number of promotions to the ranks of general and colonel to cement the loyalty of the military.

One of the main conclusions that the military drew from Tlatelolco and its aftermath was a desire not to be involved in the suppression of political opposition to the official party and the government. This desire, however, was in conflict with the growing role assigned to the military in internal security matters. During the 1970s the armed forces were called on to put down rural guerrilla activity. The government turned over control of some of the most important customs posts to the army. The military also took over responsibility for guarding vital installations such as utilities and petroleum facilities. The armed forces played a growing role in the government's antidrug efforts, especially in the 1980s and the 1990s.

As opposition to the official party grew, the tendency was for the military to be drawn further into politics. There was more violence associated with local, state, and national elections with the military being called in to maintain order in more extreme cases. The military was involved in protecting the integrity of the voting process, but the government also used it to bring about voting fraud. With its political support eroding in the 1980s and 1990s, the official party came to depend more on the military as a pillar of support.

The professionalization and modernization of the Mexican military establishment has increased steadily since the end of World War II. An expanded system of formal military education has played an important role in establishing the attitude of military subordination to civilian control.

In terms of personnel and budget, the military does not pose a heavy burden for Mexico. Military spending dropped during the postwar years, leveling off at approximately 2 percent of the national budget during the 1980s. The size of the armed forces reached a low of 40,000 in 1967. Internal and external factors later led to a steady increase in numbers to 140,000 in 1990. Despite this recent increase in size, the armed forces are still small in relation to the population when compared to that of other Latin American countries. Interservice rivalries do not play a role in driving up military expenditures; the army dominates the air force, which is part of the army, as well as the independent but small navy.

The changes currently taking place in the political scene will unavoidably affect relations between the military establishment and civilian authority. Greater democratization has the ironic effect of creating a greater potential for military involvement in politics, even if the military is reluctant to assume a greater role. The fact that the military is playing a more visible role in national affairs in such areas as the antidrug campaign and civic action does not necessarily mean that a resurgence of militarism is taking place.

—DMC

See also: Corruption; Cristero Rebellion; Drug Trafficking; Korean War; Presidents of the Twentieth Century; Revolution of 1910; World War II.

References:

Camp, Roderic Ai. *Generals in the Palacio: The Military in Modern Mexico.* New York: Oxford University Press, 1992.

Lieuwen, Edwin. *Mexican Militarism: The Political Rise and Fall of the Revolutionary Army, 1910–1940.* Albuquerque: University of New Mexico Press, 1968.

Ronfeldt, David, ed. *The Modern Mexican Military: A Reassessment.* San Diego, CA: Center for U.S.–Mexican Studies, 1984.

Monsiváis, Carlos (1938–)

Like the great "fools" in the plays of William Shakespeare, Carlos Monsiváis has used a playful spirit, sarcastic wit, and linguistic facility to mock the powerful and exalt the mundane. These qualities have made him Mexico's most potent (if self-reflexive) and most beloved (if reserved) social critic. A widely published journalist and pioneer of the "new chronicle," Monsiváis's unique ability to combine penetrating political critique and social commentary with humor, compassion, and a deep appreciation of Mexico's vibrant popular culture have won over even his nominal enemies. Numerous national and international awards testify to the esteem in which he is held by colleagues in journalism and literature. Still, his response to a public celebration in his honor at the Palace of Fine Arts in Mexico City might serve as a personal manifesto of sorts: "It really embarrasses me, eulogies are all false, only criticism is welcome."

Carlos Monsiváis Aceves was born in Mexico City on 4 May 1938. His family was lower middle class and devoutly Protestant. Reflecting back on his upbringing in an early autobiography, he confessed that "sin was the central theme of my childhood and it continues, after a fashion, to govern me still." An avid reader from an early age, he also demonstrated a remarkable affinity for spoken language, memorizing and reciting extensive passages from the Bible for Sunday School and the family's daily scriptural reading. The religious context would eventually disappear (or at least recede) but the lessons in written and spoken language are still evident in his innovative prose style, celebrated for its verbal virtuosity and attentiveness to linguistic rhythms. Aside from a residual concern with sin, the effects of his devout upbringing are hard to trace. "Yes, I believe that good exists, yes I believe that evil exits," Monsiváis told his friend and fellow new chronicler Elena Poniatowska in an interview, "but I know that those professionally consecrated to declare each week 'this is good and this is evil' end up being extremists in oppression." By his own admission, the experience of being a Protestant child in Roman Catholic Mexico was more important to his development than religious dogmas. This early Protestant experience—full of jokes like "Oh prostitute . . . I thought you said Protestant"—exacerbated by his parents' divorce (another marker of Protestantism), made him feel like an outsider in Mexican society, and, if not exactly typical, it nevertheless produced a certain empathy toward other forms of exclusion—economic, social, racial, sexual—experienced by so many Mexicans.

In his teen years, empathy with marginalized Mexicans quickly translated into an obsession with social justice. "What the PRI [Mexico's ruling party until the 2000 elec-

tions] has been for the last fifty years," he would write later, "is a veil, a cape of invisibility over the fact that this is one of the most unjust societies in the world." At fourteen, recruited by a high school history teacher, Monsiváis joined a young communist reading group where he was introduced to the marxist classics and their vitriolic critic of capitalism. An inveterate reader, he also developed an appreciation for the radical novels of American muckrakers like John Steinbeck and Upton Sinclair. Seminal Cold War events like the Rosenberg treason trial and especially the 1954 U.S.-sponsored invasion of Guatemala spurred Monsiváis to act on his radical convictions. As an organizer of the Guatemalan Friendship Committee, he helped put together a huge public demonstration that included prominent public figures like painters Diego Rivera and Frida Kahlo. Thus, by age of sixteen, Monsiváis was already moving in the highest circles of Mexico City's radical vanguard, a group that included luminaries like labor leader Demetrio Vallejo, painter David Alfaro Siqueiros, and novelist José Revueltas. Despite the leftist pretensions of President Adolfo López Mateos (1958–1964), the late 1950s and early 1960s were hard on radicals: Vallejo, Siqueiros, and Revueltas would all spend time in prison and, in 1962, *campesino* activist Ruben Jaramillo and his pregnant wife were murdered by government thugs in an act that horrified many but that insiders like Monsiváis knew to be all too common. Looking back, he admitted that "the experience of those years was definitive for me, because it taught me . . . the meaning of the expression 'living dangerously.' And not because I was risking anything . . . but because I felt necessary and in solidarity and because at the same time I understood in some distant way, that I was incapable of participating in the common jubilation."

This ambivalence about radical politics and political activism followed him to the National Autonomous University (UNAM), where he majored in economics and literature. Intellectually ambitious and bored with classes, he would never finish the degree but some of his readings in Mexican literature—Alfonso Reyes (for his insistence on Mexican cultural autonomy), Salvador Novo (for his sarcastic humor and irreverent style), Juan Rulfo (whose *Pedro Páramo* would provide the inspiration for the "new chronicle")—would have a profound impact on his later writings.

The late 1950s signaled the beginning of a renaissance in Mexican letters as writers like Octavio Paz and Carlos Fuentes turned from the narrow nationalistic concerns of the novelists of the Revolution to a more cosmopolitan vision. Their themes remained quite Mexican—Paz wrote the definitive work on national identity and Fuentes's first novel explored the dark side of Mexico City—but their stylistic innovations, incorporation of "universal" themes, and intellectual generosity provided the inspiration for a new generation of literary lions. In 1957, the nineteen-year-old Monsiváis and future novelist José Emilio Pacheco took over direction of the literary supplement to *Estaciones* and both collaborated with Carlos Fuentes on his literary journal, *Medio Siglo.* By the early 1960s, then, the precocious Monsiváis had gone from star-struck political activist to head of a literary mafia that produced and relentlessly promoted the work of newcomers like Pacheco, Salvador Elizondo, Elena Poniatowska, Sergio Pitol, Homero Aridjis, and Monsiváis himself. If they sometimes positioned themselves in opposition to more established "stars" like Octavio Paz, the sense of intellectual ferment generated by these competing mafias probably benefited everyone. Monsiváis's own "star" status in Mexico City literary circles was affirmed by the 1966 appearance of an important poetry anthology, *La poesía mexicana en el siglo XX* (Mexican Poetry in the Twentieth Century) and an autobiography (at age 28!). Nor was literature his only venue. The 1960 offer of a radio show, *Film and Criticism,* on University (UNAM) Radio, kicked off a ten-year stint as a radio broadcaster. Here, Monsiváis honed his appreciation for

cinema, his distinctive authorial voice, and his biting wit—the latter with a satirical show, *The Children's Hour,* that lasted only until the university's general secretary happened to hear a broadcast.

A 1965 trip to Harvard University to represent Mexico at the International Seminar revived Monsiváis's political energies. Although he found the seminar itself patronizing and dull, Vietnam War protests, the political activism of groups like the Students for a Democratic Society, rock music, and especially New York City's vibrant cultural scene made a huge impression. "For me, a convicted and confessed proto-*pocho* [Americanized Mexican]," he admitted soon after, "North America is always a lesson and an example."

The 1960s were a radical time in Mexico, too, as students joined with workers in protests against authoritarian politics and social injustice. These protests culminated in 1968 as the approaching Mexico City summer Olympic games—the first hosted by a "developing" country—brought things to a head. Disgusted at the massive expenditure on international public relations in a country with pressing social needs, protesters stepped up the pressure on the government. President Gustavo Díaz Ordaz responded by calling out the military and, on October 2, soldiers fired on protestors gathered in the Plaza of Three Cultures in the Tlatelolco section of Mexico City. The official figures admitted only a few casualties but independent sources suggest that nearly 400 people died. Arrests of political dissidents quickly followed. The combination of fear and repression effectively dampened political activism, radicalizing some but frightening most, but it also destroyed any illusions of reform from within Mexico's one-party system.

The Tlatelolco Massacre was recognized immediately as a watershed in Mexican political and cultural life. Younger activists became the "generation of 1968" and Monsiváis became one of its most important voices. In *Días de guardar* (Days of Remembrance,

1970), a collection of essays published shortly afterward, he wrote that "After a misfortune as unjust, irreparable, and unpunished, as the massacre of Tlatelolco, things were never again the same." A second collection published seven years later, *Amor Perdido* (Lost Love, 1977), reiterated this harsh judgment: "[Tlatelolco] established . . . that our system is paternalistic, and that it punishes; that it is boastful, and defiantly assumes the monopolization of the power to punish; that it is melodramatic, and displaces its guilt on to the punishment of others; that it is insincere and vacillating, publicly proclaiming the abolition of punishment; that it is didactic and has circular argument, and punishes the victims of punishment." And to ensure that these lessons were not lost to future generations, he edited two document collections about Tlatelolco, the first included trial transcripts of political activists (1970), and the second, recently released army records (1999).

Already recognized as an innovative stylist in Mexico City literary circles, Monsiváis's essay collections from the 1970s exposed a broad spectrum of the reading public to the "new chronicle." Indebted to the American "new journalism" of Norman Mailer and Tom Wolfe but resolutely Mexican in its rhythms and themes, the new chronicle melded conventional reporting with editorial interpretation, traditional literary devices with media techniques, to capture the "feel" and complexity of important events like Tlatelolco, popular culture, and everyday life in Mexico City. For demoralized activists, this new style reflected their confusion and ambivalence while acknowledging and validating their sacrifices. The essays in *Días de guardar*—along with fellow new chronicler Elena Poniatowska's devastating collage of eyewitness accounts and reportage, *La noche de Tlatelolco* (The Night of Tlatelolco, 1971)—ensured that official attempts to cover up the massacre would further discredit the regime.

Monsiváis has continued to be a thorn in the side of Mexican politicians. A fifteen-year stint as editor of the prestigious culture supplement to *¡Siempre!* (1972–1987) and, more recently, his widely read column in the independent newspaper *La Jornada* (1993–), along with frequent appearances on radio and television, have kept Monsiváis firmly in the public eye where his unrelenting attacks on the regime's ideological pretensions served as important correctives to an often complacent (and sometimes complicit) mainstream press. Indeed, since the 1980s, he has been one of the most important chroniclers of Mexico's emerging civil society: producing an influential book on the subject, *Entrada libre: cronicas de la sociedad que se organiza* (Free Admission: Chronicles of a Society that is Getting Organized, 1987); serving as advisor to opposition presidential candidate Cuauhtémoc Cárdenas; and engaging in public dialogues with Subcomandante Marcos, the leader of the 1994 Zapatista revolt. He has also been outspoken on issues of sexuality—machismo, abortion rights, gay rights—controversial topics in a patriarchal, mostly Roman Catholic culture like Mexico's (as they are in the patriarchal, mostly Protestant culture of the United States). As early as *Amor Perdido* (1977), he exposed the politics of machismo, noting that "those in control of society know that in the self-delusions of machismo (in the fascination of being defenseless before one's most deplorable fantasies) there lies an endless source of control." More recently, Monsiváis has turned his attention to the repression of homosexuality in Mexico. His biography of the flamboyantly gay poet, Salvador Novo, a fixture of Mexico City night life until his death in 1974—*Salvador Novo: Lo marginal en el centro* (Salvador Novo: The Marginal at the Center, 2000)—is the first serious historical study of Mexican homosexuality, and his presence at gay rights rallies has helped attract support for that fledgling movement. Asked about the situation of gays in Mexico at the start of the new century, he noted optimistically that "in a country with the repressive and homicidal intolerance of Mexico, a country with a high annual quota of murders of homosexuals . . . a movement for the revindication of the civil rights of homosexuals and of people that declare themselves homosexuals in a society that's so macho, seems to me a gain, an undoubted advance."

Important as his political commentary has been, Monsiváis is perhaps best known (and most appreciated) for his writings on Mexican popular culture. In addition to political ferment, the turbulent 1960s saw a resurgence of Mexico City night life, especially in the restaurants and nightclubs of the *zona roja* (pink zone). Inspired by this cultural explosion and well prepared by his radio experience, Monsiváis brought the new chronicle style to brilliantly idiosyncratic essays on Mexican popular culture. The published collections of these essays became instant classics in Mexican (and Latin American) cultural studies. In *Amor Perdido* and *Escenas de pudor y liviandad* (Scenes of Modesty and Frivolity, 1988), his enthusiasm for popular culture icons like macho ranchero singer José Alfredo Jiménez, radical muralist David Alfaro Siqueiros, popular songwriter Agustín Lara, labor leader Fidel Veláquez, film star Dolores del Río, and comedian Cantinflas helped spark appreciation for popular culture and bridge the cultural gap between ordinary Mexicans and intellectuals, whose enthusiasm for authentic Mexican folk art was often matched by a disdain for mass-produced culture. Likewise, a more recent collection, *Los rituals del caos* (Rituals of Chaos, 1995), demonstrated the extraordinary breadth of popular culture from the contemporary antics of Gloria Trevi, "the Mexican Madonna" to Boy Fidencio, a borderlands healer from the 1920s whose clients included the rabidly anticlerical president Plutarco Elías Calles.

—*RMB*

See also: Fuentes, Carlos; Intellectuals; Novel since 1960; Paz, Octavio; Poniatowska, Elena; Rulfo, Juan.

References:

Egan, Linda. *Carlos Monsiváis: Culture and Chronicle in Contemporary Mexico.* Tucson: University of Arizona Press, 2001.

Monsiváis, Carlos. *Mexican Postcards.* Trans. and with an Introduction by John Kraniauskas. New York: Verso, 1997.

Monterrey Group

The name is a reference to one of Mexico's most powerful groups of business elites, which is based in Monterrey, the capital city of the northern state of Nuevo León. The term "Grupo Monterrey" became widely used after 1940 and especially referred to the formidable Garza-Sada family, which is among Mexico's wealthiest and most influential. The affluence and political clout of the Monterrey Group has its roots in the nineteenth-century economic expansion that especially affected northern Mexico. Through ambitious business ventures and the careful cultivation of social ties, Monterrey entrepreneurs succeeded in building a local economic empire that weathered the Mexican Revolution and that continues to this day.

Monterrey's proximity to the United States–Mexico border, as well as the coming of the railroad, helped create trade and business opportunities that, by the turn of the century, had transformed the city into an industrial center. Sometimes referred to as the "Pittsburgh" of Mexico, Monterrey was home to Mexico's first iron and steel mill. The probusiness policies of President Porfirio Díaz (1876–1911) aided Monterrey's growth and encouraged businessmen like Isaac Garza and Francisco G. Sada to pool their resources. In this way, Monterrey became home to other large-scale enterprises, including the Cervecería Cuauhtémoc (the Cuauhtémoc Brewing Company), which remains a major Mexican business. In addition to pooling resources and enhancing their economic clout through vertical integration, Monterrey businessmen began to form a coherent elite through marriage and the cultivation of other social ties.

The Mexican Revolution of 1910 presented a new set of challenges to Monterrey's business elite. Although the city's industries weathered the fighting with relatively minor consequences, its entrepreneurs could no longer count on a stable, probusiness environment. As national politicians increasingly courted workers and spoke of social reform, the Monterrey elite became increasingly cliquish as it sought to preserve its rights. Led by the Garza-Sada clan, Monterrey's important businessmen became increasingly political. To counter government-sponsored labor groups, they established their own company unions, and in 1929 they helped form COPARMEX (Confederación Patronal de la República Mexicana), a confederation of employers that sought to confront Mexico's growing and increasingly influential labor movement. COPARMEX became the conservative voice of Mexican businessmen.

During the presidency of Lázaro Cárdenas (1934–1940), the confrontation between Monterrey's entrepreneurs and the central government came to a head. Cárdenas was determined to assert his own authority and to continue building a political base among Mexican workers. Monterrey elites were determined to hold their own against organized labor and to fight for their survival in the midst of a worldwide depression. Amid increasing unrest by Monterrey's workers, Cárdenas traveled to the city in 1935 to support the decision of the local labor arbitration board that had declared a company union illegal. City elites responded with an economic "blackout" that shut down the local economy and threatened to cause further unrest. Monterrey businessmen extended their protest to a general indictment of Cárdenas and organized labor, both of which were accused of being inspired by communist ideology. Cárdenas was eventually forced to back down, and organized labor in Monterrey was weakened considerably.

The conflict between Monterrey elites and the social and economic policies of Cárdenas persisted in the aftermath of the economic "blackout" and became a centerpiece of Mexico's 1940 presidential election. The Monterrey group challenged Manuel Avila Camacho,

candidate of the official party (eventually known as the PRI). It supported the candidacy of retired General Juan Almazán. Although Cárdenas's hand-picked candidate, Avila Camacho, defeated Almazán, the Monterrey group won an important victory within Mexico's official party. For in choosing Avila Camacho, Cárdenas was in fact responding to the demands of the Monterrey elite and confirming a determination, especially obvious after 1940, to move away from the social reforms of the 1920s and 1930s. Under Avila Camacho and his successors, the Mexican government did assume a more probusiness stance.

Members of the Monterrey Group once again benefited from state-sponsored industrial growth in the decades after 1940 while Monterrey itself solidified its position as an important industrial center within Mexico. Business elites continued to take advantage of new economic opportunities, including those created by Mexico's oil boom during the 1970s and first years of the 1980s. Under President Luis Echeverría (1970–1976), Monterrey elites also successfully weathered another populist administration by once again forming a business organization (reminiscent of COPARMEX) to oppose Echeverría's policies.

The last two decades of the twentieth century saw the Monterrey Group struggling to recover after Mexico's oil bust and a peso devaluation that left the country in a recession. The Garza-Sada clan and other Monterrey entrepreneurs were compelled to regroup. Anticipating their country's move toward the North American Free Trade Agreement, they established new links with foreign companies and markets. A good example was the Garza-Sada's Vitro Company, a maker of glass and household appliances. Through the creation of links with the American companies Whirlpool, Ford, and Dow Corning, Vitro succeeded in remaking itself into a multinational corporation. The country's movement toward the North American Free Trade Agreement and away from statist economic policies has given Monterrey entrepreneurs a new opportunity for success based on their historic links to outside markets and investment. As the twenty-first century opened, the Monterrey Group showed every sign of remaining an important force in Mexico's economy and a leading conservative voice in Mexican politics.

—*SBP*

See also: Avila Camacho, Manuel; Cárdenas, Lázaro; Economy; Labor Movements; Nuevo León (State).

References:

Cerutti, Mario. *Burguesía, capitales e industria en el norte de México: Monterrey y su ámbito regional (1850–1910)*. Monterrey: Universidad Autónoma de Nuevo León, 1992.

Nuncio, Abraham. *El Grupo Monterrey*. Mexico City: Nuevo Imagen, 1982.

Zaragoza, Alex M. *The Monterrey Elite and the Mexican State, 1880–1940*. Austin: University of Texas Press, 1988.

Morelos (State)

Morelos is a south-central Mexican state sharing borders with the Federal District (Mexico City), Puebla, Guerrero, and Mexico State. Cuernevaca is the capital. In many ways, Morelos's history has been characterized by the struggle over land and water. Beginning in the colonial period, land concentration occurred at the expense of the state's *campesinos* (peasants or rural workers) and Indian villages. Popular rebellion became a response to the steady growth of large estates, and in the early twentieth century, many peasants took up arms in the Mexican Revolution. They found a leader in Morelos's most famous native son: Emiliano Zapata.

Several native languages, including Nahuatl, Mixtec, Zapotec, and Otomí, are still spoken in Morelos, testimony to the region's large indigenous population and its rich and varied pre-Columbian history. In the centuries before the Spaniards arrived, Morelos developed in conjunction with southeastern Mexico (from which the influence of the Olmecs came) and central Mexico (which, under the Aztecs, eventually conquered the area). Morelos was also home to the ceremonial center of Xochicalco, which was a center of the Toltec culture and perhaps an ancient Maya site as well. The Spanish Conquest of Morelos began in 1521, and in 1523 Hernán Cortés captured Cuernevaca, where he established his residence. Cortés claimed most of Morelos's land as his own, and he established the first sugar mill of New Spain in Tlaltenango. Franciscan, Dominican, and Augustinian missionaries followed, introducing the Roman Catholic faith to many of Morelos's native peoples.

After Cortés, Morelos became home to several large sugar haciendas, which were worked by Indians and black slaves. Sugarcane became the main economic enterprise of colonial Morelos, and the sugar haciendas grew steadily. This expansion increased local competition for land and water, and it especially pressured native villages and their communal lands. Popular discontent resulting from the expansion of the sugar economy provided support for the rebellions of Miguel Hidalgo and José María Morelos in the early nineteenth century. Indeed, Morelos captured Cuernevaca in 1812 and also installed himself in Cuautla, a town to the east of Cuernevaca. In 1821, Agustín de Iturbide occupied Cuernevaca in the name of an independent Mexico before proceeding to Mexico City to become the new country's first leader.

Morelos did not immediately achieve statehood after Mexican Independence. Instead, it became a part of Mexico State and remained so until 1869 when Benito Juárez created the state of Morelos. Its location in central Mexico and its proximity to Mexico City ensured that Morelos would directly experience the political struggles of the nineteenth century. During the Mexican War (1846–1848), American troops occupied Cuernevaca, and with the War of Reform (1858–1861) Mexico's liberal and conservative factions vied for control of the capital city. During the 1860s, Cuernevaca was controlled by the French, who invaded the country and established an empire (1862–1867).

Morelos's sugar industry remained at the heart of the state's economy, and several laws passed during the second half of the nineteenth century facilitated the continued growth of the region's haciendas. Modernization was aided by the arrival of the railroad and by the introduction of steam-powered equipment. By the early twentieth century, Morelos was among the world's largest producers of sugar. As during the colonial period, however, such expansion occurred at the expense of Indian villages and their communal lands. The man who eventually provided a voice for these traditional village communities was Emiliano Zapata.

Born to a *campesino* family in the village of Anenecuilco, Zapata became a local leader in the struggle to protect land and water from encroachment by the state's wealthy *hacendados* (hacienda owners). He responded to Francisco Madero's call for rebellion against President Porfirio Díaz in 1910–1911, and he gathered an army that succeeded in capturing Cuautla. Zapata's victory helped force Díaz from power and bring Madero into the presidency. Zapata, who insisted on land reform as the central component of the Mexican Revolution, did not remain allied to Madero for long, however. Madero supported the *hacendados* of Morelos, who succeeded in installing Ambrosio Figueroa (a landowner from the neighboring state of Guerrero) as governor in 1911.

Zapata responded to the imposition of Figueroa and to Madero's failure to carry out meaningful reforms by breaking with the central government. By the end of 1911, he had issued his Plan of Ayala, which demanded the return of lands taken by hacienda owners and that asserted the people's right to choose their leaders. Zapata's movement attracted a large following in Morelos and it spread beyond the state. It continued to grow after Madero's overthrow and death in 1913. Attempts by the central government to suppress the Zapatista rebellion brought heavy fighting to Morelos and resulted in the destruction of many of the state's haciendas, as well as the collapse of the sugar industry. Morelos also suffered a precipitous decline in its population through death and emigration.

From 1914 to 1916 the Zapatistas controlled Morelos and they were allied with the so-called Convention government against Venustiano Carranza's Constitutionalist movement. Under Genovevo de la O and Lorenzo Vázquez, Morelos had a radical government that divided the state's sugar haciendas and redistributed land. The Revolutionary gains of Zapata's local regime were short lived, however. In 1916, Constitutionalist general Pablo González began an offensive that, by 1919, left Carranza in control of Morelos. In the same year, Zapata was ambushed and killed. His movement waned, though many of his followers continued to wage guerrilla warfare.

In 1920, the surviving leaders of Zapata's rebellion, including Gildardo Magaña (who assumed leadership of the movement after Zapata's death), adhered to the Plan of Agua Prieta, which overthrew Carranza and aided Alvaro Obregón in his ascension to the presidency. In Morelos, José G. Parres, a medic in Zapata's army, assumed control of a new state government. Parres called on the people of Morelos to submit claims for land and the state was among the first to see land distributed to *campesinos*. Some 200,000 hectares of land had been distributed in Morelos by 1929. But the agrarian reform of the 1920s was designed as much to placate the peasants as it was to make them beholden to the central government and to a new group of local political bosses who did its bidding. Indeed, Zapata's earlier land reforms were nullified and land redistribution was carefully controlled and manipulated by the leaders of Mexico's national government. While several peasants received *ejidos* (plots of land granted by the government to be cultivated communally), villages like Anenecuilco, which claimed historic rights to land, did not see those lands returned.

During the 1930s President Lázaro Cárdenas distributed an additional 70,000 hectares in Morelos, even as he brought *campesinos* into a national organization, the National Peasant Confederation (CNC). Meanwhile, the state's haciendas, which survived the Mexican Revolution in diminished form, turned to commercial agriculture. Lacking the capital to participate in the new market-based economy, many peasants became indebted and beholden to those who could provide them with machinery and access to markets beyond the state.

The politicization of Mexico's land reform program, and the increasingly heavy hand of the national government, pushed some of Morelos's *campesinos* to rebel again. In 1935 and 1938 Zapatista veteran Enrique Rodríguez led an uprising against the intrusion of the Mexican government, and in the 1940s, Rubén Jaramillo, who had also joined Zapata's army, took up arms to protest the continued exploitation of the peasants. Although Jaramillo's efforts to organize the state's *campesinos* earned him death threats, and the animosity of wealthy landowners, he remained active. He formed the Agrarian and Workers' Party of Morelos (PAOM), and during the 1950s he became a local representative of the CNC. Ultimately, however, Jaramillo supported land invasions as the only real way in which peasants could gain land. In 1962, Jaramillo was assassinated, most likely on orders from the central government.

The last decades of the twentieth century saw the continued growth of commercial agriculture in Morelos, as well as the intensification of agriculture through the use of new machinery, chemical fertilizers, and insecticides. Access to capital and outside markets became crucial to the state's farmers, and peasants were left farther behind. Many responded by emigrating to the United States or to Mexico City. Industry and tourism also became a part of Morelos's economy. Cuernevaca in particular became a major tourist destination and a modern highway linking Cuernevaca to Mexico City helped make the state's capital a popular weekend spot for Mexico City residents. While the energy of Zapata's Revolutionary

movement seemed to have faded by the end of the twentieth century, the ideals of that movement were still in evidence. Peasants continued to raise their voices, as in 1996 when a group from Tepoztlán began a march to Mexico City to protest plans for development that included a golf course, industrial park, and resort. Police forces confronted the caravan and shot and killed one of the protestors. The public outcry over this event caused the suspension of the development project.

—*SBP*

See also: Agrarian Reform/Land and Land Policy; Carranza, Venustiano; Confederación Nacional Campesina (CNC); Revolution of 1910; Zapata, Emiliano.

References:

Brunk, Samuel. *Emiliano Zapata: Revolution and Betrayal in Mexico.* Albuquerque: University of New Mexico Press, 1995.

Warman, Arturo. *We Come to Object: The Peasants of Morelos and the National State.* Trans. Stephen K. Ault. Baltimore, MD: Johns Hopkins University Press, 1980.

Womack, John. *Zapata and the Mexican Revolution.* New York: Random House, 1968.

Official state web site: http://www.morelos.gob.mx

Morones, Luis (1890–1964)

Mexico's most important labor leader from 1918 to 1928, Luis Morones was born in the Federal District of working-class parents. Morones worked in the electrical industry and soon became active in efforts to organize workers in the Mexico City area. He joined the first major labor organization to emerge after the Revolution of 1910, the Casa del Obrero Mundial (The House of the World Worker, or COM). In late 1914 as Mexico sunk into civil war between the Constitutionalist forces of Venustiano Carranza and Alvaro Obregón and the rebel factions following Emiliano Zapata and Pancho Villa, Morones was helping to establish a union for electricians in Mexico City, the Sindicato Mexicano de Electricistas (the Mexican Union of Electricians, or SME). The SME later affiliated with the Casa.

Morones's rise to union leadership had come at an opportune time. Control of Mexico City had been passing back and forth between the different Revolutionary factions. In early 1915, with the Constitutionalists in control of the city, the SME called a strike against the Mexican Telegraph and Telephone Company where Morones worked. The government, headed by President Carranza, responded by seizing the company and turning it over to the workers to manage. An assembly of workers then selected Morones to direct the operations of the company. As the economic situation continued to decline, the SME participated in the call for a strike of workers in the Federal District in July 1916. Carranza responded by declaring martial law, using troops to disperse the strikers, and closing down the Casa. Carranza even threatened to have the strike leaders executed.

In 1916 and 1917 Morones was pursuing two different approaches that would ultimately converge. First, Morones was moving away from the Casa's emphasis on "direct action" (strikes, sabotage, and worker confrontation with management and government) to what he described as "multiple action," which included political involvement as a labor weapon. This was a major departure from the anarchist-influenced attitudes of the Casa, which rejected political activity. Second, Morones was moving beyond the Federal District to a national stage in the labor movement. Morones played a prominent role in national labor congresses held in Veracruz in 1916 and in Tampico in 1917.

These two approaches converged at another national labor congress convened in Saltillo, Coahuila, in May 1918. This congress was sponsored and financed by the Carranza administration. Carranza had concluded that the formation of some sort of national labor organization was inevitable; therefore, it was important that the organization be under government control. This meeting led to the formation of the Confederación Regional Obrera Mexicana (the Regional Confederation of Mexican Workers, or CROM). The meeting elected Morones to head the organization as its secretary general. In theory, the CROM was radical and rejected political action. In fact, the CROM soon represented the more conservative elements of the labor movement, and the pragmatic and politically minded Morones was more than willing to work with the government if there were sufficient benefits for the CROM and himself. In 1919 Morones and other CROM leaders established what was essentially the political arm of the CROM, the Labor Party.

Morones and the CROM soon had an opportunity to get involved in politics. A major crisis was developing over presidential succession in 1920. The Constitution of 1917 prohibited reelection, so Carranza was not eligible to run. Carranza's principal general, Alvaro Obregón, was the leading candidate for the presidency, and Obregón believed that Carranza would support him for the position. Carranza, however, indicated his support for the civilian Ignacio Bonillas, a move interpreted by many as an effort by Carranza to retain power unofficially. Morones signed a personal agreement with Obregón, in which he promised to provide labor support for Obregón in the coming contest for power in return for Obregón's promise to implement prolabor legislation and promote the interests of the CROM. Morones then threw the support of the CROM and the recently established Labor Party behind Obregón. With the election approaching, the CROM launched strikes to pressure the Carranza regime. When supporters of Obregón revolted against Carranza, Morones furnished armed workers to help overthrow Carranza. At one point in the struggle, Morones and Obregón had to flee Mexico City together. After the overthrow and assassination of Carranza, Obregón sent Morones to the United States to lobby indirectly for U.S. recognition of Obregón's government. Morones enlisted the aid of Samuel Gompers, head of the American Federation of Labor, in this effort.

With the triumph of Obregón, Morones and the CROM were able to extend their influence over union organization. The CROM rapidly became the dominant labor organization, claiming that its membership rose from 50,000 in 1920 to 1,200,000 in 1924, the years of the Obregón administration; although these figures are undoubtedly exaggerated, they accurately reflect the growing dominance of the CROM. Morones himself was appointed to the important position of director of the federal munitions industry in the Obregón administration. The CROM and the Labor Party came increasingly under the personal control of Morones and a small number of his cronies known as the Grupo Acción (Action Group). The growing control of Morones and his political views led to a number of defections from the CROM, especially by more radical elements.

The presidential succession in 1924 also produced a political and military crisis. Obregón tapped as his successor General Plutarco Elías Calles, sparking a revolt by another longtime political ally of Obregón, Adolfo de la Huerta. As in 1920, Morones positioned the CROM and the Labor Party on the winning side—that of Calles. In 1924, Morones was also elected to the Chamber of Deputies, the lower house of the Mexican Congress. In November 1924 he was shot and seriously wounded in the Chamber of Deputies but made a complete recovery.

The Calles administration from 1924 to 1928 represented the peak of the influence of Morones and the CROM. Calles appointed Morones to his cabinet as minister of industry, trade, and labor. Morones had long aspired to this position and used it to strengthen further his personal control and the dominance of the CROM. Morones also used his labor and government positions to accumulate substantial personal wealth. He diverted union funds to his personal accounts, threatened employers with strikes if they did not pay him off, and acquired extensive property holdings in Mexico City, including the capital's largest and most luxurious hotel. Morones's control of the CROM and the Labor Party became increasingly authoritarian. By flaunting his wealth and abusing his power, Morones was becoming an increasingly controversial figure.

As the presidential elections of 1928 approached, Morones considered himself a presidential possibility. His presidential aspirations received a fatal blow when the Constitution of 1917 was amended to permit reelection of the president and Obregón announced that he would run in 1928. The new situation posed major problems for Morones and the CROM. Morones opposed amending the Constitution when the matter was first presented. With Obregón as a candidate, Morones had to decide whether to support his reelection. Morones and the Action Group put both the CROM and the Labor Party officially behind Obregón but with the provision that this endorsement could be withdrawn at any time that labor leaders thought necessary. In April 1928 the Labor Party publicly withdrew its support of Obregón, and Morones indicated that he was rethinking the whole question of political involvement by the CROM.

Obregón easily won the election, which guaranteed a president hostile to Morones and the CROM. The situation became even worse when President-elect Obregón was assassinated in July 1928. Based on the assumption that Morones and the Action Group had the most to lose if Obregón took office, suspicion immediately fell on Morones. Because Morones had close ties to outgoing President Calles, there was also suspicion that Calles may have been involved in the assassination as a way of continuing his control. Although Morones later maintained that he and Obregón had reconciled politically just before Obregón's assassination, Calles had to deal with mounting pressures from the disappointed followers of Obregón; Calles asked for and received Morones's resignation as minister of industry, trade, and labor. Other CROM leaders holding government positions also resigned.

The power of the federal government that had promoted the CROM and the career of Morones was now turned against its former allies. The Mexican Congress elected an interim president, Emilio Portes Gil. As governor of Tamaulipas, Portes Gil had tangled earlier with Morones and the CROM when Portes Gil successfully sponsored unions under his control against CROM-affiliated unions in his state. As president, Portes Gil used his power to attack Morones and the CROM. There was a congressional investigation of Morones's personal finances as well as the financial activities of the CROM. With the CROM in disfavor with the federal government, many of its affiliated unions left the CROM to form new labor combinations. Morones further alienated Calles by opposing the formation of an official Revolutionary party in the aftermath of Obregón's assassination. Morones tried to put a brave face on the situation by leaving on a six-month trip to Europe to demonstrate the strength of the CROM as well as his confidence in its future. The CROM and the personal fortunes of Morones, however, continued their decline. When the Labor Party attempted a modest return to political action in the elections of 1932, it went down to humiliating defeat in the races it contested.

The final eclipse of Morones came in 1936 in conjunction with the end of Calles's role as the dominant political figure in Mexico. Unlike Morones, who was in decline, Calles had maintained his dominant role in Mexican politics as the *Jefe Máximo* or Maximum Leader of the Revolution through a series of three puppet presidents he controlled between 1928 and 1934. Calles, however, encountered problems with his fourth puppet, Lázaro Cárdenas, who was elected president for the 1934–1940 period. Cárdenas wanted to reorganize agricultural workers, urban workers, and the official party. Cárdenas encouraged workers to organize and to strike; the wave of strikes that followed alarmed the increasingly conservative Calles, who considered the strikers "ungrateful" and the strikes a

threat to the social order. With worker support for Cárdenas growing, Calles turned to Morones and the badly weakened CROM for labor support. In the showdown that followed, Cárdenas was the clear winner. In April 1936, Cárdenas accused Calles and Morones of being involved in a plot to dynamite a train on the Mexico City–Veracruz line. He had both Calles and Morones flown into exile in the United States.

Morones was later permitted to return to Mexico and even to resume leadership of the CROM. Neither Morones nor the CROM ever figured prominently again in Mexican politics. He died in Mexico City in 1964. Historical evaluations of Morones have been greatly influenced by his authoritarian style, strong-armed organizational methods, and corrupt activities. For better or for worse, however, Morones pushed the labor movement into the political arena and helped to establish a pattern of relations between the state and organized labor that endured for the rest of the twentieth century.

—DMC

See also: Anarchism; Calles, Plutarco Elías; Cárdenas, Lázaro; Carranza, Venustiano; Confederación Regional Obrera Mexicana (CROM); Constitution of 1917; Labor Movements; Obregón, Alvaro; Portes Gil, Emilio.

References:

Ashby, Joe C. *Organized Labor and the Mexican Revolution under Lázaro Cárdenas.* Chapel Hill: University of North Carolina Press, 1967.

Clark, Marjorie Ruth. *Organized Labor in Mexico.* Chapel Hill: University of North Carolina Press, 1934.

Dulles, John W. F. *Yesterday in Mexico: A Chronicle of the Revolution, 1919–1936.* Austin: University of Texas Press, 1961.

La Botz, Dan. *The Crisis of Mexican Labor.* Westport, CT: Praeger, 1988.

Morrow, Dwight (1873–1931)

International financial expert and U.S. ambassador to Mexico in the turbulent years from 1927 to 1930, Dwight Morrow's career was shaped by two important influences. First, after missing out on an appointment to the United States Military Academy at West Point, Morrow attended Amherst College, where he became a friend of future President Calvin Coolidge. Second, after graduating from Columbia Law School, Morrow later became a partner in the internationally famous financial firm, J. P. Morgan & Company. Morrow had two major connections with Latin America prior to becoming U.S. ambassador to Mexico. First, his older brother, Brigadier General Jay Johnson Morrow, served as governor of the Panama Canal Zone from 1919 to 1924. Second, in the early 1920s Morrow helped to reorganize the chaotic finances of the Cuban government. Although the United States had the legal right to intervene in the internal affairs of Cuba, Morrow argued against such intervention to "collect debts or enforce private contracts."

President Coolidge appointed Morrow ambassador to Mexico in September 1927 at a time when relations between the United States and Mexico were at a low point. The presidency of Plutarco Elías Calles (1924–1928) had aroused controversy over a number of issues: oil, land reform, Church-State relations, and government finances. With Morrow's background as a high-powered corporate lawyer and partner in the J. P. Morgan Company, many Mexicans believed that Morrow would take a very aggressive stance in dealing with the Mexican government. One Mexico City newspaper predicted that "after Morrow, come the U.S. marines." Morrow, however, took a decidedly low-key approach. He showed an appreciation for Mexican culture and history and demonstrated a willingness to listen. Most important, Morrow soon developed a personal relationship with Calles, who invited Morrow to private breakfasts and to take trips with him in Mexico. Morrow also used visits by humorist Will Rogers and aviator Charles Lindbergh to promote better relations. Rogers and Morrow accompanied Calles on a six-day train trip to inspect irriga-

tion projects in northern Mexico. Recently returned from his solo flight over the Atlantic, Lindbergh made a dramatic nonstop flight from Washington, D.C., to Mexico City. The world's most-famous flyer got lost on the way but still arrived to be greeted by a huge crowd, including President Calles. Lindbergh later married Morrow's daughter, Anne.

The most serious issue in U.S.–Mexican relations involved the status of U.S. oil companies, which had been feuding regularly with the Mexican government since the passage of the Constitution of 1917. Article 27 of the Constitution provided for national ownership of subsoil resources, reversing the principle of private ownership that had been in place since 1884. The dispute over subsoil resources had been briefly settled in 1923 when the United States and Mexico agreed to follow the "doctrine of positive acts." Under this doctrine, oil companies could retain their subsoil rights if they took the "positive act" of developing their resources prior to 1917. Calles revived the controversy in 1925 when a new petroleum law went into effect requiring all holders of subsoil rights to have these rights "confirmed" for a shorter period of time or lose them. Morrow tried to defuse the situation by encouraging Calles to treat the issue as a legal question rather than a political or diplomatic one. Calles faced a growing civil war and a crisis over presidential succession in 1928 and saw in Morrow's proposal a face-saving way of getting out of the confrontation. With Calles controlling both the Supreme Court and the Mexican Congress, he had the Supreme Court declare the offensive provisions of the petroleum code of 1925 unconstitutional, reinstating the doctrine of positive acts. He then had the Congress pass a new petroleum code in 1927, which also reaffirmed the doctrine of positive acts. Morrow was also drawn into the growing struggle between Church and State. The Constitution of 1917 had drastically restricted the operations of the Roman Catholic Church, ranging from property ownership to education to political activity.

Calles was the first president since 1917 to enforce vigorously the anticlerical provisions of the Constitution. This led Church leaders to the unprecedented response of having the clergy go on "strike," refusing to perform religious services as of 31 July 1926. Church resistance soon evolved into a civil war known as the "Cristero Rebellion." Various Roman Catholic groups in the United States pressured the U.S. government to become involved in the controversy on behalf of the Mexican Church. Morrow, however, was reluctant to get involved, seeing the dispute as strictly an internal affair. He also realized that domestic peace could not be restored until the Church-State conflict subsided. Morrow urged Calles and his successor in the presidency, Emilio Portes Gil, to negotiate with Church officials. Negotiations proved difficult, especially after the assassination of former president and president-elect in 1928, Alvaro Obregón, by a religious fanatic. The domestic situation, however, encouraged both Church and State to reach a settlement. Negotiators for the Church stayed secretly in the apartment of the U.S. naval attaché in Mexico City. Finally, an agreement was reached in June 1929. Under the terms of the agreement, the Church agreed to call off the strike and abide by the provisions of the Constitution of 1917; the government in turn promised to ease its attack on the Church. The settlement was widely seen as a victory for the government in its long-running conflict with the Church. Morrow played a prominent role in getting the parties to reach an agreement. Morrow, however, came under criticism for his peacemaker role. Many supporters of the Church claimed that he had sold out the Church in order to get a favorable settlement of the oil dispute. Some supporters of the government criticized him for meddling in Mexico's internal affairs. Morrow himself did not see the agreement as a solution to the Church issue; instead, he viewed it as a sort of armistice between Church and State.

The agrarian reform program under Calles also produced friction in U.S.–Mexican relations. The program had resulted in the expropriation of a number of properties owned by U.S. citizens who frequently claimed that the expropriations were discriminatory and the compensation inadequate. Morrow hoped to convince Calles that the government had already distributed more land than the peasants were willing or able to cultivate properly and that land redistribution ought to be deemphasized in favor of programs that encouraged more effective cultivation of lands already distributed. Calles, however, continued with the redistribution program, leaving Morrow with little that he could do except encourage U.S. citizens to challenge the expropriations in the Mexican courts.

Morrow also became involved in the ongoing efforts to deal with Mexico's foreign debt. Successive presidential administrations had been negotiating on the foreign debt with the International Committee of Bankers on Mexico, made up of representatives of the leading U.S., British, and French banks. The U.S. banks dominated the committee, which was headed by Thomas Lamont, a longtime friend of Morrow's and a partner in J. P. Morgan & Company. The committee and the Mexican government had reached an agreement on the payment of the foreign debt in 1922, but the agreement had to be modified in 1925 because of Mexico's continuing financial difficulties. Morrow became involved in the process in 1928 when the Calles administration indicated that a further revision in the agreement was required. While Lamont initially welcomed Morrow's involvement, it soon became clear that Morrow favored a much different approach to managing Mexico's financial problems. Morrow supported a comprehensive plan for dealing with the government's entire debt, both internal and external. Morrow opposed a settlement that favored any single group of Mexico's creditors, such as the committee. He also believed that current revenues should first be devoted to meeting current expenses rather than being pledged in advance to pay a certain group of creditors as had been the case with earlier payments to the committee. In Morrow's terms, Mexico needed a "program" to pay all of its creditors not a "contract" to pay only a certain group of creditors. Morrow feared that a succession of uncoordinated agreements with different groups of creditors would only compound Mexico's financial problems.

Morrow's views on how to deal with Mexico's debt problem did not prevail. In July 1930 Lamont negotiated a revised agreement with Mexican Minister of Finance Luis Montes de Oca. Under the agreement, the debt was scaled down and payment was secured by future customs revenues. Full service on the debt was not scheduled to begin until 1936. Morrow went directly to President Pascual Ortiz Rubio to argue against the agreement, but the president indicated his support for the proposal. The Mexican Congress, however, rejected the agreement, which never went into effect. A final settlement was not reached until 1942.

Morrow's rebuff by the Mexican government on the debt question was partially a reaction against the public impression that he exercised too much influence with the Mexican government, especially on financial matters. It also reflected the fact that Morrow had only recently returned to Mexico City after an eight-month absence during which he had served as a delegate to the London Naval Conference and also had returned to the United States to campaign successfully for the Republican nomination for the U.S. Senate in New Jersey. Morrow's days as ambassador were numbered. He returned to Washington in September 1930 and resigned as ambassador. In November he won election to the Senate. He died unexpectedly on 5 October 1931 of cerebral hemorrhage.

Morrow's tenure as U.S. ambassador helped to raise public consciousness in the United States about the situation in Mexico. Critics of Morrow, however, questioned his

practical, long-term achievements. Morrow's efforts neither solved nor resolved the problems of oil and Church-State relations; both of those issues returned as major problems in the 1930s. On the land question, Morrow could point the way to a possible resolution—use of the Mexican courts—but was in no position to negotiate a major settlement. On the issue of Mexico's finances, Morrow proposed what may have been the best approach to dealing with that problem: a comprehensive plan that did not favor any particular group or groups. He was unable, however, to convince either the Mexican government or Mexico's most powerful creditor group that his approach should be implemented. Morrow's basic approach—especially his rejection of intervention—was a good indication of the general direction of U.S. policy in regard to Latin America. The United States was retreating from its interventionist policies of the first two decades of the twentieth century. Morrow became a forerunner of what would soon be called "the good neighbor policy."

—DMC

See also: Calles, Plutarco Elías; Constitution of 1917; Cristero Rebellion; Debt, Mexico's Foreign; Obregón, Alvaro; Ortiz Rubio, Pascual; Portes Gil, Emilio; Religion.
References:
Dulles, John. W. F. *Yesterday in Mexico: A Chronicle of the Revolution, 1919–1936.* Austin: University of Texas Press, 1961.
Nicolson, Harold. *Dwight Morrow.* New York: Harcourt, Brace and Company, 1935.
Smith, Robert Freeman. *The United States and Revolutionary Nationalism in Mexico, 1916–1932.* Chicago: University of Chicago Press, 1972.

Muralist Movement

Born of the turmoil from the Revolution of 1910, the Mexican muralist movement is perhaps its most brilliant progeny. Renowned poet and art critic, Octavio Paz remarked that "the Revolution revealed Mexico to us. Or better, it gave us eyes to see it. And it gave eyes to the painters." (quoted in Ades, *Art in*

Latin America, p. 151). What the painters saw, they sought to share with all Mexicans by recording their visions on the walls of public buildings throughout Mexico, Latin America, and the United States. In so doing, they gave meaning to the Revolution, helped construct a new national identity in a post-Revolutionary age, and inspired generations of public artists throughout the Americas.

The origins of the muralist movement are unclear. Certainly Dr. Atl's fascination with Renaissance public art, which he shared with future muralists like Diego Rivera, José Clemente Orozco, and David Álfaro Siqueiros, played a pivotal role. It was Atl's 1910 *Centro Artístico* that received the first official commission to paint murals on the walls of the elite National Preparatory School, where so many of Mexico's future leaders received their secondary education. (The Revolution intervened just as they finished putting up the scaffolds.) Moreover, Mexico had an ancient indigenous tradition of public murals still visible at archeological sites, and religious murals often decorated the churches and monastic cloisters of the colonial era.

But it was Alvaro Obregón's idiosyncratic secretary of education, José Vasconcelos, who made it happen. Although well known for his later philosophical musings on the "cosmic race" of racially mixed Latin Americans and an unsuccessful presidential bid, Vasconcelos began his public career as a reformer of education. He insisted that only secular public education could redeem the bodies, minds, and spirits of Mexico's impoverished and often illiterate lower classes. His biggest concern (and one of the principal Revolutionary promises) was the expansion of education to all Mexicans, especially into hitherto neglected rural areas. Vasconcelos realized that these reforms would take time. Large-scale pubic murals, however, were immediately accessible to everyone from privileged preparatory students to illiterate peasants. He theorized that murals just might provide a common cultural experience that could unite Mexicans across social barriers of class and race. In an influential 1916 tract on nation-building, *Forjando Patria* (Forging the Fatherland), anthropologist Manuel Gamio had argued that "when native and middle class share one criterion where art is concerned, we shall be culturally redeemed, and national art, one of the solid bases of national consciousness, will have become a fact" (quoted in Charlot, *The Mexican Mural Renaissance, 1920–1925,* p. 68). Vasconcelos agreed. With national consciousness itself at stake, he wasted no time.

By recruiting Mexico's most promising young artists, Vasconcelos ensured that the project would be taken seriously and attract public attention—and recruit them he did. Personal summonses were sent to budding Cubist sensation Rivera and the fiery Siqueiros in Europe, to a brooding Orozco recently returned from New York, and to the most adventuresome of the capital's young artistic talents, Fernando Leal, Ramón Alva de la Canal, Fermín Revueltas, Emilio García Cahero, and Jean Charlot (who would become the chronicler of the movement). Vasconcelos could offer only artisans' wages, but he promised official support, an audience, artistic freedom, and walls to paint. The staging ground for the mural movement was to be the National Preparatory School. The first major obstacle to developing a Mexican muralist movement was technical. Mural painting was a "lost" art, and its latest practitioners struggled to find a workable and durable method for painting on walls. Rivera pushed for encaustic, a labor intensive process that involved bees' wax, lemon resin, lavender essence, and the use of a blowtorch to burn the colors into the wall. Charlot and Alva experimented with true fresco, applying paint directly to fresh plaster so that the colors became part of the wall itself. Although it forced the painter to work quickly before the plaster dried, fresco proved a more straightforward technique than encaustic, and with the help of their mason assistants, who had practical experience painting the colorful walls of Mexico City's many cantinas and *pulquerías* (bars that sell *pulque,* the mildly alcoholic fermented juice of the maguey cactus and a great favorite of the lower classes), Charlot and Alva developed an efficient method. Recognizing the virtues of fresco, Rivera and the others quickly switched techniques.

The second major obstacle was the artists themselves. The first mural commissions were given to more established artists; Roberto Montenegro, Xavier Guerrero, and Dr. Atl were to decorate the former church of San Pedro y San Paul, which Vasconcelos wanted to convert into a school. These first murals, however, were mostly decorative and failed to solve the technical challenges posed by large-scale wall painting. (Dr. Atl's special "atl" colors faded even more quickly than oil paints.)

The younger artists working in the National Preparatory School considered these works somewhat old-fashioned. To signify the Revolutionary nature of their project, they formed a Union of Mexican Workers, Technicians, Painters and Sculptors. The union's manifesto declared: "We reject so-called Salon painting and all the ultra-intellectual salon art of the aristocracy and exalt the manifestation of monumental art because they are useful. We believe that any work of art which is alien or contrary to popular taste is bourgeois and should disappear because it perverts the aesthetic of our race" (quoted in Ades, *Art in Latin America,* p. 324). The union newspaper, *El Machete,* provided a forum for Revolutionary ideas and an artistic vehicle for the members' graphic talents.

Not that the new generation could agree among themselves. Rivera, with his European reputation and overbearing personality, often alienated younger colleagues. To add insult to injury, the less-established painters were dismissed by critics as "Dieguitos." This split was especially noticeable in their choice of subject matter. Rivera's *Creation* mural for the auditorium was a renaissance-style allegory with figures representing the arts and civic virtues topped by a radiant symbol of "primal energy." In a similar vein, latecomer Siquieros painted a huge angel, *The Spirit of the Occident Alighting on Mexico,* that represented the introduction of European culture into Mexico. Orozco also began with allegorical subjects like *Spring* and *Maternity.* Not the Dieguitos. Inspired in part by Dr. Atl's 1921 exhibition of Mexican popular arts, they took their themes directly from Mexican history and culture: Leal's *Fiesta of the Lord of Chalma,* Charlot's *Massacre in the Main Temple,* Alva's *The Raising of the Cross,* and Revuelta's *Devotion to the Virgin of Guadalupe* all reflect their preoccupation with Mexico's unique historical experience, in particular the formative years of Spanish Conquest and colonization. As work on the murals progressed, Revolutionary themes emerged, especially in the later works of Orozco and Siquieros, with suggestive titles like *The Trench, Return to the Battlefield* and *Burial of a Worker.* Although initially a source of division, in the long run, variations on these different themes—allegory, myth, history (distant and immediate), and culture—would dominate most of the murals that followed. The third obstacle was the students. The painters with their elaborate scaffolding and crews of workers disrupted school routine; students responded with jeers and practical jokes. (Frida Kahlo, a student at the time, remembered harassing future husband Rivera while he tried to paint.) Moreover, they found the more controversial murals, especially Orozco's depiction of *Christ Destroying His Cross,* offensive to good taste and religious sensibilities. As the project dragged on and the murals became increasingly controversial, the students staged a "riot," in which they defaced several murals by Orozco and Siquieros. The painters' union responded with the demand that "the members of the state bureaucracy remain true to their calling, that is not betray the Revolution by allying themselves with that most dangerous of groups, the ideological reactionaries" (quoted in Ades, *Art in Latin America,* p. 326).

They were soon disappointed. In 1924, Vasconcelos resigned as education secretary in protest over the assassination of a political opposition leader. His replacement, José Manuel Puig Casauranc had little patience for temperamental artists, however innovative and revolutionary. Orozco and Siquieros were dismissed and, a month later, a presidential decree halted most mural work at the National Preparatory School. Rivera, absorbed in a new set of murals for the Department of Education building, resigned from the union. The mural movement's formative phase had ended. The movement itself, however, was far from dead. Rivera's Department of Education murals with their vivid portrayals of Mexican daily life and revolutionary message were hugely popular. Along with his other major murals from the 1920s and 1930s, the allegorical murals at the National Agricultural School in Chapingo that exalted the fecundity of a Mexico fertilized with the blood of martyrs like Revolutionary peasant leader Emiliano Zapata, the panoramic historical murals for the Monumental Stairway of the National Palace that celebrated the triumphs and tragedies of Mexican history from the Conquest through the Revolution, and the regional historical murals for Cortés's Palace in Cuernavaca that depicted Cortes as a deformed, syphilitic exploiter of Indians and lauded Zapata's efforts to liberate the oppressed Indians set the standard for an official style that still dominates Mexican mural painting. The most prominent of the other muralists moved on to other, less contentious, sites in Mexico City, Orizaba, and Guadalajara.

By 1927, however, government contracts had all but evaporated and those that could—Rivera, Orozco, Siquieros, Charlot—looked for commissions abroad, especially in the United States. Rivera painted major murals in San Francisco, Detroit, and New York City, in which he explored the aesthetic possibilities of advanced technology. The controversy over his inclusion of Lenin (both he and Siquieros were communists) in the Rocke-

feller Center murals that resulted in their destruction only served to enhance his international reputation as an artistic revolutionary. Orozco, too, profited from his time in the United States. His apocalyptic mural for Dartmouth College drew disturbing parallels between ancient and modern forms of human sacrifice and its jarring juxtaposition of images pushed the expressive boundaries of mural painting. While Rivera and Orozco explored the mural's aesthetic possibilities, Siquieros (after a stint as a union organizer in Mexico City that landed him in prison) experimented with new technologies and techniques: everything from spray guns and waterproof cement to team painting and the incorporation of painting "accidents" like drips and erasures. These years in the United States thus proved extremely fruitful for *"los tres grandes"* (the big three) by providing them international exposure and a chance to develop their distinct artistic visions.

Lázaro Cárdenas's ascension to the presidency in 1934 cleared the way for the return of the "big three." Cárdenas espoused a more populist political program that once again stressed the importance of public education, and this commitment meant more opportunities for artists to serve the "Revolutionary" cause. The return of Rivera, Orozco, and Siquieros to Mexico thrust the mural movement back into the public eye, even as it somewhat eclipsed the work of the less well-known artists (Leal, Revueltas, Montenegro) and relative newcomers (Juan O'Gorman, Leopoldo Méndez, Pablo O'Higgins, Rufino Tamayo) who had managed to find work in the tough economic times of the early 1930s. This mature phase would last into the 1950s—Orozco died in 1949, Rivera in 1957—and produce some of the movement's greatest achievements: Rivera's *Dream of a Sunday Afternoon in the Alameda Central Park* with its humorously ironic, personal representation of Mexican history; Orozco's violent, pessimistic *Miguel Hidalgo* mural for the Governor's Palace in Guadalajara; and Siquieros's testament to the struggle for human liberation, *New Democracy*. Siquieros would continue to paint major murals into the 1960s.

This period also witnessed the emergence of a new generation of muralists. Some of these artists continued to develop mythical-historical themes: for example, José Chávez Morado's mural for the Alhóndiga de Granaditas, a central site of the independence struggle, and Juan O'Gorman's huge murals for the new library of the National Autonomous University in Mexico City. Others, such as Rufino Tamayo, rejected the nationalistic, politicized agenda of their predecessors and explored instead the power of universal symbols (although often taken from indigenous sources, as in his famous *Serpent and Jaguar* mural for the National Museum of Anthropology) and geometric shapes. Although the pace has slowed considerably in recent years, contemporary artists throughout the Americas continue to explore the possibilities of mural painting.

Assessing the muralists' legacy is difficult. Their undeniable influence over twentieth-century Mexican art and their international stature is both a blessing and a curse. Octavio Paz rightly points out the negative moral and political implications of official muralism:

> These works that call themselves revolutionary, and that, in the cases of Rivera and Siquieros, give proof of a simplistic and Manichean Marxism, were commissioned, sponsored, and paid for by a government that had never been Marxist and that had ceased to be revolutionary. The government allowed artists to paint on the walls of government buildings a pseudo-Marxist version of the history of Mexico, in black and white, because such painting helped give it the look of being progressive-minded and revolutionary. Populist and progressive nationalism has been the mask of the Mexican state. (Octavio Paz, *Essays on Mexican Art*, p. 132)

Paz's critique, however, simplifies a complex movement that was and is much more than the propaganda arm of a the Mexican state.

Even the most blatantly propagandistic of the official murals committed the government to revolutionary notions of social justice as its principal source of political legitimation. Mural art could and often did cut both ways. Orozco (and sometimes Rivera) painted disturbing versions of revolutionary struggle and mercilessly ridiculed the corruption and stupidity of politicians and generals before and after the Revolution. Siquieros spent time in prison in his seventies for attempting to undermine the government. Nor has this ambivalent quality that simultaneously celebrates and critiques changed with the passing of the big three. During the 1960s and 1970s, for example, Chicano artists in the United States painted murals that glorified their Mexican American heritage and their own struggle against oppressive government. Mexico City street artists continue to use mural art (often in portable form for demonstrations) to claim a place in the public sphere and to subvert the power of the state. As Orozco remarked, at its best: "[mural painting] is the highest, the most logical, the purest, and the strongest form of painting . . . since it cannot become a source of personal wealth, nor can it be hidden for the sake of a privileged few. It is for the people. It is for *all*" (quoted in Edwards, *Painted Walls of Mexico from Prehistoric Times until Today*, p. 261).

—*RMB*

See also: Art since 1950; Cárdenas, Lázaro; *Mestizaje* and *Indigenismo;* Murillo, Gerardo (Dr. Atl); Obregón, Alvaro; Orozco, José Clemente; Paz, Octavio; Revolution of 1910; Rivera, Diego; Siquieros, David Álfaro; Tamayo, Rufino; Vasconcelos, José; Zapata, Emiliano.

References:

Ades, Dawn. *Art in Latin America: The Modern Era, 1820–1980.* New Haven, CT: Yale University Press, 1989.

Charlot, Jean. *The Mexican Mural Renaissance, 1920–1925.* New Haven, CT: Yale University Press, 1963.

Edwards, Emily. *Painted Walls of Mexico from Prehistoric Times until Today.* Austin: University of Texas Press, 1966.

Hurlburt, Laurence P. *The Mexican Muralists in the United States.* Albuquerque: University of New Mexico Press, 1989.

Paz, Octavio. *Essays on Mexican Art.* Trans. Helen Lane. New York: Harcourt Brace & Company, 1987.

Rodríguez, Antonio. *A History of Mexican Mural Painting.* Trans. Marina Corby. New York: G. P. Putnam's Sons, 1969.

Schmeckebier, Laurence E. *Modern Mexican Art.* Westport, CT: Greenwood Press, 1971.

Murillo, Gerardo "Dr. Atl" (1875–1964)

Gerardo Murillo Cornadó, better known by his Nahuatl pseudonym, Dr. Atl, was a man of many talents—painter, political organizer, art theorist, mystic, volcanologist—and much charisma. By most accounts, he was also the godfather of twentieth-century Mexican art, the teacher-storyteller-agitator who inspired by word and deed the master painters of the Mexican muralist movement, including the "big three," José Clemente Orozco, Diego Rivera, and David Álfaro Siquieros. Unlike his muralist protégés, however, his specialty was landscapes. As befits a great Revolutionary, his preferred subjects were the great volcanoes of the central Mexican plateau: Popocatépetl and Ixtaccíhuatl.

Born in 1875 in Guadalajara, Murillo was a generation older than the "big three" and a mature artist and intellect when the Revolution of 1910 broke out. Extensive travels in Europe had produced a degree in philosophy and law, a deep appreciation for Renaissance public art, an impressionist painting style, and a commitment to social change through collective action. He was also a visitor at the 1900 Universal Exhibition (World's Fair) in Paris, for which the Mexican government of Porfirio Díaz constructed a "Aztec" palace to represent Mexico's new national image as a country with an exotic past, a modern infrastructure, and a cosmopolitan perspective. In keeping with the cosmopolitan nationalism of the time, Murillo acquired a pseudonym— Dr. Atl, from the Nahuatl (Aztec) word for water—in a baptismal ceremony conducted by Argentine poet Leopoldo Lugones. Artistic nationalism would become the hallmark of Atl's activities during the first decade of the twentieth century. By 1903, he was back in Mexico organizing exhibitions of Mexican art (including Rivera's first) and teaching at the Academy of San Carlos, the nation's most prestigious art school. In 1910, the Díaz regime staged a notoriously lavish centenary celebration of Mexican independence, for which Atl organized a hugely successful showing of independent, mostly new, Mexican artists to offset the official exhibition of Spanish art. He even designed a Tiffany glass curtain on a volcano theme for the theater in Mexico City's Palace of Fine Arts. That same year, encouraged by Minister of Education Justo Sierra, he founded a Centro Artístico charged with painting murals on the walls of a new auditorium at the elite National Preparatory School. Revolution and the demise of Díaz's government prevented the realization of the mural project and Atl returned to Europe in 1911, this time to study volcanology, exhibit his paintings (including several volcano landscapes), publish articles on Mexican art and politics, and stage a successful protest against a proposed French loan for Victoriano Huerta's government.

His experience as a polemicist proved useful when he returned to war-torn Mexico in 1913 after Huerta's ouster. During a brief tenure as director of the Academy of San Carlos, Atl attempted an artistic revolution. "I find myself in this dilemma," he said, "whether to propose that the school be scrapped, or else converted into a workshop geared for production, like any industrial workshop of today, or like all workshops of all epochs when art flowered vigorously" (quoted in Charlot, *Mexican Mural Renaissance,* p. 49). Revolution again intervened. When the advancing armies of Pancho Villa and Emiliano Zapata converged on Mexico City, Atl led a contingent of artists to Orizaba where they painted and engaged in various political activities. As Venustiano Carranza's chief of propaganda, Atl edited the Constitutionalist newspaper, *La Vanguardia,* for which he recruited talented young artists like Orozco, Siquieros, and Francisco Goitia, who would later become a renowned painter of indigenous people and culture. Nor were Atl's talents confined to art and propaganda: in 1914 he helped reestablish *La Casa del Obrero Mundial,* the first Revolutionary labor union that had been suppressed by Huerta. From its ranks, he helped assemble the "Red Battalions" to provide soldiers for the Constitutionalist cause.

In 1920, in recognition of his service to the victorious Constitutionalist cause, Atl was named director of the government's Department of Fine Arts. Seemingly tireless, he began another mural project at the Church of San Pedro y San Pablo—the use of his own "Atl colors" proved a failure and the murals faded—and staged an important exhibition of Mexican popular art, for which he published an important study, *Artes Populares de México,* further evidence of his ongoing commitment to the liberation of Mexican art from its dependence on European techniques and styles. He continued to push for an artistic revolution "that will make of painting something dynamic, instead of the static thing our ancestors knew" (quoted in Charlot, *Mexican Mural Renaissance,* p. 102). But his hold over the younger generation, especially those like Rivera and Siquieros, who had had formative European experiences of their own and who considered Atl's impressionistic landscapes somewhat dated, was gradually waning. Fresh from his Parisian success as a Cubist, Rivera felt free to publicly disparage his former mentor with the remark that "the young painters know that under the pompous sheen the bald pate is stuffed with straw, and not even the quack's beard succeeds in putting them to flight" (quoted in Charlot, *Mexican Mural Renaissance,* p. 103).

His murals an acknowledged failure and no longer at the forefront of the Mexico City art scene, Atl retired to his beloved volcanoes. When, in 1943, a new volcano, Paricutín, erupted, he set up shop nearby and spent the next few years documenting its eruption, including some experiments "aeropainting" from an airplane. But if his influence was somewhat diminished by the ascendancy of the "big three," his pivotal role in the birth of modern Mexican art was openly acknowledged even by critics like Rivera and he is generally recognized as one of Mexico's greatest landscape painters. On his death in 1964, he was buried alongside several of his protégés in Mexico City's Rotunda of Famous Men.

—*RMB*

See also: Muralist Movement; Orozco, José Clemente; Paz, Octavio; Rivera, Diego; Siquieros, David Álfaro.

References:

Charlot, Jean. *The Mexican Mural Renaissance, 1920–1925.* New Haven, CT: Yale University Press, 1963.

Edwards, Emily. *Painted Walls of Mexico from Prehistoric Times until Today.* Austin: University of Texas Press, 1966.

Rodríguez, Antonio. *A History of Mexican Mural Painting.* Trans. Marina Corby. New York: G. P. Putnam's Sons, 1969.

Schmeckebier, Laurence E. *Modern Mexican Art.* Westport, CT: Greenwood Press, 1971.

Nayarit (State)

Located in western Mexico and along the Pacific coast, Nayarit includes several small islands in the Pacific Ocean and has as its capital the city of Tepic. Most of the state's population is concentrated in the fertile Tepic Valley, although the coastal area, including the port of San Blas, experienced a revival during the latter part of the twentieth century, aided by the fishing industry and tourism. For centuries, Nayarit's sierras have been home to native groups and the Huichol, Cora, and Tepehuan languages are still spoken. The Huichol Indians in particular have preserved their traditions, and they are now a tourist attraction, drawing visitors to their communities and marketing their crafts throughout Mexico.

Francisco Cortés, nephew of the Spanish conqueror Hernán Cortés, was the first European to pass through Nayarit, which became a part of the province of Nueva Galicia. Although initial contacts between the Spaniards and the native peoples of Nayarit were peaceful, the subsequent conquest of Nueva Galicia by Nuño de Guzmán brought repression and eventually encouraged a massive Indian uprising known as the Mixtón War (1541–1542). Though the Spaniards managed to contain the uprising, many Indians took refuge in the sierras of Nayarit, where they continued their resistance to Spanish control until the early eighteenth century. Franciscan and Jesuit missionaries also aided in the pacification of native peoples, and their efforts helped keep peace in the sierras during the late colonial period.

The rich soil of the Tepic Valley encouraged the development of haciendas during the colonial period, and Nayarit also produced some gold and silver. The local economy received a boost during the second half of the eighteenth century when San Blas was established as a military base, serving in the defense of the Californias, which were threatened by the English in Canada and the Russians in Alaska. San Blas and Tepic were connected by road to Guadalajara (the capital of Nueva Galicia and later of the state of Jalisco), and goods flowing to and from the port city helped create a regional economy that encouraged development in the Tepic region.

The Guadalajara–Tepic–San Blas axis grew in importance during the early nineteenth century, aided by the temporary closure of Mexico's main Pacific port of Acapulco, owing to the disruptions of the struggle for independence. For a time, San Blas became Mexico's most important western port, linking Tepic and Guadalajara to an extensive global trade. Tepic itself attracted foreign merchants from England, Spain, Germany, France, and the United States, and foreign investment aided the growth of agriculture and industry. The sugar and tobacco industries, which remain an important part of Nayarit's economy, began in this way.

Politically, the nineteenth century was a volatile one for Nayarit. Despite growing sentiment for autonomy, the area remained under the jurisdiction first of the state of Jalisco and later of the federal government. (Nayarit did not become a state until 1917). Civil unrest plagued Nayarit as two of its wealthiest families, Barrón and Castaños, pegged their rivalry to Mexico's broader struggle between liberals and conservatives (the main political factions during the nineteenth century). Meanwhile, banditry and rebellion developed in the sierras as expanding sugar haciendas displaced older communities. From this popular struggle emerged Manuel Lozada, himself a victim of the encroaching hacienda system. Lozada became a regional leader and he made allies of sierra Indians, including the Coras and Huicholes. Until his death in 1873, Lozada fought for the return of lands taken from Nayarit's native peoples since the colonial period. Other agrarian leaders continued Lozada's struggle, but the trend was toward more loss of land, particularly during the reign of Mexico's dictator Porfirio Díaz, who ruled the country from 1876 to 1911.

During the Porfirian era, Nayarit maintained a healthy agrarian economy (producing sugar, tobacco, cotton, and coffee), although the late arrival of the railroad (1912) limited the development of mining and industry. As was typical in Mexico during this period, wealth and power became increasingly concentrated in the hands of a small, elite group. A Spanish family named Aguirre came to control over half of Nayarit's wealth, and some seven families monopolized most of the state's land, mines, and industry.

In the early phase of the Mexican Revolution, Tepic was occupied by General Martín Espinosa. Espinosa arrived from neighboring Sinaloa to claim the area for Francisco Madero, whose movement succeeded in deposing Porfirio Díaz in 1911. Espinosa continued the Revolutionary struggle in Nayarit after Madero's assassination in 1913, and the city of Tepic changed hands several times as the Revolution splintered into factions. Although Nayarit finally gained statehood in 1917 as a result of the new constitution that emerged from the Mexican Revolution of 1910, it continued to be plagued by unrest and economic dislocation. Thirty-two governors attempted to pacify the state between 1918 and 1934, and many politicians and labor and agrarian activists were killed.

The popular struggle for land reform that had gained momentum in the nineteenth century under Manuel Lozada's leadership was effectively blocked by a series of governors aided by large landowners, including the Aguirre clan. Not until the middle of the 1930s were the immense holdings of the Aguirres and other elites dismantled, creating *ejidos* (communal plots) for many inhabitants of Nayarit. The state's economy, however, was slow to recover from the disruptions of the Revolution. Despite their growth during the late colonial period and early nineteenth century, Tepic remained a fairly provincial city and San Blas had declined as a port.

The revival and modern growth of Tepic and Nayarit depended on new transportation systems developed during the twentieth century. The first of these was a railroad line, completed in 1928, that linked Tepic to Guadalajara and to the port of Mazatlán. The second was a highway, linking the same cities (and extending to Nogales, on the U.S.–Mexico border) and completed by midcentury. These transportation networks helped to integrate Nayarit and create more effective links with the rest of Mexico. They also encouraged an impressive increase in Tepic's population and aided in the revival and further growth of Nayarit's agricultural sector, which continues to export its products internationally. By the end of the twentieth century, San Blas and Nayarit's coastal area had also experienced a revival, aided by the growth of a fishing industry and by tourism. Bahia de las Banderas, an area to the south of San Blas, was built as a tourist area with American, Canadian, and Japanese money.

As the twenty-first century began, Nayarit was increasingly seen as a tourist destination. Other sectors of the state's economy were beginning to mirror modern realities. In response to the global market and the exigencies of free trade, Nayarit added the production of specialty crops, such as mango and watermelon, to its list of agricultural export goods. The fishing industry, also largely geared to export, was facing the challenges of overexploitation and water pollution. Politically, Nayarit had achieved a remarkable stability, compared to that of the past. In 1999, Antonio Echevarría Domínguez was elected as Nayarit's first non-PRI governor, thus helping to erode the political monopoly held by Mexico's Partido Revolucionario Institucional (Institutional Revolutionary Party, or PRI) since its establishment in 1929.

—SBP

See also: Jalisco (State); Partido Revolucionario Institucional (PRI).

References:

Castellón Fonseca, Francisco Javier, ed. *Nayarit al final del milenio.* Tepic, Nayarit: Universidad Autónoma de Nayarit, 1998.

Meyer, Jean. *Breve historia de Nayarit.* Mexico City: Fondo de Cultura Económica, 1997.

Official state web site: http://www.nayarit.gob.mx

Newspapers and Magazines

Mexico has had a lively and contentious press since its independence in 1821. For most of that period, however, government co-optation and repression has been the rule rather than the exception. In addition, widespread illiteracy, especially in rural areas, limited the development of regional and local newspapers. Mexico City had literacy rates of nearly 50 percent and several daily newspapers by 1900, but the rest of the country did not reach similar levels until the 1950s. Despite these obstacles, by the middle of the twentieth century most every town had its own newspaper, and newsstands had become a regular feature on urban street corners throughout Mexico. For the most part, the central government managed the news with a combination of paper subsidies, advertising and public relations expenditures, and "supplementary" income, or *embutes,* to reporters. In the 1980s and 1990s, however, independent newspapers, such as *La Jornada* and *Reforma,* began to seriously challenge the official story, a challenge that would contribute significantly to the 2000 presidential election defeat of the Partido Revolucionario Institucional (PRI), which had held power since the 1920s. Now, as it enters the first decade of the twenty-first century, the Mexican press is as free as any press can be in a world of international media conglomerates.

For an authoritarian regime, the presidential administration of Porfirio Díaz (1876–1880, 1884–1911) stimulated a surprising amount of press activity. The introduction of new printing technology at the end of the nineteenth century was one reason. In 1896, the country's first major daily newspaper, *El Imparcial,* appeared in Mexico City. Its low price—at one centavo it was well within the reach of even working-class readers—and modern design drove daily sales to well over 100,000 by 1910. Many older papers, like liberal stalwart *El Monitor Republicano,* could not compete and gradually died off. Despite its name, *El Imparcial* maintained close ties to the Porfirian regime and the "order and progress" agenda of Díaz's *científico* (technocratic) advisors. Other dailies represented different major interest groups: *El País* and *La Voz de México* were pro-Catholic papers while *El Diario del Hogar* reflected traditional liberal concerns.

The turn of the century also witnessed the birth of a new kind of journalism, the tabloid or *nota roja* (red letter). In Mexico City, the aptly named *Gaceta de Policía* (Police Gazette) regularly reported on criminal activities—the more shocking, the better—and even the mainstream dailies engaged in *nota roja* style reports in order to attract readers. *Hojas sueltas,* or single-page broadsheets, with sensationalist texts and lurid prints by graphic artists like master printmaker José Guadalupe Posada commemorated especially gruesome crimes, such as the serial murders of Mexico's "Jack the Ripper," aka "La chalaquero" (the throat-slitter). In Mexico, as elsewhere in the "modern" world, *nota roja* sensationalism effectively captured the combination of titillation and horror with which many readers confronted the wrenching social changes that accompanied modernity.

The satiric penny press—a phenomenon that took place mostly in Mexico City—reflected a more critical and humorous approach to social change. The majority of these weekly papers adopted the reformist rhetoric of *puro* (pure) liberalism associated with liberal icons such as former President Benito Juárez, mixed with just a dash of socialist concern for and solidarity with the working class. The penny press editors of papers such as *El Hijo de Ahuizote* and *El Comillo Público* voiced middle-class concerns about Díaz's abuse of power and Mexico's need for democracy and modernization, while editors of papers like *La Guacamaya* and *El Diablito Rojo* advocated for the needs and rights of the nation's working classes. Some of these papers achieved considerable popularity. *La Guacamaya,* for instance, reported sales of over 20,000 for its hottest editions and penny press editors regularly mentioned efforts by shop bosses in provincial towns to halt the reading of their papers. Special interests sometimes had their own newspapers as well, which they used to push their different agendas. The mutualist newspaper *Bien Social* (Social Good), for example, sought better working conditions for union members and an end to government repression of union activities. As this proliferation of newspapers suggests, the regime tolerated a certain amount of dissent as long as editors refrained from personal attacks on the president or his family. Nevertheless, editors crossed the line often enough to form an Incarcerated Journalists Club.

After the Revolution of 1910 (1910–1920) that ousted Porfirio Díaz, further improvements in printing and distribution technologies, along with the increased literacy rates that resulted from post-Revolutionary education policies, produced a boom for Mexican newspapers and magazines that lasted until the advent of television in the 1950s. Their spread, in turn, contributed to post-Revolutionary nation-building as shared information—whether major events, business reports, sports, or celebrity gossip—joined readers in a common national culture. This boom also sparked a revolution in related industries, such as advertising, that promoted the spread of consumer culture, yet another important national bond.

Many newspapers maintained close ties to the central government and, as might be expected, the most influential were printed in Mexico City. *El Universal,* founded in 1916 by Revolutionary politician Félix Palavicini, generously styled itself "El gran diario de México" (the great paper of Mexico) although its perspective generally reflected national interests as seen from the capital. Perspective aside, *El Universal* was the most advanced of the daily newspapers: the first paper to use international wire services, to employ national and foreign correspondents, to include Sunday comics, and to produce an evening edition, *El Universal Gráfico* (in 1922). As politically acquiescent as it was commercially innovative, *El Universal* generally echoed the opinions and policies of the central government. Even its *nota roja* tendencies were put to the service of a pro–law-and-order position on everything from street crime to political rebellion. The *Excélsior,* founded in 1917, took a similar tack and did even less to hide its cozy relationship with the official party, the PRI. Both papers routinely printed government press releases verbatim as though they were news. Not all newspapers were so dependent on government support, especially outside Mexico City. For example, Hermosillo's (Sonora) *El Imparcial,* founded in 1937, regularly reported on and defended the regional interests of the northern borderlands.

As leaders of a nominally democratic state, government officials took some pains to avoid accusations of direct censorship (except on moral grounds), opting instead for a more subtle combination of co-optation and repression to control information. The principal mechanism was a government-owned paper importer and distributor, Productora e Importadora de Papel (PIPSA). Created in 1940 to provide subsidized paper (most of it imported from the United States and Canada) at low cost, PIPSA encouraged the spread of periodicals but used its control over inexpensive paper to control the news. Newspapers that stepped too far out of line invariably encountered paper supply problems, and those that tried to use other paper sources generally failed within a few months because they could no longer compete with their subsidized rivals. If that was not incentive enough, government advertising and public relations money was essential to the financial health of most newspapers—yet another reason for editors to cooperate. To ensure that journalists also kept their criticism of government officials and policies to a minimum, they routinely received *embute* or supplementary payments as a reward for services rendered. The result of these different forms of financial coercion was a co-opted press that could be counted on to report favorably on government initiatives and to keep their investigations of touchy issues, like official corruption and political dissent, to a minimum.

There were complaints, of course. Journalist Francisco Martínez de la Vega wrote in 1953 that: "We could say that in Mexico newspapers can be free. But the sad case is that they seem determined to reject that freedom; the chains of gold are necessary so that the industry prospers and balances are satisfactory. The general tone of our press is that of a lamentable, persistent servility which makes it impossible to freely examine the country's problems." Despite these criticisms and the official declaration in 1951 of Freedom of the Press Day, journalists who did not go along with the system experienced a variety of repressive techniques from loss of employment to assault.

Like newspapers, magazines benefited from technological advances and the literacy boom. *Nota roja* tabloids like *Detectives* (in the 1930s) and *¡Alarma!* (beginning in the 1940s) continued to capitalize on sensational and melodramatic crime stories or "modern" tragedies brought on by the pressures of migration and urbanization on "traditional" cultures, but they had access to much larger audiences than their predecessors. The period from the mid-1930s until the beginning of the television age in the mid-1950s was the heyday of illustrated magazines in Mexico—glossy weeklies that combined literary texts and first-rate photography. *Hoy, Mañana, Rotofoto,* and *¡Siempre!,* the brainchildren of master editor José Pagés Llergo, sometimes pushed the limits of official tolerance as they attempted to balance support for the government and the professional demands of investigative photojournalism. *Hoy* and *Mañana* generally cooperated by providing laudatory spreads on prominent politicians and innocuous articles on Mexican culture and famous celebrities. *Rotofoto,* however, published several embarrassing photos of prominent politicians—in their swimming trunks, leering at women, etc.—and was subsequently harassed into folding after just a year. *¡Siempre!* operated somewhere in between, publishing a riveting Nacho López photo essay, "Sólo los humildes van al infierno" (Only the humble go to hell), on lower-class Mexico City residents' everyday interactions with the police while also covering endless presidential trips and providing pictures of scantily clad young women in every issue. Special interest groups developed new newspapers and magazines as well. Some of them—a short-lived 1920s feminist magazine, *Mujer,* in the 1920s and the graphically striking 1930s Communist Party paper *El Machete*—were quite innovative and critical of the status quo; others—for example, *La Prensa,* the newspaper of the opposition Partido Acción Nacional (PAN)—reflected diverse interests that were a bit closer to the mainstream of Mexican politics.

As pressure to democratize grew and television gradually replaced print journalism as the most important purveyor of news, government controls over the press relaxed considerably. The administration of President Carlos Salinas de Gortari (1988–1994) ended PIPSA paper subsidies as part of its privatization of government-run businesses and passed new press laws in 1992 that sought to end the manipulation of government advertising money and *embute* payments to journalist. These reforms were not always carried through, however, sometimes because underpaid journalists solicited government "support." Moreover, journalists were still targeted for repression and reprisals when they threatened the vested interests of corrupt politicians or narcotraffickers. The 1984 murder of respected *Excélsior* columnist Manuel Buendía by a hit man in the employ of crooked officials linked to narcotrafficking sent a powerful message to other reporters who might consider pushing their investigations too far.

Overall, however, the Mexican press has grown progressively independent since the late 1970s. The first decisive move came in 1976 when prominent journalist Julio Scherer García left *Excélsior* to found an independent weekly magazine, *Proceso,* that has maintained a critical perspective on political and social issues ever since. The left-leaning daily *La Jornada* first appeared in 1984 and provided much-needed sympathetic coverage to the opposition Partido Revolucionario Democrático (PRD) during the contentious 1988 elections and to the Zapatistas after the 1994 Chiapas revolt. While it too has occasionally run government press releases, editors always set them apart with italics to alert readers to their source. *La Jornada* has also served as a platform for the acerbic social criticism of Carlos Monsiváis, whose regular

"Por mi madre, bohemios" column documents the absurdities of Mexican politics (and life). In 1994, the longtime owner of Monterrey's *El Norte,* Junco de la Vega, began publishing a new, independent Mexico City daily, *Reforma,* which has given the conservative opposition a credible national voice. As independent news coverage became more common, established papers have joined in as well. Hermosilla's *El Imparcial,* for example, regularly runs exposés on narcotrafficking, police abuses, and corruption. Even *El Universal* has become more independent with in-depth investigations of official chicanery and urban squalor.

—RMB

See also: Monsiváis, Carlos; Photography; Radio; Television.

References:

Díaz, María Elena. "The Satiric Penny Press for Workers in Mexico, 1900–1910: A Case Study in the Politicization of Popular Culture." *Journal of Latin American Studies* 22 (1990): pp. 497–525.

Fromson, Murray. "Mexico's Struggle for a Free Press," in Richard R. Cole, ed., *Communication in Latin America: Journalism, Mass Media, and Society,* pp. 115–138. Wilmington, DE: Scholarly Resources, 1996.

Lepidus, Henry. "The History of Mexican Journalism." *The University of Missouri Bulletin* 29 (1928).

Marz, John. "Today, Tomorrow and Always: The Golden Age of Illustrated Magazines in Mexico, 1937–1960," in Gilbert Joseph, Anne Rubenstein, and Eric Zolov, eds. *Fragments of a Golden Age: The Politics of Culture in Mexico since 1940.* Durham, NC: Duke University Press, 2001.

Orme, William, ed. *A Culture of Collusion: An Inside Look at the Mexican Press.* Miami, FL: University of Miami Press, 1997.

North American Free Trade Agreement (NAFTA)

The North American Free Trade Agreement links Mexico, Canada, and the United States into one of the world's largest single markets. Officially in place as of 1994, NAFTA commits all three countries to the elimination of tariffs and other barriers to trade. The pact also includes two side agreements designed to ensure fair labor practices and environmentally sensitive economic development in each of the signatory countries. For Mexico, NAFTA is particularly significant for two reasons. First, it represents the culmination of a long-term economic relationship with the United States. Second, NAFTA is part of a historical process by which Mexico has gradually dismantled the state-run, protectionist economy that emerged out of Mexico's Revolutionary experience and which intensified in the aftermath of World War II. Since this process has involved significant changes to the Mexican Constitution of 1917, it has not occurred without protest. Indeed, many Mexicans consider NAFTA to be a "sell-out" to the United States and a significant compromise of the principles of the Mexican Revolution.

Like many Latin American countries searching for ways to bolster their vulnerable economies and promote industrialization, Mexico adopted import substitution in the aftermath of World War II. As with the nationalization of the oil industry and the creation of Petróleos Mexiconos (PEMEX) in the 1930s, the Mexican state assumed a significant role in the economy. State-run enterprises came to include a national telephone company (Telemex), a national airline (Mexicana), and a national highway system. The Mexican economic "miracle" of the 1940s and the oil boom of the 1970s appeared to endorse this approach to economic development. By the 1980s, however, it became apparent that the state-run economy was overextended. Two boom and bust cycles left Mexico with runaway inflation, a huge foreign debt, and an industry and infrastructure in a state of decline.

President Miguel de la Madrid began to reverse Mexico's economic course in the 1980s. Privatization of state-run enterprises, the revision of protectionist policies, and the promotion of more foreign investment became the new economic goals, which would be embraced by de la Madrid and his successor, Carlos Salinas de Gortari. Throughout the 1980s and continuing into the next

Demonstration in Mexico against the NAFTA agreement, November 1993 (Dorantes Sergio / Corbis Sygma)

decade, the Mexican government pushed privatization and took additional and often controversial steps intended to open the Mexican economy. In 1988, Salinas changed Mexico's 1973 Law on Foreign Investment to allow for 100 percent foreign ownership of property—a move reminiscent of the Porfiriato that made many Mexicans nervous. Perhaps the most controversial of Salinas's economic reforms involved an attempt to restructure Mexico's inefficient agricultural system. In 1991, Mexico amended Article 27 of its Constitution, ending the agrarian reform that was such a visible part of the Mexican Revolution of 1910. By giving Mexican farmers titles to plots of land or *ejidos,* and by allowing for the sale of such lands previously held in trust by the Mexican state, Salinas hoped to encourage the efficient consolidation of farmland and to open the agricultural sector to foreign investment.

Mexico's drift toward a more open economy in the 1980s and 1990s eventually culminated in NAFTA. Indeed, it was under Salinas that Mexico joined GATT, and Salinas himself took the initiative in proposing a free trade agreement with the United States (the U.S.–Canadian link had been established already through a free trade pact signed in 1988). Such an agreement promised to enhance important trade linkages that already existed between these two countries. Most Mexican exports went to the United States in the years before NAFTA, and since 1965, the two countries had been connected by the *maquiladora* program, which enabled American companies to take advantage of inexpensive Mexican labor for the assembly of goods. NAFTA commits Mexico to continuing its policies of privatization and deregulation while encouraging the country to play to its comparative advantage. In the NAFTA market, Mexico's agricultural sector will gradually be given over to specialty fruit and vegetable production, which Mexico can, among the three countries, produce at the lowest cost. Basic grains, including corn (long the staple of the Mexican diet), will become the domain of the United States and Canada with their highly mechanized agricultural systems. Under NAFTA, Mexico is also expected to be the cheapest source of unskilled and semiskilled labor for Canadian and American businesses.

Concerns over the protection of workers and of the environment surfaced in Canada, Mexico, and the United States during the negotiations that led to NAFTA. Indeed, many feared that the *maquiladora* industry, now notorious for its low wages and negative effect on environmental quality along the U.S.–Mexico border, might represent the shape of things to come under a free-trade agreement. Political pressures in all three countries resulted in the drafting of two side agreements to NAFTA. The labor agreement addresses the chief concern that low wages and poor enforcement of worker protection laws will make Mexico a haven for foreign companies in search of cheap workers. It cre-

ates a three-country labor commission to investigate complaints related to issues such as worker safety, child labor, and minimum wages. The environmental side agreement addresses the main concern that Mexico, with its fairly weak environmental laws, will become a "pollution haven" for foreign businesses. An environmental commission is charged with investigating environmental problems. This side agreement has also encouraged the United States and Mexico to address the issue of environmental degradation in the border zone. The Border Environmental Cooperation Commission (BECC) and the North American Development Bank (NADB) are the chief mechanisms for planning and funding environmental cleanup along the U.S.–Mexico border.

The preliminary results of the NAFTA side agreements are decidedly mixed. Several labor complaints were filed on behalf of Mexican workers during the first few years of the treaty, most of which addressed the problems of workers in the *maquiladora* industry. But while helping to call attention to the conditions of some Mexican workers, such complaints have also underscored the difficulties involved when an international commission with little real power attempts to oversee the enforcement of an individual country's labor laws. The difficulties are compounded in the Mexican case by domestic labor politics, with the official labor union (the Confederación de Trabajadores Mexicanos, or CTM) exerting pressure on *maquila* workers who have attempted to establish independent unions that are more responsive to workers' needs. The environmental side agreement has likewise helped call attention to Mexico's environmental problems, and citizens groups have used it to protest against attempts by the United States to weaken its own environmental legislation. Yet while this side agreement has created mechanisms for change, it is limited by practical and political constraints. The chief task of cleaning up the border zone has been hampered by a lack of funds while investigations of environmental problems have been hampered by domestic politics, particularly in Mexico and the United States.

From a strictly economic perspective, the first years of NAFTA were successful. Trade among the three countries increased dramatically, and more Mexican workers found jobs as foreign companies set up shop in Mexico. Mexico's initiation into the world of free markets and neoliberalism, however, has not been without problems. In late 1994, just as the first year of NAFTA was drawing to a close, Mexico was forced to devalue its currency and to accept a $50 billion emergency loan from the United States. This financial crash resulted from President Salinas's deliberate overvaluing of the peso, a move designed to ensure a PRI victory in 1994 elections, but one also intended to convince the United States that the Mexican economy was stable enough to be part of a regional trade bloc. Although Mexico quickly repaid the loan, the 1994 peso crash raised questions about the country's neoliberal economic policies. Such questions intensified at the end of the 1990s, when the Mexican government was forced to renationalize a handful of industries that were on the verge of bankruptcy.

Perhaps the most visible challenge to the new economic course charted by de la Madrid and culminating with NAFTA has come from the Zapatista rebels in Chiapas. Deliberately choosing the first day of NAFTA's implementation to begin their rebellion, Zapatistas declared NAFTA a "death sentence for the indigenous people of Mexico" and focused their criticism on the end of land reform and the restructuring of the agricultural system that had begun to occur as Mexico changed its economic course during the 1980s. Despite such protest and the difficulties encountered in the moves away from a protectionist system, Mexico seems determined to remain a player in the increasingly globalized economy.

—SBP

See also: Agrarian Reform/Land and Land Policy; Constitution of 1917; Debt, Mexico's Foreign; Foreign Policy; Revolution of 1910.

References:
Metz, Allen. *A NAFTA Bibliography.* Westport, CT: Greenwood Press, 1996.
Orme, William A., Jr. *Understanding NAFTA: Mexico, Free Trade, and the New North America.* Austin: University of Texas Press, 1996.
Weintraub, Sidney. *NAFTA at Three: A Progress Report.* Washington, DC: Center for Strategic and International Studies, 1997.

Novel of the Revolution

The Mexican Revolution (1910–1920) devastated the country and left nearly 2 million people dead (out of a population of only 15 million!). But for all the devastation, the Revolution represented a new beginning for Mexico, an opportunity to reimagine the national community. According to novelist Carlos Fuentes, the Revolution brought together Mexicans from all walks of life and from the remotest regions of the country for the first time:

> A country in which the geographical barriers of mountains, deserts, ravines, and sheer distances had separated one group of people from another since ancient times now came together, as the tremendous cavalcades of Villa's men and women from the north rushed down to meet Zapata's men and women from the south. In their revolutionary embrace, Mexicans finally learned how other Mexicans talked, sang, ate, and drank, dreamed and made love, cried and fought. (Fuentes, *The Buried Mirror,* p. 308)

It is hardly surprising, then, that this Revolutionary embrace has obsessed Mexican novelists ever since. It is through the great novels of the Revolution—Mariano Azuela's *Los de abajo,* Martín Luis Guzmán's *El águila y el serpiente,* Nellie Campobello's *Cartucho,* Agustín Yáñez's *Al filo del agua,* Juan Rulfo's *Pedro Páramo,* Carlos Fuentes's *La muerte de Artemio Cruz,* Elena Poniatowska's *Hasta no verte Jesús mío*—that Mexican fiction is best known to international audiences.

Although the novel of the Revolution tends to dominate national fiction (at least from an outsiders' perspective), Mexico had a strong prerevolutionary novelistic tradition: José Joaquín Fernández de Lizardi's great satirical novel, *El periquillo sarniento* (The Itching Parrot, 1816), with its *pícaro* antihero, mocked the social conventions of independence-era Mexican society. Liberal romantics like Ignacio Manuel Altamirano (1834–1895) combined politics and melodrama in their novelistic portrayals of noble liberal reformers and dastardly conservative landholders and clerics. Realists like José López Portillo y Rojas (1850–1923) portrayed the dismal lives of hacienda peons (which he blamed on their lack of ambition). Naturalists like Emilio Rabasa (1856–1930), Amado Nervo (1870–1919), and Federico Gamboa (1864–1939) brought their cosmopolitan cynicism and francophile literary style to bear on modern social problems. These diverse novelistic traditions contributed topics and techniques to the novels of the Revolution in a literary embrace every bit as invigorating as the meeting of Villa's and Zapata's armies.

As with most wars, the Mexican Revolution attracted its share of hack writers interested primarily in satisfying the reading public's demand for heroes, villains, and violence (with perhaps a dash of bittersweet romance and brutal lust). In most of these works, character development and moral subtleties take a backseat to one-dimensional protagonists and crude nationalism. Still, the Revolution's many phases and shifting alliances made choosing sides a difficult, dangerous process and straightforward patriotism impossible.

For writers of talent, however, the Revolution's inherent ambiguity proved fertile ground. As early as 1895, Heriberto Frías's (1870–1925) *Tomochic,* a novelistic participant account of the Porfirio Díaz regime's brutal repression of a rural rebellion in northern Mexico, had begun to explore the dramatic possibilities and moral dilemmas posed by collective violence. And in 1911, with the Revolution barely a year old, its first

important chronicler, Mariano Azuela (1873–1952), published a novel about Francisco Madero's successful ouster of Porfirio Díaz, *Andrés Pérez, maderista,* that denounced the self-interest at the heart of Revolutionary politics. This disgust would carry over into a series of novels—*Los caciques* (The Bosses, 1917), *Las moscas* (The Flies, 1918), *Las tribulaciones de una familia decente* (Tribulations of a Decent Family, 1919)—that exposed the corruption and selfishness of the middle and upper classes during the Revolution. "My bitterness," Azuela wrote later, "is directed against men, not against the idea—men who corrupt everything." Elite hypocrisy also appears in Azuela's masterwork, *Los de abajo* (The Underdogs, 1915), in the guise of a fawning intellectual, Luis Cervantes, whose principal contribution to the cause is high-blown Revolutionary rhetoric. *Los de abajo,* however, focuses primarily on the *campesinos* (rural workers), who did the bulk of the actual fighting. The novel revolves around the rise and fall of Demetrio Macías, the campesino leader of a Revolutionary band, from his first victory to the ambush that kills him. Azuela even has both battles occur in the same place, giving the novel a circular structure that suggests the ultimate futility of civil war—an image reinforced by horrendous scenes of destruction and brutality. The privileged classes might pursue war for personal gain but for poor *campesinos* like Demetrio it was an irresistible force of nature. One character compares the Revolution to a hurricane that sweeps everything before it. Demetrio explains it to his wife in their farewell scene by tossing a rock into a ravine: "Look at that rock," he tells her, "it just keeps rolling." For a conflict that would eventually take the lives of one in eight Mexicans, including most of its leaders, Azuela's early assessment seemed remarkably prescient—the violent phase of the Revolution would last another five years! Indeed, when *Los de abajo* finally reached a national audience in the mid-1920s, it was quickly hailed as a classic.

Subsequent classic novels of the Revolution were every bit as ambivalent about the conflict as *Los de abajo*. In 1928, Martín Luis Guzmán (1887–1976) published *El águila y el serpiente* (The Eagle and the Serpent), a semifictional account of his two years (1913–1915) with Pancho Villa's army of the north. While Azuela's novel had resembled a Greek tragedy with its circular plot and archetypal characters, *El águila y el serpiente* presented the gritty daily details of Revolution: inadequate hospitals, petty corruption, martial law, and incidental violence. Although Guzmán would later write a more flattering *Memorias de Pancho Villa* (Memoirs of Pancho Villa, 1951), in *El águila y el serpiente,* the swaggering General Villa embodies the ever-changing face of Revolution. Alternately cruel and sentimental, brutal and loyal, he appears as an elemental force, although more mechanical (and thus modern) than natural. In Guzmán's estimation:

> This man wouldn't exist if his pistol didn't exist. . . . It isn't merely an instrument of action with him; it's a fundamental part of his being, the axis of his work, and his amusement, the constant expression of his most intimate self, his soul given outward form. Between the fleshy curve of his index finger and the rigid curve of the trigger there exists a relation that comes from the contact of one being with another. When he fires, it isn't the pistol that shoots, it's the man himself. Out of his heart comes the ball as it leaves the sinister barrel. The man and the pistol are the same thing. Whoever counts on one can count on the other. Out of his pistol have come and will come his friends and his enemies. (Guzmán, *The Eagle and the Serpent,* p. 210)

Guzmán's next novel, *La sombra del caudillo* (The Shadow of the Tyrant, 1929) was just as ambivalent about the post-Revolutionary power struggles of the 1920s. Although ostensibly a work of fiction, this novel with its treacherous generals and paranoid president (modeled on Plutarco Elías Calles), provoked enough controversy to prevent its publication in Mexico until 1938.

Ambivalence about the Revolution, however, was not always expressed in overtly critical terms. In *Cartucho* (Cartridge, 1931) and *Las manos de mamá* (My Mother's Hands, 1937), Nellie Campobello (1900–1986) drew on her personal experiences to recreate the Revolution through the eyes of young girl—Campobello's age at the time—from the northern state of Chihuahua, Pancho Villa's center of operations. The result is a series of apparently disconnected anecdotes held together only by the child narrator, her mother, and the soldiers that pass through her life. In *Cartucho,* for example, she calmly relates the conversation of some of Villa's wounded soldiers at a hospital where her mother often visited:

> That dog got what was coming to him! He was sleeping in the Iberia hotel in Torreón, and we came and wrapped him in a bed pad and threw him out the window like a sack. We laughed to see him hit the ground. Then we shot him right in the heart and hanged him. We pinned a picture of Carranza to his fly and stuck a fistful of Carranza bills in his hand. (Campobello, *Cartucho,* p. 59)

Told without moral indignation or horror, these anecdotes brilliantly convey the ordinariness of Revolutionary violence for the children who grew up surrounded by atrocities. But if for Guzmán, Pancho Villa is a fascinating monstrosity; for Campobello's narrator, he's a popular hero whose many cruelties seem perfectly "natural." Both authors provoke a similar feeling of ambivalence about Revolutionary violence, but with Campobello that response takes place outside the text itself—the reader is shocked precisely because the little girl is not.

While Campobello explores the Revolution's impact on women and children, the many novels of Gregorio López y Fuentes (1897–1966) are concerned mostly with its effect on indigenous communities. In these works, ambivalence about the Revolution gives way to outright distrust. Written during the heyday of an official *indigenismo* that sought to promote the interests of Mexico's many Indian cultures, López's novels, especially *Tierra* (Land, 1932) and *El indio* (The Indian, 1935), integrate rich ethnographic description into sordid tales of Indian neglect, exploitation, and betrayal at the hands of callous whites, including many of the same Revolutionaries who publicly espoused the Indian cause. Other novelists were more critical still. For example, in *El resplandor* (Sunburst, 1937), Mauricio Magdaleno (1906–1986) confronted post-Revolutionary government Indian policy head on with a damning account of an Otomí village's futile attempt to gain access to promised farmland from the local hacienda. The Revolution's novelists were quick to acknowledge the heroic aspects of the conflict, but in most cases that heroism only made its betrayals harder to bear.

By 1940, the Revolution's glamour, ambivalent or not, had begun to subside as the social experimentation of the Lázaro Cárdenas presidency gave way to the more conservative, business-oriented administrations of Manuel Avila Camacho and Miguel Alemán. Writers and artists, too, had begun to resist the Revolution's hold on the national imagination. Just as painter Rufino Tamayo publicly rejected the Revolutionary nationalism of Diego Rivera and the muralist movement, members of a new literary movement, the *Contemporáneos,* began to call for more cosmopolitan, less nationalistic forms of expression. Their biggest influence was on poetry, nevertheless an occasional work like Jaime Torres Bodet's *Primero de enero* (First of January, 1934), an introspective inquiry into new year's resolutions and self-identity, or José Rubén Romero's *La vida inútil de Pito Pérez* (The Useless Life of Pito Pérez, 1938), about an eccentric bum with a negative view of the rest of humanity, suggested alternatives to the dominance of the Revolutionary novel.

Nevertheless, some of the best novels of the Revolution were yet to come. But while this new wave of novels would continue to express ambivalence about the Revolution

and obsess about its impact on modern Mexican society, the event itself often receded into the background. For example, in *Al filo del agua* (The Edge of the Storm, 1947), Agustín Yáñez (1904–1980) uses the impending Revolution primarily as a backdrop for his study of collective emotional and sexual repression in a small, Roman Catholic "village of black-robed women" near Guadalajara. For Yáñez, a cultural revolution prompted by new ideas about individual identity and sexuality brought in from the outside—Guadalajara, Mexico City, the United States—dissolves the village's traditional social bonds and sets the stage for the collective violence of revolution. Even the local bell-ringer, whose chimes structure the townspeople's daily routine, succumbs and "all the forces of earth combined could not stem the torrent set in motion by the power of love and death" (Yáñez, *The Edge of the Storm,* p. 209). The sequel, *Las vueltas del tiempo* (The Twists of Time, 1973), takes place after the Revolution (and the death of Calles) as Yáñez follows his characters into middle age. In both novels, the Revolution drives the plot from backstage but is mostly absent from the stories themselves.

The Revolution also provides historical context rather than dramatic focus in the works of Juan Rulfo (1918–1986). In the title story of *El llano en llamas* (The Burning Plain, 1953), the Revolution as seen through the eyes of a Revolutionary bandit, El Pichón, is nothing more than a golden opportunity to fight, loot, and rape women, all of which he continues to do long after its official end. In "Tell Them Not to Kill Me," civil unrest gives an army colonel a long-awaited chance to revenge himself on his father's murderer, whose own son refuses to intervene (except to cart away the body). In Rulfo's influential novel, *Pedro Páramo* (1955), the Revolution is easily subverted by the local hacienda owner and serves to enhance rather than challenge his power. Confronted by an angry Revolutionary with "everyone in the government is a crook, and you and your kind are nothing but a bunch of lowdown bandits and slick thieves," Pedro Páramo merely responds: "How much do you need for your revolution? . . . Maybe I can help you" (Rulfo, *Pedro Páramo,* p. 97). The Revolutionaries accept his money and eventually the leadership of one of his cronies.

By the 1960s, cynicism about the increasingly "institutionalized" Revolution was widespread among Mexican intellectuals. For a new generation of novelists, the Revolution's dramatic power more often derived from the memories of its participants than from the event itself. In *La muerte de Artemio Cruz* (The Death of Artemio Cruz, 1962), Carlos Fuentes (1928–) has the main character relive the Revolution in flashbacks—the idealism and bravery of his Revolutionary youth tainted in advance by the corruption and venality of post-Revolutionary power and wealth. "You will choose," Artemio Cruz muses on his deathbed, "in order to survive you will make choices, you will choose from the infinite array of mirrors only one, the one will reflect you irrevocably and will throw a black shadow over all the other mirrors" (Fuentes, *The Death of Artemio Cruz,* p. 200). Likewise, in the biographical novel *Hasta no verte Jesús mío* (Here's to You, Jesusa, 1969), Elena Poniatowska (1933–) recounts Jesusa Palancares's life as a *soldadera* (camp follower) during the Revolution as one of several significant stages—albeit the most dramatic— in her long life. Denied her widow's pension by President Venustiano Carranza, Jesusa retorts: "Those Revolutionaries make me feel like I've been kicked in the balls . . . I mean, if I had balls. They're just bandits, highway robbers who're protected by law" (Poniatowska, *Here's to You, Jesusa,* p. 137). Disgusted but hardly defeated, she gets on with her life. Coming the year after the government's massacre of student (and other) demonstrators at Tlatelolco, Jesusa's response in *Hasta no verte, Jesús mío* mirrored the resignation felt by most Mexicans. Clearly, in these novels, as in contemporary life, the Mexican Revolution might loom large in the historical memory but it is no longer larger than life itself.

—*RMB*

See also: Calles, Plutarcho Elías; Fuentes, Carlos; *Mestizaje* and *Indigenismo;* Muralist Movement; Novel since 1960; Poetry; Poniatowska, Elena; Revolution of 1910; Rivera, Diego; Rulfo, Juan; *Soldaderas;* Tlatelolco Massacre; Villa, Francisco "Pancho."

References:

Azuela, Mariano. *The Underdogs, a Novel of the Mexican Revolution.* Trans. E. Munguia Jr. New York: New American Library, 1963.

Brushwood, John S. *Mexico in Its Novel.* Austin: University of Texas Press, 1966.

Campobello, Nellie. *Cartucho and My Mother's Hands.* Trans. Doris Meyer and Irene Matthews. Austin: University of Texas Press, 1988.

Fuentes, Carlos. *The Buried Mirror: Reflections on Spain and the New World.* New York: Houghton Mifflin, 1992.

———. *The Death of Artemio Cruz.* Trans. Sam Hileman. New York: Farrar, Straus and Giroux, 1964.

Guzmán, Martín Luis. *The Eagle and the Serpent.* Trans. Harriet de Onis. New York: Dolphin Books, 1965.

Gyurko, Lanin A. "Twentieth-Century Fiction," in David William Foster, ed., *Mexican Literature: A History,* pp. 243–304. Austin: University of Texas Press, 1994.

Poniatowska, Elena. *Here's to You, Jesusa.* Trans. Deanna Heikkinen. New York: Farrar, Straus and Giroux, 2001.

Rulfo, Juan. *The Burning Plain and Other Stories.* Trans. George Schrade. Austin: University of Texas Press, 1967.

———. *Pedro Páramo.* Trans. Lysander Kemp. New York: Grove Press, 1959.

Yáñez, Agustín. *The Edge of the Storm.* Trans. Ethel Crinton. Austin: University of Texas Press, 1963.

Novel since 1960

In the decades immediately following the Mexican Revolution (1910–1920), the nation's best-known novelists took that seminal event as their central focus. For the 1920s and 1930s, Mariano Azuela's *Los de abajo,* Martín Luis Guzmán's *El aguila y el serpiente,* and Nellie Campobello's *Cartucho* powerfully and provocatively evoked the great heroism, tragedies, sacrifices, and betrayals of the Rev-olutionary years. In the 1940s and 1950s, Agustín Yáñez's *Al filo del agua* and Juan Rulfo's *Pedro Páramo* expanded the boundaries of the Revolutionary novel with their pene-trating psychological analyses and formal ex-perimentation. By the 1960s, Carlos Fuen-tes's *La muerte de Artemio Cruz,* Elena Garro's *Los recuerdos del porvenir,* and Elena Ponia-towska's *Hasta no verte Jesús mío* had pushed those boundaries almost to the breaking point as the Revolution became a problem of historical memory rather than lived experi-ence. After 1960, although novelists contin-ued to write about the Revolution, the genre gradually lost its dominant position in Mexi-can literature.

The shift was inevitable. As the Revolution receded further into the past, as "modern" Mexico became less of an aspiration and more of a fact (although the benefits of mod-ernization failed to reach many Mexicans), literature became less self-consciously na-tionalistic. If some of the nation's best novel-ists, such as Carlos Fuentes and Fernando del Paso, continued to obsess about issues of na-tional identity, those issues were generally connected to broader concerns. By 1960, then, the Mexican novel had come of age. As a result, it began to diversify, representing an ever-broadening spectrum of concerns, forms, and voices. Thus, at the turn of the twentieth century, it is no longer possible to identify a distinct national genre or literary style. In its place is a rich mix of genres and styles that includes everything from detective stories and historical fiction to new journal-ism and women's literature.

Even in its heyday, the novel of the Revo-lution had never completely dominated the literary scene. As early as the late 1920s, a group of Mexico City writers known as the *contemporáneos* openly challenged the nation-alist trend in Mexican literature. Although more influential in poetry, theater, and jour-nalism than in novelistic fiction, writers like future Secretary of Education Jaime Torres Bodet (1902–1974) and the multifaceted Sal-vador Novo (1904–1974) insisted on a more cosmopolitan (if still decidedly Mexican) ap-proach to literature that rejected the "crude" nationalism and social realist technique of novelists like Gregorio López y Fuentes and Rafael Muñoz, who chronicled the adven-tures of Revolutionary heroes Emiliano Zap-ata and Pancho Villa. The work of Octavio Paz (1914–1998), especially his influential 1950 essay collection *El laberinto de soledad* (Labyrinth of Solitude), blended the urban sophistication of the *contemporáneos* with the nationalist obsessions of Revolutionary nov-elists to produce a cosmopolitan nationalism that connected Mexican themes to universal concerns and vice versa. In Paz's poetry and essays and in the first novels of Carlos Fuentes (1928–), especially *La región más transparente del aire* (Where the Air Is Clear, 1958) and *La muerte de Artemio Cruz* (The Death of Artemio Cruz, 1962), this new cos-mopolitan nationalism would bring Mexican literature worldwide attention as part of the great 1960s "boom" in Latin American litera-ture that produced such internationally ac-claimed authors as Argentina's Jorge Luis Borges, Colombia's Gabriel García Márquez, and Peru's Mario Vargas Llosa.

Another important trend in midcentury Mexican literature, the novel as a form of so-cial and political engagement, enhanced the role of writer-intellectuals in the nation's po-litical and social life in a different way. The best novelists of the Revolution had also served as its conscience by pointing out its failure to better the lives of ordinary Mexi-cans and by goading Revolutionaries (during and after the Revolution) for their cruelty, corruption, and antidemocratic tendencies. Still, most of these novelists (with the excep-tion of Guzmán) stayed out of active politics and many accepted government jobs. Some writers, however, saw literature as a means to promote serious social change, especially when accompanied by political activism. José Revueltas (1914–1976), for example, served as a role model for several generations of committed Mexican writers and especially for the generation that came of age in the 1960s. While still in his idealistic twenties, essayist Carlos Monsiváis acknowledged Revueltas to be "one of my most important influences, a great writer, who because of his ideological firmness went twice to [the penal colony on] Islas Marías, who has risked jails and universal animosity and who has lived a life of exemplary anti-conformism." (quoted in Monsiváis, *Nuevos escritores mexicanos,* p. 46). This political engagement and nonconformist attitude was clearly reflected in Revueltas's fiction. An early novel, *El luto humano* (The Stone Knife, 1943), used a variety of narrative strategies, many inspired by film, to explore the solitude and suffering of six *campesinos* (rural workers) struggling desperately to escape a flooded village. Another study of human alienation, *El apando* (Solitary Confinement, 1969), sprang directly from the author's own prison experiences, especially the five-year sentence he received for his vociferous protests of the 1968 Tlatelolco Massacre of antigovernment protesters by the Federal Army. Even less troublesome writers like Rosario Castellanos (1925–1974) derived much of their fictional material and their personal mystique from social activism. Castellanos's two novels, *Balún-Canán* (The Nine Guardians, 1958) and *Oficio de tinieblas* (Office of Shadows, 1962), drew on her extensive experience as an outreach worker for the National Indian Institute in her native state of Chiapas in order to expose the historical cycles of repression and resistance that dominated the lives of Mexico's impoverished and oppressed Indians.

By the 1960s, increased prestige (whether from the international boom or a reputation for social activism) and increased readership (whether from literacy campaigns or government subsidized book prices) encouraged more and more young Mexicans to become writers. The proliferation of writer's workshops and literary presses in the major cities provided invaluable training and outlets for new work. Although some critics worried about a dilution of resources and literary quality, the end result was an explosion of new novels, many of them excellent, on an increasingly broad range of topics.

Two distinct literary trends emerged during this decade of worldwide social experimentation and student protests. The most flamboyant was the counterculture movement that took its name from Mexico's burgeoning rock and roll scene, *la onda* (the wave or the vibe). *La onda* novelists like José Agustín (1944–) and Gustavo Sainz (1940–) combined a fascination for sex, drugs, and rock and roll Mexican-style with a bent for literary experimentation, urban slang, and antiestablishment humor. In novels like *La tumba* (The Tomb, 1964) and *De perfil* (In Profile, 1966), Agustín documented the humorous but futile efforts of Mexico City's middle-class hippies to make sense of their aimless lives. The deft use of counterculture slang and a disjointed narrative style captured the absurdity of his generation's self-absorbed alienation. Likewise, in *Gazpacho* (1965), Sainz's portrayal of an urban youth culture obsessed with freedom from parental, sexual, and institutional repression emerges from a literary montage of tape recordings, telephone conversations, letters, and diaries in which real and imagined incidents mix freely. Interviewed later about his and Sainz's early work, Agustín remarked that: "We wrote about youth while we were a part of it. We used a different language, a distinct mentality, and an entirely distinct sensibility" (quoted in D'Lugo, *The Fragmented Novel in Mexico,* p. 164).

Literary experimentation also characterized the other major trend of the 1960s: *escritura* (literally "writing"). Less a youth movement like *la onda* than a commitment to innovative writing in the aftermath of the "boom," *escritura* took on many forms and had many practitioners, not all of them young. In *escritura* novels, readers are encouraged to engage directly with the text, to participate actively in its construction—a process that seeks to expose and question the author's efforts to control its meaning. For example, Juan José Arreola (1918–), already well known for his brilliant short stories ("Confabulario," 1952; "Bestiario," 1959), turned his hand to the novel with *La feria* (The Fair, 1963). Arreola's novel represents the complexities of small-town life in his native Jalisco through narrative fragments that reflect the region's myriad voices but with a sensitivity to colloquial speech that hints (to the active reader) at cultural commonalities just beneath the surface of his characters' obvious differences in life experience and social position. Already an international literary star thanks to "boom" novels like *La región más transparente del aire* and *La muerte de Artemio Cruz*, Carlos Fuentes followed suit with the appropriately titled *Cambio de piel* (Change of Skin, 1967). Although the novel revolves around two Mexico City couples on an ill-fated road trip to Vera Cruz, Fuentes ruthlessly denies the reader any sense of stability by fragmenting his narrative, refusing to distinguish reality and fantasy, having his characters play different parts, and constantly shuffling narrators. As with most *escritura* novels, Fuentes leaves it up to the individual reader to make sense of the plot (or not). The apparent surrender of authorial control, however, did not prevent writers like José Emilio Pacheco (1939–) from inserting moral concerns into their work. In *Morirás lejos* (You Will Die in a Distant Land, 1967), Pacheco uses narrative fragments from historical events like the Holocaust and generic character names like *eme* ("m") and *Alguien* (Someone) to push readers to construct their own ethical as well as aesthetic understanding of his complex novel. Even more demanding are the novels of Salvador Elizondo (1932–), especially his bafflingly hermetic *Farabeuf o la crónica de un instante* (Farabeuf or the Chronicle of an Instant, 1965) in which the bewildered reader is warned that:

It is necessary to make an effort. You should try to remember everything, right from the beginning. The tiniest incident could be of utmost importance. The most insignificant point is capable of bringing us to the discovery of a fundamental fact. It is necessary that you make a detailed, exhaustive inventory of all the objects, of all the sensations, of all the emotions that have assembled here in what is perhaps a dream. (quoted in D'Lugo, *The Fragmented Novel in Mexico*, pp. 143–144)

While Elizondo's vivid descriptions of torture (including a graphic photograph) shock the reader into engaging with the text, his incorporation of Chinese numerology and spirituality (yin and yang, for example) hint at an underlying unity available perhaps to the persistent (enlightened?) few. "It is not the novel that has died," Fuentes pointed out, "but specifically the bourgeois form of the novel and its term of reference, realism" (quoted in Duncan, *Voices, Visions, and a New Reality*, p. 3).

But even as *la onda* and *escritura* writers waged war on realism and the "authoritarian" master narratives of the bourgeois novel, the massacre of antigovernment protesters at Tlatelolco in 1968 by the Federal Army reminded them that authoritarianism had many faces, some more real (and brutal) than others. Under these circumstances, experimental novels—as likely to frustrate as to engage most readers—hardly seemed the appropriate response. Some writers, such as Pacheco and later Fuentes himself, eventually turned back to a more "realistic" (if hardly "bourgeois") style. Others, such as Arreola and Elizondo, abandoned the novel for other literary genres. The most direct response, however, was "new journalism," a style that combined innovative novelistic techniques with old-fashioned news stories whether of current events or human interest. Having pioneered the new style in *Hasta no verte Jesus mio* (Here's to You, Jesusa, 1969), a fictionalized enthno-biography of a working-class domestic, Elena Poniatowska (1933–) produced *La noche de Tlatelolco* (Massacre in Mexico, 1971). A damning collage of eyewitness accounts, photographs, and documents of the Tlatelolco Massacre, *La noche de Tlatelolco* kept the event in the public eye and contributed to a growing disillusionment with

Mexico's one-party state. *Nada, nadie. Las voces del temblor* (Nothing, Nobody: Voices of the Earthquake, 1988), which chronicled the government's failure to deal with the 1985 Mexico City earthquake, further damaged the regime's already shaky credibility. In an essay from *Días de guardar* (Days to Keep, 1970), fellow new journalist Carlos Monsiváis (1938–) lamented: "after a disgrace as unjust, irreparable, and unpunished as the Tlatelolco massacre, things were never the same." (quoted in Monsiváis, *Días de guardar*, p. 75). Although Monsiváis in subsequent essays has often worried publicly about creeping cynicism, alienation, and lethargy, his own penetrating insights and sardonic humor about everything from politics to popular culture have continued to prove a powerful antidote to official hypocrisies. More than just critique, however, new journalism reinvigorated the notion of socially and politically engaged literature inherited from activist-authors like Revueltas, whose incarceration over Tlatelolco served as a symbol of the ongoing struggle against government oppression.

As the new journalism of Poniatowska and Monsiváis suggests, Tlatelolco marked the end of an era. Although official party propagandists struggled mightily to maintain at least the pretense of consensus politics, after 1968, they fooled no one. In a 1973 essay, Monsiváis issued a call to literary arms: "From the formal point of view . . . the Mexican Revolution has died . . . thus genuine literature must fulfill a function: to determine exactly the extent of our rejection and the magnitude of our dissent . . . politically, socially, culturally, morally, etc." Novelists took up the challenge with a vengeance. The result was a "postmodern" literary landscape, too fractured and too mixed up to allow for easy classification. By 1980, the identity politics of women, gays, working-class men, borderlanders, and others had begun to produce recognizable literatures, and established genres like the historical novel and detective fiction had begun to take on new shapes and themes.

Perhaps the most monumental shift was the emergence of a literature by, for, and about women. Mid–twentieth-century Mexican letters had had more than its share of great women writers. Nellie Campobello, Rosario Castellanos, Elena Garro, Elena Poniatowska, and others provided (and still provide) generations of young Mexican women writers with inspiration, role models, and support. Still, until the 1980s, Mexican literature, like most areas of public life, was predominantly male. This was sometimes the case even with female authors. For example, in *El libro vacío* (The Empty Book, 1958), Josefina Vicents's (1911–1988) exploration of Mexico's male-dominated society, the protagonist, a colorless office worker with writer's block, refers to his wife only as "my woman" and confesses to her: "I treat you badly because your composure bothers me, because I can't tolerate your simplicity. I treat you badly because I detest people who aren't their own worst enemies" (quoted in D'Lugo, *The Fragmented Novel in Mexico*, p. 86). With attitudes like these, it is hardly surprising that women's voices were few and far between in the novels of the period. Still, as female literacy and educational opportunities for women increased during the economic boom years of the 1950s and 1960s, so did the potential audience for women's literature.

Encouraged by the 1969 success of Poniatowska's *Hasta no verte Jesús mío* with its dominant (and domineering) female protagonist and Rosario Castellano's 1975 feminist comedy, *El eterno femenino* (The Eternal Feminine), Mexican women writers set out to remedy the situation. By the 1980s, women's literature was an established genre and women's voices and concerns were amply represented. The novels of Carmen Boullosa (1954–), *Mejor desaparece* (Better It Vanishes, 1987) and *Antes* (Before, 1989), focus on the way that gender relations structure family dynamics. *Mejor desaparece,* for example, portrays the nightmare world constructed by a distant, authoritarian father unable to relate to his young daughters (all named for exotic flowers) after their mother's death (he's forgotten her name) because he cannot even distinguish among them (at one point he even burns their birth certificates). *Antes* views family dynamics in retrospect as the female narrator flashes back to her early years before the onset of puberty and the guilt, fears, obsessions, and absurdities that formed her personality. Similar concerns about female development in a male-dominated society appear in María Luisa Puga's (1944–) *Pánico o peligro* (Panic or danger, 1985), in which the protagonist, Susana, self-consciously constructs her own life narrative as a journey from dependence and insecurity to freedom and self-confidence. The unnamed female narrator of a later novel, *La forma del silencio* (The Shape of Silence, 1987), explores the broader social context of urban women's lives—constant threats of violence, official corruption, widespread cynicism and alienation—and concludes that "in this vast and chaotic universe that is the D.F. [Mexico City], they are alone" (quoted in D'Lugo, *The Fragmented Novel in Mexico,* p. 222).

With their niche securely established, some women writers began to reject or at least play down the feminist agenda implicit in most 1980s women's fiction. That strategy, deliberate or not, greatly expanded its audience. In Angeles Mastretta's (1949–) immensely popular *Arráncanme la vida* (Mexican Bolero, 1985), the heroine, Catalina Guzmán, battles to maintain her identity in the rough-and-tumble (and macho) world of post-Revolutionary politics. Still, the novel is more a celebration of one woman's gritty defiance than a call for female solidarity. Mastretta even confessed to an interviewer: "perhaps because of my children I live a very self-centered life. I don't go to the university, I don't teach. . . . And I am not very crazy about those meetings about women writers and literature. . . . I confess that because I'm a woman perhaps I write with greater facility about women, but maybe it's because I am myself" (quoted in De Beer, *Contemporary Women Writers,* pp. 239–240). Another hugely

successful novelist, Laura Esquivel (1950–), takes a similar "feminine" approach to feminism. In *Como agua para chocolate* (Like Water for Chocolate, 1989), Esquivel not only uses a stereotypical female genre, the melodrama, she also structures her love story around traditional Mexican recipes and sets much of it in the kitchen, a traditionally feminine domain. While her story, like Mastretta's, forthrightly acknowledges the gender inequalities in Mexican society, Esquivel's villain is a repressed, repressive mother while her male characters are either ineffectual or supportive. Perhaps because of their feminine approach to feminism or because both novels provided straightforward narratives or because they revived the ever-popular "novel of the revolution," *Arráncanme la vida* and *Como agua para chocolate* have become international bestsellers with English translations and, in the latter case, a feature-length film directed by Esquivel's husband, Alfonso Arau, that has attracted considerable international attention as well.

Encouraged by the success of women's fiction with its forthright discussions of gender discrimination and female sexuality, and inspired by a distinguished tradition of "gay" writers like Salvador Novo and Carlos Monsiváis, some Mexican novelists turned their attention to issues of homosexual identity. Luis Zapata's (1951–) pioneering gay novel, *Las aventuras, desventuras y sueños de Adonis García, el vampiro de la colonia Roma* (Adonis García: A Picaresque Novel, 1979), for example, uses the tape-recorded interview format—a favorite of *la onda* writers—to detail the "adventure, misadventures and dreams" of a young male prostitute who unabashedly rejects the straight life because: "i do what i wanna do when i wanna do it and that's well i think that's happiness" (quoted in D'Lugo, *The Fragmented Novel in Mexico,* p. 191). Equally unapologetic about homosexual lifestyles, José Rafael Calva's (1953–1997) *Utopia gay* (Gay Utopia, 1983) revolves around a male couple, Adrián and Carlos, anxiously awaiting the birth of their child—the reader is left wondering if Adrián's pregnancy is real or imagined—and a new utopian life in Baja California. Despite their optimistic, unrepentant tone, however, both novels explicitly address the repression of male homosexuals in Mexican society. In Zapata's *En jirones* (In Shreds, 1985), the gradual destruction of the gay protagonist-narrator caught up in an obsessive erotic relationship with a lover known only as "A" exposes the psychological dysfunction within the gay community that results from the social stigmatization of homosexuality.

Lesbian fiction followed a similar trajectory from unrepentant "celebration" of homosexual lifestyles to introspection and self-critique. Mexico's first well-known lesbian novel, Rosamaría Roffiel's (1945–) *Amora* (Love, 1989), explores female relationships—lesbian as well as straight—through the diary of its protagonist, Guadalupe, a writer for the prominent Mexico City feminist magazine, *fem*, who insists that "lesbians are common and natural women, of all colors, ages, nationalisms, and professions who simply love other women instead of loving men." "Just like the rest of the human race," she points out, "we like ice cream and tacos" (quoted in D'Lugo, *The Fragmented Novel in Mexico*, p. 199). Celebratory or not, Roffiel's novel acknowledges the difficulties that women, especially lesbians, face in a patriarchal society that ruthlessly suppresses female sexuality of any sort whether through harassment or outright violence. In this hostile environment, women learn to rely on each other and *Amora*'s heroine, Guadalupe, returns (at least temporarily) to the emotional security of her lover, Claudia. Like *Amora*, Sarah Levi Calderón's (1942–) *Dos mujeres* (Two Women, 1990) focuses on the ins and outs of a lesbian relationship. But, in Levi's novel, the protagonists, Valeria and Genovesa, are ultimately unable to sustain the intimacy of their periodic exiles (financed by Valeria's wealthy father), avoid the conventional gender roles perpetrated by popular culture, or resist the commercialization of

their own relationship, which Valeria turns into a novel. Just as in Zapata's *En jirones*, social intolerance makes loving gay relationships at least as difficult to sustain as straight ones.

Women and gays were not the only groups to take advantage of identity politics and the literary experiments of *la onda* and *escritura* writers in order to produce distinct literatures. If *la onda* writers gave voice to Mexico City's restless middle-class youth, working-class writers Armando Ramírez (1954–) and Emiliano Pérez Cruz (1955–) speak the language of the capital's tough, economically marginal neighborhoods, like Tepito, notorious for its thieves market, and Nezahualcóyotl, one of the world's largest shanty towns. Carlos Fuentes, among others, has written gritty urban novels about "Makesicko" City (as one of Fuentes's characters called the capital) but works like Ramírez's bestseller *Chin-chin el teporocho* (Chin-Chin the Wino, 1978) and Pérez's *Borracho no vale* (It's No Good Drunk, 1988) provide a distinctive working-class perspective on barrio life as well as lots of alcohol, drugs, sex, and violence. For other writers, like Luis Arturo Ramos (1947–), the vast urban metropolis becomes a site for male wanderings, although the working-class hero of his *Violeta-Perú* (1979) is too drunk and absorbed in macho fantasies to discover much of anything.

Nor are working-class urban lives the only source of inspiration and identity for late twentieth-century Mexican writers. The last two decades have seen a resurgence of local and regional literatures. Building on a distinguished tradition—the Jalisco of Juan Rulfo and Agustín Yáñez, the Chiapas of Rosario Castellanos—authors like Hernán Lara Zavala (1946–), Carlos Montemayor (1947–), and Federico Campbell (1941–) have expanded the local and regional repertoires with their evocative treatments of Yucatán, Chihuahua, and Baja California-Tijuana. For example, Lara Zavala's *Charras* (Union Leader, 1990) is not only rooted in his home state of Yucatán but documents the 1947 murder of his cousin, a prominent reformist labor leader, by state political bosses, including the governor. Another example, Montemayor's *Minas del retorno* (Returning Mines, 1982), is more poetic and mythical than political and historical. A meditation on death and the loss of historical and cultural memory, *Minas del retorno* is nevertheless firmly rooted in the Chihuahua desert "where the sound of the heat has another sound, a sound that is not of other things but, simply, of tomorrow (or morning)" (quoted in Duncan, *Voices, Visions, and a New Reality,* p. 82). Campbell works both veins with a novel, *Pretexto* (Pretext, 1979), about the repression of journalists (the author's profession) in Baja California and a collection of impressionistic short stories, *Tijuanenses* (Tijuanans, 1989), about the peculiarities of life in a border town overwhelmed by floods of migrants from central Mexico and the looming economic and cultural presence of the United States. The short novella, *Todo lo de las Focas* (Everything about Seals, 1982) for example, chronicles a young man's obsession with a beautiful blonde American woman who appears and disappears mysteriously in an airplane before dying in his car from a botched abortion on their way to the border.

If gender, sexuality, social class, and geography expanded the repertoire of literary identities, traditional literary genres benefited from the writing boom as well. None benefited more than the venerable historical novel (including, of course, the novel of the Revolution). The most consistent and consistently brilliant of modern Mexican historical novelists is probably Fernando del Paso (1935–). His early novel, *José Trigo* (1966), chronicled the 1958 railroad workers' strike; *Palinuro de Mexico* (1977), the Revolution and 1968 student movement; and *Noticias del imperio* (News of the Empire, 1987), the French intervention. More than just a chronicler, del Paso is also a droll humorist and innovative stylist whose ambitious sprawling novels play with conventional notions of historical change. Although both *José Trigo* and *Palinuro de Mexico,*

for example, deal with distinct historical events, del Paso uses the slaughter of Aztec resisters by the Spanish at Tlatelolco as the foundational event for both novels. That he wrote *José Trigo* before the 1968 massacre only adds to the many mysteries embedded in del Paso's complex texts. The versatile Carlos Fuentes also found inspiration in epic historical novels—the massive *Terra Nostra* (1975), the cynical *Cristóbal Nonato* (Christopher Unborn, 1986), the romantic *La campaña* (The Campaign, 1990)—that confront the great unresolved issues in Mexican history, such as authoritarian politics, endemic corruption, and social inequality. Like del Paso, Fuentes plays fast and loose with conventional notions of time as the boundaries between past, present, and future seem to overlap in an historical palimpsest. More recently, Homero Aridjis (1940–) has further blurred those boundaries with a series of historical novels—*1942; Vida y tiempos de Juan Cabezón de Castilla* (The Life and Times of Juan Cabezón of Castille, 1985), *El ultimo Adán* (The Last Adam, 1985), *La leyenda de los soles* (The Legends of the Suns, 1993)—that incorporate the author's environmentalist concerns with traditional myths and historical events to produce an apocalyptic vision of a seemingly unavoidable future.

Perhaps the genre that has benefited most from the post-1960s boom of the Mexican novel is the detective story. Since the advent of mass media at the turn of the nineteenth century, Mexicans (like most everyone else) have been drawn to sensational crimes and clever detectives, as attested to by popular weekly tabloids like *Detectives* (1932–1942) and *Alarma* (1951–). Since the 1960s, some of Mexico's preeminent writers have transformed the genre. New journalist and playwright, Vicente Leñero (1933–), for example, has published several novels with detective "tendencies," including *Los albañiles* (The Bricklayers, 1964), *El garabato* (The Scrawl, 1967), and *Asesinato. El doble crimen de los Flores Muñoz* (Assassination: The Double Crime of the Flores Muñoz Family, 1985). All three of Leñero's novels use the genre to interrogate modern Mexican society on a variety of subjects from corruption in the construction industry to political assassinations. All three stretch the detective story to its limits with shifting perspectives, narratives within narratives, and undigested documentary evidence (including actual reports on the real-life Flores Muñoz case) that reproduce for the reader the ambiguities and frustrations of the detective. Another prominent playwright turned novelist, Jorge Ibargüengoitia (1928–1983), uses similar strategies in his detective novels, *Las muertas* (Dead Girls, 1977) and *Dos crimenes* (Two Crimes, 1979). The first surrealistically mixes fact and fiction in a grim story about a madam and her consort who kill the prostitutes they can no longer afford to support; the second deals with a Mexico City police raid that propels the protagonist into a contested inheritance, illicit sexual liaisons, deliberate poisoning, and a mistaken murder in a small provincial town. In both stories, Ibargüengoitia subverts the cynical moralism typical of the detective novel with the cheerful amorality and aimless corruption of his characters and by denying the reader the sense of closure needed to pass judgment on them. The versatile Carlos Fuentes weighed in as well with a detective-spy novel, *La cabeza de la hidra* (Hydra Head, 1978), about international intrigue, Mexican oil politics, and assassination plots. But, as with most Fuentes novels, these geopolitical concerns are intimately connected to issues of personal and national identity, in this case the frustrated efforts of his idealistic protagonist, Félix Maldonado, to control the narrative and salvage a coherent sense of self.

If the considerable literary talents of Leñero, Ibargüengoitia, and Fuentes lent prestige to the Mexican detective genre, the many novels of Paco Ignacio Taibo II (1949–) have expanded both its audience and intellectual breadth. Like distinguished predecessors from Arthur Conan Doyle to Raymond Chandler, Taibo II has a hero, Héctor Belascoarán Shayne, the son of a Spanish anarchist (like his creator) and an Irish folksinger who abandons

a promising career as an engineer for an American company to become an alcoholic, reclusive private investigator whose greatest love is Mexico City "that inscrutable porcupine bristling with quills and soft wrinkles" (quoted in Stavans, *Antiheroes*, p. 113). In many ways Belascoarán Shayne is the stereotypical detective as cynical social commentator, but Taibo II, inspired by *la onda* writers like Agustín and Sainz, also challenges his readers' expectations with irrelevant facts, unlikely twists, and authorial asides that mirror the chaotic violence—real and metaphoric—afflicting a society in the throes of an endless modernity crisis. In one of Taibo II's earliest novels, *Días del combate* (Days of Combat, 1976), for example, the villain is a serial killer of women and importer of foreign products (including Swiss cheese) who voluntarily sends Belascoarán Shayne the journal that exposes his crimes after the detective appears on a tacky television game show dedicated to famous serial killers from history.

From the feminine feminism of Mastretta and Esquivel to the borderland existentialism of Federico Campbell to the historical environmentalism of Homero Aridjis to the postmodern detectives of Taibo II and company, contemporary Mexican novels come in too many different styles and genres to effectively categorize all of them. Despite these differences, most novelists continue to write about what it means to be Mexican in the modern world. The obsession with national identity may be firmly rooted in the nation's past but the Mexican novel at the turn of the twentieth century suggests that the issue is far from resolved and that it will continue to inspire novelists into the next century.

—*RMB*

See also: Castellanos, Rosario; Fuentes, Carlos; Gender and Sexuality; Monsiváis, Carlos; Novel of the Revolution; Paz, Octavio; Poetry; Poniatowska, Elena; Rock and Roll; Rulfo, Juan; Theater; Tlatelolco Massacre.
References:
D'Lugo, Carol Clark. *The Fragmented Novel in Mexico: The Politics of Form.* Austin: University of Texas Press, 1997.

De Beer, Gabriella. *Contemporary Women Writers: Five Voices.* Austin: University of Texas Press, 1996.

Duncan, J. Ann. *Voices, Visions, and a New Reality: Mexican Fiction Since 1970.* Pittsburgh, PA: University of Pittsburgh Press, 1986.

Monsiváis, Carlos. *Días de guardar.* Mexico: Ediciones Era, 1988.

———. *Nuevos escritores mexicanos del siglo XX presentados por sí mismos.* México: Empresas Editoriales, 1967.

García, Kay S. *Broken Bars: New Perspectives from Mexican Women Writers.* Albuquerque: University of New Mexico Press, 1994.

Gyurko, Lanin A. "Twentieth-Century Fiction," in David William Foster, ed., *Mexican Literature: A History,* pp. 243–304. Austin: University of Texas Press, 1994.

Stavans, Ilan. *Antiheroes: Mexico and Its Detective Novel.* Trans. Jesse Lytle and Jennifer Mattson. London: Associated University Presses, 1997.

Steele, Cynthia. *Politics, Gender, and the Mexican Novel, 1968–1988.* Austin: University of Texas Press, 1992.

Nuevo León (State)

The state of Nuevo León is located in northeastern Mexico and has as its capital the industrial center of Monterrey. Nuevo León's history has been shaped by its geographical position as a frontier and by its proximity to the states of Durango, Coahuila, and Tamaulipas, which have supplied the raw materials needed to fuel the state's modern economic growth. Nuevo León enjoys a reputation as a major industrial center in today's Mexico. During the twentieth century, the state has been shaped by a growing business and industrial elite that has resisted many of the reforms coming out of the Mexican Revolution and that has helped give Nuevo León its reputation for political conservatism.

Indian raids and wars characterized the entire colonial era and delayed Spanish settlement of Nuevo León. The Spanish presence was formally established in 1596 with the founding of Monterrey and, as in other northern provinces, Tlaxcalan Indians from central Mexico helped the Spaniards gain a foothold. The scarcity of natural resources helped ensure that Nuevo León would remain a frontier area, and despite the establishment of missions and military outposts, the Spanish presence in this province was always tenuous and hampered by the continuing problem of Indian raids. As it emerged from the colonial era, Nuevo León remained economically marginal and far from Mexico's center of power.

Nuevo León's proximity to the Texas border ensured that it would be shaped by events in the United States during the nineteenth century. The province was a center of fighting during the Mexican War, and U.S. forces occupied Monterrey for over a year. During the U.S. Civil War, local merchants facilitated the transfer of cotton from the U.S. South to Mexican ports, thus helping Confederate states bypass the Union blockade. Fortunes made as a result of this transborder commerce helped propel many local traders into the ranks of Nuevo León's fast-emerging economic elite. Indeed, by the latter part of the nineteenth century, the economic transformation of the province was under way, aided by the arrival of the railroad and by the emergence of industry. Monterrey began to develop its reputation as a center of business and industrial development housing a variety of new enterprises, including the famous Cuahutémoc Brewery established in 1891.

The nineteenth century was also a significant era in Nuevo León's political history, underscoring the state's traditional isolation from the center of power and revealing separatist tendencies. Local strongman Santiago Vidaurri dominated the state's political life during the 1850s and 1860s. In 1856 Vidaurri defied the central government and annexed the neighboring state of Coahuila. He maintained personal control over this larger political unit for eight years. Vidaurri's political power was augmented by his direct control of some of the customs revenues collected along the northeastern border of Mexico. In the 1860s, during the French Intervention in Mexico, Vidaurri refused to support the government of Benito Juárez and sided with the foreign invaders.

Nuevo León's economic potential and its separatist reputation made the state a focus of centralization efforts during the regime of Porfirio Díaz (1876–1911). Díaz sought to control the state through General Bernardo Reyes, who served as military commander in northeastern Mexico and as Nuevo León's governor. Reyes presided over an era of impressive economic growth, aided by foreign investment and by the continuing development of an infrastructure.

By 1900, opposition to Reyes and Díaz had emerged in Monterrey and other areas of Nuevo León. Francisco Madero's Anti-reelection Movement found supporters here, but the state experienced no real uprising in response to Madero's call for revolt in 1910. By 1913, however, Nuevo León was in the midst of an armed movement. In 1914, Venustiano Carranza's Constitutionalist forces captured Monterrey and General Antonio Villarreal took control. In a brief period of radical reform, Villarreal declared an end to debt peonage and he struck against the Roman Catholic Church by expelling all of the state's foreign clerics and declaring that churches could only be used to celebrate Constitutionalist victories. Francisco "Pancho" Villa gained some adherents in the state, and when he split with Carranza in 1914, Nuevo León was briefly divided between the two factions. After Villa's occupation of Monterrey in 1915, Carranza's forces regained control of the state and maintained their supremacy. In 1917, Nuevo León drafted a new constitution, marking an official end to the fighting.

While the armed conflict of the Revolution subsided in the state after 1915, Nuevo León, like many areas of Mexico, continued to experience unrest throughout the 1920s and 1930s. Until 1920, rebel forces occupied a southern section of the state, and the revolt of Agua Prieta, which challenged Carranza's national authority, succeeded in installing a new state governor. The economic instability of the Revolutionary period also encouraged labor agitation. After a wave of worker unrest in 1918, state leaders established a board of arbitration in an attempt to placate workers. Labor activism continued, however, and the 1920s and 1930s saw hundreds of strikes and work stoppages. Meanwhile, state elites resisted the wave of reform spearheaded by President Lázaro Cárdenas during the 1930s, and they began to encourage a shift away from Revolutionary reform.

Relative stability and impressive urban and industrial growth have characterized Nuevo León's history since the 1940s. The 1980s saw the establishment of 7,000 new businesses, and the implementation of the North American Free Trade Agreement promised to improve the economic clout of this northern state all the more. Local industrial elites, including the famous "Grupo Monterrey"—a collection of powerful economic players who enjoy considerable influence on the national level—continue to bolster Nuevo León's image of political conservatism through their support of the right-of-center Partido Acción Nacional (PAN).

—SBP

See also: Díaz, Porfirio; Monterrey Group; North American Free Trade Agreement (NAFTA); Partido de Acción Nacional (PAN); Revolution of 1910.

References:

Cavazos Garza, Israel. *Breve historia de Nuevo León.* México City: El Colegio de México, 1994.

García Valero, José Luis. *Nuevo León: Una historia compartida.* México City: Instituto de Investigaciones Dr. José María Luis Mora, 1989.

Saragoza, Alex M. *The Monterrey Elite and the Mexican State.* Austin: University of Texas Press, 1988.

Official state web site: http://www.nl.gob.mx

O

Oaxaca (State)

Oaxaca is a southern Mexican state that has as its capital the city of Oaxaca de Juárez. Oaxaca's Pacific coast region is home to the planned resort of Huatulco and to Puerto Escondido and Puerto Angel, two other tourist destinations. The state also contains part of the Tehuantepec Isthmus, a strip of land connecting the Yucatán Peninsula with southern Mexico. Oaxaca is home to a large Indian population and many of the state's inhabitants still speak native languages. During the nineteenth century, Oaxaca produced two of Mexico's most famous political figures: Benito Juárez (whose surname is incorporated into the name of the capital city) and Porfirio Díaz. The twentieth century was characterized by Oaxaca's efforts to assert its independence in the midst of Mexico's Revolution and by ongoing attempts to develop a more modern economy and integrated society.

The impressive pre-Columbian ruins of Mitla and Monte Albán are testimony to the strength of Oaxaca's Zapotec culture. The Zapotecs occupied the largest part of the state that was also inhabited by several other ethnic groups in the centuries before the Spaniards arrived. The Mixtecs, political rivals of the Zapotecs, were Oaxaca's other main native group. In the century before

Spanish contact, the Aztecs of central Mexico gained political control over part of Oaxaca, and they established the city of Huaxyacac on the site of today's capital.

The Spaniards arrived in Oaxaca in 1521 and they soon established a settlement at Huaxyacac, modifying the name of the Aztec city to "Oaxaca." Francisco de Orozco and Pedro de Alvarado led the conquest of the region's central valleys and Dominican missionaries led attempts to convert native peoples. Oaxaca's colonial economy developed slowly. It was based primarily on cochineal, a dye that, along with silver, became the key export of New Spain. Mixtec and Zapotec Indians produced cochineal, and they were compelled by the Spaniards to hand over this precious commodity for sale. Oaxaca also developed a textile industry during the colonial era, and along its Pacific coast, black slaves labored to produce sugar and cotton.

Despite Spanish dominance of the central valleys, Oaxaca remained one of the most strongly indigenous areas in the colony. Rural Indians in particular clung to their customs and languages, and there were several rebellions against Spanish demands and abuses. Such popular unrest was at least partly channeled into the rebellion of Miguel Hidalgo and José María Morelos that began Mexico's independence movement. Morelos organized an army in Oaxaca and in 1812 he occupied its capital. A guerrilla movement persisted beyond the deaths of Hidalgo and Morelos until Mexico achieved its independence from Spain in 1821.

Oaxaca gained statehood in 1824. The destruction of the independence movement, as well as the political struggles that plagued Mexico in the decades after independence, challenged the state's economy and its leaders. Mixtec, Zapotec, and other native groups added their rebellions to local and national political struggles. The Isthmus of Tehuantepec (a Zapotec stronghold) emerged as a particularly troublesome area. There, natives resisted the political authority of Oaxaca City and fought against attempts by individuals to expropriate land and precious resources (including the region's lucrative salt beds). Such unrest encouraged the national government to create a Federal Territory of Tehuantepec, which existed from 1853 to 1856.

From 1847 to 1852 and again from 1856 to 1857, the challenge of governing Oaxaca fell to Benito Juárez, himself a Zapotec Indian from the village of Guelatao. Educated as a lawyer, Juárez emerged as one of Mexico's most prominent political leaders. As governor of Oaxaca, he promoted education (including education for Indians and women). He was also temporarily successful in calming the unrest of the Tehuantepec region. Juárez's liberal views propelled him into national politics, and his desire to curtail the economic and social power of the Roman Catholic Church influenced the country's 1857 Constitution. When liberals and conservatives clashed over the Constitution of 1857 in the War of Reform (1858–1861), Juárez assumed the presidency on behalf of Mexico's liberals. After the liberal victory, he served as Mexico's president until his death in 1872.

Oaxaca's other famous native son, Porfirio Díaz, also emerged in the context of nineteenth-century political struggles. A military

man who first joined a youth battalion during the Mexican War, Díaz later became a political boss of the Ixtlán district. During the War of Reform, he joined liberal forces in battling conservatives, and during the French occupation of Mexico (1862–1867) he distinguished himself as a military leader. Hoping for an important political post in the Juárez government after the departure of the French, Díaz was passed over. He retired to his hacienda, "La Noria," and he plotted two revolts. The second of these succeeded in overthrowing Juárez's successor, Sebastián Lerdo de Tejada, in 1876, ushering in the so-called Porfiriato.

The emphasis on economic development and foreign investment that was the hallmark of the Díaz regime brought significant growth to Oaxaca. Railroad lines connected Oaxaca to Mexico City and Mexican and foreign investment led to a boom in mining and commercial agriculture. Although several investors made fortunes from mining and from the export of cotton, coffee, sugar, and other crops, Oaxaca's Indian peoples experienced a new assault on their lands. Mine workers and factory laborers also grew increasingly restive as they endured poor working conditions and witnessed the uneven prosperity that accompanied the state's economic growth. Predictably, a political opposition to Díaz had emerged by the dawn of the twentieth century.

Several areas of Oaxaca joined in Francisco I. Madero's call for rebellion against Díaz in 1910–1911. In the aftermath of Madero's victory, Benito Juárez Maza (Benito Juárez's son) briefly assumed the post of governor before his death in 1912. Several groups dissatisfied with Madero's national government rebelled in Oaxaca. On the Isthmus of Tehuantepec, José ("Ché") Gómez led a rebellion from Juchitán. Followers of Pascual Orozco and Emiliano Zapata added to the unrest. In 1913, Fidencio Hernández and Guillermo Meixueiro declared the Plan of the Sierra, beginning a movement that resisted the attempts of Mexico's Revolutionary leaders to control Oaxaca. Indeed, in 1915

Oaxaca declared itself neutral in the factional struggles of the Revolution and declared its intention to govern itself independently.

Venustiano Carranza, who became Mexico's president in 1916, challenged the so-called *soberanista* (sovereignty) movement led by Meixueiro. Carranza's forces managed to occupy Oaxaca's capital and to reorganize the state's government. The *soberanista* movement persisted, however. Only after Carranza's overthrow and death in 1920 did Meixueiro and other *soberanista* leaders mend Oaxaca's break with the central government.

During the 1920s and 1930s a series of governors sought to reconstruct the state and bolster its economy. Some land reform occurred, and there were efforts to organize workers and to integrate Oaxaca's Indian peoples into a more modern state. Oaxaca's leaders also sought to strengthen ties between more remote areas (such as the Tehuantepec Isthmus) and Oaxaca City. Oaxaca's reconstruction and growth were significantly hampered by a massive earthquake that rocked the capital and the southern section of the state in 1931.

During the last half of the twentieth century, Oaxaca's governors continued their attempts to integrate the state and develop its economy. Results were decidedly mixed. Although transportation links within the state improved, areas remained isolated and many Indian communities continued their separate existence, largely removed from regional and national events. And while commercial agriculture experienced growth, the state did not industrialize. By the late twentieth century, an ambitious plan to develop the Isthmus of Tehuantepec (historically one of the most isolated areas) was generating both optimism and resistance. The plan called for a series of road and rail links that would tie together the isthmus, opening it to commercial growth and foreign investment. Improvements in the ports of Coatzacoalcos (in Veracruz) and Salina Cruz (in Oaxaca) were also a component of the project. Although foreign investors, along with national and state leaders were eager to embrace this plan, many of Tehuantepec's inhabitants resisted. Peoples of this area, who are mostly Indian, fear the kind of change that such development might bring. A grassroots protest movement had emerged by the late 1990s, warning especially of the environmental damage that might accompany Tehuantepec's commercial development.

—SBP

See also: Carranza, Venustiano; Díaz, Porfirio; Juárez, Benito; Madero, Francisco; Orozco, Pascual; Revolution of 1910; Zapata, Emiliano.

References:

Badomín, José María. *Monografía del Estado de Oaxaca.* 4th ed. Oaxaca: n.p., 1991.

Dalton, Margarita. *Oaxaca: Una historia compartida.* Mexico City: Instituto de Investigaciones Dr. José María Luis Mora, 1990.

Iturribarría, Jorge Fernando. *Oaxaca en la historia.* Mexico City: Editorial Stylo, 1955.

Official state web site: http://www.oaxaca.gob. mx

Obregón, Alvaro (1880–1928)

President from 1920 to 1924, Alvaro Obregón was born on a hacienda in the northwestern state of Sonora on 19 February 1880. Obregón came from a large family and was educated in the towns of Huatabampo and Alamos, Sonora. After a brief period as a primary schoolteacher, he worked in a flour mill and then purchased his own farm in 1908. Unlike many early Revolutionary leaders, Obregón did not participate in the first phase of the Revolution in 1910–1911 led by Francisco Madero. His first political office was municipal president of Huatabampo in 1911. Obregón began his spectacular military career in 1912 when he successfully led a volunteer force of 300 against the rebel troops of Pascual Orozco, who had revolted against the Madero administration. When Madero was overthrown and assassinated in February 1913 by General Victoriano Huerta, Obregón refused to recognize Huerta's government and became commander of the garrison at Sonora's capital of Hermosillo.

Obregón joined the Constitutionalist forces of "First Chief" Venustiano Carranza and rose rapidly from colonel to commander of the army of the northwest. Obregón drove south from Sonora, his ultimate goal Mexico City. He was in an unofficial "race" for the national capital with his fellow Constitutionalist general, Pancho Villa, who was feuding with Carranza. Villa was also driving south from his regional base in northern Mexico. Obregón won the race when his troops entered Mexico City ahead of Villa in August 1914. Obregón's military success gave him a reputation that put him on an equal footing with Villa as well as Emiliano Zapata in the South.

The clashing personalities and political agendas of the Revolutionary leaders led to the calling of a "Revolutionary convention" in Aguascalientes in October 1914 aimed at preventing a violent split in the Revolutionary ranks. Obregón played a key role at the meeting, which Carranza pointedly refused to attend. If Obregón went over to the side of Villa and Zapata, it would have put Carranza in an impossible military position. Obregón, however, elected to stay with Carranza; rather than preventing a split in the Revolutionary ranks, the convention brought about a definitive split between Villa and Zapata on one side and Obregón and Carranza on the other.

The stage was now set for the bloodiest phase of the Mexican Revolution, in which Revolutionaries would fight other Revolutionaries. Although the initial advantage lay with Villa and Zapata, the two never successfully coordinated their military operations. Obregón reorganized his army, recaptured Mexico City, and then relentlessly drove Villa and his forces to the north in 1915. Obregón's impressive list of military victories was marred by a serious injury he suffered during one of the battles; wounded by a grenade, Obregón almost died and had to have his right arm amputated. With Villa reduced to a regional leader in the north and Zapata contained in the south, the Constitu-tionalist Revolution with its political leader Carranza and military leader Obregón had triumphed.

During 1916 and 1917 Obregón served as minister of war in Carranza's cabinet, a stark reminder to the "First Chief" of who had put him in the presidency. In late 1916 Carranza called a constitutional convention at Queré-taro to put the Revolution on a legal basis. Although Obregón did not attend the convention, he had a major influence on the new constitution that emerged. Obregón's supporters at the convention helped to make the new constitution much more radical than Carranza had wished, another indicator of the political differences dividing the Revolutionary leaders.

When Carranza took office in May 1917 as the first president elected under the new Constitution, Obregón "retired" to private life. He returned to Sonora to tend to his expanding business interests, expecting that Carranza would support his candidacy for president in 1920. Carranza, however, backed a civilian, Ignacio Bonillas, a former ambassador to the United States. Obregón saw this action as not only an extreme display of betrayal and ingratitude, but also as an effort by Carranza to impose a president which he could control from behind the scenes. Carranza tried to undercut state authorities in Sonora and attempted unsuccessfully to arrest Obregón. Governor Adolfo de la Huerta of Sonora and fellow-Sonoran General Plutarco Elías Calles revolted against the Carranza regime in April 1920, issuing the Plan of Agua Prieta. Most of the army sided with the rebels, and Carranza tried to flee Mexico City for Vera Cruz. A rebel force overtook Carranza's party and killed the president on 21 May 1920. Adolfo de la Huerta became provisional president, elections were held, and Obregón won easily, taking office as president on 1 December 1920.

Having worked its way through the presidential succession crisis, Mexico was experiencing an unusual level of political tranquility when Obregón took office. As interim president, Adolfo de la Huerta had issued a general and unconditional amnesty for all rebels, effectively neutralizing most of the supporters of Emiliano Zapata—assassinated in 1919—and Pancho Villa, who accepted his own "retirement package" of land and money from the government in 1920. The economic and financial picture was considerably less optimistic. Mexico was suffering from the accumulated financial and economic problems of years of civil wars, the dislocation of World War I, and a postwar recession in the bargain.

While Carranza had left the more radical provisions of the Constitution of 1917 unenforced, Obregón wanted to move forward on the social and economic reforms set down in the Constitution. Agrarian reform had posed a major problem for every government since 1910. While committed to land distribution, Obregón also wanted to avoid further dislocation of the economy. Landowners whose properties were expropriated and redistributed were supposed to be compensated, a difficult task given the inherited financial problems. Obregón distributed some 3 million acres of land with compensation taking the form of long-term "agrarian bonds," a method immediately challenged by the landowners. In the area of labor relations, the national labor confederation—the CROM—continued to be favored by the government in return for CROM support of government policies; the Obregón administration, however, tried to block the development of any labor organizations independent of the government.

A number of factors affecting Obregón's reform efforts came together in the Bucareli Agreements of 1923 with the United States. At stake were such issues as compensation for expropriated property, control of subsoil resources, financial claims against the government, and diplomatic recognition of the Obregón regime. In the agreements, the United States government recognized payment in long-term bonds as adequate compensation for expropriated property. The Mexican government agreed to exempt foreign holders of subsoil rights from regulation under the Constitution of 1917 if they had actively implemented their concessions prior to 1917. Two special commissions were established to handle private financial claims against the government, one dealing with the pre-1910 period and the other the post-1910 period. The United States government also agreed to extend diplomatic recognition to the Obregón administration, which, it was hoped, would make it easier for the Mexican government to obtain new loans from U.S. banks. Although the agreements represented concessions by both parties, there was strong resistance to them in the Mexican Congress and even within the Obregón administration itself. A senator was reportedly assassinated because of his opposition, and Minister of the Treasury Adolfo de la Huerta strongly opposed the agreements, a split with the president that would soon lead to open revolt.

The last portrait of Alvaro Obregón, president between 1920 and 1924 (Library of Congress)

Reform also had to take a backseat to the growing crisis over who would succeed Obregón in 1924. The choice was a particularly delicate one since Obregón would have to choose between two fellow-Sonorans, Adolfo de la Huerta and Plutarco Elías Calles. Both had outstanding Revolutionary credentials and long-standing political ties to Obregón. When Obregón designated Calles as his successor, de la Huerta soon revolted in a move that almost toppled the Obregón regime. After putting down the de la Huerta revolt, there was little opposition to Obregón's imposition of Calles, who assumed the presidency on 1 December 1924.

Obregón's "retirement" in 1924 was similar to his "retirement" in 1917. He returned to Sonora to tend to his business interests, all the time planning for a return to politics. Obregón's political intentions became clear when the Constitution was amended in 1926 to permit the reelection of presidents to nonconsecutive terms, a move obviously aimed at permitting Obregón to run for the presidency in 1928. With the support of Calles, Obregón easily won reelection in July 1928. On 17 July 1928 President-elect Obregón attended a banquet in his honor in a Mexico City suburb. During the activities surrounding the banquet, a religious fanatic shot Obregón five times; he died within a matter of minutes. The succession crisis leading up to the presidential election of 1928 had quickly and dramatically changed into the succession crisis following the presidential election of 1928.

—DMC

See also: Agrarian Reform/Land and Land Policy; Aguascalientes, Convention of; Assassinations; Calles, Plutarco Elías; Carranza, Venustiano; Confederación Regional Obrera Mexicana (CROM); Cristero Rebellion; Huerta, Victoriano; Madero, Francisco; Presidents of the Twentieth Century; Vasconcelos, José; Villa, Francisco "Pancho"; Zapata, Emiliano.

References:

Dulles, John W. F. *Yesterday in Mexico: A Chronicle of the Revolution, 1919–1936.* Austin: University of Texas Press, 1972.

Hall, Linda B. *Alvaro Obregón: Power and Revolution in Mexico, 1911–1920.* College Station: Texas A&M University Press, 1981.

———. *Oil, Banks, and Politics: The United States and Postrevolutionary Mexico, 1917–1924.* Austin: University of Texas Press, 1995.

Oil Industry

Long before the arrival of the Spaniards, indigenous peoples of the Gulf Coast of Mexico had used petroleum that had naturally seeped to the surface for incense and patching canoes. Later Spanish settlers considered these oil ponds as obstacles to ranching and farming rather than a valuable natural resource. Well into the nineteenth century, there was little commercial development of the oil deposits. When the rise of the oil industry did occur, it was greatly influenced by external forces, especially the expansion of foreign-owned railroads and the growth of the U.S. oil industry.

Beginning in the 1880s, there was a rapid expansion of Mexico's railroads, which were controlled primarily by U.S. entrepreneurs. The railroads represented both potential customers for oil products as well as a cost-effective method of transporting oil products. The boom in the U.S. oil industry, especially in Texas, soon spilled over the border to the Mexican Gulf Coast. U.S. and British firms dominated the emerging Mexican oil industry from the start. Oil pioneers such as Henry Clay Pierce of the United States and Sir Weetman Pearson of Britain (later Lord Cowdray) began as sellers of oil products rather than producers. Pierce—allied with John D. Rockefeller's Standard Oil—imported crude oil from the United States, processed it at three Mexican refineries, and sold the products in Mexico. Pearson's early efforts at oil production enjoyed limited success, but he too had to import oil from the United States for his Mexican refinery. Edward L. Doheny, who had opened the Los Angeles oil fields in the 1890s, began oil production in Mexico in 1902, but the oil was so heavy that it had to be used for paving streets rather than for fuel.

Both Pearson and Doheny invested heavily in exploration and production. Pearson's El Aguila Petroleum Company and Doheny's Huasteca Petroleum Company epitomized the expansion of the Mexican oil business under foreign control. Major oil strikes in 1908 and 1910 soon earned the region from Tampico to Tuxpan the nickname, "the Golden Lane." In May 1911—the same month that the lengthy rule of Porfirio Díaz ended—both Pearson and Doheny began exporting Mexican oil in substantial quantities.

Ironically, a major expansion of the oil industry took place between 1911 and 1920 despite the dislocation caused by the Revolution, which began in 1910. Increased oil prices helped to fuel the boom. Prices increased gradually until the outbreak of war in 1914, when they shot up dramatically; prices almost tripled as a result of the conflict. New discoveries and rising prices brought new producers to Mexico. These included major oil companies—Gulf, Texas Company, and Royal Dutch Shell—as well as hundreds of independent producers.

Although the oil industry was expanding, it was under growing pressure from the different Revolutionary factions competing for power. In addition to fighting in and near the oil fields, the oil companies had to contend with increased taxation, forced loans, confiscation of supplies, and attacks on employees. Rebel groups commandeered oil company machine shops to repair and manufacture military equipment, and some Revolutionaries even ate in oil company cafeterias.

The most important long-term problem for the oil companies was the growing government reliance on the oil industry as a source of taxes. With much of the economy in shambles, a booming oil industry was a tempting source of revenue regardless of which government was in control in Mexico City. Presidents Porfirio Díaz, Francisco Madero, Victoriano Huerta, and Venustiano Carranza all

increased taxes on the oil industry—although tax collection often proved difficult.

The debate over taxation phased over into issues of government control of the industry and national sovereignty. Foreign control of the industry was extremely controversial in an increasingly nationalistic Mexico. Managerial, technical, and skilled labor positions were normally reserved for foreigners. Even when foreigners and Mexicans performed the same jobs, foreigners were typically better paid. The companies also attempted to block the formation of unions.

The growing controversy between the government and the oil companies came to a head with the passage of a new Constitution in 1917. Article 27 of the new Constitution claimed national ownership of all subsoil resources, reversing the position the Díaz administration had taken in order to encourage foreign investment. The interpretation and implementation of Article 27 would place the government at odds with the oil companies for the next decade and have a profound negative impact on the booming oil industry.

The year 1921 proved to be a turning point in the evolution of the Mexican oil industry. Both production and prices began to decline. Oil production reached 193 million barrels in 1921; by the end of the decade, production had slid to 40 million barrels. Prices also dropped, falling almost 50 percent between 1920 and 1921 alone; this price slide continued throughout the 1920s. Major new fields were coming on line in other parts of the world, and the international oil companies now looked to Venezuela rather than Mexico as their principal source of Latin American oil.

The decline in the oil industry was also related to the continuing feud between the oil companies and the government over the issues of taxation and control of subsoil resources. The government continued to look to the oil industry as a major source of revenue but did try to take into account changes in the international oil scene. The dispute over subsoil resources was briefly settled in

1923 only to be revived again in 1925. Another agreement in 1928 returned the status to the 1923 situation; the 1928 agreement restated the "doctrine of positive acts," under which the oil companies could retain their rights regarding subsoil resources if they had taken the "positive act" of developing their resources prior to 1917. By 1928 the oil companies had already become disenchanted with the government's efforts to increase control and taxation and were looking to countries like Venezuela where the political climate was considered more friendly.

A further problem for the oil companies was the changing role of labor during the 1920s. The government and labor were forging mutually beneficial ties at a time when employment in the oil industry was declining sharply with more than 30,000 jobs lost between 1920 and 1922. The workers were competing for the remaining jobs while rival labor organizers competed to unionize the workers. This volatile situation posed yet another threat to the control of the industry by the foreign-owned companies.

The uncertainties of the 1920s soon phased into the problems of the Great Depression of the 1930s, with Mexican oil production bottoming out in 1932 at slightly less than 33 million barrels. Production then began a modest upswing, followed by improving prices in 1934. Another important structural change in the industry was that domestic consumption now accounted for a greater portion of Mexico's oil production. The government also became more actively involved in the industry. Taxes on the industry increased, and in 1934 the government started fixing prices for gasoline.

Government support for unionization was to produce the most dramatic development in the oil industry in the 1930s. In 1934 the new president, Lázaro Cárdenas, encouraged the formation of one, industrywide union for the oil industry, whose workers previously had been represented by 21 different unions. Cárdenas believed that one giant union could more effectively confront the large multinational companies that dominated the oil business. This new dominant union soon demanded a major pay raise, equal treatment for Mexican workers, and greater control over management and supervisory positions. Efforts to settle the dispute made their way to the Mexican Supreme Court, which ruled on 1 March 1938 in favor of the workers. The oil companies then provoked a national crisis by refusing to abide by the Court's ruling. On 18 March 1938, President Cárdenas issued a decree nationalizing the foreign-owned oil companies, which accounted for more than 90 percent of Mexico's total oil production.

Nationalization forced the Mexican government to reorganize the oil industry and to compete in a rapidly changing international market. The international companies whose Mexican assets had been expropriated quickly retaliated. U.S. and British companies immediately withdrew their managerial and technical personnel. They also refused to sell oil supplies to Mexico, would not lease tankers to the Mexican government, and tried to block the sale of Mexican oil in the international market. The Cárdenas government responded by swapping Mexican oil for German and Italian manufactured products, a move that alarmed the U.S. government, which had rejected pleas by the companies to intervene. To manage the nationalized properties, Cárdenas established a state corporation known as PEMEX (Petróleos Mexicanos). PEMEX soon developed a reputation for inefficiency, corruption, and politicized decision making. Despite these problems, the nationalization was highly popular in Mexico itself where it was hailed as Mexico's day of economic independence. The Cárdenas administration had correctly guessed that the international situation would prevent any strong response from the U.S. or British government and would force the oil companies to accept the Mexican government's estimate of what the nationalized properties were worth (approximately $25 million) rather than what the companies claimed they were worth (about $450 million).

With nationalization taking place on the eve of World War II, there was ample demand for Mexican oil; production, however, did not return to prenationalization levels until 1946. As part of an overall plan to promote industrialization, Mexico was also committed to developing its oil resources in response to domestic needs rather than to international market factors; thus, the oil industry was viewed primarily as a source of cheap domestic energy rather than as a generator of foreign exchange. PEMEX was also trying to transform itself into a fully integrated oil company involved in exploration, discovery, refining, and distribution. Initial exploration efforts yielded little in the way of new reserves, and PEMEX relied on heavy exploitation of existing fields, sometimes damaging long-term production.

With Antonio Bermúdez as director general from 1946 to 1958, PEMEX expanded its exploration activities, built new pipelines and refineries, reversed the decline in known reserves, and experienced an increase in crude oil production. Bermúdez increased oil exports but rejected the idea that Mexico would never again become a major exporter in the world market. PEMEX also played an important role in financing the government and the economy through its tax payments and the provision of oil products at low, subsidized prices. Basic financial and economic considerations took second place to political and social concerns in guiding PEMEX policy. The prices of oil products and the wages paid to oil workers were the responsibility of the government rather than PEMEX's management. The financial demands made on PEMEX made it difficult for the company to accumulate the capital needed to finance expansion. The union of oil workers also increased its power at the expense of PEMEX management; the union controlled the hiring of personnel, participated in contracts between PEMEX and private companies, and could even form its own "cooperatives" to compete for PEMEX contracts. The union also selected four of the nine members of

PEMEX's management council, which had overall responsibility for managing the firm. Predictably, such arrangements led to corruption and inefficiency. Union leaders benefited financially much more than union members, with some leaders even "selling" jobs to workers. PEMEX was also seen as an important source of employment, leading to a 157 percent increase in the workforce between 1947 and 1958.

The basic principles guiding PEMEX in the 1960s and early 1970s were unchanged. Primary emphasis continued on meeting domestic needs, and total production increased, particularly in terms of natural gas. One of the most important developments was the growing petrochemical sector. A law passed in 1958 made the production of "basic" petrochemicals a PEMEX monopoly but permitted production by private companies of "secondary" products. In 1960 the government issued a list of 16 products classified as "basic" and therefore restricted to production by PEMEX; in 1967 a new list classified 45 petrochemical products as "basic." The list of basic petrochemicals eventually reached 70. Even the production of secondary products by private firms was done under government supervision.

Despite the growth of the petrochemical sector, there were still some fundamental problems hampering PEMEX's activities. Exploration and drilling activities proceeded at an uneven pace, leading to overexploitation of existing fields. The financial demands made on PEMEX made it difficult to finance needed expansion. While production increased, consumption was increasing at an even faster rate. Mexico had to abandon the exportation of crude oil in 1966; it increased its imports of crude oil, and by 1971 it had become a net importer of crude.

With Mexico's postwar economic "miracle" fading by the early 1970s, the general economic and financial situation added to PEMEX's problems. Two major developments, however, were about to change the situation dramatically. The Arab oil embargo

Petroleum workers at the PEMEX oil refinery. PEMEX is Mexico's national oil company. (Richard Melloul / Corbis Sygma)

of 1973 set off a long-term increase in oil prices, and the discovery of major new oil reserves in southeastern Mexico and offshore took place in the mid-1970s.

Caught in a major financial crisis in 1976, Mexico now had to decide how to deal with its newfound oil wealth and a new position in the international oil market. New oil discoveries meant that Mexico could once again become a major exporter of oil while increasing prices for oil meant that oil could also be a major source of foreign revenue. President José López Portillo had the pleasant task of deciding how Mexico would deal with its new oil wealth. The new oil policy called for gradual development of Mexico's petroleum resources, with limits on production and exportation. Oil revenues would be gradually infused into the economy to avoid the inflation, waste, and corruption that had accompanied rapid oil wealth in countries such as Venezuela and Iran. The future appeared even brighter in 1979 when revolution in

Iran sparked an even bigger rise in oil prices. Mexico also found it easy to get loans from international agencies and commercial banks, with the loans implicitly secured by future oil revenues. There was also confidence that this plan could be successfully implemented by López Portillo, the first in a series of financial technocrats to occupy the presidency.

Unfortunately, Mexico soon experienced the perils of oil prosperity. With oil revenues and international loans, the government embarked on an unparalleled spending spree, with federal spending increasing at a rate five times the increase in the gross national product. PEMEX had long subsidized energy; the new oil wealth permitted the subsidizing of a growing list of consumer items. Much of the oil wealth went into capital-intensive projects that provided little relief for Mexico's unemployed. There was widespread corruption that reached to the top of PEMEX, whose head—Jorge Díaz Serrano—was later convicted of defrauding PEMEX of approximately $30 million. When oil prices began to decline in the early 1980s—instead of continuing to rise as the government had forecasted—Mexico found itself in another major economic and financial crisis because of its oil wealth instead of in spite of it.

Mexico had not only mismanaged its oil wealth; it had also heavily indebted itself based on a level of future oil revenues which now would not be realized. Mexico's debt crisis forced it to make major changes in its financial and economic policies, which in turn had a major effect on PEMEX and its activities. As the government drastically reduced its spending and opened the economy to greater competition, PEMEX had to adjust to the changing political and economic environment. One of the first casualties was PEMEX's involvement in petrochemicals; PEMEX began to phase out its production of "secondary" petrochemicals, selling off its plants to private firms. The list of "primary" petrochemicals—reserved for production by PEMEX—was steadily reduced from a peak of 70 in 1986 to only 8 in 1992. In January 1989 new president Carlos Salinas de Gortari—whose candidacy had been opposed by the powerful oil union—retaliated by arresting 35 union leaders. In 1992 there was a major reorganization of PEMEX into units responsible for exploration and production, refining, natural gas and basic petrochemicals, secondary petrochemicals, and international activities. New accounting and tax procedures also aimed at improving efficiency. The notoriously overstaffed PEMEX saw its workforce drop from 210,000 in 1987 to 106,000 in 1993. PEMEX also scaled back its nonoil activities in such areas as air transport and provision of medical services. The implementation of the North American Free Trade Agreement in January 1994 gave both Canadian and U.S. companies greater access to the petrochemical sector, oil goods and services, and PEMEX contracts. Most of these reforms were aimed at depoliticizing PEMEX and making it more like the giant international oil companies with which it competes. At the same time, the democratization process made PEMEX operations more susceptible to partisan politics as witnessed by the recent congressional blockage of the proposed sale of some of PEMEX's secondary petrochemical operations. PEMEX is also under growing pressure to clean up its environmental act. Environmental concerns led PEMEX to close its Mexico City refinery in 1991, and there is growing support for PEMEX to indemnify private citizens who have suffered losses from PEMEX activities in oil-producing areas.

For the near term at least, PEMEX will continue to be more than the state oil company. It will continue to be the leading symbol of Mexican economic nationalism, a cherished part of the Revolutionary heritage, and a force for social welfare not just government profit.

—*DMC*

See also: Cárdenas, Lázaro; Constitution of 1917; Corruption; Debt, Mexico's Foreign; Economy; Environmental Issues; Labor Movements; López Portillo, José; Madrid (Hurtado), Miguel de la; North American Free Trade Agreement (NAFTA); Revolution of 1910; Salinas de Gortari, Carlos.

References:
Brown, Jonathan C. *Oil and Revolution in Mexico.* Berkeley: University of California Press, 1993.
Brown, Jonathan C., and Alan Knight, eds. *The Mexican Petroleum Industry in the Twentieth Century.* Austin: University of Texas Press, 1992.
Hall, Linda B. *Oil, Banks, and Politics: The United States and Postrevolutionary Mexico, 1917–1924.* Austin: University of Texas Press, 1995.
Meyer, Lorenzo. *Mexico and the United States in the Oil Controversy, 1917–1942.* Austin: University of Texas Press, 1977.

Orozco, José Clemente (1883–1949)

Although acclaimed, along with Diego Rivera and David Siquieros, as one of "the big three" artists of the world-renowned Mexican muralist movement, José Clemente Orozco was considerably more reticent than his colleagues. While Rivera fought with the

Rockefellers and Siquieros masterminded an attempt to assassinate Soviet dissident Leon Trotsky, Orozco focused almost exclusively on his art. "There is nothing of special interest in [my life]," he wrote, "no famous exploits or heroic deeds, no extraordinary or miraculous happenings. Only the uninterrupted and tremendous effort of a Mexican painter to learn his trade and find opportunities to practice it." Despite his reticence, however, Orozco's forceful, often apocalyptic style, his ambivalent treatment of political and historical themes, and his rejection of Rivera's folkloristic tendencies produced a style very different from that of his colleagues and extremely influential in its own right.

Orozco was born on 23 November 1883, in Ciudad Guzmán in the west-central state of Jalisco. The family was well respected and moderately wealthy, but like many small-town residents during the late nineteenth century, they felt the lure of the big cities. They moved first to the state capital, Guadalajara, and, when the boy was 6 or 7, to the nation's political and artistic capital, Mexico City. In Mexico City, the vibrant images of graphic artist José Guadalupe Posada, who worked just down the street from Orozco's primary school, caught and kept the young boy's attention. Orozco reminisced later that:

> Posada used to work in full view, behind the shop windows, and on my way to school and back, four times a day, I would stop and spend a few enchanted minutes in watching him, and sometimes I even ventured to enter the shop and snatch up a bit of the metal shavings that fell from the minimum-coated metal plate as the master's graver passed over it. This was the push that first set my imagination in motion. (Orozco, *José Clemente Orozco,* p. 8)

Whether Orozco embellished a bit on the subject of Posada (who had become something of a celebrity among the muralists) is unclear, although the graphic power that dominates both men's work suggests a strong artistic affinity. What is clear is that Orozco, like his future colleague Diego Rivera, demonstrated a precocious talent and began to attend night classes in drawing at the National Academy of San Carlos, Mexico's finest art school. Three years at the School of Agriculture and four at the elite National Preparatory School only fed his obsession with painting and he reentered the academy in 1905. There, Orozco received rigorous training in the demanding techniques of European academic art. Although he would quickly reject the academy's somewhat rigid approach, he nevertheless lauded the atmosphere of "unrivalled enthusiasm."

At San Carlos, Orozco came under the influence of radical painter Gerardo Murillo, better known by his Aztec pseudonym Dr. Atl, who was encouraging Mexican artists to renounce their "colonial" status and discover "a sense of our own being and our destiny." Inspired by Dr. Atl, Orozco briefly involved himself in politics as an illustrator for a Constitutionalist newspaper, *Vanguardia,* although he would later insist with more modesty than most that "I played no part in the Revolution, I came to no harm and I ran no danger at all." He also took to the capital's streets, producing a *House of Tears* watercolor series (1911–1912) on Mexico City prostitutes. His 1916 exhibition of those pictures shocked the staid Mexico City art establishment and, in 1917, the disgusted Orozco decided to visit the United States, only to have Laredo, Texas, customs officials destroy sixty prints they considered too immoral for American sensibilities.

After three years on the margins of the San Francisco and New York art worlds, Orozco returned to Mexico in 1920. His timing was excellent. The violence and chaos of the Revolution of 1910 had abated, at least in Mexico City, and the new government of President Alvaro Obregón, eager to represent itself as the legitimate heir to the Revolutionary legacy, turned to the nation's artists for help. In 1922, Obregón's dynamic secretary of education, José Vasconcelos, summoned a cadre of politically aware

Revolutionary scenes: 1940 frescos by José Clemente Orozco in the interior of Gabino Ortiz library (Jiquilpan, Michoacán, Mexico. (The Art Archive / Dagli Orti)

young artists that included Orozco, Rivera, and Siquieros to paint the walls of the National Preparatory School, Orozco's old alma mater and the elite training ground of Mexico's future leaders. Orozco's emotionally charged murals (1922–1924, 1926–1927), with titles like *Political Junkheap, False Leaders, Mother's Farewell, Grave-digger,* and *The Trench,* mocked prerevolutionary political culture and recalled the tragic sacrifices of the Revolution that had finally destroyed it. Some provoked considerable controversy. The dramatic *Christ Destroying his Cross,* which symbolized an end to the victimhood of the downtrodden, and *The Revolutionary Trinity,* which replaced the Holy Trinity with workers, were destroyed by conservative Preparatory School students enraged at the artist's appropriation of tra-

ditional Christian symbols. (Both paintings were recreated in 1926).The withdrawal of government patronage in 1927 sent Orozco back to the United States. The murals from this period—at Pomona College, the New School for Social Research, and Dartmouth College—garnered Orozco an international reputation. Although stylistically very different, these murals demonstrate Orozco's preoccupation with universalist, epic themes: Prometheus at Pomona, world-historical figures like Gandhi and Lenin at the New School, the prophecies of Quetzacoatl at Dartmouth. His frequent companion and patron, Alma Reed, wrote that "if Father God, Zeus and Huitzilopochtli [the patron deity of the Aztecs] sit enthroned for him in the same heaven, New World art is enriched by a concept that holds an epic promise."

The Dartmouth College murals, in particular, reflected Orozco's growing ambivalence toward the possibility of human progress. Apocalyptic images like the axe-wielding Christ (an Orozco favorite) surrounded by the devastation of war in the ironically entitled, *Modern Migration of the Spirit,* and the thrashing skeleton of *Stillborn Education,* suggested a profound distrust of modernity.

On his return to Mexico in 1934, Orozco further developed this pessimistic view of modern "civilization," especially in a series of murals painted in different locations in Guadalajara (1936–1939), Mexico's second largest city. Also evident in the Guadalajara murals was Orozco's ambivalence about Mexico and its great social revolutions. The 1937 *Miguel Hidalgo* mural in the governor's palace, for example, depicted the father of Mexican independence with a fiery sword unleashing the brutal violence of an oppressed people. Orozco had tackled historical subjects before—his 1930 oil painting of Zapata with its shadowy hero lurking in the background—but his final murals, most of them in Guadalajara and Mexico City, seldom strayed from Mexico's tumultuous history. While Orozco sometimes held his pessimism in check, as in his celebratory portrayal of Hidalgo signing a decree that outlawed slavery in the 1948–1949 Guadalajara Hall of Deputies mural or the portrait of Benito Juárez in his *National Allegory* mural for Mexico City's National School for Teachers, the brutality of both exploitation and liberation was always there to remind Mexicans that their freedoms had come at a horrible price. Ironically, perhaps, for a great painter of apocalypses, Orozco died of a heart attack on 7 September 1949 while hard at work on a mural (for a Mexico City housing project) with the hopeful title, *Primavera* (Spring).

—RMB

See also: Muralist Movement; Murillo, Gerardo "Dr. Atl"; Rivera, Diego; Siquieros, David Álfaro; Vasconcelos, José.

References:

Helm, MacKinley. *Man of Fire: José Clemente Orozco; An Interpretive Memoire.* Westport, CT: Greenwood Press, 1971.

Orozco, José Clemente. *José Clemente Orozco: An Autobiography.* Trans. Robert C. Stephenson. Austin: University of Texas Press, 1962.

Reed, Alma. *Orozco.* New York: Oxford University Press, 1956.

Orozco, Pascual (1882–1915)

An important political and military leader from 1910 to 1915, Pascual Orozco was born in the northern state of Chihuahua. After a few years of primary education, Orozco went to work in his father's store but later left to become a muleteer, transporting ore shipments from mines in the area. Orozco soon owned his own string of mules and became well known in the region for his efficiency and honesty. Orozco's continued success permitted him to add a retail store to his transport activities; by 1910 Orozco was a prosperous businessman whose capital would soon be devoted to Revolution.

Orozco came from both a region and a family that was politically active and prone to Revolution. His father, Pascual Orozco Sr., supported the Revolutionary activities of the Mexican Liberal Party, one of the earliest groups to oppose the regime of President Porfirio Díaz. Both Orozco and his father became involved in the opposition to the reelection of Porfirio Díaz in 1910 that soon turned to revolution. Abraham González, leader in Chihuahua of the movement supporting Francisco Madero for the presidency in 1910, selected Orozco as military leader for his home district of Guerrero. Orozco's reputation and experience aided in recruiting forces, and Orozco launched his Revolutionary activities on 19 November 1910, the day before the date set by Madero for the Revolution to begin. Orozco's victory on November 27 at Pedernales, Chihuahua, was the first important rebel victory over regular federal forces.

Orozco soon emerged as the leader of the Revolution in the state of Chihuahua and was one of the few rebel leaders anywhere in Mexico enjoying significant success against

Mexican Revolutionary leader Pascual Orozco (Library of Congress)

Díaz's Federal Army. In February 1911 provisional President Francisco Madero joined Orozco and assumed command of military operations. Madero soon launched an attack on the town of Casas Grandes, Chihuahua, without notifying Orozco. Madero suffered a major defeat, including being wounded. Madero then recognized the leading military role of Orozco by making him the first colonel in his Revolutionary army. The rebels then focused their efforts on the key border town of Ciudad Juárez, across the Rio Grande from El Paso, Texas. The capture of Juárez would provide an important entry point for supplies from the United States as well as deal a major psychological blow to the Díaz regime.

In early May 1911 rebel forces under Orozco and Francisco "Pancho" Villa isolated Juárez and prepared to launch a final assault. Madero, however, was afraid that an attack on the border might lead to U.S. intervention and ordered his forces to move south,

away from the international boundary. Orozco disregarded the orders and attacked Juárez anyway, quickly forcing the surrender of the city on 10 May. Orozco presented Madero with the victory that signaled the end of the Díaz regime but also engaged in an act of major insubordination. After the fall of Juárez, Orozco got into another major confrontation with Madero over the fate of the federal commander at Juárez, General Juan F. Navarro. Navarro had earlier ordered the execution of some of Orozco's men, and Orozco demanded that Navarro be court-martialed for the executions. Instead, Madero saw to it that Navarro made it safely to the U.S. side of the border.

Orozco was the principal military figure in the overthrow of the Díaz regime, which opened the way for Madero to assume the presidency in November 1911. Orozco expected to be rewarded for his efforts, possibly as minister of war but at least with the governorship of Chihuahua. Madero, however, supported other people for both of those posts. Orozco became head of rural forces in Chihuahua, an important position but not in keeping with his military contributions in the Madero revolt. Orozco's name was soon linked to plots against the Madero government from both the left (Emiliano Zapata) and the right (federal General Bernardo Reyes). After an unsatisfactory meeting with President Madero on 19 January 1912, Orozco submitted his resignation as commander of Chihuahua's rural forces, but Madero refused to accept the resignation. Orozco even helped to put down an anti-Madero mutiny by troops in Juárez in early February. Orozco again submitted his resignation as commander of Chihuahua's rural forces; this time President Madero accepted the resignation.

On 3 March 1912 Orozco formally pronounced against the government of Francisco Madero. A number of factors influenced Orozco's decision to revolt. Conservative elements in Chihuahua were willing to help finance the revolt, believing that they could manipulate Orozco to protect their interests.

In a contradictory vein, other important anti-Madero rebel leaders in Chihuahua urged Orozco to assume leadership of their movement based on the view that Madero had betrayed his promises of reform. Orozco put forward his own Revolutionary "plan" on 25 March, which called for a comprehensive program of social, economic, and political reforms.

Orozco's movement enjoyed some early victories, including the defeat of a force led by Pancho Villa. An arms embargo imposed by the United States hurt the rebels both militarily and financially. A major government offensive began in early April 1912, led by the veteran federal General Victoriano Huerta. Huerta inflicted a series of defeats on Orozco's forces, culminating in the retaking of Juárez from the rebels in August. Orozco continued to wage guerrilla warfare into early 1913 when events in Mexico City produced another phase in Orozco's Revolutionary career.

In February 1913 General Victoriano Huerta, who had earlier defended the Madero administration against Orozco, overthrew Madero, who was soon assassinated. Huerta assumed the presidency but immediately encountered military resistance to his takeover, especially in northern Mexico. Needing military support, the new president then tried to win over Orozco and his followers. For his support Orozco made a series of demands, most of them financial; he also wanted promises of an early agrarian reform program, an issue which had bedeviled Madero. Huerta was happy to comply with these conditions and made Orozco a brigadier general in Huerta's army. Huerta also hoped that Orozco could be used to bring about a peace settlement with Emiliano Zapata. Huerta selected Orozco's father to be one of the peace commissioners to negotiate with Zapata; Zapata, however, had the commissioners arrested for betraying the Revolution and later had Orozco's father executed.

Orozco launched his northern campaign in May 1913, enjoying a series of victories en route to Chihuahua and winning promotion to general of brigade. Orozco soon began feuding with his fellow federal general, Salvador Mercado, who technically was Orozco's superior. Mercado and Orozco disagreed over political and military matters. This disunity hindered the federal response to a rebel offensive under Pancho Villa which began in November 1913. By January 1914 Villa and his forces controlled Chihuahua. As federal forces disintegrated, Orozco escaped capture by Villa, who had vowed to execute him. Mercado tried to place the blame for the federal defeats on Orozco, but Huerta promoted Orozco to general of division and gave him the responsibility of organizing a new northern offensive. Orozco left Mexico City with his new force in April 1914, intending to avoid major confrontations with the rebels and to establish a base for guerrilla operations in Chihuahua. The federal military position had deteriorated so badly that Orozco had no hope of achieving his goal. In July 1914 Huerta resigned and went into exile, leaving Orozco in Mexico to plot his next move.

Orozco immediately announced that he was in revolt against the new government without waiting to determine its composition or policies. While Orozco could still field a respectable force of about 4,000 men, his latest revolt did not command the popular support of his earlier pronouncements. His new movement soon encountered problems with supplies and financing; by September 1914 Orozco was no longer a major military factor in the north. A new Revolutionary conspiracy and an old partner, however, soon presented themselves.

A number of exiles from the Revolution living in the United States were interested in recruiting Orozco for another military movement in northern Mexico. At the same time General Victoriano Huerta was negotiating with agents of the German government in Europe to help finance his return to power. With substantial German backing, Huerta returned to the United States in April 1915. Huerta and Orozco joined forces to head a revolt scheduled for 28 June 1915. Huerta agreed to meet Orozco at Newman, New Mexico, near El Paso, the scene of much of the exiled Revolutionary activity. U.S. officials, however, had been monitoring Huerta's activities closely; when Huerta and Orozco met at Newman on 27 June, they were immediately arrested. Federal officials took them to El Paso where they were charged with conspiracy to violate U.S. neutrality laws. While being held at nearby Fort Bliss, Orozco escaped on 3 July. Orozco remained in the general vicinity of El Paso on the U.S. side of the border. On 30 August 1915 a posse composed of U.S. federal marshals, Texas Rangers, and U.S. Army troops killed Orozco and four companions. Orozco proved controversial even in death. Many categorized his killing as an "execution," citing the fact that Orozco and his four companions died while not a single member of the posse was even injured.

In May 1911, following the rebel victory at Ciudad Juárez, Orozco had been one of the Revolution's leading figures. In August 1915, across the river in Texas, Orozco became another former leader of the Revolution who wound up on the losing side once too often.

—DMC

See also: Assassinations; Chihuahua; Constitutionalists; Díaz, Porfirio; Madero, Francisco; Revolution of 1910; *Rurales;* Villa, Francisco "Pancho"; Zapata, Emiliano.

References:

Hall, Linda B., and Don M. Coerver. *Revolution on the Border: The United States and Mexico, 1910–1920.* Albuquerque: University of New Mexico Press, 1988.

Meyer, Michael C. *Mexican Rebel: Pascual Orozco and the Mexican Revolution, 1910–1915.* Lincoln: University of Nebraska Press, 1967.

Raat, W. Dirk. *Revoltosos: Mexico's Rebels in the United States, 1903–1923.* College Station: Texas A&M University Press, 1981.

Ortiz Rubio, Pascual (1877–1963)

President from 1930 to 1932, Pascual Ortiz Rubio was born on 10 March 1877 in Morelia, Michoacán. The son of the rector of the Colegio de San Nicolás, Ortiz Rubio received a good education, including a degree in topographical engineering from the National School of Mines in Mexico City in 1902. Ortiz Rubio became involved in politics at a young age, agitating against the reelection of President Porfirio Díaz as early as 1896. As a captain, he fought in the forces of Francisco Madero, who overthrew Díaz in 1911. Elected to the national Congress in 1912, Ortiz Rubio was arrested by the government of General Victoriano Huerta when Huerta dissolved the Congress in October 1913. After being freed, he aligned himself with the Constitutionalist forces of Venustiano Carranza, serving in a number of capacities between 1914 and 1917. He was promoted to brigadier general in 1915 and later became director of the Department of Military Engineers in the Ministry of War.

In 1917 Ortiz Rubio became governor of Michoacán; he was still governor in 1920 when supporters of General Alvaro Obregón revolted against the government of Venustiano Carranza, who was attempting to impose his successor as president. Ortiz Rubio sided with the victorious rebels, a move which resulted in him serving as minister of communications and public works in the cabinets of both Interim President Adolfo de la Huerta and President Alvaro Obregón. When Adolfo de la Huerta revolted against Obregón in 1923, Ortiz Rubio once again came down on the winning side, supporting President Obregón. Ortiz Rubio then switched from politics to diplomacy, being appointed ambassador to Germany in 1924 and ambassador to Brazil in 1926. Following the assassination of President-elect Obregón in July 1928, Ortiz Rubio returned to Mexico, supposedly to take the position of minister of the interior (internal security) in the cabinet of Interim President Emilio Portes Gil. Ortiz Rubio declined the position when he discovered that he was being considered as a presidential possibility in new elections to be held in November 1929 to serve out Obregón's term.

Posed left to right: Mrs. Henry L. Stimson, Señora Rubio, President-elect Ortiz Rubio, Secretary of State Henry L. Stimson, and Manuel Tellez, Mexican Ambassador to the United States (1929) (Library of Congress)

As a presidential possibility, Ortiz Rubio's greatest strength was also his greatest weakness: his lengthy absence from the country during most of the 1920s. While he was not current on domestic affairs, he also had not been pulled into the increasingly vicious political competition among the various Revolutionary groups. Ortiz Rubio also had solid Revolutionary credentials while his principal competition for the presidency, Aarón Sáenz, was seen by many as insufficiently committed to radical change. A Sáenz candidacy was also opposed by some powerful generals, including Minister of War Joaquín Amaro and future President General Lázaro Cárdenas. In March 1929 the newly formed official party, the Partido Nacional Revolucionario (the National Revolutionary Party, or PNR), met to nominate its candidate. The convention was hardly under way before

Sáenz—realizing that he did not have a majority of the votes—abruptly withdrew as a candidate and left the convention. The delegates then nominated Ortiz Rubio by acclamation. After a violent campaign and a vote marred by numerous irregularities, Ortiz Rubio easily defeated the civilian candidate, José Vasconcelos, who subsequently went into exile.

The ease with which Ortiz Rubio had been nominated and elected quickly disappeared during the events of his inaugural day, 5 February 1930. After the inauguration ceremonies, Ortiz Rubio was shot in the jaw and seriously wounded while leaving the National Palace. The would-be assassin was caught immediately, and officials tired unsuccessfully to link him to a pro-Church or pro-Vasconcelos conspiracy. The president later blamed the incident on conflict in the Congress, which created the atmosphere for such an attack. Ortiz Rubio did not appear again in public until 3 March 1930 and did not attend his first cabinet meeting until 20 March.

As president, Ortiz Rubio had to contend with the fact that he had been a compromise selection for the presidency and had no real political base of his own. In particular, he had to cope with the presence of former President Plutarco Elías Calles, who had preferred Sáenz to Ortiz Rubio and who was determined to dominate the political process. In the area of agrarian reform, the distribution of land continued at about the same rate as it had under the previous administrations of Emilio Portes Gil and Calles. The first major legislation implementing the prolabor provisions of the Constitution of 1917 was passed: the Federal Labor Law of 1931. The new legislation perpetuated an old trend: strengthening labor organization while simultaneously increasing government control of organized labor. While employers could be required to hire only union workers, at the same time unions had to register with the federal government and submit annual financial reports. The law also established a national arbitration board with significant influence over labor-management relations. Ortiz Rubio had to deal with the full impact of the Great Depression of the 1930s. Mexico reached a new agreement with its international creditors in July 1930, but the worsening financial condition of the government and strong domestic criticism of the agreement prevented it from being submitted for congressional approval. Ortiz Rubio also had to deal with the growing stream of Mexican nationals being repatriated, often forcibly, from the United States. Those repatriated had once been considered a vital source of labor; with unemployment worsening in the United States, they became unwanted competition for jobs and "surplus labor."

Ortiz Rubio could never escape the shadow of former president Plutarco Elías Calles, the "Maximum Leader of the Revolu-tion." When former president Emilio Portes Gil asked for Ortiz Rubio's support to run for the governorship of Tamaulipas, Ortiz Rubio replied that he knew nothing about such matters and that Portes Gil should go confer with Calles. So many politicians and officials were bypassing the president and going to Calles, the cabinet had to pass a resolution directing administration officials to consult with Calles only if ordered to do so by the president. When a new policy was implemented to deal with the financial crisis, it was publicly referred to as the "Plan Calles." The showdown between Calles and Ortiz Rubio came in August 1932 when Calles made it known that no friend of his should accept any high position in Ortiz Rubio's government. Ortiz Rubio resigned as president on 3 September 1932, citing health problems and "grave political reasons." He left the next day for self-imposed exile in the United States.

Ortiz Rubio returned to Mexico during the administration of President Lázaro Cárdenas (1934–1940), who in 1935 appointed him head of the government-owned oil company, Petro-Mex. He soon resigned, assuming the role of respected elder statesman and practicing his original profession of engineering. He died in Mexico City on 4 November 1963.

—DMC

See also: Assassinations; Calles, Plutarco Elías; Cárdenas, Lázaro; Carranza, Venustiano; Debt, Mexico's Foreign; Huerta, Victoriano; Madero, Francisco; Michoacán; Obregón, Alvaro; Partido Revolucionario Institucional (PRI); Portes Gil, Emilio; Presidents of the Twentieth Century; Revolution of 1910; Vasconcelos, José.

References:
Dulles, John W. F. *Yesterday in Mexico: A Chronicle of the Revolution, 1919–1936.* Austin: University of Texas Press, 1972.

Meyer, Lorenzo, Rafael Segovia, and Alejandra Lajous. *Historia de la Revolución Mexicana.* Vol. 12. *Los inicios de la institucionalización: la política del Maximato.* Mexico: El Colegio de Mexico, 1978.

P

Partido de Acción Nacional (PAN)

The Partido de Acción Nacional (the National Action Party, or PAN) is the second-oldest political party in Mexico. It has generally played the role of "loyal opposition" to what was for years the "official party" of Mexico, the Partido Revolucionario Institucional (the Institutional Revolutionary Party, or PRI).

The formation and early direction of the PAN owed much to Manuel Gómez Morín. Gómez Morín was a distinguished lawyer and financial expert. He was professor of law in the law school at the National University from 1919 to 1938 and was also dean of the school from 1922 to 1924. He helped to write the law establishing the Bank of Mexico in 1925, serving as its first chairman of the board. In his private practice, Gómez Morín specialized in commercial law, providing important additional contacts with the business community. He definitively parted company with the Revolutionary elite by supporting the presidential candidacy of former Minister of Education José Vasconcelos, who unsuccessfully opposed the first presidential nominee of the official party, Pascual Ortíz Rubio. In 1933–1934 he was head (rector) of the National University; he used this position to try to reduce marxist influence at the univer-

sity. The policies pursued by the presidential administration of Lázaro Cárdenas (1934–1940) alarmed Gómez Morín. Cárdenas called for the introduction of socialist education and sex education; he also stressed agrarian reform, especially the transfer of lands to communal holdings. Gómez Morín and other conservatives feared that Cárdenas intended to establish a socialist state in Mexico. In anticipation of the 1940 presidential elections, Gómez Morín took the lead in the formation of a new political party.

On 14 September 1939—less than two weeks after the start of World War II in Europe—a convention met in Mexico City to form PAN, with Gómez Morín in the lead. The most prominent component of the new party was a group of Roman Catholic activists, many of whom had been students of Gómez Morín at the university or had supported his effort to reduce socialist influence at the institution. Business interests also played a prominent role in the early years of the party. These diverse components reflected diverse views on Mexico's political situation. Catholic activists and business interests feared the establishment of a socialist state. While business interests supported a capitalist view, many of the Catholic activists were suspicious of liberal capitalism with its emphasis on individualism, materialism, and the profit motive.

PAN's diversity was evident in its uncertain response to the 1940 presidential elections. Cárdenas confused the situation by tapping as the official candidate a more conservative figure, General Manuel Avila Camacho. His principal opponent was Juan Andreu Almazán, a former Revolutionary general with ties to big business. PAN decided not to run its own candidate in 1940. Almazán never became the official candidate of the PAN. The PAN, however, did provide a limited endorsement of Almazán, and many PAN members supported his candidacy. Almazán subsequently went down to defeat in a violent election riddled with fraud. In the 1940 elections, PAN did not offer any candidates for the national Congress but did contest unsuccessfully in a few municipal elections.

From its foundation and for much of its history, PAN has carried with it the image of a proclerical and probusiness party. This image—although enduring—is misleading. While a Roman Catholic influence on the PAN was strong and obvious, it was not a clerical party. Mexican law prohibited a direct connection between the Roman Catholic Church and any political party. While a devout Catholic, Gómez Morín did not want PAN identified with the Church, fearing that it would cost the party membership. Many of the business interests that originally supported PAN soon abandoned the party when the administrations of Manuel Avila Camacho (1940–1946) and Miguel Alemán (1946–1952) adopted policies that were highly favorable to business.

In its early years, PAN enjoyed little success in elections. PAN did not run a presidential candidate in the 1946 elections but did elect four deputies to the lower house of the national Congress. In the 1952 elections, PAN ran its own presidential candidate and won five seats in the national Congress; in 1955 they won six seats. PAN's lack of electoral success was not discouraging to its leaders, who viewed electoral contests as an opportunity to educate the public about the PAN program rather than as an occasion to achieve power. PAN supported the vote for women in federal elections, the strengthening of municipal government, an independent federal judiciary, reform of the agrarian reform program, an expansion of social security, profit sharing for workers, and an end to labor union corruption. While not directly linked to the Church, PAN's program reflected the contemporary Roman Catholic thinking on social justice.

One of the demands of the PAN had been for proportional representation in Congress. Under a system of proportional representation, seats in the lower house of Congress would be awarded on the basis of the percentage of the vote won by a party in addition to seats that were based on victories in geographic districts. When the new system first went into effect in 1964, the PAN won 2 seats outright and was awarded an additional 18 seats based on proportional representation; this total of 20 seats compared with 5 held by PAN in 1961. The number of seats assigned by proportional representation and the total number of seats in the lower house of Congress were increased in 1977 and again in 1986. As a result of these changes, the size of the lower house was 500, with 200 of the seats based on proportional representation. Although there was still criticism that the government was assigning seats instead of guaranteeing free elections, the PAN increased its presence in the national Congress and opened the door for other opposition parties to do likewise.

Mexico's growing economic problems in the 1980s and 1990s provided new opportunities for the PAN. For the presidential elections in 1988, PAN put forward millionaire industrialist Manuel J. Clouthier, who epitomized a new breed of regional business leader being attracted by the PAN. Clouthier finished a disappointing third behind the PRI candidate, Carlos Salinas, and PRI defector, Cuauhtémoc Cárdenas. More encouraging were developments at the state level. PAN won the governorship of Baja California in 1989, the first governor's race officially won by an opposition candidate since the 1930s. In 1991 the PAN also won the governorships of San Luis Potosí and Guanajuato as well as a seat in the national Senate from Baja California. In the 1994 presidential elections, the PAN candidate—Diego Fernández de Cevallos—finished second to the PRI's Ernesto Zedillo. The 1997 elections provided further gains for PAN. PAN held 121 seats in the lower house of the national Congress and 33 in the Senate. In addition, PAN won governorships in Nuevo Leon and Querétaro and was making steady inroads at the municipal level.

As the presidential elections of 2000 approached, PAN had still not passed the most crucial test of its position as Mexico's most-durable second party—winning the presidency. For its presidential nominee in 2000, PAN turned to Governor Vicente Fox of Guanajuato, another regional business leader who had not been active in the PAN until the 1980s. Fox won in a three-way race with 43 percent of the popular vote. For the first time since the founding of the official party in 1929, an opposition candidate won the presidency. PAN substantially increased its representation in both the lower house of the national Congress, the Chamber of Deputies, and in the Senate but lacked a majority in either body. The PRI also continued to control most of the governorships.

The lack of a working majority in the Congress has held up many of the reforms proposed by Fox, most notably fiscal reform and treatment of the indigenous population. The PAN led the fight for democratization and became one of the biggest beneficiaries of the democratization process. Electoral success has brought criticism from longtime members of PAN that the party has lost its ideological compass; indeed, the PAN has adopted a more pragmatic approach, and Fox downplayed ideology in his 2000 campaign. PAN's cooperation with the PRI in the

1990s—especially on economic matters—also drew criticism from the PAN ranks; in 1992 several PAN leaders, including two former party presidents, resigned in protest over the growing cooperation with the PRI. With Fox in the presidency, the tables have been turned; the PAN now needs cooperation from the PRI to gets its major measures through the Congress. Congressional elections in 2003 resulted in the PRI retaining its position as the largest party in the Chamber of Deputies while the PAN suffered a decline from 2000. With no party holding a majority and all of the parties already maneuvering for the 2006 presidential elections, the limited possibilities for PAN reforms became even less likely. The future of PAN is very much tied to the democratization process; where that process is taking Mexico is yet to be determined.

—*DMC*

See also: Cárdenas, Cuauhtémoc; Cárdenas, Lázaro; Democratization Process; Elections; Fox, Vicente; Partido Revolucionario Institucional (PRI); Salinas de Gotari, Carlos; Zedillo Ponce de León, Ernesto.

References:
Domínguez, Jorge I., and James A. McCann. *Democratizing Mexico: Public Opinion and Electoral Choices.* Baltimore, MD: Johns Hopkins University Press, 1996.
Levy, Daniel C., Kathleen Bruhn, and Emilio Zebadúa. *Mexico: The Struggle for Democratic Development.* Berkeley: University of California Press, 2001.
Mabry, Donald J. *Mexico's Acción Nacional: A Catholic Alternative to Revolution.* Syracuse, NY: Syracuse University Press, 1973.

Partido Liberal Mexicano (PLM)

The Mexican Liberal Party (Partido Liberal Mexicano, or PLM) had its roots in the Liberal Clubs formed in Mexico in response to the repressive rule of President Porfirio Díaz (1877–1880, 1884–1911). Camilo Arriaga, a wealthy engineer and liberal reformer, called for a national congress of Liberal Clubs to meet in San Luis Potosí in February 1901. The First Liberal Congress convened on 5

February 1901, the anniversary of the Constitution of 1857 whose liberal provisions they felt were being ignored. The Congress passed a series of resolutions calling for the organization of the Liberal Party, the strict enforcement of the anticlerical provisions of the Constitution of 1857, respect for freedom of the press, effective suffrage, independent municipal government, and impartial administration of justice. One of the leading figures at the Congress was Ricardo Flores Magón, whose newspaper *Regeneración* became the semiofficial organ of the new Liberal Party.

The new party soon encountered two problems that would plague it throughout most of its history: internal divisions and external repression. Early on, the party developed two factions: a reform group led by Arriaga and a more radical faction led by Flores Magón. This division eventually led to major defections from the party, including Arriaga. The Díaz administration also quickly cracked down on the budding Liberal Party. Both Arriaga and Flores Magón were jailed and later forced into exile in the United States, where both Mexican and U.S. authorities continued to harass them. Mexican officials also prevented the holding of a Second Liberal Congress scheduled for February 1902.

Official harassment of the liberals in exile forced them to move from Laredo, Texas, to San Antonio, Texas, to St. Louis, Missouri. This external pressure increasingly radicalized some of the liberals, leading to a formal break between Arriaga and Flores Magón. Arriaga did not agree with the growing radicalism of Flores Magón and returned to San Antonio, Texas, to pursue a less-radical agenda. The PLM increasingly was identified with Flores Magón and his views. The split between the reformers and the radicals took concrete form in September 1905 when Ricardo Flores Magón announced the formation of the "Organizing Junta of the Mexican Liberal Party," with himself as president of the junta and his brother Enrique as treasurer.

The PLM established a military as well as a political organization. It set up Revolutionary cells in Mexico to wage guerrilla warfare against the Díaz regime. These cells primarily drew their recruits from peasants and urban workers. Members of the cells elected their own leaders, helping to broaden the base of PLM support.

On 1 July 1906, *Regeneración* published the "Program and Manifesto of the Mexican Liberal Party," which would influence Revolutionary thinking for years. Part of the Program simply called for strict enforcement of the Constitution of 1857 in such areas as civil rights and restrictions on the Roman Catholic Church. The program, however, also called for wide-ranging political, social, and economic reforms. Education would be completely secularized and made mandatory. There would be government regulation of working conditions, including an eight-hour workday, a six-day workweek, and a guaranteed minimum wage. Child labor would be prohibited. Workers had to be paid in legal tender, undercutting an important aspect of the old debt peonage system. All uncultivated lands would revert to the state for redistribution to the peasantry. There would be an agricultural credit bank to provide low-interest loans to small farmers. Communal lands that had been illegally taken would be restored to the Indian communities. Foreigners would not be permitted to own land. The prison system would also be reformed, with the emphasis on rehabilitation rather than punishment.

In September 1906 the PLM leadership moved to El Paso, Texas, in anticipation of military action by Revolutionary cells in Mexico. The few revolts that broke out were quickly suppressed by Díaz's forces. In addition, the revolts attracted the attention of U.S. authorities concerned about liberal violations of the neutrality laws. The PLM had to move its headquarters once again, leaving El Paso for Los Angeles.

In addition to Revolutionary activity, the PLM was also involved in political activity.

One of the liberal leaders, Manuel Sarabia, tried to recruit members for the PLM from among Mexicans and Mexican Americans working in the Arizona mines. In June 1907, Arizona authorities arrested Sarabia without a warrant and turned him over without extradition proceedings to Mexican federal authorities. The "kidnapping" of Sarabia became an international incident, with Mexican officials reluctantly returning him to the United States.

The oft-jailed Ricardo Flores Magón also continued to have legal problems. In June 1907, Flores Magón had started a new publication, *Revolución,* to replace *Regeneración,* which had been closed down in St. Louis by law enforcement officials. The more radical tone of *Revolución* soon attracted the attention of Los Angeles authorities, leading to the arrest of Flores Magón in August 1907. In March 1909, he was extradited to Arizona to face federal charges of launching a Revolutionary movement from Douglas, Arizona, in 1906. He was found guilty and sentenced to eighteen months in federal prison. The pursuit and harassment of liberal leaders by Mexican authorities, U.S. officials, and private investigators helped to increase popular support for the PLM but also resulted in the removal of key liberal leaders for extended periods of time.

After his release from federal prison in August 1910, Flores Magón revived his newspaper *Regeneración,* with an even more radical slant. Flores Magón and the PLM soon faced a major decision. In October 1910, Francisco Madero, a wealthy landowner from the northern state of Coahuila, issued a call for Revolution against the Díaz regime. Madero had unsuccessfully opposed Díaz's reelection earlier in 1910. Earlier, Madero had also helped to finance the PLM but had ended his financial support because of the growing radicalism of the PLM under the leadership of Flores Magón. Flores Magón had to decide whether to join Madero's struggle or to continue to wage an independent campaign against Díaz. Given the failure of liberal-backed revolts in 1906 and 1908, there were some in the ranks of the PLM who wanted to join the Madero Revolution.

Flores Magón, however, refused to align the PLM with Madero's Revolution. Flores Magón considered Madero to be insufficiently radical to implement a true revolution in Mexico. Madero stressed political reforms while Flores Magón wanted sweeping social and economic reforms as indicated in the Program of 1906. With his growing commitment to anarchism, Flores Magón believed that major changes could come only through mass movements, not by seizing control of the government. His decision to withhold his support from Madero may also have had a personal aspect. Flores Magón may very well have resented what he saw as a challenge to his revolutionary leadership by a man who had come very late to Revolutionary action. Flores Magón's influence over the PLM was so great that he was able to impose his view of the Madero Revolution on the organization. Many supporters of the PLM, however, defected to the Madero Revolution.

Even if the PLM refused to align itself with Madero, there was still pressure on Flores Magón to return to Mexico from his exile in Los Angeles and to commit the PLM to the armed struggle. The PLM's only major military involvement in the Madero revolt was a failed effort to seize Baja California in 1911. Not only did the PLM's invasion fail; it also heightened splits within the organization and created the impression of a filibustering campaign aimed at separating Baja California from Mexico. The Baja campaign would also bring new legal problems for Flores Magón. Even after the triumph of Madero's Revolution in May 1911, Flores Magón still refused any connection with Madero. Indeed, Flores Magón continued to move the PLM farther to the left on the political spectrum. In September 1911, the PLM issued a new manifesto that was openly anarchistic in its principles; among other proposals, the manifesto called for an end to private property and the establishment of communal work groups in both agriculture and industry. The manifesto also called on all Mexicans to give their support to the PLM rather than to Madero, who only offered them "political liberty."

The Baja campaign led to the arrests of both Ricardo and Enrique Flores Magón for violation of the federal neutrality laws. Both were tried and found guilty in June 1912. They were sentenced to twenty-three months in a federal penitentiary. Once again the top leadership of the PLM was in jail while crucial developments were taking place in Mexico. By the time the Flores Magón brothers were released from prison in early 1914, Madero had been overthrown and assassinated by General Victoriano Huerta. Huerta's seizure of power had led to new revolts by a number of different factions. Ricardo Flores Magón's commitment to anarchism led to his refusal to align the PLM with any of the emerging Revolutionary factions in Mexico. As a result, the PLM became increasingly irrelevant to the bloody conflict that was taking place in Mexico and would have little direct influence on the leaders who might emerge from the struggle.

Although the PLM was becoming less important to the struggle in Mexico, the organization's anarchist message was finding support among Mexicans and Mexican Americans in the U.S. southwest. The PLM was linked to raids in Texas under the Plan of San Diego, a Revolutionary movement aimed at detaching parts of the United States formerly owned by Mexico and establishing an independent nation.

The PLM leadership continued to encounter major legal problems. In June 1916 both Ricardo and Enrique Flores Magón were convicted of violating a federal law that prohibited the sending of reading materials advocating murder, assassination, or arson through the U.S. mails. The "reading materials" in question were articles from the PLM paper *Regeneración*. Out on bail while his conviction was appealed, Ricardo Flores Magón was arrested yet again in March 1918 for sending anarchist literature (copies of *Regen-*

eración) through the mails. With the United States at war, federal authorities were even more sensitive to the anarchist writings appearing in *Regeneración*. Flores Magón was convicted in July 1918 and sentenced to twenty years and a day in federal prison. Ricardo Flores Magón died in the federal penitentiary at Leavenworth, Kansas, in November 1922.

The role of the PLM leading up to and following the Revolution of 1910 largely reflected the dominant role assumed by Ricardo Flores Magón as party leader and chief propagandist. As his anarchist views became more pronounced, splits developed in the PLM between moderate leaders such as Camilo Arriaga and the more radical Flores Magón. Even the defection of the moderates did not bring peace to the leadership of the PLM because of the close identification of the party with one person. The failure of Flores Magón to align the PLM with any of the Revolutionary factions after 1910 ultimately condemned the PLM to a marginal political role in post-Revolutionary Mexico. The frequent arrests and jailings of PLM leaders also caused problems for the PLM. Even though the PLM had little military involvement in or direct political influence on events in Mexico, its Revolutionary ideas—especially the Program of 1906—had a major impact on Revolutionary thinking and on the new Constitution of 1917. The PLM also influenced opinion among Mexican and Mexican-American groups in the United States as well as the international anarchist movement in general. The PLM and its program found favor with the Chicano movement of the 1960s and 1970s in the United States and continues to appeal today to many persons at odds with mainstream politics in Mexico.

—*DMC*

See also: Anarchism; Díaz, Porfirio; Flores Magón, Ricardo; Madero, Francisco; Revolution of 1910.

References:

Albro, Ward. *Always a Rebel: Ricardo Flores Magón and the Mexican Revolution.* Fort Worth: Texas Christian University Press, 1992.

Langham, Thomas C. *Border Trials: Ricardo Flores Magón and the Mexican Liberals.* El Paso: Texas Western Press, 1981.

MacLachlan, Colin W. *Anarchism and the Mexican Revolution: The Political Trials of Ricardo Flores Magón in the United States.* Berkeley: University of California Press, 1991.

Partido Revolucionario Institucional (PRI)

The PRI (Partido Revolucionario Institucional, or National Revolutionary Party) is the current name of the political party that has run Mexico since 1929. The party emerged during a period of political crisis following the assassination of President-elect Alvaro Obregón in August 1928. President Plutarco Elías Calles was scheduled to turn the presidency over to Obregón on 1 December 1928. With Obregón's assassination, Calles confronted civil war, dissent within the army, tensions among the Revolutionary factions, and even suspicions of involvement in Obregon's death. Calles wanted to create a political organization that would bring together the various Revolutionary factions and promote political stability throughout the country.

There had been crises over presidential succession in 1920, 1924, and 1928; one of the key factors in the establishment of the PRI was the creation of a method for peaceful transfer of presidential power. After the formation of the official party, there developed a procedure whereby the outgoing president "tapped" or appointed his successor at the last moment. This practice reduced competition among potential successors and also maintained the power of the outgoing president. The president, operating through the PRI, was able to influence the nomination of candidates for political positions at all levels of government.

The close connection between the PRI and the government bureaucracies made it difficult to distinguish between what the party was doing and what the government was doing. This overlap shaped the role of elec-

tions, which, traditionally, were not contests for political power but rather a gauge of popular support for the policies being pursued by the PRI and the government.

Since its founding in 1929, the PRI has gone through a series of name changes and reorganizations. Originally called the PNR (the Partido Nacional Revolucionario or National Revolutionary Party), it was designed to impose discipline on the different Revolutionary groups. In 1938, President Lázaro Cárdenas reorganized and renamed the party the PRM (the Partido de la Revolución Mexicana or the Party of the Mexican Revolution). The renamed and reorganized party reflected the growing importance of labor and peasant organizations and was composed of four sectors: workers, peasants, the military, and "popular organizations." In 1946 the party received its current name, indicating the changing political priorities and economic policies of the postwar period.

Mexico's postwar "economic miracle" gave way to a series of economic and financial crises from the 1970s to the present that have severely undermined popular support for the PRI and have encouraged the growth of opposition political parties. The PRI committed itself to major economic and political reforms in the 1980s, but economic reform proceeded more rapidly than political reform, which faced considerable opposition from within the PRI. There was also a growing split within the PRI between the "politicians" (those who have risen through the party organization and have held political office) and the "technicians" (those who have risen through the government bureaucracy and have little party experience). Since 1976, a series of technicians with little PRI background have occupied the Mexican presidency: José López Portillo (1976–1982), Miguel de la Madrid (1982–1988), Carlos Salinas de Gortari (1988–1994), and Ernesto Zedillo (1994–2000). The PRI has reluctantly recognized opposition victories in local, state, and national congressional elections, but the disputed presidential elections of 1988 convinced many that the PRI would not give up the presidency. Political and financial scandals surrounding the administration of Carlos Salinas de Gortari further undermined the position of the PRI.

The erosion of popular support for the PRI and a series of electoral reforms in the 1980s and 1990s finally made elections a real contest for power. The July 1997 elections included contests for all of the seats in the lower house of the Mexican Congress—the Chamber of Deputies—as well as races in several key states for the governorship. For the first time, the position of mayor of Mexico City—previously an appointed position—was up for election. The elections resulted in major gains for the two principal opposition parties, the National Action Party (Partido de Acción Nacional, or PAN) and the Democratic Revolutionary Party (Partido de la Revolución Democrática, or PRD). The PRD's Cuauhtémoc Cárdenas easily won the mayor's race, making him a leading candidate for the presidency in 2000. Cárdenas had resigned from the PRI in 1988 after failing to receive the PRI nomination for the presidency and ran unsuccessfully for the presidency as an opposition candidate in 1988 and 1994. For the first time in its history, the PRI lost its majority in the Chamber of Deputies; the PRI, however, was still the largest party in the Chamber and had a majority in the upper house, the Senate. The PRI lost the governor's race in the key northern state of Nuevo León, with its capital of Monterrey, but won most of the governorships being contested. The 1997 elections ended the PRI's iron grip on the electoral process but still left it the dominant national party.

The 2000 presidential and congressional elections witnessed an even greater decline in the power of the PRI. In the Congress, the PRI barely retained its position as the largest party in the Chamber of Deputies while the PRI lost its majority in the Senate. More important, the PRI for the first time since 1929 lost the presidency; the presidential winner was Vicente Fox, the candidate of the Alliance for Change, a combination of the PAN and Mexico's small Green Party. In the 2003 congressional elections, the PRI experienced a modest increase in the seats it held in the Chamber of Deputies; it retained its position as the largest party in the Chamber but still lacked a majority. In 2003, the PRI also won the governorship of the state of Nuevo León, a traditional stronghold of the PAN.

As the PRI lost offices at the national, state, and local levels, the identification between the PRI and the government declined. This was particularly important at the national level after the PRI lost control of the presidency in December 2000. For years, critics of the PRI hopefully proclaimed that the PRI was experiencing a "crisis." After the 2000 elections, the PRI really did face a crisis. The party was badly divided as to what the "lessons" of the 2000 elections were. The party old guard—the "dinosaurs"—viewed the defeat as a confirmation of the correctness of their opposition to democratization while a group of new leaders saw the elections as a wake-up call to reshape and rejuvenate the party. The results of the 2003 elections have encouraged the new PRI leadership to believe that they have the party on the right track and that their prospects for the presidential elections in 2006 are good. Despite its political ups, downs, and ups, the PRI is still the most important party in the Mexican political system.

Changing the rules of the political game caught up with the PRI. Historically, the PRI dominated Mexican politics at the local, state, and national levels, effectively creating a one-party country. The PRI maintained control of the political system through a combination of patronage, government connections, the co-opting of leaders from its limited opposition, and even violence and repression of opposition forces. While the PRI still has access to some of these tools, its ability to control the political process has been drastically altered, especially with the loss of the presidency on 1 December 2000. At the same time, the PRI has shown a talent for reinventing itself, as its reorganizations and renamings indicate. Claims that the PRI was "dead" after the 2000 presidential elections were certainly premature. The PRI showed increased strength in the 2003 elections and remains the most powerful party in Mexican politics.

—*DMC*

See also: Assassinations; Calles, Plutarco Elías; Democratization Process; Elections; Government; Obregón, Alvaro; Partido de Acción Nacional (PAN); Presidents of the Twentieth Century.

References:

Aguilar Camín, Hector, and Lorenzo Meyer. *In the Shadow of the Mexican Revolution: Contemporary Mexican History, 1910–1989.* Austin: University of Texas Press, 1993.

Cothran, Dan A. *Political Stability and Democracy in Mexico.* Westport, CT: Praeger, 1994.

Morris, Stephen D. *Political Reformism in Mexico.* Boulder, CO: Lynne Rienner Publishers, 1995.

Story, Dale. *The Mexican Ruling Party: Stability and Authority.* New York: Praeger, 1986.

Paz, Octavio (1914–1998)

In a distinguished Mexican tradition of intellectuals in public life, Octavio Paz (1914–1998) stands out for the subtle beauty of his poetry, the critical brilliance of his essays, his long-standing commitment to democratic reform, and his intellectual independence. The unifying theme in all Paz's writings was his quest to uncover the essence of Mexican national identity and, in so doing, to know himself. "I felt myself alone," he wrote, "and that Mexico was a lonely country, isolated, far from the central flow of history. . . . Thinking about the strangeness of being Mexican, I discovered an old truth: everyone carries a stranger hidden within himself. . . . I wanted to dive within myself, to dig up this stranger, to speak with him" (quoted in Krause, "In Memory of Octavio Paz"). In practice, Paz's public quest became something of a self-fulfilling prophecy as many Mexicans learned to see themselves in his texts and to construct their identities on his terms. Certainly, his ruminations on national identity, the power

of love, and Mexico's rocky road to true democracy touched several generations of Mexicans. Nor did his influence stop at the border: Paz was awarded the 1990 Nobel Prize in Literature in recognition of the global implications of his work.

The grandson of Ireneo Paz, a distinguished liberal, soldier, novelist, and sometime confidant of Porfirio Díaz, and the son of Octavio Paz Solórzano, a Zapatista general and emissary to the United States, Octavio Paz was born on 31 March 1914, in Mixcoac (now part of Mexico City) with strong familial ties to the nineteenth-century liberal democratic tradition and the radical populism of the Revolution. Both traditions would weigh heavily on his mind throughout his long life. Family connections, studies at Mexico City's prestigious National Preparatory School, and his own remarkable talents propelled Paz to the forefront of Mexico's lively intellectual community. Extended periods abroad, especially in Paris, expanded his horizons further still. By the 1950s, Paz was a respected poet, essayist, and cosmopolitan intellectual with close ties to Europe and Latin America's most creative minds: French writers Andre Breton, Jean-Paul Sartre, and Albert Camus; Chilean poet Pablo Neruda; Argentine novelist Julio Cortázar; and Spanish film director Luis Buñuel (who spent several years in Mexican exile from Francisco Franco's fascist regime in Spain). In recognition of his international stature, he was named Mexico's ambassador to India in 1962.

The political obsessions that would dominate Paz's later career date from 2 October 1968. On that day, the Mexican government, worried about possible disruption to the Olympic games, massacred hundreds of student demonstrators peacefully assembled in Tlatelolco's Plaza de Tres Culturas. Appalled both by the brutality of the event and official efforts to cover it up, Paz publicly renounced his ambassadorship and, after a brief residence in the United States, returned to Mexico to stay. His 1970 essay, "Posdata," denounced in no uncertain terms

Poet and essayist Octavio Paz (1914–1998) (William Coupon/Corbis)

the antidemocratic methods of the ruling Partido Revolucionario Institucional. In 1971, Paz continued his attacks in a new magazine, *Plural,* and, when the government managed to have it terminated by the publisher, he founded another, the independent *Vuelta.* He would use *Vuelta* as a forum for open literary and political debate until his death on 19 April 1998.

Paz was a controversial political thinker, increasingly drawn to the liberal-democratic ideals of his grandfather's generation and deeply critical of Mexico's one-party state. He was also one of the first prominent leftist intellectuals to openly criticize the authoritarian bent of Fidel Castro, for many years the darling of progressive Latin American thinkers. But he was equally suspicious of capitalism. In a 1990 essay on poetry, "La otra voz. Poesía y fin de siglo" (The Other Voice: Poetry and the Century's End), he argued that "the market is circular, impersonal, impartial, and inflexible. . . . It knows about prices, not about values." For Paz, the market, rather than political parties and ideologies, represented the greatest contemporary threat to the arts and literature.

As a poet, Paz's great themes were love, memory, and freedom. In the coda to a 1987 poem, "Carta de creencia" (Letter of Testimony), he extolled the creative power of love:

Perhaps to love is to learn
to walk through this world.
To learn to be silent
like the oak and the linden of the fable.
To learn to see.
Your look scatters seeds.
It planted a tree.
I talk
because you shake its leaves.
(Eliot Weinberger, ed. and trans., *The Collected Poems of Octavio Paz, 1957–1987,* p. 635)

Also, in a poem from the 1970s, "Pasando en claro" (A Draft of Shadows), he recalled with some bitterness his alcoholic father's tragic death:

Between vomit and thirst,
strapped to the rack of alcohol,
my father came and went through flames.
One evening of flies and dust,
we gathered, among the rails and crossties
of a railway station, his remains.
I could never talk to him.
I meet him now in dreams,
that blurred country of the dead.
(Eliot Weinberger, ed. & trans., *The Collected Poems of Octavio Paz, 1957–1987,* p. 451)

These themes came together in his 1982 study of colonial Mexico's greatest poet, *Sor Juana Inés de la Cruz o las trampas de la fe* (Sor Juana Inés de la Cruz or the Traps of Faith), in which Paz celebrated Sor Juana's poetic gifts while lamenting the repressive intellectual environment that forced her to abandon them. Poetic and philosophical rather than strictly historical, Paz's biography drew inevitable parallels between Sor Juana's repression and his own as it reiterated his lifelong call for political and artistic freedom.

The themes of love, memory, and freedom permeated his essays as well, although here the focus was less on the poet's inner life than on his homeland. Paz's most influential work was *Labyrinth of Solitude,* a collection of essays on Mexican national identity published in 1950. This work, which quickly became a classic, plumbed the depths of the Mexican national psyche: the fashion-driven nihilism of Chicano gangsters in Los Angeles, the national obsession with masks, the macabre celebration of the Day of the Dead and other collective rituals, the psychological effects of violent conquest. The work also explored Mexico's historical development from its conflicted Spanish-Indian beginnings to its hybrid *mestizo* (racially and culturally mixed) present. Paz concluded that Mexicans lived trapped in a labyrinth of solitude. "Our indifference," he wrote, "hides life behind a death mask; our wild shout rips off this mask and shoots into the sky, where it swells, explodes, and falls back in silence and defeat. Either way, the Mexican shuts himself off from the world: from life and from death" (Paz, *Labyrinth of Solitude and Other Writings,* p. 64). According to Paz, authoritarian political and social structures reinforce that sense of solitude, which, in turn, perpetuates authoritarianism and inhibits democratic freedoms. Like his politics, Paz's interpretation of Mexican national character is controversial. For example, the masculine character of Paz's archetypical Mexican and his negative portrayal of female stereotypes like Fernando Cortés's "violated" Indian mistress, translator, and arch-traitoress La Malinche, has generated considerable criticism from feminist writers. Nevertheless, the power of his analysis continues to shape debates about Mexican national identity.

—*RMB*

See also: Intellectuals; Poetry; Tlatelolco
Massacre.

References:
Krause, Enrique. "In Memory of Octavio Paz," *The New York Review of Books,* 28 May 1998, pp. 24–25.
Paz, Octavio. *Labyrinth of Solitude and Other Writings.* Trans. Lysander Kemp, Yara Milos, and Rachel Phillips Belash. New York: Grove Press, 1985.

Weinberger, Eliot, trans. and ed. *The Collected Poems of Octavio Paz, 1957–1987.* New York: New Directions, 1987.

Wilson, Jason. *Octavio Paz.* Boston: G. K. Hall & Co., 1986.

PEMEX

See Petróleos Mexicanos

Pershing Expedition

After the overthrow of the dictatorship of General Victoriano Huerta in July 1914, U.S. President Woodrow Wilson found it hard to sort out and influence the different Revolutionary leaders contending for power in Mexico. Francisco "Pancho" Villa was Wilson's first choice for the presidency. Villa was the only major Revolutionary figure who had not denounced the U.S. Occupation of Vera Cruz in April 1914. Wilson also believed that Villa would be the Mexican leader most likely to accept guidance from the U.S. president in the ways of democracy. The "Constitutionalist" forces loyal to First Chief Venustiano Carranza, however, inflicted a series of military defeats on Villa in 1915, eliminating him as a national leader. The Wilson administration reluctantly granted diplomatic recognition to Carranza's government in October 1915.

The recognition of Carranza convinced Villa that he had been betrayed by Wilson and that Mexico had been betrayed by Carranza. This view seemed to be confirmed when the Wilson administration let Carranza use railroads on the U.S. side of the border to move troops from El Paso, Texas, to Douglas, Arizona, in late October 1915. These troops later inflicted a major defeat on Villa's forces at the border town of Agua Prieta, Sonora, on 1 November 1915. Later that same month, Villa's troops engaged in a cross-border shootout with U.S. Army forces at the twin border town of Nogales, Arizona-Sonora. There were no U.S. casualties, but an estimated 50 of Villa's soldiers were killed with many more wounded.

Although his military resources were considerably reduced and his forces scattered, Villa was still a regional power in northern Mexico with the capability of threatening the U.S.–Mexico border region. The first major incident occurred in January 1916 at Santa Ysabel, Chihuahua. A group of American employees of the Cusi Mining Company were returning to Chihuahua to renew operations interrupted by Revolutionary activity. They were traveling with the encouragement, and supposedly under the protection, of Carranza officials. On 9 January 1916, some of Villa's forces stopped their train near Santa Ysabel. The rebels systematically killed sixteen of the seventeen Americans on the train. The massacre badly shook U.S. confidence that Carranza was restoring law and order to Mexico and produced strong demands for U.S. military action, which were rejected by the Wilson administration.

In early March 1916 there were reports that Villa's forces were near the border, but U.S. officials discounted the stories. Before dawn on 9 March, some 500 of Villa's troops crossed the international boundary and attacked the town of Columbus, New Mexico, where there was a detachment of U.S. troops—350 men of the 13th Cavalry under Colonel Herbert W. Slocum—stationed outside of town. The U.S. troops reacted immediately, but the Villistas still succeeded in killing seventeen Americans and burning and looting much of the town. Villa's forces suffered an estimated 100 casualties.

U.S. forces operated under specific instructions not to cross the international boundary without prior permission from Washington, but Colonel Slocum ordered a detachment of cavalry under Major Frank Tompkins to pursue Villa's troops into Mexico. Tompkins's force of 59 men engaged in four separate actions with the Villistas, killing between 75 and 100 of the raiders on Mexican soil, and returned to the United States after about seven and one-half hours.

The Wilson administration later approved of the hot pursuit by Tompkins's cavalry and

General Pershing and General Bliss inspect the camp, with Colonel Winn, Commander of the 24th Infantry (1916). (Library of Congress)

began organizing a much larger military group—the Pershing, or Punitive, Expedition—that would be sent after Villa and his raiders. General John J. Pershing was given command of the force that was being assembled at Columbus to purse Villa and to disperse Villa's forces so that they would no longer threaten the border. The first elements of the expedition did not cross into Mexico until 15 March, long after hot pursuit was possible. Representatives from the United States and Mexico had quickly reached an agreement permitting crossings of the border in pursuit of bandits, but the agreement had not received final approval and applied only to future incidents, not to any past event. Carranza considered the presence of the expedition to be an invasion of national territory, although initially he was not prepared to resist the incursion with military force.

The expedition was organized as a provisional division with an initial strength of more than 5,000 troops and a peak strength of more than 11,000. The original emphasis was on cavalry, but later infantry, artillery, and even air units joined the expedition. The Carranza administration initially was not willing to risk a major confrontation by offering military resistance to the intervention and tried unsuccessfully to convince the U.S. government that it could deal with Villa and his forces. It did, however, refuse to cooperate with the expedition. The most critical example of this lack of cooperation was the Mexican refusal to let the expedition freely use the Mexican railways, which had figured importantly in U.S. logistical planning. The Wilson administration was especially aggravated by this refusal since it had earlier permitted Carranza to use U.S. railroads to transfer troops against Villa. Washington also directed that expedition forces avoid major population centers, further complicating the supply problem. The United States would have to supply the expedition overland in an area with few roads, in difficult terrain, and with major weather problems. In developing a system of motorized supply, the U.S. Army confronted a shortage of officers, drivers, trucks, and mechanics. By June 1916 the expedition was using more than 300 trucks of 14 different types produced by 8 different manufacturers. The U.S. Army used aircraft in combat for the first time in the expedition, dispatching the 1st Aero Squadron (also its only aero squadron) of 8 planes for reconnaissance and communications purposes. By 20 April 1916 the only two planes still operational returned to Columbus where they were unceremoniously burned by their own pilots after being classified as unfit for service.

One of the biggest fears on both sides was a military clash between the expedition and Carranza's forces. As the expedition grew in size and moved farther south, the possibility of an incident increased. By early April, the expedition had penetrated more than 300 miles into Mexico and had grown to almost 7,000 troops. Carranza sent reinforcements to the area and positioned his forces with a view to what the Pershing Expedition was doing rather than to deal with Villa and his forces. The first major encounter came at Parral, Chihuahua, on 12 April. Believing he had the permission of Carranza's officials, Major Frank Tompkins—leader of the original pursuit of Villa's forces at Columbus—led a cavalry unit into Parral to purchase supplies. Local citizens began firing on the U.S. soldiers who were also attacked by regular troops as they attempted to withdraw. The U.S. unit suffered two dead and several wounded while Mexican casualties were estimated at forty. The Carranza administration broke off discussions of a crossing agreement and began to pressure the U.S. government to withdraw the expedition.

Both Carranza and Wilson began preparing for a wider conflict neither wanted. In early May there were new but smaller raids from Mexico into Texas by forces associated with Villa. These raids provoked smaller and briefer punitive expeditions into Mexico by the U.S. Army. The Wilson administration also responded by federalizing the National Guards of Texas, New Mexico, and Arizona, and sending them to the border to support the Pershing Expedition. By June the two countries appeared to be on the brink of full-scale war. President Wilson federalized the National Guards of the other forty-five states and sent them to the border. Carranza's forces received orders to resist any movement by units of the expedition unless they were withdrawing to the north.

On 21 June there was another major clash between U.S. troops and Carranza's forces. Concerned about movements by Carranza's forces, General Pershing sent out reconnaissance patrols but gave them explicit instructions not to enter any town where Carranza's forces were present. One of the patrols violated its orders by trying to enter Carrizal, Chihuahua. The U.S. unit clashed with Carranza's troops and suffered twelve killed—among them the patrol's veteran commander—ten wounded, and twenty-four taken prisoner. Mexican casualties numbered at least seventy-four. War was avoided when Carranza announced that the U.S. prisoners would be returned and both sides agreed to submit their disagreements to a joint commission.

While the joint commission negotiated without results, the U.S. government was reevaluating the continued presence of the expedition in northern Mexico. By September 1916, General Pershing, his immediate superior, General Frederick Funston, and U.S. Army Chief of Staff Hugh Scott agreed that there was no longer any military reason for keeping the expedition in Mexico. The expense of military operations was also a consideration. The War Department estimated that the cost of the expedition and the federalized National Guards (some 110,000 troops) was approximately $15 million per month. The demobilization of National Guard units began in late fall 1916, and a phased withdrawal of the expedition from northern Mexico began on 27 January 1917. The last of the expedition's troops returned to U.S. soil on 5 February 1917. Many of the troops who marched out of Mexico—including their commander—would soon be marching off to France and to World War I. After spending $130 million and almost eleven months, the expedition had proved a partial success. It never captured Villa, who continued to be a problem until 1920, but it dispersed Villa's forces so they were no longer a threat to the U.S. border area. The Pershing Expedition and the mobilization of the National Guard provided valuable experience for the European conflict, even though the trench warfare of the Western Front was to prove far different from the guerrilla warfare of northern Mexico.

—DMC

See also: Revolution of 1910; Vera Cruz, Occupation of (1914); Zimmermann Telegram.

References:

Clendenen, Clarence C. *The United States and Pancho Villa.* Ithaca, NY: Cornell University Press, 1961.

Gilderhus, Mark T. *Diplomacy and Revolution: U.S.–Mexican Relations under Wilson and Carranza.* Tucson: University of Arizona Press, 1977.

Hall, Linda B., and Don M. Coerver. *Revolution on the Border: The United States and Mexico, 1910–1920.* Albuquerque: University of New Mexico Press, 1988.

Petróleos Mexicanos (PEMEX)

Petróleos Mexicanos (Mexican Petroleum, or PEMEX) was a government agency established in 1938 to deal with the properties of foreign-owned oil companies that were expropriated by decree of President Lázaro Cárdenas in March 1938. The foreign-owned oil companies had been at odds with a series of presidential administrations since the outbreak of Revolution in 1910, especially over issues of control of subsoil resources and taxation.

By 1938 the Mexican government had already experimented with a series of state organizations involved with the oil industry. In the early 1920s the government established a bureau, the Control de Administración del Petróleo Nacional (the Administrative Control for National Petroleum), which explored and drilled on oil lands belonging to the government. In 1925 the government set up the Administración Nacional del Petróleo (the National Petroleum Administration), which engaged in both production and refining activities. In 1934 Petróleos de México (Mexican Petroleum, or Petromex) came into existence as a mixed-capital venture. By law, the Mexican government controlled at least 40 percent of the stock in the company. Any remaining stock could be purchased by private interests, but there was a specific ban on ownership of Petromex stock by foreigners. Petromex functioned as a fully integrated oil company, although on a much smaller scale than the foreign-owned oil companies with which it competed. In early 1937 yet another agency was created, the Administración General del Petróleo Nacional (the General Administration of National Petroleum). This new agency was completely government controlled and engaged in exploration, production, and refining activities.

In the immediate aftermath of the expropriation of March 1938, Cárdenas established the Consejo de Administración del Petróleo (the Board of Petroleum Administration) to administer temporarily the assets of the foreign-owned oil companies. The board was composed of two representatives from the Ministry of the Treasury, two from the Ministry of National Economy, and three from the oil workers' union. In July 1938 two more government agencies began operations: the Distribuidora de Petróleos Nacionales (the Distributor of National Petroleum) and Petróleos Mexicanos (Mexican Petroleum, or PEMEX). The Distribuidora handled the marketing of oil products while PEMEX took over the administrative functions previously exercised by the Board of

Petroleum Administration. This division of responsibilities proved awkward, and in August 1940 President Cárdenas abolished the Distribuidora, turning over its responsibilities to PEMEX. PEMEX now exercised an effective monopoly on the Mexican oil industry. PEMEX itself was managed by a council of nine persons, five appointed by the president and four by the oil workers' union. The president also appointed the top official at PEMEX, the general director.

The world in which PEMEX had to compete was a complex and rapidly changing one. While the Mexican government promised to compensate the foreign-owned oil companies for their assets, the companies and the government became involved in a lengthy dispute over the value of the properties involved. The companies took legal action against Mexican efforts to market oil products overseas. Foreigners had dominated the managerial and technical positions in the companies, so there were few Mexicans prepared to take over operations of the companies. The companies were able to protect their oil tankers, so PEMEX immediately encountered major problems with transporting its oil. PEMEX found it difficult to obtain the oil supplies and the equipment it needed to operate. PEMEX lacked the credit and the capital required to maintain and expand operations. The beginning of World War II in Europe in September 1939 created a great demand for Mexican oil but also caused major dislocations in the international oil market. There were also management problems with the powerful oil workers' union, the Sindicato de Trabajadores Petroleros de la República Mexicana (the Union of Petroleum Workers of the Mexican Republic, or STPRM).

From its inception, PEMEX was expected to do more than simply manage the Mexican oil industry. PEMEX was supposed to be an important source of government revenue, a role that varied depending on the price of oil. PEMEX was to be an important source of employment; in its first eighteen months of operation, PEMEX increased its employees by almost 50 percent and by more than 250 percent between 1938 and 1958. PEMEX was to support and promote the social and economic goals established as national policy by the government and the official party. PEMEX was also to serve as a powerful symbol of Mexico's economic nationalism.

During most of the 1940s, PEMEX struggled to fulfill its multiple responsibilities. Problems of labor and capital continued. Primary emphasis was on meeting domestic demand for oil products; there was no significant effort to restore Mexico to its former position of major oil exporter. PEMEX helped to promote the development policy being pursued in the postwar years by providing energy at subsidized rates. PEMEX lacked the capital to engage in major new efforts at exploration so it had to depend on more intensive exploitation of existing fields; this approach often reduced the total amount of oil that could be recovered from a field. PEMEX also struggled with the organizational problems of trying to integrate fully from exploration to distribution in order to compete with the large, multinational oil corporations. In the early postwar years, private capital—including foreign—could participate in exploration, drilling, and development of wells under contract with PEMEX. In 1958 new legislation restricted private companies to service contracts with PEMEX; the law specifically prohibited PEMEX from entering into contracts that called for payment in the form of a percentage of production. This latter restriction was particularly discouraging to private investors. PEMEX did expand its distribution capacity through the construction of new refineries and pipelines.

One of the biggest problems confronting PEMEX management was its lack of control over many fundamental business decisions. Government officials—not PEMEX officials—set wages for workers in the industry and the prices that PEMEX charged for its products. The oil workers' union, the STPRM, enjoyed privileges that cut into management's decision-making powers. The STPRM—not PEMEX management—controlled the hiring of workers. The union also had the right to participate in contracts PEMEX entered into with private companies; the STPRM was able to form cooperatives, which received preferential treatment in the awarding of PEMEX contracts. A PEMEX job was considered so desirable that corrupt union officials regularly sold jobs to those seeking employment.

PEMEX was also in the forefront of the development of the petrochemical industry in Mexico. Legislation passed in 1958 gave PEMEX exclusive control over the production of what were classified as "basic petrochemicals." Private companies could produce "secondary petrochemicals," with the restriction that such companies could not be more than 40 percent foreign-owned. In 1960 the government released a list of 16 specific products that were classified as basic; in 1967 the list of basic chemicals was expanded to 45. In 1971 legislation established the Mexican Petrochemical Commission to help determine whether petrochemical products should be classified as basic or secondary. While having a monopoly on basic petrochemicals, PEMEX also produced—and subsidized for the domestic market—secondary petrochemicals. By 1970 there were 217 petrochemical plants in Mexico, of which 41 belonged to PEMEX.

During the 1960s and the early 1970s, PEMEX experienced a steady increase in production, especially in the area of natural gas. Hydrocarbon consumption, however—driven by a growing population and rapid industrialization—was increasing at a much faster rate than production. PEMEX was unable to achieve its goal of hydrocarbon self-sufficiency and was forced to increase its importation of crude oil. In the late 1960s and early 1970s, PEMEX had to stop exporting crude oil for the first time in its history. In 1965 the government set up the Mexican Petroleum Institute (the Instituto Mexicano del Petróleo, or IMP) to promote the technical expertise of PEMEX. This scientific assistance was especially important as PEMEX found it necessary to engage in much more deep drilling as well as becoming more actively involved in offshore drilling. The financial position of PEMEX deteriorated badly as extraction costs increased, oil prices declined, and the prices for PEMEX products domestically were frozen.

Despite the bleak financial and economic picture, PEMEX was on the verge of a major change in its fortunes. This change was a product of two forces—one beyond the control of PEMEX, the other directly connected with its activities. The factor beyond the control of PEMEX was the dramatic improvement in oil prices beginning with the Arab oil embargo of 1973 and continuing throughout the decade. The factor directly connected to PEMEX was the discovery of major new oil reserves in southeastern Mexico, both on land and offshore. The reserves would permit Mexico to return to the position of a major exporter of oil. Mexico was not a member of the Organization of Petroleum Exporting Countries (OPEC) because it was not a major exporter of oil at the time the organization was founded. Mexico was able to benefit from the price increases provoked by OPEC's manipulation of production but was not subject to the kind of criticism increasingly leveled at OPEC by the industrial countries. In fact, Mexico was even able to charge slightly more for its oil than the OPEC countries because of its greater proximity to major consumers, especially the United States.

It was the government—not PEMEX—which would decide how to deal with this new oil bonanza. The administration of President José López Portillo established maximum limits on daily production, overseas sales, and sales to any one country (meaning the United States). This was supposed to ensure the "digestible exploitation" of the oil wealth PEMEX would produce. PEMEX found itself indirectly subsidizing a number of consumer products, beyond its traditional direct subsidizing of energy. On the surface PEMEX's financial performance was spectacular; by 1983 PEMEX accounted for approximately 13 percent of Mexico's gross domestic product and almost 50 percent of government tax revenues. The downside was that the government was spending the additional revenue even faster than PEMEX could generate it and was borrowing heavily as well to maintain public spending. PEMEX's share of the Mexican government's foreign debt was also increasing dramatically, rising from approximately 10 percent in 1970 to almost 30 percent in 1981. Corruption connected with PEMEX also achieved new dimensions as the oil boom unfolded.

The decline in oil prices beginning in the early 1980s brought economic hard times to Mexico and greater attention to the role played by PEMEX in the economy. The near economic and financial collapse forced the government to adopt an austerity program that soon phased into the introduction of major economic and financial reforms. Critics attacked PEMEX for its inefficiency, mismanagement, and corruption. One of the first targets for reform was the powerful oil workers union, the STPRM. A presidential decree in 1984 restricted the subcontracting activities of the STPRM with PEMEX. The STPRM publicly voiced its disenchantment with the economic reforms being implemented and opposed the official candidate for the presidency in 1988, Carlos Salinas de Gortari. When Salinas assumed the presidency, he retaliated by arresting thirty-five of the top union leaders. The president made it clear that the new union leaders would be expected to support the government's economic policies or face similar treatment.

With labor subdued, President Salinas was able to undertake a major reorganization of PEMEX. PEMEX was divided into units responsible for exploration and production, refining, natural gas and basic petrochemicals, secondary petrochemicals, and international operations. New accounting and tax procedures were introduced to better determine profitability and efficiency. Employment at PEMEX dropped rapidly from 210,000 in 1987 to approximately 106,000 in 1993. These reforms were aimed at making PEMEX function more like the multinational oil companies with which it competed. Almost a decade later in late 2001, the current general director of PEMEX—Raúl Muñoz Leos—indicated that the reorganization of PEMEX in the early 1990s had not produced any substantial improvements in operations. Muñoz Leos also predicted that Mexico would soon be importing more gas, refined oil products, and petrochemicals if PEMEX was not allowed to increase its spending on exploration and production.

One of the reforms being implemented in the 1980s and the 1990s was privatization, the selling off of government enterprises to the private sector. With major government enterprises such as the national telephone system being sold off, many wondered whether privatization would be extended to PEMEX. The petrochemical activities of PEMEX were soon affected. The number of basic petrochemicals—those reserved exclusively to PEMEX for production—peaked in 1986 at seventy. The list of basic petrochemicals contracted rapidly; by 1992 it was down to only eight. PEMEX also began to sell off some its secondary petrochemical activities to private companies. The administration of President Salinas was also actively pushing for implementation of the North American Free Trade Agreement (NAFTA), designed to improve the flow of capital and trade among the countries of Mexico, Canada, and the United States. Salinas hoped that NAFTA would lead to a significant increase in foreign investment in Mexico. NAFTA posed the issue of the role of PEMEX in a freer business environment. Because of the symbolic importance of PEMEX in national life, even the reform-minded Salinas was not willing to make major changes in the role played by PEMEX in the Mexican oil industry. When NAFTA went into effect in January 1994, it provided easier access for U.S. and Canadian companies to the petrochemical sector, to provision of oil goods and services, and to PEMEX contracts. The dominant role played by PEMEX, however, was left intact.

In recent years PEMEX has come under increasing criticism for its environmental practices. In its efforts to expand operations rapidly, PEMEX often ignored the environmental consequences of its actions. Farmers in southeastern states charged that PEMEX activities so polluted their lands that they could no longer be cultivated. Growing PEMEX operations offshore brought with them the possibility of water pollution to add to pollution of soil and air. The pollution charges were often followed by claims that PEMEX was slow to pay for or refused to pay for environmental claims. The debate over NAFTA heightened concerns about the environment, focusing more unfavorable attention on PEMEX. PEMEX officials maintained that they were tightening pollution controls; the most notable example of this supposed new policy was the closing in 1991 of PEMEX's major refinery in Mexico City, a notorious polluter in the Federal District. PEMEX also claimed to have accelerated payment of compensation for pollution but also made it clear that it would pay only when environmental damage could be clearly linked to PEMEX.

The PEMEX operating in the twenty-first century is different organizationally from the PEMEX of 1938. In its proposed budget for 2002, the Fox administration described PEMEX as a "commercial enterprise" that would be judged by criteria different from those used to evaluate other public-sector activities. The new budget also called for PEMEX to have greater freedom of action in investing in new projects. Despite efforts to make PEMEX more like other multinational oil corporations, it is still very much a special case in terms of its role in the Mexican oil industry and its symbolic significance for Mexican economic nationalism. PEMEX has survived world war, price fluctuations, corruption scandals, debt crises, and peso devaluations to endure as a symbol of Mexico's hopes for economic development and independence.

—DMC

See also: Cárdenas, Lázaro; Corruption; Debt, Mexico's Foreign; Economy; Labor Movements; López Portillo, José; Madrid (Hurtado), Miguel de la; North American Free Trade Agreement (NAFTA); Salinas de Gortari, Carlos.

References:

Brown, Jonathan C., and Alan Knight, eds. *The Mexican Petroleum Industry in the Twentieth Century.* Austin: University of Texas Press, 1992.

Mancke, Richard B. *Mexican Oil and Natural Gas: Political, Strategic, and Economic Implications.* New York: Praeger Publishers, 1979.

Rippy, Merrill. *Oil and the Mexican Revolution.* Leiden, The Netherlands: E. J. Brill, 1972.

Photography

With its spectacular landscapes and vibrant cultures, Mexico has attracted some of the world's best photographers. With its gift for creative cultural appropriation, Mexico has also produced some of the world's best photographers. Any list of great twentieth-century photographers would have to include Manuel Álvarez Bravo and, more recently, Tina Modotti and Graciela Iturbide. Photojournalism has flourished as well, beginning at the turn of the century with Agustín Víctor Casasola and continuing with the innovative work of Héctor García and Nacho López at midcentury. As Mexico enters the twenty-first century, photographers in both genres have found endless sources of inspiration in its ever more tangled mixture of modern, traditional, and postmodern landscapes and cultures. The result is a proliferation of talented photographers working on a wide variety of subjects (from indigenous women to transvestites to bureaucrats), in a wide variety of locations (from rural village to urban barrio to the border), and with a wide variety of styles (from realism to surrealism to abstraction).

Photography came early to Mexico. In 1839, émigré French engraver Louis Prélier introduced the new daguerreotype in Vera Cruz just months after its Paris debut. By 1844, Mexican daguerreotypist Joaquín María Díaz González had opened a studio in Mexico City.

For educated Europeans fascinated by all things exotic in an age of colonial empires, Mexico provided a vast repository of images that appealed to all kinds of aesthetic tastes. As early as 1859, French explorer Désiré Charnay had begun to publish books of photographs of southern Mexico's spectacular pre-Columbian ruins. Other archaeologists and anthropologists, most of them foreigners, quickly followed suit. In the early years of the twenty-first century, this photographic invasion shows no signs of abating. Their impressive and extensive work has colored (and in many ways continues to color), the outside world's view of Mexico as a land of past glories, quaint people, and curious customs.

Although many Mexicans would come to appreciate this exotic image, whether for its tourist potential or as a reflection of their cultural distinctness, photography's initial appeal was its ability to democratize portraiture—a luxury previously restricted to wealthy elites with enough money to pay a professional painter. Although rather costly until the early twentieth century, photographic portraits nevertheless proved an instant and enduring attraction. Sometimes, the photographic subject was an important political figure like the ill-fated Emperor Maximilian or his nemesis Benito Juárez. On Juárez's death in 1876, for example, Cruces y Campa (the Mexico City photography studio of Antíoco Cruces and Luis Campa) produced and presumably sold 20,000 small commemorative portraits of the great liberal hero. Most of the time, however, Mexicans from all walks of life flocked to studios or sought out itinerant photographers in order to have personal and family portraits taken. In response to the huge demand, entrepreneurs opened studios throughout Mexico; even a small provincial capital like Guanajuato could boast its own master photographer,

Romualdo García. Moreover, because photography was a new technology, it had few of the restrictions of traditional craft guilds and thus offered opportunities for a new generation of artisans, such as Natalia Baquedano, whose Mexico City studio presaged the prominence of women in twentieth-century Mexican photography.

Popularity did not preclude class distinctions. For the upper classes, studio photographers like Cruces y Campa or the Valleto Brothers (Guillermo, Ricardo, Julio) offered elegantly appointed spaces and impeccable technique. Cruces, for example, had studied photography in Paris, while Campa was a painter of some repute as well as drawing master at the prestigious Academy of San Carlos in Mexico City. An integral part of a new consumer culture, these high-end studios branched out with innovative marketing strategies like hand-colored prints and postcard series of Mexican popular types for local and international consumption.

Obsessed with the modernizing potential of new technologies and with attracting foreign investors to Mexico, turn-of-the-century government technocrats also embraced photography. After a tumultuous nineteenth century, their first concern was restoring public order. In an effort to control crime, photography was used to identify convicted criminals in Mexico City jails as early as the 1850s. A decade later, concerns about the public health implications of sexual commerce led to identification cards for registered prostitutes. The photographing of Indians and the urban lower classes by ethnologists and anthropologists while less overtly disciplinary, was also linked to longstanding elite concerns about Mexico's sizeable and potentially volatile rural and urban under classes. Regardless of motive, by century's end, the photographic surveillance of "deviant" populations was a common if by no means consistent practice.

In addition to its contributions to social control, photography provided a convenient way of inventorying and representing (for potential investors) national resources, whether people, infrastructure, or natural wealth. Prominent American photographers like William Henry Jackson and Charles Waite received Mexican government commissions to photograph everything from modern railroads to traditional labor practices. The German-born Guillermo Kahlo (1872–1941), father of the famous painter Frida Kahlo, opened a Mexico City studio with help of his father-in-law and was promptly awarded a government contract to photograph the nation's past and present architectural glories for the 1910 centenary of Mexican independence.

The rise of mass daily newspapers, beginning with the government-subsidized *El Imparcial* in 1896, marked the debut of a new kind of photographer, the photojournalist. The most famous photojournalist of this first generation was undoubtedly Agustín Víctor Casasola. With a gift for ingratiating himself with the powerful and an eye for quotidian drama, Casasola tirelessly recorded the great events, important people, and everyday life of over three decades of Mexican history. Quite apart from their artistic qualities, his many images of turn-of-the-century Mexico and the Revolution of 1910 are indispensable historical documents for these watershed years, especially in conjunction with the thousands of other photographs from the period that he and his brother Miguel added to their massive collection. Indeed, some photographs from the Casasola collection—Revolutionary leaders Pancho Villa and Emiliano Zapata in the National Palace, Zapatista soldiers drinking coffee at Sanborn's restaurant, a *soladera* (camp follower) leaning from a train—have been indelibly imprinted on the minds of generations of Mexican schoolchildren and have thus become integral parts of the nation's historical memory.

The 1920s and 1930s produced another kind of photographic legacy. The arrival in Mexico City of renowned American photographer Edward Weston (1886–1958) and his partner Tina Modotti in 1923 sparked a boom in Mexican art photography that has yet to subside. Disdainful of conventional studio photography and picturesque postcard images, Weston produced elegant, hard-focus photographs that ranged widely in content from landscapes to still lifes to portraits but without recourse to sentimentality or storytelling. Weston's modernist aesthetic with its emphasis on the inherent beauty of form found a receptive audience in Mexico City's lively artistic community—dominated by the muralist movement headed by the dynamic Diego Rivera but eager to absorb stylistic innovations from newcomers like Weston, fellow American Paul Strand, French photographer Henri Cartier-Bresson, and Soviet filmmaker Sergei Eisenstein.

Weston's greatest disciple was his controversial companion, Tina Modotti (1896–1942). An Italian-born fashion model and actress who had begun an affair with Weston in Los Angeles, Modotti agreed to manage his Mexico City photography business in exchange for training in photography. She proved a quick study, at one point drawing from the never humble Weston the comment: "Tina has one picture I wish I could sign with my name—that does not happen often in my life!" Modotti's early photographs—"Folds of Cloth," "Telephone Wires," "Calla Lily," "White Roses"—with their exquisite sense of form and texture show her considerable debt to Weston's modernist style. But the radical politics she shared with fellow artists and friends like David Álfaro Siquieros, Diego Rivera, and Frida Kahlo came to play an increasingly prominent role in her artistic vision, especially after Weston's departure in 1926. In addition to images of the muralists at work and professional commissions for portraits and "folk" images, Modotti began to shoot photographs of Mexican workers—many of them for the Communist paper *El Machete*—and still lifes of Revolutionary images—hammers, sickles, guitars, sombreros, cartridge belts. Even her relatively abstract work from the late 1920s—"Mother and Child," "Hands Resting on Tool," "Mella's Typewriter"—hinted at an increasingly radical populism. Although she was recognized as a major artistic talent, these radical politics brought Modotti to the attention of Mexican authorities, especially after her companion, Cuban communist firebrand Julio Antonio Mella, was brutally gunned down in a Mexico City street by his political opponents. Accused of Mella's murder by the police, Modotti mounted a successful defense, but Mexican authorities deported her anyway. She spent most of the next decade in Stalinist Russia and fighting on the Republican side in the Spanish Civil War. A 1940 return to Mexico brought some hope of artistic resurrection but a mysterious heart attack in a Mexico City taxicab in 1942 prematurely ended her promising career. Modotti's influence on Mexican photography, however, would be profound and her artistic reputation, like that of her friend Frida Kahlo (another woman overshadowed in life by a mentor-lover), has continued to grow since her death.

At the time, however, Modotti's most important contribution to Mexican photography was probably her mentorship of a young civil servant who would soon become Mexico's best-known photographer: Manuel Álvarez Bravo (1902–2002). Although well trained in photographic techniques by German émigré photographer, Hugo Brehme (whose considerable talents lay in picturesque landscapes and quaint customs), Álvarez Bravo languished throughout most of the 1920s as an accountant in the national Comptroller's Office, first in Mexico City and later in Oaxaca. In 1924, he and his wife, Lola (1907–1993)—Lola would later to become an important photographer in her own right—encountered the work of Weston and Modotti at a public exhibition in Mexico City. Although too shy to do more than admire from a distance, Álvarez Bravo's Oaxaca pictures from the mid-1920s began to reflect a similar preoccupation with form. At the same time, the formal beauty of his ironic "Paper Games I" with its loops of paper that look suspiciously like a roll from an accountant's adding machine hints at the playfulness that would become the hallmark of his later work.

In 1927, the Álvarez Bravos returned to Mexico City and began to frequent Modotti's artistic circles. Impressed with Álvarez Bravos's early work, Modotti sent his photographs off to Weston in California, who responded that they were "of better than usual technique and of excellent viewpoint" and wondered if Modotti had taken them herself. Thus encouraged, Álvarez Bravo, over the course of the next decade, would produce some of his most memorable images: "Wooden Horse," "Two Pairs of Legs," "The Sympathetic Nervous System," "The Dreamer," "Young Girl Looking at Birds," "Optical Parabola," "The Dream," "The Dancers' Daughter," and the gruesome "Striking Worker, Assassinated" (a rare "documentary" photograph of a dead striker lying in a pool of blood). These enigmatic slices of Mexican life with their suggestive titles attracted considerable attention (if not much income) both in Mexico and abroad. By the late 1930s, Álvarez Bravo was exhibiting his photographs alongside those of renowned French photographer Henri Cartier-Bresson at Mexico City's Palace of Fine Arts and meeting with visiting artistic dignitaries like French surrealist master André Bretón. A commission from Bretón resulted in his most famous image, "Good Reputation Sleeping," which depicts a bandaged but otherwise naked women lying on blanket in the sun in front of a rough plaster wall with several spiny cactus buds strewn beside her. Like most of his pictures from this period, this image relies on hard-focus realism to produce a subtly subversive "surrealist" effect in which the clarity of the photographic image fails to define its elusive meaning. Endorsements like Bretón's garnered Álvarez Bravo international attention but little money and he spent most of the 1940s and 1950s working steadily in the thriving Mexican film industry. He returned to photography in the 1960s, focusing this time on female nudes, experimenting with new photographic techniques and textures, and helping to train a new generation of photographers.

Inspired perhaps by Modotti's example, Lola Álvarez Bravo followed her husband into photography. During the 1920s and early 1930s, she worked closely with Manuel, using the same camera and darkroom and working in a very similar style. In 1935, the Álvarez Bravos split up and Lola went from supportive wife to struggling professional photographer. Regular commissions from news magazines and government institutions like the National University's Department of Aesthetic Research and the National Institute of Fine Arts took her all over Mexico and encouraged her to explore a broad spectrum of subjects and styles. Photomontages like "The Dream of the Poor II" with its dirty street urchin sleeping under electromagnets clustered with coins reflect a political awareness typical of the radical milieu of 1930s Mexico City. Portraits of artistic celebrities like her friend Frida Kahlo or the flamboyant poet-playwright Salvador Novo demonstrate an extraordinary gift for the photographic representation of complex personalities. Lola Álvarez Bravo, however, is best known for her unsentimental but deeply empathetic images of everyday Mexican life: rural *campesinos* slaughtering a bull ("In the Mountains"), a pensive woman behind lattice shadows ("In Her Own Jail"), a kneeling blind woman in a crowded marketplace ("Indifference").

The opportunities for professional photographers were greatly enhanced by the appearance of photography magazines like *Helios, Revista Mensual Fotográfico* (1929–1936), and *Rotofoto* (1937–1938). The latter publication, celebrated by historians of photography for its innovative, satiric photojournalism— President Manuel Ávila Camacho in a very un-macho bathing suit, pictorial-interviews with rebel leaders like Saturnino Cedillo—lasted only eleven issues before a government-instigated strike forced its closure. Other, less adventurous, magazines like

Todo, Mañana, and *Siempre!* would continue to encourage first-rate photojournalism, although editors were usually careful to heed the *Rotofoto* lesson and keep their social critiques and satiric impulses tame or ambiguous enough to avoid official censure.

Despite these constraints, photojournalism thrived in midcentury Mexico. Again, foreigners working in Mexico played a key role as the five "Hermanos Mayo [Mayo Brothers]," forced to flee to Mexico after Franco's victory in the Spanish Civil War, introduced the lightweight 35 mm Leica camera, which revolutionized on-the-spot "action" photography. Armed with this new technology, first-rate photojournalists like Hector García (1928–) produced riveting images of the era's most noteworthy events, from the 1958 railway workers' strike to the 1968 Tlatelolco Massacre. Others like Nacho López went beyond the recording of important events and daily news stories to delve into seldom-seen corners of Mexican life with visual exposés of the callous corruption of the local precinct house or the squalid inhumanity of the national penitentiary. Both men struggled with unofficial censorship as most newspaper and magazine editors took care to avoid anything that might provoke official repression. By the 1970s, these struggles began to pay off as independent publications like *Uno más uno* (1977–) and *La Jornada* (1984–) provided the basis for a self-identified "new Mexican photojournalism" that operated outside the self-censoring mainstream media and contributed significantly to the political democratization of the late twentieth century.

Art photography has flourished as well. Although styles vary widely, the most notable trend is a quasi-anthropological interest in recording the magic of everyday Mexican life. Although heavily influenced by the work of Álvarez Bravo and the photojournalists, this new generation of art photographers favors a "postmodern" approach that acknowledges the photographer's involvement in the production of images and thus undermines the medium's claim to represent an objective reality. This is especially noticeable in the work of Graciela Iturbide (1942–), probably the best-known Mexican photographer of the late twentieth century. Although initially trained as a filmmaker, Iturbide became an assistant to Manuel Álvarez Bravo in the 1970s. That experience, combined with a desire to work alone (and without high overhead), pushed her toward photography. An inveterate traveler, Iturbide would become the premiere practitioner of a new kind of ethnographic photography. Her first big commission, a photographic study of the Seri Indians of Baja California, attracted considerable attention for its brilliant use of Baja's stark landscapes and complex representations of everyday life among the Seri. Images like the enigmatic María Félix—a smiling Indian woman standing on the beach in front of a painted boat and holding a string of fish—with its popular culture referent (María Félix is one of Mexico's most famous and glamorous film stars) subverted the folkloric approach of traditional anthropology. This sly subversion of anthropological "objectivity" reaches its highest level of expression in her work with the Zapotec Indians of Juchitán, Oaxaca, undertaken at the behest of painter and native son, Francisco Toledo. Aided by Toledo's local connections, Iturbide immersed herself in Juchitán society and her photographs uncovered a hidden world of powerful matriarchs like the famous "Our Lady of the Iguanas," whose composure in the face of years of exploitation suggest a self-awareness and historical sensibility too often denied indigenous subjects. A more recent series on the annual ritual slaughter of goats among the Mixtec Indians of Oaxaca—"In the Name of the Father"—ignores the immediate religious significance of the event in order to explore the aesthetics of ritualized violence and death. A similar subversion of traditional ethnographic photography is also present in the work of Mariana Yampolsky (1925–), another Álvarez Bravo assistant and photographer of rural Mexico's dying hacienda culture, and Flor Garduño (1957–), whose compelling images of indigenous women have helped popularize the new ethnographic photography.

While photographers like Iturbide, Yampolsky, and Garduño have taken new approaches to the representation of traditional cultures, Mexico's ongoing confrontation with a never quite realized modernity has inspired contemporary photographers to move beyond the conventions of midcentury photojournalism. In a series dedicated to early twentieth-century German photographer August Sander, for example, Rafael Doniz subverts the journalistic "slice-of-life" photography by deliberately posing his urban "types" in the style of early studio photographers. Pablo Ortiz Monasterio (1952–), on the other hand, undermines the picturesque tradition by juxtaposing modern trash—oil drums, plastic bags, barbed wire—with traditional images of fishermen at work and by framing his photographs in unexpected ways that call attention to their constructed nature. And Pedro Meyer (1935–) extends the urban ethnographic gaze from the blue-collar street into the white-collar office with images of bureaucrats and secretaries or indulges in over-the-top irony, as in his photograph of the huge, decrepit replica of the Statue of Liberty that looms over the world's largest slum-city, Cuidad Nezhualcoyotl.

Not content to subvert existing traditions, some photographers have opted for unabashedly contemporary subjects. Lourdes Grobet (1940–) photographs the lives of Tijuana's professional wrestlers both inside the ring and out while Yolanda Andrade (1950–) produces images of gaudily dressed drag queens and Mexico City's vibrant punk rock scene. In perhaps the most subversive move of all, José Hernández Claire (1949–) confronts the power of the professional gaze head-on with sometimes gruesome, sometimes compassionate photographs of the sightless eyes of the blind. Thus Mexican photography continues to flourish into the twenty-first century, enriched rather than cowed by the chaotic cultural hybridity that has come to characterize modern life.

—*RMB*

See also: Kahlo, Frida; Muralist Movement; Rivera, Diego; Siquieros, David Álfaro.

References:

Álvarez Bravo, Manuel. *Manuel Álvarez Bravo.* Introduced by A. D. Coleman. New York: Aperture Masters of Photography, 1987.

Debroise, Oliver. *Mexican Suite: A History of Photography in Mexico.* Trans. Stella de Sá Rego. Austin: University of Texas Press, 2001.

Iturbide, Graciela. *Graciela Iturbide.* Introduced by Cuauhtémoc Medina. New York: Phaidon, 2001.

Marz, John. *Nacho López: Mexican Photographer.* Minneapolis: University of Minnesota Press, 2003.

Modotti, Tina. *Tina Modotti.* Introduced by Margaret Hooks. New York: Aperture Masters of Photography, 1999.

Tierra y Libertad: Photographs of the Mexico, 1900–1930. Oxford: Museum of Modern Art, 1985.

Ziff, Trisha. *Between Worlds: Contemporary Mexican Photography.* New York: Impressions, 1990.

Poetry

Mexican poetry—as a literary form—has a distinguished history dating back at least as far as the Aztecs and Maya, some of whose oral poetic traditions were preserved by the Spanish friars sent to convert them to Christianity. During the colonial period (1521–1821), elite intellectual circles, although dependent for the most part on imported European high culture, produced a world-class poet in Sor Juana Inés de la Cruz (1651–1695), a Hieronymite nun whose work was celebrated throughout the Spanish empire even in her lifetime. For the most part, however, colonial Mexican poetry imitated "superior" European models or, perhaps more accurately, participated in a peripheral way in a cosmopolitan, pan-European culture filtered through a Spanish imperial system that increasingly found itself on the periphery of mainstream European culture. Colonial-era Mexican poets sometimes drew on Mexican themes, especially from the country's pre-Hispanic past, but, in the absence of a developed national consciousness, they saw little reason to challenge the primacy of imported models or the desirability of a "European" audience (at least in cultural terms).

The independence period (1810–1821) produced its share of patriotic poetic effusion, most of it in the European romantic tradition, but this nationalist poetry was of little interest to anyone outside the new nation or to most Mexicans for that matter. After all, until the beginning of the twentieth century (and some would argue not until after the Revolution), literacy rates were abysmal, many Mexicans spoke an Indian language rather than Spanish, and few felt much loyalty to their new "imagined community." As in the colonial period, appreciation for literature, and especially poetry, was generally confined to the educated classes, those with the time and inclination to ponder its subtleties and a vested interest in its political and ideological potential.

The advent of modernism as a poetic style in the last decades of the nineteenth century laid the groundwork for a distinctly Mexican poetry that nevertheless continued to draw heavily from European models. Earlier poets had labored in the shadow of a "superior" imported culture; for Mexican modernists and their successors, however, the competing claims of cosmopolitan and national literary cultures would become a source of creative tension rather than artistic inferiority. Inspired by French Parnassian poets like Charles Baudelaire and Paul Verlaine with their "cult of beauty" and obsession with formal and linguistic precision (as opposed to romantic effusion) and by innovative Spanish-language poets like Nicaraguan modernist Rubén Darío and Spanish symbolist Gustavo Adolfo Bécquer, turn-of-the-century Mexican modernist poets founded two influential literary reviews, *Revista Azul* (1894–1896) and *Revista Moderna* (1898–1911), to disseminate the new modernist aesthetic. As part of a cosmopolitan poetic tradition, their work, like that of their predecessors, reflected its

European influences but with an important difference: the Parnassian insistence on "objectivity" and the accurate representation of external "reality" encouraged Mexican modernists to shift their focus from the subjective impact of the environment on the poet—a position that reinforced their Europeanized cultural perspective on Mexico—to the objective observation and description of that environment—a position that emphasized Mexico's uniqueness vis-à-vis Europe. If that was not enough incentive, the late nineteenth-century European craze for exotic cultures provided them with whatever external justification and encouragement they might have needed for coming to grips with their own. Nor were they alone in this endeavor. Government-sponsored exhibits at world's fairs and international exhibitions in Europe and the United States used images of exotic Mexico—usually connected to Indian cultures past and present—to "sell" the country to foreign investors and potential tourists.

As might be expected, different poets grappled with Mexican reality in different ways, most more subtle than the government's crude "orientalism." Manuel Gutiérrez Nájera (1859–1895), for example, wrote about Mexico City nightlife with a poetic elegance that reflected his broad culture, refined tastes, and a melancholic disposition that sought distraction (usually without success) in the frivolous life of a big city *catrín* (dandy). In contrast, the carefully crafted, impressionistic poetry of Salvador Díaz Mirón (1853–1928) belied an active life of frequent duels, public service, and political exile in the romantic mode of Lord Byron. Modernism's most famous practitioner, Amado Nervo (1870–1919), pursued his spiritual obsessions through several poetic styles, including symbolism, Parnassian formalism, and, finally, a deceptively simple "literature without literature" that brought him international acclaim. Finally, the most eclectic of the modernists, José Juan Tablada (1871–1945), helped publicize the movement as a self-professed "decadent" who en-

joyed shocking respectable literary circles with poems like his 1898 "Black Mass." More important to the future of Mexican poetry, Tablada was also an inveterate traveler perpetually in search of the latest avant-garde movement or poetic fad. One of his "discoveries," the cryptic Japanese haiku, would become a favorite of later poets, as would his preoccupation with oriental philosophies. At their best Tablada's, haikus subtly portrayed the clash between traditional and modern aesthetics (as well between Japanese solemnity and Mexican irreverence) as is the cryptic " . . .? . . .," which read simply: "Double radiance scarcely mobile / in the nocturnal path. Perhaps an owl? / Perhaps a car . . . ?"

With the exception of Nervo's later works, modernism was an elitist enterprise directed at a select audience of fellow esthetes. Nevertheless, it also served as a high culture alternative to turn-of-the-century Mexico's dominant intellectual current, positivism, which favored a scientific-materialistic worldview and saw little use in the metaphysical musings of poets, modern or not (although French positivism did have a spiritual component). In that sense, then, modernist poetry contributed to the intellectual assault on the authoritarian Porfirio Díaz regime (1877–1880, 1884–1911) by opposition groups like the young philosophers of Mexico City's Ateneo de la juventud (Athenian Youth), who shared the modernists' disdain for official positivist ideology. To both groups, the government's positivist slogan, "Order and Progress," lacked a corresponding concern for individual and national spiritual development and thus seemed little more than a shallow imitation of Yankee materialism.

This critical perspective was especially true of later modernists such as Enrique González Martínez (1871–1952), whose famous "Tuércele el cuello al cisne" (Wring the Neck of the Swan, 1911) appeared to attack the work of earlier modernists like Rubén Darío by killing off the swan, their preferred symbol of idealized beauty, because "it doesn't feel the soul of things nor the voice of the countryside." Although González Martínez continued to write in the modernist-symbolist style (but with more attention to internal than external symbols like the swan), the propitious timing of his "manifesto"—it coincided with the outbreak of the Revolution of 1910—signaled an aesthetic rupture with the past and the dawn of new era in Mexican poetry. This sense of revolutionary rupture was reinforced by the work of Ramón López Velarde (1888–1921), whose long 1919 poem, "La suave patria" (Gentle Fatherland, 1919), provided an impressionistic and extremely personal assessment of the Revolution's impact on the provincial cities of central Mexico. López Velarde's gift for carefully crafted vignettes (usually on Mexican themes) along with his Freudian obsession with the interplay between love (*eros*) and death (*thanatos*) would become staples of twentieth-century Mexican poetry.

Even though the Revolution had a profound impact on poetry, that influence was quite different from its effect on the novel or the visual arts. Novelists like Mariano Azuela and painters like Diego Rivera produced widely disseminated masterworks on national, even nationalistic, themes in the realist mode for a popular audience. Poetry—again with exception of Nervo—had less mass appeal. Consequently, post-Revolutionary poets continued to draw inspiration from cosmopolitan models even as they turned more and more to Mexico for much of their subject matter. The creative tension between the cosmopolitan and the national would dominate their artistic visions, even more than it had the modernists.

The most radical of the new poetic movements was Estridentismo (1921–1927), which drew heavily on avant-garde European movements like French Dadaism, Italian Futurism, and Spanish Ultraism. The movement's founder, Manuel Maples Arce (1900–1981) founded short-lived but influential literary journals with names like *Ser* (Being), *Irradiador* (Radiator), and *Horizonte* (Horizon)

and wrote poems like "Urbe" (1924) that extolled the dynamism of Mexico City and its new class of industrial proletarians. (This long poem was translated into English by American novelist John Dos Pasos.) More important for its political radicalism than its poetic merits, Estridentismo nevertheless brought together some major artistic talents, including photographers Edward Weston and Tina Modotti, both of whom contributed pictures to *Horizonte*.

More significant from a poetic perspective were the Contemporáneos: Carlos Pellicer (1897–1977), José Gorostiza (1901–1973), Jaime Torres Bodet (1902–1974), Xavier Villaurrutia (1903–1950), and Salvador Novo (1904–1970) to mention only the best known. Like their predecessors, the Contemporáneos understood the importance of literary journals. Although theirs, too, were short lived—*Ulises* (1927–1928), *Contemporáneos* (1928–1931)—they provided a crucial forum for the innovative works of both Mexican and foreign poets (including major writers such as Paul Valéry and T. S. Elliott). Unlike the Estridentistas, however, the Contemporáneos rejected overtly political or socially engaged poetry, even through Pellicer, Gorostiza, and Torres Bodet had been involved in Ateneo founder José Vasconcelos's efforts to expand public education in the early 1920s, and Gorostiza and Torres Bodet went on to distinguished careers as public servants. (The former would become secretary of foreign relations; the latter, secretary of education and ambassador to France.)

As with the modernists, and despite their collective identity as a literary movement, each of the Contemporáneos had a quite distinctive style. Gorostiza acknowledged a shared "investigation of certain essences—love, life, death, [and] God" and critics accused them of cosmopolitan elitism. Members themselves admitted only to being a "group of loners" (*grupo de soledades*). This attitude is certainly reflected in their poetry.

As the oldest and most independent of the group, Carlos Pellicer was the closest in spirit and style to the modernists, especially Tablada and López Velarde. His poetry shares their interest in spirituality (a blend of occultism and mystical Christianity in his case) and expands López Velarde's fascination with the impressionistic elements of provincial Mexican life to include, not just his native state of Tabasco, but all of Latin America. Like his one-time mentor Vasconcelos and Uruguayan writer José Enrique Rodó, whose famous essay "Ariel" (1900) had galvanized a generation of Latin American intellectuals, Pellicer insisted on opposing the penetration of North American Puritan materialism (supported by frequent U.S. interventions in the region) into Latin American culture, which these writers saw as both more sensual and more spiritual if less productive in a material sense than that of its Anglo-Saxon neighbor.

José Gorostiza's work, on the other hand, appears much closer in spirit if not in style to Spanish Golden Age poetry or the Mexican poetic tradition of Sor Juana. This is especially true of his long meditation on existence and extinction, "Muerte sin fin" (Death without End, 1939). But, even this rather austere (although wordy for Gorostiza), metaphysical poem, after an obligatory lamentation of the limitations of human intelligence—"solitude in flames that conceives everything without creating it"—concludes with a sardonic and very Mexican "dance" with death: "From my insomniac eyes / my death is beckoning me / it beckons me, yes, it makes love to me / with its languid eye. / Come on, little whore with icy blush / come on, let's go to the devil!"

His fellow government minister, Jaime Torres Bodet, as prolific as Gorostiza was parsimonious, developed his poetic vision out of scenes and objects from everyday life. A modernist poet in his early years, Torres Bodet further refined the objectivist approach with the introduction of surrealist elements into his poetry in the 1930s. In this surrealist phase, ordinary occurrences of everyday life—a telephone call, the raising of a drawbridge—filtered through the perceptions of the poet become extraordinary events, the significance of which is laden with meaning but never explained. In much of his later poetry, Torres Bodet, like so many of his colleagues, turned his attention to death, a prefiguration perhaps of his eventual suicide. In a poem entitled "Nunca" (Never), he wrote: "I will never tire of my job as a man, / Man I have been and will be while it exists / Man no more: project among projects, / parched mouth glued to the pitcher, / insecure feet on the fiery dust, / Spirit and matter vulnerable / to all the trials and good fortunes. . . ."

Death certainly occupies center stage in the poetry of his younger colleague, Xavier Villarutia, not so much as a growing concern with mortality but rather a constant presence that informs every human act. "Death always takes the form of the bedroom that contains us," he wrote in "Nocturne of the Bedroom," " . . . Death is all this and more that surrounds us / and unites us and separates in turn, / that leaves us confused, stupefied, suspended, / with a wound from which no blood flows." His masterwork, "Nostalgia de la muerte" (Nostalgia for Death, 1938), further developed Villarutia's preoccupation with solitude and the desire for death. Some critics have speculated that his homosexuality, a well-known "secret," contributed to a melancholic disposition. Some of his finest poetry—and Villarutia's mastery of poetic form is uncontested—supports this contention as, for example, in the following *décima* (ten-line poem): "Yesterday I dreamed about you. Trembling / the two of us in the pleasure impure / and sterile of a dark dream. / And on your soft body / my lips went leaving / tracks, signs, wounds . . . / And your passing words / and my delirious ones / of those brief moments / prolonged our lives."

Less melancholic (at least as a poet), more sardonic, and openly homosexual, Villarutia's sometime roommate Salvador Novo wrote frankly about the devastating effects of alienation but with an ironic, reflexive sensibility that few of his colleagues could match. For example, in an "Elegy," a poetic form usually used to mourn the death of a friend, Novo writes disparagingly about his own physical appearance: "Those of us who have hands that don't belong to us, / grotesque for caresses, useless for the workshop or the shovel, / large and flaccid like a flower deprived of seed / or like a reptile that delivers up its poison / because it has nothing else to offer." Perhaps Novo's most important contribution to poetry was his ear for colloquial speech and the linguistic virtuosity—in the manner of English-American poet T. S. Elliot—to turn it into poetry. Even when Novo writes about death, he cannot resist the urge to fool around: "We've all gone on arriving at our tombs / in good time, at the proper hour, / in affordably priced ambulances / or maybe through natural and premeditated suicide. / And I can't continue sketching a perfect scenario / in which the moon would have an important role to play / because in these moments / there are trains covering all the earth / that throw out sad sighs / and leave / and the moon has nothing to do / with the brief fireflies that watch us / from a nearby and unknown blue / full of polyglot and innumerable stars."

Many critics of the time condemned the Contemporáneos as unpatriotic "reactionaries" for their cosmopolitan tastes, disinterest in nationalist art, and "decadent" (even homosexual) lifestyles. That was not case with the "new" generation of poets that formed around the literary journals, *Taller poético* (1936–1938) and *Taller* (1938–1941), in particular its two "stars," Octavio Paz (1914–1998) and Efraín Huerta (1914–1982). The *Taller* poets openly acknowledged their debt to the older generation, and indeed the poetic innovations of the modernists, Estridentistas, and especially the Contemporáneos found "mature" expression in their work. They also openly embraced the French surrealist movement and the socially engaged poetry of renowned Chilean poet, Pablo Neruda. Despite these acknowledgments,

most critics insisted that *Taller* poets had finally produced an authentically Mexican poetry that reflected national rather than international realities. The creative tension between cosmopolitan and national that had been so prominent in their predecessors, critics felt, had properly shifted in favor of the latter.

This shift is easiest to see in the poetry of Efraín Huerta with its intriguing combination of eroticism and political radicalism. This combination seemed to embody—as the work of the Contemporáneos had not—the manly Mexican spirit associated in the popular imagination with world-renowned muralist Diego Rivera or Revolutionary novelist Martín Luis Guzmán. Whether in odes to drunken girls who generously surrender their "melted hearts" or in sardonically nationalistic laments like "Juárez Avenue" that heaps calumny on "the beloved tourists 'brought by the wind', / the neurotic millionaires one hundred times divorced, / the gangsters and Miss Texas / [who] trample beauty, soil art, / who swallow up the Gettysburg Address and the poems of Walt Whitman, / the passport of Paul Robeson and the films of Charlie Chaplin, / and leave one thrown in the middle of the street / with eyes slashed. . . ." Huerta's poems seemed unquestionably, even self-consciously Mexican, despite the occasional lapse into marxist internationalism.

Octavio Paz—the most famous and revered Mexican poet since Sor Juana (whose biography he would write)—is harder to categorize. On one hand, as the grandson of a Revolutionary general and author of *Labyrinth of Solitude* (1950), a hugely influential set of essays on Mexican national identity, Paz's nationalist credentials were impeccable. On the other, his embrace of French surrealism and long diplomatic service suggested a cosmopolitan perspective reminiscent of the Contemporáneos. In poetic practice, Paz turned these contradictions to his advantage. His predecessors had exploited the creative tension between opposed forces: cosmopolitan and national, reality and illusion, love and death, solitude and solidarity. But it was Paz, more than any other poet (Mexican or otherwise), who located the "dialectical process" at the center of his poetic project. For Paz, the creative tension between opposing forces, while impossible to reconcile, could nevertheless be captured in the visionary (surrealistic) images generated by that tension. In the poem "Dawn," for example, he vividly portrays the eternal struggle between night and day from the momentary perspective of the waking sleeper-poet: "Rapid cold hands / Take off one by one / The bandages of the shadow / I open my eyes / Still / I am alive / In the center/Of a still fresh wound." Other poems like those in the collection, *Piedra del sol* (Sunstone, 1957), explore the dialectical tension inherent in linear versus circular perceptions of time. In *Piedra del sol,* the central image of an Aztec calendar stone allows the poet to ruminate about the intersection of mythical, historical, and personal perceptions of time and, by extension, the great theme of "solitude" that informs so much of twentieth-century Mexican poetry. For all its nationalist appeal, Paz's poetry brought him considerable international fame and the 1990 Nobel Prize for poetry. That external validation, in turn, put an end to accusations of literary elitism and excessive cosmopolitanism in Mexican poetry. Since Paz, poets have played a central role in the definition and production of national identity, even as their poetry has become far too diverse to permit facile classifications.

One constant has been the preoccupation with love, death, time, and solitude exemplified in the poetry of Paz's younger contemporaries: Ali Chamacero (1918–), Rubén Bonifaz Nuño (1923–), Jaime Sabines (1925–), and Marco Antonio Montes de Oca (1932–). Refracted through the poetry of these very different writers—all four noted for their mastery of poetic forms—these great "Mexican" themes would develop deeper and deeper layers of meaning, nuance, and imagery. There were even occasional glimmers of hope, of an end to soli-

tude, in their poetry. Bonifaz Nuño admitted that "I am writing so that everyone / can know where I live / in case someone wants to answer me." And Sabines acknowledged: "I don't know it for certain, but I suppose / that a woman and a man / some day will love each other." The biggest change in mainstream Mexican poetry after midcentury was the inclusion of women's voices in important literary journals. Inspired in part by Chilean poet Gabriela Mistral's frequent visits to Mexico (and her 1945 Nobel Prize for poetry), poets like Emma Godoy (1918–1989) and Guadalupe Amor (1920–), Margarita Michelena (1917–1998), and Margarita Paz Paredes (1922–1980) founded a women's literary journal, *Rueca* (Spinning Wheel, 1941–1946) to publish their work. According to Gabriel Zaid (mentioned below), "almost all [these women] began with a Catholic, literary, feminine militancy patterned after Sor Juana or Gabriela Mistral." That trajectory holds for the first woman accepted among the ranks of major twentieth-century Mexican poets: Rosario Castellanos (1925–1974), who managed the difficult trick of maintaining a feminine-feminist consciousness while still appealing to a broader audience that insisted on "universal" (rather than gender-specific) themes. In her poetry, Castellanos explores with great ambivalence, candor, and wit the personal side of race, class, and especially gender inequalities. Her most consistent theme—developed years before it became a central theme in European academic discourse—was the self's encounter with the other. In a poem from the collection *Poesía no eres tú* (You're Not Poetry, 1972), for example, Castellanos implies that only through that encounter can the self take on a sense of identity and purpose: "The other: mediator, judge, balance / between opposites, witness, / knot that binds up all that had broken / The other, muteness begging a voice / from the speaker, / claiming an ear / from the listener. / The other. With the other / humanity, dialogue, poetry begin."

With the advent of the turbulent 1960s, radical politics reemerged as a force within Mexican poetry just as it had in the 1930s with the Estridentistas. In the combative spirit of Huerta (who had kept the radical torch burning during the 1940s and 1950s while producing lively, un-propagandistic poetry), five young activist poets, including Juan Bañuelos (1932–), Eraclio Zepeda (1937–), and Jaime Labastida (1939–), published an important collection of "protest" poems, *La espiga amotinada* (The Mutinous Spike, 1960) in the first year of the new decade. It would be followed by a second collection, *Ocupación de la palabra* (Occupation of the Word, 1965), and by Bañuelos's influential *Espejo humeante* (Smoking Mirror, 1968), in which he blasted global inequities past and present including Hiroshima, U.S. racism, the Vietnam War, and the treatment of political prisoners (although without the crude didacticism of much Revolutionary poetry of the period).

After the 1968 government massacre of as many as 400 peaceful demonstrators at the Tlatelolco's Plaza of the Three Cultures in Mexico City, less radical poets also began to tackle political topics on a regular basis. For many, like Octavio Paz, who resigned his ambassadorship to India to protest the massacre, the weapon of choice was prose rather than poetry. Whatever the response, the specter of Tlatelolco would haunt Mexican poetry (and intellectual life in general) for decades after the event.

The pervasive sense of disillusion that followed the Tlatelolco Massacre would manifest itself in different ways—poetry, after all, is the most personal of literary genres—but most of those manifestations included a reflexive political awareness that shifted, sometimes rather abruptly, from deep cynicism to utopian longing even within a single poem. For example, the poetry of Isabel Fraire (1934–), celebrated for its exquisite images of natural beauty, also evinces despair over the futility of human endeavors as in the opening lines of the poem, "8 1/2": "it's not a question of making an effort and of going against / the current . . . / by which I don't *know* what I mean to say / by which I don't know / by which. . . ." For Gabriel Zaid (1934–), poetry captures the beauty and wonder of everyday life and thus serves as an antidote to the corruption and absurdity of politics (which he exposes relentlessly in his journalistic alter ego). An early poem, "Acata la hemosura (Revere Beauty)" provides a simple and elegant manifesto: "Revere beauty / and yield to it / hard heart. / Revere truth / and harden it / against the tide. / Or let it go, perhaps, / like the Spirit / faithful over the waters." In a similar, but less lighthearted vein, poetry serves novelist José Emilio Pacheco (1939–) as an agent of change that can help overcome pessimism and despair. In much of his poetry, Pacheco engages with contemporary political, social, and environmental issues in order to affirm the power of the poetic vision to transcend the twentieth century's vicious cycles of destruction, as in his poem about Tlatelolco, "1968": "A world comes apart / a world is born / the darkness draws near / but the light flares up / everything is broken and brought down / and everything shines / . . . / there's no hope / there's life and / everything is ours." Fellow novelist Homero Aridjis (1940–) also brings political concerns to his poetry. (Among other things, he is Mexico's best-known environmental advocate). Sometimes characterized as a neoromantic, Aridjis blurs the boundaries between love's transformative power in interpersonal relations (as in traditional romantic poetry) and the possibilities it raises for social justice and environmental responsibility. This tendency has been central to his poetry from the start. A poem from the early 1960s begins: "And all the things that my love contemplated / the sound and the rain—the parks and the image / appeared in her."

Any attempt to characterize recent Mexican poetry or canonize a new generation of poets is still premature. By the 1970s, Gabriel Zaid's efforts to produce two anthologies of

Mexican poetry—*Omnibus de poesía mexicana* (1971) and *Asamblea de poetas jóvenes de Mexico* (1980)—convinced him that "there was a profusion of young poets: the dynastic succession was experiencing a population explosion." The problem was not just numbers, he added, the superb quality of much of the new poetry made any choice arbitrary. The situation has only gotten "worse" since 1980.

General trends, however, can be discerned. The most obvious is a neotraditionalist poetry that emphasizes careful crafting and linguistic subtlety over innovation for its own sake. In this vein, poets like David Huerta (1949–), Efraín Bartolomé (1950–), and Juan Domingo Argüelles (1958–) produce poems that continue to address "timeless" themes (sometimes using traditional forms) in ways that often disguise the authors' considerable originality. Argüelles has insisted that "poetry that doesn't contain emotion is destined to oblivion." More sensitive to their historical roots than most, the neotraditionalists have no intention of courting oblivion by catering to the latest poetic fads or pursuing a politics of rupture and confrontation.

Another trend breaks with tradition and adapts instead a "postmodern" critique of modernity and its twin myths of "order and progress." For example, in *El pobrecito Señor X* (Poor Mister X, 1980), Ricardo Castillo (1954–) assesses the damage wrought by these myths with the observation that "Man took a luminous slope that led to Chaos / And Chaos breathed hard on the ruins of man," and, less portentously, in "Oda a las ganas" (Ode to Desire) with irreverent verses like "Peeing is the greatest engineering feat / at least as far as drainage goes. / Besides, peeing is a pleasure . . . ," a poke perhaps at the great drainage projects that enabled Mexico City "developers" to cram nearly 20 million people onto an old lake bed at the expense of the residents' mental and physical health.

Yet another trend in contemporary Mexican poetry is the multiplication and increased sophistication of women's voices. From the neomedieval mysticism of Elsa Cross (1946–) with its subtle manipulation of traditional poetic forms to the postfeminist irony of poet-novelist Carmen Boullosa (1954–) with her teasing "Letter to the Wolf"—She signs off: "Recognizing myself a prisoner / and convinced that there's no greater glory than the neck / of a virgin offering itself up to you, / nor greater goodness than that registered in your painful, /slow, / interminable / and cruel / loving attack, / I close this letter /Sincerely yours, / Carmen"—these poets have challenged conventional and typically condescending notions of women's poetry. To be sure, there's still a recognizable women's poetry in Mexico but its boundaries are no longer as obvious as they once were and it secondary status in high literary circles is a relic of distant past.

The most radical new development, however, might be the decentralization of Mexican poetry, as cultural production expands out of Mexico City to border cities like Tijuana and to Mexican communities in the United States. Performance artist Guillermo Gómez Peña, a former resident of Mexico City who moved first to Tijuana and then to the United States, expresses the new positioning in linguistic terms in his "Border Brujo": "I speak Spanish therefore you hate me / I speak in English therefore they hate me / . . . I speak in tongues therefore you desire me." As Gómez Peña's paradox suggests, the impact of these new cultural centers on Mexican poetry—especially as the border population swells and the United States becomes one of the largest Spanish-speaking countries in the world—is likely to disturb and enrich a well-established and thriving literary genre. Certainly, the great twentieth-century debate over poetic cosmopolitanism versus nationalism, far from disappearing, seems likely to heat up again in the near future.

—*RMB*

See also: Castellanos, Rosario; Intellectuals; Paz, Octavio; Theater; Tlatelolco Massacre; Vasconcelos, José.

References:

Acosta, Juvenal. *Light from a Nearby Window: Contemporary Mexican Poetry.* San Francisco, CA: City Lights Books, 1993.

Dauster, Frank. *The Double Strand: Five Contemporary Mexican Poets.* Lexington: University of Kentucky Press, 1987.

Gander, Forrest, ed. *Mouth to Mouth: Poems by Twelve Contemporary Mexican Women.* Trans. Zoe Anglesley et al. Minneapolis, MN: Milkweek Editions, 1993.

García, Adriana. "Twentieth Century Poetry," in David William Foster, ed., *Mexican Literature: A History,* pp. 171–212. Austin: University of Texas Press, 1994.

Hoeksema, Thomas, ed. *The Fertile Rhythms: Contemporary Women Poets of Mexico.* Trans. Thomas Hoeksema and Romelia Enríquez. Pittsburgh, PA: Latin American Literary Review Press, 1989.

Paz, Octavio. *Anthology of Mexican Poetry.* Trans. Samuel Beckett. Bloomington: Indiana University Press, 1958.

Paz, Octavio, ed. *New Poetry of Mexico.* New York: Dutton, 1970.

Poniatowska, Elena (1933–)

Born in Paris, raised in southern France, educated in the United States, Elena Poniatowska is probably the most cosmopolitan of Mexico's great contemporary writers. But, as with her artistic counterpart Frida Kahlo (also of mixed parentage and culture), Poniatowska's grand obsession with Mexico and Mexicans shines through all her work. Moreover, her extraordinary gift for capturing the voices of everyday people in a variety of genres—interviews, news reports, journalistic collages, testimonial novels—has made her a prominent figure in the country's intellectual and political life. Indeed, when she took time out from writing to help fellow Mexico City residents dig out from the devastating 1985 earthquake, Carlos Monsiváis, Mexico's renowned cultural critic and a great journalist in his own right, chided her with: "What is the best chronicler of Mexico doing sitting in her home? Start writing" (quoted in García, "Elena Poniatowska: Search for the Voiceless," p. 246). At the turn of the twentieth century, she shows no sign of stopping.

Although much praised for her carefully nuanced renderings of Mexican Spanish, Elena Poniatowska's first language was French and her formative years were spent in France. Poniatowska was born in Paris on 19 May 1933. Her father—scion of a Polish émigré family with aristocratic ties—and her mother—the daughter of Mexican landed gentry—had been born and raised in France as well. In 1942, Elena's mother moved to Mexico with her two daughters to escape the disruptions of World War II. (Her father stayed to fight and rejoined his family seven years later.) In Mexico, the nine-year-old Elena "absorbed Mexico through the maids, following them around as they made the beds and mopped the floors, listening to their chatter as they prepared the hot tortillas" (quoted in García, "Elena Poniatowska: Search for the Voiceless," p. 237). This informal grounding in Mexican language and culture would prove an important counterweight to her formal schooling in French and English schools in Mexico and at the Sacred Heart Convent in Philadelphia. It would also inspire her best work.

Helped by family connections and a cosmopolitan (if sketchy) education, Poniatowska began her career as an interviewer for a Mexico City newspaper, *El Excelsior* (she later moved to *Novedades*). Hard work and interviews with prominent figures like Diego Rivera, Lázaro Cárdenas, Luis Buñuel, and Fidel Castro quickly made hers a recognized voice in Mexico City's vibrant cultural life.

Natural inclination and a brief stint with American anthropologist Oscar Lewis, renowned for his oral histories of everyday Mexicans, inspired Poniatowska to shift her attentions from the glamorous world of the Mexico City literati to "ordinary" people. This shift resulted in her most important fictional work, *Hasta no verte Jesús mío* (Here's to You, Jesusa, 1969), the barely fictionalized story of a Mexico City laundrywoman, Jesusa Palancares, whose remarkable life spanned the Mexican Revolution and the dramatic changes that followed. Told in Jesusa's voice

Portuguese Nobel laureate author Jose Saramago (left) and Mexican writer Elena Poniatowska attend a cultural rally in Mexico City, 12 March 2001. (Reuters / Corbis)

and in the colorful, informal language of Mexico City's working class, *Hasta no verte Jesús mío* made Poniatowska's reputation, won the prestigious 1970 *Mazatlán* prize for literature, and established her as a powerful advocate for those excluded from the post–World War II Mexican economic "miracle." Of her controversial borrowing of another woman's voice, Poniatowska acknowledged that "It fills one with anxiety, with insecurity. One handles very fragile material, people's hearts; their names which are their honor; their work; and their time" (quoted in Jörgensen, *Elena Poniatowska: Engaging Dialogues,* p. 62). Poniatowska's gift for everyday language and her commitment to providing a voice for ordinary people resulted in powerful chronicles of two seminal events in modern Mexican history: the 1968 massacre of student (and other) demonstrators at Tlatelolco by the Federal Army and the 1985 earthquake that destroyed several downtown Mexico City neighborhoods. In both *La noche de Tlatelolco*

(The Night of Tlatelolco, 1971) and *Todo México* (All Mexico, 1990), she reconstructs the events through eyewitness accounts that document the tragedies, failures, and quiet heroism of everyday people. Both chronicles also expose the distortions behind the official stories and reveal the corruption, cruelty, and ineptitude of Mexico's Institutional Revolutionary Party (PRI). The Tlatelolco Massacre and the government's bungled earthquake response played key roles in undermining the legitimacy of the PRI and thus encouraging a gradual move toward democracy in Mexico; Poniatowska's works were instrumental in that process. Nor has her commitment to social justice wavered; she was one of the first to publicly protest the February 2000 arrest of students that ended the nine-month student strike at the National University (UNAM).

An avowed feminist, Poniatowska has also shown considerable interest in the plight of women. Sometimes, as in *Hasta no verte Jesús mío,* her protagonists are working-class women struggling to survive and construct meaningful lives on the margins of Mexican society. Two important quasi-biographical works, *Querido Diego te abraza Quiela* (Dear Diego Affectionately Quiela, 1978) and *Tinísima* (1992), however, focus on women as artists and lovers of artists. In *Querido Diego,* Russian painter Angelina Beloff, writes to her former lover Diego Rivera, the father of her son, about their life together. *Tinísima* celebrates the life of Italian born photographer, Tina Medotti, mistress of North American photographer Edward Weston, and her politically inspired wanderings through Mexico, Europe, and the Soviet Union in support of social liberation. In both works, women's difficulties in reconciling art and personal relationships takes center stage. "Women don't ask," Poniatowska argues, "and if we do it's in a voiced so low, with such timidity . . . that our own attitude invalidates the worth of our request" (quoted in García Pinto, *Historias íntimas,* p. 196). To encourage women to speak out, she started a literary workshop that publishes the works of ordinary women. In a show of feminist solidarity, she has lauded the works of her competitors. "I am sure," she insists, "that everyone knows that if one of us triumphs, the triumph is everyone's because of the possibility that it will open more bigger doors for all" (quoted in García Pinto, *Historias íntimas,* p. 198).

—*RMB*

See also: Cárdenas, Lázaro; Kahlo, Frida; Monsiváis, Carlos; Partido Revolucionario Institucional (PRI); Rivera, Diego; Tlatelolco Massacre.

References:
García, Kay S. "Elena Poniatowska: Search for the Voiceless," in Marjorie Agosín, ed., *A Dream of Light and Shadow: Portraits of Latin American Women Writers.* Albuquerque: University of New Mexico Press, 1995.
García Pinto, Magdalena. *Historias íntimas: conversaciones con diez escritoras latinoamericanas.* Hanover, NH: Ediciones del Norte, 1988.
Jörgensen, Beth E. *Elena Poniatowska: Engaging Dialogues.* Austin: University of Texas Press, 1994.

Popular Music

Mexican popular music can be divided into two general categories: "traditional" music—folk music and dance, *corridos, mariachi, norteña,* etc.—with strong historical roots in national culture, and "modern" music—*bolero* and *danzón,* rock and roll, pop music, etc.—whose primarily foreign origins mark its transnational, contemporary quality. But while these categories are useful for the purposes of classification, marketing, and self-image, things are not that really that simple. The mixed origins of traditional music make mockery of any attempt to establish its authenticity, especially when much of its purportedly historical character comes from modern institutions like 1940s *charro* (singing cowboy) films and the internationally acclaimed Ballet Folklórico (founded in 1952). At the same time, nostalgia has transformed "modern" music like composer Agustín Lara's *boleros* or 1930s *danzón* into potent symbols of a glamorous past.

Folk music and dance do indeed have deeps roots in Mexican history and culture. Any respectable survey must catalogue hundreds of regional variations of different genres with influences ranging from Afro-Caribbean in the west, to indigenous in the south, to European in the north, to Spanish colonial in the center—a process further complicated by a long history of cultural transfers among those regions. During the nineteenth century, these folk traditions were used to mark regional differences and to entertain tourists. In the late nineteenth and early twentieth centuries, as policymakers struggled to construct a coherent national culture, some of these different regional songs and dances were integrated into popular *cancioneros* (songbooks) to produce a standardized repertory of "Mexican" music. This national canon included everything from the national anthem to the Revolutionary favorite "La Adelita" to the traditional *jarabe* with its animal sounds and colorful dance routines. These songs and dances became a vital part of every Mexican schoolchild's civic education and thus an important component of national consciousness.

After the Revolution of 1910, the national government took the lead by promoting these manifestations of *mexicanidad* (mexican-ness) in the public school curriculum and by encouraging commercial radio stations like Mexico City's super-station XEW to broadcast programs of *música típica* (typical music). In addition to entertainment, these school and radio programs served an ideological function. By acknowledging and even emphasizing regional differences while at the same time stressing a common *mexicanidad,* they provided a multicultural model for the new, more inclusive nation that post-Revolutionary policymakers aspired to create from the fragmented "many Mexicos" of the past. Musicologists supported this nationalization of regional music by insisting on a common origin, the *son* (literally "sound"), from which most folk music was thought to have originated—an origin that prefigured and thus naturalized the nation-state that was to come. The culmination of these efforts occurred in 1952 with the creation of the Ballet Folklórico, which joined together *bailes típicos* (typical dances) like the picturesque colonial-era "Mexican Hat Dance" and colorful Aztec stomps as pieces of an "invented" national tradition that has visually and aurally represented Mexican culture for Mexican and international audiences ever since.

Included within the *música típica* tradition but forming an important category in its own right is the *corrido,* a narrative ballad that usually commemorates some event of local, national, or even international importance. Some scholars trace the *corrido* back to the medieval Spanish *romance,* but the first identifiable *corridos* appeared in the 1860s and 1870s. Although often performed with just guitar accompaniment, the *corrido* is also well suited to small ensembles. The *corrido* ensemble varies by region: guitar, accordion, electric bass, and sometimes drums are common in the north; while mariachi orchestras with *guitarrón,* violins, trumpets, and sometimes harp are more common farther south. The key to the *corrido*'s popularity is its unique status as a living ballad tradition through which stories of heroism and betrayal are mythologized and disseminated—orally by itinerant musicians, in published broadsheets at the turn of the century (often illustrated with dramatic prints artists like José Guadalupe Posada), or more recently on records, cassettes, compact discs, and even in music videos. In the past, *corrido* subjects included famous bandits like Chucho el Roto, border conflicts like the riveting story of Gregorio Cortéz who shot a Texas sheriff in self-defense, and Revolutionary icons like Siete Leguas, Pancho Villa's famous horse. In the years following the Revolution, *corridos* came to represent the "authentic" voice of the Mexican people with influential public figures like artists Diego Rivera and Frida Kahlo holding regular *corrido* evenings to celebrate this vital part of the nation's popular culture. Rivera even incorporated *corrido* lyrics into his famous murals for the Secretariat of Education building. As practitioners of a living tradition, *corrido* singers have also tackled more contemporary events like the 1963 assassination of president Kennedy and the 1995 debt crisis. Most recently, a new subgenre, the *nacrocorrido,* has emerged, thanks in no small part to compelling music videos with flashy pickup trucks, scowling gangsters, and sexy women; and songs like Los Tigres del Norte's "Contrabanda y traición" (Contraband and Betrayal, 1972) have already become *narcocorrido* classics.

More a musical style than a specific genre, mariachi has come to represent Mexican music to the rest of the world. Beginning as a *son* ensemble—guitars, *guitarrón* (bass guitar), violins, trumpet, and diatonic harp—in the northwestern state of Jalisco, the music of classic mariachi bands like Mariachi Vargas featured the poignant *canciones rancheras* (ranch songs) with their intense nostalgia for the simpler rural life of the northern ranches and haciendas (large estates)—a compelling

Ballet Folklórico performers (Lindsay Hebberd / Corbis)

message in a rapid modernizing, increasingly urban society. As early as 1898, Mariachi Vargas had relocated to Mexico City to become the toast of high society during the last years of Porfirio Díaz's presidency (1876–1880, 1884–1911). Post-Revolutionary governments continued to regard the group as the guardians of traditional Mexican musical values, and they were invited to play at President Lázaro Cárdenas's inauguration in 1934. Regardless of this early popularity, the widespread acceptance of mariachi as *the* national style resulted from the mid–twentieth-century craze for *charro* films that began with the 1936 classic *Allá en el rancho grande,* whose title song quickly entered the national canon. Star performers like Lucha Reyes (1908–1944), Jorge Negrete (1911–1953), Pedro Infante (1917–1957), Lola Beltrán (1932–1996), José Alfredo Jiménez (1926–1973), Vicente Fernández (1940–), and Juan Gabriel (1950–) have kept it in the limelight ever since. So have the many mariachi groups

that congregate every night in Mexico City's celebrated Garibaldi Square or in countless restaurants and plazas throughout Mexico (and the southwestern United States) to play for aficionados, diners, and tourists.

As a cultural form, mariachi has tended to reflect "traditional" patriarchal notions of patriotism, male valor, and female virtue despite the prominence of strong female performers like Reyes, Beltrán, and Las Coronelas (The Colonels), a popular 1940s all-female mariachi group. Songs like Jorge Negrete's classic version of "Yo soy mexicano" (I'm a Mexican) or Pedro Infante's breezy "Ni por favor" (No thank you) with its cavalier: "If you don't love me, so what, of love I will not die" have come to define the stereotypical macho Mexican male. Since these men were also prominent celebrities, racy stories about their womanizing and the tragedy of their untimely deaths contributed to a masculine ideal of sexual prowess and reckless daring. The fanfare and riots that accompanied Infante's 1957 public funeral give some indication of the cultural power of this macho nationalism. Sometimes, however, the macho stereotype has verged on caricature as when José Alfredo Jiménez's "La Rey" (The King) sings to the women who has abandoned him: "I know I'm on the outside now, but on the day that I die, I know you will have to cry (and cry and cry)"; or on farce as when the notoriously effeminate (if brilliant) Juan Gabriel dresses up like a poor *campesino* (peasant) and sings about "The Mexico That's Gone Forever."

Norteña music from the border region of northern Mexico and the southwestern United States is a more upbeat version of the classic mariachi style. Inspired in part by the dance music of nineteenth-century German settlers, the standard *norteña* ensemble includes a guitar, a *bajo sexto* (twelve-string guitar), and the button accordion usually played in the polka-style pioneered by Narciso Martínez (1911–1992) in the 1930s. By the 1950s, innovators like Tony de la Rosa (1931–) and the Conjunto Bernal had expanded these ensembles into larger, more musically sophisticated *conjuntos* (groups). Modern *norteña* groups tend to be either resolutely traditional, like Los Tigres del Norte, or openly pop, like "Selena" Quintanilla Perez (1971–1995), who has become something of a legend since her 1995 murder by her fan club president. Somewhere in between these extremes is *banda,* the music and dance craze of the 1990s, with its peculiar combination of traditional Mexican town band instruments like the tuba and the perky "bubble gum" style of *norteña* pop.

Mexican popular music had always been open to outside influences, especially from Europe and the Caribbean, but most of these influences were incorporated gradually into preexisting forms and styles. By the early twentieth century, however, new recording and radio technology combined with modern transportation systems, urbanization, and an expanding consumer culture, had created the conditions for a massive invasion of the latest Afro-Caribbean music and dances brought by traveling Cuban variety shows, or *Bufos Habaneros.* The coastal cities of Vera Cruz and Mérida (via Progreso) became musical centers for Afro-Caribbean music and dance, but they spread quickly to Mexico City, where popular dance halls like Salón México served to introduce Mexican men and women of all classes to the latest imported dances, like *danzón,* fox-trot, rumba, tango, mambo, cha-cha, and eventually salsa. These dance halls, then, became important sites for the performance of new identities, especially for lower-class Mexican men and women who, by shedding their traditional garb, changing their hairstyles, and engaging in public intimacy, marked their emergence as "modern" subjects and thus full-fledged citizens in a rapidly (if unevenly) modernizing society. Elite policymakers, however, linked these same dance halls to a broad spectrum of social ills including drinking, gambling, prostitution, and violence, which they contrasted with the more "wholesome" and uniquely Mexican mariachi style.

An extraordinarily popular new song genre, the *bolero,* also presented a more problematic version of *mexicanidad.* Inspired by Afro-Carribbean music and dance forms but developed in Mexico, *boleros* were urban melodramas of hopeless love and cruel betrayal set in the glamorous urban underworld of cabarets and dance halls. The undisputed king of the *bolero* was singer-songwriter Agustín Lara (1887–1970). Lara's songs about fallen women—"Santa," "Imposible," "Adventurera"—and betrayal—"Arrancame la vida" (Tear out my life), "Pervertida," "Piensa en mí" (Think of me)—exalted the seedy side of a Mexican modernity in which women were forced to sell their bodies to survive in a heartless world or abused their new freedom by heartlessly abandoning men. The prolific Lara not only wrote over 400 songs in nearly every popular song genre from tango to waltz to *canción ranchera* to *bolero,* he was also a radio and film star, and a national icon every bit as popular as Pedro Infante. At the same time, his notorious reputation as former bordello entertainer with four tempestuous marriages (in Roman Catholic Mexico), although crucial to his public persona, provided a dubious example of Mexican manhood. And if female interpreters like Vera Cruz's beloved, Toña La Negra (1912–1982), managed to subvert the *bolero*'s macho message, even a woman's perspective failed to blunt its "pathological" appeal and negative connotations. Thus, when social reformers condemned the insidious effects of popular culture, it was the "foreign" *bolero* rather than the "native" *canción ranchera* that they usually targeted. In recent years, however, *danzón* and *bolero* have become the focus of intense nostalgia for the moment when Mexicans first became modern (while still remaining culturally Mexican). Director María Novaro's acclaimed film, *Danzón,* for example, weaves *danzón* and *bolero* into a touching story of a telephone operator's journey of self-discovery (from Mexico City to Vera Cruz) with a hotel manager who sings along to Toña La Negra records and a transvestite nightclub performer who sings Agustín Lara's "Piensa en mí" while serving breakfast.

In the 1980s and 1990s, pop singers like Juan Gabriel and Luis Miguel (1970–) cleaned up the *bolero* tradition with a "new" genre, the *balada rómantica* (romantic ballad) and become international stars in the process. Juan Gabriel burst on the scene in the 1970s with an accessible style and remarkable gift for crafting songs in nearly every genre from *canción ranchera* to *bolero* to rock to *balada rómantica*. Gabriel's love songs have been recorded by nearly every major artist singing in Spanish and his *canciones rancheras* are among the most requested numbers in mariachi repertoire. More recently, Luis Miguel has been garnering international attention with global tours, a Frank Sinatra duet, and four Grammy awards. His youthful

Recording artists Paulina Rubio (L) and Thalia pose for photographs following the Latin Grammy Awards nominations show in Miami, 17 July 2001. (Reuters/Corbis)

good looks and tender love songs—from albums with titles like *Romance, Nada es igual* (Nothing's the Same), and *Amarte es un placer* (Loving You Is a Pleasure)—have transformed Lara's controversial legacy into a wholesome and marketable pop commodity.

Not all pop music performers have taken a conservative approach. Eugenia León, for example, uses the popular music tradition for political critique as in her remake of the traditional ballad "La paloma," which openly criticizes NAFTA (North American Free Trade Agreement) and American cultural imperialism. Less political but more outrageous is 1990s pop phenomenon, Gloria Trevi (1970–), whose records, films, and pinup calendars shocked conservative Mexicans. Cultural critic Carlos Monsiváis described her as "the serpent in the Garden of Eden dressed in a thong" for her on- and off-stage antics—antics that ran the gamut from undressing and whipping men during her performances to a real-life abduction scandal involving the sexual enslavement of teenage girls by her manager and companion. As Mexico struggled during the mid-1990s with endless political scandals (including several assassinations) and a grave economic crisis, Trevi's rebellious attitude seemed to capture the spirit of the age. During one performance, she confessed to her audience: "They want me to see a psychiatrist, but I'm not crazy. I'm just exasperated!"

—*RMB*

See also: Cinema from 1930 to 1960: The Golden Age; Cinema after 1960: Contemporary Mexican Film; Radio; Rivera, Diego; Rock and Roll.

References:
Burr, Ramiro. *The Billboard Guide to Tejano and Regional Mexican Music.* New York: Billboard Books, 1999.
Hernández, Mark. "Remaking the Corrido for the 1990s: Maldita Vecindad's El Barzón." *Studies in Latin American Popular Culture* 20 (2001): pp. 101–117.
Pedelty, Mark. "The Bolero: The Birth, Life, and Decline of Mexican Modernity." *Latin American Music Review* 20 (1999).
Rubenstein, Anne. "Bodies, Cities, Cinema: Pedro Infante's Death as Political Spectacle," in Gilbert Joseph, Anne Rubenstein, and Eric Zolov, eds., *Fragments of a Golden Age: The Politics of Culture in Mexico since 1940,* pp. 199–233. Durham, NC: Duke University Press, 2001.
———. "Mass Media and Popular Culture in the Postrevolutionary Era," in Michael C. Meyer and William H. Beezley, eds., *The Oxford History of Mexico,* pp. 637–670. New York: Oxford University Press, 2000.
Wald, Elijah. *Narcocorrido: A Journey into the Music of Drugs, Gun, and Guerrillas.* New York: Rayo, 2001.
Zolov, Eric. "Discovering a Land 'Mysterious and Obvious': The Renarrativizing of Postrevolutionary Mexico," in Gilbert Joseph, Anne Rubenstein, and Eric Zolov, eds., *Fragments of a Golden Age: The Politics of Culture in Mexico since 1940,* pp. 234–272. Durham, NC: Duke University Press, 2001.

Portes Gil, Emilio (1890–1978)

President from December 1928 to February 1930, Emilio Portes Gil was born in the northeastern border state of Tamaulipas in 1890. Portes Gil received his primary and secondary education at schools in Ciudad Victoria, Tamaulipas, and became a schoolteacher in 1910. He did not participate in the overthrow of the old regime of Porfirio Díaz, but the downfall of the elderly dictator encouraged Portes Gil to become involved in local politics. In 1912 he moved to Mexico City to study law, receiving his degree in 1915. Portes Gil also served in legal and administrative capacities for the Constitutionalist Department of the War and Navy, bringing him into contact with future Presidents Alvaro Obregón and Plutarco Elías Calles. In 1916 Portes Gil was elected to the first of three terms as a member of the national Congress, aided by his careful cultivation of labor support. In 1920 Portes Gil came out in favor of the Revolutionary Plan of Agua Prieta put forward by the Sonorans Plutarco Elías Calles and Adolfo de la Huerta on behalf of the presidential aspirations of General Alvaro Obregón. The triumph of the Revolutionaries led to a brief period as provisional governor of Tamaulipas for Portes Gil.

President Emilio Portes Gil, at the left, as he listens to the reading of the proclamation giving the land to the peasants at an Agrarian Community in the State of Hidalgo, 1929. (Bettmann/Corbis)

Portes Gil served in the national Congress in the early 1920s, supporting Calles in the struggle over a successor for Obregón in 1923–1924. Portes Gil was elected governor of Tamaulipas in 1925, aided primarily by strong support from labor. As governor, he continued to promote the interests of labor, preventing the corrupt national labor confederation, the CROM, from gaining control over independent local labor organizations. Portes Gil was also an enthusiastic supporter of agrarian reform. He brought labor and peasant groups together in a political party, the Partido Socialista Fronterizo (Border Socialist Party), which provided a powerful state base for him.

After the assassination of President-elect Alvaro Obregón in July 1928, outgoing President Calles appointed Portes Gil to the key cabinet position of minister of the interior (internal security). There was fierce competition over who would serve in place of the assassinated president-elect. Calles declined suggestions that he continue in office, a move which might provoke major political upheaval. There was a bumper crop of generals who wanted to be president, which virtually guaranteed that selecting a general would lead to revolts by disappointed generals. Calles opted for a civilian, Portes Gil. Under the Constitution, Congress was to elect a provisional president until new elections could be held to select someone to serve out Obregón's term (1928–1934). On 25 September 1928, the Congress unanimously elected Portes Gil to serve as provisional president. New presidential elections were to be held on 20 November 1929, with the new president to take office on 5 February 1930.

Portes Gil labored under three political liabilities as president. First, he was a provisional president who would be serving a brief term (1 December 1928 to 5 February 1930). Second, the political presence of Calles—the "Maximum Leader of the Revolution"—had to be taken into account on all major issues. Third, there was a widespread sentiment among the generals that only generals were fit to be president. This last problem soon showed itself in the rebellion of March 1929 by General José Gonzalo Escobar, one of the generals frequently mentioned as a presidential possibility. Although the rebellion was quickly crushed, with Escobar going into exile, the revolt was a clear indication that the generals were reluctant to give up their control of the National Palace.

In his inaugural address, Portes Gil indicated that he wanted to do more than merely preside over new elections for president; as provisional president he pursued much the same policies he had as governor of Tamaulipas. He accelerated the distribution of land, even though Calles thought it would be best to slow down the process. Portes Gil reduced government support for the national labor organization, the CROM, just as he had fought it at the state level. He also tried unsuccessfully to gain congressional approval for a bill implementing the prolabor provisions of the Constitution of 1917. Portes Gil also helped to conclude the Cristero Rebellion, which had broken out in 1927 as a result of the strong anticlerical measures enforced by Calles; the settlement represented a victory for the government. The fighting mostly ended, and the Roman Catholic Church agreed to abide by the constitutional restrictions imposed on its activities. In early 1929 Portes Gil also played an important role in the establishment of the new official party, the Partido Nacional Revolucionario (the National Revolutionary Party, or PNR). Following a practice he had used with the Partido Socialista Fronterizo in Tamaulipas, President Portes Gil decreed that the PNR would be financed through deductions from the wages of federal employees.

The campaign leading up to presidential elections in November 1929 was marred by violence, and the election itself produced numerous charges of irregularities. The official election results certified by the Congress gave 94 percent of the vote to the candidate of the PNR, General Pascual Ortiz Rubio. The principal opposition candidate, the civilian José Vasconcelos, declared the election results invalid and then went into exile in the United States. Even the transfer of power on 5 February 1930 produced violence. After the inaugural ceremonies, President Ortiz Rubio was shot and wounded by a would-be assassin. Political opponents accused Portes Gil of being involved in the assassination, a charge which Portes Gil—and Ortiz Rubio—denied.

Portes Gil's exit from the presidency was not the end of his political career. He served under Ortiz Rubio as minister of the interior and as president of the PNR. He was forced out as head of the PNR when Calles became concerned that Portes Gil was using the position to establish his own power base; Calles also blocked Portes Gil's efforts to return to the governorship of Tamaulipas in 1932. Despite these setbacks, he became attorney general in the cabinet of President Abelardo Rodríguez from 1932 to 1934. Under President Lázaro Cárdenas (1934–1940), Portes Gil held the prestigious position of minister of foreign relations (1934–1935) and also president of the PNR (1935–1936). Portes Gil was increasingly uneasy with the radicalism of the Cárdenas administration just as Cárdenas was becoming increasingly uneasy about the personal political ambitions of Portes Gil. In 1936 Portes Gil retired to private life for almost a decade. He returned to public life in the 1940s as a diplomat, serving as ambassador to the Dominican Republic, Ecuador, and India. Author of a number of works dealing with political and historical themes, Portes Gil died on 10 December 1978.

—DMC

See also: Assassinations; Calles, Plutarco Elías; Cárdenas, Lázaro; Confederación Regional

Obrera Mexicana (CROM); Cristero Rebellion; Morones, Luis; Morrow, Dwight; Obregón, Alvaro; Partido Revolucionario Institucional (PRI); Presidents of the Twentieth Century; Tamaulipas; Vasconcelos, José.

References:

Dulles, John W. F. *Yesterday in Mexico: A Chronicle of the Revolution, 1919–1936.* Austin: University of Texas Press, 1972.

Meyer, Lorenzo. *Historia de la Revolución Mexicana.* Vol. 13. *El conflicto social y los gobiernos del Maximato.* Mexico: El Colegio de Mexico, 1978.

Meyer, Lorenzo, Rafael Segovia, and Alejandra Lajous. *Historia de la Revolución Mexicana.* Vol. 12. *Los inicios de la institucionalización: la política del Maximato.* Mexico: El Colegio de Mexico, 1978.

Posada, José Guadalupe (1852–1913)

José Guadalupe Posada's images, especially his skeletal *calaveras,* have become perhaps the best-known example of Mexico's rich popular culture and an inspiration to generations of Mexican (and Mexican American) artists eager to develop a distinctive national style. Despite his current fame as a graphic artist, during his lifetime Posada's artistic reputation was slight. Academic artists and art critics steeped in European traditions and techniques considered his prints—most produced for penny broadsides and popular newspapers—to be crude, ephemeral, even scandalous. A moderately successful Mexico City artisan, Posada died in relative obscurity just a few weeks before the assassination of President Francisco Madero plunged Mexico back into revolution. In 1920, Posada was rediscovered by a French artist, Jean Charlot, who brought his work to the attention of renowned muralists Diego Rivera and José Clemente Orozco. Prompted by Charlot's interest, both men recalled visiting the engraver in his workshop when they were children (most historians doubt Rivera's account) and promptly claimed Posada as their most important predecessor, a truly Mexican genius untainted by the compulsion to imitate European art. One of Rivera's greatest murals, *Dream of Sunday Afternoon in the Central Alameda,* publicly acknowledged the debt; at the mural's center, Posada's *Calavera Catrina* takes her husband-creator's arm with one hand while she holds the child-Rivera's hand with the other. The muralists' enthusiastic endorsement and the undeniable power of Posada's vibrant images have guaranteed him a prominent place in the history of modern Mexican art. The artistic and commercial uses of his famous *calaveras* have spread his artistic vision far beyond the confines of his modest Mexico City workshop.

José Guadalupe Posada was born in 1852 in Aguascalientes, a provincial city of about 20,000 people in north-central Mexico. His father was a baker and family resources were scarce. At sixteen, having exhibited some skill at drawing, Posada became an apprentice in a commercial lithography shop that produced everything from magazine advertisements and party invitations to political cartoons. His budding gift for graphic satire may have aggravated local politicians because, in 1872, Posada relocated to nearby León where, for sixteen years, he ran a commercial lithography shop of his own. During these years, he married, had a son, and taught lithography at a vocational high school. In 1888, Posada moved his lithographic press to Mexico City. There he found his true artistic vocation as an illustrator for broadsheet publisher Antonio Vanegas Arroyo and the capital city's lively penny press. The Vanegas Arroyo broadsheets were colorfully dyed, single pages with an illustration, often by Posada, at the top and explanatory text at the bottom. The subject matter varied widely—oddities of nature, bullfights, religious images, sensational crimes, bandit escapades, executions, political commentary, and battles (especially during the Revolutionary years)—anything the publisher thought would sell. While the broadsides served primarily as mini-tabloids, the penny press specialized in political and social satire. Intended for a working-class audience that bore the brunt of Porfirio Díaz's

This print by José Posada shows a fierce calavera brandishing knife, and a crowd of calaveras behind him. (Library of Congress)

obsession with order, it mocked corrupt politicians, Yankee interlopers, exploitive capitalists, upper-class pretensions, and ignorant policemen. Some sources suggest that Posada may have spent time in jail when his satire crossed the line into overt criticism of the Díaz regime. (Under Díaz, Mexico City journalists were jailed often enough to form an "Incarcerated Journalists Club.") For the most part, however, Posada seemed to have known just how far he could go without inciting the authorities. Nevertheless, the constant barrage of satire from Posada and others helped undermine the legitimacy of Díaz's rule. Certainly, radical artists like Rivera and Orozco considered him the most important precursor of their artistic revolution—a crucial link between the elite art world in which they received their training and the popular culture of the Mexican working class that they hoped to represent and instruct.

Posada's influence was artistic as well as political. His prints of bandits, criminals, bullfighters, and Don Chepito Marihuano (a pretentious middle-class lecher whose mis-

adventures included failed seductions and nearly fatal bullfights) encouraged later artists to explore the seamier side of life. His brilliant use of popular graphic traditions like the *calaveras* inspired popular and academically trained artists alike to develop distinctly Mexican modes of expression. It even led social commentators like Octavio Paz to assert that Mexicans' familiarity with death set them apart from modern, death-denying societies like that of the United States. His innovative use of a variety of printing techniques—wood and lead engraving, which involved gouging out the white spaces in a print, and zinc etching, which used acid-resistant ink to draw in the black lines before bathing the block in nitric acid—provided a wealth of expressive possibilities for future artists to exploit. In sum, Posada's artistic vision with its powerful images, rich popular tradition, and innovative techniques, combined with his indisputable credentials as a true man of the people, represents a tremendous artistic legacy. His influence on the muralists in the 1920s, on artists like Leopoldo

Méndez and Pablo O'Higgins from the Workshop for Popular Graphics Arts in the 1930s, on Latino activists in the United States in the 1960s and 1970s, and (fittingly enough) on commercial artists in the late twentieth century has guaranteed that vision an audience for a long time to come.

—*RMB*

See also: Díaz, Porfirio; Muralist Movement; Orozco, José Clemente; Paz, Octavio; Rivera, Diego.

References:

Frank, Patrick. *Posada's Broadsheets: Mexican Popular Imagery, 1890–1910.* Albuquerque: University of New Mexico Press, 1998.

Tyler, Ron, ed. *Posada's Mexico.* Washington, DC: Library of Congress, 1979.

Presidents of the Twentieth Century

The Constitution of 1917 bestows on the executive branch of government considerably more power than is true in the United States. Executive power, in turn, tends to concentrate in the presidency. The development of a one-party state beginning in the 1920s has further strengthened the powers of the president. One great restraint on this accumulating power was the restriction on presidential reelection. The Constitution of 1917 originally prohibited reelection but was briefly modified to permit Alvaro Obregón to be reelected after staying out of office for one term. In 1928 the Constitution was amended, prohibiting reelection under any condition but also extending the presidential term from four years to six years. This restriction on reelection led a series of presidents to try to impose their successors for the presidency, often provoking political discord and sometimes even armed rebellion.

In the early decades of the century, being president was an uncertain and often dangerous job. President Porfirio Díaz was forced into exile in 1911. The first three Revolutionary presidents—Francisco Madero (1911–1913), Venustiano Carranza (1917–1920), and Alvaro Obregón (1920–1924)—were assassinated. Obregón's successor, Plutarco Elías Calles (1924–1928), lost out in a power struggle to his successor, Lázaro Cárdenas (1934–1940), and wound up in exile in the United States. Political and financial scandals led to what was effectively self-imposed exile for three later presidents: Luis Echeverría Alvarez (1970–1976), José López Portillo (1976–1982), and Carlos Salinas (1988–1994). Mexico's various political and military upheavals also produced eight "temporary, interim, or provisional" presidents between 1911 and 1934. Their time in office ranged from less than one hour (Pedro Lascuráin, 19 February 1913) to more than two years (Abelardo Rodríguez, 3 September 1932 to 30 November 1934).

The first Revolutionary president—Francisco Madero (1911–1913)—was basically from the nineteenth-century liberal mold, which emphasized political reform as the key to Mexico's problems. His moderate approach to socioeconomic issues such as agrarian reform and labor alarmed the conservatives and disappointed more radical elements, leading to his overthrow by General Victoriano Huerta, president from February 1913 to July 1914. To dismiss Huerta as simply "counterrevolutionary," however, is misleading. Huerta actually devoted considerable attention to education and agrarian reform. A coalition of Revolutionary factions overthrew Huerta in July 1914.

The overthrow of Huerta led to a split within the Revolutionary ranks and, ultimately, to a civil war, which made it difficult for any leader to claim effective control of the country in late 1914 and early 1915. A series of military defeats suffered by Villa in 1915 left Carranza as the only major national contender for power. As self-proclaimed "first chief," Carranza held control of the executive power and decided to institutionalize his position by calling a constitutional convention, which met in late 1916. Although Carranza carefully screened delegates to the convention, the new Constitution of 1917 was considerably more radical than he wished. Wanting to avoid another split in the Revolutionary ranks, Carranza accepted the Revolutionary document but ignored its more radical provisions relating to agrarian reform, labor and social welfare, and anticlericalism. As the first president elected under the new Constitution (1917–1920), Carranza—like Madero—believed that the emphasis should be on political reform. Carranza enthusiastically embraced the antiforeign theme of the Constitution, which coincided with his long-standing spirit of nationalism. Prevented by the Constitution from being reelected in 1920, Carranza tried to bypass his leading general, Alvaro Obregón, in favor of a civilian successor. Obregón's supporters soon revolted against the government. In May 1920, while fleeing from Mexico City to Vera Cruz, Carranza became the second Revolutionary president to be assassinated.

As president from 1920 to 1924, Obregón struggled to consolidate power, restore peace, and reorder the public finances. While wanting to move forward on the themes of the Revolution, Obregón was an astute politician who recognized the need to proceed cautiously and pragmatically. With his outstanding military record, Obregón commanded the respect of his fellow generals, whom he pacified with political and financial favors. The president also promoted the growth of organized labor while assuring that it was more closely tied to his administration. Obregón emphasized agrarian reform but engaged in only limited redistribution of land (some 3 million acres) owing to the unsettled economic situation. He did make major strides in organizing the peasants politically and binding them to his administration. Obregón made a major effort to improve public education, but the effort had a limited impact because of a shortage of funds and trained personnel. After lengthy negotiations, Obregón also received diplomatic recognition from the United States. The crisis over who would succeed Obregón in 1924

led to a split within the administration and a major military revolt in 1923, which Obregón suppressed.

The failure of the 1923 revolt put Plutarco Elías Calles in the presidency when Obregón stepped down in 1924. Calles continued the process of reducing the role of the army in political life, cutting the military budget, and encouraging greater professionalism. Calles accelerated the distribution of land to the peasants and addressed the technical side of agrarian reform by providing agricultural credit and education programs. While agrarian reform actually led to reduced agricultural production, the program had the more important political benefit of tying the peasantry to the administration. Calles was the first president to enforce vigorously the anticlerical provisions of the Constitution, provoking a major confrontation with the Roman Catholic Church and a three-year civil war. Calles also revived the struggle with the foreign-owned oil companies—settled under Obregón—by resurrecting the debate over ownership of subsoil resources.

Amid civil war and international controversy, the problem of presidential succession in 1928 appeared. With the backing of Calles, Obregón returned to the presidency over both military and civilian opposition. Obregón, however, would never start his second term; he was assassinated in July 1928. Faced with the possibility of another bloody split in the Revolutionary ranks, Calles decided to establish an institutional structure that would bring together the Revolutionary leaders while at the same time promoting the centralization of power. This new organization was known as the National Revolutionary Party, the Partido Nacional Revolucionario, or PNR. Recognizing that his continuation in the presidency could lead to major political problems, Calles opted to exercise control through a series of three puppet presidents who held office between 1928 and 1934.

Lázaro Cárdenas was supposed to be the fourth puppet of Calles. Elected to the presidency for the 1934–1940 period, Cárdenas asserted his independence from Calles and moved rapidly forward on agrarian reform and labor issues. In a struggle to control the official party, Cárdenas forced out the supporters of Calles and then reorganized and renamed the party. The new party was organized around four sectors—agrarian, labor, military, and "popular"—and was called the Party of the Mexican Revolution, the Partido de la Revolución Mexicana, or PRM. This reorganization broadened the political base of the party while also increasing the president's control over political competition. These moves produced a public split between Cárdenas and Calles, which led to Calles being forced into exile in the United States. Cárdenas accelerated the distribution of land and brought together the different local and regional peasant organizations into a national confederation, extending presidential and party control over this key group. Cárdenas also promoted the growth of a new national labor organization to replace the one associated with Calles. This new organization, in turn, was the foundation for the labor sector of the PRM. Cárdenas also devoted considerable attention to education, provoking new conflicts with conservative elements by promoting socialist and sex education in the public schools. Cárdenas brought the long-running feud with the foreign-owned oil companies to a dramatic conclusion by nationalizing the companies following a labor dispute.

Cárdenas brought the Revolutionary themes of the Constitution of 1917 to their peak but encountered a problem familiar to Mexican presidents: public finances. Mexico's financial crisis in 1937 led to a cutback in spending for social programs and the movement toward a completely new economic development approach that would shape Mexico's evolution for more than forty years. Although the transition to this new approach was made under the administration of Manuel Avila Camacho (1940–1946), it became most closely identified with the presidency of Miguel Alemán, who served from 1946 to 1952. The official party even rechristened itself, changing its name from the Party of the Mexican Revolution to the Institutional Revolutionary Party, the Partido Revolucionario Institutional, or PRI.

The new development scheme required the de-emphasis—critics claimed the abandonment—of some of the basic goals of the social revolution: agrarian reform, labor/social welfare, nationalism, and anticlericalism. The emphasis was now on industrialization, business, foreign investment, and a working arrangement with the Roman Catholic Church. The new plan thrust the central government—and the president—into a much more active role in the economy. These revised policies ushered in a period of spectacular and sustained economic growth known as the "Mexican Miracle." Unwilling to tamper with success, a series of presidents—Adolfo Ruiz Cortines (1952–1958), Adolfo López Mateos (1958–1964), and Gustavo Díaz Ordaz (1964–1970) persisted in the development scheme. There was growing opposition to this program, especially among rural elements who claimed that the countryside was being neglected. López Mateos tried to silence these critics by engaging in the largest land distribution program since Cárdenas, by extending social security to rural areas, and by subsidizing food and other basic necessities. This populist fling could not conceal the fact that the "Mexican Miracle" was losing its momentum nor correct the problems associated with the miracle: inequitable distribution of income, excessive urbanization, population pressures, and pollution.

Presidents also found it increasingly difficult to restrict political discussion and competition to the confines of the official party. There was growing disenchantment with the political dominance exercised by the PRI and the political linkage between the PRI and the government. The most spectacular example of this problem was the infamous Tlatelolco Massacre in Mexico City in October 1968 when the army and police fired on antigovernment demonstrators, killing more than 300.

President Luis Echeverría (1970–1976) had been closely connected to the Tlatelolco Massacre as Díaz Ordaz's minister of the interior, a fact which did not keep the outgoing president from tapping him as his successor. Echeverría represented a new direction in at least one way; he was the first in a series of presidents who had never run for an elected office prior to the presidential campaign and who had risen to power through the government bureaucracy rather than through the party. Presidential rhetoric moved substantially to the left under Echeverría, although talk often exceeded action. Echeverría did put additional resources into the rural sector, imposed price controls on basic commodities and a tax on luxury items, and maneuvered to make Mexico a leader of the less-developed countries. He also, however, had to face growing domestic terrorism, illegal land seizures by peasants, a declining economy, and the first in what would become a series of crises involving the value of the peso. Echeverría left office on an appropriate note—a massive devaluation of the peso which had otherwise retained its value for more than two decades.

José López Portillo, another technocrat in the presidency (1976–1982), was faced with the daunting task of dealing with Mexico's mounting social and economic woes. López Portillo received an unexpected boost from the discovery of major new oil deposits at a time when the world price for oil was rapidly increasing. Since the government owned the oil, the additional revenues could finance a variety of projects as well as serve as a basis for acquiring loans. The administration embarked on an unprecedented spending spree, financing public works, social welfare projects, expanded subsidies for consumer goods, and greater government ownership of business activities. Government spending was based on the comforting assumption that oil prices would continue to increase well into the 1980s; instead, beginning in 1981, oil

prices went into a long period of decline. The oil boom had gone bust, with López Portillo leaving office just as he had entered it—in the midst of a major financial and economic crisis.

Miguel de la Madrid, president from 1982 to 1988, was not only another technocrat but a U.S.-trained one at that. Selected as the PRI candidate for his financial expertise, Madrid won the presidency in the face of growing political opposition. The new president had no alternative but to introduce a much-needed but highly unpopular austerity program, centering on massive cuts in federal spending and an opening of the Mexican economy. The austerity program was made even more unpopular by the highly visible role played by the International Monetary Fund and the U.S. government in getting Madrid to implement it. Even nature seemed to be working against the president in September 1985 when a massive earthquake devastated Mexico City, killing an estimated 8,000 people and causing $4 billion in damage. Although the economic and financial actions taken by Madrid might have been unavoidable, there was no denying that they had led to a declining standard of living for most Mexicans. The public response to that decline was evident in the presidential elections of 1988.

The PRI nominee for the presidency in 1988 was Carlos Salinas de Gortari, another financial technocrat in the mold of Miguel de la Madrid. Salinas narrowly prevailed over strong opposition from both the left and the right amid widespread and probably accurate charges of electoral fraud. For years critics of the PRI had complained that the PRI had abandoned the basic principles of the Revolution: agrarian reform, labor/social welfare, anticlericalism, and nationalism. Building on the reforms started under Madrid, Salinas made it clear that these themes had outlived their usefulness and that Mexico needed major changes. Salinas abandoned the program of land distribution and even permitted the break-up of the traditional communal landholdings. He pressured labor leaders to keep wages down, arresting some of the most recalcitrant ones. Salinas brought a definitive end to the anticlericalism of the post-1917 period by amending the Constitution to permit Church ownership of property and the operation of Church schools. He renewed diplomatic relations with the Vatican and even had an audience with Pope John Paul II. Revolutionary nationalism and its long-standing distrust for the United States gave way to the North American Free Trade Agreement, which created an even stronger linkage between the Mexican and U.S. economies. While Salinas assembled an impressive collection of economic reforms, there was growing criticism that the president and the PRI were delaying promised political reforms.

The 1994 presidential elections proved as unsettling as those of 1988. The campaign took a dramatic turn when the PRI candidate, the energetic and popular Luis Donaldo Colosio, was assassinated in March 1994. The PRI hastily put forward Ernesto Zedillo, Colosio's campaign manager and another U.S.-trained technocrat with extensive financial credentials. Zedillo won in another close election. Zedillo continued the economic and financial policies of his predecessors but soon faced a financial crisis featuring a major devaluation of the peso. Zedillo and Salinas publicly feuded over who was to blame for the financial mess, but Zedillo was eventually able to overcome the crisis using a modified austerity program and a major international loan package. Zedillo pushed forward more vigorously on political reforms. The opposition won some governorships and a much stronger role in the national Congress, where the PRI lost its majority in the lower house for the first time since the official party was established. Zedillo also moved to democratize the PRI itself, supporting an open political contest for the presidential nomination in 2000 rather than tapping his successor as was the tradition. Mexico was entering a new era in its political development, one featuring considerably more competition for power as well as political uncertainty.

Zedillo's political reforms helped to produce a serious three-way race for the presidency in 2000. With Zedillo choosing not to tap his successor, the competition for the PRI nomination resulted in a victory for Francisco Labastida Ochoa. The two principal opposition candidates were Cuauhtémoc Cárdenas of the Partido de la Revolución Democrática (the Party of the Democratic Revolution, or PRD) and Vicente Fox of the Partido de Acción Nacional (the National Action Party, or PAN). Cárdenas and Fox tried but failed to develop a coalition. In the presidential elections held in July 2000, Fox won the presidency with 42 percent of the vote to 36 percent for Labastida and approximately 17 percent for Cárdenas. Fox's election marked the first time since the founding of the official party in 1929 that an opposition candidate had officially won the presidency. Fox's party, however, did not have a majority in either house of the national Congress, making it difficult for Fox to put together a workable majority to pass the list of reforms he proposed. The PAN had no experience in running the executive branch of government, and the PRI had no experience with playing the role of opposition party, "loyal" or otherwise. As a result, Fox had to compromise on such key issues as tax reform and indigenous rights. Fox found it difficult to maintain the political momentum of his early months in office. Much of the ultimate success or failure of Fox's administration would hinge on congressional elections to be held in 2003. The elections of 2003 strengthened the position of the PRI in the Congress, making it even more difficult for Fox to get his reforms approved. Fox will always have a place in Mexican political history as the man who beat the PRI. Whether his historical repuation will rest on more than that remains to be seen. Time is running out on Fox the reformer.

—*DMC*

See also: Agrarian Reform/Land and Land
　　Policy; Assassinations; Constitution of 1917;

Democratization Process; Militarism; North American Free Trade Agreement (NAFTA); Religion; Revolution of 1910.

References:

Aguilar Camín, Héctor, and Lorenzo Meyer. *In the Shadow of the Mexican Revolution: Contemporary Mexican History, 1910–1989.* Austin: University of Texas Press, 1993.

Camp, Roderic Ai. *Political Recruitment across Two Centuries: Mexico, 1884–1991.* Austin: University of Texas Press, 1995.

———. *Politics in Mexico.* 2d ed. New York: Oxford University Press, 1996.

Rodríguez, Victoria E., and Peter M. Ward, eds. *Opposition Government in Mexico.* Albuquerque: University of New Mexico Press, 1995.

Puebla (State)

Puebla is a central-eastern Mexican state with a capital city of the same name. Puebla's location between central Mexico and the Gulf Coast has made the region a participant in and witness to most of the major events of Mexico's past. Historically one of Mexico's most populous areas, Puebla has also been an economic and cultural center. Puebla City attracts thousands of visitors each year, and *mole poblano,* one of Mexico's most distinctive dishes, was created here during Mexico's colonial era. By the end of the twentieth century, Puebla had undergone a remarkable transformation from a rural to an urban state, and its capital city was Mexico's fourth largest urban center.

Puebla's fertile central valleys attracted a variety of peoples in the centuries before the Spanish Conquest. Cholula, the site of a great pyramid, emerged as an important religious center. It was occupied by successive waves of people, including the Toltec-Chichimecs, and was eventually identified with the worship of Quetzalcoatl (the Feathered Serpent). Puebla's more rugged northern region, known as the Sierra Norte, was also home to several native groups, most notably the Totonacs and the Huastecs.

The arrival of Hernán Cortés and the Spaniards in central Mexico found the inhabitants of Puebla's central valleys in a state of political conflict and competition. Spanish Conquest of the Puebla region began with the capture of Huejotzingo and Cholula, the latter city's capture accompanied by a massacre of thousands of Indians. The Spaniards coveted the rich agricultural lands of central Puebla, and they laid claim to those lands, insisting on Indian labor to work their holdings. Franciscan, Dominican, Augustinian, and Jesuit missionaries all played a role in converting Puebla's Indians and in establishing a strong presence for the Roman Catholic Church. In the Sierra Norte, conquest proceeded more slowly, and its native peoples resisted attempts at conversion and assimilation.

As created by the Spaniards, the Province of Puebla (known as Puebla de los Angeles) stretched well beyond the current state boundaries, toward the Gulf Coast and the Pacific Ocean. The region became an important supplier of cattle and agricultural goods for central Mexico, and by the end of the colonial era, its southwestern corner had emerged as a prime sugar area. The city of Puebla (established in 1531) became an important textile center, supplying cotton goods for all of New Spain. Puebla City also gained fame as a cultural hub and was known for its architecture, literature, and music. The city's cathedral (the tallest in Mexico) is an outstanding example of colonial architecture. Finally, the capital came to be associated with the culinary arts. Mexico's famous *mole poblano,* a rich sauce combining chiles and dark chocolate, originated in one of the city's convents, which was given the task of creating a special dish to help welcome a royal official.

The revolt of Father Miguel Hidalgo that began Mexico's Independence era brought insurgent activity to the Sierra Norte and to Puebla's southern zone. Rebel leaders in the province included Guadalupe Victoria, Vicente Guerrero, and José Francisco Osorno. In 1821, nearly a decade after Hidalgo's popular insurrection was crushed, Agustín de Iturbide (who became the first leader of independent Mexico) entered Puebla's capital and declared the region free of Spanish control. Puebla was granted statehood in 1824, and although it initially preserved its reach to the Pacific and the Gulf Coast, during the nineteenth century, Puebla lost these outlets as other states were created and boundaries redrawn. Despite its loss of territory, however, Puebla remained one of Mexico's wealthiest and most populous areas.

The first fifty years of independence were politically difficult for Puebla. The capital city and its surrounding region were strategic prizes for Mexico's political factions and for foreign invaders. American troops occupied the city during the Mexican War, and although Ignacio Zaragoza led Mexican troops in the defeat of French forces on 5 May 1862 (an event celebrated today as Cinco de Mayo), the French later besieged and gained control of Puebla City. On both occasions, Puebla's government was relocated, and insurgents within the state harassed the foreign intruders. Mexico's War of Reform (1858–1861) also brought violence to the capital and elsewhere as liberals and conservatives clashed over the country's future direction.

The latter part of the nineteenth century was a time of economic expansion for Puebla. Much of this expansion took place during the reign of Porfirio Díaz (1876–1911), which was characterized by its heavy emphasis on modernization and foreign investment. Railroad lines linking Puebla with Mexico City and the port of Vera Cruz were built, the state's textile industry grew, and coffee, sugar, and other agricultural products found new markets. By the turn of the century, Puebla was the fifth most important industrial state in Mexico, with foreign and Mexican capital providing the means for this expansion. Such growth did not bring even prosperity, however. Owners of sugar haciendas in the southern part of the state, for example, augmented their holdings at the expense of small-scale and communal lands. Peasants became laborers on sugar plantations, and many became trapped by debt. By

the turn of the century, textile workers were also feeling the negative effects of economic development. Overexpansion in this industry, coupled with a recession, brought hard times to textile factories and forced some to close. In 1906, textile workers struck for better conditions. Despite support from workers in other states, however, they gained few concessions from the Díaz administration, which held out the threat of violent repression to quiet the strikers.

The repression of dissent and creation of a stable environment for investment were priorities for Rosendo Márquez and Mucio P. Martínez, who governed the state in the last decades of the Porfiriato. Márquez built up the state's police forces and punished recalcitrant workers by drafting them into the army. Martínez gained a reputation for corruption, and he used his official position to enrich himself. As elsewhere in Mexico, the political system was far from open, and elections were subject to manipulation, often with the help of the central government. Perhaps the best example of political repression in Puebla during the Porfiriato occurred in Tehuitzingo, where a violent demonstration against a rigged election resulted in the execution, imprisonment, or exile of several rebels.

Among those who eventually emerged to challenge the dictatorship of Díaz and the behavior of his local cronies was Aquiles Serdán. A radical reformer, Serdán organized workers, students, and peasants in support of Francisco I. Madero, the *hacendado* (landowner) from Coahuila who campaigned against Díaz's reelection and who eventually called for his overthrow. In 1910, during the earliest phase of the Mexican Revolution of 1910, Serdán (who had been designated the leader of Madero's revolt in Puebla) was killed in a battle with local security forces. Serdán's brother Máximo was also killed, and his sister Carmen was injured and imprisoned. Within the next year, several rebel groups emerged throughout Puebla. Although Madero's rebellion attracted Pueblans from a variety of backgrounds, his presidency failed to consolidate this support. After Madero's overthrow and death, Puebla became a battleground for numerous Revolutionary factions, and Puebla City a prize for Venustiano Carranza, Emiliano Zapata, and Pancho Villa. Although the partisans of Zapata gained a significant following and were active in Puebla until 1919, the tide was in favor of Carranza, who gained control of the state in 1915 and whose representatives held it until Carranza's own demise in 1920.

During the period of Carranza's control, a handful of governors, including Francisco Coss, Cesáreo Castro, and Alfonso Cabrera enacted limited agrarian reform while contending with the Zapatista threat and the state's restive workers. The 1920s and 1930s brought more significant gains for workers and peasants, particularly under Leonides Andrew Almazán, who organized workers and distributed nearly 210,000 hectares of land. From 1937 to 1941, Puebla was governed by Maximino Avila Camacho, whose brother Manuel became Mexico's president in 1940. Avila Camacho focused on bringing stability to the state, and he worked with the national government to co-opt workers and peasants. He also smoothed relations with the Roman Catholic Church, which had come under attack during the Revolutionary period. Finally, the governor worked closely with businessmen to promote Puebla's economic recovery and development. Among the foreign businessmen Maximino courted was William O. Jenkins, an American consular official who had been kidnapped by Revolutionaries in 1919. Jenkins created a sugar empire near the city of Atencingo, though most of his holdings were later expropriated by President Lázaro Cárdenas.

Although Puebla had achieved a degree of political stability by the 1940s (though the University of Puebla became a site of student unrest in the 1960s and 1970s) it struggled to maintain a viable economy in the latter decades of the twentieth century. World War II increased demand for Puebla textiles and agricultural products, but in the aftermath of the war that demand slowed. In both industry and agriculture, Puebla failed to modernize and diversify. As population increased and the economy stagnated, many chose to migrate to Mexico City and the United States. Beginning in the 1960s, the state and federal governments sought to bolster Puebla's economy by investing in the construction of industrial parks. Several new industries established themselves in the vicinity of the capital, including the Volkswagen automobile company and the Mexican steel manufacturer Hlysa. Industrial growth encouraged migration to the cities (particularly Puebla City, Tehuacán, Atlixco, San Martín Texmelucan, Huauchinango, and Teziutlán) and helped transform Puebla into a highly urbanized state. Meanwhile, the Puebla countryside benefited from the Plan Puebla (announced in 1967), which brought a Green Revolution to the rural sector.

By the end of the twentieth century, Puebla had managed to create a highly diversified economy. It had also maintained its reputation as a tourist attraction, and visitors were especially drawn to the pre-Columbian pyramid of Cholula and the historic center of Puebla City (which was jolted by a major earthquake in 1999). Politically, the National Action Party (PAN) was emerging as a strong opponent to the long-dominant Partido Revolucionario Institucional (the Institutional Revolutionary Party, or PRI).

—*SBP*

See also: Avila Camacho, Manuel; Carranza, Venustiano; Díaz, Porfirio; Food; Partido de Acción Nacional (PAN); Partido Revolucionario Institucional (PRI); Revolution of 1910.

References:

LaFrance, David G. *The Mexican Revolution in Puebla, 1908–1913: The Maderista Movement and the Failure of Liberal Reform*. Wilmington, DE: Scholarly Resources, 1989.

Lomelí Vanegas, Leonardo. *Breve historia de Puebla*. Mexico City: El Colegio de Mexico, 2001.

Official state web site: http://www.puebla.gob.mx

Querétaro (State)

Located in central Mexico, Querétaro has a capital city of the same name. It includes within its borders a part of Mexico's rich agricultural region known as the Bajío. The northern section of the state (often referred to as the Sierra Gorda region) is mountainous and has historically been a producer of silver, copper, and other minerals. Although Querétaro has never been as important a mining region as the neighboring states of Guanajuato and San Luis Potosí, its location (near Mexico City and in the economic heart of central Mexico) has ensured Querétaro's participation in the major events of Mexico's history. Indeed, the capital city was the site of several notable developments, including the ratification of the Treaty of Guadalupe Hidalgo (which ended the Mexican War), the drafting of the Constitution of 1917 during the Mexican Revolution, and the formal establishment of the Partido Revolucionario Institucional (the Institutional Revolutionary Party, or PRI), which dominated Mexican politics for much of the twentieth century.

Querétaro was home to several native groups in the centuries before Spanish contact, and it was a transitional area between nomadic groups and the more urban cultures (including the Mexica-Aztecs) of central Mexico. Spanish exploration and settlement, which began in the sixteenth century, utilized Otomí Indians, who had already settled in the state's central valley. Hernando de Tapia, a Christianized Otomí, established the city of Querétaro and, along with his son, was recognized by the Spaniards as a political leader of the town and its surrounding area. Eventually, however, Spanish settlers pushed the Otomís to the fringes of the city. In the northern Sierra Gorda region, Spanish settlement was encouraged by the prospect of mineral wealth. Despite the work of outstanding missionaries such as Junípero Serra, however, native resistance continually hampered the Spanish advance in this area.

Querétaro's location, along the road from Mexico City to the wealthy mining region of Zacatecas, ensured the persistence of conflict with native groups, and Indian raids and warfare characterized the first century of Spanish settlement. Similarly, Querétaro's proximity to Mexico's other mining centers (including neighboring Guanajuato) meant that the region's economy, despite Indian resistance, would experience steady growth. By the end of the colonial period, cattle ranching, agriculture, textiles, and some silver and copper mining were a part of the local economy. Querétaro's textile industry especially grew in importance, supplying clothing items to other areas of Mexico.

When the popular insurrection that inaugurated Mexico's independence struggle began in 1810, those who had been displaced by Spanish settlement, as well as textile workers whose lives were characterized by poor working conditions and abuse, leant their support. Querétaro, and particularly the restive Sierra Gorda, was a center of the movement led by Father Miguel Hidalgo, which began in neighboring Guanajuato. Although rebels never succeeded in capturing Querétaro City, the insurgency resulted in serious damage to the region's economy. Recovery was slow, and rebel activity subsided slowly.

The political unrest and civil conflict that characterized the decades after Mexican Independence had a direct effect on Querétaro, which became a state in 1824. The long and often bloody political struggle between Mexican liberals and conservatives took its toll on local politics, and the state witnessed numerous changes in leadership. Tomás Mejía emerged as a prominent conservative figure in Querétaro, and during the War of Reform between liberals and conservatives (1858–1861), he captured the capital city. Mejía's forces also occupied the state in the 1860s, providing support for the French, who established a short-lived empire in Mexico. The city of Querétaro was the scene of the final battle between the French Loyalists and their opponents. Mejía and Emperor Maximilian (who had come from Austria to rule Mexico) were executed at Querétaro's Hill of the Bells in 1867.

In the Sierra Gorda, the pattern of popular unrest that characterized the colonial period persisted into the nineteenth century. The area's *campesinos* (peasants, many of them descendants of the state's Indian population) struggled to regain lands lost to the ever-expanding hacienda system. Beginning in 1849, they joined *campesinos* of San Luis Potosí and Gunajuato in a revolt. Tomás Mejía led in the repression of the rebellion, and many insurgents were executed or imprisoned.

The thirty-five-year dictatorship of Porfirio Díaz that preceded the Mexican Revolution of 1910 brought relative stability to Querétaro and encouraged economic expansion within the state. Francisco González Cosío (who served as governor for most of the 1880–1911 period) presided over growth in the textile industry and in agriculture and oversaw the establishment of roads, railroads, and telegraph lines. A middle class emerged as urban centers grew and textile and railroad workers began to unionize, some under the aegis of the Roman Catholic Church. Although railroad workers struck in 1909 and the Sierra Gorda remained a restive area, many of the state's residents seemed to welcome the peace of the Porfirian era.

The early phase of the Mexican Revolution brought rebellion only in the Sierra Gorda, where rebels from the neighboring states of Hidalgo, San Luis Potosí, and Guanajuato were active. After 1913, however, the entire state was increasingly drawn into the civil war and factional competition. In 1914 and 1915, Querétaro was caught between the rival factions of Venustiano Carranza and Pancho Villa. The capital city changed hands three times and governors for both factions attempted reforms. Beginning In 1916, and with Carranza triumphant in Mexico, Querétaro City hosted the congress that drafted Mexico's Constitution of 1917. Federico Montes Alanís assumed the governorship and began the process of trying to pacify the state.

Alanís faced a volatile situation. In the Sierra Gorda, an armed struggle fed by long-standing grievances over land, continued, and Porfirio Rubio (originally from Hidalgo state) emerged as a local strongman in the municipality of Jalpan. His command of armed groups in the sierra region gave him virtual political autonomy, and Jalpan operated independently of Querétaro's state government for a time. Although Rubio helped give voice to the demand for land reform in the sierras, Saturnino Osornio emerged as his counterpart in the valley regions. Osornio used his local following to propel himself into the governorship in 1931, encouraging the state's *campesinos* to organize and begin fighting for land. Particularly in the second half of the 1930s, Querétaro witnessed significant land reform.

During the last half of the twentieth century (and as in many areas of Mexico), agrarian reform was deemphasized in favor of industrial growth. Particularly since the 1960s, agribusiness and other highly mechanized enterprises have become the mainstay of the state's economy, and Querétaro has emerged as one of Mexico's most important industrial areas. Bernardo Quintana was among the entrepreneurs instrumental in fostering such development. Quintana purchased farmland in the environs of Querétaro City and converted it into an industrial park. By the end of the twentieth century, his holdings had become part of a much bigger industrial corridor that included San Juan del Río and Corregidora. Together, Querétaro City, San Juan del Río, and Corregidora contain half of the state's population and most of its wealth. Yet while Querétaro's industrial development has given the state a high economic profile, the benefits of such growth have not been evenly shared. Many of the state's industries are so mechanized that they have produced relatively few new jobs, and the concentration of growth in the industrial corridor has meant that the Sierra Gorda and southern Querétaro have been left out of the prosperity. As the new century emerged, these areas remained underdeveloped and poorly integrated.

—*SBP*

See also: Constitution of 1917; Guanajuato (State); Hidalgo (State); Partido Revolucionario Institucional (PRI); Revolution of 1910; San Luis Potosí (State).

References:
García Ugarte, Marta Eugenia. *Breve historia de Querétaro.* Mexico City: El Colegio de Mexico, 1999.
Official state web site: http://www.queretaro.gob.mx

Quintana Roo (State)

Mexico's youngest state, Quintana Roo, is located in the eastern section of the Yucatán Peninsula. It is named after Andrés Quintana Roo, a nineteenth-century statesman. Quintana Roo shares a border with the country of Belize, has an extensive Caribbean coastline, and includes several islands, including Cozumel, Cancún, and Islas Mujeres. The significant and strong presence of Maya Indians has shaped the region's history, as has Quintana Roo's isolation from central Mexico and from central control. By the late twentieth century, the state was a tourist mecca, attracting travelers and workers to Cancún and other resort areas.

Quintana Roo's Maya civilization, like that of the entire Yucatán Peninsula, proved especially resistant to Spanish incursions and missionary efforts. Spaniards made their first contact with the peninsula in 1502, and in 1511 a shipwreck off Quintana Roo's coast killed all but two of the Spanish explorers aboard. Those two survivors, Gonzalo Guerrero and Jerónimo Aguilar, lived among the Maya and adopted their ways. Beginning in the 1520s, more Spanish expeditions came to the Yucatán, and gradual but incomplete Spanish control was established. By the seventeenth century, the small town of Bacalar was the only real Spanish settlement in the area of Quintana Roo.

The lack of precious metals in Quintana Roo and the Yucatán Peninsula meant that Indian labor became the chief source of wealth for Spanish settlers. Even as the Indian population declined (primarily due to disease), Spanish demands for labor and tribute increased. The region's Maya people responded with frequent rebellions, and many fled to the more remote areas of the peninsula, thus escaping Spanish control. Quintana Roo's extensive coastline also attracted pirates, who destroyed Bacalar in 1652 (the town was rebuilt and fortified in the eighteenth century). English pirates in particular gained a foothold in this section of the Caribbean, and in an attempt to capitalize on the area's lucrative dyewood trade, they established the settlement of Belize, south of the Hondo River.

With Mexico's independence from Spain, the Yucatán Peninsula functioned as a single political unit that resisted central control and periodically asserted its independence. The region's native peoples also continued to struggle for autonomy. For the Maya, independence brought no real change in their subordinate status. Economic developments, most notably the growth of a sugar industry, also threatened the traditional subsistence farming practices of the Maya. In 1847 the Yucatán's Maya went on the offensive, beginning the Caste War, perhaps the most important event in Quintana Roo's history.

The Caste War began with assaults on non-Indians and their properties in the Yucatán Peninsula. It continued as a group of Maya rebels retreated to the remote eastern section of the peninsula (i.e., Quintana Roo). They adopted the Christian cross as a symbol, likening their struggle against non-Indians to Christ's Passion, and adopting the title of Cruzob ("people of the cross"). The Maya insurgents established the village of Chan Santa Cruz in central Quintana Roo, which became the spiritual and political center of the rebellion. From this base, the Maya continued to assert their independence of Mexico and of the provincial government of Yucatán. Periodic war against non-Indians continued and was aided by material assistance from English colonists in neighboring Belize.

The Caste War persisted into the late nineteenth century, when President Porfirio Díaz determined to end it. In this, Díaz was motivated by the Yucatán's natural resources (including sugar, cocoa, and precious woods), which promised to bring wealth and foreign investment to the peninsula. Díaz initiated a final military campaign against the Maya rebels, which finally succeeded in capturing Chan Santa Cruz. Settlement of the boundary between Mexico and Belize (which came with the agreement that aid to the rebels would cease) helped end the Caste War. Finally, the establishment of Payo

Obispo, a non-Indian settlement in southern Quintana Roo, helped populate the region and extend government control to the remote eastern section of the Yucatán. In 1902, Quintana Roo became a federal territory.

Quintana Roo's new territorial status brought direct federal control over the region. Porfirio Díaz named *jefes políticos* (political bosses) for the area, including Ignacio Bravo, the general responsible for the earlier capture of Chan Santa Cruz (renamed Santa Cruz de Bravo in his honor). Bravo oversaw the economic development of Quintana Roo and personally benefited from the extraction and marketing of its natural resources. Under Bravo, Quintana Roo also became a kind of penal colony, to which journalists, politicians, and other critics of the Díaz regime were sent.

The Mexican Revolution arrived late to Quintana Roo, with Bravo losing his status as *jefe político* only in 1912. The arrival of new officials, sent by Revolutionary leader and president, Francisco I. Madero, also resulted in the freeing of the region's political prisoners. There was no significant fighting in Quintana Roo, and Revolutionary change was imposed from without. The region's political status, moreover, was challenged during the Revolution.

From 1913 to 1915, Quintana Roo lost its territorial designation and came under the tutelage of the neighboring state of Yucatán. Salvador Alvarado, Yucatán's governor from 1915 to 1918, encouraged a variety of reforms. In Quintana Roo, he extended an olive branch to the Maya, returning Santa Cruz de Bravo to Indian control and thus allowing the Maya to reassert their leadership in central Quintana Roo. General Francisco May emerged as the Maya strongman of this section of the state. His leadership was virtually unchallenged until the 1930s, when the Mexican government reasserted its control over Santa Cruz, which was renamed Felipe Carrillo Puerto, after another Yucatán governor. Also during the 1930s, Quintana Roo's status changed twice more: in 1931 it was divided between Yucatán and Campeche before having its territorial status restored by President Lázaro Cárdenas. Cárdenas also created the territorial capital at the southern town of Payo Obispo, which gained its modern name of Chetumal.

In the decades after the Mexican Revolution, the central government paid increasing attention to Quintana Roo and its economic potential. Under Lázaro Cárdenas and territorial governor Rafael E. Melgar, the region developed an infrastructure and boosted production in the agriculture and forestry sectors. The wood products industry emerged as the region's most important. Meanwhile, railroad lines and roadways helped break Quintana Roo's historic isolation and aided in the integration of Maya communities. Another push in the area's development began at midcentury, when President Adolfo López Mateos actively promoted the territory's development. This time, hope for Quintana Roo's future was placed in tourism, and the central government sought to capitalize on the region's benign climate and attractive Caribbean coastline. Beginning in the late 1960s, federal money built the resort of Cancún, which became Mexico's largest resort area. Other areas, including Cozumel and Islas Mujeres, were also developed with tourism in mind.

The tourist industry transformed Quintana Roo, bringing development to the sparsely populated northern section and its islands. It also attracted thousands of people from other areas of Mexico, who came to fill the countless jobs created by tourism. This migration has continued, as Quintana Roo's tourist industry experienced steady growth during the latter part of the twentieth century. Indeed, by the 1990s, Quintana Roo had Mexico's highest level of inmigration. The successful transformation of Quintana Roo's economy paved the way for statehood, which had been delayed because of the region's historically low population base and because of concerns over its economic viability. In 1974 Quintana Roo became Mexico's youngest state.

Although tourism has heightened the importance of Quintana Roo, it has also presented new challenges. Environmental concerns are paramount, and the coastline and coral reefs that attract thousands of tourists and divers each year, are especially threatened. The desire to protect the state's environment and preserve its wildlife gave rise to the Sian Ka'an Biosphere Reserve in 1986. With its economy so heavily dependent on tourism, Quintana Roo is also particularly vulnerable to economic cycles outside of its control. Indeed, the only other successful enterprise to emerge in the latter twentieth century was the sugar industry, which began as a government enterprise in southern Quintana Roo during the 1970s. Finally, with its extensive coastline, the state has increasingly been drawn into the international drug trade. Narcotics are regularly shipped from South America to the United States, using Quintana Roo as a transshipment point. By the end of the twentieth century, the potential difficulties that the drug trade could bring to the state itself had become apparent. In 1999, and just days before his term as governor (and thus his legal immunity) ended, Governor Mario Villanueva vanished in an attempt to escape charges of drug trafficking that had been brought against him.

—SBP

See also: Campeche (State); Drug Trafficking; Revolution of 1910; Tourism; Yucatán (State).

References:

Careaga Viliesia, Lorena. *Quintana Roo: Una historia compartida.* Mexico City: Instituto de Investigaciones Dr. José María Luis Mora, 1990.

Dachary, Alfredo César, Daniel Navarro López, and Stella M. Arnaiz, eds. *Quintana Roo: Los retos del fin de siglo.* Chetumal, Quintana Roo: Centro de Investigaciones de Quintana Roo, 1992.

Official state web site: http://www.quintanaroo.gob.mx

R

Radio

Radio is one of the great success stories on Mexico's otherwise rocky road to modernity. A quick glance at the rapid growth of radio stations since 1930 gives some indication: from 32 radio stations in 1930, to 113 in 1940, to 195 in 1950, to 369 in 1960, to 603 in 1970, to 848 in 1980, to 1,045 by 1990. Current estimates indicate that radio now reaches as much as 98 percent of Mexico's population. More than just a statistical success, radio has played a vital role in twentieth-century nation-building by providing a sense of shared knowledge and culture that has helped to bring all Mexicans into the national mainstream in ways that the literate culture of newspapers and government decrees was never able to do. This process has been facilitated by a close if informal partnership between the state and private enterprise, a partnership that has stressed the commercial aspects of radio but has also provided spaces for government-sponsored "public radio" and other alternatives. The price of this cozy relationship, however, has been the concentration of power, first in radio networks and later in media conglomerates with close ties to the state and powerful economic interests, often at the cost of "objective" news reporting and

community service. Since the political opening of the 1990s that culminated in the defeat of the PRI (Partido Revolucionario Institucional), the party that had controlled Mexican politics since the Revolution of 1910, radio has become a somewhat more independent, if still far from radical, force in Mexican society.

The early years of radio began with a few pioneering experiments in the early 1920s and ended with established radio networks by 1940. Early on, astute policymakers and entrepreneurs recognized radio's revolutionary potential, although they did not always share the same vision of revolution. For directors of the Liga Central Mexicana de Radio (Central Mexican Radio Alliance, 1923), including radical labor leader Vicente Lombardo Toledano, radio seemed the ideal medium through which to publicize the new national project that was emerging out of the Revolution of 1910. To this end, the Liga sponsored a 1923 radio broadcast of a speech by President Alvaro Obregón, one of the first nonexperimental uses of radio in Mexican history. At the same time, entrepreneurs like Raúl Azcárraga, whose La Casa de Radio (House of Radio) company sold electronic parts, saw commercial radio as the ideal way to merge new forms of advertising—ads that stressed product image over substantive content—and the new music recording industry. In 1923, Raúl and his brother Luis convinced Mexico City's largest daily newspaper, *El Universal,* to enter into a partnership for a commercial radio station, El Universal-La Casa de Radio, with the call letters CYL. A select affair in an era when few Mexicans owned radios, CYL's inaugural broadcast opted for high culture with a distinguished lineup that included Spanish classical guitarist Andrés Segovia, Mexican composer Manuel Ponce, and Estridentista poet Manuel Maples Arce reading his poem "Radio." CYL's success soon attracted regular sponsors like the Mexico City department store chain, Sanborns, which even developed a Radio brand of carbonated beverage. Not to be left behind, the capital's largest cigarette manufacturer, El Buen Tono, a pioneer in new and creative forms of advertising since the 1880s, started a rival radio station (CYB, later XEB) and began marketing El Radio cigarettes. Given the relative scarcity of both radios and radio stations, these early efforts focused logically enough on Mexico City and other large urban areas. Programming was conservative as well, favoring either government propaganda or "easy listening" dance band music like *danzón* and fox-trot.

For communications policymakers, the first order of business was to establish guidelines and regulations for the new industry. Concerns about radio's propaganda potential and the danger of cultural imperialism, especially from the United States, were clearly reflected in this early legislation. A 1926 law, for example, permitted only Mexican nationals to own or operate radio stations. Later laws required Spanish-only broadcasts—a restriction loosened in the 1940s—and that all stations broadcasting in Mexico operate within national borders. Mexican radio laws promulgated between 1932 and 1936, went further, requiring that commercial stations broadcast at least 25 percent Mexican content, no politics or religion, and regular public service announcements (later set at 12.5 percent of programming). In the initial legislation, commercial advertising was restricted to 10 percent of programming. To encourage private investors who might be put off by these restrictions, the new laws offered generous fifty-year concessions. Global developments also played a decisive role in the shape of Mexican radio. International conferences designed to regulate global communications systems not only designated specific call letters for each country—in 1924 Mexico was given CYA-CZZ; in 1929 the letters were switched to XAA-XPZ—but also encouraged participating countries to develop a commercial rather than public radio model.

The triumph of commercial radio in Mexico was, in many ways, an Azcárraga family affair. The decisive moment in that affair came in 1930 when government regulators granted Emilio Azcárraga Vidaurreta, owner of XET in Monterrey, a license for a new radio station in Mexico City, XEW. With a 200 kilowatt transmitter, XEW was the most powerful radio station in the Western hemisphere—"La voz de América Latina desde México" (The Voice of Latin America from Mexico) according to its slogan—with an RCA affiliation and a range that included the southwestern United States and much of the Caribbean basin. By 1938, Azcárraga Vidaurreta and his associates controlled a national radio network of 15 stations that they kept supplied with prerecorded programs, shipped in from Mexico City (in part because an inadequate communications infrastructure made simultaneous broadcast extremely difficult). The formation of an industry lobby, AMERC or the Asociación Mexicana de Estaciones Radiodifusoras Comericiales (Mexican Association of Commercial Radio Stations), in 1937, along with the establishment of a rival network, XEQ, in 1938, indicated that Mexican radio had come of age in just a few short years.

The secret to XEW's dramatic success was a gift for combining a nationalist cultural agenda with popular music. Encouraged by the government's protectionist policies and local demand, Azcárraga's radio network delivered mostly Mexican music. XEW programs like the popular *Así es mi tierra* (That's My Country, 1930), for example, offered *música típica* or typical Mexican music under a comprehensive "umbrella" category that subsumed very different regional musical styles—simplifying but at the time embracing those differences. In addition to this nationalization of traditional Mexican music, XEW also developed and supported new talent. As early as 1929, singer-songwriter Agustín Lara, whose bohemian lifestyle and heart-wrenching *boleros* (romantic ballads) would make him one of Mexico's biggest celebrities, was given a weekly radio show, *La hora íntima* (The Intimate Hour) in a mutually beneficial move that provided Lara a national audience and XEW a star attraction. Much the same thing happened in the late 1930s with *charro* (cowboy) singing sensation, Pedro Infante, who went on to become one of Mexican cinema's most important stars and a national icon. In fact, the XEW stable would eventually include nearly all the greats of midcentury Mexican popular music (and musical cinema), including Jorge Negrete and Lola Beltán. Just as important as its lineup of stars was a wildly popular new genre: the *radionovela*. Melodramatic serials like *Colegio de Amor* (School of Love, 1945) brought the romantic style and narrative complexities of *historietas* (comic books) to the radio. Indeed, Yolanda Vargas Dulché, principal writer for the popular *historieta, Lágrimas, risas y amor* (Tears, Smiles, and Love), also wrote *radionovelas*. If melodrama was not enough, XEW (and its imitators) fostered listener loyalty with promotional gimmicks, like having listeners call in marriage proposals or make on-air public apologies to *novios* (boyfriends and girlfriends) and spouses.

The Mexican government got into the act as well. Government-sponsored radio stations like XEPO offered a mix of public service, propaganda, history, and culture through programs like *La Hora Nacional* (The National Hour, 1937), the nation's longest running radio show. Populist President Lázaro Cárdenas (1934–1940) was especially adept at exploiting radio's propaganda potential. Beginning with the broadcast of his inauguration speech in 1934, he regularly used radio to address the Mexican people on important issues like the expropriation of American oil companies by the Mexican government in 1938. But even the Cárdenas administration, whose programs, such as socialist education and *ejido* (communal) agriculture had anticapitalist overtones, never seriously challenged the regime's close relationship to commercial radio or the dominance of the commercial radio model.

The middle decades of the twentieth century, from 1940 to 1970, were a golden age for Mexican radio, an era of unprecedented expansion and influence. The number of radios in Mexico grew from one-half million in 1940, to 2 million in 1950, to 3 million in 1960, to 14 million by 1970. Along with this tremendous expansion of the listening audience came an even greater concentration of power in the hand of a few radio networks. The biggest player by far was still the Azcárraga group. In 1941, XEW and its principal competitor, XEQ, merged to become Radio Programas de México (RPM), a network which controlled half the radio stations in Mexico and several in Caribbean basin. Moreover, during World War II, the propaganda arm of the U.S. government, the CIAA (Office of the Coordinator of Inter-American Affairs) bought huge chunks of airtime on the nationalistic RPM stations in order to drum up Mexican support for the Allied cause. This infusion of war dollars further bolstered RPM's already dominant market share.

Programming generally followed the successful formula developed during the 1930s: a mix of *música típica,* musical celebrities, and *radionovelas.* Competitors, however, sometimes adopted different formats in order to compete. After its 1942 debut, Radio Mil, XEOY, developed market niches in sports and news. Beginning in 1947, XEX successfully marketed a wholesome, family values image—including a "blacklist" of offensive songs (among them many of Lara's *boleros*)—in order to differentiate itself from the dominant RPM network.

Not everyone, however, was happy with the monopolistic character of Mexican radio during this period or so willing to adjust to the status quo. The spread of repeater stations in the early 1950s, for example, threatened local broadcasters, who appealed to the government, pleading regional autonomy in radio programming. Dependent on national radio networks to help disseminate policy and news, government officials declined to intervene. Even the on-again, off-again tension between commercial broadcasters and the state over program content resulted in nothing more than a commitment by commercial broadcasters to increase public service programming to 12.5 percent and half-hearted government efforts to revive XEEP, Radio Educación.

Domination by radio networks like RPM continued after 1970 and the number of radio stations continued to climb from 603 in 1970 to 1,045 by 1990. Nevertheless, the rise of television began to erode radio's dominant position in the communications industry (but not the overall position of the Azcárraga group, which monopolized television even more effectively than it did radio). Mexican radio continued to expand, especially into U.S. Spanish-speaking markets, but radio's percentage of overall advertising revenues declined, reaching a low of 9 percent in 1995. These changes affected programming as live television began to supplant live radio and the popularity of the *radionovela* declined dramatically in the face of its televised rival, the *telenovela*. As these older programs faded, new formats like talk radio became increasingly popular. The introduction of new technologies like stereo FM, which had captured 65 percent of the market by 1985—although AM recovered somewhat with the introduction of stereo AM in 1990—and the inauguration of satellite transmissions in the early 1990s, provided an innovative spark

that kept radio from losing still more ground to television. More recent technological advances like Digital Audio Broadcasting (DAB) with its compact disc quality sound suggest that this trend will continue.

Other aspects of Mexican radio changed as well after 1970. In the wake of late 1970s electoral reforms, full-fledged political advertising emerged from the shadow of "apolitical" public service announcements that usually lauded government or PRI initiatives. News programming began to play an even more important role than before, although it was (and still is) driven by the reporting of international wire services like the Associated Press that tend to focus on national events at the expense of local coverage. Regardless, as PRI hegemony waned during the 1990s, popular demand for more "objective" coverage led to the development of a more professional, less overtly progovernment approach to news reporting. This less-compromised news style and the presence of more English-language stations has signaled an end to the government's special arrangement with commercial radio networks.

The reemergence of public radio in recent years also bodes well for more independent radio programming. College radio has been around since 1937, when Radio UNAM, XEUN, began broadcasting at the Universidad Nacional Autónoma de México (UNAM) in Mexico City. Innovative approaches that included well-regarded programs on cinema and popular music by cultural critic Carlos Monsiváis flourished during much of the 1970s, but the pace of innovation slowed considerably as government funding grew more scarce in the wake of repeated economic crises. Public radio did manage some successes during the 1980s with a federally sponsored radio network, Grupo IMER (Instituto Mexicano de la Radio), devoted to traditional Mexican music, and Radio Cultural Indigenista (RCI) stations like XEZV—"La voz de la montaña" (The voice of the mountain) in Guerrrero—intended to help preserve indigenous languages and culture. In more recent years, independent radio stations like Radio Cultural Campesino (RCC) in Vera Cruz have taken to using community staffers to cover local issues and cultural events. These efforts, as well as the growth of low-tech, short-wave stations like XEJM that emphasize literacy programs, hold out hope that future Mexican radio can do something more than cater to consumer desires.

—RMB

See also: Monsiváis, Carlos; Popular Music; Television.

References:

Hayes, Joy Elizabeth. *Radio Nation: Communication, Popular Culture, and Nationalism in Mexico, 1920–1945.* Tucson: University of Arizona Press, 2000.

Miller, Michael Nelson. *Red, White, and Green: The Maturing of Mexicanidad, 1940–1946.* El Paso: Texas Western Press, 1998.

Rubenstein, Anne. "Mass Media and Popular Culture in the Postrevolutionary Era," in Michael C. Meyer and William H. Beezley, eds., *The Oxford History of Mexico,* pp. 637–670. New York: Oxford University Press, 2000.

Religion

Since the Spanish conquests of the 1520s, religion in Mexico has revolved around Roman Catholicism and Church-State relations. The Catholicism brought from Spain was a militant one, which the Spaniards were literally willing to spread by the sword. The conversion of the native population led to a blending of Roman Catholicism and various native religious influences that are visible even today. The Roman Catholic Church in colonial Mexico became a powerful institution. It exercised a virtual monopoly on education, functioned as a major instrument of social control, and even played an important economic role as it accumulated property and donations from the faithful. There was no concept of separation of Church and State. As a result of concessions from the Papacy, the Spanish Crown effectively converted the Roman Catholic Church into a department of government. Likewise, there was no concept of religious toleration; Catholicism was the official religion to the exclusion of all others.

After Mexico achieved independence in 1821, the Roman Catholic Church and its relation to the State came under almost immediate attack from reformers who saw the Church as the main obstacle to the modernization of the country. The political struggle over the Church's role continued for decades, culminating in the reform Constitution of 1857, which eliminated the privileged legal position of the Church and required it to liquidate its property. Resistance to the new constitution led to a three-year civil war that produced even greater restrictions on the Church, including the confiscation of all Church property and the suppression of religious orders. During the period of domination by Porfirio Díaz (1876–1911), the Church regained much of its social position but made only a modest recovery of its former economic role by having members of the laity nominally control properties used by the Church. The politically astute Díaz tried to keep the Church in line by encouraging Protestant missionary activity but with little success. These changes did not reflect any change in the legal status of the Church. The old reform laws were still on the books; they simply were not enforced.

The onset of the Revolution of 1910 threatened the informal working relationship of the Díaz era. The Church had actually been expanding its activities in response to a growing spirit of social activism that had started in the late nineteenth century. The early years of the Revolution brought few problems for the Church. It was the enactment of a new Constitution in 1917 that challenged the Church's position in Mexican society. The Revolutionary Constitution of 1917 placed a number of restrictions on the Church and its operations. The Constitution prohibited Church involvement in primary education as well as Church ownership or management of any property. Members of the clergy were not permitted to vote, hold office, or engage in political activities. Public religious ceremonies were not permitted, and the clergy were not even allowed to wear clerical garb in public. The Constitution gave state legislatures the power to regulate the number of clergy by licensing them. The enforcement—or nonenforcement—of these constitutional provisions would determine relations between Church and State into the 1990s.

Under the presidential administrations of Venustiano Carranza (1917–1920) and Alvaro Obregón (1920–1924), Church-State conflict was kept to a minimum by limited enforcement of the anticlerical provisions of the Constitution. The basis for a bitter conflict, however, was being laid. The emerging Revolutionary State saw the Church as a competitor in terms of both ideology (or at least formation of social values) and the organization of the masses (labor unions, peasant cooperatives, women and youth groups). After the strongly anticlerical Plutarco Elías Calles became president, a violent confrontation soon took place. Calles vigorously enforced the anticlerical provisions of the Constitution of 1917 and even attempted to set up a schismatic "Mexican Catholic Church" under government control. He also encouraged state governments to crack down on the Roman Catholic Church, especially through their power to license priests. The Church responded by announcing a suspension of services in July 1926.

What happened next surprised both Calles and Church leaders. A small-scale civil war, known as the Cristero Rebellion, developed, which lasted until 1929. The assassination of President-elect Alvaro Obregón in July 1928 by a religious fanatic also heightened Church-State tensions. Both parties saw the conflict as a threat to their respective positions and reached an agreement in June 1929 in which the Roman Catholic Church publicly agreed to abide by the restrictive provisions of the Constitution of 1917 while the government agreed privately to less rigorous enforcement. This agreement was the beginning of a working arrangement that would guide Church-State relations into the 1990s.

The administration of President Lázaro Cárdenas (1934–1940) brought a brief period of renewed conflict between Church and State over the issue of education. Cárdenas introduced sex education and socialist education into the Mexican public school system, which provoked a strong response from both the Roman Catholic Church and conservative elements. Cárdenas later deemphasized both of these policies and brought about a lessening of enforcement of anticlerical measures by both federal and state officials. The Church reciprocated by publicly supporting Cárdenas's controversial expropriation of foreign-owned oil companies in 1938, even encouraging the faithful to make financial contributions to the government to help pay for the nationalization.

Cárdenas's successor, Manuel Avila Camacho, brought Church-State cooperation to a new level. Avila Camacho openly courted the Church's support and proclaimed after his election, "I am a believer." A small but significant example of the greater cooperation was Avila Camacho's allowing chaplains in the army for the first time in the Revolutionary era. The Catholic hierarchy publicly supported Avila Camacho's domestic and foreign policies. Although the government was lax in its enforcement of constitutional restrictions, Avila Camacho would not support any major changes in the anticlerical provisions of the Constitution of 1917.

There was a corresponding easing of Church-State tensions at the local and regional levels during the 1930s and 1940s. While these changes sometimes were in response to actions at the national level, they also were a product of grassroots accommodation independent from the Church hierarchy or federal officials.

The spirit of accommodation continued into the 1950s and the 1960s. Factors were operating, however, which would eventually lead to a change in the Church and in Church-State relations. Mexico's postwar population growth and urbanization forced the Church to reorganize dioceses, establish new urban parishes, and rely more on the laity in its social activism. The Second Vatican Council, which opened its sessions in 1962, led to major changes in the worldwide Roman Catholic Church, which would eventually influence the activities of the Church in Mexico. The Council called for a greater emphasis on Church involvement in secular affairs and a corresponding commitment to social justice. Most Mexican bishops took a moderate approach to implementing this new social doctrine, rejecting the increasingly popular "liberation theology" with its marxist and Revolutionary connotations. This new direction, however, brought with it in Mexico the potential of Church conflict with the State over such basic issues as economic development, human rights, and democratization.

Mexico's growing economic, financial, and political problems in the late 1970s and early 1980s brought additional changes in the Church and in Church-State relations. Bishops in southern Mexico criticized the political and economic systems that exploited the peasantry while bishops in the north publicly criticized rampant electoral fraud. Mexico's financial and economic problems forced Presidents Miguel de la Madrid and Carlos Salinas to introduce major changes in the policies that had guided Mexican development since the 1940s. This growing reform movement spilled over into Church-State relations.

The questionable presidential election of 1988 tainted the new president, Carlos Salinas, and the official party, the PRI. Despite this handicap, Salinas was determined to continue with the reforms, extending them to Church-State relations. Salinas considered the old-style anticlericalism as embodied in the Constitution to be outmoded. Better and more visible relations with the Roman Catholic Church would improve his administration's image with foreign lenders and investors whose support was crucial to the success of economic and financial reforms. During the 1988 presidential campaign, Salinas met privately with a number of high-ranking Church officials. In January 1989, shortly after his inauguration, Salinas invited the Vatican representative and four leading Mexican bishops to lunch with him at his official residence, Los Pinos. In February 1990 Salinas appointed a high-profile "personal envoy" to the Vatican, Agustín Téllez Cruces, former president of Mexico's Supreme Court of Justice. When Pope John Paul II made his second visit to Mexico in May 1990, Salinas publicly—but in a "strictly personal" capacity—greeted him at the Mexico City airport. The pope's visit involved a series of technical violations of the constitutional restrictions on public religious ceremonies, which officials at all levels overlooked. As Salinas moved closer to the Church, the Church moved closer to Salinas by supporting his efforts at debt relief and his principal domestic program, the National Solidarity Program, aimed at improving socioeconomic conditions at the local level. Salinas even returned the Pope's visit, having a special audience with the Pope during a European trip in 1991.

While Church and State moved closer, the two basic issues of constitutional reforms and formal diplomatic relations were yet to be addressed. In January 1992 the Congress amended the anticlerical provisions of the Constitution of 1917. Religious instruction would now be permitted in private schools. Public religious ceremonies were legalized. "Religious associations" received legal status and were permitted to own property. Members of the clergy were given the right to vote, although they were still prohibited from holding public office. Another amendment lifted the ban on religious orders. In September 1992 Mexico and the Vatican formally established diplomatic relations. Although constitutional amendments and diplomatic relations did a great deal to "normalize" relations between Church and State, problem areas continued to appear. The assassination of Cardinal Juan Jesús Posadas Ocampo in May 1993 soured relations between the Church and Salinas, leading several bishops to criticize publicly both the government and the military for corruption in the antidrug campaign. The Zapatista revolt in Chiapas in January 1994 thrust the Church into the role of mediator in the person of Bishop Samuel Ruiz. Many members of the clergy continued to criticize the government for the socioeconomic consequences of its policies as well as for the lack of progress in democratization. The Church's growing emphasis on social justice made it increasingly difficult to draw the line between social activism and political involvement.

The fourth visit of Pope John Paul II to Mexico in January 1999 highlighted the uncertain and evolving relationship between Church and State. In rapid succession, the Pope criticized the excesses of neoliberal economic measures such as Mexico had recently implemented, met with President Ernesto Zedillo, celebrated mass at a Mexico City racetrack before an estimated crowd of one million people, and called on the government to meet the "legitimate aspirations" of Mexico's indigenous people. After spending much of the nineteenth and twentieth centuries in a bitter political struggle, both Church and State entered the twenty-first century trying to adjust to their new relationship as well as meeting the needs of a rapidly changing society in which they functioned.

—DMC

See also: Constitution of 1917; Cristero Rebellion; Democratization; Drug Trafficking; Economy; North American Free Trade Agreement (NAFTA); Revolution of 1910; Ruiz, Bishop Samuel.

References:

Camp, Roderic Ai. *Crossing Swords: Religion and Politics in Mexico*. New York: Oxford University Press, 1997.

Grayson, George W. *The Church in Contemporary Mexico*. Washington, DC: Center for Strategic and International Studies, 1992.

Reich, Peter Lester. *Mexico's Hidden Revolution: The Catholic Church in Law and Politics since 1929*. Notre Dame, IN: University of Notre Dame Press, 1995.

Tangeman, Michael. *Mexico at the Crossroads: Politics, the Church, and the Poor*. Maryknoll, NY: Orbis Books, 1995.

Revolution of 1910

In November 1910 the first great social revolution of the twentieth century began in Mexico. The Revolution brought forth a number of different leaders pursuing different goals. Early Revolutionary presidents—Francisco Madero and Venustiano Carranza—emphasized the need for political reform. The two most famous military leaders—Francisco "Pancho" Villa and Emiliano Zapata—responded to the growing demands of the peasants and urban workers for major social and economic reforms. There were also demands for curbs on the social control and political influence exercised by the Roman Catholic Church. Almost all of the Revolutionaries reflected a growing sense of nationalism and called for a reduction in the important role played by foreigners in the economy. For many, the Revolution did not involve the pursuit of long-term national goals; the chaos of the Revolution was simply a chance for personal advancement. Almost a decade of fighting and civil war took place before the fundamental goals of the Revolution were set down in the Constitution of 1917. It would take another two decades for the Constitution to be fully implemented.

The immediate target of the Revolution was General Porfirio Díaz, who had dominated national politics since the 1870s. After leading a revolution of his own in 1876, he became president in 1877, emphasizing the principal of no reelection. Díaz originally honored his no-reelection pledge by stepping down from the presidency when his term expired in 1880 but was later reelected in 1884, 1888, 1892, 1896, 1900, 1904, and 1910. Díaz justified his continuation in power by citing the political stability and economic development experienced by Mexico under his administration.

There was no denying that Mexico needed political stability when Díaz started his long stay in the presidency. In the fifty-five years between Mexico's independence in 1821 and Díaz's rise to power, the presidency had change hands on seventy-five different occa-

Mexican military officers stand around a table in a planning room. (Library of Congress)

sions. Díaz employed a mix of coercion and conciliation to bring his political opponents in line. Law and order ultimately depended on the army and the rural police force, which had reputations for dispensing summary justice. Díaz and his political allies rigged elections at all levels of government. Press criticism of the regime was met with force or bribery. Political and economic favors were extended to those who supported the regime.

Díaz wanted his administration to play an active role in economic development, especially industrialization. He believed that Mexico lacked the capital and technology to industrialize, so it would be necessary to make Mexico attractive to foreign investors. The attractions of political stability, government subsidies, and a friendly court system brought extensive foreign investment, particularly after 1900. Foreign investors—especially from the United States and Britain—soon dominated transportation, mining, and the oil industry.

Díaz's policies for land and agriculture proved especially controversial. Long before Díaz came to power, Mexico had a major problem with land being concentrated in the hands of a small minority of the population; under Díaz the concentration of land became worse. Díaz compensated private land companies for surveying federal lands by awarding them one-third of the land surveyed, with an option to buy the remaining two-thirds at low prices. This approach soon transferred extensive public lands into a limited number of private hands; by the mid-1890s these survey companies had gained control of 20 percent of Mexico's total land area. As more land passed into the control of a small minority, the vast majority of the rural population—primarily native—experienced a decline in real wages and standard of living. Agricultural policy stressed the growth of commercial agriculture geared to the export market. As production shifted to export crops such as sugar and coffee, Mexico had to

Group of Mexicans with cannon during the Mexican Revolution (Library of Congress)

import foodstuffs, even basic commodities such as corn.

Urban workers also enjoyed few of the benefits of the modernization process taking place around them. Working conditions in urban areas were harsh, with a twelve-hour workday and a six-day workweek typical. Efforts to unionize met with opposition not only from management but also from political and legal authorities. The courts typically viewed unions as "illegal associations," and political authorities used the police and sometimes even the army to suppress union activities.

Although the development policies pursued by Díaz had produced some impressive results, the benefits of the new prosperity were shared by only a small elite, perhaps 10 percent of Mexico's total population. A downturn in the international economy in 1907 was quickly transferred to Mexico; even the elite benefiting directly from the

government's development policies suffered from this downturn. Mexico experienced a major crisis in food production and distribution in 1909 and 1910. Antiforeign sentiment was on the rise as the result of a major increase in foreign investment in the first decade of the twentieth century. Although eighty years old, Díaz was planning on yet another reelection in 1910.

Díaz's lengthy rule had supposedly brought an end to the political unrest caused by presidential elections. The presidential election of 1910, however, provided the immediate background to the Revolution. There was little indication that the presidential candidacy of a member of the elite, Francisco Madero, would lead to Revolution. Madero originally supported the reelection of Díaz in 1910 but called on the aging dictator to permit a free selection of the vice-president, who would presumably succeed the aging president. When it became evident

Mexicans aim rifles from a mountain during the Mexican Revolution. (Library of Congress)

that Díaz would not permit any choice, Madero chose to run for the presidency himself. Díaz initially welcomed Madero's candidacy as a harmless threat that would provide a democratic appearance to the election. When Madero became the focal point of anti-Díaz forces, Díaz jailed Madero until after the presidential elections, which resulted in a predictably overwhelming victory for Díaz. Díaz then released Madero, who promptly fled to San Antonio, Texas, to plot revolution.

Madero set forth his Revolutionary program in the Plan of San Luis Potosí, named for the Mexican city in which he had been jailed. The plan provided a good indication of the direction and the future problems of Madero, who was concerned primarily with Mexico's political difficulties and the transition to a new government. Madero's plan offered little to peasants demanding the return of their traditional lands or to urban laborers seeking better working conditions. The plan nullified the 1910 elections and appointed Madero provisional president until new elec-

tions could be held. There was even a specific starting time for the Revolution: 6:00 p.m. on 20 November 1910. Madero's intention was to lead a rebellion, not a social revolution.

Although Madero's initial effort to lead the Revolution failed and he returned to San Antonio, numerous rebellions occurred throughout Mexico under Madero's banner. Emiliano Zapata revolted in the south in the name of agrarian reform. More important was the revolt in the north under the leadership of Pascual Orozco and Pancho Villa. Madero returned to Mexico in February 1911 and resumed nominal leadership of the rebel movement. The northern rebels focused their attention on the capture of the border town of Ciudad Juárez, across the Rio Grande from El Paso, Texas. The capture of Juárez would deal a major psychological blow to the Díaz regime and give the rebels control of an entry point to import war materials. On 10 May 1911 rebel forces led by Pascual Orozco and Pancho Villa captured Juárez. Díaz recognized that the end of an era

Carranzista rebels near Chihuahua (Mexican Revolution).
(Library of Congress)

was at hand and agreed to resign before the end of May; in return, Madero promised to keep Díaz's Federal Army and bureaucracy intact, a concession that would ultimately cost Madero his life. Díaz resigned on 25 May 1911 and went into exile in Europe. In new presidential elections held in October, Madero won an overwhelming victory over a group of minor candidates and took office on 6 November 1911.

The election of Madero was the beginning, rather than the end, of the Revolution. Many years of bloody fighting lay ahead, years that would lead to the deaths of hundreds of thousands of Mexicans, including Madero and Orozco. The worst of the fighting was over by 1916, and a new Constitution went into effect in early 1917. Even then, the Revolutionary violence had not come to an end. The first two presidents elected under the new Constitution—Venustiano Carranza and Alvaro Obregón—were both later assassinated, as were Villa and Zapata, who resisted the new constitutional governments just as they had fought against Díaz. The Revolutionary themes of the new Constitution would not be fully developed until the mid-1930s; by the 1940s there was already criticism that the Revolution was dead as Mexico embarked on a new era of modernization and industrialization. Political

and economic reforms in the 1980s signaled an end to the pursuit of the traditional themes of the Revolution: agrarian reform, anticlericalism, labor, and antiforeign sentiment.

Various political groups and parties have attempted to appropriate the Revolution of 1910 as their own. The "official party"—the Institutional Revolutionary Party, or PRI—has both claimed credit for implementing the ideals of the Revolution as well as received constant criticism for abandoning them. The Revolution was always an idea as much as it was a historical process. The "idea" of the Revolution is still very much at the center of Mexican politics today.

—DMC

See also: Díaz, Porfirio; Presidents of the
   Twentieth Century; *Soldaderas;* Villa, Francisco
   "Pancho"; Zapata, Emiliano.
References:
Hart, John M. *Revolutionary Mexico: The Coming and
   Process of the Mexican Revolution.* Berkeley:
   University of California Press, 1987.
Knight, Alan. *The Mexican Revolution: Counter-
   revolution and Reconstruction.* 2 vols. New York:
   Cambridge University Press, 1986.
Ruiz, Ramón E. *The Great Rebellion: Mexico,
   1905–1924.* New York: Norton, 1980.

Rivera, Diego (1886–1957)

Flamboyant, self-aggrandizing, and prodigiously talented, Diego Rivera is probably Mexico's best-known artist. As with so many of his contemporaries, his career is inextricably bound up with the Revolution of 1910. Before the Revolution, Rivera enjoyed considerable success in the hothouse art scene of early twentieth-century Paris as a member of the cubist school of painters along with such luminaries as Pablo Picasso and Georges Braque. After the Revolution, he was enticed back to Mexico by Secretary of Education José Vasconcelos to lend his prestige to an ambitious public mural program intended to interpret Mexico's history and culture in a form accessible to all Mexicans. The combination of Rivera's contentious personality, radical political views, and extraordinary mastery of the large-scale mural form ensured a huge international audience for the muralist movement. Although muralist movements represented a passing fad in Europe and North America, Rivera continues to exert a tremendous influence on Mexican, Latin American, and Mexican American artists. His public murals are still admired by thousands of visitors every day.

José Diego María Rivera was born on 13 December 1886, in Guanajuato, the most important of Mexico's colonial silver mining centers. Both parents taught school and the family was solidly middle class. His father's liberal ideas apparently alienated conservative local elites and, when Diego was six, the Riveras relocated to Mexico City. His mother, however, remained staunchly Roman Catholic and the boy was sent to private religious schools. Already something of a prodigy, the eleven-year-old Diego began to attend art classes at the National Academy of San Carlos, Mexico's premiere art school. Later in life, Rivera would complain about the stifling academic training he received there, but by most standards he thrived (at least if regular scholarships and prizes are any measure of success). Certainly his instructors, including world-renowned landscape painter José María Velasco, were the best Mexico had to offer. In 1905, his studies concluded, Rivera joined a modernist group, *Savia Moderna* (Modern Sap), which rejected the sentimentalism of nineteenth-century academic painting as well as the positivism of President Porfirio Díaz's *científico* advisors and their pretensions to the scientific administration of Mexican society.

Before the group's attempts to subvert entrenched ideologies could attract the attention of authorities, Rivera received a four-year scholarship to study art in Europe. Aside from a brief trip back for an Independence centennial exhibition of his painting at the Academy of San Carlos—inaugurated by Díaz's wife, Carmen Romero Rubio de Díaz—Rivera would remain in Europe until 1921. There he studied old Spanish masters like El Greco, Velásquez, and Goya and absorbed the latest advances in European art from Gustave Courbet, Edouard Manet, and Paul Cézanne to Pablo Picasso, Georges Braque, and Piet Mondrian. His most important painting from this period, *Zapatista Landscape: The Guerrilla* (1915), done in the fractured idiom of cubism, demonstrated not only stylistic mastery but also a sympathetic understanding of the momentous events unfolding in Mexico at the time. The picture's radical sympathies (Emiliano Zapata was the most socially "progressive" revolutionary) would become clearer once Rivera returned to Mexico in 1921.

The Revolution was over, for all intents and purposes, by the time Rivera returned. His purpose was to ensure, through a public and politicized art, that it fulfilled its many promises, especially those given to Mexico's long-suffering masses. Under the patronage of a dynamic education secretary, José Vasconcelos, Rivera joined with other Mexican artists, such as José Clemente Orozco, David Siquieros, Fernando Leal, Jean Charlot, and Roberto Montenegro, to initiate the muralist movement. These muralists sought to educate all Mexicans, literate and illiterate alike, through huge, colorful public murals on historical and allegorical themes that they painted on important public buildings, including, in Rivera's case, the Department of Education and the National Palace. Nor was Rivera content with artistic statements: he joined the Mexican Communist Party in 1922 and actively participated in Party activities until 1929, when its leaders expelled him for allegedly supporting Stalin's rival, Trotsky, who would later take up residence in Mexico with Rivera's help. A committed Marxist-Leninist (even outside the official party), Rivera would espouse radical causes throughout his career.

Painted for the auditorium at Mexico City's elite National Preparatory School, Rivera's first major mural, *Creation* (1922–1923), was an uncontroversial creation allegory—the preferred genre of Vasconcelos—with Mexican national types presented in a

Renaissance fresco style somewhere between Giotto and Michelangelo with just a trace of cubist geometry. His next major project (1923–1928), this time for the courtyard of the renovated Department of Education, was considerably more daring. In the Department of Education murals, Rivera painted scenes from Mexican rural and urban working-class life along with popular celebrations like Day of the Dead. This glorification of popular cul-

Diego Rivera (1886–1957), ca. 1944 (Bettmann/Corbis)

ture and life was controversial in itself, but Rivera went further, depicting the exploitation of Mexican workers by the decadent upper classes and stressing radical Revolutionary promises like land redistribution and rural education. To reinforce these broad political themes, Rivera painted in a portrait of Zapata, the Bolshevik hammer and sickle, his wife-to-be Frida Kahlo distributing arms to workers, and snippets of Revolutionary songs or *corridos* with titles like "This is the Way the Proletarian Revolution Will Be" and "Corrido of the Agrarian Revolution." "For the first time in the history of art," Rivera said later, " . . . Mexican mural painting made the masses the hero of monumental art." Rivera's astonishing capacity for hard work—twelve- to eighteen-hour workdays were typical—ensured that these monuments to the masses would be many.

The mural cycle for the National School of Agriculture at Chapingo (1924–1926) combined the mythical qualities of *Creation* and radical politics of the Department of Education murals to celebrate the birth, fertility, and liberating potential of social revolution. To stress the generative power of revolution, at the center of the largest mural, *The Liberated Earth and Natural Forces Controlled by Humanity,* Rivera painted a voluptuous earth goddess (modeled on his second wife, Guadalupe Marín). The National Palace murals (1929–1935) moved from revolutionary myth to Mexican history with a huge central panel crowded with the nation's many heroes and villains. Mexico's rich history dominated much of Rivera's subsequent work: the murals for Hernán Cortés's palace in Cuernavaca (1930) depicted the conquest and exploitation of Native Americans and their redemption by Zapata; and his last great mural, *Dream of a Sunday Afternoon in the Alameda Central Park* (1947–1948) placed the painter (as a child), wife Frida Kahlo, precursor José Guadalupe Posada, and a skeletal Calavera Catrina (as mother Mexico) at the center of a vivid panorama of Mexican history.

Mexico was his grand passion, but Rivera had other loves, too. A series of murals in San Francisco, Detroit, and New York City showed his appreciation of modern technology's transformative power and aesthetic beauty. Rivera understood, as Marx had, that despite its many flaws, capitalism had tremendous creative potential. Financed by automobile magnate Edsel Ford (son of Henry), his *Detroit Industry* murals for the Detroit Institute of Arts (1932–1933) revealed the beauty and power of modern factories and glorified the collective aspects of factory work. The Detroit murals had raised some hackles among local conservatives, but Edsel's enthusiastic support blunted their criticisms. Another commission, this time for the Rockefeller Center (1933), caused an international incident when Rivera insisted on including a portrait of Lenin in his *Man at the Crossroads* mural. When Rivera refused to remove it, the Rockefellers had the mural destroyed. (Rivera would later recreate it in Mexico City).

Nor were Rivera's loves limited to his art. His third wife and fourth wife (their stormy relationship involved two marriages), Frida Kahlo, affectionately called him *Sapo-rana,* toad-frog, but despite that "handicap" and his considerable size (over 6 feet tall and 300 pounds), Rivera proved irresistible to women. Married five times, Rivera also conducted several semipublic affairs with dancers, artists, and even Frida's sister. Rivera's flamboyant personality, coupled with his controversial political activities, kept him in the public spotlight until his death in 1957. His prodigious talent has attracted audiences ever since.

—*RMB*

See also: Kahlo, Frida; Orozco, José Clemente; Muralist Movement; Posada, José Guadalupe; Revolution of 1910; Siquieros, David Álfaro; Vasconcelos, José; Zapata, Emiliano.

References:

Craven, David. *Diego Rivera as Epic Modernist.* New York: G. K. Hall & Co., 1997.

Marnham, Patrick. *Dreaming with His Eyes Open: A Life of Diego Rivera.* New York: Alfred A. Knopf, 1998.

Wolfe, Betram D. *The Fabulous Life of Diego Rivera.* New York: Stein and Day, 1963.

Rock and Roll

As in most modern societies, rock and roll has been a source of controversy in Mexico. For many, mostly older, Mexicans, rock culture and its *rebeldes sin causa* (rebels without a cause) represent a disruptive force that undermines social stability by encouraging substance abuse, sexual promiscuity, and disrespect for authority. For cultural nationalists, rock and roll threatens to supplant a rich and varied Mexican musical heritage that runs the gamut from local "folk" styles to mainstream genres like *mariachi* and *norteño*. At the same time, as a North American and British import (especially in its early years), rock music symbolizes modernity to authorities and parents as well as their rebellious children. From this perspective, rock and roll, properly controlled by government regulation and music industry self-policing, represents a positive cultural influence that promotes modern values and, in this capacity, it has sometimes received official support. Mexican rockers, caught between a predominantly English-speaking, cosmopolitan musical culture and their desire to produce an authentic Mexican rock and roll, have vacillated between imitation and, less often, innovation. In recent years, however, especially with the 1990s *roc en español*, Mexican rock has come into its own and has even begun to exert an international influence.

Controversy surrounded rock and roll in Mexico from the first North American and British "invasions" of the 1950s and 1960s. Confronted with North American films like *Blackboard Jungle, Rock around the Clock, The Wild One* and *Rebels without a Cause* which linked rock music, juvenile delinquency, macho posturing, and unrestrained female sexuality, Mexican audiences responded with a mixture of enthusiasm, shock, and disgust. Groups like the League of Decency and the Mexican Society of Authors and Composers lobbied government officials to censor objectionable films and the music that energized them. Establishment journalists went even further, falsely accusing Elvis Presley of saying "I'd rather kiss three black girls than a Mexican" and producing an explosion of anti–North American sentiment. Young *rebeldes sin causa,* however, found the mix irresistible and, at the 1959 Mexico City premiere of Elvis Presley's King Creole, they initiated a riot during which gangs of boys assaulted girls with shouts of "Meat! Meat! Meeaat!" and tore up the theater before being brutally ejected by riot police. The Mexican Congress responded with a 1960 Federal Law of Radio and Television that ordered media "to avoid noxious or disturbing influences on the harmonious development of children and youth . . . [and] to exalt the values of Mexican nationality" (quoted in Zolov, *Refried Elvis,* pp. 48 and 59). Authorities seldom enforced the law, but it nevertheless served as an effective warning to media executives interested in promoting rock music.

Inspired by their North American (and later British) counterparts, young Mexican musicians began to produce their own rock and roll. Mexican rock, especially in its formative stages, was derivative—mostly cover versions of imported rock tunes, first in Spanish, later in English—and confined by and large to middle- and upper-class youth with more access to expensive, hard-to-find foreign records. Recording for both domestic and international labels, groups like Los Rebeldes de Rock and Los Teen Tops launched the "Grand Era" of Mexican rock (1959–1964) with performances of Spanish language *refritos* (covers) of English-language hits and star turns in movies like *Twist, The Youth Craze* (1962), and *Youth Take Over* (1964). Mexican fan magazines provided crucial support, including biographical details on the latest rock stars, lyrics to hit songs, and a squeaky clean image to reassure anxious parents and government censors. The 1964 British "invasion" brought a new edgier style to Mexico and initiated the first of many debates about an authentic Mexican *rocanrol.* Performers and audiences favored English as the authentic, international rock and roll language and used it to rebel against the Mexican music favored by their parents' generation and the cultural nationalism of intellectuals and government propagandists. Government efforts to block the sale and performance of imported new rock backfired as bands from the U.S.–Mexico border region gained a national audience with English-language cover versions of the new music and their firsthand experience with youth culture in the United States. By the late 1960s, Mexican groups responded to these new trends with original material of their own. But even the rockers of *La Onda Chica* (The Chicano Vibe, 1969–1973)—La Revolución de Emiliano Zapata, División del Norte, Peace and Love, Three Souls in My Mind—sang their originals primarily in English despite some blatantly nationalistic group names.

The rock invasion also had a profound impact on Mexican society in general, as many youth adopted *jipi* (hippie) fashions from their North American counterparts: exchanging shoes for sandals, growing their hair long, and expressing a new-found appreciation of Mexico's indigenous cultures. The government responded with a mixture of tolerance and repression. Notoriously straight-laced President Gustavo Díaz Ordaz, whose own son Alfredo exhibited *jipi* tendencies, went on record with: "Everyone is free to let his beard, hair or sideburns grow if he wants to, to dress well or badly as he sees fit, so long as he does not harm others' rights or break the law" (quoted in Zolov, *Refried Elvis,* p. 116). But he also oversaw the closure of most of Mexico City's mainstream rock clubs on the grounds that they corrupted youth and perverted national culture. Still, despite government repression, and abetted by transnational record companies eager to supply Mexico's growing appetite for rock and roll, Mexican rock music thrived. Two events—the 1968 Tlatelolco Massacre of nearly 400 protesters (mostly young univer-

sity students) and a controversial 1971 outdoor concert at Avándaro attended by over 200,000 fans—changed the face of Mexican rock and roll. Government crackdowns on student activism, rock concerts, and mass media promotions of foreign music, forced rock underground into makeshift urban venues or *hoyos fonquis* (funky holes). Bands like TRI, the latest incarnation of Three Souls in My Mind, became vocal critics of Mexico's one-party state (the PRI) and its repressive policies. With the rise of lower-class Mexican punk rock in the 1980s, Mexico finally developed an original Spanish-language rock style. (It is somewhat ironic that just as Mexican rock was declaring its independence, Mexican folk music, inspired by the Cuban-based New Song movement and Simon and Garfunkel's rendition of "El condor pasa," was enthusiastically supported by the government and the radical left as an authentic representation of Mexican culture and, for the more commercially inclined, as an exportable commodity.) Middle-class youth, previously the rock and roll trendsetters, followed cautiously along.

By the late 1980s, Mexican rock had reemerged from the lower-class *barrios* (neighborhoods) more popular and more original than ever as the neoliberal policies of President Carlos Salinas de Gortari opened Mexican markets to foreign imports (including music), and media executives recognized the commercial potential of the new *roc en español.* Mexican rockers like Maná, Los Caifanes, Café Tacuba, and Maldita Vecindad y los Hijos del Quinto Patio (Damned Neighborhood and the Sons of the Tenement) have responded to this opening with an eclectic approach to musical styles—everything from *norteño* to ska—that defies categorization, rejects pretensions to authenticity, and crosses musical and cultural borders with ease. In the words of Café Tacuba guitarist, José Rangel: "We had a lot of information from the outside, a lot of information from the inside. There is not one Mexican culture, but lots of them living together in parallel, in different layers. You can go deep into your roots and not be able to see what's around you. I think we're trying to do both" (quoted in *Boston Globe,* 19 November 1999). With the Latino population now the largest minority group in the United States—30 million in 2000—the market for *roc en español* is expanding rapidly. Maná's "Sueños Líquidos [Wet Dreams]" won a gold record in 1995 for selling over 500,000 copies in the United States and their 1999 "MTV Unplugged" album sold 700,000 copies in the United States and Latin America in just its first week! In an increasingly transnational world, the Mexican experience might just be the future of rock and roll.

—*RMB*

See also: Díaz Ordaz, Gustavo; Popular Music; Tlatelolco Massacre.

References:

Hernández, Mark. "Remaking the Corrido for the 1990s: Maldita Vecindad's El Barzón." *Studies in Latin American Popular Culture* 20 (2001): pp. 101–117.

Martínez, Rubén. "Corazón del Rocanrol," in *The Other Side: Notes from the New L.A., Mexico City, and Beyond.* New York: Vintage Books, 1992.

Zolov, Eric. *Refried Elvis: The Rise of the Mexican Counterculture.* Berkeley: University of California Press, 1999.

Rodríguez, Abelardo (1889–1967)

President of Mexico from 1932 to 1934, Abelardo Rodríguez was born in Guaymas, Sonora, on 12 May 1889. With a primary-school education, Rodríguez worked as a laborer, including a period of time at the famous Cananea copper mines. He lived in the United States from 1906 to 1913, returning to Mexico in 1913 to fight against the dictatorship of General Victoriano Huerta, who had overthrown President Francisco Madero. Rodríguez joined the Constitutionalist forces under Venustiano Carranza as a lieutenant. He rose quickly through the ranks, serving with two Sonoran generals, Benjamín Hill and Alvaro Obregón. In 1920 when Carranza attempted to impose his successor as president, Rodríguez joined the successful rebellion supporting the candidacy of General Obregón. Also in 1920, Rodríguez was promoted to the rank of brigadier general.

Rodríguez held a variety of military commands in the early 1920s, culminating in his appointment as military commander of Baja California Norte. From 1923 to 1929, he also served as governor of Baja California Norte. As governor, Rodríguez passed a number of important measures. He established a minimum wage and encouraged the formation of labor unions. His administration also stressed education, road construction, and irrigation projects. In response to criticism that Asian immigrants were taking jobs from local workers, Rodríguez tried to block the entrance of additional Asian laborers into the area and required local employers to have a workforce that was at least 50 percent Mexican. With Prohibition in effect in the United States, Rodríguez encouraged the development of the border town of Tijuana as a tourist attraction. He had a personal financial stake in the development of Tijuana, which led to Rodríguez becoming a prominent business figure as well as a key political and military official. His investments ranged from fishing to cement, and Rodríguez was a wealthy man by the time he resigned as governor in December 1929.

After a brief European tour to study business techniques and aviation, Rodríguez returned to Mexico and served in a number of positions in the cabinet of President Pascual Ortiz Rubio. He started as subsecretary of war in 1931; in early 1932, he became secretary of industry, commerce, and labor. Rodríguez became minister of war in August 1932 as a major political crisis was coming to a head over the interference of former President Plutarco Elías Calles in the affairs of the administration of Pascual Ortiz Rubio. When Ortiz Rubio resigned on 3 September 1932, the Congress elected Rodríguez to serve out the remainder of Ortiz Rubio's term, which was to end on 1 December 1934.

As president, Rodríguez's actions were under the constant supervision and frequent interference of Calles who continued to

President Abelardo Rodríguez (center) leaves the White House after lunching with President Roosevelt; Washington, D.C., January 1935. (Bettmann/Corbis)

dominate the political scene. Agrarian reform had slowed down in 1933 because of administrative and legal problems; during 1934 Rodríguez substantially accelerated distribution of land, resulting in about 2 million acres being distributed from 1932 to 1934. In the area of labor relations, Rodríguez established a separate ministry of labor, splitting labor affairs from the ministry of industry and commerce. He also pressed for a variable minimum wage, which went into effect in September 1933. Church-State relations took a turn for the worse under the Rodríguez administration. As part of an effort to reorganize and centralize education, there was a simultaneous effort to introduce socialist education and sex education into the schools. This provoked a major controversy with the Roman Catholic Church and conser-

vative elements in general that would carry over into the administration of Lázaro Cárdenas. When Pope Pius XI publicly criticized the anticlerical program of the government, Rodríguez responded by expelling the papal representative from Mexico. With encouragement from the central government, state governments restricted Church activities, especially by limiting the number of priests who could operate in each state as the Constitution of 1917 permitted.

One of the most important functions of the Rodríguez administration was to assure the peaceful transfer of power to the next president, who would take office on 1 December 1934. Rodríguez supported the candidacy of General Lázaro Cárdenas, whom he appointed to his cabinet as minister of war in December 1932. Cárdenas was also acceptable to the "Maximum Leader of the Revolution," former President Calles. Cárdenas received the nomination of the official party, the National Revolutionary Party, and went on to win easily in the elections of July 1934. Cárdenas assumed the presidency on 1 December 1934 without incident. In evaluating the Rodríguez administration, it is hard to distinguish between what he did and what Calles wanted done. Rodríguez did show an independent streak at times; he blocked a meeting between the U.S. ambassador and Calles, fired the minister of finance without consulting Calles, and criticized his own officials when they consulted with Calles without the president's permission.

After leaving the presidency, Rodríguez continued to function in both the private and public arenas. He remained an important and wealthy figure in business affairs in the states of Sonora and Baja California Norte. During World War II, he served as military commander of the Military Zone of the Gulf. From 1943 to 1948, Rodríguez was governor of Sonora; he resigned in April 1948 citing health reasons. He died on 13 February 1967.

—DMC

See also: Baja California Norte; Calles, Plutarco Elías; Cárdenas, Lázaro; Huerta, Victoriano; Immigration/Emigration; Obregón, Alvaro; Presidents of the Twentieth Century; Tourism.
References:
Dulles, John W. F. *Yesterday in Mexico: A Chronicle of the Revolution, 1919–1936.* Austin: University of Texas Press, 1972.
Meyer, Lorenzo, Rafael Segovia, and Alejandra Lajous. *Historia de la Revolución Mexicana.* Vol. 12. *Los inicios de la institucionalización: la política del Maximato.* Mexico: El Colegio de Mexico, 1978.

Ruíz, Bishop Samuel (1924–)

Bishop of Chiapas from 1960 to 1999, Samuel Ruíz García was one of the most visible representatives of the Mexican Roman Catholic Church during the last half of the twentieth century. He was also among the most controversial, vilified by his critics as the "Red Bishop" (a reference to Ruíz's alleged ties to socialist ideas) and eulogized as "Tatic" ("dear father") by the Maya Indians of Chiapas. His family background and religious training (which occurred in the context of the Cold War) suggested that Ruíz would be a conservative cleric. But his appointment as Bishop of Chiapas radicalized him and ensured that Ruíz would be a prominent figure in events surrounding the Zapatista rebellion of 1994.

Ruíz was born in 1924, on the eve of the Cristero Rebellion, a Church-State struggle that arose in the aftermath of the Mexican Revolution. Ruíz's birthplace, the state of Guanajuato, was a center of the religious conflict precipitated by the government's attempts to undermine the historically strong position of the Roman Catholic Church. Ruíz's parents were devout supporters of the Roman Catholic Church who refused to send their children to the public, secular schools established by the Mexican state. Moreover, Ruíz's father, a former migrant farmworker, was a member of the conservative lay organization, Catholic Action (Acción Católica).

Samuel Ruíz's formal religious training began at the Seminary of León in Guanajuato, which he entered at the age of fifteen. His studies eventually took him to Rome, where he was ordained a priest. Ruíz completed his religious education (obtaining a doctoral degree in Scripture) as the Cold War began, and his tenure in Rome coincided with that of Pius XII, a conservative pope known for his virulent anticommunism. When he returned to Guanajuato in the 1950s, Ruíz entered the service of a Mexican church that endorsed Pius's conservatism. He gave every indication of upholding that tradition when he was named Bishop of Chiapas in 1959. Indeed, his first pastoral letter pointedly criticized communism as an "atheistic doctrine." Somewhat ironically, Ruíz's designation as Bishop occurred during the papacy of Pope John XXIII, who worked to liberalize the Roman Catholic Church, making it more responsive to popular needs and encouraging Church activism on behalf of social justice and human rights.

Ruíz arrived in Chiapas at the age of thirty-five and began his ministry among the state's diverse population of poor Indians and wealthier cattlemen and coffee plantation owners. He witnessed firsthand the concentration of wealth in the hands of an elite that worked closely with Mexico's official Institutional Revolutionary Party (PRI) to control the state's economic and political life. Within a few years of working in Chiapas, Ruíz had become sensitized to the poverty and political repression that affected the lives of the state's large Indian population. His attendance at Vatican Council II, an ecumenical council convened by John XXIII in the early 1960s, introduced Ruíz to a "new" Church that was less traditional and more attuned to social problems. In 1968, Ruíz also took part in the Second General Conference of Latin American Bishops (CELAM), where he joined other progressive bishops in debating the problems faced by Latin America's poor. By the end of the 1960s, Ruíz's beliefs and approach had shifted dramatically. He was critical of capitalism, dedicated to the idea of Church activism on behalf of the poor, and increasingly identified with Liberation Theology, a marxist-inspired doctrine that encouraged the Church's direct participation in the struggle against oppression. It was in this spirit that Ruíz, based in the highland community of San Cristóbal de las Casas, dedicated himself to helping Chiapas's poorest inhabitants.

Ruíz's attempts to plant the seeds of a new Church were especially well received in eastern Chiapas, and particularly in the Lacandón Forest. Many indigenous people had earlier taken refuge in the Lacandón after being expelled from their lands in other parts of the state (a result of the continuing concentration of land that favored the cattle and coffee industries). During the 1970s, after declaring the area a biosphere reserve, the Mexican government began evicting people from the Lacandón, a move that encouraged the growth of peasant organizations. Ruíz encouraged the establishment of such organizations, and he sent priests and other volunteers into the Lacandón to support peasant activism. At the same time, Ruíz became a vocal advocate of indigenous rights, helping in the establishment of economic programs (including peasant cooperatives) and social programs (including health care) that targeted Chiapas's Indian peoples.

Bishop Ruíz's activism increased throughout the 1970s and 1980s, even as the Mexican government was responding to agrarian unrest in Chiapas by augmenting the military presence in that state. In 1974, Ruíz provided a forum for the discussion of Indian concerns by organizing the First Indigenous Congress of Chiapas. In 1989, in response to escalating violence against Chiapas's Indians, he established the Bartolomé de las Casas Human Rights Center (named after the first Spanish bishop of Chiapas). As the negotiations that led to the North American Free Trade Agreement (NAFTA) proceeded throughout the 1980s, and as President Carlos Salinas de Gortari (1988–1994) eliminated agrarian reform in an attempt to open the country's agricultural sector to large-scale investment, Bishop Ruíz became a prominent voice of dissent. He lamented the changes in Mexico's agrarian policy, and in 1993, when Pope John Paul II paid a visit to Mexico, Ruíz issued a pastoral letter that criticized neoliberal economic policies and that underscored the difficulties such policies presented for Mexico's Indians. At the same time, Ruíz was a public and vocal opponent of a Mexican system that he identified as corrupt and responsible for human rights abuses.

Not surprisingly, Samuel Ruíz quickly became the object of criticism, by both the Mexican government and the Roman Catholic Church. By the 1980s, he was commonly referred to as the "Red Bishop" by his opponents, who accused him of provoking Chiapas's Indians into violent action. Meanwhile, a conservative Church hierarchy attempted to have Ruíz removed from his post, and the Vatican (under Pope John Paul II) placed him under investigation for his views. Popular protests by the Bishop's Indian followers, as well as the support of international organizations such as Amnesty International, helped to postpone Ruíz's departure. Ruíz remained a controversial figure, and in 1994 the Zapatista rebellion propelled him into the national and international spotlight.

The Zapatista rebellion (named after Emiliano Zapata, a key figure of the Mexican Revolution) began as a protest against the neoliberal economic policies of the Mexican government and developed into a rebellion on behalf of indigenous rights. After a round of violence, in which the Mexican military tried to crush the movement, negotiations began. In 1996, the rebels and the government agreed on the San Andrés Accords, which granted a degree of autonomy to Mexico's Indian communities. Shortly thereafter, however, the Mexican government reneged on the agreement, stating fears of Indian separatism. As the new century began, there was a stalemate in Chiapas, punctuated by violence and characterized by the Zapatistas' continuing struggle to achieve recognition and official support for indigenous rights.

From the beginning of the Zapatista rebellion, Ruíz was accused by his conservative enemies and by the Mexican government (including President Ernesto Zedillo, who called Ruíz a "theologian of violence") of aiding and abetting the rebels. In 1995, the Vatican responded to such concerns by naming Raúl Vera López as co-Bishop of Chiapas, an attempt to undercut Ruíz's authority in the state. Ruíz denied any role in orchestrating the Zapatista rebellion, and he became the chief mediator between the government and the rebels. In 1997, a right-wing paramilitary squad that included conservative Roman Catholics and Protestant Evangelicals made an attempt on Ruíz's life and shot and wounded Ruíz's sister. Several Catholic churches identified with Ruíz were closed down, and in December 1997 forty-five worshippers in the village of Acteal were massacred.

Ruíz condemned the violence, which was allegedly supported by the Federal Army and the PRI. Citing government back-pedaling on the San Andrés Accords and accusing Mexican leaders of unwillingness to negotiate in good faith with the Zapatistas, Ruíz resigned his position as mediator in 1998, the same year in which he was nominated for the Nobel Peace Prize. In 1999, he also resigned as Bishop of Chiapas. At the same time, Bishop Raúl Vera López (who took sympathy with the plight of Chiapas's Indians and thus failed to fulfill his role as a conservative counter to Ruíz) was transferred to the northeastern state of Coahuila, far from the conflict in Chiapas.

Although he did not preside over a definitive end to the Zapatista conflict, Samuel Ruíz made a significant contribution to the cause of indigenous rights in Chiapas and indeed, in all of Mexico. His commitment to improving the lives of Indians was genuine and stemmed from firsthand experience with their particular plight. His willingness to criticize the corruption and unfairness of Mexico's political and economic systems, and his energetic work on behalf of human rights, were also remarkable, and they proved Ruíz's dedication to using the traditional institution of the Roman Catholic Church to affect significant social change.

—*SBP*

See also: Chiapas (State); Lacandón; Zapatista National Liberation Army (EZLN).

References:

Collier, George A., and Elizabeth Lowery Quaratiello. *Basta! Land and the Zapatista Rebellion in Chiapas.* Oakland, CA: Food First Books, 1994.

Fazio, Carlos. *Samuel Ruíz: El Caminante.* Mexico: Esposa Calpe Mexicana, 1994.

Harvey, Neil. *The Chiapas Rebellion: The Struggle for Land and Democracy.* Durham, NC: Duke University Press, 1998.

Katzenberger, Elaine, ed. *First World, Ha Ha Ha!: The Zapatista Challenge.* San Francisco: City Lights, 1995.

Ross, John. *Rebellion from the Roots: Indian Uprising in Chiapas.* Monroe, ME: Common Courage Press, 1995.

Ruiz Cortines, Adolfo (1890–1973)

President from 1952 to 1958, Adolfo Ruiz Cortines was born in the port city of Vera Cruz. He cut short his formal education in order to support his widowed mother, taking a bookkeeping job in a local commercial firm. In 1912 he moved to Mexico City, where he found employment with the engineering firm of Alfredo Robles Domínguez, who became his first important political contact. In 1913 when President Francisco Madero was overthrown and murdered, both Ruiz Cortines and Robles Domínguez joined the opposition to the military dictatorship of General Victoriano Huerta. They joined the Constitutionalist forces under the leadership of Venustiano Carranza. Ruiz Cortines served in Carranza's secret service in Mexico City, which was under Huerta's control. When Huerta was forced out in July 1914, Carranza appointed Robles Domínguez governor of the Federal District which included Mexico City. Robles Domínguez, in turn, selected Ruiz Cortines to be his principal administrative aide. When General Heriberto Jara took over as the new governor of the Federal District, Ruiz Cortines continued as his aide. In November 1914 he accompanied Jara to Vera Cruz, which was being restored to Mexican control after occupation by the United States since April 1914. In the civil war of 1915–1916, Ruiz Cortines remained on the Constitutionalist side. He saw some combat, but his primary value was as an administrator, including the position of military paymaster. Although valued for his administrative talents, Ruiz Cortines never became one of the Revolutionary generals.

In 1920 Adolfo de la Huerta and Plutarco Elías Calles led a successful revolt against President Venustiano Carranza on behalf of the presidential ambitions of General Alvaro Obregón. Ruiz Cortines supported the rebels. During Adolfo de la Huerta's interim presidency, Ruiz Cortines served as private secretary to General Jacinto B. Treviño, secretary of industry and commerce. In 1921 Ruiz Cortines took a position in the newly created federal Department of Statistics, where he remained for the next fourteen years. In 1935 he became chief of staff for the Federal District; at that time he formed a friendship with his fellow-Veracruzano, Miguel Alemán, that would shape the rest of his career. When Alemán became manager for the presidential campaign of Manuel Avila Camacho in 1940, Ruiz Cortines became the campaign treasurer. After becoming president, Avila Camacho appointed Alemán secretary of the interior (internal security); Alemán in turn appointed Ruiz Cortines to the number-two position in the secretariat, where he served until 1944. Ruiz Cortines became governor of the state of Veracruz in 1944, taking time off to serve as campaign manager for Alemán's successful bid for the presidency in 1946. He resigned as governor in 1948 to become now-President Alemán's secretary of the interior.

As the presidential elections of 1952 approached, the official party needed a candidate to restore public confidence after the free-spending and corrupt administration of Miguel Alemán. The sober, austere former bookkeeper, Adolfo Ruiz Cortines, was a logical choice. His reputation for honesty dated back to the early years of the Revolution when he had served as an army paymaster and later had provided an accurate inventory of the assets that President Carranza had fled the capital with in 1920. Although Ruiz Cortines held a prominent position in the Alemán cabinet, he escaped the corruption scandal that enveloped the Alemán administration. The election was marked by violence and fraud, but as the nominee of the official party, there was no doubt that Ruiz Cortines would emerge the winner.

As president, Ruiz Cortines had to deal with major problems involving government finances: an inherited budget deficit, trade deficits, inflation, and corruption. He basically implemented what later presidents would call an "austerity program": curbing spending, reducing inflation, and launching an anticorruption campaign. One of his most dramatic measures was the devaluation of the peso from 8.65 pesos to the dollar to 12.5 pesos to the dollar. The devaluation had the desired results: a reduction of imports, an increase in exports, greater investment, and an increase in tourism. The administration recognized the harsh results of the devaluation but predicted that the devaluation of 1954 would keep the value of the peso stable for a lengthy period of time. The prediction proved accurate; Mexico did not devalue the peso again until 1976.

Ruiz Cortines maintained the basic policies that had been in place since the late 1930s. The emphasis continued to be on industrialization, which the federal government heavily financed despite its financial constraints. The devaluation of the peso provided an opportunity for industrialization to move beyond import substitution into the area of greater exports. Road construction remained a priority, with the system of state and federal roads almost doubling during his administration. Electrical power capacity also increased, and the state oil monopoly—PEMEX—expanded its refining and distribution activities. The government maintained its tight control over the labor movement. The Ruiz Cortines administration tried to ease worker discontent by authorizing wage increases and an increase in the federal minimum wage, but most workers still found it hard to keep up with inflation. There was also a major expansion in social security benefits. The government's conciliatory policy toward the Roman Catholic Church continued, with First Lady María Izaguirre de Ruiz Cortines sponsoring a drive for improvements to the Shrine of the Virgin of Guadalupe. Despite financial problems, there was a modest increase in funding for education.

In the area of agrarian reform, the long-term decline in the amount of land redistrib-

Adolfo Ruiz Cortines (right of speaker with hand raised) during a presidential campaign rally in Acapulco, March 1952 (Bettmann/Corbis)

uted continued under Ruiz Cortines. The president, however, was greatly concerned about the agrarian sector; in particular, he was concerned about the level of agricultural production and its link to inflation. Rather than expropriation and redistribution, Ruiz Cortines focused on expanding the area under cultivation. This was accomplished primarily through the extension of irrigation to new areas, with medium and large land-holdings receiving the greatest attention. Agrarian loans helped to finance the modernization of agriculture. Ruiz Cortines also guaranteed prices for agricultural products and provided subsidies for basic foodstuffs. Although agricultural production increased and prices stabilized, Mexico still had to resort to the importation of agricultural products to meet its domestic needs.

Despite its financial and economic problems, the administration of Ruiz Cortines was able to maintain economic growth, bring federal spending under control, and curb inflation. The vision of a modern, urban, industrial Mexico seemed closer at hand, at least for residents of Mexico City, which was already experiencing the problems of rapid growth. The anticorruption campaign produced some embarrassing resignations of politicians and generals, but corruption remained a fundamental part of the political structure. The official party continued to be split between supporters and opponents of the government's development policy, and Mexico's continuing "economic miracle" still was not filtering down to the lower classes. In December 1958, Adolfo Ruiz Cortines—"the puritan among the plutocrats"—stepped down from the presidency and essentially withdrew from public life. He died in Vera Cruz in December 1973.

—DMC

See also: Agrarian Reform/Land and Land Policy; Alemán, Miguel; Avila Camacho, Manuel; Corruption; Import-Substitution Industrialization (ISI); Korean War; Mexico City; Partido Revolucionario Institucional (PRI); Presidents of the Twentieth Century.

References:
Pellicer de Brody, Olga, and Esteban L. Mancilla. *Historia de la Revolución Mexicana. Periodo 1952–1960.* Vol. 23. *El entendimiento con los Estados Unidos y la gestación del desarrollo estabilizador.* Mexico City: El Colegio de México, 1978.
Pellicer de Brody, Olga, and José Luis Reyna. *Historia de la Revolución Mexicana. Periodo 1952–1960.* Vol. 22. *El afianzamiento de la estabilidad política.* Mexico City: El Colegio de México, 1978.

Rulfo, Juan (1918–1986)

Juan Rulfo is the mystery man of twentieth-century Mexican letters. A tragic childhood, his reclusive personality, miniscule output, and cryptic style have all contributed to this elusive image. Of Mexico's great twentieth-century writers, he is the most resolutely Mexican in both the setting and themes of his two masterpieces: the collected short stories of *El llano en llamas* (The Burning Plain and Other Stories) and the short novel *Pedro Páramo.* For poet-essayist Octavio Paz, "Juan Rulfo is the only Mexican novelist to have provided us an image—rather than a mere description—of our physical surroundings . . . he has incarnated his intuitions and his personal obsessions in stone, in dust, in desert sand" (Paz, *Alternating Current,* pp. 15–16).

Rulfo's remarkable evocations of the Mexican landscape derive in large part from a childhood spent in the economically depressed desert lowlands of Jalisco in north-central Mexico. Born 16 May 1918 in the small village of Apulco and raised in the nearby town of San Gabriel, he experienced firsthand the traumatic years that followed the Mexican Revolution (1910–1920). Rural Jalisco was at the center of the Cristero Rebellion against the antichurch decrees of the Revolutionary government and Rulfo's family found itself caught in the middle. In 1925, his father was murdered; his mother died of heart attack two years later. In 1928, relatives placed him in the Luis Silva school for orphans in Guadalajara—a cheap form of "boarding school" education in an economically depressed era. The trauma of these early years would emerge in the central themes of Rulfo's mature works: solitude, human helplessness in the hands of fate, and an abiding obsession with death. The title of his first published story, "La vida no es muy seria en sus cosas" (Life Shouldn't Be Taken too Seriously), suggests that Rulfo had indeed arrived early in life at his pessimistic view of the human experience.

Fortunately for Rulfo, these formative years also provided opportunities for education and an escape from destitution. As he tells it, his first exposure to literature—mostly adventure stories—came from a priest's library stored in his grandmother's house to keep it safe from the depredations of government troops. Four years in the orphanage, distressing though they must have been, provided an educational foundation solid enough to permit him to enroll in the University of Guadalajara (although a student strike prevented his attendance) and law school at the prestigious National Autonomous University in Mexico City. Financial pressures and boredom with the legal profession ended his academic career after just two years. Still, he had acquired sufficient education to secure a series of decent jobs with the Mexican immigration service, Goodyear Rubber (in sales and publicity), the Papaloapan Irrigation Commission, and the National Institute for Indigenous Affairs (as education department director). Married and with four children to support, Rulfo kept a day job throughout his life and continued to refer to writing as a "pastime" even after he was awarded the National Literary Prize, Mexico's highest literary honor, in 1970. Coupled with a certain social awkwardness, professional modesty, and a marked reluctance to publish, his reticence about writing added an element of mystery to his considerable reputation as one of the most unique and important voices in twentieth-century Mexican and Latin American letters.

That reputation is based on two brilliant books. Published in 1953, the stories in *El llano en llamas* (The Burning Plain) attracted immediate and favorable attention. Rulfo's stark portraits of rural Mexico and its people offered a dramatic contrast to action-packed novels of the Mexican Revolution that had captivated readers of the previous generation. Here, the main protagonist is the harsh, arid environment of the author's native Jalisco. In "Luvina," a drunken narrator describes the town's incessant wind "that scratches like it had nails: you hear it morning and night, hour after hour without stopping, scraping the walls, tearing off strips of earth, digging with its sharp shovel under the doors, until you feel it boiling inside of you as if it were going to remove the hinges of your very bones" (Rulfo, *The Burning Plain,* p. 112). "So much land all for nothing," a character remarks in another story (p. 13).

The harshness of Jalisco's arid environment both reflects and produces the hard, violent lives of its mostly poor inhabitants. The Mexican Revolution as seen through the eyes of a Revolutionary bandit, El Pichón, in the story "The Burning Plain" is nothing more than a golden opportunity to fight, loot, and rape women. In "Tell Them Not to Kill Me," the civil unrest gives an army colonel a long-awaited chance to revenge himself on his father's murderer whose own son refuses to intervene (except to cart away the body). In Rulfo's world, violence also becomes part of everyday life: a farmhand is accused of murdering his employer but cannot remember what happened ("In the Morning"), a man conspires with his sister-in-law to walk her husband to death on a holy pilgrimage ("Talpa"), a man murders a religious charlatan and buries him in the yard ("Anacleto Morones").

Under these harsh conditions, Rulfo's protagonists can only endure. For example, the narrator of "Macario," a retarded boy (of undetermined age) who can never get enough to eat, gives a matter-of-fact account of everyday violence that demonstrates a stoic acceptance of fate typical of Rulfo's characters:

> I am sitting by the sewer waiting for the frogs to come out. While we were having supper last night they started making a great racket and they didn't stop singing till dawn. Godmother says so too—the cries of the frogs scared her sleep away. And now she would really like to sleep. That's why she ordered me to sit here, by the sewer, with a board in my hand to whack to smithereens every frog that may come hoping out. (p. 3)

The poor *campesinos* (farmers) given worthless land by the government in "They Gave Us Land" or the young boy whose sister Tacha will likely follow their older sisters into prostitution after a flood takes the cow and calf that represented her dowry in "We're Very Poor," share Macario's (and probably the author's) existential perspective on the human experience.

Undergirding this grim vision is a deceptively simple prose style and an innovative use of form. Commenting on a first novel he later destroyed, Rulfo confessed that:

> Practicing ways to free myself of all that rhetoric and bombast, I started cutting down, working with simpler characters. Of course I went over to the opposite extreme, into complete simplicity. But that was because I was using characters like the country people of Jalisco, who speak a very pure brand of sixteenth-century Spanish. Their vocabulary is very spare. In fact, they practically don't speak at all. (quoted in Harss and Dohmann, *Into the Mainstream*, p. 256)

But if his prose style aspires to rustic simplicity, the same cannot be said of his manipulation of form. Indeed, Rulfo demonstrates considerable mastery of a broad spectrum of modern novelistic techniques: narrative fragments, shifting points of view, interior monologues, flashbacks, time shifts, etc. This subtle combination of simple prose and complex formal experimentation attracted consider-

able attention in Mexico and throughout the Spanish-speaking world. It also won him a prestigious fellowship at the Centro Mexicano de Escritores (Mexican Writer's Center) in 1953.

Two years later, Rulfo published his second book, the short novel, *Pedro Páramo*. Critics had trouble with the book at first. However, beginning with the "boom" in Latin American literature that would last into the 1960s and produce world-renowned novelists like Gabriel García Márquez, Mario Vargas Llosa, and Carlos Fuentes, Rulfo's novel was generally recognized as one of the great masterpieces of twentieth-century world literature. In this tragic tale of a son's return home to visit his father, Rulfo expanded on the themes and techniques he had developed in his short stories. Again, the environment looms large. Even the book's title (also the father's name) suggests a rocky wasteland: in Spanish, the name Pedro (*piedra*) signifies stone and *Páramo* means wasteland. As a traveler tells the returning son, Juan Preciado, "that town's the hottest place in the world . . . when someone dies in Comala, after he arrives in Hell he goes back to get his blanket" (Rulfo, *Pedro Páramo*, p. 3). Violence too is endemic to Comala. Pedro Páramo is a ruthless *cacique* (local strongman) who kills his rivals in politics and love, tyrannizes the town, buys off Revolutionaries, and dies at the hands of an angry illegitimate son who blames him for the death of his wife. But in Rulfo, even the strong are victims of their fate. Pedro Páramo lives his life obsessed with a childhood love, Susana San Juan, who pines for a dead husband (murdered on orders from Pedro Páramo) and who escapes into insanity after their marriage. The novel ends fittingly with Pedro Páramo's last futile attempt to control his destiny: "He struck a feeble blow against the ground and then crumbled as if he were a heap of stones" (p. 123).

The disturbing themes in *Pedro Páramo* are complemented by a fragmented narrative style that distorts time, space, and reality itself. It's not until the midpoint of the novel, for example, that the reader discovers that most of the characters are already dead, including the principal narrator Juan Preciado ("killed by murmurs" according to an unidentified voice). If that were not enough, the shifting narrative voices—Juan Preciado, Susana San Juan, the author, etc.—and the withholding of a linear narrative, deliberately blur the lines between imagination and reality and between life and death. "The dead," Rulfo insisted in an interview, "live outside space and time. That gave me the freedom to do what I wanted with the characters. I could have them come in, then simply fade out" (quoted in Harss and Dohmann, *Into the Mainstream*, p. 270).

On one level, *Pedro Páramo* seems unavoidably Mexican. Certainly, the rustic setting, historical references, and obsession with death refer to enduring images in Mexican popular culture: manly *charros* (cowboys), bandit Revolutionaries, and the gaudy annual celebration of the Day of the Dead with its sugar skulls. Yet, despite its deep roots in Mexican culture, Rulfo's work also reflects a wide reading in world literature—Scandinavian, U.S., Russian, French—and a solid grounding in classical myths like Oedipus and Ulysses. It is likely this tension between local-historical and universal-mythic themes—Latin American "boom" writers would later call it "magic realism"—that made (and will continue to make) Rulfo an influential figure in Mexican, Latin American, and world literature. In recognition of his achievements, he was elected a member of the Mexican Academy of Letters in 1980, five years before his death in Mexico City on 7 January 1986.

—*RMB*

See also: Cristero Rebellion; Fuentes, Carlos; Novel of the Revolution; Paz, Octavio.

References:

Harss, Luis, and Barbara Dohmann. *Into the Mainstream: Conversations with Latin American Writers.* New York: Harper & Row Publishers, 1967.

Leal, Luis. *Juan Rulfo.* Boston: Twayne Publishers, 1983.

Paz, Octavio. *Alternating Current.* Trans. Helen R. Lane. New York: Viking Press, 1973.

Rulfo, Juan. *The Burning Plain and Other Stories.* Trans. George Schrade. Austin: University of Texas Press, 1967.

———. *Pedro Páramo.* Trans. Lysander Kemp. New York: Grove Press, 1959.

Rural Labor

The stereotype of Mexican rural labor is the poverty-stricken peasant working the land of the great estate or hacienda. Historically, for many Mexicans, this stereotype has been an accurate reflection of their lives. Beyond this image, however, lies a much more complicated rural-labor structure. This structure includes debt peons, tenant farmers, sharecroppers, *rancheros*, temporary or seasonal workers, *ejiditarios*, and members of agrarian communities. These different classifications reflect differences in landholding patterns and labor relations. Rural labor conditions have also varied considerably in terms of time and region. In Mexico, rural workers have traditionally lived in villages; the individual family farm that is such a basic feature of U.S. agricultural history has never played a significant role in the Mexican agricultural scheme.

One of the most enduring forms of rural labor was debt peonage, which originated in the sixteenth century and lasted well into the twentieth century. Large landowners bound workers to them by giving them advances on wages or goods; the workers then had to "work off" the debt. The landowners, of course, saw to it that the debt peons were never completely free of debt by continuing to make advances. Often these advances were not in real money but in scrip or in credit that was good only at the estate store, the *tienda de raya*, which was similar to the "company store" in U.S. history. During the colonial period, debt could be inherited, so succeeding generations could be drawn into the debt-peonage system. Legally, debt peons were not bound to the estate they were indebted to, but a lack of economic alternatives often meant that they in fact were bound to the land. Debt peons might be temporary seasonal workers or permanently reside on the great estates. Those who lived on the great estates (the *acasillados*) often had access to small plots of land they could work for their own benefit and received an allotment of maize. The Constitution of 1857, the Constitution of 1917, and the Federal Labor Law of 1931 all outlawed debt peonage. The repeated "outlawing" of the institution was proof of its durability. Recent historical research has somewhat softened the unrelentingly harsh traditional view of debt peonage. Many rural workers voluntarily sought out debt peonage, especially if it involved residential status that provided greater security than being a free, seasonal worker.

Tenant farming and sharecropping also represented important forms of rural labor. Tenant farmers rented lands from the great estates and kept all of the production; sharecroppers used part of the lands of the great estates in return for dividing the crop produced with the landowner. Tenants and sharecroppers also often served as seasonal workers for the owners of the great estates whose lands they used. To reduce costs, the large landowners wanted to reduce the number of permanent, residential workers on their estates (the *acasillados*); tenant farming and sharecropping allowed them to do this. The use of tenant farming and sharecropping also transferred part of the risk of agricultural production from the estate owners to the tenants and sharecroppers. Some landholders also hoped that tenant or sharecropping arrangements might reduce the possibility of land disputes with local peasants. Tenants were required to pay a fixed rent regardless of production—or lack of it. Both tenant farmers and sharecroppers usually worked the less-productive lands of the great estates. They typically grew crops for personal or local consumption rather than for sale in a broader market; for example, tenants and sharecroppers generally grew corn rather than wheat. Tenants and sharecroppers

were not bound to the great estates in the same way that debt peons were, but they still depended on access to estate lands for their economic survival.

The *ranchero* group of rural workers most closely resembles the U.S. experience of smaller, family-run farms. The *rancheros* often comprised a sort of rural middle class between the landless peasants and the large landholders. While few of the *rancheros* qualified as prosperous farmers, they did own their own land (a *rancho,* or small, rural property) and often rented lands from nearby estates. Most *rancheros* depended on their families for labor, but many also hired seasonal workers. *Rancheros* sometimes supplemented their income by working on the great estates. Much of what the *rancheros* grew was for their own consumption, but some of their produce was for sale in local markets. *Ranchos* were sometimes found grouped together; such a settlement pattern was often referred to as a *ranchería.* The land and agricultural policies of the Porfirian era (1876–1911)—with their emphasis on large landholdings and commercial agriculture—largely worked against the interests of the *rancheros.* Likewise, the policies followed by Revolutionary governments after 1910 often ignored the *rancheros* in favor of emphasizing collective holdings, or *ejidos.*

The Constitution of 1917 and later agrarian legislation led to additional changes in the rural-labor scheme. The new Constitution officially recognized the existence of the *ejido,* or rural communal landholding, which had been under attack since 1856. The *ejido* member—the *ejiditario*—was a rural worker and also a rural landholder but not a landowner. The government gave the land to the *ejido* for administration; *ejido* members had the right to use the land but did not have title to the property. There were two types of *ejido*s: individual and collective. An individual *ejido* may sound like a contradiction in terms, but it became and has remained the most important form of communal ownership. In an individual *ejido,* the land is communally owned but is divided among individual families who work their particular parcel and derive all of the profits from their production. The collective *ejido* features communal ownership and cooperative working of the land; there technically is no subdivision of the land given to the *ejido*. The profits of production are shared equally among the members of the collective *ejido*. Historically, the vast majority of *ejido* holdings have been individual rather than collective; only two presidents emphasized collective holdings: Lázaro Cárdenas (1934–1940) and Luis Echeverría (1970–1976). A variation of the *ejido* is the "agrarian community," which involves the legal recognition of the traditional communal landholdings of native groups which successfully resisted efforts since the mid-nineteenth century to convert them to private holdings.

The use of the *ejido* as a mechanism for land distribution did substantially reduce the number of rural workers who were landless peasants. Access to *ejido* lands, however, did not necessarily raise the standard of living of the rural workers nor did it guarantee their economic survival. Many of the *ejidos* were created on marginal lands that could not support agricultural activity on a regular basis without technical and financial assistance from the government—which was not always provided. Mexico's post–World War II development policy assigned a low priority to improving the *ejido* system. Members of the *ejidos* responded to their economic problems in ways that undermined the very concept of the *ejido*. Some collective *ejidos* began to divide their lands while members of individual *ejidos* began to rent—and sometimes even sell—their individual parcels. *Ejido* members often supplemented their income by providing labor to the booming private commercial agricultural operations. The large-scale urbanization taking place after 1945 reflected the declining situation in the countryside as well as the supposed attractions of the cities. As late as 1980 more than half of those who earned a living in the agricultural sector were still landless workers. The *ejido* was a political success; it bound the peasantry to the govern-

ment and the official party, the Partido Revolucionario Institucional (the Institutional Revolutionary Party, or PRI). Its economic impact, however, was far more problematic.

Organizing the rural labor force has proved more difficult than organizing industrial workers, a feature Mexico shares with a number of other nations, including the United States. The Revolution of 1910 led to the creation of a number of local, state, and regional organizations of rural workers. It was not until 1938 that a major national organization of rural laborers emerged, the Confederación Nacional Campesina (the National Peasants' Confederation, or CNC). The creation of the CNC reflected both the agrarian reform policies of President Cárdenas as well as his efforts to reorganize the official party. The CNC was designed to promote the mobilization of rural workers while simultaneously insuring that the mobilization stayed under government control. The CNC soon evolved into a principal pillar of support for the official party and came under even tighter government control.

The economic and financial difficulties of the 1980s led to major reforms that further reworked the rural-labor scheme. The neoliberal reforms pursued by President Carlos Salinas de Gortari (1988–1994) had a major impact on the agricultural sector and rural labor. The implementation of constitutional reforms and a new agrarian law in 1992 provided for the end to government redistribution of land and gave *ejido* members the right to sell, rent, sharecrop, or mortgage their land. *Ejidos* now had the right to disband and seek individual land titles for their members. *Ejiditarios* could enter into joint ventures with private entrepreneurs, including foreigners. These reforms were soon followed by Mexico's approval of the North American Free Trade Agreement, which went into effect in 1994. Salinas hoped that these measures would accelerate the modernization of Mexican agriculture, integrate Mexico into the world market, and attract foreign investment into Mexico's agricultural sector. If fully carried out, these reforms could lead to the disappearance of the *ejiditario* as a separate category of rural worker.

By the end of the twentieth century, agrarian reform—and its impact on the rural worker—had clearly run its course. The vision of a future rural Mexico embodied in the reforms of the 1990s will undoubtedly affect and reduce the rural workforce. General trends in agriculture, such as mechanization and larger holdings, were affecting the rural population long before the reforms of the 1990s. Some rural workers—such as the Zapatistas in Chiapas in 1994—have chosen to resist these changes, but a much larger number of rural workers have responded by joining the migration to the cities in search of a completely different living and lifestyle.

—*DMC*

Mexican rurales *in Gomez Palacio. ca. 1910 (Library of Congress)*

See also: Agrarian Reform/Land and Land Policy; Cárdenas, Lázaro; Confederación Nacional Campesina (CNC); Echeverría Alvarez, Luis; Import Substitution Industrialization (ISI); Salinas de Gortari, Carlos; Zapatista National Liberation Army (EZLN).

References:

Barry, Tom. *Zapata's Revenge: Free Trade and the Farm Crisis in Mexico.* Boston: South End Press, 1995.

DeWalt, Billie R., Martha W. Rees, and Arthur D. Murphy. *The End of Agrarian Reform in Mexico: Past Lessons, Future Prospects.* San Diego: Center for U.S.–Mexican Studies, University of California, San Diego, 1994.

Tutino, John. *From Insurrection to Revolution in Mexico: Social Bases of Agrarian Violence, 1750–1940.* Princeton, NJ: Princeton University Press, 1986.

Rurales

The lack of law and order in the countryside was a major problem for Mexican authorities throughout most of the nineteenth century. When liberal reformers gained control of the central government in the 1850s, their program of modernization included ending the banditry and disorder that characterized many rural areas. The central government originally hoped that state governments would bear some of the expense of organizing and maintaining rural police forces. In 1855, José M. LaFragua, minister of the interior, called for a joint program involving the federal government and the various state governments to promote law and order in villages and in the countryside. Lacking the necessary finances, state governments did little to answer the minister's call. In 1857 an executive decree called for another joint federal-state program of rural policing. Only two understaffed police units had been organized when a three-year civil war between liberals and conservatives broke out, putting a halt to the plan. In 1861 the liberal government of Benito Juárez officially created an exclusively federal rural police force, soon known as the *Rurales.* Modeled on Spain's *Guardia Civil,* this force would put down banditry in the countryside and also help extend the power of the central government into rural areas. Once again, civil war and then foreign intervention, which did not end until 1867, prevented the program from being effectively implemented.

The period from 1857 to 1867 was one of decentralization of power and new opportunities for lawlessness in the countryside. For most of the period, there were two different governments—liberal and conservative—trying to run Mexico, with state and local leaders, both political and military, often ignoring both of the central governments. With bandits turning Revolutionaries and then returning to banditry, it was hard to distinguish between banditry and political disorder. Back in control of the federal government in 1867, Benito Juárez resurrected the *Rurales*. The *Rurales* previously suffered from dual control; the minister of the interior had administrative responsibility for the group while the minister of war supervised its field operations. In 1867 Juárez put the *Rurales* exclusively under the control of the minister of the interior. This move indicated both the political and police functions that the *Rurales* would pursue; it also heightened the ability of the *Rurales* to serve as a counterbalance to the army. Juárez also expanded the *Rurales,* putting about 1,500 men into the field. The *Rurales* were still not a true national constabulary because they concentrated on policing the major roads around Mexico City. In expanding their ranks, the *Rurales* took in many of the very bandits they were supposedly pursuing.

The *Rurales* reached their peak during the lengthy presidency of General Porfirio Díaz (1877–1880, 1884–1911). Dedicated to the promotion of economic development, Díaz realized that Mexico had to deal with its image of lawlessness and political instability in order to attract foreign investors. Díaz saw the *Rurales* as an important tool in creating a new image of a law-abiding and progressive country. The *Rurales* expanded to approximately 3,000 men and constituted a true national police force. Unlike the regular army, which often resorted to conscription, the *Rurales* were an all-volunteer organization. Some bandits continued to join the force, but most of its members were artisans or peasants. The regime found it difficult to attract and retain volunteers for the four-year term of enlistment. The reenlistment rate was less than 10 percent. Desertion was a major problem; some 25 percent of all *Rurales* deserted, most in the first year. Authorities discharged another 15 percent as unfit for service. Problems of retention, desertion, and discipline grew worse after 1900; in the years

immediately preceding the Revolution of 1910, only 13 percent of the *Rurales* served out their four-year term.

Corruption was also a major problem affecting the efficiency of the *Rurales*. Unit commanders padded their rosters, enabling them to skim off funds sent to them to pay their "phantom" *Rurales*. Supply officers frequently sold arms and equipment to civilians. *Rurales* were also required to pay for their horses and uniforms, opening another avenue of abuse.

Despite these problems, the Díaz regime actively promoted the image of the *Rurales* as a ruthless and efficient constabulary that could out-ride and out-shoot any bandits or rebels. The *Rurales* cut a dashing figure in their *charro* (Mexican cowboy) outfits, which featured tight-fitting pants, bolero jacket, and wide-brimmed sombrero. This attire was also popular with some of Mexico's leading bandits, which only added to the mystique and the macho image of the *Rurales*. That few of them were crack shots and even fewer skillful horsemen was not as important as the high-profile public image of the *Rurales,* which brought favorable comparisons with such organizations as the Royal Canadian Mounted Police and the Texas Rangers. The image was more important than the reality in instilling fear and respect in outlaws and political opponents of the regime.

Although the *Rurales* evolved into a national constabulary, most of them were concentrated in central Mexico. This concentration reflected both political and economic considerations. Díaz did not want the *Rurales* to grow too large, which might threaten his control of the organization as well as the loyalty of the *Rurales* to his government. The location of the *Rurales* was also very much influenced by the economic development taking place. *Rurales* guarded railroad depots and rode on trains, which had become the most visible symbols of Porfirian modernization. The *Rurales* protected company payroll shipments and enforced labor discipline for both rural and, increasingly, factory workers. The

Rurales also helped to ensure that Díaz's choices for state and local offices were duly "elected" as ordered.

When a number of revolts took place against the regime in 1910 and 1911, the *Rurales* generally remained loyal to Díaz; but, numbering only some 2,400, they could not make a significant military contribution to the defense of the old regime. In May 1911 Díaz resigned and went into exile in Europe. The new Revolutionary president, Francisco Madero, not only retained but also expanded the *Rurales*. Many of the rebels who fought for Madero wanted full-time government employment for their service to the Revolution. Madero decided to incorporate many of these job seekers into an expanded force of *Rurales*. In addition rural disorder continued even after Díaz resigned, so there was a real need for an expanded force. The most famous Revolutionary incorporated into the *Rurales* was Pascual Orozco, the key Revolutionary general in Madero's victories in northern Mexico. Orozco became commander of the *Rurales* in the northern state of Chihuahua, a crucial area for the future direction of the Revolution. Orozco, however, was disenchanted with his appointment, believing he deserved to be minister of war in Madero's cabinet. The expansion of the *Rurales* was so rapid and haphazard that the Madero administration could not even keep track of how many troops were enrolled. Madero envisioned a rural force that would eventually total more than 18,000. If Madero had turned his vision into reality, the *Rurales* would have been a larger force than the Federal Army when the Revolution started in 1910. In February 1913 *Rurales* joined with elements of the Federal Army to defend un-successfully the Madero government against a coup that eventually was under the leadership of General Victoriano Huerta, a product of Díaz's Federal Army.

The overthrow of Madero led to Huerta's assumption of the presidency and a new series of revolts against the central government. Faced with the task of trying to pacify the countryside, Huerta tried to reorganize the *Rurales*. He removed them from the control of the minister of the interior and put them under army supervision. When this move led to massive desertions, Huerta incorporated the remains of the old *Rurales* into the army and ordered the organization of a completely new rural force. By July 1914 this new force totaled 6,000. This emerging organization played only a minimal role in defending the presidency of Huerta, who resigned and went into exile in July 1914. The following month Revolutionary forces disarmed and discharged the remaining *Rurales*. Although other groups were later referred to as *"Rurales,"* they were not historically connected to the rural federal police force created in 1861 and officially disbanded in August 1914. The *Rurales* ultimately became victims of the very disorder they were created to suppress.

—DMC

See also: Díaz, Porfirio; Huerta, Victoriano; Madero, Francisco; Orozco, Pascual; Revolution of 1910.

References:

Benjamin, Thomas, and William McNellie, eds. *Other Mexicos: Essays on Regional Mexican History, 1876–1911.* Albuquerque: University of New Mexico Press, 1984.

Vanderwood, Paul J. *Disorder and Progress: Bandits, Police, and Mexican Development.* Wilmington, DE: Scholarly Resources, 1992.

S

Salinas de Gortari, Carlos (1948–)

President from 1988 to 1994, Carlos Salinas de Gortari was born into a wealthy and politically well-connected family from the northern state of Nuevo León. His father, Raul Salinas Lozano, had master's degrees from American University and Harvard University and had been secretary of industry and commerce during the administration of Adolfo López Mateos (1958–1964). Carlos's uncle, Antonio Ortiz Mena, served as secretary of the treasury from 1958 to 1970. With this type of family background, Carlos Salinas was well prepared for his rapid rise from financial technocrat to president of the republic.

After primary and secondary education in public schools, Salinas studied economics at the National Autonomous University of Mexico, where he received his degree in 1969. While he was interested in politics at an early age, there was no indication that Salinas was involved in the student protests of 1968 that ended in violence. Following in his father's footsteps, he earned a series of degrees from Harvard University in the 1970s: a master's degree in public administration in 1974, a master's degree in political economy and government in 1975, and a doctorate in political economy in 1978.

While still pursuing his graduate work at Harvard, Salinas began working in the General Office for International Financial Affairs in the Mexican Ministry of Finance. At the Ministry of Finance, Salinas met another rising star, Miguel de la Madrid. When Madrid became head of the Ministry of Planning and Budget in 1979, he took Salinas with him. Salinas helped to formulate the National Development Plan for the administration of President José López Portillo, who was riding the crest of Mexico's oil boom at the time. When the time came for López Portillo to pick his successor, the oil boom had turned to bust, and the outgoing president tapped Miguel de la Madrid as the official party candidate for the presidency. Miguel de la Madrid then selected Salinas as his campaign director, despite the fact that Salinas had no campaign experience. After Madrid became president, he appointed Salinas to Madrid's old position of head of the Ministry of Planning and Budget. In that position, Salinas played a central role in developing the financial and economic policies pursued by the Madrid administration from 1982 to 1988. With the financial crisis continuing, Madrid turned to his fellow financial technocrat, Salinas, when the time came to select the official party's presidential candidate in the 1988 elections.

Salinas was thrown into the presidential race at a difficult time. For the first time in years, the official candidate faced stiff opposition from both the left and the right. Cuauhtémoc Cárdenas, son of legendary president Lázaro Cárdenas, split from the official party and became the candidate of the leftist coalition, the National Democratic Front. On the right, the National Action Party put forward a strong candidate in millionaire industrialist, Manuel Clouthier. There was even opposition to Salinas from within the official party itself where the old-line politicians resented yet another financial technocrat receiving the nomination. Salinas had served as Madrid's campaign manager in 1982 but had never run for elective office in his own right. Salinas campaigned extensively (some 100,000 miles of travel) but not very effectively. Amid widespread charges of electoral fraud, the official results showed Salinas the winner with 51.7 percent of the vote; in contrast, in the 1982 elections, Madrid polled 72 percent of the vote, which was one of the weakest showings ever by a candidate of the official party.

Although lacking a mandate and even legitimacy, Salinas was determined to push forward with a program of reforms he believed within a generation would place Mexico among the advanced, industrialized nations of the world. To achieve this grand goal, Salinas felt that he had to bring a definitive end to some of the basic themes that the official party had been pursuing—often with diminishing enthusiasm—for decades: anticlericalism, support for labor, agrarian reform, economic nationalism, and import substitution industrialization.

Salinas began his administration in spectacular fashion, striking at some of the more notorious figures of corruption in Mexican society. His first target was the head of the powerful oil workers' union, Joaquín Hernández Galicia, accused of fraud and corruption involving union activities. Many in-terpreted the arrest as not just an attack on corruption but also a warning to union leaders to support Salinas's economic policies. Salinas also jailed one of Mexico's leading businessmen, Eduardo Legorreta, for stock fraud and violation of banking laws. Salinas also supported a heightened attack on drug trafficking, leading to the capture of one of Mexico's most prominent drug lords, Félix Gallardo.

The new administration's top priority was the economy. Salinas expanded on the economic and financial policies of the Madrid administration, which the new president had had a major role in shaping. Salinas believed that the central government's excessive role in the economy had been a leading factor in Mexico's decline and moved to privatize most of the more than 1,000 business activities in which the government had become involved. Salinas presided over the sell-off of hundreds of companies, including the banks nationalized by José López Portillo in 1982 as well as the national telephone company, Teléfonos de México (TELMEX). Most of the privatized firms went to Mexican investors rather than foreign investors, with the proceeds helping to pay off the government's financial obligations and improve the country's infrastructure. After years of negotiation, the Salinas administration also reached an agreement restructuring the foreign debt, which lowered both the principal and interest payments of the government. There was a further reduction of government restrictions on foreign investment, opening most sectors of the economy to 100 percent foreign ownership. The government offered tax breaks on repatriated money that had been lost through capital flight, an estimated $84 billion in the ten years prior to the Salinas administration. There were also reductions in the personal income tax and the value-added tax.

One of the most controversial of the Salinas reforms involved the agricultural sector. Land redistribution and the promotion of communal holdings (*ejidos*) had been central features of agricultural policy since the

1920s. Salinas turned agricultural policy upside-down by maintaining that land redistribution and the *ejidos* had become perpetuators of rural poverty rather than cures for it. Salinas ended the official government commitment to land redistribution and had the Constitution amended to permit *ejido* members to rent, sell, or mortgage their lands. The government ended its subsidies to the agricultural sector for seed, water, electricity, and fertilizer; it also reduced price supports for crops. These reforms were aimed not only at modernizing the agricultural sector but also at making it more attractive to foreign investors.

One of the most popular of Salinas's reforms was the creation of the National Solidarity Program (Programa Nacional de Solidaridad, or PRONASOL). PRONASOL provided federal funding for local projects without the usual accompanying federal restrictions. The local community was able to establish spending priorities and allocate funds to such projects as roads, schools, and public health.

Church-State relations also felt the impact of Salinas's reform efforts. Some of the Salinas reforms merely made public law what had been private practice for decades. Public religious ceremonies were legalized, foreign priests were permitted to operate officially, and the clergy were given the right to vote. Church organizations received legal recognition and were allowed to own property. Salinas—nominally as a private citizen—had an audience with Pope John Paul II in 1990, and Mexico established formal diplomatic relations with the Vatican in 1992 for the first time in 130 years.

Salinas saw his personal political fortunes as well as the economic prospects for Mexico as increasingly linked to the proposed North American Free Trade Agreement (NAFTA) with the United States and Canada. Mexico started reducing its tariffs as part of the austerity program under Madrid. Salinas continued trade liberalization and saw NAFTA as a logical element in his economic development policy; it would also serve as a method of insuring closer relations with the United States, which Salinas deemed crucial to Mexico's development. NAFTA would provide the additional trade, technology, and investment needed to make Mexico competitive in a world that was dividing into regional trading blocs at the same time that the globalization of the economy was taking place.

Salinas had little time to enjoy the approval of NAFTA in late 1993. On the day that NAFTA went into effect—1 January 1994—rebellion broke out in the poverty-stricken southern state of Chiapas. The Mexican army moved quickly to contain the situation, and the fighting soon ended. The revolt was a direct challenge to the supposed benefits of NAFTA as well as an indication of the neglect of rural areas and indigenous peoples. On 23 March 1994 Mexico's international credibility suffered another shock with the assassination of Luis Donaldo Colosio, Salinas's selection as the official party candidate for the presidency in the elections scheduled for July. While there was no evidence of any broad-ranging political conspiracy behind the assassination, some critics tried to link Salinas to the assassination, citing growing tensions between Salinas and his designated successor. Salinas hastily tapped a new successor, Ernesto Zedillo, who was Colosio's campaign manager and a presidential possibility for the 2000 elections. A few months later, José Francisco Ruiz Massieu, the number two man in the official party, was also assassinated. Salinas's older brother, Raul, soon was linked to the assassination of Ruiz Massieu, at least in the public mind. Zedillo prevailed in the presidential election but had the lowest percentage (48 percent) of any candidate ever put forward by the official party.

Although 1994 had been a year of financial and political trials, Carlos Salinas left the presidency on 1 December 1994 with considerable national support and international prestige. With his reforms in place and NAFTA in effect, Salinas was supposed to

President Carlos Salinas makes his solidarity trip to Tetla, Tlaxcala, Mexico, September 1993. (Keith Dannemiller/Corbis Saba)

move on to head the World Trade Organization. Instead, in a few weeks Mexico would be in the midst of another major financial crisis which called into question the Salinas reforms, and the former president would soon have to go into self-imposed exile as an unprecedented national scandal broke around his family.

When Salinas turned the presidency over to Zedillo, it appeared that for the first time since 1970 there would be a change in presidential administrations without an accompanying financial crisis. Instead, within less than three weeks, the peso collapsed, followed quickly by a collapse of the Mexican stock market. Much of the foreign capital invested under Salinas quickly left the country as Mexico plunged into a recession. A shaken President Zedillo tried to blame the financial crisis on his predecessor, who promptly accused Zedillo of mismanaging the economy. The spectacle of a former president and a current president publicly feuding was un-

heard of in Mexican politics. Even more shocking was the arrest of Carlos Salinas's older brother, Raúl, on 28 February 1995 on charges that he engineered the assassination of José Francisco Ruiz Massieu, who also happened to be Carlos and Raúl's former brother-in-law. "First Brother" Raúl was also later charged with "illegal enrichment" for charging hefty fees to provide access to government leaders. Officials also connected Raúl to two of Mexico's biggest drug cartels. Carlos Salinas claimed that Raúl's arrest was politically motivated and went on a hunger strike in protest. After secret negotiations with President Zedillo, Carlos Salinas went into self-imposed exile. His exile wanderings took him to the United States, Canada, and Cuba before he settled in for the long term in Ireland. Another casualty of Salinas's fall from grace was his marriage. He divorced his wife, Cecilia, and married one of his former top aides as president. Brother Raúl was convicted for his role in the Massieu killing and was given the maximum sentence of fifty years in prison.

Carlos Salinas was only forty-six years old when he left the presidency with what was considered to be an even brighter future as head of the World Trade Organization. Within a matter of months, he was in disgrace, in exile, and no longer a candidate for the trade position. Having promised to make Mexico a "first-world" country, Salinas had failed to uplift the Mexican masses and was blamed for a major financial crisis and economic downturn. The scandal surrounding Salinas has largely obscured the important impact he had on Mexico in the 1980s and 1990s. He definitively laid to rest some of the most important themes of the Mexican Revolution and terminated completely Mexico's basic postwar development policy. Salinas believed that it would take several presidential administrations for his reforms to take full effect, and the presidential elections of 1994 and 2000 put in the presidency persons who were committed to Salinas's basic policy even though one (Zedillo) publicly feuded with Salinas and the other (Vicente Fox) was from another political party. Salinas's most lasting monument may well be the North American Free Trade Agreement and the important changes it carries with it politically, economically, and socially.

—DMC

See also: Agrarian Reform/Land and Land Policy; Cárdenas, Cuauhtémoc; Corruption; Drug Trafficking; Fox, Vicente; Import Substitution Industrialization (ISI); Madrid (Hurtado), Miguel de la; Marcos, Subcomandante; North American Free Trade Agreement (NAFTA); Partido de Acción Nacional (PAN); Partido Revolucionario Institucional (PRI); Presidents of the Twentieth Century; Religion; Zedillo Ponce de León, Ernesto.

References:

Bailey, John J. *Governing Mexico: The Statecraft of Crisis Management.* New York: St. Martin's, 1988.

Russell, Philip L. *Mexico under Salinas.* Austin, TX: Mexico Resource Center, 1994.

Schultz, Donald E., and Edward J. Williams, eds. *Mexico Faces the 21st Century.* New York: Praeger, 1995.

San Luis Potosí (State)

Located in central-eastern Mexico, San Luis Potosí has a capital city of the same name. Its central geographic location has made the state a link between northern and southern Mexico and it has served as a passage from the Gulf Coast to the interior. The area emerged during the Spanish colonial period as a rich mining center, and though output of gold and silver slowly diminished during the nineteenth century, San Luis Potosí remains a producer of copper, lead, zinc, and other metals. During the twentieth century, the state was a main theater of the Mexican Revolution of 1910, producing some of its most important intellectual precursors. San Luis Potosí was also home to Saturnino Cedillo, one of the most prominent *caciques,* or political bosses, to emerge from the Revolution.

When the Spaniards arrived in the area that is now San Luis Potosí, they encountered a variety of Indian peoples, including the Huastec and Chichimec groups. As in most areas of Mexico, the Spanish advance included the work of missionaries, and it generated conflict with some native groups. Particularly in the center and north, Spaniards faced a long pacification campaign owing to the resistance of the Chichimec tribes. That campaign lasted for most of the sixteenth century and included Spanish attempts to use sedentary and Christianized Tlaxcalan Indians from central Mexico as a tool of peaceful conquest.

The city of San Luis Potosí, which emerged on the east side of the Sierra Madre Oriental, was officially established as a Spanish settlement in 1592, displacing Indian groups already settled in the area. Its founding was linked to the discovery of mines, and it soon became the hub of a rich silver region that also included Guanajuato, Querétaro, and Zacatecas. Charcas, San Pedro, Monte, Pozas, and Real de Catorce were the mines that helped make San Luis Potosí one of Mexico's wealthiest provinces during the colonial period. Mining also spurred the growth of cattle ranching and agriculture, and wealth became concentrated among the owners of mines and haciendas. By the end of the colonial period, disputes over land and other resources were emerging, foreshadowing a problem that would persist into the twentieth century.

The movement of Miguel Hidalgo that began Mexico's independence struggle did not bring significant destruction to San Luis Potosí. Although some who had been deprived of their lands during the colonial period joined the Hidalgo insurgency (which began in neighboring Guanajuato), their rebellion was quickly crushed with the help of wealthy miners and *hacendados* (hacienda owners). With Mexico's final break from Spain, the area achieved statehood. Despite the disruptions of independence, the city of San Luis Potosí maintained its position as an important economic center, and it served as an important link between central Mexico and the important port of Tampico, in the Gulf of Mexico.

Because of its central location, San Luis Potosí was also a strategic prize for liberals and conservatives, the dominant political factions of the nineteenth century. The civil unrest generated by the competition between these two groups thus directly affected the state and particularly its capital city. When the French occupied Mexico in the 1860s, liberal president Benito Juárez briefly established his government in the city of San Luis Potosí before it was occupied by forces loyal to the French. The nineteenth century was also a volatile one in the sierras of the southeast. There, Indian groups and *campesinos* (peasants) grew increasingly restive as they lost ready access to lands, wood, water, and other resources. Rebellion was frequent in this corner of the state.

Like many areas of Mexico, San Luis Potosí experienced impressive economic growth in the last three decades of the nineteenth century. Foreign investment, encouraged by the national policies of President Porfirio Díaz (1876–1911), especially spurred growth in mining, which came to be dominated by the American Smelting Company, owned by the Guggenheim family. At El Ébano, in the southeastern section of the state, foreign money helped initiate the exploitation of oil, adding a new and strategically important sector to San Luis Potosí's economy. Overseeing much of this economic boom, and the accompanying growth of the state's infrastructure, was Carlos Díez Gutiérrez, who governed with only one interruption from 1877 to 1898. Díez Gutiérrez, an early supporter of Porfirio Díaz, enjoyed the backing of the state's wealthiest groups, to which he himself belonged.

The limits of San Luis Potosí's growth were apparent as early as 1879, when the Indian community of Tamazunchale (in the state's troublesome southeastern section) began a rebellion to recover lands taken over by wealthy hacienda owners. The conflict lasted until 1881 despite government repression and the execution of many rebel leaders. Meanwhile, the state witnessed a growth of activism in urban areas, where railroad workers and miners organized and struck for better pay and working conditions. By the early twentieth century, the capital city was also emerging as a center of liberal thought and opposition to the regime of Porfirio Díaz. Juan Sarabia, Camilo Arriaga, and Antonio Díaz Soto y Gama were among the prominent intellectuals who published opposition papers and organized a formal challenge to Mexico's dictatorial political system. In 1901, San Luis Potosí was the site of a national liberal convention that brought together opposition groups from other areas of Mexico. Arriaga, who hosted this convention, was arrested for his political activities, and he soon joined other exiles in San Antonio, Texas, in calling for the overthrow of Porfirio Díaz and the implementation of a program of significant social reform.

Not surprisingly, given the significance of land and resource disputes, the growth of a viable workers' movement, and the efforts of intellectuals like Arriaga, San Luis Potosí was a center of the rebellion of 1910–1911 that finally deposed Porfirio Díaz. Miners, railroad workers, and landowners of modest means all joined the rebellion, as did Indians and *campesinos*. This early phase of the Mexican Revolution of 1910, led by Coahuilan Francisco I. Madero, encouraged the emergence of an agrarian movement in southeastern San Luis Potosí. By 1912, Alberto Carrera Torres had emerged as a leader of this movement. The Cedillo brothers (Cleofas, Magdaleno, and Saturnino), whose family had directly experienced the effects of land concentration in the municipality of Ciudad del Maíz, joined Carrera Torres.

The rebel movement that grew around Carrera Torres and the Cedillo brothers helped to determine the path of the Revolution in San Luis Potosí. After Madero's death and as the Revolution broke into factions, Carrera Torres and the Cedillos sided with Pancho Villa, paving the way for Villa's control of the state in 1914 and 1915. When Villa's rival Venustiano Carranza captured San Luis Potosí, Carrera Torres and the Cedillo brothers retreated to their southeastern domain, where they waged guerrilla warfare against the Carranza regime and its local representative, Governor Juan Barragán. Although Carrera Torres and Cleofas and Magdaleno Cedillo soon lost their lives, Saturnino Cedillo and his followers, who continued to insist on agrarian reform, remained a force to be reckoned with. Indeed, after Carranza's own overthrow and death in 1920, the Mexican government under Alvaro Obregón recognized Cedillo's authority in Ciudad del Maíz, thus officially acknowledging his political strength.

Beginning in 1919 and continuing through the 1920s, San Luis Potosí had two governors, both of whom focused on reforms that benefited workers and *campesinos*. Rafael Nieto and Aurelio Manrique encouraged the growth of the state's worker's movement, and they began the process of land reform. Nieto also distinguished himself by granting the vote to women in San Luis Potosí decades before national suffrage was granted to them.

From 1927 to 1931 Saturnino Cedillo served a term as governor, continuing the distribution of land in his native state. Cedillo's significant following in San Luis Potosí compelled the national government to share its power. In return, Cedillo kept peace within his state, successfully muting the Cristero Rebellion of 1926–1929 and crushing other challenges to the post-Revolutionary state. Cedillo also served two terms as Mexico's secretary of agriculture under Presidents Pascual Ortiz Rubio and Lázaro Cárdenas.

Although the Mexican government took care to cultivate the San Luis Potosí strongman, the broader trend was toward a political centralization that would not tolerate the kind of local autonomy that Cedillo represented. In 1938, Lázaro Cárdenas, who was increasingly at odds with Cedillo, arrived in the capital of San Luis Potosí and ordered him to lay down his arms. Cedillo refused, and he began a rebellion that cost him his life. Military generals governed the state in the years after this rebellion, and in 1943 another civilian, Gonzálo N. Santos, assumed the governorship with the blessing of Mexico's official party (the PRI). The Santos administration coincided with a period of relative economic prosperity. World War II increased demand from the United States for products from San Luis Potosí and other areas of Mexico while the *bracero* program brought some of the state's *campesinos* to the United States, where they helped alleviate a wartime labor shortage.

Santos developed a reputation as an authoritarian leader, and although he served only one term as San Luis Potosí's governor, he continued to impose himself on local politics well into the 1950s. Opposition to Santos emerged, particularly in the capital, and especially among members of the professional classes. The University of San Luis Potosí was a center of such opposition, which came to include in its ranks Dr. Salvador Nava. In 1961, when the PRI attempted to impose as governor Manuel López Dávila, Nava launched his own opposition campaign. López

Dávila ultimately assumed office, but only with the direct intervention of the Mexican government. Soldiers were sent to guard his inauguration, and several opposition leaders were arrested. Nava and his followers regrouped, and in 1985 they protested the results of municipal elections in the city of San Luis Potosí. The protest movement grew, precipitating another bloody clash with police. In 1987, such popular activism compelled the renunciation of Governor Florencio Salazar.

Although the last decades of the twentieth century were politically volatile, they were also characterized by economic growth and modernization. San Luis Potosí emerged as a region of intensive agriculture, and during the 1970s and 1980s, the national government sponsored a large irrigation project that benefited the state's southeastern section. By the end of the twentieth century, San Luis Potosí was exporting its agricultural goods, as well as its wood products. Like many Mexican states that have adopted intensive agriculture, San Luis Potosí has begun to feel the consequences of this model of development. Erosion and deforestation are growing problems. Steady growth in population has added to the strain and has encouraged emigration. As the new century dawned, many residents of San Luis Potosí were leaving Mexico for the United States, hoping for better economic opportunities.

—*SBP*

See also: Agrarian Reform / Land and Land Policy; *Bracero* Program; Partido Liberal Mexicano (PLM); Partido Revolucionario Institucional (PRI); Revolution of 1910.

References:

Ankerson, Dudley. *Agrarian Warlord: Saturnino Cedillo and the Mexican Revolution in San Luis Potosí.* DeKalb: Northern Illinois University Press, 1984.

Falcón, Romana. *Revolución y caciquismo: San Luis Potosí, 1910–1938.* Mexico City: El Colegio de Mexico, 1984.

Monroy, María Isabel, and Tomás Calvillo Una. *Breve historia de San Luis Potosí.* Mexico City: El Colegio de Mexico, 1997.

Official state web site: http://www.slp.gob.mx

Sinaloa (State)

Sinaloa is a northwestern Mexican state bordered on the west by the Gulf of California and on the east by the Sierra Madre Occidental. Its capital city is Culiacán, and the state also includes the port city and tourist resort of Mazatlán. Like its northern neighbor Sonora and the Baja California peninsula, Sinaloa remained on the periphery of colonial Mexico and it developed important commercial ties outside Mexico before being integrated into the Mexican nation. During the twentieth century, Sinaloa emerged as a center of Mexico's agricultural export economy as well as a key producer of drugs for the international narcotics trade.

On the eve of Spanish contact, Sinaloa was home to several Indian groups, including the Cahita, whose language is still spoken by some Sinaloans in the northern part of the state. The Yaqui and Mayo Indians, who played a prominent role in the history of the Mexican northwest, also inhabited Sinaloa. To help contain and subdue Sinaloa's native population, the Spaniards established *presidios,* including the *presidio* at Mazatlán, which was also intended to protect the Mexican colony and the Spanish empire from the designs of Dutch and English pirates. Missions also emerged and both Jesuits and Franciscans sought to convert native peoples and to protect them from Spanish colonists, who encroached on Indian lands and demanded Indian labor. Conflicts between Indians and colonists frequently resulted in rebellion, particularly by members of the Yaqui tribe. Increasingly, Sinaloa's Indians lost their land and were reduced to working the lands of others.

By the late colonial period, Sinaloa's economy revolved around silver mining and a flourishing maritime trade that stretched along the Pacific coast. Sinaloan silver supplied markets in Europe and Asia, and agricultural goods were traded with upper California. After independence and for a period of approximately six years, Sinaloa and Sonora (which had been joined into one administrative unit during the eighteenth century) were linked together as the "Occidente" State. In 1830 the two areas were separated and Sinaloa emerged as a separate state with its capital at Culiacán. Sinaloa's economy continued to grow and was largely based on the export of wheat and other agricultural goods supplied by Sinaloa's expanding haciendas, which were often worked by Indians. Sinaloa's government aided the process of land concentration and agricultural expansion by passing laws that divided communal (i.e., Indian) lands and that prohibited the Roman Catholic Church from securing land through mortmain.

During the early nineteenth century, Mazatlán emerged as a key port on the Pacific and the Mexican government established a customs office and stationed federal soldiers to guard the port. The federal government's increasing interest in Sinaloa's maritime trade was not welcomed by some of the state's leaders, including Manuel María de la Vega, who served as governor during the early nineteenth century. De la Vega and other Culiacán elites challenged Mazatlán's official monopoly on foreign trade by establishing a rival port at Altata and by levying new taxes on Mazatlán commerce. This showdown with the central government was ultimately unsuccessful, and de la Vega and his followers saw their power undercut with the closing of Altata and the temporary transfer of Sinaloa's political capital to Mazatlán.

As in many areas of Mexico, the late nineteenth and early twentieth centuries brought economic modernization and growth to Sinaloa. Under the often-repressive leadership of Colonel Francisco Cañedo, a supporter of Mexico's president and dictator Porfirio Díaz (1876–1911), Sinaloa experienced impressive growth in mining. Large-scale commercial agriculture also took hold, and wealthy Mexicans and foreigners took advantage of Porfirian laws to acquire and develop Sinaloan lands. This was often done at the expense of Sinaloa's Yaqui and Mayo Indians, who clung to what remained of their ancestral properties. At the same time, railroad lines helped end the state's isolation from the rest of Mexico, and Sinaloa's commercial links to the outside world continued to grow. The sugar industry in particular fostered such connections, providing a main export crop that left Mexico through the ports of Mazatlán and Altata.

The Mexican Revolution of 1910 brought a considerable amount of unrest and economic destruction to Sinaloa. In this part of the Mexican north, the grievances of Indian groups also worked their way into the Revolution. Mayo Indians joined the Madero revolt of 1910–1911 in an attempt to reclaim tribal lands that had been gradually lost since the arrival of the Spaniards, and under the leadership of Felipe Bachamo they later sided with Pancho Villa. Sinaloa also experienced its last Indian rebellion in 1915 when Mayos of the Fuerte River Valley killed several *yoris* (non-Indians) and sacked their lands.

In the aftermath of the Mexican Revolution, some Sinaloans (including Indians) benefited from agrarian reform. Under President Lázaro Cárdenas during the 1930s and again under President Luis Echeverría during the 1970s, some of Sinaloa's large estates were expropriated and redistributed as *ejidos* (communal plots of land). Agrarian reform also brought irrigation works to previously uncultivated lands, thus expanding Sinaloa's already-lucrative agricultural sector. In the 1990s, Sinaloa opened its third port at Topolobampo, which joined Mazatlán and Altata as transit points for the state's agricultural goods.

Land reform and development during the twentieth century was limited largely to Sinaloa's lowlands, including the Fuerte, Sinaloa, and Culiacán River Valleys. The sierra region in eastern Sinaloa, by contrast, witnessed little change, despite President Echeverría's ambitious plan to bring land reform, schools, and other public services to this area during the 1970s. Once the center of the state's lucrative mining economy, the sierra region was the poorest section of

Sinaloa. That poverty provided an opening for the international narcotics trade, and the sierras produced drugs, particularly marijuana, for that trade.

As the twentieth century drew to a close, Sinaloa had two reputations: as one of Mexico's most productive agricultural regions and as Mexico's most violent state. As an agricultural powerhouse, Sinaloa produces nearly one-third of all vegetables sold in Mexico, and its produce is marketed in Asia, Europe, and the United States. The state has also become an important food-processing center. Sinaloa's violent reputation is linked to the drug trade and most of Mexico's major drug smugglers hail from this state. The local trade in heroin, marijuana, and cocaine flourishes, and many poor Sinaloans find that work on a drug crop pays more than most other jobs. Once largely confined to the sierras, cultivation of drug crops has now spread to the lowlands, and some farmers have lost their lands to drug lords. Meanwhile, drug-related violence has become a part of many Sinaloans' lives. Controlling the violence and corruption that comes hand-in-hand with the international drug trade is perhaps the biggest challenge faced by Sinaloa as it enters the twenty-first century.

—*SBP*

See also: Baja California Norte and Baja
  California Sur (States); Drug Trafficking;
  Sonora (State).

References:

Ortega Noriega, Sergio. *Breve historia de Sinaloa.*
  Mexico City: El Colegio de Mexico/Fondo de
  Cultura Económica, 1999.
Voss, Stuart F. *On the Periphery of Nineteenth-Century
  Mexico: Sonora and Sinaloa 1810–1877.* Tucson:
  University of Arizona Press, 1982.
Official state web site:
  http://www.sinaloa.gob.mx

Siquieros, David Álfaro (1896–1974)

David Álfaro Siquieros was the most revolutionary of the "big three" Mexican muralists. Although Diego Rivera was also a polit-ical radical and talented propagandist and José Clemente Orozco was a modernist innovator and apocalyptic visionary, neither artist demonstrated Siquieros's uncompromising commitment to artistic and social revolution. His artistic commitment would lead him to experiment endlessly with new materials and techniques and to publicly confront his less adventuresome colleagues. His political commitment would send him into exile and prison on several occasions. For Siquieros, the two commitments were inseparable.

Siquieros was born on 29 December 1896 in Chihuahua, Mexico. His family was of the respectable provincial elite and provided him a solidly Roman Catholic elementary education. It was not until his years as a student at Mexico City's elite schools, the National Preparatory School and the Art Academy of San Carlos, that his revolutionary tendencies attracted notice. At age fourteen, Siquieros joined in student protests against the Academy's conservative approach to art training and became a protégé of activist painter Gerardo Murillo, who took the name Dr. Atl to signify his commitment to a truly Mexican art. Under Dr. Atl's tutelage, Siquieros learned to do more than "throw stones at things or people," as his colleague Jean Charlot later expressed it.

Siquieros's brief career as a student activist was interrupted by the Revolution. In 1914, after a brief stint as a propagandist (along with Orozco) for Dr. Atl's newspaper, *La Vanguardia,* he joined the Constitutionalist army, fought in several battles, and, by the end of the Revolution's military phase in 1918, he had attained the rank of captain. The Revolution over, Carranza awarded him a government stipend to pursue his interrupted art studies in Europe. There, Siquieros met up with Rivera, who introduced him to the vibrant Parisian art scene and accompanied him to Italy to see the great Renaissance murals of Giotto, Masaccio, and Michelangelo. It was in Italy, that Siquieros encountered the Futurists, a group of artists and art theorists whose exaltation of all things modern would inspire his own artistic philosophy.

In 1921, this whirlwind introduction to the latest trends in early twentieth-century European art produced Siquieros's artistic manifesto: "Three Appeals for a Modern Direction to the New Generation of American Painters and Sculptors." The first appeal was to reject "those *decadent influences* from Europe which poison our youth and prevent us from seeing *fundamental values*" and to *"Let us live our marvelous dynamic age!"* The second called for a shift from a decorative to constructive spirit that emphasizes *"the magnificent geometrical structure of form"* over secondary considerations like color and line. The third insisted that American artists abandon "the relativity of *'national art'* for a universal art must invariably reflect our own *racial* and *regional* physiognomy" (quoted in Ades, *Art in Latin America: The Modern Era, 1820–1980*, pp. 322–323 [his emphasis]). This manifesto with its paradoxical call for an art that would be American and universal, fundamental and dynamic, traditional and modern, held great appeal for the new post-Revolutionary generation of Mexican (and Latin American) artists. It also provided Siquieros a blueprint for his own career.

An opportunity to realize this ambitious program came quickly in the form of a summons from Secretary of Education José Vasconcelos to participate in a state-sponsored "plastic renaissance" of Mexican art. Siquieros replied: "I find myself in total agreement with your basic idea: 'To create a new civilization extracted from the very bowels of Mexico,' and firmly believe that our youth will rally to this banner" (quoted in Hurlburt, *The Mexican Muralists in the United States*, p. 197). By December 1922, he was back in Mexico City as a member of the budding muralist movement, a group of artists that included Rivera and Orozco, commissioned to provide murals for the National Preparatory School. Siquieros's principal contribution was political, especially the founding of the Union of Mexican Workers, Technicians, Painters and Sculptors (he was secretary general) and its newspaper, *El Machete*. The union's manifesto, probably written by Siquieros, declared that "while our society is in a transitional stage between the destruction of an old order and the introduction of a new order, the creators of beauty must turn their work into clear ideological propaganda for the people, and make art, which at present is mere individualist masturbation, something of beauty, education, and purpose for everyone" (quoted in Ades, *Art in Latin America: The Modern Era, 1820–1980*, p. 324). It was in this period, too, that Siquieros, along with Rivera, joined the Communist Party. Rivera's commitment to party doctrine would often waver; Siquieros remained a devout, often dogmatic party member all his life. Siquieros's artistic contributions, at this stage in the muralist movement, were relatively minor but controversial enough to suffer defacement, along with Orozco's, at the hands of conservative preparatory school students. One mural, an unfinished depiction of the *Burial of a Worker* hinted at new directions but Vasconcelos's resignation prevented him from completing it. The new education secretary José Manuel Puig Casauranc, disturbed by the critical turn in Orozco's and Siquieros's work at the same time when the government was actively suppressing striking workers, dismissed both men in 1924. Orozco would return to finish his murals, Siquieros returned his attention to politics. From 1925 until his imprisonment in 1930, he devoted his considerable energies to union organizing and served as secretary general of the Confederacion Sindical Unitaria de Mexico. While confined in Taxco, Siquieros took up painting again and produced some remarkable paintings, such as his claustrophobic portraits of a *Proletarian Mother* and *Peasant Mother*, that mixed an indigenous style inspired in part by Aztec sculpture with a Revolutionary political message; and several portraits of Emiliano

Zapata, who had become the symbol of Revolutionary aspirations in an increasingly conservative era. In Taxco, he also honed his theories on Revolutionary art in discussions with renowned Soviet film director Sergei Eisenstein, who observed that "between the emotional explosion and the disciplined intellect, Siquieros strikes a blow with his brush with the implacable certainty of a pneumatic drill on the path leading to the final goal which he always has in sight" (quoted in de Micheli, *Siquieros*, p. 2).

Stymied by the political climate in Mexico, in 1932 Siquieros accepted an offer to teach mural painting at the Chouinard School of Art in Los Angeles. There he embarked on a series of experiments with team painting, new technologies like spray guns and waterproof cement, and art as propaganda. The experiments continued in Argentina and New York as Siquieros explored the use of slide projectors, photographs, plastic paints, optical illusions, parade floats, and even the incorporation of painting "accidents" like erasures, spots and drippings. (The American painter Jackson Pollock, who would achieve considerable fame for his drip paintings, was one of the students in Siquieros's Experimental Workshop in New York.) As a theorist and propagandist, he was dogmatic as ever. On a brief return to Mexico in 1934–1935, he attacked Rivera for "counterrevolutionary" tendencies, including his "archeological" use of traditional painting techniques like fresco. In response, Rivera pulled a gun at a public debate and demanded the chance to defend himself, allegedly with the quip: "Siquieros talks, Rivera paints."

Siquieros's travels also helped develop his radical political vision. The Los Angeles collective mural, *Tropical America* (1932), for example, depicted an imperial eagle hovering over a crucified Indian. Two of his best-known paintings from the late 1930s, *Echo of a Scream* (1937) with its wailing child surrounded by industrial devastation and *Ethnography* (1939) with its masked Indian peasant stripped of identity, demonstrated the human costs of modernity. In 1937, appalled by the rise of fascism in Europe, Siquieros volunteered to serve in the Republican army in Spain's bloody civil war and eventually rose to the rank of Lieutenant Colonel. With the Republic's defeat by General Francisco Franco's fascist forces two years later, he returned to Mexico.

In the relatively congenial political climate of Lázaro Cárdenas's presidency, Siquieros began (with three collaborators) a new mural for the headquarters of the Mexican Electricians Union, *Portrait of the Bourgeoisie*, that reflected his artistic and political development. The mural exposed the contradictions of a global capitalism that had produced fascist dictatorships (the central figure is mechanical talking parrot powered by money) and imperialist wars in a hyperrealist style that integrated elements of the commercial poster, documentary photography (including pictures from *Life* and *Look* magazines), photomontage, and film. However, his political activities, in particular his role in the attempted assassination of Soviet dissident Leon Trotsky, led to a trial and his exile to Chile in 1940. During his Chilean exile, in a mural with the unambiguous title, *Death to the Invader*, Siquieros developed what would become an important theme in his later work: the last Aztec ruler, Cuauhtémoc, as the first link in a symbolic chain of heroic resistance to oppression, in which he included the heroes of Mexican and Chilean independence. He took up the theme again on his return to Mexico City in 1944 with *Cuauhtémoc against the Myth* (1944) and *Cuauhtémoc Reborn* (1951–1961). These dramatic murals with their foreshortened forms, fluid lines, brilliant colors, and clear political message mark the crystallization of Siquieros's mural style—an artistic and political style he would constantly modify but never substantially change.

The same was true of his political themes. The *New Democracy* (1944) mural and his extravagant final mural-sculpture, *March of Humanity* (1964–1968), took a more optimistic

Self-portrait of muralist David Álfaro Siquieros, 1945 (The Art Archive / Museum of Modern Art Mexico / Dagli Orti)

tone that stressed the ultimate triumph of social justice without downplaying the grimness of the struggle. With three times the area of Michelangelo's Sistine Chapel, *March of Humanity* required its own building and the help of over fifty assistants but, scale aside, the underlying message had changed little. In a similar fashion, his immense *From Porfirio's Dictatorship to the Revolution* (1957–1967) told a national story of redemption and glorified the Revolutionary struggle that had played such a powerful role in Siquieros's own life.

Although imprisoned from 1960 to 1964 for "social dissolution" as a result of his ongoing political activities, Siquieros received considerable official recognition in his final years. In 1966, the Mexican government awarded him its National Prize for Art and, on his death in 1974, a place in Mexico City's Rotunda of Famous Men. Asked to explain his last mural, Siquieros replied: "They are crowds, immense crowds setting out from a distant past of misery and oppression and moving forward toward industrialization, emancipation, and progress" (quoted in Micheli, *Siquieros,* p. 21). It was to this vision that he dedicated his life and art.

—*RMB*

See also: Cárdenas, Lázaro; Muralist Movement; Orozco, José Clemente; Revolution of 1910; Rivera, Diego; Vasconcelos, José; Zapata, Emiliano.

References:

Ades, Dawn. *Art in Latin America: The Modern Era, 1820–1980.* New Haven, CT: Yale University Press, 1989.

Hurlburt, Laurence P. *The Mexican Muralists in the United States.* Albuquerque: University of New Mexico Press, 1989.

Micheli, Mario de. *Siquieros.* Trans. Ron Strom. New York: Harry N. Abrams, Inc., 1968.

Rodríguez, Antonio. *A History of Mexican Mural Painting*. Trans. Marina Corby. New York: G. P. Putnam's Sons, 1969.

Soldaderas

Soldaderas were women who followed Mexican soldiers during times of war, providing for their needs. The word is derived from the Spanish term for soldier's pay, *soldada,* and it reflects the Spanish custom whereby this pay was given to another person who then used it to obtain the soldier's food and supplies. "Soldadera" is most commonly used to refer to women who supported soldiers during the Mexican Revolution of 1910. *Soldaderas* performed a variety of tasks, including cooking and tending to wounds. Each *soldadera* was usually tied to a single soldier, so that the relationship between the two was often intimate. *Soldaderas* appear throughout Mexico's history, and until the end of the Mexican Revolution, when the Mexican military was finally modernized to include a quartermaster corps. Also known as *coronelas, Adelitas,* and camp followers, *soldaderas* had a range of experiences, and occasionally engaged in fighting.

Because of the frequency of armed conflict in Mexico's history, *soldaderas* have been present since the conquest period. Several Spanish women followed their male relatives during Hernán Cortés's campaign to subdue the Aztecs, and many Indian women took part in both resisting and aiding the Spanish Conquest. During Mexico's struggle for independence, women served troops fighting against Spanish control, as well as those fighting to preserve that control. As a new country, Mexico continued the tradition of giving soldiers money to pay others for provisions and services. Thus, *soldaderas* were present in the many wars and rebellions that characterized Mexico's nineteenth-century history. Women served in the Mexican War (1846–1848) and they aided soldiers in the defeat of invading French forces at Puebla in 1862.

Soldaderas were most prevalent in the Mexican Revolution that began in 1910 with a rebellion against President Porfirio Díaz. Thousands of women (most from the lower classes) left their homes to assist troops in the various Revolutionary armies. In addition to providing companionship (and even bearing a soldier's child) *soldaderas* performed a variety of tasks, including burying the dead, procuring food, washing clothes, and even smuggling munitions. Some *soldaderas* engaged in battle and a few disguised themselves as men and sometimes assumed positions of leadership. A few of these achieved a degree of fame. Margarita Neri, a Mayan Indian from Quintana Roo, became an officer and commanded Indian troops in southern Mexico.

While some women were coerced into joining Revolutionary troops, others actively pursued the role of camp follower. In a society that did not yet accept women as full citizens, the experience of being a *soldadera* was often life changing. Yet despite the important role played by *soldaderas* and the sacrifices they made (many lost their lives), not all Revolutionary leaders welcomed them. Pancho Villa held a particular disdain for camp followers and wished to eliminate them in order to establish a more modern army. Indeed, as the Revolution ended, Mexico's new leaders pursued the creation of a professional army, one in which *soldaderas* had no part.

Despite the official tendency to ignore the *soldaderas'* contributions, their legacy lived on in *corridos* (folk songs), literature, art, and film. One of the most famous *corridos* emerging from the Revolution was "Adelita," which became so popular that camp followers became known as *Adelitas.* Mexican muralists also depicted *soldaderas* in their illustrations of Mexico's history and its Revolution. Diego Rivera, David Álfaro Siqueiros, Rufino Tamayo, and José Clemente Orozco all illustrated *soldaderas.* Interestingly, in both *corridos* and murals, *soldaderas* were most often celebrated for their loyalty, beauty, and submissiveness to men.

In a similar way, several novelists of the Revolution incorporated the figure of the *soldadera* into their narratives. In Mariano

Las Soldaderas *(camp followers) by Clemente Orozco; oil, 1929 (The Art Archive/Museum of Modern Art Mexico/Dagli Orti)*

Azuela's classic book, *Los de abajo* (The Underdogs), two types of *soldaderas* are depicted: the camp follower and the female warrior. Azuela's treatment of the characters that represent each type is revealing. The silent and beautiful camp follower emerges as a martyr while the more assertive woman who participates in the fighting is depicted as vulgar and evil. Azuela's portrayals seem to indicate an uneasy relationship with women who experienced an unprecedented level of mobility (and even freedom) during the Revolutionary era.

Just as the often-problematic figure of the *soldadera* secured a place in Mexico's cultural history, so too did the image of the female camp follower accompany Mexican immigrants who came to the United States during and after the Revolution. That image made its way into a handful of American films, including *The Alamo* (1960) and *Viva Zapata* (1952). The *soldadera* also played a role during the Chicano movement of the 1960s and 1970s. The figure of the Mexican *soldadera,* often depicted with a gun and portrayed as an active soldier, was used to help recruit women and enlist them in the struggle for equal rights for Mexican Americans. Chicano festivals often included a dance known as "Las Adelitas," which was performed by women.

—*SBP*

See also: Chicano/a; Muralist Movement; Novel of the Revolution; Revolution of 1910; Women's Movement.

References:

Alatorre, Angeles Mendieta. *La mujer en la revolución mexicana.* Mexico City: Instituto Nacional de Estudios Históricos de la Revolución Mexicana, 1961.

Azuela, Mariano. *The Underdogs.* Trans. E. Munguía Jr. New York: Signet, 1962.

Salas, Elizabeth. *Soldaderas in the Mexican Military: Myth and History.* Austin: University of Texas Press, 1990.

Sonora (State)

Northwestern Mexican state bounded on the west by the Gulf of California and on the north by the United States. Along with the capital city of Hermosillo, Sonora is home to the important port city of Guaymas and the border town of Nogales, situated just across from the Arizona city of the same name. Until the late nineteenth century, Sonora's history was characterized by isolation from the rest of Mexico and by an ongoing struggle to populate the area in the face of Indian raids and rebellions. During the twentieth century Sonora was a center of the Mexican Revolution of 1910, and in its aftermath the state developed a lucrative agro-export economy.

Precolonial Sonora was home to several major Indian groups, including the Pima, Papago, Opata, Yaqui, and Mayo. Spanish explorers frequently passed through Sonora on their way north, and they came into contact with these groups. Jesuit missionaries worked among Sonora's native peoples during most of the colonial period and were replaced by the Franciscans during the eighteenth century. Spanish settlers drifted into the area more slowly, discouraged by its isolation and by the ongoing threat of raids by nonsedentary Indians, most notably the Apaches. By the middle of the seventeenth century, however, Sonora was attracting more settlers because of the emergence of gold and silver mining. For Sonora's native peoples, the colonial era was one of decreasing options, as they were caught between the demands of missionaries and settlers, both of whom threatened their lands, their water (a scarce commodity in this arid region), and their autonomy. Many Indians responded with rebellion, which remained a part of Sonora's history into the twentieth century.

Briefly linked to neighboring Sinaloa after Mexican independence, Sonora became an independent state in 1830. During the nineteenth century, Sonora experienced some expansion of its economy, as agriculture grew and mining continued to attract investors, both Mexican and foreign. Sonoran wheat became part of a Pacific coast trade, and the port of Guaymas linked Sonora to the United States and beyond. The state's agricultural growth was tied to the expansion of the hacienda system, and Yaquis, Mayos, Pimas, and Opatas provided a labor force. Such development was not always peaceful, however, and Sonoran Indians remained restive in the face of steady encroachments on their lands and autonomy. At the same time, Sonora struggled to contain Apache raids that encouraged many Sonorans to leave and that threatened to depopulate the Sonora-Arizona frontier.

Sonora's isolation from the rest of Mexico, and its vulnerability as a frontier area, was further underscored during the Mexican War when Guaymas was bombarded and occupied by United States troops. A slice of Sonora was sold to the United States under the Gadsden Treaty of 1853. Sonora was also a target for filibustering expeditions during the nineteenth century and rumors abounded of American desires to annex the entire state.

Beginning in the 1850s, Ignacio Pesqueira emerged as an important political figure in Sonora. A participant in the struggle against the Apaches, Pesqueria became governor and presided over a lengthy campaign to pacify the state and improve its infrastructure. Although he successfully resisted continuing American attempts to annex Sonora, his efforts against the Apaches met with mixed results. The Yaqui and Mayo likewise remained restive and Yaqui leader José María Leyva Cajeme led a movement to create a separate Yaqui state. The Yaqui rebellion was inherited by Pesqueira's successors and by President Porfiro Díaz, who governed Mexico from the late nineteenth century until the beginning of the Mexican Revolution in 1910.

During the Porfiriato, the federal government began to aid Sonora in the fight against the Apaches and in attempts to end uprisings by the Yaqui and Mayo Indians. Cajeme was captured and executed in 1887 and on the eve of the Mexican Revolution, a war of extermination was still being waged against both native groups. Although the Mayo were effectively subdued by the combined efforts of federal and Sonoran troops, the Yaqui remained a contentious presence. Many Yaqui were forcibly relocated to the Yucatán, where they were put to work on henequen plantations.

In the decades before the Mexican Revolution of 1910, Sonora experienced significant growth, particularly in mining and agriculture. Copper and silver mining attracted foreign, especially American, investment, and Porfirian land policies that tended to encourage land concentration helped stimulate the large-scale production of export crops, such as garbanzos, in the Yaqui and Mayo River Valleys. Sonora's growth strengthened its connection to the United States, and by the beginning of the twentieth century, the Sonora-Arizona border zone was especially well integrated, with family and business networks stretching across the international line. The economic importance of this border area was especially apparent in 1906, when copper miners in Cananea, Sonora, staged a strike for better pay and working conditions. Porfirio Díaz suppressed the strike with the help of the Arizona Rangers.

Sonora was a major theater of the Mexican Revolution and it produced several Revolutionary leaders, including Adolfo de la Huerta, Alvaro Obregón, and Plutarco Elías Calles. In the early phase of the Revolution, Obregón helped secure the state against the insurgency of Pascual Orozco, which threatened the new national regime of Francisco I. Madero. After Madero was overthrown and killed, Obregón and Calles participated in the rebellion that eventually brought victory to the Constitutionalist movement of Venustiano Carranza. Several years later, with the Plan of Agua Prieta, the Sonoran leaders directed the effort to depose Carranza. Through the Revolution and leaders like de la Huerta, Calles, and Obregón, Sonora secured for itself a central place in Mexico's post-Revolutionary state.

Mobilized to protect their lands since the colonial period, Sonora's Yaqui Indians were easily enlisted in the Mexican Revolution, forming their own battalions and contributing their own leaders to Revolutionary armies. Promises that their lands would be restored and their autonomy respected, however, were lost in the aftermath of the Revolution, particularly with the growth of commercial farming in the Yaqui River Valley. As competition for land increased, the Yaqui were once again the victims of government-sponsored repression. In 1926 and 1927 the Yaqui staged their last armed uprising, a move that resulted in a brutal massacre and another deportation of Yaquis to the Yucatán. During the 1930s, the Yaqui claimed a temporary victory when they were officially given one-half million hectares of land (representing half of the territory that the Yaqui claimed as their own) by the government of President Lázaro Cárdenas. This effectively ended the Yaqui military threat, though it did not guarantee Yaqui autonomy. Indeed, the continued growth of capital-intensive commercial agriculture, encouraged by the Mexican government, undercut demands for Yaqui labor and compelled the Yaqui to take part in an economy that contradicted their traditional ways. Gradually, the Yaqui became dependent on the Mexican government, especially as federal control was established over the waters of the Yaqui River.

With the important exception of the Yaqui conflict, the 1920s and 1930s brought relative stability and economic prosperity to Sonora. With Adolfo de la Huerta, Alvaro Obregón, and Plutarco Elías Calles serving terms as Mexico's president from 1920 to 1935, the state received important concessions and gained privileged access to government credit and funding. At the same time, Sonoran governors ruled with a strong hand and demands for labor and agrarian reform were muted. Although President Lázaro Cárdenas gave land to some 12,000 *campesinos* during the late 1930s, more sweeping agrarian reform was resisted by cattle ranchers and by those engaged in commercial agriculture.

The period from Word War II to the early 1980s saw continued economic prosperity. Sonoran agriculture was bolstered by the expansion of irrigation, and new technology contributed to a Green Revolution. The state's cattle industry also benefited from modernization. Wealthy companies and private individuals gained the most from these developments, and many *ejidatarios* (the beneficiaries of land reform) were compelled to sell their lands to those with the resources for large-scale agriculture. In this way, land became concentrated in fewer hands, particularly in the fertile Yaqui and Mayo River Valleys. In response to the economic and political monopoly held by a small group of wealthy farmers, leftist groups emerged. President Luis Echeverría reacted to this challenge by building on the work of Lázaro Cárdenas, expropriating more land and establishing more *ejidos*. Nevertheless, large-scale agriculture and cattle ranching maintained their central position in the Sonoran economy.

During the last two decades of the twentieth century, Sonora began to struggle with the consequences of intensive agriculture. The depletion of water and exhaustion of land have led to a decline in this sector of the economy. The North American Free Trade Agreement, which took effect in 1994 has also contributed to economic dislocation, as market forces increasingly determine what Sonoran farmers can and cannot grow. One Mexican historian recently described Sonora's economy as having no "locomotive": the heyday of commercial agriculture appears to be over, and nothing has yet arisen to take its place.

Like most Mexican border states, Sonora has also been host to the *maquiladora* industry since the 1960s. Foreign-owned *maquila* plants, which take advantage of cheap Mexican labor to assemble goods for reexport, are concentrated on the Sonora–U.S. border, in Nogales, Naco, Agua Prieta, and other cities. Although the *maquiladora* industry has attracted Mexican workers to the border zone and provided many with a viable economic alternative, its ability to bring long-term growth to individual states like Sonora is questionable. In addition, the *maquila* industry has contributed to the environmental deterioration that is now evident throughout the U.S.–Mexico border zone. The twin cities of Nogales, Sonora, and Nogales, Arizona, are emblematic of the problem. A steady growth in population and industry has depleted and contaminated the water supply and has resulted in a steady deterioration of air quality. Health problems, including cancer and birth defects, abound in the Nogales area and are a grim reminder of the effects of rapid and unregulated growth.

Like most border states, Sonora also witnessed the growth of the drug trade (along with its violence and corruption) during the latter part of the twentieth century. The state is a transit point for cocaine, marijuana, and other illegal drugs that make their way to the United States on a regular basis. Despite the efforts of both Mexico and the United States to halt this illegal traffic, Sonora remained a center of drug-related activity as the twenty-first century began.

—*SBP*

See also: Calles, Plutarco Elías; de la Huerta, Adolfo; Drug Trafficking; Environmental Issues; Labor Movements; Obregón, Alvaro.

References:

Acuña, Rodolfo. *Sonoran Strongman: Ignacio Pesqueira and His Times.* Tucson: University of Arizona Press, 1974.

Almada, Ignacio. *Breve historia de Sonora.* Mexico City: El Colegio de Mexico/Fideicomiso Historia de las Américas, 2000.

Bantjes, Adrian. *As if Jesus Walked on Earth: Cardenismo, Sonora, and the Mexican Revolution.* Wilmington, DE: Scholarly Resources, 1998.

Hu-DeHart, Evelyn. *Yaqui Resistance and Survival: The Struggle for Land and Autonomy 1821–1910.* Madison: University of Wisconsin Press, 1984.

Ingram, Helen, Nancy K. Laney, and David M. Gillilan. *Divided Waters: Bridging the U.S.–Mexico Border.* Tucson: University of Arizona Press, 1995.

Tinker Salas, Miguel. *In the Shadow of Eagles: Sonora and the Transformation of the Border during the Porfiriato.* Berkeley: University of California Press, 1997.

Voss, Stuart F. *On the Periphery of Nineteenth-Century Mexico: Sonora and Sinaloa 1810–1877.* Tucson: University of Arizona Press, 1982.

Official state web site: http://www.sonora.gob.mx

Sports

Mexican sports boast two distinct historical traditions. Traditional sports, such as bullfighting, *charreada* (rodeo), horse racing, and long-distance running, have deep roots in Spanish colonial and, in the latter case, indigenous society. Modern sports such as baseball, soccer, basketball, boxing, *lucha libre,* jai alai, and bicycle racing are mostly late nineteenth- and early twentieth-century imports. As in most countries, Mexican sports generally have been dominated by men, although many sports have women competing as amateurs and professionals. Sports have also played an important role in nationalist ideology. Traditional sports have often been seen as representing *mexicanidad* (authentic Mexican cultural ethnicity) in both its positive and negative aspects while modern sports have often been linked state-sponsored social reform efforts intended to promote the mental and physical well-being of Mexico's citizens.

The colonial origins of traditional sports have often made them seem more authentically Mexican than their more modern counterparts. Authenticity in this case, however, has not always been seen as a positive quality. Bullfighting, the most popular of traditional sports, has also been the object of heated debate. For one thing, bullfighting is closely linked to Spanish culture and thus Mexico's colonial status. This interpretation has been reinforced by frequent cultural interchanges that stress Spain's dominance of the sport. The best early twentieth-century Mexican matadors, such as Rodolfo Gaona, Fermín Espinosa, and Carlos Arruza, headed for Spain early in their careers and seldom returned to Mexico to fight. In addition to Spanish domination in the sport, bullfighting provides a parable of colonial social hierarchies with poorer Mexicans automatically taking their place in the hot sun while the more privileged lounge in the shade—a parable some see as preserving the onerous social inequalities of the past. For its most virulent critics, it represents—along with its even more disreputable counterparts, cockfighting and dogfighting—a visible symbol of cruelty, brutality, and violence that caters to and stimulates the worst, most barbaric elements of the Mexican psyche. Liberal politicians like presidents Benito Juárez, Porfirio Díaz (in his first two terms), Manuel González, and Venustiano Carranza periodically and ineffectively banned bullfighting (1867–1887, 1916–1920) in an effort to wean the potentially volatile masses from their violent and disorderly ways. Despite these efforts, bullfighting remains quite popular in Mexico where aficionados claim that the national style, which uses smaller, more active bulls, better captures the true tragic spirit of the bull's sacrifice than the flashier, matador-dominated Spanish style.

Unlike bullfighting, *charreada,* or rodeo, has generally been lauded as a truly Mexican sport. While bullfighting derives its drama from the bull's "sacrifice," *charreada* glorifies the practical skills of northern Mexico's ranching culture: riding, roping, branding, and breaking horses, along with demonstrations of male courage and endurance in bull and bronco riding, such as the dangerous *paso de la muerte* (pass of death), which involves first mounting and then riding a wild horse. For its critics, bullfighting has exalted male arrogance, violence, and the will to domination, while *charreada* has represented an alternative, more responsible machismo that stresses male courage, stoic endurance, and practical abilities. It also includes women's events that highlight their equestrian and roping skills. Moreover, it tends to be a family and community-oriented sport with local *charreadas* occurring throughout western and northern Mexico on a regular basis. These positive aspects of *charreada* culture have provided the inspiration for mariachi music (from the northwestern state of Jalisco) and the immensely popular *charro* (singing cowboy) movies of Mexican cinema's golden age (1930–1960). In turn, these cultural manifestations with their intense nostalgia for the simpler rural life of the ranches and haciendas have marked the *charreada* as the quintessential Mexican sport.

Horse racing also has deep historical roots in Mexico. Until the turn of the century, it was generally associated with festival celebrations and nearly always involved informal gambling. Some races took on legendary proportions and famous race horses were celebrated in popular *corridos* (narrative ballads) such as "El caballo bayo" (The bay stallion) and "Caballo prieto azabache" (The jet-black stallion). Beginning in 1895, sports promoters like the American Robert C. Pate introduced paramutual racing to Mexico City with modern tracks and controlled betting. At first, this new approach to horse racing appealed mostly to the upper classes and modern racetracks became the place to be seen for fashionable Mexican bourgeoisie intent on imitating in the sporting style of their American and English counterparts at the Kentucky Derby in Churchill Downs. Despite early setbacks (exacerbated by the Revolution of 1910), the association of modern horse racing with glamour, modernity, and controlled risk did much to increase its popularity among Mexicans of all classes and it is now firmly entrenched as a national sport.

Long-distance running occupies a unique place in Mexican sports history. Despite the association of modern sports like soccer, basketball, and jai alai with ritual indigenous ball games, Indian sports mostly disappeared from the sports scene (although some are still practiced locally). As long-distance and marathon running emerged on the international sports scene as one of the more glamorous Olympic sports, Mexico discovered its own indigenous running culture among the Tarahumara Indians. Their relative isolation in the deep *barrancas* (canyons) of the arid northern states had fostered high-altitude, long-distance running as a means of communication among remote, widely dispersed communities. In the past few years, these practical skills have translated into international prominence as Tarahumara runners have begun to compete successfully in high-altitude long-distance races such as the gruelling Leadville 100 mile run in the Colorado Rockies.

While traditional sports such as bullfighting have symbolized Mexico's problematic past, modern sports have been linked since their inception to various social reform efforts on the part of both government officials and private employers. Concerned about issues of citizenship and productivity, social reformers sought to redeem the Mexican working class by offering men an alternative to the cantina and the cockfight—where they might also gather to discuss politics—and by offering women (although to a much lesser extent) a chance to break free from traditional routines. Workers responded with a mixture of enthusiasm and resistance as they embraced the social aspects of competitive team sports and the machismo of boxing and *lucha libre* while bending the "rules" against drinking, gambling, and carousing to suit their own needs and experiences.

During the era of president Porfirio Díaz (1876–1911), Mexico experienced a considerable influx of foreign investment as American and British companies in particular received generous incentives to construct and run railroads, open mines, and lend money. In addition to their technology, capital, and expertise, these firms also brought "modern" sports. Extremely popular team sports such as soccer and baseball helped inculcate modern labor practices in workers, especially the unskilled workers from "backward" rural areas who took the least desirable jobs. Through these sports, workers learned to balance individual achievements with teamwork and to compete vigorously within a set of rules and in a controlled space. At the same time, the games proved attractive to workers because they represented their new "modern" identities, cost relatively little, and provided entertainment and social opportunities for players and fans alike. After the Revolution of 1910, these qualities made modern sports especially attractive to post-Revolutionary governments seeking ways to redeem (rather than repress) the nation's workers. Government sponsorship of modern sports—whether by sponsoring leagues, providing equipment, building playing fields, or adding sports to the public school curriculum—greatly enhanced their accessibility and popularity.

The most modern sport of all, bicycling, enjoyed considerable popularity not among workers—for whom the expenses involved were prohibitive—but among the bourgeoisie of the early twentieth century. The introduction of pneumatic tires and safety bicycles by Columbia Bicycle Company in the 1890s made bicycles more enjoyable and less dangerous. For the middle classes, bicycles represented the best aspects of modernization: efficiency, speed, hygiene, health, and machinery. For the lower classes, they seemed pointless, pretentious, and slightly decadent, especially for young women. Over the course of the twentieth century, Mexican bicycling developed professional organizations and competed in international competitions but the sport has yet to develop an extensive following beyond the middle classes.

Baseball, on the other hand, is extremely popular among all classes of Mexican society. In the last decades of the nineteenth century, as American economic and political influence grew, baseball replaced the English sport of cricket as the bat-and-ball sport of choice in Mexico City. About the same time, Cuban workers introduced baseball into Yucatán, as did American railroad workers in northern Mexico. With its elaborate rules, emphasis on teamwork, and specialized skills, baseball was the quintessential modern sport and it spread rapidly throughout the country. By 1925, Mexico had its first semipro league, and by 1940 it had its first national professional league. Mexican baseball has always maintained strong ties to its American roots. In the years just after World War II, the head of the Mexican League, Jorge Pasquel, challenged the national balance of power by "robbing" American players returning home from the war with higher salaries than American teams were willing to pay. On the other side of the border, during the 1980s, the brilliant career of Dodger's pitcher Fernando Valenzuela offered some relief from the anti-immigration fervor of the Reagan years.

Soccer was introduced by British miners around 1900 in the central Mexican state of Hidalgo and quickly became the most popular sport in Mexico. The first soccer organization, the Pachuca Athletic Club (founded in 1902), was mostly an English affair, but the sport spread quickly throughout Mexico, fostering community loyalties—Pachuca is still a major soccer center—and sparking community rivalries. More egalitarian in structure and more flowing than baseball, soccer appealed to modern values like teamwork but without the rigid specializations of its American rival; perhaps for that reason (or perhaps simply because it was not American) it held special appeal for Mexican workers. As early as 1921, president Alvaro Obregón was staging soccer tournaments to celebrate Independence Day (September 16)—an indication of its status as *the* national sport. The rise of professional leagues in the 1950s made Mexico an important center of world soccer. In 1970, Mexico hosted its first World Cup (won by Italy) and, in 1986, its second (won by Argentina).

Members of Mexico's soccer team celebrate their victory at the Pan American Games, 7 August 1999. Mexico defeated Honduras 3–1 to win the gold medal, while Honduras took the silver. Players are (left to right): Alvaro Ortiz, Joaquin Beltran, Adrian Sanchez. Player on far right is unidentified. (Reuters/Corbis)

Although generally ranked among the top teams in the world and a major source of international soccer players, the Mexican national team has yet to make it into the finals. A second-round loss to archrival the United States in the 2002 World Cup in Korea was especially heartbreaking, despite the presence of several Mexican American players on the U.S. team.

Other modern sports have developed niche audiences in Mexico. Beginning with a YMCA league in 1912, basketball has become increasingly popular, especially in rural Mexico. National, state, and local governments built basketball courts in some of the nation's remotest rural communities to promote modern lifestyles and physical fitness. Basketball courts proved especially popular in the mountainous areas of southern Mexico where uneven terrain and maintenance ex-

penses made it difficult to build soccer or baseball fields. As a recent consequence, transnational leagues have appeared in which teams and players travel between Oaxaca and Los Angeles to compete in tournaments and to keep migrants connected to their Mexican communities. Occasional NBA exhibitions and the global popularity of stars like Michael Jordan and Shaquille O'Neal have raised basketball's profile in urban areas in recent years. Jai alai (handball), a Basque import, has also maintained a solid niche in Mexican sports since its introduction in the 1890s and especially after the construction of permanent fronton court in Mexico City in 1929. Like basketball, jai alai's popularity in Mexico has sometimes been attributed to its supposed links to indigenous ritual ball games—a self-fulfilling prophecy of sorts as players and fans accept these alleged primordial links as part of the games' appeal. The experience of migrant workers in the United States as well as the increased availability of cable and satellite television has even begun to attract select audiences to American football—rejected by Mexican audiences in the early twentieth century as too brutal and boring—but mostly as a spectator sport.

Second in popularity only to soccer, boxing is much more controversial. Team sports like soccer, baseball, and basketball have considerable ideological appeal for modernizing elites. Boxing, which exalts individual physical dominance and transforms controlled competition into (barely) controlled violence, is a different story altogether. Another product of the turn-of-the-century American sports invasion, boxing was introduced to Mexican audiences through exhibition matches by some of the era's greatest fighters, including Billy Clark and Jack Dempsey. Mexican boxing took off in the 1940s as fighters like the legendary junior welterweight Kid Azteca became household names. The riots that broke out in 1957 when El Ratón Macías lost the bantamweight title reinforced social reformers' concerns about boxing's brutalizing tendencies but did little to diminish its popularity or the growing international reputation of Mexican boxing. When the hard-punching Julio Cesar Chávez lost his world junior welterweight crown after five years as champion in 1996, for example, it was to a young second-generation Mexican American boxer, Oscar de la Hoya. Inspired by great fighters like Chávez and de la Hoya, Mexican boxing has continued to thrive. In 2001, eight Mexican fighters held world championships in different weight divisions.

Lucha libre (professional wrestling) is probably the most distinctly Mexican of all national sports. Nevertheless, it expresses a decidedly ambivalent *mexicanidad* that disturbs rather than reinforces official ideologies and reformist pretensions. Its emergence as a spectator sport dates to the 1930s influence of the Empresa Mexicana de Lucha Libre (The Mexican Professional Wrestling Company). *Lucha libre* proved especially popular with the urban working class, and the audience, unlike other sports, included large numbers of women. Its appeal was as much theatrical as athletic with masked wrestlers divided into bad *rudos* and good *técnicos* (literally roughs and technicians) and "plots" that bordered on political parody. *Rudos* schemed and cheated while *técnicos* struggled to maintain their integrity before giving in and adopting *rudo* tactics. The inevitability of corruption and the knowledge that the result might well have been decided ahead of time made *lucha libre* a caricature of Mexican political life—different from reality only in that the good guys usually won. Although its was banned from television from 1957 to 1991, wrestlers like El Santo and Blue Demon were major celebrities with movie contracts, fan magazines, and even their own comic books. The height of the *lucha libre* craze came in 1960s, when it ranked as Mexico's second most popular spectator sport after soccer. With the return to television in the 1990s, *lucha libre* lost much of its live audience as manufactured media celebrities began to supplant trained wrestlers and the sport began to resemble its American counterpart. The commercialization of *lucha libre* was somewhat offset by the 1987 emergence of Superbarrio Gomez, a masked wrestler, as the spokesperson for the *Asamblea de Barrios* (Neighborhoods Assembly), a coalition group put together to lobby for the homeless after the 1985 Mexico City earthquake. Superbarrio's continued presence on the political scene—including a run for the presidency of the United States in 2000—suggests that this uniquely Mexican sport still manages to disturb the status quo.

—*RMB*

See also: Cinema from 1930 to 1960: The Golden Age; Cinema after 1960: Contemporary Mexican Film; Popular Music; Radio; Television.

References:

Arbena, Joseph L., ed. *Sport and Society in Latin America: Diffusion, Dependency, and the Rise of Mass Culture.* New York: Greenwood, 1988.

Arbena, Joseph L., and David G. LaFrance, eds. *Sport in Latin America and the Caribbean.* Wilmington, DE: Scholarly Resources, 2002.

Beezley, William H. *Judas at the Jockey Club and Other Episodes of Porfirian Mexico.* Lincoln: University of Nebraska Press, 1987.

Levi, Heather. "Masked Media: The Adventures of Lucha Libre on the Small Screen," in Gilbert Joseph, Anne Rubenstein, and Eric Zolov, eds., *Fragments of a Golden Age: The Politics of Culture in Mexico since 1940,* pp. 330–372. Durham, NC: Duke University Press, 2001.

Rubenstein, Anne. "Mass Media and Popular Culture in the Postrevolutionary Era," in Michael C. Meyer and William H. Beezley, eds., *The Oxford History of Mexico,* pp. 637–670. New York: Oxford University Press, 2000.

Schell, William. "Lions, Bulls, and Baseball: Colonel R. C. Pace and Modern Sports Promotion in Mexico." *Journal of Sports History* 20 (1993): pp. 259–275.

T

Tabasco (State)

Located along the Gulf of Mexico, Tabasco shares borders with the states of Campeche, Chiapas, and Veracruz, and with the country of Guatemala. Over half of Tabasco's territory is covered with water, and the state has the highest level of precipitation in Mexico. The region's major rivers are the Grijalva and Usumacinta, which have historically served as avenues of communication and transportation. For much of its history, Tabasco was something of a backwater, lacking in significant wealth and struggling to maintain a viable economy. This changed during the latter part of the twentieth century when the state's significant oil reserves were discovered. Contemporary Tabasco plays a crucial role in Mexico as a supplier of oil, and its modern history continues to be shaped by this dominant economic activity.

The Olmec, Maya, and Toltec cultures all influenced the region of Tabasco in the centuries before Spanish contact, and the Chontal Indians (a Mayan group) were especially prominent on the eve of Spanish colonization. Spaniards first arrived in Tabasco in 1518, when Juan de Grijalva led an expedition to the mouth of the river that now bears his name. On a second expedition led by Hernán Cortés, a group of Chontal Indians were subdued, and they offered a gift of Indian slaves to the Spaniards. Among this group of slaves was a woman known as Malintzín, who spoke both Mayan and Nahuatl. As "Doña Marina" (or "La Malinche"), she became Cortés's interpreter and mistress.

The Spaniards found conquest of Tabasco's coastal areas easier than its interior, and most of their settlements were established along the region's rivers. Spanish towns included San Juan Bautista or Villahermosa, located along the Grijalva River and destined to be the capital of the future state of Tabasco. Many of Tabasco's native peoples strongly resisted Spanish control. Their lives were radically altered, however, by disease and population decline, labor and tribute demands, and by intermarriage with the Spanish population. Tabasco's colonial society was also shaped by African slaves brought to the area to meet increasing labor demands. The local economy benefited from the region's abundant forests, which provided precious woods. Cattle and cocoa haciendas also emerged.

For a brief period after Mexican independence, Tabasco was a part of Yucatán. It quickly achieved statehood, however, in 1824. Not a particularly wealthy area, Tabasco remained economically dependent on its natural resources, and industry was limited to cotton textiles and the production of the fermented beverage known as *aguardiente*. By the late nineteenth century, the state's timber industry was expanding, and Tabasco exported wood and wood products (including dyewood and gum), as well as coffee, sugar, tobacco, and fruits. The region's timber barons increased their control over the land, often at the expense of native groups. By the turn of the century, Francisco Bulnes and Policarpo Valenzuela were two of Tabasco's largest landowners. Both men controlled large areas of forest land, and they extended their control to the waterways that were used to transport harvested trees. Bulnes and Valenzuela also enjoyed a close relationship with Porfirio Díaz, who was Mexico's dictator from 1876 to 1911.

Politically, the nineteenth century was a volatile one, and Tabasco experienced the unrest associated with the struggle between Mexico's liberal and conservative factions. From Independence to the beginning of Porfirio Díaz's reign, the state government changed hands countless times. In addition, Tabasco was threatened twice by foreign invaders. The first threat came from the United States, which sent Matthew Perry to gain control of the Grijalva waterway during the Mexican War. American forces briefly held San Juan Bautista/Villahermosa. During the 1860s, the French also sought control over Tabasco, but their advance into this corner of Mexico was halted. Although the French managed to establish an empire in Mexico, Tabasco sustained an independent government under Gregorio Méndez Magaña.

Simón Sarlat Nova and Abraham Bandala dominated the political life of Porfirian Tabasco. Bandala's sixteen years as governor especially generated resentment, as did the collusion of local politicians with the state's economic elite. The exploitation of hacienda workers (a problem since the colonial era) added to the discontent. By the turn of the century, opposition to the Díaz regime and its local manifestation took several forms. Journalists were especially vocal in their criticism of Díaz and Bandala. Their ranks included Dr. Manuel Mestre Ghigliazza, whose activism led to a jail sentence. The Mexican Liberal Party (PLM) was also active in Tabasco. One of its adherents, Ignacio Gutiérrez, led an uprising against Díaz in 1909. Finally, Francisco I. Madero's Anti-reelection Movement gained supporters, including Manuel Mestre, who assumed the governorship after Díaz's fall. Ignacio Gutiérrez also joined Madero, distinguishing himself on the battlefield during Madero's revolt against Díaz, before being killed in 1911.

After Madero's own death, many Tabasco Revolutionaries sided with Venustiano Carranza. But politics remained divisive, and rebel leaders from the Los Ríos region clashed with those from the area known as Chontalpa. To help pacify the state, Carranza designated Francisco Múgica as its governor. Múgica brought limited reform to Tabasco, including measures designed to undercut the power of the Roman Catholic Church. One prominent figure in Múgica's administration was Tomás Garrido Canabal, a native of Chiapas. Garrido had served as a chief legal official for the radical government of Salvador Alvarado in Yucatán before coming to Tabasco to serve in the same capacity. In 1922, with the help of the central government, he became Tabasco's governor.

Garrido consolidated his power and emerged as Tabasco's strongman, holding power until 1935. His radical reforms helped give Tabasco a reputation as a "laboratory of the Revolution." Strongly anticlerical, Garrido significantly undermined the position of the Roman Catholic Church, limiting the number of priests and converting many churches into schools. He embraced "rationalist" education, which rejected religious dogma and emphasized nationalism in the creation of a new generation of Mexican citizens. Garrido also organized workers, teachers, and *campesinos* (peasants) into leagues loyal to him, and he encouraged the establishment of the "Red Shirts," young supporters of the Revolution who demonstrated in support of Garrido's policies. Finally, Garrido conducted a campaign against vice, which included efforts to halt the production and consumption of alcohol.

When Lázaro Cárdenas assumed the Mexican presidency in 1934, Garrido was brought in to the national government as secretary of agriculture. He held the post only briefly, becoming entangled in a political dispute between Cárdenas and former president Plutarco Elías Calles, which compelled Garrido's resignation. Forced into exile, Garrido returned to Mexico in 1942, just one year before his death. With Garrido's exit, Tabasco began to move away from radical reform, and by midcentury, the focus was clearly on economic development.

Tabasco's modernization was aided by the construction of railway lines connecting the state with Veracruz and Campeche and by the completion of a Gulf Coast highway. Development of the state's jungle areas was encouraged by Mexico's "March to the Sea" program, which sought to open land in the country's coastal areas in order to relieve population pressures in central Mexico. Federal money supported projects designed to control the waters of the Grijalva and Usumacinta Rivers, and drainage and irrigation projects sought to expand the state's agricultural sector. Tabasco's economic profile changed most dramatically in the 1970s, however, when the discovery of large oil reserves intensified the development of oil fields. The state's newfound wealth attracted thousands of workers from other areas of Mexico, encouraged dramatic growth in Villahermosa, and firmly established Mexico's state-owned oil company, PEMEX (Petroleos Mexicanos), as a key economic (and political) player.

Although Mexico benefited from Tabasco's oil reserves, many in the state resisted the encroachment on agricultural lands and the environmental destruction (including acid rain) that accompanied oil production. In 1976 the state's fishermen banded together in the Riverine Pact in an attempt to

halt further drilling and to demand compensation for damages caused by PEMEX. In the 1980s, Governor Enrique González Pedrera brokered an agreement in which PEMEX promised to provide money to offset environmental destruction, and to share oil wealth with Tabasco's fishermen and farmers. Little change occurred, however, and protests against PEMEX (often endorsed by Mexico's left-of-center political party, the PRD) continued as the twentieth century drew to a close. At the beginning of the twenty-first century, Tabasco was still a major oil producer. Its economy, and the long-term fate of the state's ecosystem, will depend on how officials pursue the development of one of Mexico's most lucrative natural resources.

—SBP

See also: Oil Industry; Petróleos Mexicanos (PEMEX); Revolution of 1910.
References:
González Calzada, Manuel. *Historia de la revolución mexicana en Tabasco.* Mexico City: Instituto Nacional de Estudios Históricos de la Revolución Mexicana, 1972.
Martínez Assad, Carlos. *Breve historia de Tabasco.* Mexico City: El Colegio de Mexico, 1996.
———. *El laboratorio de la revolución: El Tabasco garridista.* Mexico City: Siglo XXI Editores, 1979.
Official state web site: http://www.tabasco.gob.mx

Tamaulipas (State)

Located in northeastern Mexico, Tamaulipas is adjacent to the Gulf of Mexico and shares a border with the United States. Its population is concentrated along the U.S.–Mexico frontier, specifically in the cities of Matamoros, Reynosa, and Nuevo Laredo. The capital city of Ciudad Victoria, and the port city of Tampico also have large concentrations of people. The center of the state, by contrast, is sparsely inhabited. As the twentieth century drew to a close, the northern border zone was perhaps the most dynamic (and most troubled) area of the state. Linked together by one of Mexico's major border crossings, Nuevo Laredo, and its sister city of Laredo, Texas, have become a particularly outstanding example of the cultural, economic, and political melding that now characterizes this international frontier. At the same time, the border zone has inherited significant environmental problems linked to Mexico's *maquiladora* industry.

Prior to Spanish contact, the area that is now Tamaulipas was part of a broader culture zone known as the Huasteca. Sedentary groups were present in the southern part of the state while a variety of nomadic groups inhabited the northern section. Early Spanish expeditions to Mexico's Gulf Coast region brought contact with the Huasteca, and Tamaulipas became part of the Province of Pánuco. The first governor of this province, Nuño Beltrán de Guzmán, saw its native peoples as commodities, and he traded Indians to Cuba and the Antilles for horses and other items. Franciscan missionaries began their work in Tamaulipas in 1544, when they attempted to colonize the southern section with the help of sedentary Olives Indians from the sierras. "Tamaulipas" may be derived from the phrase "land of the Olives."

As Spaniards gradually moved into the Huasteca, establishing ranches and utilizing native peoples as a labor force, the area to the north remained volatile, and Olives Indians helped to wage war against the nomadic peoples there. Not until the eighteenth century was northern Tamaulipas colonized (becoming part of the renamed province of Nuevo Santander), partly in response to the threat of French and English explorers operating in the coastal region. Presidios were established to protect Spanish settlers against Indian raiders and a string of settlements and missions extended Spain's reach to the Rio Grande. On the eve of Mexico's independence, however, northern Tamaulipas was far from secure. Apache and Comanche raiders were the biggest threat, and they continued their depredations well into the nineteenth century.

Tamaulipas achieved statehood in 1824 even though it continued to struggle with its northern frontier, which was home to filibusters, contraband traders, and cattle rustlers. Tamaulipas's border with Texas also ensured that it would be drawn into the Mexican War, and the state lost one-third of its territory in that conflict. During the 1860s, the port of Tampico (earlier occupied by American soldiers) was a target for the French who invaded and occupied Mexico.

Tamaulipas's economy was limited by the state's aridity and inhospitable terrain: cattle ranching was the main activity for much of the nineteenth century. Tamaulipas also remained sparsely settled, and foreigners were welcomed in an attempt to fill unpopulated areas. Most foreigners, however, were drawn not into the state's interior but to the border city of Matamoros and the port city of Tampico. Tamaulipas finally began to experience a diversification of its economy during the late nineteenth and early twentieth centuries, when an infusion of capital and foreign investment gave rise to an intensive commercial agriculture that was marketed to the world. Henequen, a crop introduced from the Yucatán and used to make twine and rope, was among the products produced for export. Mining, which had enjoyed a limited success during the colonial period was revived and Tamaulipas produced copper and zinc for export. Mexico's oil industry also emerged at this time, attracting additional foreign investors to the Gulf Coast region of Tamaulipas. As its economic base expanded, so did the state's infrastructure. Railroads linked Tamaulipas's northern border and its port city of Tampico with central Mexico, and Tampico itself was the object of improvements that made it a rival to Vera Cruz, a major port located farther to the south.

As the twentieth century began, Tamaulipas hosted several rebel groups and organizations that challenged the long-standing dictatorship of Porfirio Díaz. The Mexican Liberal Party, or PLM, gained adherents in Tampico and along the northern border. In response to Francisco I. Madero's call for an end to the dictatorship, several Maderista clubs emerged.

Emilio and Francisco Vázquez Gómez, who began as supporters of Madero and then led their own movement, were natives of Tamaulipas. During the Mexican Revolution of 1910, Tamaulipas was an important scene of fighting and competition among Revolutionaries and counterrevolutionaries. The state was also the center of a major clash between the United States and Mexico in 1914. The conflict began when American soldiers, who had gone ashore at Tampico to obtain gasoline, were briefly detained by Mexican forces. Using the incident as an excuse to invade and occupy both Tampico and Vera Cruz, the United States helped contribute to the downfall of Victoriano Huerta (who had failed to gain U.S. recognition as Mexico's president).

During the 1920s and in the aftermath of the Mexican Revolution, Emilio Portes Gil served as the governor of Tamaulipas. Portes Gil worked within the state to establish a political party that would incorporate workers, the middle class, *campesinos,* and landowners into its ranks. This party became the model for Mexico's long-standing Institutional Revolutionary Party (PRI), and Portes Gil later served a brief term as Mexico's president. Tamaulipas also experienced some changes in its economy in the decades after the Revolution. Agrarian reform reached a peak in the 1930s when President Lázaro Cárdenas redistributed lands and carved out several *ejidos* (communal plots). Irrigation was expanded with the help of the central government, a development that especially benefited northern Tamaulipas and brought more people to this area. Mexico's expropriation of oil fields in 1938 had a significant effect on the state as well; foreign investors in the oil-rich Tampico region were compelled to cede their lands to the Mexican government. Despite the disruptions of the Revolutionary era, Tampico's oil industry survived, and it remains an important component of Tamaulipas's economy. By the end of the twentieth century, the state had also become a leading supplier of natural gas in Mexico,

with production centered on the border city of Reynosa.

Cattle ranching and commercial agriculture have continued to be an important part of the Tamaulipas economy. During World War II the state became a major producer of cotton and helped supply the United States. Despite the environmental problems caused by intensive cultivation (Tampico's cotton production, for example, was declining by the end of the twentieth century as a result of soil erosion) government-funded irrigation works allowed for continued expansion of the agricultural sector. Tamaulipas produces a variety of crops (including henequen, sugar, sorghum, and citrus fruits) that are sold not only in Mexico, but also in the international market.

Like many north Mexican states, Tamaulipas's border zone experienced a significant transformation during the latter part of the twentieth century. At the heart of this transformation has been the *maquiladora* industry, which gives foreign (mostly American) companies access to low-wage Mexican workers who assemble goods for reexport. This industry has drawn workers to the Tamaulipas border in increasing numbers, and Matamoros and Reynosa have emerged as the state's two major *maquila* zones. Although many Mexicans have been drawn to the *maquila* plants in search of economic opportunity, the negative consequences of the industry were readily apparent on the eve of the twenty-first century. Indeed, as the North American Free Trade Agreement was being negotiated during the 1990s, labor and environmental groups used Mexico's *maquila* industry to argue that unregulated free trade would simply transform Mexico into a country of poorly paid and poorly treated workers while allowing foreign companies to pollute the environment, taking advantage of the weaker enforcement of environmental laws in Mexico. Matamoros, with its sister city of Brownsville, Texas, became a center of the environmental controversy, when investigations in this area revealed that industrial chemicals were being illegally dumped in the Rio Grande, posing a public health threat to residents on both sides of the international line. Indeed, Matamoros-Brownsville has a high incidence of birth defects (including spina bifida) that have been linked to industrial pollution.

—SBP

See also: Environmental Issues; North American Free Trade Agreement (NAFTA); Oil Industry; Portes Gil, Emilio; Vera Cruz, Occupation of (1914).

References:

Herrera Pérez, Octavio. *Breve historia de Tamaulipas.* Mexico City: El Colegio de Mexico, 1999.

Official state web site: http://www.tamaulipas.gob.mx

Tamayo, Rufino (1899–1991)

Although Rufino Tamayo was of the same generation as Mexico's renowned twentieth-century muralists—José Clemente Orozco, Diego Rivera, David Álfaro Siqueiros—he was a very different kind of painter. While the "big three" focused their attention on radical political agendas, mythical-historical panoramas, and the construction of a post-Revolutionary Mexican national identity, Tamayo looked inward to create "painting that subjects the object to an intense questioning concerning its plastic properties and one that is an investigation of the relations between colors, lines, and volumes" (quoted in Paz, *Essays on Mexican Art,* p. 218). His paintings and even his murals betray an introspective temperament more concerned with the juxtaposition of enigmatic symbols and subtle variations of color and texture than with the manipulation of political consciousness. Tamayo's willingness to openly buck the dominant artistic culture encouraged and inspired a new generation of Mexican artists like José Luis Cuevas, Pedro Coronel, and Alberto Gironella, who shared his disillusionment with muralism.

It is ironic, perhaps, that the unpolitical Tamayo was one of the few major artists of his generation to actually experience the deprivations of poverty and racism. Born in 1899 into a Zapotec Indian family from Oaxaca, the heartland of indigenous Mexico, Tamayo was orphaned at twelve and sent to live with relatives in Mexico City. When he was not helping his aunt sell produce in La Merced market, he attended drawing classes at the prestigious art Academy of San Carlos (the "big three" were also students). Too young to participate in Revolutionary activity like Siqueiros and Orozco, Tamayo became a disciple of Roberto Montenegro, who, in the words of one critic, taught his pupils how to "clothe the Indian spirit with European trappings" (quoted in Charlot, *The Mexican Mural Renaissance,* p. 96). If Montenegro's lessons were insufficient, a stint as chief of the Department of Ethnographic Drawing at the National Archeological Museum after the Revolution generated a wealth of indigenous images for his already prodigious imagination. Tamayo's special gift, according to French surrealist André Breton, would be "to reopen the lines of communication which painting, as a universal language, should be providing between the continents . . . [and] to extract the essence of eternal Mexico" (quoted in Ades, *Art in Latin America,* p. 218). These early experiences helped foster that gift.

In an era dominated by murals, Tamayo advocated for easel painting. His early works were strongly influenced by European artists like Cézanne, Braque, and Picasso, but already quite distinctive. "My painting," Tamayo insisted, "tries to reduce form to its essence." It achieved that effect with intensely colored and carefully textured representations of people, animals, and a limited repertoire of natural and inanimate objects, like fruit, stringed instruments, and furniture that at times appear two-dimensional. For example, an early *Woman in Grey* (1931) depicts a seated nude woman with vaguely indigenous features in a blockish style that resembles both Gauguin and Siqueiros and with just a hint of perspective to convey a sense of substance. Other pictures like *Chair with Fruit* (1929) and *The Blue Chair* (1931) show traces of Matisse and Cézanne in the handling of domestic objects and demonstrate the subtle manipulation of color, texture, and flattened perspective that would become Tamayo's trademark. "Essentialist" images and brilliant coloration also appeared in Tamayo's murals. His first fresco, *Song and Music* (1933), in a staircase at the National Conservatory, depicted women singing and playing mandolins. And even when the subject was political as in *Revolutionary Soldiers and Workers Attacking Capitalism* (1938), *The Birth of a Nation* (1952), or *Mexico Today* (1953), Tamayo emphasized symbolic power over political message, geometric shapes over realistic representation, subtly of color over careful draftsmanship, ambiguity of meaning over conceptual clarity.

Although quite successful in Mexico City with major exhibitions, mural commissions, a teaching appointment at the San Carlos Academy, and the directorship of the Education Ministry's Department of Fine Arts, Tamayo moved to New York City in 1936. It would serve as his headquarters until 1951. In New York, Tamayo and his new wife, concert pianist Olga Flores Rivas, became fixtures of the city's vibrant art community. He taught at the elite Dalton School of Art, exchanged ideas with important new artists like Ben Shahn and Joan Miró, and developed an international reputation with frequent shows in New York, Paris, and Mexico City. As his art matured, his style became increasingly enigmatic: sometimes representational as in *Niña Bonita* (1937), *Girl Attacked by a Strange Bird* (1947), and *Sleeping Musicians* (1950); at other times, almost abstract as in later works like *Woman in Grey* (1959), *Black Venus* (1965), and the Mexico City mural *Day and Night* (1955). Some paintings from this period like *Woman Reaching for the Moon* (1946) with its dramatic depth (something missing in earlier work) suggest the influence of artists like Paul Klee, famous for using geometric shapes in painting and sculpture, and Pablo Picasso,

Rufino Tamayo (1899–1991), ca. 1959 (Hulton-Deutsch/ Corbis)

whose major 1939–1940 show at New York's Museum of Modern Art Tamayo found especially inspirational.

His international reputation firmly established, in 1951, Tamayo shifted his base back to Mexico City. The government responded with a series of mural commissions on themes like *The Birth of the Nation* (1952) and *Mexico Today* (1953), which in Tamayo's hands took on symbolic rather than political meaning. In a less revolutionary time, his gift for producing mural art that seemed both Mexican and universal was embraced by patrons and critics weary of nationalistic murals and art for the masses. He produced several murals in Mexico and abroad including an *America* (1955) for a Texas bank that depicts the basic elements of the conquest—cross, plumed serpent, conquistador, prone woman—but without the evidence of violence or exploitation that was typical of earlier muralists. This turn toward the mythical and iconic—Tamayo would call it reducing form to its essence—

was also evident in his later paintings. For example, the subtly textured and colored *Empty Fruit Bowl* (1976) pares the still life, typically a luxuriant genre, to a simple table and bowl, and the mysterious *Great Galaxy* (1978) presents a stylized human figure—black with a simple skeleton visible as in an X-ray—regards a cluster of shimmering white triangles that hover just above a blue horizon. Any fears of mortality on Tamayo's part were premature; he would not face the final mystery until 1991, at age 92.

—*RMB*

See also: Art since 1950; Orozco, José Clemente; Paz, Octavio; Rivera, Diego; Siquieros, David Álfaro.

References:

Ades, Dawn. *Art in Latin America: The Modern Era, 1820–1980.* New Haven, CT: Yale University Press, 1989.

Edwards, Emily. *Painted Walls of Mexico from Prehistoric Times until Today.* Austin: University of Texas Press, 1966.

Lynch, James B., Jr. *Rufino Tamayo: Fifty Years of His Painting.* Washington, DC: The Phillips Collection, 1978.

Paz, Octavio. *Essays on Mexican Art.* Trans. Helen Lane. New York: Harcourt Brace & Company, 1987.

Rodríguez, Antonio. *A History of Mexican Mural Painting.* Trans. Marina Corby. New York: G. P. Putnam's Sons, 1969.

Television

In Mexico, as in much of the rest of the world, television has become an integral part of most people's everyday lives. From the indulged children of the upper middle class who imitate the conspicuous consumption of their fictional *telenovela* (soap opera) counterparts to the rural Indian women who use those same shows to make sense of wrenching social changes, television helps structure the way Mexicans envision and respond to life in the modern world. Moreover, the introduction of cable television and satellite dishes has ensured that even the remotest ranchos and villages can participate fully in national and international mass culture. The consequences of this unprecedented media assault are just beginning to be felt, as "traditional" cultures based on locally oriented belief systems and practices come to grips with "modern" attitudes and lifestyles. Television has had an impact on political life as well. Until the 1990s, Mexican television was dominated by the Azcárraga family's media empire, Televisa, which maintained close ties with the Partido Revolucionario Institucional (PRI), the political party that had monopolized politics since the end of the Revolution of 1910. The rise of a rival network in the 1990s, TV Azteca, signaled an end to Televisa's monopoly and helped foster the more open political debates that resulted in the PRI's defeat in the 2000 presidential elections at the hands of the media-friendly opposition candidate, Vicente Fox.

The meteoric rise of commercial television between 1950 and 1970 coincided with the so-called Mexican miracle, the post–World War II economic boom that resulted from the fortuitous combination of an expanding global economy, protectionist policies for Mexican industry, and foreign investment capital. While the bulk of the miracle's benefits went to big corporations and corrupt government officials, enough wealth trickled down to produce a sizeable middle and working class willing and able to partake in the new consumer culture. Commercial television with its powerful combination of compelling images and verbal inducements was the perfect medium through which to develop and disseminate this culture. Success came quickly: the nation's first television station began broadcasting in Mexico City in 1950; ten years later, twenty states could boast least one channel; by 1963, Mexicans owned more than a million television sets.

Another key to television's success was its cozy relationship with the national government. The relationship was first perfected in commercial radio, which had developed hand-in-hand with the PRI. (The Partido Nacional Revolucionario, the first incarnation the PRI, was established in 1929; just one year later, Azcárraga family patriarch Emilio Azcárraga Vidaurreta was granted a license for his flagship station, XEW.) At first, the administration of President Miguel Alemán chose to bypass the already powerful Azcárraga radio network, granting the first broadcast license instead to one of the president's close friends and associates, Rómulo O'Farril, who returned the favor by launching his new station in 1950 with a speech by the president. By 1955, however, the cash-strapped O'Farril had accepted a merger offer from fellow media mogul, Emilio Azcárraga Vidaurreta, which led to the creation of Telesistema Mexicano (TSM). Under Azcárraga family leadership, TSM held a virtual monopoly over Mexican television until the 1990s. Nor did its influence stop at the national borders. As early as 1961, the company expanded into the United States with the purchase of a San Antonio television station, the beginning of the Spanish International Network (SIN), and later—after SIN was found in violation of U.S. antitrust laws—of the international television network, Univisión.

TSM zealously maintained its monopoly by adapting the latest technologies like color broadcasting (1966) and by following the proven formula developed by the Azcárraga radio networks: a stable of in-house stars (including most of Mexican cinema's major celebrities) and an entertainment mix that included musical variety shows, sports, comedy and telenovelas. This last genre—derived from the radionovela and the historieta (comic book)—revolutionized Mexican television and gave it a distinctive style.

The first Mexican telenovela, Ángeles de la calle (Street Angels), appeared in 1951, but the genre really took off with the 1957 series, Senda prohibida (Forbidden Path). It has been going strong ever since. The telenovela formula typically involves thirty- or sixty-minute episodes, sometimes airing as often as five times a week. Unlike their American counterparts, however, few extend beyond a few months. Most are family melodramas

with an emphasis on female characters and love stories. The families are frequently (but not always) wealthy and the plots are complex with occasional fantastic twists to sort things out. Critics insist that telenovelas suffer from stereotypical characters like the cruel stepmother or handsome playboy and unrealistic, hackneyed plots like the long-suffering but true-hearted heroine who finally gets her man. But if they leave something to be desired as self-contained works of television art, telenovelas do encourage viewers to participate by bringing their own experiences to stock characters and plots in ways that more "sophisticated" programs do not. In this context, the apparently unimaginative repetition of the typical telenovela is merely the vehicle for a creative process that occurs not on the television screen but at the point of reception, where viewers engage with these stock characters and plots to produce more nuanced and personalized interpretations. For a country like Mexico, where people experience the tension between "traditional" and "modern" expectations and practices on a daily basis, telenovelas play a crucial role in helping them to negotiate and even to enjoy those tensions.

This creative aspect of telenovelas has certainly contributed to their immense popularity in Mexico and abroad. The height of the telenovela craze occurred during the 1980s, when the most popular shows managed an average ratings share of nearly 50 percent. Declining quality and the introduction of cable and satellite options reduced market share to the low 30s during the 1990s. Nevertheless, they are still hugely popular with the second highest television ratings after soccer. The attraction extends far beyond Mexico. For example, when the late 1970s telenovela, Los ricos también lloran (The Rich Also Cry) was exported to Europe and Latin America in the 1980s, and to Russia and Vietnam in the 1990s, the resulting exposure made its star, Veronica Castro, a global celebrity. Telenovelas continue to represent one of Mexico's most important economic and cultural exports. During the 1970s and 1980s, the Mexican government even got into the act, sponsoring a series of family-planning *telenovelas* that drew much lower but still respectable market shares and contributed to public health campaigns designed to reduce the nation's high fertility rates.

The golden age of the *telenovela*—from about 1970 to 1990—was also the height of the Azcárraga monopoly of Mexican television. In 1972, four short years of competition from Televisión Independiente de México ended when the network merged with TSM to form a new media conglomerate, Televisa. That same year Emilio Azcárraga Vidaurreta died and his son Emilio Azcárraga Milmo took over the family empire. Azcárraga Milmo consolidated Televisa's position in much the same way his father had two decades earlier with a combination of new technologies, such as satellite, cable, and video; modern business practices like syndication and video distribution; and just enough new and expanded programming like sports and made-for-TV movies to keep his audience tuned in and content. Not that the new programming was particularly innovative. In a speech in honor of Veronica Castro, Azcárraga Milmo summarized his entertainment philosophy: "Mexico is a country of people of modest means, very screwed . . . that aren't going to quit getting screwed. Television has an obligation to bring diversion to these people and to take them out of their sad reality and difficult future." Needless to say, this call for the pacification (and political demobilization) of "screwed" Mexicans raised hackles among critics of Azcárraga domination of television and PRI domination of politics, but even they admitted its effectiveness. One key to Televisa's popularity was its constant appeal to national loyalties and its successful promotion of Mexican television in the face of cultural onslaughts from the United States. In Azcárraga Milmo's final public statement, he declared that "our programming will always be for the popular classes, so I ask them to watch us, to support

us and that they don't go away feeling defrauded, but proud of what we are doing in Spanish." Even opponents acknowledged that Televisa under Azcárraga Milmo impeded "the strong pressure of North American businesses that want to control Mexico's space."

Nevertheless, Televisa's message was rife with internal contradictions. On the one hand, its public statements advocated rather conservative notions of family values, albeit centered on family television viewing. At the same time, there were no guarantees that viewers would get the message or accept its ideological presumptions. For example, in rural Yucatán, the popular *telenovela, María Mercedes (para servirle a Ud.)* (María Mercedes at your service, 1992–1993), a tongue-in-cheek melodrama about a hopelessly good girl who finally gets a rich husband despite the machinations of his family, became the central topic of small-town conversation and an important site for the negotiation of modern identities, especially among Mayan Indian women. Even more disturbing have been controversial talk shows like *Cristina* (with Cuban host, Cristina Saralegui) that challenge social norms with free-ranging and fairly graphic conversations about gender relations and sexuality.

The 1990s brought new assaults on the Televisa monopoly that somewhat diluted its still considerable influence. During the 1988 elections, Televisa openly supported the PRI presidential candidate, Carlos Salinas de Gortari, with Azcárraga Milmo openly declaring himself "a soldier of the PRI and of the president" and donating millions of pesos to the Salinas campaign. The voting fraud scandal that marred the elections, along with Televisa's coverage of the scandal, brought sharp criticism on both the PRI and the network. This criticism intensified with Televisa's blatant partisanship in the 1994 presidential elections and especially the reporting of the network's popular television news show, *24 Horas,* on the 1994 Chiapas uprising. Nor was this criticism confined to politics. In 1993, Guadalaja Mayor César Coll, a member of the opposition party (PAN), staged a public television smashing to protest against "pornographic" Televisa programs, an action that exposed the hypocritical aspects of the network's commitment to family values. Despite this building criticism, however, Televisa still controlled 80 percent of the Mexican television market in 1995.

The massive 1982 peso devaluation and the austerity programs that followed opened the Mexican economy to privatization and foreign competition. Both of these trends would somewhat undermine Televisa's cozy relations with the PRI and its monopoly on Mexican television. By the 1990s, cable and satellite television and increased video distribution provided considerably more variety than even Televisa could supply. Much of that competition came from American programs and films with high production values and costs that raised the stakes for Mexican producers. Even more important was the appearance of a major competitor, TV Azteca, made possible by the 1993 sell-off of the government's television assets to Ricardo Salinas Pliego. The 1994 North American Free Trade Agreement (NAFTA) further opened Mexican television markets, including an NBC deal for TV Azteca (although the arrangement ended with mutual recriminations and lawsuits three years later). The new network quickly established its credibility and undermined its rival's, with a 1994 interview of opposition presidential candidate Cuauhtémoc Cárdenas. Televisa responded with an interview of its own but the damage had already been done. An attempt to link TV Azteca to Raúl Salinas de Gortari—the notoriously corrupt and massively unpopular brother of the former president—backfired when Televisa's own links were revealed as well.

Whatever the legitimacy of its claims to provide more objective news, TV Azteca really made its reputation with innovative programming. Its first major effort was *Ciudad Desnuda* (Naked City, 1995), a sensationalistic news program devoted to the exposure of urban criminality and violence, and, by im-

plication, the failure of Salinas-era modernization efforts. Still more challenging, the *telenovela, Nada Personal* (Nothing Personal, 1996) revolved around an intricate web of political corruption and assassinations at a time when Mexico was still reeling from a trio of shocking political murders involving a presidential candidate, the secretary of the PRI, and the archbishop of Guadalajara. TV Azteca even tampered with the classic *telenovela* melodrama with *Mirada de mujer* (A Woman's Look, 1997–1998), the story of a middle-aged woman trying to deal with her separation from a philandering husband. If that were not enough, the network raided Televisa's stars for its own programs and broadcast irreverent American cartoons like *Beavis and Butthead* and *Los Simpons,* whose stock character, the bee man, parodied the antics of Univisión variety shows like *Sábado Gigante* and *Siempre en Domingo.*

Despite the competition, however, Televisa continues to thrive. Most of TV Azteca's programming has been derivative rather than innovative and its inroads into Televisa's viewing audience have leveled off in recent years. The company has also modernized and expanded its operations. When Emilio Azcárraga Milmo died in 1997, he left a multibillion dollar industry to son Emilio Azcárraga Jean, who responded with a much-needed financial restructuring, an international direct TV deal for Latin America (with O Globo de Brasil and Rupert Murdoch's Telecommunications International), and an Eco news channel that restored some of Televisa's dominance in that crucial area. The cozy relationship with the PRI may be a thing of the past but as Mexican television enters the twenty-first century, the Azcárraga family media empire has lost little of its clout and influence.

—*RMB*

See also: Comic Books; Newspapers and
   Magazines; Partido Revolucionario
   Institucional (PRI); Radio.
References:
Greene, Alison. "Cablevision (nation) in Rural
   Yucatán: Performing Modernity and
   Mexicanidad in the Early 1990s," in Gilbert

Joseph, Anne Rubenstein, and Eric Zolov, eds., *Fragments of a Golden Age: The Politics of Culture in Mexico since 1940,* pp. 415–451. Durham, NC: Duke University Press, 2001.

Hernández, Omar, and Emile McAnany. "Cultural Identities in the Free Trade Age: A Look at Mexican Television," in Gilbert Joseph, Anne Rubenstein, and Eric Zolov, eds., *Fragments of a Golden Age: The Politics of Culture in Mexico since 1940,* pp. 389–414. Durham, NC: Duke University Press, 2001.

Rubenstein, Anne. "Mass Media and Popular Culture in the Postrevolutionary Era," in Michael C. Meyer and William H. Beezley, eds., *The Oxford History of Mexico,* pp. 637–670. New York: Oxford University Press, 2000.

Sinclair, John. *Latin American Television: A Global View.* Oxford: Oxford University Press, 1999.

Theater

Theater has always found a receptive audience in Mexico. By most accounts, indigenous groups living in the area that would become New Spain and then Mexico had a rich theatrical tradition linked primarily to religious rituals. The introduction of Spanish-Catholic cultural forms further encouraged this theatrical bent. Local theater, whether incorporated into religious ritual or as "mere" entertainment, naturally reflected local traditions and still does. Most urban centers of any size in Mexico have had active theaters and enthusiastic audiences since the early colonial period. The development of a distinct national theater, however, came much later. According to most scholars, professionally produced, distinctly Mexican theater emerged only after the Revolution of 1910. Since that time, however, Mexican theater has been widely acclaimed as one of the most original and best developed in the Spanish-speaking world.

Any attempt to recover the vibrant popular theater of the colonial period is probably futile because so little of it was written down and the few descriptions that have survived are woefully inadequate (if tantalizing). Even the "cultured" theater of the era—the *autos* and *comedias* of poetess-nun Sor Juana Inés de la Cruz or the plays of Mexican-born playwright Juan Ruiz de Alarcón—is more literary artifact than living theatrical tradition. Moreover, the theater tradition that has been preserved or recovered is decidedly European and indeed Ruiz de Alarcón is considered one of the great Spanish Golden Age dramatists despite his Mexican birth. Independence in 1821 did little to change this outward orientation as Mexican playwrights continued to work firmly within the European romantic tradition. Fernando Calderón (1809–1845), for example, set most of his plays in the European Middle Ages. Even though Manuel Eduardo de Gorostiza (1789–1851), the best Mexican-born playwright of the period, cleverly satirized the excessive romanticism of his peers in the well-regarded *Contigo, pan y cebolla* (With You, Bread and Onion, 1832), like Ruiz, he spent the bulk of his career in Spain rather than Mexico.

Despite these limitations, the romantic love affair with exotic themes and settings did produce a *costumbrista* theater (theater of local customs) that encouraged playwrights like Ignacio Rodríguez Galván (1816–1842) to set their works in Mexican and other New World locales even if they generally favored the pre-Hispanic or colonial past over the national period. Regardless of these quasi-nationalist themes, professional theater was dominated by traveling foreign theater companies and even local producers (and presumably audiences) insisted that actors speak Castilian (from Castile in central Spain) rather than Mexican Spanish. As with the colonial period, historical sources from the early and mid-nineteenth century give some indication of a thriving popular theater that ran the gamut from satirical puppet shows to folk rituals with theatrical elements like the still popular *las posadas,* the annual Christmas drama of Joseph and Mary's search for lodging. As before, the connection between professional and popular theater was tenuous at best.

Despite changes in other literary genres like the novel and poetry, romantic conventions continued to dominate theater into the early twentieth century. Mexican playwrights like José Peón y Contreras (1843–1907) and Manuel José Othón (1848–1906) often wrote on national themes but almost always in imitation of their Spanish counterparts. The first years of the new century saw few changes as touring foreign theater companies continued to set the standard even if an occasional Mexican play made it into production. For example, Federico Gamboa (1864–1939), author of *Santa,* a notorious and extremely popular novel about prostitution, sometimes wrote for the theater, but he tended to save his literary innovations for other genres.

The great national drama of the Revolution of 1910 had a profound impact on theater. Combined with the growth of a broad-based consumer culture, especially in urban areas, revolutionary changes in Mexican society broadened the audience for popular theater, fostered the expansion of traditional or folk theater, and encouraged experimentation in professional theater. The modernization of some sectors of the Mexican economy during the Porfiriato—thirty-five years of relative political stability under authoritarian ruler Porfirio Díaz—had produced a sizeable urban working class with enough discretionary income to support the vaudeville-like *carpa* (tent) shows that provided popular entertainers with receptive audiences and enough income to hone their talents. These entertainers, among them the great comedian Cantinflas, created an indisputably Mexican theatrical style based on colloquial speech rhythms and carefully constructed stock characters from popular theater, characters like the hapless *pelado* (bum) who nevertheless manages to outwit his social superiors. Revolutionary rhetoric that exalted hard-working proletarians gave this decidedly working-class form of entertainment a respectable veneer despite its irreverence for authority and a proclivity for scantily clad female dancers.

More respectable were the new theater companies set up—often with official support—to preserve and promote Mexico's rich indigenous heritage. The Revolutionary project sought to embrace all the hitherto excluded groups in Mexican society and that included the nation's many different Indian groups. (There are nearly 60 distinct Indian language groups in Mexico.) An important symbol of this new redemptive spirit was the valorization of indigenous culture by groups like Teatro Folklórico (Folk Theater) and Teatro del Murciélago (Theater of the Bat) in the early 1920s, which attempted to recreate the rituals, dances, and songs of indigenous folk theater for national audiences.

The Revolutionary enthusiasm of the 1920s also produced a more explicitly political theater intended to commemorate the sacrifices of the Revolution and propagate its spirit. Teatro de Ahora (Theater of Now), in particular, explored theater's radical potential often with original work by Mexican playwrights like Juan Bustillo Oro (1904–1989). His play, *San Miguel de las Espinas. Trilogía dramática de un pedazo de tierra mexicana* (Saint Michael of the Spines. Dramatic Trilogy about a Piece of Mexican Land, 1933), combined operatic realism in the style of Verdi with experimental techniques like the integration of a Greek-style chorus and narrator in order to capture the collective aspects of the epic Revolutionary drama as experienced by poor *campesinos* (rural workers).

Other less-politicized theater groups like El Grupo de los Siete Autores (The Group of Seven Authors, 1925) concentrated on modernizing Mexican theater by weaning audiences from the romantic commercial fare offered by Spanish touring companies and by introducing Mexican Spanish into mainstream theater productions. Two poets, Xavier Villaurrutia and Salvador Novo, associated with another literary group known as the Contemporáneos, created a short-lived but extremely influential Teatro Ulises (Ulysses Theater, 1928) that introduced cultured Mexican audiences to the latest European and American theatrical innovations by staging the "modern" plays of Eugene O'Neill and Jean Cocteau. These efforts were subsequently taken up by other groups, especially the government-supported Teatro de orientación (Theater of Orientation, 1932–1934, 1938–1939), who helped consolidate the modernization of mainstream theater. Innovations in small theater production by Japanese director Seki Sano in the 1940s, added to this mix by introducing new ideas, training actors in new techniques (especially the Stanislavsky method), and incorporating set designs by important artists like Carlos Mérida and Rufino Tamayo.

Although these efforts focused on modernizing rather than nationalizing Mexican theater, they nonetheless provided a strong foundation for its future development. The producers, directors, actors, and playwrights trained in these different venues were the ones who would spearhead the development of a distinctly Mexican theater. The first Mexican playwright to attract significant national (and even international) attention was Rodolfo Usigli (1905–1979). In his biting critique of Mexican post-Revolutionary politics, El gesticulador (The Gesticulator, published in 1938 but first performed in 1947), a university professor takes on the identity of a famous Revolutionary general, becomes a politician, and quickly masters the empty posturing required of his new position. Equally biting is Usigli's Corona de sombra (Shadow Crown, 1943), which uses historical events—in this case the failed Mexican empire of Austrian Archduke Maximilian (1864–1867)—to critique hierarchies of power in post-Revolutionary Mexico (a project he gives a mythical twist in the rest of the Corona trilogy, which centers on Cuauhtémoc and the Virgin of Guadalupe).

Usigli's successes were mostly individual but they provided an important impetus for the further institutionalization of Mexican theater. This process culminated in 1947 with the founding of the Instituto Nacional de Bellas Artes (National Institute of Fine Arts, INBA), Mexico's first permanent, professional, state-sponsored theater. Under director-playwright Emilio Carballido (1925–), the INBA provided a stable venue for the production of new works by Mexican playwrights and for the training of a new generation of directors, actors, and technicians. Carbillido's innovative plays, such as La hebra de oro (The Golden Thread, 1955) and Yo también hablo de la rosa (I Too Talk about the Rose, 1965), which explore the intersection of mundane and fantastic in everyday life, provided literary inspiration as well. If the creation of a national theater provided a venue for new works and a training ground for new talent, the appointment of Usigli as professor of theater at the National University signified its arrival as an academic discipline. So did Carbillado's new professional theater journal, Tramoya. Usigli's successor at the National University, fellow playwright, Luisa Josefina Hernández (1928–), helped expand the boundaries of theater beyond "male" obsessions with political intrigue in plays like Los frutos caídos (Fallen Fruit, 1956), with its damning critique of middle-class Mexican family life.

With this strong foundation in place, pioneers like poet Salvador Novo (1904–1970) returned to the theater as playwrights. Written in the 1960s, toward the end of his literary career, Novo's witty farces like Yocasta, o casi (Yocasta or Almost, 1961) and La guerra de las gordas (War of the Fatties, 1963) proved quite popular, especially with audiences tired of the challenges posed by more academic and avant-garde works. Under these auspicious circumstances, a younger generation of talented playwrights—Luis Basurto (1920–1990), Sergio Magaña (1924–1990), Jorge Ibargüengoitia (1928–1983), Hugo Argüelles (1932–)—emerged that would ensure the survival of the new Mexican theater into the twenty-first century. Characterizing the work of an entire generation is impossible but one common trait is an ironic mode that sometimes borders on sarcasm especially in relation to politics. The introduction to Ibargüengoitia's El Atentado (The Offense,

1978), for example, advises the audience that "any resemblance between this work and actual historical events is not an accident but a national disgrace." Another common trait was a tacit agreement to work within a fairly elastic set of theatrical conventions that included realistic modes of representation (even when events seemed fantastical, action fragmented, or the symbolism intense).

These "conventional" goals were not shared by the entire theater community. The most vocal dissent came from a group called Poesía en Voz Alta (Poetry Out Loud). Founded in 1956 and supported by literary stars like Octavio Paz and Juan José Arreola, Poesía en Voz Alta was an eclectic experimental theater that drew on everything from popular culture—puppet shows, circuses, music halls, tent shows—to Spanish golden age drama to European avant-garde theater (including Spanish poet-playwright Federico García Lorca's one-act plays) and involved the collaboration of writers, musicians, artists, and actors. One of the most important contributors, novelist Elena Garro (1920–), wrote plays like *La mudanza* (The Move, 1959) in a poetic, magical realist style that would later become the rage among Latin American novelists like Gabriel García Márquez and Isabel Allende. By the mid-1960s, this rebellion against theatrical convention had turned into a full-fledged movement with plays like Oscar Villegas's (1943–) take on generational and institutional conflict, *El Renacimiento* (The Renaissance, 1968); La Onda novelist José Agustín's (1944–) multimedia experiment *Abolición de la propriedad* (Abolition of Property, 1969); and Maruxa Vilalta's (1932–) absurdist take on urban life in *Nada como el piso 16* (Nothing Like the 16th Floor, 1977).

In the late 1960s and early 1970s, important novelists turned to theater and added considerable prestige and some excellent plays to the burgeoning Mexican theater scene. The most important convert was Vicente Leñero (1933–), noted author of *Los albañiles* (The Masons, 1964), who began writing "documentary" plays in the mid-1960s. Although hampered by struggles with the government over funding, Leñero's plays, such as *El Juicio* (The Trial, 1972) about the trial of Obregón's assassins, *Martirio de Morelos* (1983), which portrays the human side of the independence hero, and especially *Nadie sabe nada* (1988), which deals directly with collusion between the government and the press, sought to develop the audience's critical-historical awareness without falling into the crude didacticism of earlier radical theater. While less overtly political than Leñero's work, the plays of world-renowned novelist Carlos Fuentes—*Todos los gatos son pardos* (All Cats Are Colored, 1970), which deals with cycles of violence in Mexican history beginning with the conquest and ending at the 1968 Tlatelolco Massacre, and *El tuerto es rey* (The One-Eyed Man Is King, 1970), a parable about blindness and the human condition—demonstrated a similar concern with deconstructing the myths of modern Mexican society and awakening the critical consciousness of viewers.

By the 1970s, Mexican theater had achieved an impressive breadth of purpose and a diverse body of work. Most of its themes and approaches carried over to the 1980s although often in different combinations. At the level of production and funding, government sponsorship continued to play an important role in Mexican theater, especially during the boom years of the José López Portillo presidency (1976–1982) in which oil revenues helped finance the opening of the Teatro de la Nación (National Theater) under the direction of veteran producer-director Carlos Solórzano. The subsequent bust and peso devaluation that followed certainly affected theater production in Mexico but government support has helped sustain first-rate national theater despite considerable economic adversity. The combination of continuity and change, however, was best illustrated by the plays produced during this period. For example, a founding member of the self-proclaimed Nueva Dramaturgia

(New Dramaturgy), Victor Hugo Rascón Banda (1948–), continued to write "political" works like *Los illegales* (The Illegals, 1980) about undocumented Mexican workers in the United States but also incorporated themes from mass culture in a montage play done in collaboration with a University of Veracruz theater group, *Máscara versus Caballera* (Mask versus Gentlewoman, 1985) about the consumerist mythologies surrounding professional wrestlers.

The eclecticism of Nueva Dramaturgia playwrights like Rascón Banda provided a conceptual bridge into the postmodern theater of the 1980s with its rejection of the modernist narrative of national development (including in the theater) and indiscriminate mixing of theatrical styles and techniques. In veteran playwright-director Emilio Carballido's *Tiempo de ladrones* (Time of Thieves, 1983), a nineteenth-century theater impresario voices his opposition to the notion of a national theater with: "Mexican plays are of the most detestable kind. And I'm not going to force the public to see them just because the government is going to subsidize the season." If this pronouncement has a certain ambivalence in Carballido's play, the breakdown of any pretense to a national style in recent years suggests that Mexican theater reached an important milestone in the 1980s that some critics read as Balkanization but that others saw as liberation from the constraints of endlessly rewriting the national allegory.

Regardless, the postmodern era has seen an explosion of different theater styles, a breakdown in the boundaries between commercial and popular theater, and some signs of a break in Mexico City's stranglehold on most theatrical production. Given the long history of Mexico City's cultural dominance in all things artistic, it should come as no surprise that resistance to that domination should surface most strongly on the U.S.–Mexico border. In 1986, an important collection of border plays hinted at the development of a new regional theater with only ten-uous connection to the capital. *Tres de la frontera, tres* (Three from the Border, Three, 1986) highlighted three regional playwrights, Francisco Ortega Rodríguez, Guillermo Sergio Alanís O., Irma Guadalupe Olivares Avila, who dealt with different aspects of *fronterizo* (borderlands) culture. In contrast to Rascón Banda's *Los ilegales*, which chronicled the adversity faced by undocumented workers in the United States, Alanís O's *De acá, de este lado* (From There, From This Side) dramatized the local "push" factors that encouraged Mexican borderlanders to venture to the "other side" and its destructive effect on *fronterizo* society.

In addition to the growth of regional theater, marginality of another sort has appeared in the heart of Mexico City with the stirring of a gay theater exemplified by Alberto Arteaga Olguín's (1945–) *M.M.: Un mito* (M.M.: A Myth, 1984) in which American pop icon Marilyn Monroe is performed by a Mexican drag queen who began his/her career as La Malinche (Hernán Cortés's translator-concubine who has come to symbolize cultural betrayal). In Arteaga's play, a long-standing popular theater tradition, drag performance, becomes part and parcel of a "serious" theater production, blurring the line between the two.

Genre bending and decentralization are the defining characteristics of the current explosion of street theater throughout Mexico. Street theater is often directed as much at tourists as at local audiences and the theatrical fare is a fairly conventional mix of mime, slapstick, and comedic banter. Nevertheless the quality is sometimes exceptional and the interactive nature of the theatrical encounter lends itself to everything from scatological humor to political satire. The proliferation of *Teatros de vecindad* (Neighborhood theater) in marginal urban neighborhoods, on the other hand, is unabashedly directed at increasing political awareness about a broad range of issues from tenant rights to gang violence. So, too, is the work of groups like Teatro Campesino de Tabasco (Peasant Theater of

Tabasco), although they prefer to achieve that awareness more through the inclusion of local people in theater productions, often of traditional tales like *La Llorona,* rather than by bringing in prepackaged political messages from the outside.

Most recently, performance art—with its potent combination of innovative theater and "star" performers—has attracted considerable attention. Higher profile if just as subversive as *vecindad* and *campesino* theater, the work of performers like Astrid Hadad and Guillermo Gómez Peña (1955–) has pushed postmodern theater to its absurdist limits by collapsing already crumbling genre boundaries and by calling into question some of Mexican theater's most cherished "truths." In her Mexico City nightclub act, Hadad plays loosely with potent Mexican cultural symbols like ranchera music, peasant dresses, and sacred bleeding hearts while delivering irony-laden monologues about the "joys of cultural penetration." As a self-proclaimed Chicano artist living in the United States (although he freely admits to being born and raised in Mexico City), Gómez Peña is even less respectful. In acts like *Border Brujo* (Border Witch, 1988–1990), he juggles a dizzying array of cultural stereotypes that call into question nationalist culture on both sides of the U.S.–Mexico border. His principal character, the shamanistic border *brujo* puts it succinctly: "I speak Spanish therefore you hate me / I speak English therefore they hate me / I speak in tongues therefore you desire me." With performer-director-playwrights like Hadad and Gómez Peña leading the way, the future of Mexican theater is both profoundly unsettled and extraordinarily exciting.

—*RMB*

See also: Cantínflas; Novel Since 1960; Poetry.
References:
Burgess, Ron. *The New Dramatists of Mexico, 1967–1985.* Lexington: University of Kentucky Press, 1991.
Nigro, Kirsten F. "Twentieth-Century Theater," in David William Foster, ed., *Mexican Literature: A History,* pp.213–242. Austin: University of Texas Press, 1994.

Tlatelolco Massacre

On 2 October 1968 at the Plaza of the Three Cultures in the Tlatelolco District of Mexico City, army troops and riot police clashed with protesters. This clash had as its immediate cause the student movement of 1968. The conflict also reflected the convergence of a number of other, long-term factors.

The student movement of 1968 grew out of worsening relations between secondary and university students on the one hand and the administration of President Gustavo Díaz Ordaz on the other. University students were concerned about the quality of education that they were receiving and their job prospects after graduation. Student concerns about the economy were shared by growing numbers in the lower and middle classes who were struggling with the end of the postwar economic boom known as the "Mexican Miracle." Students and nonstudents alike were demanding the democratization of the political system and the official party, the Institutional Revolutionary Party (Partido Revolucionario Institucional, or PRI). A final volatile element in the political mix was Mexico's hosting of the Summer Olympic Games scheduled for October 1968. Mexico was the first developing nation to host the Olympics, and the international media focus on Mexico was intense. President Díaz Ordaz was determined to use the Olympics to showcase the virtues of PRI rule, and security concerns were extremely high.

The first major clash between security forces and the students came on 23 July 1968. The confrontation began as a fight between students at two Mexico City schools. Authorities called out the hated *Granaderos*— riot police with a reputation for abusing civilians—who quickly stopped the fighting but who also started a rapid escalation in violence. On 26 July the *Granaderos* clashed once again with student demonstrators. On 30 July army troops used a bazooka to blast open the door of one secondary school; this attack led to the first student deaths in the growing movement.

Army assault troops take cover from rooftop fire in Tlatelolco Plaza, 3 October 1968. (Bettmann/Corbis)

Major demonstrations took place at the National University and the National Polytechnic Institute in Mexico City, followed by the organization of a National Student Strike Committee (Consejo Nacional de Huelga, or CNH) to coordinate student opposition to the government. The students took to the streets to try to win over nonstudents to the cause of political reform. On 27 August a massive demonstration attracted an estimated 400,000 to the Zócalo, Mexico City's main plaza. The government was willing to negotiate with the students, but efforts at negotiation ended over student demands that the negotiations be public. Student protesters and critics of the regime hoped that President Díaz Ordaz would use his annual state of the union message on 1 September to make a conciliatory gesture. Instead, the president denounced the student movement and threatened to use military force if necessary. He also identified educational reform as the fundamental problem behind the demonstrations, ignoring the growing role of democratization in driving the movement.

The confrontation escalated steadily in September. On 13 September there was another massive protest at the Zócalo. Although President Díaz Ordaz had said that university autonomy would be respected, army troops occupied first the campus of the National University and then the campus of the National Polytechnic Institute. Hundreds of students were arrested at both universities, and some even killed during the takeover of the Polytechnic.

The climax of this escalation came on 2 October at a rally at the Plaza of the Three Cultures in Tlatelolco. An estimated 5,000 to 10,000 demonstrators turned out in response to a call by the National Student Strike Committee. After the meeting had been under way for about an hour, some 5,000 army troops and several hundred police moved in to break up the rally. The demonstrators refused to disband when ordered to do so, and the police used force to try to disperse the crowd. Shots were then fired. The official government version maintained that snipers in nearby high-rise buildings had opened fire, and the police and army then returned fire. The antigovernment version was that the troops and police initiated the shooting without any provocation. Regardless of the version of how the shooting started, the demonstrators—as well as many spectators—were soon caught up in a devastating crossfire from the heavily armed troops who had surrounded the plaza. Official government figures placed the dead at 43, but most believe that a more accurate figure would be 300 to 400. In addition, some 2,000 were arrested.

Although the "Tlatelolco Massacre" became a watershed in Mexican political history, its immediate results were not so dramatic, particularly its impact on the Olympics. The Olympic Games opened ten days later on schedule without any major demonstrations or protests. Security at the games was extensive but discrete. International interest in the massacre was minimal in a year that saw violence between student demonstrators and police in a number of nations, including the United States. The massacre brought an end to the student movement of 1968; in early December, the National Student Strike Committee formally called off the strike and then disbanded. From the standpoint of President Díaz Ordaz, he had silenced his domestic critics. The president's attitude toward the massacre can be seen in the person he chose to succeed him. Díaz Ordaz tapped as his presidential successor, Luis Echeverría, who as Díaz Ordaz's minister of the interior was deeply implicated in the events at Tlatelolco.

Efforts to assign responsibility for the massacre have provoked various versions of events but have provided a basic list of possible villains. President Díaz Ordaz had the ultimate responsibility for what took place, but one version maintains that the president was not even in Mexico City at the time to give the necessary orders. Minister of the Interior Echeverría, given his position, has to bear a large part of the blame for what happened. The principal "actor" in the Tlatelolco Massacre was most likely the minister of defense, Army General Marcelino García Barragán, who was generally believed to have given the order to clear the plaza of demonstrators. At a press conference after the massacre, García Barragán explained the army's role by saying that the police had asked for military assistance in breaking up a gun fight between two student groups. The president, his administration, the military, and the police forces were all discredited by the action at the Plaza of the Three Cultures. In particular the erosion of the PRI's political legitimacy and popular support accelerated. As president, Echeverría made energetic efforts to regain the support of the students but never escaped the shadow cast by Tlatelolco.

The massacre at Tlatelolco continues to be a live issue in Mexican politics. There are continuing efforts to have the government make a complete disclosure about the events surrounding the massacre. The democratization process—which the Tlatelolco Massacre helped to promote—raised hopes of greater access to official records dealing with the incident. The passing away of the political generation involved in the massacre gave a greater sense of urgency to the search for information. For example, the death in October 2000 of Fernando Gutiérrez Barrios—the head of the Federal Security Directorate in October 1968 whose agents were responsible for arresting student leaders at Tlatelolco—emphasized the need to get information from those most directly involved in the massacre. The fallout from the massacre forced the PRI to start the lengthy process of rethinking its views on the preservation of an authoritarian, one-party state. Tlatelolco proved a political watershed that flowed all the way to the inauguration of the non-PRI president, Vicente Fox, in December 2000.

—*DMC*

See also: Democratization Process; Díaz Ordaz, Gustavo; Echeverría, Luis; Militarism; Partido Revolucionario Institucional (PRI); Poniatowska, Elena.

References:

Camp, Roderic Ai. *Generals in the Palacio: The Military in Modern Mexico.* New York: Oxford University Press, 1992.

Poniatowska, Elena. *Massacre in Mexico.* New York: Viking Press, 1975.

Ramírez, Ramón. *El movimiento estudiantil de México.* 2 vols. Mexico City: Ediciones Era, 1969.

Tlaxcala (State)

Located in central Mexico, Tlaxcala is the country's smallest state. It is also particularly challenged by the scarcity of natural resources, including water. The city of Tlaxcala serves as the state's capital, and other major urban centers are Apizaco, Huamantla, Santa Ana Chiautempán, and Tlaxco. Tlaxcala has a rich Indian heritage, and the state's name is derived from the Tlaxcalan culture, which played an impor-

tant role in Spanish colonization of Mexico. Dwarfed by the state of Puebla (which nearly surrounds it) and by Mexico's Federal District (with which it shares a border), Tlaxcala has struggled for much of its history to achieve political autonomy and economic viability.

In the centuries before Spanish contact, Tlaxcala was home to a variety of Indian groups. Cacaxtla and Xichoténcatl (just outside of today's capital city) were particularly important ceremonial centers, distinguished by their pyramids and murals, which are well preserved. The Tlaxcalan culture had emerged in the central part of the state by the twelfth century. Tlaxcala's native peoples fought a constant battle to preserve their independence in the face of challenges from the Aztecs of central Mexico and the Indians of Cholula in neighboring Puebla.

Although they initially resisted the Spaniards, the Tlaxcalan Indians soon forged an alliance with the Europeans, aiding in the final defeat of the Aztecs at Tenochtitlán (today's Mexico City). Tlaxcalans continued to aid the Spaniards in the colonization of Mexico, and Tlaxcalan settlements emerged in San Luis Potosí, Zacatecas, Durango, and Coahuila. Tlaxcalans derived special privileges from their relationship with the Spaniards. They were allowed to preserve their own government and they successfully represented Indian demands during the colonial era. Indian lands were also respected, at least initially.

Despite their alliance with the Spanish administration, the Tlaxcalans were increasingly affected by the colonial relationship. Population decline (caused by disease and migration to other areas of New Spain) and intermarriage with the Spanish population altered Tlaxcalan society, and these same factors ensured the transfer of traditional Indian lands. Tlaxcala's native peoples did not escape tribute demands either, and many were drafted as workers on major projects, such as the construction of Puebla's cathedral. Over time, many Indians also became a source of labor on Spanish haciendas and in textile factories owned by Spaniards in the towns of Tlaxcala and Apizaco. Additionally, the Roman Catholic Church touched the lives of some Indians, as Franciscan missionaries arrived to gain converts. The Church recognized an apparition of the Virgin Mary at Ocatlán in 1541 and ordered the construction of a sanctuary to commemorate the event.

Although Tlaxcala's native peoples could only partly resist the encroachments of the Spaniards, its leaders tended to favor the colonial arrangement as a way of protecting against the ambitions of neighboring Puebla, which sought to expand into the smaller territory. Thus Mexico's struggle for independence, beginning in the early nineteenth century, was resisted by many Indian (and non-Indian) elites. The new state of Puebla (established in 1824) did seek to annex Tlaxcala, which remained a federal territory until 1856 when it was finally granted statehood. Political autonomy was only part of the battle, however. The small state struggled to build a viable economy and its major products, wool and *pulque* (a beverage made from the fermented juices of the maguey plant) failed to compete in Mexico's markets. Meanwhile, Puebla's wealthy entrepreneurs acquired haciendas and textile factories in Tlaxcala.

The nineteenth century was also marked by political instability in Tlaxcala. The designs of Puebla elites, and Tlaxcala's central location and proximity to Mexico City contributed to unrest. During Mexico's War of Reform (1858–1861), Tlaxcala was the scene of numerous battles. The competing liberal and conservative factions both established governments in the state: the liberal government in the capital and the conservative regime in Huamantla. The 1860s brought additional disturbances, as invading French forces (who helped establish a French empire in Mexico) occupied Tlaxcala City, forcing the state government to retreat. The French were expelled in 1867 and Tlaxcala was reclaimed by the insurgent forces of Miguel Lira y Ortega, who then became the state's governor.

The last decades of the nineteenth century marked a transition to greater stability and prosperity. Under the leadership of Lira y Ortega and of Próspero Cahuantzi, Tlaxcala achieved economic growth, aided by the railroad, and encouraged by the national policies of Porfirio Díaz (1876–1911). Although some Tlaxcalans lost their lands during this period, the state did not experience a great movement of land into the hands of a wealthy few (as was the case in many areas of Mexico). Taxation, rather than loss of land, was thus the more important factor in generating the opposition that contributed to rebellion and revolution. Under Cahuantzi, an Indian *campesino* (peasant) who held power for twenty-six years, landowners of limited means struggled against increasing taxes. In 1899 thousands of smallholders protested yet another increase in property levies and were violently repressed. Cahuantzi's selective application of taxes also caused division among elites.

When the Mexican Revolution began in 1910, it built on the discontent of Tlaxcala's *campesinos* and workers, particularly in the densely populated (and heavily Indian) central-southern region of the state. Isidro Ortiz and Juan Cuamatzi were among the earliest leaders of the Revolution, and they were influenced by the radical ideas of Aquiles Serdán in Puebla. Although Cuamatzi was soon captured and shot, Cahuantzi's government soon fell, along with the national regime of Porfirio Díaz. Supporters of Mexico's new president, Francisco Madero, consolidated their power in Tlaxcala, and Antonio Hidalgo became governor. Hidalgo attempted radical reforms, including the return of communal lands, and he met elite resistance, which simply intensified after the overthrow of the Madero government. The state's Revolutionaries regrouped under Máximo Rojas, Domingo Arenas, and Pedro Morales. Arenas, a textile worker, emerged as a leading champion of land reform. He initially sided with the movement of Morelos rebel Emiliano Zapata and then became a general in Venustiano Carranza's Constitutionalist army. Arenas helped to redistribute land in both Tlaxcala and Puebla before his death in 1917. His followers, including brother Cirilo Arenas, continued their rebellion against Carranza, who resisted radical reforms.

In the aftermath of Carranza's own demise, and during the 1920s and 1930s, Tlaxcala experienced a period of social reform. Rafael Apango, Ignacio Mendoza, Adrián Vázquez, and Isidro Candia (all leaders who represented the popular classes of rural Tlaxcala) redistributed lands and used agrarian reform to co-opt Tlaxcala's *campesinos*. Land reform eventually affected the *pulque* haciendas of northern Tlaxcala, which had been particularly resistant to reform. Apango, Mendoza, Vázquez, and Candia also strengthened the state's ties with the central government and organized workers. After 1940, as Mexico shifted away from its period of Revolutionary change, Tlaxcala's leaders became more conservative, neglecting the continuing demands for land reform that persisted into the 1980s and that worsened with population growth and overexploitation of resources. The state's leaders placed a greater emphasis on industry, and industrial zones (including a Tlaxcala-Puebla industrial corridor) emerged.

The last decades of the twentieth century were characterized by increasing urbanization and by the migration, particularly of Indian peoples, to the cities. Environmental problems, including water pollution and the encroachment of urban zones into agricultural areas, accompanied such change. Tlaxcala's economic modernization also encouraged an erosion of the state's Indian culture, so that fewer people continue to speak the native languages of their ancestors. Beginning in the 1980s, however, the state government embraced a plan to preserve Tlaxcala's rich Indian heritage, a policy that was aided by the discovery and restoration of the great murals of Cacaxtla.

—*SBP*

See also: Carranza, Venustiano; Díaz, Porfirio; Puebla (State); Revolution of 1910; Zapata, Emiliano.

References:
Rendón Garcini, Ricardo. *Breve historia de Tlaxcala.* Mexico City: El Colegio de Mexico, 1996.
Official state web site: http://www.tlaxcala.gob.mx

Tourism

Tourism has long played an important role in the Mexican economy and continues to figure prominently in Mexico's long-term development plans. Tourism has achieved its economic importance for a number of reasons. First, it trails only oil and manufacturing exports as a generator of foreign exchange. Second, tourism is relatively labor intensive. Mexico's growing population created the need to generate a large number of new jobs on a consistent basis; the tourism industry could help to absorb the growing numbers of unskilled and semiskilled workers. Third, tourism provided an opportunity to disperse development and population to nonindustrial regions. This would help relieve the problem of rapid urbanization in a few cities—Mexico City, Guadalajara, Monterrey—that accompanied the drive for industrialization after World War II. Fourth, Mexico possessed a wide variety of potential historical, cultural, and entertainment activities. Finally, Mexico was literally well positioned to take advantage of the boom in international travel from the United States.

Mexico had attracted foreign travelers throughout its history, but it was not until the 1920s that tourism began to emerge as a major industry. This early development was connected primarily with tourism along the U.S.–Mexican border. The nature of the development was sometimes embarrassing to Mexican officials and business people. With Prohibition in effect in the United States, many of the U.S. visitors came to border towns such as Tijuana and Ciudad Juárez for a drink or to partake of what would have been considered "vices" on the U.S. side of the border: gambling, drugs, and prostitution.

The growth of tourism was restricted by infrastructure problems. Suitable hotel accommodations were often not available, and transportation was limited. Mexico scarcely had a road "system." Rail transportation was more dependable but also lacked coverage and was still not particularly fast. The train ride from Laredo to Mexico City took thirty-six hours in the late 1920s. There was steamship service to major Mexican ports such as Vera Cruz and Acapulco, but it was often difficult to travel inland from coastal areas. In the 1930s the Mexican government began to invest heavily in rural infrastructure projects such as roads, water, electricity, and public health. This emphasis on infrastructure development was not designed specifically to stimulate tourism, but it did indirectly have that result by facilitating transportation and making certain rural areas more attractive to tourists. Limited air travel from the United States to Mexico was also available by the 1930s but would not be a major factor for some time.

The post–World War II period saw a major upswing in tourism, especially from the United States. The Mexican government continued to invest heavily in infrastructure developments that helped to promote tourism. During the 1950s the expanding transportation system continued to funnel tourists through Mexico City as the major roads, railroads, and airlines all converged in the capital. The Mexican government made a more direct commitment to tourism with the establishment in the mid-1950s of the Fondo Nacional para el Turismo (the National Tourism Fund, or FONATUR). FONATUR provided financing for a variety of tourism-related activities. The growing importance of tourism in Mexico's development scheme was confirmed by the creation of a cabinet-level position, secretary of tourism. The government also operated its own airline, Aeronaves de México or AeroMéxico, which helped promote tourism.

While the national government was promoting tourism, the impact of increased tourism tended to be regional and local. The government did not have sufficient funds for a broad financing of tourist development. The involvement of the government in promoting tourism also guaranteed that political considerations would play an important role in funding decisions. Acapulco was a major beneficiary of government funding for infrastructure development; there were regular flights between Mexico City and Acapulco as well as a four-lane toll road linking the capital and the booming resort. Former President Miguel Alemán (1946–1952) had extensive real estate holdings in Acapulco; he also served as director general of the National Board of Tourism from 1958 until his death in 1983. Other potential tourist areas, such as Oaxaca and the Yucatán, would have to wait their turn.

By the late 1960s the Mexican government began to place greater emphasis on integrally planned, government-sponsored resort development. After a computer survey of potential resort sites, the government selected Cancún on the Caribbean coast. Within a decade Cancún was a booming tourist resort primarily catering to foreigners who arrived by air. The government promoted similar developments on the Pacific Coast at Ixtapa-Zihuatanejo, Bahías de Huatulco, and at Loreto and Los Cabos in Baja California.

While these new seaside resorts tended to focus attention on foreign tourists, the growing Mexican middle class accounted for much of the tourism boom. In 1986 there were approximately 4.5 million foreign visitors to Mexico; this compares with some 22 million Mexicans who traveled in their own country for leisure purposes. While the new integrated seaside resorts served primarily foreigners, more traditional resorts such as Acapulco, Mazatlán, and even Puerto Vallarta catered primarily to Mexican travelers. Even in border towns such as Tijuana, Reynosa, and Ciudad Juárez, Mexicans accounted for the overwhelming percentage of tourists, averaging almost 90 percent.

The 1980s brought major changes to the Mexican tourist industry. The economic reforms of the 1980s led to a broad retreat of the government from the economy, including the tourist sector. Financing for tourist development would increasingly depend on foreign investment and private domestic capital. There was also growing criticism of the social costs of tourist development. There had been little prior thought given to the environmental impact of tourism. Acapulco—once a premiere seaside resort—found its tourist business threatened by increasing pollution of its bay and beaches. The tourist industry delivered on its promise as a generator of jobs; by the mid-1980s, some 1.7 million workers were in the tourist industry. There was, however, criticism of the types of jobs being created; most were for low pay, poor benefits, and often were only seasonal employment. One of the goals of promoting tourism was to promote economic development in rural areas that would not be helped much by the government's broader economic program of stimulating industrialization. While tourism did serve this purpose, it also had the effect of attracting rural dwellers to areas that were poorly prepared to deal with a rapidly expanding population. The ongoing financial and economic crises of the 1980s and 1990s also hurt the spending power of the expanding Mexican middle class, which had earlier helped to fuel a domestic upswing in tourism.

Much of Mexico's tourism still revolves around the "sun, sand, and sea" resorts of the Pacific Coast and the Caribbean. There have been efforts in recent years to develop what has become known as "alternative tourism." One of the earliest forms of this alternative tourism was "ecotourism," which would take advantage of Mexico's unusual natural resources in a protected and sustainable way. Such tourism requires minimal capital investment and is more likely to directly benefit the local community. The concept of alternative tourism has continued to expand to include a wide range of activities ranging from archeological explorations to extreme sports. This alternative tourism has been growing at a much faster rate than tourism as a whole, but it still makes up only a small part of Mexico's larger tourist picture. There are also concerns that its rapid growth may make it difficult to protect the very resources that are being used.

In the early twenty-first century, tourism continues to play a important role in the Mexican economy, particularly in generating foreign exchange and jobs. In 2001 tourism ranked behind only oil and manufacturing exports as a generator of foreign exchange, and almost two million people were employed in the tourist industry. The terrorist attacks on the United States in September 2001 and an international recession did not severely impact the Mexican tourist industry. Over the long term (1980 to 2002), Mexico's share of international tourists and tourist income has declined because of greater international competition in the tourist industry. The administration of President Vicente Fox (2000–2006) has put forward a program called "Agenda 21 for Mexican Tourism," which has as its main goal "the sustainable development of tourist activity." Fox hopes to get local and state governments, as well as private groups, more actively involved in the promotion of tourism. It is still too early to determine whether the program represents a major departure in Mexico's approach to tourism or—even if it does—whether Fox will be successful in promoting tourism with the emphasis on sustainability and accountability. Whatever the fate of "Agenda 21," tourism will continue to figure prominently in Mexico's economy.

—*DMC*

See also: Alemán, Miguel; Economy; Government; Transportation.

References:

De Kadt, Emanuel, ed. *Tourism: Passport to Development?* New York: Oxford University Press, 1979.

Theobald, William F., ed. *Global Tourism: The Next Decade*. Oxford: Butterworth-Heinemann, 1995.

http://www.sectur.gob.mx.

Transportation

Transportation—or lack of it—has profoundly influenced the political, economic, social, and cultural development of Mexico. In the early decades of independence, Mexican transportation was made up of dirt roads, horses, mules, carts, and wagons; even these methods of transport were beyond the means of most Mexicans, for whom transportation meant walking. Lack of government funding at all levels meant that the few roads were poorly built and maintained. Mountainous terrain, tropical lowlands, and adverse weather conditions affected transportation in various parts of the country. While Mexico had a number of rivers, few of them were sufficiently navigable to serve as important transportation routes. Mexico had an extensive coastline, but much of the population was located at considerable distances from the coasts in the central plateau. The nation's political leaders—whether liberal or conservative—recognized the need for major improvements in transportation, but political instability and a lack of financial resources kept Mexico's roads and ports at a primitive level. For Mexican society, the underdeveloped transportation system fostered localism in politics, restricted the development of a national market, and promoted social and cultural isolation.

Like many in the nineteenth century, Mexicans embraced the railroads as the solution to their transportation problems and a guarantee of economic development. As early as the 1830s, the central government issued a concession for a railroad that would connect the capital of Mexico City with the country's leading port, Vera Cruz. This initial effort at railroad construction was hardly encouraging. The project was plagued by financial problems, failed concessions, civil war, and foreign invasions.

There were huge cost overruns, and the line was not finished until 1873.

These early problems with railroad construction led to the conviction that the federal government would have to play a leading role in railroad construction. After a brief period in the late 1870s of state governments trying to promote railroad construction, in 1880 the federal government stepped in and helped to set off a true railroad boom. New legislation passed that year established the general guidelines under which the federal government would become involved in railroad promotion; one of the most important provisions of the new legislation was that the federal government would provide subsidies to companies receiving federal concessions. The two most significant concessions were to foreign investors to construct railroads from Mexico City to Ciudad Juárez (the Mexican Central) and to Nuevo Laredo (the Mexican National). From the viewpoint of the investors, these rail lines represented a logical extension of the U.S. rail system that was expanding along the U.S.–Mexican border.

The rapid expansion of the railroad system during the rule of Porfirio Díaz (1877–1880, 1884–1911) had a profound impact on Mexico. While the expansion had a limited impact on passenger service, it had a major effect on freight services; shipping costs declined substantially, leading to a major increase in the tonnage carried by Mexican railroads. Railroad expansion opened new job opportunities for some Mexicans, but it also led to greater concentration of landownership at the expense of Indian villages and the public lands. The nature of the railroad expansion—especially the dominant role played by foreigners—also lessened the potential benefits to the Mexican economy. The railroads were heavily dependent on foreign capital, foreign equipment, foreign technology, foreign management expertise, and even foreign markets. Profits—which were often hard to come by—were typically remitted overseas. Railroad expansion did not provide a strong impetus to Mexican entrepreneurship as many had hoped or expected; it did, however, lead to greater government involvement in the economy and to greater importance for bureaucratic "technicians." Federal financing for railroads led to less federal involvement in the construction and maintenance of roads, which increasingly became the responsibility of state and local governments. The railroad boom did strengthen the position of the central government in relation to state and local governments, especially in the ability of the central government to move troops more easily to trouble spots. The railroads started the process of breaking down local and regional isolation, but that would be a long-term process that would last well into the twentieth century. The Díaz administration addressed the concern over foreign control of the rail system by purchasing controlling interest in the major lines and organizing them in 1908 into the Ferrocarriles Nacionales de México (the National Railroads of Mexico).

Closely connected to the expansion of the railroads was the improvement in port facilities in the late nineteenth century. Important ports served as terminals for the rail system, which was geared to the export trade. The federal government provided funding for the expansion and improvement of both Pacific and Gulf Coast ports as well as subsidies to promote Mexican merchant shipping. Despite government financial support, Mexican shipping activities were still restricted almost completely to coastal trade; Mexico's foreign trade was dominated by non-Mexican shippers, especially from the United States.

Railroads played an important role in the Revolution of 1910. Because of the poor road system, large Revolutionary armies depended heavily on the railroads for transport and supply. At the same time, railroads became the targets of Revolutionary factions trying to weaken their rivals. The Revolution led to significant destruction of rail lines, bridges, and railroad equipment. After the worst fighting came to an end, the central government turned its attention to repairing and reviving existing rail lines, but there was little expansion in the overall system during the rest of the century. Mexico's rail system expanded more during the boom years of 1881–1884 (approximately 5,000 kilometers) than it did during the period from 1935 to 1995 (approximately 3,000 kilometers).

Beginning in the mid-1920s the federal government began to emphasize road construction as the key to Mexico's transportation problems. The government was particularly concerned with rural roads as part of a broader program of agrarian reform and agricultural modernization. Federal investment in roads increased steadily until the mid-1940s and remained significant after that period. The expansion of the road network stimulated agriculture, manufacturing, and commerce; it also helped to support the government's new development approach after World War II—import substitution industrialization. The government also kept the cost of gasoline artificially low, a result of the nationalization of the foreign-owned oil companies in 1938.

In the 1950s and 1960s, air transport became more important in Mexico's transportation scheme. Although smaller airport facilities multiplied quickly, commercial traffic was dominated by a few major cities: Mexico City, Guadalajara, and Monterrey. Domestic and international flights increased, but most Mexicans still found air travel prohibitively expensive, and air freight was not highly developed. While there were a number of private airlines, the Mexican government operated its own airline, Aeronaves de México, or Aeromexico.

The series of financial and economic crises that began in the 1970s and the economic reforms they spawned affected the transportation industry, as it did virtually every aspect of the Mexican economy. The financial problems of the federal government and the austerity programs that followed quickly appeared in road construction and especially maintenance. The federal government was responsible for 100 percent of construction costs for federal roads, 50 percent of construction costs for state roads, and 30 percent of costs for local roads. The World Bank reported that by the mid-1990s more than 60 percent of Mexico's public roads were in poor condition. The administration of President Carlos Salinas de Gortari (1988–1994) adjusted to declining federal spending and deteriorating public roads by granting concessions to the private sector for the construction of toll roads. The new toll roads were in better condition than the public roads but also proved more expensive to construct than planned. As a result, high tolls limited the amount of traffic that would be diverted from public roads. The financial crisis of 1994–1995 forced the federal government to establish a government-backed trust fund that took over the assets and liabilities of the private toll-road companies.

Activities in road construction and operation reflected the changing approach of the federal government toward transportation in general. President Ernesto Zedillo (1994–2000) indicated the direction of government policy in 1995 in his "National Plan for the Modernization of the Transport Sector." The heart of the plan was deregulation, privatization, and decentralization. Deregulation of transportation was part of a broader program of government deregulation of the economy. Privatization would get the private sector more actively involved in the construction, operation, and maintenance of transport. Under decentralization, the federal government intended to turn over more of the responsibility for transportation to state and local governments. The privatization of transportation moved forward quickly in the late 1990s. By 1999 most of the state-owned railroads had been sold off to private companies. The process of privatizing the administration of Mexico's seaports was also quickly implemented. There was also an active pro-gram of privatizing the administration of government-owned airports. A typical example of this was the sale in 1999 of a concession to operate 12 airports to a group led by two Spanish companies and a Mexican company; included in the sale were airports at Guadalajara—Mexico's second biggest city—and Puerto Vallarta, a popular tourist stop. Decentralization of roads proved less successful. Most state and local governments lacked sufficient funds to maintain their existing systems, much less take on the responsibility for additional roads. There was also the ongoing problem of what to do with the toll roads that had come under government control; although these former private toll roads were of recent construction, financial problems had caused them to fall behind very quickly in terms of maintenance.

Changes in transportation have had a profound impact on Mexico's political, economic, and social development during the twentieth century. Politically, improved transportation greatly facilitated the centralization of power being promoted in the decades after the Revolution of 1910. At a minimum, better transportation permitted more rapid deployment and employment of military forces when state control was challenged; a recent example of this was the Zapatista rebellion in Chiapas in 1994, which was quickly contained militarily by a rapid movement of forces. Improved transportation has promoted economic integration into both a national and international market. Socially, expanded transportation has broken down the local and regional identities that characterized much of Mexico's history. Although the transportation systems experienced major changes in the 1990s, additional changes will be needed to provide Mexico with the transportation facilities it needs in the twenty-first century. The full implications of decentralization and privatization still have not been determined, especially in terms of road construction and maintenance. The relative roles of the public and private sectors in transportation are constantly evolving, as the toll roads issue indicates. Finally, Mexico will need to identify transportation improvements that can more directly benefit the lower classes, such as urban transport.

—DMC

See also: Environmental Issues; Government; Import Substitution Industrialization (ISI); Revolution of 1910; Salinas de Gortari, Carlos; Zedillo Ponce de León, Ernesto.

References:

Coatsworth, John H. *Growth against Development: The Economic Impact of Railroads in Porfirian Mexico.* DeKalb: Northern Illinois University Press, 1981.

Giugale, Marcelo M., Olivier Lafourcade, and Vinh H. Nguyen, eds. *Mexico: A Comprehensive Development Agenda for the New Era.* Washington, DC: The World Bank, 2001.

Reynolds, Clark W. *The Mexican Economy: Twentieth-Century Structure and Growth.* New Haven, CT: Yale University Press, 1970.

U

United States, Relations with

Mexico and the United States have a long history of often-contentious relations. While there has been talk of a "special relationship" between the two countries since the 1820s, that relationship has always been influenced by the major differences in wealth and power between the two countries. When Mexico came into existence as an independent nation in 1821, it was immediately under pressure on its northern frontier from U.S. expansion, especially in the Texas area. The Mexican government tried to avoid the loss of Texas by inviting Americans to settle there and become loyal Mexican citizens. The American population soon greatly outnumbered the Mexican population, alarming authorities in Mexico City. When the Mexican government attempted to tighten its control of the area, it led to revolution and the establishment of an independent Republic of Texas in 1836. Mexico refused to recognize the independence of Texas and warned that annexation by the United States would mean war. In 1845, the United States annexed Texas, leading to a break in diplomatic relations and ultimately war in 1846. The war proved a disaster for Mexico, which lost almost half of its national territory to the United States. This "Mexican Cession" area included all or part of the current states of New Mexico, Arizona, California, Nevada, Utah, and Colorado.

During the 1850s and 1860s, the United States was largely preoccupied with its own internal problems but did succeed in purchasing some additional land in northern Mexico in 1853 that would later form part of the states of New Mexico and Arizona. After the end of the U.S. Civil War in 1865, U.S. interest in Mexico increasingly focused on economic penetration rather than territorial expansion. During the administration of Mexican President Porfirio Díaz (1877–1880, 1884–1911), Americans achieved a major role in such high-profile businesses as railroads, mining, oil, and land development. U.S. investment was especially extensive between 1900 and 1910; by 1910, U.S. investors accounted for more than half of all foreign investment ($1.6 billion of a total of $3 billion). The growing integration of the Mexican economy into the United States economy was reflected in the growth of consular services on both sides of the border. By 1910, there were thirty-one Mexican consulates in the United States and twenty-five U.S. consulates in Mexico. A large number of U.S. citizens also resided in Mexico; by 1910 Mexico City alone had some 10,000

Americans, the largest foreign community in the capital.

The outbreak of Revolution in 1910 posed a threat to U.S. lives and property in Mexico as well as a major danger to the U.S. border region. Most of the early fighting took place in northern Mexico, close to the international boundary. The key battle that led to victory for the Revolutionaries took place at Ciudad Juárez—across the Rio Grande from El Paso, Texas—in May 1911. The attack resulted in six killed and fifteen wounded on the U.S. side of the border. The Revolution also created a lengthy period of political instability and general lawlessness that posed a threat to U.S. lives and property throughout Mexico. The United States recognized the first government to come out of the Revolution, that of Francisco Madero. After the overthrow and assassination of Madero in February 1913, the United States did not recognize any government in Mexico until October 1915. Madero's replacement in the presidency was Victoriano Huerta, an old-line Porfirian general who was believed to have ordered the murder of Madero. U.S. policy under President Woodrow Wilson (1913–1921) escalated from trying to get Huerta to resign to outright military intervention in April 1914 when U.S. forces occupied the key Mexican port of Vera Cruz on the Gulf Coast. Wilson also partially lifted an arms embargo to let Huerta's opponents purchase arms in the United States. Huerta resigned and went into exile in July 1914.

Instead of bringing peace, the resignation of Huerta ushered in the bloodiest period of the Revolution in 1915–1916. The different Revolutionary groups began fighting among themselves. This factional fighting pitted the forces of Francisco "Pancho" Villa and Emiliano Zapata against those of Venustiano Carranza and Alvaro Obregón. With Villa suffering a series of defeats in 1915 and with Zapata isolated in the south, the Wilson administration extended recognition to Carranza in October 1915. The recognition of Carranza angered Villa, who was still a force

to be reckoned with in northern Mexico. In January 1916 Villa's forces massacred a group of Americans in Chihuahua, killing sixteen. This was followed by an even bolder stroke in March 1916, when some of Villa's forces crossed the border and attacked the town of Columbus, New Mexico, killing seventeen Americans. The Columbus attack provoked a major military response from the United States. Under the leadership of General John J. Pershing, an expedition was launched to capture Villa and disperse his forces so they would no longer threaten the border. The Pershing expedition reached a peak strength of more than 11,000 troops and remained in northern Mexico until February 1917.

The withdrawal of the Pershing Expedition removed a major point of contention between Mexico and the United States, but relations continued to be tense between 1917 and 1920. Mexico implemented a new Constitution in 1917, which many Americans saw as a threat to their property interests. There was also a bitter disagreement over taxation of U.S. enterprises. Carranza was the first president elected under the new Constitution, and he continued to follow a highly nationalistic policy, which alienated the Wilson administration. The U.S. entry into World War I in April 1917 provoked further controversy between Carranza and Wilson. While Wilson attempted to line up the Latin American nations behind the United States, Carranza proclaimed Mexico's neutrality in the conflict. The overthrow and assassination of Carranza in 1920 by supporters of Alvaro Obregón ended the squabbling between Carranza and Wilson but also threw U.S.–Mexico relations into a state of uncertainty.

One of the primary diplomatic goals of the new administration of Alvaro Obregón was to obtain recognition from the United States, which was withholding recognition pending an agreement on U.S. property rights in Mexico. In 1923 the two countries reached agreements that provided recognition for Obregón and satisfied the U.S. government on the property issue. Despite the devastation of revolution and the dislocation of world war, economic ties between Mexico and the United States continued to be close during the 1920s. Obregón and his successor, Plutarco Elías Calles (1924–1928)—although criticized by U.S. investors and officials for their "socialist" and "Bolshevik" policies—in fact maintained the close linkage of the Mexican economy with the U.S. economy. The onset of the Great Depression of the 1930s demonstrated how closely linked the two economies had become. During the boom times of the 1920s, many Mexicans had found employment in the United States; when the downturn came, the flow of labor was reversed. Many Mexicans lost their jobs and voluntarily returned to Mexico, but most—more than 300,000 from 1930 to 1933—were forcibly repatriated. U.S.–Mexico relations in the 1930s appeared to bottom out when Mexican president Lázaro Cárdenas (1934–1940) nationalized the foreign-owned oil companies in 1938.

While the oil nationalization epitomized the economic nationalism of the Revolutionary era, it coincided with a shift in policy by the Mexican government that would bring even closer economic relations between the two countries. A domestic economic crisis and the changing international situation were forcing the Cárdenas administration to move toward a new development scheme in which industrialization would be given emphasis over agrarian reform. With World War II approaching, the U.S. government was concerned with hemispheric defense and access to Mexico's natural resources. After the United States entered the war in December 1941, Mexico responded by breaking relations with Japan. In May 1942 Mexico declared war on the Axis powers after German submarines sank two Mexican oil tankers.

During the war years, the United States and Mexico cooperated closely on economic and military matters. Mexico played an important role in supplying the United States with strategic materials, such as oil and copper, agricultural products, and even workers

under a closely regulated system. The United States helped Mexico to modernize its military, and Mexico even provided a fighter squadron that fought in the Philippines.

Economic ties remained strong after 1945, but military cooperation declined rapidly. Mexico hoped for U.S. assistance in continuing its economic development program, but the United States was primarily concerned with strategic considerations in Europe, Asia, and the Middle East. Although official U.S. aid was in short supply, private U.S. capital flowed into Mexico in the postwar years despite greater restrictions by the Mexican government. Tourism from the United States also came to figure prominently in the Mexican economy. The United States continued its long-established role as Mexico's principal trading partner.

As Mexico's postwar "economic miracle" began to fade by 1970, the administration of Mexican President Luis Echeverría (1970–1976) pursued new economic and foreign policies that lessened Mexico's dependence on the United States. New restrictions on foreign investment in 1973 led to a decline in U.S. investment. Echeverría tried with modest success to broaden Mexico's international trade contacts. Although Echeverría's presidency ended in financial disarray, major new oil discoveries helped to give his successor, José López Portillo (1976–1982), a powerful basis for greater Mexican independence in its relations with the United States. López Portillo, however, frittered away his opportunity in a wave of corruption and mismanagement. By 1982 Mexico was in the midst of a major financial crisis brought on by declining oil prices and excessive international borrowing. The United States played a major role in the financial bailout of Mexico that followed.

After 1982, a series of Mexican presidents—Miguel de la Madrid (1982–1988), Carlos Salinas de Gortari (1988–1994), and Ernesto Zedillo (1994–2000)—enacted major reforms that opened the Mexican economy to foreign trade and investment and led to even stronger economic ties to the

United States. The principal example of this new openness was the North American Free Trade Agreement (NAFTA), which went into effect in 1994. NAFTA pointed the way toward an even greater degree of economic integration between the two countries.

With the Cold War ended and U.S.–Mexico economic ties increasing, the biggest point of friction between the United States and Mexico was the drug trade. Mexico was a principal transit point and source for drugs moving into the United States. The situation was worsened by accumulating evidence that Mexican officials at all levels of government were deeply involved in the trade. Mexico criticized the United States for placing too much emphasis on stopping the supply of drugs coming out of Mexico and not enough emphasis on reducing the demand for drugs in the United States.

In the early twenty-first century, Mexico and the United States find their diplomatic agendas increasingly affected by their economic relationship. As the two become more integrated economically, the "special relationship" will have to adjust accordingly.

—DMC

See also: Boundary Conflicts; *Bracero* Program; Constitution of 1917; Drug Trafficking; Economy; Foreign Policy; Immigration/Emigration; Korean War; North American Free Trade Agreement (NAFTA); Oil Industry; Revolution of 1910; Tourism; Villa, Francisco "Pancho"; World War II.

References:

Hall, Linda B., and Don M. Coerver. *Revolution on the Border: The United States and Mexico, 1910–1920.* Albuquerque: University of New Mexico Press, 1988.

Langley, Lester D. *Mexico and the United States: The Fragile Relationship.* Boston: Twayne Publishers, 1991.

Raat, W. Dirk. *Mexico and the United States: Ambivalent Vistas.* Athens: University of Georgia Press, 1992.

Urbanization

Both the indigenous and the Hispanic heritages of Mexico have a strong urban tradition. Pre-Hispanic Mexico featured a number of major urban centers. The well-planned center at Teotihuacan at its peak around 600 had an estimated population of approximately 125,000, making it one of the biggest cities in the world at the time. The Aztec capital of Tenochtitlán—on the site of present-day Mexico City—had a population of approximately 200,000 at the time the Spaniards arrived in 1519. Many of the major indigenous centers were later depopulated as a result of the Spanish Conquest and the rapid decline in the native population owing to disease. The conquering Spaniards had a highly developed urban tradition that traced its roots to the period of Roman occupation of the Iberian Peninsula. For the Spaniards, the municipality was the basic political unit and the natural center for political, social, economic, and cultural activities. Even the landed elite spent most of their time in urban areas, leaving their estates to be run by resident administrators. Social services and educational facilities were found almost exclusively in urban areas. Social mobility was largely equated with moving to the city. Mexico City quickly emerged as the dominant urban center of Mexico, despite the destruction of much of the city during the conquest and an appalling decline in the native population. Despite its dominant position, Mexico City actually had a smaller population (130,000) in the late colonial period than at its peak as the Aztec capital of Tenochtitlán.

After independence in 1821, cities retained their importance in the political and economic scheme. The regionalism that characterized—and destabilized—Mexico in the years after independence often reflected efforts by urban elites to maintain their local and regional influence and power. Efforts at centralization provoked political instability as municipal leaders tried to maintain their autonomy in the face of pressure from Mexico City. During the administration of President Porfirio Díaz (1877–1880, 1884–1911), the central government was more effective in extending its control over municipal governments. Díaz also promoted a "modernization" of Mexico's major cities; this effort at modernization was mainly an effort to make Mexican cities look more like those in the United States and Western Europe. The major cities took on such trappings of modernity as electricity, telephones, trolleys, planned residential developments, and public parks. An expanding railroad network helped to connect the growing cities, and even a limited number of automobiles appeared on the improving roads. The cities provided a comfortable setting for the Porfirian elite and the expanding middle class, but the majority of city dwellers lived in poverty and led a precarious economic existence. Despite the growing attractiveness of the cities, Mexico was still overwhelmingly a rural country in 1900, with only about 10 percent of the population living in major urban areas. The most populous urban area—Mexico City—had a population of about 350,000.

The outbreak of Revolution in 1910 provoked major population shifts. Many rural dwellers migrated to the cities in search of greater security. During the 1920s and 1930s, the central government attempted to make rural life more attractive through an expanding agrarian reform program. The shift in economic development policies beginning in World War II greatly accelerated the movement from rural areas to urban areas; the new emphasis on industrialization (import substitution industrialization, or ISI) brought with it a growing urbanization. ISI was based on a vision of a future Mexico that was modern, urban, and industrial. Although urbanization was taking place on a nationwide basis, it was particularly intense in Mexico City and Monterrey, the principal centers of industrial activity. The concentration of industrial activity in Mexico City was the product of government planning; by 1970 more than 40 percent of Mexico's industrial production was located in the capital. This disproportionate level of industrial activity led to a disproportionate migration from rural areas to Mexico City; the capital's population increased at an average rate of 5 percent per year between 1940 and 1970, reaching a total population of more than 8 million by 1970. This explosive growth led the government to attempt—with limited success—to disperse industrial activity and its accompanying urbanization throughout the country. Mexico's four largest cities— Mexico City, Guadalajara, Monterrey, and Puebla—accounted for almost one-fourth of the national population.

This explosive urban growth was a combination of the perceived attractions of urban life combined with the declining social and economic conditions in the countryside. The rapidly growing urban areas found it difficult to provide the services that had attracted many migrants in the first place. There were major problems with such basic services as education, housing, water, electricity, sewage, transportation, and public health. Those who came looking for a better economic life often found only part-time employment or employment in the "underground" or informal economy. Once the flow from the rural areas to the cities had started, it was hard to reverse. Rural migrants often encountered disappointment in the cities, but there was little in the countryside to attract their return.

Since the 1960s, a new region of urbanization has come to the forefront: the U.S.– Mexican border. For most of its history, the border region featured a sparse population and limited economic opportunities. During the late nineteenth century, the area began to see an increase in population and economic activity in connection with American investment and the expansion of the economy in the southwestern United States. This connection was to continue throughout the twentieth century. The border towns not only offered improved economic opportunities; they also served as a jumping-off point for Mexican workers migrating to the United States for employment. Mexican workers returning from the United States often stayed in border towns either permanently or until

Men and women work at tables at one of the many maquiladora *plants in Tijuana. The plants developed out of the U.S. need for cheap Mexican labor and new trade agreements. (Annie Griffiths Belt/Corbis)*

their next trip to the United States. When U.S. officials forcibly returned Mexican workers, as they did in the 1930s and 1950s, they typically were returned to Mexican border towns. Border urbanization received a major boost with the advent of the Border Industrialization Program (BIP) in 1965. BIP gave rise to the *maquiladora* system of assembly plants along the border. These plants began to attract large numbers of workers from the interior of Mexico, creating a rapid urbanization of the border region. Border cities experienced the same problems as urban areas in other parts of Mexico, with the added burden that many of the problems had an international character given the series of twin cities stretching from the Gulf of Mexico to the Pacific Ocean. Air and water problems in Ciudad Juárez, Chihuahua, became problems in El Paso, Texas, across the Rio Grande. Historically, the cities on the U.S. side of the border had a larger population than those on the Mexican side. By the

early 1990s, the situation had reversed itself; with the exception of the Tijuana–San Diego twins, the twin cities on the Mexican side were larger than their U.S. counterparts.

The migration to the cities and a generally high rate of population growth has turned Mexico into a highly urbanized country since World War II. By 2000, urban centers contained about 75 percent of Mexico's population; the greater Mexico City area alone accounted for about 18 percent of the total national population. Internal migration is no longer just rural to urban; movement from one urban area to another makes up an increasingly important aspect of population flows. Urbanization continues to outpace infrastructure development and provision of services in most urban areas. Housing shortages continue to be a major problem, and few municipalities have or enforce urban development plans. Poverty is increasingly an urban phenomenon; the World Bank estimates that 63 percent of Mexico's poor live in urban areas. The rising incidence of crime is associated with a higher rate of urbanization; at one point, crime in Mexico City reached a point that led the U.S. State Department to issue a warning to Americans traveling to the city. Water and sanitation continue to be major problems. Only about one-third of the solid waste generated in urban areas is disposed of properly. Air pollution is a growing problem for many Mexican cities. Lack of urban transport is a major financial burden for the poor, who often live in areas poorly served by public transportation and have to travel great distances. Public health programs are hard pressed to keep up with the expanding urban population.

As part of the reforms of the 1980s and 1990s, a general decentralization process was initiated. This process has given additional powers and responsibilities to municipal governments, but local government still is hampered by a shortage of revenue sources. State governments still exercise considerable control over municipal activities, including the setting of tax rates; federal funding for municipalities is funneled through state governments, further restricting local decision making. Many municipal administrations still suffer from poor financial management, a shortage of skilled staff, and a lack of conti-

nuity in planning. Further complicating efforts to manage the urbanization process is the rapid growth in medium-sized cities (100,000 to 1 million inhabitants). According to World Bank figures, the number of medium-sized cities increased from 10 in 1970 to 55 in 1990. These medium-sized cities often have even greater difficulty in meeting the demands of the urbanization process. Although Mexico's general rate of population growth has declined since the 1970s, coping with the process of urbanization will continue to take up a major portion of the attention and resources of all levels of government.

—DMC

See also: Agrarian Reform / Land and Land Policy; Economy; Government; Import Substitution Industrialization (ISI); Mexico City; Monterrey Group.

References:

Giugale, Marcelo M., Olivier Lafourcade, and Vinh H. Nguyen, eds. *Mexico: A Comprehensive Development Agenda for the New Era.* Washington, DC: The World Bank, 2001.

Herzog, Lawrence A. *Where North Meets South: Cities, Space, and Politics on the U.S.–Mexico Border.* Austin: University of Texas Press, 1990.

Joseph, Gilbert M., and Mark D. Szuchman, eds. *I Saw a City Invincible: Urban Portraits of Latin America.* Wilmington, DE: Scholarly Resources, 1996.

Vasconcelos, José (1882–1959)

Of all the great public figures that emerged from the chaotic years of the Mexican Revolution, José Vasconcelos is perhaps the most controversial. A philosopher activist turned establishment lawyer (for an American firm), he played an active role in several different phases of the Mexican Revolution and served for four influential years as Alvaro Obregón's high-profile secretary of education. During his tenure as secretary of education, he helped inaugurate a new era in Mexican education that included the first important efforts to bring education to the long-neglected Mexican countryside and the beginnings of the world-renowned muralist movement. His widely read philosophical works that exalted Latin America's mixed-race peoples as the "cosmic race" of the future proved a potent antidote to European and American racism and became a prominent component of new, more inclusive, nationalist ideologies throughout the region. Political differences with Obregón and his successor, Plutarco Elías Calles, and a 1929 presidential bid that failed in the midst of massive electoral fraud embittered Vasconcelos. Disgusted at the corruption and anticlerical policies of the official party, he became increasingly conservative—pro-Spanish, pro-

Catholic, even pro-Fascist—and increasingly critical of the regime. This seemingly drastic philosophical and political shift, coupled with a mercurial temperament, have contributed to a complex legacy. Most often Vasconcelos is revered as the founder of modern Mexican education and the philosopher of the cosmic race but reviled as a conservative malcontent whose political disappointments caused him to betray his earlier progressive ideals.

Vasconcelos was born in Oaxaca on 28 February 1882 into a respectable middle-class family. The family moved to the U.S.–Mexico border when he was still very young; first to Sasabe, Sonora (across from Sasabe, Arizona), and then to Piedras Negras, Coahuila (across from Eagle Pass, Texas). On the border, Vasconcelos—later to become Mexico's first secretary of education—encountered the American school system firsthand. In his memoirs, he notes that his parents enrolled him in school in Eagle Pass because "on the other side of the border, the Yankees matched their concern with material progress with careful attention to education." Despite constant taunting from prejudiced Anglo classmates and an occasional fistfight, he thrived in school, mastering English and honing his debating skills in defense of Mexican national honor. Family moves to Mexico

City, Toluca, and Campeche further expanded his knowledge of his homeland but the acute sense of cultural difference between "Anglo-Saxon" America and "Latin" Mexico acquired on the border would have a profound influence on his later intellectual development.

Philosophy was his first love but, thanks to a Porfirian education system dominated by a positivist emphasis on technical and scientific learning, Vasconcelos had to settle for law school in Mexico City. Nevertheless, his 1905 thesis on the "dynamic theory of law," which explored the spiritual side of law, indicated a certain degree of independence from positivist thought. As a founding member of the Ateneo de la Juventud, he formed part of an intellectual circle of young scholars that included future luminaries like philosopher Antonio Caso, essayist Alfonso Reyes, novelist Martín Luis Guzmán, and painter Diego Rivera. The Ateneo sought to develop a "spiritual" aesthetics that would transcend the crass materialism of positivism. Despite its elitist tendencies and artistic (rather than Revolutionary) character, this philosophical assault on the official ideology of the Porfirio Díaz's in-house intellectuals, the *científicos* (men of science or technocrats), proved surprisingly effective in undermining the regime's credibility. In particular, the Ateneo's much-publicized disgust at the extravagant 1910 independence centennial celebrations helped turn public opinion against the president. Throughout this period of intellectual ferment and despite his rejection of both American arrogance and Porfirian materialism, Vasconcelos worked quite successfully as a lawyer for an American commercial law firm in Mexico City—one of many paradoxes in his complex life.

Involvement with politics in support of Francisco Madero's 1910 presidential bid transformed Vasconcelos from successful lawyer and part-time philosopher to political activist and public intellectual. As the editor of Madero campaign's newspaper, *El Antireeleccionista* (The Anti-Reelectionist), Vasconcelos became the public voice of the movement whose slogan, "Effective Suffrage, No Reelection," still appears on official Mexican government documents. When an aggravated Porfirio Díaz clamped down on the Madero campaign, arresting its candidate and harassing his supporters, Vasconcelos fled to the United States, the first of many trips into exile. Madero's eventual triumph brought him back to Mexico City and his legal career. Madero's subsequent assassination thrust him back into politics, first as the Constitutionalist representative to the Nicaragua Falls Conference, where he helped negotiate the withdrawal of U.S. troops from Vera Cruz and then as the opposition Conventionalist minister of public education. The Constitutionalist's eventual triumph sent him back into American exile. Carranza's overthrow saw his return, this time as interim President Adolfo de la Huerta's rector for the National University. As rector, he proved a tireless advocate of public education for all Mexicans and a persuasive lobbyist for a constitutional amendment authorizing a national department of education.

In 1921, President Alvaro Obregón, eager to promote the Revolution's oft-stated commitment to public education, appointed Vasconcelos as Mexico's first secretary of education. His response to the daunting challenge of educating a mostly illiterate country in the wake of a devastating ten-year civil war—primary school attendance dropped from 880,000 to 740,000 between 1910 and 1920—would ensure him a prominent place in Mexican history. Under his guidance, the Secretariat of Education was divided into three divisions: schools, libraries, and fine arts. A charismatic visionary, Vasconcelos's three-pronged approach to education reform reflected his philosophical concerns about the nation's spiritual as well as educational needs. Although appreciative of his early experience with American education, he distrusted the latest "pragmatic" methods advocated by American educator John Dewey and argued instead for an education based on European classics such as the Odyssey and Don Quixote that would nourish the spirit rather than focus on practical skills.

To meet the urgent needs of urban dwellers in a financially strapped era, he called for volunteers to teach reading and devised informal organizations like the Children's Army of 5,000 fourth, fifth, and sixth graders to recognize their efforts. For the nation's long-neglected rural areas, he sent schoolteachers, who he hoped would bring "civilization" to the countryside much as the early Spanish missionaries had brought Catholicism to pagan Mexico. Like the earlier Spanish effort, this rural "cultural mission" program was strongly integrationist, which, for Indian communities, meant pressure to assimilate into a national culture that was both *mestizo* (mixed race) and Spanish-speaking. Both programs generated considerable controversy. Many Mexican educators argued that European classics had little meaning for the Mexican lower classes who would benefit much more from better hygiene and improved farming techniques. Others protested Vasconcelos's pro-Spanish, pro-Catholic approach, which they considered objectionable in light of Mexico's suffering under Spanish colonial rule (although they, too, usually endorsed his integrationist approach to Indians). These objections would eventually prevail: even though his successors would continue to acknowledge the importance of Vasconcelos's initial vision, Mexican education would become increasingly practical and anticlerical. Regardless, during his four-year tenure, the Secretariat of Education oversaw the construction of over a thousand rural schools—the first serious effort to provide rural education in the nation's history.

Innovations from the other departments in the Secretariat of Education would also have a lasting effect. The libraries' department, for example, not only built nearly two thousand libraries throughout Mexico but also produced millions of literacy readers and workbooks along with a line of inexpensive "classics" of world literature, the cornerstone of Vasconcelos's attempt to reinvigorate and broaden the spirit of Mexican culture. But it was the fine arts department's sponsorship of the muralist movement that garnered the most attention both in Mexico and abroad. Although the "big three" muralists—Diego Rivera, José Clemente Orozco, David Álfaro Siqueiros—soon abandoned the allegoristic style favored by Vasconcelos, their vibrant vision of Mexico's history and culture rendered on the walls of important public buildings throughout the country captured the public imagination and intrigued the world. Rivera's highly politicized murals for the Secretariat of Education building in Mexico City might have annoyed their sponsor but, like the rural education program, their ideological importance—as a symbol of Mexican national pride and the "Revolutionary" government's commitment to social progress—was incalculable.

An opinionated visionary rather than a cooperative bureaucrat, Vasconcelos resigned as secretary of education in 1924 to run an unsuccessful campaign for governor of Oaxaca, the state where he was born. Having broken with the ruling party to run for public office, he opted for exile in California after his defeat. A year later, Vasconcelos published the most influential of his many books, *La raza cósmica* (The Cosmic Race). An eccentric work with references to everything from Atlantis and Theosophy to Mendelian genetics and Marxism, *La raza cósmica* nevertheless resonated with Latin Americans who resented European racial theories that denigrated the region's racially mixed populations as biologically inferior. During the colonial and early national periods, the Spaniards and *criollos* ("white" Latin Americans of Spanish descent) who monopolized political power shared European racist attitudes toward the mostly *mestizo* and Indian lower classes. But, during the course of the nineteenth century, as policymakers sought to integrate their heterogeneous societies into modern nation-states, these attitudes had proven counterproductive. For Mexican policymakers, ten years of violent social revolution testified to the limits of Eurocentric ideologies that rejected large sectors of the national population as congenitally unfit for citizenship. Eccentric or not, *La raza cósmica*'s rewriting of European racial theory suggested new, more inclusive alternatives. According to Vasconcelos, the domination of the white race was nearly over: "The Yankees will end up building the last great empire of a single race, the final empire of White supremacy. Meanwhile, we [Latin America] will continue to suffer the vast chaos of an ethnic stock in formation." But, out of that vast chaos, he insisted, would come a "cosmic" race: "In Spanish America . . . is going to emerge . . . the definitive race, the synthetical race, the integral race, made up of the genius and the blood of all peoples and, for that reason, more capable of true brotherhood and of a truly universal vision" (Vasconcelos, *La raza cósmica*, p. 18). For Mexicans in the 1920s (and for Chicano activists in the 1970s) in search of an antidote to European and American racism, the cosmic race was a godsend. Not only did it insist on the virtues of race mixture (invoking Mendel's notion of hybrid vigor), it also placed Mexico (and the rest of Latin America) at the forefront of human evolution as the crucible of a cosmic race that would transcend the crude materialism of the Yankee. Less popular and often ignored was Vasconcelos's reverence for Spanish-Catholic culture and his insistence that less dynamic races—Africans, Asians, Indians—would eventually fade away. The appearance of these themes in later works like *Indología* (1926) and *Breve historia de México* (1937) made them considerably less popular and less influential than *La raza cósmica*.

Still committed to political change, Vasconcelos returned to Mexico in 1929 after Obregón's assassination to run for president against Pascual Ortiz Rubio, the candidate of the newly formed National Revolutionary Party (PNR), the precursor of the PRI. Well-known throughout Mexico and especially popular with the middle classes and university students, he ran a strong campaign. Concerned PNR officials had to resort to censorship, intimidation, violence, and massive election fraud to ensure Ortiz Rubio's victory. The defeated Vasconcelos returned to exile in the United States but not before producing the "Plan de Guaymas" and calling on the Mexican people to revolt in the name of democracy. Convinced that military repression and the collusion of American ambassador Dwight Morrow had contributed to his defeat, he became increasingly disenchanted with Mexican politics and spent the next ten years working on four volumes of memoirs and a controversial *Brief History of Mexico* that stressed the Spanish contribution to Mexican civilization.

Despite his alienation, when his visa expired in 1938, Vasconcelos elected to return to Mexico. In recognition of his public service and no longer fearful of a political challenge, president Manuel Avila Camacho made him head of the National Library in 1940 and subsequent presidents allowed him to continue in government service despite his outspoken support of European fascists like Italy's Benito Mussolini and Spain's Francisco Franco. His growing preoccupation with Catholicism and his virulent anticommunism further distanced him from the nation's intellectual mainstream. Nevertheless, after his death in 1959, Vasconcelos was buried with honors by a grateful if not always understanding nation.

—*RMB*

See also: Anthropology and Archeology; Architecture; Calles, Plutarco Elías; Intellectuals; Madero, Francisco; *Mestizaje* and *Indigenismo;* Muralist Movement; Novel of the Revolution; Obregón, Alvaro; Orozco, José Clemente; Revolution of 1910; Rivera, Diego; Siquieros, David Álfaro.

References:

Marentes, Luis A. *José Vasconcelos and the Writing of the Mexican Revolution.* New York: Twayne Publishers, 2000.

Vasconcelos, José. *The Cosmic Race/La raza cósmica.* Los Angeles: Centro de Publicaciones, California State University, 1979.

————. *A Mexican Ulysses: An Autobiography*. Trans. William Rex Crawford. Bloomington: Indiana University Press, 1963.

Velázquez Sánchez, Fidel (1900–1997)

Mexico's most durable labor leader, Fidel Velázquez Sánchez was born in the state of Mexico to a poor farm family. Like many rural children, he combined primary education with work in the fields. As a child Velázquez was wounded and his father killed as a result of a land dispute. Velázquez moved to Mexico City in 1916 where he worked in the dairy industry. He began his career as a labor leader by organizing his fellow dairy workers into the Union of Milkmen in the early 1920s. He then extended his unionizing activities to workers in the growing number of small industries in the Mexico City area as well as to municipal employees. This diverse group of workers was linked to the Federación de Sindicatos Obreros del Distrito Federal (the Federation of Workers' Unions of the Federal District, or FSODF). The FSODF, in turn, was part of the most powerful national labor organization of the 1920s, the Confederación Regional Obrera Mexicana (the Regional Confederation of Mexican Workers, or CROM).

Under the leadership of Luis Morones, the CROM had forged a close alliance with the government, but the organization was increasingly criticized for its corruption, abuse of power, and authoritarian leadership. Velázquez led a growing group of reformers within the CROM who were willing to challenge the leadership of Morones. The CROM's role in the presidential election of 1928 provided the background for Velázquez and others to break with the CROM. Morones himself had considered running for the presidency in 1928 until former president Alvaro Obregón announced his candidacy. The CROM damaged its position by first supporting the candidacy of Obregón and then later withdrawing its support. When President-elect Obregón was assassinated in August 1928, many of Obregón's supporters accused Morones of being involved in the assassination. Velázquez seized the opportunity to lead a number of the most important Mexico City unions out of the CROM; in 1929 he helped to form the Federación Sindical de Trabajadores del Distrito Federal (the Federated Union of Workers of the Federal District, or FSTDF).

With Morones and the CROM out of favor with the new administration of interim President Emilio Portes Gil (1928–1930), Velázquez had an unusually favorable opportunity to advance his interests. He served as the labor representative on the Federal District's commission on conciliation and arbitration, a federal agency which determined whether unions would be officially recognized and decided whether strikes would be considered legal or not. Velázquez skillfully used this position to promote membership in the FSTDF. In 1933 Velázquez joined with another CROM defector, Vicente Lombardo Toledano, to establish a major new national labor organization, the Confederación General de Obreros y Campesinos de México (the General Confederation of Workers and Peasants of Mexico, or CGOCM). Lombardo had broken earlier with Morones and formed the "Purified CROM," a collection of unions that had left the original CROM. The heart of the new CGOCM was the Purified CROM of Lombardo Toledano and the FSTDF of Fidel Velázquez. The creation of the CGOCM was the beginning of working relationship between Lombardo and Velázquez that would see Velázquez playing the lesser role for almost a decade. Lombardo held the top position in the organization, that of general secretary, while Velázquez served on the executive board.

Velázquez became a major figure in the power struggle between former president Plutarco Elías Calles and President Lázaro Cárdenas (1934–1940). After stepping down from the presidency in 1928, Calles dominated politics through a series of three puppet presidents between 1928 and 1934. Calles thought that Cárdenas would be his fourth puppet, but Cárdenas provoked a political crisis by trying to assert his independence. In searching for allies in the labor movement, Calles depended on the much-weakened CROM still under the control of Morones while Cárdenas relied on unions loyal to Velázquez and Lombardo. Velázquez and Lombardo responded by establishing a new and even larger labor organization, the Comité Nacional de Defensa Proletaria (the National Committee for Proletarian Defense, or CNDP). Unions controlled by Velázquez were particularly important in mounting public demonstrations in support of Cárdenas, including a march by some 80,000 workers in Mexico City in December 1935.

The CNDP represented a transition to an even larger and more powerful labor organization, the Confederación de Trabajadores de México (the Mexican Workers' Federation, or CTM), which was established in early 1936. There was little argument over who should head the new organization; Lombardo was the easy choice for general secretary of the CTM. Velázquez was not yet prepared to challenge Lombardo for overall leadership, but he was determined to have the important position of organizational secretary. When it appeared that another person might get the post, Velázquez's supporters threatened to leave the CTM. To avoid the walkout, CTM voters approved Velázquez as the organizational secretary. Using his new position, Velázquez was able to strengthen the FSTDF and his control of it. He was also in a position to lay the groundwork for his future rise to the position of general secretary.

Velázquez and Lombardo also worked together to form a new international labor organization in which they would both hold positions. With government financial assistance, the two leaders sponsored a meeting in Mexico City in September 1938 that drew labor representatives from thirteen Latin American countries. This convention established the Confederación de Trabajadores de America Latina (the Confederation of Latin American Workers, or CTAL). The top leadership roles in the new organization went to Lombardo and Velázquez. Lombardo became its first president while Velázquez received the second most-important post of general secretary.

Velázquez's labor experience had taught him the importance of a labor organization having close ties with the government. In the 1920s he witnessed the rapid rise of the CROM under Morones when that organization enjoyed the strong support of Presidents Alvaro Obregón (1920–1924) and Plutarco Elías Calles (1924–1928); Velázquez also saw the rapid decline of the CROM after 1928 once that organization lost government support. The unions Velázquez had helped to organize involved low-skilled workers who were numerous but who lacked power in economic bargaining; Velázquez recognized the importance of being able to call on government support in such a situation. Lombardo shared Velázquez's views on the need for a labor-government alliance. The opportunity for forging such an alliance soon appeared. In 1938 President Cárdenas reorganized the official party along corporate lines, creating four "sectors": labor, peasant, military, and popular. The CTM was to be the heart of the labor sector. This partnership between the CTM and the official party gave the CTM a preferential position among labor organizations and in labor-management disputes, but it was done at the cost of the CTM being the junior partner in the relationship. The downside of the alliance soon became apparent when Cárdenas blocked the CTM from further efforts to organize peasants and government employees; both of these groups were organized into federations outside of the CTM. The ban on organizing government employees was particularly hard on Velázquez given his already-existing control over workers in the Federal District.

As early as 1938, the Mexican government began to shift the stress of its development plan to more rapid industrialization. Wartime demands accentuated this policy. Velázquez supported the government's efforts to freeze wages and avoid strikes as essential aspects of this policy. In 1941 Velázquez replaced Lombardo as secretary general of the CTM, a position he held until 1947. In 1942 Velázquez offered to enter into a "solidarity" pact with business calling for peaceful settlement of labor-management problems to promote the war effort. Although business rejected the pact, the CTM under Velázquez tried to follow a "no-strike" pledge anyway. In 1945 Velázquez did sign an industrial labor pact pledging to continue the wartime collaboration with business in order to facilitate the government's development scheme. The CTM's contribution to postwar industrialization was essentially unchanged from its wartime role; the CTM's main concern was to keep wages low and to maintain labor peace.

In 1947 Velázquez stepped down as general secretary of the CTM. His successor—Fernando Amplia—was a longtime ally of Velázquez. Amplia took definitive action to end the long-running competition between Velázquez and Lombardo over who would be the dominant influence in the CTM. With the approval of Velázquez, Amplia ousted Lombardo and his supporters from the CTM, withdrew the CTM from the international labor organization headed by Lombardo (the CTAL), and prohibited CTM members from supporting a new political party just established by Lombardo. Velázquez even helped to establish a new international labor organization, the Organización Regional Interamericana del Trabajao (the Inter-American Regional Labor Organization, or ORIT) as a rival to Lombardo's CTAL. Velázquez's ties to the official party—the Partido Revolucionario Institucional (the Institutional Revolutionary Party, or PRI)—also grew stronger. Velázquez was a close ally of President Miguel Alemán (1946–1952), who was the principal champion of the new industrial development approach. Velázquez approved of Alemán's imposition of new

leaders for the unions representing the railway workers, the petroleum workers, and the miners; these unions had earlier defected from the CTM. Velázquez also served as the PRI senator from the Federal District to the national Congress between 1946 and 1952.

In 1950 Velázquez returned as general secretary of the CTM, a position he would hold continuously until his death in 1997. The CTM became one of the principal sources of support for government policy while Velázquez became an indispensable part of the PRI elite. The connection was easy to defend as the government's development scheme appeared to be working in the 1950s and 1960s; Velázquez served another term as PRI senator from the Federal District between 1958 and 1964. By the 1970s Mexico's era of rapid growth had ended, and major doubts developed about continuing the postwar development scheme endorsed by Velázquez and the CTM leadership. Mexico encountered a series of economic upheavals between 1970 and 1982, culminating in the debt crisis of 1982. Velázquez maintained his support of the government and the PRI despite growing internal criticism of his policies and even personal concerns about the government's response to the economic and financial crises. Velázquez expressed his doubts—sometimes in public—about the neoliberal policies being followed by Presidents Miguel de la Madrid (1982–1988), Carlos Salinas de Gortari (1988–1994), and Ernesto Zedillo (1994–2000). Nevertheless, he signed a series of "pacts" with the government and business pledging labor support for the new measures. Velázquez was also identified with the "dinosaur" faction of the PRI, which opposed efforts at democratization both within the PRI and in the broader context of Mexican politics. The death of Velázquez in 1997 meant not only the end of a lengthy career; it represented a genuine end to an era in the Mexican labor movement and the alliance between labor and government. Although new leadership has taken over the CTM, it is unlikely that any leader will emerge who can show the power and the durability that "Don Fidel" did. Fundamental changes in Mexico's political and economic structure will make it difficult for any labor leader to duplicate the role played by Fidel Velázquez and the CTM in the second half of the twentieth century.

—*DMC*

See also: Alemán, Miguel; Avila Camacho, Manuel; Calles, Plutarco Elías; Cárdenas, Lázaro; Confederación de Trabajadores de México (CTM); Confederación Regional Obrera Mexicana (CROM); Import Substitution Industrialization (ISI); Lombardo Toledano, Vicente; Madrid (Hurtado), Miguel de la; Morones, Luis; Partido Revolucionario Institucional (PRI); Salinas de Gortari, Carlos; Zedillo Ponce de León, Ernesto.

References:
Caulfield, Norman. *Mexican Workers and the State: From the Porfiriato to NAFTA.* Fort Worth: Texas Christian University Press, 1998.
La Botz, Dan. *The Crisis of Mexican Labor.* New York: Praeger, 1988.
Middlebrook, Kevin J. *The Paradox of Revolution: Labor, the State, and Authoritarianism in Mexico.* Baltimore: Johns Hopkins University Press, 1995.

Vera Cruz, Occupation of (1914)

In an effort to promote democracy in Mexico, U.S. President Woodrow Wilson (1913–1921) developed a policy of actively trying to remove General Victoriano Huerta from the presidency. Huerta had come to power in February 1913 through the overthrow and assassination of the democratically elected President Francisco Madero. The Wilson administration was increasing pressure on Huerta when a minor incident took place at the Mexican oil center of Tampico in April 1914. Huerta's forces briefly detained a small group of U.S. sailors who had landed in a restricted area. Huerta's officials quickly apologized and released the sailors. U.S. authorities considered the apology inadequate and demanded a twenty-one gun salute. As the U.S. government wrangled over the nature of the salute with a government it did not recognize, Wilson asked Congress for

permission to use military force to obtain redress. Before Congress could respond, the Wilson administration learned that a ship bearing military supplies for Huerta was about to land at Vera Cruz. The president ordered U.S. forces to seize the customs house and dock facilities to prevent the arrival of the arms. Wilson did not expect any substantial opposition to the landing and even believed that many Mexicans would welcome intervention as a way of getting rid of the unpopular Huerta.

U.S. military and naval officials had only three hours to plan and launch the intervention at Vera Cruz. On 21 April 1914 the initial U.S. landing party of 787 officers and men came ashore and quickly gained control of the customs house and docks. Huerta had earlier withdrawn most of his troops, leaving the city defended primarily by the municipal militia and some local citizens using army weapons. Fighting soon began, with U.S. forces suffering four killed and twenty wounded on the first day. The unexpected resistance by Mexican forces and the absence of any Mexican officials with whom to deal led to a major change in U.S. plans. The original goal of confining the intervention to the dock area was expanded to include an occupation of the entire city. More troops came ashore, bringing the total to 6,000 by the end of the second day. In less than 48 hours, U.S. forces completed the occupation of Veracruz.

Total U.S. losses in the invasion and occupation were 19 killed and 71 wounded. No accurate count of Mexican casualties existed, primarily because the tropical climate required that the bodies be rapidly burned. There were probably at least 200 Mexicans killed and another 300 wounded; many of the casualties on the Mexican side were civilians accidentally killed in the house-to-house fighting.

Mexico experienced a number of foreign invasions in the nineteenth century, and Mexican federal law provided for harsh punishment for any official cooperating with a foreign invader. As a result Mexican officials

Marines and sailors from the U.S. Marine Corps and the U.S. Navy force snipers to retreat during a period of political unrest in Vera Cruz in Mexico in May 1914. The marines and sailors occupied the city for about six months. (Bettmann/Corbis)

refused initially to negotiate with U.S. officials and later to cooperate in the administration of the city. U.S. authorities hoped to operate through local Mexican officials, but Rear Admiral Frank Fletcher had to declare martial law, with U.S. officers assuming all government functions. To support the occupation, the U.S. government sent an infantry brigade under General Frederick Funston, who assumed overall command of operations at Vera Cruz.

Although President Wilson had earlier linked the end of the occupation with the removal of Huerta, the occupation continued after Huerta resigned on 15 July 1914. With Huerta out, various Revolutionary factions were contending for power, and Wilson still hoped to influence the course of political events in Mexico. In addition American forces had seized a significant amount of military supplies in Vera Cruz; with civil war impending, the decision to relinquish control of

the city and the supplies would have an important effect on who would rule Mexico. In September, the Wilson administration indicated to the government of Venustiano Carranza in Mexico City that U.S. forces would be withdrawn, but the withdrawal stalled over U.S. concerns about what would happen to the few local citizens who had cooperated with the occupation. Under growing political and military pressure himself, Carranza on 9 November issued a blanket amnesty for all Mexicans who had served the occupation government. The entire American force of some 7,000 troops was evacuated on 23 November 1914.

—DMC

See also: Huerta, Victoriano; Madero, Francisco; Pershing Expedition; Zimmermann Telegram.

References:

Eisenhower, John S. D. *Intervention: The United States and the Mexican Revolution, 1913–1917.* New York: W. W. Norton & Company, 1993.

Quirk, Robert E. *An Affair of Honor: Woodrow Wilson and the Occupation of Veracruz.* New York: W. W. Norton & Company, 1967.

Sweetman, Jack. *The Landing at Veracruz: 1914.* Annapolis, MD: Naval Institute Press, 1987.

Veracruz (State)

Veracruz is situated along Mexico's Gulf Coast and has as its capital the city of Xalapa. The state is home to Mexico's main commercial port and is Mexico's leading producer of cattle. It also contains significant oil reserves. Veracruz houses Mexico's only nuclear power plant, which was built in the 1970s and which, by the 1980s, had encouraged a significant antinuclear movement within and beyond the state. The history of Veracruz has been heavily influenced by the state's location and particularly by the importance of the port city of Vera Cruz.

The pre-Columbian heritage of Veracruz is still evident in the state's large Indian population and in the many indigenous languages (including Maya) that are still spoken there. Veracruz also contains three major pre-Columbian sites: El Tajín, Tres Zapotes, and Cempoala. The state was home to three major native cultures in the centuries before Spanish contact: the Olmec (considered Mexico's "mother culture"), the Totonac (builders of El Tajín and Cempoala), and the Huastec.

Spanish colonization of the Veracruz region began in 1518 with the expedition of Juan de Grijalva and Pedro Alvarado. They were followed a year later by Hernán Cortés, who claimed the Gulf Coast region for the Spanish Crown. One of the first cities established by the Spaniards was Villa Rica de la Vera Cruz, the port city. It was later renamed "Vera Cruz Llave" in honor of General Ignacio de la Llave, who governed the state during the nineteenth century. The port of Vera Cruz (as well as the small island of San Juan de Ullúa, just off the coast) quickly became a key link between Spain and the colony of New Spain as mule trains carried goods shipped to the port overland to Mexico City.

This commerce also aided the growth of three other cities in Veracruz: Xalapa, Orizaba, and Córdoba. Although epidemics encouraged by the coastal climate, difficulties in docking ships, and piracy compelled four changes in the port city's location, Villa Rica de la Vera Cruz maintained its position as a major port throughout the colonial era.

With the growth of the Spanish population and the arrival of missionaries, the native peoples of Veracruz saw their lives permanently altered. Many lost their lands to the colonizers, and many more became laborers on Spanish haciendas and in Spanish-owned textile mills. In the northern region, known as the Huasteca, many Indians experienced the violent conquest of Nuño de Guzmán, who sold native peoples to the islands of the Caribbean. Blacks were also a part of the colonial society of Veracruz. Sugarcane became a major crop in the area, and black slaves were brought in to help with sugar production. As the black population grew, Veracruz witnessed several slave rebellions. One of the most significant was led by Yanga, a slave who helped establish a runaway settlement near the city of Córdoba. Yanga and his followers raided central Veracruz for nearly thirty years, resisting Spanish attempts to subdue them. Intermarriage and mixing with the broader population gradually caused Yanga's community to lose its distinctiveness as a runaway settlement. With time, the community was legally recognized as the town of San Lorenzo de los Negros.

Mexico's independence era, which began with the rebellion of Miguel Hidalgo in 1810 and concluded with Mexico's formal separation from Spain in 1821, brought instability to the Veracruz region. Hidalgo's followers, including José María Morelos, sought to control the flow of goods (and thus to support their insurgency) between the port of Vera Cruz and central Mexico. In the aftermath of the Hidalgo revolt, and as Mexico's more conservative elements moved toward a break with Spain, the inhabitants of Orizaba, Xalapa, and Córdoba wavered in their independence sentiments, though they eventually leant it their support. Meanwhile, the port of Vera Cruz, home to many Spanish merchants, staunchly opposed independence. Indeed, the port city had to be forcibly liberated from Spanish control. The offshore fortress of San Juan de Ulúa remained under Spanish control until 1825, when Antonio López de Santa Anna, Mexican commander of the port of Vera Cruz, finally claimed it for the new country of Mexico. Santa Anna would serve as one of Veracruz's governors in the aftermath of independence and statehood (granted in 1824). He would also continue to play a major role in Mexican politics during the first half of the nineteenth century.

Independence and statehood were not guarantees of stability, especially for the port city, which witnessed foreign invasion, bombardment, and occupation in the decades after independence. In an attempt to reconquer Mexico, Spanish troops under Isidro Barradas attacked the port in 1829. From 1838 to 1839 the French blockaded and bombarded the city of Vera Cruz and its environs in the Pastry War (ostensibly waged to help a French pastry chef collect on damages caused to his property during the independence era). From 1847 to 1848, at the height of the Mexican War, the port of Vera Cruz was again under siege, and American troops occupied several areas of the state. During the War of Reform that pitted Mexican liberals and conservatives against each other, the port witnessed additional unrest as conservatives attempted to dislodge the liberal government of Benito Juárez, which had been established in Vera Cruz after the conservatives captured Mexico City. The port was once more occupied by foreign troops during the 1860s when the French intervened in Mexico and established an empire.

Veracruz enjoyed more stability during the latter part of the nineteenth century. As railroads connected the port city to Xalapa, Córdoba, and Orizaba, the state began to enjoy a prosperous era, particularly as foreign investment helped to expand local production of coffee, tobacco, sugar, and other crops. Mexico's young oil industry, aided by American and English investors, centered in the Gulf Coast region and brought additional growth. Veracruz's modernization was likewise facilitated by the ambitious economic agenda of President Porfirio Díaz (1876–1911) and by governors Luis Mier y Terán, Juan de la Luz Enríquez, and Teodoro Dehesa.

By the turn of the century, Veracruz was again experiencing instability related to the dislocations and uneven prosperity that accompanied its economic development. The state's increasingly vocal workers contributed to the unrest, and textile workers were especially restive as they struggled with long hours, low wages, and poor working conditions. Laborers at the Rio Blanco textile mill finally struck in 1907. They were brutally suppressed under President Díaz's orders, and nearly 100 died at the hands of federal soldiers and the rural police. The Río Blanco incident underscored the brutality of the Porfirian regime and further eroded its credibility.

The strategic and economic importance of Veracruz, particularly its port city, ensured that the state would directly experience the violence and disruptions of the Mexican Revolution. Although the rebellion of Francisco I. Madero, which began the Revolutionary era, brought little change to Veracruz, several armed groups were active. In the aftermath of Madero's death, rebel leaders such as Cándido Aguilar made initial steps toward land reform and benefits for workers. As the Revolution split into various factions, the port of Vera Cruz (including revenue from its customs house) became a strategic prize, as well as a place of refuge. From April 1914 to November 1915, the United States occupied the port. This occupation was precipitated by a diplomatic incident at Tampico and encouraged by the desire of the American government to weaken the regime of Victoriano Huerta.

The 1920s and 1930s brought popular mobilization and radical (though not always lasting) reform to Veracruz under governors Adalberto Tejada and Heriberto Jara. Tejada united the state's agrarian leaders and redistributed a significant amount of land, and both governors courted the working class. Textile workers, with their history of militancy, especially benefited from change, as their working hours were reduced and their bargaining power in the factories increased (albeit under the ultimate authority of the Mexican government and its official umbrella union). The state's oil industry was also a target of reform. When the Mexican government and foreign oil companies clashed over ownership of the country's oil resources, Veracruz oil workers participated in the strikes that led up to Mexico's nationalization of the oil industry in 1938. Mexico's oil workers became employees of the new national oil company, PEMEX (Petroleos Mexicanos).

Veracruz was also a center of a major revolt against the Mexican government that began in 1923. In December of that year, ex-President Adolfo de la Huerta challenged President Alvaro Obregón's selection of Plutarco Elías Calles as his successor. De la Huerta announced his revolt in the port city of Vera Cruz and included in his declaration a criticism of the local regime of Adalberto Tejada. The de la Huerta movement rapidly gained support and succeeded in capturing territory within the state, even as it gained adherents elsewhere in Mexico. Tejada, however, enjoyed strong support from workers and campesinos (peasants) who within two months had helped the governor defeat the de la Huerta rebellion.

Veracruz witnessed a renewed emphasis on economic modernization in the aftermath of the Revolutionary period. Governors Miguel Alemán Valdés (a future Mexican president) Jorge Cerdán, and Adolfo Ruíz Cortines (also a future president) especially encouraged development. The state's infrastructure was improved, education expanded, and modern technology used to bolster agricultural production and improve the cattle industry. By midcentury, cattle ranchers had emerged as one of the state's most powerful groups. Using national laws that protected cattle ranches against agrarian reform, ranchers consolidated their power. They also used violence to expand their holdings at the expense of subsistence farmers, including Indians. By the end of the twentieth century, Veracruz was Mexico's main producer of cattle.

Underneath Veracruz's economic growth and the dynamism of the cattle industry, however, was a growing social inequality. By 1990, Veracruz had the second highest poverty level in Mexico. It was also facing environmental problems, particularly deforestation, because of the uncontrolled expansion of cattle ranching. Meanwhile, the state failed to produce the industrial jobs needed for its expanding urban population. As the twenty-first century opened, thousands were leaving Veracruz in search of economic opportunities not available in their home state.

—SBP

See also: Alemán, Miguel; de la Huerta, Adolfo; Díaz, Porfirio; Environmental Issues; Huerta, Victoriano; Madero, Francisco; Oil Industry; Petróleos Mexicanos (PEMEX); Ruíz Cortines, Adolfo; Vera Cruz, Occupation of (1914).

References:
Blázquez Domínguez, Carmen. *Breve historia de Veracruz.* Mexico City: El Colegio de Mexico, 2000.
García-Gorena, Velma. *Mothers and the Mexican Antinuclear Power Movement.* Tucson: University of Arizona Press, 1999.
Koth, Karl B. *Waking the Dictator: Veracruz, the Struggle for Federalism, and the Mexican Revolution, 1870–1927.* Calgary: University of Calgary Press, 2002.
Official state web site: http://www.veracruz.gob.mx

Villa, Francisco "Pancho" (1878–1923)

One of the most famous folk heroes to come out of the Revolution of 1910, Francisco "Pancho" Villa proved a controversial figure both in life and in death. Born in 1878 on one

Francisco "Pancho" Villa leads other Mexican rebels on horseback. Early twentieth century. (Hulton-Deutsch/Corbis)

of the largest haciendas in the state of Durango, Villa was the son of poor sharecroppers who worked the lands of the great estate. Baptized Doroteo Arango, Villa took the name he would become famous under after turning bandit at the age of sixteen. There is disagreement over why Villa became a bandit, but the rural population often romanticized bandits for their resistance to authority. Villa acquired a reputation as a "Mexican Robin Hood" while leading a group involved in robbery, rustling, and murder.

When Revolution broke out in 1910, Villa became one of the better known rebel leaders in the north, where most of the fighting took place. A supporter of Francisco Madero, Villa played a major role in the capture of the border town of Ciudad Juárez, which quickly led to the resignation of President Porfirio Díaz. Immediately after the victory, Villa joined in a brief mutiny against Madero over Madero's leniency toward the defeated federal commander at Juárez. Villa then returned to civilian life, but as a businessman rather than a bandit.

Villa saw his military career resurrected in 1912 when Pascual Orozco—the other hero of the victory at Juárez—revolted against Madero, who had been elected to the presidency in late 1911. Appointed a brigadier general by Madero, Villa helped to put down the Orozco revolt but incurred the wrath of the principal leader of Madero's forces, General Victoriano Huerta. Huerta—an old-line federal general who disliked and distrusted Villa—ordered the arrest and execution of Villa. Although saved from execution by Madero's orders, Villa wound up in a military prison in Mexico City. In December 1912, Villa escaped and made his way into exile in El Paso, Texas, where he planned his return to Mexico.

The overthrow and assassination of Madero in late February 1913 by General

Huerta revived Villa's career as a Revolutionary. Villa soon returned to northern Mexico and began the organization of what would ultimately become the largest of the Revolutionary armies, the Division of the North. Villa directed his activities at an old antagonist: General Victoriano Huerta, who had assumed the presidency of Mexico. Villa nominally accepted the Revolutionary leadership of Venustiano Carranza, governor of Coahuila, who assumed the position of "First Chief" of the Constitutionalist army. Villa, however, wanted freedom of action in his military campaign and distrusted the Revolutionary commitment of Carranza, who was a wealthy landowner who had been part of the old system under Porfirio Díaz. Villa's forces played a key role in the ultimate defeat of Huerta, who resigned and went into exile in July 1914.

With the overthrow of Huerta, the various Revolutionary factions then began a struggle among themselves for political dominance. An effort to reconcile Revolutionary differences at a convention held in October 1914 failed. The Revolution, then, entered its most violent phase with the forces of Carranza and his ablest general, Alvaro Obregón, facing the troops of Villa and Emiliano Zapata, the famous agrarian leader from the state of Morelos. While Villa enjoyed initial military success in late 1914, Obregon's forces inflicted a series of major defeats on Villa in 1915, driving him back to his base of power in the north and reducing him to the role of a regional military problem.

Villa still demonstrated a capacity to cause trouble for Carranza and Obregón. Villa's power base in Chihuahua made him a potential threat to the U.S.–Mexican border. While relations between the United States and Villa had generally been good, they quickly turned sour after the United States granted diplomatic recognition to the Carranza government in October 1915. In January 1916 Villa's troops stopped a train at Santa Ysabel, Chihuahua, and systematically executed sixteen Americans who were returning after the Carranza administration's assurances of safety to renew mining operations. Villa's forces made an even more daring raid across the border in March 1916, attacking Columbus, New Mexico. The United States launched a massive military response in the form of a punitive expedition under the command of General John J. Pershing. Although Villa eluded capture, his forces were driven from the border region, further reducing Villa's military capabilities. Between 1917 and 1920, Villa retained enough military power to periodically embarrass the Carranza administration, but Villa had essentially lost his position as a national political force.

The overthrow and assassination of Carranza in 1920 by supporters of Obregón led to a political deal between Villa and the Obregón group that would bring to an official end Villa's career as a Revolutionary leader. In exchange for a hacienda for himself and land for his men, Villa disbanded what remained of his military force and promised to refrain from political activity. Villa spent a mostly quiet retirement but was drawn into the growing controversy over who would succeed Obregón as president in 1924. The target of earlier unsuccessful assassination attempts, Villa died in a hail of bullets in July 1923. Suspicion immediately fell on Obregón and his designated successor as president, Plutarco Elías Calles. Subsequent investigation indicated that this early suspicion was most likely justified, although there is no definitive answer as to who ordered the killing of Villa.

For many years Villa was excluded from the official list of Revolutionary heroes recognized by subsequent governments. It was not until 1966 that he received official recognition for his contributions to the Revolution and not until 1976 that his remains were transferred from Chihuahua to an honored location in the Monument to the Revolution in Mexico City for burial alongside other official heroes of Mexican history. Villa was the stuff of myths, myths which he embraced and promoted. While historians and politicians continue to debate Villa's Revolutionary credentials, he remains a potent mythic figure for those seeking social change in Mexico.

—*DMC*

See also: Assassinations; Chihuahua; Díaz, Porfirio; Durango; Militarism; Revolution of 1910; Sonora; Zapata, Emiliano.

References:
Guzmán, Martín Luis. *Memoirs of Pancho Villa.* Austin: University of Texas Press, 1966.
Hall, Linda B., and Don M. Coerver. *Revolution on the Border: The United States and Mexico, 1910–1920.* Albuquerque: University of New Mexico Press, 1988.
Katz, Friedrich. *The Life and Times of Pancho Villa.* Palo Alto, CA: Stanford University Press, 1998.

Virgin of Guadalupe

The Virgin of Guadalupe—the 1531 apparition of the Virgin Mary to a humble Indian man just outside Mexico City—is an important religious symbol throughout the Americas; she is also inextricably linked to Mexican national identity. The great Mexican poet Octavio Paz once wrote that "the Mexican people, after two centuries of experiments and defeats, have faith only in the Virgin of Guadalupe and the National Lottery." A popular saying holds that while not all Mexicans are Catholic, all are *guadalupanos* (adherents of the Virgin of Guadalupe). Testimonials like these are reinforced by the thousands of Virgin of Guadalupe images that appear throughout Mexico, Latin America, and the southwestern United States on everything from religious candles and wall plaques to T-shirts and the tattooed backs of Chicano gangsters.

For many people in the Americas, the image of the Virgin of Guadalupe carries a powerful religious meaning. In the standard account of her apparition, she asks a recently converted, poor Indian laborer, Juan Diego: "Am I not here, your mother? Are you not under my shadow and protection? Am I not your foundation of life? Are you not in the folds of my mantle, in the crossing of my arms? Is there anything else you need?" These reassuring questions make her a compelling symbol of compassion in societies that still suffer from severe social inequalities. Her choice of a poor Indian as her advocate and her own dark-skinned visage inspire a sense of spiritual inclusiveness in societies that still discriminate against people of color.

For most Mexicans, the Virgin of Guadalupe represents the national soul. The green, red, and white of the Virgin are reflected in the national flag that often frames her miraculous image and her motto, "*Non fecit taliter omni nationi*" (God has done the same for no other nation), reinforces the deep sense of national pride that Mexicans attach to her presence. That pride is far from abstract. Each day, individuals and pilgrim groups from all walks of life make their way to her sanctuary to offer thanks, fulfill *promesas* (vows), strengthen group loyalties, and reaffirm their collective national identity. Each year on her feast day, December 12, that steady stream of pilgrims becomes a flood, as people from throughout Mexico (and the world) take part in a massive celebration that ranges from Roman Catholic masses and mariachi singers inside the basilica to Indian dances and magic performances just outside the church doors. The veneration of the Virgin of Guadalupe thus provides a space for Mexicans to set aside differences of race, class, and creed and to recognize the intangible threads that bind them together as Mexicans.

The reasons for this extraordinary allegiance are closely linked to Mexico's complex history, but the historical origins of the Mexican Guadalupe cult are shrouded in mystery. According to legend, the Virgin appeared in 1531, just ten years after the Spanish Conquest, to the Indian bearer Juan Diego at Tepeyac, a few miles north of Mexico City. She instructed him to go to the bishop, Fray Juan de Zumárraga, to request that a church be built there in her honor. Not surprisingly, the bishop twice dismissed the

This inexpensive print in the "popular" style of José Guadalupe Posada shows an image of Our Lady of Guadalupe on an altar surrounded by potted plants and candles. (Library of Congress)

poor Indian's story, and on the second occasion demanded some proof of its veracity. Embarrassed by the bishop's doubts and distracted by a sick uncle, Juan Diego sought in vain to avoid a further encounter. But the Virgin appeared a third time to chide him gently for his neglect, reassure him of his uncle's recovery, and provide him with the necessary proof of her appearance, Castillian roses from Spain, which he gathered in his *tilma* or cloak. On his third visit to Zumárraga, the bishop's servants forced him to wait for hours, harassing him about the flowers concealed in his *tilma,* until he finally managed to attract the bishop's attention. When Juan Diego revealed the roses, the painted image of the Virgin of Guadalupe miraculously ap-

peared on his *tilma.* At this sign from heaven, the bishop fell to his knees and promised to fulfill her request.

Perhaps because it paints a reassuring, even conciliatory portrait of the violent conquest of Mexico and its devastating aftermath, the legend has attracted considerable popular and religious support. It has also attracted the attention of devout scientists, who marvel at the durability of the Virgin's image (which is painted on the crude cactus fiber cloth of the period), the position of the stars on her cloak, and the images of Juan Diego, Zumárraga, and the bishop's servants that they can discern in the irises of her eyes.

Historians are more skeptical. Although a Guadalupe cult apparently flourished at Tepeyac as early as the mid-sixteenth century, it was probably modeled on the cult of the Virgin of Guadalupe of Estremadura, Spain's dark-skinned virgin and a favorite of the conquistadors. The location of the cult at Tepeyac, on an Aztec religious site dedicated to the goddess Tonantzín, was typical of Spanish efforts to turn Indian sacred spaces to Catholic purposes. The earliest sources indicate that a statue rather than the *tilma* was the central focus of worship and while historical sources mention miracles attached to statue and *tilma,* there is no mention of miraculous apparitions, even in the writings of Bishop Zumárraga himself. Regardless of its historical antecedents, the Guadalupe cult flourished, attracting the support of everyone from poor Indians to the viceroy (the Spanish king's highest ranking official in what was then called New Spain).

It was not until the 1648 publication of Miguel Sánchez's *Image of the Virgin Mary, Mother of God of Guadalupe, Who Miraculously Appeared in Mexico City* that the story of Juan Diego, Bishop Zumárraga, and the Virgin of Guadalupe was first set down in print. The timing of his book was fortuitous. Sánchez was a learned and devout priest of the Mexico City archdiocese; he was also a *criollo* (a person of Spanish descent born in the New World) and a patriot. His book clearly established the New World origins of the Virgin of Guadalupe and thus offered spiritual emancipation from Spain to Mexican *creoles* who resented their colonial status in economics, politics, culture, and religion. Her miraculous interventions in the devastating 1629 floods and the 1736 epidemic that killed at least 40,000 people in Mexico City further buttressed her position as Mexico's principal patroness, a status confirmed by papal bull in 1754. By the middle of the seventeenth century, then, the Virgin of Guadalupe had become a powerful symbol of national identity that brought together Mexicans of all races and classes. When the time came for political independence, her image would play a central role.

That time came in 1810, when Spain, preoccupied with Napoleon's invasion, could no longer control its American colonies. On September 16 of that year, a *criollo* parish priest, Father Miguel Hidalgo y Costilla, gave his famous "Grito de Dolores" (Shout from Dolores), the call to Mexican independence. Father Hidalgo ended with an invocation to the Virgin and a warning to the Spanish colonial government: "Long live the Virgin of Guadalupe! Death to bad government! Death to the gachupines (Spaniards)!" On that same day, Hidalgo emerged from the church of the nearby town of Atotonilco with a banner of the Virgin of Guadalupe around which he rallied his improvised army of poor Indian and mestizo *campesinos* (peasants) for what would prove to be a violent, short-lived, and unsuccessful attempt at independence. Within the year, Hidalgo had been excommunicated and shot. Another parish priest, Father José María Morelos y Pavón, a *mestizo* and former student of Hidalgo's, took up the banner, proclaiming that "every man above the age of ten carry in his hat a cockade . . . which will proclaim him a devotee of the image of Guadalupe, soldier and defender of her cult." Like Hidalgo, Morelos became a martyr to the independence cause. One of his lieutenants, however, took the name Guadalupe Victoria and went on to become Mexico's first president. The man who defeated him, Agustín de Iturbide, a *criollo* officer in the Spanish army who with Guadalupe Victoria's help finally proclaimed Mexican independence in 1821, would preside as emperor (for a brief ten months) over the newly formed Knights of Guadalupe. Another of Iturbide's independence-era collaborators, Santa Anna, would eventually rise to the rank of Grand Master of the National and Distinguished Order of Guadalupe in addition to his service as president on eleven different occasions. As these examples suggest, during the struggle for independence, the Virgin of Guadalupe transcended her religious role as the nation's spiritual mother to become a potent symbol in the tumultuous world of Mexican politics.

In an emerging nation, deeply divided by political differences and social inequalities, the Virgin of Guadalupe held out hope for peace, reconciliation, and a more inclusive society. As happened at independence, politicians of all stripes did their best to harness those hopes to their different causes. Anticlerical liberals like President Benito Juárez, intent on pushing the Roman Catholic Church out of Mexican political and economic life, tended to steer clear of religious symbols of nationhood. However, his rival Maximilian, the French-supported emperor of Mexico, paid public homage at the shrine of Guadalupe in a futile effort to legitimize his rule. At the end of an eventful nineteenth century, the great liberal general and perennial president, Porfirio Díaz, overcame his political prejudices and encouraged Pope Pius X to elevate the shrine to the status of basilica in 1904. Then, a hundred years after Hidalgo's revolt, the troops of Emiliano Zapata carried her standard in their Revolutionary struggle against Díaz and his successors to claim a national space for Mexico's hard-pressed *campesinos* (rural workers). After the Revolution of 1910, even rabid anticlericals like Plutarco Elías Calles, sought to co-opt rather than oppose the Guadalupe cult by allowing a spectacular tricentennial celebration in 1931, hard on the heels of the vicious Cristero Rebellion that had pitted government forces against self-proclaimed "soldiers of Christ." Indeed the Mexican government's official reconciliation with the Roman Catholic Church in 1992 after 130 years owes much to the Virgin's national prominence. It comes as no surprise that Pope John Paul II's 1999 pastoral visit to Mexico was highlighted by a mass at the Basilica of Guadalupe.

—RMB

See also: Calles, Plutarco Elías; Cristero Rebellion; Díaz, Porfirio; Paz, Octavio; Zapata, Emiliano.

References:

Brading, David. *Mexican Phoenix: Our Lady of Guadalupe, Image and Tradition, 1531–2000.* London: Cambridge University Press, 2001.

Lafaye, Jacques. 1976. *Quetzalcoatl and Guadalupe: The Formation of Mexican National Consciousness, 1531–1813.* Trans. Benjamin Keen. Chicago: University of Chicago Press, 1976.

Poole, Stafford. *Our Lady of Guadalupe: The Origins and Sources of a Mexican National Symbol, 1531–1797.* Tucson: University of Arizona Press, 1995.

Women's Movement

For much of Mexico's history, political participation and political activism have been the province of men. Cultural norms that stress women's role as homemaker and mother have discouraged female political participation while class and, to a certain extent, racial divisions among Mexican women have hampered the development of a viable women's movement. As the chief beneficiaries of expanded educational opportunities during the latter part of the nineteenth century, middle- and upper-class women were the first to argue for a general improvement in women's status. Many used journalism to voice demands for better education, improved conditions for working women, and an end to laws that considered Mexican women to be second-class citizens, dependent on male relatives. By the turn of the century, a handful of women's groups had emerged. In addition, many women joined the movement against the dictatorship of Porfirio Diaz, often as members of the Partido Liberal Mexicano—the first Mexican political party to support the concept of equal rights for women.

The Mexican Revolution of 1910 was instrumental in expanding the horizons of women of all classes. While some women ventured outside of the home to serve as *soldaderas* or camp followers, others used the opportunity to push for suffrage. Yet while the Constitution of 1917 granted working women protection and benefits, and while Revolutionary leaders such as Venustiano Carranza responded to demands for the legalization of divorce and the expansion of women's economic rights, many other male politicians balked on the issue of suffrage. The view of Mexican women as the chief supporters of the Roman Catholic Church helped generate the perception that Mexican women were inherently conservative. For many male supporters of the Revolution, women's suffrage would undermine the liberal gains of that Revolution and would especially threaten attempts to curtail the power of the Church in Mexican society. Indeed, Mexican women played a prominent role in the Cristero Rebellion of the 1920s, establishing women's groups that sought to protect the position of the Roman Catholic Church and providing logistical support for pro-Church rebels. Women's participation in the Cristero Rebellion ensured that male politicians would continue to provide only lukewarm support for women's rights and for the idea of gender equality. While Mexican women continued to organize on behalf of suffrage and other issues into the 1930s, they made few concrete gains at the national level.

Despite such obstacles to the women's rights movement, feminism gained important visibility in the Yucatán during the Revolutionary era. In 1916 this Mexican state was host to Mexico's first two feminist congresses, which enjoyed the support of socialist Governors Salvador Alvarado and Felipe Carrillo Puerto. The congresses provided Mexican women with the opportunity to discuss a variety of issues, including suffrage, employment opportunities, and the expansion of women's education. Yet despite the expectations created by the two congresses, delegates could not breach a serious divide: that between radical and more conservative delegates. Members of Catholic women's groups in particular resisted significant changes for women, arguing that some ideas, such as sex education, were inappropriate and even immoral. In general, conservative delegates tended to endorse changes that enhanced, rather than challenged, women's traditional role as wife and mother. The significant philosophical divisions among delegates ensured that Mexico's first feminist congresses would have a limited effect. Nevertheless, a more radical feminism continued to find a forum in the Yucatán during the 1920s, with Governor Carrillo Puerto and his sister Elvia encouraging women's activism through the formation of the *Ligas Feministas* (Women's Leagues). Under the governorship of Carrillo, Yucatecan women were also granted suffrage and access to contraceptive information.

On the national level, the women's movement regained momentum during the 1930s, a period corresponding to the presidency of Lázaro Cárdenas. Cárdenas's socialist leanings predisposed him to support the cause of women's rights, and he moved to incorporate women into the National Revolutionary Party (PNR), forerunner of the Institutional Revolutionary Party (PRI). For their part, Mexican women, many of whom were now members of well-organized groups with international links, used their increasing political clout to demand a suffrage amendment to the Constitution. Introduced in 1937, the amendment to Article 34 worked its way through Congress and was ratified by a majority of Mexican states. Political struggles and divisions surrounding the presidential election of 1940, however, stalled the suffrage movement once again. Women had to wait until the post–World War II era, when they were finally granted the right to vote, first in municipal elections (1946) and then on the national level (1953). Significantly, women's suffrage was granted only after Mexico's Church-State conflict had been resolved.

Since the granting of suffrage, many Mexican women have found a voice in the party organizations that play a prominent role in Mexican politics. Many women have succeeded in translating such participation into office-holding, and in today's Mexico, women run for office on all levels, participate in Congress, and are appointed to high-level positions. At the same time, Mexican women continue to work among themselves to advance an agenda that is decidedly feminist. Increasingly, Mexican feminists are successfully bridging the class lines that have historically hampered the development of a coherent, popular women's movement.

The popular feminism that is characteristic of today's Mexico emerged during the 1970s, and particularly among professional women, students, and members of the middle class. It grew out of a search for the fundamental causes of women's inequality in Mexican society. Consciousness-raising groups sought to engage women in the debate over inequality, and feminists embraced several sensitive issues, including the legalization of abortion and violence against women. Women's activism gained an added boost when economic crisis hit the country in the 1980s. As homemakers and mothers, Mexican women often bore the brunt of inflation and the decline in social services that accompanied this economic bust. The economic downturn also forced many women to search for jobs, and demands for political representation accompanied women's increased participation in the economy. Mexico City's massive earthquake in 1985 also gave birth to Mexico's only all-female labor union, "19 de septiembre." This seamstresses' union has embraced a feminist agenda, and it has succeeded in remaining apart from the official, state-controlled labor movement.

In the 1990s, Mexican feminists have continued to embrace controversial issues, including reproductive and sexual freedom and affirmative action. Mexico's women also continue to increase their level of political activity. Women have been at the forefront of the country's struggle for democracy and have played a prominent role in the push for an end to the one-party political system that has characterized Mexico since the Revolution. Although persistent cultural norms and the reluctance of males to accept gender equality continue to shape women's lives and to hamper female activists, the Mexican women's movement that began at the end of the nineteenth century shows no signs of turning back.

—SBP

See also: Cristero Rebellion; Revolution of 1910; *Soldaderas;* Virgin of Guadalupe.

References:

Macías, Anna. *Against All Odds: The Feminist Movement in Mexico to 1940.* Westport, CT: Greenwood Press, 1982.

Ramos Escandón, Carmen. "Women's Movements, Feminism, and Mexican Politics," in Jane S. Jaquette, ed., *The Women's Movement in Latin America: Participation and Democracy,* pp. 199–221. Boulder, CO: Westview Press, 1994.

Soto, Shirlene. *Emergence of the Modern Mexican Woman: Her Participation in Revolution and Struggle for Equality, 1910–1940.* Denver: Arden Press, 1990.

World War II

When World War II began in Europe in September 1939, Mexico was in a state of change politically, economically, and diplo-

matically. The controversial administration of President Lázaro Cárdenas (1934–1940) was coming to an end, and there was considerable uneasiness over the approaching presidential elections in 1940. Mexico was recovering from a financial and economic crisis that had developed in 1937, and Cárdenas was attempting to redirect Mexico's development policy to one emphasizing industrialization. There was still no resolution of the diplomatic problems arising out of Mexico's expropriation of the foreign-owned oil companies in 1938.

Mexico's new president following the 1940 elections was the moderate General Manuel Avila Camacho, who had served as Cárdenas's minister of war. Avila Camacho's presidency (1940–1946) would encompass the entire wartime period. While the Mexican people were initially divided over which side to support in the conflict, Avila Camacho followed a strongly pro-Allied course. After U.S. entry into the war in December 1941, Mexico quickly broke diplomatic relations with the Axis powers (Germany, Japan, and Italy); there was, however, little domestic support for a declaration of war. It was not until two Mexican oil tankers were sunk by German submarines that Mexico declared war in May 1942.

Mexico's military involvement in the war meant closer relations with the United States. The United States wanted bases for its troops in Mexico while Mexico wanted economic and military aid. The United States never got the type of base agreement it wanted, but there was close cooperation between the two countries in military matters. Mexico received military aid under the U.S. Lend-Lease Program, and the two nations established a joint defense committee to coordinate military activities. Mexico also established an obligatory military service law, affecting men between the ages of 18 and 45. Mexico was one of only two Latin American countries (Brazil being the other) to furnish combat troops; Mexico sent the 201st Fighter Squadron, which served in the Pacific and suffered losses of two killed in training and five in combat. A more important form of military cooperation was the U.S.–Mexico agreement permitting the United States to draft Mexican citizens residing in the United States and to recruit in Mexico itself. As a result, some 250,000 Mexicans served in the U.S. armed forces during the war, with 14,000 seeing combat.

Mexico's wartime response also involved internal-security measures. Mexico adopted a program of surveillance, relocation, and deportation aimed at Axis nationals. The Mexican government forcibly relocated Japanese and Japanese-Mexicans living in coastal areas and along the U.S. border. Several German agents were detained, and Axis nationals who could not prove Mexican citizenship were deported.

Mexico's most important role in the war was economic. Mexico provided a variety of strategic materials needed for the war effort: copper, oil, lead, mercury, and zinc. Mexico also imposed price controls on these items, making it cheaper for the United States to acquire them. Agricultural products also figured prominently in Mexican exports. By 1943 the United States accounted for 90 percent of Mexico's foreign trade. Mexico even helped relieve labor shortages in the United States by agreeing to the *bracero* program, a government-regulated system of contract labor under which Mexican workers found employment in the United States. Originally conceived of to meet the need for agricultural laborers in the U.S. southwest, the program was expanded in 1943 to include nonagricultural labor as well. Some 300,000 Mexicans worked under the program during the war years. The war had negative economic consequences for Mexico as well; austerity measures, inflation, and rationing affected the daily lives of Mexicans. In June 1944 the Avila Camacho administration even ended the traditional *siesta,* the afternoon closing of offices and businesses.

The war also helped the Mexican government to pursue its new development policy emphasizing industrialization. Cut off from many of its normal sources of foreign capital and manufactured goods, the Avila Camacho administration viewed forcing the pace of industrialization as not only desirable but unavoidable. The international situation largely limited foreign involvement in this process to U.S. investors and government agencies, forging even closer economic ties between the two countries.

World War II had a profound long-term impact on Mexico and U.S.–Mexico relations. The war confirmed and accelerated domestic and foreign policies that operated until the 1980s. The war was particularly important in promoting the government's new development approach with its emphasis on creating rather than redistributing wealth. Development increasingly came to mean rapid industrialization based on import substitution. While the close military ties between Mexico and the United States did not survive the war, the already-close economic connection would become even more pronounced. The *bracero* program—conceived of to meet a wartime need—continued until 1964. The war even had the ironic effect of reducing the role of the Mexican military in political affairs. Avila Camacho eliminated the military sector from the official party and reduced the percentage of the national budget allotted to the military (partially compensated for by U.S. military assistance). He even secured the election of the first civilian president of the post-Revolutionary period as his successor in 1946, Miguel Alemán. Alemán had served as Avila Camacho's minister of the interior (internal security) and would continue the policies accelerated by the war into the postwar period. The foundations for what would later be known as the "Mexican economic miracle" had been firmly established during the war years.

—*DMC*

See also: *Bracero* Program; Immigration/
Emigration; Korean War; Militarism; United
States, Relations with.

References:

Camp, Roderic Ai. *Generals in the Palacio: The Military in Modern Mexico.* New York: Oxford University Press, 1992.

Craig, Richard B. *The Bracero Program: Interest Groups and Foreign Policy.* Austin: University of Texas Press, 1971.

Niblo, Stephen R. *War, Diplomacy, and Development: the United States and Mexico, 1938–1954.* Wilmington, DE: Scholarly Resources, 1995.

Torres Ramírez, Blanca. *México en la segunda guerra mundial.* Mexico City: El Colegio de México, 1979.

Y

Yucatán (State)

The state of Yucatán is carved out of the northern part of the Yucatán Peninsula, which juts into the Gulf of Mexico and the Caribbean Sea. The geography of the Peninsula is especially difficult; the soil is poor, and water scarce. The Yucatán depends heavily on its seasonal rains. The Peninsula's ancient history was dominated by the Maya culture, one of the most sophisticated in the Americas. Today, tourists are drawn to Mayan ruins, including Chichén Itzá, which once served as an important ceremonial center. The Maya language is still spoken in the Yucatán, and Maya culture has been remarkably persistent, though it has experienced significant changes since the colonial period. During the nineteenth century, Yucatán experienced a remarkable economic transformation, which helped make the state one of Mexico's wealthiest. The twentieth century revealed the limits of that wealth and compelled the state's leaders to change course.

The Spaniards had a particularly difficult time conquering the Yucatán. Upon their arrival, the Maya were no longer concentrated in large urban centers. This lack of centralization, and the ability of the Maya to wage guerrilla warfare in the region's inhospitable terrain, severely hampered the Spaniards, who were also disappointed to find no precious metals here. The Maya especially resisted conversion to Christianity. The tenacity with which they clung to their own spiritual beliefs and practices incurred the wrath of the Yucatán's Franciscan missionaries, and in 1562 many Indians were tortured into confessing idolatrous practices. Although the Yucatán's Maya regularly responded to Spanish pressures through flight and rebellion, they could not escape the effects of the Spanish presence. Disease, forced relocation, and labor and tribute demands all took their toll.

Even as the Spaniards struggled to gain mastery over the region's native peoples, they were establishing a capital and commercial center at Mérida (the current capital of Yucatán State). Valladolid, Campeche, and Salamanca de Bacalar emerged as other important urban centers on the Peninsula. A colonial economy with small-scale agriculture and cattle ranching emerged, but the most important products were indigo (used in the colonial dye trade) and cotton blankets and beeswax, which helped supply other areas of New Spain. All three of these items were produced with Indian labor.

Mexico's struggle for independence played itself out in a fairly peaceful manner in the Yucatán as the region's political elites clashed over the issue of whether to retain ties with Spain. One of the most important figures in this struggle was Lorenzo de Zavala, whose liberal ideas attracted many, and who argued against the highly centralized colonial system. The Yucatán, always located far from the seat of colonial power, emerged from independence with a determination to preserve its autonomy from an equally distant Mexican government. Indeed, the Yucatán's leaders twice declared their separation from Mexico, and from 1840 to 1846 the Peninsula was in fact independent.

Although the independence period brought calls for an end to the exploitation of the Yucatán's Indian peoples, they had limited rights in the new country of Mexico, and many still paid tribute. The Maya also persisted in their own struggle for autonomy. Beginning in 1847, the peninsula experienced a great Maya uprising, known as the Caste War. This rebellion enlisted rural workers in a strike against the tribute system and against non-Indians. The Maya (as well as *mestizos,* or people of mixed Indian-Spanish blood) laid siege to Mérida in 1848, and at one point they controlled most of the peninsula. Thousands of people died in the Caste War, and countless more Maya were forcibly relocated to Cuba. Although the initial revolt had been suppressed by 1854, Maya rebels retreated to Quintana Roo (the easternmost section of the Yucatán Peninsula). From this base, they remained independent of Mexican control until the early twentieth century.

The Yucatán's economic profile changed markedly during the nineteenth century as sugar and then henequen emerged as commercial crops. The sugar industry, which dominated the first half of the century, disrupted the agricultural activities of the region's native peoples, helping to contribute to the Caste War. After midcentury, henequen or sisal became the dominant cash crop. The sisal industry was supported by coercive Indian labor and was dependent on capital investment from the United States. The International Harvester Company cor-

nered the Yucatán's sisal market and supplied the growing American demand for the binder twine that was made from sisal. Binder twine was utilized in Cyrus McCormack's recently invented mechanical reaper-binder machine, which revolutionized American agriculture.

Henequen transformed Yucatán's economy and society. Land was increasingly concentrated in the hands of a few wealthy plantation owners, and increasing numbers of Indians were compelled to provide labor for this industry. Railroad lines were built to link the plantations to the growing port of Progreso, through which sisal products were exported. Sisal also affected the state's politics. Olegario Molina became Yucatán's most powerful plantation owner and he governed the state from 1902 to 1910, working with International Harvester to retain control over the market for the state's lucrative product.

The Mexican Revolution of 1910, which sought the overthrow of President Porfirio Díaz, generated some rebel activity within the state. The Anti-reelection Movement led by Francisco Madero (who would eventually replace Díaz) gained some supporters in Yucatán, including José María Pino Suárez, the man who became Madero's vice-president. Workers and peasants participated in several small-scale revolts at the beginning of the Revolution, but there was no great popular rebellion. Instead, Revolutionary changes were gradually imposed from above by two of the state's outstanding governors: Salvador Alvarado and Felipe Carrillo Puerto. Alvarado governed from 1915 to 1918. He broke the economic stranglehold of International Harvester and liberated peasants from their condition of semislavery on the plantations. Alvarado also organized workers and passed a state labor law that became a model for the federal government's own labor law.

Felipe Carrillo Puerto served as the state's governor from 1922 to 1924. A socialist, Carrillo Puerto worked to organize peasants, distribute land, and establish socialist schools. His sister Elvia organized Yucatán's women and helped the Yucatán become a center of a nascent feminist movement, which promoted contraception, sex education, divorce rights, and women's suffrage. The resistance of the state's henequen plantation owners to land reform, however, cost Carrillo Puerto his life in 1924. It was left to the Mexican government, under President Lázaro Cárdenas, to break up Yucatán's henequen plantations. Cárdenas personally supervised this, arriving in Yucatán in 1937 with the military to carry out sweeping agrarian reform. Some large-scale henequen producers remained, but Yucatán now emerged with many smaller *ejidos* (communal lands or plots cultivated by a community) that were carved out of the old plantations.

Yucatán's sisal industry continued to be central part of the economy well into the twentieth century. Yet while the two world wars aided that industry by increasing the demand for sisal products, they also helped reveal the weakness of the state's one-crop economy. After 1960, and especially as synthetic fibers replaced sisal in the manufacture of rope and other products, the state of Yucatán was forced to look for economic alternatives. Both the state and the federal government participated in this diversification, and Yucatán's infrastructure grew to support production of a variety of goods for export, including citrus fruits. In the 1980s, twenty-one businessmen from Mérida's sizeable Syrian-Lebanese population (a population that had begun to emerge during the nineteenth century as the state's prosperity attracted immigrants to the capital city) formed the Grupo Yucatán to promote foreign investment. Their efforts led to the establishment of industrial parks and *maquiladoras* (foreign assembly plants located on Mexican soil and utilizing Mexican labor), which remain an important part of the state's economy.

As Yucatán modernized its infrastructure and extended a welcome to foreign investment and industry, more of the state's rural inhabitants began to relocate to the cities. Mérida in particular experienced remarkable growth during the late twentieth century. Meanwhile, the state's rural areas (no longer home to prosperous sisal plantations) were increasingly characterized by poverty and underdevelopment. Rural Yucatán also retained its heavy Indian population, even as greater numbers of Maya speakers were migrating to Mérida to provide a labor force for the state's *maquiladora* plants.

—SBP

See also: Revolution of 1910; Women's Movement.

References:

Clendinnen, Inga. *Ambivalent Conquests: Maya and Spaniard in Yucatán, 1517–1570*. New York: Cambridge University Press, 1982.

Joseph, Gilbert. *Revolution from Without: Yucatán, Mexico, and the United States, 1880–1924*. Durham, NC: Duke University Press, 1980.

Quezada, Sergio. *Breve historia de Yucatán*. Mexico City: El Colegio de Mexico, 2001.

Valdéz, Nelson. *The Caste War of Yucatán*. Rev. ed. Palo Alto, CA: Stanford University Press, 2001.

Official state web site: http://www.yucatan.gob.mx

Z

Zacatecas (State)

Located in north central Mexico, Zacatecas was a center of development during the colonial era. Its capital city (also called Zacatecas) was second only to Mexico City in terms of population and wealth. Although the city of Zacatecas retains some of its colonial splendor (its historic center was designated a World Heritage Site by UNESCO in 1993), the state's fortunes waned during the twentieth century. Zacatecas is now one of the poorest and least-developed states in Mexico. Indeed, by the 1990s, Zacatecas had the highest number of emigrants per capita in Mexico, with many of the state's inhabitants leaving to seek better wages elsewhere in Mexico and in the United States.

During the beginning of the Spanish colonial period, Zacatecas was on the northern frontier of Spanish settlement and was home to native groups including the Cazcanes, Zacatecos, and Guachichiles. These tribes, particularly the Cazcanes, provided fierce resistance to the Spanish advance. From 1540 to 1544 Indians on New Spain's northern frontier reacted to their poor treatment at the hands of the Spaniards in the bloody Mixtón War. Native resistance continued for most of the sixteenth century, but Zacatecas's Indians declined in number and many of their original settlements dispersed. Most Indians became tribute-payers and laborers who helped extract Mexico's wealth for the benefit of Spanish settlers and the Spanish Crown.

The Spanish determination to control the northern frontier rested on the promise of mineral wealth. Zacatecas fulfilled this promise when major silver deposits were discovered in the 1540s. The Zacatecas silver boom helped transform the Mexican north, stimulating growth in agriculture and cattle ranching and giving rise to a road network that linked Zacatecas to central Mexico. More broadly, Zacatecas silver became part of a global exchange of goods that linked Mexico to Europe and Asia. Mining also helped shape a new society in Zacatecas, with Indians from other areas of Mexico coming to work in the mines (usually as part of a coercive labor system). Blacks (many of whom had served as domestic servants to the Spaniards) were often enlisted as mining administrators and cultural "middlemen" who oversaw Indian workers.

The struggle for independence in Mexico had a disruptive effect on mining, and during the first half of the nineteenth century, mining production declined as did the quality of silver being extracted. Silver mining remained an important part of the Zacatecas (and northern Mexican) economy, however, and it even attracted outside investment: British entrepreneurs invested in the mines at Vetagrande, Fresnillo, and Sombrerete. Cattle ranching followed mining as Zacatecas's most important economic sector, and agriculture lingered behind, hampered by the arid, mountainous terrain.

Zacatecas became a state in 1823 and it retained as its capital the colonial city of the same name. Its central location and proximity to Mexico's capital ensured that it would be caught up in the political conflicts of the nineteenth century. During the Mexican War, Zacatecas was briefly threatened with a U.S. invasion. It joined other north-central states in raising an army that would later be used to resist the French Intervention in Mexico (1862–1867). In 1876, when Porfirio Díaz revolted against the central government, he found support in Trinidad García de la Cadena, a former governor of Zacatecas who, upon Díaz's triumph and installation as president, assumed the governorship for a second time. García de la Cadena gained a reputation as a progressive governor, but he also resisted Díaz's attempts to encroach on state autonomy. His independent stance cost him the governorship and, ultimately, his life.

Under the dictatorial rule of Díaz, many areas of Mexico experienced impressive levels of economic growth. Zacatecas was not among them. Although the construction of railroad lines linked the state more directly to the United States and to other areas of Mexico, the economy itself remained stuck in its colonial pattern, as if waiting for the silver mines to boom once again. Lead, copper, and tin were added to the list of lucrative metals extracted from Zacatecas mines, but this sector of the economy was particularly vulnerable to recession. Zacatecas's agriculture was likewise unreliable, hampered generally by the state's arid climate and more specifically by a drought and frosts that plagued farmers as the nineteenth century drew to a close. Cattle ranching also remained a center of the Zacatecas economy,

and it seemed to enjoy more consistent success than other sectors.

Zacatecas was a main theater of the Mexican Revolution. Its strategic location between Mexico City and northern Mexico (a region that was home to Venustiano Carranza, Pancho Villa, and other rebel leaders) made the state central to the operations of Revolutionaries and counterrevolutionaries. Francisco Madero's initial call for a revolt against Porfirio Díaz in 1910–1911 was echoed in the local movement of José Luis Moya, which brought some changes to the state and encouraged political activism. With Madero's overthrow and assassination, the government forces of Victoriano Huerta captured and briefly held the capital of Zacatecas while supporters of Venustiano Carranza's nascent Constitutionalist movement established a rival capital in Sombrerete. The forces of Pancho Villa eventually helped to recapture Zacatecas's capital, but the state's Revolutionaries then broke into rival factions, some supporting Villa and others supporting Carranza. As on the national level, Carranza's Constitutionalist movement ultimately prevailed and in 1916 a Constitutionalist governor, Enrique Estrada, assumed control of Zacatecas.

Carranza's national victory was not the end of unrest in Zacatecas. The state had a strong branch of the National Catholic Party, which encouraged defiance of the anticlerical initiatives of Mexico's post-Revolutionary state. Zacatecas thus became a center of the Church-State struggle known as the Cristero Rebellion (1926–1929), a conflict that brought another round of violence to several areas of Mexico. In the decades after the Revolution, Zacatecas also experienced agitation from small-scale farmers and landless *campesinos* (peasants), whose protests brought only limited land reform during the 1930s. By the 1970s, however, a viable movement that protested against the concentration of wealth in Zacatecas had emerged. Adding their own voices to the protests of local *campesinos,* students and professors established the Frente Popular de Zacatecas (Zacatecas Popular Front). President Luis Echeverría responded to the agitation with another round of land reform that gave plots to some 4,000 peasants.

The popular unrest that characterized Zacatecas in the several decades after the Mexican Revolution took place in the context of a faltering economy. Mining, once the main source of Zacatecas's wealth, suffered a decline during the Revolutionary years and remained vulnerable to fluctuations in the international market. Another dip occurred after World War II; despite (or perhaps because of) the nationalization of the mining industry in 1961, productivity in Zacatecas's mines experienced a general decline. Agriculture, the other foundation of the state's economy, experienced a similar struggle during the twentieth century. Since most of Zacatecas is characterized by a dry climate, marginal land, and a scarcity of water, the agricultural sector has always faced significant obstacles. After World War II, the government poured money into irrigation works and other infrastructure projects, and from 1986 to 1992 the "Plan Zacatecas" sought to create an external market for agricultural products and encourage productivity through the use of fertilizer and better seeds.

Though the mining, agriculture, and cattle ranching sectors experienced some growth as a result of such initiatives, many Zacatecans struggled to make a living. At the same time, government attempts to create industrial jobs within the state faltered. Faced with few choices, Zacatecans responded to the economic situation by leaving for other parts of Mexico and for the United States. The exodus has been remarkable, and it is estimated that 600,000 to 1 million Zacatecans now live in the United States. Whole towns have been all but emptied by such migration and those who have remained in Zacatecas are often dependent on money sent from relatives living elsewhere. As the twenty-first century began, the government of Zacatecas was working with successful emigrants to fund development projects with the hope of discouraging further migration from the state.

—SBP

See also: Cristero Rebellion; Immigration/ Emigration.

References:

Flores Olague, Jesús, Mercedes de Vega, et al. *Breve historia de Zacatecas.* Mexico City: El Colegio de Mexico/Fideicomiso Historia de las Américas, Fondo de Cultura Económica, 1996.

Official state web site: http://www.zacatecas. gob.mx

Zapata, Emiliano (1879–1919)

There is perhaps no better-known figure in Mexico's modern history than Emiliano Zapata. The subject of countless books, hero of folk songs, and enduring symbol of the Mexican Revolution, Zapata continues to capture the popular imagination. His image is easily recognized by Mexicans and non-Mexicans, and his likeness often appears on political propaganda. For many Mexicans, Zapata is the figure who best represents Revolutionary Mexico, and his fight for land reform symbolizes the essence of the Revolution. His legacy has persisted into the late twentieth century with the emergence of the Zapatista National Liberation Army, a rebel group in the state of Chiapas that adopted Zapata's image to bolster its struggle for land and indigenous rights.

The year of Zapata's birth is a matter of dispute, but he was probably born in 1879, in Anenecuilco, a village in the south-central state of Morelos. He was one of ten children. His family could trace its roots in Morelos and Anenecuilco back to Mexico's struggle for independence. By the time of Zapata's birth, the family was of modest means and Emiliano inherited some land. He also worked as a muleteer and a horse trainer. In keeping with the family's long history of political activism, Zapata was elected president of the Anenecuilco village council in 1909.

Zapata reached maturity and began his political career in Morelos during a particularly

Emiliano Zapata, seated center, with his staff (Library of Congress)

volatile time. Like many areas of Mexico, Morelos was experiencing an ongoing struggle over land and other resources. The struggle dated back to the nineteenth century but intensified during the reign of Porfirio Díaz (1876–1911) and especially as owners of the state's sugar haciendas sought to expand their holdings at the expense of peasants and small landowners. Under Díaz's crony Pablo Escandón, who served as governor on the eve of the Revolution, Morelos *campesinos* (peasants), including those in Anenecuilco, gradually lost their land and their identity as members of self-governing villages. The young Zapata gained visibility as a participant in the struggle for land; visibility that would bring him his first conflicts with local authorities. By 1910, he had begun taking matters into his own hands, arming men in his native village and extending his influence into the surrounding area. After Francisco Madero's call for revolt against the Díaz regime, Zapata

helped establish and became leader of a small band of Morelos rebels. In May 1911, this band succeeded in capturing the town of Cuautla. This victory helped seal the fate of the Díaz regime and bring Madero to the presidential seat.

Zapata's alliance with Madero was always a tenuous one, based on the unfounded hope that Madero, a wealthy landowner from northern Mexico, would support measures to help those dispossessed of their lands. Madero quickly revealed that his commitment was to moderate political reform, and Morelos's wealthy planters maneuvered to reinforce their power and to block any attempt at land reform. His alliance with Madero soon broken, Zapata determined to stage his own revolution. In November 1911 he issued the Plan of Ayala, composed with the help of Otilio Montaño, a schoolteacher from the village of Ayala, Morelos. The plan refused to recognize Madero's authority in

Mexico, demanded the people's right to choose their own leaders, and most important, called for land reform. Zapata insisted on the return of lands stolen by hacienda owners and the expropriation of one-third of all hacienda properties. The Plan of Ayala also threatened to confiscate the property of Zapata's opponents.

The promise of land reform increased Zapata's support within his native state. With the ouster and assassination of Madero in February 1913, and the ascension to power of General Victoriano Huerta, that support extended further and came to include *campesinos* from several states in central and southern Mexico. Zapata assumed leadership of a rebel army, the Liberating Army of the Center and South, which was opposed to Huerta and united under the Plan of Ayala. Opposition to the Huerta regime took several forms and encouraged the emergence of a handful of regional leaders, including Venustiano Carranza and Francisco "Pancho" Villa, both from northern Mexico. As Zapata maneuvered to remain part of the Revolutionary equation and to advance the cause of agrarian reform, he chose an alliance with Villa, rejecting Carranza's more moderate commitment to change.

The Zapatista capture of Mexico City in November 1914 held out hope for Zapata's cause. In Morelos, Zapata worked with his adviser Manuel Palafox to implement land reform and to return authority to the village councils. Their reform efforts were only partly successful, and a series of military victories by the Carranza faction in 1915 and 1916 threatened the survival of both Zapata and Villa. Tensions within the Zapata-Villa camp, moreover, signaled the decline of that alliance.

By 1917, Zapata had turned to a new adviser, Gildardo Magaña for help in seeking alliances with other Revolutionary leaders opposed to Carranza. But the Zapatista movement continued to weaken, beset by military defeats, defections from the ranks, and competing interests within Morelos and the Zapatista movement itself. In an attempt

to take advantage of a rift between Carrancista officers Pablo González and Jesús Guajardo, Zapata walked into a trap. On his way to talk with Guajardo about a possible alliance, Zapata was gunned down at the Hacienda Chinameca in Morelos on 10 April 1919. Through a public display of his remains in Cuautla, Carranza hoped to convince Morelians that Zapata was truly dead and to defeat the Zapatista movement once and for all. Instead, Zapata became a powerful martyr. His movement, although weakened and localized, continued in Morelos, and claims that its leader was still alive persisted long after Zapata's death.

In the end, Zapata was a leader who was remarkably successful at the regional level but who failed to transform his local authority into national power. Ultimately, his village-based movement was eclipsed by a national Revolution that increasingly reflected the needs of an urban, industrial Mexico. Nevertheless, the demand for radical agrarian reform that was at the heart of the Morelos Revolution and the Zapatista insurgency was included in Mexico's Constitution of 1917. Land reform, to be carried out incrementally and with varying degrees of success by several Mexican presidents during the 1920s and 1930s, became, rightly or wrongly, a great symbol of the triumph of the Mexican Revolution. During the latter part of the twentieth century, as the Mexican government embraced neoliberal economic programs, moving away from land reform, the figure of Zapata assumed a new importance. That many Mexicans still consider the end of land reform to be a betrayal of one of the basic principles of the Mexican Revolution is a testament to the enduring legacy of Emiliano Zapata.

—*SBP*

See also: Agrarian Reform / Land and Land
  Policy; Morelos (State); Revolution of 1910;
  Villa, Francisco "Pancho"; Zapatista National
  Liberation Army (EZLN).

References:

Brunk, Samuel. *Emiliano Zapata!: Revolution and
  Betrayal in Mexico.* Albuquerque: University of
  New Mexico Press, 1995.

Warman, Arturo. *"We Come to Object": The Peasants of Morelos and the National State.* Baltimore: Johns Hopkins University Press, 1980.

Womack, John, Jr. *Zapata and the Mexican Revolution.* New York: Random House, 1968.

Zapatista National Liberation Army (EZLN)

On 1 January 1994, rebels in the southernmost state of Chiapas began what is perhaps Mexico's most significant popular uprising since the Mexican Revolution. Dubbing themselves "Zapatistas," in memory of Revolutionary leader Emiliano Zapata, Chiapas rebels seized four towns, including the highland city of San Cristóbal de las Casas. Peasants responded to the uprising by invading privately owned lands, and the Zapatista National Liberation Army (Ejército Zapatista de Liberación Nacional, or EZLN) took Absalón Castellanos Domínguez hostage. One of Chiapas's most influential cattle ranchers, Castellanos had served as the state's governor during the 1980s and was considered responsible for human rights abuses during his term. President Carlos Salinas de Gortari responded to the uprising with a military offensive that claimed significant casualties and helped generate public outrage as reports of the detention, torture, and murder of suspected Zapatista sympathizers surfaced. The outcry forced Salinas to call off the offensive and go to the bargaining table. Talks resulted in the freeing of Castellanos and in a pledge from the Mexican government to improve socioeconomic conditions in Chiapas's Indian communities.

The Zapatista rebellion has occurred in the context of a Mexico that is trying to become a player in the global economy. Deliberately timed to coincide with the first day of the North American Free Trade Agreement (NAFTA), the rebellion has as its cornerstone the idea that neoliberal economic policies are detrimental to the people of Mexico, particularly to indigenous people. Indeed, the leader of the uprising, Subcomandante Marcos, has called NAFTA "a death certificate for the ethnic people of Mexico." In the 1994 negotiations, the Zapatistas asked for a repeal of President Salinas's agrarian reforms, which were designed to open up Mexico's agricultural sector to large-scale investment and to end the system of *ejidos,* or communally cultivated farms.

Although anti-NAFTA sentiment served as an official rallying cry for the 1994 uprising, the Zapatista movement has taken place in a state with significant problems that predate the neoliberal reforms of the Salinas administration. Chiapas is acknowledged by many to be the poorest state in Mexico, with high illiteracy and infant mortality rates, and a scarcity of houses, doctors, roads, and other basic services. Despite the poverty of its people, however, Chiapas has tremendous natural resources. It is Mexico's largest generator of hydroelectric energy and has been a major producer of oil and gas for over a decade. The state has a large indigenous population, the majority of whom are descendants of the Maya. Historically, the economy has been characterized by the concentration of wealth, primarily land, in the hands of a few wealthy cattle ranchers and coffee growers. Chiapas's indigenous groups have typically provided the labor force for the large estates. In the aftermath of the Mexican Revolution, the state's economic elite developed close ties with Mexico's official Institutional Revolutionary Party (PRI), and it helped deliver the vote for that party. The local PRI "machine" became associated with corruption and abuse of the indigenous population.

Zapatista recruitment has been particularly successful in the eastern part of the state, including the Lacandón Forest, which has served as the base for the rebel movement. It is in this area that Emiliano Zapata's struggle for land during the Mexican Revolution has a particular relevance. During the 1950s, settlers, including indigenous people expelled from lands in other parts of the state, began streaming into the Lacandón. Utilizing Article 27 of the Constitution, they

Commanders of the EZLN listen during the closing ceremony of the third indigenous congress in the town of Nurio in the state of Michoacán on 4 March 2001. (Reuters / Corbis)

were successful in legalizing their claims to new lands. In the 1970s, the government tried to brake the continuing flow of settlers into the Lacandón and when a large part of the jungle was declared a biosphere reserve, evictions began. Many Zapatistas recall the struggle of their families to remain in the Lacandón. For them, Salinas's repeal of Article 27, ending agrarian reform, was a crowning blow. The agrarian strife of the 1970s gave birth to peasant organizations in Chiapas and the Lacandón. Some of these groups were organized by Bishop Samuel Ruíz, a supporter of Liberation Theology. Although most of these grassroots organizations were repressed or eliminated, the EZLN was able to benefit from this earlier activism when it emerged in the early 1980s.

The Zapatista movement began in the Lacandón with the arrival of Subcomandante Marcos and other activists from outside of Chiapas. Marcos and the founders of the EZLN, although they protect their identities with masks and bandanas, are generally believed to have ties to the student and rebel movements that emerged in Mexico during the 1960s and 1970s. Indeed, the Mexican government has "revealed" Marcos's identity as Adolfo Guillén, a former university student and philosophy professor. The popular appeal of the Zapatista movement and of the charismatic and mysterious Marcos has extended beyond the borders of Chiapas. From the start, the EZLN has used the internet to broadcast its movement, and Marcos has appealed to the international community, hosting celebrities and political figures and participating in international symposia on neoliberalism and human rights.

The Mexican government and the Zapatistas have held several rounds of negotiations since the 1994 uprising. In 1996, rebels and the government of President Ernesto Zedillo agreed to the San Andrés Accords, which pledge relative autonomy for Mexico's indigenous communities, allowing Indians to form local governments according to their customs, providing for education in native languages, and promising "adequate" representation of indigenous peoples in local and national legislatures. Several months after signing these accords, Zedillo reneged, fearing the effect of Indian separatism on the country. The San Andrés Accords and the issue of indigenous rights remain a sticking point between rebels and the Mexican government. Some Indian groups in Chiapas have taken matters into their own hands, attempting to establish autonomous Indian communities.

As the 1990s drew to a close, there was an uneasy stalemate in Chiapas. The Federal Army had a significant presence in the state and was conducting what many observers described as a low-intensity campaign against suspected Zapatista sympathizers. Right-wing paramilitary groups known as "White Guards" and sponsored by local landowners were aiding this campaign. Beginning in 1996, the Mexican government began expelling foreign visitors from Chiapas in an apparent attempt to detract international interest from the situation. In December of 1997, Chiapas and the Zapatista movement were once again in the spotlight when a paramilitary group in the town of Acteal massacred forty-five men, women, and children. This event renewed the pressure on Zedillo to address Chiapas's problems and to answer allegations of human rights abuses. As Mexico enters the next millennium, the Zapatista rebellion serves as a reminder that poverty, land reform, and indigenous rights are issues central to the country's history.

—SBP

See also: Agrarian Reform/Land and Land Policy; Chiapas (State); Constitution of 1917; North American Free Trade Agreement (NAFTA).

References:

Collier, George A., and Elizabeth Lowery Quaratiello. *Basta! Land and the Zapatista Rebellion in Chiapas.* Oakland, CA: Food First Books, 1994.

Harvey, Neil. *The Chiapas Rebellion: The Struggle for Land and Democracy.* Durham, NC: Duke University Press, 1998.

Katzenberger, Elaine, ed. *First World, Ha Ha, Ha!: The Zapatista Challenge.* San Francisco: City Lights, 1995.

Ross, John. *Rebellion from the Roots: Indian Uprising in Chiapas.* Monroe, ME: Common Courage Press, 1995.

Zedillo Ponce de León, Ernesto (1951–)

President from 1994 to 2000, Ernesto Zedillo Ponce de León was born in Mexico City but soon moved to the northern border town of Mexicali. He attended public schools in Mexicali until he returned to Mexico City at age 14. In 1969 Zedillo began his studies in economics at the National Polytechnic Institute, receiving his degree in 1972. During his studies at the Institute, he also worked at the National Bank of the Army and Navy as well as the Secretariat of the Presidency. Following graduation Zedillo studied in England for a year on scholarship and then pursued his master's and doctoral degrees in economics at Yale University from 1974 to 1978. Prophetically, his doctoral dissertation dealt with the risks of Mexico financing its economic growth by relying on external debt and the exportation of oil.

After completing his doctorate, Zedillo received a position at the Bank of Mexico, where he worked with Leopoldo Solís, one of Mexico's leading economists and a former professor of future President Carlos Salinas de Gortari. At the Bank, Zedillo helped to formulate the plans for modernizing Mexico's economy. He also helped to establish the Exchange Risk Coverage Trust Fund (Fideicomiso para la Cobertura de Riesgos Cambiarios, or FICORA), an agency which helped many Mexican companies stay in business by restructuring their debt. In 1987 Zedillo became subsecretary in the increasingly important Secretariat of Programming and Budget, an agency which would produce three consecutive presidents: Miguel de la Madrid, Carlos Salinas de Gortari, and Zedillo. As subsecretary Zedillo helped to

Inauguration of President Ernesto Zedillo (Keith Dannemiller / Corbis Saba)

develop the "Economic Solidarity Pact," an agreement bringing together business, labor, and agricultural interests which helped to curb inflation. When Carlos Salinas became president in 1988, Zedillo became secretary of programming and budget, a position previously held by Salinas. As secretary, Zedillo was responsible for developing the overall budgets for fiscal years 1989–1992 as well as the National Development Plan.

In 1992 the Secretariat of Programming and Budget merged with the Secretariat of Finance, resulting in the abolition of Zedillo's position. Zedillo quickly received another cabinet position, secretary of public education. While Zedillo had long been personally interested in education, the new position was not as prestigious and influential as the one at Programming and Budget. Many interpreted his new assignment as a demotion and an indication that Zedillo would not be a serious contender for the presidential nomination in 1994. Zedillo, however, displayed great en-

ergy in his new post. He helped to develop and implement the National Agreement for the Modernization of Basic Education, which resulted in a major overhaul of Mexico's public education system. In keeping with his economic views of a reduced role for government, Zedillo also pursued a decentralization of education that had long been dominated by the federal government. He also promoted special education programs that targeted the less-developed regions of the country and Mexico's poorest groups. Zedillo's efforts to have textbooks revised to reflect the new views on economic development provoked a major public controversy, but his overall performance as secretary was impressive.

Although Zedillo had impeccable credentials as a financial technocrat and had conducted himself well as secretary of public education, he did not receive the presidential nomination of the official party, the Institutional Revolutionary Party (Partido Revolucionario Institucional, or PRI). The nomination, instead, went to the more populist Luis Donaldo Colosio. Colosio, however, appointed Zedillo as the general manager of his presidential campaign. Colosio waged an effective campaign that seemed to be reviving the fading political fortunes of the PRI. The presidential campaign, however, took a dramatic turn. While campaigning in the border town of Tijuana, Colosio was assassinated on 23 March 1994, thrusting Zedillo into the national spotlight. Zedillo was the only major PRI politician who met the party's time restriction on being out of public office prior to receiving the nomination; Zedillo had resigned in November 1993 to serve as Colosio's campaign director. Zedillo also had the type of government background that appealed to outgoing President Carlos Salinas, who had followed much the same path to the presidency. Thus Zedillo was tapped as the new PRI nominee for the presidency.

As a presidential candidate, Zedillo labored under some major handicaps. He had never run for an elective office. His two principal opponents—the leftist Cuauhtémoc Cárdenas and the conservative Diego Fernández Cevallos—had been on the campaign trail for months when Zedillo received the nomination. The austere, restrained Zedillo was also a sharp contrast to the energetic, populist Colosio. Zedillo did not distinguish himself during Mexico's first televised presidential debate in May 1994. Despite these early problems, Zedillo could count on the well-established political machine of the PRI, which was especially strong in rural areas. The circumstances surrounding Zedillo's nomination helped to generate sympathy for his candidacy. In addition to sympathy, another emotion was also in play—fear. Mexicans had never experienced an administration without an official party president, and many were unnerved by the prospect of an inexperienced opposition party in control of the presidency. There were also some indications that Mexico was emerging from the worst of its financial and economic problems. In a

closely monitored election, Zedillo came in first with 49 percent of the vote, followed by the conservative Diego Fernández de Cevallos with 26 percent of the vote. The big loser in the election was the leftist candidate, Cuauhtémoc Cárdenas, who received less than 17 percent of the vote. Zedillo's vote total was the lowest ever for a PRI candidate, but under the electoral rules of the time, the winning candidate did not have to get a majority of the votes. Adding to Zedillo's credibility was the fact that the elections saw the biggest voter turnout in modern Mexican history.

While there were few doubts about the legitimacy of Zedillo's administration, there were soon plenty of doubts about the competence of the new president in the face of a major, new financial crisis. Less than three weeks after his inauguration, Zedillo had to confront a major devaluation of the peso, followed by a collapse of the Mexican stock market and massive capital flight. Despite his extensive background in economics and finance, Zedillo did not seem to have a plan for dealing with the crisis. Zedillo compounded the problem by trying to pass the blame for the crisis on to his predecessor, Carlos Salinas. Salinas retaliated by accusing Zedillo of mismanaging the economy. This kind of public bickering between a current president and his predecessor was unheard of in Mexican politics and only added to the political and economic uncertainty. Zedillo's reaction to the situation had some precedent in recent Mexican history where outgoing presidents had taken unpleasant but dramatic financial action before leaving office, such as Luis Echeverría had done with the peso devaluation of 1976 and José López Portillo had done with the nationalization of the banks in 1982. Zedillo felt—with some justification—that he had been left a financial time bomb by Salinas in the form of a deferred devaluation and a large amount of short-term government bonds that were coming due in early 1995. Adding to the embarrassment was the fact that Zedillo had to resort to a $20 billion bailout arranged by the U.S. government to work his way through the crisis. Zedillo had to implement the toughest austerity program since the debt crisis of 1982, plunging Mexico into a deep recession at the same time that inflation was on the rise.

Zedillo was also bedeviled by another inheritance from the Salinas administration: a growing scandal involving the previous president's older brother, Raúl Salinas. Criminal investigations connected Raúl Salinas to murder, drug-trafficking, and extensive government corruption. When authorities arrested Raúl on 28 February 1995 on charges that he conspired in the murder of PRI official José Francisco Ruiz Massieu, brother Carlos came to his defense, claiming that the arrest was politically motivated. Relations between Carlos Salinas and President Zedillo became so tense that Salinas wound up in self-imposed exile in Ireland. The scandal took an even darker turn in March when Mario Ruiz Massieu—who was in charge of investigating the murder of his brother, José Francisco— fled the country amid charges that he had been obstructing a thorough investigation of his brother's death and that he received payoffs from drug dealers. Mario in turn was arrested by U.S. authorities en route to Spain for carrying large amounts of undeclared cash. Mario fought off efforts by the Mexican government to extradite him, only to be later accused of stashing more than $9 million in drug money in Texas bank accounts. The scandal saw a shocking resolution in 1999 when Raúl Salinas was given the maximum sentence of fifty years for conspiring in the murder of José Francisco Ruiz Massieu, and Mario Ruiz Massieu committed suicide while still under detention in the United States. The Salinas-Massieu international soap opera went far beyond being an embarrassment for the Zedillo administration. It raised major issues of competency and corruption in Zedillo's presidency and undercut the president's ability to cope with the financial and economic crisis.

Amid the political and financial problems, Zedillo attempted to press on with the economic reforms that the government had been pursuing for over a decade. The liberalization of trade continued with Mexico's signing of a free-trade agreement in June 2000 with the "Triangle of the North": El Salvador, Guatemala, and Honduras. Zedillo tried with less success to continue the program of privatization, proposing that the electric power industry be opened to private investment. In this case Zedillo's political reforms came in conflict with his economic reforms. The growing power of opposition parties in the Congress delayed action on Zedillo's proposal.

One of the major tests for the Zedillo administration was political reform. Presidents Miguel de la Madrid and Carlos Salinas had linked economic reforms with political reforms, but the economic reforms had moved forward much more rapidly than the political. Salinas did not conceal the fact that he was putting more emphasis on economic reforms than political reforms, believing that political instability would result if political reforms outpaced economic reforms. Zedillo had emphasized from the beginning of his administration that political reform would be a top priority and proceeded to deliver on the promise. In pushing forward with democratization, Zedillo had to contend with major opposition from within his own party.

After extensive consultation and negotiation with various political parties and organizations, Zedillo supported a package of electoral reforms in 1996 that were later approved by the Mexican Congress. These reforms called for greater autonomy for the Federal Election Institute, which was responsible for conducting elections, the election of the mayor of Mexico City (previously an appointed position), and tighter controls on campaign spending. Elections in 1997 soon demonstrated the effectiveness of these reforms. Cuauhtémoc Cárdenas—twice defeated for the presidency—won election as mayor of Mexico City while his party—the Democratic Revolutionary Party—won a majority on the Mexico City council. In congressional elections, the PRI won only 239 out of the 500 seats in the Chamber of Deputies, the first time it failed to have a majority in the lower house of the Congress. The PRI retained control of the Senate because of the limited number of seats being contested, but opposition parties wound up controlling 40 percent of the seats.

Zedillo also presided over a greater democratization of the PRI itself. Zedillo announced that he would not "tap" his successor as had been the practice in the past. Instead he permitted an open contest for the presidential nomination, which went to his Secretary of the Interior Francisco Labastida Ochoa. Unfortunately for Zedillo, the only way that he could prove beyond doubt his commitment to democratization was to lead the PRI to defeat in the 2000 presidential elections. Critics of democratization had argued for years that the PRI might let opposition parties enjoy victories in local, state, and congressional elections but would never surrender the presidency. The 2000 election results demonstrated that democratization had taken effect and had also taken a toll, at least on the PRI. For the first time since the establishment of the official party in 1929, an opposition candidate won the presidency: the National Action Party's Vicente Fox Quesada. Zedillo not only became a lame duck president; he also lost effective leadership of his own party. PRI leaders were badly divided over what lessons should be learned from the 2000 election and which direction the party should take in the future. Instead of accepting the hazards of political competition, many PRI leaders bitterly and publicly denounced Zedillo for leading them to electoral defeat. Zedillo had passed the ultimate test of democratization and had won a special place in Mexico's political evolution, only to wind up being praised by his political enemies and scorned by his former supporters. Former President Carlos Salinas, in a book published just before Zedillo left office, continued his public bashing of Zedillo. Salinas not only re-

peated his charge that Zedillo botched the peso devaluation, thus causing the economic crisis of 1995, but also accused Zedillo of leaking word of the devaluation in advance to a small group of Mexican businessmen who personally profited from the financial maneuver. Zedillo maintained a low profile during the transition to the administration of his flamboyant successor, Vicente Fox Quesada. Still the financial technocrat, former President Zedillo soon left for Washington where he met with top officials of the World Bank and the International Monetary Fund. The United Nations also announced that Zedillo would chair a new committee to study the problem of development financing. An ex-president at the age of 48, Zedillo might yet play a role in the rapidly changing world of Mexican politics.

—*DMC*

See also: Cárdenas, Cuauhtémoc; Corruption; Democratization Process; Drug Trafficking; Madrid (Hurtado), Miguel de la; Mexico City; Partido de Acción Nacional (PAN); Partido Revolucionario Institucional (PRI); Presidents of the Twentieth Century; Salinas de Gortari, Carlos.

References:
Camp, Roderic Ai. *Politics in Mexico.* 2d ed. New York: Oxford University Press, 1996.
Morris, Stephen D. *Political Reformism in Mexico.* Boulder, CO: Lynne Rienner Publishers, 1995.
Schulz, Donald E., and Edward J. Williams, eds. *Mexico Faces the 21st Century.* Westport, CT: Greenwood Press, 1995.
Presidencia de la República (México): http://www.presidencia.gob.mx/

Zimmermann Telegram

The forces that would ultimately result in the sending and interception of the Zimmermann Telegram in early 1917 had been at work in Mexico for many years. During the administration of President Porfirio Díaz (1877–1880, 1884–1911), German investments in, and trade with, Mexico increased, although Germany never posed a serious threat to the dominant economic position of the United States. Long before 1917 Germany also was considering the possibility of Mexico serving as a point of contention between the United States and Japan. A "gentlemen's agreement" between the United States and Japan in 1907 had prohibited the entry of Japanese workers directly into the United States; the agreement resulted in a rapid increase in Japanese immigrants to Mexico, which could serve as a transit point to the United States. German officials even believed that Mexico might serve as a launching area for an attack by Japan on the United States.

With the outbreak of Revolution in 1910, Germany continued to view Mexico as a useful tool against the United States. Germany originally supported the Revolutionary government of Francisco Madero (1911–1913), who was seen as following a foreign policy that was not dominated by U.S. interests. Germany, however, became increasingly critical of Madero, who was considered too weak to control Mexico. The German ambassador in Mexico City, Paul von Hintze, was an early supporter of General Victoriano Huerta, who overthrew Madero in February 1913. Although the United States opposed recognition of the Huerta regime, Germany recognized Huerta but only after the British government had done so. When Huerta proved incapable of defeating the different Revolutionary factions, Hintze then worked to ease Huerta out of the presidency. When Huerta resigned and went into exile in July 1914, he left on a German ship. After arriving in European exile, Huerta began negotiations with German agents for assistance in returning to power.

In August 1914 war began in Europe, and Germany searched for ways to interrupt the flow of war materials from U.S. factories to the Allies; these methods ranged from purchasing U.S. arms producers to submarine warfare. The provoking of military conflict between the United States and Mexico became a major feature of German policy; such a conflict would interrupt the movement of war supplies and make U.S. intervention in

the European war more difficult. Germany also decided to provide the exiled Huerta with military and financial assistance in an effort to return to the presidency. Huerta, however, was arrested by U.S. authorities when he attempted to launch his Revolution from the El Paso area; he died in U.S. custody in January 1916. The Germans also cultivated exiled General Félix Díaz, who had joined with Huerta in the overthrow of the Madero government in 1913, but Díaz lost interest after the arrest of Huerta. The Germans had also been developing ties with another Revolutionary leader, Francisco "Pancho" Villa. There is strong evidence that German agents funneled money to Villa for arms purchases, but there is no direct evidence linking Germany to Villa's attack on Columbus, New Mexico, in March 1916, which prompted the United States to launch the Pershing Expedition in pursuit of Villa. Certainly the Columbus attack produced the type of results the Germans wanted. Most of the mobile force of the U.S. Army and the entire U.S. National Guard of more than 100,000 men were located in northern Mexico or along the U.S.–Mexican border. Although there were direct conflicts between U.S. forces and regular Mexican federal forces, a full-scale war was avoided.

Germany had supported a series of Revolutionary factions that failed to prevail against the government of Venustiano Carranza, which had been recognized by the United States in October 1915. By 1916 it was in the interest of both the Carranza regime and Germany to improve relations. For the Germans, Carranza represented the only viable hope for interrupting the flow of U.S. arms to Europe. Carranza's nationalism was provoking more confrontations with the United States, and the Mexican leader could use European support as a counterbalance. By late 1916 Carranza wanted closer commercial relations with Germany as well as German assistance in upgrading the Mexican army. Carranza also indicated an interest in purchasing German submarines for the Mexican navy and in constructing a major radio station for direct contact between Mexico and Germany. The Mexican government had even offered to let German submarines operate out of Mexican bases.

It was in this context of increasing friction between Mexico and the United States and closer ties between Mexico and Germany that the Zimmermann Telegram appeared. In November 1916, Arthur Zimmermann became Germany's foreign secretary after a lengthy career in his country's diplomatic and consular services. Despite his diplomatic background, Zimmermann assumed his position with the conviction that Germany would have to renew unrestricted submarine warfare, which had been followed at the beginning of the war but later abandoned under U.S. pressure. Zimmermann assumed that the resumption of unrestricted submarine warfare would probably lead to U.S. entry into the war on the side of the Allies. To limit the U.S. contribution to the European war effort, Zimmermann decided to promote a military conflict between Mexico and Japan on the one hand and the United States on the other.

On 16 January 1917 Zimmermann outlined his proposal in a coded telegram to the German ambassador in Mexico, Heinrich von Eckardt. In the telegram Zimmermann indicated that Germany would renew unrestricted submarine warfare on 1 February 1917. In the event that the United States entered the war, the ambassador was to propose a military alliance with Mexico in which they would wage war together and make peace together. Germany would provide "generous financial support" and aid Mexico in recovering the "lost territory" of Texas, New Mexico, and Arizona. Eckardt was also directed to suggest to President Carranza that Mexico encourage Japan to join in the military alliance against the United States. Zimmermann concluded the telegram by directing Eckardt to point out to President Carranza that Germany's "ruthless employment of our submarines" would make England sue for peace in a few months.

Officials in the German Foreign Office worried about the impact on the United States and U.S. neutrality if the contents of the telegram became known. Their concerns proved justified. British intelligence had broken the code that the Germans used to send the message and had intercepted the telegram in Mexico. The British did not immediately turn the telegram over to U.S. officials or publicize it because they did not want it known that they had broken the German code. The British also hoped that the renewal of unrestricted submarine warfare would be enough to bring the United States into the war. The United States did break relations with Germany but did not declare war. The British then turned the decoded telegram over to U.S. officials on 24 February. President Wilson later authorized the release of the telegram to the U.S. press, which published it under sensational headlines on 1 March.

When the telegram was first released, many critics of the Wilson administration denounced it as a forgery, attributing it to either the U.S. or British governments. Zimmermann then provided an additional shock; the German foreign minister publicly admitted that he had sent the telegram. Zimmermann's admission was apparently based on his belief that the United States could prove that the telegram was authentic and that its publication would provoke sober reflection rather than outrage in the United States. The official response of the Carranza administration was to deny that it had ever been offered an alliance by Germany; Carranza also refused to break relations with Germany as the U.S. government was pressuring him to do. Later in a secret meeting with Ambassador Eckardt, Carranza officially turned down the offer of an alliance at the time but held open an alliance as a future possibility in the event of war between Mexico and the United States.

U.S. officials at the time and historians since have attributed considerable significance to the Zimmermann Telegram in provoking public support in the United States for entrance into the war, which the United States officially entered in early April 1917. Despite the diplomatic uproar over the telegram, the telegram did not produce a change in Mexico's policy toward the war. The Carranza administration maintained its position of neutrality throughout the conflict, much to the dismay of the Wilson administration, which constantly pressured Mexico to abandon its neutrality. Even after the telegram fiasco, Germany made another offer of a military alliance with Mexico, which Carranza turned down in August 1917 but with the provision that he hoped for German aid in the event of a U.S. attack on Mexico. The German secret service moved its North American headquarters to Mexico after U.S. entry into the war. The Germans even prepared a base for submarines on Mexico's Gulf Coast, but no warships were ever sent to the base. Although the activities of the German secret service in Mexico were largely unproductive, they did help to convince U.S. officials that Carranza's supposed neutrality was designed to conceal a pro-German policy.

Although the Zimmermann Telegram shocked U.S. officials, it in fact represented the latest in a series of attempts to embroil Mexico and the United States in a major military conflict, especially along the U.S.–Mexican border. The proposal contained in the telegram makes considerably more sense when placed against the background of what German officials considered the "failure" of the Pershing Expedition into northern Mexico. Indeed, the last elements of the expedition were leaving Mexico just as the storm over the telegram was about to break. The telegram, however, came to epitomize the failure of Germany's global strategy as it applied to Mexico.

—*DMC*

See also: Carranza, Venustiano; Foreign Policy; Madero, Francisco; Pershing Expedition; Revolution of 1910; United States, Relations with; Vera Cruz, Occupation of (1914); Villa, Francisco "Pancho."

References:

Coerver, Don M., and Linda B. Hall. *Texas and the Mexican Revolution: A Study in State and National Border Policy, 1910–1920.* San Antonio, TX: Trinity University Press, 1984.

Katz, Friedrich. *The Secret War in Mexico: Europe, the United States and the Mexican Revolution.* Chicago: University of Chicago Press, 1981.

Tuchman, Barbara W. *The Zimmermann Telegram.* New York: Viking Press, 1958.

BIBLIOGRAPHY

Aguilar Camín, Hector, and Lorenzo Meyer. *In the Shadow of the Mexican Revolution: Contemporary Mexican History, 1910–1989*. Austin: University of Texas Press, 1993.

Albro, Ward. *Always a Rebel: Ricardo Flores Magón and the Mexican Revolution*. Fort Worth: Texas Christian University Press, 1992.

Ashby, Joe C. *Organized Labor and the Mexican Revolution under Lázaro Cárdenas*. Chapel Hill: University of North Carolina Press, 1967.

Bailey, David. *Viva Cristo Rey!: The Cristero Rebellion and the Church-State Conflict in Mexico*. Austin: University of Texas Press, 1974.

Bailey, John J. *Governing Mexico: The Statecraft of Crisis Management*. New York: St. Martin's, 1988.

Barry, Tom. *The Challenge of Cross-Border Environmentalism: The U.S.–Mexico Case*. Albuquerque, NM, and Bisbee, AZ: Resource Center Press/Border Ecology Project, 1994.

———. *Zapata's Revenge: Free Trade and the Farm Crisis in Mexico*. Boston: South End Press, 1995.

Bazant, Jan. *Historia de la deuda exterior de México (1823–1946)*. Mexico: El Colegio De México, 1968.

Beals, Carleton. *Porfirio Díaz: Dictator of Mexico*. Philadelphia: J. B. Lippincott, 1932.

Benjamin, Thomas, and William McNellie, eds. *Other Mexicos: Essays on Regional Mexican History, 1876–1911*. Albuquerque: University of New Mexico Press, 1984.

Bethell, Leslie, ed. *The Cambridge History of Latin America*. Vol. 6. *Part I. Economy and Society*. Cambridge: Cambridge University Press, 1994.

Brown, Jonathan C. *Oil and Revolution in Mexico*. Berkeley: University of California Press, 1993.

Brown, Jonathan C., and Alan Knight, eds. *The Mexican Petroleum Industry in the Twentieth Century*. Austin: University of Texas Press, 1992.

Butler, Edgar W., and Jorge A. Bustamante, eds. *Sucesión Presidencial: The 1988 Mexican Presidential Election*. Boulder, CO: Westview Press, 1990.

Calavita, Kitty. *Inside the State: The Bracero Program, Immigration, and the I.N.S.* New York: Routledge, 1992.

Camp, Roderic Ai. *Crossing Swords: Religion and Politics in Mexico*. New York: Oxford University Press, 1997.

———. *Generals in the Palacio: The Military in Modern Mexico*. New York: Oxford University Press, 1992.

———. *Mexican Political Biographies, 1884–1935*. Austin: University of Texas Press, 1991.

———. *Political Recruitment across Two Centuries: Mexico, 1884–1991*. Austin: University of Texas Press, 1995.

———. *Politics in Mexico*. 2d ed. New York: Oxford University Press, 1996.

Cardoso, Lawrence A. *Mexican Emigration to the United States, 1897–1931: Socio-Economic Patterns*. Tucson: University of Arizona Press, 1980.

Carr, Barry. *Marxism and Communism in Twentieth-Century Mexico*. Lincoln: University of Nebraska Press, 1992.

Caulfield, Norman. *Mexican Workers and the State: From the Porfiriato to NAFTA*. Fort Worth: Texas Christian University Press, 1998.

Clark, Marjorie Ruth. *Organized Labor in Mexico*. Chapel Hill: University of North Carolina Press, 1934.

Clendenen, Clarence C. *The United States and Pancho Villa*. Ithaca, NY: Cornell University Press, 1961.

Coatsworth, John H. *Growth against Development: The Economic Impact of Railroads in Porfirian Mexico*. DeKalb: Northern Illinois University Press, 1981.

Coerver, Don M., and Linda B. Hall. *Texas and the Mexican Revolution: A Study in State and National*

Border Policy 1910–1920. San Antonio, TX: Trinity University Press, 1984.

Collier, Ruth Berins. *The Contradictory Alliance: State-Labor Relations and Regime Change in Mexico.* Berkeley: University of California Press, 1992.

Córdova, Arnaldo. *La Revolución en crisis: La aventura del maximato.* Mexico City: Cal y Arena, 1995.

Cothran, Dan A. *Political Stability and Democracy in Mexico.* Westport, CT: Praeger, 1994.

Craig, Richard B. *The Bracero Program: Interest Groups and Foreign Policy.* Austin: University of Texas Press, 1971.

Cumberland, Charles C. *The Mexican Revolution: The Constitutionalist Years.* Austin: University of Texas Press, 1972.

———. *Mexican Revolution: Genesis under Madero.* Austin: University of Texas Press, 1952.

Davis, Diane E. *Urban Leviathan: Mexico City in the Twentieth Century.* Philadelphia: Temple University Press, 1994.

De Kadt, Emanuel, ed. *Tourism: Passport to Development?* New York: Oxford University Press, 1979.

DeWalt, Billie R., Martha W. Rees, and Arthur D. Murphy. *The End of Agrarian Reform in Mexico: Past Lessons, Future Prospects.* San Diego: Center for U.S.–Mexican Studies, University of California, San Diego, 1994.

Domínguez, Jorge I., and James A. McCann. *Democratizing Mexico: Public Opinion and Electoral Choices.* Baltimore, MD: Johns Hopkins University Press, 1996.

Dulles, John W. F. *Yesterday in Mexico: A Chronicle of the Revolution, 1919–1936.* Austin: University of Texas Press, 1961.

García, Juan Ramón. *Operation Wetback: The Mass Deportation of Mexican Undocumented Workers in 1954.* Westport, CT: Greenwood Press, 1980.

Gilderhus, Mark T. *Diplomacy and Revolution: U.S.–Mexican Relations under Wilson and Carranza.* Tucson: University of Arizona Press, 1977.

Giugale, Marcelo M., Olivier Lafourcade, and Vinh H. Nguyen, eds. *Mexico: A Comprehensive Development Agenda for the New Era.* Washington, DC: The World Bank, 2001.

González, Guadalupe, and Marta Tienda. *The Drug Connection in U.S.–Mexican Relations.* San Diego: Center for U.S.–Mexican Studies, University of California, San Diego, 1989.

Grayson, George W. *The Church in Contemporary Mexico.* Washington, DC: Center for Strategic and International Studies, 1992.

———. *Mexico: From Corporatism to Pluralism?* Fort Worth, TX: Harcourt Brace & Company, 1998.

Grieb, Kenneth J. *The United States and Huerta.* Lincoln: University of Nebraska Press, 1969.

Guadalupe Garcia, Clara. *Rojo: del asesinato político en México.* Mexico City: Plaza & Janés, 1997.

Guzmán, Martín Luis. *Memoirs of Pancho Villa.* Austin: University of Texas Press, 1966.

Haber, Stephen H. *Industry and Underdevelopment: The Industrialization of Mexico, 1890–1940.* Palo Alto, CA: Stanford University Press, 1989.

Hall, Linda B. *Alvaro Obregón: Power and Revolution in Mexico, 1911–1920.* College Station: Texas A&M University Press, 1981.

———. *Oil, Banks, and Politics: The United States and Postrevolutionary Mexico, 1917–1924.* Austin: University of Texas Press, 1995.

Hall, Linda B., and Don M. Coerver. *Revolution on the Border: The United States and Mexico, 1910–1920.* Albuquerque: University of New Mexico Press, 1988.

Hamilton, Nora. *The Limits of State Autonomy: Post-Revolutionary Mexico.* Princeton, NJ: Princeton University Press, 1982.

Hamnett, Brian. *Juárez.* New York: Longman, 1994.

Hansen, Roger D. *The Politics of Mexican Development.* Baltimore: Johns Hopkins University Press, 1971.

Hart, John M. *Anarchism and the Mexican Working Class, 1860–1931.* Austin: University of Texas Press, 1978.

———. *Revolutionary Mexico: The Coming and Process of the Mexican Revolution.* Berkeley: University of California Press, 1987.

Harvey, Neil. *The Chiapas Rebellion: The Struggle for Land and Democracy.* Durham, NC: Duke University Press, 1998.

———. *The New Agrarian Movement in Mexico, 1979–1990.* London: Institute of Latin American Studies, 1990.

Hellman, Judith Adler. *Mexico in Crisis.* 2d ed. New York: Holmes & Meier Publishers, Inc., 1988.

Henderson, Peter V. N. *In the Absence of Don Porfirio: Francisco León de la Barra and the Mexican Revolution.* Wilmington, DE: Scholarly Resources, 2000.

Herzog, Lawrence A. *Where North Meets South: Cities, Space, and Politics on the U.S.–Mexico Border.* Austin: University of Texas Press, 1990.

Hodges, Donald C. *Mexican Anarchism after the Revolution.* Austin: University of Texas Press, 1995.

Hoffman, Abraham. *Unwanted Mexican Americans in the Great Depression: Repatriation Pressures, 1929–1939.* Tucson: University of Arizona Press, 1974.

Joseph, Gilbert M., and Mark D. Szuchman, eds. *I Saw a City Invincible: Urban Portraits of Latin America.* Wilmington, DE: Scholarly Resources, 1996.

Kandell, Jonathan. *La Capital: The Biography of Mexico City.* New York: Random House, 1988.

Katz, Friedrich. *The Life and Times of Pancho Villa.* Palo Alto, CA: Stanford University Press, 1998.

———. *The Secret War in Mexico: Europe, the United States, and the Mexican Revolution.* Chicago: University of Chicago Press, 1981.

Kiser, George C., and Martha Woody Kiser, eds. *Mexican Workers in the United States: Historical and Political Perspectives.* Albuquerque: University of New Mexico Press, 1979.

Knight, Alan. *The Mexican Revolution Counterrevolution and Reconstruction.* 2 vols. Cambridge: Cambridge University Press, 1986.

La Botz, Dan. *The Crisis of Mexican Labor.* New York: Praeger, 1988.

LaFrance, David G. *The Mexican Revolution in Puebla, 1908–1913: The Maderista Movement and the Failure of Liberal Reform.* Wilmington, DE: Scholarly Resources Books, 1989.

Langham, Thomas C. *Border Trials: Ricardo Flores Magón and the Mexican Liberals.* El Paso: Texas Western Press, 1981.

Langley, Lester D. *Mexico and the United States: The Fragile Relationship.* Boston: Twayne Publishers, 1991.

Levy, Daniel C., Kathleen Bruhn, and Emilio Zebadúa. *Mexico: The Struggle for Democratic Development.* Berkeley: University of California Press, 2001.

Lieuwen, Edwin. *Mexican Militarism: The Political Rise and Fall of the Revolutionary Army, 1910–1940.* Albuquerque: University of New Mexico Press, 1968.

Liss, Sheldon B. *A Century of Disagreement: The Chamizal Conflict, 1864–1964.* Washington, DC: University Press, 1965.

Mabry, Donald J. *Mexico's Acción Nacional: A Catholic Alternative to Revolution.* Syracuse, NY: Syracuse University Press, 1973.

Macías, Anna. *Against All Odds: The Feminist Movement in Mexico to 1940.* Westport, CT: Greenwood Press, 1982.

MacLachlan, Colin M. *Anarchism and the Mexican Revolution: The Political Trials of Ricardo Flores Magón in the United States.* Berkeley: University of California Press, 1991.

Mancke, Richard B. *Mexican Oil and Natural Gas: Political, Strategic, and Economic Implications.* New York: Praeger Publishers, 1979.

Markiewicz, Dana. *The Mexican Revolution and the Limits of Agrarian Reform.* Boulder, CO: Lynne Rienner, 1993.

Martínez, Oscar J. *Troublesome Border.* Tucson: University of Arizona, 1988.

Meyer, Jean, Enrique Krauze, and Cayetano Reyes. *Historia de la Revolución Mexicana, Periodo 1924–1928.* Vol. 11. *Estado y Sociedad con Calles.* Mexico City: El Colegio de México, 1977.

Meyer, Lorenzo. *Historia de la Revolución Mexicana.* Vol. 13. *El conflicto social y los gobiernos del Maximato.* Mexico: El Colegio de Mexico, 1978.

———. *Mexico and the United States in the Oil Controversy, 1917–1942.* Austin: University of Texas Press, 1977.

Meyer, Lorenzo, Rafael Segovia, and Alejandra Lajous. *Historia de la Revolución Mexicana.* Vol. 12. *Los inicios de la institucionalización: la política del Maximato.* Mexico: El Colegio de Mexico, 1978.

Meyer, Michael C. *Huerta: A Political Portrait.* Lincoln: University of Nebraska Press, 1972.

———. *Mexican Rebel: Pascual Orozco and the Mexican Revolution, 1910–1915.* Lincoln: University of Nebraska Press, 1967.

Middlebrook, Kevin J. *The Paradox of Revolution: Labor, the State, and Authoritarianism in Mexico.* Baltimore, MD: Johns Hopkins University Press, 1995.

Middlebrook, Kevin J., ed. *Unions, Workers, and the State in Mexico.* San Diego: University of California, San Diego, 1991.

Millon, Robert P. *Mexican Marxist: Vicente Lombardo Toledano.* Chapel Hill: University of North Carolina Press, 1966.

Monsiváis, Carlos. *Días de guardar* (Days to Keep). Trans. Robert Buffington. Mexico: Ediciones Era, 1988, p. 75.

———. *Nuevos escritores mexicanos del siglo XX presentados por sí mismos* (New Mexican Writers of the 20th Century Presented by Themselves). Trans. Robert Buffington. México: Empresas Editoriales, 1967.

Morris, Stephen D. *Corruption and Politics in Contemporary Mexico.* Tuscaloosa: University of Alabama Press, 1991.

———. *Political Reformism in Mexico.* Boulder, CO: Lynne Rienner Publishers, 1995.

Mueller, Jerry E. *Restless River: International Law and the Behavior of the Rio Grande.* El Paso: Texas Western Press, 1975.

Newell G., Roberto, and Luis Rubio F. *Mexico's Dilemma: The Political Origins of Economic Crisis.* Boulder, CO: Westview Press, 1984.

Niblo, Stephen R. *Mexico in the 1940s: Modernity, Politics, and Corruption.* Wilmington, DE: Scholarly Resources, 1999.

———. *War, Diplomacy, and Development: The United States and Mexico, 1938–1954.* Wilmington, DE: Scholarly Resources, 1995.

Nicolson, Harold. *Dwight Morrow.* New York: Harcourt, Brace and Company, 1935.

Niemeyer, E. V. *Revolution at Querétaro: The Mexican Constitutional Convention of 1916–1917.* Austin: University of Texas Press, 1974.

Ojeda, Mario. *Alcances y límites de la política exterior de México.* México: El Colegio de México: 1976.

Orme, William A. *Understanding NAFTA: Mexico, Free Trade, and the New North America.* Austin: University of Texas Press, 1996.

Pellicer de Brody, Olga, and Esteban L. Mancilla. *Historia de la Revolución Mexicana. Periodo 1952–1960.* Vol. 23. *El entendimiento con los Estados Unidos y la gestación del desarrollo estabilizador.* Mexico City: El Colegio de México, 1978.

Pellicer de Brody, Olga, and José Luis Reyna. *Historia de la Revolución Mexicana. Periodo 1952–1960.* Vol. 22. *El afianzamiento de la estabilidad política.* Mexico City: El Colegio de México, 1978.

Perry, Laurens Ballard. *Juárez and Díaz: Machine Politics in Mexico.* DeKalb: Northern Illinois University Press, 1978.

Poniatowska, Elena. *Massacre in Mexico.* New York: Viking Press, 1975.

Quirk, Robert. *The Mexican Revolution and the Catholic Church, 1910–1929.* Bloomington: University of Indiana Press, 1973.

Raat, W. Dirk. *Mexico and the United States: Ambivalent Vistas.* Athens: University of Georgia Press, 1992.

———. *Revoltosos: Mexico's Rebels in the United States, 1903–1923.* College Station: Texas A&M University Press, 1981.

Ramírez, Ramón. *El movimiento estudiantil de México.* 2 vols. Mexico City: Ediciones Era, 1969.

Randall, Laura, ed. *Reforming Mexico's Agrarian Reform.* Armonk, NY: M. E. Sharpe, 1996.

Reich, Peter Lester. *Mexico's Hidden Revolution: The Catholic Church in Law and Politics since 1929.* Notre Dame, IN: University of Notre Dame Press, 1995.

Reisler, Mark. *By the Sweat of Their Brow: Mexican Immigrant Labor in the United States, 1900–1940.* Westport, CT: Greenwood Press, 1976.

Reynolds, Clark W. *The Mexican Economy: Twentieth-Century Structure and Growth.* New Haven, CT: Yale University Press, 1970.

Richmond, Douglas W. *Venustiano Carranza's Nationalist Struggle, 1893–1920.* Lincoln: University of Nebraska Press, 1983.

Riding, Alan. *Distant Neighbors: A Portrait of the Mexicans.* New York: Alfred A. Knopf, 1985.

Rippy, Merrill. *Oil and the Mexican Revolution.* Leiden, The Netherlands: E. J. Brill, 1972.

Rodríguez, Victoria E., and Peter M. Ward, eds. *Opposition Government in Mexico.* Albuquerque: University of New Mexico Press, 1995.

Roeder, Ralph. *Juárez and His Mexico: A Biographical History.* 2 vols. New York: Viking Press, 1947.

Roett, Riordan, ed. *Mexico's External Relations in the 1990s.* Boulder, CO: Lynne Rienner Publishers, 1991.

Ronfeldt, David, ed. *The Modern Mexican Military: A Reassessment.* San Diego, CA: Center for U.S.–Mexican Studies, 1984.

Ross, Stanley R. *Francisco I. Madero, Apostle of Mexican Democracy.* New York: Columbia University Press, 1955.

Roxborough, Ian. *Unions and Politics in Mexico: The Case of the Automobile Industry.* Cambridge: Cambridge University Press, 1984.

Ruiz, Ramón E. *The Great Rebellion: Mexico, 1905–1924.* New York: Norton, 1980.

Russell, Philip L. *Mexico under Salinas.* Austin, TX: Mexico Resource Center, 1994.

Sanderson, Susan Walsh. *Land Reform in Mexico, 1910–1980.* Orlando, FL: Academic Press, 1984.

Schmidt, Samuel. *The Deterioration of the Mexican Presidency: The Years of Luis Echeverría.* Tucson: University of Arizona Press, 1991.

Schmitt, Karl M. *Communism in Mexico: A Study in Political Frustration.* Austin: University of Texas Press, 1965.

Scholes, Walter V. *Mexican Politics during the Juárez Regime, 1855–1872.* Columbia: University of Missouri Press, 1957.

Schuler, Friedrich E. *Mexico between Hitler and Roosevelt: Mexican Foreign Relations in the Age of Lázaro Cárdenas.* Albuquerque: University of New Mexico Press, 1998.

Schultz, Donald E., and Edward J. Williams, eds. *Mexico Faces the 21st Century.* New York: Praeger, 1995.

Shannon, Elaine. *Desperados: Latin Drug Lords, U.S. Lawmen, and the War America Can't Win.* New York: Viking, 1988.

Simonian, Lane. *Defending the Land of the Jaguar: A History of Conservation in Mexico.* Austin: University of Texas Press, 1995.

Simpson, Eyler N. *The Ejido: Mexico's Way Out*. Chapel Hill: University of North Carolina Press, 1937.

Smith, Peter H., ed. *Drug Policy in the Americas*. Boulder, CO: Westview Press, 1992.

Smith, Robert Freeman. *The United States and Revolutionary Nationalism in Mexico, 1916–1932*. Chicago: University of Chicago Press, 1972.

Snyder, Richard. *Politics after Neoliberalism: Reregulation in Mexico*. Cambridge: Cambridge University Press, 2001.

Soto, Shirlene. *Emergence of the Modern Mexican Woman: Her Participation in the Revolution and Struggle for Equality, 1910–1940*. Denver: Arden Press, 1990.

Story, Dale. *The Mexican Ruling Party: Stability and Authority*. New York: Praeger, 1986.

Tangeman, Michael. *Mexico at the Crossroads: Politics, the Church, and the Poor*. Maryknoll, NY: Orbis Books, 1995.

Tannenbaum, Frank. *The Mexican Agrarian Revolution*. New York: MacMillan, 1929.

Theobald, William F., ed. *Global Tourism: The Next Decade*. Oxford: Butterworth-Heinemann, 1995.

Torres, Blanca. *Historia de la Revolución Mexicana, Periodo 1940–1952*. Vol. 21. *Hacia la utopía industrial*. Mexico City: El Colegio de México, 1984.

Torres Ramírez, Blanca. *México en la segunda guerra mundial*. Mexico City: El Colegio de México, 1979.

Tuchman, Barbara W. *The Zimmermann Telegram*. New York: Viking Press, 1958.

Turlington, Edgar. *Mexico and Her Foreign Creditors*. New York: Columbia University Press, 1930.

Tutino, John. *From Insurrection to Revolution in Mexico: Social Bases of Agrarian Violence, 1750–1940*. Princeton, NJ: Princeton University Press, 1986.

Vanderwood, Paul J. *Disorder and Progress: Bandits, Police, and Mexican Development*. Wilmington, DE: Scholarly Resources, 1992.

Vaughan, Mary Kay. *Cultural Politics in Revolution: Teachers, Peasants, and Schools in Mexico, 1930–1940*. Tucson: University of Arizona Press, 1997.

———. *The State, Education, and Social Class in Mexico, 1880–1928*. DeKalb: Northern Illinois University Press, 1982.

Weber, David J., ed. *Foreigners in Their Native Land: Historical Roots of the Mexican Americans*. Albuquerque: University of New Mexico Press, 1973.

Zorrilla, Luis G. *Relaciones de México con la República de Centro América y con Guatemala*. Mexico City: Porrúa, 1984.

INDEX

CPSIA information can be obtained at www.ICGtesting.com
Printed in the USA
BVOW01*2001071213

338434BV00012B/255/P